Wealdstone Football Club

Roger Slater

Statistics compiled by Roger Slater, Peter Worby and Alan Lawrence

Juma

First published in 2002 by
Juma
Trafalgar Works
44 Wellington Street
Sheffield S1 4HD
Tel. 0114 272 0915
Fax. 0114 278 6550
Email:juma@btconnect.com

ISBN 1 872204 06 6

Printed by Juma.

The Weald Stone

In early Saxon times, the "Great Weald" or "Great Wold" was an area of thick woodland that covered the northern region of Middlesex. The word "weald" meaning "forest". The whole of the area was uninhabited until the 6th century, when Saxon farmers began felling trees to clear the ground for crops and cattle.

The landmark "Weald Stone" itself, some three feet tall, two feet thick and five feet wide is believed to be a Sarsen stone and, geologically, it is not of local origin. Sarsen stones were sandstone deposits of the great glaciers of the last ice-age, 10,000 years ago. Large versions were dragged, possibly from the Marlborough Downs, were dragged some 20 miles to Salisbury plain and were used to form the outer circle of Stonehenge.

There are various theories about the use of the Sarsen stone's at Stonehenge – for solar alignments or sepulchral associations. There is also a legend about the smaller stones, that they may have been used by ancient Britons to mark track ways, to help guide the spirits of deceased tribal chieftains to their final resting place. With this theory in mind, it is believed that very early inhabitants of the region brought the "Weald Stone" to the area for religious purposes. The stone was later used as a direction stone and boundary marker.

The stone of antiquity, from which the village of Wealdstone derives it's name currently lies outside a Public House, now know as The Weald Stone Inn, yet this building is better known historically by its former name, The Red Lion. It is at least the third Inn or similar building on the same site the first, which was in existence in 1741, faced what is now known as College Road. As an ancient relic, the Weald Stone has a documented history in the Borough archives, going back to the reign of Henry VIII where there are Court Scrolls that make reference to the "Weld Ston"

The Development of Wealdstone

The Census of 1086, known as the 'Domesday Book', records that the Manor of Harrow measured 100 hides of land with 49 teams of oxen on 70 plough lands. A hide of land was reckoned to be enough to support one family and teams of oxen were usually referred to as ploughs (8 oxen per team).

Harrow was recorded as having pasture for livestock but not meadow. Harrow formed one of the Estates of the Gore Hundred – ancient divisions of the county of Middlesex. The population at the time was recorded as being '7 men' (presumably referring to landowners and/or freemen, although this is not clear) and 6-700 people resident including 1 priest and 7 knights.

Wealdstone developed in the neighbourhood of the ancient stone, known as the 'Weald Stone'. The original settlement of Weald Stone was a cluster of houses around the stone.

The present town of Wealdstone began to form about 1850, though for many years the new village was known as Harrow Station or Station End. (Not to be confused with the present Harrow on the Hill station). It was soon after the place name "Wealdstone" had been bestowed that initial steps to provide the village with a permanent church were taken.

The parish of Holy Trinity was created in 1881 out of the parishes of Harrow, Pinner and Harrow Weald. The parish of Harrow Weald was itself only created in 1844. Until 1844 Pinner Church and St Mary's Harrow on the Hill were responsible for the whole of the Harrow area. In fact the population of the new parish of Wealdstone, including those parts of Pinner and Harrow that it encompassed, contained only 1,200 people, mostly of 'the working class'.

The arrival of new factories and industry (such as Whitefriars Glass) contributed to an increase in the local population – around 1,200 churchgoers were recorded at the time.

By 1903 the local population had increased and more factories opened (Kodak had arrived in 1891 and Windsor & Newton in 1903) and the town was then recorded as having 481 houses and 2,504 people.

By the year 2000, the population of the London Borough of Harrow, including Wealdstone, had risen to over 220,000.

To the memory of those representatives of Wealdstone Football Club who lost their lives in two World Wars.

1914-1918

Andrews, P.	A fine goal scorer capped in 1911 by the County and a regular player for a number of years.
Bellchambers, C. F.	A former player and Official at the time of the 'formation' of the club in 1899. Previously involved with predecessors of the club.
Bird, C.	A player in the seasons leading up to the War
Bowells, H.	Played in the last match of the club in 1905 and to return for the first game of the reformed club in 1909.
Bradberry, R. W.	A former reserve player and relation of goalkeeper T W Bradberry.
Cozens, W.	Captain of the side in 1899, playing alongside his brother, both having turned the fortunes of Wealdstone Athletic in 1895.
Goodage, R.	A former player.
Howman, W.	A former player and relation of A Team Vice Captain in 1913-14 H Howman.
Martin, F.	Joined the club as it reformed in 1909, and 1st XI Vice Captain in 1913/14
Robertson, G.	A former player who also joined the club as it reformed in 1909

1939 – 1945

Baldwin K.	A fine goal scorer, A Chelsea Amateur and a former Schoolboy international
Bidewell R.	Another former player who had remained with the club until his call up.
Bunce C. E.	A former Captain and an outstanding player who would have gone on to better things had he returned from the Far East.
Burton W.A.	A former player from the pre-war period.
Parr W. W.	A professional player with a long career that guested for Wealdstone in the early wartime matches.
Walker E.	Initially a Reserve and then first team goalkeeper until he joined the Royal Navy in 1940. Killed at the age of 24.
Winterbottom W. A	A former player and Committee Member.

Also to the memory of those Players, Supporters and Officials connected with Wealdstone Football Club who have passed away since its inception and to those people who have passed away since adding their contributions to this history.

Rest In Peace

Wealdstone FC Grounds 1887 – 1991

1. The Oaks FC, originally accessed from Ferndale Terrace 1887. 2. Marlborough Hill 1890. 3. Greenhill Farm, later Smiths Farm 1891. 4. Now the junction of Angel Road and Welldon Crescent 1895. 5. Harrow Rec, home of the merged Harrow Athletic 1895. 6. Wealdstone Rec, home of Wealdstone Athletic 1896. 7. Headstone Drive / Marlborough Hill 1899. 8. New College Farm 1903. 9. Wealdstone Rec 1905. 10. New College Farm 1909. 11. Belmont Road Ground 1911. 12. Lower Mead 1922 – 1991.

THE OAKS FC

1887 Works team of Cogswell & Harrison formed as the company moved to Wealdstone. Played friendly matches only.

THE OAKS (WEALDSTONE) FC

1888 The club was often referred to as the Wealdstone team, the name first appeared in print as The Oaks (Wealdstone) FC in December 1888.

WEALDSTONE FC

1889 By the beginning of the 1889-90 season, The Oaks was removed from the name and Wealdstone FC appeared for the first time.

1892-93 Wealdstone FC also entered the Middlesex Junior Cup for the first time. Middlesex Junior Cup Runner Up

WEALDSTONE JUNIORS FC

1893-1895 Formed / joined by a number of members of the original Wealdstone FC prior to the amalgamation with Harrow Athletic FC.

HARROW ATHLETIC FC

1894 Wealdstone FC amalgamated with Harrow Athletic FC in April 1894 Harrow Athletic entered the Middlesex Senior Cup.

WEALDSTONE ATHLETIC FC

1895 Wealdstone Athletic were formed as a breakaway from Harrow Athletic FC in conjunction with some of the players of other Wealdstone sides in September 1895. After one year, the club ceased playing football, reverting to an Athletic Club, the players involved in the formation of Wealdstone Rovers FC.

WEALDSTONE ROVERS FC

1896-1898 As a result of the break away from Wealdstone Athletic FC, Harrow Athletic FC re-formed. A number of former Wealdstone players joined Wealdstone Juniors FC and a number of others helped in the formation of Wealdstone Rovers FC

WEALDSTONE JUNIORS FC

1897–1898 Formed late in 1897, there was no connection with the previous club on the same name.

WEALDSTONE WANDERERS FC

1897-1899 Wealdstone Wanderers FC formed at the same time, one of the first matches played was a match between the Wanderers and their newly formed neighbours, Wealdstone Juniors FC.

WEALDSTONE ALBION

1898–1899 Wealdstone Juniors were renamed for the start of the 1898 season, and incorporating players from the other local sides, Wealdstone Albion was formed to become a Founder Member of the Willesden & District League Division II

WEALDSTONE FC

1899 Wealdstone Albion FC dropped the 'Albion' and became Wealdstone FC also being joined by the remaining players from Wealdstone Wanderers FC and Wealdstone Rovers FC. Played in the Willesden and District League Division II as Wealdstone FC for the first time.

1900-01 Joined Willesden and District League Division I

1903-04 Willesden & District League Runner Up
First entered London Junior Cup and Middlesex Junior Cup

1904-05 Willesden & District League Champions

WEALDSTONE CHURCH ATHLETIC FC

1905-08 Wealdstone Football Club ceased playing, fixtures completed by Wealdstone Church Athletic FC which had formed a number of years earlier. They were members of the Harrow & Wembley & District League and they played in both leagues for the remainder of the season. Subsequently the side dropped out of the Harrow & Wembley & District League for seasons 1906-07 and 1907-08.

WEALDSTONE FC

1908-09 Split away from Wealdstone Church Athletic FC and rejoined Willesden & District League Division I.
Wealdstone Church Athletic FC reverted to the Harrow & Wembley & District League.

1909-10 North West London League Champions (Reserves)
Wealdstone (Wednesday) FC was formed as part of the main club and ran for a couple of years.

1910-11 Willesden & District League (Premier Division) Runner Up

1911-12 Middlesex Junior Cup Runner Up
London League Division II Runner Up
London Junior Cup Runner Up

1912-13 Willesden & District League (Division I) Champions
London League Division II Champions ('A' Team)
Middlesex Junior Cup Winners

1913-14 First season in Senior Football.
Wealdstone FC entered the English Cup (FA Cup) for the first time
Wealdstone FC entered the FA Amateur Cup for the first time
Wealdstone FC entered the London Senior Cup & Middlesex Senior Cup
Joined the London League Division I

1914-18 All Football ceased for the duration of the First World War

1918-19 Wealdstone United formed from players from a number of local clubs to play Friendlies after the end of the War.

1919-20 Wealdstone FC reformed and joined the London and Middlesex Senior Leagues.
Wealdstone Old Boys FC was formed by players now to old for the main club and other local sides, returning from the War.
Wealdstone Juniors FC also reformed but were not part of Wealdstone FC

1920-21 Middlesex Senior League Winners

1921-22 Middlesex Senior League Winners

1922-23 Wealdstone teams joined the Spartan League (Divisions I & II)
Harrow Charity Cup Winners
Spartan League Division I Runner Up
Wealdstone FC (Wednesday Section) reformed

1923-24 Harrow Charity Cup Winners
Middlesex Senior Cup Runner Up

1924-25 Spartan League Division II Champions
Harrow Charity Cup Winners (Reserves)

1926-27 Harrow Charity Cup Winners (Reserves)
Harrow Charity Shield Winners (Wednesday Section)
Harrow & District League Champions (Wednesday Section)
Hounslow & District League Runner Up (Wednesday Section)

1927-28 Harrow & District League Champions (Wednesday Section)

1928-29 Joined Athenian League
Athenian League Division II Champions
Harrow Charity Cup Winners

1929-30 Middlesex Senior Cup Winners
Middlesex Senior Charity Cup Winners

1930-31 Middlesex Senior Charity Cup Winners

1931-32	Athenian League Reserve Section Runner Up
1933-34	Harrow Charity Cup Winners
1934-35	Harrow Charity Cup Winners
1935-36	Athenian League Division II Winners
	Harrow Charity Cup Winners
	Middlesex Intermediate Cup Runner Up
1936-37	Harrow Charity Cup Winners
	Athenian League Reserve Section Runner Up
1937-38	Middlesex Senior Cup Winners
	Middlesex Senior Charity Cup Winners
	Athenian League Reserve Section Runner Up
1938-39	Middlesex Senior Charity Cup Winners
	Middlesex Senior Cup Runner Up
	Harrow Charity Cup Winners
1939-40	Athenian League abandoned on outbreak of war, Wealdstone had not played a game at this time. Cups & Friendlies played for the season.
	Middlesex Sports Red Cross Cup Winners
	London Senior Cup Runner Up
1940-41	Joined the wartime Hertfordshire & Middlesex League
	Middlesex Senior Cup Winners
	Middlesex Sports Red Cross Cup Winners
	Cambridge Hospital Cup Winners
1941-42	Middlesex Senior Cup Winners
	Middlesex Sports Red Cross Cup Winners
1942-43	Middlesex Senior Cup Winners
1945-46	Middlesex Senior Cup Winners
	Harrow Charity Cup Winners
	Pinner and Northwood Hospital Cup Winners
	Wealdstone Football Club Cup Winners
1946-47	Athenian League reformed
	Harrow Charity Cup Runner Up
1947-48	Middlesex Intermediate Cup Winners (Reserves)
1948-49	Wycombe Hospital Cup Runner Up
1949-50	Middlesex Senior Charity Cup Winners
	Wealdstone Football Club Cup Winners
	Harrow, Wembley & District League Division I Winners ('A' Team - Unbeaten)
1950-51	Middlesex Charity Cup Runner Up
1951-52	Athenian League Champions
	London Senior Cup Runner Up
	Middlesex Charity Cup Runner Up
1952-53	Athenian League Runner Up
	Middlesex Challenge Cup Runner Up
	Athenian League Reserve Section Challenge Cup Winners
1953-54	West Middlesex Six-a-Side Runner Up
1955-56	Middlesex Senior Charity Cup Runner Up
1956-57	Westminster Hospital Challenge Cup Winners
1957-58	North West Middlesex Invitation Cup Winners
	Westminster Hospital Challenge Cup Winners (Reserves)
	Harrow Youth League Senior Challenge Cup (Colts)
1958-59	Athenian League Runner Up (lost title on goal average)
	Middlesex Senior Cup Winners
	North West Middlesex Invitation Cup Runner Up
	Harrow Youth League Senior Challenge Cup (Colts)
1959-60	North West Middlesex Invitation Cup Winners
	Athenian League Reserve Section Runner Up
	Athenian League Reserve Section Challenge Cup Winners
	London Intermediate Cup Winners
	Harrow Charity Cup Winners ('A' Team)
	Harrow Youth League Winners (Colts)
	Harrow Youth League Senior Challenge Cup Winners (Colts)
1960-61	Athenian League Runner Up
	London Senior Cup Runner Up
	Harrow Youth League Senior Challenge Cup Winners (Colts)
1961-62	Middlesex Senior Cup Runner Up
	AFA Invitation Cup Runner Up
	London Senior Cup Winners (shared with Wimbledon FC after a 1-1 draw)
	Harrow Youth League Winners (Colts)
	Middlesex Senior Youth Cup Runner Up (Colts)
1962-63	Middlesex Senior Cup Winners

	Middlesex Charity Cup Runner Up
	Battle Of Britain Trophy Runner Up
1963-64	Middlesex Senior Cup Winners
	Middlesex Charity Cup Winners
	London Charity Cup Winners
	Mithras Floodlit Cup Winners
	Hitchin Centenary Cup Winners
	Battle Of Britain Trophy Winners
1964-65	Joined Isthmian League
	Isthmian League Reserve Section Runner Up
1965-66	FA Amateur Cup Winners
	Middlesex Senior Cup Runner Up
	Hitchin Centenary Cup Runner Up
1966-67	Alaway Memorial Trophy Winners
	East Anglian Cup Runner Up
	Harrow Senior Charity Cup ('A' Team)
1967-68	Middlesex Senior Cup Winners
	Middlesex Charity Cup Winners (Shared with Wembley FC)
	Bucks Border League Champions
	London Intermediate Cup Runner Up (Reserves)
1968-69	Presidents Cup Winners
	Isthmian League Reserve Division Runner Up
1969-70	Middlesex Senior Cup Runner Up
	Presidents Cup Winners
1970-71	Presidents Cup Winners
1971-72	Joined Southern League Division One North
1972-73	Transferred to Division One South
1973-74	Southern League Division One South Champions
	Promoted to Premier Division
1979-80	Founder members of Alliance Premier League
1981-82	Rejoined Southern League
	Southern League Southern Division Champions
	Southern League Champions after beating Midland Division Champions Nuneaton Borough.
1982-83	Rejoined Alliance Premier League
1984-85	Alliance Premier League Champions
	FA Trophy Winners
	Middlesex Senior Cup Winners
1986-87	Alliance Premier League renamed Conference
1988-89	Rejoined Southern League
1995-96	Rejoined Isthmian League, in Division Three
1996-97	Isthmian League Division Three Champions
	Associate Members Trophy Runner Up
1997-98	Promoted to Division One
1998-99	Achieved promotion to the Premier Division but were denied by Ground Grading.
2001-2002	Middlesex Charity Cup Runner Up
	PASE U19 Conference National Cup (U19 Youth Team) Runner Up

During the research for the book, particularly trying to trace some of our former players who are now overseas, I came across Wayne Roach, 'Stones former goalkeeper, now resident in New Zealand, and in particular, a friend he had interested in Wealdstone FC.

He too had written a book on the centenary of his yacht club. At a time when there was so much I had to do, his comments and advice were greatly appreciated. As time has progressed they have been proven to be true and the message is included here to give a little insight into the writing and production of this book.

The trouble is, the first 50 years are easy-peasy, because everyone's dead, and you can actually make some progress getting it all straight, and anyway, they won't come back and nag you if you didn't spell their middle names properly. In many ways they are more interesting because you can form your own opinions about a more innocent, but no less dedicated group of people.

The last 50 years, and in particular the last 25 will in some ways, be the hardest, despite the greater bulk of information. In the main this will be because most are still alive and ALL will have an opinion and feel all hurt and injured it you don't `pop around for a cuppa and look at their scrap books'.

Almost everyone still alive will regard their efforts and input to be of PRIME importance, despite the fact that your researches may turn up information from (for arguments sake) 50 years ago which will show that if certain hopelessly dedicated people (now dead) had not dragged the club out of the mire by sheer force of will, the geezers who are now ear bashing you would not have any club to celebrate.

Many books cover the first 50-75 years in a breathless rush, (partly because it's easier than doing any decent research) and spend the last 30-odd years congratulating the current crop of committee members for being such jolly good top-hole sports.

I took the view (of the kiwi yacht clubs) that the entire 100 years or so was of equal importance, and that the current members and participants/fans were only a reflection of similar dedication that had occurred all down the years.

Given what I now know of the Victorian/Edwardian sportsmen (and even into the 1930's and 1940's), I would say that they were far more dedicated than we are today, particularly to the `ideals' of sport and sportsmanship as true amateurs. The whole `club' scenario was, in pre-television mass-media days, more part of the community and a way of life. (and they didn't need McDonalds, TDK, Sharp or any such crap on their shirts to survive did they?).

The upshot of that line of thought was that the yacht club books were, as far as possible, a history of the CLUB, rather than a vehicle for mug-shots of the last 20 years of good guys and current committee members. It upset one or two people who were angry that I didn't run photos of them dressed up in drag, as scarecrows or hula maidens at the 1975 Shipwrecks Ball (pass the sick bag, Alice!) but it was better for it.

Also, I believe it plays fair by all those long dead club members, who each in turn, kept it all going year after year, so we can have a present and a future.

Under no circumstances believe any old coots that `still have all his marbles and know all about the history of the club'. During my early researches I was caught time and time again by believing these lovely old guys who talked up a storm. Most of it, while essentially correct (i.e. it happened), were hopelessly muddled as to times and dates, often getting several events and people wound together into one great-sounding (but flawed) seamless yarn.

In trying to recall events of over 60 years ago, it is nothing for people to be 5 or 6 years out and have a recollection of things that don't quite gel with your rudimentary knowledge of the event. Particularly when they were children and at the time, and were taking in and remembering important events through a child's eyes. If you know nothing about his period yourself, it is too easy to take it all on as the gospel.

I found the only way was to hit the newspaper/magazine archives, and set the dates as hard and fast signposts, clearly fixing events and people in place. Then, armed with a good understanding of the period/event, go to the old guys for the `colour' and anecdote. That way you can gently unravel the items that did not occur and even better, re-place them in their correct context.

Once you do that, you can often `open doors' in memories that have not been opened for years, purely because for the last 40 years or so, their muddled version of events has been the only one they have used. In these situations, once unravelled, you can sometimes get some truly remarkable information as they too become delighted recalling with the stuff they had completely forgotten.

That's when it really is good fun and worthwhile so have fun, the sympathy is still there.

Regards, Robin Elliott

For the last couple of years or so the original e-mail of the above has been pinned to the wall above my computer, and it has been read many times. Now, as you're reading this, the book is finished and the e-mail has been filed away with all of the other letters, mails, faxes and notes that have accumulated.

A great quantity of old programmes, accounts, contracts, photographs, newspaper articles and much assorted documentation has been loaned to me to help with the book, and a lot of has also been given (via me) to the club to preserve a little more of our history.

For all of this and the general assistance received from contributors fans and friends it was greatly appreciated and it was a great help.

I will not name everyone who has helped, as the list would almost be a book in itself, suffice to say that there have been people without whom this book would not have been completed - those people who helped search out contacts and former players and officials in the early days were particularly useful, and to each of you I offer my thanks.

Just a few that I must thank in person. Rosemary Luck, daughter of the former Club Secretary 'Chippy' who provided an immense amount of information through her late father's records. Peter Worby who helped with the majority of the stats and also Alan Lawrence who helped fill in the war years – we have not managed a complete record, but at least those at the back of the book are a far more comprehensive record than (to date) exists elsewhere.

This book would not have been possible if fans throughout the club's history had not kept records, press cuttings and memories and to each contributor named within, a special thank you for taking the time to add your thoughts.

Thanks too to all of those people who have lent photographs from their collections. Again to numerous to name, but these along with various programmes and documents I hope will add more than a little interest in the past of our club.

Lastly, thanks to the Harrow Observer for reporting on a vast majority of the club's fixtures over more than a century, ably backed in the early years by the Harrow Gazette, and also to the other publications whose copy has been used herein.

Thanks also to all those who have at various times proof read sections of the book, and to Steve Paull for the overall review, and a final thank you to Mike Bondy at MJB Research who has managed to find some of the records and results that were missing from the early years.

There have been times when progress has been very difficult and also occasions tinged with sadness as a few of the older contributors have passed away since their comments were recorded. I hope that the contributions of these people will stand as a fitting tribute to them and their time with our club, and the part they played in our history, and to those that are still alive, their contributions as well should be part of the history of Wealdstone Football Club for ever.

If anyone feels that they would like to carry on the record for the next fifty or one hundred years, I have one small piece of advice.

Start Now.

Roger Slater

FOREWORD

My first visit to Lower Mead was in the 1960's when Flower Power was reaching it's dizzy heights. Kaftans were all the rage and I was becoming increasingly aware of my Middlesex roots.

In 1965, the unthinking happened when a Conservative British government – meant to conserve British heritage, both national and local, I wrongly assumed – 'abolished' where I lived. Middlesex.

Of course they hadn't but it was a good few years later that I discovered the truth, ironically by another Conservative Government, this time Mrs Thatcher's, that only the Middlesex County Council had been abolished but the County of Middlesex – an entirely different and separate entity – would remain for posterity and eternity, as no Government could axe something that they hadn't originally created.

So, now, as we approach the Middlesex Millennium (AD 704 – AD2004) 1300 years of our County, this is a fitting time to pay tribute to one of the most loyal and devoted clubs and a band of followers so proud of their town community and Middlesex roots.

The 'Stones crest says it all, for not only do the Three Lions of England adorn the shield but they also stretch themselves as if pointing to the Middlesex colours of Saxon Crown and three Seaxes. If you went to an heraldic expert and said "We are a football club from Middlesex – can you design a badge for us?" he would come up with exactly what the Wealdstone FC coat of arms is.

Even the name Wealdstone is rich in Middlesex heritage, for in those days of yore, over a thousand years ago, the whole of northern Middlesex (and what people now describe as North London) was covered by the Great Forest of Middlesex. Peppered with little farms, hamlets and villages, each filled with Middle Saxons, living their lives.

Although the name Wealdstone isn't documented until around 1754, it was around this spot between Harrow Weald and Harrow on the Hill and Greenhill that the origins of the modern village was to spring up.

It was the coming of railroads thrusting themselves like a spider's web through the Capital County and the rest of Britain that gave oxygen to the growth of Wealdstone.

The original weald stone could have (as described previously) derived from an ancient even religious burial route as far back as the Ancient Britons (now known to most people as the Welsh) or the stone could have been a boundary marker in the Great Middlesex Forest, for a 'Weald' was exactly that – a forest or woodland.

One of the last vestiges of the Great Forest of Middlesex can be seen along the Uxbridge Road, turning left up towards Stanmore and across to Mill Hill, or if you really want to view large tracts of it, then Hampstead Heath and Primrose Hill are still pure Middlesex Weald.

I write all of this because we should all be proud of and protect our roots, as it is in the annals of Middlesex history where Wealdstone the name and identity began.

What Wealdstone FC accomplishes every day of the week is to carry on this unique community spirit and Middlesex legacy of well over a thousand years. Every time they play a match they are promoting part of our own Middlesex history and their distinct Wealdstone identity.

Their legion of fans and supporters demonstrate the kind of devotion and loyalty that most clubs can only envy. These modern day Middle Saxons have trudged long miles to claim sponsored funds to keep the club going. They have tangled with the red tape of Government and their quangos to justify their need to secure funding for a new ground, and they have suffered everything from disappointment to anger at the loss of their 'home' and the cost of litigation and to recover money rightfully theirs.

They even had to play out of their home County before tireless working from a number of people has hopefully ensured their return.

For, if ever their was truth in the old maxim if at first you don't succeed, try again, it is the news that Wealdstone have claimed back a part of Middlesex territory and lands to continue to play not just football, but to encompass other sports and recreations in the name of Wealdstone and Middlesex.

Tears of despondency have turned to smiles of joy now that the funding is in place for the club's new home. The Stones, who have been cruelly served by fate have now found Lady Luck grinning down on them.

I am more than proud to be Patron of Wealdstone Football Club. Words cannot be found to describe how much I admire every single person who has kept this great club not just alive, but on the verge of more glory.

The Stones are the epitomy of a true community and the old clichés of "it's my honour and privilege" aren't adequate when paying tribute to the men and women of Wealdstone in Middlesex, who have added their names to a roll of sporting honour that dates back over a century to when the first organised sport became the bastion of local pride.

Congratulations to you all, and to Roge for giving me the chance to write this foreword.

Russell Grant
Wealdstone FC Patron and Wealdstone and Middlesex Patriot.

More information on the County of Middlesex past and present, including regular updates on The Stones can be found by visiting http;//www.capitalcounty.com, the County Of Middlesex website.

CONTENTS

INTRODUCTION

It is has been generally accepted that Wealdstone Football Club as we know it today played its first match on October 7th 1899, winning by six goals to one against another 'new' local side, Northwood FC, while the reserves won by a margin of twelve goals to one away to Queens Park Olympic in their second friendly match of the season. Reports on both of these matches are featured later.

There is no doubt either that this is not the beginning of Wealdstone FC, more likely is that it is at least the third incarnation of the club as records indicate that there was a club as early as the 1887 season, and certainly for at least two years prior to this latest 'formation'. From details included when the club's Golden Jubilee Handbook was written, there are references to earlier clubs, not least in letters previously sent to the Harrow Observer by former players. There are also references to Cogswell and Harrison and indications of their involvement in the formation of the original club:

"The employees of a firm of gunsmiths, Messrs Cogswell and Harrison, appear to have been the pioneers of organised football in Wealdstone. The firm came to the district from Birmingham in 1887, and its Managing Director, Mr Edgar Harrison took great interest in his employees 'football activities. Two local rivals for his works team were Wealdstone Mission FC and The Oaks, which was a side made up of the clerical staff of Cogswell and Harrison".

In fact, the centenary brochure of Cogswell and Harrison also makes mention of the formation of the club:

Edgar Harrison (1858-1938) Chairman of Cogswell and Harrison 1896-1938 and original patron of Wealdstone Football Club

As an example of their spirit, the Harrow employees became the pioneers of organised football in the area laying the basis for what is now known as the Wealdstone Football Club.

We can sense the size and camaraderie of the Harrow staff since Cogswell & Harrison was able to muster two teams: the Works teams and a team called 'The Oaks' made up from its clerical staff.

Mr Edgar Harrison, who at the time lived in Hindes Road, actively supported the football activities of the Company and patronised the club. A foreman called Mr Meadows was elected Secretary.

Two games were played between the works team and The Oaks, on 19th November and 3rd December 1887. The Oaks won the first 3-0 and also the return 1-0 on Cogswell & Harrison's own ground. The enthusiasm and commitment of both teams was exemplary.

The two teams for the first match were:
The Oaks: T Hole, S Gill, W Stepehnson, G Browne, W Parker, H Darville, H Jones, A Norris, S Matthews, H Waghorn, J Poole.

C&H Works Team: F Hughes, C White, G Norton, J Walker, T Blake, G Gibson, S Simons, J Collins, T Smallwood, G Dickenson, A Norman.,

A number of the players from both sides were to continue their careers under the various guises of Wealdstone FC.

For over one hundred years, what was thought to be the first 'first team' fixture of the Wealdstone Club was a friendly, a 'preseason' match against Northwood played away from home on October 7th 1899, but the local paper of Friday October 13th 1899 reporting on this first fixture stated:

This match took place on Saturday in fine weather. Wealdstone were playing several new men. Cozens won the toss, and elected to play with the sun on his back, Northwood having the benefit of a slight decline. The 'Stones got possession immediately from the kick off, and Cozens opened the scoring with a fine shot from the extreme right, and S Dear scored a second a few minutes later, from a neat pass from his partner

The game was now very fast, Northwood getting down occasionally, although not allowed to become really dangerous. E Dear next scored goal number three, with a fast shot that the goalkeeper fumbled, and a few minutes later S Dear scored again from a corner from the left. These reverses woke the homesters up, and they attacked, several chances being thrown away by bad shooting, Bellchambers clearing finely on one occasion, however, but the visitors scoring once more, S Dear again doing the needful, the whistle sounded half time. The score; Wealdstone 5 Northwood 0.

Immediately on the re-start the 'Stones got down through Livy, but the homesters now seemed more organised and repulsed them, and each side in turn pressed, but for some smart work by the whole of the forwards, Cozens was enabled to score the sixth goal. Give and take play ensued, Bellchambers bringing off several smart clearances, but at length from a rebound, after hitting the upright, Northwood were enabled to score their only goal, and shortly after the whistle went leaving Wealdstone winners by the score of 6-1.

The Wealdstone forwards played splendidly, as indeed did the whole of the team, seeing that it was partially experimental, they trying new men at inside-left, left back and right half. S Dear and Cozens were the pick of the team, those two scoring five of the goals. Bellchambers was very safe.

Wealdstone; Bellchambers; W Cozens; Johnson; Matthews; Payne; White; H Cozens; Livy; E Dear; S Dear; Hillier."

In the opening paragraph, there is reference to a number of new men being used at inside-left, left back and right half. Therefore some of the players were 'existing' players for the club. There is also a reference to the same colours being used – the same as what?

The references made in Club records and in various handbooks over the years made some links to a number of previous clubs and in the early 1890's a cup-tie against a Tottenham Hotspur nursery team.

An amalgamation with another local team, Harrow Athletic has also been mentioned.

I hope what follows will untangle some of these links and give a clearer indication of the History of Wealdstone Football Club.

THE VERY EARLIEST DAYS OF WEALDSTONE FOOTBALL CLUB

Prior to the arrival in Wealdstone of Cogswell and Harrison in 1887, there appears to have been little football in what was at the time a village with some 6000 occupants. If you read the newspapers of the time the village is often referred to as dirty and smelly and even an unpleasant place should you ever have cause to find yourself there!

Harrow however, just a couple of miles away, had a number of teams at this time. Both Harrow Town Football Club and Harrow Rovers soon became opponents of the works teams shortly after the move.

There were two 'works' teams. One, made up from the manual workers in the company that played as Cogswell and Harrison The second was known as "The Oaks" and this team was made up of clerical staff from the company. "The Oaks" played on fields opposite the factory, near Row's Farm, between Ferndale Terrace and Station Road. The Bridge Schools in Station Road were later built on the site of this farm, although it was not long before the team had moved to a field adjacent to Marlborough Hill.

It may be that as the team owned no ground, they moved around a number of local pitches probably made available by farmers and landowners. They were also known to have played on a pitch adjacent to Nibthwaite Road, on Greenhill Farm. Extracts from the Harrow Map of 1890 show the sites as they would have been at the time, as the village of Wealdstone began to expand.

The earliest mention of a match was a brief report of a match played on 1st October 1887, which resulted in a 1-0 friendly defeat to a team called Grosvenor. More friendly no doubt than the match the following week when The Oaks were soundly beaten by eight goals to nil at Marlborough Hill by the better established and more experienced Harrow Rovers. Possibly the first victory was to come in the November, against the works team of Cogswell and Harrison, again played at Marlborough Hill on Saturday, November 19th, 1887. "The Oaks" held a two goal lead at half-time and added a further goal after the change of ends.

The teams in that fixture were;
"The Oaks"; T. Hole; S. Gill, W. Stephenson, G. Browns, W. Parker, H. M. Darville; H. Jones, A. Norris, S. Matthews, H. Waghorn, J. Poole.
Cogswell and Harrison; F. Hughes; C. White, G. Norton; J. Walker, T. Blake, G. Gibson; S. Simons, J. Collins, T. Smallwood, G. Dickenson, A. Norman.

Mr S Simons, at this time representing the works team, was to contribute to an article headed "Nearly Fifty Years On" in the Harrow Observer published on June 3rd 1938 recounting a player's memories of the club at this time.

Alive and active in supporting the contemporary Wealdstone side, Mr S Simons, it reported was known to have joined *"the old Wealdstone FC when he moved to Harrow in 1877"*, as a 19 year old. As we now know, this actually refers to him joining the Cogswell & Harrison works team, as he is recorded to have played in the two matches against The Oaks. Later on he was, with a number of his team-mates to join both The Oaks and the first Wealdstone FC at the end of the 1880's

Certainly prior to the formation of the two teams from the gun makers, almost all local football at this time seems to have centred around the various 'House Matches' at Harrow School and the exploits of the Old Harrovians – the first local side to play in the FA Cup.

Mr Simons recounted to a local reporter, *"In those days we only had 14 playing members, and it was sometimes very difficult to get a team together. We paid our own subscriptions, for our clothes and everything else and to fulfil an away fixture meant several shillings from our meagre pocket money of those days."*

A return match was played between these two teams on Cogswell and Harrison's ground on December 3rd, 1887, "The Oaks" again being the victors, but this time by the reduced margin of 1-0. Mr H M (Harry) Darville, mentioned in The Oaks team, later became a player for both Harrow Athletic and Wealdstone Athletic and subsequently Wealdstone FC where he also held office as a Club Official.

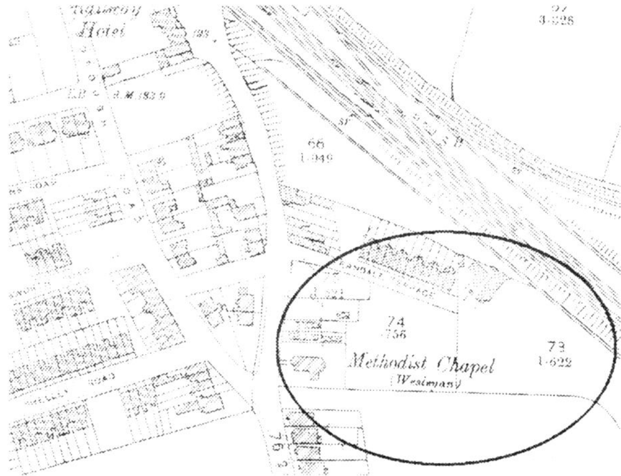

Ferndale Terrace circa 1890, showing the Cogswell and Harrison factory - the large building adjacent to the railway, where a few years later a stray spark from a passing train was to burn the factory down. The field numbered 74 (behind the Wesleyan Chapel) is the most likely site of The Oaks football pitch. The path at the bottom right was later to become Rosslyn Crescent.

On The 24th February 1888 The Oaks Football Club held a concert in the Wealdstone Schoolrooms, a successful event over which Mr E J Lilley presided, and a large attendance enjoyed the numerous performances. Mr E J Lilley was another to figure greatly in the formation of Wealdstone FC.

There are also a number of references towards the end of the 1880's to '*the Wealdstone team*' and these all indicate that as all the players came from the village, The Oaks were considered to be the village representative side.

In April, Mr E J Lilley was again to feature in the local news, but this time because, *On Tuesday morning, Mr E J Lilley was driving through Wealdstone, his horse took fright opposite Unity Villas, and, running over the kerb, threw him out, breaking his leg a few inches above the ankle.* Thankfully the injury was soon set and there was no further damage, which may well have prevented the formation of Wealdstone FC.

On December 8th 1888 the Harrow Gazette carried a match report, and for the first time The Oaks (Wealdstone) FC was recorded as the team name;

Harrow Rovers v The Oaks (Wealdstone) FC

This match was played at Wealdstone on Saturday last, and after a pleasant game, marred only by the bad condition of the ground, The Rovers proved victors by five goals to one. The Oaks won the toss, and The Rovers starting the ball, some fast play ensued, both goal-keepers having to use their hands, Warden however after a good run scored the first goal for the Rovers, Goshawk adding a second soon after. Ends now being changed, the Rovers had the better of the game, and from a series of runs down the wing added three more goals – two by Warden and one by Goshawk.

Just before time The Oaks rallied a little, and their first and only goal was scored by Jones, who played well throughout. S Gill and A Darville also doing good service for the backs.

Teams; Harrow Rovers; H Kent (goal), C Tyler, S Smith (backs), H Woodbridge, A E Dear, W Fletcher (half-backs), P Warden, G E Goshawk (right wing), A J Kay (centre), E Smith, A E Cooke (left wing) The Oaks; J Harding (goal), H Hills, S Gill (backs), A Darville, T Hole, R Branston (half-backs), S Matthews, A Morris (right wing), H Darville (centre), H Jones, W Bentley (left wing). Umpires; Messrs H Gibson and F W Stevens.

By March the following year, 1889, 'The Oaks' were no more, and 'Wealdstone Football Club' had replaced them. The first recorded 'event' of Wealdstone Football Club was another concert, this time held in the Boys School, and again the genial president was Mr E J Lilley.

It has not been possible to locate a report or any details of the first match of the club other than the date and score. The match was played on 5th October 1889 and the result was a six to nil defeat away to Harrow Town FC. This is recorded in the minutes of the AGM of Harrow Town FC in November of the same year.

The following week saw another defeat, this time by two goals to one to another local side, Victoria Hall, who featured in their line up former 'Oaks' players A Darville, R Branston and H Darville all of whom were to join the 'new' Wealdstone Club shortly afterwards

Not only were the players 'entertainers' on the field – the Harrow Gazette, late in November, records two Public performances of The Wealdstone Minstrels. Among those performing, Mr S Gill, Mr H Darville, Mr A Morris, Mr W H Crook and Mr A Darville, all of whom featured in the match report in the same issue. This report also seems to have been the first victory of a club known as Wealdstone FC. The result was a victory over Harrow Colts by three goals to two. Unfortunately, the scorers are not recorded as the match was reported by the Harrow paper, only the 'colts' scorers being listed!

The colts must have been the lesser of the local sides at the time, as in this season, Wealdstone managed to lose to each of the other 'Harrow Clubs', the best performance coming against a Harrow Town side decimated by influenza, with a 2-1 defeat.

The abilities of The Wealdstone Minstrels was to further benefit the club when in the November of 1890, a benefit concert was arranged at The Railway Hotel in Wealdstone. The fundraising was to aid a player, Mr Fred Pearce who had met with a severe accident whilst playing and had not been able to continue his occupation.

A fixture card for the 1890-91 season gives the names of the following officials;
PATRONS; Messrs. J. Lilley, E. Harrison, J. Smithers, R. Blackwell, and F.S. Blackwell;
COMMITTEE; Messrs., G. Horton, J. Poole A. Darville, H. Hills, and W. Crook
TREASURER; Mr· R· Meadows
SECRETARY; Mr. T. A. Dickenson
CAPTAIN; Mr. S. Gill; VICE-CAPTAIN · Mr. S. Simons

The colours were given as white shirts and blue knickers and among that season's opponents were Harrow Town, Southall, Wembley, Greenhill Hall Rovers, St. Albans and Watford Rovers.

On the 21st of January 1891, Wealdstone FC were to visit another new local club for the first time, Harrow Athletic FC, who as part of the Athletic Club had only been formed the previous summer. The athletic club football team was an amalgamation of a number of the local sides who had proved such difficult opponents in the past. Played at Harrow Recreation Ground, the match created a great deal of local interest;

This match drew a great many people to the Recreation Ground on Saturday afternoon last. That it was of particular interest was demonstrated by the fact that it engrossed the attention of nearly everybody on the ground, notwithstanding that a contest was taking place nearby between the Old Harrovians and the Clarence Club.

It says much for Wealdstone that before the match it was freely stated that they would win. The Athletic did not put what was their strongest team into the field but the absentees were so few that practically there was very little to regret by the partisans of the Harrow Club.

Soon after the game started – within a minute or two the Harrovians scored a goal, thanks to Cook, to whom the ball was passed, just in front of the poles. This point was the signal for great cheering, and it must have been felt, especially as the Harrow team were playing against the wind, that an easy victory was in store for the home players. But this was not to be.

The Wealdstone team contained some very smart men who soon put a very different aspect upon the game. Although they did not score in the first half, they made some very good attempts to do so, and the fact that they did not succeed was due to the splendid keeping of Mr MacMillan. This gentleman has not been long in Harrow, and consequently little was known of him on the ground.

There was indeed a little smiling to see such an elderly goalkeeper, but presently it began to be whispered that 'he was an old International' and had played for Wales against England and Scotland, and then amusement gave way to respect.

There can be no doubt that Mr MacMillan warded off defeat for his side, as again and again the ball came straight to him, and each time he capably dealt with it.

In the second half of the game, the ball did pass him, from a kick by P Smith, but this was hardly to be wondered at, for the scuffle took place very close to the goal, and when he tried to stop the ball, he slipped. This goal was scored towards the end of the game, and made both sides equal.

As no point was scored by either side afterwards, the game ended in a draw, which appeared to everyone on the grounds very satisfactory. One unpleasant incident only marred the contest. An onlooker had the bad taste to call a Wealdstone player 'a scoundrel' for an alleged foul, and narrowly escaped a thrashing, which would not have been undeserved. The Wealdstonians were proud, and rightly so, of the result.

Wealdstone continued to progress as a club through the early 1890's playing friendly matches, home and away against a number of local clubs. Some church based, such as both the Watford and Wealdstone Mission clubs, some by Schools (Aldenham, Harrow) some by area (Stanville, Stanmore) and others against 'works' teams such as Soho (Crosse & Blackwell's) such as the following match on 29th October 1892, recorded by the Harrow Gazette;

This match was played on the Wealdstone ground on Saturday last, Darville winning the toss, took advantage of a slight breeze, and at 3;35 Soho started the ball, which was at once taken down by the 'Stones left, and within a minute of the kick-off, Smith, from a centre by Simons, had put the ball through.

On restarting, the left was again conspicuous and Bentley, gaining possession, gave a well-timed pass to Norris and he scored number two for Wealdstone. Two goals within three minutes was rather sharp work, but the Wealdstone forwards kept the pace up, continually having shots at goal, but the ball was either saved or sent behind.

A corner kick for Wealdstone was well placed by Simons, but the ball was cleared and 'hands' relieved Soho for a time. Lea next found an opening, and he made the best possible use of it, scoring the third goal, which was quickly followed by a fourth from Smith, a splendid screw shot from almost off the line.

A miss-kick by Pearce let in the Soho forwards, and a goal seemed certain, but the ball was sent outside the post. Midfield play followed for a short time, and then Bentley made the score five love.

The Soho custodian now had an anxious time, several corners being taken, but without any further result. Some tricky play by the Wealdstone forwards resulted in a penalty kick, but, to the astonishment of all, Darville lifted the ball over the bar and half-time soon arrived.

The second half was rather more even, but Wealdstone always held the upper hand. Two more goals were added (Norris and Poole), and a pleasant game resulted in a win for them by seven to nil. Their forwards were in fine form and combined much better than their opponents, while the defence was always there when wanted. Coleman and Blackwell played well for Soho.

Wealdstone; W Bates (goal), H Darville and J Pearce (backs), G Poole, G Lea and J Lavender (half-backs), P H Smith, J Poole (right), A F Norris (centre), S Simons and W Bentley (left).

I wonder if the Mr Blackwell that played so well for the Soho team was a member of the family that founded and owned the business

A little later, in February 1893, another match with Harrow Athletic took place, but the atmosphere was somewhat different, as the report states

We regret that the match was played with so much feeling, as it marred what should have been a friendly match. The partisans of Harrow complaining strongly of the rough play of their opponents. As an impartial eye-witness of the game, much of the grumbling was uncalled for, certainly the Harrow men fell over like nine pins in the early part of the game ......

The game ended in favour of Harrow by two goals to nil and we cannot help but hope that the next time these two sides meet it will be in a far more friendly spirit, in order to prevent the loss of what should be an ever increasingly interesting game.

Judging by the report, the local rivalry between the main Harrow club and Wealdstone FC seems to date back to at least 1893. This was the season that also saw the first success in the Middlesex Junior Cup. In the Quarter-final, played in late February, Wealdstone were drawn away to Uxbridge, the match resulting in a draw. The following week, the replay was played at Wealdstone in front of five hundred people;

.............in front of a large crowd restrained by a rope around the pitch. A pleasing situation as with such a large number present an inconvenient state of things must have existed.

Wealdstone won the match by 2-0. The first goal by a method since outlawed by the rules;

...........The Reds then broke away, but Isabell relieved. Bentley and Stevens changed places and immediately after Smith made a good run and shot. Norwood only partially cleared, and Bentley rushing up sent man and ball through, amidst loud cheering..........

The Uxbridge team had lost a player to injury very early on and the result became a foregone conclusion, albeit the Wealdstone team squandered many scoring chances. The report did judge the effectiveness of the Uxbridge forwards, recording that the Wealdstone custodian was only called upon three times in the entire game to make saves.

The semi-final was played on Saturday the 18th March 1893, was played at Southall. The match had been scheduled for a week earlier but no suitable pitch could be found. The delay had robbed Wealdstone of two of their better half-backs, Bentley and Isabell, but it had no effect as Wealdstone ran out winners against Old Argyle by 4 goals to 2, despite losing 2-1 at the interval. The victory meant Wealdstone were to take their place in the Middlesex Junior Cup Final, on April 8th. The first final achieved by the club, it was recorded by the Harrow and Wealdstone Press;

Middlesex Junior Cup Final - Saturday 8th April 1893 - Wealdstone FC versus Robin Hood FC

Saturday was a most unfortunate day for Wealdstone, for having made a brilliant career all through the courses of the Middlesex Junior Cup, they suffered an ignominious defeat in the final.

It was a sad blow to the local football enthusiasts, for they really believed the "'Stones" were the best team. Outsiders thought the same, and perhaps the result would have been different had Robin Hood competed with the original 'Stones, instead of 'The Cripples'.

About half the members of the Wealdstone team were suffering more or less; one was recovering from influenza, others had severe colds, and not a few were only resuming their former gate after the contest with the Uxbridge reserves.

This was the kind of team that left Wealdstone for Tottenham on Saturday to play the final with the smart men of the Robin Hood.

Winning the toss, Darville decided to kick up hill and against the wind, perhaps not too wise a selection, for the Robin Hood, with this advantage, at once began to press 'Stones severely.

Fortunately, Hills, the goalkeeper was in good form, and kept out some hot shots. the 'Stones defended very well in the first half, but did not do much attacking.

The left wing (Simons and Stevens) made some pretty passing runs at times, but they did not come to anything, as either the ball was centred and the backs kicked it away, or it was forced outside.

Smith worked very hard, but he was too well looked after to get dangerous, and could not get any of his runs in. It was close on half-time before any scoring was done. Gilderson then doing the trick for "The Robins".

It was thought that the 'Stones had a good chance, playing downhill, but the wind had turned round about half time, and was against them again.

The only men who played anything like football were Bentley, Hills and Lea, Bentley especially playing well; the fact is, the majority were not in a condition to play such an important match.

Gilderson added a second goal from a good run, and soon after a third was put past Hills, who had no chance with either. The Cripples had to retire without scoring a goal, whilst Robin Hood came off victorious with three.

The Wealdstone team; W Hills (goal), H M Darville (capt.) and F Pearce (backs), G Lea, E Isabell and W Bentley (half-backs), P H Smith, A J Norris, D Justice, A H Stevens and S Simons, (forwards)

The Harrow Gazette took a slightly different view,

This final tie was decided at Northumberland Park, Tottenham in the presence of about 1000 spectators.

The Robins started the ball about a quarter past four, and at once attacked in grand style, and on several occasions looked like scoring.

The 'Stones' defence was splendid for some time, but the others, continuing to press, had the satisfaction of a goal from a kick by Gilderson. Give and take play ensued, but neither side further scored up to half time.

In the second half the Robins had the best of play, scoring two more goals, and at the close of the match proved the winners by three goals to nil.

The Wealdstone team was as follows; H Hills (goal), H W Darville (captain) and F Pearce (backs), G Lea, E Isabell and W Bentley (half-backs), P H Smith and A Norris (right wing), D Justice (centre), A H Stevens and S Simons (left wing).

Though beaten, the 'Stones may well be proud of their record in such an early stage of their existence, and should look forward to renewed and greater successes next year.

Wealdstone had indeed done well as Robin Hood F.C. was at the time a nursery club of Tottenham Hotspur. It is also recorded

Wealdstone Football Club 1893 Middlesex Junior Cup Finalists
Back; M Isabel, A Darville, F Pearce, E Stevens, Middle; A Norris, H Darville (capt.) P Smith Front; J Poole, G Poole, T Dickenson, W Bentley, S Simons (Second from the right of the bowler-hatted officials behind the team is Mr Harry Bentley, licensee of The Queens Arms, Wealdstone, later to become changing rooms for the club).

that in this match the Wealdstone players wore distinguishing red sashes, as both teams were playing in white shirts.

It had been a good season. The club had played 19 matches of which there were twelve wins and four draws, scoring 50 goals and conceding only 19, of which six were conceded in the cup competition. The 'end of season review' announced that because of the considerable interest generated in the club, the committee hoped new players would be attracted as the club wanted to run a reserve team for the following season. An open meeting was held in The Railway Hotel where anyone interested was asked to attend. The club also announced plans to hold a concert at the Wealdstone Public Hall in May to raise funds for the club. The article closed with the following paragraph;

Lastly, but not least, the club now take this opportunity of thanking their numerous supporters for their attendance at both home and 'foreign' matches. One might go for miles round before they would come across a junior club with so many staunch supporters as Wealdstone.

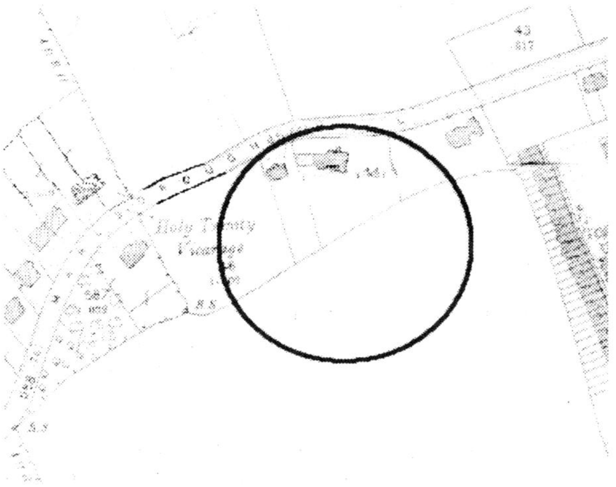

Marlborough Hill from around 1890. To the right, the houses are in Milton Road. The majority of the buildings shown on Marlborough Hill are obviously houses. The small building in the 'strip of land' may well have been the changing rooms. (Later replaced by Torver Road and Rutland Road)

Details of the 1893-94 season show that the club's ground was at Greenhill, the dressing rooms being at the "Havelock Arms" - now the site of Burger King. The opening match was a 0-0 draw against Watford Church Institute and was unremarkable, although very even, but for one incident;

A penalty kick was given against the 'Stones which occurred in this way;

The majority of the 'Stones team appealed for 'hands', but the player, having his back to the referee, that gentleman was not in a position to see the infringement, consequently the free kick was not given. Hughes however, seeing it was such a clear case of hands, without waiting for the referee's decision, foolishly picked the ball up to throw it to where the foul had taken place.

The Institute then themselves appealed for a penalty, which was allowed.

Hills the goalkeeper, came six yards out of his goal, but to the surprise of all, Slaughter sent the ball slowly rolling past the posts............

The club had been successful in attracting enough new players to run a second team. The published fixture list showed that from September 30th 1893 to the 31st of March 1894, Cup-ties permitting, there would be a Wealdstone team 'at home' every Saturday

There were a number of new opponents, selected to take on the 'Reserve' side, from Otterleigh (Stanmore), and Hollands (Kensal Rise), a number of the Watford area sides, West Herts reserves and Watford Ramblers included, and also second team fixtures against local clubs, Wealdstone Mission and Harrow Athletic reserves

In the December of 1893, on the 23rd another scheduled 'first team' match was played between Harrow Athletic and Wealdstone, and again the match caused much local interest. This match was played on The Recreation Ground and drew the largest crowd of the season, a fact not to be wondered at when the rivalry of the two teams is considered. The ground unfortunately was in a very bad state and after the play was transformed into a miniature bog.

When the men lined up it was seen that Harrow were without the services of Smith and Rosevere whilst Wealdstone were starting with ten men As soon as the game commenced the supporters of each side began the usual shouting, and never ceased until the teams had left the field.

Harrow took the ball into the Wealdstone half and after some time Kavanagh shot over the bar. Soon after the Athletics obtained a corner, but the backs cleared and the Harrow defence was tried. Though the eleventh man had turned up, only for a few minutes did play stay in the Harrow end, as Lee and Kavanagh made a fine run, the former putting the ball just past the post.

Harrow pressed, Hunt, Creuse and Kavanagh all taking shots, but could not beat Hills, who defended his goal in fine style. From a free kick for hands, Page put the ball through but as no one else had touched it this was fruitless. After a run by Hunt, Kavanagh sent the ball between the posts but off side neutralised the point.

Wealdstone then got away, but Woodbridge stopped the rush and sent well forward. Pearce miss kicked and let in Kinlock who was making for goal with no one to stop him, when Darville brought him down with a deliberate foul.

No goals had been scored by half time, and as the weather was dull no time was lost in crossing over. In the second half Wealdstone were completely penned in, the forwards being unable to get past the Harrow halves until the game was nearly finished.

A quarter of an hour before time, Hunt, with a flying shot, scored the only goal of the match and Harrow were victorious by one goal to nil. The Athletic forwards were the heaviest set that had appeared this season and this contributed largely to their success.

The half-backs played very well, and Kay spoilt those smart runs for which Smith is noted nearly every time. Fletcher only handled the ball once.

Wealdstone were unfortunate in having to play on such a heavy ground, as they are not as used to it like the Athletics and consequently long before time they were all 'pumped out'. Hills was the best man in the team and had the others paid as much attention to the game as he did, Wealdstone might have stood a better chance.

Harrow Athletic; goal; Fletcher, backs; Jones and Woodbridge, half-backs; Kay, Page and Salt, forwards; Hunt, Kinlock, Creuse, Lee and Kavanagh.

Wealdstone; goal; Hills, backs; Darville and Pearce, half-backs; Dove, Burcham, A Doctor, forwards; Simons, Bentley, Williamson, Stevens and Smith.

The Evening News and Post commented in early December that;

'The Wealdstone FC is stronger this season, and is running a second team. They have played only three matches at home and have not yet suffered defeat. Their record is Played 8, matches won 6 drawn 2, goals for 23 against 4.

The Wealdstone Reserves, by defeating Harrow Athletic Reserves, have taken their record to played 8 won 6, lost 2, goals for 18, against 11.

There was also a comment on biased reporting from a Watford paper after the previous week's match, away at Rickmansworth;

A Watford contemporary had the following announcement last week; "The Institute, without Heath (who was playing for the reserves) and Burr, managed to defeat Wealdstone by two goals to nil."

Might I ask when this happened? Certainly not this season. Perhaps the scribe has been doing a Rip Van Winkle. Wealdstone as yet preserves an unbroken record. the 'Stones have never been able to spell defeat this season so far.

The Rickmansworth team are sore over their defeat, and for the want of some more tangible excuses, have induced a Watford periodical to publish not only an unfair but an absolutely untrue account of the match. Wealdstone treats the matter with silent contempt.

The March of 1894 also saw the first fixture played by Wealdstone FC against The Wealdstone Mission, also founded by Mr Edgar Harrison of Cogswell and Harrison.

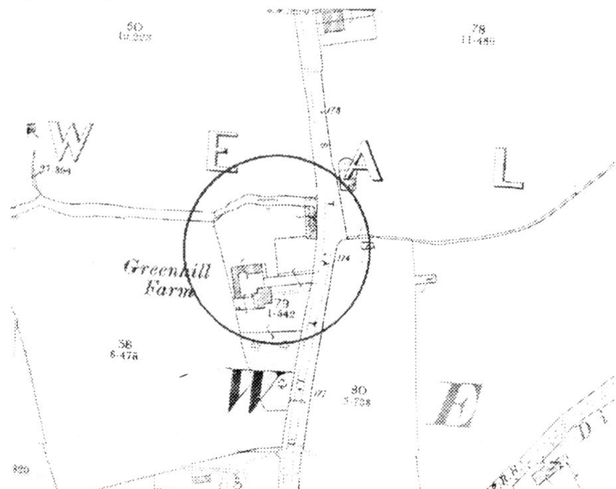

Greenhill Farm which was to become the third home, and the first where a club called Wealdstone FC was to have played 'adjacent to what is now Nibthwaite Road. This was the path going from the centre of the map to the left, eventually being made up into Nibthwaite Road as it is today.

Mentioned previously, the article by Mr S Simons, published in 1938 recounted his memories as a player at this time. Below the photograph of the Wealdstone FC team of 1893 it mentioned that seven members of the team shown were at the time still alive and active in supporting the then present Wealdstone side. It is also known and confirmed in the article, that in 1894/5 Wealdstone and Harrow Athletic amalgamated to form a new club, and according to the article, this club continued until the formation of the 'new' Wealdstone Football Club in 1899, although we now know that this is not the case.

He remembered;

There was one instance of a player's keenness, which is hard to beat - we had a fixture at Hayes and on this particular occasion we started off in our horse-break without one of our best players.

We all expected to have to play a man short but to our surprise the missing player arrived at the ground about five minutes after we all did. He had run and walked cross-country all the way from Harrow to Hayes, and then played as good a game as usual!

Although we cannot be certain, it seems likely that this match was played on November 11th, 1893, Wealdstone beating Hayes on their own ground in the second round of the Middlesex Junior Cup before 200 spectators. The score was 5-0, all the goals being scored in the second half.

The third round of this competition was played at Wealdstone on January 13th, 1894, when Uxbridge Reserves won 2-1 It is recorded that C. Ferry, a Wealdstone player, broke a leg in this match

Another comment on the foundation of the club came a year or so earlier on the 5th of February 1937. The Harrow Observer published and article based on a letter from Mr. Percy Smith headed " Wealdstone 45 years ago" which puts the date at 1891 or 1892. He wrote,

"As I sit on Saturday afternoons at Lower Mead, Station Road, watching the admirable football now provided by the Wealdstone Football Club, I often compare the game as it is now played with the conditions some 45 years ago, when 15 of us first started the club.

We used to play on a field at the end of Hindes Road, no goal nets, no covered or uncovered stands and no gates - free to all and sundry - our colours where Black and White stripes, and well do I remember going with others to Gamages to purchase the shirts.

Meetings were held at The Railway Hotel, by the bridge.

There were no leagues then, and our principal matches apart from the Middlesex competition were against surrounding villages and towns, such as Stanmore, Rickmansworth, Uxbridge, Watford, City business houses such as Clarence (Maples) Vulcan (Schoolbreds), Grove House (Spencer Turner) - but the greatest event was meeting our neighbours, Harrow Athletic, whom we played twice every season, once on the 'Rec' and once at home.

Our players consisted of Hills, goal, Isabel and Pearce (backs), Harry Darville, (Captain and a splendid athlete), Walter Bentley and Walter Cook (half-backs), Simons (Harrow bowler) and Stevens (right wing), Arthur Darville (centre) Norris and myself

(wing), other members were Jack Williamson, Dickenson, Joe Lavender, Perry, etc."

Even in these very early days Wealdstone had an 'away' following, as the letter continues;

"I should like to record that the considerable enthusiasm our matches aroused amongst the villagers, and in away matches horse drawn charabancs and other vehicles (no motors then) full of supporters, used to accompany the team, every one of whom was born and lived in Greenhill and Wealdstone"

Mr. Smith had some interesting comments to make on the standard of play those days, and he made comparisons with the football of the late 1930's.

"Football nowadays to me seems far more skilful and faster." he writes, "whereas in the early days it was more a question of stamina and brawn. What are now called fouls were laughed at then; in fact, a club's greatest asset was a centre forward renowned not for skill but strength, who could bundle the opponents' goalkeeper through the goal whenever the ball was in its vicinity - it was then quite legitimate.

Nearly all the players in those days wore caps. I remember Harry Darville (our captain) used to wear a Rugby Cap with a tassel, and how proud he was of it – by this, I suppose we used to do very little heading" "The clubs greatest feat was getting into the final of the Middlesex Junior Cup, played at Northumberland Park, Tottenham.

Our opponents were a team called Robin Hood, a Tottenham team who beat us 3-1. I remember the Daily Chronicle in referring to the game stating how unfair it was that we should have to play in what was almost our opponents' home ground, many of the players being more or less Spurs reserve team, but of course it was purely a question of gate.

Personally, I have cause to remember the match, as I was laid up for several weeks afterwards as a result of a kick in the groin, which thus ended my football career".

It is certain that this club was a forerunner of the present side and there is a defined link to the present club but on September 8th 1894, this 'early' Wealdstone FC were to amalgamate with Harrow Athletic.

The local paper recorded this decision and added the expectation that it would greatly strengthen the Athletic Club which would now run three teams for the forthcoming season. The comment continued that with a good list of fixtures it was expected that the forthcoming season would be even more successful than the last.

The following week's paper carried the announcement of the first fixture to be played by the 'combined' Harrow Athletic FC, a gentleman's match between two teams representing Mr C Page and Mr G E Kay, both members of the club. Between them, the two teams included six players from the Wealdstone side of 1893. This was followed a week later by the first competitive friendly against Bowes Park, with five of the Wealdstone side appearing in the match and another, Mr S Simons no less, featuring as referee!

The Harrow Athletic side won by three goals to nil, the goals scored by Hartley (2) and Fisk, but the comment locally was that; *although it is early to judge, a number of the Athletic players will have to improve if they are to feature regularly in the starting line up this season.*

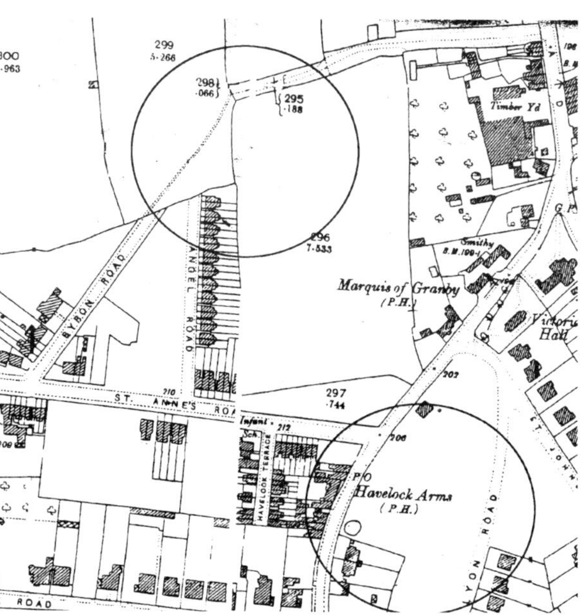

On the corner of Angel Road and what is now Welldon Crescent, the 1893 home of Wealdstone FC. At this time though, Welldon Crescent was no more than a track, and Angel Road and Byron Road were also only partially made up.

At the end of March 1895, this combined side was to be drawn against the 2nd Scots Guards in a semi-final tie of the Middlesex Senior Cup. Against both the team and the "Up Guards and at 'em" battle cry of their supporters Harrow Athletic were not expected to fair well.

The Harrow Gazette recorded;

This was the cry which many supporters of the Guards used on Saturday last in an attempt to spur their team on to victory, and while the Guards responded to the cry again and again, they found that in this waterloo of football, they were not dealing with men of Napoleonic calibre, but with footmen worthy of their steel...........

The report goes on to effuse on the capabilities of the Athletic team on that day, in front of a crowd of 2000 people, as the result was to be a 0-0 draw, the comment from the supporters at the Southall ground where the match was played was a general opinion that it had been the best match ever played on the ground.

The team that day was Page, Woodbridge, Smith, Barker, Darville, Carter, Hunt, Stogden, Parker, Kavanagh, Bosworth-Smith.

The match was the zenith of the amalgamation between Harrow Athletic and Wealdstone FC as the following week, the replay was lost by a margin of ten goals to one. Another week on, the 'Athletic lost in the final of the West Middlesex Cup to the 8th Hussars.

On April 25th 1895, a meeting was held at The Railway Hotel, Wealdstone, at which the formation of Wealdstone Athletic was confirmed. The meeting was recorded in The Wealdstone, Harrow and Wembley Observer, which noted that the Officers of the new Athletic Club were to include Mr J E Lilley, J Poole, Russell Bradberry, C Hills, H Hills, J Parker and A Norris, all previously members of the Harrow Athletic Club and a number formerly members of Wealdstone FC.

The Harrow Athletic team of 1894 that amalgamated with Wealdstone FC
Back; G E Kay, C E Cater, H Woodbridge, J H Carew-Hunt, H Hills, W Bentley
Front; W E Kavanagh, J E Page, S H Smith (capt.), H M Darville, E A A Cooke

The Railway Hotel was to become the headquarters of the club, and Wealdstone Athletic FC was formed as part of this new club. The minutes of the following meeting informed the club that: *Mr Durrant's offer of a field at £12 0s 0d per annum was accepted, Mr J E Lilley was also elected President and a number of well known local people were to be asked to act as Vice-Presidents. Mr J W Clench was elected Secretary with Mr C Rowley as his assistant.*

Arrangements were made for the coming season, and a good team it is expected will be forthcoming.

The Harrow Athletic Club were also to continue and a number of the former Wealdstone players did (at least initially) remain with Harrow Athletic for the forthcoming season. (The Harrow Athletic Club was to run up to and beyond the Second World War as a local Hockey Club and Cricket Club as well as a football team.)

This club also became the first local side to win a match against 'senior' opposition, when in October of 1895, Harrow Athletic beat a Tottenham Hotspur side by three goals to one (a Barker hat trick), although the Tottenham side was not their strongest owing to their playing an FA Cup-tie on the same day.

The Wealdstone Athletic Club was not well starred from the beginning – a section in the local paper, in a note from 'referee' expressed hope that the club would be a strong one and the remaining players who had previously left to join Harrow Athletic would return 'to play in their own country'. His comment went on: *to relish the return of the stirring local derby matches against Harrow Athletic that had been played two years previously at Greenhill - I for one shall be heartily glad to hear the old cry again 'Play up 'Stones'.*

The first match of this new club was against Eagle Wanderers at the end of September.

The first match of the Wealdstone Athletic Club was played on their ground at Wealdstone on Saturday last. The game was started at 4:30pm when the team lined up as follows;

A Gibson, goal, F Little and Gill, backs, halves; W Beckley, G Smith and Cooper, forwards; A Beckley, G Wells, W Meadows, Poole and A N Other.

The Wanderers kicked off but were immediately robbed of the ball by Smith, and the Wealdstone forwards, by very pretty play, took the sphere up to the Wanderers goal but missed the sticks by a few inches.

The Wanderers got possession and had a shy at the Wealdstone fortress, but their centre shot wide. The Wealdstone team again took up the running and had another turn at the Wanderers goal, but nothing came of it. Meadows getting possession took the ball up, but his shot was spoiled by the Wanderers left back.

The Wanderers then took the ball up on the right and scored their first goal by a rattling shot. This seemed to wake them up, for on the leather being again started, the Wanderers obtained possession and by making straight up, they scored their second goal from a bully. Wealdstone now had hard luck in not scoring they having a number of shots that missed by inches only. Meadows putting in a beauty, which struck the bar and bounced over.

The pace had been too fast for Wealdstone and the Wanderers now had the best of play. Working the ball up, they secured another goal. This put the Wealdstone men on their mettle and they gave the Wanderers custodian a warm time and they succeeded in placing the first goal to their credit. (The scorer is unknown).

At half time the score was 3 to 1. On resuming, the game was very even, the ball travelling from one end to the other. the 'Stones had hard luck in not scoring several times, and the game eventually resulted in a win for the Wanderers by four goals to one.

A number of players were to join the club around this time in an effort to strengthen the side, but in the early part of the season, little was to change as defeat followed defeat with only occasional breaks in between.

There were also a number of problems with the club as a whole, indeed, a report from early November for a match against Wembley states that *The home men turned up as advertised (a splendid performance for the 'Stones to begin with)....*and this was not the only occasion, as the following week, true to form Wealdstone could only field nine men against Stanmore.

In fact it was not until late in November that the fortunes changed at all, when two brothers joined the club. H and W Cozens were certainly to improve the fortunes of Wealdstone Athletic and both were to remain involved in the club up until the fixture with Northwood in 1899 and beyond. These two also inspired a rare win against Bushey by two goals to nil at the end of November.

The following April saw a Committee Meeting of the club. A report on the evenings events stated that: *..owing to the condition of the ground, the football matches had not been as successful as expected. In fact several of the better players refused to take part in the matches in consequence of the amount of water between the goal posts. The final matches had had to be played on an adjoining field.*

Thus began the demise for the second time of a forerunner of Wealdstone FC as the following season sees no records of the club having played, nor do they feature in the fixture lists of the other local sides.

There are reports however of a new side, Wealdstone Rovers which by nature of its members seem to have been formed from the Athletic. The Wealdstone Rovers side for their first match in September featured H and W Cozens, Gibson, Beckley, Poole and Livy all of whom were members of the Athletic team of the previous season, indeed four had been on the committee.

This first match also showed a far better turn of fortune as it resulted in a win by five goals to nil for the Rovers. This was the first season for League football in Harrow with Harrow Athletic joining the London League. They secured their first League win in their first match, beating Clapton Clifton in front of 650 people.

Wealdstone Rovers also played matches against Harrow Athletic and 'F Little's XI'. He was a member of the Harrow Athletic club with some connection to other local sides. As no formal fixtures had been arranged, two matches were played at Easter and Christmas 1896. The first of these seems to have passed off without incident resulting in a 1-1 draw, but the second match brought the following comment from 'referee';

I am very glad to say that scenes such as those witnessed on Christmas Day are a very rare occurrence in this district and it is well for the popularity of the game that it is so.

The proceedings of Christmas Day involved the conduct of supporters towards the referee and I must say at once that the offenders (and I am very sorry to say it) hailed from the Wealdstone district.

A match was played between an eleven got up by Mr F Little and the Wealdstone Rovers. I cannot give the Rovers team but I must confess at times they played some smart football, and did fairly well against the strong combination opposed to them.

A great deal of feeling was exhibited during the game and some of the decisions of the referee were received very badly by the 'Stones' supporters.

An appeal for hands was given against the Rovers and the whistle was blown, but the players would not or did not hear, and when the ball had been out of play the referee ordered it back to where the infringement took place.

This action (which I consider quite proper) being received with a loud outburst of hooting from a certain section of the spectators, these idiotic yells being backed up by language of the most filthy description and threats of personal violence.

I am very sorry for the Rovers team, who in no way were led by the utterances of their supporters. They deserve better support than that accorded them by the rabble on Christmas Day.

Wealdstone Juniors continued through the following season, but October 1897 also saw the formation of another local side in the village of Wealdstone, Wealdstone Wanderers FC, who played friendly matches throughout the season.

A number of their players were drawn from the other local sides and it seems that they may have caused the Wealdstone Rovers side to stop playing towards the end of 1897.

The results that have been found seem to show that up to October / November 1897 Wealdstone Rovers played fairly regularly but from then on, only the Wealdstone Wanderers matches appear to have been recorded.

One match played at the end of January 1898 was between Wealdstone Wanderers and Wealdstone Juniors;

A match between these two newly formed clubs was played on the latter's ground on Saturday last, and resulted in a win for the Wanderers by three goals to nil.

Armstrong having beaten Bellchambers in the spin of a coin, G Norman set the ball rolling at 3:15pm. Dear getting away was soon brought up by Hayes. The Juniors soon settled down, and the way they made matters hum around the Wanderers' goal it seemed as if they were going to win easily, but owing to the backs, and Brown at centre half being in fine form, they rarely got to the goalkeeper.

At least Dear getting away well, passing out to Norman, that player, just as he was getting away, was pulled up for offside.

The Wanderers now they had settled down fairly monopolised all the play, Smither saving well from all the forwards.

At last, Dear getting away well and passing to Norman left that player with an open goal, but owing to the ground being very slippery and heavy, he was unable to get his footing, and Smither, rushing out saved what seemed to be a certain goal.

From now until half time, the play slowed down a bit. The juniors, though playing up better were never allowed to become dangerous, their forwards rarely passing the backs who were playing a fine game.

Bellchambers broke up the attacks time after time with splendid kicks, very often sending half the length of the field, while Dear and Booker, well fed by the other forwards, were very conspicuous on the right, Smither saving in grand style time after time.

The whistle blew half time with the score sheet blank. From the re-start the Juniors at once got away only to find Brown impassable, who, with fine tackling and splendid kicking was playing a fine game, and sending on to Booker, that player racing away forced a corner which was cleared by the Juniors, who were now for the most part on the defensive.

Corner after corner was taken by Dear, but the Wanderers, try as they would could not score until Dear getting right away centred and had the satisfaction of seeing H Norman place the ball between the uprights.

From the kick off, spurred by this success the Wanderers at once went away, Barratt having hard lines in not scoring, while shortly after Smither saved well from Dear and Booker. From a goal kick the Juniors tried to get away, but were well stopped by Brown and Bellchambers.

At last Dear, receiving the ball some 30 yards from goal and dribbling past four opponents sent in a lovely cross-shot, giving Smither no possible chance, and succeeded in scoring number 2.

From now the Juniors were fairly beaten, but good play from the backs prevented them from scoring. Later a corner was well placed from Dear and H Norman getting his head to it, succeeded in scoring number 3.

Wealdstone Wanderers; A House, W Bellchambers, W Perry, T Butland, H Brown, J Butland, T Booker, E Dear, G Norman, H Barratt, H Norman.

Wealdstone Juniors; Smither, Matthews, Thompson, Leadale, Hayes, Baldwin, James, Sherlock, White, Hillier, Armstrong

Looking with hindsight at the line-ups above, the connections with Wealdstone FC are obvious as the majority of the players in the match were to be part of the next few years of Wealdstone FC.

THE FIRST LEAGUE SEASON

At the end of the season, Wealdstone Juniors changed their name to Wealdstone Albion FC and became founder members of the Willesden and District League Division II, where they were expected to compete with the Wealdstone Wanderers FC.

The Wanderers side never joined the league though, although they played a match against the Albion at the beginning of September, winning by 8–0. (There is little mention of the team for the remainder of the season though and as the season progressed, players from the Wanderers began to appear in the Albion line up).

The Harrow Observer reported on the prospects of two local sides, Messrs Moffat, Hillier, Mathews, White and Woodward prominent for The Albion who were to play at Marlborough Hill, and The Wanderers, to play at Hindes Road, featured E Dear, W Bellchambers, W Perry and G & H Norman all of whom later becoming players of Wealdstone FC.

As the season progressed a number of other local players were encouraged to join both sides, and of these, the Welch brothers, the Cozens brothers and Royce, Dymock, Kirby, Baldwin and Kay were to feature for Wealdstone FC.

For the 1899 – 1900 season, Wealdstone Albion FC and the remnants of Wealdstone Wanderers and Wealdstone Rovers amalgamated into one and Wealdstone FC as we know it today was formed. The reference to 'new players' mentioned above, by inference indicated that some of the players had played for the club before, and it seems that this was a reference to the previous guises, most recently Wealdstone Albion FC.

The date given previously as the foundation of the present club, certainly commemorates the first season of a new "Wealdstone FC", but the club had been in existence in some form for the previous twelve seasons, and had already been playing League football for one season in the Willesden and District League Division II.

A common factor throughout the changes was the presence of a number of the Officials and players from the previous seasons and players from the various 'former clubs', including Edgar Harrison and J E Lilley, the later having been President or Chairman under numerous previous identities.

The friendly match against Northwood on October 7th 1899 was still fixture for a new club albeit Wealdstone had been in existence for a number of years, as a newspaper report from late August welcomed the formation of the new Northwood team, their first fixture being a defeat by 4-0 to Amersham the week previous. An earlier Northwood club, a rival of the original Wealdstone FC, had folded some years earlier.

Aside from the first team of the new Wealdstone club, there were sufficient players interested and involved to immediately form a reserve team, and on the day that the first team travelled to Northwood, the reserves took part in a match against Queens Park Olympic. Again, the local paper reports;

This one sided match was played at West End Lane, on Saturday, and resulted in an easy victory for the visitors by 12 goals to nil. The first half of the game was very even, the visitors scoring twice, but on changing ends the latter had matters all their own way, putting on ten more.

The Wealdstone team was represented by; Farnborough, goal; Dymock and W Welch, backs; H Welch, Keetch and W Welch, half-backs; Moffat, Key, Royce, Baldwin and Kirby, forwards."

This was thought to be the first match for the reformed reserve team as well but further information has since come to light, which records a match played by the reserves the previous week against a team called White Feather, in Willesden.

There is no record of the match report and the result is unknown, but the team is recorded as follows;

Farnborough, goal; Hawkins and Dymock, backs; Burfitt, Snelling and H Welch, half-backs; Key, Merridew, Royce, Baldwin and W Welch, forwards; reserves; Almond and Buckley

In the first three matches, first and reserve team, of the 'new' Wealdstone FC, thirty players were used. Of these seventeen had played the previous year for Wealdstone Albion, five had represented the Wanderers and three more, Wealdstone Rovers. The remaining five were 'new' players to the club.

As the club as we know it today started its first League season as Wealdstone FC, the Wealdstone Mission team was still in existence. It had its meeting place in a corrugated iron building on a site at the comer of Rosslyn Crescent, near the Cogswell and Harrison gun factory in Ferndale Terrace, and played on the ground once occupied by The Oaks FC. Edgar Harrison also took a keen interest in the work of the Wealdstone Mission until the Mission building was demolished in 1904 when the new Wesleyan Methodist Church was built in Locket Road. At this time the members of the Wealdstone Mission FC joined the present Wealdstone F.C. and another local side that was later to play a part in the clubs history, Wealdstone Church Athletic FC.

There are grounds then to re-establish the foundation of the club as early as 1887 with the inception of The Oaks. This club became Wealdstone FC in 1889, although it was to merge with Harrow Athletic (1894) and one year later re-form as Wealdstone Athletic (1895), the subsequent formations and amalgamations and incorporations of Wealdstone Rovers (1896-1898), Wealdstone Wanderers (1897-1899) and Wealdstone Juniors (1897) were all instrumental in the first league season as Wealdstone Albion (1898) and then finally Wealdstone FC (1899).

FINALLY, WEALDSTONE FC

The Wealdstone FC of 1899–1900 was a team from a village with a population of no more than 6,500 and far smaller than either Harrow or Wealdstone are 100 years further on.

Local solicitor and Club President, Mr J E Lilley supplied the new home ground. He allowed the club to use fields situated where a map today shows Marlborough Hill and Headstone Drive.

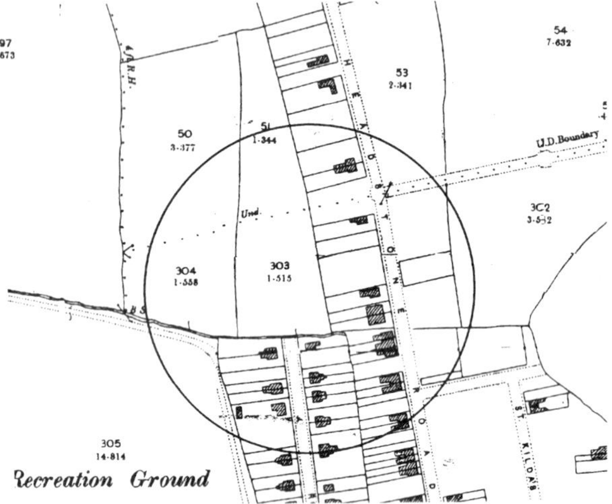

The map of the time showed Headstone Road, running from top to bottom (later known as Harrow View) and the track that was Marlborough Hill that finished at the edge of the fields owned by the club's benefactor.

Mr W T Bellchambers was the club Chairman and Mr T Matthews held the joint post of Secretary and Treasurer.

Dressing Room facilities were at The Queens Arms in Wealdstone by invitation of the landlord, and those players detailed in the match reports above, playing in Black and White Hoops in the Willesden and District League Division II at least laid the foundations of the present club.

One week after the friendly win at Northwood, Wealdstone were in action again, against opponents from their league, albeit in a friendly. Roundwood Swifts, then leading the Willesden and District Division II table were the hosts. It was another resounding win for the 'Stones with S Dear recording a further hat trick for the new club, following his hat trick the previous week;

"Wealdstone v Roundwood Swifts October 14th 1899

This match was played on the Swifts ground, Dog Lane, Stonebridge on Saturday last. Wealdstone won the toss and set the homesters to face the sun and a slight incline.

Immediately from the kick off S Dear secured, and worked down, but the home defence cleared only to see them come again, S Dear opening the scoring from close quarters. The ball was continually out of play, owing to the smallness of the ground - and the long grass - made accurate passing impossible.

From the kick off Poole got possession and sent a cross to Cozens who was declared offside however. From the "free" the Swifts managed to force a corner, which proved abortive and S Dear and Cozens getting away, the former put the 'Stones two up.

The visitors were having most of the play, the Swifts only attacking occasionally, and Cozens and Johnson being very safe, Bellchambers was only troubled on two or three occasions. A corner at the other end looked dangerous, but nothing came of it, another few minutes later being cleared also, but at length Poole scored again and half time sounded Wealdstone 3 Roundwood Swifts 0.

With the slope in their favour the homesters had somewhat more of the play, Bellchambers having to save a hot drive from the left, but a fine piece of passing by the whole of the forwards, resulted in S Dear scoring number 4. Still keeping up the pressure, Poole scored No 5 after E Dear had scored an off-side goal, and, Matthews narrowly missed a few minutes later, a corner being conceded, of which nothing came, and then the Swifts rushed down but Johnson sent back. The visitors struggled desperately, but shot behind.

Offside against Matthews relieved somewhat, but a corner again S Dear scored number 6.

This concluded the scoring and time found the 'Stones easy winners by six goals to love. For the winners, S Dear was the pick of the forwards all of whom combined well considering the ground, the halves worked hard, and both Cozens and Johnson cleared well, Bellchambers had little to do, but did that little well.

Wealdstone team; Bellchambers, W. Cozens, Johnson, Welsh, Payne, White, H. Cozens, S. Dear, E. Dear, Matthews and Poole."

The first league fixture of this first season as Wealdstone FC was scheduled to be played on 21st October against Maida-Hill, at home. Perhaps as an indication of what was to happen in the future, even that was not to work out as planned as the visitors failed to arrive. That meant that the first league fixture as the modern day Wealdstone FC became an away fixture, played against the Metropolitan Railway on 28th October 1899, at Neasden.

Wealdstone were to have opened their Willesden League list with a match against Maida-Hill, at home on Oct 21st, but as seen in last weeks issue the visitors failed to appear, so that the 'Stones made their initial appearance on Saturday, when they journeyed to Neasden to meet the Metropolitan Railway.

Wealdstone kicked off uphill, the Met. Having won the toss, and the game opened very fast, Wealdstone being the first to press, they obtaining a corner, which proved abortive. The 'Mets' then had a spell and forced a corner, which likewise came to nothing.

After 20 minutes play, E Dear opened the scoring for Wealdstone, first striking the crossbar, and scoring from the rebound. Despite several good shots the 'Stones failed to improve their score, E Dear and H Cozens having hard lines, and half time arrived with the score Wealdstone 1 Metropolitan Railway 0.

The game became somewhat rough on the restart, S Dear putting Wealdstone two up within five minutes. The 'Mets' then made a fierce onslaught and succeeded in getting the ball past Bellchambers.

Still keeping up the pressure the 'Mets' shot the ball into the goalkeepers hands and appealed for a goal, claiming the goalkeeper was over the line, but the referee was unable to decide, so the ball was thrown up, and from the bully, H Cozens made a splendid run down, and passed out to the left, the opposing back conceding a corner which, however, was cleared.

With a fine shot Pool scored number three. The Mets then broke away, and Elkin missed an easy chance, and the 'Stones coming again forced a corner, and, one of the homesters handling inside the 12-yard line, H Cozens scored from the resultant penalty.

Fouls were plentiful just about now, both sides being to blame, but there was no more scoring, and time found Wealdstone winners of their first League match by four goals to one.

The 'Stones were very slack at times, for whom E Dear, S Dear and H Cozens were the pick. Bellchambers was very smart in goal. The opposing custodian also played splendidly.

Wealdstone team; Bellchambers, W. Cozens, Johnson, Welsh, Payne, White, H. Cozens, S. Dear, E. Dear, Matthews and Pool.

The early 1900's saw Wealdstone Football Club attempt to establish itself in the community and in the league, and although the club had started well, there was no silverware won in the early years.

Having played its first season in the Willesden and District League Division II, where it lay in third place for most of the season, the following season saw the club take its place in Division I, finishing 6th out of ten, the second division having been disbanded.

The opponents in the league at this time were Harrow Athletic, still surviving after the period of amalgamation with Wealdstone, Harrow Weald, Wembley, Northwood, Shepherds Bush, Roundwood Rangers, Ealing St Johns, Haven Green, Willesden Highfield and Roxeth Brigade Old Boys.

The 1900 – 1901 season also records the first 'Representative Honours' for Wealdstone players. W Cozens, H Livy, William Welch and Keetch were selected to play in the league side against the North West London League and Alliance. Livy, Welch and the goalkeeper (at the time), T Matthews were also selected to play for the Rest Of The League side against Champions, Brigade Old Boys.

During the 1900 – 1901 season another Wealdstone side appeared as Wealdstone Juniors. It is not certain this was again part of the main club, but there were players common to both sides. One fixture in October 1900, gives the line up as;

W Montague, G Elmslie, G Pople, A Kendle, H Rogers, S Nightingale, A Dodd, A Cane, R White, C Roots and H Harton. Records show that at least five of these players were to appear in the Wealdstone first team.

For the 1901 – 1902 season there was another ground move, this time to the Wealdstone Recreation Ground, a move that brought about an improvement in the fortunes of the club. The local paper was pleased to report that since its formation, things had never looked so rosy for the club as at present.

The previous seasons success was deemed remarkable and *"showed in the ranks many players of real merit and in addition for the coming season the club has signed on several new players, including one from Clapton Orient!"*

The first match of the 1902-03 season as part of the entertainment at a local fete;

The Wealdstone Club brought off its first match this season on Saturday, when it encountered a team representing the Great Central Loco'.

The match was played at Wealdstone, but not on the club's pitch. At the invitation of Professor Fleet and with the sanction of the association, the match was played at Home Field, in connection with the fete and carnival held there.

The condition of the pitch was not all that could be desired, the grass was long and consequently impeded the ball a great deal. A sharp wind was also blowing across the ground.

In spite of these drawbacks however, the 'home' team played in excellent fashion and succeeded in beating their opponents without having a goal scored against them.

Shortly after the kick off Wealdstone went down into the visitors territory, where they remained for quite a quarter of an hour! Many attempts were made at the goal, but the backs in the first half were firm and kept the ball at bay.

From a throw in, Welch, of the home team, sent the ball into the goalmouth and it went between the posts, but the point was not allowed. A few moments after this Livy was in possession of the ball, and centred well, but the wind altered its course, and it just grazed the left post. This was followed by a succession of corners at the visitor's end, but no goals were registered.

However the homesters were not disappointed in the next attempt at goal. Brown was in good position for scoring, the ball was passed on to him and he drove it into the net.

Not long after the whistle sounded for half-time, the score remaining unchanged. The visitors seemed to put more energy into their play on the resumption of the game, but the homesters were too much for them.

In a few minutes the second point for Wealdstone was scored and this was followed by the repetition of the pressing tactics exhibited during the greater portion of the first half, and before time was reached, three further points were added by Wealdstone.

Wealdstone; Barratt, goal, Cozens and Hawkins, backs, W Carmalt, Welch and Rowe, halves and Dawes, C Brown, Todd, Glidle and Livy, forwards.

It was not until 1903 – 1904 that the club re-entered the major cup competitions, the London Junior Cup and at the same time, the Middlesex Junior Cup, as the club still had Junior status.

It was the first season that brought success in the league. Wealdstone led the table for the majority of the season, their first defeat coming in February, but they were eventually to finish as runner up to Willesden Invicta who won the league on the last day of the season.

The following year, season 1904–05 started well with a comprehensive victory over promoted Cameron Rangers, the Champions of Division 2 the previous year. 'Stones featured some new additions to the squad and despite a strong challenge, wore down their opponents and won by 5-1.

Win after win followed in the league, and despite having been knocked out of both the London Junior and Middlesex Junior Cup's, Wealdstone led the league from the start.

A match in February was to emphasise their superiority;

After sharing the points with Harrow United at Neasden, the Willesden Radicals came to Wealdstone last week in search of league points.

That they might succeed against the 'Stones was quite possible, as the home team were short of Wolters, Keetch, Stevens and Petley, and had to play throughout with only ten men.

Keeping an eye on the championship of the league, the 'Stones played up determinedly, and at half time had scored six goals to the one by the Radicals. Keeping up the pressure, the homesters added no fewer than eight points in the second half without response, the final result being 14-1 in favour of Wealdstone.

For the home team, Lines, who grabbed five of the goals was in particularly fine form. Gibson in goal, and Welch, at back had so little to do that they joined in the attack, and were both credited with two goals!

The other scorers were Bowells (2), Dawes (2) and Brown Wealdstone remain at the head of the table with fourteen points from seven games played.

The club did not drop a league point until March 4th, in a 2–2 draw with Ealing St Johns as Wealdstone went on to secure the Championship for the first time in their short history,

1905 also saw the first change in the club colours. Having previously played in Black and White Stripes, this season the kit changed to Green Shirts with White Sleeves and Collars, which was the kit worn up until the First World War.

The league success was not repeated in the cups, as Wealdstone were defeated in both the London and Middlesex competitions;

"Holborn Circus v Wealdstone 20th January 1905

Whatever hopes the Wealdstone Club had of annexing the London Junior Cup were extinguished on Saturday last, when they went down before Holborn Circus at Acton by two goals to none.

The progress of the 'Stones in the cup has been marked by bad luck both on and off the field and in the draws, having been drawn away from home in every match save one. The task set them in the sixth round was acknowledged by all to be a very difficult one, especially after the frosts of the previous week, the 'Stones having played their best games on muddy pitches.

Leaving nothing to chance, 18 players journeyed to Acton, the following team eventually turning out; C E Gibson, goal, W Welch captain, and T Matthews, backs, F Wolters, Keetch and Gregory, halves, E Davies, H Bowell, H Lines, A J Buckley and J Brown, forwards.

To everyone's surprise the referee ruled the ground to be fit enough for a cup-tie, and the game was started with but half of the Wealdstone team readily dressed. Straight from the kick off the 'Stones attacked, and their numerous supporters round the ropes had great hopes of an early score. The home team however, gradually pressed them back into their own half, and Gibson was called upon to save a good shot.

Coming again the homesters looked like scoring but a free kick relieved the pressure. From this the ball came out to the left wing and Brown getting possession raced away but only to put behind.

Thus early in the game the referee showed crude ideas of the offside rule, and the home forwards, taking advantage of his weakness, lay well up, and only the good form shown by Gibson prevented them from scoring.

Getting the ball from a goal kick Brown took it down, but Lines, taking his pass was given offside, a decision that was received very badly.

Playing now with only ten men, Wolters being off the field owing to a kick, the visitors played up with more dash than had previously shown, but they had great difficulty keeping their feet on the hard ground. How the ground affected the play was seen when a good centre by Davies was missed by both Lines and Buckley, when but a touch would have put it through.

After some even play in midfield, halftime came with the score blank.

Edward Dawes, who played for Wealdstone from 1901 and was ever present in the Championship season, scoring 9 goals. He was one of the first players to leave at the end of the season to join Wealdstone Church Athletic.

The second half was much the same as the first, as far as the play went, except that the Circus team scored twice, both of the points being more than doubtful. The first goal was scored from a clear offside position, while later on Gibson, in saving, was injured, the referee not stopping the game, enabled the home team to score their second point.

Shortly after this full time came, much to the relief of everyone on the ground. For Wealdstone, the defence was, as usual, very

safe, but the halves and forwards had great difficulty in keeping their feet on the slippery ground, and were not able to force home their attacks".

It is interesting to see that almost 100 years ago, there was as much contention caused by the application of the offside law as there is now and even in those more gentlemanly days, referees were not beyond criticism.

As was the custom at the time, alongside the report, a table announced the fixtures for the following day, in this case Wealdstone were to play a Willesden and District League game against Clare Hampstead.

The selected team and reserve as well as details of the meeting and travel accompanied the fixture details for 'away' matches. In many cases this was how the players found out that they had been selected!

More onerous for the club (although it is unlikely that it caused much concern at the time), was contained in the paragraph immediately above the Wealdstone side.

It was confirmation of the Wealdstone Church Athletic team to play in a Wembley and Harrow District match against a team called Lexicon. The listed team included full backs Dodd and Cozens, E G C Bellchambers among the 'halves' and H H Richardson and G E Elmslie among the forwards, each of them a former Wealdstone player.

In winning the Championship of the Willesden and District League, 'Stones shared in the local success with Wealdstone Church Athletic FC who had won the Wembley and District League.

The Observer again reported at the end of March, that in celebration, a Football Club Smoking Concert had been held, and this was to play a greater part in the history of Wealdstone FC than anyone was to realise. The report read;

"The Railway Hotel was the meeting place of footballers in the district on Saturday night, when Wealdstone Football Club held a most successful smoking concert.

The Chair was occupied by Mr A Murray, himself a footballer of no mean ability, noted throughout Wealdstone and the neighbourhood as a good half back. Supporting the Chairman were Messrs E E Beckley (Hon Secretary), J Harris and G White, whilst in the room could be seen many familiar faces in the football world including Messrs H Bowell, J Brown, Saunders, Gregory, W Carmalt and members of the Wealdstone Church FC.

The late arrival of the pianist delayed the start, but despite this the concert went from start to finish with a smoothness, which was most creditable to the Committee.

The toast of 'The Visitors' was proposed by Mr E E Beckley who congratulated the Church FC on having won the Wembley and District League, and Mr G Elmslie, Secretary of the Wealdstone Church FC, gave a similar courteous reply.

The toast of The Chairman having been drunk with musical honours, Mr Murray proposed Wealdstone Football Club. In a few well-chosen words, he congratulated the club on winning the Championship of the Willesden And District League, not yet

Wealdstone Church Athletic FC 1904 – 1905, Winners of the Harrow, Wembley & District League. Back Row; W Carter, T Biggs, F A Pluck, A Dodd, W Montague. Centre Row; A Keedle, G E Elmslie, E Bellchambers, A Lane, A Smith. Front Row; S E White, F Theobold, E Biggs, J Wicks, H Richardson. (Six of the side had previously represented Wealdstone).

having sustained a defeat in that competition.

The vocal items were huge successes, and encores were frequent. The humorous selections naturally claimed most attention and the comedians included such popular favourites as Mr Charlie Sherlock and Mr Harry Jeanes, who gave several songs. Mr W J Beckley played a capital violin solo and Mr Tit Baldwin showed a wonderful skill with the bones."

In light of what was to happen the following year when the club became defunct again, (only for the fixtures to be completed by Wealdstone Church Athletic FC), was it pure good fortune that the two clubs had spent such an evening together, and more so that Mr Elmslie was able to toast the club. After all, that family was to go on and become such a part of Wealdstone FC just a few years later.

At the start of Wealdstone's season as champions all was not well. Many of the players that had been successful had left the club, a number joining the Church Athletic.

After losing a number of matches early in the season, and with the new players not 'gelling' well into the side, the club was in disarray and, as reported, *it had become the subject of some derision locally due to the tardiness of the players that remained.*

By the beginning of October the support too, had dwindled away. For a Cup match at home to Sudbury Institute, the Harrow Gazette recorded that only a sparse crowd attended the College Road ground.

A week or two later, in mid October 1905, the Harrow Observer carried the following report on the next Wealdstone fixture;

Wealdstone v Leyton Athletic

This match was played on the College Farm ground on Saturday last, to decide who should survive the first round of the London Junior Cup

Wealdstone commenced with the slope against them and during the first half Leyton had most of the play, the score at the interval was Leyton 1 Wealdstone 0.

During the second half Wealdstone tried most strenuously to equalise, but all their efforts were unsuccessful. They had the play in the lower half of the field for fully thirty minutes during this half, and though often extremely near they never gained their object.

Towards the close of play the visitors got away and Cannington shot from a weak save by the home custodian and the game concluded Leyton 2 Wealdstone 0.

Wealdstone kept up their reputation for losing matches. This is the fourth consecutive match played at home with the encouraging result of lost 3 drawn 1. Perhaps they would not fare any worse if they could so arrange matters that their players would all be on the field when the match commences, and not, as last Saturday, come dribbling onto the field in units up to half time.

I understand that the visitors had heard a rumour as to the rough play Wealdstone were capable of, yet they confessed at the conclusion that they had not expected all that they got.

G Butler worked extremely hard in the forward line during the second half, but his efforts were not supported by his colleagues as they might have been, or the conclusion may have favoured Wealdstone.

The backs were very sure on Saturday, Gregory being especially good. His accurately placed shots would often be very serviceable to the forward line, as some of these gentlemen do not seem to know when to shoot, and when they do, well, the goalkeeper does not need to trouble himself.

The 'odd dozen' round the field were exceedingly turbulent on Saturday, and many of their remarks directed at the referee were more pointed than polite. They got the impression that this person was favouring the visitors. I do not know who constitute the Committee of Wealdstone FC but I suggest they wake up!

The last paragraph seems to have been sound advice but judging by the newspaper the following week it was too late, the club was destined to fail once again.

Under the local news heading of 'Wealdstone' there appeared a paragraph reporting a sudden death of an infant – this in truth would equally have served as a heading for the paragraph below, as the sixth league season of this latest Wealdstone Football Club was destined to be its last;

Defunct

It is with deep regret that we have to record the demise of what used to be the well known Wealdstone Football Club.

Since the commencement of the present season the signs have been ominous; the dilatoriness of the players in arriving on the field at the start of the game, the thin line of spectators who dotted the line of demarcation along one side of the ground, all betokened a sad falling off of interest. This is more to be regretted as the club were very strong last season, and headed the list of the First Division of the Willesden and District League, thus winning the cup and Medals after a very successful season.

This year they expected to enhance their chances by new blood, but as often is the case this failed to act, as the players, not knowing each other, could not combine with the facility necessary to good football, and consequently lost every match.

So now, we believe by unanimous consent of the players and Committee, they have disbanded completely, and probably, we shall notice players of the team in the lists of other teams.

Wealdstone Church Athletic were at the time lying in third place, unbeaten in the Wembley and Harrow District League. The club immediately applied to join the Willesden & District League, making a step up in standard, in the stead of the now defunct Wealdstone FC.

One month later their membership was accepted and they then completed the remaining Wealdstone FC League fixtures.

As the season progressed, more of the previous Wealdstone players were to appear for the club, some in the Willesden League, others 'as reserves' in the Wembley & Harrow League.

In mid November, the club were congratulated on having secured their place in the league. Hopes were high that they would be as successful as they had been in the Wembley and Harrow League.

Their first match was against Victoria Halls. They won by a comfortable 4 goals to one and they followed this with a victory by 2-1 over Old Lyonians, indicating that they would have no problem in making the step. In fact by mid December their record (in both Leagues and Cup matches) showed that they had played 15 games, winning 13 with 1 draw and 1 defeat, scoring 63 goals while conceding only 13.

By the season's end, the Wealdstone Church Athletic side finished in third place in the Willesden League and in the Wembley and District League, they finished in ninth place.

A number of former Wealdstone players were also to be involved in a match before the end of this season, albeit in a friendly match set up as Bank Holiday entertainment.

The local paper gave a report under the heading of Novel Match - United v Old Harrow Athletic players, and that's what it was. The Harrow United team of the day playing against a team of former Harrow Athletic players, a number of players from both teams having previously represented Wealdstone FC.

Harrow United won out 5-0, the score being 1-0 at half time but the fitness of the Veteran players let them down in the second half.

The teams that day were; (Former and future Wealdstone players in bold)

Harrow United; H Barrett, goal ***P Steadman*** *and F Jones, backs, W Cashen, W Carmalt and H Barnett, halves,* ***P Barnes, A Skilton, F Theobold,*** *Parkes and J Roberts, forwards.*

Old Harrow Athletic; C Sherward, goal, ***W E Kavanagh*** *and* ***H Woodbridge,*** *backs, D Hawkins,* ***H Darville****, and H Titchener, halves,* ***A W Parker****, F Eden, J Knight, A Nash and* ***F G Cobb****, forwards.*

In June 1906 the Church Athletic Club elected their Officers for the forthcoming year and this further strengthened the ties with Wealdstone FC.

The Officers elected were Rev H Chapman, President (subsequently President of Wealdstone FC until 1921), Mr J E Lilley (President at the formation of The Oaks FC in 1878, The Oaks (Wealdstone) in 1888, the first Wealdstone FC in 1889, Wealdstone Athletic FC in 1895 and first President of Wealdstone FC from 1899), A Wolters, A Forster, E E Beckley (Committee member of Wealdstone FC from 1899), E A Borer, vice presidents, Mr S White, Captain, (Former Captain of Wealdstone FC who was Captain of the reformed club in 1909), Mr F Pluck, Vice Captain (retained as a player and Hon. Secretary in the reformed Wealdstone Club). Messrs Lane, Whittle Spooner, Montague and Latham formed the Committee (Lane, Spooner and Latham later played for Wealdstone FC).

The prospects of the club were also noted before the 1906-1907 season started;

The Wealdstone Church Athletic was the team that finished third in the Willesden and District League last season, and their prospects are distinctly encouraging for the coming winter.

Contrary to the practise last year, only one team will be run for 1906-07, and this will have the effect of strengthening the personnel of the team. Another alteration is in the venue of play, and the matches, instead of on a Private Ground (New College Farm in Locket Road) will be played on the Wealdstone Recreation Ground.

Some good playing talent has come into the ranks, with the addition of Robertson and Martin, formerly of the Wealdstone Juniors, a club that also went to the wall last season. Robertson is to figure in the forward line and in the defence Martin will be included. (Both subsequently played for Wealdstone FC after it reformed)

The record of the first team last year – 31 played, 20 won, 7 lost and 4 drawn should be equalled if not beaten this season. The Church Athletic commences the season with every prospect of successful, and interesting football.

So yet again, Wealdstone FC was not to be seen on the fixture lists of local football, although the club did continue. A number of memberships were held, but it seems these also passed over to the Wealdstone Church Athletic FC along with the playing duties.

As previously noted, the Church Athletic side contained a good number of Wealdstone FC players and the club itself, a number of Wealdstone FC Officials. In both cases these seem to have been the more reliable members and not those that had caused the Wealdstone team to resign during the previous season.

The three seasons in which Wealdstone Church Athletic played the Wealdstone fixtures were somewhat unremarkable.

After the 1905–1906 season, the Athletic withdrew from the Harrow Wembley & District League to concentrate on the Willesden League, though they had nothing more than an average season, followed by more of the same in 1907 – 1908.

At Easter in 1908 they were invited to join a Football Carnival at the Old Lyonians Club.

The occasion was spoiled a little by wintry weather despite predictions of a bright clear weekend, as the report on the football tournament read;

Frequent storms of sleet, hail and snow were the order of the day. The tournament consisted of a series of six a side football matches and were decided in nearly every instance under conditions that were all against a good exposition of the game, but many of the players distinguished themselves with good performances. The turf was rendered somewhat treacherous by the heavy downfall but the players contested their matches in a very sportsmanlike manner, the referee's tasks being very light.

The first match down for decision was Wealdstone Athletic v Harrow Weslyans, and the former emerged successful by seven points to three. Harrow Association easily put paid to Allens Athletic account by administering a 12–1 defeat.

Wembley Institute registered a 20–13 win over Stanmore and the Old Lyonians got the better of Wealdstone Juniors by 15 points to 2.

The result of the Harrow Association v Wealdstone Athletic encounter was a draw, each side obtaining 11 points, and the spin of a coin favoured the Association team. They entered the final to face Old Lyonians who had overcome Wembley Institute, the hosts winning in the final moments.

With the Wealdstone influence still prominent in the 'Athletic' club it was to no-one's surprise when the following year the Wealdstone club returned in its own right, replacing the Wealdstone Church Athletic team in the Willesden and District League, the Church Athletic returning to the Wembley and District League.

ANOTHER BEGINNING

It was at the start of the 1908-09 season that Wealdstone FC returned to the field of play in their own right, rejoining the Willesden and District League Div I.

The Observer carried the following preview on September 4th 1908;

This season sees a new era in the fortunes of the Wealdstone Football Club. The committee have secured the College Farm Ground in Locket Road, and they hope to be able to run a team worthy of the town of Wealdstone.

Of course, to do this, it is absolutely essential for supporters of the club to rally round in large numbers on Saturday afternoons (when the small charge of 2d will be made) so as to place the club on a good, sound financial footing and to allow scope for improvements.

The club are also issuing Honorary Members Tickets for 2s 6d and as a very attractive list of fixtures has been arranged it is expected that these will find a ready sale. Tickets may be obtained from all members of the committee.

The Officers elected are; President; the Rev. H Chapman, Captain; S E White, vice-Captain F Martin, Committee; Messrs; H Kane, W Akers, J Keedle, H C Hird, L E White and J Martin and the valuable services of Mr FA Pluck are again available as Honorary Secretary.

The club have entered the Willesden and District League, London Junior Cup and West Middlesex Junior Cup.

Tomorrow (Saturday) on the College Farm Ground, the team will meet West London Old Boys, a strong team of seniors who went through last season in invincible manner.

The Wealdstone Team will turn out as follows; Pluck, goal, Martin and Spooner, backs, Bellchambers, Cane and Miller, halves, White (Captain), Bowells, Lane, Theobold and Roberts, forwards.

The referee will be W Howe and Kick off will be 3:30pm sharp.

The line up showed the background to the formation of the club. Only Bowells remained from the last match played by the preceding club as a number of players had already moved on to new clubs before Wealdstone FC withdrew from the league. Pluck, Bellchambers, White and Theobold who had previously represented the club, before they too had departed to Wealdstone Church Athletic FC rejoined him.

The Committee were trying their utmost to ensure that the new club was successful both on and off the field, and a number of attractive fixtures were proposed to try and entice the local support to return to the club and to increase in numbers. The omens were good, as the reformed Wealdstone Football Club ran out winners in their first match against West London Old Boys.

The Wealdstone side opened their season on Saturday in first class style, beating a good team from West London by two goals to nil.

The form displayed by most of the players was highly satisfactory, and augurs well for a successful season. A goodly attendance of spectators was present and the Committee hope the Supporters will turn up in still greater numbers, as they have gone to considerable expense to give an interesting afternoons sport to their patrons.

A great feature this season will be that spectators can view all games without getting their feet wet, as the Committee have secured a large number of boards for standing purposes.

Tomorrow, Rotherhithe Invicta (Winners of the Blackheath and District League, runner up of the Lewisham League and semi-finalists of the Charlton District Cup) will make their first appearance before a Wealdstone crowd.

The anticipation of a visit from 'new' opposition however far outweighed the actual ability and performance on the day as Rotherhithe were not as strong as anticipated. The very brief report after the match went as follows;

Wealdstone were disappointed on Saturday with the strength of the Rotherhithe team, the visitors displaying farcical form. The homesters were quickly all over them, Lane, Bowells and F Cane quickly getting through. The Invicta goalie saved several good shots and was the only man to show anything like good form. Seven goals were scored in the second half and Wealdstone ran out winners by eleven goals to nil.

Wealdstone had started the season well, and a fixture arranged with Old Lyonians in late November was eagerly awaited. The report in the Harrow Observer and Gazette also gave another insight to the Wealdstone area of the time;

Considerable interest was shown in this fixture on the Harrow Recreation Ground, in the Willesden & District League.

Much friendly rivalry exists between the two teams, but the odds were laid on the boys from the factory land, and as they appeared on the line in their brilliant green jerseys they looked a formidable lot.

A large crowd lined the ropes, mainly Wealdstone supporters, who were prepared to back their fancy. It was not forgotten though that the Lyons had made rapid progress during the season.

The start was sensational, for before Wealdstone had awoke to what was happening the "Garibaldis" had, by some brilliant passing on the part of Cave and Cory, and admirable support by the half-backs, rushed through THREE goals to the consternation of Pluck, who was in charge of the goal.

These reverses were not pleasant, and Wealdstone made a determined onslaught on Carber's charge to the frantic cheers of the crowd and the ringing of the Wealdstone Muffin Bell.

Theobold – who we believe has played for Watford – was very noticeable in the front rank of the visitors, but Carter had an easy task. With this balance against them Wealdstone had an uphill task in the second half, but though having the best of play, could not break through the admirable defence of the Lyons, and the game ended in a very creditable win for the Old Boys.

(It has not been possible to trace whether the reporter was correct in the belief that Theobold had played for Watford, but there is no reason to expect it not to be true. He had previously played for Pinner with his brother who also played for Wealdstone.

The reference to the 'Wealdstone Muffin Bell' seems to be a reference to exactly that – the bell rung out by the Muffin Man when selling his wares through the streets of Wealdstone. It is mentioned once or twice in reports and it seems that the bell and owner were followers of the team).

There were mixed fortunes for the club, and they were rarely 'out of the public eye' during the season, sometimes for the right reasons and sometimes not. A match in the Divisional Semi Final of the Middlesex Junior Cup saw Wealdstone play host to Kilburn. There were a number of occasions when supporters and players alike disagreed with the decisions of what was described as a poor referee, none more so than when the visitors were awarded a penalty, the referee apparently the only person present who knew the cause. The visitors scored the only goal of the match and the protests continued.

Two weeks later, at the beginning of February, the Western Committee of the Middlesex FA met at Ealing to discuss the events of the day. The result was that the Wealdstone ground was shut for a period of six weeks, and the team prohibited from playing any match within a two-mile radius of the ground, in consequence of the bad behaviour of the spectators at the cup-tie. Two players, F Cane and F Wolters were also banned. F Cane until the end of the season for using foul language to the referee and F Wolters for one month for misconduct on the field.

The ban and the weather meant that the club cancelled a number of fixtures and only played a few more in April. It left a shortfall financially and to redress the balance, a fundraising match was arranged for the end of the 1908-09 season.

In late April Mr P G Skilton, at this time still involved in local football in Harrow, agreed to raise a team to play a Wealdstone side on Wednesday May 3rd 1909, at Wealdstone Recreation Ground with a 6:00pm Kick Off. Tickets of admission were sold and the proceeds went towards the Wealdstone Club, but it must be remembered that at this time there were no floodlights, so an evening kick off was something of a rarity! Little is known of the match, teams or outcome except to say that *'by the second half the spectators had difficulty seeing the attacking play and some players also had the same trouble which resulted in a number of corners for both teams, and a number of half saves'*

In 1909-10, Wealdstone FC fielded a Reserve side in the North West London League, winning this competition. This was to signal the start of a number of successes for the club leading up to the First World War.

The fundraising efforts had been well rewarded during the previous season, as, during the close season at the end of May 1909, the Wembley and Harrow District League decided to start a Wednesday section. Wealdstone were one of seven teams along with Uxbridge Unity, Watford Wednesday, Northwood, Roxeth Institute, Harrow and Rickmansworth duly elected as founders of this League. It had been suggested as a means of allowing more people to play football in the Borough as at the time organised football and other sports were banned on Sundays. Wednesdays were suggested as an ideal solution as most shops and businesses closed for a half day on a Wednesday afternoon!

Pre-empting the wandering of later years, another move took place at the start of the 1910-11 season, this time to a field at the end of Belmont Road, described at the time to have a good path leading to the field – something strange to us these days but of great importance at the time – Northwood FC for example announced they were to play at a ground in Dene Road and were to build a new path from the road in the hope that this would attract more ladies to watch! No doubt at the time, the clothing styles did not lend themselves to a walk along a muddy path or across a field!

This season also saw the first individual players at the club receive County representative honours, F Theobold was selected to play for Middlesex Juniors against Kent Juniors early in the season, and a little later, P Andrews was also selected. Achieving his third match selection against Berks and Bucks Juniors, P Andrews was entitled him to his Junior County Badge. This match appears to have been the first representative match hosted by Wealdstone FC as it was played at the Belmont Road ground on Saturday March 18th 1911.

The team that day was; Mullins (Teddington) goal, Dykes (Polytechnic) and Ward (St Stephens Old Boys) backs, Reid (Ealing St Johns), Smith (Fulham Amateurs), and Randall (Centel), half-backs, Taylor (Teddington), Steeles (Roxeth Institute), Ford (Fulham Amateurs), Andrews (Wealdstone) and Haynes (Wembley Institute), forwards.

It was a successful season for the club as a whole as had been predicted before the start of the season.

Pinner again were a strong side and were the Champions of the Willesden and District League, Wealdstone finishing as runner up. Wealdstone also reached the semi-final of the London Junior Cup, where they were beaten by Silvertown Rubber Works;

This London Junior Cup semi-final was played at Shepherds Bush on Saturday last.

Wealdstone were at full strength, and received plenty of vocal support from the large band of enthusiasts who accompanied the team.

Andrews at last set Howman going, a good run resulting in the ball going behind. From the goal kick the Works attacked again, and Bradbury, being out of range, O'Brien saved what seemed to be a certain goal.

White put in a nice centre, which was cleared and the Works team had one of their men off the field for some time through injury. Bradberry had been kept well employed and saved finely on a number of occasions.

At the interval, the score sheet was still blank. Wealdstone pressed at the restart but met with a sturdy defence. A foul was given against Wealdstone and Murrell put the Works one up. Page soon after had hard luck with a good shot, and Houchin scored the Works second from close range. Wealdstone now pressed to the finish, Cane going very near with a beauty, and the whistle went with a win for the Works by 2-0. Wealdstone are to be congratulated for putting up such a good fight against their redoubtable opponents.

Next Saturday, Wealdstone will play Wealdstone Mission Social Club in the fourth round of the West Middlesex Cup at Belmont Road kick off 3:30pm.

T Bradberry, goal, E Bellchambers and F Martin, backs, P O'Brien, F Cane and H Miller, halves, S E White F Tow, G Page, P Andrews and H Richardson, forwards.

The report on the Annual General Meeting of the club, opened as the 14th albeit the club had only returned to the playing arena some four years previously, highlighted the success of the club both on and off the field.

In some 33 matches played by the First XI, twenty two had been won, six lost and five drawn, and scoring 88 goals, conceding 41.

P Andrews had created a goal scoring record in the season, scoring 21 times, the brothers P and J Shadwick had also contributed well, each scoring on ten occasions.

The gate receipts had amassed the grand total of £26, with a net balance in hand of £6 5s again a record. From this and our previous knowledge of the admission of 2d it seems that there was a good number of supporters following the 'Stones, certainly at home.

We can assume there were ten home League games and probably five in the cup which means that an average paying gate of around 210 would have attended these matches, not including those Members and Ticket Holders whose payment would not have counted to the gate. This was actually mentioned in that the committee decided that Vice Presidents who had not paid up their subscriptions would be prevented from gaining their free admission to the ground!

Flushed with this success, the AGM also decided that for the following season, there would be two Wealdstone Football Club teams. Not as previously a First XI and a Reserve side, both would compete equally.

One was to be entered for the Division II of the West London League, the London Junior Cup, the Middlesex Junior Cup and the Middlesex Charity Cup. The other would compete in Division I of the Willesden and District League or if that could not be achieved, Division I of the Wembley and Harrow League, and also in the West London Charity Cup.

Mr T Bradberry was elected Captain of the 'first' team and Mr F Cane his Vice- Captain, a Mr C Heard became Treasurer and Mr G E Elmslie (formerly associated with Wealdstone Church Athletic FC above) was appointed to the position of Secretary with Mr Pitt his assistant.

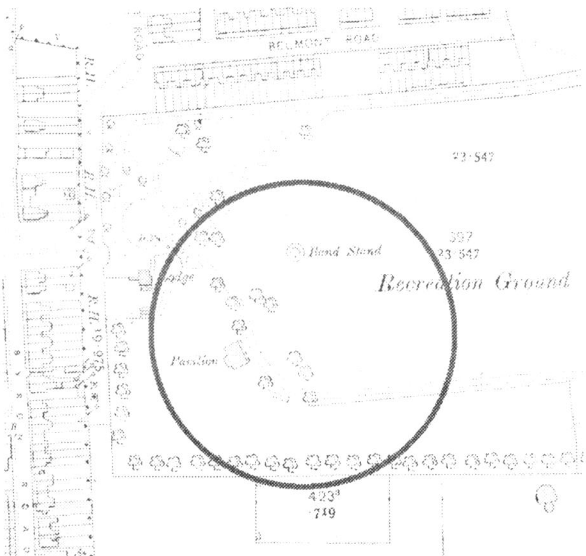

Wealdstone Recreation Ground from a map of 1910, the ground was occasionally used by the 'Stones in the early 1900's before becoming the regular ground in the 1910 season. From the map, the Pavilion that was the dressing room for the teams, and the bandstand are clearly shown.

As the 1912 -1913 season progressed it was evident that it was to be a successful one for Wealdstone, and in fact for both Wealdstone teams.

In the October an offer was received and duly accepted for the visit of Chelsea Football Club who agreed to play a friendly match at Wealdstone for a guarantee of £3 0s 0d.

It seems that it was also the first time that a Match Programme had been produced, for the match played on November 3rd, and it was unsurprisingly a record gate for Wealdstone at that time, a massive £5 3s 7d being taken!

As we know the admission was 3d (including a programme), then the gate would have been around 410.

Today, a copy of this programme (should one exist) would be worth in excess of twenty times the total gate for this match!

Wealdstone v Chelsea

Defeated, but by no means disgraced could truly be said of the 'Stones, when on Saturday they met a strong Chelsea eleven, composed of Professionals with the exception of H Bull, a budding young Amateur, who filled the right half position.

The team included Read who has figured in English First League Football this season, Buchanan, whom the Chelsea Officials are anxious to see shape, after an injury received while playing against Watford, Ford and McLeod, whilst Bevan took the place of Harwood who was transferred from Southend United.

Being the first time a Professional side visited Wealdstone, local football folk turned out in large numbers at Belmont Road, and received a good exhibition of their favourite winter pastime for their three pence.

The home club kicked off but Chelsea were the first to press, and Bradberry soon realised that he had forwards against him that knew the art of shooting, and he cleared twice, being heartily applauded.

Wealdstone seemed to be suffering from nervousness in the first half, their kicking being very rash at times, and of course, by pursuing such tactics seldom seemed likely to score. Mallett tested Denoon with a fine shot just inside the post, which produced a corner, but Kirby placed the kick badly.

The Chelsea forwards were very smart, treating the crowd to some splendid combination, which somewhat upset the home defenders. White made one or two spirited runs and once almost got away on his own when McKenzie managed to turn the ball of his toe.

The Stamford Bridge team were the best side up to the interval although Walker was always on the alert to snap up a chance or two for the 'Stones, but unfortunately not so many as should have done came his way, giving the centre forward little opportunity to show his ability.

Chelsea were in the 'Stones half a good deal but Bevan missed badly when close in, but Bull made amends for this error shortly afterwards scoring with a ground shot, which Bradberry went at full length to save, the ball going over his arm.

Wealdstone made an attempt to get on equal terms, but Denoon ran out, picked up and sent down the field, the visiting forwards working the ball near Bradberry, eventually gaining a corner, which Martin cleared.

At half time, the local club were losing by the only goal scored. Upon the restart, Chelsea went away with the rush, which seemed sure to bring about the downfall of the 'Stones citadel a second time, but the pressure was relieved for a few minutes, Bradberry kicking down the field. They came back again by some pretty work, Bevan obtained the ball and scored the goal of the match with a capital shot.

After this last reverse, Wealdstone played up splendidly, and severely taxed the pro's defence for some time. Mallett put in a rattling shot, which the goalie saved, this being followed by one from Muller, which also failed. Kirby played much better in this period, and on two or three occasions beat the opposing wing-back, only to see his centres intercepted by Buchanan, who was putting in some good head work.

It was somewhat surprising at this juncture to see Chelsea resort to the 'one back' game, and this in no way helped baulk 'Stones in their efforts to score. Play was once again around Bradberry, who left his charge and picked the ball up from an opposing forwards foot and cleared in masterly fashion.

Striving hard, the home team gave a polished exhibition against their redoubtable professional opponents, Andrews being unfortunate with a nice shot. They forced a corner, which McKenzie headed away, Wilkie receiving on the extreme left, and racing away, he was beaten by Bellchambers in the nick of time.

Wealdstone certainly deserved to score, but in Denoon, found an extremely hard nut to crack. Miller had a chance to take good aim, but shot long before there was any real need, consequently sending wide. White beat McKenzie and centred splendidly, and Buchanan nearly headed into his own goal, but nothing was gained by the resultant Corner Kick.

The exchange up to the finish continued to be fast, but no more scoring resulted, thus leaving Chelsea winners of this fine and interesting match by two goals to nil. To be beaten only once in each half reflects great credit on Bradberry and the backs, and taken all round, the Stone came out very creditably. Tomorrow Harrow Weald are the visitors in the Middlesex Junior Cup.

Wealdstone; T Bradberry, E Bellchambers, F Martin, F Rogers, F Cane, H Miller, S E White, A E Mallett, W Balkwill, P Andrews, R Kirby.

The remainder of the season saw success on a number of fronts for the club, and at the AGM the Officers were pleased to report that the Wealdstone teams between them had won the Middlesex Junior Cup and the London League Division II.

The two sides had played a total of 51 competitive matches, winning 39 with six draws and six defeats, this season scoring 167 goals with only 62 conceded.

After such a successful season the committee decided that the club would continue to run two teams for the following season, although one would now be known as the 'A' team to distinguish the sides.

There was still a problem with pitches however and the Willesden and District League side withdrew from the league having only played (and won) one match by the end of December. The London League side though, did continue and completed the season finishing in second place.

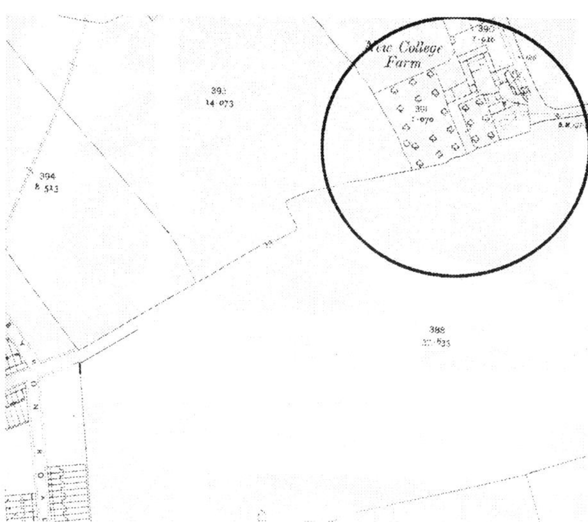

New College Farm, another ground from the early 1900's, before and after the Church Athletic Club's involvement The map extract is taken from 1912, when there was still nothing more than a path to the farm from the junction of Byron Road and Locket Road in the bottom left hand corner of the extract.

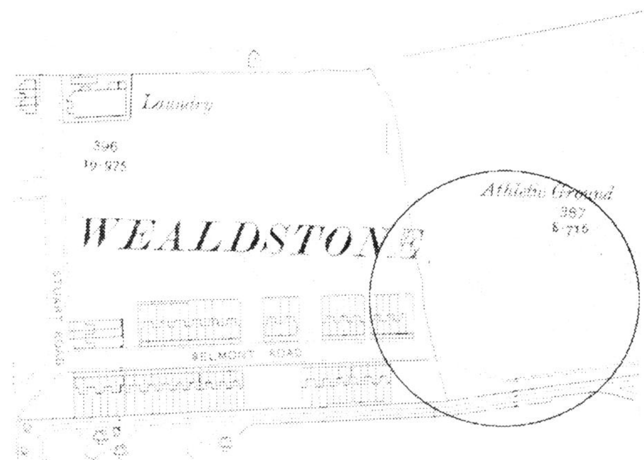

Another extract from the map of 1912, the Belmont Road Ground, to become Wealdstone's home either side of World War I. Belmont Road at this time only ran about 350 yards, before opening directly onto the Recreation Ground.

The following season, both teams were re-entered in their leagues, and with some success as both leagues were won as well as the Middlesex Junior Cup. In league matches, the combined record was Played 26, won 20, drawn 3 lost 3, scoring 92 goals and conceding only 21.

The committee decided that it was time for the club to progress, and having won both leagues and the Junior Cup, Wealdstone were to compete the following season in Senior Football for the first time. The Committee having entered the club in, and been accepted for the English Cup (the FA Cup), the FA Amateur Cup, the London Senior Cup and the Middlesex Senior Cup as well as the London League Division I. The Wealdstone A Team was to compete in the London Junior Cup, .the Middlesex Junior Cup and the West Middlesex League Division I. (It subsequently transpired that Wealdstone fielded a team in the Willesden and District Premier Division, in place of their membership of the West Middlesex League Division I.)

Wealdstone FC 1912 – 1913. winners of Middlesex Junior Cup, London League Div II, Willesden & District League Div I

Back Row; W Watson (Com), H Rolfe, F Rogers, H Bellchambers, H Howman (Vice Capt A Team), F Martin (Vice Capt), S E White, J Hinchcliffe (Com). Centre Row; R C Harding (Com), A Little (Trainer), C Bird, H E S Southwood, A Harding, H A Stevenson, J Mines, H Miller, W Deeley (Com), W Bellchambers (Com). Front Row; G E Elmslie (Hon Sec), W Howman, P Andrews, J J Shadwick (Capt A Team), T B Bradberry (Capt), W Balkwill, G Page, G Fox, H C Hird (Hon Treas.)

P Andrews was elected Captain as T Bradberry did not wish to continue, the remaining officers were re-elected.

Flushed with their success the club also secured the ground at Belmont Road for another season, and gained permission for some improvements to be made, including the drainage of the pitch.

Season 1912–1913 turned out to be the club's last in Junior football. It also saw Wealdstone win the Middlesex Junior Cup, a 3 -1 victory over NLP securing the trophy to celebrate a treble, as Wealdstone had also won both the Willesden & District Premier Division and the London League Division 2.

The Junior Cup Final was tinged with sadness as HES Southwood, a reserve player playing only his third first team match received an injury when he was kicked behind the knee. He was treated in hospital and sent home, but the injury to his leg worsened and by the time the team took the field again, against West Norwood in the league, his leg had had to be amputated at the knee.

The next season commenced with two teams as the club looked set to go from strength to strength in its first season in Senior Football. There were also the added attractions of the first matches in both the English Cup (now known as the FA Cup), and also the FA Amateur Cup.

On Friday September 19th 1913, The Observer reported;

Wealdstone v Page Green Old Boys

Wealdstone's career in the English Cup came to an end almost before it commenced, when, on their own ground at Belmont Road, on Saturday, before a large body of supporters, they were defeated by Page Green Old Boys by three goals to nil.

Many of their supporters anticipated with a fair amount of confidence that Wealdstone would survive this Preliminary, but they were to say the least, disappointed.

Wealdstone took the field as follows; T Bradberry, E Bellchambers and F Martin, F Rogers, H Rolfe and H Miller, F Butler, P Andrews (capt.), W Balkwill, F Theobold and G Fox, while the visitors were H Aston, W Simons and C B Debb, F Brewer, H F Carble, and C H Edwards, I G Carter, C Hannaford, F Beeth, W P H Love and A G Grant.

To commence with, Wealdstone had both wind and sun against them, and the former was an advantage of which Page Green made full use.

Five minutes from the start, Bradberry was called upon to make a save, and he having cleared nicely, play became once more easy, but never slow.

After 15 minutes play, Wealdstone had what was thought a fine chance for Fox, who was easily the fastest man on the field, flew along the left and almost from touch put in a cross which it should have been the easiest thing in the world to convert, but somehow or other Miller put wide.

Beeth, the Page centre broke forward and looked decidedly dangerous, but Martin did his work well, and later in saving he headed behind, but the corner proved to be of no avail.

Balkwill here looked dangerous, but offside spoiled his effort. Fox again received and covering half the field, centred right into the top corner of the goal, but the goalie proved too smart for Balkwill. This was about the best run Fox had for he was too closely marked to do anything.

Wealdstone's captain, Andrews got in a very smart shot, and although the goalie failed to hold it, he managed to clear. Almost immediately Beeth received and beating the backs, scored just out of Bradberry's reach. There followed a bombardment of the home goal, Love miss kicked with only Bradberry to beat and the latter player just turned a shot from Beeth around the post. Theobold did some very good work, but he, like Balkwill could not penetrate the Page backs, who played splendidly and half time arrived with Wealdstone one down.

Page forced a corner from the kick off, and Bradberry just managed to come out of a scrimmage best. Grant on the visitors left was continually dangerous while Carter on the other wing got in several warm shots, and shortly afterwards Bradberry was laid out through a heavy fall when jumping to punch.

The best shot of the match for the homesters was put in by Theobold only to be met by the vigilant goalie. On the ball coming to the other end, Beeth hit the post with a low drive and upon the rebound Castle steadied and gave Bradberry little chance with a shot in the top of the net.

Two minutes later Grant touched into goal making it 3-0 with five minutes to go, and this proved the extent of the scoring. The home team where quite outplayed, owing mainly to the better combination of Page Green, in fact Wealdstone shaped very poorly altogether, passes being very badly placed time after time.

However, the season is early and practise will no doubt work wonders with the material the team possesses.

It was on 18th October 1913 that Wealdstone were again to make a Cup Debut, this time in the FA Amateur Cup. The report from the Harrow Observer was as follows;

Wealdstone v Sutton Court

This match was played at Wealdstone in the Amateur Cup before a good crowd, and after a fast game with never a dull moment in it, Wealdstone retired winners by the substantial margin of five goals to one.

As is usual, Wealdstone pressed at the start and were nearly through in the first few minutes. The visitors centre forward then got going and his long forward passes were well taken by his wing men, but the home backs were very safe, Martin's dash and Bellchambers steadiness spoiling many pretty combined efforts. P Andrews had plenty to do at centre half and did it well.

After about a quarter of an hour Wealdstone opened the scoring Balkwill putting the finishing touch to a bout of passing. From the kick off the visitors made desperate efforts to equalise and gave Martin a sultry time. Bradberry in goal was kept busy for some time, but he was in tip-top form and anticipated every effort before it was made.

Shortly before half time, the equaliser came, the visitors centre forward netting the ball at close range from an obviously offside position. The referee however ignored the appeals of players and spectators.

No further scoring took place before half time, although

Shadwick had hard luck in hitting the upright with a fine shot, and Miller missed by inches from 30 yards out. From the restart play ruled very even for some ten minutes, but the home team redoubled their efforts, and White at outside right, after splendid combination with Shadwick, slung across a perfect centre, which Balkwill made no mistake with.

Keeping up the pressure, White again got through and put on number three with a glorious shot just underneath the bar. White then popped across another centre and Shadwell headed number four. The visitors outside right got in one or two clever runs and Bradberry had to negotiate one or two fine attempts from long range, but long shots never beat Bradberry, and he disposed of them in his usual masterly manner.

Back came the home forwards and P Andrews sent in a pile driver that missed by inches. There was no stopping the home forwards, and well backed by their halves they swarmed around their opponents goal, and D Andrews, securing close in, made no mistake with number five.

No further scoring took place although in the last five minutes, Fox put in two terrific shots that would have beaten most goalkeepers. Wealdstone are to be heartily congratulated on their smart performance. It is the best thing they have done in Senior football, and their victory is more meritorious when we take into consideration that three such fine players as Kirby, Theobold and Rogers were out of the team.

Everyone played well with Sid White the star turn. His pace and judgement were a revelation. He had a good partner in Shadwick, who passed beautifully and made many clever openings. Balkwill in the centre was a lot quicker than usual and showed improvements in every way, his two goals being splendid efforts.

D Andrews at inside-left dribbled well and has good control of the ball, and although new to Senior football, stayed the pace well. Fox was well hunted but seldom caught and played his usual clever hustling game and had hard luck in not scoring.

Andrews and Miller at half-backs were the hardest working members of the team, being opposed to fast trickiest of forwards, who required a good deal of watching, hence the other half back was not quite a Rogers, but played a useful plucky game, and should come on well with a little more experience.

The backs were seldom at fault, and a slip here or there from one of them only gave the opportunity for a show of brilliance from the other. Bradberry was Bradberry – he defies criticism.

Sutton Court are a clever team, with plenty of experience and did not deserve to be beaten by five goals to one. Their forwards were fast and tricky and clever, particularly the centre and outside right, and their defence was sound.

Youth and Training beat them. The last half hour was their bad time and they did not quite stay the pace. The fresh condition of the home team at the end of a very fast game was remarkable and proved the value of training.

So a victory then in the first Amateur Cup-tie played by the club, to perhaps wipe away some of the disappointment of the previous defeat in the first FA Cup-tie.

Just before the end of the season Wealdstone had played 8 matches (of 10) in the Willesden and District League Premier Division having won three and lost four, and were sitting in third place where they eventually finished. For one player, there was still the opportunity to gain a representative honour.

On Easter Monday 1914, the Willesden and District League team were to play the Marylebone and Paddington League on the ground of the Hyde and Kingsbury Club. Selected to play for the Willesden and District League were A Robertson of Wealdstone and P Deeley, then playing for Harrow Weald who was to join Wealdstone after the war.

Over the same weekend, and with the ever-changing situation in Europe well known, the War Department had arranged a display in Harrow by the local Brigade Voluntary Aid Detachment. (It was part of the recruitment drive as a number of the local volunteers had joined a Naval Auxiliary Reserve and numbers were not as high as wished.) The demonstration took two parts – the first a simulation of a mine accident – acknowledged as not very common in Harrow - but it was the second that is worthy of inclusion;

A Football Accident

The second portion of the display comprised Stretcher drill under Sergeant Ketley, and bandaging by the Nursing Division under Miss Pitcairn, and the latter performance was most creditable, being warmly applauded by the audience who closely inspected the work. The concluding scene was the collapse of a Football Stand, arranged by Corporals Hutt and Manson, and the very common accident was realistically carried out.

The good-humoured crowd assembled, the teams entered from the back of the hall, and the enthusiasm of the crowd caused the collapse of the stand.

There were of course Brigade men on hand who administered first aid and removed the injured.

As the company passed out of the hall they inspected the ambulance station fitted up in the adjacent room, under charge of Corporal Oram, where everything was neat and orderly and ready for an emergency.

The end of the season saw the club established and looking forward to the next series of matches in Senior football, but the AGM gave the club a little unwanted publicity in June. A letter appeared in the Harrow Observer questioning the way the club was run;

Sirs,

Hearing by accident the Wealdstone Football Club were holding a General Meeting on Thursday last, I presented myself for admittance, and was astonished by being asked for a ticket of admission. I had not the necessary ticket in my possession, butprobably owing to the fact that I was known to a number of the members present, I was admitted.

Having some doubt as to my presence being in order, at the commencement of the meeting I asked the Chairman if it was a public meeting and I was fairly taken aback when he said it was not, and that any person not having a ticket had no right to be in the room.

I immediately left, after expressing my doubts as to the policy of such a proceeding. If the public are considered good enough to pay their money to witness matches and thereby help to support the club, surely they should have the opportunity of learning, through the medium of a public meeting, the position of the club, both financially, and from a playing point of view.

When the Committee of the Wealdstone Football Club have reached that stage where the criticism of the public is abhorrent, then the future of the club is somewhat doubtful. I should like to hear the views of other supporters of such an extraordinary action.

I am Sir, Yours Faithfully, H T Rogers.

The name of Rogers was involved with Wealdstone on many fronts up to and beyond the First and Second World Wars, indeed at the time there was a Rogers playing for the First XI and another became goalkeeper immediately after the First World War. It is a matter of intrigue as to whether Mr H T Rogers was related to any of these people. Perhaps he may have had a vested interest in what was to be said, but there was no reply and the matter was overtaken by the course of events.

There was little else of note to report from Wealdstone's first foray into the world of senior football and the Summer progressed with the normal references to the next season, and the confirmation of which competitions were to be entered. This was put to one side in early August.

On August 4th 1914, War was declared and before the club could commence their second season as seniors, in common with all other clubs, Wealdstone FC closed down for the duration.

THE NEW DAWN

At the end of the First World War, in November 1918, a number of players returned to the area from overseas but the clubs they had previously served were still mothballed. There were no Leagues in place and little football available, so a number of 'new' clubs sprung up in their place and regular friendly matches were played in the hope that some of the old established clubs would reform for the following season.

A number of Wealdstone players appeared in these matches for the Young Men's Football Club (YMFC later to become the YMCA) and for 'Wealdstone United'. Matches were played against various Services teams, The Brigade and The Rangers, as well as similar sides from the surrounding areas such as Highgate and Stonebridge Oakwell.

Another name to come to the fore at this time was that of Mr Jabez Barnes, who was associated with the Ministry at the Methodist Church in Wealdstone. He, for a number of years, had been involved in an unofficial capacity at Wealdstone FC and was to continue as the club reformed. He was also involved in the setting up of the YMCA at this time, where he was elected President. At the end of the war, he was a local magistrate!

A report on one of the friendly matches played by YMFC tells us that after the match the YMFC team were entertained to tea at the Alpine Restaurant by Mr Jabez Barnes. There is also mention of the New Year festivities in celebration of both the end of the war and the first year of the YMCA.

Jabez Barnes, the popular President, provided a sumptuous, though wartime repast to which about 60 people sat down. A hearty tea was served to the participants of a football match earlier in the afternoon, and merriment ruled from start to finish!

At the Annual General Meeting of Wealdstone FC on 20th June 1919, it was unanimously decided to revive the club on its original pre-war lines. Negotiations were preceding with a view to the tenancy of a well-appointed ground, formerly occupied by Gamages Athletic Club, as the ground in Belmont Road was unavailable after the war. This however was resolved and the club did indeed kick off the new season on its original Belmont Road ground.

The club entered teams in the London League and Middlesex Senior League for the 1919-20 season, and also re-entered the English Cup and the London and Middlesex Senior cups.

It was noted at the time that;

With the majority of the old players returning and the inclusion of some new blood, a successful season is promised. It is also hoped that local sportsmen will rally round to help the Senior Club in the district, and help the Committee in their endeavour to provide football worthy of the town.

On the 23rd of August a trial match was played. The Harrow Observer was pleased to report that the match showed that a good amount of talent was available. It went on to say that there was a good level of youth and promising recruits as well as some good experienced (former) players.

On the 30th of August, the first league match was to be played, a London League fixture against Catford Southend, played at the Belmont Road ground.

The Wealdstone team for that match was;

G Jacobs, H Kirby, J Smerdon, J Durham, F Harbud, F C Hardy, W Gallagher, H Wentworth, T Theobold, R Kirby and W Ward.

The match was played before a crowd of 450.

The visitors won the toss and took advantage of both wind and slope. Following the kick off the visitors were first to get together, and they kept the home defenders busy for the first ten minutes.

A huge kick by Smerdon relieved the situation, and Wentworth went close with a high cross shot. The visitors were not to be denied, and racing to the other end, forced a corner. This being well placed, Bowen scored close in.

The home side quickly retaliated, Theobold and Kirby showing good form on the left. The ball travelled end to end at a very fast pace, both sets of defenders doing good work.

A smart passing run by Theobold and Kirby left the former in a favourable position, a terrific drive only being partially saved by the goalkeeper, Gallagher dashed in and equalised.

A ding-dong struggle ensued up until half time.

On resuming the home side were soon in evidence, and kept up a strong attack on the visitors goal, but poor shooting spoilt many a good opening. Both teams were feeling the effects of their early efforts and the game became scrappy.

A draw seemed the likely result when Ward, taking an advantage of a miss kick by a visiting back scored a fine goal. This put some life into the players and Catford made strenuous efforts to equalise.

Hardy, at back for the homesters was a rare stumbling block, repeatedly checking the visiting forwards.

Two minutes from time Harbud got in a splendid drive, the visiting goalie allowing the ball to twist from his grasp and into the net, thus giving Wealdstone the victory by the substantial margin of 3 goals to 1.

The local team thoroughly deserved their win and their display was proof of the good team the committee have got together.

The following week a similar team was selected for a match against Chiswick Town in the Middlesex Senior League. The match was advertised with a kick off of 3:30pm and Admission was 5d (including tax).

Doug Brown
Supporter from 1912-1920's

"My only connection with Wealdstone FC was as a Schoolboy supporter. I moved from Claremont Road to Aberdeen Road in 1912, from where most of my spectating was done.

In those days the ground was situated at the end of Belmont Road, which was quite short and ran then alongside Wealdstone Rec and cemetery. A footpath continued across a smaller field and then onto the pitch itself, which was a mown field and very muddy at times. The players often emerged very muddy indeed.

As a Schoolboy I remember getting very excited during the game and shouting loudly as we knew who the players were, as most could be seen about town - I remember that 'Taff' Deeley was a local Blacksmith.

I seem to remember that the team kit was kept in Fewings General Shop on the corner of Belmont Road and Stuart Road.

Of the players I remember best, the first two names that come to mind were the two fullbacks, Smerdon and Burrows. They were two very uncompromising characters that had deadly sliding tackles. Very impressive in muddy conditions.

Next came Badger Kirby who was a very active centre forward and scored a lot of goals. There were the halfbacks, Frank Harbud and Theobold, both accomplished players with upright stances.

The goalkeeper was named Haskell, he was rather a slight figure for a goalkeeper. Arty I' Anson was another – a fair-haired winger, left, I think. There was another good local player, Harry Millar, a halfback who I think played for Harrow Weald as well.

At half time, Mr. Jabez Barnes always came on to the field – there was no half time rest! – with refreshments for the players. I always thought it was a slice of lemon, but I may be wrong. He always wore formal clothes with spats. To me he looked slightly comical and out of place. He was connected with the Primitive Methodist Church, which was situated in the High Road on the corner of Gordon Road.

Another man who was on the management side was Mr. Elmslie. He was the Manager of W H Smith and Sons shop opposite the railway station. He was a charming and cheerful man and he seemed to know everybody. "

It was a successful start to the season, as the first team progressed in Senior football and the 'A' team started with four wins in the Middlesex League scoring 22 goals and conceding only two, but the record was lost on the 18th October in a defeat against Zenith Carburetors.

The first team on the same day played away to Kingstonians in a London Senior Cup-tie;

In this London Senior Cup-tie at Kingston, the Wealdstone team were unlucky to lose by two clear goals. Kingston won the toss and set the 'Stones to face a stiff breeze.

The home team attacked early but Burroughs replied. Stock made good progress on the right but his first shot lacked sting. Kingston returned the attack and gave the visiting defence an anxious time, weak shooting spoiling many good openings.

Theobold was noted for some pretty work, his good passes being a feature of the play, while at the other end Daniels made a sad mess of a glorious chance, shooting by the post with an open goal.

Play ruled even, both sets of defenders showing to advantage. Harbud was responsible for some clever headwork, and the home centre forward was kept in subjection. Wealdstone were by now having more of the game, and Kirby had hard luck when he hit the upright, and again, when the home goalie fell on a teaser.

After halftime Kingston were swarming forward round the visitors' goal but Howman was very safe between the sticks. At the other end Wentworth went very close with a fast grounder, while Burroughs hit the bar with a shot the home goalie completely misjudged.

The home left wing was a constant source of danger, and Howman affected a great save from Crick. Wright got clear away on the right, and passed squarely to Henson, who had no difficulty in scoring.

Wealdstone tried hard to recover the position but nothing came off for them. Within ten minutes of the end, Daniels beat Howman with a good shot and put the issue beyond doubt, a well fought game ending with a 2-0 win for the homesters.

Wealdstone FC 1919-1920. Unfortunately, we do not have names to put to the faces.

It was the first season that a Wealdstone match was played in front of a crowd of over 1000, as the match on 31st December in the London League against Stirling Athletic gained the honour.

Early in 1920 Wealdstone played against a side who have been rivals for a number of years, running out comfortable 2-0 winners in the London League against Grays Athletic. It was noted that both teams were leg weary after a strenuous Christmas programme, the game suffered accordingly.

At the end of this first post war season, 'Stones had continued to acquit themselves well and in late March they hosted the Middlesex League leaders, Handley Page, taking the honours with a victory by three goals to two.

Three of the Wealdstone players that day had also been selected for 'County Honours'. Kirby, Harbud and Theobold being selected by Middlesex to play on the Easter Tour to Ostend, Antwerp and Brussels. Kirby also played on the following Thursday for the Middlesex League against Millwall Reserves.

During the close season, on 1st June 1920 the Annual General Meeting of the club was held at the YMCA Concert Hall, again 'loaned' to the club for the evening by Jabez Barnes.

Mr W H Whittaker presided, being supported by Messrs A J Halsey, Hon. Secretary and Treasurer and Mr J L Smerdon, Assistant Secretary.

The financial statement, which showed a substantial balance of £ 29, was unanimously adopted, and the committee were congratulated on such a successful season and financial result the Secretary in submitting his report stated that the first team had Won 19; Lost 11 and Drawn 9 matches out of 39 played, and had scored 93 goals against 61 conceded.

The 'A' Team had won 18 Lost 8 and Drawn 1 game out of 27 played and had scored in all 90 goals to 34. The first team had finished third in the Middlesex League and fourth in the London League, the 'A' team also finishing third in their Middlesex League. It was proposed for the following season that the club should enter the Middlesex League, the First Division of the London League, The Football Association Cup, the Amateur Cup, the Middlesex Senior Cup, the Middlesex Senior Charity Cup and the London Senior Cup.

Mr Jabez Barnes congratulated the club on its play during the year, and offered to assist the club in every possible way and the following Officers were elected by ballot; President; The Rev H Chapman, Hon Secretary and Treasurer Mr A J Halsey, Assistant Secretary Mr J L Smerdon, Committee; W Peace, W H Whittaker, T Bradbury, W Balkwill, A Bryan, H Rogers, C Sherlock, F Cane, J Hinchcliffe and Captain H Miles.

The meeting was well attended by football supporters, the club's prospects are exceedingly bright for the next year.

Mr Jabez Barnes offered the club the use of the Concert Hall and three Tennis Courts during the summer, an offer gladly accepted.

According to the balance sheet, the gate money for the season amounted to £202 15s 2d which meant that with a known admission charge of 5d, some 9730 people had watched Wealdstone at home!

It also seems that this was the first season where an award was made to the Wealdstone FC Player of The Year.

What we are certain of is that the first recipient of the award was Harry Miller who had played for the club prior to World War 1 and had become Captain when the club restarted in 1919.

Harry Miller pictured in 1913.

The uncertainty stems from a report in a newspaper in 1969 that says the award was made to Harry Miller in 1929, some years after he had in fact retired.

The following season saw Wealdstone drawn against local rivals Harrow Weald, away, in the Amateur Cup. This game was to create an excellent atmosphere locally,

The match between Harrow Weald and Wealdstone in the Preliminary Round of The Amateur Cup excited a good deal of interest in local football circles, and a crowd of about 1600 gathered on the Alma Road ground to witness the encounter. Wealdstone were the favourites, but Harrow Weald was expected to make a hard fight of it. A keen and exciting game ended in a draw, 1-1 but on the run of the play, the home team just deserved to win it.

The teams lined up as follows Harrow Weald; H Miall, G Martin and V Ulph, B Bunker, L Courting and H H Simper, F J Thorne, Page, T Beech, D Ward and D Morgan.

Wealdstone; R Bates, J Smerdon and J Burroughs, C Durham, Bowman and H Miller, A Smith, E Theobold, R Kirby, F Theobold and W Hobbs.

Playing uphill, the home team put up a hard game in the first half and at both ends there were many exciting incidents. Thorne was early conspicuous for an excellent centre of which full advantage was not taken, and shortly after Miall cleared well following a Wealdstone attack. Smith placed a corner with splendid judgement, but the ball went dangerously across the goal mouth, and fell behind.

E Theobold gave a nice pass to Smith who sent in a fine shot which Miall held and cleared and a pretty piece of combination between E Theobold, Kirby, Smith and Hobbs followed and culminated in a shot from Smith, which just went over the bar.

A free kick was accurately placed by Miller, but Miall saved in confident style at the expense of a corner. Courtin, Harrow Weald's centre half, was playing a magnificent game and was always a source of worry to the opposing forwards while on occasions he also supported his own forwards. Martin and Ulph too, were conspicuous for some good defensive work.

From the Harrow Weald Amateur Cup game in 1920

During a Weald attack, Smerdon was penalised for a foul in the penalty area but with the resultant kick Beach placed wide.

Thorne made a fine run on the right and his shot was well saved by Bates who was playing a cool and safe game in goal. Ward, Thorne and Courtin were frequently notable for good work but in spite of their efforts they could not find a loophole in the Wealdstone defence.

On one occasion, Thorne got away on the right and centring beautifully a goal appeared certain, but somehow the visiting defenders cleared.

At half time, no score had been registered. Harrow Weald pressed hotly after the kick off and in five minutes had opened the scoring through Morgan, who succeeded in putting the ball in the Wealdstone net during a scrimmage.

Wealdstone went away at once and from a corner, beautifully placed by Hobbs, F Theobold headed in and equalised. Shortly after another corner was forced by F Theobold but the ball went behind.

Page was injured during a dangerous raid on the Wealdstone goal, but he pluckily resumed and soon after was conspicuous with a hard shot, which bates saved at the expense of a corner. During this half Harrow Weald pressed most of the time without adding to their score.

No decision had been reached when the final whistle blew and an extra half hour was played. Thorne had hard luck with a hard shot that just skimmed the bar and when time was called there had been no further scoring and a replay will therefore be necessary on the Belmont Road ground.

The replay the following week was played in front of a crowd of over 1800 and again was a keenly fought contest. Wealdstone scored first through Shadwick, only for 'Weald to equalise early in the second half with a 20 yard shot from Ward.

Wealdstone were to eventually win through an own goal scored by Harrow Weald defender, Ulph who deflected a shot when trying to clear in the first period of extra time, although 'Stones also missed a penalty shortly afterwards.

That season was to bring Wealdstone another League success. Having been challenging for the Middlesex League title all season with Gnome Athletic, Wealdstone ended the April with a crucial win, four goals to nil against Croydon South End.

The press, however, were not entirely happy. The report stated that it was a most unsatisfactory match and Wealdstone should have won by a far bigger margin – Croydon South End were in fact bottom of the table and had conceded over 100 goals in 20 matches

The paper went on to point out that the Championship was still open, and it could be that goal average would be the deciding factor. Wealdstone's players however, seemed to have other ideas.

On the 30th of April they were to play local rivals, Old Lyonians, away from home at Harrow Recreation Ground, and then in the final game of the season, the following Wednesday evening they were to host league leaders Gnome Athletic.

With just these two games to go, the top of the league table read;

	P	W	L	D	F	A	P
Gnome Athletic	21	17	4	0	70	25	34
Wealdstone	**20**	**14**	**3**	**3**	**52**	**23**	**31**
Hyde and Kingsbury	21	13	6	2	70	37	28

The match against Old Lyonians was reported as follows;

Never before during the football season now closing has there been such a gathering on the Harrow Recreation Ground, as that which assembled on last Saturday afternoon to witness the encounter between Wealdstone and the Old Lyonians in the Middlesex League, the playing pitch being completely encircled by an enthusiastic crowd which in places was six to seven deep.

A good game was anticipated, with Wealdstone the favourites, and as it turned out, the visitors more than justified their victory by three clear goals.

Throughout the season Wealdstone have shown consistent form, and have proved themselves on the whole a reliable team, while on the other hand the Lyonians have been models of inconsistency – they have on occasions showed excellent form and have beaten with ease the teams at the head of the table, yet on others they have had to fight hard against the teams at the foot.

On Saturday the were outclassed by the superior team and the game for the most part resolved itself into a battle between the Wealdstone forwards and the Old Lyonians defenders.

The home teams vanguard, who missed Massey, their pivot, rarely made a concerted movement toward the Wealdstone goal, their efforts being mostly of an individual character, and were easily held by the reliable line of halves against them. The Lyonians defence put up a brave show with Viccajee the shining light and both Heard and Cory had a gruelling afternoon of it.

In bright sunshine but with a stiff breeze blowing the teams lined up as follows; Lyonians; Cory, Heard, Viccajee, Chatham, Bates, Page, Cave, O'Brien, Woodbridge, Kinsey and Dawson.

Wealdstone; Bates, Borroughs, Smerdon, Durham, Harbud, Miller, Smith, E Theobold, Kirby, F Theobold and Latham.

The Wealdstone forwards who dominated the play throughout the first half were at once on the aggressive, and rapidly forced a corner on the left hand side. Kirby threatened danger in the goalmouth a few seconds later but Viccajee made a good clearance and then Heard cleared when E Theobold and Kirby were making ominous tracts towards Cory.

The first shot at goal came from Smith who following an effective combination between Kirby and E Theobold, received from the latter and sent in a beautiful hard shot which skimmed the bar and went behind. From E Theobold, Cory got the ball just in time, and then to the delight of the Lyons supporters, their right wing came into action.

Cave's centre was met by Smerdon and the visiting forwards again advanced towards Cory in the home goal. Woodbridge endeavoured to get his forwards moving without result and the ball was sent out to Latham who with F Theobold forced the ball into the Lyonian goalmouth.

After Cory had saved from Kirby, the leather went to E Theobold who could have breasted it into the net with ease but in the excitement his hands came into play first and he punched the ball in!

The opening goal was as a result of a pretty display of understanding between E Theobold and Kirby, and from his colleagues final pass Kirby beat the Lyonian defence for speed and scored. The Wealdstone forwards, continuing to play clever football, continued to enjoy the advantage and Cory experienced many anxious moments while Viccajee and Heard defended in fine style.

Dawson made energetic efforts to force the ball to the Wealdstone end, and assisted by Kinsey who had also been

putting in good work in the defence, got well on the way, the ball being passed eventually to Woodbridge from whose effort the visiting defence cleared.

Bates was called upon to make his first save of the match from O'Brien and a few seconds later saved again, but these Lyonians attacks were few and far between during this half. Heard was forced to concede a corner when the position for the Lyons was dangerous position and from Smith's well placed kick E Theobold headed just over. Dawson was then in action again and forced a corner which Harbud cleared.

Smith amused the crowd and perplexed the several opponents with his tricky foot movements and feints, and when the half time whistle blew the visitors were still prevalent. Play had been somewhat one sided but the Lyonian defence had put up a good display against an exceedingly clever forward line who were on the top of their form.

With the wind favouring them in the second half the Lyons had more of the play, but although they threatened the Wealdstone goal they were never very dangerous, and Bates hardly had one direct shot to hold.

Dawson was the dangerous man in the Lyons forwards and from one of his efforts Bates ran out to clear. He failed to obtain the ball however and Woodbridge made a good attempt to hook the ball into the net from a difficult position, but he was about a yard the wrong side of the post.

At the other end Wealdstone were awarded a penalty, which was taken by Miller, and Cory had but little difficulty in anticipating the direction of the shot and making a good save.

Excitement increased towards the end with the Lyons pressing hard for an equaliser. They forced several corners and from one, accurately placed by Chatham, Bates leapt to the ball and cleared before it could threaten further danger.

Following this Lyonian activity Smith sped away on the Wealdstone right and Kirby added the finishing touch to the little wingers' final shot, thus putting Wealdstone two up. Again their forwards attacked and clever play by F Theobold who beat about three opponents culminated in his scoring the third goal for his side.

The Lyonians played up pluckily and forced the ball to the Wealdstone goal where more than one corner was forced, and Woodbridge headed over from Chatham before the final whistle blew.

The game had been interesting enough particularly in the second half when the sides where more evenly matched, and Wealdstone, who played delightfully throughout thoroughly deserved their win.

So it was then that the season was to be decided in the final match. Wealdstone needing a victory over their visitors and league leaders Gnome Athletic, one point in front with just this one game to play.

The report in the local news section of the paper seems to have been written by the same person as the Old Lyonians report....

Before the largest crowd that has witnessed a football match on the Belmont Road ground this season, Wealdstone won a fast and exciting game on Wednesday, beating Gnome Athletic by two goals to nil.

Reproduced from a photocopy, the above picture appeared in the Harrow Observer on 18/01/1962, depicting the Wealdstone team that won the Middlesex League in 1920–21. Back Row; R Wartnaby (trainer), C Durham, W Burton, F W Harbud, R Bates, J Smerdon, W Gallagher, A I Son, W Balkwill (trainer). Front Row; A Smith, E Theobold, H Miller, F Theobold, C Latham. The picture was taken at Wealdstone Recreation Ground.

The match was to decide the Championship of the Middlesex league, and the local team evidently had this well in mind, every player being on the top of his form. The game was to some extent spoilt by the tactics of a number of the visitors but the referee had matters well under control and his decisions were always impartial.

Kirby kicked off but the determined rush was soon checked and a "free" was given against Durham for accidental hands, which resulted in the visiting left half striking the ball against the cross bar with terrific force.

An exciting scrimmage ensued Miller eventually clearing with a strong kick, which set Latham away, and his final effort missed the target by inches.

Smith soon after had hard luck after outwitting three opponents, and Latham forced a corner but the wind carried the ball over the line. The visitors then took up the running and attacked in force, Burroughs being obliged to concede a corner, which was well cleared by Smerdon.

A nice shot by the visiting centre forward missed by inches, and Bates brought off two fine saves in as many minutes.

Smith raced away and delighted the crowd with some tricky footwork his final shot being cleared by the goalie. A ding-dong struggle ensued and half time arrived with both goals intact.

The second half opened with a sensational rush towards Bates but Smerdon dashed in and cleared with a tremendous kick. The first goal came as a result of a foul on E Theobold. Durham took the kick and F Theobold headed in from close range.

The homesters then gave the visitors a gruelling time, but found their defence sound, the play of the right back being especially brilliant, clearing time after time from the goal line when the goalkeeper was beaten.

A "free" against Harbud looked dangerous but Miller affected an excellent save and then E Theobold was again fouled. Durham took the kick to F Theobold who scored with a splen-

did low drive.

Occasional breakaways by the visitors looked dangerous, but they could not penetrate the home defence. Bates fisted out from a host of players when a goal seemed almost certain.

The homesters again attacked and free kicks were numerous, but the defence proved stubborn and no more goals were scored. Wealdstone deserved their victory and are to be congratulated on their Championship.

Just below the match report was an announcement from the Vice President and Club Secretary, stating that there was to be a Celebration dinner to which all the players and officials would be invited as guests, and at the same time asking for all supporters who wished to attend to send a postcard indicating their intentions.

It also asked them to buy a ticket for themselves and a guest, as this would alleviate the need to ask for subscriptions to pay for the event.

Some three weeks later the AGM of the football club was held and all present were pleased to accept the reports and balance sheet at the end of a most successful season.

A Mr Whittaker was unanimously elected Chairman and the treasurers report showed that receipts were £1109 10s 8d, with a balance in hand of £93 10s 5d, making the season the most successful in the history of the club. The Secretary reported that it had been the first Championship of the Middlesex League for the club, and it was therefore the first Senior Competition that had been won.

The Middlesex League team had played a total of 36 matches winning 24 and drawing and losing 6 each. 87 goals had been scored and 41 conceded, but the club also reported that the London League team had not done so well, playing 33 matches and winning only 8 to 21 defeats.

It was at this AGM that Mr C E Brady was elected to the position of President and it was noted that the Chairman (Mr Whittaker) and the Secretary (Mr Halsey) were responsible to Mr Jabez Barnes for the sum of £400 for the purchase of the ground in Station Road.

(In the early part of June the Harrow Observer also reported on the development of a new football stadium at Wembley, to cost £1,000,000, and to become the home of the English Cup. The ground was to have a capacity of 127,000 with 35,000 seated and a further 10,000 ring seats. A number of organisations were financing the project, including the Football Association, and for their contribution they were to be guaranteed the use of Wembley for cup finals and Internationals for a set number of years).

Late in August, a Celebration Dinner was held, attended by the mayor and a number of Councillors and local dignitaries, as well as officials of the Middlesex League, who presented the shield and medals. The Harrow Observer too joined the celebratory atmosphere with its report, which went as follows;

The Wealdstone Football Club, after a particularly successful season, brought honour to the locality that they represent, by winning, with clean and sporting football, the Championship of the Middlesex League, and to celebrate this noteworthy performance a celebration dinner was held at the Central Hall where the Shield and Medals were presented.

The occasion was well attended and the atmosphere of enthusiasm prevailed among all present, a spirit being in evidence which augers well for the club in the season about to open.

The League Officials present were further pleased to welcome the Championship Shield back to the County after some twenty years, as the name was somewhat a misnomer, the majority of clubs playing in the league being from surrounding counties.

The Chairman of the League, when he presented the Shield also spoke at length about the club and its spectators;

The continued health and prosperity of the club are important, more earnestly because they are Champions of the Middlesex League.

He continued that it was important to him that the club should maintain the reputation it had made for itself since the war. It had had a reputation before the war, but he would not compare the past with the present.

The club had a reputation now, and the crowd too had a reputation separate and distinct, (which brought a good deal of laughter). The members of the club were a jolly good set of players, and they had never had any complaints against them during the years they had been members of the league.

The club, he understood, had played under a certain handicap for last season or the season before the conduct of some of the spectators left something to be desired, and to be capable of playing the best football in amateur spheres in that atmosphere and also of gradually improving that atmosphere was something to be proud of. Club Secretary Mr Halsey responded and gave a brief history of the club, noting that in the 1913-14 season, the first in Senior Football and in the Middlesex League the club had finished third.

Then unfortunately came the war period, and the club were very proud that their players joined up as keenly as they joined the football team. Some thirty players joined and they lost eight of them. In season 1919-20 they were again third in the league, and then in the last season they won it. It was noted that all of the players had signed on again for the new season.

Mr H C Hird proposed a toast to the visitors, and noted that 12 to 16 years ago at a football match they would not have found half as many spectators as there were present that night (100). In regard to Mr Clarke's remarks about the conduct of the spectators, the club would like to assure him that at the present time they were as good as gold.

They had a certain number that made a lot of noise, but taking them generally, they were just as well behaved and just as polite and nice as any other crowd that visited any class of football in the British Isles today.

They admired their players and were proud of them because they were all picked from their own village and not from all over the country as some clubs did.

The accounts showed a cash credit of £80 but there was a credit note to the value of £300. Therefore the club was £220 in debt, however Mr C E Brady, the club President said that they had had an expensive season with another before them and a new ground to take over. The intention was to have

Wealdstone Football Club, 1921 – 1922 Middlesex Senior League Champions

Front Row; E Theobold, G Martin, A Wilson, E Wright, H Miller (Capt), A I' Anson, G Davenport, D Morgan, E Pearce, Centre Row; W H Pearce, F Perry, H C Hird, R Wartnaby, J Smerdon, J Burroughs, F Harbud, P Deeley, W Gallagher, S Brett, A J Halsey, H Bowman, A Twitchen. Back Row; F Cane, S White, C E Brady, H Samuels, A Haskell, W Burton, A Bryan, C V Elmslie, C Austin

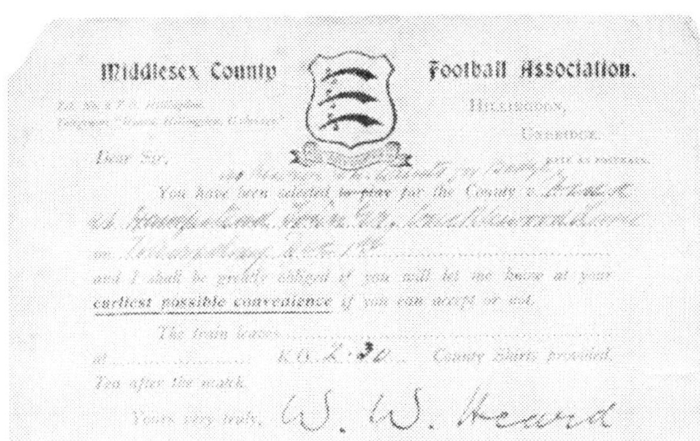
Middlesex County Football Association.

Dear Sir,

You have been selected to play for the County v.

and I shall be greatly obliged if you will let me know at your earliest possible convenience if you can accept or not.

The team leaves

at K.O. 2.30 County Shirts provided.

Tea after the match.

Yours very truly, W. W. Heard

The original card received by Harry Miller inviting him to play for the Middlesex County team, postmarked 4 Nov 1921

raised sufficient money to start work on the new ground after September 29th, so that they could get into the ground by Christmas, and he added £10 to the £90 raised that evening by donation.

The club intended to start the following season as the last at Belmont Road. The new ground that had been purchased by the club behind the Veterinary Hospital in Station Road, and described *"as a most central position, which should result in larger gates"* was to be ready during the season. The initial agreement was for Wealdstone FC to rent the ground for 13 years at a cost of £350, with an option to purchase the freehold if the funds could be found. The purchase price of the ground was set at £1,650. (This was later raised as a loan to complete the purchase).

By May of 1922, the Middlesex Senior League had been won for the second year in succession – only the second team to do this following Waltham in 1906-07 and 1907-08 – this time almost at a canter. Wealdstone having been in control of their matches and season alike for long periods.

The match programme for the last game of the season informed supporters of the intention to move, finally, to Lower Mead and also to apply to join the Athenian League for the forthcoming season. The application was to prove unsuccessful for the following season and the club opted to join the Spartan League where it was to remain for six years.

In July, it was reported that the club had retained all of the players from the previous season and had also recruited a new forward, R H Peel from local football, but the club had been unsuccessful in trying to complete the return of former centre forward R Kirby who had been playing at Hampstead Town, but he chose to sign on as an amateur at Watford.

At around the same time, the club were pleased to announce the completion or the works at Lower Mead, with the laying of paths and the building of terraces finally completed. The last action had been to lay a memorial to the players of the club who lost their lives in the first war.

The club in fact wrote to The Duke Of York in an attempt to encourage him to lay the memorial stone, but it was reported that this request, although met with a pleasing and courteous reply, had been unsuccessful.

The 1921-22 season started in a similar way to the previous, Wealdstone dominated their early fixtures, starting with a 3-0 victory away to Willesden and the report effused that if they and won by a much larger margin, it would have been no more than they deserved.

In mid September it was announced that work had started on the Lower Mead Field, at the rear of the Vetinary Clinic and Greenwood Farm in Station Road. The work on the new ground though, did not progress as well as had been intended; drainage of the ground being particularly difficult, and with limited funds available, the club was to remain at Belmont Road for the whole season, while work continued on the new ground.

A map of the Greenhill Farm area from 1920, with an original sketch of Lower Mead overlaid on the site. In later years, parts of the site were sold off to raise money and most notably, High Mead was built.

MOVING TO LOWER MEAD

One of the players in the side at the time of the move to Lower Mead was William (Bill) Gallagher, who played his first game for the 'Stones in the 1910 – 1911 season. Some ten years later he was appointed Trainer, a position he held at the club for over 30 years.

The first match at the new ground was to be a Trial Match, to select players for the forthcoming season, on 16th August 1922 with a kick of at 6:20pm. The opposing teams on the evening were to consist entirely of new players, and admission was to be free although there was to be a collection in aid of the St John's Ambulance Brigade.

The building of barriers and pay boxes was to commence immediately after the trial game, and there were to be four entrances to the ground. Final works on the ground were proceeding apace and it was expected that an admirable ground would be available for the season.

Near the entrance a pavilion had been erected which contained simple dressing room accommodation, a tea and refreshment room, committee room and the Secretary's Office. On the left hand side of the field, a covered stand thirty yards long with four tiers of seats, which would accommodate 400 people, was being erected.

The playing field was to be wired off and beyond the wire there was to be a cinder track and beyond that, Railway Sleepers were placed *"for the benefit of supporters on the fringes of the crowd"*

It was announced that the club would play two friendly fixtures to 'open' the ground, against Clapton Orient and Arsenal and the first serious match would be against Berkhamstead in the first round of the English Cup. Members tickets for that first season were put on sale for 7s 0d. The trial match caused quite a stir at the time, not because of the football but because of the crowd. The Harrow Observer reported;

The firm hold which football has upon a large section of the public was well indicated at the first trial match for the Wealdstone Football Club, which took place on the new ground, Lower Mead, Station Road, last Wednesday evening when there was an attendance of fully 2000.

The match was well contested and a number of new players were identified. The final score was Blues 2, Stripes 2, the goals having been scored by Booth (Stripes) equalised by Stock (Blues) and Gleinster (Blues) equalised by Booth with his second.

Wealdstone 0 Clapton Orient Reserves 6

Lessons learned by the Wealdstone team during the progress of this match against Clapton Orient, which was watched by just under 2000 spectators will, surely compensate to some extent for their heavy defeat by six goals to nil in their first fixture of the season on the Lower Mead ground on Saturday afternoon.

Capable as they no doubt are of putting up a good game against the strongest Amateur combinations, they were no match for the Reserve XI of the Second Division club, who controlled the exchanges from start to finish, and who would probably have run up a greater score had their shooting been as accurate as the rest of their play.

Wealdstone played pluckily against their superior opponents, but their attacks on the Orient goal were infrequent and sporadic, and resulted chiefly from wing efforts to which Wilson was particularly successful on the right.

The play of the professionals against the Amateurs was an object lesson in tackling, combination and accurate passing, and the finesse of the Orient players alone made the match worth watching although they were too strong for the homesters to produce an exhilarating contest.

At least the game provided useful practise for Wealdstone players, and seeing it was nothing more than the opening of the season trial, their defeat by a trained professional team should not be taken too seriously.

Not the start at Lower Mead then that had possibly been hoped for but the 2000 odd crowd was well entertained as the report went on;

At the start, the home players appeared nervous, and in the first minute a delightful combination resulted in Haskell having to clear. In the next minute, he saved again, and from the rebound, the Orient opened the scoring, less than five minutes from the kick off.

The next goal was not so easily obtained, although when it did come it was of the lucky variety. Williams, their inside-right, sent in a long shot which travelled along the ground until within a few feet of Haskell when it bounced clean over his head into the net. Lee the outside right headed the third and the score at half time was 3-0 in the Orients favour.

Wealdstone, outplayed as they were, had two chances worthy of mention, F Spencer headed just over from a free by E Theobold and E Theobold, following a miss-kick by an opposing back wasted a great opportunity by kicking feebly wide from close in with only the goalie to beat.

A corner accurately placed by Wilson also caused the Orient defence some anxiety before they could clear their lines.

The visitors scored their fourth goal a few minutes after the resumption, and following this came Wealdstone's best effort of the match. Their attack was more effective and they came close to scoring on at least three noteworthy occasions.

The first was when F Spencer meeting a nice centre from Wilson tested French, the goalie, and compelled him to carry beyond the legitimate distance to clear. He was consequently penalised but the free kick taken by Edwards from a yard or two from the goal line was unsuccessful.

The second occasion was due to good work by Wilson, who from near the line sent the ball accurately across the goalmouth where Spencer misjudged the flight in an attempt to reach it with his head. The narrowest escape however followed a corner conceded by French from a warm shot by Edwards, which was delightfully placed by Edwards.

Wilson ran in and with French at the other end of the goal, sent in a hard drive, which appeared a certain scorer, when an Orient defender intercepted the ball and the position was saved. This was the sum total of Wealdstone's scoring opportunities, although later Wilson created a splendid individual effort from the half way line.

With the exception of Deeley, the Orient forwards did not have much difficulty with the home half back line, but Martin and Spencer proved harder nuts to crack.

A few minutes from the end it looked as though Wealdstone would escape with nothing more than a four goal defeat, but in the last minute a fifth goal came, which Haskell, apparently handicapped by the sun, made no attempt to save. From the kick off Williams waltzed through the defence with the utmost ease to add the sixth.

Such strong opposition was hardly a fair test for the Wealdstone team playing together for the first time and it would be unreasonable to form too definite judgements as to the players' capabilities.

The game however, showed up Martin and Spencer to great advantage at the back. Deeley was the strongest of the halves and Wilson the most effective forward. Edwards accomplished one or two movements but was overshadowed by Worboys, the best half back on the field, in fact the Orient halves were generally much too good for the Wealdstone line and their forwards too good for the home halves.

Wealdstone; A H Haskell, G Martin, V Spencer, F Gibbons, E Randall, P Deeley, E Wilson, E Theobold (Captain), E Pool, F Spencer, A Edwards.

Clapton Orient; French, S Tonner, Bradberry, Worboys, Townrow, J Tonner, W Lee, Williams, Jones, Raby, Nunn.

The following week, in the second match at Lower Mead, Wealdstone faced an Arsenal team, and pushed them all the way, finally losing 2-1 in front of a crowd of over 2000. The Wealdstone side had been strengthen by the return of Millar and Harbud to the half back line and F Theobold to the forwards, the Wealdstone goal, the first at Lower Mead, was scored by club captain E Theobold.

Before the game, Lieutenant General Sir Francis Lloyd had unveiled a Memorial Plaque in the ground, adjacent to the Pavilion, in memory of those eight members of the Wealdstone Club that had lost their lives in the First World War.

Presented to the club amongst a collection of documents from H A 'Chippy' Luck, an Official of the club for over fifty years was this original receipt for the purchase of Lower Mead. It reads; *Received from the Wealdstone Football Club, the sum of Three Hundred Pounds on account of Sixteen Hundred and Fifty Pounds being purchase money of the freehold of Lower Mead Field Greenhill. Subject to contract to be entered into for tenancy with an option to purchase on terms as mutually agreed. It is signed Jabez Barnes and dated 26/8/20.*

This plaque, although later moved, was to remain displayed at Lower Mead until the ground was eventually demolished. The local public confirmed the feelings of a local reporter and agreed that *the tribute that has been paid by the Wealdstone Club is worthy of the affection that the club still retains for the memory of its departed servants.*

The closing words of the speech by Lieutenant General Sir Francis Lloyd at the unveiling were to instruct the two teams to go out and play the game that they (those named on the plaque) loved so well............

In early October, Wealdstone entertained Polytechnic in the Amateur Cup, eventually running out winners by 2-0, both goals being scored in the last three minutes, after some stalwart defending by the Polytechnic team. Wealdstone had also by this time secured the return of 'Badger' Kirby to the forward line. He celebrated by scoring the second goal.

More interesting however was the mention of the Guests of Honour at the game among a crowd in excess of 1600 – Mr Oswald Mosley MP and Lady Cynthia Mosley, both of whom were to follow the fortunes of Wealdstone for a number of years. This was only one of a number of visits they made to Lower Mead.

The following year showed again the strength of support for Wealdstone FC as in mid August, the club was pleased to announce that all of the playing members from the previous season had signed on again, including club captain H Miller who was to enter his 18th season with the club.

The brothers E and F Theobold were also to return, both having represented the club for a number of years, and two trial matches were announced on the Monday and Wednesday the 21st and 23rd of August.

Both matches were played between mainly new players trialing for the club and the total attendance at the two games was in excess of 4000, an astounding figure when you consider that just prior to the war, a crowd of 300 was considered to be large.

This was the season of Wealdstone's greatest victory, or at least victory by the greatest number of goals. A number of newspapers carried reference to the match concerned, when Wealdstone created a sensation as well as a club record at the time. On Saturday October 13th 1923 they scored 22 goals against the 12th London Regiment (The Rangers) in the Amateur Cup.

The local paper carried comment that indicated the score could have reached as high as 40 goals to nil had Wealdstone been so inclined, but it also mentioned the quality of the opposition

..........gallant fellows as their war record shows, but they are aspiring to achieve levels of football above their class as these results show, for only two weeks ago they were beaten by 19-0 by Wood Green in the FA Cup.

The actual match report did little but commend the remarkable feat of goal scoring, mentioning that C Mason scored seven, A Edwards scored six, A Mascall four, R G Hall three, P J Deeley scored one and there was an own goal from Curtis, The half time score was 9-0.

The Wealdstone side that day contained a number of reserve players, no doubt, as the club was aware of the 'strength' of their opposition; H Beard, H Deeley, G Martin, E Theobold, F Harbud, P J Deeley, W Wright, A Mascall, C Mason, A Edwards and R G Hall, playing in what to this day is the largest victory recorded by Wealdstone FC.

It was the first season that Wealdstone had had a Supporters Club, although little is known of the structure, the Harrow Observer reported in the following May

Supporters Clubs would appear to be finding favour in football circles, ands well they might, for where ever they have been tried, they have proved to be of great advantage to the football club to which they owe their allegiance.

In this district, Wealdstone led the way at the beginning of last season and the supporters thus organised have provided both encouragement to the teams and services to the officials....

By the middle of June, the Wealdstone Supporters Club had been formed. To ensure that everyone knew the aims of the Supporters Club, an introduction was given by Mr Fox who had recently relinquished the Chairmanship of St Albans City Supporters Club.

He stated that, *The first duty of Supporters Club members is to attend matches, and they at St Albans had been very successful in arranging excursions.*

If they got 500 or 600 supporters 'on foreign soil' it was wonderful what the effect was on the players.

He also called upon the members to look out for new players. St Albans had had from Wealdstone, one of the best players the club had ever had, Billy Hughes.

There were many boys who could play football and it was the supporters' duty to recommend them to the Committee.

Another thing that the supporters could do was to give a player a good word when he's doing well, but not to give him a bad word if he was playing badly.

Other things that Supporters Club's could do was too organise whist drives, concerts and dances as there was money to be got in that way.

The first officers of the Wealdstone Supporters Club were then appointed; Mr Halsey became Secretary and Treasurer, and Mr Mackintosh was elected Chairman. Messrs Sweatman, Blakey, Keys, Tilley, Norton, Braid, Howell and Thame along with Mrs Sweatman and Mrs Knight were elected to the Committee. It was not long before fundraising events were to come to the fore, to assist in paying initially the lease and the loan and eventually the purchase price of the Lower Mead ground.

The end of that same season saw some controversy with problems associated with the Harrow Charity Cup – the competition organisers falling foul of an FA Rule preventing the playing of any matches in the competition after May 3rd and the semi-finals, in which Wealdstone were involved being scheduled for the 8th May. There was a great deal of too-ing and fro-ing which resulted in the semi-final match between Harrow and Greenhill FC and Harrow Weald FC, due to be played at Lower Mead, being played as a friendly, this was decided the day before the match was to take place, and all the proceeds were split between the Harrow Hospice and St Johns Ambulance.

Subsequently Wealdstone withdrew from the competition, as it seems it was they that had highlighted the rule. It was eventually agreed that the matches could be completed at the start of the following season, Wealdstone rejoined to take their place in the semi-finals, eventually going on to win the competition.

All this resulted in a full column in the local newspaper – far more coverage than any match during the season!

In early June of 1924, there were a number of small items reported, all of which were to show an insight into club's and football's futures.

The first was a small Spartan League item as a result of their AGM – two clubs were elected to the league for the following season having finished as Champions and runner up of the Great Western league, and both clubs having defeated the Wealdstone side on their own grounds in the previous season.

The two clubs were Botwell Mission, later to become Hayes and Staines Lagonda.

There was surprise that this season's Spartan League Champions, Leavesden Mental Hospital, had to resign from the league *"owing to the uncertainty of their financial position, the club being precluded from taking a gate"*.

They were old members of the league, but they *"had incurred considerable unpopularity from a spectators' point of view last season"*.

Immediately below this, appeared the following;

As was indicated at the Annual General Meeting of the Wealdstone Club last week, they require to save some £200 a year if they are to acquire possession of Lower Mead, Station Road, as their own property at the expiration of the ten years that remain of their lease.

All sportsmen will wish them success in their efforts, for Lower Mead is obviously the finest site in the neighbourhood for the home of an ambitious senior football club. No doubt the committee will be considering ways and means of raising the amount.

In many cases, a small finance committee, with the set object of effecting economies and watching the expenditure has produced wonderful results, but whatever is done it should command the support of all who follow the games at Lower Mead.

At the same meeting Mr C V Elmslie acknowledged the assistance he had received from players – he struck the right note in referring to those attached to other local clubs who, at the last minute perhaps, helped him out of a difficulty in agreeing to play for the Wealdstone Club.

It shows an excellent spirit when players who are not regular members of a team respond so readily to an appeal of that description. Wealdstone are doing the correct thing in keeping their eyes on promising junior players in the District, and I agree with Mr Elmslie that such players should consider it an honour to be asked to play for the towns senior club.I look for-

July / August 1922	
To erecting Stand, 150 feet long as per plans and as per contract,	£ 210 0s 0d
To erecting Pavilion as per plans, as per contract	£ 270 0s 0d
To Extras	
To supplying and fixing Gas and Water supplies and fittings as per tender	£ 44 10s 0d
To supplying Two new pavilion baths	£ 12 0s 0d
To supplying and fixing sink, with draining boards complete with water supply and waste,	
Supply and fix counter with shelf and front and with boarded ends and flap entrance	£ 7 8s 0d
To supply and fit two table tops, each 14 feet long with three trestles	£ 4 0s 0d
Supply four forms for tables 14' long and supply one form for home Dressing Room	£ 2 10s 0d
For supplying three Yale type locks for front door	£ 1 0s 0d
Supply materials and erect two latrines at rear of Pavilion for players, complete with seats and pails with boarded screens in front of each and supply and fit two fence enclosures at each end of pavilion with leafed doors hung with fasteners. Excavate and wheel away for two soakaways and supply and fit in two yards of sifted ashes to each soakaway and put in drainage to same	£ 18 0s 0d
Supply and erect Public latrines 28 feet long in front with 5 foot screens, 13 boards high and with 24 foot back with 8 foot section 11 boards high	£ 14 5s 0d
Supply and erect 2 long enclosures at each end of the stand, 28 feet long and 22 feet wide with part roofed enclosure to each and form Box in 1 enclosure and double entrance with wide gate and lock and key	£ 25 0s 0d
To ten off extra lengths of stand at pro rata	£ 14 0s 0d
To excavating and removing earth from Roadway, filling in with old concrete and filling in and levelling off with ashes, 3 mans time at £1.14.8 each	£ 5 4s 0d
Supply 4x2 for entrance gangways and posts; 92 feet x 2 _	19s 2d
Supply 2 dozen Veritas mantles 13/-, 5 burners 4/9, 5 shades @ 2/-	£ 2 6s 9d
Committee Room	
Supply and fit 1 6' by 1'8" by 1'8" locker complete with lock and key	£ 1 0s 0d
Supply and fit 16' run of seating	16s 0d
Extend partitions to roof in Committee Room with asbestos sheeting, labour and materials	£ 2 15s 0d
Supply and fit 3 wire guards for windows	£ 3 5s 0d
Casing in Meter complete with lock and key	16s 6d
Total	£ 642 10s 5d
Deposit	£ 150 0s 0d
Due	£ 492 10s 5d

The original bill (reproduced above) from Government Contractors Dr to G O Davies and Sons showed the amount of work that had been carried out on the new Lower Mead ground.

ward to a time when every member of the Wealdstone team will be a local product.

Around the same time, the first Trustees of the club were confirmed, as part of the negotiations with The Wealdstone and District Building Society for the mortgage for the eventual freehold of the ground.

Those named in the agreement were Charles Brady, Algernon George, William Pitts, Clarence Elmslie, Thomas Harris, William Cunningham, Ernest Bellchambers, Frederick Cane, Herbert Hird, William Peace, Campbell Austin, Arthur Halsey, Frederick Perry, Ronald Borrisow and William Whittaker.

The club entered into the arrangement with the building society to allow them to purchase Lower Mead for the sum of £1700, repayable over a period of twenty years. The agreement was signed and sealed on 25th March 1925.

Later that year in the August, the policy or recruiting local talent was further emphasised with the organisation of two trial matches for new young players early in August, and off the field,

There were one or two other minor problems to be sorted out at this time as well. The entrance to the ground had bridged a small drainage ditch and it seems that in fencing this off, the club had encroached on their neighbour's land, a householder by the name of Dundas. This matter was resolved when the club agreed to allow Mr Dundas to move the fencing and posts, an offer which he declined as it would have cost as much to move them as they were worth.

The club had also by this time introduced a policy of Training, and after the first 'pre-season' session they were pleased to announce that all of the previous seasons players had again returned, accompanied by the addition of a left winger, J R Weaver, recruited from Walthamstow Town.

The Lower Mead ground had suffered in the four years since it had been a farm, and over the summer, a number of supporters assisted in 'repairing' the pitch. More serious was the need for better drainage as a whole on the ground, and some levelling work. A local groundsman, Charles Lewin, was invited to inspect and tender for the works.

The pitch at this time had a slope in excess of six feet from end to end. This was to be reduced to a maximum of two feet nine inches, the spare soil carried away. Also strips of turf twelve feet wide were to be removed across the pitch, excavated and re-laid on ashes before re-turfing.

At the same time, along one side of the ground, a drainage ditch was to be excavated to a depth of two feet nine inches, and four inch agricultural open jointed drainpipes were to be laid in, this then being covered with rough material, old tins, crocks and clinker, then covered with rough house ashes, then filled to leave an open ditch.

The club had suffered no little anxiety and expense in maintaining the surface. As a result of the energetic efforts over the close season, the pitch was reported to have an excellent appearance for the start of the new season, which was to open at the end of the month with a fixture at home to Botwell Mission.

It was reported that for the first time, the club had decided to appoint a full time groundsman to maintain the pitch and this was expected to prove a very wise move.

The pitch may well have improved but the fortunes of the Wealdstone sides were very different.

Up until the Christmas period, the first team were struggling a little in the Spartan League table, although their games must have been entertaining judging by the goals scored – after eleven matches a new striker, N Groves had claimed 24 goals and four more in the reserves, where the top scorer was E Wilson with 17 (plus two for the first team) while James Williams was close behind with fifteen.

The reserves at this time carried all before them, being comfortably top of Division 2 of the Spartan League, the Reserves Section.

The Boxing day newspaper also carried a report of another high scoring game, this time the first team winning 7-1 at home against Maidenhead. There was one item in the report, however, that surely could not be repeated today. The report reads;

One of the most sporting incidents that have been witnessed at Lower Mead occurred, when following a struggle in the Maidenhead goalmouth, the ball passed over the goal line, apparently off of a defender, the referee pointed to the centre The visiting goalkeeper protested but the referee adhered to his decision. Groves, the Wealdstone centre forward intervened in support of the objection, and indicted that he had handled the ball in the struggle. The referee then awarded a free kick to Maidenhead instead of a goal to Wealdstone.

Groves' spontaneous admission was warmly applauded by the visiting players and supporters.

This incident was quickly followed by a legitimate point when Hall, receiving from Groves made a solo dart toward the visitors' goal and although attended by a defender, retained his command of the ball and scored with a good shot.

Who knows whether he would have made such an admission if the scores had been level at the time!

Having been in command of their division for so long Wealdstone Reserves suffered a dip in form towards the end of the season. It was a result of the misfortune of others, when Lyons Athletic were beaten by Chesham Reserves, that Wealdstone remained with a chance of the division title. They had two games remaining and had to win both to secure the title.

They had also continued their good performances in the Harrow Charity Cup and they retained the Trophy having won the previous season's competition. (They therefore won the same trophy twice in one year).

The final victory was a convincing one, by four goals to nil over Preston, a young club formed after the First World War

The two league games resulted in a 6-1 victory over Bush Hill Park, and this was followed by a 1-0 win over Apsley, the three games having taken place over six days, only thirteen players (including two goalkeepers) being used.

Eventually finishing as Second Division Champions, Wealdstone had won 20 out of 26 league matches with 1 draw, in the process scoring 85 goals and conceding only 35, and finishing three points clear of second placed Lyons Athletic.

The first team were less successful, finishing in tenth place (of

One of a number of ways the club used to attract fans to Lower Mead in the 1920's. This occasion was April 28th 1923 when Champions Chesham visited Lower Mead on the day that the first F A Cup Final was played at the new Wembley Stadium.

fourteen) in the Spartan League Division One, where Chesham were champions with 21 wins, 4 draws and one defeat.

The 1923 -1924 season was a little better for the first team, but not so successful for the reserves, both teams eventually finishing in seventh place in their respective Divisions.

Off the field the fundraising by the Ways and Means and Programmes Committee had almost exactly reached its target for this season by raising £ 299 0s 81/2d. The major contributors to this had been the Wealdstone FC Fete, which had raised a profit of £128, dances which had raised £46, programmes £96 and the bar £20.

The reserves had better fortune over the next two seasons as well, retaining the Harrow Charity Cup in 1923-24 and again in 1924-25 when they were also crowned as Champions of the Spartan League Division II.

The first team had had three mediocre seasons, their only success reaching the final of the Middlesex Senior Cup in 1923-24.

At the beginning of the 1926/27 season Wealdstone had the opportunity to avenge the defeat in the first game at Lower Mead, when they were beaten 6-0 by Clapton Orient. This season the result was somewhat different, 'Stones running out winners by 2-0, as the Harrow Observer reported;

If the quality of football played by the Clapton Orient A eleven which visited Lower Mead in the opening match of the season on Saturday had attained the standards expected of the nursery team of a Second Division club, Wealdstone's victory by two goals to nil would have been a more noteworthy achievement than it actually was.

This is in no way meant to disparage the performance of the Wealdstone team as a whole, for they were the superior team throughout all the challenges, but to subdue any false impressions that the first victory of the season may have had on followers of the club.

The heat was intense and this may have been some way responsible for the disappointing attendance, but it did not seem to have any effect on the performance of the players.

Wealdstone, with three new players in the team, A Berry in goal, F Thorne late of Harrow Weald and Watford Old Boys, outside right, and D Dooleavy at inside-right, were captained by A Dowling.

R Tansley, who was selected to play at centre forward was unable to play owing to an injury received in the trial, and Champion led the attack.

They were soon on their mettle, and notably good play was seen on the left wing where Church was frequently conspicuous for smart work. Well served by both H Smith, R Smith and Champion he frequently had the opposing half back line beaten, and delivered well-placed centres.

After the game had been in progress for about 30 minutes, Champion manoeuvred the ball cleverly in the goalmouth, drawing one defender and beating him and then another until the defence was in a tangle. When his opportunity seemed to be slipping away he parted with the ball to H Smith who with a clear opening dispatched the ball into the net.

Ten minutes later Wealdstone went further ahead, following an enterprising movement on the left wing. H Smith delivered a hard shot, which, with the help of his knee, West, the goalkeeper, saved. The ball however, rebounded to Champion, who promptly drove it back into the net well out of reach.

Both goals were good ones and Wealdstone had earned their lead at half time. Neither side scored in the second half though Orient, kicking towards the Pavilion made desperate efforts to improve their position, without making much impression on the home defence.

Berry, in the home goal, had more to do during this period but he was not unduly tested, although on one occasion in taking a ball that skidded low across the box he showed good judgement and skill. Later, after the ball had struck the crossbar and bounced down, he collected it and affected a timely clearance.

Church on one occasion was in a good position near the Orient goal, but the visiting defence swooped down upon him and squeezed him out. Champion too, found himself well placed from a dart through, but his shot was saved.

Thorn, who was not very prevalent, sent in a perfect shot from the wing, the ball glancing against the crossbar and rebounded into the goalmouth, Champion there, received it and delivered a spirited shot which was cleverly saved by West.

The game, considering the conditions was an interesting one, and the enterprise of the club deserved better patronage than it received.

Wealdstone; A Berry, W W Pratt, A Dyrning, J Williams, E Randall, R Smith, F Thorne, D Dooleavy, A Champion, H Smith, A Chapple.

Clapton Orient; West, Ashton, E Bryant, A E Bowcott, Oxford, W Ashfield, H Martin, T Medlarch, T Brookes, Hill, Booth

Possibly not the excellent victory that the supporters may have hoped, but a victory none the less, and Wealdstone's first against a professional team.

It was to be the start of another successful season at Lower Mead with a number of high scoring games played, none less than the Amateur Cup victory over RAF Uxbridge by nine goals to three at the end of November.

The club were pleased to report that the ground had taken the heavy rain well, and there was no question of the match not being played as it had the week previous.

Among the Wealdstone goals was one described as particularly sensational – a 40-yard shot that travelled at some great speed and completely deceived the visiting goalkeeper. This obviously disturbed the RAF Uxbridge team, as within minutes Wealdstone had scored twice more!

The goalscoring feats continued. The high point was the perfect Christmas present for 'Stones fans, when the first team recorded a Boxing Day victory by 16-2 against Hertford Town, having previously beaten them by six goals to one and in this match, Townley equalled the record of scoring seven goals in a match (first recorded against The Rangers). It all went a long way to ensuring that the club scored over 100 league goals in a season for the first time.

The success of the club was to rob them of the Spartan League title, as fixture congestion caused by long runs in all the cups and some postponements due to bad weather meant as many as three games were played each week at the end of the season.

The reserves were good enough to regain the Harrow Charity Cup from holders RAF Northolt and thus recorded their fourth win in the competition in five years, as recorded by the reporter from the Harrow Observer;

In blazing sun almost on a par with Midsummer, Wealdstone Reserves beat RAF Northolt at Lower Mead on Saturday afternoon (7/5/27), in the Final of the Harrow Charity Cup. A small crowd witnessed an interesting game in which the cup-tie spirit was conspicuous by its absence!

The weather no doubt affected the players, but nevertheless a little spirit might have been exhibited by the participants, and a little more effort and enterprise shown.

The RAF while not having the greater of the play finished their efforts better and the crosses, which Rogers had to deal with, were far more difficult than those sent in by the home forwards, whose shooting was wild to a painful degree.

Not the best of entertainment, but Wealdstone ran out eventual winners by 3-0 goals from Mascall (2) and, Bayles.

The fixture congestion was to cause the cancellation of a Charity Match in which Wealdstone had been invited to play. The match was to have raised funds for the local hospital and the teams were to compete for Gold Medals – the opponents were to be a London League club, but who has not been recorded. All this was to help to raise the £3000 per year that the hospital needed to cover its costs.

The Spartan League season ended for the first team with two fixtures against Colchester United. The first, played at Lower Mead was won by Colchester. Wealdstone won the second surprisingly after the disruption to the team.

Visiting Colchester in the final match of the season on Saturday, Wealdstone had their revenge for the defeat at Lower Mead the previous week.

The Wealdstone team had been subjected to considerable reorganisation as E Ryder was selected to play for the Spartan League against Maidenhead United, the League Champions, and H Smith and E Wilson were also unable to play. Deeley took the right back position and Pratt was at centre half. R Groves, a junior player, led the forwards and L Groves was on the left wing in place of Lee who missed his train.

Considering all this the best of the afternoon's game was quite a good one, and Wealdstone's victory was well deserved. In spite of the re-arrangement the forwards showed attractive combination and soon settled down to a pleasing game. I' Anson and Tansley played with perfect understanding on he right wing, and R Groves, who has a strong kick, proved a useful and promising leader of the attack, opening up the game in good style.

Downing adapted himself well to the Outside Left position, and L Groves centred and shot with accuracy. Though not so convincing as at right back, Pratt put in some capital work at centre half. Williams was confident but R Smith's form was again disappointing. Deeley and Kelly were safe at the back, and Berry made no mistake in goal.

Colchester opened the scoring through Barrell ands shortly afterwards Downing equalised. Wealdstone then took the lead through R Groves who added another about 15 minutes before the interval. Wealdstone leading by three goals to one at half time.

After a period of even play in the second half, Downing scored Wealdstone's fourth goal and Collins was successful for Colchester who made strenuous efforts to improve their position. Hands against Deeley in the penalty area provided them with an opportunity but the kick was saved by Berry at the expense of a corner. Five minutes from the end, Colchester obtained their third goal from their Outside Right.

Wealdstone; W Berry, H Deeley, L Kemp, J Williams, W Pratt, R Smith, A I' Anson, R Tansley, R Groves, A Downing, L Groves.

At the Annual General Meeting of the club, the Committee were pleased to confirm that the season had been more successful than the previous year,

In 1926 Wealdstone had been beaten in the second qualifying round of the FA Cup. In 1927 they had reached the third qualifying round before losing to Waterlows. In the Amateur Cup last season they had been beaten in the first qualifying round, this

last season they had reached the first round proper.

In the Middlesex Senior Cup in 1926 they had lost in the first round, this season they had lost in the semi-final to Uxbridge Town. In the London Senior Cup they had previously lost to Yiewsley in the first Qualifying Round, but again this year had improved, losing in the final Qualifying Round to Barking.

In the Middlesex Cup they had again lost in the semi-final, this time to Barnet. In spite of this and the congestion, they had finished a good fourth in the Spartan League, one point behind the runner up and only four points behind the winners.

They had played 28 league matches, won 18 lost seven and drawn three and had scored 100 goals against 67 conceded gaining 39 points.

The reserves, as well as regaining the Harrow Charity Cup had finished third in the Spartan League Division II, playing 24 matches, winning 14, losing 7 and drawing three, scoring 81 goals against 63, attaining 31 points.

The top goalscorers in all competitions were Hoskins with 52, Tansley with 48, Champion with 31 and H Smith with 24. The fixture congestion was detailed as at the end of the season, no fewer than 24 matches were played in 32 days – out of these, 16 were won and two drawn.

The local paper for the first week of May shows that matches were played nightly the previous week, the matches on Monday and Wednesday being two of the best of the season. Some of the home players had played in four matches in five days!

The treasurers report showed that receipts amounted to £1545 0s 4d which included the balance from the previous year of £32 and additionally, £441 11s 6d had been received from cup-tie gates, £ 374 14s 6d from League and Friendly fixtures, £80 8s 6d from 'away' Cup gates. The assets of the club were also listed at £2142 15s 1d, which was made up of a number of items including the ground at £1600 and £256 9s which was the value of the Pavilion and Stand and fittings. There was still a liability of £300 on the second mortgage and £1000 to the Wealdstone Building Society on the original ground purchase.

Honours for the season went to the Wednesday section. Reformed to allow more people to play football, possibly at a slightly lower standard, they had won the Harrow and District League and been runner up in the Hounslow and District League, also winning the Harrow Charity Shield for the first time.

At their AGM, the President, C V Elmslie, and Hon Treasurer H A Luck were pleased to announce that the club had played 48 matches, winning 36 and drawing 4. 118 goals had been scored and only 47 conceded and it had been the most successful season for the club.

There was to be another Wealdstone FC Fete at Lower Mead, something that had been introduced to raise money to buy the Lower Mead ground.

The Supporters Club and Club Committee ran these under the title at this time of the Ways and Means and Programmes Committee. This year it was their fundraising of £288 5s 6d that had allowed the club to remain solvent.

The Fete was planned for June 18th but was far short of a success due to terrible weather on the day, a downpour having limited the attendance and therefore the amount of money raised, where in the previous year, 6000 people had attended, this year only about a third of that number paid admission. There were still a number of popular attractions. D Grey, a local showman of the time had provided Roundabouts, Chairplanes and Swings.

The Committee had also organised a number of sideshows and competitions. For one of these the prize was a live pig, which escaped during the afternoon causing a great deal of amusement before it was recaptured.

The Donkey Derby had again aroused interest but in the conditions the entry was smaller than in previous years and unfortunately, the open air dancing in the evening was severely curtailed by the downpour at 8:00pm. Ever resourceful, the Committee immediately rescheduled the popular event for July 2nd. Tickets for this alone were to cost 1/-. Due to the conditions, the event failed to cover its costs, but undaunted, the club rescheduled another event for August 13th and added a number of additional attractions. These were to include a Motor Cycle Gymkhana, which was to conclude with a Motor Cycle Football Match on the Lower Mead pitch for one hour! There were also events that local Motor Cyclists could enter such as an obstacle race, with an entry fee of 1/-.

The club were also hoping to have a Military Tattoo to close the day's events, and to ensure the maximum profit from the day, they were inviting tenders from local tobacconists, confectioners, fruiterers and the like to rent space to sell their wares from stalls.

The slogan at the time was to raise money to keep Lower Mead as an open space and there was still some £1500 required to allow the club to discharge all their liabilities and own the ground.

A number of friends of the club came forward in the meantime to offer donations as insurance against further bad weather and as it proved, just as well. The Harrow Observer reported;

In order to retrieve the loss made by Wealdstone Football Club when poor weather spoilt their Annual Fete, a number of Club Members had organised a further event and a Motor Cycle Gymkhana for last weekend at Lower Mead.

The bad luck, which has dogged the club in its social events this year, however struck again, and rain fell heavily throughout the afternoon and evening. The arrangements had been admirably made and given fine weather a financial success would undoubtedly have been achieved.

Daring motor cyclists had been advertised and with a number of sideshows and attractions all augured well for the admittance of a record crowd. As it was, at four pm when people should have been streaming in, there were less than 100 people in the ground.

Before the commencement of the programme members of the Watford Auto Cycle Club revived the somewhat flagging interest of the crowd by skilful riding in a preliminary game of football, and the spectators were much amused by the participation off Mr L Hoskins, who, attired as a Policeman, rode onto the ground on a Donkey.

His steed however viewed the Motor Cycles askance and in spite of the remonstrations of his rider, insisted in returning to the refreshment pavilion.

The Motor Cycle Football Match which took place later,

between two teams representing Watford and the 'Stones was an event replete with thrills. The play was carried out at a fast pace serious collisions seemed at all times imminent. After a spectacular run down the field, in which the forwards moved at about thirty miles per hour, Watford opened the scoring.

Soon afterwards one of the 'Stones made a retirement for a technical adjustment, but his team equalised after a breathless melee in the goalmouth. A save by the Watford goalkeeper proved but a prelude to a further score from the 'Stones, and at half time, the game changed over with the score 2-1.

By this time the muddy conditions of the pitch made skids frequent and the utmost skill of the riders on their machines was required, and after a fast and furious second half, 'Stones were winners by three goals to two.

The proposed Stunt Display was cancelled due to the condition of the pitch – I wonder what groundsman would allow a similar event one month before the season's start these days! Yet more surprising, there was to be another Motor Cycle football match to be rescheduled for the September, i.e. during the football season.

A number of important appointments were made at this time. Billy Williams was appointed as Trainer to the second eleven. He retained the position into the late 1950's, working alongside Bill Gallagher and after the Second World War he was often called upon by the Middlesex County FA to assist them.

Also, a number of people were elected Life Members of Wealdstone FC. Herbert H Hird, a former Chairman and long serving Committee member was elected to this position to join W H Peace and C E Brady, elected a season or so earlier. All were instrumental in ensuring the future of the club on a daily basis, and were all instrumental in the purchase of Lower Mead. They formed part of an ever growing list that included E G C Bellchambers, C W Elliot, and H Howman, being joined the following season by A J Halsey, Dr Margaret Brady and G W Pitts and subsequently by F W Harbud, H A 'Chippy' Luck and W Rich.

The next season was to be more promising, continuing in the same goalscoring vein (albeit without silverware) from the previous year. 'Stones opened the season with another victory over a professional club, this time defeating a strong Fulham team by the odd goal in nine, having come back during the second half from a three-two deficit to be five-three in front some five minutes later.

There were a number of high scoring games during the season – an 8-2 victory over Polytechnic in the league in September was followed by a run of poor form and results, inconsistency being the failing of the side. They returned to winning ways against Uxbridge Town in the Amateur Cup by three goals to two.

Later in October there was the prospect of a visit to Hendon Town in the next round for what turned out to be an extraordinary match in difficult conditions, as the Observer was to report;

Worse conditions could hardly be imagined than those suffered by Wealdstone in their visit to Hendon Town on Saturday, Wealdstone winners by six goals to four. Not only was there incessant rain but fog and darkness descended necessitating a temporary suspension of play, and the pitch was a quagmire.

Although Wealdstone took the lead twice during the first half, Hendon did not concede ground and quickly equalised on both occasions. The visitors gradually went ahead however and led by three goals to two at half time.

In the second half Wealdstone soon demonstrated their superiority by scoring two more goals, and after the enforced interval caused by darkness, only the skill of Standish in the Hendon goal prevented the home side suffering a greater reverse.

Wealdstone made no changes to the formation that had done so well at Slough the week before and the formation again did itself justice. The quality of football was good despite the conditions, and although there was no lack of keenness, fouling was pleasingly absent.

Berry, in the Wealdstone goal was not busy, but what he did was done well. He was admirably covered by Bowtle and Downing who were both sound, their kicking and tackling being accurate and sound despite the conditions. Pratt was effective at right half and allowed Edwards, the old Wealdstone player, little room.

R Smith also gave a sound display but Ryder was not happy on the sodden ground and did not do himself justice. The forwards combined well throughout, and were far more effective than the Hendon attack, being quicker on the ball and superior in their finishing.

Maskell was to the fore with clever and enterprising wing work, and Bradshaw was again constructive and hard working. In the centre, Tansley was in a resourceful mood and scored three of the Wealdstone goals. Collins confirmed the favourable impression he made last week, rendering good all round service, and with Eagle readily supporting him, the pair made a satisfactory left wing.

There was a sensational opening, Ryder sending the ball immediately across to Collins who deposited it in the goal. It seems impossible to convince players of the folly of stopping to make appeals to the referee. It rarely does any good and often presents the opposing side with a goal. It did so again on Saturday, for Hendon were able to equalise through Edwards who got the opening in consequence of the defenders directing their attentions to an appeal for offside instead of tackling the man.

After the game had been in progress for 25 minutes, Tansley received the ball from Smith, cleverly eluded two opponents and scored with a low drive.

Just before the interval Hendon again equalised through Evans, who converted a centre from the right wing. Wealdstone however, went ahead before half time, Tansley accepting a centre from Maskell and scoring having outwitted the home goalkeeper. Ten minutes after the resumption Tansley completed his hat trick following good play by Maskell.

The light became very bad at this juncture and it was difficult to follow the movement, which led to Hatton scoring for Hendon with a shot from the right wing. As a culmination to a pleasing operation by the inside forwards, Wealdstone's fifth goal was obtained by Eagle, who ran in to score with a ground shot.

So bad was the light that Mr T Taylor, the referee stopped play and consulted the captains. The Hendon players were under the impression that the closure had been applied and left the field for the pleasant shelter of the Dressing Room.

The Wealdstone team and the referee remained on the field, and with the light improving, the official ordered the resumption of the play. The home players were loath to leave the dressing room, and it was several minutes before they returned to the field of play, minus, at first, their goalkeeper.

During the closing stages Wealdstone dominated the play, pressing continuously, with Standish defending brilliantly in the home goal. His saves included one from a penalty kick entrusted to Ryder.

Collins completed the scoring for Wealdstone and Clinkel, the inside-left, replied for Hendon. Tansley and Tarrant, the Hendon right back were off the field with injuries when time was called

Wealdstone; W Berry, M Bowtle, A Downing, W W Pratt, K Ryder, R Smith, T Maskell, A Bradshaw, R Tansley, F Collins, A Eagle.

In February, Wealdstone were to meet Old Lyonians, their former rivals in the Middlesex Senior Cup, and as with the previous matches between the two sides, the tie was fiercely competitive and played in front of a great number of spectators.

The first match ended in a draw, three all after extra time, having been played in pouring rain and Wealdstone having finished the game under a fifteen minute onslaught from the Old Lyonians forwards, and with only nine men on the pitch.

In the second game, played at Pinner View, Wealdstone took the lead only to fall behind 2-1, then recovering to a 3-2 position before Old Lyonians again scored twice to lead 4–3. Eventually finishing the ninety minutes at 4–4. Wealdstone went on to score the final goal five minutes from the end of extra time.

In March, there were more professional visitors to Lower Mead when a strong Tottenham Hotspur side visited.

The match report detailed it as an interesting game that finished in...

...a win for the Spurs by three goals to one. The football played reached a high standard with the visitors giving a delightful exhibition of skill full ball control and accurate passing, but the home team were by no means eclipsed.

During the first half kept their more experienced opponents at bay as a result of sound defensive work by A Downing and A Stocks ably supported by R Groves.

In the second half the Spurs scored three goals and Wealdstone replied with one, and during the closing stages Wealdstone rallied and but for the skill of Smith in the visitors goal, they would have got level before the end. It is of interest to note that nine professionals appeared in the Tottenham team.

The club had another good season, the first team finishing in fourth place again, while the reserves finished their season in sixth place. The top four of the Senior Section was;

	P	W	D	L	F	A	Pts
Botwell Mission	28	22	2	4	106	46	46
Walthamstow Avenue	28	21	2	5	106	48	44
Chesham United	28	18	5	5	101	44	41
Wealdstone	**28**	**17**	**3**	**8**	**90**	**62**	**37**

This was to be the club's last season in the Spartan League, as Summerstown FC were forced to withdraw from the Athenian League. Their ground had been acquired for building. At the AGM of the Athenian League, Wealdstone FC were duly elected to take their place, and they subsequently arranged to purchase the Stand from Summerstown FC to replace the far smaller original one at Lower Mead.

There was a surprising plea from the club to help finance the purchase of the ground, the stand and the additional expenses of the Athenian League.

Stanley L Green
Supporter 1920's

When I first lived in Harrow as a boy, our house in Nibthwaite Road backed onto the ground of Wealdstone FC. Although I was an adherent to the Rugby code newly introduced then, to the Harrow County School, living on top of the ground naturally brought me into close contact with the club.

Most afternoon's I would walk through the hedge at the bottom of my garden and save myself sixpence I would have had to pay for admission.

In 1925/26 when I first came to live in Harrow, the school boasted of two Old Gaytonians playing for the Wealdstone first XI, they were the Groves brothers, Reginald and Leslie, more affectionately known as "Navvy".

Another name which comes to mind from this era is Campbell, he was a tough, chunky halfback and there was the goalkeeper, Norman. I knew this character well because at that time he had transferred from the Tufnell Park FC to join Wealdstone. Tufnell Park was where my family had moved from.

The original pavilion and changing rooms at 'Lower Mead' was a one storey'd wooden building standing just away from the pitch at the Station Road end and the 'Stand' was a low roofed wooden structure with about four rows of benches inside. It ran the length of the pitch on the 'Hindes Road' side.

I wonder how many people remember the old rambling Victorian house and its outbuildings fronting on to Station Road and backing on to the football pitch?

This was the house and property of a fellow named Probyn (who was a well known Vetinary surgeon), which eventually would be smothered by the Dominion Cinema, and all the other shops built in that are at the time.

I can recall many occasions of my friends and I exploring the buildings and grounds and being chased away! There may too be those who remember the second pitch, which ran alongside the main one.

This second pitch backed directly onto my own back garden and ran almost the length of the lower part of Nibthwaite Road.

Of course this parcel of land has long since gone and houses and flats now stand where once my friends and I kicked a ball into goal in the evenings after the groundsman had gone home.

This second pitch (rather a mud-heap) was situated perilously near a pond at the lower touchline. It was interesting as it was here that every other Wednesday afternoon, Wealdstone Wednesday used to play.

It was a side made up of local tradesmen mostly, who played on their half day off. One fellow was a long legged string bean named Mills. He used to play at right or left back and he worked as an assistant at the Greengrocers Shop in Station Road.

Another player was Walsh, Some of the spectators at these games used to call him 'Banger' and when I recall him in action in those days it is not difficult to realise why he earnt the name.

Despite this though, he eventually graduated to the Wealdstone Reserves and first team and served the club for many years.

On the senior pitch before (in those days) the Spartan League matches the club would provide musical entertainment for the few hundred attending the match. It varied from season to season but I recall so well a pair of coronet players who used to blow their hearts out for us every Saturday afternoon.

Their piece de resistance was a sort of 'echo duet' played to the tune of 'O Sole Mio'. One player would take up a position by one corner flag and the other would place himself diagonally opposite. Then one would blow away on his horn and then in the distance far across the field his partner would echo his playing.

This was great stuff for a boy of my tender age but if the truth is known I expect those present were sick to death of hearing it week after week and were impatient to see their heroes emerge in their black and white hoops from the old wooden pavilion.

In what was described by a sceptical press as "the latest stunt", posters were put up around Wealdstone with the headline "Wanted - 1000 New Members!" and the text ran as a request for people to become members and support the club.

In a conversation later, C V Elmslie stated that these posters had caused a great deal of comment and interest locally, the club were assured of good regular support for the forthcoming season. Further development of the ground was also going at a pace and Sports Notes in the Harrow Observer recorded in mid August that...

...there was a considerable amount of effort at Lower Mead where the original stand is to be replaced. The new stand has a capacity for some 500 - 600 people, and the erection is well towards completion.

The stand is a very substantial affair of steel frameworks and was purchased from the now defunct Summerstown FC, so that many Wealdstone supporters will be familiar with it. In re-erection the stand has been specially constructed to allow a dressing room for both home and visiting teams, and the referee, being built in underneath, complete with large plunge baths fed from an outside Boiler House.

A roomy enclosure adjoining the stand, new pay boxes and larger flood-gates with increased parking space for cars and cycles are other improvements to be introduced while some 600 loads of material will be used to increase the popular 'banking' behind the goal.

Wealdstone lost their first Athenian League match, at home to Enfield, by three goals to four, but the club enjoyed moderate success in new company, eventually finishing in eighth place out of fourteen teams, but with more goals scored than any other team.

There had been much speculation as to how Wealdstone would fare having 'moved up' in standard, and a good crowd in excess of 1500 was present at Lower Mead for the first Athenian League match.

Wealdstone had shown well early on, taking a two-goal lead through Clark after some fifteen minutes, but Enfield were soon on level terms, then taking the lead on the half hour and scoring their fourth goal before half time.

Groves scored Wealdstone's third in the second half, but 'Stones were unable to equalise, although their performance had shown that they would be able to compete at this level.

It was to be another high scoring season, buoyed by victories over bottom club Cheshunt, beaten 7-3 at Lower Mead and 9-2 away and a 10-1 victory over Windsor and Eton at home and 5-1 away.

The victory over Windsor and Eton at home had come at Christmas time on the back of three consecutive defeats, which was the worst run the club had during the season.

Wealdstone opened the scoring after five minutes, added two more on the half hour and another before half time. The fifth followed midway through the second half and the remaining goals came in the last ten minutes as the Windsor defence, under pressure for so long, crumbled.

Wealdstone were so dominant in the game, reports stated that they should have doubled their score and they also managed to miss a penalty during the second half!

	P	W	D	L	F	A	Pts
Leyton	26	19	5	2	78	33	43
Hampstead Town	26	16	3	7	64	39	35
Sutton United	26	13	7	6	73	50	33
Southall	26	12	5	9	66	47	29
Enfield	26	11	7	8	47	51	29
Bromley	26	11	6	9	68	63	28
Barnet	26	12	3	11	67	55	27
Wealdstone	**26**	**11**	**3**	**12**	**81**	**63**	**25**
Redhill	26	9	6	11	70	59	24

The reserves fared even better in their first season, eventually winning the reserves Championship, and also being the highest scorers in their Division.

Improving on the first team's record, there was only one club that conceded fewer goals than the reserves, league runner up, Redhill.

The top of the reserves final table was as follows;

	P	W	D	L	F	A	Pts
Wealdstone	**26**	**18**	**3**	**5**	**97**	**47**	**39**
Redhill	26	18	1	7	73	43	37
Barnet	26	15	5	6	94	65	35

The greater interest in the club that was evident with their elevation to the Athenian League was confirmed at the AGM at the end of that first season, when the attendance was more than double that of the previous years meeting.

Further confirmation that the profile of the club had been raised came from a no doubt less welcome source. It seems that no Income Tax had been paid by the club since the move to Lower Mead.

The assessments were received in the July, but the amount due was not cut and dried until the November, when various allowances for the development of the facilities at the ground and such like were taken into account.

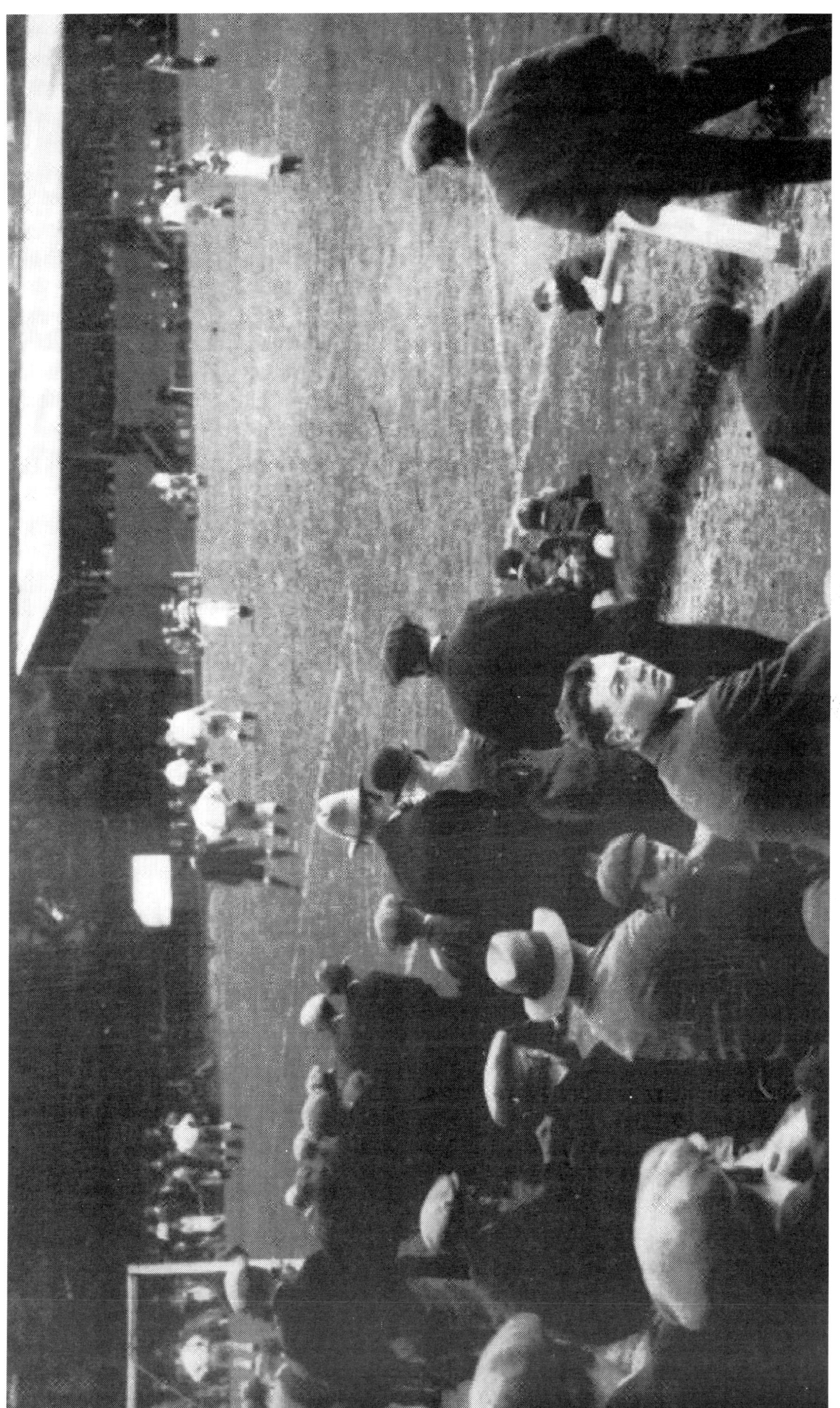

An early action photograph from Lower Mead. We cannot date it accurately, but it seems that one side is playing in Black and White hoped shirts, the Wealdstone kit up until 1929-30. The stand is also in place that was bought from Summerstown FC and re-assembled in 1928.

The amount eventually agreed was £152 18s 8d, and there is a letter confirming the same addressed to HM Inspector of Taxes, politely informing him that the money would be forwarded as soon as there was sufficient in Club Funds!

I doubt these days that the matter would be so leniently treated. The club also produced accounts for the following two seasons showing that there was no tax liability as for both seasons they had made a loss, due in part to the purchase of the ground outright.

The next season, 1929-1930 was certainly eventful.

Early in November, Wealdstone were to travel to Staines for an amateur cup-tie. Suffering a number of injuries, three reserve team players travelled with the first team, two expecting to play which they duly did. However three of their team mates were delayed in their journey and 'Stones started the match with only eight players on the field. Two more arrived after some ten minutes play, but the third did not arrive until after half time.

Staines too had a problem, losing a defender before half time and playing the remainder of the match with ten men! The weakened Wealdstone side eventually ran out winners by four goals to one.

Continuing with the goalscoring feats of the time, just before Christmas Wealdstone were drawn away to Erith and Belvedere FC in the London Senior Cup. The first match had seemed to be going the way of the home side, as they led 4-2 late in the second half, but Wealdstone rallied and forced a creditable draw.

The following week at Lower Mead, Erith had arrived late, causing the kick off to be delayed. They also had travelled without their goalkeeper, their outside left, Brooker taking his place. No doubt then, that when the match eventually kicked off Wealdstone must have felt their chances were good, but those thoughts were quickly dispersed as Erith and Belvedere went into a four goal lead by half time.

The second half saw a better performance from the home side and they did manage to pull back the deficit. In near darkness ten minutes from the end of the game, Wealdstone equalised, but not before their third goal had been disallowed because of a defenders handball, the referee insisting that a penalty be taken, and Champion who had scored the disallowed goal duly stepped up to score from the spot.

With ever increasing darkness, the referee allowed extra time to start and then immediately abandoned the match as it had become impossible for players and spectators alike to see what was happening. The game then was to enter a third match.

Later that week, on Christmas Day and Boxing Day, Wealdstone played home and away against Hampstead Town, later becoming Golders Green FC and later still Hendon FC, for the first time.

These regular fixtures continued for some 40 years and often were memorable events and in this first meeting Wealdstone dominated both games. Although they could only draw the Christmas Day fixture at Lower Mead they won by three goals to two the following day.

The reserves also played similar fixtures with similar results, drawing 1-1 at Hampstead on Christmas Day and winning 4-1 at Lower Mead on Boxing Day.

The third game against Erith and Belvedere was played the following Saturday, again at Lower Mead. This time Erith travelled with a reserve goalkeeper and both fullbacks were also reserves.

Wealdstone scored through Hopkins after ten minutes. It was the first time in the tie that they had been in the lead. Hopkins went on to score a first half hat trick, Smith adding the fourth goal and, in the second half, Hoskins added a fifth to give Wealdstone a resounding win.

The three games had seen twenty-one goals scored between the two teams.In the space of four days, Wealdstone had won twice and drawn once to maintain a good record in their first Athenian League season.

The Golden Jubilee handbook reported for the 1929/30 season that *"anyone who saw the two FA Cup matches with Dulwich Hamlet will certainly remember them"*

Wealdstone had already beaten Walthamstow Avenue, St Albans City, Apsley and Chesham United at home in the competition, and were then drawn to play Dulwich Hamlet at Champion Hill in the fourth qualifying round. The match was to record fourteen goals, both sides scoring seven, in front of a record attendance that was not to be beaten for a number of years.

Wealdstone's Dogged Recovery

The eagerly awaited match between Wealdstone and Dulwich Hamlet in the final qualifying round of the FA Cup competition was played at Dulwich on Saturday and resulted in a draw, 7-7. The game was dramatic and exciting from the start and both teams played good football in spite of the heavy rain and the sodden-ness of the pitch.

Wealdstone did very well to draw with as strong a side as Dulwich on their own ground. They are to be congratulated on the fine way in which they were to turn the game round, once in the first half when Dulwich were leading by three goals to nothing and again in the last ten minutes of the second half when the score was 7–5 against them.

Playing down the hill, Dulwich attacked from the start and for the first quarter were always on the offensive. Clever forward play near the Wealdstone goal left Lee in possession with only the goalkeeper to beat but Dunn threw himself forward and smothered the shot in a manner worthy of Howard Baker himself. Before Dunn could recover, the ball fell to another Dulwich forward, but his shot was cleverly stopped in the goalmouth by Davies and the ball was eventually cleared.

A breakaway by Wealdstone led their backs into the error of standing too far up the field and when the ball was cleared it came down the slope too fast for them to catch it and Copas raced through and scored with a hard low shot which gave Dunn no chance.

Dulwich continued to attack and several shots from the inside forwards hit the crossbar and the side posts before Davies, attempting to clear a shot from Lee when he may have better left the ball to Dunn, deflected a ground shot into the corner of the goal.

The third Dulwich goal which came soon afterwards was scored by a Wealdstone defender, Turner, who miss kicked in trying to clear a shot from Murray across the goalmouth.

Wealdstone, after a shaky start, began to settle down and they attacked in their turn. Maskell took the ball up field and placed it accurately in the centre, where Hoskins coolly steadied it before shooting into the corner of the net.

Wealdstone scored again before half time from another centre by Maskell, which Hugo, one of the Dulwich backs miss kicked into his own goal. Before half time a shot from Hester beat the Dulwich goalkeeper but a goal was not allowed on the grounds that the offside rule had been infringed.

Wealdstone continued to attack at the beginning of the second half and had most of the play for the first few minutes, then Copas increased the Hamlet's lead while at the other end Hester dropped the ball into the goalmouth and Hugo, in an attempt to clear, kicked it through his own goal again. This was the fourth goal so far scored by a defender against his own side.

A few minutes later Hoskins was fouled as he was running through the Dulwich defence and Hannam took the penalty kick to make the score equal at four all. Both sides then attacked in turn and a very good shot by Smith, was stopped by a Dulwich back when the goalkeeper was out of position.

Hoskins had to leave the field for a time through injury and Davies also required attention, leaving Wealdstone with nine men. The Dulwich forwards began to play more together and a goal scored by Lee from fifteen yards out was followed by another making the score 6-4 in favour of Dulwich.

At the other end, Cooper, the goalkeeper stopped a free kick by Hannam by falling on his knee and managed to clear from among a crowd of attackers. Wealdstone continued to press and a centre was well placed by Maskell, and Champion in tackling a defender who was slow in clearing was left with an open goal. From a corner taken by Hannam, Smith's shot just missed the side post.

The Dulwich inside forwards again got going and from a perfect forward pass Lee obtained possession of the ball, and though half tackled, ran through and scored with a good shot. With only a few minutes left to go and the score at 7-5 in their favour the game looked safe for Dulwich. Wealdstone, however, continued to attack and in the growing dusk Champion headed a beautiful goal from a high centre from Maskell.

The last goal which quickly followed was obtained by Wealdstone from one of the best combined efforts of the game. Hoster placed the ball to Hannam who was unable to shoot but managed to put the ball across the goalmouth. The Dulwich goalkeeper failed to gather it cleanly and Hoskins, well on the spot, dabbed it through.

Wealdstone; R V Dunn, R Groves, C Davies, T J Turner, H R Smith, D Short, T Maskell, R H Hannam, L Hoskins, A Champion, S Hoster.

Dulwich Hamlet; C Cooper, G Robinson, A Hugo, C Murray, A H Hamer, A Atkin, L Morrish, K J Spalton, V Lee, G T Copas, F Minshull.

Dulwich were missing their England International goalkeeper, Solly, and Kall, the international Inside-right. Wealdstone were missing their captain and centre forward Clarke, although Hoskins had played well in his place, but there cannot have been a spectator present who would ever forget the game and after such an incredible tie, it was no surprise when the national papers became more interested in the replay.

The report from the Daily Express, under the headline *Solly's Great Day At Wealdstone* by Spotter read;

Wealdstone FC 1929 – 1930 winners of the Middlesex Senior Cup and the Middlesex Charity Cup. Names are unavailable for this photograph although we do know that the goalkeeper is F Poulson who was to serve the club for a number of years. The team that won the two trophies was; goal, F Poulson, backs, R Groves and C Davies, halves, T J Turner, H R Smith, and D J Short, forwards, T Maskell, E H Hannam, S L Hoskins, R L Clark and S Hester

When Dulwich Hamlet and Wealdstone met in the fourth qualifying round of the FA Cup at Champion Hill on Saturday, they shared equally no fewer than fourteen goals. With the memory of that extraordinary score on my mind, one turned up for the Replay at Lower Mead, Wealdstone yesterday prepared for fireworks. We got them.

The Hamlet won this spirited tie by two goals to one, but in my opinion they were fortunate to do so. They crossed over a goal up, scored by F Minshull from long range after 30 minutes. They deserved this success for they were the better team up to the interval. But it was a different story throughout the second half. Wealdstone sailed into battle with such determination that Dulwich were almost constantly on the defence.

Justice was done when, after 20 minutes E H Hannam equalised. A fine run by L Hoskins ended in A Solly landing himself at the centre forward's feet. Solly stopped Hoskins but the ball rolled away to Hannam who netted.

Then it was a duel between the Wealdstone attack and the Hamlet defence, with a personal argument between Solly and Hoskins as the big attraction. Solly rushed out many times to meet the Wealdstone man's rushes. He managed to grab the ball each time and, in addition made numerous splendid saves from other Wealdstone forwards. Solly saved the game for the Hamlet.

Despite Wealdstone's continued pressure, however, it was Dulwich who claimed the winning goal. G T Copas secured the ball during a goalmouth scrimmage and had an easy task to drive it past R V Dunn. Wealdstone fought on to the end, but Solly, S Knight and W Edgar kept them out. Wealdstone were awarded a penalty kick in the first half but Hannam drove the ball straight at Solly, who cleared. If that kick had been successful Wealdstone and not Dulwich might have had the pleasure of entertaining Plymouth Argyle in the fifth round.

The club were successful however in the Middlesex competitions, both County cups finding their way to Lower Mead. In the Senior Cup Wealdstone drew 2-2 with Hayward Sports at Hampstead Town, before winning the replay 3-1 on the same ground and in the County Charity Cup, Hampstead town themselves were beaten 3-1.

In the League, the first team finished fifth, but the reserves had a poor season, finishing fourth from the bottom of the table. Financially, things were not quite as good, as the Annual Accounts presented at the AGM showed an expenditure over the season of £3621 3s 8d of which £204 3s was paid in wages and £1929 0s 10d had been repaid against the mortgage and loans. This left the club with an overdraft of £1950 at the bank.

Worse was to follow when it was declared that the club still had liabilities in unpaid accounts to £101 14s and outstanding loans to C E Brady, J H Bailey and C V Elmslie of £50, £120 and £55 respectively.

The assets were listed as cash in hand of £7 12s 5d, The Ground, Stand and Buildings £2000 and the Mower £5, a further deficit of £264 1s 7d.

THE NINETEEN THIRTIES

The club held its Annual Fete in early May of 1930 and yet again there was a special attraction. This time there was to be a Baseball match between England and Canada, which had been arranged by the Kodak Baseball Club, as well as all of the normal sideshows and a Funfair. The money raised was a welcome addition to the club funds, as there were expenses committed for works on the ground during the summer and little money available to pay for them.

The club had certainly been successful on the field, but although the first team had played 54 matches, more than 20 were cup-ties. Whilst these may have been expected to be a boost to the club financially, in this season they had been a drain and were in the most part unprofitable.

At the start of the 1931–1932 season, there were to be a number of changes in the team. Not this time the addition of successful trialists to the existing squad, but as was reported before the seasons opening match against Cheshunt a number of the players that had been instrumental in winning the two trophies the previous season would no longer be available.

R L Clark, a former captain who played left back or forward, was unable to return due to his business commitments; Vice captain D short had left to join St Albans City; R H Hannam, the right half, was unable to start the season; and worse still the club were seemingly without a goalkeeper, first choice F Poulson looking likely to join Clapton Orient and R V Dunn was to play for The Army.

The last trial of the pre-season included a number of players from local clubs who were to join the squad for the coming year and although F Poulson signed on for Clapton Orient after a successful trial, he was still able to take his position in goal for the start of the season.

The new players certainly seemed to inspire the 'Stones in the early part of the season. In the first match against Cheshunt, the report detailed how in front of over 1000 supporters, 'Stones had wasted a number of chances in the first half, the half time score being one all, but the second half was a different matter – 'Stones scored seven second half goals with new man C Bowyer scoring five in an eventual 8-2 victory. The reserves, too, had an early run of form, as the Harrow Observer was to report;

Four matches have been played at Lower Mead this season, two for each team, and forty goals have been scored there – that should be enough for the most voracious appetite...

The paper went on to compliment the club on a wonderful match programme and also mentioned a feature on the club's captain at the time, Harold Smith. The match programme from Saturday September 20th 1930 featured him as the first in a series of 'Player Profiles' it read;

Harold Smith, our popular centre half has been with us for seven seasons. He was discovered playing Inside-left for Wealdstone Wednesday and was a member of the successful Watford St Mary's team. He played with the reserves as a forward, and since he gained his place in the first team, he has fulfilled many positions with success.

He has been playing centre half for several seasons, and in that position he has few equals in the Athenian League. He is a player who thrives on work and goes all the way. He is Captain of the team today.

Harold Smith

Although we don't know his actual age, it must be judged from the above that he was in his mid to late twenties, which made it more surprising that, later in the season, his prominence was noted by others as well and he was to move on and join the professional ranks at Notts County.

As he was an amateur, there was no transfer or fee involved, merely a matter of the professional club inviting him to join. He was quite at liberty to accept in the way non-contract players these days can be approached after a seven day notification by another club.

This was though, a time when gentlemen were involved in both the amateur and professional game, and Notts County therefore chose to compensate Wealdstone for the loss of their club captain.

The first 'official' transfer fee received by Wealdstone from another club is duly recorded as £10 0s 0d, a full set of shirts for the first team and confirmation that Notts County would bring down a full first team for a friendly match later in the season.

The Harrow Observer also kept Wealdstone fans in touch with the career of Harold Smith. It reported in early March, Harold having left the club in the early part of the season, that;

Many supporters of the Wealdstone Club will follow with interest the career of Harold Smith who left the club some months ago to join the professional ranks of Notts County.

Smith, I am able to say, is making excellent progress, and has created a highly favourable impression in Third League football.

His play has frequently been praised by the critics, and, as an example, I quote the following from the Report of the match against Gillingham on Saturday last; "Losely, the Gillingham centre forward, had a poor match against the much improved centre half, Smith, who outshone Dewsey and Kemp in the Notts County half back line.

As the season went on, the goals continued to flow and for the second season in succession, Wealdstone FC were successful in the County cup competitions.

The Easter weekend saw home and away matches against local rivals, Uxbridge. At Lower Mead on Good Friday morning, what was expected to be an exciting match was, in the first half at least, spoilt by the poor weather, with rain falling throughout the match.

At half time, the teams changed ends with the score at 0-0, although there had been a number of chances created at both ends.

The second half saw a complete change in fortunes, as observed by the reporter from the local paper;

Wealdstone began the second half in impressive style and were soon a goal to the good. Turner placed the ball across the goal-mouth and Maskell was there to accept the opportunity. Then Brown provided an excellent pass for Bowyer to score number two.

Uxbridge were then dangerous for a short spell without results. Wealdstone's third goal was then obtained by Wilson as a sequel to a centre from Maskell, who added number four soon afterwards with a fast drive.

Uxbridge's only goal accrued from a scramble in the goal-mouth, Underwood shooting home through a crowd of players.

Maskell scored another for Wealdstone, his second of the match and then Bowyer got the sixth, the majority of Wealdstone's goals were easily obtained, and better shots and keener pressure in the first half proved unproductive.

Wealdstone won the match on Easter Monday at Uxbridge by the odd-goal in five. The match was tied at 2-2 after some thirty five minutes when the Official referee eventually arrived, the match having started under the authority of one of the Linesman.

Wealdstone went on to score the winning goal midway through the second half to complete their weekend double.

Ever mindful of the profile of the club, and to develop the opportunities that arose from the 'ownership' of Lower Mead, the Committee were pleased to ensure that as many games as possible were played on the ground – although there was rarely a fee applied, often the refreshments to the crowd were provided by the host club, and a slight revenue earned there.

This Easter in particular was no different. On Easter Saturday, Hayes played Hayward Sports in the County Cup semi-final, and on Easter Monday, an International Match was staged between the English Railways team and their counterparts from the French Railways.

On April 29th, the promised match with Notts County was staged and the following report appeared in the Harrow paper;

A crowd of about 2300 saw Notts County, the Southern Section Third Division Champions, engage with Wealdstone, the local Athenian Leaguers. This fixture was a sporting gesture on behalf of the Champions in recognition of having recruited Harold Smith from the local side early in the season.

Smith, who up until November was Wealdstone's centre half and captain, soon made good on turning professional. After three games with the 'County Reserves, he secured his place in the first team and retained it for the remainder of the season by his consistent good form.

Mr H Henshall, the Notts County manager told an Observer representative that Smith had done remarkably well and Notts County would wish to have a few more like him from Wealdstone!

The County paid Wealdstone the respect of fielding as representative a team as was available, three inside forwards and the left back being unable to play due to injuries. Wealdstone turned out in new colours, Black and White halves replacing the usual Royal Blue.

The cheer, which greeted the County players as they took the field, was obviously largely a personal one for Smith, who captained them for the occasion, and the cheering was resumed when he shook hands with C Davies, the home captain, and won the toss.

As was to be expected the County side proved the superior side, but Wealdstone did well to score three goals in response to the eight scored by their opponents. The County's positional play, combination and deadly shooting was a pleasure to watch.

They were evidently out for goals throughout and lost not a single chance of shooting, so much so in fact that Poulson, the home goalkeeper was continually in action throughout the first half, and earned the appreciation of the spectators by many clever saves.

The County's 5-1 lead at the interval was largely due to the opportunism of their clever young inside-left, Hall, whose accurate first time shooting was an object lesson to the home forwards. He scored four goals in this period and Nelson the other while Bowyer, from an opening made by Groves, obtained Wealdstone's solitary goal with a well-placed shot.

After Taylor had scored the sixth for the County almost immediately after the resumption, Maskell reduced the deficit, Groves again providing the opportunity. More steadiness in front of goal, particularly from Hoskins and Wilson would have enabled Wealdstone to narrow the margin of goals against them, for they had a good share of the exchanges in this second period.

Shorland, the home right back put through his own goal for the County's seventh goal, and centre forward Lovatt scored the eighth. Hoskins, after many unsuccessful attempts, scored for Wealdstone in the closing stages. Poulson was the hero of the losing side, with Groves, Brown and Davies the pick of the remainder.

Smith was naturally the centre of attention in the County side, and the spectators were quick to note his positional play and the accuracy of his passes.

Wealdstone; F Poulson, C Davies, J Shorland, C G Brown, C E Woodham, T J Turner, T Maskell, E Wilson, L R Hoskins, C Bowyer, L G Groves.

Notts County; Ferguson, Mills, Thorpe, Dossey, Smith, Jakeman, Taylor, Nelson, Lovatt, Hall, Halden.

The final league match at home to Barking continued the goal scoring feats that had been achieved during the season by Wealdstone teams. Yet again, not without its unusual elements;

Wealdstone concluded their Athenian League fixtures at Lower Mead on Saturday, with a convincing win over barking by ten goals to nil.......

....from the start, Wealdstone pressed, and Bowyer, making his first appearance at centre forward, scored the opening goal after ten minutes, putting the finishing touch to an accurate pass from Maskell

Wealdstone were again in the vicinity of the visitors' goalmouth in the next minute, but Bowyer finished badly after defeating two opponents as he shot wide. The Barking goal had many narrow escapes in the ensuing play, on one occasion Smith the goalkeeper, made a brilliant save in stopping and holding a stinging shot from Groves.

Brown was keeping Maskell and Wilson well supplied with passes, and these two were a constant source of danger with their clever combinations and Wealdstone's next goal came ten minutes before the interval when Woodham scored with a fine shot from about twenty yards out. Bowyer then added the third before the interval from a penalty awarded for handling.

When the game resumed, Wilson scored number four with a capital shot. Shortly afterwards from close in Groves shot over from almost under the crossbar and from the goal kick, Champion prepared the way for Bowyer to score the fifth goal for Wealdstone. The same player also obtained the sixth.

Immediately afterwards Groves scored the seventh, and the eighth goal, the best of the match, was to the credit of Maskell, who beat the goalkeeper with a terrific drive. After Champion added the ninth goal there was a regrettable incident.

When a free kick had been awarded against Barking for what the referee ruled was a foul, a Barking back rushed across and seemed to aim a blow at Bowyer. It appeared the referee ordered the Barking player from the field, but Davies, the Wealdstone Captain interceded on his behalf and he was thereupon allowed to remain.

An Official of the Barking Club also encroached on the field of play and ignoring protests from the stand took part in the argument to the astonishment of the spectators.

At the restart, Bowyer then scored his fifth and Wealdstone's tenth goal of the match.

Wealdstone; F Poulson, J Shorland, C Davies, C G Brown, G E Woodham, T J Turner, T Maskell, E C Wilson, C Bowyer, A Champion, L Groves.

The following week, Wealdstone retained the Middlesex Charity Cup with a three goals to two win over Hampstead Town at Finchley. The match itself was unremarkable although by all reports a good sporting fixture, but as though there was always to be some incident or controversy surrounding the club, the presentation of the Trophy was not without incident;

The presentation of the cup was marred by an unusual demonstration of hostility towards the winning team. Mr W W Heard Hon Secretary of the Middlesex FA was subject to many interruptions and prolonged boo-ings that he had difficulty in making his speech introducing Councillor A T Pike who was to present the trophy.

Mr Heard said he thought (the supporters) would agree with him that they had witnessed a very good sporting game. This remark was met with several shouts of dissent and boos.

After several attempts to resume his speech, Mr Heard said "I can tell you this. I don't care two pence whether you agree with me or not, I have my own opinions, and I am quite sure that when I go into the Dressing room to talk to the players they will tell me that they enjoyed the game."

Councillor Pike, in presenting the trophy to C Davies, the Captain of the Wealdstone team, congratulated the club in winning for the second year in succession. He thanked both teams for the good game that had been played, and he was interrupted several times.

The interruptions resumed when Davies spoke in acknowledgement. He congratulated Hampstead (who were conspicuous by their absence from the presentation ceremony) on the sporting game they had played in this year's final as in the last one, he also expressed a wish that the two teams should meet again in next years final.

The Annual General Meeting, which took place at the beginning of June 1931, was able to report on one of the most successful seasons in the club's history. In the report from the club secretary, C V Elmslie he reported that he and his fellow officers had become optimistic about the future as they had experienced a good season, one of the outstanding events being the visit of Notts County to Lower Mead as part of the arrangement that saw Harold Smith leave the club.

Wealdstone v Barnet Dec 31 1931

Mr Elmslie also reported that the club had increased their stature in the eyes of the Football Association, as they had now been exempted from the Preliminary Round of the Amateur Cup. He went on to add that to put everyone's mind at rest, he had already entered the club into the FA Cup for the forthcoming season, having forgotten the previous year!

The players were congratulated on the esprit de corps that ran through the club as a whole and this was to be built on in the coming season with the social side of the club coming to the fore.

Turning to the financial side, he said that the club had not had a more successful season. Although receipts were down by £200, this was mainly because fifteen less matches had been played.

This in turn meant the club was in a position to pay of a number of debts and they were also in a position to consider putting into action a number of plans for development at Lower Mead.

Both teams had been in great goalscoring form during the season, the first team scoring 79 goals in the league, finishing fifth, with only the Champions, Barnet scoring more, and sixty of those 79 goals were scored at home!

The reserves finished third in their Division, scoring 119 goals in the process, far more than any other club in the league.

Season 1931–1932 also saw a good number of goals scored in matches at home, none more so that the FA Cup Extra Preliminary Round, where Wealdstone, in front of a crowd of over 1200, beat Thame Athletic by twelve goals to four.

The match was not as one sided as the score line suggested. It was again due in part to the exploits of Bowyer who scored a double hat trick, that Wealdstone were to win so convincingly;

Wealdstone assumed the offensive right from the kick off and only five minutes had elapsed when Bowyer opened the scoring. A Thame defender was penalised for handball and although the spot kick was saved, Bowyer scored from the rebound. Three minutes later he scored his second after fine individual work.

Although Wealdstone continued to dominate the play, Thame were seen in several commendable if unsuccessful attacks. Bowyer however, completed his hat trick in the twenty seventh minute during a goal mouth scramble.

Two minutes later, Turner scored the fourth with a capital first time shot, and before the interval Morgan converted a centre from Maskell, and Bowyer put the finishing touches to clever work by Maskell and Morgan.

A surprise was in store for those who expected Wealdstone to have things all their own way in the second half, for within three minutes of the restart, Woodbridge obtained a clever goal for the visitors. Prestwich showed good skill in scoring Wealdstone's seventh goal soon afterwards, but it was not long before Clark outwitted the whole of the Wealdstone defence to score another good goal for the visitors.

Encouraged by this success, Thame played like an entirely different team and scored a further two goals through Josey and Chowins.

For a time, Thame were definitely superior, but after Bowyer had scored Wealdstone's eighth goal a quarter of an hour from the end, the visitors fell away considerably. In this period Groves, Morgan, Bowyer (penalty) and Prestwich carried Wealdstone's total to twelve.

Wealdstone; F R Poulson, A Loveday, C Davies, T J Turner, B Darville, A G Butcher, T Maskell, R C Prestwich, J M Morgan, C Bowyer and L Groves.

The reserves had more consistent success during the season, leading the table for a long period before finally finishing second to Enfield in the Reserve Section, the first team eventually finishing in sixth place.

The final matches of the season for Wealdstone Reserves showed very mixed fortunes, as in their final league match with the title already decided, Wealdstone introduced the two outstanding schoolboy footballers from the District.

The experiment in the league was a success, Wealdstone winning the match by six goals to one over a Southall team. The two schoolboys, D Wiggins of Alperton and J Smith of Ruislip, having previously distinguished themselves in representative schools football played well enough to suggest that they may be involved in the following seasons, both scoring during the match. Wiggins, a forward forcing a number of saves from the Southall goalkeeper.

Their last game of the season, the following week, was the Middlesex Junior Charity Cup. The side was strengthened with the return of regular players and the addition of one or two first teamers, but to no avail, the reserves losing three one to Hampton.

Some of the money available from the previous season was put to good use at the end of this, when for the first time, the club were able to hold the AGM in the Pavilion at Lower Mead, rather than renting or borrowing a local hall. All this due to the improvements made to the Pavilion over the year although they had to borrow the chairs from the Harrow Presbyterian Church for the evening!

The reports during the evening congratulated the teams, the reserves on an excellent League season, and the first team on their improvement during the second half of the season – in fact it was felt that if the team had performed as well in the early part of the season as at the end, they would have won the league by a good margin.

A number of players had received County Honours during the season, including top scorer Bowyer, who had scored 40 goals for the first team and reserves.

Mr C V Elmslie during his report was to describe ...*a beastly state of affairs after he thanked the local church for the loan of the chairs, which showed the good feeling that existed between the two bodies, but he did feel in other matters the club had been too charitable.*

He went on...*I think we are just beginning to realise that charity begins at home.*

The Harrow and District Football League was granted the use of the ground several times last season, and I now challenge the league to prove that one single club connected with the league has ever endeavoured in any shape or form to send one player to the Wealdstone club.

I think it is a beastly state of affairs, particularly when we are being asked on all sides why we do not play local footballers.

We have tried to foster a good spirit between this Club and junior sides in the neighbourhood, and all I can trace in return is an invitation to their annual dinner! I do not think this is quite equitable.

The Wealdstone club has never tried to steal a player from local football, and it has never approached a single player. In return for our sporting attitudes towards local football we have received nothing. It is time we expected at least, courteous treatment.

I am not referring to the officials of the league but to the clubs themselves. As far as I am concerned next year there will be a slight change in the usual procedure.

Mr Elmslie went on to question if the local public appreciated Lower Mead and what it could mean to them. Leagues and Clubs requested the use of the ground, but as soon as the club suggested a donation, there was more often than not a certain amount of foot shuffling.

The financial state of the club was still good and the club as a whole was congratulated on the way it was now managing its affairs, as this had again led to the availability of funds to improve the ground and its surroundings.

R J Pluck
Supporter since 1922

My memories go back quite a long way, in fact to the early part of the twentieth century around 1906, when my uncle, Fred Pluck started playing in goal for the 'Stones'. He appears in one of the Team Photographs.

At a later date, about ten years or so later, Fred's younger brother Bill played on the wing.

My first recollection of the 'Stones was in the early thirties when my Dad first took me to Lower Mead.

At that time, the pitch was surrounded by a post and wire fence, with duckboards for the spectators to stand on.

The area where High Mead was later built still belonged to the club. During the 'off season' there used to be a fairground appearing where High Mead now is.

The following season Wealdstone were pleased to retain the majority of the players from the previous year, the notable exceptions at the start of the season were F Poulson and C Bowyer, goalkeeper and top scorer respectively, and this played a part in the poor form of the team.

In the August, things began to look decidedly less rosy. A letter was received from H M Customs and Excise with regard to the Members Scheme operated by the club.

It detailed the requirements to pay Entertainment Duty on the sums received from members, as, without further payment, members could gain admission to an entertainment provided by the club.

This potential cost was to be backdated to season 1921 – 1922 when the scheme first operated, the club were given fourteen days to calculate and present their accounts for the charge to be levied.

They were offered the opportunity to determine a percentage of this charge. If it could be proved that the payment made by members did not solely allow admission free of further charge to an entertainment, the proportion applicable was to be determined and detailed within seven days.

All of these presentations, along with the fixture list for the following season were to be forwarded to the Commissioner of Customs and Excise.

The membership scheme was immediately suspended until the club had resolved the situation. Thankfully this was not too long in coming, although it did restrict the funds available at the time.

A number of letters detailing the amount of Membership (the total paid in memberships for the previous season was £9 5s 0d) and the conditions of membership were duly presented and eventually, on 3rd December 1932 a further letter was received that stated

With reference to your letter of 26th August last, I am directed to inform you that, so long as the present conditions of issue of membership tickets, the present rate of duty continue to apply, the duty payable on such tickets is NIL.

Any increase in the payment made for membership must, of course, be notified to this office....

Thankfully that was the end of the matter, and memberships were immediately offered for the remainder of that season.

Having been expected to build on a successful end to the previous year, it was both a surprise and a disappointment that the first team was to finish the season tenth out of fourteen. The reserves did fare a little better, finishing in fourth place.

In the June of 1933, it was again the Wealdstone Fete that was to bring the club to the fore, and in good weather there were three main attractions for the crowd in the afternoon.

These were a Children's Sports, for which there were over 300 participants, a Tug Of War between four local teams. (Hamilton's Brush Works were defeated by the Co-Operative Society and the Harrow Post Office defeated Forward Works. The Co-Operative Society won the final in two straight pulls).

The third attraction was a Fire Display by the Harrow Fire Brigade, including demonstrations of life saving.

The report also mentioned the excellent organisation and the contributions made by members of the Committee and their wives in providing refreshments to augment the occasion.

Although the club had been fairly consistent in success since joining the Athenian League in 1928, the mid thirties were to become difficult times on the field for the first team at least.

In the season 1933–1934, Wealdstone were to finish in thirteenth place (out of fourteen), in 1934-1935, they were to finish fourteenth and the following season, back to thirteenth place.

It was a different story for the reserves however, as they finished third and then fifth in their section, but in 1935 – 1936 they were Champions of the Athenian League Reserve Section, Redhill Reserves being runner up.

In finishing fifth, the reserves scored 90 goals during the season, far more than their competition, yet the following season as Champions they scored only 68 goals!

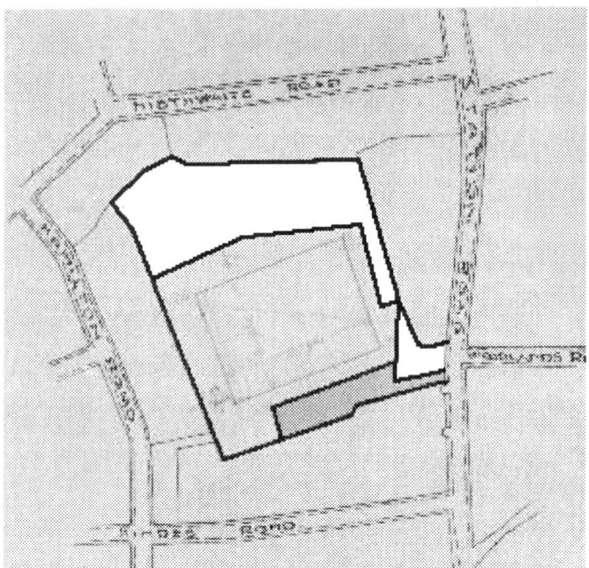

The two areas shown in white were those sold off in 1934 for the sum of £3350, the area at the top became part of High Mead, and the flats were developed there at this time.

Off the field there were a number of changes taking place. The club were to realise some of their earlier investment in the Lower Mead site. Having originally had plans for a Bowling Green and Tennis Courts on the far side of the ground, opposite the Pavilion, the club decided instead to sell off this area, and another adjacent to Station Road.

They received the sum of £3350 for these two pieces of land, (a substantial amount when you realise at the time the club had £62 9s in the bank!) and this was sufficient to discharge the remainder of the original mortgage and pay off a number of other debts. There was enough left to allow for some development work to be carried out within the club.

The dark grey area, (on the map above) the access road and the car park, were sold off in 1935 and leased back to the club on a ninety-nine year lease. This area was to become a substantial part of the deal when the ground and surrounding areas were sold on in 1991.

Prior to the sell off and the subsequent building works, there was another opportunity for the club to promote their place in the local community.

In the summer of 1934, an open air service was held on the pitch at Lower Mead by the Salvation Army, although there is no record known of the popularity or attendance. It was one of a number of different uses to which the ground was put.

Locally, there were also some changes taking place that would affect a number of the sporting clubs in the area.

As stated previously, the 'Wednesday' clubs had been formed to allow more people to join organised clubs and still support their senior sides, as Sunday football was not permitted either in Middlesex or by the Council. This was to change in November 1934 when Harrow Councillors voted to facilitate Sunday sports at all sports grounds. Causing the demise of the Wednesday leagues and teams, this in turn allowed more people to play, and thus more players to come to the attention of Wealdstone and the other senior sides.

At around the same time, the work commenced on the building

The farmhouse, demolished to make way for the cinema. A builder also purchased the farmhouse, Smiths Farm and the surrounding field adjoining Station Road at the time, soon becoming the parade of shops and cinema that stand on Station Road today.

of High Mead and the flats, and also the new Plaza Cinema at the Station Road end of the ground. The local paper reported on the steady advance of the building work at the ground, and effused about the better view that would result from the high banking being built along the side of the ground. It meant that there would be banking on three of the four sides.

Watching was not always enough, as was proven by a small article in the Observer in April of 1935. It referenced a Court hearing in which John Hearn (21) and Peter Hearn (19), both of Milton Road, Wealdstone, both pleaded guilty to the charge of playing football in the street! P.C. 337X said that the defendants and a number of other lads were kicking a full sized football about and a number of passers by were annoyed.

He had managed to catch these two defendants and they were each ordered to pay 4s costs!

The AGM on June 12th 1935 was able to report on the best financial position in the history of the club, as well as identifying a number of changes to the ground for the benefit of the spectators;

During the summer months, many improvements and alterations are to be carried out on the ground and when the 1935-1936 season opens, supporters of the club will be pleasantly surprised with all that has been done for their benefit.

There will be covered terracing accommodation for 1200 persons behind the top goal, at no increased charge, and where the entrance is at the moment, will be a commodious Car Park, running the entire length of the stand to the rear. The Car Park will be used jointly by arrangement with the new Plaza Cinema, and it will be possible to enter the ground from this point.

The main entrance to the ground will be from Higher-mead. Behind the bottom goal and abutting on to the Cinema and shops will be an 8 foot concrete retaining wall and this will be surmounted by a fence 4ft 6ins high, thus ensuring spectators a clear and uninterrupted view of the game.

There will be little change in the stand and club enclosures with the exception that they will be given a lick or two of paint so as to present a spick and span appearance. It is hoped that with voluntary efforts, to complete the terracing all round the ground by the end of the season

There will be three twelve feet wide floodgates to expedite the emptying of the ground after matches. Every effort is being made to make the ground one of the finest in the south of England. It will be capable of holding 12000 spectators.

The report went on to commiserate with the first team and congratulate the reserve team on their performance, in spite of the calls on players made by the first team, the new club policy of using the reserve team to play trialists - it resulted this season in 82 players representing the reserves throughout the year!

The cash statement indicated receipts of £4200 5s 11d, the ground account receiving £3383 2s 6d, mainly from the sale of the additional land; league and friendly match receipts totalling £273 6s 8d, cup receipts totalling £179 12s 7d.

The expenditure showed that the outstanding Mortgage and other loans on the ground, and bank charges totalled £2353 17s 5d and the wages for the season (no players here as we were very much an amateur club) £213 8s 4d.

This left cash on deposit at £400 0s 0d and cash in hand at £177 12s 2d, both of which were to pay for the improvements at the ground during the summer and the following season.

As the new season started, (somewhat remarkable as it was the first season for fifteen years that the first team opened their season away from home), Lower Mead had been transformed. There was some sadness that the ground had lost some of its rural beauty, but this was outweighed by the fact that the comfort and convenience of the supporters had been greatly improved.

The value of the ground as an asset had also been increased by the works which included the addition of the Elmslie Stand, so named in memory of C V Elmslie who had died in June 1935, having been involved in the running of the club as Secretary and Treasurer for many years.

The car park had been fenced off from the ground, and new entrances added in High Mead, the banking was under way for the terraces on High Mead and behind the goal at the Cinema end. It was even suggested that when these works were complete the capacity would be in the region of 20,000!

The season itself was to follow a similar pattern to the previous year, the first team starting well in the cup competitions and falling away in the league, but the reserves improved still further, winning the Championship of the Athenian League Division II.

A Christmas Greeting (1935) from the Club. The players illustrated are; J Wheatley, A Nurton, J Barrett, J Wilson and D Scott.

The first team were behind in games for most of the season. By the end of October, they had only played two league matches, most games being cup-ties, and this continued until December. It meant that there was a fixture pile up at the end of the season, and this, too, did not help the first team's cause.

At the AGM, the first team were in fact congratulated on the sporting way in which they faced defeat! The Committee insisted it was placed on record that the Sportsmanlike behaviour of the first team in facing adversity had often drawn spontaneous applause from their victorious opponents.

For the reserves, it was a different story, as they only lost four games in all competitions during the season. As well as their League Championship, they also retained the Harrow Charity Cup, having held it successively for three years and having won it in nine of the previous thirteen years. They were also the losing finalists in the Middlesex Intermediate Cup.

They had played 26 matches, winning 18, and in all competitions they had scored 105 goals, conceding only 47.

A former player and active Committee member at this time was Mr E G C Bellchambers, who retired on this evening, and in light of his service to the club since its modern day inception, he was made a Life Member.

He had captained Wealdstone Reserves from 1900 to 1908, the First XI from 1909 to 1911, subsequently serving on the Committee after World War 1 and again from 1924 to 1936.

One important change made at this time was with the Selection Committee for the teams. Previously, there had been seven members of this committee, but it was agreed that to get seven people to agree on team selection was almost impossible. It was mentioned that the Selection Committee picked the team on the preceding Monday, whereas the critics picked theirs on the following Saturday night.

The vote was duly carried and the committee reduced to the two Match Secretaries and another gentleman to be selected by these two. The Trainers and Coaches at this time were only responsible for training and for the 'tactics' and performance of the team selected by the committee.

The playing staff for season 1936-37 was to include a number of well remembered players, Charlie Bunce for example, was to go on and become one of the most prolific goalscorers in the club's history until he was killed during WWII. He played alongside some notable men.

Right back Arthur Loveday was to play for England twice during the season, against both Scotland and Ireland, while left back Bob Ellis was to play for England against Wales. Syd Bidewell, who was to sign for Chelsea in May 1937, was a regular and many of the players were well remembered for a number of years, not least Jackie Wilson, Ken Potts, Stan Friday and Bill Showler, who was to become a Club Official when his playing days ended.

The early part of the season continued the goal feast of recent years at the club. The opening fixture was an 8-0 win over Uxbridge. This was followed by 9-0 victories over Old Lyonians in the FA Amateur Cup and 7-0 over C.W.S. (Silvertown) in the London Senior Cup.

Although the first team won no silverware, it was a better season. Having had to apply (successfully) for re-election to the

Athenian League, having finished in the bottom two for the previous two seasons, 'Stones finished in third place and had in fact led the League up to Christmas. The reserves too had a good year. As defending Champions in their League they were to finish second to Walthamstow Avenue.

Wealdstone had also had a good run in the Amateur Cup. Following the victory over Old Lyonians, there were victories over Ealing Association, Hounslow, Hayesco, Frosts Athletic (Norwich), Chesham United and Uxbridge before their eventual defeat after a replay by Dulwich Hamlet.

The AGM was pleased to record the success of the two sides, and also that all of the players with the exception of Syd Bidewell, were to return.

More works were proposed on the Lower Mead ground; this time the whole of the playing surface was to be levelled off and new drainage installed, at a cost of £1250. This did mean, however, that it would not be possible to let out the pitch during the summer.

This allied with the cost of the work meant that the club would start the following season with a debt of around £500 albeit in one of the finest grounds in Middlesex.

As well as the reversal of fortunes in the league, the first team had also reached the third round of the Amateur Cup, losing in a replay to the eventual winners, Dulwich Hamlet, after a 1-1 draw at home, nine matches having been played in the competition.

The record for the season in all matches showed 42 played with 27 won and four drawn, scoring 117 goals and conceding 65.

Captain, Charlie Bunce, was by far the most prolific scoring 47 goals during the season. Jackie Wilson scored 22 and Syd Bidewell scored 12.

The reserves again retained the Harrow Charity Cup. Their record showed that they played 34 matches, winning 24, with 2 drawn, scoring 127 goals and conceding 65. They also had outstanding goalscorers, in F Masters who chipped in with 46 (plus 3 for the first team), Mills with 24 and J Roche 13(+2) the next.

Vice Presidents subscriptions were increased from 10s 6d to 15s, and memberships raised from 7s 6d to 10s 6d. season Tickets for the following season were to cost 7s 6d.

For the following season, 1937-1938, the local paper was pleased to report that a number of new players had been signed, and these would strengthen an already strong squad, which should make the season one of the best in the club history.

They were also pleased to report on the success of the Drainage and Levelling works at the ground, which had removed the seven feet slope from end to end. Thousands of tons of earth were removed, and 26000 new turves were laid with the 2000 best turves from the original surface.

At the same time the white hoop fence was installed around the playing surface to replace the ropes. The cinder track was also laid.

The report went on to mention that the club officials and players had kept together during the close season by running a cricket team, playing Sunday matches against a number of local sides.

Wealdstone FC Cricket Team 1937 – 1938

The next game was to be against Wealdstone Corinthians, another side playing local football as well, the selected team was; L Fraser (capt.), L D'Arcy, E Walker, R Ellis, A Loveday, W Showler, S Friday, A Reeves, D Scott, A Downing, R Brewin and S White.

The season was to start in the same vein as the previous year, with an 8-0 win, this time over Enfield, although a week later in the return, the result was a 3-3 draw.

There were in excess of 3000 spectators at Lower Mead for the first game, and they were treated to a match where six goals were scored in the second half, five of them in a fifteen minute period. All in all, it was considered to be one of the best Wealdstone XI's ever to start a season.

As a Thank You to the club after they had signed Syd Bidewell, Chelsea were to visit again early in September 1937;

A crowd approaching 3000 saw a team from Chelsea defeat Wealdstone by two goals to one at Lower Mead last Wednesday.

The match was the result of Inside-right Syd Bidewell having signed professional forms for Chelsea during the summer.

Chelsea paid Wealdstone a nice compliment by sending a strong team, which included Jackson and Law, the Scottish Internationals, and also Barraclough, Miller and Mayes, all of whom have played for the first eleven. Foss the old Southall player was included in the eleven and Bidewell was given the honour of captaining the side.

Wealdstone were at full strength with the exception of Ette, who was unable to get away from business. Reeves returned at left half, Wilson came in at inside-left and Lloyd crossed over to inside-right.

Naturally, with their greater experience, Chelsea were the more polished side, but Wealdstone throughout gave a fine display, and on the run of the game there was not much in the professionals favour.

As was only to be expected, Chelsea finished much the better and had far more goalscoring opportunities. On the other hand, with a less capable goalkeeper to beat than Jackson, Wealdstone would have scored more than one goal. In addition in the second half both Lloyd and Wilson missed badly with only the goalkeeper to beat.

Chelsea scored the only goal in the first half, and on this occasion, the ball was deflected into the net by Ellis in trying to clear. Wealdstone had more of the play in the second half, but the forwards were unable to finish.

Twenty minutes from the end Chelsea were two up, Mayes scoring from a corner. Immediately afterwards Lloyd cleverly drew the defence and Wilson shot hard for goal. Jackson partially saved the shot, but before he could recover Bunce raced in from outside right where he had gone owing to an injury, and crashed the ball into the net.

From then until the end there was a great deal of excitement and on several occasions Wealdstone came very close to equalising. Walker played a brilliant game in goal, making many fine saves. Loveday and Ellis played strongly, covering each other well.

The half-backs worked untiringly and there was little to choose between them for each gave of his best. The forwards were good individually but lacked cohesion, Downing, Lloyd and Bunce were the pick.

Wealdstone; E Walker, A Loveday, R Ellis, W Showler, S Friday, A G Reeves, C Brown, J Lloyd, C Bunce, J Wilson, A Downing.

Chelsea; Jackson, White, Law, Alexander, Mayes, Miller, Byrne, Bidewell, Sherbourne, Foss, Barraclough.

Despite the early promise, Wealdstone were to finish the season in fourth spot again, but there was success as the first team won both the Middlesex Senior Cup and the Middlesex Charity Cup in the space of a few weeks.

The Senior Cup was clinched with a 3-1 victory over Tufnell Park after being 1-0 down at half time, the match played at Golders Green FC. Three weeks later, the 'Stones beat Golders Green FC 4-0 in the Final of the Charity Cup, played at Lower Mead.

In the two competitions, Wealdstone had played seven matches, scoring 32 goals and conceding six.

In early May, on the Saturday preceding the Charity Cup Final, Wealdstone 'warmed up' with a friendly fixture against Tottenham Hotspur Reserves, running out winners by two goals to nil.

'Stones scored an early goal in the first half, through Bunce, but for the remainder of the half they were treated to an exhibition of ball control and passing in a strong wind. The Tottenham combination side coped well with the conditions, although unable to score.

The second half saw 'Stones score again on the hour, although they spent much of the half defending, the report commenting that but for the woeful shooting of the Tottenham forwards, the result could have been different.

Walthamstow Avenue were again winners of the Athenian League, with Barnet and Romford close behind, and it was a similar picture for the reserves, again finishing runner up to Walthamstow Avenue, and Southall finishing rooted to the bottom of both divisions.

The first team's record was played 45 won 24, drawn 8, with 115 goals scored and 71 against. Charlie Bunce was again top scorer, his tally thirty this season. The reserves had scored 105 goals winning 18 of the 31 games played with six draws, and T Morris was top scorer with 14.

The following season, 1938 – 1939, was again to start impressively. Wealdstone were top of the League at Christmas, but it was not to last, 'Stones finally finishing in third place, with Walthamstow Avenue again the winners and Romford runner up.

There were a number of good victories on the way, not least a 9-2 win over Tooting and Mitcham. The first team were to retain the Middlesex Charity Cup, but couldn't complete the double,

Wealdstone Football Club 1937-38
Winners of the Middlesex Senior Charity Cup and Middlesex Charity Cup
Back row; L Clark (Match Secretary), F Thame (Asst Match Sec), T Morris, W Showler, R Lewis, A Loveday, R Ellis, D Scott, W Gallagher (trainer), W Williams (Reserve Trainer) H A Luck, (Hon Secretary), S White
Front Row; J Rogers (Hon treasurer), C Brown, H Dyke, S Friday, C Bunce (Captain), J Wilson, K Potts.

losing in the final of the Middlesex Senior Cup, beaten 4-0 by Golders Green, a reverse of the previous season's result.

Wealdstone were also a little lucky to have progressed in the Charity Cup, as in their first round match against Finchley, the visitors took the field with only nine men. 'Stones took the lead against the 'nine', and scored another goal while Finchley played with only ten men. After about twenty minutes, both teams were at full strength and an extremely spirited match ensued, the final score being 3-2 to Wealdstone.

This match was the first time Charlie Barker was to appear at full back – his only previous appearance in the first team had been at outside left, although he had been a full back in the reserves since joining the club. He made an impression on all those present, as recorded in the Harrow Observer;

Barker created a particularly good impression by his display at right back. His kicking was strong and clean, his tackling thorough and he was quick to recover when beaten. He extricated the defence from a number of sticky situations and is evidently a most resourceful player.

Charlie was to go on and become one of the best known and most appreciated players of his era, playing for the club for a number of years. He was to become an excellent penalty taker, taking over 140 for the club and missing on only four occasions. His shot was so hard from the spot that on at least two occasions, opposing goalkeepers who had attempted a save damaged their hands sufficiently to prevent them completing the match!

The reserves league season was similar, they eventually finished third as well, Walthamstow Avenue Reserves winning the Division and Barking finishing runner up.

Their 'star' player was Gilbert Gaze, who during the season, like Charlie Barker, progressed into the first team. On 6th of May of 1939, another professional club visited Lower Mead for a friendly, this time Watford were the visitors in the first match between the two clubs, as reported in the local paper;

The match attracted considerable local interest, and a good crowd witnessed an entertaining game played in a good sporting spirit. Although the match lacked the atmosphere of a cup-tie, the players did sufficient to prevent it becoming a go as you please exhibition affair and there was enough to interest the spectators from start to finish.

Wealdstone pleased their supporters, and played so well as a team it was difficult to understand how they had lost form so badly in their last four league matches, costing them the chance to finish runner up.

Watford, who fielded their full first team, gave a good exhibition of professional play, but their marksmanship was by no means convincing. In comparison Wealdstone were the better marksmen and the visiting goalkeeper had to give of his best, he may not have handled the ball so many times as Lewis, but the shots that reached him were generally of a more difficult nature and he made a number of spectacular saves.

Watford were better in defence than attack and had a great advantage in having three half-backs who were above average height. Armstrong at centre half and Reed at right half dwarfed the Wealdstone forwards and had little difficulty in getting the ball when it was in the air, but the defence as a whole could not afford to take liberties with the Wealdstone forwards.

Watford set the pace at the start, but Wealdstone soon replied, McHugh saving a point-blank shot from Bunce. Wealdstone took the lead after eight minutes from a free kick for 'hands'.

From just outside the penalty area, Scott drove the ball hard at McHugh, who caught it only to see the ball spin out of his hands and into the goal. Wealdstone held their own in the half hour which preceded Watford's equaliser, most of their attacks coming from the left wing.

Five minutes before the interval, G Lewis found a gap in the Wealdstone defence and broke through the middle. His namesake, R Lewis saved his shot but failed to prevent the ball from rebounding to the Watford leader, who scored in the resulting scrimmage.

Bunce, Schofield, Wilson and Gaze each tested McHugh with good shots in the second half, and though Watford tried hard to score in the closing stages, the home defenders gave nothing away.

Wealdstone; R Lewis, A Loveday, R Ellis, L Green, R Bidewell, D Scott, G Gaze, K Baldwin, C Bunce, J Wilson, F Schofield.

Watford; McHugh, O'Brien, J Lewis, Reed, Armstrong, Woodward, Jones, Barnett, G Lewis, Evans, Davies.

Some Personal Reminiscences
By THE PRESIDENT Mr. C. E. Brady edited from the Golden Jubilee Handbook

Practically the whole of the playing staff of the Wealdstone Football Club volunteered for service at the' outbreak of war in 1914, and when the club resuscitated itself directly after the cessation of hostilities it had lost in the war about one-third of its players

The team played on an undulating field at the end of Belmont-Road, Wealdstone, a site which has long since been covered with houses. Someone living near the ground let the players have the use of buckets of water after the matches.

Immediately after the war I had the honour to be appointed chairman of the club. Had I foreseen the anxieties, risks, expense, and trouble I might have hesitated.

Tom Bradberry was the moving spirit of the club in its early days. Some of its prominent players were the two Theobalds, 'Miller Durham, Harbud, Kirby, and Gallagher Jabez Barnes, a Y.M.C.A. man, and a strict Sabbatarian, took an interest in the club. He gave them acid drops at half times, together with a cheery word.

On his initiative, and with his help, we bought the field of which Lower Mead is a part.

Most of the purchase money remained on mortgage and £300 was advanced on War Loan for the balance. Ultimately, I took this over, as Mr. Barnes would not permit any work of any kind on the ground on Sundays.

We erected a temporary building at the east end of the ground for dressing accommodation. We got a local builder to put up a wooden building on the north side, which looked like an elongated cowshed.

The club agreed to pay him interest on the purchase price and to give him the "stand" takings until our indebtedness was discharged. Opportunity arising, we got a building society to advance a consider-able sum of money on the security of the ground and buildings, and we then paid the builder.

This eased the situation at the time,' but we had some difficulty in meeting current expenses. We held "fairs" on the ground and we also launched a "Save Lower Mead" appeal.

On one occasion there was an incident, which I doubt if dear old Jabez Barnes would have allowed me to call providential.

We were desperately hard up to meet current expenses. Whilst at the ground one day, one of our members came along and said he "wanted a bob" from me. I gave it him and asked him what it was for. He told me I had drawn a horse in some race (I think it was the Cambridgeshire). I asked him the name of the horse. It was "Charlie's Mount." I had never "drawn " a horse in a sweepstake before, so I decided to put 10/-. on it.

Although the price was 100 to 1 against it, I was only able to get 40 to 1 not being acquainted with the book-making world. "Charlie's Mount" came first! I got back my stake and £20. Of course, the club thought it ought to have the money. So it got it. A little windfall of £20 also coming to me at that time secured the club sufficient to reduce its current debts by £40.

Then a well-known and much-esteemed club, known as Summerstown FC, had to wind up, as the lease of its ground expired and it could not get another one. We bought their grandstand at a reduced figure.

We had it removed and set up on our ground at a cost of some £200. It is there today and was extended last season. Dressing rooms, match officials' accommodation, baths, etc., have also been added and improved. The committee considered matters, and it came to the conclusion that it would be well to get the debt transferred, if possible at a lower rate of interest. I obtained an introduction to the principal manager of Lloyds Bank in Lombard-street.

He was very businesslike, but very kindly disposed, and the bank advanced this a large sum of money on the security of the ground and buildings, and on a personal guarantee by myself. The manager frankly stated that in the event of default the 'bank would not seize the ground, which if they did would lose them most of their Wealdstone customers but would come upon me - he explained to me the doctrine of subrogation. The occasion did not arise.

At first the ground was un-drained and it sloped down to what became the main entrance to the ground and the car park. In wet weather the ground had little "lakes" over it and was thoroughly sodden.

The "mole" system of drainage relieved matters. But before and after this, dear old W. W. Heard (known affectionately as Billy Heard) helped us all he could and insisted on representative matches being played on our ground. Mr. Heard's successor as honorary secretary of the Middlesex County Football Association, Mr. George R. Hawes, is no less considerate, but he has not, so far as we are concerned, such a difficult job.

At the end of about 18 years, there was an offer for the northern part of our ground, This portion was absolutely useless to the club and to anyone else as it' stood. We sold it for sufficient to discharge our debt to the bank and all outstanding debts. We had the whole ground dug up and leveled - 6ft. in depth transferred from one half to the other, and we surmounted the troubles naturally arising from this hurried between-the-season's work.

By the start of the 1939–1940 season, Wealdstone were confident of winning the Athenian League for the first time, not only because of the improvement made over previous seasons, but also aided by the fact that both Walthamstow Avenue and Romford had been successful in their applications to join the Isthmian League.

This meant that both winners and runner up were no longer in contention and it also meant that for the first time, Wealdstone were honoured to be invited to take on the Rest Of The League team in the seasons opening match;

The Wealdstone team showed a couple of changes from the previous season, Charlie Barker had come into the side to replace R Ellis who had left and joined Enfield FC, on the day representing the League XI, and C Brown formerly of Uxbridge who had impressed in the Trial match, played at right wing.

The 'Rest' team as was expected were the stronger throughout the match, eventually running out winners by four goals to three. Wealdstone had given a good account of themselves, opening the scoring after 20 minutes play when Wilson headed the ball against the post and Baldwin was on hand to head in the rebound.

The 'Rest' equalised with a goal from a free kick scored by Murphy of Hitchin Town, but Bunce was soon able to restore Wealdstone's lead with a header off of the underside of the bar. The lead lasted only until half time, when the unfortunate Barker was to head an own goal to equalise.

The second half saw the visitors start brighter and pressure the 'Stones defence, during which time S Friday received a bad cut above his eye and he had to leave the field. This however being a friendly match, a substitute was used, possibly for the first time ever in a Wealdstone game, R Bidewell joining the fray. The League took the lead for the first time shortly afterwards, a low shot after a breakaway from Kelleher, of Barnet, Barker making up for his earlier error, scoring Wealdstone's equaliser with a well struck penalty, but the League were to score again just before time, when Osborne of Tooting and Mitcham scored from close range.

Wealdstone; R Lewis, A W Loveday, C Barker, L Green, S Friday, D Scott, C Brown, K Baldwin, C E Bunce, J Wilson, F Schofield.

The Rest; P T Bartaby (Bromley), L A Gray (Bromley), R Ellis (Enfield), A Lovell (Golders Green), V J Weeks (Bromley), L N Hockday (Leyton), H Farrow (Hayes), R D Murphy (Hitchin Town), J F Osborne (Tooting and Mitcham), D Kelleher (Barnet), L Griggs (Bromley).

Amid rumblings of discontent on the continent, the season opened the following week with an FA Cup-tie at Lower Mead, against Old Johnians, in the Extra Preliminary round. It was a comfortable win recorded by the Harrow Observer;

Wealdstone did not experience much difficulty in defeating the Old Johnians at Lower Mead on Saturday. The final score was seven goals to three in Wealdstone's favour.

Wealdstone made two changes from the side fielded the previous week, S Friday was unable to play because of business reasons, Scott went to centre half and Baldwin dropped back to right half. Nicholson from the reserves filled Baldwin's normal position and Gaze came in at outside right in place of Brown.

Owing to calls of National Service the Old Johnians were compelled to field a scratch team and added to this, they experienced transport difficulties, with the result that the game was an hour late in starting.

Not a great deal of good football was seen. Wealdstone seemed to sense that the opposition would not extend them and accordingly played well within themselves, while the Old Johnians were content to adopt kick and rush methods in the hope of getting near enough for a shot on goal. Lewis had no chance with the three shots that beat him, and all through, played in his usual confident style.

Loveday played a cool and calculating game at right back, and Barker, his partner vastly improved on his for of the previous week. The halfbacks kept a tight rein on the opponents' forwards and at the same time fed their own forwards freely.

The forwards are still not that smooth combination of last season. Bunce worked untiringly and had a hand in most of the goals scored. Wilson and Nicholson supported him splendidly and the latter gave a highly creditable display. Gaze was a distinct improvement on Brown and sent across many well-placed centres. In the first half Schofield persisted in shooting at goal at every opportunity and invariably he drove the ball high over the bar. In the second half he scored two excellent goals and then lapsed back into his old ways again.

At half time, Wealdstone were leading by 3-2, Wilson (two) and Bunce scoring. On the resumption three goals were scored by Wealdstone in ten minutes, Schofield netting twice in succession, whilst Wilson completed a successful match by obtaining the other two and making his own total four.

Wealdstone; R Lewis, A Loveday, C Barker, K Baldwin, D Scott, L Green, A Gaze, R Nicholson, C Bunce, J Wilson, F Schofield.

The day prior to the match had seen the news that Adolf Hitler had sent his troops across the Polish border. The following day, Prime Minister Neville Chamberlain voiced his nation's disapproval of Germany's actions and war was declared.

By the time the match report was published, Harrow had an Emergency Defence Committee and in common with the majority of organised sports, the Athenian League had been suspended and eventually cancelled.

What had promised to be one of the best seasons in the club's history, with a real chance of league honours, had been snatched away almost before it had started.

THE WAR YEARS

As the war did not develop as had been anticipated and the hostilities at this time and in the next few weeks were very distant, based entirely on mainland Europe, it was not long before football was played again.

A number of local leagues and competitions were established to replace the usual league and cup competitions. The committee at Wealdstone however had decided at this time not to join one of the new competitions but to arrange a list of friendly fixtures. The first of these was to be against their League rivals, Southall, at Lower Mead, on the 16th September. Again the match was reported by the Harrow Observer;

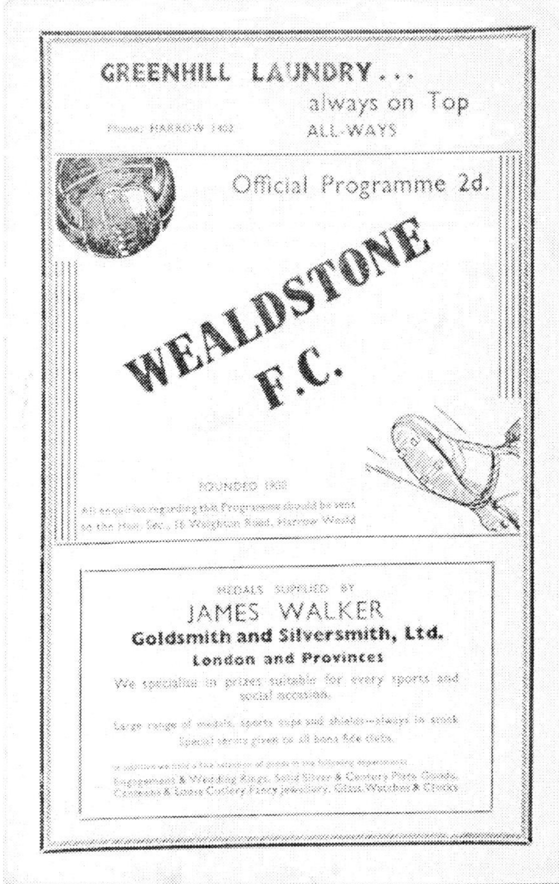

Wealdstone v Southall. September 16th 1939.

Wealdstone FC played its first wartime fixture on Saturday, against Southall. Competitive football having been abandoned it was a friendly fixture won rather easily by eight goals to four. The game was quite interesting and provided the crowd with a much-needed respite from the matters of war, and it gave them as far as goals were concerned, full value for their money.

With the exception of Friday who was on ARP Duty, Bidewell filling in, Wealdstone were able to field a full side and they played in a manner, which delighted their supporters.

The report went on to state that *'Stones forwards had played with tremendous vigour, and had it not been for the Southall goalkeeper, another Lewis, the score would have been much higher. Bunce had led the 'Stones attack well, ably assisted by Wilson and Baldwin.*

Wealdstone faced the sun in the first half and the opening exchanges were evenly contested. When Wealdstone did attack, Lewis was at once brought into the action and within a few seconds he saved a stinging shot from Scott, turned a header from Bunce around the post and dived full length to save a shot from Baldwin.

The pressure could not last however without result, and after some ten minutes play, pretty work by the Wealdstone left wing culminated in a fine centre from Schofield which Bunce converted.

Southall then started to attack in earnest but uncertainty in front of goal nullified their efforts. In a breakaway, Schofield for Wealdstone beat several players and finished off a splendid dash with a stinging shot, which skimmed the crossbar. Southall however managed to equalise after thirty minutes, Morrod the inside-left going through on his own.

Wilson then put Wealdstone ahead with a shot that never rose higher than a foot from the ground and this started a riot of goals. Kennett, the Southall Outside right put his side level again with a shot that Lewis appeared to miss-judge and almost immediately afterwards Wealdstone retaliated through Baldwin, who scored again before the interval to give Wealdstone a 4-2 lead.

In the second half the play was mostly in Wealdstone's favour, Wilson exciting the crowd by beating three opponents before deftly turning the ball neatly into the goal. Bunce concluded a good days work by scoring three more of his own, while Southall's other goals were scored by Morrod and Hill.

Wealdstone; R Lewis, A W Loveday, C Barker, L Green, R Bidewell, D Scott, A G Gaze, K Baldwin, C E Bunce, J Wilson, F Schofield.

The anticipated strength of the Wealdstone side became evident as the weeks passed. Although not in a league, the opposition for Wealdstone in friendlies was of a good standard, but for a long time, none were good enough. Victories came week after week with Golders Green losing 2-1, then Hitchin Town (8-0), followed home and away by Chesham United. Wealdstone won by eight goals to one at Chesham, and then the following week won by 7-2 at Lower Mead.

It was in the first of the two Chesham matches that Wealdstone made use of a guest player, a common act during the war years as players in the forces were based and moving around the UK, often before going overseas.

The first of this ilk to appear for Wealdstone was W (Bill) Parr, an amateur International who played regularly for Dulwich Hamlet and had also played for Blackpool. His debut at Chesham was described as successful, not really surprising as he scored three times in the second half!

Matches against Kingstonians, Hayes, Nunhead and Metropolitan Police were also arranged and again Wealdstone were dominant. In fact, the first defeat of the war was not to occur until 4th November, Wealdstone going down by five goals to two to Brentford Reserves. This was only a minor 'blip' however, the team immediately returning to winning ways thereafter.

In early January, Chelsea Reserves were visitors to Lower Mead. The Chelsea side was to have included Jackson, the current Scotland goalkeeper, but Woodley who was England goalkeeper at the time replaced him. There were a number of other players who had appeared in the first team.

The game was described as the best exhibition of football ever seen at Lower Mead, in particular the positioning and the confident and polished display of the visiting goalkeeper suggested that the amateurs of Wealdstone would be hard pressed to score. Score they did however, F Schofield and C Bunce scoring the two Wealdstone goals in an excellent 2-1 victory.

As a sign of the times, it was to be the last game for a number of the Wealdstone team; both Bidewell and Haydon were called up and reported for military service on the Monday after the game. The victories continued in games over Wycombe Wanderers, Woking and Brigg Sports and it wasn't until Easter that Wealdstone next failed to win.

There were three attractive fixtures played over the break, Wealdstone gaining two wins and a draw from three games. They shared six goals with Crystal Palace at Selhurst Park on the Good Friday, before returning home to face Nunhead on the Saturday at Lower Mead.

Wealdstone won the match by six goals to one, but it was remembered for the tremendous sporting spirit in which the match had been played. This was shown no better than by two similar incidents, when injured players were replaced by others with the agreement of both teams. This of course in the days before substitutes were permitted.

For Wealdstone, L Green had started the match having seemingly recovered from injury, but there was a recurrence and after four minutes he was replaced by Edmonds, who played the reminder of the match at centre half.

This was later followed by a similar incident when Cornell, the Nunhead goalkeeper suffered fractured ribs in a collision with one of his own players, – he was taken to hospital and replaced by their regular goalkeeper, Murray, who had been watching from the stand!

The final game of the Easter break was the return with Crystal Palace at Lower Mead on the Monday this time a weakened 'Stones side running out winners by three goals to two. Due to an injury, D Scott also missed his first game for almost three years on the Monday.

Wealdstone created club history in this season by reaching the final of the London Senior Cup, beating Bromley 7-4 in the quarter final and then a strong Barnet team 2-1 in the semi-final. It was the club's first final in the competition, and they met their former League rivals Walthamstow Avenue at West Ham's Upton Park ground.

Two weeks before the final, Wealdstone scored their biggest win of the season, a ten – nil victory over Gillingham, at the time professionals in the Southern League. Gillingham had not expected such strong opposition and had sent a weakened team.

The match was seen as some form of comic relief after the cup-tie atmosphere of the previous two matches and the report went on;

If the spectators did not get value for money from the football played by the visitors, then they certainly did from Wealdstone, and the number of goals scored and other amusing incidents.

Hardly a member of the visiting team gave any indication of footballing ability. The team lacked any sort of combination and was quite incapable of offering a challenge to the home team. Rarely have I known a football crowd to treat a game so much as a rollicking comedy.

Such was their dominance that three of Wealdstone's six goals in the first half were gained while they were a man short, Dyke having suffered an injury and left the field, and it was twenty minutes before Nicholson came on to replace him!

The result brought the season's goal tally to 154, Bunce at this stage having scored 49, and Barker having scored 10 penalties.

The London Senior Cup Final was a different matter, and despite a large following, Wealdstone were beaten by five goals to nil.

Afterwards, a party of over fifty players, supporters and officials ate together, and Club captain, Charlie Bunce, promised that the side were not downhearted, and would retain the Middlesex Sports Red Cross (Charity) Cup the following week.

'Stones went on to beat Golders Green by 4-1 in the final. The competition had raised the sum of £400 for the British Red Cross and the County 'Boot Fund' had also benefited, £40 having been spent by sending football boots to all parts of the world for servicemen in the Middlesex Regiments.

Some 3000 people were had watched the final, admitted for a cost of 1/- to watch, and after expenses, an additional sum of £128 was handed over.

The reserves had played league football during the first 'wartime' season. The hastily organised West Middlesex Combination had consisted of nine teams, Wealdstone and local rivals Edgware Town, Harrow Town, Pinner and Wood Green Town included. The Wealdstone side had finished fourth.

At the end of the season, Wealdstone hosted a Six-a-Side competition at Lower Mead, again in aid of the British Red Cross. Sixteen teams had entered and two pitches were marked out on the playing surface.

After a tournament lasting four hours, and to the satisfaction of the majority of spectators, the Wealdstone A team, made up of first team players were the winners.

The 'rules' were modified on the day to ensure a winner, four points being awarded for a goal in any match and one point for a corner so that if a match were tied, there would still be a winner!

Wealdstone 'A' had played Wealdstone 'B' in the semi-final and had won by 23 points to 2, (five goals and three corners to two corners!). In the final, Wealdstone A met Hayes, winning by 21 points to six, Wealdstone having scored five goals again, to Hayes' nil.

As the season drew to a close, the AGM recorded that it had been the best ever, both on the field and financially. Although the war had caused the Leagues to be suspended, the high quality opposition attracted to Lower Mead by the Committee for friendlies had ensured the gates were higher than normal.

This was aided by the excellent record of the first team. After the defeat by Brentford Reserves they had then won 16 consecutive matches, before the draw at Crystal Palace spoilt the run.

The playing record for the season was as follows;

	P	W	D	L	F	A
v Rest Of League	1	0	0	1	3	4
FA Cup	1	1	0	0	8	2
London Senior Cup	5	4	0	1	19	12
Middlesex Red Cross Cup	4	4	0	0	25	4
Friendlies	31	26	3	2	137	59
Total	**42**	**35**	**3**	**4**	**192**	**81**

Charlie Bunce had scored 58 goals in 40 matches and Ken Baldwin had scored 40 goals in 41. Five others also scoring more than ten. Charlie also announced at the meeting that like a number of other players, he had enlisted and therefore would only be available occasionally, if at all, for the following season.

Unfortunately, he was captured and taken prisoner by the Japanese in Malaya. He died at the age of thirty as a Prisoner of War. He had scored 174 goals in his career with St Albans and Wealdstone.

Bill Parr had scored 12 goals in his 19 appearances for the club, before service took him overseas. He was not to play for the club again, although he did play for both Arsenal and Blackpool occasionally before he was killed, serving with the RAF in March 1942.

Alan Lawrence
Supporter 1940's and 1950's

An Uncle took me to my first game at Lower Mead in the early years of the war. It was actually when Wealdstone played Gillingham in a friendly in 1940. I remember it well because Wealdstone won 10-0 and my uncle, who had a very loud voice shouted "Keep it on the island" every time anyone kicked the ball into touch.

Otherwise I remember little about the game other than my uncle telling me that 'Scotty' was laughing all over his face - it must've been after the 'Stones scored the tenth! 'Scotty' was of course Dave Scott. I recently looked up the match report in the Harrow Observer archives - it confirmed the result was 10-0 and the Wealdstone side that day included Bill Parr, George Bunce and Ken Baldwin, all three of whom were later to lose their lives in the war.

I started going regularly to Wealdstone the next year in 1941, when I went along with my pals, and certain matches during these early days stick in my memory - when Wealdstone won the Middlesex Senior Cup at Lower Mead, and when Harold Charlton broke his leg - that had quite an effect on me for a long time, and of course the Red Cross Cup Final at Wembley - I still have my program and entrance ticket stub, it cost just one shilling to get in!

There were many strange games and results during these times - I saw Wealdstone win 6-0 and then lose 6-1 in successive weeks to Finchley, and there was one game when they beat Barnet 9-7! That was in the wartime Herts and Middlesex League, which, it seemed, was always topped by Walthamstow Avenue, from Essex!

There were regular appeals in the program for Clothing Coupons - people were giving up their ration allocation for the club to buy new kit, and there were also the letters from players serving overseas in the forces.

One of the saddest times was hearing that Ken Baldwin had lost his life. Although one of three players from that win against Gillingham to lose his life, he stuck in my memory as he had still been a regular when I watched the 'Stones with my friends. He had become a great favourite of mine, and played regularly up to the end of the 1943-44 season.

Wealdstone FC 1940/41;
Winners of the Middlesex Senior Cup, the Cambridge Hospital Cup and the Middlesex Charity Cup.
Back Row; H Luck, (Hon. Secretary) G Upchurch, L Dolding, M Doherty, B Leeming, P Bunyan, F Harbud (Hon Treasurer), B Gallagher (Trainer).
Front Row; R Nicholson, L Green, A Loveday, H Charlton, F Butterworth, B Dyke.

With the call on players from the first team as well as a number of players often unavailable through military service, the club decided to disband the reserves for the 1940-1941 season. To replace them, an agreement was reached with Brookshill whereby they would play at Lower Mead on alternate Saturdays, and there would be a mutual exchange of players between the two clubs. This was similar to the previous arrangement with Sudbury, who had disbanded altogether.

As the season started, the war had begun to take its toll on the Wealdstone squad. For the opening match of the season, only 4 players remained from the side that had been so successful the previous year, and out of the new players only three had previously played for the reserves. A number of promising youngsters had been engaged after impressing in the Trial matches, and Wealdstone started the season with a pre-season Friendly match, winning at home to Erith and Belvedere.

For the season itself, Wealdstone had joined the newly formed Herts and Middlesex Combination league and started this new Wartime League Programme with a 5-0 win over Golders Green. This game was disrupted when the air raid sirens were sounded during the second half, but as described by the local paper, "after a brief interruption the all clear was given and the match continued!" Wealdstone's form continued to impress the following week when they played the reverse fixture, this time winning by seven goals to nil.

One of the stars of the Wealdstone side at this time was Len Dolding. He was born in India and by the age of seven he had travelled back and forth between England and India five times, before settling to school in Margate. He captained Cliftonville School's Cricket and Football teams.

His footballing ability developed further during his time at Wealdstone and he won three consecutive Middlesex Cup winners medals while at the club. He also played for Queens Park Rangers as an amateur before joining Chelsea to play on a professional basis. He also served in the RAF during the war.

In his time at Chelsea, he formed a good understanding with Tommy Lawton before moving on to join Norwich City. He was on the MCC ground staff at Lords and he became the first Wealdstone player to take part in a test match, when he acted as Twelfth Man for England against New Zealand in the second test in June 1949!

The following season saw 'Stones lose two more players to call ups, F Butterworth joining L Green in the RAF, but Charlie Barker declared that he would be available most Saturdays throughout the season.

Again, it was the cup competitions that saw Wealdstone gain most success, making progress in the Middlesex cups and also in the Herts and Middlesex League Cup. The league form had been a little less impressive, 'Stones having gained seven wins and eleven defeats from eighteen matches by mid April.

In January the team were pleased to run out in a new kit, their first since before the war and the first that had been purchased after a collection and donations of clothing coupons from the supporters, all clothing being rationed at the time.

At the beginning of April the highest crowd at Lower Mead during the season watched Wealdstone retain the Middlesex Senior Cup in a thrilling victory over Finchley by four goals to one.

The Harrow Observer reported;

Finchley were the first to be dangerous with pressure from the start and Doherty was called upon to save a number of shots, which he did with confidence. Throughout the match his work was outstandingly good. From a corner Haskow, Finchley's right-winger placed the ball accurately and Young, the centre forward threw himself at the ball in a determined effort, but Doherty saved at the expense of another corner.

After 20 minutes of keen and attractive football a corner was conceded by Finchley. From the kick, taken by Charlton, Thomson headed the ball to Morris who lightly touched it on to Russell, for that player to open the scoring.

Later, a delightful movement, in which Morris, Dolding and Russell were associated, provided the latter with another chance which he took to score with a rasping shot. Wealdstone led 2-0 at half time.

The second half opened with a series of thrills, Two corners were conceded by Finchley and off the second, taken by Dolding the ball was cleared by a Finchley defender but Leeming however, returned the ball to the Finchley area, where Russell took it on the bounce and scored another goal.

At this period two players were injured and both had to leave the ground for treatment. Charlton of Wealdstone was taken off to hospital with a broken tibia. (He had been one of the first players to become a regular in the first team after joining the club when Brookshill played as Wealdstone Reserves.)

Afterwards, receiving a through pass from Morris, Lewis was brought down in the Finchley area, and Barker scored from the penalty to further increase Wealdstone's lead.

A spectacular effort on behalf of Finchley was made by Withers, their left back, who, securing the ball in his own penalty area ran the length of the field skilfully evading three Wealdstone defenders. He finished up by sending a hard shot across the goalmouth. Finchley scored five minutes from the end when W Boston sent the ball out to F Boston who scored with an accurate shot.

After the match medals were presented to both sides, and Wealdstone's Tom Morris, now a Flight Sergeant in the RAF made a sporting gesture when he handed his winners medal to the father of Hugh Dyke.

Hugh had played in all the previous rounds of the competition until he was called up, Morris taking his place in the final.

The following Saturday Wealdstone continued their better Cup Form when they beat Golders Green by two goals to one in the Quarter Final of the League Cup, going on to meet Southall in the semi-final.

The semi-final though was to see Wealdstone exit the competition, losing a replay at Southall by six goals to nil. They had had numerous chances to win the first encounter though, at one point leading by three goals to one before eventually drawing 4-4 after extra time.

The reserves had a more successful season in the Harrow and Wembley league, finishing in fifth place having won 12 and drawn three of twenty two matches played, but there was still at the start of June one outstanding first team fixture, the Middlesex Red Cross Cup Final, to be played at Wembley Stadium.

A Spectator Tells Of When Wealdstone Played at Wembley
Edited from the Golden Jubilee Handbook

In comfort would not be a very apt slogan if applied to the rush-hour train service between Harrow and Baker Street, for, although the authorities seem to run as many trains as can be accommodated on the tracks available, "standing room only" is all too often the order of the day. But when I reached Baker Street station, on my homeward journey on the evening of Wednesday, June 3rd, 1942, it seemed to me that "all Harrow" hoped to travel down by the same train.

It was the evening when the final of the Middlesex Senior Red Cross Cup was to be played at Wembley Stadium—the first time a County Cup match had ever been played on the famous Wembley turf, and, I believe, the first amateur football match to be staged there.

The finalists were the R.A.F. (Uxbridge) and Wealdstone, and when the train in which I had been very much wedged in left Wembley Park station there were seats available for all comers.

There was none of the big-match atmosphere to be found on the walk to the Stadium. Pirate programmes were prominent, and were being bought by the unwary, and there were the usual shouts of "Wear your colours."

In the Stadium itself there was the Central Band of the Royal Air Force playing on the field in front of the Royal Box. In fact, the stage seemed set for an International match, or, perhaps, a "real" cup final. There was one outstanding difference, however—there were fewer than 100,000 people present! Nevertheless, I was one of several thousands.

The match had received a good advance Press and most of the writers seemed to expect the redoubtable R.A.F. team—in previous rounds of -the cup the R.A.F. had scored 13 goals and had conceded only two—to win comfortably. Wealdstone, too, had scored 13 goals, but their defence had conceded eight, and it was generally thought that the "big names " in the R.A.F. eleven would score freely, particularly as their players were experienced in playing before comparatively large crowds.

So I was not alone among Wealdstone supporters in feeling that I should be quite satisfied so long as " our" men gave their opponents "a run for their money." In fact, I must admit to feeling not a little despondent when I saw the names of the R.A.F. -players in the programme.

They had Cpl. Clack (Brentford) in goal, and Cpl. Forder (Crystal Palace) and L.A.C. Dale (Portsmouth) as the backs, the halfback line, too, looked impressive—Cpl. McGregor (Manchester City). Sgt. Vattse (Rochdale), and L.A.C. Johnson (Newcastle United). There was a formidable appearance about the forward line, which was led by Sgt. Clements (Casuals and Corinthians), an amateur international with a reputation for sharp shooting. His inside partners were Cpl. Harris (Swansea Town), a son of the former Newcastle United player, and Cpl. Mullinger (Aston Villa). L.A.C. Gibson (Watford) was on the right wing, while the outside-left was an old friend of Wealdstone's—Lester Finch (Barnet and England), one of the best-known and most popular players of his time, who was then a Flight Sergeant.

Mick Doherty was in goal for Wealdstone and the backs covering him were Charlie Barker and Tom Kay. Reg Stanton, George Upchurch. and Brian Leeming were the halves, and the forward line, reading from the left, was; Len Folding, Bobby Wilson, Jack Russell, Flt. Sgt. Tony Morris, and Jimmie Moore.

The teams received a great reception as, lead by their chief officials, they emerged from the dressing rooms. The match is still no doubt fresh in the memories of those Wealdstone supporters who were at Wembley Stadium on that June evening—and I am sure that every follower of the club who was able to be there was among the crowd —and I do not intend, therefore, to make more than just a few observations about the play.

Clements put the R.A.F. eleven in the lead after 25 minutes' play, Doherty, who had previously made some daring and brilliant saves, being beaten by what might be truly described as an "unstoppable" shot.

Russell equalised for Wealdstone after 20 minutes' play in the second half;' this goal encouraged the 'Stones to even greater efforts, but it was the R.A.F. who scored the next goal. Clements breaking through the Wealdstone defence to score with another fine shot.

Were Wealdstone downhearted? For the answer to that question I quote from the Harrow Observer representative's report of the match. "Then came the thrill of the game." he wrote. "Straight from the line-up, Wealdstone attacked vigorously.

An R.A.F. defender, trying to clear, obligingly tapped the ball past Clack to bring the scores level again."

There was no further scoring and extra time was played. During this period, it may he recorded, the professional side fell away badly, almost every man appearing to be tired out. Wealdstone, on the other hand, found renewed energy and scored three times without reply. Tom Morris netted twice, the other goal coming from Jack Russell.

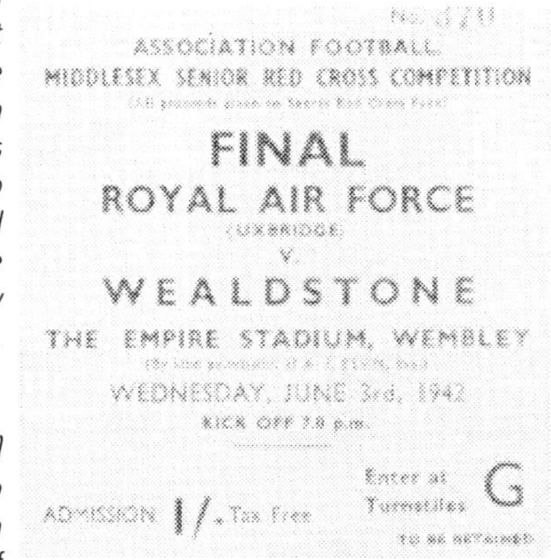
ASSOCIATION FOOTBALL
MIDDLESEX SENIOR RED CROSS COMPETITION
FINAL
ROYAL AIR FORCE
(UXBRIDGE)
v.
WEALDSTONE
THE EMPIRE STADIUM, WEMBLEY
WEDNESDAY, JUNE 3rd, 1942
KICK OFF 7.0 p.m.
ADMISSION 1/- Tax Free
Enter at Turnstiles G
TO BE RETAINED

It was a splendid finale to a great game, and the Wealdstone men were acclaimed as they went up to receive the cup and medals from the hands of Capt. (now Sir) Leslie Bowker, O.B.E. M.C.

Mr. (later Sir) Arthur J. Elvin, who placed the Stadium at the disposal of the Middlesex Football Association for the match, enter-tained the players and officials of both teams after the game.

As a spectator at the match, I had already had my entertainment.

Jack Russell
Player 1941-1944

I was born in South Wales in 1916, and my connection with the club started in 1941, aged 25 when I joined as a player. The Golden Jubilee Handbook kindly describes me as 'the club's outstanding centre forward in wartime football'! and I later transferred to Hendon and Finchley.

I have wonderful memories of trainer, Bill Gallagher, who was coming to the end of his thirty years with the club when I was playing, but we immediately managed to strike up a rapport and he was a great support during my time there. It was the first time I'd played for a club where the Trainer wore a white coat!

There was no 'Pro' football in the war – only us amateurs. With people in 'the services' you never knew who was going to turn up from week to week. A lot of the players were with us for a long time but couldn't play every week. I had a trial for Wales as an amateur as well. They picked the whole of the other team except the chap that was marking me, but I still couldn't get in.

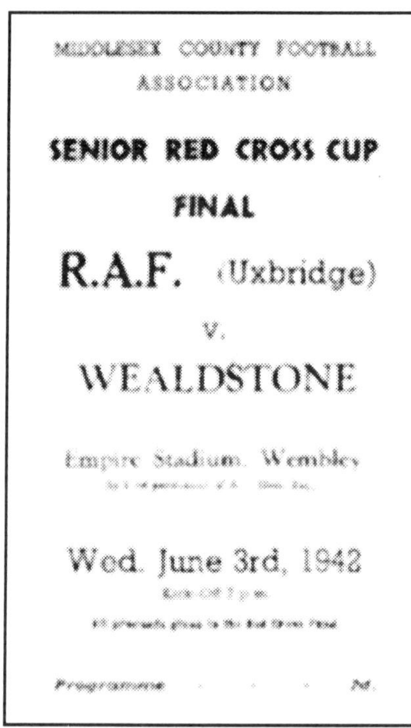

MIDDLESEX COUNTY FOOTBALL ASSOCIATION

SENIOR RED CROSS CUP

FINAL

R.A.F. (Uxbridge)

v.

WEALDSTONE

Empire Stadium, Wembley

Wed. June 3rd, 1942

Programme d.

I broke my wrist just before the war playing football and didn't know. Then I did it again playing cricket and it never set properly. When I got called up, they wouldn't take me as I couldn't hold a rifle!

I think the highlight must be the Red Cross Cup Final of 1942, played at Wembley Stadium. The opposition were R.A.F. Uxbridge - a team made up of nine professionals, all from English Football League Clubs, and the other two were Amateur Internationals.

They were strong favourites and everyone expected them to win.

The match was played in June, it was a very hot evening and there was quite a crowd there including a lot of servicemen in uniform, however, we lasted the pace well, although we went a goal behind in the first half.

I scored with a shot in the second half – that was the second goal scored by an amateur at Wembley. The first had been the goal we conceded. All those professionals in their side and the goal had been scored by a bloke from Corinthians!

I equalised but I think the R.A.F. soon went in front again only for one of their team to score an own goal to make the score 2-2 at the end, so we had to play extra time.

We seemed much stronger then and I scored another goal and (Flight Sergeant) Tom Morris, playing for us scored another two, and we won 5 -2 after extra time.

I remember the Central Band of the R.A.F. playing and that made the day even more memorable.

Although I went on and played for other senior clubs, I always look back on my time at Wealdstone as my happiest memories, and I had such great respect for Charlie Barker who was a tremendous and inspirational captain.

The report on the match from the Harrow Observer of June 4th 1942 reads;

WEALDSTONE TRIUMPH AT THE STADIUM - FORMIDABLE RAF TEAM DEFEATED

Showing a complete disregard for "Wembley Nerves" and all-star opponents, Wealdstone defeated the RAF Uxbridge team at Wembley Stadium on Wednesday night 5-2. It was a near thing at one time, and extra time had to be played before Wealdstone could clinch it.

This is Wealdstone's second Cup this season, their other trophy being the Middlesex Senior Cup.

Stamina won them the game, for during the extra time, the RAF team, comprising largely of professionals and one English International faded out almost completely, and in the end apart from occasional spurts from the RAF forwards, Wealdstone were doing all the attacking.

It was definitely a victory of combination over individual skills as Wealdstone showed they could swing the ball about and some of their passing movements, particularly in the early part of the game were masterly.

Consider for a moment what the Wealdstone forward line was facing – Moore had to hold Finch (England and Barnet) and he certainly did his best. Morris faced Mullinger (Aston Villa), Russell was up against Clements (Casuals and Corinthians) while Wilson and Dolding on the left had to tackle Harris (Swansea) and Gibson (Watford).

Right from the start, both goalkeepers were called upon to bring off some splendid saves, and Clack in particular showed his Brentford form and saved the RAF many a goal.

On both sides however there was far too much passing back to the goalkeeper, instead of making clean clearances and on one occasion this proved disastrous for the RAF.

After some dazzling exchanges, broken by a good deal of lose kicking, the airmen took the lead after 25 minutes play. Clements running in to take up a pass from Gibson. Doherty, who had been playing well never stood a chance.

That was all the scoring in the first half and 20 minutes of the second, during which the RAF had gone on the defensive, had gone by before Russell equalized with a grand shot.

Russell played a fine game throughout and was always ready to seize any chance. The equalizer brightened the game considerably and Wealdstone began to attack vigorously but it was the RAF who scored, Clements getting away alone and breaking through.

Then came the thrill of the game. Straight from the line-up the Wealdstone team attacked vigorously. An RAF back, trying to clear, obligingly tapped the ball past Clack to bring the scores level again.

At this point, Gibson, the RAF Outside Right who had left the field some 20 minutes earlier with an injured foot, returned. Wealdstone kept on their toes, but the match proper ended with the score 2-2 During extra time Wealdstone had most of the play and Morris (2) and Russell made sure with three clear goals.

Wealdstone; M Doherty, T Kay, C Barker, B Leeming, G Upchurch, R Stanton, J Moore, Flt-Sgt Morris, J Russell, R Wilson, and L Dolding.

RAF (Uxbridge); Cpl Clack (Brentford), Cpl Forder (Crystal Palace), IAC Dale (Portsmouth), Cpl McGregor (Manchester City), Sgt Vause (Rochdale), IAC Johnson (Newcastle), IAC Gibson (Watford), Cpl Harris (Swansea), Sgt Clements (Casuals and Corinthians), Cpl Mullingay (Aston Villa) and Flt Sgt Finch (England)

At the AGM of the club a few weeks later, the Chairman reflected on the League season, the club finishing a poor eleventh after third place in the previous year, but then went on to cover the victories in both Middlesex Competitions.

The Middlesex FA presented the club with a commemorative trophy marking the win at Wembley, as Wealdstone had become the first Amateur Club to play and win there.

The meeting was tinged with sadness though. Former Club member and player, W W (Bill) Parr had been killed on active service and P Hansard and Charlie Bunce had been reported missing In action.

Jimmy Moore
Player 1938 – 1949

I started playing at Wealdstone in about 1938, just before the war. They were a good set of blokes then and we all knew each other. Most of us worked in Kodak and we were all together all the time, we had a bit of fun and that.

Playing in the war was totally different though, some 'Pro's came and played, Bill Parr and all. I wasn't able to play all the time during the war but I got away a bit. I served with the rough boys, the big boys – SAS as a Physical Training Instructor.

It made a bloody mess of my football but at least I got the opportunity to come back on leave and sometimes at weekends – I carried on with the Wealdstone – backwards and forwards.

After the war things changed as well. We used to go out together in the evenings, but after the war they all got married off you see and it buggered it up slightly but I stayed together with Charlie Barker and Charlie Edmunds. When I finished playing for Wealdstone at 34, Barker, myself & Edmunds went to Edgware and St Albans and we played there for a few years. Wealdstone were getting younger people in so we just finished.

Charlie Barker definitely was a character and centre forward Ginger - can't remember his real name – he was a nasty bugger – if you didn't give him the ball he'd shout "what the bloody hell you doing" and I'd shout back to him "bugger off".

He was only playing for a few weeks on and off but he was a great centre forward, then he went off and we never saw him again. Don't know what happened to him. He disappeared. He was a joker as well but he was a bloody good centre forward and Reg Hill - the Goalkeeper – used to wear glasses when he was playing!

I often look back at the mementoes and cuttings, they're good memories. When we played near Wembley, Charlie Edmunds and Charlie Barker and me always went off to the Dogs ! We'd lose all our money.

We weren't supposed to be paid but there was 'Boot Money' – about £3 10/- and then expenses, but we'd still lose it. Pro's were only getting five or six pounds, so with our jobs we were better off than they were! Mind you the club could afford it – the crowds - It was always chock a block when we played.

It was soon announced that Charlie Bunce too had died. In the match programme for October 2nd 1943 v Barnet, the club printed the following;

"His name will be remembered with pride and affection"

The passing of Charles Edward Bunce is a tragic blow to the world of Amateur Football. He joined this club in 1936 from St Albans and his coming was the start of the most successful period in our history.

His charming personality, allied with superb skill and a rigid observance of all the laws of the game endeared him to all his colleagues both on the field and off. He was an inspiration to the team at all times. His last game for us was on June 8th 1940 and he scored 174 goals during the four seasons in which he played. In representative matches he played for The Athenian League, Isthmian League, Hertfordshire, London Amateurs and South v North, the Amateur International Trial game. Had he wished he could have played regularly for West Ham United.

He joined the Suffolk Regiment in 1940 and went to the Far East. He was reported missing after Singapore and after a long period of suspense news was received that he was a prisoner of war in Malaya. He passed away in June.

There will be a minutes silence today followed by The Last Post and Reveille played by buglers of the Harrow Sea Cadets.

Charlie Bunce

Janet Kay
Wife of the late Tom Kay, Player 1940-1948

My husband Tom Kay played for Wealdstone Football Club between 1940 and 1948, and he had some happy memories of his time there.

I have some faded old press cuttings and a photograph or two and I remember the Annual Dinner dances, in particular the one at The Gayton Rooms in Harrow when Dennis Compton was the guest of honour, Leslie Compton also turned up.

I remember some sadder times during the war, when we were told that Charlie Bunce was a Prisoner of war, and also that Charlie Barker had been wounded, and later when we found out that Charlie Bunce had died.

At one time, late in the war, Tom's two brothers also turned out for the 'Stones, and all three played together on a couple of occasions.

Wealdstone had some good players at the time, Dave Scott and Brian Leeming, Bert Dyke and of course Len Dolding, he was a lovely player and a lovely man and he later joined Chelsea, before being killed in a car crash.

I remember when we played Walthamstow Avenue - it was always such a hard game and they had the great Jim Lewis in their side - he was an amateur International, and then of course, the Red Cross Cup Final at Wembley Stadium.

Wealdstone played R.A.F. Uxbridge who were the favourites - they had nine professionals in their side and the other two were Amateur Internationals, one was Lester Finch of Barnet - he ran rings round Wealdstone in the first half, but in the second half Tom got a hold of him and of course Wealdstone went on to win in extra time.

There was another occasion at Southall when an old Ex-pro did for one of Tom's brothers, only for Tom to go on and 'even the score' - Tom really clattered him and Wealdstone went on to win that day as well, and that was all that mattered!!

Tom died aged 69 in 1984, still well and truly involved in football - two days before his death he was coaching and training the Park Street team.

The following season saw Wealdstone struggle as a club on and off the field. Call-ups had begun to decimate the Wealdstone side and on occasions the club found it difficult to put out a side.

This was not better demonstrated than by an away fixture at Barnet, where the home club loaned Wealdstone two players, making their number up to 10. Wealdstone suffered a defeat by 9–1.

In all matches, Wealdstone had only recorded two victories by the end of January. Although February brought some respite with a run of four wins, Wealdstone were to finish bottom of the league with five wins and one draw from 22 games. There was still a loyal band of supporters who, even in these hard times supported the club – the match report from the first game of 1943 starts;

Enthusiastic applause from the band of loyal supporters who have remained faithful to Wealdstone throughout their long run of defeats greeted the club's triumph at Lower Mead on Saturday when in the Herts and Middlesex league they beat Southall by three goals to one.

The reserves fared better though, finishing the season in third place with 13 wins and two draws from 20 matches.

There was news from overseas during the season, with some of the club's former players taking the time to send their good wishes to the club whilst on military service overseas;

Wealdstone v Tufnell Park 18/09/1943
Ernie Walker our former goalkeeper writes;

I am unable to tell you where I am but the climate is very hot. The life is very boring sometimes but we do have a little excitement when we come across a Jerry.

While I was at Scotland I played for the Fleet and we had some very good games, but now while I am at see I miss my football very much.

I quite realise how much I enjoyed playing for Wealdstone in the past and I hope that when this war is over I will be able to come back and render the club many years more service. I don't know how the club faired last season, but I hope you have a successful season this year and that it may also bring peace. Give my regards to the Committee and players and the Trainers.

Wealdstone v Tufnell Park 18/09/1943
Fred Hayden writes;

At last after attending to the more important mail- you know what wives are - I have the chance to write to you. I suppose you know by now that I'm in Sicily with the Eighth so I have travelled quite a lot since I last saw you all last. Although the campaign didn't last very long I can say that repaid a few debts I owed, one especially for Charlie Bunce, and another for Bill Parr. Things now are very quiet and we are at rest at the moment.

I guess by when you receive this the football season will be well on its way, so all my best wishes to the old club for a good season, hoping that next season will be in more peaceful times.

As the boys say we have just won the semi-final, knocking out Mussolini and the Final is pretty soon against Hitler, we are giving him ground advantage I believe (Ha ha!!)

Must close now, remember me to all the chaps and tell old Bill Gallagher that I'll be able to out do him when I come home.

Wealdstone v Grays 16/10/1943
H Dyke writes;

As you probably heard from my father, I sailed from England 2 days after you played Hounslow in the cup, unfortunately I wasn't given any leave consequently I could not come up and see you. This transfer was a great surprise to me, fortunately moving from Bromley to Scotland I managed to spend a day at home.

You are probably aware that I'm somewhere in the blue Mediterranean as we took part in the invasions of Pantellaria and Sicily. At the moment we are in port resting from our exertions! - We do not know what is going to happen to us but I am hoping that we shall soon join a convoy that will take us home.

We called at quite a few interesting places, among them being much bombed Malta where we played a couple of games of football.

I am afraid that the conditions under which we played were not quite like home, the actual pitch was of a hard core stuff similar to our tennis courts, except that on some occasions when tackled, clouds of dust arose, also the heat was terrific - even hotter than we get at home when our season starts.

I recently received some Observers from home and I read of your victory over Finchley in the cup final.

One of the fellows with me has been playing for Finchley occasionally since the war started, and so of course I was pleased with your performance, unfortunately he produced the Finchley local paper which was headed Wealdstone Lucky In Cup Final - Finchley have 60% of play but lose!

Of course as neither of us was there we were unable to pass any opinion.

Please remember me to all my friends.
Cheerio, all the very best,

Wealdstone v St Albans 30/10/1943
Corporal Jack Wilson writes;

I would like you to convey my best regards to all my friends at Wealdstone, your committee and team and let them know that I am keeping quite fit and well and looking forward to the day we all re-unite at Wealdstone.

I am playing plenty of Football and Hockey and represent the Battalion at both of these games. The soccer league starts next month so we shall not be long before we start the ball rolling here again.

It was a hard job to get used to these hard grounds which are used on the 'Rock' (Gibraltar) after playing on Wealdstone's pitch and then playing here is like playing on a grass pitch and then playing on a tarmac road, so you can just imagine the difference can't you? But still, football is played here and its up to a quite high standard.

I should think its up to the standard of the Athenian League soccer before the war, of course you realise that the Pro's these teams have got now a days can't you, and there are quite a few on the 'rock' I can tell you!

I don't think I have much more news to tell you, although I think I could write a book on the Guard Mountings we have here, the spit and polish is back with us once more.

It takes us 48 hours to prepare for a 24 hour guard what with all the blanchoing and cleaning brasses. Both sides!

Scrubbing equipment and ironing your shirts and shorts, you can guess what we all have to got through here.

I will close with the best wishes and best of luck to Wealdstone FC for the coming season.

Wealdstone v Golders Green 25/12/1943
Letter from Fred Haydon. North Africa;

Very sorry to hear about Charlie Bunce, some blow. I also see by the local that 'Lew' got a packet out here, he will be very likely sent home, that seems to be the usual procedure.

Rather a queer start the old club have made, I have a chap in my platoon who hails from Barnet, and he's a red hot supporter, so I'm one up on him even if it was a cricket score. We have some rare old tussles, so for God's sake don't let them beat you.

Tell Charlie Barker its difficult to get home from here, no matter who signs the pass! Ha-ha, as for myself I'm in the pink, maybe a bit slimmer but North Africa doesn't hold the chances as Sicily. There is no comparison.

I am going to Tunis tomorrow, makes a nice break to see a few up to date shows. Merry Xmas. Yours, Fred.

In the same match programme the club were also able to announce that news had been received of Percy Hansard who had been posted missing for many months, he was a prisoner of war in Japan.

Others were not so fortunate and there was further reason for sadness in the club during January 1943 with the death of the well-known and popular Wealdstone player Robert Wilson.

He had joined the club in 1938 playing mainly in the reserves, but since rejoining in 1941 and playing in the first team he was rated as one of the best young prospects, playing an important role over the previous seasons.

Having served in the RASC, his Army duties had allowed him to play again and he starred at Wembley in the Red Cross Cup Final.

His appearances had been limited during the current season and he died after contracting Pneumonia after an operation.

Again it was a cup competition that was to provide Wealdstone's greatest moments of the season, and again it was the Middlesex Senior Cup. In March, Wealdstone traveled to Hounslow in the semi-final of the competition with all but the most dedicated fan expecting a defeat – Hounslow were riding high in the Middlesex Senior League with 29 points from 18 games while Wealdstone had gained only 11 points from 22 games in the Herts and Middlesex League.

As cup holders though Wealdstone were not to be underestimated and a battling performance saw them come through as winners by two goals to one, to qualify to play Finchley (again) in the final.

At the same time, Wealdstone played a quarter final of the league cup away to Wood Green and having arrived with ten men, they were loaned a player by the hosts. Wealdstone then proceeded to win the match by two goals to one, scoring the winner with only three minutes remaining.

It was very much the done thing at the time where possible to 'loan' players to make up even sides for a match and this was shown really to Wealdstone's advantage in a reserve match in April 1943.

Arriving to play the Worcester Regiment with only ten men, the army side loaned Wealdstone a centre forward who had not been picked to play for his own team. Williams, the army man had obviously decided to impress on his teammates the error of not picking him as he helped Wealdstone record a win by five goals to four. Nothing special in that though, until you see that Williams had scored four of Wealdstone's five goals!

After losing in the semi-final of the League Cup and failing to collect another point in their remaining League fixtures, Wealdstone approached their last game of the season, the Middlesex Senior Cup Final with some trepidation.

The match finished as a 3–3 draw after extra time and Wealdstone retained the cup with a 3–0 win in the final replay to at least end the season on a high note.

It was the fiftieth anniversary of the first cup final contested by a Wealdstone Team, the Middlesex Junior Cup Final of 1893 being the first. In the fifty years between, Wealdstone had contested 29 cup finals and had been victorious on 23 occasions.

R J Pluck
Supporter since 1922

My Dad and I supported the club into the forties when I managed to get into the side. I played a lot in the reserves, with a few appearances in the first team, along with those as 12th man or traveling reserve to games as it was then called.

Unfortunately I was called up in 1943 but I managed to play until September 1944 when a posting finished my career with the 'Stones.

The next year showed a slight improvement in the league and there was certainly some entertainment for the supporters as early as October when Barnet were the visitors to Lower Mead.

Spectators at Lower Mead on Saturday had good value for their money when 16 goals were scored in the Herts and Middlesex league match between Wealdstone and Barnet. Both teams gave a great display of football, Wealdstone winning by 9-7.

From the kick off Barnet went away and Saw scored for them within three minutes. After a spell of give and take exchanges Wealdstone were awarded a penalty for a foul on Morris and Barker converted the kick.

Both goalkeepers were called upon in turn before Morris scored for Wealdstone from a pass by Preston and Barnet then took a turn and Saw restored the balance, to be followed immediately by another goal for the home team from Parrish. Wealdstone then forced a corner, and then Saw scored two quick goals for Barnet, but Morris not to be outdone in goalscoring twice put the ball in the net for Wealdstone from passes by Hardie and Baldwin made up the half dozen to give Wealdstone a lead of 6-4 at half time.

In the second half Barnet took up the attack and forced a corner, Haynes attempted to clear but put the ball through his own goal to make the score 6-5. Barnet were awarded a free kick about six yards outside the penalty area and Wilmore scored directly from the kick to equalise.

Both teams went all out for the lead that fell to Wealdstone through Baldwin who took up a nice pass from Preston. Morris was then given offside when in a good position and from the free kick Saw broke through and scored the seventh goal for Barnet.

Barnet then secured a couple of corners before Morris scored No 8 for Wealdstone from a pass by Baldwin to be followed by a final one from Hardie. The inclusion of Barker, Baldwin and Green in the home team made a great difference. All three players gave a good display..............Morris at centre forward made a great leader and scored four goals and Preston at Outside left has the makings of a good winger.

Wealdstone; L East, T Kay, C Barker, L Green, W Saunders, G Parrish, G Hardie, K Baldwin, W/O Morris, L Haynes, S Preston

There had been a Harrow Open Air Festival for a number of years, solely to raise funds for St Dustan's, a charitable organisation known throughout the world for its work with the armed forces who suffered blindness as a result of action or injury.

This year, the festival had not been held and in the October, Wealdstone FC hosted an International football match to raise funds in its place. The two teams were from Norway and Canada, and were made up from Allied servicemen from these countries based in the UK at the time.

It was in this season that Wealdstone were to suffer the record defeat in a match with Edgware Town FC. The Harrow Observer reported Wealdstone's 'black day' as follows;

Total Eclipse at Edgware

There was no doubt whatsoever about Wealdstone's exit from the London Senior Cup at Edgware on Saturday, when the Town scored on fourteen occasions without reply.

Undoubtedly the heavy going and their inability to be at full strength greatly handicapped Wealdstone as the ground soon churned up into a quagmire and the visitors found the greatest difficulty in retaining their balance, whereas Edgware in such conditions were in their element.

Early on there were fast and exciting moments at both ends and after ten minutes Edgware opened the scoring in a most unusual manner.

From a corner Cooke came out to fist clear but the ball struck the back of his hand and rebounded into the net. Following further pressure a centre from the left was easily converted. Edgware's third goal was obtained from a corner.

In leaping up for the ball Cooke's legs slipped from under him and with the goalkeeper prostrate the town scored easily. At

26

PROGRAMME. PRICE 1d.

EDGWARE TOWN F.C.

MEMBERS MIDDX.SENIOR LEAGUE AND HARROW,WEMBLEY AND DISTRICT LEAGUE
LONDON SENIOR CUP.

EDGWARE TOWN V WEALDSTONE

SATURDAY 9th DECEMBER,1944.

K.O. 2.45 p.m.

EDGWARE TOWN.

R.Owens (1)
R.Scott (2) S. Bailey (3)
A.Langston (4) E.West (5) J.Griffin (6)
D.Allbone (7) R.Ade (8) S.Kay (9) D. Wade (10) E.Hornsby (11)

0

A. Hardy. F/L.D.Jones. J.Russell. G.Garrigan. F/L.K.Emmett.
W.Hancock. G. Parish L. Green.
E.Upton. W.Christmas.
H.Beck.

WEALDSTONE.

Next Week's Fixtures 16th December, 1944.
Middx. Sen. Cup. Edgware Town V Tufnell Park at White Lion, K.O. 3 - 0 p.m.

Friendly. Manor Farm V Edgware Town A.

NOTES.

The 1st XI had a comparatively easy win last Sat. when they defeated Handley Page 7 - 2 at Hendon. Up to half time the home team were holding their own 2 - 2 but with the aid of the wind the Town exerted a little pressure and the issue was never in doubt. Unfortunately for both teams G. Graves and an Handley Page player had to leave the game early in the second half for medical attention due to a mid-air collision necessitating several stiches. This injury will put George out of todays all important game and may in fact cause several last minute changes, especially if Don Wade does not put in an appearance.

We have great pleasure in welcoming Wealdstone as todays visitors and it is to be regretted that with the recent rains the ground will be rather heavy. However, this handicap should not prevent senior teams of repute providing us with an hour and a halfs good entertainment.

We extend a particular welcome to W. Hancock who, several seasons ago wore the Town's colours. Our all-conquering Reserves in beating Canons Park in the Middx. Jun. Cup last Sat. have now brought their total number of goals scored to well over the century for the season todate. They are today visiting N.F.S. in a rearranged league fixture at Hendon and we hope they maintain their 100% record. As a mark of honour for their achievements the Reserves have been elected together with three other clubs to represent the H.W.& D. League in the Middx Jun. Red Cross Cup.

The 'A' team have no game today so we welcome them to the White Lion as spectators for a change.

half time Edgware were leading by only 3–0, the feature of the half being the splendid defensive work shown by Parrish.

In the second period came the avalanche of goals, the Edgware forwards in irresistible form put on eleven more. As can be judged from the score, Owens in the home goal was seldom troubled.

Hornsby (five) Whytock (four) Ade, Kay (two each) and Cooke (own goal) made up the grand total for Edgware. A more overwhelming reverse than this for Wealdstone cannot be recalled. Edgware made two changes from the team that beat Wood Green the previous week. Hornsby proved a perfect winger on the left and showed no signs of his long stay in a Military Hospital, while S Kay at inside-left was brilliant.

Among the numerous supporters from Lower Mead was Tom Kay, the popular full back. He is expecting to be fit again in about a fortnight. Coxon was a spectator due to a knee injury and to complete Wealdstone's cup of misfortune, Poxon arrived to late to take part.

Wealdstone; H Cooke, W Christmas, E Upton, L Green, G Parrish, W Hancock, K Emmott, G Garrigan, J Russell, D Jones, K Hawson.

Edgware; Owens, Scott, Bailey, Langston, West, Griffin, Albone, Ade, Whytock, Kay, Hornsby.

There was no success for Wealdstone in the cups during the 1943–1944 season, their best effort was losing another semi-final in the Herts and Middlesex League Cup, this time to Clapton, by five goals to three. From 36 matches played, eleven were won and five drawn, 93 goals scored while 117 were conceded.

Jack Russell continued to cement his place in the record books by again being the top scorer with 26 goals, followed by Flight Sergeant and later Warrant Officer T Morris with 15.

There was another 'International' at Lower Mead. A match between Wealdstone FC and Austrian FC had been organised. The visitors were described as the Free Austrian patriots helping in the liberation of their land.

There was also a mention later in the programme of another effect of the war;

Our club, ever since it has been at its present ground has always provided hot tea at a small price to spectators. For three years, the local Food Controller licensed the continuance of this practise with one or two other small items.

Suddenly, without any apparent reason the catering licence has limited the supply of tea to the players and officials only. An appeal; was made to the District Food Controller, London, and although opposed by the local food controller, spectators will have gathered from the local press that the club's appeal has been successful and spectators can still get tea at matches.

The following season, 1944-1945 was unremarkable, Wealdstone's best efforts improving little in the league. Their endeavours in the cup competitions saw them lose two semi-finals, to Southall 3-1 in the Middlesex Senior Cup and to Golders Green in the Middlesex Red Cross Cup by 3-2.

The season did see the return to football of Leytonstone, former rivals of Wealdstone and in the January of 1945 a friendly was arranged at the ground of the latter.

It was to be a stark reminder of the effect of the war, the newspaper reports identifying that *"the ground was in a deplorable condition. The blitz had left its mark on the Stand and the surrounding buildings, the pitch had got well out of hand and the goals had no nets".*

It was reported however that a good competitive match took place between the two sides, Wealdstone by no means at full strength losing by the odd goal in seven, but again not before an unusual interruption.

It seems that during the match *"a Flying Bomb raid started and one of these fell dangerously close to the ground!"* It is not reported as to whether the match was interrupted.

Altogether Wealdstone played 42 matches, winning 13 with 5 drawn, scoring 84 goals and conceding 129. Jack Russell again was top scorer with 24 goals.

The reserves had suffered fixture congestion due to poor weather. To alleviate this the club had agreed to play league matches for double points. One such game was played against D H Ultra at Lower Mead late in January 1945, Wealdstone Reserves running out winners by 5-1.

They enjoyed a greater level of success than the first team over the season, finishing in third place in the Harrow League and top scorer H Jennings with 29 goals was one of a number of promising young players in the reserves ranks.

There was sadness during the season firstly with the news that Ernie Walker was reported 'Missing In Action', whilst serving in the Royal Navy. Although mainly a reserve team player, Walker had played a number of matches in goal for the first team deputising for Reg Lewis, eventually replacing him until he joined the Navy in November 1940.

He was regarded as a youngster of considerable promise but unfortunately he was never to return to the club.

Another great loss was reported in April of 1945, when it was announced that Ken Baldwin, forward and former schoolboy international, who had signed as an amateur with Chelsea before the war had been killed in Germany.

He had gone to Normandy with the Liberation Army and had been wounded at Falaise Gap, from where he was repatriated to recover.

Once fit he had played for Wealdstone, appearing five times before returning to France where he served with the Royal Artillery.

Subsequently he took part in the Rhine crossing where he met his death, Wealdstone players marking his death in a Red Cross Cup match where the players all wore black armbands and observed a silence as a mark of respect.

With the overall situation of war evolving on an almost daily basis, it was in May of 1945 Lower Mead was to feature in a front page story and headline in local papers, this time though with good news.

It was the 'Stand Down' of the Harrow Civil Defence Services. Accompanied by the pre Service Units and The Home Guard thousands of people took part in a parade and service at Wealdstone's Lower Mead ground.

Programme of

Youth Sports Meeting

and Dog Show

TO BE HELD AT

LOWER MEAD STATION ROAD WEALDSTONE

(Rear of Dominion Cinema)

On SATURDAY JULY 22nd 1944

GATES OPEN 2.30 p.m. COMMENCE 3 p.m.

ORGANISED BY THE WEALDSTONE FOOTBALL CLUB
ASSISTED BY

Dog Show
W. H. Lapwood, F.L.S., M.M.
810, Kenton Lane,
Harrow Weald

Sports
P. E. Carden,
77, Salisbury Road
Harrow, Middlesex.

AND OFFICERS OF THE COMPETING ORGANISATIONS

Prizes will be presented by

MRS. I. M. HOCKING,
Group Commandant of the Women's Junior Air Corps (Harrow Group)

and

LT. COMMANDER E. E. HERMAN, R.N.V.R.

PRICE SIXPENCE

In common with most other seasons and close seasons, Wealdstone again staged some other events at Lower Mead. The programme above for a Youth Sports Day and Dog Show held in July 1944.

This was the only official function organised in Harrow for the Victory Day celebrations.

There were some celebration events organised by the club itself, the main one of these being a Fun Fair and Dog Show organised for the beginning of July. There were a number of sideshows, games and events for adults and children alike and the event ran from 2:00pm until dusk.

There were displays by the local Sea Cadets, sixteen separate sections in the dog show and competitions to find a Mr V E Day and such like. The event was well attended throughout the day, everything being organised by the club and in particular an 'Event Committee' comprising of J Roach, D Wiltshire, C W Elliot, D Finney and P E Carden.

Peter Roach

Son of Jack Roach, Goalkeeper 1920's and then Vice-Chairman, subsequently Player himself from 1949-1951

My father Jack Roach played as goalkeeper in the 1920's, although I never saw him play.

I was born in 1933 by which time my father had become a committee member and subsequently he became Vice-Chairman. He was later particularly concerned with keeping the club going through the war years in the Hertfordshire and Middlesex League.

I grew up at Lower Mead really, because my father was always there. There were some great players at the time, Charlie Bunce, Bert Dyke, Jimmy Moore, Charlie Barker and Charlie Edmunds. The famous fullbacks, Loveday and Ellis.

I remember a particular match at Bromley during the war years - we traveled with only nine players! One of the Committee and the coach driver made up the team alongside the likes of Jimmy Moore.

We also used to sell the coach tickets from our house for away games so there were plenty of supporters around, and we used to have fairs to raise money at Lower Mead every year - I used to get a ride on the Cossack's horses - we always had Cossack's, and my father always ran the bar in a hut on the left hand side of the Elmslie Stand end before the club House was built.

I think my most memorable match of this time would be the replay of the Amateur Cup in about 1948-49 against Leytonstone. I think we drew 1-1 away, an excellent result as Leytonstone were one of the top clubs at that time.

Then we lost the replay 1-0 to a Leon Joseph goal in front of a crowd of over 13,000.

During 1949 I was fortunate enough to play in a cup final at Lower Mead for Harrow YMCA against Willesden Foods and we won 3-2. Frank Harbud, an official of the club at the time saw the game and asked me to join Wealdstone and play for the A Team.

I joined the training in the 1949-50 season under Bill Gallagher, and I can remember going on a run under the control of Charlie Barker and Charlie Edmunds.

After a few minutes they both stopped for a cigarette and told the rest of us to go round the block and to rejoin them later!

Unfortunately, soon after, National Service caught up with me and I didn't return to the club.

THE POST WAR YEARS

The Athenian League Council met on April 23rd 1945 and the decision was immediately taken to restart the League for the forthcoming season with the same member clubs as the last pre-war season.

This meant that a number of the wartime leagues and emergency competitions, such as the Herts and Middlesex League, which had maintained football at a good standard coupled with much needed entertainment during the war, were to be disbanded.

Wealdstone joined the other thirteen members of the last Athenian League, from season 1939–40 in signifying their readiness to compete, although it was accepted that in the first year there would be a number of changes as players returned from overseas.

One significant change in the league itself was the appointment of a Match secretary, who would be responsible for forming the fixture list for the whole league, clubs previously having arranged their own fixtures.

This position was ably filled by Mr H P Lawrence, an official of Hendon FC, who had held the same position in the Herts and Middlesex league.

Wealdstone itself though was still a far cry from the Wealdstone of today. This was highlighted by the welcome in the Hitchin Town match programme for the visit of the 'Stones on 1st September 1945, it read; *the visit of Wealdstone will be interesting. Our friends from the village near Pinner.......*

It was to be a successful season for Wealdstone, starting poorly in the league, the results improved as the season wore on. With players returning from overseas the side was not as settled as it might have been. The by now traditional Christmas home and away fixtures against Golders Green had been retained, this year Wealdstone winning both, 4-0 at home on Christmas morning and the following day, 3-2 at Claremont Road.

Within twenty minutes of the start of their Christmas morning match with Golders Green, Wealdstone had scored four times without reply. No further goals were scored by either side although the home team held the initiative until the end.

After only four minutes, centre forward Gaze ran in and scored after Roberts the Golders Green goalkeeper having fumbled the ball saving a hard shot from Dyke. The centre forward increased the lead when he scored from a well placed centre from Williams playing his first game for Wealdstone. After Dyke scored the third, Garrigan shot through a crowd of players to make the score 4-0.

Up until that time the visitors had been eclipsed by the thrustful Wealdstone side, but when their forwards broke away, McDonald saved point blank from the outside right..........

He dealt confidently with anything that came his way and he was adequately covered by Upton, Edmonds and Barker, Wealdstone acclimatising themselves better to the heavy ground than did their opponents, and they well deserved to take both points.

The following day, Golders Green played better but were unable to stop Wealdstone, although they equalised twice before Barker scored a penalty a few minutes from the end to give 'Stones the win. The following Saturday and the good run of form was to continue with a 6-0 win over Enfield, a large crowd enthused as Wealdstone scored five times in the first half.

Two weeks later, Wealdstone were drawn at home to Rayners Lane in the Middlesex Senior Cup.

Wealdstone got the better of Rayners Lane by 4-3 after a thrilling ninety minutes of typical Cup-tie football culminating in a dramatic finish.

From a long throw-in, Buller opened the scoring for Wealdstone early in the game, and Dyke went through on his own to put them two up. Rayners Lane fought back and Wiggins scored with a cross shot. Dyke then put Wealdstone further ahead when he gathered a lose ball near the centre and cleverly worked his way clean through the Lane defence.

It was a faultless piece of footwork and Dyke well deserved the ovation he received. At the interval Wealdstone lead by 3-1.

On resuming the Lane gave a spirited display and all but saved the game. Surrey converted a penalty kick and in a further onslaught, McDonald, the Wealdstone keeper came to the rescue by neatly tipping the ball over the bar from Jennings.

With the defence appealing for offside Sproate placed the visitors on level terms, and then came the dramatic climax. In an all out attempt by Rayners Lane the ball rebounded from the post and was promptly netted, but whilst the Lane were dancing with joy and congratulating each other, the referee disallowed the goal on the grounds of offside.

Quick to seize the opportunity Barker immediately punted the ball up field where it was pushed through to Ward, and the winger, leaving the backs standing, went on to win the game for Wealdstone only a matter of minutes from time.

Rayners Lane, fortunate not to have been further behind at the interval can nevertheless consider themselves unlucky losers after such a gallant fight.

Wealdstone then must consider themselves a little lucky to have won this first round match, particularly as they went on to beat Wood Green Town 7-1 in the second round, Pinner (5-1) in the semi-final and Edgware Town (2-0) in the final to secure their first post war trophy win.

Mr H H Harrison, at this time a member of the committee (later to become Chairman of the club) had also promised the hospitality of his Public House, The Plough In Kenton should the team be successful in the final, and as they were, a dinner was held attended by some notable guests including W J (Bill) Edrich, the Middlesex and England cricketer and Harold Gittins, a sports cartoonist with the London Evening News.

'Stones gained further success in beating Pinner by 3-1 in the final of the Pinner and Northwood Hospital Cup, and after a committee proposal, Wealdstone also inaugurated the Wealdstone Football Club Cup.

It was proposed that a footballers bed be endowed at Harrow Hospital in memory of the Wealdstone players and officials that had lost their lives in the war and an annual match be played for the Wealdstone FC Cup, all proceeds of the match going to the upkeep of the bed.

Mr H H Harrison and Mr W G Leadbetter donated a handsome trophy, and Golders Green were duly engaged as opponents for

Wealdstone FC 1945-46, Winners of the Middlesex Senior Cup, Harrow Charity Cup, Pinner and Northwood Hospital Cup Winners, Wealdstone Football Club Cup Winners

the first competition, Wealdstone running out winners by 4-0, Gaze and Dyke both scoring twice.

In total forty-six matches had been played, twenty-one of these were won and fourteen drawn, and the first team had won three cups and finished sixth in the league.

Bert Dyke had scored 18 times in 37 games, while Gilbert Gaze scored 16 goals in only 14 appearances. The season was not as successful for the reserves however who only gained eight points during the whole season and they were firmly rooted at the bottom of the table, although they did gain some consolation in winning the Harrow Charity Cup.

At the AGM of the club it was announced that a profit of just over £22 had been made, a drop on the previous year (£58) mainly due to increased travelling costs and the appointment of a full time groundsman, the services of the part time groundsman also being retained.

It was also decided that the club would increase the admission fee for the next season, from 7d to 9d in common with most other Athenian League clubs!

An unremarkable season was to follow in 1946 – 1947. The first team did manage to improve its League position, finally finishing in fourth place, level on 30 points with third placed Bromley.

The season itself had started brightly for both the first and reserve teams, but a very harsh winter, which saw no football played at all for six or seven weeks due to frozen pitches, stalled the progress of both sides. It also meant that the season would be extended, eventually finishing in the second week of June although there was still a great deal of fixture congestion.

Wealdstone had risen, early in November to second place to Hendon (formerly Golders Green FC) in the table on goal average, both sides having played ten matches, Wealdstone with six wins and two draws, Hendon with seven wins and three defeats. The two clubs retained the top two positions until Christmas when, as usual (but this season with a little more at stake) they were to meet on Christmas Day and Boxing Day.

Hendon well deserved their victory at Lower Mead on Christmas Day. A large crowd was treated to a fine display by the visiting side that played fast attractive football. Owen the Hendon left-winger scored two goals in the first half to give his side a decisive interval lead.

After the change of ends Bryant added a third goal before Moore reduced Wealdstone's arrears six minutes from time. Bryant however scored Hendon's fourth goal with just one minute remaining.

In the return match on Boxing Day, Wealdstone made amends for their failure of the previous day and their 2-0 victory put them back to the top of the table. Both sides made changes and the pitch was somewhat firmer than the pitch at Lower Mead had been, the conditions more favourable to Wealdstone's style of play.

After a quarter of a hour Dyke held on to a through pass and ran on to score with a good shot, while with a minute remaining before the interval, Hardie cut inside and left Kemp, the Hendon goalkeeper, no chance following a well placed centre by Boston. The Hendon defenders were pinned in their own area for almost all of the second period, but their defence held out.

Wealdstone in fact were to retain the lead at the head of the table until the last few weeks when indifferent results in their last five matches saw Sutton, who won 1-0 at Lower Mead in the last game of the season, win the title.

Games in hand for Barnet and Bromley then saw those two clubs overtake Wealdstone as the season drew to a close.

There had been one further highlight during the season, when the BBC decided for the first time to show 'live' amateur football. The match selected was between Wealdstone and Barnet on October 19th 1946, which Barnet won by three goals to two.

Wealdstone deserved at least a point from the fast and thrilling match in the Athenian League at Barnet on Saturday, when the home team triumphed by three goals to two. Parts of the exchanges were included in the television programme for the day and with this added attraction the ground was packed to capacity.

Prior to the start, Edmonds and Kelleher, the rival captains and the referee Mr A V Boorer appeared before the cameras situated at the half way line. After formal introductions, the toss for the choice of ends taking place on the touchline provided a most unusual sight for the spectators, and with Kelleher guessing correctly, Barnet elected to kick up the slope and the game developed steadily into a keen struggle for supremacy, with fast end to end play.

Midway through the first half an attractive Wealdstone movement ended in Gaze passing the ball admirably to Moore, for the winger to run in and score with a low drive. Wealdstone's lead was well merited and they held onto it until the interval.

Directly on returning Phipps equalised for Barnet and this brought a period of sustained pressure from the home team. Wealdstone defended grandly but Kellerher put Barnet ahead from 25 yards range with a beautifully placed cross drive.

The visitors fought back but Powell defeated all attempts to beat him. The last 20 minutes proved the most exciting of all and produced two further goals, neither of which was televised, the service having closed down on account of bad light and a steady downpour of rain.

After Hill had miraculously saved at the feet of Kellerher, in the very next attack the veteran Finch drove in a lovely goal from the right wing. Right on time, Moore crowned a splendid afternoons work with a swift ground shot from the edge of the penalty area, which Powell never saw.

Wealdstone; R A Hill, F Haydon, C A Barker, S W Young, C A Edmonds, T E Pratt, J Moore, J Fowler, A G Gaze, H Dyke, F Boston.

It was to be three seasons later when Wealdstone were to feature on television again.

It was a poor season for the first team in the cup competitions, a number of early exits resulting in no 'silverware' and even the Wealdstone FC Hospital Cup, inaugurated the previous season was lost, Harrow Town inflicting a 5-1 defeat to win the trophy.

It was a better season for Harrow Town generally in the meetings between the sides, a record crowd of over 3200 saw 'Town beat Wealdstone at Earlsmead in the first qualifying round of the FA Cup by 4-3, after leading 3-0 at half time. Wealdstone's comeback not quite good enough.

The reserves though did manage to improve on their previous season's record. Starting their league season with four wins and a draw from five league games, they had increased the previous year's points tally by the first weekend in October, eventually finishing in seventh place. They were also losing semi-finalists in the league cup beaten 4-2 by Finchley reserves and the lost in the final of the Harrow Charity Cup, 2-1 to Northwood Town.

There were a number of signs of the war still present in and around London. This was evident in some of the friendly fixtures still being played by local clubs, various Army, RAF and Navy teams putting on creditable displays, and in some cases still bolstered by 'professional' players on National Service.

Wealdstone too were to host friendly matches, and one of these in April of 1947, was possibly Wealdstone's first fixture against truly International opposition. (Austrian FC, the opposition a few years earlier, were a British based team at the time).

Had Wealdstone not changed their policy and tried to emulate their opponents artistry they might well have been more successful in their friendly match with Carpathians at Lower Mead on Easter Monday.

The Carpathians, an eleven drawn from the 3rd Polish Carpathian Infantry Division, a section of the Polish Second Corps, have lost only two of their 20-odd matches played since they arrived in the country from Italy. Their team at Lower Mead included two internationals, Habowski at centre forward and Kulawik (inside-left).

The Poles delighted a large crowd with their fast close passing. In the early stages Wealdstone held their own, but then they appeared to try their skill at the close passing game. In this they were not successful and the additional work they gave themselves left them with a very tired team well before the end.

The Carpathians' first goal came after 30 minutes play and was scored by Janduda. After Jakubiec had put the Poles further ahead, Barker scored for Wealdstone from a penalty kick. There was no addition to the score until Sitko beat Hill to score a few minutes from the close to give the Poles a win by 3 goals to 1.

Wealdstone's main strength was in the middle line. Edmonds kept a tight check on the international Habowski, while both Pratt and Young were in great form. Hill was sound in goal, and Haydon and Barker did well until they tired. Individually Hunt, Gaze and Dyke were prominent at times.

Wealdstone; R A Hill, F Haydon, C A Barker, S W Young, C A Edmonds, T E Pratt, G Hardie, D Hunt, A G Gaze, H Dyke, S J Beasley.

Off the field, it was in financial terms a record season, the club showing a profit of £454, a sharp improvement on the £22 of the previous season.

It was a good season for a number of players as C A P Edmonds, H Dyke, A Hardie, G Hardie, A Stevens, R Jocelyn and G Upton were selected for the County in a number of matches.

There was also another first, in that it was the first season Wealdstone FC players had been covered by insurance for injury.

The policy was such that after one week's incapacitation, players would receive £5 per week. Six players received payments during the season, at a time when they were not paid for playing, they were L McDonald, S W Young, R Fowler, F Boston, D Scott and C Barker.

After such a difficult season with regard to the weather, it was noted that there was little work to do to repair the ground although one area of banking had been concreted to make a permanent terrace. A fund was started, with a target of £100 to allow the installation of concrete terracing on the banking all round the ground.

Wealdstone FC 1947
Standing; E Norton (Match Secretary), H A Luck (Hon. Secretary), C A P Edmonds (Captain), H Dyke, F Haydon, L McDonald, C A Barker, E Francis, F W Harbud (Hon. Treasurer), W Gallagher (Trainer), H H Harrison (Chairman). Seated; R Nicholson, W G Hill, A G Gaze, R H Atwood, W H Ray.

The following season saw a bright start in the league, but again, this solid foundation went to waste as results slipped away as the season went on. The first team falling one place to finish in fifth place, while the reserves finished third.

The FA Cup was to prove the most attractive in the early part of the season, starting with a preliminary qualifying round match at home to Enfield;

The eagerly awaited FA Cup match with Enfield drew a large crowd as expected, queues forming at the entrances over an hour before kick off. Enfield were far more prominent in the early stages than latter, and they failed to take full advantage of the openings created. Play opened briskly and despite a brief heavy downpour, continued at a fast pace throughout, the spectators being treated to all the thrills associated with cup-ties.

The visitors were paying dearly for their missed chances early on, and the latter part of the half found Bennett constantly in action. After 30 minutes a clever move by Moore led to Wealdstone opening their account.

The winger instead of lobbing the ball into the goalmouth in the orthodox manner made a perfect pass across field to the unmarked Ray on the other flank. This upset the calculations of the Enfield defence and Ray had little difficulty in scoring from close range.

NOTICE TO CYCLISTS

Supporters with cycles must enter the ground through the cyclists gate and all cycles must be put in the open space by the main gates. Cycles will not be permitted in any other part of the ground.

The Club will not be responsible for the loss of, or damage to cycles or cycling equipment. The cyclists' gate is the large gate next to the Hut in the Car Park.

From the match programme, Season 1947-48

In the second half, Wealdstone were well on top, the cracking pace telling on the visitors, and midway through the half they deservedly increased their lead, Bryant netting after a bout of sustained pressure, despite the protests from the visitors, convinced that the Wealdstone forward had been in an offside position.

Two weeks later in the first qualifying round, Wealdstone were drawn at home to Finchley;

The fighting qualities of Wealdstone can rarely have been seen to better advantage than on Saturday, when a 3-0 half time deficit was turned into a thrilling 5-4 victory in extra time, at the expense of hitherto unbeaten Finchley.

In the opening half Finchley had things much their own way and lost little time in establishing a commanding lead. They were the better side throughout this period being quicker on the ball, which at times ran consistently well for them and it caused little surprise when Neary opened their account following a corner kick. Worse for Wealdstone was to follow, for they failed to strike their form, the forwards being disjointed while the defence, subjected to intense pressure, looked far from impregnable.

A couple of slips by the rear guard allowed the visitors to go further ahead, first, Hill got up well to an inswinging corner kick but allowed the ball to elude his grasp and it fell to the feet of Hanwell who drove it into the net.

Neary got a third after the goalkeeper had left his charge in an effort to stave off disaster, so the position at half way was indeed black for Wealdstone, three down and their undefeated record in danger, the largest crowd for many a season was dumbfounded.

The second half saw a complete transformation, Edmonds rallying his men for a stern fight against great odds. First Barker reduced the arrears with a well-taken penalty kick and then a minute later amid great applause, Dyke scored with a lovely drive.

Finchley broke away and Cook again place them in a favourable position by making the score 4-2, but Wealdstone were now coming into their own and goals from Attwood and Ray levelled matters when all seemed lost.

Two leg weary sides were left to battle out 30 minutes of extra time, but it was a very bad stroke of luck that struck Finchley when Milne suffered a leg injury, which prevented him taking any further part in the game. This popular player who had gone through most of the game with his head swathed in bandages as the result of an unintentional kick on the forehead, received a sympathetic ovation as he was carried from the field by both trainers.

Despite their depleted ranks Finchley made Wealdstone fight all the way for the winning goal, which came after 20 minutes of extra time, Bryant receiving the ball from Dyke made no mistake from short range. Wealdstone ran out worthy winners of this cup-tie played under ideal conditions in the best sporting spirit.

Wealdstone; R A Hill, F J Haydon, C A Barker, W G Hill, C A Edmonds, E T Francis, J A Moore, H H Dyke, B L Bryant, R H Attwood, W H Ray.

At the end of October, the next round was away to Edgware Town and the local paper reported the sadness that a game so evenly contested for 80 minutes was decided by a disputed goal. The game finished with a player from both sides being dismissed from the field, all this in front of a record crowd.

About ten minutes from the end, from a clearance by the Wealdstone defence the ball fell to Ray who centred smartly. A tussle developed in the Edgware goalmouth, Trueman in goal appeared to have the ball covered when Attwood forced his way through and deposited the ball into the back of the net.

Edgware players and supporters in the vicinity held that the ball had been punched in, but the referee was firm in his decision and the goal stood. Uproar followed and it had scarcely subsided when Hardy (Edgware) and Moore (Wealdstone) were at loggerheads and the referee ordered them both off.......

Sadly, on December 2nd, the death was reported of Mr William Hedley who had been Chairman of the club from 1912 to 1922 and was instrumental in recommending the purchase of Lower Mead. He was 73 years old.

He became a Trustee of the club in 1925 until his death. He had been a player with Enfield FC and had represented them against the Brussels Racing Club in 1897 in the Belgian capital.

The success of the club had been reflected in the gates, which showed a good increase on the previous year, and again a record profit had been made over the season. This was the first in excess of £1,000, with a final figure on the balance sheet of £1,078.

During the season, the club had for the first time sought the services of a 'Coach', the teams being selected by Committee's and Mr J James was to take over in December. This was felt to have been a success and his services were retained for the following season.

On the playing front, it was decided that for the following year the club would try and attract the services of some younger players, alongside the first and reserve teams to form an 'A' Team to compete in the Harrow Wembley and District League.

For the first time, also, a Club Badge had been produced and the AGM reported that it would soon be on sale to supporters. The badge was approximately 1 1/4" in diameter, and it featured an enamelled Club Crest with the words 'Wealdstone Football Club Founded 1900' around the edge. Two versions were made, one with a pin and the other with a lapel clip.

The design incorporated the three Lions of England, the three Seaxes and Crown of Middlesex with the remaining quadrants featuring a football on a green background and the club colours of Blue & White Quarters.

Frank Harbud also had the honour of Life Membership bestowed on him at the end of the 1947 – 1948 season, in recognition of his long service. He had been a player in the Belmont Road days, had been Club Captain, Reserve and First Team Secretaries and eventually Honorary Treasurer.

Dorothy Roberts
Worked in the tea bar in the 1940's and 1950's

My family had quite a long connection with the club - my father was Charlie Elliot who had been on the Committee and was the club groundsman before and after the war. He lived in Headstone Lane and always used to travel the one stop by train to Harrow and Wealdstone for matches and meetings.

We helped out with the 'Annual Fete' as well as the football, and when I later worked on the tea bar I used to go the same way. I worked with Eve Salmon and Norman but in all those years we never did get to see much of the football.

Charlie also used to represent the Bus company as a runner - he did a lot of Cross-country when he was younger and even entered some Veterans races, then when he gave up the running he got involved with training the Wealdstone players.

The tea bar was at the side of the ground, but in those days we used to get three or four thousand supporters for almost every game - the tea Bar was very small and Norman used to look after all the tea urns along the back while Eve and I served - can you imagine making hundreds and hundreds of cups of tea in a little cabin?? Imagine the Big games where we may have done thousands of cups!! Its no wonder it was always so hot inside!!

During the War of course it was even more difficult - we had difficulty at times in getting hold of Tea and Milk and Sugar because of the rationing, but normally, Norman had been able to find some!

We actually got a special ration I think because we were a club, but I'm sure once or twice we appealed to supporters for some of their ration vouchers - The club did the same thing to get some clothing vouchers to provide the team with a new kit - then of course there was the Black Market - I don't really know if that's where all of the tea and everything came from but I'm sure it helped!

Club Chairman H H Harrison listening to the speaker during the Drumhead Ceremony at Lower Mead in August 1948.

A LITTLE MORE SUCCESS

Just prior to the start of the 1948 season, Lower Mead hosted another activity not related to football. As part of the 'celebrations' for Mons week, a Drumhead Ceremony was held on the Lower Mead pitch, just three weeks before the new season was due to start.

The 1948-1949 season started as had the previous season with mixed form in the league, and as the months progressed cup fixtures started to take more importance, none more so than the Amateur Cup.

Even in the first round, Wealdstone recorded a major achievement, beating Walthamstow Avenue 2-0 at Lower Mead even though the pitch was in a terrible state as Gittins was to record in the Evening News (opposite).

The weather was also to play a part in the league season as well. After a period of rain calling off matches due to waterlogging, late November and early December were beset with fog.

Wealdstone fans were caught out in November for an away fixture at Southall, as the Harrow Observer commented;

The team coach left Lower Mead in bright sunshine to be followed shortly afterwards by coaches of supporters, eager to see Wealdstone's two debutant players, Latimer, a goalkeeper and Gordon Norman.

The coaches ran into thick fog shortly after they crossed the Western Avenue. The convoy continued their journey only to be met at Southall at half past two by a recently chalked sign informing them that the referee had called of the match at 2:10pm.

It was not to finish there however as by this time the fog had descended still further and the Wealdstone contingent then spent the whole of the afternoon making the return journey to Harrow!

It did give two players in particular a rest that they may well have welcomed, as in the following week, Charlie Barker was selected to play for the FA XI against the Royal Navy. Both he and Hugh Dyke having been selected for the FA XI against Oxford University in the week previous.

Mike Turner
Supporter since the early 1940's

My father Fred Turner was a supporter and had been a Vice President before the war, so as soon as I was old enough, I accompanied him to matches.

I was in the record crowd of over 13,000 for Leytonstone's visit in the cup in 1949, but I was never sure it was a record as I also remember the Colchester match in the FA Cup at about the same time, which I'm sure was another 'full house' at Lower Mead.

I actively supported the 'Stones until I left home and started work and then I only saw them, with Dad, on a limited number

of occasions up to the 1970's. Since them I've been an armchair supporter.

I remember some great players - Tommy McGee who also played for Portsmouth as an amateur, The Royal Navy, England Amateur and the 'Stones - he was a really classy full-back and a perfect gentleman both on and off the field.

Another great was Edgar Francis, a Welsh International wing half and of course Charlie Townsend - an absolute credit to both the club and himself and a character as well.

More individual honours were to follow immediately as Charlie Barker was selected to play for England against 'The Rest' team, which was to include Fred Haydon.

The Amateur Cup run was to continue with a tie against the Metropolitan Police, a fixture that Wealdstone were confident that they could win.

The result at Lower Mead was a 1-1 draw, however 'Stones were victorious in the replay at Imber Court by 3-1.

Round three then saw another home tie – this time against Thameside Amateur FC, the Kent side having progressed from the earliest rounds of the competition, their achievements had been well reported in the national press. In fact the success was made all the more creditable as their home ground was not an enclosed pitch, so they had had to play every tie away from home. Their run was to end at Lower Mead however, Wealdstone winning comfortably by two clear goals.

The fourth round saw Wealdstone drawn away to Leytonstone, the Amateur Cup holders and strong favourites again.

Wealdstone accomplished the best feat of the day on Saturday in the Fourth Round of the Amateur Cup, when they held Leytonstone, favourites and holders for the past two years to a goalless draw. After 120 minutes of pulsating football, a draw was the fair result of a grand game that did credit to both sides.

In no way abashed by the home side's formidable Cup record this season, Wealdstone started confidently and held their own throughout. At the same time they owed a tremendous amount to Rowe, an international goalkeeper in almost everything he did.

His flawless handling and skilful positioning gave confidence to the whole team and he never looked like being beaten. By the end of the game, there appeared to be no space at all in between the two goal posts he guarded.

Haydon, Edmonds and Barker all played with fearless dash against a clever forward line and in the first half particularly the cool head of Edmonds in more senses than one held Leytonstone up time and time again. He was never beaten in the air and gave T E Bailey the centre forward and Essex cricketer no rope at all.

Francis too had a good afternoon, prompting many attacks with shrewd passes. On the other flank Hill battled gamely and emerged with credit. All the forwards played spiritedly, but as a line they never moved with the grace and understanding that characterised Leytonstone's attack, and they were without much sting in front of goal.

Dyke's clever ball control was always a potential menace, however, and he all but sealed a fine afternoon's performance with a wonder goal towards the end of the 90-minute period. Receiving the ball some 30 yards out, he made a gap in the Leytonstone defence by sheer body swerve, only to shoot a little hastily and the ball trickled just a few inches the wrong side of the post.

Ground conditions were ideal for great football and helped by a strong wind, Wealdstone started spiritedly, and Dyke twice nearly scored in the early stages. Leytonstone quickly retaliated and Joseph and Smith were prominent in attacks that ended with Rowe making smart saves. End to end play followed for the remainder of the first half with Leytonstone taking more opportunities to shoot.

Wealdstone resumed strongly and for quite a long period seemed to have the edge on their opponents, Smith came right into the picture for them for the first time and in forward movement Hardie and Franklin also played a good part. They were still reluctant to shoot however and the most dangerous shots came from the other side. Joseph particularly testing Rowe with hard drives. Noble and Bailey were less accurate and both blazed the ball over the bar when well placed.

Playing extra time in their third consecutive Cup-tie, Wealdstone, not unnaturally perhaps, lasted better than their opponents, and in the first period especially, opened the game out skilfully with long ranging passes to the right. Hardie showed plenty of dash in taking advantage of them, but none of his centres quite found their man.

Not until the last few minutes did Leytonstone begin to wear Wealdstone down and then Barker and Haydon were content to hold out with hard kicking to touch, and await the replay at Lower Mead on Saturday.

Wealdstone; R F Rowe, F J H Haydon, C A Barker, B S Hill, C A Edmonds, E T Francis, G R Hardie, R S Franklin, E W Smith, H Dyke, L Weston.

Leytonstone; D H Jarvis, L J Wallis, A W Nichols, J R T Groves, C R Hockday, J J M Kavanagh, F W Smith, A W Noble, T E Bailey, I E Nichols, L Joseph.

With the promise of a semi-final tie at the home of Arsenal FC, Highbury, for the winners a record crowd was expected for the replay at Lower Mead.

The club announced that admission would be 1/- and additionally that 'No cycles will be allowed inside the ground'.

The previous ground record was the 11,500 that had watched the cup-tie with Leytonstone the previous season, but on this March Saturday, this record was to be well beaten. Crowds were evident queuing from the early afternoon, the gates were shut well before kick off with a record attendance of 13,504, paying a total of £675, an attendance record that still stands today.

The dream was set to end though. The Wealdstone side again started brightly and at half time the score remained 0-0, but the visitors were to score their first goal through Bailey minutes into the second half. This knocked Wealdstone back and they went on to concede three more goals in the next fourteen minutes, the visitors eventually winning 4-0.

Aside from this there was to be no great success in any of the other cup competitions.

Although the club were invited to compete for the Wycombe Memorial Hospital Cup at the end of the season they were beaten by three goals to two by Wycombe Wanderers, in front of a crowd of 3,372, the trophies being presented on the day by Lord Carrington.

The league playing record of the first team finished as P 42 W 20 D 7 L 15, scoring 84 goals and conceding 74, finishing in fourth place in the Athenian League.

At the annual dinner at the end of the season, the club were to announce plans to further develop the Lower Mead ground, with the addition of a large assembly hall, lounge and bar, billiard room and a stage for entertainments.

All of this development coincided with additional terracing and covered seating inside the ground itself. The intention was to make the ground the centre of local football and the best amateur ground in the county.

There were a number of fundraising schemes put into place and the plans of the development were being prepared to Harrow Council for planning approval.

At the same time, the Council were looking at the ground and associated land as development potential – with the Chairman of Harrow Council present at the dinner, Club Asst. Secretary, W G Leadbetter stated

'Wealdstone are aware that the Council has its eyes on the ground, but we are confident that Mr Brady (Club Chairman) can convince the Council that there are many far better places in Harrow to build offices...'

There were still some notable performances in the league, one in particular was an early season fixture against the previous seasons Champions Barnet, who were summarily despatched by 7-1 at home. On the down side, the two fixtures against Bromley resulted in a 10-0 deficit, seven of the goals being conceded away from home.

An agreement was reached with Chelsea FC during this season for an exchange of players, and one of these was Eddie Smith. He became the club's top scorer during the season with 33 goals. Of the others, Gordon Norman and Bert Hill had also become regulars in the first team. The intention was for younger players to come to the 'Stones and progress through the grades to a higher standard of football.

There was no suggestion of Wealdstone becoming a nursery team for their West London neighbours, as Wealdstone still retained the opportunity to not play a 'Chelsea' player or indeed to decline to accept a player from Chelsea at any time.

Alan Franks
Supporter 1946 –1956, Shareholder.

I first saw Wealdstone in 1946 (East was in goal, and Bert Dyke was to the fore). Until 1956 when I moved I saw them play regularly. Certainly in over 50 years I have never seen a better penalty taker than Charlie Barker. No goalkeeper ever touched one of his penalties and I don't remember him ever missing!

Another memory is of a match with Barnet in 1947 when they were the top team, Cup Winners etc. My memory may be fading but I think we beat them 7-1 and Eddie Smith got all or most of the goals. Neither I, nor anyone else at Lower Mead had ever seen or heard of him before. I was surprised that he never 'went further' as a professional.

Later on Townsend and Lindsay too could have had professional careers but they stayed with the 'Stones..........

The reserves finished with a record of P 37, W20, D 6, L 11, with the team scoring 91 goals and conceding 59. It was the first time in the club's history that an 'A' team had been run, with the intention of bringing younger players to the club and then developing them through the ranks to the first team.

One such player to graduate during the first season was a young player from Chelsea, Gordon Lieven, who did in fact represent all three levels of the club during the season.

The AGM was able to report that the Council had granted the planning application for the extension of the main stand to house 170 people and for the new club hall to be built. Less enthusiasm was evident when the club proposed to increase membership fees and subscriptions to help meet the cost, the proposal being rejected by a majority of one vote.

Robert Marjoram
Player 1946-1949. Brothers Thomas and Richard also played for the club at the same time.

I was the first Marjoram to join the club, in late 1946. I'd played Representative Football during the war for The Royal Signals and after de-mob returned to my previous employ at H.M. Stationary Office in Headstone Drive, Wealdstone.

I played in trial matches and joined Wealdstone as a centre half for the reserve team. I also had two younger brothers, Thomas and Richard who were keen footballers and I introduced them to the club soon after de-mob and they became prominent members of the reserve team too!

Tom was working on the railways and was unable to play regularly on Saturdays owing to his variable shift work patterns. After joining Wealdstone, he was advised and given an intro-

duction to Kodak Ltd for future employment. He accepted the post with Kodak and remained there until his untimely death aged 57.

We three became a defensive trio for the Wealdstone Reserves and we were subsequently selected to play for Middlesex Juniors v Kent in the counties Junior cup final at Bromley F.C. - we went on to win 3-1 - I was lucky to play as I had played nine games for the first team and was therefore only one appearance from being classed as a 'Senior' player.

I became a centre forward and after a successful spell, moved on to Hayes F.C. with my brother Richard prior to his retirement through injury sustained during the war and Tom subsequently moved on to Harrow Town F.C.

Working at H.M. Stationary Office, I knew several people associated with Wealdstone F.C. - the club treasurer Reg Lemmings and first team trainer Bill Gallagher were both work colleagues and there were some notable players of their time too, Edgar Francis was a fine wing half and a Welsh International, there was Charlie Edmunds who was a real stopper of a centre half, Charlie Barker - the Penalty king who hit the ball so hard and a superb winger in Jimmy Moore.

I have one particular memory of a nostalgic home match, I believe against Edgware. After the game as we changed I was told that a spectator was asking for me - I met him and he said "Sorry, wrong chap" - he was actually looking for another brother, Leslie with whom he had served in the war, but he was killed serving as a rear gunner on a Sunderland Flying Boat. This gentleman gave me a wonderful photograph of the R.A.F. Pembroke Dock football team with Leslie as centre forward.

The football was very different then, there was no floodlighting or substitutes - I for one would not have been happy to be banished to the bench, and if a player was injured he'd go up front 'out of the way' and try and cause their defence a problem or two whilst everyone else played on.

The balls were made of leather - not like these lightweight PVC spheres that are used today and we had real leather boots above our ankles as well!

The Wealdstone 'End of Season' dinners at this time were also memorable. They were always so popular and we had many sporting personalities attending - I remember Leslie and Dennis Compton who lived in Harrow, Bill Edrich and Godfrey Evans in particular. There was also the Athenian League Dinner - a very austere occasion at The Connaught Rooms - there was always attempts at 'player poaching' so the club officials were always very wary and protective of their players.

Over 80 now and looking back I well remember the match at Hounslow, and my hat trick in what was my first senior amateur appearance - I was summoned by telegram to play on the Friday evening and in the morning I had moved into my first flat in Hanwell!

After a busy close season where work commenced on the extension and the new clubhouse, the pitch was completely reseeded.

Wealdstone entered their Jubilee season in 1949 – 1950 on good form and with the stage prepared for a season of celebrations fundraising and social events off the field. On the field, the players too made this another memorable season in the history of the club.

At the beginning of the season a true friendly match was played as part of the clubs celebrations, a team from Schaffhausen FC of Switzerland entertained at Lower Mead and afterwards to dinner at the Railway Hotel.

There was a large attendance at Lower Mead for the match which was won 2–1 by the visitors, Charlie Barker scoring the Wealdstone goal from a penalty.

From the reports it seems that the pre-season rustiness was still very evident in the Wealdstone side, which had still created more than enough chances to win the match.

The Swiss goalkeeper was barracked often by the home fans, the frustration his frequent time wasting!

The FA Cup was to occupy most people's thought early in the season at Wealdstone. Among their league matches was their first fixture, away to Hendon on September 17th, which 'Stones won by 4–0. A fortnight later and the second qualifying round saw a goalless draw at Enfield, before 'Stones won the replay by 2–0.

The third qualifying round was a stiffer test, away to Isthmian League St Albans City, where Wealdstone won a difficult match by 1–0. The fourth qualifying round saw another difficult match against local rivals Edgware Town on their own ground and this was to be the second time Wealdstone FC appeared on live television.

The occasion was reported in the Harrow Observer;

A record crowd both inside and outside the ground, for this match was televised, saw Wealdstone break Edgware Town's unbeaten record this season by winning 1–0 in the final qualifying round (South Eastern Section) of the FA Cup on Saturday.

It was a thrilling game between two sides that have exceptionally good records this season. Neither, it is true, ever obtained the poise to play notably skilful football. That was hardly to be expected in a 'needle' cup-tie of this type, but by displaying superior method both in attack and defence, Wealdstone deserved their narrow win.

Next came the professionals of Colchester United. The Southern League leaders visiting Lower Mead early in November, in the Final Qualifying Round (National) of the competition.

After five FA Cup-ties Wealdstone were confident, they had not even conceded a goal yet in the competition and for the first time they had been drawn at home.

Phil Carden
described the scene in the Golden Jubilee Handbook;

The effect of the Colchester 'nerve war' on the Wealdstone players was very different from that on the players of (some of Colchester's previous opponents). Ted Fenton (Colchester Manager) certainly spoke freely to the press of his team's chances of success, but in the dressing room at Lower Mead on training nights, Charlie Barker and his colleagues were also evolving plans.

The day – November 12th – dawned dull over Lower Mead and district. Heavy rain fell just before the kick off, and, although it had been expected that a record attendance would be registered, fewer than 10,000 spectators were present to witness the match. The game was seen by others, for the BBC

SATURDAY—October 29

11.0-12.0 NEWSREEL
(Composite edition)

* * *

2.40-4.25 app. ASSOCIATION FOOTBALL
(F.A. Cup Third Qualifying Round)
Edgware Town v. Wealdstone
A visit to Edgware Town football ground to see the whole of this afternoon's Cup Tie
Commentators:
Jimmy Jewell and Peter Lleyd

* * *

8.30 MUSIC-HALL
with
Derek Roy
Norman Thomas
and his Plantation Four
The Draggazi Trio
Jack Daly
Molly Raynor
Jackie Ross
Leslie Roberts Music-Hall Maids
Eric Robinson
and his Augmented Orchestra
Produced by Richard Afton

9.30 FAMILY AFFAIR
by Eric Maschwitz
from an idea by Betty Farmer
being the first instalment of the Connover family at home
1—'Henry Breaks the News
Linda............Heather Thatcher
Henry............Michael Shepley
Tony............Denis Gordon
Marion............Sarn A'Deane
Bunty............Betty Blackler
Martin............David Preston
Maggie............Madoline Thomas
Miss Cherry.....Daphne Oxenford
Settings by Richard R. Greenough
Produced by Michael Mills
You are invited to meet the Connover family again next Saturday evening at 9.30 p.m.

10.0 NEWSREEL
(Repeat of Friday's edition)

10.15-10.30 NEWS (sound only)

WEATHER CHART
At the close of evening programmes viewers see the latest weather charts specially prepared by the Meteorological Office

From The Radio Times, 21st October 1949

The Lower Mead TV Gantry, a temporary structure in place for the match v Colchester.

Television cameras were in action for the entire match, in fact, the viewers joined the crowd at Lower Mead half an hour before kick off.

The Harrow Observer and Harold Gittins from the Evening News again describe the match;

Scenes of great enthusiasm marked Wealdstone's surprise but thoroughly merited single goal win over Colchester United, the Southern League leaders at Lower Mead on Saturday. The spectators, who had been kept in a continuous state of audible excitement throughout the game, surged onto the pitch immediately the final whistle blew.

The victorious players, after being heartily congratulated by their professional opponents, were besieged by the crowd and had some difficulty in making their way to the dressing rooms. It was a tribute worthy of a win that must stand high in the club's history.

Though on balance the visitors had slightly the better of exchanges and in the closing stages were distinctly unfortunate not to score once or twice, there could be no real quarrel with the result.

Adapting themselves much more readily to the treacherous and heavy ground in the first half, Wealdstone showed a liveliness of spirit that out-matched the visitors' superior technical skill. It was as though Colchester realised the urgency of their position too late. When they did they found themselves against an indomitable defence.

Barker performed a great service for his side by winning the toss. A strong wind behind them in the first half gave impetus to the Wealdstone attack and handicapped the visitors. The wind dropped later and in the second half Wiltshire was easily able to clear the half way line with his goal kicks – a feat denied to Wright early on.

Wealdstone made the going from the start and within a few minutes even Barker had a shot at goal.

Colchester was a long time in getting the ball away, and when they did Foxall was easily stopped by Haydon.

Thrills abounded and after a centre had crossed the Wealdstone goal without a Colchester forward being able to connect, Dyke split the Colchester defence open, but the ball ran just too far. Smith was doing fine work on the left.

Foxall shot hopelessly wide when well placed just before the vital goal came in the 28th minute. Smith pushed the ball through a defence that appeared to be waiting for the whistle to blow. Rogers chased it and, though tackled by Wright, continued to push the ball past him and Saunders had only to run up and tap it over the line. Rogers was hurt and for some time changed places with Smith.

After this Wealdstone played with terrific spirit and Roberts force Wright to save smartly. When Colchester retaliated, Foxall beat three men, only to see Curry shoot wide, whilst a fine shot by Hillman went close.

Colchester was more determined in the second half, and adopted Wealdstone's more direct tactics. Both goals had thrilling escapes and Cutting once got the ball past Wiltshire but from an offside position.

Wealdstone replied with some storming football, and mid way through the half showed that if anyone was going to tire, it was not they. They were in fact the more dangerous side near of goal, Roberts making some particularly fine efforts.

For the final ten minutes Colchester exerted all they knew to break up the dogged Wealdstone defence, but they only brought out the best in Wiltshire, though they hotly claimed a goal when he once dropped the ball on the line. To the end however Wealdstone refused to concentrate exclusively on defence.

Danny Wiltshire saves from a Colchester forward as Charlie Barker and Fred Haydon watch on.

Wiltshire in action again, punching away a cross.

The fullest praise must go to Wiltshire and the fine trio in front of him, Barker, Haydon and Shailer.

The two backs tackled, kicked and covered brilliantly throughout, Francis and Norman were equally active in attack and defence.

The part played by the forward line cannot be overestimated. For the entire 90 minutes they never allowed the Colchester defence to relax, Roberts, perhaps regarded as the weak link, played with particular courage and resource and deserved at least one goal. Smith and Saunders were dangerous wingers, and Rogers and Dyke were nearly always prominent.

Colchester had a grand half back line and all the forwards and Foxall in particular, showed class but over-elaborated.

Wealdstone; D Wiltshire, F J H Haydon, C A Barker, G Norman, G Shailer, E T Francis, W Saunders, H Dyke, W Roberts, P A R Rogers, E W Smith.

Colchester; G Wright, Kettle, D Beach, H Bearryman, R Stewart, W Layton, D Hillman, R Curry, V Keeble, F Cutting, S Foxall.

It was a great victory for the Wealdstone side, and the fans celebrated long after the match with the players. Danny Wiltshire and the defence had played superbly to preserve Wealdstpone's lead.

An anonymous supporter at the time wrote the following to celebrate 'Stones victory over Colchester,

WEALDSTONE v GOALESSTER

Years may come and pass us by,
But in our hearts will never lie
A memory of that certain day
When Wealdstone went on the field of play.
While adding honours to their name
Enrolled upon their scroll of fame.
The chances of a Wealdstone win,
To say the least seemed very thin,
The writers in the Daily News
Quite freely stated all their views –
"United" for the first round proper,
but, sad to say, they came a cropper.
For playing in the English Cup,
The 'Stones were very soon one up.
And though they then were much despised,
Colchester never equalised.
A pass by Rogers, Saunders touch
Just got the goal that meant so much.
No credit goes to just one man,
All working to a certain plan,
Though the play was often keen
Both sides kept it very clean.
Each team deserves special praise.
Considering those Cup-tie nerves
Ten, twenty, fifty years from now
Men will relate with wrinkled brow,
Of Wealdstone's great and gallant stand
By Charlie Barker and his band.
As greybeards shake their heads they'll say
"You don't see things like that today"

The next round was to see 'Stones drawn away for the fifth time in six rounds, this time to Third Division South side Port Vale. Sitting in eighth place in the division, they were in fact only two points behind the team in second place with a game in hand, having not been beaten in any of nine home matches during the season.

They were however second only to Watford across the whole league for the lowest number of goals conceded – 10, of which only 3 were at home.

"Hard Luck Wealdstone" ran the headline in the Evening Standard on the day the cup Draw was made, the comment column opened

Hard luck Wealdstone, amateur heroes of the last round of the FA Cup. For the next round, the first round proper – these conquerors of the professional side Colchester United have to go north to play Third Division Port Vale.

A tremendous task for them.

Mr G J Orange however writing in the Evening News was able to give 'Stones fans a more re-assuring message;

Wealdstone for their grand show in beating Colchester United in the last round have been given rather poor reward. They have been given a journey to Hanley, to play Port Vale, who has not been beaten at home this year by any Club. But Wealdstone may make a great fight of it and in the cup you never really know...

There was very little from any other sports writer to give Wealdstone a chance at all, the dressing room at Lower Mead the day after the draw was made held a similar thought.

Charlie Barker and his team were however soon planning to make the fullest use of their outside chance of victory which they felt was within their grasp.

Leaving as little to chance as possible, the Wealdstone team were to travel with a party of officials on the Friday evening, staying in the North Stafford Hotel, Stoke-on-Trent overnight before making the short journey to Hanley on the morning of the game.

Meeting at Euston, there was already some good news for the travelling party when centre forward Bill Roberts announced that his wife had given birth to their son that very afternoon.

On arrival in Stoke, Wealdstone were met by the Manager and Hon secretary of Port Vale FC, Messrs G Hodgson and N J Jones who escorted them to their Hotel.

They also arranged for Eddie Smith to have a fitness test at the ground, and for the squad to be entertained on the Saturday morning with a visit to a pottery.

The 'Stones supporters travelled some by coach, a six hour journey that left Lower Mead before 7:00am on the Saturday Morning and also by train.

The train had left Euston at 10:00am calling at Willesden Junction, Wembley Central, Harrow and Wealdstone and Watford Junction, due to arrive at Hanley at 1:20pm for a 2:15pm kick off. The full fare was 19/- from Wembley and 18/9 from Wealdstone, a special train having been laid on for the occasion.

The players arrived at the ground an hour before kick off, just as four coach loads of Wealdstone fans arrived, which gave

PORT VALE FOOTBALL CLUB CO. LTD.
Bryan Street, Hanley, Stoke-on-Trent

OFFICIAL PROGRAMME—2d.
Saturday, November 26th, 1949

CLUB NOTES.

NEW GROUND FUND.

Many supporters have sent contributions to the 100,000 shillings fund, some accompanied by good wishes and helpful suggestions.

One writer this week asks for Ballot Boxes to be placed at the entrances to receive contributions from supporters who don't want to be troubled to send letters to the Town Hall but who nevertheless wish to help the fund.

To meet this need Ballot Boxes have been provided at all entrances and the amount contributed will be announced next week. THANK YOU!

DELAYED LICENCE.

We ask supporters not to worry about the Licensing Officer's decision announced last week. This decision, for many reasons, is not accepted as final by the club and further steps are being taken to bring the facts of the case to the notice of the Minister.

In this connection we are indebted to the "Evening Sentinel" for publishing the speeches of Ald. Greaves and Ald. Austin, made at Thursday's Council meeting. Ald. Greaves is an Architect and knows more about building trade conditions, materials and housing than most members of the Council. His statement is incontrovertible. Thanks, Alderman Greaves!

WEALDSTONE.

Our opponents in the cup-tie today have an excellent record, six matches won without a goal against, and it will be necessary for the Vale to be on their best behaviour to secure victory. We hope

(continued on next page

The welcome to Wealdstone FC on the bottom of the programme front and inside reads "Our opponents in the cup-tie today have an excellent record, six matches won without a goal against, and it will be necessary for the Vale to be on their best behaviour to secure victory. We hope that they will not be unduly alarmed by the bad condition of the dressing room due to subsidence. They will at least, understand why we are pressing for permission to build a new ground at Burslem. In any case we give them a hearty welcome to Hanley.

them great heart as they made their way into the dressing room for their final tactical talk with Bill Gallagher and to loosen up.

Fighting all the way, though owing a tremendous amount to the courageous and skilful goalkeeping of D Wiltshire, Wealdstone went out of the FA Cup competition full of credit when they played Port Vale, at Hanley, Staffordshire on Saturday. A rather tragic goal score after 25 minutes following a free kick was the only score.

Wiltshire was the hero of the match and left the field to the congratulations of the Port Vale players and an appreciative roar from the crowd of 15,300. He made at least two dozen memorable saves from shots fired at him from all angles in what was afterwards described as the best goalkeeping display for years.

Wealdstone nevertheless, were no one-man band. They played some delightful football, especially in the first half, when at times they outplayed their professional rivals by sheer artistry.

Even in the second half, disorganised by an injury that kept Francis limping on the left wing, they refused to wilt under the pressure, and left the field with heads held high.

To vie throughout in stamina with such strong opponents under gruelling conditions harshened by heavy going was a credit to all eleven players.

Port Vale opened with a confidence springing from an unbeaten home record, But it was soon Wealdstone who were making the running. Playing crisp open football, they kept the ball in their opponents half and Dyke and Saunders engineered several movements, which almost put Roberts through.

Rogers then came into the picture with the best forward run of the match. Picking up the ball on the half way line, he dribbled his way past three defenders to the extreme left before sending in a tricky high shot that King was barely able to tip over the crossbar for a corner.

Saunders perfectly placed kick was scrambled away, but Wealdstone were soon on back and Dyke tried a hook shot, which King again saved smartly.

Port Vale began to make progress with cleverly placed passes to the wings, and were unlucky not to score when a header by pinchbeck struck the crossbar with Wiltshire beaten. The goal came after 25 minutes play. Wiltshire brilliantly saved a hard shot by Hulligan, but he could only turn the ball away to the right wing, where it was secured by Allen.

The winger was pushed off the ball and a free kick was awarded. Allen took the kick himself and lobbed the ball right back into the goalmouth. Wiltshire appeared to be hampered as he rose to punch the ball away, and Pinchbeck scrambled the ball past him into the net.

Wiltshire retaliated with spirit but Port Vale maintained the initiative, Hulligan being prominent in several dangerous attacks. By no means done with, Wealdstone hit back just before the interval, and on two occasions fruitlessly threw the Port Vale defence into a state of near panic.

An injury to Francis's ankle forced him to move to the left wing after the interval, Rogers dropping back to left half and Smith moving inside. Neither this nor their goal deficit broke Wealdstone's spirit, and in an early attack Dyke fired in a good shot that King did well to hold.

Port Vale however, were always on top in the second half though the Wealdstone defence stood firm under relentless pressure.

Shots were rained in on Wiltshire, but he was invincible, though aided by fortune on occasions. One point blank save from Pinchbeck almost challenged belief, and in a despairing effort to beat him, Allen shot well over the bar from a penalty kick.

Game to the end, Wealdstone made one last rally, but were held up by a foul about 45 yards out. Barker went up to take the kick, but his shot, though hard and accurate was safely held by King.

Then came the final whistle with Wealdstone beaten but still uncowed.

About 500 Wealdstone supporters, travelling by special train and coaches contributed to the gate of over £900. Their long journey was well rewarded and they returned in good heart.

Port Vale; King, Hamlett, Butler, McGarry, Cheadle, Todd, Allen, Martin, Pinchbeck, Polk, Hulligan.

Wealdstone; D Wiltshire, F Haydon, C Barker, G Norman, G

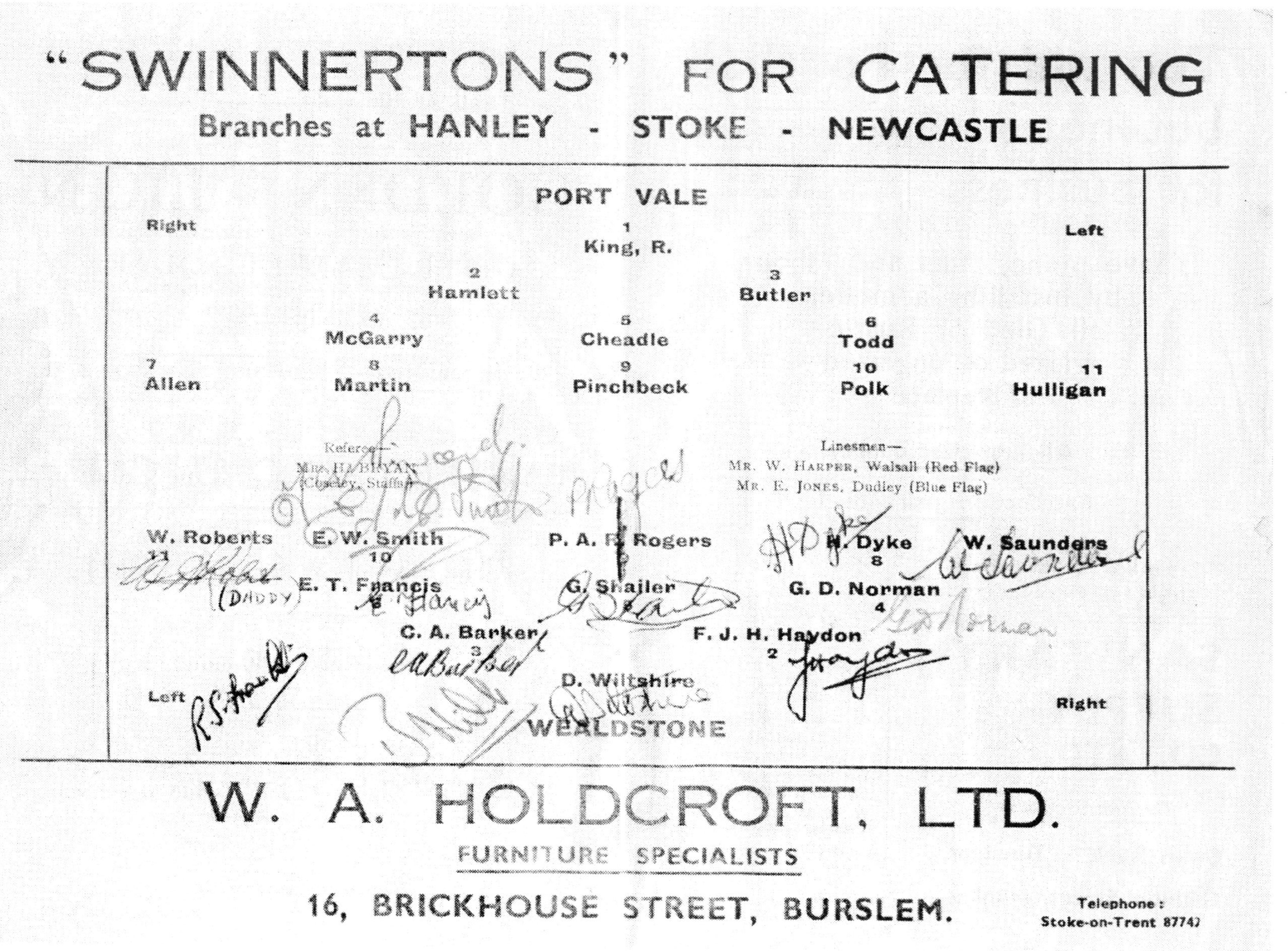

"SWINNERTONS" FOR CATERING

Branches at HANLEY - STOKE - NEWCASTLE

PORT VALE

Right | Left

1 King, R.

2 Hamlett | 3 Butler

4 McGarry | 5 Cheadle | 6 Todd

7 Allen | 8 Martin | 9 Pinchbeck | 10 Polk | 11 Hulligan

Referee—
Mr. H. Bryan,
Coseley, Staffs.

Linesmen—
Mr. W. Harper, Walsall (Red Flag)
Mr. E. Jones, Dudley (Blue Flag)

W. Roberts 11 | E. W. Smith 10 | P. A. R. Rogers | H. Dyke 8 | W. Saunders

E. T. Francis 6 | G. Shailer 5 | G. D. Norman 4

C. A. Barker 3 | F. J. H. Haydon 2

D. Wiltshire

WEALDSTONE

Left | Right

W. A. HOLDCROFT, LTD.

FURNITURE SPECIALISTS

16, BRICKHOUSE STREET, BURSLEM.

Telephone: Stoke-on-Trent 8774)

The centre page team sheet from the Port Vale FC v Wealdstone FC FA Cup-tie in November 1949, autographed by the Wealdstone side.

Shailer, E Francis, W Saunders, H Dyke, W Roberts, P Rogers, E Smith

Rosemary Luck,
Daughter of Harold 'Chippy' Luck (formerly Hon. Secretary and Treasurer connected with the club from 1926-1971)

My father was connected with the club for nearly fifty years firstly as a player and then as an official in various capacities, Treasurer, Secretary for 21 years and then Chairman and President before he retired in 1971, and as a result of my fathers involvement I too support Wealdstone.

I'm told my brother and sister and I were first taken Lower Mead when I was five, but I think we were more interested in running up and down the stairs than in the games themselves!

As we became older all three of us regularly sold programmes - this was in the days when it was quite normal to sell a thousand or more and on some of the bigger days we could sell several thousand.

My sister and I also used to help with the refreshments on training nights and on match days and the players taught me how to play snooker and table tennis as well as enjoying the club's social side.

For a long period I watched the club home and away and remember some memorable matches, particularly when we beat Colchester one nil in the F.A. Cup in 1949-50, the match was to be the second complete match televised by the BBC, the first having been our win in the previous round against Edgware.

Wealdstone was a big part of our lives – we all went down because Dad was so involved. Then it became more of an interest and I traveled with the players on the coaches.

During the War, we played in the Herts & Middlesex League. There were no coaches then – everyone had to make their own was as best as they could and often you would turn up with only nine or ten players. Normally the 'home' team would lend a player to make the sides even. The football was then just an entertainment.

HH Harrison was the Chairman. We all used to call him 'Fearless' - not in hearing mind you. I once travelled to a game in his car. There were a few others and he had a disagreement with one of them – then he stopped the car and made the other person get out!

The most harrowing game was the Colchester game – I spent the last ten minutes with my head in my hands crying with the tension. They were so 'on top' of us at the time. We had scored and were hanging on – we thought the whistle was never going to blow.

Then we went up by train to see the 'Stones play at Port Vale - we'd chartered a special train I think, and the same season we played the holders Leytonstone in the 4th round of the Amateur Cup with excellent support in a crowd of over 13,000.

The excitement of the FA Cup had occupied the thoughts of players and fans alike, but after the match at Port Vale, the reality of what was becoming an otherwise poor season struck home.

Within a few weeks, Wealdstone were defeated 4-1 at Salisbury in the Amateur Cup in front of a crowd of over 5,500.Their league form had also been poor, resulting in the 'Stones falling to the bottom of the Athenian League table early in January of 1950.

In the Dressing Room
By W. F. SHOWLER (Hon Secretary) Edited from the Golden Jubilee Handbook

Mr. Showler will be remembered by many as being one of the finest right-halves the club has had. He is now doing equally good work as an official of the club, being in charge of the first team. In this article he tells something of his task.

The hour is 2.57 p.m. and kick-off is timed for 3 o'clock.
In each goalmouth players are having their preliminary ball practice, while the spectators impatiently await the appearance of the referee.

Somewhere in the vicinity of the dressing rooms two team secretaries, in common with hundreds of their kind throughout the country -at this time, breathe sighs of relief, happy in the knowledge that they each have a complete team on the field of play and-with three minutes to spare. Lucky chaps, these two secretaries.

What of their less fortunate brothers, some of whom are anxiously watching a couple of reserves hurriedly changing to rush on to the field in place of two of the selected team who -have failed to put in an appearance?

Pity the poor team secretary, too, who is confronted by his goalkeeper with the news that he has omitted to pack his football boots—size 10 and there is not another pair larger than size 8 anywhere in the club! These are just two of dozens of snags which can and do arise in those vital minutes before the start of a game.

I write in this strain because, having now had some experience in the position, I feel that the team secretary's primary job is to ensure that the team as selected by the selection committee is on the field of play in good time, happy, contented, and prepared to give of its best for the full 90 minutes of play.

There are many points to be considered in order to achieve this happy state. - Firstly, strict attention to details regarding times, traveling arrangements, etc. This is particularly important when -members of the team are living a considerable distance from the locality of the ground or are away from home on National Service. Personal contact and a knowledge of the characteristics of each individual player are most essential.

Having played senior amateur football for some 15 seasons, I have personally had a first-rate opportunity to study the various types of men who normally comprise a football team.

These are many and varied. One man is easily disheartened when the ball is not running well for him and needs words of encouragement. Another only requires to be, told that his immediate opponent is having a good game and is immediately stung to extra effort.

Still another type is the man who knows when he is up against apparently superior opposition and can be relied upon to work out his own salvation.

This latter type is usually the man who causes the ream secretary the least worry. He invariably arrives at the ground in ample time. His playing kit, which he had methodically packed the previous evening, is neat and correct. Boots clean and per-

fectly studded, ankle bandages neatly rolled, a spare pair of laces in case of accident. In fact, everything in apple-pie order.

Contrast him with the real headache; the player who arrives 10 minutes before the kick-off time, boots caked with the previous Saturday's mud, two studs missing, and a broken lace. Within two minutes of his arrival, the dressing room is in a state of turmoil with perhaps three people rushing about endeavoring to get one player on the field (in presentable order) at the same time as his teammates. Not that one is a better player than the other, but how much easier would be the mind of the team secretary with II of the first type. I feel that no such amateur team exists!

It may appear to the reader that the position of the team secretary carries with it a burden of worry and trouble. That is so, up to a point, but in effect the team secretary is the liaison between the club committee, the trainer, and the players. Without the confidence and co-operation of the committee his work can be most difficult or even impossible.

I am happy to say in my particular case that every reasonable request in connection with the comfort or welfare of Wealdstone players, either as a team or individually, which comes before the club committee, receives prompt and sympathetic attention. Furthermore, I am fortunate in working with a trainer who is devoted to his job and goes to endless trouble to ensure the fitness of the players.

These conditions certainly make the work of the team secretary easier, but however much help and co-operation are forthcoming, nothing can prevent illness or injury that may deplete an otherwise good team. To be successful, therefore, a team secretary must have a large helping of good luck.

THE NINETEEN FIFTIES

The start of 1950 saw the club introduce a number of new fundraising ideas, to finance some of the work already completed on the ground. This was necessitated by the members' decision not to increase subscriptions, all under the guise of the Golden Jubilee Fund.

One of these initiatives was the Mile Of Shillings. This was a scheme to lay a path of shillings for one mile by lapping the Lower Mead pitch that was to have raised around £10000 towards the club's target, the intention being to complete a path of 200,000 shillings.

Later in the season, a Boxing Match was to be held in the open air at Lower Mead. Bad weather saw this was washed out but luckily the club had insured the event and so it still made a profit!

Another fundraiser was a Midnight Matinee organised at the local Granada cinema. This was a tremendous success in terms of entertainment but was a financial failure. It featured Kenneth Horne and Richard Murdoch, supported by Peter Cavanagh, Joyce Golding, Jean Metcalfe and Owen Walters and his Broadcasting Orchestra.

It was not until the end of the season that the club's fortunes began to look up on the field of play either. Improving form in the league and 'catching up' on games postponed because of the FA Cup exploits saw Wealdstone rise to fifth place, having played 26 matches, winning 11 and drawing 7, scoring 55 goals against 42 conceded.

There was only one cup success, that in the Middlesex Charity Cup, where wins over Enfield 1-0, Uxbridge Town 2-1, and then Finchley in the final by 3-1 saw the trophy returned to Lower Mead.

The first team had also won the Wealdstone FC Cup, an invitation having been extended to Maidstone United, who were beaten at Lower Mead on the 13th of May. This match was to be Fred Haydon's last for the club as he was about to move to South Africa.

The reserves finished third in their division but the 'A' team surpassed their seniors, winning the Harrow, Wembley and District League Senior Division with an unbeaten record. They had played 22 Won 18 Drawn 4, scoring 65 goals and conceding only 16 in a league that included Chelsea Youth, Harrow St Mary's II and Northwood II among others.

A number of players gained representative honours during the season. Danny Wiltshire was selected for the England Trials, Edgar Francis and Charlie Barker were selected to play for the Athenian League XI and Francis, Dyke, Gordon Norman and Bertie Smith played for Middlesex.

The reserves too were rewarded for their season, finishing third in the Athenian League Reserve Section, with G Padina selected to play for the Athenian League Reserve XI.

Charlie Barker, Wealdstone Captain laying his contribution to start the 'Mile of Shillings' watched by (left to right) C Thomas, D Wiltshire, W Saunders, G Shailer, A Benningfield, W Roberts, E Smith, H Dyke, G Norman, F Haydon and H H Harrison, Club Chairman.

In their second year however, the greatest success was gained by the 'A' Team. They won the Senior Division of the Harrow, Wembley and District League with an undefeated record, winning sixteen league games and drawing the remaining four.

The Wealdstone Squad at the end of the Jubilee Season.

To mark the end of the Jubilee season, an invitation match was held, Maidstone United being invited to compete for the Wealdstone Cup, the hosts however ran out easy winners by 6-1, the trophies were presented by a well known British Film and Stage actress, Miss Margot Grahame.

Eddie Smith and Bertie Hill, both of whom had joined the club as part of the arrangement with Chelsea FC were to sign professional forms with the West London club, this seen as proving the success of the scheme for all concerned as both players had figured regularly in the Wealdstone first team, Smith as top scorer.

Lower Mead of the Future
By JACK HOLT Edited from the Golden Jubilee Handbook

Jack Holt was the member of the committee responsible for the upkeep of the ground, a position for which he had special qualifications. Mr. Holt divulges here something of the club's plans for making Lower Mead one of the finest amateur football grounds in the country.

Those of our supporters and friends who have been interested enough in the Wealdstone Football Club to buy a copy of the Jubilee Handbook will, I am sure, be keen enough to want to know something of the club's plans for the future of what is already a first-class football ground.

In that belief, therefore, and not over-looking the fact that this (Golden Jubilee Handbook) is largely a volume of reminiscences of highlights of the past 50 years, I have endeavored to convey a broad outline of the committee's plan of development at Lower Mead.

A very comprehensive scheme has been evolved; the scheme has inevitably to be divided into two sections. First comes our plan for the early future, and I want to stress that the ground improvements envisaged under this section have been so arranged that they will comprise a part of the complete development scheme.

It will be readily appreciated that there are several factors that make it impossible for us to go straight ahead with the scheme in its entirety —building restrictions and lack of adequate financial resources being among them. Nevertheless, we feel that we shall be able to make steady progress towards our ultimate ambition. Much depends, of course, on our ability to provide attractive and successful football in order that we may ensure continued support.

Some of the ground improvements have already been carried out. The extensive concrete terracing has proved its worth. In addition to enhancing greatly the comfort of spectators, it has enabled us to pack another 2,000 people into the ground, conclusive evidence of this being forthcoming on the occasion of our fourth-round Amateur Cup-tie with Leytonstone in the 1948-49 season when 13,504 paid for admission.

Work on other parts of the terraces is to be carried out as soon as possible. The stand has been extended to accommodate another 170 people. New railings now enclose the playing field; in addition to bettering the appearance of the ground, the railings will, it is hoped, deter youngsters from going on to the playing field at the conclusion of matches, a practice which in the past has caused no small amount of damage to the turf.

Improved accommodation has also been provided for referees and linesmen. Recent improvements also include an extension to the stand that has given us an additional room for the use of visiting club's officials on match days. More space under the stand has been allotted to our popular and capable trainer, Bill Gallagher, who now takes great pride in the sanctum in which he keeps so many "magic" bottles, together with the various lamps for the treatment of players, which he manipulates with such skill.

Many of you will remember that following our 2-0 success over Walthamstow Avenue in the Amateur Cup in the 1948-49 season. Harold Gittins' cartoon on the match in the Evening News was highly complimentary to Bert Dyke, but that it also implied that our playing pitch at Lower Mead was in bad shape.

We accepted the hint. During the close season the field was thoroughly scarified, new material introduced into the soil to obtain porosity, and the bed remade and re-seeded. This operation was both drastic and costly. Further expense has since been incurred on the field, but we are now confident that ground conditions will be much improved in this and subsequent seasons.

And now for a few words about what must be regarded as the most impressive part of our plan for the reasonably early future. This is the erection of a large and, we hope, very handsome building at Lower Mead.

The plans of the proposed structure have been approved by Middlesex County Council and Harrow Urban District Council, but the authority of the Ministry of Education to go ahead with the scheme has not yet been obtained. Consequently, it may be rather longer than we had anticipated before our plans come to fruition.

Our present premises are quite inadequate it we are to achieve our desire to make Lower Mead a social centre with the accent on youth. The new building will be used to a large extent to enable youngsters of the district to come along, not only to improve their football skill, but also - and no less important - their general fitness.

They will receive first-class coaching from a qualified instructor, and they will also enjoy the facilities of a gymnasium. Naturally, we hope that the amenities to be made available will benefit the playing strength of the Wealdstone Football Club in due course.

It is intended that the new building will also afford opportunity for relaxation and recreation. Dances, whist drives, and concerts, and there will also be facilities for billiards, snooker, and table tennis. Another feature will be a pleasant lounge where members can settle down to enjoy refreshment and a chat.

This is indeed a bold experiment and one, which will demand your full support if it is to be achieved. I can assure you, however, that the committee is confident that members and supporters generally will agree that the proposed social centre constitutes a very real need of the community and that it will prove to be a very appropriate way in which to commemorate the club's golden jubilee.

In conclusion, I should like to add a word or two about our even more distant programme of development. The main part of this calls for a reinforced concrete and brickwork structure abutting the car park for almost its full length and comprising a stand to accommodate five or six times as many people as can be seated in our existing stand. It is planned to have larger dressing rooms, together with ample accommodation for training rooms and offices, thus leaving the new hall that I have described above to be used solely for recreational activities.

The full scheme may appear to be very ambitious and one that is likely to prove very difficult to accomplish, it is both of these things. But with the necessary support and encouragement we believe that our plans will be realised.

Peter Rogers
Player late 1940's-1951

I joined Wealdstone as one of 'The Chelsea Boys', Wealdstone having an agreement at the time to be a nursery club for the Stamford Bridge team.

I was playing in a trial game at Stamford Bridge, and Wealdstone officials Harry Luck, Frank Harbud and John Rogers (no relation) and Jim Holt were watching and they asked the Chelsea officials if they could sign-on the inside forward who looked like an Italian Ice Cream salesman, and I became one of the first players to sign, along with Hill, Eddie Smith and Gordon Norman who went on to captain the side.

I played for a few seasons, including playing in the side that beat Colchester 1-0. Edgar Francis and I traveled to the game together by bus as usual. The atmosphere in the ground was terrific - there was a crowd I think around 9,000. The dressing room wasn't really all that different from any other game although I was quite nervous, I was just quietly telling myself that I'd be all right and I'd have a good game, and I wasn't to be frightened of making a mistake.

The early part of the game passed very quickly, but near the end, I remember we were hanging on for grim death against Colchester's pressure and I received the ball around the half way line and I turned toward the stand side and smashed the ball into the High Street to waste a few more seconds! There were no yellow cards or time added on in those days!

When the final whistle blew, Mr. Harrison, the Chairman - a very large man - ran onto the ground he engulfed me saying; "We've done it, Peter".

A great moment.

After the game we went to Wembley Monarchs Ice Hockey and then off dancing, although I think a few of the team went off to Mr. Harrison's pub to celebrate.

I remember we were presented on the stage of the cinema after that win, but we had some great players, Danny Wiltshire should've played for England - I'll never know why he didn't, and there was Charlie Barker, Fred Hayden and 'Ginger' Smith who did sign as a 'pro' with Watford. Edgar Francis was a very influential member of our team - he was one of the best players I had the good fortune to play with. He was certainly one of the best players of our era.

A little later, for the Port Vale game, the team traveled up by train on the Friday, staying overnight in a hotel - I roomed with Danny Wiltshire, and then after breakfast on the day of the game we were taken on a tour of one of the potteries.

After lunch we made our way to the ground and again the dressing room was much as normal, the odd word spoken here and there. I think we were quite confident of our ability and certainly not over awed. There was no 'hype' like you have at today's games.

The game started very evenly until Edgar Francis was injured, and he moved out to the wing as there were no substitutes allowed then, but we still weren't overrun. Every player ran himself into the ground and Danny Wiltshire was great in goal.

One thing I'll never forget was a section of our supporters calling my name and waving from the stand - I waved back - they just wanted us to know how much they appreciated our efforts, and even on the train journey home they kept coming down to talk to us.

In those days we played in front of thousands every week, and it was very rare to get 'stick' from them.

I left the club to play for St. Albans and then after a while I rejoined the club, only to break my knee during a game. I can't remember who we were playing, only that we were kicking to the Cinema End and it was during the first half.

I went forward and played on until half time, and then just after the club sent me off to Harley Street where the damage was diagnosed. The Wealdstone officials all visited me in the London Hospital and then in Banstead when I was transferred there to recuperate.

As an aside, I met my future wife there. She was nursing me, and we've been very happily married ever since.

When I had recovered the club asked me to help out coaching the 'A' side and I was sent on coaching courses before eventually managing and coaching the club for three seasons, finish-

Training on the beach at Brighton

ing runner up to Hendon by one point in the league, and losing to Enfield in the London Senior cup final at Highbury. I think Enfield also beat us in the final of the Middlesex Senior Cup that year as well.

I used to do the coaching on my own; it was mainly fitness work, although the club sometimes hired a gym for 'ball work'. Every Thursday we used to have a meeting in the dressing room after training to discuss the previous Saturday's match.

The players used to hear my views and then I would hear theirs - as Charlie Townsend was in the Army but still a very important member of the club, I used to write to him about the meetings and games.

Sometimes we used to travel to Brighton when we were preparing for the cup games, and to make a change we trained on the beach. We all used to have a Brine Bath, then a meal together and then we'd come home. It was all voluntary and we used to pay our own way. One week one of the lads, John Saunders 'obtained' a removals van so we could all go down in that!

We all climbed in the back and off we went it was great fun although I for one was never sure where the van came from.

After he games we'd all be in the bath together singing - Keep Right On To The End Of The Road and then George Mowle used to throw parties for us.

There was Peter Parfitt - he just loved playing for Wealdstone and he was another reason that the three years I was running the club as manager and coach was the best time I ever spent in football.

It was a wonderful feeling that I can't really explain - just a once in a lifetime memory. I was with Hendon, Marlow, St. Albans, Reading and various other clubs in Cornwall and Sussex but nothing could compare with those years.

Wealdstone Goalkeeper F T Edgehill saves from Leytonstone's Vic Groves in the Amateur Cup

Most of us still keep in touch from those days - maybe we all thought how much we enjoyed those years. That mystical magic, one hears so many people talk about team spirit when a club's having a good run - how long does that last? Our feeling's always undying it will last and last.

The 1950–1951 season was unremarkable in every way, more so when compared to the cup exploits the previous season. A number of players had moved on and this disrupted the side as new players settled in. Indeed after the first match of the season, a defeat away to Barking, the comment from the Harrow Observer was...

...on this showing, Wealdstone have a hard task ahead and there will be plenty of competition for first team places....

In the league, Wealdstone finished in ninth place, the league having been expanded to sixteen clubs with the addition of Cambridge Town and Walton and Hersham. Wealdstone's record was P30 W11 D5 L14 for 27 points and with 52 goals both scored and conceded.

The most notable victory in the season was to come on Boxing Day v Hendon. Having lost 3-1 at Lower Mead on Christmas Day and with a team weakened by a number of injuries in that match, Wealdstone managed to win the return fixture by 5-2.

The FA Cup promised far more than it delivered – having won 3-1 at Hertford Town in the Preliminary Qualifying Round, St Albans who had been beaten in the previous years Cup run were drawn to visit Lower Mead.

This time winning comfortably by 5-1. The FA Amateur Cup saw Wealdstone drawn in the first round to face holders Leytonstone again, losing 3-2 away from home.

The only slight success was to come in the Middlesex Charity Cup, where 'Stones did manage to reach the final before losing 3-2 to Finchley, the final played at Hayes FC.

In among the few bright spots for Wealdstone and the fans were three friendly matches, two played as part of the Festival of Britain celebrations. Wealdstone lost 2-4 to the Watford first team and then secured a 4-1 victory over the RAF, both matches played at Lower Mead.

The third match was a benefit for the long serving trainer Bill Gallagher. The match was played against a Chelsea XI and Wealdstone won 4-1. The benefit fund yielding a total of £141. There was one significant change at Wealdstone during the season. That was, for the first time, the appointment of a Trainer and Coach for the first team in George Milton.

The improvement in players' fitness and tactical awareness was not to show great benefit during the current season but it must have played a part the following year.

The reserves too had a moderate season, finishing seventh in the Athenian League Reserve Section although they did reach the final of the Reserve Challenge Cup, losing 1-0 to Tooting and Mitcham Reserves. The 'A' Team suffered even more. In a season disrupted badly by the weather, Wealdstone in common with a number of other Clubs failed to complete their fixtures.

In a season of rising costs, the AGM announced that the club

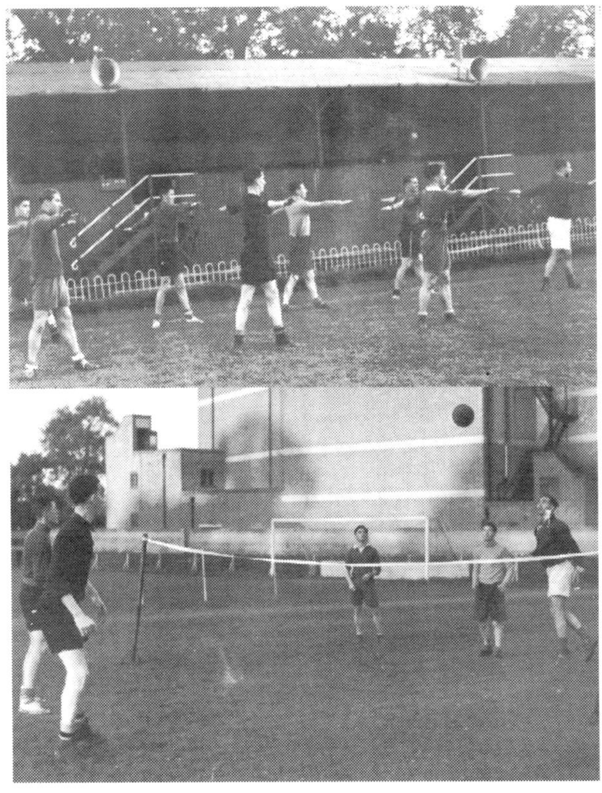

An early training session at Lower Mead

had made a loss of £481, principally because compared with the previous season cup-tie gate receipts were more than £1500 lower. It was noted that a Leather Football which at the start of the season cost £2 5s 0d was now costing £4 10s 0d.

It was decided to increase the admission in common with other Athenian League Clubs from nine pence to one shilling, and members' subscriptions were increased from 15/- to £1, Vice President subscriptions increasing from one guinea to 25/-.

Alan Lawrence
Supporter 1940's and 1950's

The club continued successfully after the war, and the Christmas games home and away, against Golders Green and then when the name changed, Hendon, were always a must.

I well remember the Amateur Cup-tie against Leytonstone when the crowd was over 11,000, then the next time they met the crown was over 13,000! In the early 1950's I started to play regularly for Harrow Town with many former Wealdstone players, Tom Marjoram, Eric Bicknell, Ron Franklin and Bert Dyke. Bert and Ken Baldwin were two of the best players to play for the club at this time.

After completing my National Service in 1956, I decided to try my luck as a player at Lower Mead - there was quite a crowd of us who responded to an advert in the Harrow Observer, and there was no trial match, we just started training early on, run by Edgar Francis. None of the previous seasons Wealdstone players attended although Ken Harrison who had scored in an Amateur Cup Final at Wembley was there with us at the time.

As the season approached, trial matches were held, and I played out of position in one and was then not selected for the next, so I left the club and joined Kodak - shortly after we played a pre-season friendly against Wealdstone and won 4-1.

Many of the Wealdstone players worked at Kodak and quite a few played for the firm before finally retiring - I was lucky enough to play with Charlie Barker and George and Alec Hardie and Gordon Lievans, and we played an inter department 5-a side tournament against a team that included Viv Evans and Charlie Townsend.

Unusually for the start of the 1951–52 season, Wealdstone's pre-season trials were held at the British Rail sports ground in Headstone Lane. This was because of the close season installation of new drains and to allow the newly seeded Lower Mead a little longer to 'bed in'. It also meant that the 'home' season started an additional week later than usual.

As in previous years, a number of new players were trailed. This season these were more from other clubs rather than from local football. A number of these new players were considered good enough to go straight into the Wealdstone first team, most notable, two Polish players were added to the squad, Henryk Mikrut and Henryk Wegrzyk.

The team started well scoring fifteen goals in the first four league games, wins away to Barnet and home to Walton and Hersham both 2-0, and Hitchin and Leyton by 6-0 and 5-2 respectively. It was not until Bromley won at Lower Mead on September 8th that a point was dropped. This was followed by one defeat in the next three months and by Christmas, Wealdstone found themselves in 5th place in the league table with four games in hand on each of the teams above them. Wins in all four would have seen them catch Hendon at the top of the table.

One thing stood out in the early season form. The influence both Mikrut and Wegrzyk on the team.

On the 20th October Wealdstone were at home to Tooting and Mitcham in the Athenian League,

A brilliant start was largely responsible for Wealdstone's 5-1 victory over Tooting and Mitcham before another big crowd at Lower Mead on Saturday.

Almost up to the kick off there was some doubt as to whether Mikrut would be fit to play and Palmer was standing by as a substitute, but the Polish centre forward quickly demonstrated his fitness by scoring a splendid hat trick, his first for the club after only fourteen minutes. McGee returned to the Wealdstone side in place of Ward and there was another sailor newcomer to the side in Ferris who took Garden's place at inside-left.

Winning the toss, Wealdstone started with a sparkle that matched the sunny autumnal afternoon. Beautifully precise forward movements soon had the Tooting defence at sea and goals came quickly. White's persistence brought the first, refusing to give in, in a tangled encounter with the Tooting left back, Thomson, he eventually got clear to send over a high dropping centre which Benningfield tapped to Mikrut who easily scored.

The Wealdstone pressure continued and after a delightful movement between Wegrzyk and white had ended with Thomson heading off the line from Mikrut, the same two players combined again to provide the centre forward with his second goal.

Mikrut completed his hat trick with a great opportunists goal. As Selwood was shepherding a through pass by Norman towards the goal line Mikrut made a sudden burst and hooked the ball off his toe. It crashed past the astonished Hall in goal, giving him no chance to save.

This for was too good to be true and gradually Tooting came more into the picture. Their wingers, Webb and Bennett who was given too much scope by Norman's wanderings were dangerous, but a number of clever movements failed because of a mixture of woefully weak shooting and Wiltshire's alertness in goal.

Tooting looked the better side in the opening stages of the second half and got a goal when a corner kick was headed into the net by Bennett. For a time they seemed likely to narrow the margin still more, but eventually Wealdstone came right back into their own and Mikrut scored a fourth goal, which was followed by one from Ferris.

With the possible exception of Norman who wandered too much, and Benningfield, all the home players touched their best form. Wegrzyk was the inspiring genius of a clever forward line and put in the two best shots of the match.

Wastell often earned applause for his terrier-like tackling and Edmonds whilst less obtrusive maintained his remarkable record of not allowing an opposing centre forward to score this season.

Wealdstone; D Wiltshire, T McGhee, C Barker, G Norman, C Edmonds, J Wastell, P White, H Wegrzyk, H Mikrut, R Ferris, A Benningfield.

A slight hiccup in form around Christmas saw both games over the holiday with league leaders Hendon drawn, and following a win at Hayes, Wealdstone drew the return fixture with Tooting and Mitcham. That fixture, played on 12th January was the turning point in that it saw the last point Wealdstone were to drop in the league all season, their remaining thirteen games resulting in wins.

The Hayes match was Charlie Barker's last game for the club. Returning from injury he had played at centre forward and had scored, but while injured, Wealdstone had signed Ron Gadsden who had made the left back spot his own.

Charles Albert Barker

Born in January 1915 first played football during his schooldays. He was captain of Alperton School and also of London Boys against the South Of England.

His senior football career started at Hounslow Grove in the Hounslow League later joining Shahinian FC. A match against Wealdstone in the Middlesex Senior Charity Cup resulted in Charlie having a trial at the start of the 1938–1939 season. Joining Wealdstone, he first played in the reserves, initially playing in the first team at outside left before reverting to full back.

He enlisted with the Royal Engineers in July 1940, serving overseas and taking part in the D-Day landings, playing football whenever the opportunity arose, be it at Wealdstone, for the Army or as a guest player for Norwich City.

He was able to skipper Wealdstone in the Red Cross Cup Final at Wembley in 1942, when 'Stones became the first amateur side to play at and win at the famous stadium. He was described as a brilliant full back, though he gained few representative honours, his all round play was backed by a very powerful shot.

He was the club's penalty taker and in a 14 year career with the club, he missed only four out of 140 taken. In total in his career he scored 136 for Wealdstone, 9 for St Albans and 5 for Edgware Town to achieve the 150 mark. He was selected for an England Trial and eventually did achieve selection for the County and the Athenian League teams.

There was to be some success in the cups. A good run in the FA Cup, resulted in 'Stones eventually losing in the final qualifying round away to Tonbridge, 2-0.

The Amateur Cup saw a home defeat to Corinthian Casuals the following week, but the London Senior Cup saw Wealdstone reach the final for the second time.

Winning 3–0 at Bromley in the first round, 'Stones then won 1–0 at Dagenham. Another 1–0 win at home to Southall saw 'Stones drawn to face Hounslow Town in the semi-final to be played at the home of Queens Park Rangers, Loftus Road. In front of an excellent crowd of over 8000, Wealdstone emerged victorious by 2-1, Mikrut and Bennett scoring 'Stones goals and securing a place in the Final against Finchley, to be played at Highbury.

In the league, Wealdstone's run of wins did not see them break away at the top of the table, in fact it was not until a 2-1 win over Southall on Easter Monday, April 14th did Wealdstone head the table (on goal difference) for the first time.

It was a neck and neck tussle with Hendon throughout the season, and it was not until the last game, when Hayes visited Lower Mead that the title was decided. Wealdstone were top on goal difference, Hendon having completed their fixtures. One point would guarantee the Championship, and even a 1-0 defeat would see 'Stones as Champions, but any other defeat would see the title slip away.

Giving a brilliant display both in attack and defence, Wealdstone made certain of the Athenian League Championship by beating Hayes by 6-2 on Saturday. From the moment Mikrut kicked off, after Brown, the Hayes International full back had beaten Norman in the toss, the home players showed irresistible form and not a trace of nerves.

They immediately clicked into gear like a well-oiled machine and the Hayes defence was overrun time and time again. Mikrut, who revelled in the heavy ground conditions gave them the lead with a grand header from an accurate centre by Bennett after only five minutes play, and Hayes were never again in the game during the first half. Wegrzyk was in particularly brilliant form and went close with several flashing drives and skilful headers before he got the goal he deserved.

This directly followed a goal kick by Wiltshire, Mikrut and Nuth, the Hayes centre half rose together for the ball but missed and Wegrzyk dashed through to take possession. Taking the ball in his stride, he streaked towards the goal and when within striking distance, sent in a shot which Culver had no hope of saving.

Wealdstone became even more inspired and goals by each of the wingers, Bennett and White made the score 4-0 by the interval. Had this score been doubled there could have been no complaints, so superior were Wealdstone in speed, craft and shooting ability.

Any possibility of a Hayes recovery was killed off soon after half time. Bennett putting the seal to a splendid display by completing his hat trick to make the score 6-0. Only then did Wealdstone relax their tremendous effort and allow Hayes more of the game.

It was a proud moment for Norman, the young Wealdstone captain, and when the final whistle blew the crowd gave the team a rousing reception.

It was Wealdstone's 23rd victory in 30 games during which they were only beaten three times, and scored 81 goals conceding 29.

Wealdstone had won the Championship with a record number of points, 50 from a possible maximum of 60. A number of the crowd of over 6000 stayed on to watch the presentations after the game in the clubhouse.

Club Chairman H H Harrison presented each player with a combined Tea and Coffee Pot. He told the players that he and been so confident he had gone out and bought the gifts well in advance of the match. Each player was also presented with a Tankard, these the gift of an anonymous spectator. The following Monday the team were the guests of the Granada Cinema, each being invited onto the stage and announced to the audience in turn. The exceptions R Gadsden and F Bennett, who the previous evening had flown to Hong Kong as part of the Athenian League team.

There was one match still to play, however. The following Saturday, Wealdstone were to play Finchley in the final of the London Senior Cup. There was certain to be excellent support as at the beginning of the week over twenty coaches had been booked to ferry supporters to the match. It was to be an anticlimax, Finchley winning the match by 1-0 in front of 11,919 spectators, Wealdstone failing to find the form that had seen them secure the Championship seven days earlier.

Gordon Norman
Player 1948-52

I was very lucky when I was at Wealdstone. There were some great fixtures and great memories.

In 1948-49 we played against Leytonstone in the Amateur Cup. I didn't play in the first match as I was playing in a representative match for the County. I played in the replay. It was tremen-

Pictured immediately after the game, The Athenian League Champions 1951 – 52, Wealdstone FC Back; FA Bennett, R F Gadsden, E T Ward (did not play in final match), H Wegrzyk, H Mikrut, T McGhee, C A P Edmonds. Front; P C J White, J Wastell, G Norman, D Wiltshire, J Wall

dous. A great game. Everyone lifted their performance for matches like that. It was great to play in front of over 14,000 people.

The following season we had the FA Cup run. We beat Edgware away - the match was televised. We ran and ran for 90 minutes. At the end of the game I sat in the dressing room for a long time. I was absolutely shattered. Again the crowd was superb really shouting and rallying the team. It really gave everyone a lift.

Then we played Colchester. A fast battle on a muddy pitch but we won that as well. It was a shame that when we went to Port vale in the next round Edgar Francis got injured. They were unbeaten at home and with Edgar a passenger we only lost 1-0. Danny Wiltshire in goal was outstanding and we defended stoically but Cliff pinchbeck scored. Ronnie Allan the England international played for Port Vale that day.

We were just an Amateur team and they were professionals but we played well in front of a train load of our supporters.

Even as Amateurs we got 'boot money'. I suppose it was not really allowed but we got £4 to £6 per game, plus expenses.

In 1951 we won the Athenian League Championship. Hendon and Wealdstone had broken away at the top of the table. I think we won the last 13 games home and away to win the title! There were some great players in that side too. The two Poles Wegrzyk and Mikrut and Phil White who went off to Leyton Orient. He had a long career there.

Tommy McGhee was one of the fullbacks at the time. He was in the navy and used to travel up from Portsmouth to play. He eventually signed for Portsmouth.

There were Charlie Edmunds and Charlie Barker too – he got an International Trial at 38 years old! Johnnie Wall and Frank Bennett also played a big part in that team. I think we won the title with a big win over Hayes, 5 or 6–2.

The crowds were astounding. A 4,000 crowd was just run of the mill in those days – if it was a good game in the league you'd expect 6,000 at least.

They were three very good seasons but then I went to play for my works side. I did return a few seasons later but we weren't as successful. They are still some good memories though.

Alan Couch
Supporter and Club Official since the mid 1940's

I can still remember the first match I ever saw al Lower Mead, in March 1946, when Wealdstone drew 3–3 with Finchley in an Athenian League match, and then in 1948 Wealdstone signed Eddie Smith as an amateur, on loan from Chelsea.

I recall his first two matches for the 'Stones. His first was at Redhill in the league where Wealdstone won 4–0 and he had scored twice. The following Saturday he made his 'home debut' against Barnet and he scored six times in a 7–1 victory!

Later, in March 1949, I was one of the 13,504 crowd that saw Wealdstone lose by four goals to nil against Leytonstone in an FA Amateur Cup replay – two of our opponents goals scored by Trevor Bailey, an England and Essex cricketer, later to become a famous Test Match commentator.

Other memories around this time were the defeat of Colchester United (at the time, famous cup 'Giant Killers') in the 4th Qualifying round of the FA Cup, in November 1949. Wealdstone won 1-0 and this still remains as one of the greatest performances by the club ever. It's difficult to compare the amateur days with the modern professional set-up, but to me season 1951–1952 was the highlight of the amateur days.

The Wealdstone side at that time included the two Polish amateur internationals, Henryk Mikrut and Henryk Wegrzyk and together with Phil White, a speedy winger who had the beating of most full backs, they won the Athenian League title for the first and only time. They'd scored most of the seasons goals between them and it was great to see them in action. It was a truly unforgettable season.

The reserves too had done well, finishing as worthy runner up to Bromley in the Athenian League Reserve Section. They had been challenging at the top of the table for most of the season.

They did gain a little more satisfaction by beating the Champions at Lower Mead in their last league game.

Jack Rollin
Former Player, Author, Book Compiler and Vice president of Aldershot Town FC

I had the most modest of careers at Wealdstone, but the club did play a significant role in my connection with football. The first match I ever saw was at Wealdstone, on Christmas Day 1942 against Golders Green, it was the year I returned from evacuation in Devon. I remember the outstanding player was Golders Green's outside-right Roy Stroud but my favourite was Len Dolding who later played for Chelsea and died so tragically at an early age.

The first senior club ever to invite me to play was Wealdstone, ten years later in the 1951-52 season, while I was stationed at RAF Fighter Command HQ at Bentley Priory, Stanmore. We had a right back on the camp who played for the reserves, his name escapes me now, but left-winger Vince Hopkins an Irish lad was the one who got me interested in the club.

Vince was a real will-o-the-wisp, so small he could sleep in a telephone box – and did! We often left him in the billet taking most of the springs from his bed and leaving him in it with the covers on, undetected. Nobody really knew what he did in the RAF.

Wealdstone were very good to him, and got him a flat and a job when he was released from the services, I followed his career for a time and he moved to Finchley, I believe.

One game I remember at Lower Mead as a spectator was during the war. 'Stones were playing a friendly against a team called The Thrusters, I believe.

Wealdstone whacked them into double figures and the visiting goalkeeper was so unnerved, he ran out of the ground at the final whistle!

A celebration Dinner and Dance was held at the Tithe Farm Hotel in South Harrow. The club were also presented with a congratulatory resolution from Harrow Council, embossed on velum. It read;

The Council, on behalf of the residents of the district as a whole, hereby places on record its pleasure, and extends its cordial congratulations to the Wealdstone Football Club, upon the club's outstanding achievement in winning the

Championship of the Athenian League for the 1951–1952 football season.

The Council pays tribute to the club's magnificent team spirit, and to the splendid support and encouragement given by the President, Vice-Presidents, Chairman, Officials and Supporters of the club, which undoubtedly have contributed largely to the club's success.

It was an unusual resolution to be placed on record but it was agreed unanimously by the Council. The certificate was presented at a public meeting.

Wealdstone had also reached the final of the Middlesex Charity Cup to face Southall, but due to fixture congestion this match was held over to the start of the following season.

The 'A' team had suffered again, with their pitch being unplayable for long periods and this caused the club to resign from the Harrow Wembley and District League. It was not to be the end of the team however as the club intended to run them as a Strollers XI the following year.

As always looking to progress, it was announced at the AGM that the club would compete in the new London Challenge Cup in the following season, this competition also featuring the professional London sides and it was hoped that this would again be successful for the club.

The first teams overall record for the past season was P46, W35, D4, L7 scoring 114 goals with only 43 conceded and joint top scorers were Henryk Mikrut and Henryk Wegrzyk, both with 27 goals.

Lionel Brill
Supporter 1950's and 60's

I haven't attended many recent matches. Coin, marriage and growing family etc, but Wealdstone's is the first result I look for on a Sunday, even now, and of course Ron and Frank Wilson keep me up to date.

I guess I saw my first match immediately after the War when the Athenian League resumed. I can remember the centre forward – the local milkman, Gilbert Gaze and the 'No 10' was a distant relative, named Bert Dyke.

At that time the Christmas matches were always big games – the local derbies against Hendon, which I seem to recall we lost more often than not, and of course winning the Athenian League in 1951-52.

One match that does stand out was against a Nigerian Team who played in bare feet, I don't recall the date or result.......

My favourite player must be Henryk Wegrzyk who scored some really outstanding goals, he could really strike a ball. I can still recall one goal he scored at Ilford against Walthamstow Avenue in the Amateur Cup, a second replay. Their goalkeeper, Gerula?, another Polish player, was still diving when the ball passed him coming back out of the net. (Or so it seemed!)

The new season started with victories for both the first team and reserves over Cambridge Town, the first XI winning 4–1 away, having missed two first half penalties and the reserves winning 5–0 at home. Both matches had in fact seen Wealdstone leading by only 1-0 at half time.

There were some new players on show, A Comben and L Hussey coming into the first team, replacing Gordon Norman who had left to join his works team, Briggs Sports and J Wall who had also moved on.

The following Wednesday saw Wealdstone face the Athenian League in the traditional Champions v The Rest fixture, winning 2–0, as reported in the Harrow Observer;

Wealdstone set the seal on their record-breaking season by handsomely defeating the Rest of the League after a splendid game at Lower Mead on Wednesday. From start to finish they gave a heart-warming display, strong in every department and with every man really fit they directed the play for about three quarters of the game with a neat balance of individual skill and polished team work.

Hussey and Comben quickly established themselves as favourites with the crowd, and to Hussey fell the distinction of scoring both goals, in the second half. The first was made by White, deputising for Mikrut who was off the field after a collision with Topp. He collected a loose ball and made ground rapidly before slipping it forward to Hussey who from close range beat Bennett with an unstoppable shot.

From an almost identical position, Hussey scored again right on time following a dazzling movement between Hussey Comben and Wegrzyk. Wealdstone came close to scoring in the first half when Comben forced his way through The Rest defence to send in a fine shot that Bennett saved brilliantly. Several headers by Mikrut also went close.

Wealdstone's supremacy was completely established in the second half, and after their opening goal they almost cantered to victory. McGhee and Gadsden always played with a speed and resource, which combined with hard tackling, held up almost every attack and Edmonds held the lively Stroud well. In Wastell and Comben, Wealdstone must have two of the most tenacious and constructive wing halves in amateur football.

Wealdstone; D Wiltshire, T McGhee, R Gadsden, A Comben, C Edmonds, J Wastell, P White, H Wegrzyk, H Mikrut, L Hussey, F Bennett.

The Rest; E Bennett (Southall), S Hudson (Hayes), E Hardy (Southall), L Topp (Hendon), K Yenson (Leyton), A Crook (Walton and Hersham), R Evans (Hendon), J Sorenson (Sutton United), R Stroud (Hendon), A Ault (Finchley), E Johnson (Walton and Hersham).

The following Saturday, the ease of these first fixtures of the season was soon forgotten as Finchley were the visitors to Lower Mead.

Playing in front of over 5,500 fans, Finchley defended stoically from the start, the supporters becoming more and more disgruntled as the match progressed, and more so when they took the lead from a breakaway.

Former Wealdstone centre forward Hugh Dyke ran through the 'Stones defence and passed the ball to England International and Tottenham Hotspur's outside left, Robb, who scored from close range.

In the second half, Wealdstone forced Finchley into greater defensive exploits, but with 'Stones pushing forward more room was left for the Finchley forwards and Head scored their second goal.

Wealdstone however continued to press and Wegrzyk reduced

the arrears midway through the second half, Bennett then scoring an equaliser much to the relief of players and fans alike.

The Harrow Observer commented that Wealdstone would find themselves up against many tough and defensive opponents during the coming season, but that they had showed that they had great courage and stamina as well as ability and skill.

The early season cup-ties also saw Wealdstone in winning form. Early in October a 4-0 victory away to Windsor and Eton of the Metropolitan League saw 'Stones make early progress in the FA Cup, but they were to lose 1-0 against local rivals Hendon in the next round.

'Stones also won 3-1 at Crystal Palace against a strong professional side in the London Challenge Cup, only to lose in the second round by the same score at Brentford.

It certainly was to be a hard season overall, but Wealdstone had started well in the league. Their first defeat came in October, despite this they steadily climbed the table, by December taking over at the top of the Athenian League after an excellent home victory over Redhill by 4-1. This completed a double for the season and was more satisfying than usual as Redhill were somewhat a 'bogey' team having won in both previous visits to Lower Mead.

The Christmas fixtures were nicely set up, both Hendon and Wealdstone challenging at the top of the table. On Christmas day the largest league crowd of the season at Lower Mead saw 'Stones run out winners by 2-0. Some 7,300 people were in the ground and it was noted that a number of enquiries had been received from women supporters during the game eager to know the score!

Wealdstone and Hendon continued to lead the league table, into the new year but in February, all eyes turned again to the Amateur Cup, Wealdstone securing an excellent 0-0 draw away to Walthamstow Avenue, who returned to Lower Mead two weeks later for the replay.

With a difficult away tie at Southall awaiting the winners, Wealdstone were successful in front of a crowd of 9,220 Henryk Mikrut scoring in the 56th minute. An 'all Polish' affair as Wegrzyk had collected the ball from distance, and shot hard, only for S Gerula, another Pole in the Walthamstow goal to parry the ball, and Mikrut ran in to score.

Walthamstow were to get their revenge a few weeks later however, in the semi-final of the London Senior Cup, played at Hendon's Claremont Road ground, while Hendon were away to Enfield almost certainly securing the Athenian League title.

A dramatic breakaway goal in the last few seconds at the Claremont Road ground gave them a 2–1 victory over Wealdstone and entry into the final of the London Senior Cup.

The goal was a bitter blow from which Wealdstone, who for most of the second replay had looked the better side, had no chance to recover. Extra time had seemed inevitable when Wastell was dispossessed in midfield; the ball was flashed right into the Wealdstone half and whipped into the centre by Lewis.

The Wealdstone defenders, for the second time were caught unawares and before they had time to recover Lucas had crashed the ball past the helpless Wiltshire.

This unfortunately ended Wealdstone's last hope of winning a major honour this season – Hendon's 4–2 victory at Enfield virtually assuring them of the Athenian League championship.

Yet the result could have been so different. Undeterred by losing the toss both for choice of colours and choice of ends, Wealdstone played like Champions, sound in defence and rapid and skilful in attack. Only the alert anticipation of Gerula prevented them from obtaining a comfortable early lead, but after many good efforts they went ahead with the best goal of the match.

Wegrzyk and White combined well in midfield and when the winger tapped the ball back inside, Comben dashed through to take it. He made ground rapidly before putting over a perfect centre, which Bennett banged into the net with a first time shot.

With Wastell and Comben dominating the midfield play and Lewis again held by Edmonds. Wealdstone seemed to have the goal well under control when misfortune hit them hard. Gadsden who had been playing splendidly, miss-kicked a spinning ball to put Fielder away. Caught on the turn, the Wealdstone defenders were unable to cover his centre and Lewis hooked the ball into the net from close range. On the balance of play the Avenue were more than fortunate to be on terms.

The second half opened on a thrilling note when Wealdstone broke away from a goalmouth melee in which Avenue appealed unsuccessfully for a penalty for handling against Gadsden.

The Avenue defence was outwitted and Ayres was left with the task of putting the ball into an empty goal. He placed the ball wide and Wealdstone never had as good a chance again though on another occasion Ayres broke through, a defender brought him down as he was about to shoot but the referee turned a deaf ear to Wealdstone's appeals for a penalty.

Avenue too, had their chance when Wiltshire could only deflect a shot from Lewis to Camis, who obligingly hit him with the return shot.

Wealdstone; D Wiltshire, F Haydon, R Gadsden, A Comben, C Edmonds, J Wastell, P White, H Wegrzyk, R Ayres, H Mikrut, F Bennett.

Walthamstow Avenue; S Gerula, D Young, D McLelland, E Harper, D Saunders, G Rayner, G Fielder, G Lucas, J Lewis, D Hall, K Camis.

The Hendon result did seal the Athenian League Championship for them, Wealdstone finishing the season as worthy runner up after a 4–2 victory at Hayes and then a third defeat of the season to Southall, (who after the Amateur Cup win had also beaten Wealdstone in the final of the Middlesex Challenge Cup) by three goals to two.

There was better news from Lower Mead, where Wealdstone Reserves had sealed the Athenian League Reserve Section Challenge Cup with a home win, 1-0 over Sutton United, Doak scoring with a half lob-shot. The victorious team was

P Prunty, P Rogers, A Nairn, J Gaughan, E Francis, P Bloxham, P Doak, F Williams, W Roberts, T Morris, V Hopkins.

The reserves also finished their league season in similar style to the first team, eventually finishing in fifth place, one point behind Leyton in third, but ten and thirteen points respectively behind Tooting and the Champions, Finchley.

At the AGM, the club reported that the first team had a final record of P 48 W 27 D 8 L 13 scoring 91 goals with 59 conceded, and for the second successive year, Wegrzyk and Mikrut were joint top scorers, this time with 18 goals each. The reserves had played 33 matches, winning 18 and losing ten, scoring 79 goals in total.

The club had made a loss of £520 on the year. There had been a lot of work done in the ground. The drainage, reseeding the pitch, the 'cinema end' terracing and cover had both been improved and these had cost the club over £1200 during the season.

An additional entertainment tax of £100 had also been levied and the club had received £700 less from the Football Association as less progress had been made in the cups. Otherwise the weather had meant that three home matches had been played on rainy afternoons and this had substantially reduced the gate on these occasions.

There was some disquiet from the members over the signing and resigning of players. The members felt that the newspaper should be used as a means of publicising new signings. The club replied that this was not possible. Players could sign for any number of clubs as Amateurs and there was little way of knowing if they would really join the club until they appeared in a match.

It was felt that announcing signings could alert other Clubs who may also be interested in a particular player. This had in fact happened the previous season, when a player was expected for a match only to play elsewhere.

The question had been raised by a member, concerned at rumours that a number of the better Wealdstone players had left the club. The answers on the evening were a little vague, the club President C E Brady said that all bar one of last season's side had re-signed, while Secretary, 'Chippy' Luck said that he felt the majority had re-signed. As it turned out on 15th of August, neither was correct.

Twenty newly signed players made their debut before a crowd of close on a thousand spectators in public trial match at Lower Mead on Saturday.

While it is difficult to assess from one trial game whether a player will prove a valuable acquisition, on Saturday's showing, Wealdstone can claim to have captured one or two useful players, while a number of the others may well reach first team standard with the right coaching.

Probably not the positive outlook that Wealdstone fans and the club would have preferred but there were a number of players who were to figure in the first team during the coming season, the most notable being Ken Bodfish, an outside right who the previous season had played against Wealdstone in the Amateur Cup, for Moor Green, and Cyril May a sound left half from the Queens Park Rangers 'A' Team.

Cyril 'Trigger' May
Player 1953

I suppose one of the best memories was that day at Arsenal – we had a good side, Peter Rogers, Ken Bodfish. Arthur Littlejohn – he was a hard player, he didn't mess around, but playing in front of 8000 people and at Highbury – amazing!

Mr Harrison called me in – he often always used to – just to ask me what was going to happen. All I could tell him was that it would be '4 all' at half time and if we couldn't manage that, at least we'd all kick the same way.

George Milton was the same. His wife and son used to come along as well, she told me once that George thought the world of me – he tried to make me stay for another year as an amateur because he thought I'd get capped, but I wasn't sure. I had friends at QPR – scouts had come to see me from Brentford and Tottenham as well. Looking back, I think he was probably right.

There was Phil White too – he was a great player – they used to call him Stanley Matthews because he could turn you on a sixpence. He smoked like a trooper as well, and he loved the pictures. He'd go in the afternoon and in the evening!

There was one day we played at Walthamstow, I think it was the Challenge Cup – they had 10 internationals in their side. My firm, where I was working wouldn't let me off to get to the game.

Anyway, I was really looking forward to the game and I didn't know what I could do. Then there was a phone call and I was called into the office. It was a call from the club and somehow they'd arranged that I could have the time off to play, but I didn't have my boots or anything.

I still didn't know how I was going to get to the game though, then Mr Harrison turned up to collect me in his Rolls Royce and he took me to get my boots on the way! Took me to The Plough in Kenton – he owned it – he got me some lunch and then he took me to the ground. Imagine the ribbing I got from the players when I turned up in the Chairman's Rolls!.

Fred Haydon couldn't believe his eyes, I can hear him now "What's going on then, Trig? How do you get special treatment?"

Its great to look back, Christmas morning against Hendon we played in front of 10,000 – it was like a small war! We won 4-2 on Christmas morning and then lost 2–0 away on Boxing Day. I admired their player, Laurie Tott, at the time. A right half and international, what a great player he was. We always had a fair old tussle.

A new reserve goalkeeper also joined from the trial, J Muller and another local player W Millard also signed. Neither of these youngsters had previously played at this level. T O'Connor signed from Bushey and Oxhey FC.

For the first league match the following week, against Southall, there was a very new look to the Wealdstone Team,

D Wiltshire, T McGhee, A Nairn, A Payne, A Littlejohn, E Francis, K Bodfish, T O'Connor, W Roberts, L Hussey, V Hopkins.

Only two of the previous seasons first team had dropped to the reserves, while three made the step up. The reserve team also featured five new players from the trials.

So it was to be for the new season. One exception however was Henryk Mikrut who had left the club to join his local side, Epsom, but he returned at the start of September!

The second match of the season was a benefit match. Wealdstone hosted Slough Town in the Printers Charity Benefit Cup. Proceeds from this match were to go to the Lloyd

Memorial (Caxton) home for Printing and Allied Trades. Admission was one shilling to the ground, with Stand Admission one shilling and three pence extra.

The effort was designed to help liquidate a debt of £28,000, which had arisen through the rebuilding of the Home on two occasions. It was to be a greater benefit than first thought, as the match ended in a draw and there was a replay held at Slough's ground at the end of the season!

'Stones started better than expected, their defeat against Southall on the opening day being their only one early in the season. In October, Wealdstone were to face Southall again in an FA Cup-tie at Lower Mead.

Clinging rather desperately to a lead they had thoroughly earned in the first half, Wealdstone beat Southall by two goals to one before a big crowd at Lower Mead on Saturday.

The powerful Southall side gave a courageous display after losing their inside right, Frost, just before the interval. Fighting back from a 2-0 deficit they scored through their International recruit, Cutbush and in the closing spell made nearly all the running.

Yet they were lucky to have the chance to get so near to saving the game. Playing storming and at times brilliant football in the first half, Wealdstone completely outplayed their bigger opponents and a 4-0 lead at half time would scarcely have flattered them.

Bennett, the England goalkeeper can seldom have had a more hair-raising half. Hopping desperately from side to side of his goal, he rarely made clean contact with the ball, and was twice hopelessly beaten by shots that hit the goalposts.

At other times the ball was blocked by defenders whilst he was out of position and on one occasion a Wealdstone forward obliged by getting in the way of a certain goal. During this period Wealdstone played some brilliant football, Hussey repeatedly opening up the defence with shrewd passes and Hopkins driving Harlow into panic clearances.

Wealdstone took the lead after seven minutes play, when Bodfish had already missed two possible chances. Securing the ball after a clearance by McGhee, Hussey sent in a terrific surprise shot from 30 yards and Bennett did not even attempt a save as the ball entered the net from the underside of the crossbar. Soon afterwards, Rogers, who unfortunately did not strike up the understanding with Bodfish that he had had with Millard previously, was unlucky to see a good shot strike the angle of crossbar and post.

Desperately clearing a succession of dangerous goalmouth incidents Southall were eventually forced into conceding a penalty from which Hussey easily scored and Southall's plight seemed helpless when just before the interval Frost left the field with an injured leg after a tussle with Wiltshire.

The second half was a different story as Wealdstone tired badly, having taken too much out of themselves in the first half. Southall's ten men rose gallantly to the occasion and, as so often happens, played better than they had with a full team. Cutbush's goal came when Wealdstone laid the offside trap once too often and he eluded it to beat Wiltshire with a low cross drive. He remained the visitors most dangerous forward with parker well subdued by Littlejohn and Reynolds, though given too much rope at times seldom getting the better of McGhee.

Wealdstone could barely keep their feet at the end, but held out for a victory earned much earlier on. It was revenge for a reverse by the same margin on the first day of the season, Wealdstone's only one so far.

Wealdstone; D Wiltshire, T McGhee, F Haydon, A Payne, T

E Bennett, Southall and England Goalkeeper gathers the ball in the cup-tie. P Rogers, Wealdstone inside-right, is held off by R Sloane, the Southall right back. J Harlow of Southall also stands guard, whilst L Hussey, Wealdstone inside-left, is seen running up to help. H Mikrut is obscured by Sloane.

Littlejohn, C May, K Bodfish, P Rogers, H Mikrut, L Hussey, V Hopkins.

The season was progressing far better than anyone at Wealdstone had hoped at home, with less success away from Lower Mead, but a lack of strength in depth was eventually to take toll on the first team results.

It was a time of change for football as a whole. Having up until this time played midweek matches early in the season and with early kick off's due to fading light, the introduction of floodlights had allowed late evening matches to be staged.

At amateur level there were of course no lights at this stage, but Wealdstone had entered the London Challenge Cup, and this season they were to face Arsenal at Highbury on Monday 2nd November 1953, under floodlights. This was the first match to involve Wealdstone, played under floodlights.

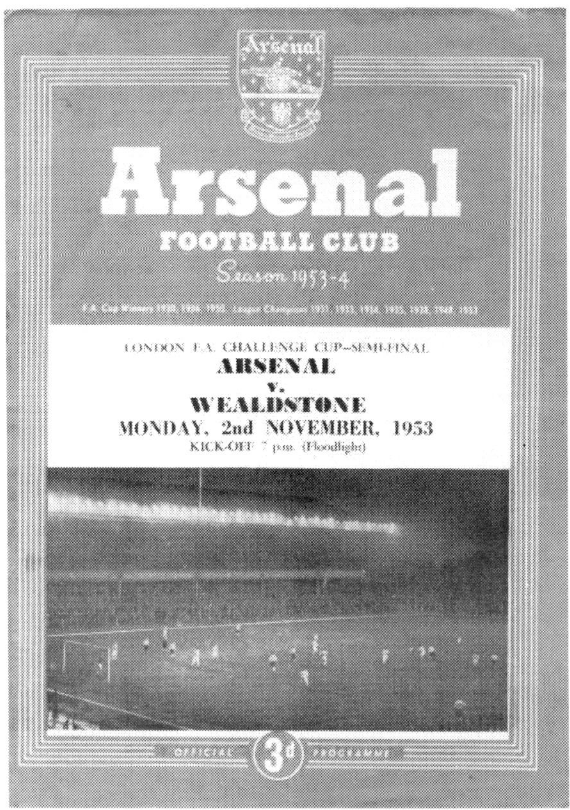

It was one of the first 'starts' for the new goalkeeper, J Muller who was to retain his place for the rest of the season. 'Stones lost the match by four goals to one, Hopkins scoring the Wealdstone goal from a penalty. Arsenal had played a strong side, captained by L Smith, the England left back.

An injury crisis was slowly robbing Wealdstone of their first team and the best of its reserves. Results soon began to suffer as a result. On 19th December, the first round of the Amateur Cup saw Hendon visit Lower Mead.

The match finished in a 3–3 draw but Wealdstone had played with four injured forwards watching from the stand and defenders E Bicknell and A Nairn pressed into action up front. The next two league games were also the usual Christmas fixtures between the two clubs and the cup replay was to take place on January 2nd.

Suffice to say this was not a successful period for the club.

By April, the season had completely fallen apart, Wealdstone were due to play at Walton and Hersham before leaving on an Easter Tour to Cornwall, seeking their first point away from home since a draw at Sutton in the second league match of the season.

It had become a true relegation battle as Wealdstone had slipped into the bottom three in the table in February and remained firmly entrenched. The tour did at least provide some relief from the rigours of the Athenian League.

Wealdstone opened their Easter Tour with a fine 8–3 victory over Falmouth Town on Good Friday, but on Saturday were beaten 3–0 after a good game with Truro City.

The Friday match was marred by the fact that K Bodfish, who had given a brilliant display at outside right, broke his wrist when falling after completing his hat trick.

Although losing the toss and kicking against the wind, Wealdstone were soon playing scintillating football and were two goals up within ten minutes of the start. Trehearne being the scorer on both occasions, though the second was deflected by a defender.

Wealdstone continued to attack and after Kenny had broken away to score his first goal for the Senior side, Bodfish made the half time score 4–0 with a clever overhead hook shot from a corner.

Starting the second half in the same bright manner, Wealdstone had taken the score to 6–0 and Kenny had completed his hat trick before Allen replied with Falmouth's first goal.

A good pass from Franklin led to the second goal from Bodfish and then came his last goal and unfortunate mishap. In the last three minutes, Falmouth scored twice to make the score line a fairer reflection of a game that was always interesting.

Wealdstone; J Muller, P J Rogers, E Francis, A Payne, G Wilkinson, R Franklin, K Bodfish, T O'Connor, G Kenny, S Trehearne, R Stewart.

For the match with Truro, Wealdstone brought in J Warrick at left back and made him captain for the day. This was to mark the fact that he had previously played for St Austell and had come to Wealdstone from Cornwall. He responded with his best display for the club so far. The only other change was that E Bicknell replaced K Bodfish.

Wealdstone again gave a good exhibition of fast, first time passing but failed in front of goal and by half time Truro had a two goal lead.

Wealdstone continued to play attractively in the second half but still could not score, and although the score line flattered them, Truro deserved their win.

The Wealdstone party of 14 players and six Officials left Harrow by Coach on Thursday and after dinner at Salisbury went on to Exeter where the night was spent. On Saturday evening all were the guests of the Truro club at a dance, and on Sunday morning the players played golf at Falmouth. In the afternoon there was a launch trip down the River Fal. The return journey on Monday was made via Salisbury and Bagshot.

Returning home things were little better in the league. A match

A packed terrace at Lower Mead in January 1954 for the visit of Barnet

against Hayes saw the return of McGhee, Mikrut and Payne to allow Wealdstone to field their strongest side for a number of months.

After a bright start it became apparent that these returning players were not fully fit – Mikrut in particular was noted to be at no more than half pace.

However, on a pitch that had a lot of surface water, Wealdstone took a three goal lead in thirteen minutes, only to later concede four goals and to equalise at 4–4 from a hotly disputed goal minutes from the end.

Finishing in 12th place out of 14 was the honour bestowed on both the first team and the reserves, the first team above Barnet and Enfield and the reserves above Sutton and Redhill. The league records too were similar, the first team having played 26 W 8 D 4 L 14, scoring 51 goals and conceding 60 while the reserves amassed 8 wins, D 3 L 15, scoring 56 goals and conceding 71.

There was a little better news off the field, when on 16th July, Wealdstone FC were proud to have their new Pavilion opened by Mr Doug Insole, Captain of Essex County Cricket Club.

He was accompanied by Mr T E Bailey, the England and Essex all rounder who three seasons previously had played against the 'Stones in the Amateur Cup for the victorious Corinthian Casuals. Mr J Bailey the Essex fast bowler was present.

The new pavilion comprised an excellent Dance Hall and Bar, a Billiard Room with two full size tables, a Board Room and Cloak Rooms.

A few weeks later saw the club hold the Annual General Meeting.

This for the first time was held in its own Clubhouse, and this in turn led to an extremely harmonious atmosphere from the large attendance. No doubt further buoyed by the news that the club had also made a profit of £100 during the season although a mortgage of £3000 had been raised to finance the building of the new hall.

This sum had been needed to make up the shortfall in the cost of the building and it was noted that all twelve trustees of the club had signed to offer their security against the mortgage. Each had also sent their good wishes for the future!

Tommy McGhee
Player 1950's

I played for Wealdstone while I was serving with the Royal Navy, eventually leaving to sign as a pro at Portsmouth.

Wealdstone were a wonderful club. Everyone was very friendly. The support was always very good and there were some wonderful players and characters.

One was the jovial old trainer, Mr Gallagher. He was blessed with a great knowledge of the game. The players that stood out were Danny Wiltshire in goal and Charlie Edmunds. Phil White too went pro at Leyton Orient I believe and to have the two Polish lads, well!

Missing Tommy McGhee who had turned professional with Portsmouth, Ken Bodfish who had returned to Birmingham, Peter Rogers who had joined St Albans and G Wilkinson who had joined Leyton, Wealdstone again brought in new players for the new season.

The first fixture, away to Sutton United resulted in a 5-0 defeat. It was little consolation that J Muller the goalkeeper would soon return from his holiday – the Harrow Observer commented that although the score line may have flattered the home side, it was evident that the defence would need to be strengthened to prevent Wealdstone letting in a record number of goals.

Slightly better news was that A Littlejohn and L Hussey were now training again after suffering long-term injuries in the previous season.

It was not until October 16th that Wealdstone managed to win for the first time in the league, beating Leyton by two goals to one and although playing better, it was to be the tale of the season, Wealdstone winning only four league games during the season and finishing firmly bottom of the Athenian League.

In fact their next two wins were the highlights of the first team season, in early December beating reigning Champions Finchley by 3-1 and their next, on the 9th April, losing 2-1 at half time to Walton and Hersham, 'Stones played an excellent second half to run out winners by 4-2.

The reserves too had had a poor season, improving their league position by only one place over the previous year, winning just one more match.

The brightest spot of the season came right at the end, when the club organised a benefit match for W Wiltshire, who had been incapacitated and could not work. He had served on the Club Committee for a number of years, and the match was organised to help him in a time of need.

Former stars of Wealdstone returned to shine at Lower Mead on Wednesday last and delighted an enthusiastic crowd beating an All Professional QPR team by 6-2.

The occasion was a memorable one. A surprisingly large crowd in view of the heavy rain which had ceased only minutes before the match began, and transport difficulties caused by the only recently finished Bus Strike gave their former favourites a rousing reception. The players representing Wealdstone's richest talent before during and after their championship year, rose to the occasion with a scintillating display.

Despite the score and the fact that the Rangers obtained the last goal, the game was not uneven, Wealdstone's strength lay-

ing in the supreme cleverness of their forwards.

Representative of the older players, Bert Dyke led them with great skill, his admirable positioning concealing a lack of pace and Eddie Smith, whose hair seemed nearer Vermillion than ever, schemed and dribbled admirably, his graceful corkscrew headers recalling a hat full of goals scored in days gone by.

Then there was Henryk Wegrzyk with frequent reminders that his right foot was the most lethal seen at Lower Mead since the war, swinging out perfect passes to his old partner, Phil White. And there was White, responding maestro like by ringing the changes on perfect centres, fierce shots and the shrewder of return inside passes. Finally Frank Bennett, eel-like and as elusive as ever, brought out his best form.

With players in this mood and fast, hard tackling wing-halves in Johnny Wall and Paddy Glennon to prompt them, goals were bound to follow, and come they did. Every one a good one.

In fact Rangers scored first, a corner by Tomkys being deflected into the net in a May - Quinn heading encounter. Wealdstone's reply was swift; Smith beat three men in a swerving dribble before passing to white that, from the fringe of the penalty area cracked in a shot which tore fiercely at the rigging of the goal. Soon afterwards, another Smith - White move ended with Bennett slipping the ball past Tzen to make the score 2-1.

Play continued lively and full of incident until the interval with Rangers failing to accept good chances to draw level and Wegrzyk getting in one grand shot which grazed the crossbar.

Wealdstone's third goal was a masterpiece. A long cross-field pass by Wegrzyk found White unmarked and the winger sped along with Glennon in close support. At the right moment White slipped the ball forward to Glennon whose short centre to Dyke was wept into the net.

For a time QPR seemed to be getting the upper hand, but then Wealdstone finished in a blaze of glory with three fine goals. Wegrzyk got two of them, the first after a shot from Smith had crashed down from the cross bar, and the second followed a good run by Dyke. Then White rounded things off with a superb shot from a fairly oblique angle. Finally, almost on the stroke of time, Tomkys ran through the Wealdstone defence to leave his captain, Smith, with the task of tapping the ball into an empty net.

Wealdstone's defence was a little inferior to the attack. Reeves showed what great strides he has made and was an ideal partner for Gadsden, the two doing so well that Wiltshire had comparatively few chances of revealing his prowess. Wall was as diligent and tenacious as ever and Glennon was quite at home in distinguished company.

Wealdstone; D Wiltshire (Maidstone), W Reeves (Yiewsley), R Gadsden (Hayes), J Glennon, C May (QPR), J Wall (Crystal Palace), P White (Leyton Orient), H Wegrzyk (Finchley), E Smith (Northampton Town), F Bennett (Carshalton).

QPR; Tzen, Colgan, Woods, Clickson, Powell, Angell, Pounder, Smith, Fidler, Quinn, Tomkys

There had been a number of fundraising dances and whist drives held in the new Pavilion at Lower Mead and these were to continue. During the close season, however they were further supported when the Wealdstone Fete was re-introduced, this time as "A Cavalcade of Entertainment" held on the Lower Mead pitch in mid-June.

The event lasted for six hours, being opened by Miss Jill Manners, an actress famous at the time.

For once the event was blessed with a full days sunshine. There were a number of events for both adults and children to enjoy, including a Punch and Judy stall and a 'Beat The Goalie', the goalkeepers on the day being R Glennon and D Mulley from the Wealdstone first team.

There was also a fancy dress boat race between the Wealdstone squad and a team from Hamilton Brush Works, both teams dressed as women. In common with the teams results during the previous season, this match was lost as well.

There was a weightlifting competition and a dancing display, A pipe band, and fancy dress where one entrant dressed as a Wealdstone player and carried a placard, which read "Support Your Local Club, Wealdstone".

The evening saw the entertainments aimed more at adults. A prettiest ankle competition was held, followed by open air dancing.

It turned out to be a very successful day, and the money raised was put towards paying off the mortgage taken out to build the new Pavilion.

There was sadness during the summer, with the death of Bill Gallagher who had loyally served Wealdstone FC as Player and Coach for 43 years. He had received numerous offers from professional clubs, but always chose to remain with the 'Stones.

He had played senior football as a 16 year old in Ireland, before first appearing for Wealdstone in 1912, playing at Belmont Road, and he went on to play regularly as a full back, centre half or centre forward, and he did on one occasion play an entire match in goal.

He was most successful as a centre forward averaging two goals per game in this position and he scored the last Wealdstone goal at Belmont Road before the club moved to Lower Mead in 1923. He was awarded the Military Medal during World War 1.

He won 16 medals as a player in various league and cup competitions, and on the move to Lower Mead became the club's trainer. He was in charge of the reserve team for a number of years before being promoted to run the first team, all the while acting as Trainer to the Middlesex County FA, The Athenian League and (during the war) the Herts and Middlesex League.

The AGM of the club was able to report that a new Trainer had been employed. Mr Maurice Welham joining the club from Bognor Town, where his record in the two previous seasons had been impressive.

He had also been the Trainer for the Royal Navy team. His intention was to strengthen the side as soon as possible holding additional trials for younger players.

It was hoped that the club would improve their position under him, but he had to act quickly, as in a tough start to the season Wealdstone were to play five games in the first 12 days, as well as having to play in the Extra Preliminary rounds of both the FA Cup and Amateur Cup due to their previous poor performances.

Arthur Littlejohn
Player 1949-1956

I joined the club as a player in 1949, and I played in the 'Strollers', the 'reserves' and subsequently the First XI, and I was given the honour of captaining the First XI on a number of occasions, in fact all of my Senior football career was with Wealdstone, having only played for Chelsea Central Boys Club as a youngster.

I also made some representative appearances, for Combined Services during my National Service, and also for the Middlesex County Junior and Senior sides whilst with Wealdstone.

In fact there was one game against Essex where the Middlesex team included Bob Marjoram, who had also played for Wealdstone before joining Hayes, and one Fred Titmus from Hendon playing at inside right!

I didn't miss many matches during my years with the club, but I doubt if you'd need two hands to count the number of goals I scored!!

One of the things I remember about Wealdstone was the Blanket Collections held for injured players on mach days, to supplement our incomes whilst we were off work, I once shared one of these with Henryk Mikrut and the few pounds helped out!

There was one occasion when I arrived at Lower Mead for training in the evening, I walked into the dressing room to find the communal bath had been filled with seaweed courtesy of Charlie Barker, I believe, in an effort to give us all a refreshing 'brine bath'!

One of the matches that meant the most to me was the one against Arsenal on 2nd November 1953 in the London FA Challenge Cup Semi-Final. I didn't have a particularly good game, but to play at Highbury under floodlights was really something special. Running this a close second would have to be the game against Headington United in the F.A. Cup, played in the same week!

There were some great players at the time, but one I remember in particular was Bill Hudson, the father of Alan Hudson who later played for Arsenal and Chelsea.

More recently there has been one player whom I admired long before I realised his Wealdstone connection, and that is Stuart Pearce, but my favourite from my own time with the club would have to be Edgar Francis, he was a wonderful and modest man and a great model for anyone to follow.

With trials well in progress and the 1955-56 season only a week away, Mr Welham however left to take over the Licence of a Pub and Hotel in Guilford. Acting quickly the club moved to re-appoint George Milton who had run the club successfully from 1950 to 1953, winning the Athenian League Championship in 1952.

A number of players returned to the club, some from injury others from other Clubs at the start of the season and things looked very bright for Wealdstone.

Unfortunately it wasn't to last – after 15 minutes of the first match, this season at home to Sutton United, the goalkeeper J Muller dislocated a finger and had to leave the field. Stephens the back immediately took over in goal, but 'Stones were soon trailing and in the second half Viv Evans took his place between the posts.

Sutton took great advantage of their numerical superiority and ran out winners by five goals to nil for the second time in successive seasons.

Even with Henryk Mikrut, Henryk Wegrzyk and Abel Comben all returning to the club, there was little they could do, as in the next two matches 'Stones were beaten again, away to Barnet and Enfield by 3-2 and 4-0 respectively.

It was again to be the story of the early part of the season as by the time the club faced Hounslow in the fifth game, five of the starting line up from the first game were unavailable through injury. To make thing worse, two more left the field in that game, although Wealdstone eventually earned a 2-2 draw.

In six league Games, Wealdstone had won one, beating Southall, drawn two and lost three to find themselves near the foot of the Athenian League table. There was to be some relief from the rigours of the league in late September when Wealdstone faced Harrow Town in the first qualifying round of the FA Cup.

Panic stricken by a defensive blunder which gave Wealdstone the lead after only two minutes play at Earlsmead on Saturday, Harrow Town never looked like recovering and were ultimately beaten by seven clear goals. True, they only conceded one goal in the second half and that following a rather harsh penalty decision, but in this period Wealdstone clearly eased up. Even so, they would have added to their score with better shooting.

Conditions were ideal for the match, but the hopes of the crowd of 2,530 paying a record amount of £123, that the thriller of 1946, when Town won 4-3 would be repeated, were soon doomed to disappointment.

Harrow Town contributed to their own disaster by the last minute gamble of introducing a complete newcomer, D Kay at centre half. This led to A Lees going to right back to replace A Lee, another newcomer who was hurt at work in the morning. Kay could scarcely have made a more ill starred debut. Almost the first time he was in action was to rise to a harmless enough centre from Evans, and to deflect it well beyond Burgin's reach.

At once a defence that had looked shaky to start with abandoned itself to panic. Kicking became wild and tackling and marking irresolute, while even the usually confident Burgin grew nervy and frequently dropped the ball.

As a result, Wealdstone carved them to pieces for a time and had virtually won after only ten minutes play, the score by that time being 0-3. Evans scored the second goal with a hard, low drive after clever work by Bowen and then clever combination between Saffery and Harper enabled Bowen himself to tap the ball in from Harpers pass.

Little was seen of the Town forwards at this stage, though Ward was persistent and Zubiena made one good run. After Burgin had splendidly saved a fierce drive from Wegrzyk, there was a lull until just before the interval when Wealdstone put on a brilliant burst to score three times in little more than a minute.

Evans started this revel with an individualist goal after a splendid run down the wing, Kay again blundered badly by allowing Harper to dispossess him almost on the goal-line and score and then Evans completed his hat trick with the Town defence all at sixes and sevens.

After the interval Town had a fairer share of the midfield play but could not rally hard enough to make more than fleeting impressions on the Wealdstone defence. Indeed Muller was not once seriously troubled in the whole match. Alone of the home forwards, Zubiena showed progressiveness and Case was entirely neglected. At time the ball was moved about well but too squarely for real headway to be made.

With Wealdstone concentrating on "exhibition stuff" play became desultory and unrecognisable as a Cup-tie. Fire returned temporarily when Wegrzyk made it seven from the penalty spot, but Bowen contrived the miss of the match in the next minute.

Just before the end an overworked Burgin fished the ball out of the net for the tenth time but as on two previous occasions the goal was disallowed.

Harrow Town; K Burgin, A Lees, J Crowley, J Ryan, D Kay, R Franklin, H Case, H James, A Zubiena, K Aldridge, C Ward.

Wealdstone; J Muller, B Bodimeade, J Randall, A Comben, G Halward, J Glennon, G Saffrey, H Wegrzyk, I Harper, J Bowen, V Evans.

Although there were a few victories in the cup competitions, Wealdstone's league form had remained patchy at the very least. By the first week of March, 'Stones had climbed to 8th in the Athenian League table with nine wins from 22 games.

This record was somewhat different from the beginning of the previous month, as the victory on March 3rd was their fourth consecutive league win, their best run of the season. This game did offer one of the strangest reasons for a players unavailability however, as the Harrow Observer reported'...

..."with Mulley at right back for Reeves, who was again chasing the runner K Norris with a newsreel camera......"

It seems that the Wealdstone defender was an integral part of some early Outside Broadcast sports filming, quite literally keeping pace with the day's news!

As the season came to a close, Wealdstone first lost to Wembley by 3-1 in the semi-final of the Middlesex Senior Cup and then 'Stones beat Edgware Town by 4-1 at the White Lion Ground, to reach the Middlesex Senior Charity Cup Final, where they were to play the Athenian League runner up, Hounslow Town.

Before the match could be played, the Committee had made an appeal for funds as the season, whilst an improvement on the field had been disastrous financially. In the match programme, the following was printed...

Viv Evans slides in to score against Rayners Lane

Rising costs of maintenance, kit and all the many items, which a football club needs, together with the fact that our attendances have not been good, has made it absolutely necessary for an appeal to go out to all our members and supporters for financial assistance. The position is extremely serious."

Attendances had been hit by bad weather as well as by poor form, and the local paper also commented that...

...league matches these days have little attraction anywhere, and this strengthens the case for a fusion of the Athenian and Isthmian League's with a system of promotion and relegation.

The major loss though was due to the early exit from the major cup competitions in the early stages. The bigger gates came as teams progressed through the rounds.

Even in the FA Cup, two of the three victories were away from home with small crowds. The club had invited Portsmouth and Leyton Orient to play matches at Lower Mead, both having former Wealdstone players in their current sides, but both had declined the requests.

The last home game of the season did bring a high point. It was Wealdstone's highest score of the season, an 8–1 win against Finchley. It had been a good season for the goalscorers anyway – the seventh of the match against Finchley being the team's 100th goal in all matches, and the eighth took the league total to 64 in 28 games. Less impressive was the 60 goals conceded in the league.

The Finchley game was also unusual in that each of Wealdstone's five forwards had scored in the match.

One week before the Middlesex Charity Cup Final there was more sadness for the club, with the announcement of the death of Mr C E Brady, who had become Vice President of the club in 1912 and President in 1921, a position he held until his death 35 years later.

Never a mere figurehead, Mr Brady continued to preside over the committee meetings until 1939. After the war he chaired the annual general meetings of the club and with Frank Harbud, he was the last surviving committee member from the clubs days at Belmont Road.

There was nothing he liked more than attending matches and he was often at Lower Mead, when great age and illness would have made this an intolerable strain on almost any other man.

The final league table saw Wealdstone in tenth place in the Athenian League and a poor 12th in the Reserve Section, but the club hoped to be at full strength for the cup final.

Wealdstone rightly considered themselves unlucky to be beaten 1–0 by Hounslow in the Charity Cup Final at Hayes on the Saturday. Handicapped by an injury to their Captain, Comben, early in the game, they were still the more thrust-full and skilful side, and it was only a bad slip by Farmer five minutes from time that gave Hounslow the vital goal.

There had been some improvement on the field, but it was not enough to secure a Trophy for the club.

Financially, although there had been some response to the appeal, Members had donated £92 and loaned a further £ 495, there was still a deficit to be made up.

Wealdstone v HMSO at Pushball

Even after the economies made by the club, they had still lost £721 overall, almost double the £394 lost the previous season.

It was announced at the AGM that further efforts were to be made to achieve solvency the following season. These measures were to include the club dispensing with the services of George Milton as Trainer and the disbandment of the Strollers team.

There were also to be some increases in admission in common with other Athenian League clubs, from 1/- to 1/3. Membership fees and subscriptions were also raised by 5/- each.

H 'Chippy' Luck was appointed Chairman after 21 years as Honorary Secretary, as H H Harrison, the Chairman for the previous 12 years was appointed President to succeed the late Mr C E Brady.

The Lower Mead Fete was again to play a part in reducing the club debts, and in common with the previous year a number of events were held to attract people to the day. The opening this year was done by Mr Bill Kitchen, a former Wembley Speedway rider and there was also a Push Ball competition, where a ball approximately six feet in diameter had to be moved to score goals on the football pitch, the overall strength of the player being far more important that their skill!

Wealdstone FC beat Her Majesty's Stationary Office FC and Harrow Town FC beat Wembley FC in the semi-finals, Wealdstone FC eventually beating Harrow Town FC in the final by 4-2 after being two goals down at half time.

For the second year in succession, the event had been blessed by good weather and the respectable sum of £120 was made as profit for the club.

Aside from the events being held almost weekly in the new clubhouse, Wealdstone were actively trying to raise money from any source, and despite both Clubs declining during the previous season, Leyton Orient and Portsmouth were both to visit Lower Mead for Friendly matches during 1956–1957.

At the same time, Wealdstone had also agreed to play an away friendly with Harrow Town FC to help their fundraising and their challenge for the Spartan League title.

There were some new faces in the 'Stones line up, perceived to be the most notable were the signings of Derek Toombs, a strong young centre forward from Edgware Town, and F Mensah, a young Nigerian forward. He was described as a real personality and had been spotted by the club playing for the British Rail team against Middlesex at Lower Mead the previous season.

'Stones started the season with a 3–1 win away to Enfield – a reason for great pleasure as in the previous three seasons, Wealdstone had only won away from home twice!

There were again a lot of goals around at the start of the season – Wealdstone twice conceding five goals, 5–1 at Walton and Hersham and 5–2 to Finchley, but their second win was top be a 5–1 victory over Leyton, all of this by the beginning of September.

There was an interesting fixture at Lower Mead on September 5th 1956, again covered by the Harrow Observer;

Although beaten by 10-1 by a strong Athenian League side at Lower Mead, the Uganda Touring team made a pleasing impression by their keen, clean play.

Playing barefooted in the first half as they had hoped, the tourists were unable to keep any sort of foothold on the soggy pitch and they found the leaden white ball difficult to move. As a result, the Athenian League team ran through them at will and crossed over with a half time 8-0 lead.

Things were vastly different after the interval. Now booted and quite unaffected by the big score against them, the Ugandans began to play really clever and cohesive football, which often had the Athenian defence at full stretch. Only some spectacular saves by Pearson prevented them from scoring more than once, through Seruwaggi, and they had more than a fair share of play.

Given constant encouragement by a crowd of about 2000, they fought hard until the end, and as Mr W A Warren, the Athenian League Secretary told them afterwards, they might have further extended their opponents had they worn boots throughout the match! Darey and Cannon both scored first half hat tricks, the other goals coming from Evans and Champelovier. Champelovier again scored the ninth and Spector who missed several good chances scored the tenth.

The Ugandans had C Peagram, the former Corinthian Casual in goal and his big kicking was one of the features of the play. Throughout the match the tourists conceded only one free kick.

Athenian League; W Pearson (Sutton), G Taylor (Hounslow), J Randall (Wealdstone), L L Topp (Hendon), J Adams (Hendon), D Evans (Hounslow), R Cannon (Barnet), L Champelovier (Hayes), J Darey (Hendon), J Rawlings (Hendon), M Spector (Hendon).

Brian Henderson
Supporter and Official

I first went to Wealdstone F.C. at the age of 9. I lived at Poets Corner, which was a 'Stones throw from the ground, and I helped G Gaze on his milk round and eventually watched him play.

Players came and went and it was eventually call up time for me to go into the Army. I lost track of what happened with the club until I saw they were playing Port Vale in the F.A. Cup in 1949, when they lost 1-0. I was soon to leave the forces and began following them again.

There were many characters back then, such as Eric Metcalfe, the man in blue. He had been given all the players old shirts to

Wealdstone FC 1956-57;
Back Row; J Glennon, H Wegrzyk, W Reeves, G Wood, G Halward, J Randall, Front Row; J Wall, J Coster, A Comben (Captain), G Furness, V Evans

make his suit, which he proudly wore on match days.

I had served behind the bar by this time and became friendly with Johnny Ryan. He asked me to become a committee member and at that time, you had to serve a year on the social club before you were able to join the football committee.

My memories of different games are plenty and the few that stand out as being particularly memorable are when the Hastings players walked off the pitch (did they disagree with a sending off?) and also when the visiting African team played the first half in boots and the second half with none.

Wealdstone were congratulated in mid October when the club appointed Mr Jimmy Bain as 'Teams Manager'. He was the first person to hold such a title in the club's history. He had recently retired from professional football after 21 years as Assistant Manager at Brentford, where he had formerly been a player. A centre half he had joined the club from Manchester United and was captain of the London side during their most successful period, in the 1929-1930 season the club created a record winning every home league match.

Unfortunately, It wasn't to be a successful start at Wealdstone, the first team managing to lose 8 consecutive matches in league and cup competitions up to Christmas when they beat Hendon in the traditional Christmas Day fixture. They lost the Boxing Day return.

During this period, Wealdstone's most colourful and best known supporter, Mr Eric Metcalffe, who always dressed from head to foot in blue and white and was normally found behind the goal passed on to Hendon the Wooden Spoon held by Wealdstone (and worn by Eric) for twelve months.

It was a traditional token identifying that Wealdstone had finished bottom of the Athenian League, and the spoon, with a hand painted Wealdstone Crest had been attached to the Blue and White suit worn by Eric. As, in the previous season, Hitchin Town had finished bottom and relieved Wealdstone of the dubious honour, the spoon had been duly decorated with their Club crest, and the presentation was made after their visit to Lower Mead in November.

Club Chairman, Mr H A 'Chippy' Luck made the presentation as the players of the two teams shared a meal after the match. It was sportingly accepted by Hitchin, also defeated in the afternoon, who promised to pass it on in the future. They also made comment that were they to have the misfortune to earn it three times, it would at least be a useful adjunct to their Soccer Museum!

Eve Salmon
Worked in the tea bar in the 1950's

My memories of Wealdstone FC go back to the fifties when my then boyfriend and now husband of 46 years' sister asked me if I would like to take her place and help out with the refreshments at Lower Mead. I was glad to help as it was a good place to go on a Saturday afternoon, and what I earned would help with the repayments on my bicycle!

The man in charge was George Roberts and there was another man who helped out - his name was Les and he lived in Locket road - I can't recall his surname. George's wife, Dorothy also came along - she'd worked there for a couple of years, and as I remember I was paid the princely sum of 10 Shillings for a first team match and 7/6 for the reserves, although many times at reserve games we didn't take 7/6!!

One game not to be forgotten was against Walthamstow in a cup match - I earned 12/6 that day as we'd been so busy - I nearly needed Securicor to take me home!!

I missed a couple of seasons in the mid-fifties when I married and then I went back in 1957, when my daughter was a year old. I'd finished paying for the bike by then but my earnings were still the same! I used to go over to Sybil's Department Store and find something in the Baby department to take home!

I remember toward the end of matches I always had to run to the local Cake Shop opposite the 'Granada' and get a box of 'fancies' (cakes) for the players. Well, I did get out of the washing up so it wasn't so bad!!

I ended up going full circle really, I ended up working in the Harrow Medical Centre for 14 years, so meeting up with so many of the people I'd handed out cuppa's to, but this time I was handing out prescriptions, but it was very nice meeting up with everyone again.

I still make a good cup of tea, too.......

As the New Year progressed things continued to disappoint at the club, their first draw of the season bringing their first point of the New Year – that was a 2-2 draw with Sutton United at the end of February.

In the meantime though, dissatisfaction had seen the resignation of a number of players, mostly with first team experience and as a result a number of changes were made on the field.

There was better news though of some other former players as it was reported that...

...'two of George Wood's rivals for the Goalkeeping duties at Wealdstone during pre-season had found them selves as opponents in a Corinthian League match, Brian Stevens keeping goal for Epson against Peter Monk and Edgware Town'

There was more news of another former 'Stones goalkeeper. Suffering a period of injuries, an Irishman and goalkeeper Pascal O'Toole had been recommended to the club by Sutton United. He had played a couple of games for the reserves and was then dropped for one game, promptly disappearing.

He resurfaced at the end of the season keeping goal for Cork Athletic against Waterford in the Eire Cup Final, and this season had been the reserve goalkeeper for the League of Eire team against the English Football League.

Among the changes was the return of Ken Bodfish and the addition of J Birch from Kingstonian. At the same time a number of other regulars were to make way, the most notable H Wegrzyk, J Coster and J Glennon, none of whom were to feature for any Wealdstone side for a month.

Continuing the fundraising, Wealdstone FC asked the Middlesex FA for permission to play for a new trophy, replacing the Wealdstone Hospital Cup, which in common with those from Wycombe and Cambridge was no longer competed for.

The County FA agreed, and the competition was sanctioned, the North West Middlesex Invitation Cup. In this first season, it was to be competed for by Wealdstone, Wembley, Harrow Town and Edgware Town. The competition was to be drawn into two semi-finals and a final, each to be played on a home and away basis, the aggregate score counting towards progression.

By the beginning of March, the club decided that with poor results and dwindling crowds they had to assure the fans that something would be done to rectify the situation. The following statement appeared in the match programme for the fixture against fellow strugglers, Walton and Hersham. It seems that it had an immediate effect on the players, as Wealdstone ran out winners by eight goals to two, by far their best performance of the season.

The very bad playing record of the teams has quite naturally caused great concern among our members and supporters. It has also caused the committee considerable anxiety.

Some of our members and supporters have written to the Hon. Secretary making criticisms and suggestions. All these letters have been considered and answered. We realise that in addition to those who have written to us there are many others worried about the teams' poor results.

Other members have written to the Press. The Committee feels that to reply to members and supporters' criticisms through the Press could well be inconclusive and would not be satisfactory and have therefore decided to make these comments.

The season started without a professional Coach and without an 'A' team because of our financial position. A working arrangement with HMSO Press FC through Mr Jim Pyers, a member of our committee, gave us facilities for trying out players.

Early results were not satisfactory and on October 22nd Mr Jim Blain was appointed Coach and given a place on the selection committee with power to vote. Although the financial position had not improved the committee took this step to endeavour to achieve better results. In January, the committee made the following decisions;

- *To intensify the efforts of team building with the object of regaining our former prestige.*
- *To start negotiations at once to obtain a ground for next season to enable us to run an 'A' team.*
- *To invite local players to apply for trials to be held during April (Approx. 30 applications have been received).*
- *To get a link with the local schools so that the most promising boys would be, on leaving, persuaded to join us. This has been achieved and we now have a representative from the Harrow Schools Parents Association (Mr Emerson) on the committee.*

Much of the criticism has been levelled quite naturally, at the selection committee. They have a difficult and thankless task in endeavouring to find a winning side and have not spared themselves in their efforts. Criticism contained in letters sent to us has been, we hope, satisfactorily answered.

In Mr Lacey's letter, which appeared in the Harrow Observer, he states that the club management is complacent. As to this we can fairly state that this is not true and that the entire committee are deeply concerned and disturbed with the lack of success and all that it entails.

When it is borne in mind that members of the committee are guarantors at the bank it must be appreciated that great efforts have been and are being made to get satisfactory results on the field of play, which automatically would improve our financial position.

We think it would be agreed that we have had players injured during the course of the season and others not available through various reasons and that some of the players we all thought assets to the side did not find their form in spite of being persevered with.

In conclusion we would like to thank all our members and supporters who have regularly attended our matches despite our lack of success and to assure them that we shall not spare our efforts to achieve the success we all so much desire.

There is no doubt that three goals in the first five minutes and a further five in the last half hour of the match against Walton had calmed the atmosphere in the ground, and the actions of the committee were to be commended by most present. It also seemed that the statement had had a positive effect on the team as the Walton victory was the first of three consecutive wins, 'Stones bets run of the season.

At the same time, there was a further example of the luck that befell Wealdstone on occasions.

The reserves, travelling to Walton and Hersham for a reverse friendly fixture, arrived to find their opponents missing one player.

Sportingly, Wealdstone loaned J Murphy who had appeared at left half or left back for Wealdstone to the home side, who played him at inside-left for the match. He scored four of Walton and Hersham's goals in a 7-3 victory!

The North West Middlesex Cup saw Wealdstone drawn to play Harrow Town, the matches to be played over Easter starting at Earlsmead. The match went true to form – although Wealdstone were the senior side and was expected to win, they could only score once and a late equaliser from the penalty spot was enough to set up the return match at Lower Mead.

Before the return match at Lower Mead, another friendly was played, Grange Farm from Wales being the visitors for the second year in succession. The Monday though, saw another trophy chance that was to escape Wealdstone, as Harrow Town won comfortably at Lower Mead to reach the final of the North West Middlesex competition.

Worse was to come when in the last game of the season, Barnet, wooden spoonist's at the bottom of the Athenian League and second bottom of the Reserve Section were the visitors to Lower Mead. They completed a seasons double over the home side, winning by 5-1 after Phipps their veteran centre forward completed a hat trick in the first fifteen minutes.

Surprisingly, it was announced at the AGM that Wealdstone FC could show a profit on the balance sheet at the end of the season for the first time in three years.

Although announced as a result of economies, increased subscription charges and membership fees, all set off against further falling income and reduced gates, the profit was shown as £241. Closer inspection of the balance sheet however shows that this included a £300 donation from the Social Club.

The cash in hand was listed as £43, and the overdraft 'was perilously close to the £553 limit set by the bank' so things were not quite as rosy as suggested.

The club also announced at the AGM that Mr Len Goulden, former England player and Watford Manager, had been employed as Coach and also that the 'A' team would indeed be re-introduced for the forthcoming season, along with a Youth side, meaning Wealdstone were to run four teams for the first time.

There was a more positive atmosphere at the start of the 1957–1958 season. The Harrow Observer had run a feature on the new fitness and training methods being employed at the club and the report of the pre-season trials was good.

Of thirty three players used, 19 were new to the club and a number of these were expected to be retained. The 'probable's' in the trial included the whole left flank of the previous years team, and this no doubt assisted left wing Viv Evans as he collected a first half hat trick in a 6–1 win.

For the next week, the changes were evident. It was only this left flank, four players in total that were to be retained for the opening league match with Cambridge City at Lower Mead. In fact a further change was made before the match kicked off as Harper resigned from the club, and Wealdstone started with only three players from the previous season in their line up.

A very tight and difficult match ensued, and Wealdstone were leading by 2-1 at half time. The visitors equalised early in the second half but to no avail as Wealdstone went on to win by 5 goals to two with three scored in the last fifteen minutes, the last of which seemed to have been scored by Viv Evans with his elbows.

The following week saw wins away to Redhill 2–1 with Charlie Townsend scoring both goals and Hayes 3–0 after being reduced to ten men through injury to Randall, gave Wealdstone a better start than they had had for a number of years.

The return of Harper after less than a week away also buoyed the club. The reserves too had a similar start also winning their first three matches to give the club a 100% record.

It wasn't until their fifth league game that 'Stones were to drop a point in a 1–1 draw away to Hitchin Town. It saw them lose their place at the top of the table to Hendon on goal difference. The reserves followed suit by also drawing with their Hitchin Town counterparts, thus losing their 100% record as well.

The excellent start was not to last though, as the club suffered one or two injuries and yet more new faces were added to the line up. 'Stones for began to fade and in November, not a single match was won. They did achieve a draw against Uxbridge in the FA Amateur Cup with only nine fit men, only to lose the replay at Lower Mead by 2–1.

Strangely, with so many clubs involved in cup-ties, this poor run of form didn't damage the league position too greatly, as in early December Wealdstone were still in second spot in the

WEALDSTONE F.C.: Standing — Packham, Fogden, Wood, Coster, Randall, Hannam. Sitting — Knox, Glennon, Harper, Conroy, Evans.

Happy Days for Wealdstone

WEALDSTONE, the popular Middlesex club, have had to struggle hard in the last three seasons, but now their prospects look much brighter.

The loss of several of the crack players who helped them to win the Athenian League championship in 1951-52 was a severe handicap.

Dan Wiltshire, still one of the most dependable and experienced goalkeepers in amateur Soccer, moved to Maidstone; right-back Tommy McGhee signed as a professional for Portsmouth; England left-back Ron Gadsden returned to Hayes; their captain, Gordon Norman, went to Briggs Sports; outside-right Phil White became a Leyton Orient professional; and Polish international inside-left Henrik Wegrzyk joined Sittingbourne.

But after many trials towards the end of last season Wealdstone found a team well-balanced enough to gain a convincing League win over Amateur Cup semi-finalists, Hayes.

When that promising young goalkeeper, Derek East, was forced to give up the game on medical grounds, they found an experienced successor in George Wood, from Enfield.

At right-back, 22-year-old Don Packham, from Uxbridge, played so well, when Bill Reeves was injured, that he won a regular place in the side.

He forms a most reliable partnership with that tall veteran, John Randall, whose stylish defensive play helped Middlesex in their Southern Counties Amateur Championship successes.

John has also played for the Athenian League, and for Berks and Bucks, when he assisted Aylesbury United.

Gordon Norman, now returned to the club, fills the centre-half position.

Norman played for England schoolboys at Hampden Park, and originally joined Wealdstone in 1951, after a season with Ilford.

Right-half Abel Comben, formerly with Wycombe, Aylesbury and Hayes, is a most experienced player. He has turned out for Berks and Bucks and Middlesex.

And left-half 21-year-old John Harrison, from Ruislip Manor, has been playing well enough to keep former Navy half-back, Paddy Glennon, out of the team.

George Knox, 23-year-old Queen's Park Rangers' amateur, has been leading the attack splendidly.

On his right-wing, Ken Bodfish—who, on securing a position at De Havilands rejoined the club from Moor Green—has developed a productive partnership with 21-year-old Mike Conroy, who has played in five youth internationals, and has captained Middlesex schoolboys.

Two seasoned men form the left-wing—Ivor Harper, who played for Berks and Bucks when with Aylesbury, and speedy 23-year-old Vivian Evans, Middlesex and Athenian League.

In the next campaign Royal Navy backs John Valentine and Ted Farmer will be fighting for places in the side.

Wealdstone are fortunate in having a loyal committee, with big Bert Harrison as president, Harry Luck as chairman, Jack Rogers as vice-chairman, Bill Leadbetter as honorary secretary, Johnnie Ryan as publicity chief and Jimmy Bain (Brentford) as team manager.

This committee has adopted a wise policy.

With M. A. Emerson, the secretary of the Parents' Association of Harrow Schools as liaison officer, it has taken under its aegis all the schools in the district.

So every player who leaves school has a trial with the club.

23

Charles Buchan's Football Monthly. June 1957. No 70

Athenian League. A hard fought victory by 4-2 over Enfield strengthening their position but it was not to last.

The Christmas games did allow Wealdstone to earn three points out of four, a 2–2 draw at Lower Mead on Christmas Day followed by a 2–1 victory at Hendon on Boxing Day went someway to levelling the slate after Hendon had dumped Wealdstone out of the FA Cup earlier in the season.

For the remainder of the season in the league, some good victories were interspersed with misfortune and unsteadiness leading to defeat. The side lacked the consistency of a team borne from a side that had played together for a long time. The final statistics however did show an improvement, Wealdstone finishing in 8th place.

George Mowle
Player 1950's,

I first watched the Stones in 1944 and followed them for a couple of years, then as a player, I joined the Stones from Barnet - -on my first visit back playing for Wealdstone I scored the winning goal. I always remember that one!

I played for them in the late 1950's for almost five seasons and I've followed their fortunes ever since. I think I made around 150 appearances. A lot of us from that era still keep in touch as well, and we do occasionally meet up.

I can still see Eric the Cabbie in his Blue & White suit. Stood behind the goal ringing his bell throughout the matches – great support.

There was a little more success in at least one Cup Competition however. Having inaugurated the North West Middlesex Invitation Cup the previous season, losing in the semi-final, this seasons competition saw Wealdstone visit Wembley in the first leg of their tie on February 8th 1958.

There was an air of sadness surrounding the game though, as both teams wore black armbands as a mark of respect to the Manchester United players that had been killed in the Munich air crash a few days previous. The crowd of over 2000 joining the players in a minute's silence before the kick off.

After a week of freezing conditions, an overnight thaw had made the pitch very heavy, conditions which suited the Wealdstone players far more than their hosts, Wealdstone eventually running out winners by 7-3.

In the same week it was announced that the club were to hold an 'Open Meeting' on 19th February to discuss the formation of a new Wealdstone FC Supporters Club.

An appeal had been made by the club for a volunteer organizer, and the Committee interviewed Mr Tom Verrall and asked him to 'get on with the job'. This first meeting was to be exploratory to judge the potential support, but it appeared that already 60 people had indicted their interest in joining.

A fortnight later, the Harrow Observer reported...

With the Mayor of Harrow, Alderman H granger as President, Wealdstone FC Supporters Club has now been formed. The immediate objective is to get 500 members by the end of the year.

An inaugural meeting was held at the Lower Mead Social Club on Wednesday of last week when it was unanimously agreed to form the club and invite the Mayor, whose interest in football is well known, to become President. His acceptance was received by return of post.

Officers and a Committee were elected and the Chairman, H A Luck, gave the Football Club's official welcome and promise of assistance.

Subscriptions were fixed at 2 shillings a year for adults and 1 shilling a year for pensioners and juniors up to the age of 16. Rules are being drawn up and a 'supporters' badge is being designed by the Supporters Club Treasurer, Mr Eric Metcalfe who is familiar to all Wealdstone followers as 'the man in blue' who attends all matches home and away in full regalia.

Over 30 members were at once enrolled and the Committee were busy signing on others at the match against Walton and Hersham on Saturday.

The Officers elected were; Alderman H Grainger – President, Mr C Cluck - Vice-president, Mr T Law – Chairman, Mr A Johnson – Vice-Chairman, Mr T Verrall – Secretary, Mr E Metcalfe – Treasurer, Mrs Raven, Messrs S Burrows, D Turner, N Vincent, R Thorne and W Waterlow, Committee.

Ten days later the Supporters Club announced that they had enrolled their 250th member and by mid March, with over 300 members, the first function was announced.

This was to be a Dance and Cabaret in the Lower Mead Social Club on Friday April 25th, tickets were available for half-a-crown, and were soon selling well.

On Easter Monday, Wealdstone played the return leg of their North West Middlesex Cup semi-final against Wembley, and leading 7–3 from the first leg, Wealdstone expected to go through comfortably. They were however troubled by a weakened Wembley side before finally winning 4–1 to go through 11–4 on aggregate.

League form was still indifferent and inconsistent, exemplified by a fixture away to Walton and Hersham. Wealdstone were behind at half time by 4–3 and to all onlookers, were expected to lose by more as the second half progressed.

A complete change saw Wealdstone take the initiative in the second half, convincing most onlookers that they were the most likely winners, equalising quickly and then having a goal disallowed that would have seen them take the lead.

'Stones though could not find the net and Walton took the lead with six minutes to go, by 5–4 only for Wealdstone to equalise, then having another goal disallowed that would have seen them take the lead again, only for the Wealdstone goalkeeper, A Brown, to miss-judge a gently rolling ball, allowing a Walton forward to score with the last kick of the game for a 6–5 win.

The season finished on a high note. Facing Harrow Town in the two leg Final of the North West Middlesex Invitation Cup, 'Stones recorded a creditable draw at Earlsmead, 1–1, then went on to win at Lower Mead 3–2 after extra time, the fitness of the Wealdstone players being the deciding factor.

With gates having increased slightly over the season, poor results in the 'major' cups resulted in the club losing £91 on the season, against a profit of £241 the previous year. This was now causing great concern as the club had a deficit of £1,192 at the bank.

Much as the Committee hoped that better results in the cups would increase income to alleviate the situation, they were also looking to reduce their overall costs. The Supporters Club had helped in this area, their first effort on behalf of the club being to redecorate the ground, painting the grandstand in the process.

Another Wealdstone Fete, this time organised by the Supporters Club was being planned for July.

On the playing side the inconsistencies were put down to (among other things) injuries, which resulted at one point in four out of five goalkeepers being injured.

Mr Len Goulden who had been appointed Coach at the start of the season had generously offered to continue unpaid as the financial position came to light but eventually he too had had to leave the club due to Business commitments, Edgar Francis and Peter Rogers taking over.

The 'A' Team had been the most successful, comfortably winning their section of the Harrow and Wembley League and several of their players had progressed into the reserves during the season.

The newly formed colts – Wealdstone FC had taken over the Harrow Schools team during the season – had collected their first trophy, the Harrow Youth League Senior Challenge Cup, beating Shaftesbury Rovers after extra time in the final at Harrow Town FC, Dempsey and Pottle scoring the colts goals.

Terry Shannon
Player 1957-1960,

I'd played for my school team, and for Harrow Schools from the Under 11's to, as it was then, the Over 15's, mainly in the left back and left half positions which was funny really, as I was predominantly a right footed player!

'Mr. Emerson' whose son, Melvin, played in all of the Harrow teams in that period was connected with Wealdstone, and he somehow persuaded the club to start a 'colts' team. They did, and they used the entire Harrow Over 15's side to play!

We won the cup in our first season and also came runner up in the league.

The following season we won both the league and the cup. I graduated into the 'A' team and then the reserves and finally into the Senior Team, unfortunately only for a few games before work commitments took me away from football altogether.

I remember as a boy, watching Wealdstone win the Athenian League and I ran onto the pitch with all the other boys, my favourite player then was Mikrut at centre forward - he was the best header of a ball I've ever seen.

Later, when I played, my favourites were Charlie Townsend and Viv Evans, I always remember Charlie being very vocal on the playing field but very quiet and gentle off it.

A couple of years after leaving Wealdstone, coming away from a meeting in Kenton, four young lads approached me and asked for my autograph, they also asked who I was playing for, saying that they followed my progress at Wealdstone.

I must say I left them with a lump in my throat and a sadness that I had not extended my playing career with the club. I still look back on that time with great pleasure and I wish the club a happy and successful future.

A better start on the field the following season laid a firm footing for what seemed likely to be a good year and by late September 'Stones were well placed near the top of the Athenian League.

A league visit to Maidstone, the previous season's runner up with former Stone Danny Wiltshire in goal amplified the improvements Wealdstone had made, when they ran our easy winners by 4–0, inflicting the Kent club's heaviest defeat since they joined the league.

Maidstone had been struggling to score to such an extent that they introduced a 15 year old England trialist, Michael Broad into their side at outside left for the match. As reported at the time.

Almost everything he did was rich in promise, but his colleagues were hopelessly disjointed and un-progressive near goal............

A week later it seemed that the Gods were smiling on Wealdstone. The financial position well known and the FA Competitions an important source of funds, Wealdstone were drawn at home to face Hayes in the second qualifying round.

Lucky Wealdstone, unlucky Hayes! With Hayes deservedly leading by 4-1 after 82 minutes play, referee H E Stokes blew one short sharp blast on his whistle and the game was abandoned. Leaving a thoroughly beaten Wealdstone side living to fight another day.

Was the referee's decision justified? Hayes officials indignantly thought not. They conceded that this step may well have been taken half an hour earlier when a torrential storm all but flooded the already saturated pitch. Yet they felt that having gone so far the game should have been taken to an admittedly farcical conclusion, with the players unable to propel the ball more than a few feet through mud and puddles.

On the Wednesday following it became evident just how lucky Wealdstone had been, as they went on to win the replayed tie 2-1, both goals being penalties and the second hotly disputed. It was Wealdstone that were to progress and play Yiewsley in the third qualifying round.

Johnny Moran
Player 1958 -1963,

I played for Wealdstone for almost six seasons, and although I don't know how many appearances I made, or even how many goals I scored, I do know that I was the club penalty taker during this time, and I only missed one! (It was at Sutton United and I'll never forget it!)

I came to Wealdstone from Wembley FC, and when I left I joined Barnet, then Hendon and Finchley but I have always thought of Wealdstone as 'my' club.

During my time with the 'Stones, I played for Middlesex, the Athenian League, FA XI's and I was a reserve twice for England, against West Germany and Scotland, and I also played as an amateur for QPR Reserves for three years!!

There are so many memories, but in particular the sing-songs we always had coming home from away games, always led by 'Banger' Walsh and his pal, George, who was Charlie Sells' father in law. The Yo-Yo Song, The Winkle Song, My Brother Sylvest, - win or lose it didn't matter, we would always sing on the way home, and funnily enough I don't think I've ever heard any of those songs sung since those days.

We had a couple of 'club tours' as well, one to either Belgium or Holland where we ended up in a 'dubious' nightclub. One of the lads, (I think it was Brian Henderson) put a big note over the bar to buy a round, but, just at that moment the police raided the joint - the bar grill went down immediately and we all made for the back door as fast as we could dragging the protesting Brian along with us - He still talks about the money that place owes him!

There was a young guy called Ben who worked with me on the printing machines at H.M. Stationary office at Wealdstone and he also worked part-time at Wealdstone Mortuary, as well as helping out on the massage table for the club .He used to work quite a lot with red ink, which is extremely difficult to get out once it's under your finger nails.

I remember a couple of occasions when, with new players at his mercy on the massage table, Ben would tell the tale about "the chap they brought in to the mortuary this morning, who had been knocked down by a bus - there was blood everywhere......." he'd then casually show his hands in front of the player on the table as he added " Sorry, I didn't have time to wash!!".

They always went as white as a sheet, and a couple even ran out of the dressing room screaming!

There's one match I remember where we were at home, playing Hayes at Lower Mead and we were losing 1-4 when there was a tremendous downpour of rain and the referee abandoned the match with only about ten minutes to go. The match was replayed shortly afterwards and we won 2-1 and the Hayes players were still talking about that referee years later!

The reserves too had started well in their division. With the cricket season now over, Peter Parfitt of Middlesex and England had rejoined the club, scoring five of Wealdstone's goals in a 10–5 victory over BSP, Mick Hughes (4) and Mick Fisher being the other scorers.

It was a busy time for the Wealdstone FC Trainer, Freddie Welch. He was a coach to Wealdstone Amateur Boxing Club. He was honoured when selected as a 'second' for London in an international amateur boxing match versus Moscow at the Royal Albert Hall.

Luck again played a part for Wealdstone in the FA Amateur Cup. Drawn at home to Ruislip Manor, although on balance of play being the better side, Wealdstone were losing by two goals with only ten minutes remaining. Charlie Sells then scored a 'breakaway' goal to make the score 1–2 before a curious penalty was awarded to Wealdstone, the linesman spotting a handball that the referee, who was well up with play, had failed to spot.

Moran stepped up and scored with some ease to equalise and force yet another replay, which Wealdstone went on to win 4–0.

In common with other seasons, October was fast becoming a month of cup-ties, but this season Wealdstone were drawing and winning rather then losing, as had been the case in recent seasons.

After the eventful victory over Hayes, Wealdstone were drawn

Wealdstone FC Reserves 1958; Winners of the Westminster Hospital Cup;
Back Row; Peter Rogers, Tony Conniff, Matt Farrell, Roy Gibbons, Brian Green, Derek Kay, Mike Dunk, Ted Dew,
Front Row; Jim Pyers, Nial McLaughlan, George Mowle, Reg Ware, Clive Stone, Ben Freeman

away to professional Yiewsley in the divisional qualifying final of the FA Cup, a club they hadn't beaten in any competition since 1953.

Yiewsley started the stronger and they took the lead in the first half, but despite a lot of pressure, Wealdstone's defence held firm and didn't concede any more goals. The second half saw a more confident Wealdstone take the game to their opponents, and they scored twice to achieve a 2-1 win through Sells and Nichols.

On the same afternoon the reserves also progressed in a cup match, theirs the Middlesex Junior Cup at Lower Mead where they faced a Pinner reserves team.

A strong Wealdstone Reserves side gave the Pinner side no chance in the Middlesex Junior Cup at Lower Mead and beat them 11-0.

Although outplayed throughout, Pinner thoroughly earned the applause they were given for a sporting exhibition and there was special praise for the plucky goalkeeping by Vassalo, who was in no way to blame for this defeat.

Peter Parfitt, the Middlesex cricketer was again on the mark, scoring five goals for the second week in succession. Three of his goals came in the first half, when Davies, Matthews and Nash also scored, Parfitt (2) Mathews, Nash and Deanus took the total to eleven after the interval.

Wealdstone; E Finch, G Mowle, R Ware, A Comben, J Hall, R Gibbons, J Matthews, F Deanus, G Nash, P Parfitt, J Davies.

The first team were drawn at home again in the FA Cup, this time to the professionals of Headington United of the Southern League who ran out winners by four goals to two in a closely competitive match, most people considering that a one goal advantage would have been more accurate.

There was some good news as the income had briefly relieved the pressure on the club and there was still the opportunity of further income in the FA A Amateur Cup later on.

While the first team slipped to defeat at home, the reserves won the first trophy of the season, winning the Westminster Hospital Challenge Cup Final, delayed from the previous season, beating Walton and Hersham Reserves by three goals to one, the third and eventually winning goal scored again by Peter Parfitt.

In fact it seemed that all of the Wealdstone teams had little trouble in front of goal, as the Wealdstone 'A' team won a Middlesex Junior Cup-tie by 13–1 against Corona, Fred Deanus helping himself to five goals, Keen (4), Conniff (3) and Howard completing the scoring. The Colts won 7–2 on the same day, to give the club three wins and one defeat scoring 25 goals and conceding 8.

Wealdstone finished the year on a high, four wins and one draw gaining the club nine valuable league points while there was further success in the London Senior Cup.

Then it became a happy Christmas as well, the club drawing with Hendon at Lower Mead on Christmas day 3–3 and winning at Claremont Road the following morning 4–3 in a farcical match played in ankle deep mud.

To complete a successful Christmas all round, Wealdstone Reserves beat Enfield 6–1 to complete a league double and the 'A' team advanced to the fifth round of the Middlesex Junior Cup by beating Southall 'A' by 6–1 at Headstone Lane, the Railway sports Ground having become their home base.

The Supporters Club had also been making progress with a consistent flow of memberships. At the first AGM, Secretary Tom Verrall announced that the club's fortunes were being followed by members far and wide including America, Canada, Ceylon and Egypt.

These were included in a membership of over 750, and they had already contributed a full 'continental' kit to the Wealdstone first team as well as completing numerous jobs in the ground.

There was now a new target in sight – that of the installation of floodlights for training at Lower Mead, the area behind the Elmslie Stand to be cleared to allow training under lights without damaging the main pitch.

In fact the membership continued to increase and later in the season Cardew Robinson attended a Wealdstone fixture as usual. He was invited to join the Supporters Club, which he accepted, becoming number 900 on the membership list, and he also became Vice-president.

Mr & Mrs Tom and Julia Verrall
Supporters and founders of The Supporters Club

I was a follower for a few years and then after an appeal by the club Chairman for someone to try and form a Supporters' Club I offered to try and arrange something.

With the help of some volunteers, led by Jock Law, Sam Burrows & Barbara Robson we formed a committee to run a Supporters club. My wife Julia joined with me to gets things going and she decided to open a couple of tea huts to supply spectators with refreshments.

With the help of Mrs. Law two tea huts were opened on the ground for the benefit of supporters at matches and it was from this that a Supporters' Club was formed and the response from this was great.

It was decided that arrangement be made to provide transport for supporters to away matches and it was usually that three or four coaches were available for Club Members. Meanwhile, many jobs were done by committee members to improve their comfort on match days such as the cleaning up of seats for the benefits of spectators and all of the work was done voluntarily with no cost to the club.

One great helper was a member called Eric Metcalfe who was in charge of the coaches and he always had a supply of sweets that he gave to the children on the coaches and his top hat and rattles were a feature everywhere.

Another feature of the Supporters' Club was the formation of a Social Club and many grand concerts and evenings were given by a group of club members such as Chuck Adams and some female members who provided first-class entertainment for members in general.

It was generally agreed by other Clubs that Wealdstone FC was first-class in all respects and the club Officers such as Danny, Ken and Mrs. Wiltshire were a great asset in forming a great Club. This of course helped in attracting players to the club!

I would say that my favourite player was THE WEALDSTONE CLUB itself and I am proud of being the Founder President of the Wealdstone FC Supporters' Club and regret that my visits recently been rather low due to ill health.

Both Julia and I are Life Members of the Football Club and proud of the fact.

As Easter came and went, Wealdstone recorded three league victories, scoring twelve goals and conceding only three to join Barnet in second place in the Athenian League, Maidstone, the leaders four points in front with three matches remaining.

Wealdstone and Barnet both had nine matches still to play, having had some cup success earlier in the season. This success still lead to fixture congestion at the end of the season, and despite a one week extension to the season granted by the FA after the death of a Birmingham City full-back, Wealdstone found themselves with seven matches in fourteen days including the Middlesex Senior Cup Final!

Wealdstone continued to tussle for the league honours but did manage to defeat Enfield in the Middlesex Senior Cup Final by three goals to one in persistent rain. This, like the league matches at the time was a struggle, many of the players finding it difficult to play so often.

The summer weekends though were brightened up with regular trips to the seafront at Brighton, more a social event than serious football but light training in the sea air gave everyone a lift.

As if it wasn't enough that there were so many league fixtures and reserve fixtures being played at Lower Mead, the ground was 'rented out' to the Harrow referee's association who held a charity match against the Showbiz XI in front of 1800 people.

It was the setting for a match as part of the television coverage for the FA Cup Final, a match being staged between the T V All-stars and a National Boys Clubs XI, selected by the singer Frankie Vaughan.

Mike and Bernie Winters, Harry Fowler, Alfie Bass, Jess Conrad, Pete Murray, Lonny Donnegan and Anthony Newly were some of the 'stars' taking part. The match was refereed by Tommy Docherty, the Scotland and Arsenal full back.

It was no doubt a very busy day for the groundsman as in the evening, Wealdstone had an Athenian League match, kicking off at 6pm, well after the televised FA Cup Final had finished.

A late 50's Fun-day at Lower Mead. The teams shown include a number of players and officials: Left at the rear, G Knapp, Centre: 1st Facing: Edgar Francis, two behind him, Viv Evans and W (Bill) Roberts. The right hand team: Jim Pyers, Ken Wiltshire, R Kelly, C Hurford and A Adams.

The battle at the top of the table with Barnet continued until the last day of the season. Wealdstone new exactly what they had to do in the last match, away to Sutton United, even a 1–0 defeat would have been sufficient to secure the title for a second time, but it was not to be. A very tired Wealdstone team lost by 3–2, and thus lost the title on goal average by 1/25th of a goal!

Reg Ware
Supporter and Player

I started watching Wealdstone back in the late 1940's. I grew up in Wealdstone, but never had enough money to ride a bus, so it was a mile and a half walk to the ground from Toorack Road.

If we were quiet we could watch the first half from the top of the steps above the shops next to the Dominion Cinema. Then, as soon as the gates opened up at half time, we were able to get in and see the second half from the terraces.

If we were really lucky, there was a programme discarded somewhere, which was then used to get autographs at the end of the game. We were right there, with 'The Man In Blue' behind the goal.

One of the early highlights was seeing Eddie Smith's first game for the club when he scored six goals. Forward Bert Dyke and Goalkeeper Les McDonald lived in Toorack Road, so we almost felt part of the team!

After being de-mobbed from the RAF, I started to play for the 'A' Team under Jimmy Pyers, who also worked in the Stationary Office where I was apprenticed.

We had a cup final in the first few weeks which was left over from the previous season, and we won the London Hospitals Cup.

Eventually, I played in the reserves and then I had a few games in the first team at the end of the 1958-59 season. Then a woman came into my life, and her family emigrated to the USA. I joined them in July of 1959 and I'm still here living in Florida and watching all the football I can on TV.

Jim Hall
Player 1958-1962

I joined Wealdstone at the start of the 1958-1959 season from Enfield as a centre half, and I played regularly for three seasons, until in 1962 I left and had short spells at Carshalton and Edgware, before returning to Lower Mead the same season.

I was fortunate on my return to still be considered a squad member and I was happy playing reserve team football with the occasional appearance in the first team, and I managed to play a variety of positions including Goalkeeper during this time.

When I was at Enfield, they had seven current internationals in their first team squad, so my appearances had become limited to covering when players were injured or on International duty but at least this improved my game, playing with such good players when I did get the opportunity, that Wealdstone were interested in signing me!

The local paper ran a small piece when I joined Wealdstone, stating how "Enfield's Loss is Wealdstone's Gain" and also saying I'd "got fed up with the closed shop policy at Enfield" which upset them, and me as it wasn't true, and In my second or third game, Enfield were the visitors - I got a lot of stick that day!!

All of my memories of Wealdstone are happy. The players, Coaches, Committee and Supporters were always very friendly and the support from the terraces during matches was tremendous.

There were so many matches that stick in the mind, and other occasions such as being selected to play for Middlesex and the club tour of Amsterdam and on a personal note, having played with and against some of the many quality players in the Athenian League at that time.

My greatest memory is of the whole of the 1958-1959 season. The highlights after a fairly ordinary start to the campaign was the winning streak that took us to the top of the league, neck and neck with Barnet, needing to do no worse than lose 1-0 at Sutton in our last game of the season to win the title, Barnet having already finished their matches.

We fell behind twice and levelled twice only to concede a third goal in the last minute or two, suffering a 3-2 defeat, and missing out on the league title by point zero, zero something of a goal, Barnet winning the title without playing that day.

There was Champagne waiting in the dressing room for us. It may be still waiting there!

In all my time with the club there was only one disappointment - in the Official Handbook at the end of that season, in 1959, there were 'Pen Pictures' of all the players and I was named as Jimmy HILL not Hall. I never did have the chin.............

Such was the spirit among the players that even after a long hard season, they were intent in staying together as a club, and so it was the Wealdstone FC Cricket team was re-formed, playing a number of matches throughout the summer, filling vacant dates on their opponents ground on a number of Sunday afternoons.

There were a number of first team players that were already competent Club cricketers to aid the side and there was the hope that on occasions they would be further strengthened by the addition of Peter Parfitt, of Middlesex and England.

The close season was a happier one at Wealdstone, the AGM able to report a better season financially and in terms of results.

The greatest topic of discussion was a proposal for a three up and three down relegation between the Athenian and Corinthian leagues.

The Athenian League members had by vote agreed, but Wealdstone Chairman H A Luck made no bones about the fact that Wealdstone did not vote in favour of the proposal.

He pointed out that there was a 'break' in the agreement after three years, so that if the clubs so wished, the scheme would be scrapped and the clubs would all return to their 'original' leagues!

The following season promised a great deal as the majority of the Wealdstone team had remained with the club, an after winning two of the first three league matches of the season the club were in buoyant mood. It was not to last though as this signalled a long run of indifferent performances and defeats, and what (in hindsight) may be considered panic moves by the selection committee.

So it was in September that the Harrow Observer reported...

Only four members of the Wealdstone team that won 2-0 at Walton and Hersham three weeks ago survive for the return fixture this coming Saturday.

The selection committee took this drastic action after disappointing displays against Hounslow and Enfield.

Dropped are Captain, Roy Hurrell, Derek Kay, John Saunders, Matt Farrell and Brian Moore, whilst from the earlier team Ted Culver and George Mowle have already been relegated to the reserves.

In the general whirligig, Arthur Ash, unable to regain his place at the end of last season and beginning of this becomes right back and captain. He is partnered by M Quinn who last Saturday played for Millwall Reserves. Len Hills leads the attack and Tony Conniff is preferred to Massey.

Much as these changes were quite drastic, in the short term they had the desired effect, Wealdstone running out winners by 3-1 in the match.

The Lower Mead ground was so highly considered among amateur grounds at the time that it was always one of the first choices when representative matches were being arranged.

This sequence continued when the Athenian League side played and beat a Caribbean XI by 7–2, Johnny Moran, the 'Stones striker scoring two goals in the second half, one, a great shot and the second a neat header.

The 'Stones strangely up and down start to the season continued though. In the last week of October another win was recorded, 3–1 over Finchley, with two goals in the last couple of minutes securing the points – this was their first win since late September when they beat the same side 2–1 on their own ground.

Results were poor right up until Christmas and were not improved by the annual fixtures against Hendon, this year a draw at Lower Mead by 2-2 was followed by a farcical defeat at Claremont Road by 1-0, in conditions that were if anything totally unplayable.

Parts of the pitch were underwater at the kick off, and the whole pitch soon became a quagmire as more rain fell. Worse still, there were times when it became so dark it was almost impossible to determine who was who!

The New Year saw Wealdstone in the first round proper of the Amateur Cup for the first time in a number of years, but it was still a major disappointment when the club fell at the first hurdle, losing to Bromley.

Consistency had been a problem for the 'Stones on the field before Christmas, but it cannot have been helped by the number of team changes, trying to find a successful mix.

Indeed as a result of the Bromley fixture John Saunders became the fourth Captain to lose his place since the start of the season! He was one of a number of changes the following week when Wealdstone were to face Willesden in the Middlesex Senior Cup.

The inconsistencies showed again though, as Wealdstone lost and were knocked out of three cup competitions in consecutive weeks.

Captain George Mowle holds the North West Middlesex Challenge Cup aloft after the wins against Harrow Town. Behind him is Reserve forward Peter Hatton, scorer of four goals.

At the end of the month of January, Wealdstone had suffered five consecutive defeats adding the two in the league to those in the cup, and yet they were not slipping too far out of contention in the Athenian League.

February saw an immediate improvement with three good wins, beating Grays 6-0, then inconsecutive weeks beating Hornchurch and Upminster 4-2 away and then 2-1 at home. The latter could only be described as a lucky win though, the winning goal being scored by Matt Farrell, who receiving the ball in an offside position controlled it with his arm, neither linesman or referee noticing!

This left Wealdstone second in the table behind Barnet, a position they maintained the following week with a 1-0 win at Leyton. In truth this was a somewhat false position, most clubs had better goal average and games in hand due to more success in the cups.

Wealdstone Reserves had similar form early on but their task was made all the more difficult by a number of Representative Call-ups as well as a regular loss of players to the first team. Their fortunes were a little better in the cup competitions, a single goal against Green and Silley Weir securing a place in the London Intermediate Cup semi-final. The following week a 2-1 win against Ford United Reserves, who were unbeaten until this time, saw 'Stones reach the final.

For the first team, Johnny Moran received a representative call up, being selected as a reserve for England against Germany. This honour came on the back of a number of good performances for the FA XI including the previous week he had scored twice at Maidstone.

The first team finished their league fixtures early in April with a 1–0 win over Barnet (who were still expected to win the league) at Lower Mead.

The following week facing Edgware Town in the semi-final of the North West Middlesex Invitation Cup, struggling to a 3-0 win at Lower Mead and then winning the return match at Edgware by 9-0.

Viv Evans scored twice at Edgware, the first of the two, his 100th goal for the club. It meant at least that the first team had the opportunity to finish their season with a trophy of their own, while the reserves had continued to improve in the league and had two cup finals to contemplate.

Finishing strongly, the reserves had secured the runner up spot behind Hayes, some four points adrift while the first team finished 4th, equal on points with third placed Enfield but well behind eventual champions Hounslow Town and Barnet whose form had faded badly at the end of the season.

The first team won the North West Middlesex Invitation Cup beating Harrow Town by 3–1 at home and 5–1 away in the two-legged final, and the reserves duly won the Athenian League Reserve Section Challenge Cup beating Grays 4–0, before completing their 'double' beating Wimbledon Reserves in the final of the London Intermediate Cup by 1–0.

In a period of nine days, the first team and reserve Cup winners (twice) were joined by two more. The 'A' team, primarily a team playing to keep players fit and available for the other sides, won the Harrow Senior Charity Cup and the colts won the Harrow Youth League Cup for the third year in a row which was a record in itself. The colts also went on to complete a double, winning the Harrow Youth League title as well.

It was to be a successful week at the end of a season where the form of all the Wealdstone sides had fluctuated and perhaps had not, despite the cup wins, delivered all that was promised.

At the beginning of June it was announced that Wealdstone FC were to go on an overseas tour for the first time, twelve players and nine officials travelling to Luxembourg for three matches over a weekend. Hounslow Town were also to travel playing matches against the same opposition.

Only a few seconds prevented Wealdstone from returning from their visit to Luxembourg completely victorious on Monday. They were leading Joeuf 2-1 in the last minute when the home side broke through to score an equaliser. There was not time left to restart the game even.

Although not at full strength, Wealdstone returned with a better record than Hendon, the Amateur Cup holders who made the same trip a fortnight ago, and Hounslow Town, the Athenian League Champions, who shared the plane with Wealdstone and only won one of their three games.

Luxembourg officials rated Wealdstone as the best footballing side they had met on such visits, Mr J Ryan, the Wealdstone Press Secretary told the Observer.

The Wealdstone Squad in Luxembourg; Back Row; The Coach Driver, Roy Hurrell, Charlie Townsend, Ted Culver, Geoff Riddy, Ray Hooper, Don Aldridge. Front Row; Charlie Sells, Mick Hughes, Viv Evans, Tony Conniff, John Saunders, Jim Pyers (1st Team Secretary) Bill Leadbetter (Club Secretary)

In the first game, played on a poor pitch after they had driven about 60 miles through rain and hail, Wealdstone beat Jarny 3-2 Tony Conniff scoring twice from centre forward and sells adding the other goal.

On Saturday a match played against Audon in almost tropical heat was a real battle with tempers getting high at times. This time Sells scored twice and Conniff once for Wealdstone to win. In the final game, Viv Evans, Captain for all three games scored both goals.

Between games the party did a good deal of sightseeing quite apart from having to travel considerable distances from their hotel to all three matches. The players returned with the customary pennants and plaques to London Airport on Monday night.

The AGM was able to report that although the gate income had dropped, a number of actions taken to reduce the debt shown on the balance sheet had shown benefit.

A profit of £322 on the season had brought the club assets to a position some £64 below its liabilities, a far stronger position than it had been in for a number of years.

There was still a long way to go as some £4,600 was still to be repaid but this had reduced by a third in the previous five years. It was again helped by a share out from the FA and Amateur Cup funds. The Amateur Cup contributing £137 this season on its own.

Wages were still the greatest expenditure, totalling £866. For the following season, admission was to increase from 1s 3d to 1s 6d, and membership was to increase to £1 15s from £1 10s.

Jim Pyers
Player 1949-1953, 'A' Team Secretary 1958-1964

The Stand and Dressing Rooms at Lower Mead were bought from Sommerstown FC (London) in the 1930's and the Turnstiles came from Hurst Park racecourse when it closed down, later Harrow Council stipulated when the Floodlights were installed in 1962 that they had to be taken down at the end of each season to placate local objections - it was soon found to be non-workable!

There were some characters and well known faces (and voices) behind the scenes as well, with the educated voice of Phil Carden on the tannoy in the forties and fifties, with announcements of the club news and teams and music to entertain, the team regularly running out to a song of which I believe the words were;

Here we are, here we are, Here we are again,
-Forget about the weather - Never mind the rain,
Now we're all together, Here we are again
-All good friends and Jolly Good Company!

The Sunday Mornings at Lower Mead became a tradition as well. Every Sunday the dressing rooms would be open to Wealdstone and local junior teams - all the 'walking wounded' alike.

Bill Gallagher, Billy Williams and Ernie Pitt, the First, Reserve and 'A' Team Trainers would be there to treat all that came in, and when they finished it was all into the old clubhouse beside the Main Stand to be welcomed by the Wiltshire family - Danny (senior) Bill and Stan serving at the bar and everyone there dissecting the previous Saturdays game's over a pint or two. I always wondered what they talked about in the summer!

There was always a special welcome to new players when they joined Wealdstone as well from Les Hill. He was just a supporter, but he became responsible for the jugs of tea in the Dressing Room on match days and training nights, and he was always quick to make the new players feel at home with a cup or two.

On the playing front, I think my favourite player was Charlie Townsend. Off the field he's such a shy character, but on the field he was a regular tiger. Shouting instructions - Hold It - Help Him - Move It - and occasionally with the odd rude word

Wealdstone FC 1959-60;
Back Row; Banger Walsh (Trainer), Charlie Townsend, Bill Fowler, Ron King, John Saunders, Peter Rogers (Coach),
Front Row; Jimmy Pyers (1st Team Secretary), George Mowle, Ken Aldridge, Viv Evans, Charlie Sells, Matt Farrell, Don Aldridge, Peter Parfitt

thrown in. He had a tremendous 'football brain' and the skills to match - he always wanted to win.

An example of his shyness was his return to the clubhouse on the Saturday evening of his first England Cap (April 29th 1961) There was the usual entertainment of music and dancing in the club and it was full of people, but a watch was being kept in the car park for his arrival as he'd promised to come in after the game. When the door opened and he entered, the band struck up 'For He's A Jolly Good Fellow' - Charlie almost turned round and left, but in his usual unassuming way he just walked the length of the dance floor to the bar and ordered a drink.

It was strange looking back, as Charlie was nearly released in his first season with the club - The 'A' team played away in Bushey, and Charlie was to be our opponent, someone had already tipped us off about him, so it was a great opportunity to have a look at him.

The day after the game my father and I went to his house to sign him and he joined the club, playing at first in the reserves as a forward which was his position at the time, and being a little unremarkable - certainly less than we'd hoped for.

We considered releasing him at the end of the season until one Saturday when there was no game for Charlie, and he went to watch the first team. As he got to the ground Edgar Francis approached him and said that one of the team - I don't remember who - had had an accident and wouldn't be able to play. Edgar asked Charlie if he would like to step in which he did, in 'midfield' where he went on to play for the next dozen or more years!

A G Johnson
Supporter since 1930's

After sixty years it would take me months to put to words my memories of the good matches and to name one of hundreds of good players that have played for the club from Baldwin and Bunce in the 1930s

I have fond memories of Eric the Wealdstone taxi driver who never missed a game home or away and was known to all home and away supporters as the man in the Blue and White suit and top hat.

We always have had great support, but remember the 40's 50's and 60's when it was nothing to see the turn-out of at least four coaches to away games and at least 14 coaches to away cup-ties.

I also have fond memories of Frank Harbud who played for Wealdstone at wing half and finished his time as bagman. My wife and I used to travel with Frank on the team coach to all away games.

The players were always close to the fans as well – I used to drink with Henryk Mikrut in the now forgotten pub "The Marques of Granby" next to Debenhams on Saturday evenings after the game.

Everything was different - Watching players such as Charlie Barker and Charlie Edmonds training during the week (running around the streets of Harrow) was a common sight. My wife and I used to enjoy the family nights on Saturday evenings when the club was at Lower Mead, especially one of our Wedding Anniversaries when I won 3 prizes in the raffle two of which we still have after all these years -. A glass bowl and a potato chipper - the third prize was returned and re-raffled.

The most memorable game must be when we beat Colchester United in the FA cup the Wealdstone team being managed by our old player Peter Rogers. He spent a lot of the match running around the outside of the pitch coaching our players!

Other great games were Wealdstone's two cup games at Wembley. The Television matches and the wartime matches against Spurs, Arsenal and West Ham. I also remember Jackie Milburn coming into the club house at Lower Mead after Newcastle had won the cup. It was full of champagne and we all had a drink out of it! He came down to show his appreciation of Wealdstone supporters attitude when they visited Newcastle. In the previous round, their supporters had been refused entrance to Hendon FC's social club!

I could with the aid of records go on writing forever about a great Club who used to mean a great deal to the people of Harrow and Wealdstone and hopefully will in the future.

THE NINETEEN SIXTIES

The 1960-61 season started well for Wealdstone, winning 5-3 at Barnet to open the season and then winning at home 4-1 and 2-1 against Finchley and Hayes respectively.

A defeat at Sutton by the odd goal in three was the first setback, then came another away fixture with Hornchurch and Upminster.

Although beaten twice by Wealdstone the previous year, Hornchurch and Upminster had ended the season undefeated in their last 17 league matches, and they started far better on the day, quickly taking a 2-0 lead which they held until half time.

Wealdstone though, were a better side than in the previous season, and settling into their stride in the second half, and with Charlie Sells and Viv Evans showing excellent form, 'Stones fought back to win by four goals to two.

Wealdstone were also honoured by being the first club fully affiliated to the Football Association to be invited to take part in the Amateur Football Association Invitation Cup. In Mid September they played their first fixture in the competition, against Pegasus, the combined Oxford and Cambridge University team.

'Stones ran out by three goals to one after extra tome, but there was a tinge of sadness to the occasion as the Wealdstone players had worn black armbands throughout the match in memory of Henryk Mikrut, who had recently died in his early thirties.

The last match of September was a league fixture away to the reigning Champions, Hounslow Town. Having been beaten at home 5-4 by the same opponents a fortnight earlier, 'Stones were out for revenge, and they duly won the match by 4-2 to go level with Hendon and Sutton United at the top of the Athenian League.

Wealdstone had led 2-0 just after half time but were reduced to ten men when Don Aldridge left the field with a knee injury. Hounslow scored twice to equalise and with twenty minutes still to play, it seemed they were likely to go on and win, but a fighting display from the ten man 'Stones led to Townsend and Sells scoring twice more to seal the important victory.

There were yet more honours for Wealdstone players as well, as Charlie Townsend was selected as Reserve for England and

Wealdstone v Pegasus.

SPOTTED !

Tipped off by a supporter that there was a brilliant outside - left playing in Sunday football, a Hayes official went to see him in action on Sunday. The outside-left was, surely enough, in cracking form and scored a hat-trick. Alas for Hayes . . . the player's name was Vivian Evans.

And Evans was chosen for Wales on Monday.

From the Harrow Observer 10/11/60

at the same time Viv Evans was selected for Wales although this was not an international as Wales were to face a Combined Universities team.

He won a half cap for the call up, having previously missed an opportunity for a full cap as he was representing Middlesex Wanderers on tour in Nigeria! Charlie Sells was chosen for the Athenian League team alongside Charlie Townsend and Matt Farrell was to play centre forward for Middlesex against London University.

The beginning of November saw Wealdstone score twice in each half at home against Redhill to run out winners by 4-1, a victory which saw Wealdstone top the Athenian League outright.

The pitch was in poor condition and was described as 'becoming more and more like a glue pot as the match continued' Redhill coping better as the conditions worsened but by then the match was well beyond their reach, as Wealdstone had so dominated the first hour.

Brian Curtis
Supporter since the 1950's

I was born in 1944 and attended the now demolished Belmont Secondary School in Fisher Road, Wealdstone. I believe my first match was a trial game - Blues v Whites - in the mid 1950's.

I cannot remember the year, but I can remember the Wealdstone team; Ted Culver in goal, Roy Hurrell and John Randall, backs, Charlie Townsend, Ray Kingsland, John Saunders, halves and Colin Moore, Charlie Sells, Matt Farrell, Ivor Harper and Viv Evans, forwards.

Colin Moore was an old fashioned winger, hugging the touchline and providing crosses for the forwards. My school friends and I went to stand opposite the main stand, midway between the half way line and the Elmslie Stand. Colin used to parade his tricks in front of us for one half and we started an unofficial 'Colin Moore Fan Club'. We didn't have too many members as he wasn't the most popular player but we regularly applauded his skills and chanted his name.

One day our idol fell from grace. Colin was injured, not badly, but right in front of us. The trainer made his way from in front of the stand, bucket, water and sponge in hand. Having reached Colin, he was just about to administer the treatment when Colin cried out "Not the water, no, not the water!".

We all wondered what was in the water but we decided that Colin was a bit of a wimp.

Bill Emerson was the Secretary of the club for many years. He also used to announce the teams over the P A System, often giving wrong names, and once even the wrong opposition. He was always working hard for the club and it was all part of the Saturday entertainment.

His son Mel also used to play for Wealdstone. He was a centre half who was master of the mistimed tackle, and he usually played in the reserves. The man he was trying to replace at the time was Ron King, who was quite old, but he was good, very good.

Having now graduated to the Members Enclosure with Wealdstone Officials, I always remember a match in which Bill Emerson proceeded to highlight the few errors of Ron King in an effort to 'promote' his son as the replacement. By the end of the game I think all those around would have agreed, just to enjoy some peace and quiet.

I also remember Peter Parfitt and the 'retribution' tackle. Actually, it was more like assault on a Redhill player who had continually fouled Viv Evans.

Peter was an enthusiastic player who later became one of England cricket's best players. In the match against Redhill, a tall full back was unable to stop Viv Evans and he was fouling him quite often.]

Viv was eventually injured. Peter waited, not for too long, until this player dwelt on the ball in front of the main stand.

He then proceeded to fly through the air and hit the opponent somewhere in the thigh region and he despatched him into the railings! (The actual distance grows as the memory fades but it was yards!).

Peter didn't even wait for the referee to remove him from the field, he just ran off down the tunnel.

Wealdstone for once were able to maintain their form in some of the early rounds of the cup competitions. In early December Wealdstone travelled to Wood Green Town in the final qualifying round of the Amateur Cup.

'Stones completely outclassed their opponents, scoring four times in each half, to secure a tie in the first round proper at home to Enfield.

It was a match played under the most dismal of conditions, rain falling continuously, against the unhappy background of acrimony between the two clubs over Wealdstone's successful protest about the shortness of the pitch, and it was played before the tiniest of crowds, Tottenham Hotspur entertaining Burnley just down the road.

It seems that the pitch was found to be some yards short of the required length, and for whatever reason this had been determined from an Ordinance Survey map. Wealdstone had protested, and the result of the protest was that the pitch was altered prior to the match.

The following week Wealdstone completed the first half of their Athenian League programme with a convincing 4-1 win over Enfield at Lower Mead.

In doing so, the club also achieved its 'half century of goals scored' in just fifteen matches.

Victory not only kept Wealdstone at the top of the table, but it did much to wipe out the memory of the humiliating 5-0 defeat at Enfield in September, Enfield being the only side to beat 'Stones by more than the odd goal in any match so far.

It was a bitterly cold day but with battle seriously joined from the kick off both goalkeepers were soon warmed up, Fowler playing especially well as Thomas and Agar led their side into attack. It was this pair that schemed their side into the lead after only 17 minutes, Agar's final shot giving Fowler no chance to save.

Not long afterwards, Evans got his head to a corner by Moran and was unlucky to see the ball strike the crossbar, Flavell clearing off the line soon afterwards. It was not until the 34th minute that 'Stones drew level, obstructed inside the penalty area, Ken Aldridge took the free kick himself and his perfectly placed lob was headed fiercely into the far top corner of the net by Evans.

In fast end to end exchanges before the interval, both sides had their escapes, Hyde once hitting the crossbar when well placed and Hannam clearing off the line following a fine movement between Sells and Farrell.

Making a great burst from the kick off, Wealdstone all but took the lead immediately, Farrell getting through to shoot wide. This mattered little for Wealdstone went ahead within a minute. Again Farrell went through, this time with Evans in support, Farrell slipped the ball through at just the right second and Evans crashed it right footed past a helpless Dawson.

This was the real turning point and Wealdstone's confidence was seldom seriously disturbed though Enfield won a number of corners and looked dangerous at times. With almost an hour gone, Moran caught the Enfield defence flat footed with a fine through pass and Farrell, seizing on it, put a shot well to Dawson's left before Flavell could tackle.

The scoring ended with a fourth fine goal on 73 minutes, Moran rising high above the Enfield defence to head a corner from Aldridge past Dawson, who got his fingers to the fast flying ball but could not hold it.

So the teams are left to await next months Amateur Cup-tie with both sides having beaten the other by a considerable margin, and Wealdstone at home to Dulwich Hamlet in the London Senior Cup this Saturday look to the Christmas games with Hendon for light on their Championship prospects.

Wealdstone; W Fowler, G Mowle, M Quinn, C Townsend, R King, P Parfitt, K Aldridge, C Sells, M Farrell, J Moran, V Evans.

The Dulwich match saw Wealdstone continue their good form and high scoring in the cup competitions, beating the home side by 6-2, but the Christmas showdown with Hendon was a disappointment due to the weather.

The Christmas Day match at Lower Mead was abandoned and the match the following day ended as a 4-4 draw, allowing Hendon to maintain their one point lead at the top of the table.

January started with a Middlesex Senior Cup-tie, a fixture against Chalfont National and Wealdstone again were the high scoring winners, by 8-0. Four of the goals were scored by Matt Farrell, bringing his total for the season to date to 32, only one behind Eddie Smith's season record of 33!

There were then two shock defeats in the league, Wealdstone travelled to bottom of the table Finchley where they were beaten 3-2 which dented the Championship challenge, and the much vaunted Amateur Cup-tie with Enfield resulted in a home defeat by 2-1.

There was another victory in the London Senior Cup the following week, Wealdstone bouncing back from the Amateur Cup disappointment by beating Kingstonian by 7-0. Wealdstone also reached the semi-final of the Middlesex Senior Cup with a solid 3–0 victory at Lower Mead over Uxbridge.

Still battling away at the top of the league, 'Stones continued to score some success in the cups. In early March 'Stones reached the final of the London Senior Cup for the third time by beating Carshalton Athletic 4-1. In the same week that it was announced that the club were to install floodlights for the start of the following season.

The following week, the Middlesex Charity Cup-tie saw Wealdstone face Harrow Town, who had defeated them by 2-1 in the FA Cup earlier in the season.

Despite equalising twice, Harrow Town were eventually beaten by 6–2, as Wealdstone gained their revenge in bright sunshine. The crowd was over 2,200 and as this was the Charity Cup, the main benefactor was the Middlesex FA Benevolent fund; each Club's share of the proceeds was £37.

The Trainers Bench; L to R; Jim Pyers (first team Secretary), Edgar Francis (Assistant Coach), Vince Burgess (Coach), Jack Rogers (Deputy Chairman), Fred 'Banger' Welch (Trainer).

Mark Snell
Supporter

Vince Burgess as Manager is another never to be forgotten.

He always had a cigarette in his hand and at half time he used to disappear into the bar, often not coming out until well into the second half!

I'm told that down at training, the likes of Lindsay and Townsend used to run training. If Burgess ever came out they'd make a comment about needing a left back or such like. He'd return to the bar and come out later letting them know who he'd signed! He could always poach players. Mostly school teachers I believe.

As the season progressed into March and April, Wealdstone, Hendon and Barnet all continued their challenges at the top of the league. At the end of April Wealdstone were beaten at home by Sutton United, seemingly ending the 'Stones chance.

The following Monday however the race was on again as Hendon drew with Hitchin Town. This left the situation both open and complicated in the last week, as reported by the Harrow Observer;

That draw left the Athenian League Championship more open than ever, with all three clubs still in with a chance. Nor need tonight's clash between Barnet and Hendon at Underhill necessarily settle it unless Hendon win by a really clear-cut margin. (If they do, Wealdstone will have to run up a cricket score against Hitchin on Saturday night to wrest the title away from them on goal average).

Probably a goal average decision is the most likely outcome. In which case Wealdstone might be in the position of losing the title by that unsatisfactory means twice in three seasons. There is an infinity of mathematical situations that could arise and a high scoring win for Barnet may suit Wealdstone best. There would then remain the last stiff hurdle.

Hendon though went on to win 2-0 and 'Stones could only manage a 0-0 draw with Hitchin Town two days later, thus finishing as runner up. A win by 6-0 would have given them the title on goal average.

The following Saturday there was more disappointment when, for the third time Wealdstone lost the Final of the London Senior Cup, this time going down to Enfield by 3-0.

Enfield had become a bogey side during the season, winning the first league encounter by 5-0, winning 2-1 at Lower Mead in the 1st round of the Amateur Cup, and then this 3-0 victory in the London Senior Cup Final. 'Stones only success was the return league encounter, won by 4-1.

There should have been a further meeting between the clubs in the semi-final of the Middlesex Charity Cup but this match was abandoned at 0-0 after 52 minutes in torrential rain. The re-arranged tie was held over to the following season.

The Wealdstone colts though fared better winning the Harrow Youth League Cup for the fourth season in a row, Byford and Carpenter scoring after Warwick Rovers had taken the lead.

As June came along the Committee decided to release Peter Rogers, the first team Coach without giving a reason, after three years. Those three years had seen the club finish as Athenian League runner up twice. They had won the Middlesex Senior Cup and had lost in the final of the London Senior Cup.

At the AGM the club announced that Vince Burgess, formerly of Harrow Town would be replacing Peter Rogers and at the same time it was announced that he had taken over at Hendon, thus joining the league champions from the runner up.

For the second year in succession a small profit had been made, this time £47, and a further payment of £400 to the FA to pay off their loan had also been made.

As part of the celebrations for the club's Diamond Jubilee, the Supporters Club were pressing ahead with the installation of Floodlighting, and a fundraising appeal was launched to help meet the cost.

Supporters Club members digging the trenches for the installation of Floodlights.

There were a number of planning restrictions around the use and the installation of these lights, and the club also appealed against a number of these, while at the same time appealing to the supporters to provide the labour for the work.

Another introduction for the Diamond Jubilee season was the introduction of a Sportsman Of The Year Trophy, won on this first occasion by Ted Culver, the reserve team goalkeeper. Ted had been the first team keeper for two seasons before losing his place.

On the field the following season, a bright start earned Wealdstone three wins and a draw from their first six games, fourth in the table behind unbeaten Enfield, while the reserves were in mid table after two wins and two draws, again from six matches.

There were some new faces in the Wealdstone side, some players having left to join their former trainer at Hendon. A number of changes were made while the club sought the correct balance. This lead to inconsistencies again in the results, amplified in the last week of September.

Bob John
Supporter since the 1950's

I first visited Wealdstone FC in 1956. One match that comes to mind was probably the first match I ever saw. A lot of the kids at the time were wearing 'Davy Crockett' hats which were popular at the time.

Wealdstone played Hounslow Town in the old Athenian League and won 3-1 I think, at home. I remember the left back, Bill Reeves scoring with a shot from a full forty yards. He was a very tough no nonsense player.

Matt Farrell
Player 1958 -1963,

I played for Wealdstone over five seasons, but I never did find out the exact number of games I played - I do know however that I scored over 100 goals for the club.

I was very fortunate to play for Wealdstone at a time when Amateur Football was at a very high standard and was very well supported, especially in Middlesex. The club has always been served very well by a great band of helpers, and the supporters always got behind the team to create a great atmosphere.

There are three matches which really stand out in my memories but surpassingly and unfortunately, Wealdstone didn't win any of them!

The first was in season 1958-59 away to Sutton United in the last game of the season. we were in a situation that we could afford to lose one nil and still be Athenian League Champions on goal average.
Sutton scored first, but I equalised shortly afterwards then Sutton went ahead again and Wealdstone equalised again only for Sutton to score a third goal and hold on for the win.

That meant that Barnet had won the league - by 0.003 of a goal!

A couple of years later, on December 27th 1960 at Lower Mead Wealdstone played Hendon - It was traditional for local rivals Wealdstone and Hendon to play home and away at Christmas.

The game at Hendon on Christmas Day had been rained off and so for this game the ground at Lower Mead was packed solid with an 'unofficial' crowd of around 6,000. The atmosphere was electric, but at half time the scores were still nil-nil.

After the interval things started to happen and the crowd was enthralled by a marvelous end to end game that finished in a four all draw!

Myself and 'Chubby' Aldridge were happy to have shared Wealdstone's goals and most people thought it was the best local derby they had ever witnessed.

Later in 1961, on May 13th we traveled to Highbury to play the London Senior Cup Final against Enfield. Due to injuries we were forced to make changes for this major game and we were unable to play to our usual settled pattern of play.

We were well beaten 3-0 by a very strong Enfield team. To have got this far and then not to perform to our best was very disappointing for everyone involved with the club.

That same season I was lucky enough to play with a very strong squad of players and I was able to break the club goal scoring record as I netted 46 goals and that didn't include any penalties!

I have still got an engraved plaque and a pewter mug from the supporters and the club to remind me of the occasion and they will always remind me of the good times I had at Wealdstone.

The best players at the time would have to be Charlie Townsend and Viv Evans. Both were very consistent and dedicated players and they were both very loyal to Wealdstone. Viv was a very strong and fast goal-scoring winger and he was surpassingly good in the air considering his small stature.

Charlie Townsend was very skillful and read the game quicker that the average player. He was well known to the spectators to make shouted comments during the game such as " don't forget lads, we're playing in blue and white today!" when passes went to the opposition, and "They'll build a block of flats on this ground next week if we keep playing like this" - little did he know how near the truth he was.

After a draw with Barnet at Lower Mead in the FA Cup three

Matt Farrell scores in a win over Enfield watched by Charlie Sells (WFC), Ray Kingsland, Roy Agar and Fred Flavell (EFC) and Johnny Moran (WFC).

vastly different results were reported in the Harrow Observer on the same day;

Three down in the first fifteen minutes, Wealdstone afterwards put up a great struggle before being beaten 6-3 by Brentford in the first round of the London Senior Cup under floodlights at Griffin Park on Monday.

Indeed with the score at 4-3 midway through the second half, Wealdstone appeared to have an even chance and looked the more aggressive side as the pace slowed after a fast and furious first period................

The Second report read;

With three clear chances and King injured for most of the game, Barnet at Underhill humiliated Wealdstone to the extent of nine clear goals on Thursday.

Barnet were hardly flattered by the score, which would have been even bigger but for some bad misses and a determined display by Fowler who refused to be daunted by the fact that he received virtually no cover.......

...and the third;

Ascending rapidly from the ridiculous to the sublime, Wealdstone thrashed Athenian League Champions Hendon by five clear goals on their own newly laid pitch at Claremont Road, Moran (2), Farrell (2) and Rowley sharing the goals, three of which came in a four minute spell in the second half.

There was to be further disruption however as Matt Farrell and John Saunders resigned from the club intending like others to join Hendon, but Wealdstone blocked the transfers pending a decision from the Athenian League. The club released a statement saying that the transfers were blocked as in neither case had the request come from the (Hendon) Club Secretary, which was a league rule.

The problem had arisen as a number of the successful Hendon side had left the club and joined Enfield when the Coach and Secretary had resigned. There were also a number of claims and counter claims of poaching between the two Clubs and this had further unsettled a number of players who had remained at Wealdstone, notably Charlie Townsend and George Riddy who were named by Wealdstone as having also been approached by a scout.

As a result in November it was announced that both Matt Farrell and John Saunders were banned from playing for any Athenian League club other than Wealdstone until the end of the year, the league upholding Wealdstone's appeal that irregular approaches had been made to the players.

Wealdstone again made the first round proper of the Amateur Cup, this time with a 5-0 victory over Aveley, from the Delphian League.

Wealdstone had also reached third in the league by this time, despite lacking consistency in their performances, and the following week, scoring another five goals, Sutton United were defeated at Lower Mead. It was Wealdstone's second league double of the season and seemed at last to have lain to rest the Sutton United tag as a 'bogey' team.

Disappointing Christmas performances, this season (rarely) against Hayes rather than Hendon were followed by a 5-0

'Stones win, away to Grays Athletic. Ken Merry scored a hat trick to bring his goal tally to 12 since signing from Southall the previous September. It was a good foundation for the followings weeks' London Senior Cup-tie at home to Barking.

By one of the most mysterious and remarkable goals ever seen at Lower Mead, Wealdstone beat luckless Barking, bottom club of the Isthmian League, 2-1 in the first round of the London Senior Cup on Saturday.

Time was running out with the score at one goal each when a strong Wealdstone attack ended with merry smacking the ball past the Barking goalkeeper, Martin. It looked a goal all the way, but stuck in the mud short of the line!

Then, to general astonishment, Hennen, the left back raced up and hammered the ball into his own net!

Apparently, he thought the referee had awarded a goal, but it was an unaccountable action by any means and cost his side the chance of a replay.

The match had been in doubt all morning after heavy rain, but the referee took a fork out onto the pitch for his inspection and subsequently ruled it playable!

Wealdstone's fortune and form were to hols a little longer as well. The following week, Wealdstone were at home to Uxbridge in the Middlesex Senior Cup.

When Coggin crashed the ball into the net after a great effort by Ault had hit the post, Uxbridge seemed well poised to knock Wealdstone out of the Middlesex Senior Cup in the first round proper at Lower Mead, for there were only ten minutes left and the visitors now held a 2-1 lead.

Two minutes later, Merry helped a scoring shot from Peel over the line and with three minutes left for play, Evans, who had been fouled on the edge of the penalty area somehow headed Knox's free kick through a crowd of players and into the net. Wealdstone securing a 3–2 victory.

By the end of January, the floodlight installation had been completed. Wycombe Wanderers were to take part in the first match to be played under the lights to celebrate the installation.

Heavy rain, which began over an hour before the match started and persisted relentlessly throughout the evening restricted the attendance for the inauguration of Wealdstone's floodlights to just over 1200 on Tuesday.

It was a memorable occasion nevertheless with Wealdstone and Wycombe Wanderers rising above the difficult conditions to provide highly entertaining football before drawing 1-1 in the AFA Invitation Cup.

In a goalless first half, Wealdstone missed the greatest chance when Rowley, presented with an open goal by Evans, smashed the ball against the cross bar.

Afterwards Wealdstone had the better of the play but when Holmes headed Wycombe into the lead from a corner by Worley, it seemed that they would be the first team to win under the lights. But Wealdstone fought back strongly and with only a few minutes left, Evans who had switched wings with Rowley cracked in a great equaliser.

Before the match, Mr H A Lucit, Wealdstone Chairman, thanked the Supporters Club for its splendid gesture in providing the lights and welcomed guests from the FA, the AFA, the Middlesex FA and the Athenian and Isthmian League's.

The lights were then formally handed over to the club by Mr Jock Campbell, Supporters Club treasurer and switched on by Mr R Kelly, who completed all the fittings after the contractors had installed the pylons.

Wealdstone's team was; W Fowler, G Mowle, M Quinn, C Townsend, R King, A Knox, A Peel, G Rowley, G Davies, K Merry, V Evans.

Taken from the steps on the ABC Cinema, Wealdstone's first match under floodlights at Lower Mead.

Late in February, Wealdstone's high scoring season saw the 100th goal scored. Having been 4–1 down well into the second half of their Athenian League match with Leyton at Lower Mead, 'Stones recovered to score four times although only the first three were to count, the fourth ruled out for offside. It was the equalising goal that was the 100th scored during the season.

In mid March, Wealdstone travelled to Weston Road, Southall to face Hayes in the Middlesex Senior Cup semi-final. Hayes had won both league encounters over Christmas, but Wealdstone were able to exact revenge winning an exciting game by 5–2, to reach the final against Enfield.

The end of March saw the inconsistencies return. A 7–1 defeat away to Hitchin Town and the Middlesex Senior Cup Final defeat by 4-1 to Enfield were followed by Wealdstone's best performance of the season.

Smashing through Bromley's grimly organised defensive barrier thrice just after the half hour, Wealdstone took full advantage of a strong wind to cross over with a 3–0 lead. And although the Isthmian League Champions scored two shock goals in the second half, they never really looked like a match for a side that went on to win the London Senior Cup third round replay 5–2 after a 1–1 draw at Bromley a fortnight earlier.

This was one of Wealdstone's best displays of the season with Townsend repeatedly switching wing half positions with Knox in the first half, the complete master, and Peel also playing with match winning brilliance.

From the outset Bromley dedicated themselves to defence in the face of a fierce wind and from Wealdstone's point of view it seemed essential that they must be at least two goals in front by the interval.

Although Bromley seldom left their own half, it was a full half hour before they conceded a goal, near as Wealdstone went on several occasions. Then at last Townsend, in one of his switches to left half, put Evans away and from the wingers centre, Jarmin atoned for earlier errors by crashing the ball past a helpless Price.

Hardly had the sheering ceased when Knox, back in the number five position, essayed a hard, low drive, which Price, diving far too late, allowed to pass beneath his body into the net.

Now Wealdstone really threatened to run rampant and Peel, always impervious to the most desperate efforts of Nelson and Norman to check him, waltzed round three defenders before slipping the ball to Merry, who easily converted from close range.

Facing driving sleet at the start of the second half, Wealdstone lost their poise and rhythm for a time, but were still largely untroubled by a Bromley attack which now had Nottage limping at outside right. Yet, taking heart at last, Bromley drew closer with a header by Fry and then appeared to get back into the game with a real chance as Nottage hooked the ball past Fowler during a break away.

But it was purely a temporary falter on Wealdstone's part. As the floodlights were switched on their superiority returned and Bromley's hopes were blasted when Evans moved into the centre to force the ball past Price, who cannot have had many busier matches this season.

Peel set the final seal on a triumph in which he had played so outstanding a part when Moran's hard shot from a narrow angle was knocked into the air by price to fall on the line, for Peel to race in and add the last decisive touch.

With a 6;30 kick off the match was watched by 2,211 people and Wealdstone now meet Enfield in the semi-final, the winners to play Wimbledon who the previous evening overwhelmed Hayes 6-0 on the Kingstonian ground.

Wealdstone; W Fowler, G Mowle, J Low, C Townsend, R King, A Knox, A Peel, D Jarmin, K Merry, J Moran, V Evans.

The match was followed by what was described as the clubs worst of the season, thankfully only in a friendly when they lost for the third time in the season to Maidenhead United, 2-1 at Lower Mead.

Against all expectations, Wealdstone thoroughly deserved their 3-1 win over Enfield in the semi-final, to reach their third post war London Senior Cup Final. Enfield only a few weeks earlier had beaten 'Stones 4-1 in the Middlesex Senior Cup Final and they started hot favourites to repeat the victory.

Just a few days before the final there was sadness at Lower Mead, the club Secretary, W (Bill) Leadbetter had died suddenly in Peru. He had been in touch with the club regularly during his three weeks in South America, and had been expected back for the Saturday final, the match reported by the Harrow Observer;

Within five minutes of defeat, Wealdstone were later a hands breadth of victory in the final of the London Senior Cup at Dulwich on Saturday. But extra time brought no addition to the 90 minute score of 1-1 and they will share with Wimbledon the handsome trophy for a year. As Evans won the toss, Wealdstone will be the holders for the first six months.

For Wealdstone there was modified jubilation but some sadness too, since they should have won in view of the fact that Wimbledon had four players absent on the England tour and three others injured, but fate took a hand to redress the balance, Jack Morley injured after 16 minutes, was almost a passenger for the rest of the match.

He almost became the hero in extra time; he received a pass from Evans and stabbed the ball towards the far post. It looked a goal all the way, but Wealdstone's shouts of exultation were strangled as McAlpine hurled himself sideways and getting half a hand to the ball, deflected it for a corner.

Earlier Wimbledon had looked winners when with only five minutes to go they were clinging, without great strain, to a surprise lead given to them by Moore almost immediately after the interval.

With Morley hardly able to move, Moran out of form and Knox and Merry mainly operating defensively, there was no thrust or sting in the Wealdstone attack and it seemed the dismal record of nor scoring in the three previous finals was to be maintained.

Only the wingers, Evans and Peel, offered a real threat to the Wimbledon defence and it was these two that saved the day. Knox created the opening by sending Evans away on the left.

He lobbed the ball high into the middle and with McAlpine and Morley both failing to get a touch it dropped down and Peel, bouncing like an India rubber ball, forced a hard header into the net.

Even then Wimbledon all but snatched victory when Moore with Fowler advancing and three defenders breathing down his neck, put wide.

Wealdstone; W Fowler, J Low, R Good, S Cazely, R King, J Morley, A Peel, A Knox, K Merry, J Moran, V Evans.

Wimbledon; E McAlpine, G Coote, D Willis, J Wallis, A McGuiness, E Murphy, E Adams, G Hamm, E Reynolds, M Moore, N Williams.

At the end of season Dinner and Dance, Viv Evans collected the Leadbetter Trophy, formerly the Player of The Year Trophy, renamed in honour of the late Club Secretary. The trophy itself was a carved wooden football on a stand originally presented to the club by Hong Kong FC.

There were also a number of speeches led by Supporters Club President Cardew Robinson. He praised the club as a whole for the progress made during his thirty year association, the first team for their success in the London Senior Cup and finally, new club captain Charlie Townsend, who had cemented his place in the England line up.

The new club secretary, Ken Wiltshire also proposed 'the Supporters Club' and noted

Wealdstone FC are notably proud that they had been the first Amateur Club to play on the green turf of Wembley Stadium; they were the first club in Europe to have a complete match televised; and now, thanks to the efforts of the Supporters Club, they were the first Athenian League Club to have floodlights.

Over the Whitsun weekend, Wealdstone were again off on tour, this time to Amsterdam in Holland. Wealdstone played two matches, the first expected to be the harder match was against H R C Den Helder (second in the Senior Amateur League). Wealdstone in fact won that match by 4-1, Ken Merry and Tony Knox both scoring two goals.

After a day's sightseeing, Wealdstone looked tired in the second match but shared four goals (Alan Young scoring twice) with Permerend (first in the Senior Amateur League). The teams were; M Gillhooley (W Fowler), G Mowle, R Good, C Townsend, M Emerson, J Hall, G Knox, A Knox (A Young), K Merry, J Moran and V Evans, those bracketed were the changes for the second match.

As Press Secretary, John Ryan recounted in the tour in the 1962-63 handbook;

A party of 21 players and officials left Lower Mead on Whit Saturday at 8:00am and made their way by Coach and Train to Harwich, then by boat to the Hook.

Once aboard Bill Fowler suggested and persuaded everyone to follow him and George Mowle to the bar for the usual buying of duty free cigarettes, and Roger (Good) getting something for his mum. On arrival at the Hook after a count up, one was found to be missing. After about half an hour he was found in the smallest room on board asleep.

Arrived at central Station Amsterdam, and then on to the Hotel Fleeizig. Rooms were sorted out and then a first class evening meal.

Our first game against Den Helder we won 4-1, about 20 miles from our headquarters, then a tour of the Dutch fleet, a first class game and the usual hospitality afterwards. Our old friend from Maidenhead Jimmy Price acted as coach for this game.

Our second game against Permerend (drawn 2-2) was a very close one, with the travelling and heat etc telling on our boys. We earned a well-deserved draw.

Times we'll remember? George Mowle mixing one of his unusual drinks, after shave lotion, and Ben Trueman, Ken Merry and Mike Gillhooly having a different brand of milk delivered.

Visits to Billy's place, Charlie Townsend trying his strength with a hand cart, Viv Evans acting as a courier in Canal Street. Jimmy Pyers and Fred Walsh going to bed early in case they missed the kick off and Viv, Ken, Charlie, Mike and Bill all getting their hand in and acting as Harbour Masters on the pier.

Once again our lads gave all they had and the brand of football served up was high standard. The name of Wealdstone ranks high in Holland.

John Burrows
Supporter late 1940's on

I suppose that as a football mad 9-10 year-old with a father (the late Sam Burrows) a devout Wealdstone FC follower, it was almost inevitable that I would become a Lower Mead regular.

In those days, just after the second world war leisure choices were much simpler and virtually no television to tempt us to stay in on cold and wet days.

There was however another factor that persuaded me to visit Lower Mead and that was the Dominion Fish and Chip Restaurant - for me the best fish and chips in the world! Situated right outside the ground.

After completing my time at Junior School, the rest of my education was in Harrow. Thus a midweek evening game at home August / September or April / May only could be combined with mouth-watering fish and chips, bread and butter and tea, all served for 1/9d (just under 9 "new" pence) - pure heaven!

Of course Lower Mead is no more; I believe the fish and chip location, albeit the proprietors of the above days have long departed, still survives, it's a funny old game they say!

At the end of season AGM, the club were pleased to announce that a further profit had been made of £226. This was mainly due to the increased revenue from the cup matches and additional floodlight friendly matches played since the lights had been installed.

It was considered a good season on the field. The club had finished up as joint holders of the London Senior Cup, the first team were third in the Athenian League and hadn't been outside the top three all season.

They were finalists in the Middlesex Senior Cup, semi-finalists in the Charity Cup, and as had been shown in a number of friendlies, they were more than capable in holding their own with senior opposition.

Somewhat strange then, the changes also discussed and made at the meeting;

Eric 'The Man In Blue' Metcalfe heads the queue at the new tea bar built in 1961

The Wealdstone FC Entertainments Team 1961
L to R: Chic Adams (Referee Committee), Dick Batty (A Team Trainer), Ken Wiltshire (Club Secretary), Jim Pyers (A Team Secretary), Bill Green (Referee) and Reggie Ling (Committee).

Against the strong advice of officials, members at the Wealdstone AGM voted that in future the coach should be responsible for picking the first team. Last season this was as usual in the hands of a committee of three, Mr J Holt, Mr F W Harbud and Mr W Roberts in consultation with the coach, Mr V Burgess.

Moving the change, later accepted by 46 votes to 27, Mr R A McMillar said he in no way criticised either the selection committee or the coach but he felt the club should follow the example of other clubs and make one man, the one they paid, responsible.

He added that at the moment it seemed the coach was little more than a glorified PT Instructor.

Mr T Law, Supporters Club Chairman, added that he felt with three selectors, favouritism could creep in. With a Coach responsible, if things went wrong they could sack him.

Strongly opposing the suggestion, Mr Jack Rogers, deputy Chairman, said that as a member of the committee for thirty years he felt this would be a dangerous and retrograde step. In fact the committee already had the power to appoint the coach as the sole selector. The present system was that the coach put forward his suggested team and the three members discussed it.

Last season there appeared to have been no disagreements.

Moreover they should remember that there was more than one team to pick.

Considerable discussion followed mainly in favour of the change, though Mr M A Emerson, selector of the colts side, declared there was more danger of favouritism in one man selection than three.

The suggestion that the proposal should also include the reserves by the reserve team coach was defeated.

There was another change for the forthcoming season with the introduction for the first time of a true pre-season match. In past years in common with most other clubs, a number of closed trials were held. Finally two squads selected to play a public trials match – from these two teams the opening side was then selected.

Wealdstone and Harrow Town had held their closed trials during training and then arranged a public trial match against each other played at Lower Mead. Wealdstone started the stronger and ran out winners by 4–0, using 17 players in the match, all of whom were retained for the forthcoming season.

The season started the following week with a league match away to Walton and Hersham. There were a couple of further additions to the Wealdstone squad, Hugh Lindsay returning to the club after a couple of seasons at Kingstonian. He was joined by Dave Richards, a Welsh International trialist, who also signed from the Surrey club.

They were to make quite an impact in their first game, as 'Stones trailed by the odd goal at half time, then starting the second half with three goals in nine minutes, and two more before twenty minutes had passed, to take a 5-1 lead.

Hugh Lindsay had scored three and Dave Richards and Viv Evans one each before 'Stones relaxed. The final score realised a 5–2 win.

It was a successful start to the season for Wealdstone. Despite a defeat by 1–0 to Southall in their first home league game, this was followed by four wins; beating Hendon (2–1), Sutton away (3–2), Finchley away (2–0) and finally Grays at home 6–0 to top the league by the end of September.

They had also beaten Harrow Town 2-0 at Earlsmead in the FA Cup, the only other defeat in this period coming at home to Chelsea in the Battle Of Britain Trophy.

After a highly entertaining match, Chelsea beat Wealdstone 3-1 on Tuesday.

Chelsea paid the organisers, the RAF Association and Wealdstone the compliment of playing their full league side, apart from a change at wing half. Ironically it was Wealdstone that were unable to parade their brightest stars, Charlie Townsend and Hugh Lindsay being pronounced unfit.

Earlier in the day it had been announced that both were retained in the England side to meet Eire in Dublin on Sunday week.

Both were badly missed for their constructive ability and attack was left largely to the energy of Evans and Smith.

The defence worked so heroically and well that it was not until the stroke of half time that Chelsea took the lead, Bridges heading through when Shellito rounded off a great run with a perfect centre.

The latter part of the half had been played in a fierce thunderstorm but the drenched spectators were rewarded for their hardiness seven minutes after the interval.

Evans then put Wealdstone on terms with much the best goal of the match, as he flung himself at a corner by Peel to head the ball into the net off of the far post.

Tambling restored Chelsea's lead during a scrimmage a few minutes later but the game remained open until near the end when Bridges clinched the issue by netting from close range.

In the interval, Fowler had made a succession of gallant saves and the defence, in which Richards and Good were outstanding, had fought to its last gasp.

Chelsea meanwhile played attractively from one end of the field to the other, lacking only punch. Both teams were applauded off the field as Bobby Tambling the Chelsea captain went to collect the trophy from Miss Jill Browne, a television actress.

Before the game the players were presented to The Mayor of Harrow, Alderman C E Jordan and Group Captain J F Ellis, donor of the trophy. The attendance was 3200 and gross takings were £284 7s 9d

Wealdstone; W Fowler, J Low, R Good, D Richards, R King, A Knox, A Peel, W Smith, D Norman, K Merry, V Evans.

Chelsea; Bonnetti, Shellito, McReadie, More, Mortimer, Harris, Murray, Tambling, Bridges, Moore, Blunstone.

At the end of September Wealdstone's ability to triumph over adversity came again to the fore, as in a fixture with Hornchurch, Bill Fowler collapsed after only nine minutes.

He was replaced in goal by Viv Evans and Wealdstone went on to win with 10 men, by 4–2, falling to second place in the league on goal difference to Barnet, Wealdstone having scored 22 goals and conceded 8 in seven matches, Barnet having scored three more.

There was no further progress though in the FA Cup, Enfield, opponents at Lower Mead the following week were continuing to be the bogey side for the 'Stones, this time running out winners by 5–1.

The club's league form continued to be good, but they really were saving the highlights for their professional opponents. After the defeat to Chelsea, Wealdstone faced West Ham United at Lower Mead in the London Challenge Cup.

After one of the most spirited displays in the club's long history, Wealdstone crushed West Ham United 4-1 in the second round of the Challenge Cup, and they now entertain Arsenal in the semi-final.

It was a match of many thrills for the 3000 spectators who gave Wealdstone a richly deserved ovation as they trooped off the field at the end.

For the professionals, who fielded their Combination side with five players with Football League experience, there was little but humiliation.

On level terms at the interval after conceding the first goal, they looked set to win and began the second half with confidence. This quickly vanished in the face of Wealdstone's tremendous verve and long before the end they were a whipped team.

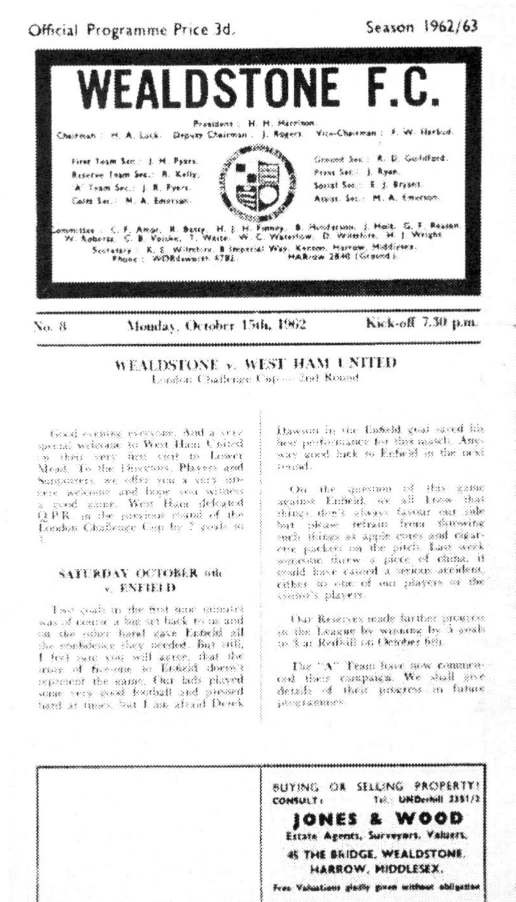

Official Programme Price 3d. Season 1962/63

WEALDSTONE F.C.

President: H. H. Harrison.
Chairman: H. A. Luck. Deputy Chairman: J. Rogers. Vice-Chairman: F. W. Harbud.
First Team Sec.: J. H. Pyers. Ground Sec.: R. D. Guildford.
Reserve Team Sec.: R. Kelly. Press Sec.: J. Ryan.
'A' Team Sec.: J. R. Pyers. Social Sec.: E. J. Bryant.
Colts Sec.: M. A. Emerson. Assist. Sec.: M. A. Emerson.
Committee: C. F. Amor, R. Basey, H. [illegible] Finney, B. Henderson, J. Holt, G. F. Reason, W. Roberts, C. B. Voisin, T. Waite, W. C. Waterlow, D. Wiltshire, H. J. Wright.
Secretary: K. S. Wiltshire, 8 Imperial Way, Kenton, Harrow, Middlesex.
Phone: WORdsworth 6782. HARrow 2840 (Ground).

No. 8 Monday, October 15th, 1962 Kick-off 7.30 p.m.

WEALDSTONE v. WEST HAM UNITED
London Challenge Cup — 2nd Round

Good evening everyone. And a very special welcome to West Ham United on their very first visit to Lower Mead. To the Directors, Players and Supporters, we offer you a very sincere welcome and hope you witness a good game. West Ham defeated Q.P.R. in the previous round of the London Challenge Cup by [illegible] goals to [illegible].

SATURDAY OCTOBER 6th v. ENFIELD

Two goals in the first nine minutes was of course a big set back to us and on the other hand gave Enfield all the confidence they needed. But still, I feel sure you will agree, that the score of five-one to Enfield doesn't represent the game. Our lads played some very good football and pressed hard at times, but I am afraid Derek Dawson in the Enfield goal saved his best performance for this match. Anyway good luck to Enfield in the next round.

On the question of this game against Enfield, we all know that things don't always favour our side but please refrain from throwing such things as apple cores and cigarette packets on the pitch. Last week someone threw a piece of china, it could have caused a serious accident, either to one of our players or the visitor's players.

Our Reserves made further progress in the League by winning by [illegible] goals to [illegible] at Redhill on October 6th.

The "A" Team have now commenced their campaign. We shall give details of their progress in future programmes.

Wealdstone's main hero was Hugh Lindsay who scored two of the goals and made another for Phil West who also scored twice. At his brilliant best Lindsay repeatedly had the West Ham defence back pedalling helplessly in the hope of divining which way his twinkling feet were going to take the ball.

They rarely guessed right!

Wealdstone had taken the lead when Lyall fouled Peel and his free kick was headed onto West who scored, and Wealdstone could have extended their lead a minute later when Evans broke through but lobbed over the bar.

Lindsay had scored the second twelve minutes after the interval, this time from a Peel corner, and victory was assured in the 72nd and 74th minutes, Lindsay scoring with a low shot and then crossing for West to side foot home.

Wealdstone; W Fowler, J Low, R Good, D Richards, R King, A Knox, A Peel, H Lindsay, P West, K Merry, V Evans.

West Ham United; Dickie, Kirkup, Lyall, Landsdown, Bickley, Charles, Dear, Hugo, Sealy, Sissons, Crawford.

The semi-final against Arsenal was played in front of a crowd of 5500, Wealdstone lacking firepower and a little luck having hit the woodwork on three occasions, went behind to an 80th minute goal.

Arsenal however had been handicapped by the loss of their goalkeeper in the first ten minutes, but it was not until the very last kick of the match that Wealdstone equalised when Evans headed down to West who scored from close range.

The referee blew for the goal and pointed to the centre circle but there was no time left for the visitors to kick off and the match went to a replay, won 3–1 by Arsenal the following Monday evening.

At the beginning of December the club wrote to all members and then to the Harrow Observer telling them of the improvement planned for Lower Mead.

These included repairs to the terracing and the erection of a new covered stand at the Dominion Cinema end of the ground, a new car park and training facility behind the Elmslie End and a number of changes in the social club, such as the billiard room being turned into a new bar. There was to be some extension to the existing grandstand.

Unfortunately the announcement and the associated appeal for funds came about at the same time as the Amateur Cup. Wealdstone again failing to impress on the field, beaten with some ease by Letchworth.

What had started so well was fast becoming another average season, as with this defeat there was little chance of overtaking Enfield at the top of the Athenian League. The only major trophy left to defend was the half share in the London Senior Cup from the previous season.

Little did anyone know what was to happen after Christmas. Wealdstone played as usual over the holiday but they were not to play again until 16th of February when they played away to Ford United in the second round of the London Senior Cup, drawing 1–1.

Most of the southeast had been covered with a layer of snow and ice, pitches frozen for almost seven weeks, practically wiping out all sport at all levels!

It was two weeks before the replay could be staged, which Wealdstone won by 2–1 and despite a defeat at Hornchurch in the league, Wealdstone saw in March in second place in the league. Albeit with only a slight chance of returning to the top of the table.

Even with the season extended through May, the club was still to play twice and even three times a week to fit in all the remaining fixtures.

Another defeat against lowly Carshalton (beaten 11-0 by Southall the previous week) convinced all but the most biased supporter that Wealdstone's league chance had finally gone in mid April. They were still second, five points behind Enfield but having played two matches more. Barnet, also with two games in hand were only three points behind Wealdstone in third place.

Arthur Peel
Player 1961-1964

I came from Manchester originally, and came south to further my football career. I played for Wealdstone from 1961 to 1964 and there were some great highlights during those years, winning the Middlesex Senior Cup, the Middlesex Charity Cup and the London Senior Cup (jointly with Wimbledon).

I was privileged to play with some great players such as Viv Evans, Charlie Townsend, Ron King, Tony Knox and many, many more.

There was one game that has a particular memory - it was just after 'the big freeze up' of 1963, and we were to play away at Barnet.

The pitch had been frozen solid in the morning, and Barnet had tried to thaw the pitch out by burning car tyres on the surface - dozens of then spread all over the surface. They succeeded in getting the game under way but at he game progressed we found this horrible black 'goo' sticking to us every time we fell over or tackled etc.

At the end of the game every single piece of kit, our socks, shirts and shorts had to be thrown away. It just was not possible to clean - the 'goo' had started to set! It even took us all as players ages to clean it off in the bath afterwards.
I always wondered how many strips were un-usable after being worn in Barnet's matches after our game. But its still funny looking back on it after so long.

We played a game against Arsenal (07/10/63) and drew 1-1- they had put out some good players in their side. Afterwards, Billy Wright, the Arsenal manager at the time threw a major 'wobbly' in the dressing room, which we could hear it through two sets of closed doors!

We also played a very strong Chelsea side, (04/09/62), that was in the Battle of Britain Cup, and we beat them in front of a crowd, which was, according to local newspaper reports, well over 3,000. The support then was even better than Wealdstone's support today! They were always exceptional.

Lower Mead was selected one of a number of venues for a Youth International Tournament. In late April, Belgium faced Czechoslovakia under floodlights and as was becoming the custom at Lower Mead for floodlight matches, in heavy rain. The Belgian side eventually running out winners in front of 2000 spectators by 2–0.

A month later and the season still in progress, Wealdstone faced Enfield, normally their bogey side, in the Middlesex Senior Cup Final at Finchley FC, again witnessed by the Harrow Observer;

What had promised to be a travesty of a match was transformed into a signal triumph for a makeshift but amazingly gallant Wealdstone side. With only two first team players in their normal positions, they beat the holders 2-0 to win the trophy for the eighth time.

Refusal by the FA to release the three internationals although they had no further matches to play (Townsend, Lindsay and Ashworth), and refusal by Enfield to postpone the match, allied to injuries to Evans, Jones and reserve centre half Emerson, left the 'Stones coach with an apparently insoluble problem, yet by brilliant improvisation and shrewd tactics he produced a combination that by relentless effort reduced Enfield to utter frustration.

Only Fowler and Good remained in situ, Richards captained the side from right back, Merry appeared as centre half for the first time, 'A' team centre forward Knox became an excellent right half and Peel moved to inside-right to become player of the night, though it really was a team effort.

Wealdstone's tactics were to play four half-backs diagonally across the field to blunt Enfield's scoring and keep defeat within respectable limits.

Their success was beyond their wildest hopes, Enfield helping to encompass their own disaster by starting at too leisurely a pace although having the wind in their favour.

On 37 minutes Hughes slipped a perfect pass to Smith and his cross was met by Houston who hit the ball hard and low into the net to open the scoring, a lead maintained incredibly until half time.

Surviving barrages at the start of the second half, right on the hour Houston flicked a glorious pass to Jones who took it in his stride and his shot was hit well wide of the helpless Dawson.

Enfield was confounded though one goal may well have been followed by others but Wealdstone denied them short range shots, Fowler handling all others superbly.

There was a fantastic climax as supporters swarmed on the pitch believing the final whistle to have blown, but it had not and they were moved to ring the edge of the pitch.

Then the floodlights failed and there was another brief hold up, but at last a still disbelieving Richards climbed the steps to receive the trophy. It was a triumph that will be talked about for years and brought honour to all those who shared it.

Wealdstone; W Fowler, D Richards, R Good, G Knox, K Merry, S Cazely, W Smith, A Peel, P Houston, M Hughes, C Jones.

The three Wealdstone players called up by England were playing in the FA Centenary Amateur Tournament at Gateshead. Hugh Lindsay had played in all three matches, beating France losing to West Germany and beating Holland.

Charlie Townsend had been injured in training but recovered to take part in the win over Holland where he scored, and they were joined by John Ashworth who was called in to the squad after impressing playing for Portsmouth against Middlesborough!

The season was still not over however, but a defeat against Barnet saw Wealdstone finish in third place in the league, before defeating Finchley in the Middlesex Charity Cup semi-final, by 2–1, to meet Hayes in the final carried over to the following season.

Expecting a break before the end of season tour, it was only a week or so later that Wealdstone left for a tour of Eire. Leaving on the Friday morning, that evening they played Bohemians at Dalymount Park, Dublin, winning by 3-2 with one goal by Viv Evans and two by Tony Knox, guesting from Hendon. On the Sunday they played a Drogheda Representative side, losing by 3-1 Hugh Lindsay scoring Wealdstone's goal from a free kick.

Stephen Burke
Bohemians FC, Ireland

I have yet to meet anyone who saw Wealdstone's visit, but I have been able to piece together the following from my notes and the odd conversation; (the game was played at Dalymount Park, Friday 31st May, 1963)

Bohemians 2, Wealdstone 3

The "Irish Press" of Saturday 1st June,
"This Game Did Not Please"

It bordered on the ridiculous. Wealdstone, the Athenian League side, arrived half an hour late after their plane was held up. The game had been due to start at 8 p.m. "The crowd then became impatient when Bohemians delayed the start of the second half and most of the second half was played in near darkness until the referee asked for the second time, for the lights to be switched on.

Evans, Wealdstone's left winger, put the visitors 1-0 up from what seemed an offside position, beating the advancing Bohemian keeper, John Kelly, and their inside-left, Knox, made it 2-0 before Bohemians' centre forward O'Brien headed a goal.

Straight from the second half kick-off Maguire equalised off a Willie Browne pass. After 60 minutes Knox scrambled home what would prove to be the winner, but the game could have gone either way.

The "Irish Times" reported attendance a very poor attendance (how right they were, I was able to find from Bohemian Club records that the Gate receipts were just £31 15s 06d). .

None of these national newspapers gave team line-ups, but I do have probable line-ups from the "Irish Times";

Bohemians - John Kelly; J. Nolan, Billy Young; Mick Dalton, Willie Browne, Con McKnight; H Reid, Des Maguire, Michael O'Brien; Mick Conroy; John Millington.

Wealdstone - Bill Fowler; John Low, Roger Good; Charlie Townsend; Johnny Ashworth; Dave Richards; Arthur Peel; Hugh Lindsay; Ken Merry; Cliff Jones; Vivian Evans and Tony Knox

Obviously Knox must have played in place of one of the above. Of the Bohemian probable line-up, two were guests from local non-league clubs; J. Nolan (TEK United) and H Reid (St Brendan's), John Kelly was a Republic of Ireland amateur international as were Willie Browne, Billy Young and Mick Dalton.

Browne was in fact also a full international and was the last amateur to appear for the Republic's full international side; he won 3 caps. Mick Conroy was a brother to Terry Conroy (Stoke City and Republic of Ireland).

In a run-down on the Wealdstone team one newspaper (I don't know which as these details are from an old player's scrap-book);

Wealdstone were the first amateur team to play in a cup final at Wembley and Wealdstone included 4 English amateur internationals - Charlie Townsend (who is on Spurs Books), Arthur Peel (who has played for Spurs) Johnny Ashworth (on Portsmouth's books) and Hugh Lindsay; 3 Welsh internationals - Dave Richards, Cliff Jones and Vivian Evans. Roger Good had a trial for England and Bill Fowler in goal was once on WBA's books and played for 2 years in Germany.

I see from my notes that the "Irish Independent" of Monday 3rd June reported on a match at Lourdes Stadium (in Drogheda) when a strong Drogheda Select XI beat Wealdstone 3-1 on the Sunday.

At the end of a fair season, one trophy had been won and another final was still to be played. Financially the fixtures against professional clubs had bolstered the coffers and there was progress being made on the ground alterations. Reserve player George Knox was awarded the Sportsman of The Year trophy.

The weather conditions that had caused such a long lay off mid-season were described as the worst in memory but everyone had worked hard to ensure that all the matches were later staged.

It was decided to dispense with the 'A' team, but to replace it with another Colts side as this had played its part in the development of players for the first and reserve teams.

The new season started with an away win, 1–0 at Grays Athletic, new signing Brian Jenkins scoring the goal, but it was not the best of Wealdstone performances.

It was followed by a poor run of form which saw 'Stones in the lower half of the table with a record of Played 6 won 1 drawn 1 lost 4 by mid October. It was not all through bad however as the side was frequently depleted by international calls, often in successive weeks.

First, two Olympic Qualifying matches, home and away with Iceland, had ruled out Lindsay, Townsend and Ashworth and then the same three players were selected to play for England, each match taking place on a Saturday afternoon.

After a home defeat to Finchley by 4–2, the Comments column in the Harrow Observer reported;

One might have thought the news had gone round that £5 note were being distributed free in Station Road, so steady was the drift to the exits long before then end of Wealdstone's match with Finchley on Saturday.

Disappointment and disillusion could go little further though Finchley could share part of the blame for their monotonous offside tactics. It can be fairly said that Wealdstone are having neither luck nor the run of the ball at the moment but again it must be repeated that they are already a jaded side.

Under the circumstances the coach Mr Vince Burgess may be thought moderate in resting only Dave Richards, Bill Fowler and Bill Creasy for Tuesdays match against Loughborough Colleges in the far from vital Hitchin Centenary Cup.

But the fact is that changes cannot easily be contemplated when the fact is faced that the reserves are bottom of the table with only one point.............

A couple of weeks later and Loughborough had been beaten but league form was no better. Wealdstone continued their fall to the bottom of the league table with a defeat at Dagenham.

There had also been a disappointing exit from the FA Cup, losing to Hertford Town having had by far the better of their opponents throughout. This was backed up by the statistic that Wealdstone had won eighteen corners in the match and conceded none, but unfortunately they had conceded the only goal.

There was at least one bright spot that showed there was still some potential in the side;

A hat trick by Charlie Townsend, his first for the club inspired Wealdstone to a 4–2 win over Leyton Orient in the battle Of Britain Trophy at Lower Mead.

Fielding a reserve side including former 'Stone Phil White and England Amateur goalkeeper Pinner. Orient fought back from 2-0 down at the interval to equalise after 20 minutes of the second half, but a brilliant opportunist goal by Townsend restored Wealdstone's lead and six minutes from the end he scored again from the penalty spot in exemplary style.

Although playing some brilliant football, Wealdstone were a little fortunate to be 2-0 up at half time. Devine volleyed home a cross by Lindsay who had received from Evans after 11 minutes and right on the half hour Townsend raced onto a long pass from Bell and took advantage of Pinner's fumble to force home a second.

Between times at least five Orient shots had been stopped on the line by defenders and there were several more similar incidents before Scott shot wide from a penalty awarded against Ashworth.

Orient equalised in the second half with goals from white and Pearce, but with twenty minutes to go Townsend hammered a poor clearance by Pinner straight into the net and then the penalty for a foul on Lindsay was similarly despatched.

Wealdstone; R Durdle, W Creasey, R Good, C Townsend, J Ashworth, D Richards, A Peel, H Lindsay, H Devine, D Bell, V Evans.

Phil White had been signed for Orient by Alec Stock in 1953. His first game for Wealdstone had come at the end of the 1950-51 season, when he appeared in the Middlesex Cup final defeat (2-3) to Finchley.

Prior to his departure for Orient before the 1953-54 season, he made 82 appearances for Wealdstone, scoring over 20 goals.

He was nurtured by Orient and played mainly in the reserves over the next two seasons, before establishing himself in the first team in the 1955-56 season.

He retired after the 1963-64 season, still as an Orient player having made 233 appearances, scoring 28 goals. He had suffered a bad leg injury which meant he missed a whole season and he never fully regained his fitness.

It is widely believed that had he played for a more glamorous club, he would almost certainly have gained International honours.

It was Phil's choice however to remain at the Orient. In 1956 the club were offered and accepted a £15,000 bid from Liverpool, but he chose to remain in London.

By mid November Wealdstone had improved slightly, having won 2 and drawn three of ten league games but for the home match with Carshalton they welcomed back Matt Farrell, who had left Hendon at the end of the previous season, and in fact hadn't played since.

He certainly made an immediate impact scoring with his first touch in the first few seconds of the match, sweeping a shot past the Carshalton goalkeeper from a long pass from Arthur Peel.

It was a match full of incident as Carshalton equalised within a couple of minutes and were 3–2 in front at the interval. Soon after the start of the second half, Wealdstone had equalised and then scored what proved to be the winner after 61 minutes with a headed own goal. Two minutes later Griffiths the Carshalton centre forward was sent off for something he said to the referee.

Ashworth was then adjudged to have handled and Carshalton were awarded a penalty, but the tame shot was easily saved by Durdle.

Then with the light fading at the end of the match a mysterious second penalty was awarded to the visitors, awarded for what only the referee considered to be a foul 'committed' outside the penalty area. Up stepped Carshalton's Holden whose much better attempt was again well saved by Durdle sealing a Wealdstone victory by 4-3.

Roger Durdle
Player 1963 – 1964

I joined Wealdstone in 1963 having spent two years on the ground staff at Fulham as an apprentice – as a goalkeeper.

I remember playing with Charlie Townsend, John Ashworth, Dave Richards and Roger Goode. I don't remember too much about particular games apart from one memorable game against Carshalton when I saved two penalties at Lower Mead.

Regrettably I didn't stay that long at Lower Mead and I went and played for Wembley, however my time at Lower Mead did get me started in the Construction Industry where I still am today. The club President at the time was Jack Holt – he was commercial manager at George Wimpey!

I also remember getting paid £2 a game I think - at a time when I was only earning £8 per week in full time employment! - probably shouldn't be saying this as we were of course amateurs in those days.

The reserves too had improved their form and a 5-0 win at Hornchurch following a draw and another win saw them slowly climbing the table. The first team won again the following week, 4-0 away to Vauxhall Motors in the Amateur Cup, finishing the month of November far more optimistically than it had started.

The improved form continued through Christmas and into the

New Year for a match with Grays Athletic, played in less than perfect conditions.

So far as could be discerned through the eerie fog that enveloped the pitch, threatening moment by moment to bring the whole insubstantial pageant to an end, Wealdstone neared the peak of their form in thrashing Grays 5-0.

While visibility remained passable, Viv Evans was seen to score an excellent goal following a typical piece of Charlie Townsend brilliance in the first half. Afterwards, reports relayed from the fog enshrouded Dominion end and subsequently confirmed by the participants, were that Matt Farrell had smashed in three more from close range, numbers two and three sandwiching an opportunistic effort from Hugh Lindsay.

What could be determined from a mid point was that Grays who had not previously conceded more than two goals in a match and were one of three clubs sharing third place in the table had been outplayed in every department.

Amplifying the conditions, Hugh Lindsay's goal was described;

Presumably disguised as one of the cleaner fog patches (as Wealdstone played in all white) Lindsay seized on a short goal kick intended for a defender and as Fox waited for the return ball, it thundered past his ear into the net.

Matt Farrell's re-signing had certainly been part of the improvement as his three goals in this match brought his tally to nine in five games since his return.

Wealdstone 's league form continued to improve and although knocked out of the major cup competitions fairly early on, there was still the opportunity for 'Stones to win a trophy to add to the Battle of Britain Trophy won early in the season with the Middlesex Competitions and also the Mithras Floodlit Cup.

The last week of March was another successful one with 'Stones beating Southall 2-1 to reach the final of the Middlesex Charity Cup against Hayes.

Goals from Farrell (2), Lindsay, Haydon and Bremer gave them a 5-0 win over Bishops Stortford in the East Anglian Cup semi-final first leg after a goalless first half (Wealdstone won the second leg by 4-0), and then with Matt Farrell unavailable, Wealdstone beat Hornchurch 7-2 in the league, recording their biggest victory of the season. Viv Evans had returned in Farrell's place after illness and scored four of the goals.

The Middlesex Senior Cup semi-final saw Wealdstone deprive the holders of their trophy, winning 3-1 against Enfield, one of the seasons Amateur Cup Finalists, to reach the final against Finchley. Wealdstone fielded almost a full strength team after the weakened side put out in the previous years final, only Fowler and Farrell unable to take part.

Enfield opened the scoring against the run of play, Wealdstone then scoring three times more without reply before 'Stones Mickey Doyle conceded an own goal to make the score 3-2 at the interval. On the hour, Enfield equalised again and the match was forced into extra time with 'Stones eventually running out winners by 6 goals to four to win the trophy for the second year in succession and the ninth time overall.

Playing league fixtures on Saturdays, Wealdstone's midweek fixtures at the end of the season were taken up with cup matches. The Tuesday following the win over Enfield saw the first leg of the Mithras Cup Final, 'Stones earning a creditable 1-1 draw away to Maidenhead.

The second leg a fortnight later at Lower Mead was played on a near waterlogged pitch. Wealdstone were soon able to take a 2-0 lead, both goals scored by Terry Haydon, the son of former Wealdstone player Fred. Terry had been seconded back to England on business and had recently joined Wealdstone following in his father's footsteps.

Maidenhead equalised but it was another new face in the Wealdstone side, Bernie Bremer, who scored the third and winning goal on the night to give Wealdstone the trophy.

A few days later and it was another cup final at Lower Mead, this time the Middlesex Charity Cup, against holders Hayes.

Hayes took an early lead, but Wealdstone replied three times to secure the trophy, Bremer, an own goal and Haydon the scorers. Four days later and Lower Mead was to host its third final in a fortnight, the Middlesex Senior Cup Final, against Athenian League runner up, Finchley.

Rounding off an otherwise disappointing season with a flourish, Wealdstone won their second trophy of the week, retaining the Senior Cup with a 2-0 win over Finchley, runner up in the Athenian League. Haydon again featured as a goal scorer and he passed the ball to Charlie Townsend to score the second.

Four trophies secured in what had started off as a very poor season, and two finals, the Hitchin Centenary Cup against Stevenage and the London Charity Cup against Barnet still to play!

The AGM was a busy affair with a number of points to be discussed, not least a proposal that the club should change its name to Harrow Football Club.

The reasoning behind the proposal was that when Wealdstone was formed the club represented the village that bore the same name. By 1964 it had become part of one of the largest boroughs with a population of 210,000.

The following year Harrow was to be incorporated as part of Greater London with representation on the GLC.

The proposal was heavily defeated, only five members supporting the change.

Charlie Townsend was presented with the Leadbetter Trophy as Sportsman of The Year in recognition of his service to the club and his International and Olympic selection, all of which bestowed honour on the club as well.

It was also announced that the club had been accepted as members of the Isthmian League for the first time. This meant that they would no longer take part in the Mithras Cup or East Anglian Cup but they would still compete in the Middlesex and London competitions.

The old problem of keeping good reserves had again proved a headache. An increasing gap between the colts and reserves sides had not improved the situation so it was decided again to revive the 'A' team under the leadership of Edgar Francis.

To ensure that this was an effective move, the side would not as before be a 'Strollers' XI but they would compete in the newly formed Surrey Combination, a league made up of Athenian and Isthmian League clubs.

After the disappointment against Hertford Town in the FA Cup, worse was to follow, as for season 1964-1965 Wealdstone were excluded from the competition as their application had not been posted in time!

After a public trial match won by the 'probable' team by 6–2, Wealdstone's final preparation for their first Isthmian League fixture was a behind closed doors friendly against Redhill.

With eight forwards fighting for five available places in the starting line up, Wealdstone's all out attack proved too strong for their opponents, running out winners by 8–0, Bell scoring twice and Jones once in the first half, Bremer (2), Farrell, Connell and Townsend scoring in the second period.

For their first fixture in the Isthmian League, Wealdstone entertained Tooting and Mitcham FC.

Making an encouraging start to their Isthmian League career, Wealdstone scored through Hugh Lindsay in the third minute and went on to win by 2–1 in front of a sun bathing crowd of 2000 at Lower Mead.

On balance of play, a draw might have been a farer result, but Wealdstone earned the points for a hard fight in the face of a leg injury to Townsend in the first half.

He remained on the field for most of the match and created the winning goal with a typically brilliant bit of football, but he was little more than a passenger for most of the second half, limping off before the end.

Both defences were considerably superior to the attacks and as a result both goalkeepers had a moderately easy afternoon though one brilliant second half save by Fowler from Viney was probably worth the extra point to his side.

Doyle was at his best, striking his best form despite missing both pre-season trials, and Ashworth directing operations with complete confidence as well as blotting out Gowland.

At the other end Jones failed to reproduce the form of the trials and Haydon had probably his most disappointing match for the club so far.

Wealdstone made a great start, two sharp thrusts from the start were cleared but Wealdstone were quickly in front. When a clearance went to Doyle the right back spotted Lindsay on the wing and a perfect pass was neatly gathered. Lindsay then cleverly rounded Filliary and beat Geearts with a hard shot from a narrow angle.
Almost at once, Leonard appeared to have a chance to reply but the lively ball rebounded too quickly to his knee and ran wide.

Wealdstone almost increased their lead when Jones, receiving from Evans, surprised Geearts with a fierce low drive from about 30 yards out. The ball spun out of the keepers' hands and along the line but there was no Wealdstone forward in sight and the Tooting defence had plenty of time to clear.

Leonard blasted a shot wide for Tooting and Lindsay got the ball into the net again from a clever hook by Jones but was ruled offside, and both sides slowed down before the interval.

Tooting dominated the early stages of the second half just as Wealdstone had done the first and they were as quickly rewarded, Wealdstone failing to clear a corner from Charman, and Green having an easy task to lift the ball into the roof of the net.

Haydon had a more difficult chance at the other end but put his shot far too high and Tooting appeared to be getting on top when the injured Townsend switched the game back into Wealdstone's favour.

Catching the defence in a complete muddle, he chipped the ball to Bell who wasted no time in smacking it into the net.

Wealdstone; W Fowler, M Doyle, R Good, C Townsend, J Ashworth, D Richards, D Bell, T Haydon, C Jones, H Lindsay, V Evans.

With the club pleased with its start, the following Tuesday they hosted Athenian League Champions Barnet in the held over final of the London Charity Cup. Barnet took the lead in the 52nd minute but were unable to hold on as Farrell and Haydon scored to give Wealdstone the victory in a side with four changes from the previous Saturday.

It was a busy week for the 'Stones as on the Wednesday they faced an away match in the league at Kingstonian which they lost by 2–1. Then, on the Saturday another away match which resulted in a 2–2 draw at Ilford, Wealdstone 10th of 20 clubs with one win, one draw and one defeat from their first three Isthmian League matches.

Wealdstone certainly held their own in the first months of their Isthmian League career, challenging at the top of the table for a long period. In fact after twelve league matches, 'Stones were in second place, one point behind Enfield on 18, with eight wins and two draws to their credit, having scored 35 goals.

Their goalscoring was becoming a notable habit – adding the London Charity Cup Final, held over from the previous season and friendlies with Redhill and Loughborough University, Wealdstone had scored 51 goals in 15 matches. There were a number of good wins, both Woking and Loughborough falling by 6–0 and Wycombe Wanderers (away) and St Albans beaten by 3–0.

November consisted mainly of cup fixtures, but there was a major shock as the month started with a home Middlesex Senior Cup-tie with C.A.V.

Suffering perhaps the biggest humiliation in their long history, Wealdstone, eight times winners and holders, lost possession of the Middlesex Senior Cup, when C.A.V. an Acton works team only admitted to the competition this season after 31 years as juniors deservedly beat 'Stones 2-1 at Lower Mead.

There could be no excuses although they played with only ten men for all but 23 minutes, finished with nine, and the visitors' first goal was a freak, direct from a corner. The fact was they should have established command before Evans, the hardest trier of them all was sent off the field.

Evans had already been hurt in one heavy tackle when he was brought down in the penalty area by Marren as he was heading for goal. The referee Mr R P Wall, unhesitatingly pointed to the spot but even as he did so, Evans was picking himself up and he seemed to aim a blow at Marren.

It landed, the right back collapsed. the linesman reported the incident and Mr Wall had no alternative but to send Evans off, though Evans said afterwards it was purely a warning action and he had not realised Marren was close enough for the blow to land. If that was not enough, Connell, deputed to take the kick, put the shot wide.

It was not to be Wealdstone's afternoon, conceding a goal direct from a corner nine minutes into the second half and going further behind twenty minutes later. Farrell restored some hope with 14 minutes to go but it was not enough.

Nothing Wealdstone could do availed, and as the match ended C.A.V. players were mobbed off the field by second and third team players whose matches had been postponed in honour of the occasion.

A splendid half back line, competent backs and enthusiastic forwards had won the day against opponents who took their task too lightly from the start and offered their opponents every opportunity to play above themselves.

Wealdstone; W Fowler, M Doyle, R Good, C Townsend, M Emerson, L McKendry, A Wyatt, J Connell, M Farrell, H Lindsay, V Evans

C.A.V. D Wynn, M Marren, P Perry, B Laing, K Foster, R Durrant, J Seymour, R Brogan, G McGrath, J Walsh, G Hallimond.

The following week, Wealdstone got back to winning ways with Townsend and Lindsay absent on England duty. The side was still good enough to beat Enfield 2–0 in the London Senior Cup. Victories away to Dagenham and Didcot in the London Challenge and Amateur Cup competitions helped to wipe away the memory of the C.A.V tie before a defeat in their first floodlit league game saw Wealdstone falter in the league.

There were also problems off the field, three of Wealdstone's regular players resigning from the club. Matt Farrell, Roger Good and Clive Jones all attempting to join Maidenhead.

The 'Stones refused clearance for the players to leave, the second time that they had done this with Matt Farrell and the matter was referred to the FA. All three players however appeared for Maidenhead in a match at Barnet, winning 4-2, Matt Farrell scoring a hat trick.

Eventually, the FA revoked all three players' registrations at Maidenhead, and Wealdstone finally agreed to their release which allowed the three to join Hemel Hempstead Town for the remainder of the season.

First team league form was still slipping slightly, and two defeats, 3–6 at Lower Mead and 2–1 in the return, against Hendon at Christmas didn't improve the situation. The second match it seems was more remarkable for the way in which it was played.

*So hard and treacherous was the Claremont Road pitch last Saturday that both sides agreed on a non-aggression pact before the match started. This was honourably kept by both sides and as a result there was no heavy tackling...........*was how the Harrow Observer started its match report!

Things were a little better for the reserves though, as they continued their victorious run, winning every match between 17th October and the end of the year. By mid January the run reached 14 consecutive victories with a 2-1 win over Kingstonian Reserves.

The same week a number of changes saw Wealdstone' first team secure a 4 –2 win over Hitchin Town in the first leg of the Hitchin Centenary Cup Final, held over from the previous season and to complete a ht-trick the Wealdstone 'A' team recorded their biggest win of the season, 16–0 against Epsom and Ewell, centre forward Lawford scoring ten of the goals.

Eric Metcalfe and the supporters at Bishop Auckland with their banner

It was to prove a good 'warm up' for the Amateur Cup-tie at the end of the month, Wealdstone making the long trek to visit Bishop Auckland.

A number of supporters also made the trip, arriving in time for an early breakfast before parading around the streets with a banner containing all of the names of the Wealdstone players. They then welcomed the Wealdstone team on their arrival at the ground before watching the match and enjoying the evening as guests of the local Working Men's Club, the party finally returning to Harrow at 6 am on the Sunday.

It must have been a pleasant trip as the result went in Wealdstone's favour.

Conquering a treacherous, snowbound pitch as well as opponents richly steeped in Amateur Cup tradition, Wealdstone played with increasing skill and unquenchable spirit to beat Bishop Auckland, ten times Amateur Cup holders, in the second round on Saturday.

First to score after 17 minutes, they shrugged aside the rebuff of a shock equaliser two minutes later, snatched back the lead and pressed with increasing momentum but little luck until the interval; held all their opponents' efforts to pull the game out of the fire in the second half and were almost coasting home 4-1 when the home side had the last word, scoring again with only seconds left to play.

Two inches of snow covered the pitch as the match started, and the Bishops were first to look dangerous, Doyle doing well to halt one attack at the expense of a corner and Scott bringing Fowler to his knees with a sharp low shot.

Soon, Wealdstone were forcing there way down the slope to make full use of their wingers. Given plenty of space Wyatt and Bremer responded by showing the backs a clean pair of heels on more than one occasion and Wealdstone gradually began to take command.

Wyatt forced a corner which Lindsay lifted high over the goal-mouth and when Bremer headed it down into the area the defence was still too confused to clear and Ashworth, who had come up for the kill, seized a sharp chance to drive the ball into the net.

Two minutes later however, Wealdstone were retreating in depth and when Richards conceded a free kick the goal area became a confused mass of bodies. Eventually, the ball was cleared to midfield, but a quick exchange of passes between Redhead and Scott gave Heatherington the chance to equalise.

This unwelcome reply did little to check Wealdstone's mounting confidence and soon Bremer and Wyatt were bewildering the Bishop's defence again. Only indifferent finishing and desperate defence combined with good goalkeeping denying them tangible reward for their skills. Wyatt indeed twice had shots blocked on the line.

Another goal soon came and Bremer had a big part in it, gathering a perfect pass from Lindsay and taking it almost to the line before pulling it back, right to his partners right boot. The defence was caught flat-footed and Lindsay's fierce drive skidded along the ground, well out of the goalkeepers reach.

That was after 38 minutes play and as the interval approached, Wealdstone seemed to appreciate with increasing urgency that a one goal lead might be inadequate with the slope to conquer in the second half, but try as they would, they could not score again, Kirkbride, Siddle and Hull repeatedly extricating their side from perilous situations.

With the home forwards making little or no impression on a now confident defence in the second half, Hull tried to take a hand with a blistering shot from well out, but Fowler brilliantly turned it over the cross bar and Wealdstone with Lindsay hitting his passes with almost uncanny precision were soon looking the far more dangerous side once again.

Almost on the hour Townsend made his side's passage into the third round almost certain. Moving quickly to a centre by Wyatt he breasted the ball down and turned in the same movement to hit the ball just as it hit the ground. Kirkland was stood helpless on the goal line as the ball flew into the right hand corner of the net.

12 minutes from the end, Childs in swinger hit the unlucky Siddle and the ball glanced past Kirkbride and over the line. Iceton kicked the ball away and afterwards claimed a 'save' but the linesman was right on the spot and flagged a goal.

Bishops were by now well beaten and over half the crowd left, missing the final goal from Scott, making a good solo run and beating Fowler with a low shot.

The ball was re-touched only once after the kick off and soon the entire Wealdstone team was rushing over to give a victory sign to their little knot of travelling supporters. Their superiority was handsomely admitted by home officials and spectators. The fans' only complaint appeared to be the number of free kicks their side had been awarded.

It was not a rough game and there was only one appearance by one trainer on the field. The attendance was 1,772 and the receipts £210.

Wealdstone; W Fowler, M Doyle, S McPhee, D Richards, J Ashworth, L McKendry, A Wyatt, C Townsend, R Childs, H Lindsay, B Bremer.

Wealdstone were still faltering in the league, their form not able to match that of the early part of the season, so it became more important for the club to continue their exploits in the Amateur Cup, the 'holy grail' that for so long had evaded them.

The draw saw 'Stones set to visit Alvechurch. They were expected to do well against 'the Worcestershire village side' but in front of a crowd of 7,028 'Stones were defeated.

Wealdstone scored first but then they were given a footballing lesson by the home team, Wealdstone missing a penalty and conceding four goals on their way to an inglorious defeat.

Viv Evans pictured in 1957

By early March, 'Stones had slipped to seventh place in the Isthmian League table and there was little left to compete for. A victory by 3-1 over Hitchin in the second leg of the Centenary Cup Final at least secured that trophy albeit almost a year late.

It was this time when Viv Evans left the club. Having been a regular first team player for eleven years, he had lost his place and joined Hemel Hempstead Town, already fielding three former 'Stones.

Viv had scored over 200 first team goals at Wealdstone and also had a number of Welsh trials, achieving representative honours for Middlesex and the Athenian League. He represented the club in almost every position, at least once having played in goal!

His career spanned over sixteen years from 1954 as his departure to Hemel and then Maidenhead United saw a season at each before he returned to Wealdstone.

Kenny Gee
Player and Reserve Team Manager

I joined Wealdstone at the same time as Viv Evans. We both played our first match in the reserves, away to Sutton United and we won 5-1. Viv got three goals and I got the other two.

The following week we both played for the first team, and Viv scored again. It was the start of a great record that he set. He never got dropped from the first XI until he retired from Senior football (the first time!). It's a great record and he was a great player and a nice chap.

The season seemed to peter out early for Wealdstone, their few cup matches allowing league fixtures to be 'fitted in' early on. A number of friendlies were arranged, both to keep the first team players fit and involved and to entertain the home support when the reserves were away.

One of these saw Amateur Cup conquerors, Alvechurch, visit for a return match. Wealdstone this time ran out winners by three goals to two, scoring the winner with the last kick of the match, but many felt Alvechurch deserved to win again, having led 2-1 with only ten minutes to go.

Again they had given a fast, skilful and invigorating display coming from behind after Dillsworth opened the scoring after 20 minutes, a lead that 'Stones only held for two minutes. Childs and Smith were Wealdstone's other goal scorers.

There was still a good deal to celebrate at the end of the season though, as the reserves had continued their good run of league form in their first Isthmian League season, finishing runner up to Hendon.

Their league record for the season was played 30 won 22 drawn 3 lost 5, scoring 97 goals with 42 conceded. The first team finally finished in eighth place.

A special meeting of the club had also been called by a number of members to vote on a resolution of No Confidence in the current administration and committee. Over 100 members had signed the petition to call the meeting and it had been caused by the resignation of three of the committee after the remainder had re-appointed Vince Burgess as coach for the following season.

The resolution, read out at the meeting was;

This meeting feels that the governing committee of the club are out of touch with the feelings and aspirations of the members that it represents, that, through lacking foresight, muddled thinking, and years of ineffectual administration culminating in the recent re-appointment of Mr Vince Burgess as coach for the forthcoming season – the committee have failed to reflect the wishes of the majority of its members; and therefore this meeting has 'no confidence' in the committee as presently constructed.

The vote saw only 40 people support the resolution while some 150 voted against it.

At the beginning of June a party of 25 left Lower Mead on a seven-day tour to Italy, with one match to be played at Alassio on the Italian Riviera.

Flying from Heathrow to Genoa and then travelling by coach, the party arrived early on the Friday morning. That afternoon, the club officials visited the Municipal Stadium to see the pitch, only to find a general state of disrepair and the posts not in place.

After a search the secretary and President of the club was found and questioned about the proposed match on the Sunday. The response was that the Town Mayor had forbidden the match taking place as there was a local festival on the same afternoon, and he didn't want the match to be a distraction!

It was eventually rescheduled for the following Wednesday evening, the Wealdstone players spending their time touring and on the beach in the meantime.

Perhaps the relaxing atmosphere had too great an effect on the touring side as they went on to lose by 4–1 against opponents who had included four Italian Under 23 Internationals as guests in their side.

The Tour Party in Italy
Back:?, Dick Kelly, Jim Cooley, ?, ?, Len McKendry, John Connell, Banger Walsh, Charlie Townsend, Bernie Bremer, Micky Doyle, Ken Wiltshire.
Front: Barrett (1),?, Vin Burgess, Jim Pyers, Barrett (2), Hugh Lindsay, Bobby Childs, Dave Richards,?,?

It was to be a busy close season as, not for the first time, a meeting was held at Harrow Council between Wealdstone FC, the Mayor Councillor H T Mote, Council officers and officials of Harrow Town FC. This time though, there were two reasons for the meeting.

The first was to gain the support of both clubs to raise a joint team to play a Watford XI at Lower Mead in aid of the Mayors Charity fund, this was duly arranged, but the second reason no doubt would have caused a far greater depth of conversation. It was proposed by the Mayor's office that the two clubs should amalgamate! The Council would be supportive of the amalgamation and would assist in the ongoing development of the stadium, Lower Mead proposed as the home.

The report commented that that this had been in the minds of some people for a long time and that is where it was to remain!

Thankfully the club AGM also passed with no further dissention, the members and club re-united in looking forward to a second Isthmian League season.

Charlie Townsend, John Ashworth and Hugh Lindsay

Steve Batty
Supporter since 1965

My father, Richard, was a Reserve and A Team player and a Committee member at Wealdstone. I started accompanying him to matches in 1965 when I was 5 years old.

Our crowd for home matches was myself, my father, Jim Pyers and another friend of my dad's, Alan Johnson. We always used to stand in front of the Main Stand, just beside one of the dugouts.

One evening game, Alan said to me "Do you want to keep the ball after the game?" Being an impressionable 6 or 7 year old I replied " Yes Please!!" Nothing more was mentioned.

Just as the referee blew the final whistle, purely by chance, the ball bounced over the fence into Alan's hands "There you go" he said and gave me the ball.

Magic.

Needless to say, I couldn't actually keep it, but that was it. I was hooked and I've been watching ever since. - All I need now is a similar piece of 'Magic' for my own sons.

A number of pre-season matches had been arranged, where more than just a trialist's side was to take the field. These started with a match against Edgware Town (won 3-0) and were followed at Hampton, (won 4-3). The first home fixture was to be against Rothwell Town.

Semi professional Rothwell had won the United Counties League the previous season and a strong match was expected, Wealdstone fielding a strong side with one or two newcomers added to the previous seasons line up.

Winning by 6-1 (Bremer 2, Childs 3, Allen) Wealdstone had impressed those who watched but there was a more serious subject of discussion. News that Charlie Townsend had left the club disappointing many that attended.

After 10 years he had left to join Hendon – he had been asked to play against Rothwell but had chosen to watch as Hendon took on Wimbledon in a friendly.

It was generally felt that he would be sorely missed, having amassed 22 caps for England as an International and Great Britain as an Olympic player.

The new season started in earnest the following week with a 2-1 win away at Maidstone and there was better news of Charlie Townsend as well – he was now 'undecided' about his future and had not played for any club in the first match of the new season!

In fact he represented the Isthmian League in a match against Wimbledon on the following Tuesday evening and had been listed in the programme as a Wealdstone player, having been taken to the game by the 'Stones secretary, Dick Kelly.

Two home games followed with poor results, a defeat to Enfield and a draw against Barking mirroring the previous seasons first three results, but another away win 4-1 at Kingstonian lifted the spirits, more so as it saw the return of Townsend, his proposed move to Hendon having not been completed.

An FA Cup victory at Hertford was followed by two more in the league, 4-0 against Dulwich and 6 –1 at home to Clapton, Childs and Cooley both scoring hat tricks.

As if this was not enough, the match between a combined Wealdstone and Harrow Town team against Watford had also been played, Watford leading twice in the first half, Wealdstone's Bremer and then Childs restoring equality, before another 'Stones player, Mackenzie scored a second half winner, the result being 3–2.

The combined side was; C Davidson, M Reynolds, A Holloway (all Harrow Town), D Richards, M Doyle (both Wealdstone), M Boist (Harrow Town), B Allen, D Sidley, R Childs (sub E Mackenzie) E Dillsworth and B Bremer (all Wealdstone).

After the victory away to Hertford, Wealdstone were drawn to meet Harlow Town in the second qualifying round of the FA Cup, at Lower Mead, Wealdstone moving into a 2-0 lead before Harlow pulled a goal back. Wealdstone then went on to score three times more in the last 20 minutes to secure a 5-1 win and a tie against Stevenage.

It was to be a memorable season for cup adventures as a whole, the Amateur Cup run the pinnacle but an early taste of cup excitement came from the FA Cup-tie with Stevenage;

Never in front until a 35 yard free kick from Hugh Lindsay screamed into the net in the last minute, Wealdstone achieved a fantastic 6-5 win over Stevenage in the third qualifying round of the FA Cup.

Saving a seemingly lost cause, Lindsay had completed a hat trick in seven minutes and scored for the fourth time after the professionals had held and lost the lead four times. Small wonder a section of the 2,539 crowd erupted onto the field to cheer their heroes off.

Stevenage afterwards attributed their defeat to the referee, Mr D S Adey, who ordered the former Spurs and England forward, Brooks, off the field for bad language just before the interval.

The fact is though, that without him, Stevenage were leading 5-3 with only seven minutes to go, they then collapsed before a magnificent rally that was slow to build but irresistible when it got under way.

Normally sympathy may be felt for a team that had come so close, but Stevenage merited none. Some of their tackling was nothing short of brutal, the wingers, Bremer and Allen being the special target. All this marred a match that exploded into action with three goals in the first seven minutes.

With Goymer still unfit and Childs failing a late test, Wealdstone began apprehensively the ball quickly being played three times to the young goalkeeper, Smith and this did nothing for his confidence. After two minutes he was beaten by a low shot by Sheriffs after a clearance by McKendry was charged down

Wealdstone were soon back on terms, a clever overhead kick by Dillsworth being thumped home by Cooley before, after seven minutes, Stevenage were back in front again, Cashmore going through unchallenged and walker at the far post nodding home the centre.

As Wealdstone stormed back the visitors panicked into a profusion of corners and free kicks and Dillsworth made the score 2-2 forcing the ball home from close range after Cooley's shot had been blocked.

That was after 21 minutes and Stevenage were still under pressure 13 minutes later when a good shot by England from 30 yards beat Smith to put Wealdstone behind for the third time.

With the interval near came Brooks dismissal.

After a bad foul on Allen, Townsend lobbed the ball into the penalty area and Mr Adey ruled that a forward had been fouled. The decision seemed harsh and there were vehement protests before Lindsay was able to take the kick and lash the ball past Peacock. The protest redoubled and Brook was sent off.

Re-appearing with his leg heavily bandaged after the first half 'marking' Bremer was badly brought down right at the start of the second half.

Another name was taken and Stevenage had lost their impartial friend, yet Wealdstone seemed quite unable to capitalize on their numerical advantage and Stevenage took up the running.

England was especially dangerous and when Doyle pulled him down just inside the area, Cashmore easily scored from the penalty spot. Almost immediately Sheriff was unlucky to see a hard shot bounce off Smith for a corner.

With Wealdstone still off the boil a fifth goal by Walker after 63 minutes looked to be decisive.

Townsend and Lindsay were continuously at work probing for openings and at last a duel effort between Cooley and Dillsworth induced the game's third penalty.

Lindsay's powerful kick heralded a few minutes of glory and triumph, the equalising goal being cleverly hooked in by Lindsay, before his decisive free kick.

Wealdstone; R Smith, M Doyle, D Richards, C Townsend, J Ashworth, L McKendry, B Allen, J Cooley, E Dillsworth, H Lindsay, B Bremer.

Graham Clark
Supporter since 1960

As a 14 year old this was my first experience of the 'big match' atmosphere, having watched Wealdstone since 1960. In the previous rounds we had beaten Hertford Town and Harlow Town but the crowds were nothing like the 3000 plus this afternoon.

The match had everything a partisan or impartial supporter could want. There were 11 goals, three penalties, a sending off, six bookings and Wealdstone coming back from 5-3 down to win the game with a Hughie Lindsay free kick in the dying seconds.

The memory or standing behind the goal – at five all – and seeing Hughie embark on his 35 yard run up, and power his shot, which hit the top of the net, still rising as it passed the goalkeeper has lived with me since the game.

It was amazing. It firmly committed me to following the 'Stones through thick and thin.

The next FA Cup opponents were also next in the league, Oxford City securing a draw at Lower Mead in the league before falling 2-0 in the cup allowing Wealdstone to progress. For the second time in the club's history, they had reached the first round proper, this time drawn away to Millwall.

Club Secretary Ken Wiltshire clears a patch of the snow for the local referee J L Jackson to inspect the ground underneath before the match with Tow Law Town.

It was a daunting prospect, Millwall at the time were unbeaten at home and had the best record in any division of the Football League, having gained 20 points from twelve matches.

It was a difficult and hard match, played in front of 11,794 supporters, Millwall taking a 2-0 lead into the interval.

Soon after Cooley smashed a hard drive past Alex Stepney in the Millwall goal. Wealdstone spending the greater part of the second half on all out attack. In fact with ten minutes to go it was still 2-1 although their third headed goal of the match on 82 minutes put the result beyond doubt in Millwall's favour.

Cup exploits seemed to concentrate Wealdstone's minds and the league form slipped somewhat. In the run up to Christmas it did again improve with four wins in five matches.

The New Year started with a series of cup-ties and further success for the club, beating Hitchin 4–1 in the Amateur Cup, following that with a 4–0 win at Ford United in the London Senior Cup and home wins over Wingate (3–0) in the Middlesex Senior Cup and Tow Law Town 2–1 again in the Amateur Cup.

The match against Tow Law was particularly difficult, the Northern League side battling and more than playing their part in a spirited, unyielding struggle in difficult conditions. Their grim defending after they equalised Wealdstone's tenth minute goal seemingly destined to see the tie go to a replay at their Durham home.

The day before and the Lower Mead pitch had a 2" covering of snow, cleared by volunteer supporters after the referee declared that the match could go ahead if the pitch was cleared.

Wealdstone had taken the lead when, after 10 minutes, Lindsay was unceremoniously brought down some 30 yards from goal. Townsend ran over the ball at the free kick and Lindsay followed through with a venomous shot that left the keeper rooted to his goal line.

Tow Law Town equalised, also from a free kick after 35 minutes and it wasn't until the 78th minute that Wealdstone restored their lead, the winning goal coming from Wortley.
Their first away draw in the competition saw Wealdstone set to visit either Barking or Ferryhill in the last 16, their first tie having been postponed due to the weather.

Barking won the re-arranged tie so Wealdstone were to visit their fellow Isthmian League side at Vicarage Fields.

It was an incident packed match, described in the match report as one where the referee was booking and sending players off for what would normally be met with a wagging finger!

Wealdstone took an early lead when Cooley crossed, Lindsay dummied and wrong footed the defender, the ball ran wide allowing Allen to cross from the other side and Childs scored with a header.

Cooley again was involved after 20 minutes, when the Barking goalkeeper collected a through ball as he ran in. Unable to stop his attempt for the ball on a difficult surface, he caught the goalkeeper above the right eye. Cooley turned top apologize but was manhandled away by the home defenders, no doubt concerned as the previous week they had seen their regular goalkeeper carried off with concussion.

The keeper left the field to receive attention, and although he was off only five minutes, it was long enough for Townsend to extend Wealdstone's lead scoring the second goal, scoring with a volley from fully thirty yards. Barking did manage to pull a

Wealdstone goalkeeper Arthur Paisley saves from M Elder, while Eddie Dillsworth looks on.

ers grasp and dropped over the line to give the visitors a fifteenth minute lead.

Better finishing may have allowed Leatherhead to increase their lead against a lethargic Wealdstone side, but with fifteen minutes to go, Townsend scored an equaliser. As a corner came over, Leatherhead's ten man defence unsighted O'Malley in goal and the ball dropped for Townsend to score with a low shot.

Leatherhead hung on defiantly but to no avail as with two minutes to go, Townsend floated in a cross which Cooley met, his shot leaving the goalkeeper no chance.

goal back just before half time, Hunt scoring from close range.

The referee visited both dressing rooms during half time, warning both teams against further instances on the field but his warnings seemed to go unheeded, Wealdstone soon awarded a penalty for a foul on Childs. Lindsay usually so certain with his kicks, managed to strike the ball the wrong side of the post having sent the goalkeeper the wrong way.

After 65 minutes Barking's Craddock was sent off for another foul on Dillsworth, nudging him as the ball ran out of play. Then Sedgley followed for Wealdstone after a heading duel.

The match then seemed to settle down a little and late on, a cross from Allen found Childs at the far post and he scored Wealdstone's third goal on the day.

'Stones luck was to hold as the draw was announced for the last eight, a home tie against the winners of the Hayes v Leatherhead replay. The last two remaining Athenian League clubs the two least feared in the competition. Leatherhead finally becoming the opponents.

The pressure of fifty years of failure seemed to weigh heavy on Wealdstone's shoulders as they made very hard work of the match against Leatherhead, finally running out winners by 2-1 in front of a crowd in excess of 5,000 at Lower Mead.

They had been stunned into almost silence as Leatherhead lead 1-0 from a freak goal, Wealdstone rarely looking capable of breaking down their opponents.

The goal came when Brazier the Leatherhead captain shot hard from 40 yards straight at debutant Paisley in the Wealdstone goal. The crowd gasped as the shot slipped from the goalkeep-

Wealdstone had made history with one of their poorest displays in living memory but had reached the semi-final of the Amateur Cup, their third semi-final of the season along with the Middlesex Senior Cup and the London Senior Cup.

The Amateur Cup semi-final was played at Stamford Bridge, home of Chelsea FC in front of a crowd of 14,225. The opponents were the conquerors from a season earlier, Alvechurch.

A magnificent defensive display, particularly from Ashworth and Dillsworth helped Wealdstone establish their superiority although Alvechurch too defended stoically.

Chances were limited; Allen and Childs having the best for Wealdstone but midway through the first half Alvechurch were awarded a penalty. Paisley, in goal for Wealdstone again as Goymer was still injured (it was the third season in succession he had been injured and unable to play in a semi-final) stepped up to have a word with the taker, Cocking, as he placed the ball.

He told later that the forward had suggested that if he missed, his team did not deserve to go to Wembley, and miss it he did. A poor penalty was struck tamely, allowing Paisley to make the save and Ashworth rushed in to clear the ball for a throw.

As half time approached, Townsend and Lindsay created chances for Wealdstone and Cooley also had a shot blocked but the score at the interval was 0-0. The second half saw Wealdstone create two early chances but then Alvechurch took over and had their greatest period of superiority, Paisley saving a good shot from Mason.

After 77 minutes, Wealdstone, whose occasional attacks had seemed more likely to bear fruit, scored in well-rehearsed

The Wealdstone crowd at Stamford Bridge for the FA Amateur Cup semi final.

fashion. Lindsay's pass found Allen and his cross to the back of the goal would normally have met the inrushing Cooley. On this occasion Cooley was slow starting but did enough to distract the goalkeeper whose late attempt to clear the ball only aided it on its way into the net.

For the last few minutes, play was even, Wealdstone having a chance to extend their lead through Childs and Alvechurch forcing Paisley into a couple of good saves, but Wealdstone it was that were to reach the Wembley final, the second appearance at the famous stadium for the club, and one where they hoped to match the side of 1942 by winning their final.

Edgar Fry
Supporter since the early 1940's

I'm afraid I'm hazy on dates, but one of my early memories is of Eric the Bell Man who dressed in Blue & White top hat and Wealdstone shirt with a placard round his neck. He was a well-known figure, striding down towards Lower Mead with a trail of young kids in tow, like the Pied Piper and once in the ground when "'Stones" scored he would vigorously ring his bell much to our delight and to the annoyance of rival fans.

I think one of my memorable matches was the Amateur Cup semi-final at Stamford Bridge (Amateur Cup) against Alvechurch (1966). We scored the only goal about 10 minutes to go. Charlie Sells (I think) put what was meant to be a cross, the Keeper came, missed, and the ball ended in the net, then there were the last finger biting minutes, the final whistle and we were at Wembley at last.

In my early days supporting, I used to stand with an old boy I knew who remembered the ground "'Stones" had before Lower Mead and he always referred to Lower Mead as the new ground. He was constantly running down and moaning about the players, but when one scored he would nudge me in the ribs and say, "there you are - I told you so, the best player on the pitch".

When I started going to Wealdstone, I was about twelve, the ground used to be packed, three or four deep all round, but as kids we found ourselves pushed to the front by the fence behind the goal. It was great; I've been hooked ever since.

Before the Amateur Cup Final could be played there were a number of other fixtures to complete. 'Stones lost their London Senior Cup semi-final 2-0 at Leytonstone, Hugh Lindsay sent off in the match but he and Wealdstone came back with a vengeance in their next match, beating Hitchin 6-1, Lindsay scoring three. Three more victories in the next four league games also improved the league position and maintained the confidence of the side as the final approached.

Magnificently unperturbed by conceding a shock goal in the fifth minute to the holders and firm favourites, Hendon, Wealdstone strode imperiously to a 3-1 victory in their first appearance in the FA Amateur Cup Final at Wembley Stadium on Saturday. With gathering confidence they almost played Hendon into the ground yet it was not until three minutes from the end that they took the lead for the first time.

Then, from the 16th corner they had forced from an unhappy Hendon defence Townsend dropped the ball accurately into the centre of the goalmouth. Cooley used his full height to beat Riddy in the air and nod the ball down to Bremer, who sent the crowd delirious with delight as he swept the ball past Swannell from close range.

Desperately, Hendon fought back to regain their grip on the trophy they had so worthily won last year and momentarily, Wealdstone seemed in danger of panic, but twice Dillsworth made cool, almost insolent interceptions before slipping the ball to Goymer, and his side swept back to score another great goal.

This last decisive moment began when Townsend intercepted a clearance by Swannell. Swiftly, the ball went from Townsend to Allen, from Allen to Childs and then back to Townsend and back to Childs again. This time, Lindsay was brought into the movement and he shot so fiercely that Swannell could not hold the ball and Childs following through, hammered the rebound into the net.

Childs second goal came well into injury time and soon afterwards Ashworth and the rest of the team were receiving the 45,000 crowd's generous acclaim as they moved off the pitch to receive the trophy and medals from Earl Alexander of Tunis.

Opponents and critics alike were afterwards unanimous and unstilted in their praise for a great team effort that had left Wealdstone wholly deserving winners of one of the best Amateur Cup Finals played at Wembley, and it was left to Wealdstone Captain, John Ashworth to award the premier honours to the England link men, Townsend and Lindsay.

Hendon's tactics were to blot out these two as much as possible but they could catch neither as they set up attack after attack, which would have brought earlier reward with sharper shooting from the other forwards.

As it was, Hendon were repeatedly pushed back and after the

Captain, John Ashworth presents England International Charlie Townsend to Earl Alexander of Tunis before the Amateur Cup Final. Coach Vince Burgess is wearing the blazer.

opening ten minutes attacked mainly in breakaways. Even in the first half when honours were shared, they were so concerned with defence that twice the only forward in the Wealdstone half was caught offside only a few feet over the line.

From the kick off Wealdstone were on the attack, Lindsay fouled by Cantwell, but attempts by Townsend and Dillsworth to turn the kick to advantage, failed. Almost immediately Bremer rounded Hogwood and slipped the ball to Lindsay but his shot was deflected for a corner. The cross was driven in low but when it rebounded to Sedgley, his shot was wide.

Wealdstone were looking anything but second favourites but found themselves a goal down when Hyde raced down the left and forced Ashworth to concede a corner. Taken by Hyde himself this was headed away by Ashworth but only to an unmarked Riddy and the former Wealdstone centre half hit the ball low and hard into the net.

Wealdstone were almost immediately back on the attack, Lindsay shooting too high before Bremer earned a corner on fifteen minutes. Cooley got his head to the ball but it hit Swannell's legs and rolled to safety.

As Wealdstone kept up the pressure a centre from the right by Cooley beat Swannell who looked anything but England's number one amateur goalkeeper, and Hogwood headed hastily away for another corner. Two more followed quickly as Hendon showed signs of panic.

Wealdstone should have drawn level when Swannell fumbled a powerful drive from Lindsay but Childs arrived on the scene a fraction of a second too late. Another Lindsay special was expected when Cantwell again pulled him down just outside the penalty area but instead, Townsend took the kick and lobbed the ball just over the angle of crossbar and post.

Little now was seen of the Hendon attack that badly needed the midfield generalship and genius of Quail, but Wealdstone's growing authority almost received a setback when Evans broke clear only to shoot too high from a fine position.

Hendon earned their second corner on half an hour, but they soon had ten men in defence again. Even this could not save them and five minutes before the interval, Bremer tricked Riddy before slipping the ball to Childs, whose low, curling shot took Swannell completely by surprise as it sped into the corner of the net.

The second half began with a flurry of Wealdstone attacks in one of which Swannell brilliantly turned away a fierce drive from Lindsay.

Three corners in two minutes were all cleared before at last Hendon got back into the game with two runs by Churchill. Sedgley foiled him each time and the only danger was when Riddy got his head to his side's third corner but the ball flew too high.

Wealdstone were immediately hammering away at the other end, but Childs was now limping with a recurrence of his old ankle injury but he kept going and helped in a movement, which ended when Swannell again made a fine save from Lindsay.

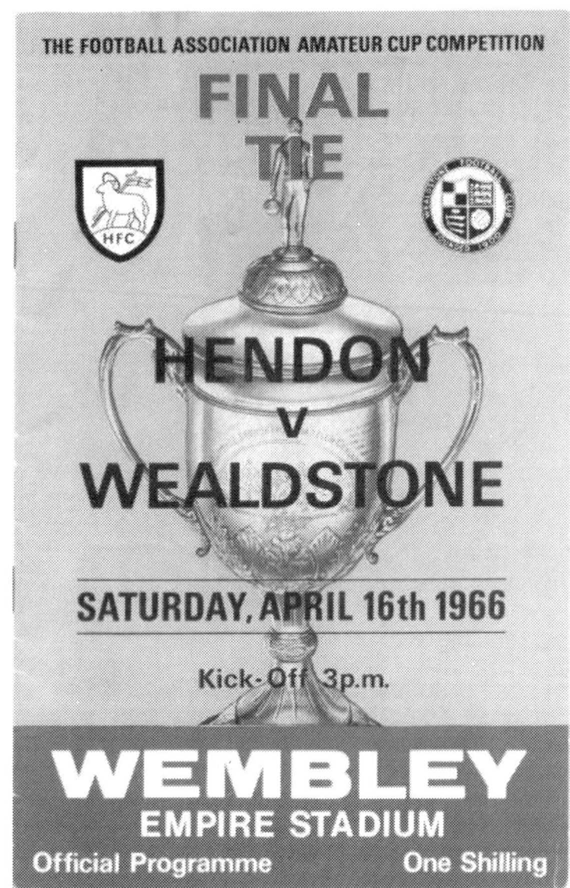

The Match Programme from the Amateur Cup Final. Wealdstone's second winning visit to Wembley Stadium.

After 70 minutes there was a premature cheer as Childs headed Lindsay's centre on to Allen who slipped the ball into the net, but he was offside and Hendon recovered their breath to launch a counter attack in which Sleap who had earlier injured Childs was injured himself.

Rain was making the pitch, which was under a thick mantle of snow only 36 hours earlier, even heavier and it was beginning to look like a battlefield with Shacklock and Sedgley prone and several other players limping.

As Hendon still struggled they gained their fourth and last corner but they were now looking like a beaten side and when Shacklock who had been off the field receiving treatment returned, it was only to be a spectator as Wealdstone rode to a notable victory, a victory earned by superior skill as well as greater stamina, and, perhaps above all, unquenchable courage when at times it seemed every effort was in vain.

Apart from one or two slips, Ashworth played the dominant defensive role that played so big a part in his side's progress to the final while Doyle and Sedgley have never served it better and content with a comparatively inconspicuous role Dillsworth did all that was asked of him.

In attack, Cooley simply justified the coach's faith in him with a strong performance that never allowed the Hendon defence to settle, and Childs, by seizing two chances had a memorable afternoon and a plucky one considering the number of heavy tackles he had to endure.

Hendon; J Swannell, D Hogwood, M Cooper, D Shacklock, G Riddy, R Cantwell, L Churchill, J Evans, D Swain, R Sleap, D Hyde.

Wealdstone; Brian Goymer, Mickey Doyle, Gordon Sedgley, Charlie Townsend, John Ashworth, Eddie Dillsworth, Brian Allen, Bobby Childs, Jim Cooley, Hugh Lindsay, Bernie Bremer.

It was a triple celebration for Eddie Dillsworth as the Sierra Leone born Eddie won the Amateur Cup on his 21st birthday and he became the first African born player to play in (and win) a Wembley final.

Dave Mizney
Supporter since 1960's to 1980's

I remember at the Amateur Cup Final in 1966, John Ashworth handing the cup to Eric – the No1 supporter – to hold it up to the crowd. A wonderful gesture.

John Ashworth
Player 1963- 66

I joined the club in 1963 straight from the Royal Navy. At that time Wealdstone were still in the Athenian League. I was made Captain during 1964 and I had a great relationship with the Manager, Vince Burgess as well as Ken Wiltshire, Johnny Ryan, Dick Kelly and the many, many supporters who followed us everywhere.

There were some great characters and great footballers involved – Charlie Townsend, Hughie Lindsay, Bobby Childs, Jim Cooley and the rest of the boys. April 16th 1966 seems to remain quite clearly in my mind. It was the day we defeated the 'arch enemy', Hendon! What a great day, a great end to a great cup run. Lifting the cup? What a great end to a season!

Dave Bassett
Opponent 1966-74 and subsequently a Football League and Premiership Manager

I first came across Wealdstone as a player in the 1965-66 season when I played for Hendon, my first game was Boxing Day, at home, and we (Hendon) won 1-0, but I missed out on the Amateur Cup Final through injury.

Jimmy Quail broke his leg in the Quarter Final against Wycombe Wanderers, and like a pratt I was playing Sunday football as well the next day and I did the same thing!

There were some great players at that time in both clubs, but I particularly remember Charlie Townsend and Hughie Lindsay - Hughie always used to get a Christmas present from Alf D'Arcy - without fail he'd try and knock him out, but that was part and parcel of the battles at that time.

Only once did it ever carry over into the bar - normally we'd all have a drink and promise to get one back in the next game, but there was one where I 'caught' Brian Goymer and he got a bit arsey in the bar after but it was nothing serious.

After the game, the team returned to Harrow where they made a special appearance on the stage of the Granada Cinema during the evening's performance, before attending a Civic Dinner at the Clarendon restaurant.

The film on that evening was "The Intelligence Men" with Morecambe & Wise, but the biggest cheer came when Eric Metcalffe (the man in blue and white) and his bell led the team onto the stage.

Wealdstone FC Amateur Cup Winners 1965-66
Bobby Childs, Hugh Lindsay, Eddie Dillsworth, Gordon Sedgley, John Ashworth with the Amateur Cup, Jim Cooley, Charlie Townsend, Brian Goymer, Brian Allen, Bernie Bremer and Mickey Doyle.

Following this they took the short journey to Lower Mead and were met by the fans for a celebration dance.

It was possibly the shortest route ever to a cup final as well! With a number of home draws, only one away match and the final at Wembley, Wealdstone had in fact travelled no more than 70 miles in winning the competition.

(The following season for example, Wealdstone played five ties, finally being beaten in the third round, having already travelled over 1000 miles.)

Although it was the fifth time that the two sides had met over the season, it wasn't to be the last, as in early May the sides met again at Clarendon Road in a Middlesex Senior Cup semi-final replay, Wealdstone again running out winners, by 4-2 after a draw at Lower Mead. In the two legged final Wealdstone lost 2-0 and 2-1 to Enfield.

Stephen Yearley
Supporter since 1960's

My first introduction to football was in 1966 when I was 13 years old and for some reason a family friend took me to Wembley to see the Amateur Cup Final between Wealdstone and Hendon.

I was told I was supporting Wealdstone. We won and although my view was restricted and we stood next to a large man who continually rang a loud bell throughout I thoroughly enjoyed myself. I must add that prior to the game I had not been interested in football and I had hardly kicked a ball in earnest at all.

I also remember standing outside Harrow & Wealdstone Station watching the players go past with the cup, on top of an open top bus if my memory serves me well. Then a few weeks England won the World Cup and I was hooked on football for life.

Mike Scofield
Supporter, 1966

My Grandfather Cecil Scofield, used to live in Headstone Drive & he took my Cousin Alan & me to different grounds all over North London to watch football. Arsenal, Chelsea, Tottenham, Watford (mostly), Fulham, QPR, Wealdstone, Wembley (Vale Farm, not Stadium !).

He was the original football lover, who wanted to see a good game, no matter who won.

I remember going to the old original ground behind the ABC cinema with him, for an FA Cup qualifying game in 1960's against Ford United (I think). The ground was absolutely packed - must have been 2,000 or so I would think - & the Ford keeper had a magnificent game. It ended 0-0, but a good game.

He always used to say what a good club Wealdstone were & how if I could not get taken on by any of the league clubs when I reached 15 (he was convinced I would make the grade, but of course I did not) I should go down to Wealdstone who played a good standard of football.

That great day out at the Amateur Cup Final was the culmination of a good season of watching amateur football for me (aged 10 at the time). I had moved to Hemel Hempstead who were doing very well in the Athenian League (never saw them play Wealdstone, who must have been in the Isthmian League at the time) & I had not missed a home match.

Since they had been knocked out of the cup, I had kept myself up to date with the progress of other teams, & decided very late on that I would go to the game, after seeing the TV preview the night before the game.

My parents dropped me off at Wembley Park, on their way to Alperton to visit relatives & I decided that my Hemel Hempstead green & white scarf made me a Hendon supporter for the day.

Strange really, when I had already been introduced to Wealdstone & had been to a game at the old home ground behind the cinema against Ford United a season or so before! I remember thinking that this was the kind of ground that Hemel Hempstead needed. Real terracing, not just the big grassy banks behind each goal at Crabtree Lane.

I did not have a ticket, but asked a tout how much he wanted for his, & since there was only about 10 minutes to go till kick-off, he just gave me one! It was a very expensive seat in the blue coloured posh seats to the right of the Royal Box.

Sat next to me, were three chaps in suits, who were Wealdstone supporters & they were very kind & spoke to me about how come such a young boy was there on his own. I just told them, very matter of fact, that my Dad did not like football, so I came on my own. They thought this was very funny, which I did not really understand.

I remember Hendon taking the lead, & me thinking that I had chosen the right colours to wear. As the game wore on however, it became clear that Wealdstone were the better team, & of course, Eddie Dillsworth (the chaps next to me insisted on calling him Eddie Dillsworthy) drove them on to a famous victory.

I got caught up in the excitement of it all as my new friends, went completely mad as the winning goal went in, & decided that since this was Grandad's team, I really should be cheering for them.

I remember quite clearly, that one of them actually threw his trilby hat into the air at the end of the game. Never seen that before or since except in comic's.

N.V. Bunker
Supporter since 1948

There was one supporter and member named Eric Metcalfe, now deceased who use to dress up in his blue and white shirt and trousers and his top hat and carry his hand-bell, which he used to ring to encourage the team. There is a picture of him in the 1961-62 Club handbook of which I have a copy.

My main memory is of the 1966 Amateur Cup Final as I was on the Football Club Committee season 1965-66. I still have the card they gave us with the names of the Officials, Committee, players and the Itinerary such as departure time of the players' coach and committee coach and all that was to happen during the day and evening. A wonderful day.

League form also improved a little at the end of the season, with both teams eventually finishing sixth in their respective divisions and there were more individual honours for the cup winners with Eddie Dillsworth selected to play for the Isthmian League side, John Ashworth, Hugh Lindsay and Charlie Townsend selected for England. Hugh Lindsay was presented with a trophy as 'Amateur International of the Year' by Soccer Star magazine.

As usual, there was a tour organised for Whitsun and this year the destination was Guernsey in the Channel Islands.

A crowd of over 800 turned out to watch Wealdstone take on a Guernsey Select XI. Searle scored for the 'Stones after five minutes and then Wortley headed in a Lindsay centre on the half hour. Allen took over from Searle in the second half, and further goals from Wortley and Bremer saw Wealdstone complete a comfortable 4-0 win. Missing from the tour though was cup winning captain, John Ashworth who had already resigned from the club to pursue his career elsewhere.

Gordon Sedgley
Player 1966

I have many happy memories of the club although I only had one full season there as a player. It was very important for me, as I was a member of the side that won the Amateur Cup. The following season I was asked to return to Enfield, which I did, and that too turned out to be fortunate, as for the second time I played in a team that won the Amateur Cup. Two winners medals in two seasons, which was remarkable as I was only an average player.

I always remember the Wealdstone support. It was particularly good when we played local rivals like Hendon FC who we beat in the final, and our manager; Vin Burgess who had a pretty laid back style. He almost always took training wearing a collar and tie. Secretary Dick Kelly too was well respected by everyone at the club and in amateur football in general.

As in most teams there were different types of player – our captain, John Ashworth who had been in the navy and played for Portsmouth FC whilst stationed there. He was a marvellous header of the ball and had the longest neck and loudest voice I have ever seen and heard.

Hugh Lindsay I also remember. He was only slight in build but he had one of the hardest dead ball kicks ever. I would say that he was the best player I have ever played with or against. Both of them were heavy smokers and like the rest of us liked a drink, but it certainly didn't seem to affect their ability.

There were some memorable matches that season too. Our FA Cup game against Millwall FC at The Den. Alex Stepney played in goal for them and soon after was transferred to Manchester United so we must have made him look good! True to reputation, the Millwall fans were very volatile and I don't think I ever felt as threatened as I did that day at the Den.

The Amateur Cup semi-final at Stamford Bridge was memorable as Brian Goymer had been injured in a previous match and a young reserve goalkeeper by the name of Arthur Paisley had to play. He saved a penalty to get us to Wembley.

In the final we were considered the underdogs as Hendon had almost a whole team of Amateur Internationals. Our defender Eddie Dillsworth celebrated his 21st birthday on cup final day and he and everyone else played above expectations. We fully deserved to win the match.

In the photo, John Ashworth is sitting on my shoulder. The other player supporting him is Jim Cooley. It was Jim that told me before the match that if you wanted your picture in the papers, you had to hold the captain up with the cup!

Stan Pearce
Player 1965 – 66

I have many happy memories of Wealdstone Football Club both watching and playing for the club in the 1965/66 season.

One match stands out for me and that was a reserve team match played against Hendon reserves. The game saw the arrival of Keith Searle; playing in front of a reasonable crowd was a thrill for somebody who had just turned 18, the experience was wonderful. That evening saw Keith score four goals, each goal taken superbly. I used to play on the right wing and put in three crosses for Keith who put them all away. We eventually ran out winners 5-1.

It was a great pleasure to be involved with the 'Stones. The players both in the reserves and first team were of a very high standard, always taking time to encourage the young players, non-more so than Charles Townsend and Hughy Lindsay.

The experiences I had at Wealdstone helped shape my own football career. When I left Wealdstone I played for Kingsbury Town for three years. During that time I got married and moved down to Brighton where I still live. I have spent the last thirty years coaching and playing at senior level clubs.

At Saltdean I came into contact with Bob Marchini. Bob was Wealdstone through and through. The players from the 1966 cup final side will always remember Bob for the meals they had at his restaurant in Brighton whilst training on the beach; a true supporter of the 'Stones, a part of their history.

I thank you Wealdstone for the experience, a 'happy band of brothers.

After the previous couple of years, the AGM was a far more settled affair. This time there were no dissenting calls with regard to coach Vince Burgess – as can be imagined he was given great credit for the Amateur Cup win and finally laying the 'ghost' that had haunted the club for so long.

A profit had been made of over £1,870, helped by a £1,525 share of the Wembley gate receipts, which totalled £18,862. This was soon used though as plans to cover the Cinema End terrace were with Harrow Council and approval was expected shortly.

There was also a plan to build a Multi Storey car park where the existing car park stood to increase capacity but this idea was eventually rejected although the original Lower Mead pavilion was demolished to make way.

At the Annual Dinner, the mayor of Harrow Councillor E G Buckle and his predecessor, Councillor Mote both spoke of the honour the club had brought to the Borough as a whole by winning the Amateur Cup and amid the extended gratification, awards were also made to the Chairman, Jack Rogers and his wife (a table lamp surrounded by miniature Amateur Cup trophies) and Secretary Ken Wiltshire (a table lighter) as mementoes of the season's success.

There was an award too for Keith Searle, who although he had not made the 'final' team, he had made a number of successful appearances in the forward line during the season. The club felt he had earnt the Leadbetter Trophy.

There were a number of new signings as the new season approached and the cup final team was never to play together again – the only occasion in which the full eleven had was in the replayed Middlesex Cup semi-final away to Hendon. Gordon

Sedgley (Enfield), John Ashworth (Hendon) and Jim Cooley (Chesham) had left the club, Sedgley at Enfield making his debut in their second match of the new season, at home to Wealdstone.

Three of the new signings made their debut's in Wealdstone's opening match, George Riddy, Hendon's cup final centre half occupied the same position for Wealdstone and he was joined by Robert Drake, also from Hendon and Tony McTurk.

It was the first competitive Wealdstone match in which substitutes were allowed and McTurk was the 'Stones first. He replaced Drake fifteen minutes from the end of the match, a 2-2 draw with Corinthian Casuals.

Despite his place in the club history, the appearance was not to be the start of an auspicious career. This was his only first team appearance for the club and he soon left.

It was not the greatest of starts for the club either, as the home draw was followed by a defeat at Enfield and a series of indifferent results followed.

By early November, Wealdstone occupied 10th place out of twenty in the league, having played 19 matches, winning and losing seven each and drawing five.

'Stones recorded another 'first' in the meantime, hosting the amateur champions of Libya, Hilal, in a match where a commentary was transmitted live to the visitor's home country.

A mixed Wealdstone side took the field, including Arthur Paisley, the goalkeeper who had played a part in the previous season's cup run and Wilkinson the reserve centre half, making his debut.

Another debutant was Miguel O'ria who had been signed before the season started from Athletico Madrid, then had to wait for his International clearance, only just received from FIFA.

There were other new signings introduced in the game, Fulkes at centre forward joining from Hitchin Town and the returning Arthur Peel also appeared as a substitute.

Falling behind early on Wealdstone proved too strong for the Libyans, 'Stones running out winners by three goals to one.

Something of a record must also have been created by the Officials for the match, the referee, Sid Jackson was a former Harrow Town player and the two linesmen, Ted Ward and Trevor Blake had both previously played for Wealdstone.

November also saw the first trophy of the season, Wealdstone beating Middlesex Wanderers to claim the Alaway Brothers Memorial Trophy. It was a match that also saw the return of Hugh Lindsay and he had an immediate impact scoring two goals in Wealdstone's 3-2 victory against a Wanderers side that included eight internationals including most of the current England side, Townsend and Lindsay excepted.

There was no similar success though in the final of the Hitchin Centenary Cup, held over from the previous season, as Wealdstone lost to Hillingdon Borough. The cup exploits too were not to be repeated as a first round home defeat to Nuneaton ended Wealdstone's interest as it started in the FA Cup.

Another first at Christmas was a fixture postponed by a player. The Isthmian League rules included the following;

"The referee in conjunction with the two captains shall have the power to decide as to the fit condition of the ground in all matches" the match against Hendon on Boxing Day afternoon, Charlie Townsend felt that the pitch was playable while Roy Sleap the Hendon captain did not. The match was postponed leaving over 300 supporters already in the ground and the Wealdstone officials astounded and appalled.

The New Year started with the Amateur Cup, Wealdstone the holders set to make their first defence at home to Stowmarket. The Suffolk side visited Lower Mead as underdogs but held the holders to a 1-1 draw, which they then repeated in the replay at their own ground. The match went to a third instalment, played at Layer Road, the Colchester United ground as a neutral venue.

Wealdstone scored after 11 minutes, but again Stowmarket equalised from a penalty on half time. In injury time in the second half it was still 1-1 and Wealdstone had a lucky escape as Byford handled when shooting from close range and this was spotted by the referee. In extra time Wealdstone took the lead in the 100th minute and scored again minutes later before Stowmarket pulled one back.

The final score though was a 5-2 victory for Wealdstone who progressed to the second round in front of a crowd of 2,411 making the total for the three matches 6,731. There were plenty of plaudits for Gillingham in the Stowmarket goal though as he had conceded only 3 goals in the first 310 minutes of the tie only to be beaten four times in the last twenty.

The second round saw a long trek to Brook Sports in Batley, West Yorkshire. Wealdstone rewarded for the journey with a comfortable 3-0 win although the draw again was unkind, a trip to Lancashire league side Skelmersdale in round three finally proving too much for Wealdstone who were beaten 1-0.

The league form was still indifferent as a record of ten wins and ten defeats from 25 matches showed and this was amplified by some high scoring defeats (6-2 at home to Enfield) and similarly high scoring wins.

Celebrating the first anniversary of their Amateur Cup triumph, Wealdstone recovered some of their faded glory by crushing championship chasing Wycombe Wanderers 7-0 before an incredulous crowd at Lower Mead on Saturday.

It was a double celebration for Eddie Dillsworth, one of Wealdstone's heroes when he spent the afternoon of his 20th birthday at Wembley Stadium, but on Saturday, the eve of his 21st he was relegated to 12th man. Dillsworth's chance came when Hugh Lindsay who had been showing every sign of returning to his real form, limped of the field with a damaged leg at the interval and didn't return.

No substitute can have seized his unexpected opportunity with more brilliance. Dancing up and down the Wycombe territory like a feather-footed Collossus, Dillsworth crashed in a hat trick inside 25 minutes and then delivered the final blow to his reeling opponents in the dying minutes of the game.

Almost with his first kick, Dillsworth banged a shot past Maskell to make the score 3-0, Wycombe having failed to clear Townsend's free kick, and in the 69th minute he seized on a slip by Rundle and, racing up to Baker, beat him brilliantly to score again from close in.

That was from the right wing. A minute later he was over on the left and almost in his own half when the ball came loose. Wycombe stood appealing for offside but, flagged on by the linesman, Dillsworth covered almost half the length of the field before flashing another cross-shot into the net and so completing his second hat trick for the club.

By this time Wycombe were losing their heads and after speaking to Rundle for a ferocious tackle on Childs the referee booked another Wycombe defender.

Taking the free kick himself, Childs crashed the ball into the defensive wall, whence it bounced past Maskell for the sixth goal. It was his last contribution to the match as he immediately left the field with a badly bruised shoulder, leaving Wealdstone to play the last thirteen minutes with only ten men.

In this period Wycombe should have scored twice through Merrick but Dillsworth had the last word, again bobbing up in the middle to seize the chance when Wycombe defenders failed to clear. Approaching the game with confidence following a 4-2 mid-week win over Hendon, Wycombe were not as outplayed as the score suggests, but they were never really in with a chance once Lindsay had given Wealdstone an 80 second lead.

Played onside when a defender deflected Bremer's pass Lindsay went on smoothly to score and although Wycombe afterwards ran hard they made so little impression on a firm Wealdstone defence that most of their scoring efforts came from right half Gale and these were competently dealt with by Blythe, who played with ever increasing confidence and surety of touch.

Finding out that the ball was beginning to run for them at last, Wealdstone maintained the pressure with some intricate forward movements and increased their lead in the 20th minute when combination between Quick, Bremer and Lindsay ended with Childs side-footing the latter's knee-high pass into the net.

In the 36th minute, Lindsay collided with Maskell and as they both fell to the ground, the goalkeeper rolled on the leg that the England International injured earlier in the season. Off the field for four minutes he returned but could not run and had to retire. at half time.

All the Wealdstone team showed improved form, with Dave Leonard having his best game for several weeks and coping well with Worley, Wycombe's most dangerous forward.

Wealdstone; M Blythe, M Doyle, D Leonard, C Townsend, A Quick, R Warman, K Searle, R Harper, R Childs, H Lindsay, B Bremer, Sub; E Dillsworth.

John Jones
Supporter

One great memory is of Eddie Dillsworth taking on Wycombe Wanderers almost single handedly. We won 7-0 that day and I remember one of their fans trying to hit the linesman with a brass bell. (I encouraged him 'cos I don't like Linesmen either!)

Another great day was when we lost at Millwall in the sixties in the FA Cup. The crowd there gave Eddie racial abuse throughout and although we lost, we did so with honour. He played his heart out and even their fans cheered him when, just before the final whistle, two hulking Millwall players tried to 'finish him off' with a full blooded sandwich. As they converged on him, he stood there, then at the last second jumped out of the way. The two defenders hit each other and were both out cold receiving treatment when the final whistle went.

Alongside the match report in the local paper was a small piece about another local footballer, Bobby Moss, a former Harrow Schools and Parkfield Youth winger who, on the same day had made his first team debut for Fulham in a friendly with Kilmarnock. Some years later, Bobby was to join Wealdstone.

Wealdstone's results were a little better at the end of the season than at the beginning. They also reached the final of the East Anglian Cup with a 4-1 win in the semi-final over Dagenham, although the final was lost away to holders Kings Lynn by 3-2.

Their final home league match also resulted in a good win, by 4-0 over Dulwich Hamlet with Eddie Dilsworth, the hero only a few weeks earlier missing. He had in fact asked the permission of the club to play for Lincoln City in the Football League against Luton Town on the Saturday but this had been denied. He chose to play anyway and was immediately suspended for the rest of the season by Wealdstone. This turned out to be a two match suspension, as due to injuries, coach Vince Burgess was forced to include him again a week later!

One of the two matches he missed? A friendly with a full strength Luton Town side at Lower Mead, which finished in a 1-1 draw.

The first team finished in a disappointing twelfth place in the league, eventually finishing with a record of played 38 won 13 and lost 17, but there was a little more to cheer as the season ended when the Wealdstone 'A' team won the Harrow Senior Charity Cup beating Victoria 4-1 at Ruislip.

There was little else to cheer as the AGM announced a loss on the season of £2,260 due to falling gates and an increase in the costs of the ground works.

To try and improve the situation, two professional clubs had been invited to take part in Public Trial matches for the forthcoming season, Leyton Orient and Bedford Town confirmed as the visitors. Due to the cash flow situation yet again, the 'A' team was to be scrapped.

Eddie Dillsworth
Player 1964 - 1967

I remember joining the club as a wing half. I think my first game was against Hendon and Dave Bassett, we met a few times after that as well on and off the field. We were friends then and met up with Allen Batsford and Brian Hall and it was those guys that later convinced me to sign for Chelmsford.

I scored on my debut and then didn't play in the next game, but the one after I scored two. I didn't score in the next game and I was dropped, then I missed another game and came back scoring three in my fourth game, so in four matches I'd scored six goals! I kept being dropped for Matt Farrell to play, so I went to see the Manager and I told him I didn't want to play up front anymore, so I said I'd try playing at the back. That's why it happened at Millwall and it seemed to work.

I wasn't aware of too much during the game other than the odd chant, but I was focused on my game. There was one incident near the end when I saw two players coming in to clatter me, but I pulled the ball back and they both missed. That created a bit of noise! I think if we'd have had someone up front to put the ball in the net we'd have won that day..........

The Amateur Cup Final was on my 21st birthday but its strange, I didn't really appreciate what it meant at the time but I can remember the noise on the day. I was too young to appreciate everything that it meant.

I remember there was the game at Wycombe the following year as well. I'd got injured playing for a Sunday team and I'd missed a few games then I came back at Wycombe, as Substitute and I scored four goals in a 7–0 win!

Missing Charlie Townsend who was on a three match tour of Sweden, Ireland and Iceland with the British Olympic squad, and Bobby Childs and Keith Searle, the club's top scorers in the previous season who had both left the club, a much changed Wealdstone side faced Orient in the first trial and gained a creditable draw 3–3.

Yet more changes for the second trial resulted in a 4–1 defeat away to Southall and this was a pattern that continued as the season started.

For the second season in succession, the FA Cup interest ended as soon as it started, this time with a 2–0 defeat at local rival, Wembley, who were locally quoted as 3/1 underdogs and who played part of the match with ten men!

Wealdstone's officials were also less than gracious in defeat, firstly stating that they had lost the match rather than Wembley had won it. Then when pressed, they blamed the defeat on Wembley's pitch where they said the long grass had slowed the ball down!

The following match saw a 1–0 win over Oxford City and the debut of John Hutchinson, praised by team mates and supporters alike for his memorable part in the match and he was to become a regular in the first team almost immediately.

He also played a part the following week in a 3–1 victory over Dulwich Hamlet in a match where it was felt that had a boxing rather than a football referee been in charge, he would have declared Dulwich "unable to defend themselves" at half time and stopped the contest such was the first half battering that had taken place.

After the interval it seems that the Wealdstone team as a whole adopted a somewhat condescending attitude to their visitors and spent the remainder of the match trying to engineer a goal for Hutchinson.

Wealdstone had added an element of steel to their performances and with some success – the next match away to St Albans resulted in a 1–0 win and a report that started;

A bruising, brawling match with an inept referee ended in Wealdstone's second away win of the season and a move into sixth place in the Isthmian League, but the match was marred from the start by lethal tackling by [former Stone] Mickey Doyle on John Hutchinson, Mickey Blythe and Bobby Warman.

Wealdstone were not the only side with a physical element to their play. By early October, they had risen to second place in the league table, four points behind Enfield and were to visit bottom club Maidstone the following Saturday;

If the FA had ordered Wealdstone to play this match on one leg and instructed goalkeeper Andy Williams not to handle the ball, it would still have been a massacre, for these teenage innocents of Maidstone are incapable of giving the Lower Mead reserve side a game.

John McCormack, Charlie Townsend and David Swain contrived to miss a number of chances, and despite goals being disallowed, Wealdstone still managed to record a 6-0 away win, later in the season winning the return by 7-1.

Keeping their form going, Wealdstone followed their win at Maidstone with a 5–1 victory over Clapton, a 2–2 draw at Sutton and a victory 2–0 at Ilford, maintaining the pressure on league leaders, Enfield.

By the start of December Wealdstone had gone 22 matches unbeaten, the match at Wembley in the FA Cup being their last defeat. They were to face Wembley again in the Presidents Trophy 1st leg and despite fielding a weakened side, they were able to extend their run to 23, scrambling a second equaliser a few minutes from time.

A week later and there was another new competition to be played for, Wealdstone having entered the Bucks Border Floodlight League for the first time. The visitors for this first match were Wellingborough.

The power of no longer 'secret weapon' Lindsay and a moment of inattention by Andy Williams left the result of this match as a tough draw.

Indeed, so tough in fact that Wellingborough had words with the referee at half time about the power of the Wealdstone tackling.

Early Wealdstone attacks produced a good save by Frost from Derek Smart and then from Charlie Townsend before the visitors stormed away for Jeffries to test Williams on the quarter hour. The first Lindsay free kick after a foul by Marriott was a tame affair but Marriott made his contribution when he felled Slade on 24 minutes. Wellingborough lined up, Lindsay took the free kick and 'nuff said.

Brian Gill, making a tough debut against the semi-professionals wasted a pass to Smart but the Wellingborough attack were getting into gear and Williams smothering the ball, was injured in a melee with left winger Capel.

At 30 minutes it should have been 1–1 as Miller was gifted a chance to level but fluffed his shot, with the odd reply from Wealdstone of McGuiness galloping out of defence to shoot wide.

A further Wellingborough raid brought a wide from Bennett and then a great save by Williams from Marriott, who refused to be upset by the Wealdstone off-side trap used more in anxiety than anything else. Miller too made light of the plan, having no less than six chances of one sort or another inside some 90 seconds before Bates came charging in to blast wide.

Gill started the adventures after the interval down the right but on 52 minutes a Townsend – Slade move broke down sadly and Miller, moving down the right shot from 20 yards.

Williams watched the ball, then "took my eyes off it" as it came in at the far post and the ensuing scramble left the in-running Capel a simple prod to score.

Jeffries almost made it 1–2 seconds afterwards as Wellingborough really became menacing, Bennett earned a corner, the nippy Capel swung the kick just wide of the far post and then it was Bennett again with a Lindsay style free kick that bounced of McGuiness for Miller to shoot wide.

When Dyte fouled Denny Montague in centre-field, Wealdstone came back into the picture. Townsend lobbed forward and Gill got a touch, ending stretched in the penalty area, as the ball bobbled across, Smart volleyed in.

The goal added aggression to the Wellingborough drive and Gill was chopped down. The Townsend free kick went by the post, and McNamee came close to being booked as he took command in the middle.

A nervous moment on 69 minutes saw Montague foul and concede a free kick. Taken quickly, there was no danger and Swain set off on a solo run. He lost and regained the ball before shooting into the side netting, before Wellingborough levelled again. It was Montague again, giving away his and Wealdstone's second penalty of the season on 72 minutes. The battered Bates made no mistake and all the chips were down.

This was the last round for both sides and Williams and Frost were constantly on the move, Williams with the busy Caper from both wings and Frost troubled by Swain. On 82 minutes, Swain and Smart tried a double attack and Smart lashed the ball in unmarked from the left, only for the referee to give a free kick.

Wealdstone; A Williams, B Warman, D Leonard, C Townsend, T McGuiness, T Slade, B Gill, H Lindsay, D Swain, D Montague, D Smart, Sub; J Hutchinson.

The unbeaten record though was to be broken by Wembley in the second leg of the Presidents Memorial Trophy, Wembley winning at Lower Mead on the 19th December.

Approaching the Christmas fixtures, things looked very bright for Wealdstone but losing a further three league points in the traditional fixtures against Hendon and a defeat at Woking all but ended Wealdstone's title hopes.

John Torpey
Supporter since the 1960's

Imagine Tony Adams transferring to Spurs, then coming back to Highbury for a North London derby, and scoring a spectacular own goal in front of the North Bank. Farfetched? Well back in 1968, the non-league equivalent of this nightmare scenario occurred in a Wealdstone vs. Hendon Isthmian League derby game at Lower Mead.

Wealdstone had built well upon their Amateur Cup winning side of '66, retaining the nucleus of the victorious side, and bringing in players of the highest calibre including goalkeeper Andy Williams, winger Johnny Hutchison, and prolific goalscorer Keith Searle. The 'Stones were having a fantastic season and had embarked on a long unbeaten run of some 20 plus matches.

Wealdstone vs. Hendon matches were of course always keenly contested, but this one had extra spice. The 'Stones Amateur Cup winning captain, centre half John Ashworth had transferred to the enemy, and was back at Lower Mead for the first time. As I recall, the game took place shortly after the 1968 New Year.

As a schoolboy, I took my place at the front of the Elmslie end, standing slightly to the left of the goal. This was a Tuesday evening, floodlit game, and with the crowd larger than usual, the atmosphere was that little bit special, the banging on the corrugated iron of the stand along with the increased vocal support amplified in the winter's night air.

As I recall, the game was closely fought, and the result could have gone either way. During the first half with the 'Stones attacking the Elmslie End, something quite unexpected happened.

'Stones were putting Hendon under extreme pressure and John Ashworth completely misjudged the direction of a headed clearance he needed to make from a Wealdstone cross, and the ball flew spectacularly past his own keeper, the England Amateur international John Swannell.

The uproar and abuse that ensued, was unbelievable, and my friends and I enthusiastically joined in. I had had a fantastic view of the incident, and along with a few George Duck specials remains my most abiding memory of 25 years of watching the 'Stones at Lower Mead.

Oh by the way, the result was a 2-2 draw, which was almost academic after the events of that unforgettable first half.

January again saw the club start on the Amateur Cup trail, and this season, more than many others 'trail' was the correct description, Wealdstone drawn away to Torpoint in Cornwall.

Dave Neighbour
Supporter 1960's

I had many happy memories at Wealdstone FC during the sixties as a supporter, until work moved me to Bath where I now live, and support the local side.

I remember Barbara Robson who was in charge of the supporters club and ran all of the away coaches to all the matches. I remember once we were drawn in a cup match away to Torpoint, Cornwall and we had to travel all night to the match!!

It rained and there was sleet all night and not many of us slept on the coach. During the early hours of the morning we were following a lorry and it shed its spare tyre which hit and damaged our coach and we could not go on until a replacement coach had been hired to complete our journey.

We arrived in time for the match but the conditions were terrible - we had a snowstorm throughout the first half! It was so bad that the referee made the teams turn round at half time and carry on the second half without a break - he said afterwards that he would have abandoned the match if the supporters (ours) had not traveled so far. We won the match so it made the long journey there and back worthwhile.

I did go back to Lower Mead a while ago when Wealdstone played Bath in The Alliance Premier League - I had very mixed emotions about who to support, and I was very sorry to see the club leave Lower Mead - It was a great club to support.

In conditions that would normally see any match abandoned, the fixture at Torpoint started! The weather was so bad in the South of England, which this match was one of very few played at all, and it was mastery of the conditions that eventually saw 'Stones run out winners by 4-2.

"We were robbed," claimed Torpoint Secretary Les Cardew after his team had slithered out of the FA Amateur Cup in the Sportsfield mud. He claimed the Linesman was at fault when Wealdstone scored their first and their fourth goals.

But Wealdstone, who grabbed four goals in the first half, held out with a grim defensive display in the second. Although Torpoint were the fitter side, they lacked the necessary penetration in the vital stages of the match. They also had certain defensive weaknesses, which Wealdstone ruthlessly exposed.

Wealdstone romped into the lead after only ten minutes, outside-left Hugh Lindsay crossed superbly for David Swain to push the ball home from close range. The Isthmian League side now threw everything into an avalanche of attack and Torpoint goalkeeper Colin Bradford was not handling the greasy ball safely.

Gradually, the Cornish side hit back and talented winger Dave Ewings forced reserve right back Pettit into numerous errors. A thirty-five yard free kick was punched into the net, apparently by a Torpoint forward, but the referee disallowed the goal and the home side's jubilation was short lived. Ewings sent in two cracking pile drivers, which Andy Williams was glad to punch to safety. Torpoint were now applying tremendous pressure and only the grim determination of Wealdstone kept the marauding forwards at bay.

Finally, the pressure paid off. Tony McGuinness floored David Babb just inside the penalty area and Stephens equalised with the spot kick on 24 minutes. Torpoint were now playing with confidence but it was Wealdstone who regained the lead against the run of play. After 30 minutes, Lindsay took a long free kick, the ball was slipped back by Swain and Bremer made it 2-1.

With rain pouring down, conditions were now appalling, but the football was exhilarating end to end stuff. Gradually, Wealdstone began to assert their superiority and Bremer nearly scored when Bradford saved. Bremer did help to make it three after 41 minutes, he swung a precision cross from the right, and Swain rose high to head it past Bradford.

Wealdstone made it 4-1 only one minute before half time. Slade chipped the ball through to John McCormack who scored the softest goal imaginable, but plucky Torpoint continued to fight hard in the second half. They were rewarded with a second goal on 51 minutes.

The dynamic Barry Stephens drove a tremendous free kick goalwards and Dave Underhay headed home in spectacular style. It was now all Torpoint. Wealdstone had obviously decided that they would settle for a defensive policy in the second half.

After the match Wealdstone coach Vince Burgess said "we are relieved to be in the second round. Considering the punishing conditions it was a great match and well worth coming 250 miles"

Wealdstone; Williams, Pettit, Leonard, Townsend, McGuinness, Slade, Bremer, McCormack, Swain, Montague, Lindsay.

After Christmas their Isthmian League form was still indifferent although a good run of results saw them finish as Champions in the Berks and Bucks Border League and the victory over Torpoint was to see the start of another Amateur Cup run for Wealdstone.

It was followed by a home victory over Kingstonian (2-0) and then an away tie with Eastwood Town, the first match a 1-1 draw before 'Stones won the replay at Lower Mead by 4-1.

Bob John
Supporter since the 1950's

In 1968 I remember going to Eastwood Town away in the Amateur Cup and missing the coach home! The pitch was very basic, with just a rope separating the supporters from the players. I went with the Murphy brothers and we were all drunk by the end of the match – that's why we ended up missing the coach!

The Quarter final was another home tie with Barking, Wealdstone winning 3-1 to reach a semi-final tie against Chesham to be played at Craven Cottage, Wealdstone favourites to reach Wembley for the second time.

A changed side and a changed pattern of play though, saw Wealdstone defeated 2-0 by the team that started the competition as 1000-1 outsiders, to end the dream for another year.

The match was described as one of the major upsets in Amateur football history on the afternoon. Chesham adapted to the windy conditions far better than Wealdstone, and the result had caused major consternation among supporters.

Questions 'were asked' by means of an open letter in the Harrow Observer, questioning the plans made in preparation for the match and how or why the players were instructed to play by the coach, Vince Burgess.

The following week, this letter was questioned in another from a supporter who felt that it was wrong to expect the players to play as instructed by the coach, as the team had enough talent at its disposal to be allowed to make their own decisions!

The training methods were also queried by supporters who felt that the 'Stones team had become stale and nervous by overtraining during the week preceding the match.

Comment was passed on the use of wingers in the match, why most of the forwards were pulled back to help the defence leaving only one or two men forward.

Vince Burgess was advised to ignore all his fancy schemes and get back to the fundamentals, such as wing play to draw defence's out of the middle, to instill running off the ball and quick interchange of positions and to keep the forwards up the field utilising the first time clearances from the defence.

The letter finished with the following paragraph;

All these points, we, who understand football through years of

John McCormack, Wealdstone inside-right heads over the bar in the first tie with Eastwood Town.

watching other teams do it, well know they often mean a lot of running about, but I know they can be deadly in upsetting opponents, and I am sure Wealdstone FC can remain a great force in Amateur football.

The Middlesex Trophies also saw some good performances, Wealdstone winning the Senior Cup and sharing the Charity Cup with Wembley.

The Senior Cup Final was two legged, with Hayes the opponents. The first leg was to be influenced totally by Charlie Townsend.

As was reported at the time;

Charlie was involved in the majority of the play during the match, commanding the midfield during the first half, while tracking Hayes' 42 goal inside forward John Couzens to such an extent that he was out of the game.

Three minutes into the match, Dave Leonard collected the ball and overlapped, passing to Hutchinson and his cross found Townsend fully 35 yards from goal in midfield. His first time curling shot was described as no more than a blur when it passed the Hayes goalkeeper, rooted to the spot, to give Wealdstone the lead.

After 31 minutes, the result was sealed when Hutchinson broke away again. A shout from Townsend resulted in a pass finding him twenty yards from goal, and this time a slightly lower volley again gave Roope in the Hayes goal no chance, Wealdstone taking a 2-1 lead into the second leg.

Before the second leg was played, Wealdstone had two matches with Watford to finish their season in the Berks and Bucks Border League. In the first, at Vicarage Road, Watford fielded mainly a reserve side, and 'Stones came away with a 1-0 victory which meant that only a draw was required in the return at Lower Mead to at least ensure a share of the title.

Watford brought a far stronger team, including no less than six regular first team players and £30,000 winger Stuart Scullion. Wealdstone though, played up to their opposition and in one of their best performances of the season won by 3–2 to seal the Championship, Townsend, Montague and Phillips playing outstandingly in midfield in an excellent team performance.

After only four minutes Watford opened up the home defence through Welbourne, but Pearce eased the ball just wide.

From a Leonard clearance, Hutchinson sped away and a precise ball inside found Bremer. As Hanson came out to challenge, Bremer did his 'change legs' act and stabbed the ball past the wrong-footed keeper for his fourth goal in two matches.

Watford though took only 30 seconds to wipe out this lead, Scullion hammering a splendid shot past Williams from 20 yards. End to end play ensued, Hutchinson and Welbourne having chances at opposite ends before Williams saved well from Pearce, heading in a Scullion cross.

Townsend too was having an inspired half, and off he went again to drive at Hanson. The ball came back to Kieron Somers, rebounded, and the lanky leader hit in the second chance with both Hanson and Gareth Hand stretched out in their area.

It was a really remarkable Wealdstone show. They were taking on the best side to visit Lower Mead this season and were playing up and beyond them. With five minutes of the half left though, Watford gave an example of class. Left-winger Low accelerated through the middle and as Williams came out to the edge of the area to cover, sent an immaculate shot over him and in to equalise.

A minute before the break though another Low cannon shot left Williams, who had been limping, flat out with a leg injury. Finally he had to come off and Bremer took over in goal. As the injury time mounted, Wealdstone went down to nine men as Packer landed a cracking tackle on Lindsay's shin and he too left the field!

There always seemed the chance of a title settling win in the second half if Bremer could be covered, but on 67 minutes he made his own bid for independence, holding one shot casually and then covering another like a mother hen watching it go past the post. Townsend bobbed up in midfield, Phillips and Leonard had watched Scullion so carefully and solidly that the winger had retreated to midfield himself, to collect a pass from Lindsay, hitting wide from 20 yards.

Townsend's rifle though had now found the range and in the same minute, McGuinness gifted a pass to almost the same spot and the Wealdstone skipper hit a glorious shot that swerved and then dipped past the waiting Hanson to land neatly in the back of the net. Scullion then came back into the attack to shoot, only to see Bremer punch his shot away – Bernie said afterwards that he was trying to catch it.

Wealdstone; A Williams, A Phillips, D Leonard, C Townsend, T McGuinness, D Montague, B Bremer, T Slade, K Somers, H Lindsay, J Hutchinson, Sub; M Clary

Watford; Hanson, Packer, Hand, Galloway, Rivers, Eddy, Scullion, Farrall, Welbourne, Pearce, Low, Sub; Cooper.

The following Saturday saw the second leg of the Middlesex Senior Cup Final at Hayes. In a match disrupted by spasmodic thunder and rain and some 'odd' refereeing, Wealdstone eventually ran out winners by 1–0, an aggregate of 3–1 securing the trophy for the tenth time.

'Stones had had a good goal disallowed for offside and seen a player hooked down from behind, only to concede the free kick in referee Mr Burns' last match, one he seemed to want to be memorable.

The coup de grace came in the final few minutes when Hayes defender Tweed brought down Kieron Somers in he penalty area. With the linesman flagging, the referee refused to give a penalty and when Townsend spoke his mind, he was booked for the first time in his eleven year Wealdstone and England career, for not coming towards him when called!

Wealdstone had made four changes from the twelve, M Blythe, R Williams, B Harper and D Petit coming in for A Williams, A Phillips, J Hutchinson and M Clary. To finish a busy week, there was another match to play on the Sunday.

As Parliament debated the Sport on Sundays bill to allow competitive and professional matches to be played on Sundays, Wealdstone staged a Sunday Match at Lower Mead in aid of the players tour fund, the target this year, a Whitsun tour to Spain.

The match was played against Johnny Haynes All Stars. The final score was 7–7, Johnny Haynes having scored four and made two more of the visitors goals, aided ably by Dave Sexton, Jimmy Hill and Terry Mancini among others.

Ken Nicholas of Maidstone also scored three of the visitors goals and although Wealdstone scored first, they trailed by 1-3, 3-4 and 4-7, before equalising each time. Wealdstone scored through Poole, Townsend, Somers, McCormack and Clary (3) to leave a 1628 crowd more than pleased with their afternoon's entertainment.

The season had not quite finished as Wealdstone again had a busy week coming up. Their home match on the Thursday against Corinthian Casuals, the last league game of the season was won 3-0, then in another experimental match, Wealdstone faced Hayes again on the Sunday morning in the Middlesex Charity Cup semi-final.

The match finished, as was described by the Harrow Observer, as 0-0 after ENDLESS time, a complete bore-draw having disappointed the 1004 spectators.

The report continued;

Everyone thought that last Saturday was a poor cup final but the 1004 spectators who watched this Sunday morning performance won't agree, for if ever their was justification for going home and beating wife / parent / dog or cat, this sprawling stupid mess of a match was it.

As it meandered into half hour of extra time, it kept one pattern. A chance meant a mistake by the opposing side that you had to miss to level affairs, and the longer the event lasted the worse it became.

It almost seemed as the players had lost interest. Wealdstone won through in the replay (3-0) to meet Wembley in the competition final, played on 23rd May.

Wealdstone's three round path to the final and then the final itself had seen 450 minutes of football played. It cannot have been a surprise to anyone present when Wealdstone equalised ten minutes before the end of extra time to make the final score 2-2, both Wealdstone and Wembley sharing the trophy as joint winners.

Wembley had four matches against Wealdstone during the season and had not been beaten once despite their 'lower' status.

Vince Burgess had resigned from the club, and by the end of the season it was announced that he had taken over at Hitchin Town. Dave Underwood had been announced as the new Wealdstone coach. This had placated some of the concerns from supporters about the way the team was being run. It was thought generally that this team had run its course and changes would be needed for the next season.

It had been a long hard season with some 75 first team matches being played, including four cup replays and only one friendly.

The season though was disappointing after a promising start as injuries to key players had caused problems. Now that it was finally over, there was still the eight day Spanish tour to be enjoyed, and enjoyed it was.

Charlie Townsend commented that it was the most enjoyable tour he had ever been on including those with England and Middlesex Wanderers.

It was a very relaxed eight days with only one match to play, a 2-0 defeat at Lloret Del Mar but the match was played with very much an exhibition spirit. The only real complaint was that it had been too hot to try and equalise!

One near casualty of the trip though was goalkeeper Andy Williams. He was unaccustomed to the Spanish principles of the Civil Guards, the police, who whistled to control traffic, tourists and as necessary, cattle.

He derided them on one occasion and was promptly 'arrested' and whipped into the local town hall. The alarmed remainder of the touring party however, were pleased to see him emerge after a caution just five minutes later.

Bob John
Supporter since the 1950's

I remember too going to Lloret-del-Mar in Spain 'on tour'. 'Stones had a friendly set up against a local side on the Costa Brava, but after some problems, and because of the heat, the match didn't kick off until 11:00pm.

Dave Swain the ex-Hendon forward was playing for us and I remember he was a bit 'worse for wear'. How he got through the whole match without falling over was beyond me. It was some game though.

The AGM reported that the club had made a healthy profit of £2,387 during the season, the Amateur Cup run primarily responsible for the increased income on the field, while the Thursday afternoon market operations had been the major contributor off the field.

This not only covered the loss from the previous season, but, along with £500 from the Supporters Club, the money was to go toward a bill of over £2000 to upgrade the floodlights and re-wall and re-paint the Elmslie Stand.

P. Culverhouse
Supporter in the 1960s/70s

I was a regular supporter in the 1960s/70s and occasionally I still visit now. My memories are of the guy who used to dress up in blue and white with the bell. I have many memories from the 60's and early '70s. The win over Stevenage 6-5. Wembley matches versus Hendon & Enfield etc.

As for my favourite players, this is difficult as there are too many; 1. Charlie Townsend 2. Hugh Lindsay - what a shot! 3. Viv Evans - great little player. 4. Bernie Bremner - not even he knew what he was going to do.

The first match under new coach Dave Underwood, opening the 1968-1969 season was a friendly against Chelsea Reserves, a side that featured no less than seven players with first team experience, and Wealdstone held them to 0-0 at half time.

The fitter Chelsea team went on to score three in the second half. Supporters though were disappointed as the score-line flattered Chelsea and with better finishing Wealdstone should at least have been on equal terms. The wholesale changes wanted by so many had failed to materialise and it looked as though a hard season was ahead.

A better start than expected ensued, Wealdstone winning three and drawing three of their first seven league matches as changes were made while the club sought a settled side. The eighth match was at home to Kingstonian and was played in front of 2,100 spectators;

In a fantastic turn-around in the last nine minutes on Wednesday night, Wealdstone scored twice to draw level with the red army of Kingstonian and then Denny Montague hit the winner from the penalty spot with only thirty seconds to left!

It was certainly crowd pleasing, more so as the match had been spoiled by some weak refereeing. Former 'Stones, John McCormack and Dave Leonard had been instrumental in giving Kingstonian a 2-0 lead in the second half before on 81 minutes Dave Bromley scored from a corner.

The equaliser was a remarkable goal in itself, Hugh Lindsay collecting the ball wide on the left and from fully forty yards he unleashed a shot at knee height that shot straight across the goal into the far corner with no one moving!

Last minute victories seemed to be becoming the 'norm' as shortly afterwards, Southern League Dunstable were beaten three two as 'Stones scored goals in the last few minutes in the FA Cup as well.

Also in the FA Cup, two goals in the first three minutes put Wealdstone well on the way to a 3-1 victory at home to another Southern League side, Banbury as the side and the new players settled in.

The league form continued well, and by mid October 'Stones had played 15 matches, winning nine and drawing three, holding fourth place with 21 points, although again injuries were to take their toll.

Another victory over Aylesbury in the FA Cup had seen 'Stones continue their progress in that competition. In the week before the next round of the FA Cup, away at Slough, Wealdstone had to field very much a scratch side away to Bletchley in the M1 Floodlight League.

Having searched desperately for players to make up the side. They ended up with a goalkeeper Edwards, who was in fact a winger at Ruislip Rangers and he had never before played under floodlights.

Further boosted by what was described as an Oscar winning performance, the 'veteran' Viv Evans returned to the club to play in the reserves. He scored one goal and then, as described by Dave Underwood...

...he produced the best dying swan since Pavlova to collapse in the penalty area three minutes from time to get a totally undeserved penalty that was duly scored.

Wealdstone in fact ran out winners by 4-1 from a game (and a side) where the most optimistic prediction had been a draw.

In mid November, Wealdstone visited Barking for a league match and won 2–0 with probably the 'latest' two goals the club would ever score. The Barking inside-left, John Wilsonham had tried every possible way to unsettle the 'Stones goalkeeper, Andy Williams, but all his antics to prevent Williams clearing the ball achieved was for the referee to add on time.

During this time, in the 96th and 98th minutes, Wealdstone scored the only two goals of the afternoon, Hutchinson and Searle the scorers.

It all looked promising when Wealdstone met St Albans at home in the first round proper of the FA Cup, but a 1–1 draw was the final score. The replay took on greater importance though as the draw for the second round had been made. The winners were to play at home to Walsall.

It was an old Wealdstone failing that cost them the tie, as starting the second half slowly, they were stung by the only goal of the match, and missed the opportunity to face Football League opposition again.

Just before Christmas, Wealdstone were to endure another marathon cup-tie in the first round of the Amateur Cup. Drawn away, Wealdstone were to face Hartford Town and former 'Stone Bobby Warman. The first match at Hertford though ended 0-0.

In the replay, Wealdstone led three times but the match remained deadlocked after extra time and a second replay was to take place. After the toss was won for venue, this too was to take place at Lower Mead.

Hertford Town scored first and Wealdstone were fortunate to be awarded a penalty on 80 minutes from which they equalised. No further goals were scored in extra time so the match went to a third replay, this time at the neutral Vale Farm where again Hertford Town were the better side, but still the deadlock could not be broken.

The fourth replay was played at Hertfordingbury Park and finally saw a result. After 43 minutes, Colin Franks collected the ball in midfield, he swung a pass out to Charlie Townsend on the right wing and his pass found John Hutchinson precisely. He moved the ball inside to Dave Swain.

The forward turned a full 360 degrees before blasting the ball inside the far post for the only goal of the match, the deciding goal being scored 497 minutes from the start of the tie although Hertford did have a second half equaliser disallowed for offside!

The next round saw a much quicker result, Wealdstone beating Cirencester 2-1 at Lower Mead, the victory meaning a tie in the last 16 at home to Hayes, a match that saw 'Stones victorious by the only goal. The quarter final saw 'Stones drawn away to North Shields at the end of February.

North Shields moved into the semi-finals of the Amateur Cup at Middlesborough on Saturday week, a team without right, and a sad, sad reminder to all that a bad side can always out-clog a good one, for this match at Appleby Park on Saturday was an absolute travesty of what the Amateur Cup is meant to be about.

In an opening half of sustained and rarely punished violence, and with some 5,000 making the ground a bull ring, they clobbered Bernie Bremer with a crude tackle by John Twaddle – with a hamstring injury he hobbled off after 27 minutes. Three minutes later, Brain Joicey, their centre forward, charged straight into Wealdstone 'keeper Andy Williams who needed treatment, while the cost to North Shields was a free kick instead of a goal kick and so it ranged on.

The match blew up on just three minutes past the hour with a bizarre episode in the Wealdstone area. A long ball sliced into the crowded box, hit Tony McGuinness' hand, and referee Eric Foulkes from Sheffield awarded a penalty. After protests, he consulted his linesman, upheld his decision and then sent Williams off. Charlie Townsend took over in goal and George Thompson blasted the penalty over the bar, dashing in bull-like with his head up.

And here is where the match became more and more amazing.

With ten men, Wealdstone kept rolling the tough North Shields side back until 17 minutes from the end. Micky Lister, on the Shields' right, took a corner and as it curved into the area, Joicey obstructed Townsend, Cassidy pushed Dave Bromley (who was dashing in to cover) away, and Richie Hall bundled Townsend, ball and all, into the net. This time, despite protests, Mr Foulkes did not consult his linesman as he awarded a goal and rushed back to the half way line. It was, for a first class referee with 21 years experience, a remarkable decision.

So it was for another season, a chance of the major prize in Amateur football had been taken away.

The following Tuesday, Wealdstone were at home again in the league for a match against Sutton United. Unremarkable in itself, it was an evening when Wealdstone's Dave Bromley wrote himself into the record books, scoring all four goals in a 2-2 draw!

On 56 minutes he deflected a Trevor Bladon shot past Andy Williams to give the visitors the lead. On 69 minutes, he equalised with a header from a Hugh Lindsay cross, but he then gave Sutton the lead when he helped in a Larry Pritchard shot on 80 minutes. His final goal of the evening was another header from a Hugh Lindsay corner on 82 minutes to equalise for the second time.

Stephen Bird
Supporter since the 1960's

My father was responsible for getting me interested in Wealdstone in the first place. He had supported the 'Stones since the early 50's when he moved to the area, and then when I was 8 in 1967 he decided that I was old enough to go with him.

My first game at Lower Mead was v Dulwich Hamlet - we won 3-1 but I'm afraid I can't tell you the teams or the scorers, Dad rarely bought a programme although I do remember writing them down in a long lost Letts School Diary!!

For that one match we went in the stand but thereafter we stood on the High Mead terrace and I usually stood down by the fence where dad could keep an eye on me.

The team in those days included such players as Charlie Townsend, Hugh Lindsay, Dave Swain and the goalkeeper, Andy Williams but my favourite was Kieron Somers who later came to prominence with Wimbledon in the FA Cup in the 1970's.

My first away match was a major disappointment - the Amateur Cup semi-final defeat to Chesham United at Craven Cottage.

I remember Chelsea were also at home that day, and we were in one of the coaches that got stuck in the traffic through Hammersmith. The driver eventually dropped us about a mile up the Fulham Palace Road and we walked the rest of the way, arriving at the ground about half way through the first half, only to be told it was a terrible game and Kieron Somers was dreadfully off form, but thankfully we hadn't missed any goals!!

Unfortunately we had settled in our places in plenty of time to see Chesham United score both of their goals and to see Wealdstone lose to a club a couple of Divisions Lower down the leagues and that was something that was to become all too familiar in later years.

There was one other strange memory of the time. I think it was an Isthmian League game against St. Albans, a 2-2 draw - was it 1969? - When Dave Bullock managed to score all four goals!!

Dad stopped coming in 1971-he didn't like the idea of the club turning semi-professional, although by that time it was the way things were going generally.

A week later and an era was to end at Wealdstone, when Charlie Townsend resigned from the club after twelve years, deciding to hang up his boots for the remainder of the season, although he was to play again the following year.

Edited from FA News March 1969
Charlie joined Wealdstone, his first senior club at the age of 19. He started his senior career as a centre forward, but he had not the height to compete with tall centre halves for the high balls.

His responsibilities as leader, too, somewhat cramped his style and, after a couple of seasons, he converted to wing half, where his terrier like determination to chase every ball was more usefully employed.

His early training as a centre forward stood him in good stead however, for during his career he successfully played not only as a wing half, but also as the link man in 4-2-4 formations, and front lines of 4-3-3. Occasionally too, he has played as a pure defender.

When the England Amateur team decided to adopt 4-2-4, at Whitley Bay for the International Tournament in 1963, Charlie Townsend and Hugh Lindsay, two young but experienced internationals coupled up as an ideal international pairing.

Lindsay provided skill and shrewdness, while Charlie gave a non-stop performance of energy and vigour. Mentally and physically, each was the perfect foil to the other. As one member of the Amateur Selection Committee said " If Lindsay and Townsend were off form, we lost. If they were on form, we won".

The list of honours and achievements are no indication of Charlie's happy and light hearted behaviour when on tour abroad. On a tour to Italy, The Netherlands and Germany in 1962, the organisation is Italy was, to say the least, unsatisfactory.

A three hour wait at Rome Airport was followed by a hair raising six hour journey through the Appenine's in an antique bus.

At the end of the nightmare trip, the party was lodged in a very inferior hotel where the first meal – breakfast – was, by English standards, ruined by the cooking.

This grim situation was saved when Charlie led some of the players into the kitchen, and to the amusement of the hotel staff, proceeded to demonstrate exactly how the eggs and bacon should have been cooked.

Jane Toon,
Daughter of Charlie Townsend

I spoke to my dad last night about some of his memories while at Wealdstone, and I am now acting as his personal secretary!

Charlie was actually Rodney, (that's his real name although he has always been known as Charlie) he was a Wealdstone player from 1957 to 1970 and was Club Captain for a while. An England International and Olympic Footballer, he made over 600 appearances for Wealdstone, one of which was the Amateur Cup Final win in 1966.

Charlie Townsend leading out the side at Lower Mead Charlie accumulated over 30 Amateur International caps while with Wealdstone. He had also played in the preliminary rounds of the Olympic Qualifying Tournaments of 1964 and 1968, and in representative matches for the Isthmian League and the FA.

It was a bit unexpected as Wealdstone were the underdogs, but when Mum used to leave for Church on a Sunday, Dad always used to ask her to 'ask him up there' to let Wealdstone win the cup. Mum said "OK but you'd better give me half a crown for the collection and we'll see what we can do"

Dad kept giving Mum the collection money every Sunday and lo and behold, Wealdstone did it !

Brian Curtis
Supporter since the 1950's

Charlie Townsend was my favourite player. I doubt if there has ever been a better player in the history of the 'Stones. His touch, passing ability and his gift of creating space were not bettered.

I remember seeing him play for England against Spain at White City and he was outstanding. Even if he played, as he often did, with poor Wealdstone teams, his level of performance seldom dropped.

At the end of March, Wealdstone also managed another record; a 2-2 draw with Barking in the London Senior Cup became the tenth Cup match Wealdstone had drawn during the season.

Wealdstone's challenge for league honours continued but despite winning their last home match 4–3 against Clapton, they were destined to finish fifth in the table, although the reserves had maintained their good form throughout the season to finish as runner up in their division.

There was one piece of Silverware still up for grabs, Wealdstone and Wembley due to meet in the two-legged Presidents Memorial Trophy.

The first leg at Wembley resulted in a 0–0 draw, Wealdstone's superiority only matched by John Ritchie's inability to score, missing four clear chances in the game.

The second leg at Lower Mead was made more memorable perhaps by the appearance for Wealdstone of one Tommy Steele (nee Hicks). Whether it was an attempt to increase the crowd or not remains to be seen, but playing as a roving right winger, He certainly had an impact on the result. The match started with 'Stones well on top but stoic defending preserved the stalemate before...

......an inspired piece of play by Tommy Steele gave Wealdstone the lead. Receiving a return pass from Swain, the hirsute winger sprinted down the right flank, turned on half a sixpence and floated over a glorious centre, which Messer couldn't quite reach, and Lavin, chesting the ball down successfully, pierced the red shirted ranks on the goal line. Seven minutes later Steele repeated the trick with a succinct through ball to Swain but the centre forward stumbled.....

Hugh Lindsay scored the winner with five minutes to go for the very makeshift Wealdstone side, and with a minute to go, Wealdstone were awarded a penalty that was taken by Steele but pushed away to safety by the Wembley keeper.

The 'Stones team was Bill Fowler returning in goal, Bernie Bremer, Gary Hand, T Smith, D Murphy, D Underwood jnr, Tommy Steele, H Lindsay, D Swain, K Searle and J Lavin making up the starting line up, with J Ritchie as the substitute.

Another tour was planned, this time to Majorca, to face the local amateur side, Collerance FC. The match took place though, with Hendon, also on tour playing in place of Wealdstone. Hendon went on to win by 4-1.

The Wealdstone team arrived too late on the island after delays to make the match but the players still enjoyed the tour although no football was played.

During the close season, the AGM was again able to report a profit, the additional cup replays generating an extra £1,000 of income.

Alongside the usual presentations and the county honours received by players, there was another first for the club, when deputy Chairman Frank Harbud was made the first ever Life Vice President of the Middlesex FA, Harry Luck was elected as a County Vice President and Ken Wiltshire was elected to the county committee.

On the playing front, there was a surprise as pre-season training started, not with a new player but with a new coach, Manager Dave Underwood having employed the services of mile runner Pat Butler to improve the speed and stamina of the players.

The 1969-1970 pre-season programme saw matches won against Slough Town, Paget Rangers and Dagenham and the season started in earnest with a home match against Maidstone.

An accomplished performance saw 'Stones run out 3-0 winners.

The Tuesday evening saw a visit to Loakes Park and Wycombe Wanderers who had won 5–0 on the previous Saturday. With the two clubs at the top of the table, an excellent match was the result, Wycombe taking a 2–0 lead on 53 minutes only for Wealdstone to score twice in 90 seconds and almost snatch a winner.

On performances alone it looked as though a better season was under way. A 6–1 win at Bromley followed by another draw left Wealdstone one point behind the leaders. A defeat in the next match, 1–0 at home to Sutton United was overshadowed by the news that Hugh Lindsay had resigned from the club to join Hampton, unhappy that he was to be 'replaced', the club signing John Connell from Enfield. Dave Bromley and Player of the Year Dave Leonard also moved on, indicating some unrest behind the scenes.

A month later and the club fast approaching crisis point, as striker Keith Searle and recently re-signed Gordon Sedgley also both resigned. John Connelly also having returned to his former club and league results too were slipping.

The FA Cup saw 'Stones draw at home with Aylesbury and then win the replay 3–1 to face Banbury in the next round, Wealdstone winning 1–0 at Lower Mead.

This match had started with a one-minute silence to the memory of Supporters Club former Chairman, Jock Law. He had been taken ill while driving on the Wednesday and had died in Chertsey Hospital the following day.

He was the first Chairman of the Supporters Club, holding the office from 1957 until 1966 when he resigned, although he remained on the committee. With his wife, they ran the Catering hut in the ground. Jock was made a Life Member of the football club in the mid sixties.

The much-changed Wealdstone team started to settle down and their FA Cup run continued with a 4-0 home win over Dunstable, a number of the younger players becoming regulars in the first team, but defeat in the next round at home to Enfield caused concern at all levels in the club.

Defeat also in the London Senior Cup at Ilford, in a match that the reserves would have been expected to win caused pressure to mount on the coaching staff and Dave Underwood in particular.

It wasn't helped by the departure of one of the most promising players, John Hutchinson. He had played for the 'A' team and reserves before breaking into the first team, leaving to join Wycombe Wanderers in November.

A week later, and England International Howard Moxon, signed to strengthen the back line and to add experience to the squad threatened to leave the club.

The week before the Amateur Cup-tie at home to Vauxhall Motors saw the final straw. The club committee met on the Thursday evening, and after a stormy meeting, an official statement was released to say the Dave Underwood had left the club "by mutual consent". Club Captain Howard Moxon was to take over for the remainder of the season.

Underwood himself was less convinced that there was agreement. In an interview with the Harrow Observer he said that he felt the goal that finished him was Enfield's FA Cup winner. From then on he felt that the spirit of the club had gone.

From the club's perspective it was suggested that the slide downwards had started when Charlie Townsend had been forced to play in the back four the previous season prior to leaving. The resignation of a number of other players had also added weight to the argument.

It had been hoped that a number of these players may return under new coach Moxon, but there was to be one further departure on the same evening, Dave Swain wishing to join Enfield although he missed only one game before returning.

Surprisingly, after a week of turmoil, Wealdstone did manage to win their match against Vauxhall Motors, the visitors taking an early lead before Wealdstone replied with three goals. (One crafted by Viv Evans, recalled to the starting line up. His cross met by new player coach Moxon to head Wealdstone into the lead on half an hour).

Vauxhall scored again ten minutes from the end to set up an exciting finish but Wealdstone hung on to claim the victory.

Indifferent results did not bode well for the club, worsened by two defeats to Hendon over Christmas, but there were some brighter spots as the New Year started.

A victory over Bromley in the second round of the Amateur Cup also lifted spirits. A lucky point away to Walthamstow Avenue and the news that on the same day former Wealdstone youngster Colin Franks scored his first goal for Watford in a 1–0 FA Cup win over Stoke kept a little momentum going.

The club was eliminated from the Amateur Cup at the end of January, suffering a 1-0 defeat away to Wycombe Wanderers returning to play a home league game the following week against Clapton in front of only 450 fans;

Two opportunist goals by Lincoln Peddie tell only part of the story of him home league debut for Wealdstone. Lower Mead was an anti-climatic place to be after last week, but Peddie's speed and control prompted constant sparks where none could have been expected.

Peddie's zeal was infectious, and the team were always looking for goals, despite putting the result beyond doubt well before the end. Tow goals in two minutes midway through the first half signalled the start of an even greater assault, and the third goal was Wealdstone's 26th goal in six home matches against Clapton.

Wealdstone's assets were strength and speed, useful armament on a soft and treacherous pitch, which made it impossible for defenders to turn quickly. Their directness gave them an advantage which clumsy Clapton never looked likely to challenge, yet they showed real potential whenever their speedy flankers Kempton and Bull received worthwhile service down the wings.

Early on it was the combined efforts of Clapton that looked likely to open the scoring, but Wealdstone responded with their best move of the match, Williams throwing out to his brother Rob, to set Swain, Ritchie, Bremer and finally Peddie goalwards, the wingers final cross just eluding the advancing line of blue shirts.

The next attack on 21 minutes though, brought Wealdstone's opener. After Hoare conceded a corner, Hand's kick found the well-placed Peddie who, despite only half hitting his shot from eight yards gave it enough direction to wrong foot the defence.

The match had barely restarted before Bremer, commanding in midfield, slipped a pass to Dave Swain who in turn fed Doyle making a brilliant overlap down his favourite wing. He cut in and passed to John Ritchie, but Clapton's luckless Hoare saved his young opponent the trouble of scoring by turning the ball into his own net to give 'Stones a 2-0 lead.

John Ritchie in action

Montague also went close but the match was all but over as a contest eight minutes into the second half in which Dave Bullock, on for Hand at half time went closest from twenty yards before Swain passed to Bremer. He planted a perfect ball down the middle and Peddie, with a dazzling body swerve around the Clapton keeper, Moore, did the rest, coolly slotting home from ten yards.

Moments later he almost got a hat trick with another will-o'-the-wisp act which took him past three men before he lost himself in his own maze and let the ball run out of play.

Wealdstone; A Williams, M Doyle, H Moxon, R Williams, M Barnard, D Montague, B Bremer, G Hand, D Swain, J Ritchie, L Peddie, Sub; D Bullock.

It was the week in which full-back Mickey Doyle got his first England cap, coming on as a substitute with three minutes to go against Ireland when Phil Fry was injured. He didn't touch the ball in his time on the field but the cap still counts!

Wealdstone's form was still inconsistent, a loss in the next match away to St Albans was followed by three victories then another defeat was followed by a win, seven draws and two defeats in ten matches.

There was still unrest though as Bernie Bremer, scoring two goals and making two in the 4–0 win over Finchley in the Middlesex Senior Cup semi-final resigned from the club two weeks later. The news broke on the morning of the match with Enfield.

'Stones too were without the services of Howard Moxon who was on holiday, yet showing great spirit, Wealdstone won the match 3–2! And Bremer soon returned to remain with the club until the end of the season.

Fans too turned out on occasions, one of these being a benefit match for Peter Parfitt played at the end of March. It was a promise made by the club six years earlier to the wing half who put cricket before soccer to play for Middlesex and England. A Wealdstone team beat the Peter Parfitt XI by four goals to one in front of 1,800 spectators, contributing £240 to the benefit fund.

Charlie Townsend returned to play for his former team-mate, as did former coach Dave Underwood who shared the goal-keeping duties with England International Ron Springett. Jimmy Hill made another appearance, as did Cliff Jones and Bill Perry and Bill Holden of Blackpool. Ian St John was also present but unable to play as he had played the previous afternoon for Liverpool.

Over the Easter Weekend, Wealdstone also entertained foreign opposition for a friendly, FC Amsterdam visiting Lower Mead, and winning by 2–0. It was all that left to entertain the fans it seems, as there was no interest in the league, Wealdstone set to finish in mid table, and the only trophy's left to compete for, the Presidents Memorial Trophy and the Middlesex Senior Cup, both two legged finals were not to be played for another month.

League crowds dropped further after the Enfield game and by the time Wealdstone hosted Leytonstone in April. Thankfully only 400 people witnessed a match that the Harrow Observer described as follows;

Take two teams in mid-table with nothing left to gain and the end of a season near, and you should get a shapeless fag end of a match. And that dear readers describes Wednesday night at Lower Mead perfectly!

At the end of April, four matches remained and Wealdstone contrived to slip to a 2–1 home defeat in the first, the first leg of the Presidents Memorial Trophy at home to Wembley, but the following week 1,800 saw Wealdstone defeat visitors Enfield in the first leg of the Middlesex Senior Cup Final.

A week further on, and Wealdstone won 2–0 at Wembley to retain the Presidents Trophy on a 3–2 aggregate and as if to sum up the 'up and down' season that preceded it, Wealdstone then visited Enfield where they were defeated by 3–0 to lose the Senior Cup by the same aggregate score. Andy Williams also became the first holder of the Supporter Club's Jock Law Trophy, after his performances in goal during a difficult year.

The customary end of season tour saw 'Stones visit Majorca, the only match resulting in a 3–0 defeat to the local side. The tour ended on a sour note when Dave Swain was in a car accident that resulted in hospitalisation and a number of stitches in head, leg and shoulder injuries.

Gordon Ellen
Supporter since 1935

Having lived in Harrow throughout most of my 74 years my support of Wealdstone goes back to when I was 8 years old and at that time being a pupil of Bridge Schools which, as you no doubt may know, is now the Civic Centre.

One thing however that has always stood out has been the support. Not as great now as it was in the 40's 50's and 60's but still a loyal following.

Howard Moxon in action

Alan Humphries had taken over as coach before the end of the season and was retained for the forthcoming season. Former player coach Howard Moxon remaining as a player with the club.

One of Humphries' first duties during the close season was to receive the resignation of Mickey Doyle, who had signed for Slough Town. It was to be the first of many.

As the new season was about to start Bernie Bremer finally left for Wycombe Wanderers, cutting the last remaining link with the Amateur Cup winning side of 1966. His departure left Wealdstone with only three first team players remaining from the previous season.

Only Dave Bullock, John Draper and Micky Barnard remained, following a season where the club had had three coaches, watched crowds drop dramatically and to top it all, they had lost £1,770 on the season.

Howard Moxon had taken over at Enfield and club captain Dave Swain had played in two of the pre-season matches (scoring against Guilford) before announcing his resignation and his intention to join Slough Town.

Andy Williams
Goalkeeper seasons 1967-70

I made approximately 120 appearances over 3 seasons, and thankfully there were no own goals! I have great memories of the close contact between the players and supporters, in particularly those who would travel to away games during those seasons, approaching the time when the club was to turn professional.

The Manager - Vince Burgess – another memory was him taking training sessions in the club house - dressed in his blazer! And other players from the squad like Dave Underwood entertaining us, particularly with his experiences in the professional game with Fulham F.C. and Charity Games involving personalities like Tommy Steele and Johnny Haynes.

Then there was Trainer Bob Croucher and the Reserve Team Manager, Edgar Francis who had been with the club for a long while.

I was very proud to receive the "Jock Law" Trophy as Player of the Year in 1969-70, it is one of a number of fond memories of Wealdstone as a real club both on and off the pitch and I was lucky enough to play alongside Hughie Lindsay - an outstanding player and a fine influence in my time at the club.

It was no surprise when the season started poorly with a defeat by 2–0 at Tooting and Mitcham. This was followed by a home defeat 6–1 to Wycombe Wanderers before a 2-1 win against Dulwich temporarily lifted the gloom.

A number of new players were brought in and tried, some with more success than others. By mid September, even Charlie Townsend had returned although in his first match back he couldn't prevent a 3-1 home defeat to Barking. The following Tuesday, he did aid Wealdstone in a 1-1 draw with Kingstonian, Wealdstone's only third point of the season, seven of the previous eight league matches having been lost.

There had also been one win in the FA Cup, against Hatfield by 2-0 to secure a visit to near neighbours, Wembley which also resulted in a 2-0 win.

A draw with Tooting in the league gave the club and spectators alike some hope that the worst was over but a draw at Spartan League Leighton Town in the FA Cup and then defeat 1-0 in the replay at Lower Mead showed that there was still plenty of work to do.

More new signings and the return of Gary Hand from Enfield boosted the 'Stones at the end of October, some making an immediate impact;

Three soaring headers from new signing John Hazell from Woking, signed late on Thursday night along with Alan Pentecost from Sutton, gave Wealdstone their first away league win of the season on Saturday.

The addition of a tall Head conscious leader to the Wealdstone line worked wonders and Pentecost too worried and probed and took considerable pressure off the sorely tried defence. Coach Alan Humphries said " I didn't think much of the first half, so I told them to split, five up and five back, and it didn't look bad at all".

It did in five minutes when, with dreadful chaos on the Wealdstone line and with keeper Alan Thomas stretched out on it, Haywood forced the ball over to give Corinthian Casuals the lead. The immediate response was for Charlie Townsend to get through on the left but he was unable to control the ball enough for the narrow angle.

On the 14 minute mark it was level as Hazell rose well to nod down past Willis, Shuflebotham rushing in to touch the ball over the line, and soon Hazell was back in action with a neat header from a Mick Barnard free kick that Willis took at the foot of the post.

The first half ended with two remarkably near things. First Elias hit a crossfield pass way over Thomas's goal when it seemed easier to score and then Ritchie, curving inside his back hit a screamer of a drive that went narrowly over the angle.

On the hour, Pentecost sent a swirling centre into the middle and Hazell met it perfectly to put Wealdstone ahead. With just the two new men in the centre, Wealdstone were now building up round them, but Rob Williams broke the pattern with a massive drive that Wallis gathered.

Townsend too tried a long range effort, a 25 yarder that curled over the bar from the left. He was spot on though, on 72 minutes as his corner reached the far post and the inevitable Hazell headed in for 1-3.

This goal sealed it all up and first Johnny Wilson and then Ritchie had good efforts, before Ritchie tried again the move that had failed in the first half. This time his shot was from 22 yards and it swerved brilliantly into the top corner, a really unstoppable effort.

Shufflebotham offered Jones a free shot at goal with a bad attempt at a clearance but Jones shot wide, then Pentecost almost wrapped it up with a diving header that just skimmed the bar in the last seconds.

Wealdstone; A Thomas, T Mahon, M Bernard, R Williams, J Shufflebotham, G Olson, J Wilson, C Townsend, J Hazell, J Ritchie, A Pentecost, Sub B Bennett.

It was to take more than one win to bring the crowds back though, and the evening match against Chesham was played in front of only 319 spectators.

At least those who were there saw Gary Hand return as well as Hazell and Pentecost, signed the previous week. They also saw 'Stones win by three goals to one, Hazell, Chalker and Ritchie scoring the goals.

An indifferent season for the reserves had also started to improve and in a midweek friendly, they had entertained the Lower Mead crowd with a 7-2 victory over the United States Navy.

Freddie 'Banger' Walsh also received a tribute in the local paper at Christmas, both for his involvement at Wealdstone and his coaching at Harrow ABC Boxing Club.

At 69 he was reserve team trainer, a position he had held for most of his forty year involvement with the club. He signed as a player in 1927 after spells with Rickmansworth, Harrow Town and Wealdstone Wednesday, joining the club in the London League.

He remembered;

The reserves as it was used to play off Belmont Road and the changing rooms were a shop. Once changed, players walked down the pavement and climbed over a stile to get to the pitch.

He played as a hard tackling half-back for six seasons, earning the nick name ' Banger' for his direct style and then after the death of his predecessor, Bill Gallagher, he took over as trainer to the first team.

Just before Christmas there was another change at Wealdstone when Alan Humphries was named as Manager.

Having been coach since the end of the previous season, he became the first Team Manager in the club's history, taking on sole responsibility for team matters, where in the past there had been a committee, although the role of this had reduced significantly in recent years.

It was a decision made with an eye on the future and the intention of the club to join the ranks of professional football. A full committee meeting of the club was held on 26th January 1971, and that meeting made the final decision to turn professional.

Almost as a celebration, Wealdstone faced and beat Enfield, the Amateur and Anglo Italian Cup holders 1-0 at Lower Mead in front of 945 people, the largest gate for a long while, only to follow up with a 1-1 Christmas Day draw with Hendon in front of 975!

The final hurdle to entering the professional ranks was in mid March when the club had to attend a meeting of the Southern League to be told the terms on which Wealdstone's application to join would be accepted.

At 4pm on Sunday 14th March, in the Great Western Hotel, Paddington, Ken Wiltshire, Alan Humphries and Brian Henderson heard the news that Wealdstone, along with 12 other clubs had been accepted into the Southern League.

From this point on, it was surprising that Wealdstone managed to play at all never mind win matches. The whole Amateur squad was expected to be released and a number of new signings were muted and began to appear at the club.

Manager Alan Humphries had been guaranteed a budget of £5,000 towards his squad for the next season and he was already on the look out for players.

On the field there were a number of good results, but not always met with a gracious response, Kingstonian for example were beaten 2–1 on their own ground, but were more concerned with running down Wealdstone's decision to leave the Isthmian League, commenting that they would want only one of the Wealdstone squad.

After a very poor start in the league, one win and one draw from their opening nine matches, Wealdstone had done well to recover to 13th out of 20 teams with just a few matches remaining at the end of the season, one of these saw another 'record' as 'Stones contrived to lose 2-1 at Ilford, recording their first ever Isthmian League defeat by the club.

For the home match with Corinthian Casuals the club released the full Official Statement on turning professional. It was printed in the match program and read as follows;

As you may know by now, we have decided to join the Southern League and thus become a semi-professional club after 71 years as an amateur side.

The decision was taken by the committee of the Wealdstone Football Club after a long and arduous investigation into the pro's and con's of both games.

It was felt by the majority of the committee that what was needed at Lower Mead was competitive football with promotion and relegation, thus stimulating interest in the game.

Unfortunately we were not getting that in the Isthmian League, and because we could not see that in the foreseeable future, a move was made to accept the Southern League invitation.

Although the final zoning of the first two divisions has not been decided, the demarcation line has and it is certain that we will be in the Northern area, the line being drawn from north of the Thames to Bristol.

Thus, the majority of our opponents will be easily reached by motorways. The farthest north is Burton, some two and a half hours (120 miles) journey by the M1. There is however a journey into Wales.

The Southern League invited 32 clubs outside of their league to talks with a view to offering them a place in a newly designed league with the promise of a Football Alliance from which a club could earn, through ability on promotions, a place in the Football League proper. The new league would then form part of the pyramid into the Football League.

In the future proposals there will be promotion and relegation from the Southern in the Alliance and then into the Football League proper. This new Southern League would then be the gateway into the Football League for any club that progressed through its playing ability.

A club need only play one professional in its side to qualify and it will give a greater control on its playing staff by placing them under contracts and selling them if the need arises.

Better and more attractive matches; (i) The non-league Trophy; (ii) The London Challenge Cup (this privilege is no longer open automatically to the semi finalists of the London Senior Cup) (iii) There are better opportunities to get exemption from the Preliminary rounds of the FA Cup (iv) The Southern League Trophy. The fixture lists will be compiled for the whole season, thus giving clubs better publicity time for its games.

One may argue that the standards of some of the first division Southern League clubs are not as good as some Isthmian League sides, and that some of the facilities are not as good either. This one would agree, but at the same time, most of the Premier Division clubs' facilities and playing standards are good. Surely it would be the object to progress into that division and onto the Football League proper if possible.

We have seen the importance of the Amateur Cup and the London Senior Cup go down over the years, and with the tightening up of the Amateur status, the senior amateur game will have to make some serious changes if it is to survive.

That is why we have looked into this in earnest and we have decided to tender our resignation from the amateur game, a game that we have been proud to compete in, in the past, but in which we feel there is no future.

We felt that having been invited to join the Southern League which is going to be asked to play its part in forming a part of the Football Pyramid within the Football League, and that another opportunity may not come our way again, we made application to join and were accepted.

Ken Wiltshire,
Hon Secretary.

Wealdstone's last home match as amateurs saw them entertain Woking, and an opportunist second half display of shooting gave them a story book ending and an Isthmian League double, having previously won the reverse fixture.

Seven minutes into the second half, Rob Williams passed to Alan Pentecost who blasted an unstoppable shot high into the net from the edge of the box to give 'Stones the lead.

On 70 minutes a poor back pass was intercepted by John Ritchie. He tapped home the second goal past the stranded goalkeeper, Collyer. Eighteen minutes later, Ritchie again rose to head in a Townsend cross to make the final score 3–0.

A night of celebration was added to when captain for the evening, Charlie Townsend was presented with the Supporters Club Jock Law trophy.

The last amateur match was away and it looked for a long time as though Wealdstone would record another victory and record their first league win over hosts, Hendon, John Ritchie having given Wealdstone a first half lead. It was not to be however, as the home side equalised on 70 minutes to ensure a draw.

There was some sad news with the retirement of both Jack Rogers the club Chairman and Chippy Luck, neither of whom agreed fully with the move away from the amateur football roots of the club. Although not disagreeing totally, both felt that the time was right to step down and allow younger men to take over.

Jack Rogers had been connected with the club since 1931, first as a supporter but then holding almost every office in the club until he was elected Chairman in 1963.

Harry 'Chippy' Luck joined the club in 1925, brought in to run the 'Save Lower Mead' campaign. The club were in financial difficulty and at risk of losing their recently acquired ground, successful as the club were to remain there until 1990!

He had also been treasurer of Wealdstone Wednesdays and joined the main club committee in 1928, seven years later becoming Club Secretary, a position he held until 1956. He became President in 1963. Both however did express their serious reservations with regard to the cost of becoming a professional team. Neither felt the gates were high enough and the club did not have many other means of revenue.

Hillingdon Borough were set as an example, having an average crowd of between 800 and 1000 in the Premier Division, but it was only their 'other' fundraising that increased the income over the costs.

An expected wage bill of over £200 per week was beyond Wealdstone's means. When the running costs were added on, an income of over £400 per week was required. Again far more than Wealdstone could raise on past performance.

Rob Williams
Player 1967-1971

I joined Wealdstone in 1967 having played for Lloyd's Bank, my employers at the time and captained Wealdstone 1970/71 season but when the club entered the Southern League I decided that the travelling would be too much, bearing in mind my bank responsibilities.

I joined Wycombe Wanderers in 1971 and played alongside other ex-Wealdstone players - John Hutchinson, Keith Searle, Bernie Bremner and Dave Bullock winning the Isthmian League and having successful cup runs.

I have many happy members of Wealdstone FC, the Lower Mead Singers and "Chicken George" (Young). I will always remember my debut. It was when Wealdstone legend Charlie Townsend was away playing for England and I had only been in senior football for a couple of months.

The first half went very quickly and although not seeing much of the ball, I thought I put in a reasonable performance. With 20 minutes to go I "went completely" and suddenly the ball kept coming at me! I hardly had the strength to kick the ball 10 yards; eventually I passed to my own side to the ironic cheers of the crowd. In the local paper the following Thursday (scoop) wrote, "As for debut boy Williams, he was simply dreadful"!

Other fond memories are of Edgar Francis, the reserve team manager when I joined - he appreciated my somewhat over enthusiastic approach to tackling, Vince Burgess taking training with track suit over collar and tie and popping into the bar for a Guinness whilst we were doing sit ups and Dave Underwood and games against the All Star XI - Jimmy Hill, Johnny Haynes etc. Alan Humphries telling tales of his times at Fulham and joining Johnny Haynes for a drink with Alan at various Chelsea pubs after East London games. He also called special training in the morning before an F.A. Cup match - John Ritchie and Gerry Olsen clashed heads during the session and spent the afternoon being stitched up in hospital.

Hugh Lindsay was my favourite player, although an international, he always had time to talk to and encourage younger players such as myself.

As Wealdstone was my first senior club I have always had a soft spot for it. I am very pleased that the club is now recovering after its problems.

Steve Paull
Supporter since the 60's

In our last amateur season, John Ritchie didn't score for over three months – November to March - and was then signed by Arsenal – I think he went on to play in the UEFA Cup.

Les Boyle,
Player, A Team Manager and Official from 1946

I was born in Essex and moved to Ireland where I played Gaelic Football in my schooldays. When I came back to the Wealdstone area in 1935, that's why I took up as a goalkeeper. I went to watch Wealdstone as often as I could before I was called up in 1939. I had a fine football career in the Army and I played on Ninian Park and at Aldershot.

I came out of the Army in 1946 and joined Wealdstone at the start of the season, playing mostly in the reserves, but I did play several times in the first team before I moved to Harrow Borough until an injury finished my playing career.

In the early sixties I was asked to run the Wealdstone 'A' team, playing on South Harrow Recreation ground. I'll always remember one of the groundsmen. He hated Wealdstone and whenever he would he would put us on the worst pitch!

Crystal Palace were in the same league as us, so the boys really enjoyed playing on their first team pitch. When it came to the return match I asked if we could play at Lower Mead.

They gave us a night fixture, under floodlights and the boys responded very well against a very talented Palace team. Many of the Palace team went on to play for the first team, including Steve Kember.

In the early sixties I was made Reserve Team Manager and it was good to be involved in the club when the first team went to the Amateur Cup Final at Wembley. The club chairman, Jack Rogers had taken a price of 66/1 with his bookmaker and he won a lot of money that day.

There is one story that springs to mind, told to me by Ken Wiltshire. Over in Ireland for the International with Charlie Townsend and Hugh Lindsay in the England side, the hospitality was so good in the Irish Club that they left only twenty minutes to get to Dalymount Park.

It so happened that Roger Casements body was being re-buried in Dublin on the same Saturday, so the streets were lined with people and police.

When they asked the taxi driver to get them to the ground, he relied that they would have to go up a street that was closed. In so doing they got to the end of the road and were at the head of the funeral cortege.

The taxi driver told Frank Harbud to keep taking his hat off and to bow to the crowd - In those days Frank always wore a hard black top hat.

Bernie Bremer
Player 1962 – 1970

I didn't miss many matches in my time at the club, certainly between 1964 and 1970 and the Amateur Cup Final at Wembley of course stands out.

One player stands out too. Hughie Lindsay. Not just because he introduced me to a higher class of football with Wealdstone (I was a pupil at his school) but because he epitomised to me what football was about, albeit in quite a diminutive frame.

He had vision, energy, control, superb passing and shooting with either foot. And he was a nice bloke with it.

Gordon Allen and Mark Snell
Supporters, reminiscing together!

Gordon started watching Stones in 1933, Mark in 1946, taken along by his Grandfather, such were the crowds, he used to be lifted over the fence to watch the game.

There have been some wonderful players at Wealdstone in 'our time' and starting at the back we'll remember a few of them;

There have been a number of good goalkeepers over the years – Arthur Paisley, who stepped into the Amateur Cup semi final for example. He famously went up to the penalty taker before the kick and said "you better not miss this because you'll look a pratt" Miss it he did.
Another great was Rowe the England amateur international. He looked to be a great goalkeeper – everything about him looked the part, but he didn't stay for very long. It seemed from Wealdstone's point of view that he only did one thing wrong, and that was that the ball ended up in the net too often!

Later on there was a goalkeeper called Martindale, another great player, although he never received the plaudits that Danny Wiltshire got. He was another that should have got into the England side but he was prevented by Bennett of Southall.

Just after the war we had Tommy McGhee – an excellent full back before he joined Portsmouth.

Charlie Barker too, a tremendous shot for a full back and think how heavy the ball was then. He was always the penalty taker, I don't ever remember him missing one but I suppose he must have.

Another full back was Arthur Loveday.

I remember him in the cup tie with Leytonstone. It was a very muddy pitch and defending a corner I think, Arthur took a moment to wipe the mud from his face. The kick was taken and squared towards Arthur . The ball hit his hand and the referee awarded a penalty that went some way to deciding the match. Arthur never forgot that.

It was a good sire too, Charlie Edmonds at Centre Half as well. They played so well together.

In the half backs as they were then, we had Jimmy Wastell, the flying winger and Cyril Trigger May who went on to QPR. Abel Comben played in some of the successful years as well. Peter Parfitt also filled a role – he was a very aggressive player. He wasn't dirty but he did have a challenge about him.

Of course in 1966 it was Eddie Dillsworth who stood out, his legs seemed able to stretch any where.

Edgar Francis another who played for a number of years and then gave great service to the club as a coach and involved with the running of the sides.

Charlie Townsend stands out as a great player, but (don't tell him this!) he did occasionally let his head drop if things were not going his way. Laurie Tott at Hendon was in the England side and he kept Charlie out for a long while, but Charlie still gained a good collection of 'Caps'.

The first forwards I remember are Bert Dyke and Charlie Bunce. Bert was a tremendous player. I watched him get the ball from kick off and dribble through the whole defence to score. Eddie 'Ginger' Smith also scored a great deal of goals in a short time with us.

There was a whole forward line that stood out – Phil White who went on to Leyton Orient, Wegrzyk and Mikrut.

Mikrut was tremendous header of the ball.. One memory of him was when I was standing at the Elmslie End, the ball arrived at his feet on the penalty spot and he was so surprised, he seemed to stand there until someone shouted 'Kick the bloody thing'. He did and he scored which also seemed to surprise him.

Alan Benningfield on the left wing at the same time was one of a number of good wingers. W W Parr and Viv Evans are others that spring to mind. Viv played in just about every position for the club as well.

Bernie Bremer and Arthur Peel are two more that stand out. I remember one game where Arthur took a free kick, which (except Arthur apparently) everyone realised was indirect. Arthur shot anyway. The ball hit the crossbar, bounced down and against the goalkeeper and went in. I think it was only Arthur that didn't realise it wouldn't have been a goal if it had gone straight in!

There was Hugh Lindsay too. Always looked so frail but what a tremendous striker of the ball. His best game must have been the match with Stevenage.

That winning free kick in the last minute. Magnificent.

I remember the ball being about half way between the goal area and half way line, but it might be like the fisherman's story – every time it is told the distance becomes greater!

Off the field, there was Ken Wiltshire. He was the face of Wealdstone and he would do anything for the club. He didn't mind who he upset to do it either, as long as it was for Wealdstone.

TURNING PROFESSIONAL

Wealdstone, beginning their 1971–72 season as professionals for the first time held their AGM almost without mention of the decision to leave the Amateur ranks, a decision that seemed for a while to split the club in two.

The only comment made came from the floor, one unnamed supporter expressing his dissatisfaction that the decision had been made by the committee with no reference to the members at a special meeting, but Ken Wiltshire replied that the membership had been consulted in a number of discussions and conversations.

Alan Humphries, the manager informed the meeting that to date (early July) nine professionals had been signed, two more were on trial at pre-season training, and there were four amateurs in the first team squad. He also informed the members that the intention was to reduce the age of the reserve team squad to bring younger players through, as there was no point in having reserves that would not be good enough for the first team.

In light of the loss of Harry Luck and Jack Rogers, Harry was made a life Vice President of the club, and the Cinema End Stand was renamed in honour of the departing Chairman, as The Rogers Stand.

A number of pre-season friendlies were also organised and many of the new signings were to be seen in these including Gary Townend, formerly of Leyton Orient, Hillingdon Borough and Worthing, Trevor Watson, formerly Fulham and Hillingdon Borough, Derek Gibbs, formerly Chelsea and Leyton Orient, Dave Cockell, formerly Queens Park Rangers and Crawley Town and Cliff Jones formerly of Spurs and Wales.

The first competitive match as a professional club was to be played at home in the league stage of the Southern League Cup, against Banbury, who had visited Lower Mead twice in the previous three seasons in the FA Cup without success.

One of the most hazardous parts of a sports writer's job is to return to his office after the first match of the season and predict the future for a club. This task becomes all the more onerous when the club has just embraced professionalism and capably dealt with the opposition.

It would be very easy to write a glowing account of 'Stones excellent, often highly entertaining victory in this Southern League Cup Qualifying Match. There was the tonic of the first goal of the season after ten minutes, a dazzling display by Welsh wizard Cliff Jones, some clever midfield build-up and one quite outstanding free kick set-piece, the obvious brainchild of manager Alan Humphries, which will have more than one defence in trouble this season.

Ultimately there was a reasonably resounding victory, which

A promotional flyer produced by the club to attract sponsorship for the first season in professional football.

must have satisfied most of the 1350 paying customers. Yet, truth to tell, 'Stones will have to do better. During pre-season games they looked so strong, but they too often creaked uneasily at the back. Banbury's one goal came from an appalling defensive error with too many players static at the same time, and when they had a second disallowed, the defence again was all at sixes and sevens.

So wrote Phil Sugden to open his match report of this fine first day victory. With an almost gale force wind at their backs in the first half, and in their faces for the second, Wealdstone had won the match by three goals to one, Jones' weaving run and accurate pass finished off by Townend after ten minutes. On 38 minutes Jones scored himself from Bielkus' corner, to give Wealdstone a 2-0 half time lead.

Banbury pulled one back on 59 minutes, but Wealdstone restored their advantage shortly afterwards with a glorious goal from Cliff Jones, his second. He received a good pass from Cockell and then weaved through three defenders before unleashing a right foot shot into the far corner of the visitors net. Wealdstone's side for that first professional match was;

John Barr in goal, who went on to make 108 (1) appearances for the side between 1971-73,
Tommy Mahon, the only amateur in the side, 21 appearances 1971,
Dave Bielkus, who made five appearances,
Dave Cockell who made 74 (1) appearances 1971-72,
Derek Gibbs who made four appearances,
Bill Bailey who made 23 (4) appearances 1971-72, scoring twice,
Trevor Watson who made 42 (1) appearances 1971-72, scoring twice,
Micky Brown who made 92 appearances scoring 44 goals 1971-73,
Gary Townend who made 31 (3) appearances scoring ten goals between 1971-72,
John Furie 72 (2) appearances and 1 goal, 1971-72 and
Cliff Jones 16 appearances and 5 goals, 1971.
It was a new side in a new league and there were a number of changes as the season progressed.

By the start of September, Wealdstone had re-signed amateur Gary Hand from Enfield and another amateur, centre half Jackie Oliver from Watford. Both started the next match away to Dunstable which saw Wealdstone secure another win, by 2-0.

The side had managed to top their 'league' in the Southern League Cup qualifying competition, but in the league, things were more difficult, scoring twice and conceding six goals in two opening defeats.

The second of these at Kings Lynn exposed more than defensive frailty, as Wealdstone scored all three goals in a 2-1 defeat. Wealdstone had taken the lead on four minutes through Townend but on 65 minutes, Bailey scored past his own goalkeeper to equalise before Barr himself could only help a corner into the net to seal the result.

Wealdstone visited Harrow Borough in the first round of the FA Cup and came away with a 1-0 victory, but this was brief relief.

Worse was to come as they were then drawn away to 'the amateurs' of Boreham Wood where they were held 1-1 by a home side that had only amassed eight points from ten league matches.

The replay was a different matter though, as Boreham Wood ran out worthy 2-0 winners at Lower Mead and the Harrow Observer ran the headline " The night shame came to Lower Mead".

A league record that showed Won 1 Drawn 2 Lost 4 did little to quell the disquiet and after such a dismal FA Cup performance better things were expected of the teams visit to Wellingborough a few days later.

This will surely go down as one of the most wretched performances for a long, long time, surpassing even the shock FA Cup defeat four days earlier. So bereft of ideas up front, and totally inept in defence were 'Stones that they made Wellingborough – themselves only a moderate side – look far more competent than they really were.

The aptly named Dog and Duck ground, Wealdstone were the lame ducks in the heavy rain, proved to be the burial ground of what was hoped would be a revival after the Boreham Wood debacle. Much as Wealdstone started brightly they could not score, nor sustain the effort and as the match continued their display worsened.

The match was followed by three more defeats to bring the run to twelve matches without a victory as 'Stones struggled to find their feet in the professional ranks, the run only ending with a 1-0 win at Kingstonian, as if to prove for the second year in succession that the change from Amateur to professional football was a justified one.

There were some brighter spots though, as finding themselves without a match on a November Saturday, they took on Premier League leaders, Barnet, in a friendly and were unfortunate to lose by the odd goal in three. Most observers commented that if Wealdstone had shown as much spirit and ability in the league as they had in this match they would be making a serious challenge for promotion rather than fighting at the bottom of the Division 1 North table!

One name missing from the Wealdstone line up for the Barnet match was that of Cliff Jones. On the Friday before the game he had become the first professional 'transfer' from Wealdstone, Cambridge City paying £200 for his registration.

Later in the month it was all smiles around Lower Mead, as for the first time since late August Wealdstone had won at home, even after falling two goals behind in seventeen minutes to Kettering Town. 'Stones had battled their way back into the match and won far more convincingly than the 3-2 scoreline suggested.

Full of confidence, Wealdstone travelled to Bletchley midweek and came away with a 1-0 victory in another match that they had dominated. Even the Bletchley Manager after the game was quotes as saying "Wealdstone were a very good side and should have scored eight!"

It was not to last though, as leading up to Christmas a 5-0 home defeat to Stourbridge saw the return of the dismal and disappointing performance headlines. As the New Year broke, Wealdstone, still looking for the correct mix, managed three more wins but these too flattered to deceive and were soon followed by a run of poor results.

By March, it was suggested that Alan Humphries would 'move upstairs' and become General Manager with responsibilities more for fundraising than team matters, while a new man was sought for the footballing side. Coach Nick Farmer and the players Management Committee took on the selection and run-

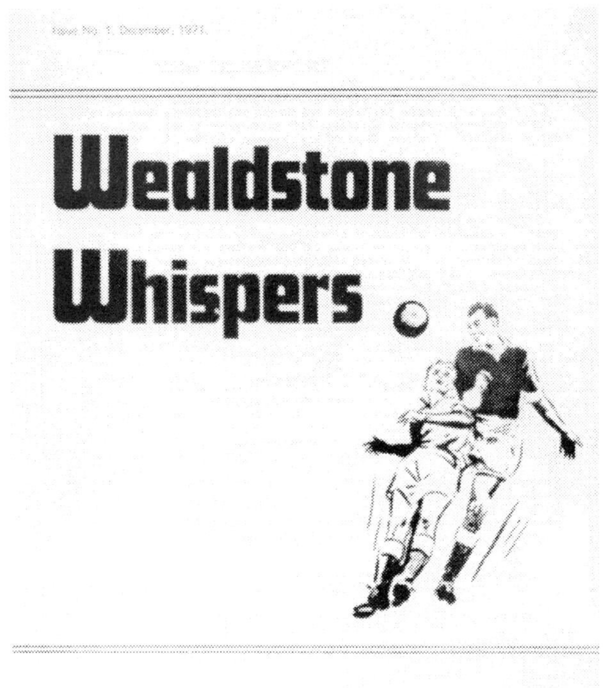

The first issue of Wealdstone Whispers produced in December 1971.

ning of the side in the meantime ands there were signs again of an immediate improvement. Alan Humphries however left the club.

Saving one of their best performances of the season for one of their hardest matches, Wealdstone hosted league leaders Corby Town and were unfortunate not to win, the match ending in a 1–1 draw, a fine result after all the off field disruption during the week.

As if to highlight the changes made during the season, only five of the side that faced Corby had played at the start of the season, the likes of Eddie Presland, Bill Byrne and Terry Dyson having been brought in to strengthen the 'Stones team. Another excellent performance also saw 'Stones record another win, at home to Barry Town. Micky Brown recorded the club's first professional hat trick in the match. He was joined on the scoresheet by recent signing Bill Byrne, who had scored his third goal in three matches since joining the club. It was Barry's heaviest defeat (and their 20th) of the season, and yet they had surprised 'Stones early on and taken the lead.

On the terraces, the 'Stones unique support had seen the first issue of 'Wealdstone Whispers', the first 'fanzine' produced by the Supporters Club. Put together by Ray Corner, Peter Fuller, Laurie Trott and Sheila Pope, all members of the Supporters Club committee at the time, the magazine was short lived but did offer the supporters an insight and updated news on the club.

This was later followed by two more fanzines, *'Long Ball Down The Middle'* and *'The Elmslie Ender'* which was by far the most........passionate is probably the word.

Sid Prosser was named as the new Manager by the end of the month and with three matches over Easter he chose to see as many of the side play as possible. His first job was to produce the retained list determining the players that would remain with the club, being offered terms for the following year.

Five players were offered new terms, John Barr, John Furie, Dixie Hale, Terry Dyson and Dave Cockell while Micky Brown, John Pearce, Ray Whittaker and Bill Byrne had already been engaged for the following season, (of those nine only four had figured in the first match). Eddie Presland was also retained after the club realised they had made a mistake and left him off the original list.

The season ended on a high at home at least, with a win by 5-2 over Lockheed Leamington took their point's tally to 33 from 33 matches, one per game. The score would have been greater but for the performance of the Lockheed goalkeeper, Chris Lightfoot, who saved well on a number of occasions. Micky Brown managed to score another two goals to take his tally for the season to 26, but it was another good performance from John Barr in goal that ensured he received the Player of the Year trophy.

Sid Prosser was making plans for the future as the season ended offering the experienced Viv Evans, who had captained the reserves through the season a scouting role, his task being to keep a flow of good young players through the clubs ranks and into the first team.

The first professional season had ended and Wealdstone took stock of their position. Realising that they had had more to learn than they previously though, they were at least satisfied they had made the right decision and could look forward to the future.

The only drawback at the end of the first season was a major one. The first exploits as a professional club had caused a loss of over £6,000 in the first year, although some of this was a one off cost in setting up a paid side.

It rang true with the comments the previous year from Jack Rogers and Chippy Luck that the professional game came at a cost Wealdstone could ill afford. One of the greatest differences they encountered was the distance travelled to league fixtures. In the past the most recorded was in the region of 1,000 miles but this year in the league alone Wealdstone had travelled 3,226 miles, the longest trip being a midweek away to Barry Town, some 316 miles.

Brian Curtis
Supporter since the 1950's

Over 40 odd years, I have met many fans and made friends with a number of other Wealdstone supporters. I will not go into any further detail other than to recall a supporter who used to stand adjacent to the Members enclosure in the late 1970's.

He used to 'rally' the 'Stones with a cry of "All together – One at a time!". It must be one of the most contradicting cries ever.

The close season saw Wealdstone move Divisions, into the Southern Section of the league with Dunstable and Bletchley, to increase the Division to 22 clubs.

The club were also accepted into the FA Trophy competition for the first time and they announced that they were also to field a side in the Mid Surrey Professional Midweek Floodlight League.

Paul Webb
Supporter 1960's-1970's

I haven't watched the 'Stones since I was a teenager in the mid seventies. I remember seeing Cliff Jones, Terry Dyson and

Johhny Haynes playing, but the one player who seemed to have his picture in the Harrow Observer every week was Micky Brown.........

As pre-season approached, the club were able to announce the first new signings, 20 year old George Duck joining the club from Southend, 18 year old Les Broughey joining from Spurs and Phil Woods a 28 year old centre half signed from St Albans.

Bill Byrne was to have left the club to emigrate to South Africa but a change in his plans also meant that he would remain at Wealdstone for the forthcoming season.

Another new signing announced shortly afterwards was at the time considered to be the most important, Eric Burgess joining the club from the Colchester United back four.

He appeared in 48 of their 52 matches the previous season and was offered a new contract by the Football League club but he rejected the terms as he had taken up a new position as a Sports Executive and wished to remain part-time.

His brother too had a Wealdstone connection, having played for the club as an amateur before joining his then side, St Albans.

Before the new season started, Wealdstone again used the Lower Mead ground in their fundraising activities – this time, holding a Pop Concert, featuring Stone The Crows, Atomic Rooster, The Roy Young Band among other with DJ John Peel as compere.

The day was a success as far as the weather and the music went, but financially it was a disaster.

The Harrow Observer reported that despite the concert being organised to "Save the Club" Wealdstone were not too down-hearted despite a £1000 loss on the event, and they intended to stage another even the following year.

The publicity had been good before the event, and the weather too had been kind, but the expected crowd did not materialise. There was good coverage In the music press as well before and after the event and both New Musical Express and Melody Maker reporting on the concert. A crowd of over 3,500 had attended but this was against a target of 10,000.

Defiantly the club proposed the following year to have the top group of the day and to have the whole event organised by Robert Stigwood Productions, one of the leading promoters of the time.

This was all to fall by the wayside however when at the AGM the true figures came out showing that in fact the concert had actually lost over £4,000, and this was on top of the £6,000 loss from the first professional season of the club.

As the new season began, Wealdstone soon adjusted to the Southern Division and started brightly in the league and the cup competitions. Early September saw three wins in eight days, the third of these a 1-0 home victory over Premier Division Waterlooville, Wealdstone's first ever match in the FA Trophy, the club having been too late to enter the previous season.

A few weeks later, the second tie in the competition saw Wealdstone away to Andover. Wealdstone had given permission for the club goalkeeper John Barr to travel to the match from his holiday in Cornwall. It was a decision which almost cost the club dear, as he was held up in heavy traffic, and arrived at the ground 15 minutes after the kick off.

Substitute John Beyer started the match in goal and after 25 minutes, when Barr replaced him, 'Stones were 2–0 behind, having conceded the first goal on 30 seconds and the second on 20 minutes.

In disarray for the first twenty five minutes, the arrival of Barr instilled confidence throughout the team and he was only called on to save once in the remainder of the first half!

By thirty one minutes the scores were level, George Duck scoring both, the first with a shot from outside the box and the second, a header from a Bill Byrne chip.

The second half continued in the same vein, Duck completing his hat trick on 61 minutes and Alick Brown scoring a fourth. It capped a good week for the 'Stones as on the previous Wednesday they had been unfortunate only to draw to a hotly disputed equaliser at Millwall in the London Challenge Cup.

A further Trophy win at Winchester added to the expectation at Lower Mead, but despite the good start, 'Stones season was to slip away. Defeat (1–3) at Banbury saw the end of the Trophy run, the league form also suffered, no more so that in a 3–2 home defeat to Dorchester Town in November, - they had previously won only one of thirteen matches.

Dorchester came to Lower Mead with one of the worst defensive records in the Southern League and the fans turned out almost gleefully to watch the slaughter of the innocents, and of course, to welcome former England star Johnny Haynes on his debut for the 'Stones.

It appeared that all would be right for the supporters at half time when Wealdstone led by 2–1, Haynes, without rushing about too much, having revealed touches of his former mastery, and victory very much on the cards.

One of the adverts placed to publicise the open air concert

"As if it was not warm enough on Saturday afternoon, some of the more enthusiastic fans started dancing."

Alas, the best laid plans...... Wealdstone suddenly lost their touch and the visitors scored two more goals. They retired from the fray with two points they scarcely expected to win and dealt the home side's promotion chances a very severe knock.

Haynes had signed from Durban City and was to play until the end of January, before returning to Durban to play for a further season.

There were changes to be made and new players appeared, Paul Fairclough starting with an impressive debut in a 4–1 win at home to Trowbridge in mid December. This win was only enough to improve Wealdstone's position to mid table, the recent run of poor results taking their toll on a good start. Six home points dropped in a month prevented 'Stones from continuing their challenge.

Off the field, there was a proposal from Brentford FC that Wealdstone should become and official nursery club of their third division neighbours. The proposal was considered by the management committee and rejected as it meant that Wealdstone would no longer be able to compete in the FA Cup. It also came in a week where Waterlooville were instructed by the Southern League that they had to sever all ties with Portsmouth or they would be expelled from the Southern League – a further risk that 'Stones were not prepared to take.

January became George Duck's month as early season form returned to Lower Mead. In the space of four days, a 5–1 defeat of Bexley United was followed by a 4–0 victory over Salisbury, and continuing his personal run of goals, George Duck had scored a hat trick in each match.

The standing ovation he received at the end of the Salisbury match saluting the fact that by 12th January he had already scored 26 goals in the season.

It was a month when Wealdstone tried an experiment – a Sunday afternoon match. Despite reservations, the match against Bognor Regis Town attracted the fourth biggest crowd of the season, over 1600, and this was despite the lack of publicity from the Harrow Observer.

Chris Kinnear had also been brought in but despite some good victories there was not quite enough to re-ignite the promotion challenge.

It was the season that Fred 'Banger' Walsh retired having been at Wealdstone for 48 years, initially joining as a player before taking on the duties of reserve and then first team trainer.

Dan Helen

Long-time supporter, Football Committee 1970-72

For many, many years the real character amongst the supporters was "The Man in Blue" through the 1950s, 60s and 70s. He never seemed to miss a game home or away, decked in blue and white from his top-hat to his toes and of course his large hand bell yet Eric Metcalfe was known far and wide.

So many memories of great games, the amateur Cup in 1966 winning the Gola League up at Kettering in 1985 followed by the Trophy win over Boston a few weeks later.

So many memories that it is hard to pick out one. But one that always comes to mind is the 6-5 win over Stevenage at Lower Mead. 3-3 at half time when they had a player sent off (Johnny Brooks) yet they were 5-3 up well into the second half until Hugh Lindsay hit the amazing hat trick.

I can still picture the winner in the last few minutes - a free kick at least 35 yards out and it hit the roof of the net at the cinema end with the goalie just blinking!

I started to support WFC in 1958 having moved from West London. My visits from then on to Craven Cottage started to decrease, having been very surprised at the quality of football played at Lower Mead. I also liked the close bond between supporters and players and the many social events attended by all.

I was elected to the football committee in 1970 and served for 2 years, including year we took the decision to move from the one division Isthmian to the Southern League (a move I voted for). If memory serves me right the decision at the board meeting (held every Monday night) was only carried by about 4 or 5 votes, the football committee comprised 12 elected members, plus about 10 officers of the club.

Terry Dyson leads out Johnny Haynes on his Lower Mead debut.

During this period it was a great thrill for me to see my hero from Craven Cottage Johnny Haynes sign and make his debut for us in November 1972. I saw him make his debut for Fulham on Boxing Day 1952 and rated him one of England's finest and the best passer of a ball I have seen. (How we could do with him now - of course I mean England!).

These were the great days and I try and focus on these rather than the black days when we literally "lost" Lower Mead (or gave it away).

Although at the end of their second professional season, Wealdstone had retained amateur links through non-contract players and by being run as a 'club' by a committee.

This era was finally to come to an end on the 30th April 1973, when the Management Committee and all its sub-committees were disbanded formally.

With immediate effect the club was to be governed by eight people. These people were to be instrumental in the formation of a Limited Company during the close season. They were to become the first Directors of the club. (At this stage it was in title alone, as it was to take another full year before the Limited Company was finally formed.)

They were nominated by Don Brown, who remained as the Club Chairman. The Directors were Ken Wiltshire (General Secretary), Harry Benjamin (Financial Secretary), Bill Emerson (Asst. General Secretary), Colin Pope (Public Relations Officer), John Ward (Fixture Secretary), John Harding (Accountant and Financial Adviser), Brian McNally (Property Adviser). There was also to be a General Purposes Committee headed by Frank Harbud.

Prior to the end of the season, another new signing was made, John Smith joining the club from Winchester. He appeared in four matches, scoring twice before the end of the season and he was expected to feature prominently the following year. It was not to be though, as in May, he left for trials with the Philadelphia Eagles of the (American) National Football League as a place-kicker. He was subsequently offered a contract worth £12,000 to play from May to December – a phenomenal amount in comparison to his earnings at Wealdstone, although he was expected to return at the end of the NFL season in December.

This also remained a disappointment as he made a career for himself in the USA as a player before later appearing on Channel 4 as the co-presenter of their weekly American Football coverage.

Season 1973–1974 started well for Wealdstone, the side achieving six wins out of the first seven games, including three wins out of three in the league.

This all happened without the services of the club Captain, Eric Burgess who was on holiday – he returned for the match at Bletchley at the end of August.

This match also saw Chic Brodie take over in goal from Ray McKenzie and Johnny Henderson replaced Alick Brown in the forward line, while John McCormick continued to impress in midfield.

A 4–1 win at Bletchley followed by a 2–0 win at Marlow in the FA Cup continued 'Stones run of excellent form on the pitch, despite the lack of funds off the field, but in early September it seemed that a solution had been found for these problems as well.

The Harrow Observer front page of September 7th 1973 gave people the news that Wealdstone had a plan to build offices and a Multi Storey Car Park on the Lower Mead site, in conjunction with a development by EMI that was expected to earn the club an income of £20,000 per year. The story continued;

If this ambition is fulfilled it will mean a dramatic change from rags to riches. At the club's AGM on Friday members were told of an £11,000 loss on the 1972 - 1973 season. This included over £4,000 loss on a Pop Concert, which it had been hoped would revive the club's dwindling fortunes.

Plans are gradually taking shape to turn Lower Mead into one of the finest Stadiums in non-league soccer, at the same time making Wealdstone rich beyond it's wildest dreams.

Press officer Colin Pope said "Following months of negotiations with EMI who own the adjacent ABC cinema, Wealdstone are in the final stages of preparing plans for an office complex with a multi-storey car park on part of the stadium.

It would mean that the pitch would be turned around by 90 degrees and space age facilities including lush dressing rooms and offices, a new social club with a separate ballroom, with squash courts and sauna baths provided.

The remodelled ground will have the capacity of 16,000 with a new 2,000 seat stand incorporated with as much terracing as presently exists. The over riding factor is the rents from the office block would mean a revenue in excess of £20,000 per year to Wealdstone FC!

The club has already reached agreement with Harrow Borough FC to share their ground for two years while the work is carried out, (Harrow Borough are presently playing at Lower Mead while their own pitch is reseeded ready for the New Year).

The whole scheme is dependant on EMI gaining the required Planning approvals, but Wealdstone's advisors feel that EMI would not have already expended so much money and effort if they felt the project had a less than reasonable chance of being accepted in its entirety. The provision of a Public Car Park will help as this is sorely needed in the centre of Harrow."

Perhaps though, the last paragraph was the most relevant – it was a comment from the Chief Planning Officer who said that only preliminary discussions had been held, no application had been submitted and he was surprised that the club had referred to the proposals in the match programme.

Although these plans were eventually to be shelved, at the time they should have been a boost to the club, but after a promising start, September saw a dismal run of results with an away draw with Chesham in the FA Cup followed by a 4-2 defeat in the replay, a defeat at Ramsgate and then by 4–0 to Spurs in the London Challenge Cup, Terry Dyson welcomed back to his former club by the fans.

It may have been a blessing in disguise. This poor run coincided with Cup matches. By the beginning of November, a 2–0 win over fellow promotion rivals, Poole Town, put 'Stones second in the league. This was followed by a 1–0 win at Wimbledon in the fifth meeting between the clubs, this time gaining a second round place in the FA Trophy.

Off the field, the fuel crisis had led to the resignation of Chairman Don Brown. He had to devote the majority of his time to his business interests nationwide, which limited the time he had available for Wealdstone FC. He was replaced by David Martle.

The good run of league form continued and 'Stones were challenging for promotion through the winter, but the first match in February was memorable for more than the result!

One of the most sensational games seen at Lower Mead saw Hasting United captain John Ripley lead the Sussex side off the field four minutes into the second half, after John Jefferson had been sent off by referee D R Waterman.

The incident occurred after full-back Harry Cunningham had handled for the second time in 48 minutes and Wealdstone were awarded their third penalty, all three scored by George Duck. All three were obvious, but the third was the most blatant, for Cunningham pulled down a Henderson shot with two hands when a goal seemed certain. Jefferson protested too much and was at first booked and then sent off.

For a minute or so he refused to leave the field and the referee was more than lenient with at least two other players who pushed and jostled him near the goal line. Jefferson finally walked off and Ripley at once took his team off.

A touchline conference (a heated argument is perhaps a truer version of what happened) lasted two or three minutes with Wealdstone Manager Sid Prosser and substitute Terry Dyson joining those to ensure sanity.

Eventually, still protesting vigorously, Ripley led his men back on and four minutes after the handball, Duck was able to take the penalty, to establish at the time, a 3–0 lead. Prior to this match, Hastings had only conceded twelve goals in as many games away from home.

They had been beaten 2–1 at Lower Mead in December in the league and had made few friends then, but they will not have added any more names to their fan club after this FA Trophy tie.

George Duck scored four goals, three penalties and one a header, John Henderson scoring the fifth in a 5–2 victory, Hastings having played better with ten than they had previously with eleven, taking advantage of a couple of lapses in the concentration of 'Stones defenders.

Nick Woolford
Supporter since 1966

I have been a supporter of Wealdstone FC and a regular on the terraces since 1966. Prior to that I used to go to Highbury to watch the Arsenal but that started to get expensive and as I began courting it got a bit difficult to explain why I needed all of Saturday afternoon and most of Saturday evening to watch a 90 minute football match !

Living in Harrow (close to Harrow-on-the-Hill Underground Station) and attending the Salvatorian College in Wealdstone meant that my journey to school passed the hallowed turf of Lower Mead and so it seemed quite natural for me to gravitate to that stadium to satisfy my desire to watch live football on a Saturday afternoon !

The first few years proved to be a bit spasmodic and uneventful, and it was not until the club changed status from Amateur to Semi-Professional that I really started to get involved with the club and attend as many home matches as was possible.

In those early semi-pro days, one of the first matches that I can recall was an International (!) versus a German side from Elmsbuttel. I made the mistake of taking my wife (the girl I had courted earlier and who is at least partly responsible for my change of allegiance from Arsenal to Wealdstone) and she wanted to sit so I had to join her in the grandstand (!!) rather than take my usual place on the second step of the Elmslie Stand.

I have a very clear memory of Beryl shouting "Elmsbuttel, Elmsbuttel, Yah Yah Yah !"

Much to my disgust and the amazement of the Elmsbuttel players. Needless to say I do not remember the score from that game !!

My fond memories are of the George Duck era with the Hastings F.A.Cup game being clearest of all. I recall laughing till I nearly cried at the antics of the Hastings manager at taking his players off the field when the third penalty was awarded and put away by George.

Furthermore we got a mention on Grandstand that afternoon.

By mid March Wealdstone were set to face league leaders Poole Town in the return fixture at Poole. A 3–2 win greatly increased their chance of winning the league and therefore gaining promotion to the Premier Division.

Played on a Sunday, it was the home side's first home defeat for four months and the standard of Wealdstone's play was such that at times the whole of the 1,100 crowd often applauded their possession.

A 3–0 win in midweek saw Wealdstone take over as league leaders. They followed this with four more wins, at home to Crawley and Canterbury and away at Bognor and Andover to cement their position at the top.

Sid Prosser had resigned as Manager and by the end of March, Eddie Presland had taken over for the run in. 'Stones finally clinched the title with a 2–0 win at Gravesend in mid April, just three weeks after he took over.

Swept along on the tumultuous tide of sheer emotion from the massed ranks of their supporters, Wealdstone turned in a performance of towering ability, a virtuoso display fit for a connoisseur at Gravesend on Monday to win the Championship in glorious style.

As the referee blew the final whistle, everyone of the Wealdstone players were buried beneath an avalanche of fervent supporters, as the pitch became a seething mass of people. Denied success for many seasons, all the heart aches and disappointments of the past were dissolved as Wealdstone's fans – the envy of every Club in the league – gave vent to their feelings.

Long after the game ended, players were being enticed half naked out of the dressing room to take yet one more bow, and then came Eddie Presland's turn. White faced and barely able to conceal his joy, manager for only three weeks after a splendid season among the action, he was carried down the tunnel.

This is not merely a good 'Stones side, but a great one. As Gravesend Manager Tony Sitford said, "you have to beat these guys twice to get goal-side and likely as not, they'll be back for another go. Their character shows up as much as their skill, and when you have both of those assets, you have the complete team."

Wealdstone had won the title using only eighteen players all season and that number included goalkeeper Chic Brodie who had been released long before the end of the year, Barnes who only made four appearances and Baker who made only one..

The side at Gravesend was; Ray McKenzie, Chris Kinnear, John Watson, Eric Burgess, John McCormick, Jim Godfrey, Paul Fairclough, Ray Fulton, Bill Byrne, George Duck and John Henderson, Terry Dyson was the substitute. The other two play-

Wealdstone FC 1973-74 Southern League Division One South Champions
Back; Jim Spark (Club Doctor), Bill Byrne, Keith Bristow, Alick Brown, Paul Fairclough, Roy McKenzie, Jim Godfrey, Eric Burgess, John Henderson, George Duck, Eddie Presland (Manager), Fred King (Trainer)
Front; Ray Fulton, John Watson, John McCormick, Chris Kinnear, Terry Dyson.

ers used that season were Alick Brown and Manager, Eddie Presland.

The run of results continued through to the end of the season as 'Stones made it eight wins on the trot beating Basingstoke at home and Metropolitan Police away and in five of those games they kept clean sheets. A 1-1 draw with Trowbridge was followed by a 3-0 defeat of Bexley, George Duck scoring all three – his fifth hat trick of the season, bringing his seasons tally to 62 goals.

The final match was another draw with Trowbridge; this time 3-3 and 'Stones had won the league with an 11 point advantage over runner up, Bath City, to achieve promotion to the Southern League Premier Division.

The strength of the squad was acknowledged by the club during the summer as all of the previous season's professional players were retained, and the two amateurs, Bill Byrne and Chris Kinnear also re-signed, despite offers to both from other Clubs.

It also gave Manager Eddie Presland the opportunity to stamp his mark on the team in the style of play that was to be adopted.

In June 1974 it was announced in the local papers that Wealdstone were to play a 4-2-4 formation for their first season in the senior league *"to give full reign to their free scoring forwards, which was the talk of the league last season"*. Eddie Presland was quoted as saying that there were few additions required – one was to be an additional striker to supplement Bill Byrne, George Duck and John Henderson.

Both Chris Kinnear and Bill Byrne were to sign professional forms before the start of the season, as a number of Pro clubs showed interest. There were three new signings, the Evans twins from Trowbridge, both had impressed in fixtures between the clubs in the previous season, and John Morton who had played in the FA Trophy Final for Dartford, the previous season's Premier League Champions.

With the clubs status as a Limited Company confirmed there were also some changes off the field. For three years the club as a professional side had lost over £25,000. An immediate result of the promotion was additional cost for the playing staff.

To counter this admission was increased by 33%, from 30p to 40p per match, with an additional 10p to transfer to the Stand. A ground season Ticket was introduced, and this was to cost £8.40 and offered a saving of almost £3.00 as it covered the 21 home Southern League and 7 home Midweek League fixtures.

A season Ticket for the Main Stand cost £9.50, and this was a saving of £4.50 over the season.

Shares were also to be made available in the new public Limited Company for the first time. Letters introducing the 'idea' had been distributed at the end of the previous season. The club had received requests from many parts of the Home Counties as well as Devon, Cornwall, Wales and the Midlands. Others had also come from overseas.

Once the Articles of Association had been ratified by the Football Association, the club were able to make 10,000 shares of £1.00 available to the public.

As the new season got underway, a comfortable 7-1 win over Bury Town in the league cup showed the benefit of the new 4-2-4 system, but this was against weak opposition and in some quarters 'Stones were criticised as people felt a score of 10 or 11 would have been more realistic!

In September it was announced that after a meeting of the Football League in London, there was a very good chance that the following season would see the introduction of a new

National League, expected to be known as the Football Alliance.

The proposal from Wigan Athletic, seconded by Yeovil Town was for a league of 20 clubs, being the top ten each from the Northern and Southern Premier Leagues. This was seen as another incentive for 'Stones to do well in the league, as it was expected to be a stepping stone for promotion to the Football League itself.

Financially the new league was to benefit clubs as it was expected to be included on the Football Pools and therefore would earn revenue for its competing teams.

By October the team's form had dropped – no more so than a 1-0 defeat to Finchley in the FA Trophy showed, and when 'Stones dropped three points in five days new signings became imminent.

By the end of November after such a good start 'Stones found themselves in 7th place in the league.

At the start of December, 'Stones were to go on a mid season (social rather than football) tour to the Channel Islands, where they did play one match against First Tower FC. This match was to feature another 'signing' albeit a surprising one, as Chairman David Martle played the entire match at sweeper as 'Stones cruised to a 4-1 win.

It was the start of improved form for the team as a whole. A run of six games unbeaten over the New Year period lifted 'Stones to fifth, and back with an outside chance of honours. The run extended to nine games until consecutive defeats followed the departure of John McCormick, who retired to become a publican.

February saw another change and an addition to the Wealdstone Club, with the first appearance of Wealdstone Ladies. Their first competitive match resulted in a 3-2 win away from home against Weston in the Lee Valley League. Kim Rafferty (2) and Lynn Irvine the scorers.

Wealdstone finished the season with another series of wins, this time not enough to challenge but enough to see the side finish a creditable eighth in the league, although the 'carrot' of the Football Alliance was not set to start for a few more years.

In mid April, 'Stones hosted a testimonial match for Eric Burgess, against Wolverhampton Wanderers;

Wolves came in strength to Lower Mead with a team, which would have steamrollered most league sides, so what they did to Wealdstone mattered little. A crowd of over 4000 turned up to see the testimonial game.

What had been expected to be a normal testimonial turned out to be a cracking match. Indeed, it seemed as though wolves had come to get two First Division points by the way they played.

What was most astounding was Wolves' discipline. Even when they were 4-1 up the boss (Bill McGarry) was calling for more and even more in this comparatively friendly game. And they went looking for them, this of course is professional soccer at its best!

Wealdstone did well. They raised their game, helped by the evergreen jimmy Greaves, who still has lots to offer in midfield, and quick burster Mark Lazarus. Roy McKenzie had no chance with the four goals put past him in the first half, and Wealdstone's only reply was from the penalty spot, when, after being hauled down by Palmer, Duck rose from the floor to send a fine shot past Phil Parkes.

Adriaan Eglite replaced Bobby Moss for Wealdstone in the second half, and Duck brought 'Stones back into the game with a wonderful header from a Mark Lazarus cross. Eric Burgess also brought cheers from the crowd when he came on himself ten minutes from the end, but then Kenny Hibbet settled it scoring the fifth with only a minute to go.

The club looked again for ways to cut costs during the close season, and also for ways of improving the fitness of the squad as a whole, especially when not directly involved in the first team. To this end it was decided to introduce a Youth Team to play in the Chiltern Youth League.

This would aid the development of the younger players and with an 'over-age' rule it also meant that the club could play a first team squad member returning from injury or suspension. For the supporters, it also meant that there was football at Lower Mead every week for those who didn't travel 'away'.

Bert Dyke and Les MacDonald were to take on the duties of Manager and Coach (although Eddie Presland remained in overall control) and the squad was to train with the first team twice a week.

In June there was a Seventy Fifth Anniversary Dinner of the club, attended by over 200 people. Ted Crocker, then Secretary of the Football Association complimented the club on their achievement in the Premier Division after only three years as a professional club.

The new season started with a practice match away to Boston and in front of a large number of travelling fans, a disappointing Wealdstone side with only one new face (John Lewis, signed from Romford) was beaten 4-2. Things failed to improve despite the return of a number of key players as 'Stones made a stumbling start to the new campaign.

A draw at home to Harrow Borough followed by defeat at Hendon saw 'Stones eliminated pre-season from the Middlesex Charity Cup. A home draw with Stourbridge was followed by a 2-1 victory over Maidstone but a 2-0 defeat away to Dunstable was reported with a quote from Manager Eddie Presland;

I was disgusted. Words fail me. This was the worst performance I can remember, especially in the second half and the first was not much better. Had I paid to see this rubbish I would have asked for my money back.

There was some improvement though and also a victory for the Youth Team in their first match, a 3-1 win over Pitshangar but it was the FA Cup rather than the league that was to bring better fortune to Wealdstone.

The FA Cup record in recent years had not been impressive, Wealdstone often losing to competition from lower leagues, and this year a draw at home to Woking was little more than was expected. The following Tuesday, the replay seemed to be going the same way;

The time was 8:50pm and Wealdstone were 3-1 down, being outplayed by a side not even their best friends would call competent, and they were just 15 minutes from being bundled out of the FA Cup by an Isthmian side that have not won in ten games.

By 9:05, Wealdstone had somehow (and it was not abundantly clear how) drawn level and were hanging on for dear life. At 9:06pm a glorious header from Woking's No 10 Steve Cosham, one of the best players on view, was passing just under Wealdstone's cross bar when Ray Fulton flung himself across the goal to head clear. More was still to come as with three minutes remaining, Cosham thundered a shot against the post.

This then was the backcloth to an incredible cup replay at Kingfield. A match which Wealdstone were never in front until extra time, when their superior stamina told, and Woking, torn apart by some cruel luck, ran out of heart.

This was Ray Fulton's finest hour. With deference to the rest of the team the final score could well have been Woking 3 Ray Fulton 5, for the ginger haired Wealdstone midfield man scored two superb goals, kicked one off the line in the first half and then kept his side in the cup with the header at the end! He also made a superb goal for Jim Godfrey in the last quarter of extra time.

In point of fact, the game probably hinged on the substitution of Paul Fairclough for Adriaan Eglite with 22 minutes to go, Jim Godfrey moving up front. It was an immediate success with Fairclough's presence giving extra depth to the defence.

Woking of course only had themselves to blame for not going through to the next round, as, indeed had Wealdstone had the same number of chances we should have been indignant at anything less than 5–1.

Twice in the first ten minutes Alan Morton fluffed chances but the disturbing aspect of the first half was that although Wealdstone played some reasonable stuff, they weren't creating chances – in fact throughout the whole game they rarely got two strikers in the box at the same time.

It was no surprise when Woking went ahead on twenty minutes, Morton striking a magnificent goal from the edge of the box, yet totally against the run of play, Fulton scored an equally good equaliser five minutes later, belting in a cross from Kinnear, out by the right corner flag. Ten minutes later and Woking regained the lead through Cosham, who shot through a ruck of players, the half ended with Wealdstone having only really set up the one chance that Fulton accepted.

The ignominy of inglorious defeat quickly loomed for Wealdstone in the second half when Morton and Cosham combined splendidly down the left and Cosham was brought down by Godfrey in full flight, the same [player scoring from the resulting penalty.

At this point Wealdstone were in total disarray and few in the crowd would have given a brass farthing for their chances of survival, but full credit to them for coming back midway through the half, when they appeared to have resigned themselves to their fate.

Byrne led the revival with 14 minutes to go when he swivelled neatly just inside the box to lash a right footer past Spittle and almost immediately afterwards Fulton had the large Wealdstone contingent invading the pitch when, with his "donkey" right foot, he shot through a crowded goalmouth to bring the scores level.

Midway through the first half of extra time, Godfrey, now leading the attack, was brought down from behind and Duck gave Spittle no chance from the spot, so after 98 minutes play, Wealdstone were in front for the first time.

The match was finally settled in the 115th minute. Fulton, who since the substitution of Fairclough had dropped back to left back, overlapped superbly and took the ball to the bye-line before crossing low and hard and Godfrey brilliantly hooked the ball just wide of the goalkeeper's left hand and inside the post.

That Wealdstone failed so dramatically to really take apart a very poor side is another indication of their appalling inconsistency. For some strange reason, too many players have too many off days, and this was certainly the case on Tuesday.

Wealdstone; Morton, Kinnear, O'Kane, Godfrey, McCormick, Fulton, Lewis, Moss, Byrne, Duck, Eglite, Sub; Fairclough.

The following round saw 'Stones win 2–0 at Burnham and this was followed with a 2–0 victory over Dagenham which went someway to allay the memory of the early defeats in previous years.

During the cup run there was some improvement and consistency in the league form, highlighted when Wealdstone again 'rose to the occasion' against top opposition, beating high flying Weymouth at Lower Mead by 3–1, when they could have been 4-0 up at half time.

The next opponents in the FA Cup were Sussex County League side, Southwick, the victors going through to the first round proper of the competition. They had already performed above their status in beating Southern League Division One sides Guilford and Dorking and Basingstoke. Their run was to end though as Wealdstone beat them by 3–1 to enter the draw where they were paired with Football League side, Aldershot Town.

Early November saw Wealdstone in action in the FA Trophy as well, and a 4–0 win over Oxford extended their unbeaten run to 10 games. The improvement in league form had seen 'Stones rise from the bottom of the league table to 15th with 11 points from 11 games, 4 wins and 4 defeats, and having both scored and conceded 18 goals.

The unbeaten run was to end in dramatic style at Aldershot, as the home side ran out victors by 4-3

Marauding Wealdstone gave Aldershot the fright of their third division lives with a rampaging, defiant performance that took them to the brink of an upset in the enthralling FA Cup-tie. Matching the home side for long periods in every department, pace, skill, power and fitness,

'Stones only finally failed because their opponents were that little bit more deadly in the six yard box. In fact the margin between the two sides was so fractional that if 'Stones had not lost centre half John McCormick with injury at half time, then the second half seven goal spree could so easily have gone their way.

As it was 'Stones, who burned with determination and fire every time Aldershot seemed to have stamped their hopes into ashes, proved on the day that they can live with the best that the lower reaches of the league can throw at them.

Having frustrated Aldershot throughout the first half they fell behind after 55 minutes, sprung back within two minutes when George Duck equalised, were stunned again by a two goal in four minute burst, hauled themselves back into contention with a John Lewis goal, conceded a disputed fourth, but refusing to lie down, grabbed a third through George Duck, before in the final moments reducing the 5,221 crowd to desperate whistling for time.

Their worst moments came in the opening minutes when tentative work at the back let in Shots to test Morton with a series of blistering drives. Any thought that 'Stones would be pulverised faded as Ray Fulton, Bobby Moss and John Lewis crunched into every 50-50 ball in the middle and Paul Fairclough, John Watson and Chris Kinnear got a grip on Shots' mobile front four.

Ominously too for the home side George Duck and Bill Byrne began winning the ball in the air of Richardson and Jopling. Having weathered the early storm, the visitors began playing the cleverer, more intricate football against their more direct opponents.

Both defences creaked and moaned, and Moss, polished and versatile, headed just wide from a corner after a quarter of an hour and then five minutes later, he turned defender to clear off the line.

As the game ground to a stalemate, Aldershot suddenly turned the screw in a bid to gain a half time lead, when after 38 minutes Bell skated down the left and whipped over a wicked lob which seemed to deceive Morton until he arched his back and plucked the ball out of the air at the second attempt. Kinnear too joined the aerobatics by spectacularly heading clear from under Howarth's nose as the prolific striker closed in for the kill.

At half time, Adriaan Eglite came on up front and Bill Byrne stepped into the breach at the back and this change may have been crucial. 'Stones began the second half with a flourish when Duck forced Johnson to go full stretch to grasp his arching header and then he saw the keeper turn aside a perfectly struck drive, but it was Aldershot that opened the scoring after Byrne stopped a counter attack at the expense of a corner. As the kick came over Morton under pressure could only punch the ball out to Richardson who rifled it past Fulton on the goal line.

Unbowed, 'Stones bounced back after 57 minutes when Moss was chopped down and Duck confidently sent Johnson the wrong way with the penalty. The dream of a draw evaporated when Fairclough upended Warnock in the opposite area after 64 minutes and although Morton got both hands to the penalty he could not stop it screaming in.

Aldershot surged to an apparently unassailable lead after 67 minutes when their tactics of testing 'Stones with long raking crosses paid off as the ball evaded Byrne and flew over to Howarth to bullet his header into goal.

Back came Wealdstone and just as it seemed Aldershot may take control Duck fired the ball forward to Lewis who strode through an inviting hole in the defence and clipped the ball past Johnson. This badly rattled Aldershot who huffed and puffed in the face of the non-leaguers battling fight back and they were lucky to clinch the tie with ten minutes left when Morton appeared to be impeded as he went to gather the ball before it spun out for Howarth to poke it over the line.

Somehow Wealdstone plumbed the depths of their talent to retrieve that hammer blow when Eglite made tracks down the right and crossed deep for Moss to connect with a header Johnson couldn't hold, allowing duck to make it 4-3.

Wealdstone; Morton, Kinnear, Fairclough, McCormack, (sub; Eglite 45mins), Watson, Moss, Lewis, Fulton, Duck, Byrne, Henderson

It was a tremendous performance from 'Stones. They had come so close to causing a real FA Cup shock, but one certainty was that no-one involved could have given any more. The reception from the fans and in the press celebrated an excellent performance. The club also received a letter of thanks from the Hampshire Police, congratulating the club on the excellent conduct and enthusiasm shown by the fans at the Recreation Ground!

The following Tuesday evening, Gravesend were the visitors to Lower Mead and they were to catch the brunt of Wealdstone's disappointment as the home side recorded their best win as a professional club in a 7–1 thrashing, taking a three goal lead inside fifteen minutes.

The league performances had become more consistent and continued to bring points, allowing 'Stones to rise to 5th place with a win over Tonbridge in front of 1200 fans, but they were beaten by Leatherhead in the FA Trophy losing the replay 1-0 after a 2–2 draw at Lower Mead.

As the New Year started though, the inconsistency returned to a Wealdstone side that had little bar respectability to play for and a series of defeats saw the club slip quickly down the table. By the end of January, a defeat at Bedford Town by 2–1 had the Harrow Observer considering Wealdstone to be reasonable relegation candidates.

Having had a run of six wins, four draws and three defeats in thirteen league games leading to the Tonbridge victory and fifth place, 'Stones had managed only one win and seven defeats in the following eight league games.

At the end of February, 'Stones were languishing third from bottom in the league table and the financial situation was limiting the money available to strengthen the side.

Not for the first time however, the Supporters Club were able to step in and help by a donation to the club of £400 which went someway towards allowing the club to sign Danny Light from Dover.

It didn't seem to be enough though as by mid March, another run of defeats had seen Wealdstone slip to 2nd from bottom and they looked almost certain to be relegated with a series of difficult fixtures remaining.

Even Manager Eddie Presland had had enough. At Maidstone his patience finally snapped and he gave the team "the biggest rollicking since I took over" he said "I told them they were cheating me, the fans, each other and I said things I didn't think I'd ever say to people but it had got to the stage where it had to be completely honest.

These are the same players that did so well in the first half of the season – they are the same players but they have not been playing as they can. They have not been giving it all they could"

It had an immediate impact, surprising both second placed Maidstone and a number of Wealdstone fans who heard it, but the team all but pulverised the home side, unluckily only coming home with a point after a 1–1 draw. The Maidstone manager stating that his player had fouled John Morton in the 'Stones goal when scoring the equaliser, and he felt that 'Stones had done more than enough to win the match.

Another draw against Bedford and a win by 2-1 over Yeovil closed the gap on those above, but with eight matches to go, 'Stones were still 21st in the table but a 4-1 defeat in the relegation derby at Hillingdon Borough finally saw the patience of the board snap and the hard decision to dismiss Eddie Presland, who had been with the club for five years as player and then manager, was made.

Adriaan Eglite
Player 1974 - 1976

I came over from Holland where I had played for Ajax and I had been a Dutch Youth International at U18's. I also played for Ilford, Kingstonian and Hertford Town in England where I remain. I was only with the club for part of two seasons, but I enjoyed it. I remember the headlines after my first evening match - "Coco the Clown turns on his tricks for the 'Stones!"

There were some great characters, particularly John (Willie) Watson and Bill Byrne and some big matches. Those against Wimbledon were always big games!

Just one question. Why did we always have to play Dover away on a cold wet winter's evening in December?

Paul Fairclough
Player 1972 - 1976

Some off the field memories - 'Stones had a Director called Harry Benjamin, and I was a school teacher at Roxeth Manor school, Press officer Colin Pope also had some involvement in a Travel Agents. Harry worked out and excellent deal for us to fly from Heathrow - all the kids looked identical in matching Track Suits - we were met in Amsterdam, and Harry put us into a Hostel, right smack in the middle of the Red light district.

There were matches organised and visits to the Ajax stadiums everything, but as you can imagine it got a bit out of hand with all these 13 and 14 year olds staying in the middle of the red light area. We wended up being kicked out of the hotel the night before we were due to leave.

I was convinced that was going to be the end of my teaching career. I certainly called Harry some names. There was a great bond of secrecy between the people on that trip never to tell what really happened, so this may bring back more than a few memories!

I went to Wealdstone because I was teaching at the Manor, it wasn't as if I joined the club and then found a job. Harrow Borough never even came into the equation, despite the location, because they were just a small club. Wealdstone were the big side.

When the weather was bad we used to use a hall - the Territorial Army - for training. The first time we went, Sid Prosser, the Manager, let us finish off with a game. The first time a window got broken and the Commander gave Sid a hard time about it. We all got told off and told never to do it again...........

Lo and behold, the next time we came down they'd covered the windows to stop them getting broken, but sure enough, another window did get broken. By this time Sid had steam coming out of his ears. He decided his next plan was to deck the whole hall out with camouflage nets a yard in from the walls, just to stop the damage, but there was still a gap. Sid had been down there hours fitting them all and it came to the game.

Two chairs for posts at each goal and I really belted the ball at this chair. It went underneath the netting and hit this huge clock and smashed it! Well, we all ran - every player ran out of the hall and ran all the way back to the club. By the time we got back it had become a bit of a joke and as we got back the lads picked me up on their shoulders and carried me into the club!. Sid found out and called me into the office and cleaned me, he called me all the names he could think of.

We used to have some parties as well. When I was living in Ealing, I'd arranged a party - I was single and I'd laid on a load of women as well. It was a bit lively. Chic Brodie was so excited about the party, he got to the pub early that afternoon and got stoned out of his head - he collapsed inside the toilet and we had to break the door down to get him out!

The party was a great success as you can imagine, but my girlfriend at the time found out and she went round and found out which girls where there, who they had been with and all sorts.

At the next home game, she came down to the ground and went into the bar and told all the players wives and girlfriends about this party.

We went out and played this game, terrified. All the wives and girlfriend s were ashen faced in the front of the stand, and none of the players would come within twenty yards of it. We played the whole game with no width at all just so the players didn't have to go over by where all the wives and girlfriends were sitting........

Terry Dyson used to have a party piece with a coin. He do it successfully all the time. He'd get a coin and flick it up in the air, catch it on his foot, flick it up onto his chest and then slide it down either into his blazer or shirt pocket!

John Watson and Ray Fulton were outrageous. The Terrible Twins! Some of the things those two got up to, and Ray going everywhere with a ventriloquists dummy, I'm sure he was round the twist.

There was one game where John played fullback. He went down the line and got fouled by this guy. He then chased him the length of the field and 'tackled' him. The guy is on the floor and John has picked him up by the hair as Ray has run over. It was always the same if you fouled one the other would even the score. Willie is still the same now with that glint of madness in his eye.............

I got scared at Wealdstone too, I played sweeper alongside John McCormick - this opponent was giving us a hard time both physically and verbally, and John was getting quite animated about it. Anyway he said to me "look, when there's a corner, just stand next to him, and when the corner comes over just stick your elbow in his mouth" - I wasn't that type of player at all but when the corner came over I just did what I was told. There was a crack, teeth came out and this guy collapsed on the floor. "Well done" said John. We played them again a few months later and he didn't come near me!

There are fond memories of Wealdstone. It was the first time I won any major awards. The people were always good to us as well, Dave Martle, Colin Pope and all. I went on another one of Harry Benjamin's dodgy deals, a holiday to Gibraltar. I ended up playing football over there and getting stones and all sorts thrown at us from the stands...........

The football was good too.

The new manager was named as Geoff Coleman formerly of Nuneaton Borough. This was expected to introduce a new era of professionalism both on and off the field. More importantly, the immediate concern was to ensure that Wealdstone were not relegated.

Wealdstone gained points in a number of matches but with so few to play and so little time it was always going to be very difficult for Coleman to change the club's fortunes.

It seemed at the end of April that things had reached an all time low, when in a match described as *bringing the reputation of the game to its knees in a malice ridden shambles*, Wealdstone lost 4–1 at Wimbledon, three players from each side were sent off.

Bobby Moss, John Watson and Danny Light were sent off with Wimbledon's Glen Aitken, Selwyn Rice and John Leslie. All were dismissed for fighting, Moss and Aitken for a pointless exchange in the 44th minute and the others in a brawl that involved a dozen players fifteen minutes from time.

'Stones had taken an early lead in front of the 2,181 fans and a number of league officials, present to award the Championship Shield to the home club.

Even Wimbledon Manager Allen Batsford became involved, arguing with the Linesman as players continued their 'battle'. It was said to be a fitting epitaph to a graveyard of a season for Wealdstone that after a first half where they had played well, despite the dismissals, the second half saw them tamely give up.

Worse was to come for the supporters as the coach was attacked on the way home, and a number of the windows were smashed and for the team as the result meant that Wealdstone would finish fourth from bottom – in a relegation position – with 33 points from 42 matches, but they would have to wait until the league AGM in June to find out their fate, dependent on the futures of other clubs.

Dave Bassett
Opponent 1966-74 and subsequently a Football League and Premiership Manager

In the early seventies when I was at Wimbledon, Johnny Watson and I had a bit of a barney and were both sent off and I think we had a bit of a go in the tunnel as well but it was soon forgotten. I still see Johnny - he often picks me up in his cab in London and he never charges me so he can't hold a grudge. It was always a battle - neither of us giving any ground nor expecting any - we used to kick the crap out of each other on the pitch but we'd always have a beer afterwards!

I do remember once, we were playing at Plough Lane, Wealdstone winning 1-0, and as we were coming out of the penalty box George Duck put his arm round me to as though to 'commiserate' and he punched me straight under the chin, then he kept hold of me and carried me to the half way line before he let go so no one knew what had happened!!

John Morton
Player 1974 - 1977

I joined from Dartford after we had won the Southern league Championship and were runner up in the Trophy. Eddie Presland signed me and of course his coach was the unforgettable Terry Dyson.

They complimented each other very well. I remember after Bill Nicholson left Spurs that the TV showed clips of the famous double side. One clip showed Terry scoring and Kenneth Wolstenholme came out with the phrase "Dyson, what a player!". That evening, at training, every time someone did something special "What a player" resounded around Lower Mead.

There were some great players there and some memorable matches. One, a 1-0 win over Wimbledon prior to their great FA Cup run when over 3,000 packed Lower Mead.

There were the FA Cup games against Aldershot and Reading where we had two players sent off and lost 1-0 to an awful side. It's interesting that in the recent book 'Robin Friday, the greatest footballer you never saw' that match isn't recorded. I remember it well, as on collecting a ball at the near post Robin Friday ran up my back and over my head. He was merely chided by that famous referee Eric Read.

One game I missed through injury was the match at Plough Lane when the home side were to be presented with the Championship.

All the League and local dignitaries were there to see both sides have three players sent off and a very open 8-a-side match ensued. The battles between Dave Bassett and John Watson were legendary.

I made a lot of friends and I'm still in touch with a number of players from Wealdstone and my non-league days. Its one aspect of the game that I cherish.

Wealdstone's place in the Premier League was retained by re-election more because of the changes at Dunstable than by their own merits, but it at least allowed Geoff Coleman to start to build for the following season.

The first announcement was of the 'pre-season' programme which would see 'Stones play at home to Torquay United, Luton Town and Croydon and travel to Leytonstone before the league season got underway.

John Hitchenor
Supporter since 1975

A Manchester City supporter from an early age, when at work in London I used to support them when they visited the Metropolis. This meant that I had several hours to fill in after Saturday morning working.

My boss at that time said "John, I can't understand you spending all this time waiting around when you could be watching Wealdstone". He said it on a number of occasions and eventually I went along to Lower Mead in January 1975. I made note in my diary that Wealdstone played Grantham in the Southern League Premier Division. They won 1–0.

Whilst not giving up on 'City, I managed a few more Wealdstone matches that season and went along to Aldershot following a run in the FA Cup. My diary recorded that the ground was very countrified, plenty of trees.

Wealdstone acquitted themselves well, finally losing 4–3, Duck (2) and Lewis the scorers. They lost the centre half at half time, injured and Byrne dropped back to fill in. I stood among the Aldershot supporters and they were very impressed by our 'non-league' standard of play, even though we were trailing throughout the match............

Sacha Loban
Regular Supporter 1960 – 1974, now in Singapore.

Hello Wealdstone fans everywhere....

thanks to the wonders of cyberspace. I can attempt to rekindle a glorious love affair that started around 1960 when I was six...my first visit to Lower Mead!

Won't bore y'all with details/life history etc right now...But as kid turned to boy etc. Wealdstone FC became a passion. I was a regular at Lower Mead between about 1960-1974...moved on abroad etc. currently in Singapore!

I'm really full of admiration for you people though against all odds etc! But WFC fans were always a bit special.. Anyone on any of the 5 coachloads we took to BIshop Auckland 1965? Oh No - it's flashback time. I see it now...

The extraordinary case of Wycombe Wanderers fans circa 1967. Away fans; coachloads of grannies/aunties and grandpas with thermos flasks and travel rugs, Home fans; heavy duty 'skins' with a few regular geezers. What a shock at my first visit to Loakes Park!!

What is it about the Southwest. (nothing to do??) Why were Bath City and Yeovil people always looking for a fight?

Gravesend and Northfleet away. Last match of season. Massed ranks of WFC fans in their "kop" end and a great rendition of "You'll Never Walk Alone" as we clinch promotion. The "choir" was 7 deep!.

Snowballs v John Swannell and Hendon FC. on Boxing Day in the sixties. Cup marathons.(Hertford Town !!)...

OK..OK..I'll stop...but please appreciate that now that I've found others with the same disease I need to "testify"

Oh yes...The Bishop Auckland Supporters club provided us with a cooked meal when we arrived! Keep your Euro Super Leagues. - a meat and tater pie a bottle of stout and a bit of banter with the Geordies!

All best to WFC fans everywhere. Keep the Faith!

Graham Smith
Supporter since 1961

I started going to Lower Mead in January 1961. I cannot remember which was the first game, but it could well have been the Middlesex Senior Cup game against Chalfont National when Wealdstone won 8-0 or the London Senior Cup match against Kingstonian, this time 'Stones turning out 7-0 victors.

Wealdstone were in the Athenian League then and there were some great players at the club at the time - England International Charlie Townsend, Welsh International Viv Evans and Matt Farrell. In March of that year 'Stones beat Harrow Town (to be renamed Harrow Borough) 6-2 in the Middlesex Charity Cup. In 1962 Hugh Lindsay joined and he had one of the hardest shots in non-league football scoring many great goals. Following on from Peter Parfitt he was also a good cricketer, playing in the league for the Kenton Cricket Club First XI.

The greatest memory of the sixties came on Saturday April 16th. 1966 as 'Stones reached the Final of the F.A. Amateur Cup.

My cousin's husband took me to Wembley in his car, unfortunately he was a Hendon supporter. Wealdstone, the underdogs, won 3-1 after being 1-0 down and getting two goals in the last three minutes. Bobby Childs who has now passed away scored twice with Bernie Bremer getting the other.

The whole day seemed to go so fast and I was proud to have been there. I remember going to the Dominion Cinema that evening as the team were presenting the cup, it was a very emotional evening and everyone was so happy.

A couple of years later and Colin Franks was in the Wealdstone line up before he went on to play for Watford. Wealdstone also had the Tottenham player Cliff Jones who was in the "Double" side and then a year later his team mate at Spurs Terry Dyson signed. These were among the biggest signings in Wealdstone's history at the time, as the club was still Amateur.

Then George Duck arrived at Lower Mead and became one of the most prolific scorers 'Stones have ever had.

In January 1973 another massive signing, but it was only for a couple of games and that was the ex England and Fulham player Johnny Haynes. I remember him being 5 moves ahead of everybody else.

It was around this time that I got friendly with the physio Jim Spark and was allowed in the dressing room to help and see what went on, and this I suppose was really just the start of what I was going to do in later years.

I remember one game at Lower Mead in February 1974 when 'Stones played Hastings in the F.A. Trophy. The referee had just awarded a third penalty to the home side when a Hastings player protested so much that he was sent off and the manager ordered his whole team off the pitch. After about five minutes they went back and George Duck was allowed to score his third penalty. Wealdstone won 5-2 with George Duck getting four (three from the spot). This was the season that they won the Southern League (South).

A very sad day in February 1975 when arriving at Lower Mead as usual I asked for my pass that Jim Spark used to leave by the gate for me, but this time the pass was not there.

I went through the turnstile and tried to look for Jim but I could not find him anywhere. I asked an Official by the dressing room only to be told that while he was helping his landlady into an ambulance the previous Thursday he collapsed and died, I was devastated!!. That was the second death in the Club that week as John Murray died a few days earlier in the week.

The 1976–1977 season started with similar form to the previous season, which could at best be described as 'mixed'.

The first win came on the last Saturday in August, a 2-0 victory away to Margate, when the club only had twelve fit players to chose from after a speight of early season injuries added to the unavailability of Watson, Moss and Light after the sendings off in the match at Wimbledon the previous year.

To cap it all, Manager Geoff Coleman was also missing, having just gone under the surgeon's knife at Northwick Park Hospital. He had torn an Achilles tendon on the previous Thursday while training with the squad.

Perhaps it was an omen of the season to come as, despite a good pre-season and an early away win (it had taken 30 weeks

Wealdstone in Minehead

As an Old Wealdstonian, I am constantly reminded of that fact each time I visit the toilets in Minehead.

Scrawled across the wall above my head on an otherwise clean wall, are letters one foot high and taking up to eight feet in length, sprayed in green paint, "Wealdstone Rules OK."

H. J. R. CROSS
Chapel Court
Porlock,
Somerset.

to record an away win the previous season) the next three matches brought a 2–1 defeat at Minehead, a 2–0 defeat at home to Bath and then an embarrassing 5–1 defeat at Wimbledon, although this year both sides finished with a full compliment of players.

Another similarity with the previous year was another big victory, not quite a record this time, but in midweek after the defeat at Wimbledon, A P Leamington were the unfortunate visitors to Lower Mead, suffering a defeat by 7–2, although none of the Wealdstone 'strikers' managed to get on the score-sheet, the goals coming from Ray Fulton (2), Bill Byrne, Chris Kinnear, Danny Light and Bobby Moss (2) scoring the goals.

The goals continued to come the following Saturday as well as Wealdstone returned to the FA Cup trail with a 5–1 win over Clapton. In the league, another defeat was suffered at Nuneaton, though this was followed by a 4–2 victory over league leaders Telford, Player Manager Geoff Hurst and all.

It was another former international centre forward that 'undid' the 'Stones in the following game as Derek Dougan's Kettering side won 3–0. Again, the FA Cup was to figure highly in Wealdstone's season and victories over Kingstonian and Dulwich, both 2–0 sandwiched a league defeat at Burton Albion, the home side featuring Ian Moore, the third international striker faced in consecutive matches!

The cup was high on the agenda for the Youth Team at this time, and one tie recorded probably the highest aggregate of any 'match' involving the club – their FA Youth Cup-tie with Kingstonian took three matches before Kingstonian won, the scores being 5–5, then 3–3 and finally 3–2.

A run of better form followed the victory over Dulwich with a 3–1 win in the FA Trophy over Wellingborough, a similar scoreline in the league match against Dover and then a battling 3–2 win in the fourth qualifying round of the FA Cup over Bishops Stortford. A 1 –1 draw at Atherstone meant the 'Stones went into the match against Reading in the FA Cup 1st Round proper on a five game unbeaten run.

One maddening moment of unprecedented hesitation cost rampaging Wealdstone this intriguing and at times unbelievable FA Cup-tie against Reading.

Poor Wealdstone! They saw an hour's superiority checked by a gift-wrapped goal and finally killed off by the sending off of two defenders within a frantic minute. For nearly 60 minutes Wealdstone mauled their Football League hosts with precision and skilled play, then in the 59th minute tragedy struck.

Defender Alan Fursden was brushed off the ball in his own penalty area by Robin Friday and although the ball beat goalkeeper John Morton, it was easily blocked on the line by Lennie Prince, but the Wealdstone player literally froze and John Murray rushed in to crash tackle and the ball bounced into the net.

This was only the beginning of the end of a nightmare, although the Lower Mead lads received an insight when Dave Parratt was stretchered off after only ten minutes to be replaced by John Arnold.

With a goal under their belt Reading began to unloosen and 'Stones countered this with new determination and grit to ensure a frantic, hair raising last half hour. Watson was booked for a trip on Friday and Fursden followed him into the book for a similar offence. Then he felled Hiron – a foul made to look more serious than it was – and he was shown the red card. With the 5,767 crowd baying for blood, Arnolds who had been booked earlier foolishly launched himself at Carnaby and he too saw red.

Astonishingly, Wealdstone's nine men carried the game to retreating Reading in the last ten minutes. Indeed Duck and Moss both had chances to snatch a shock equaliser in injury time.

It was not to be however and Wealdstone's involvement in the competition was ended. For the second year beaten by Football League opposition by one goal away from home. Like the previous year, league form was still indifferent and as the New Year started, Wealdstone found themselves in seventeenth position with 13 points from 16 games.

At the start of February, form had not improved and for the second time in under a year, Wealdstone sacked their Manager.

This time, Coach Alan Fogarty was appointed as a Caretaker Manager. One point from the next two league matches indicated how difficult a task lay ahead as for the second year in succession Wealdstone were threatened with relegation.

In mid February, 'Stones found themselves with 15 points from 22 matches, fourth from bottom of the table and as in the previous season, two defeats and two draws from the next four matches saw 'Stones slip into the bottom two. Even their first win in three months failed to lift the side as it was followed by another two defeats before George Duck's 200th goal for the club secured a 2–1 win over Burton Albion.

This almost started a mini revival by recent standards as 'Stones then won two and drew one of their next four matches to offer a glimmer of hope that relegation could be avoided.

A number of the youth players were also drafted into the squad and this did inadvertently set another record, as, using the 'overage player' rule, Wealdstone's youth team coach came out of retirement 24 years after making his first appearance for the club. Not only did Viv Evans play in the match at Lower Mead against Cambridge City Youth, but also he scored two goals in the 80th and 86th minutes, helping gain a fine 4–1 victory!

Another two wins and two draws from four matches improved Wealdstone's chances of escaping relegation and Premier League status was finally assured with a 2–1 win away to Chelmsford City in a match that saw the home side's relegation confirmed.

It was not the most memorable of victories it was the result of two first half own goals and a penalty save by Chris Lightfoot, the home side's only response an 85th minute consolation from Jimmy Greaves. It was enough for Alan Fogarty to be awarded a contract for the following season, Wealdstone eventually finishing ninth from bottom of the Southern League, only 'safe' by four points.

The close season saw 'Stones announce that they were to run a

Reserve side the following season, competing in the Suburban League and that this would replace the Youth Team although Belmont United were 'adopted' as the clubs representatives in the Chiltern Youth league. It was felt that more senior players could develop at this level with the addition of some of the better youth players and that this would support the first team better. Terry Woodrow, a former manager of Bishops Stortford was duly appointed Assistant Manager and he was to take responsibility for the reserve team.

On the playing side, Fred Barwick was the only significant signing in the close season as manager Alan Fogarty brought the strength up to 14 – when asked he said that was all that the club could afford and at least their was now a reserve team to 'make up the numbers' but the injuries had stated to take their toll before a ball had been kicked. When the players turned up at Hamilton's Brush Works for the first pre-season training session, the gates were locked. John Watson climbed over to find the groundsman and on climbing back, stood on a football and he twisted his knee, damaging the ligaments!

By September there had been a better start in the league than in recent seasons but there were still problems behind the scenes.

In mid September Terry Woodrow was to leave the club after a 'clash of personalities' between himself and Manager Alan Fogarty and Tony Caruana was appointed his successor.

It came in a period of some stability on the field as Wealdstone had an 11 match unbeaten run in all competitions up to mid November, all leading up to the FA Cup-tie at home (for the first time to league opposition) against Hereford United. It was to be a very one-sided tie, Hereford having numerous chances to win the match but a battling 'Stones team thwarted them at every quarter. The replay the following Wednesday evening at Edgar Street was a different matter.

Brilliant Wealdstone wiped out the shock of conceding a goal after 86 seconds to pull off a magnificent giant killing, defeating third division Hereford United on their own ground on Wednesday evening.

The Southern League club looked set for a hiding when Kevin Sheedy netted for Hereford with their first serious attack, but they came back in tremendous style to book a second round home tie with Fourth Division Reading, making the second round for the first time in the club's history.

Jubilant Wealdstone manager Alan Fogarty said afterwards "I am absolutely over the moon. The boys played their hearts out and thoroughly deserved to win. We won on merit. The goals were superb and I'll be buying everyone a well earned drink on the way home!" John Sillett, the Hereford manager said, "It was a nightmare. I have never been so deflated in my life"

Wealdstone stuck to their guns to extend their unbeaten run to 15 games, but Hereford had a dream start after 86 seconds. Stephens collected a throw in and squared the ball to Sheedy who planted a 20-yard drive in the back of the net. The 17 year old Eire youth international came close with a couple of similar efforts on Saturday at Lower Mead and shouldn't really have been given the shooting space here.

Pat Ferry and George Duck were left to plough a furrow in the United half for the first thirty minutes, but Wealdstone gradually grew in confidence and got men forward to support them. Wealdstone rocked their opponents with a goal out of the blue on 37 minutes; Furphy drove a low free kick into the Hereford penalty area and Pat Ferry beat the defence to the ball and turned it into the net.

Five minutes later and the home fans were stunned into silence when Wealdstone grabbed their second goal. Furphy was again involved. He centred deep into the Hereford goalmouth and Bobby Moss out-jumped everybody to head powerfully home.

The Hereford players looked on in disbelief as Ferry scored again for Wealdstone in the 58th minute. Furphy, who had an outstanding game and had a hand in all three goals floated a free kick to the near post and Ferry glanced in a great header that had Mellor beaten all the way.

Hereford threw everything into attack in the last half hour and reduced arrears when Steve Davey turned the ball home from close range in the 66th minute, but Wealdstone held out well under pressure and survived eight corners in the last 15 minutes. Goalkeeper Chris Lightfoot produced some fine saves to foil Davey, Holmes and Carter and the crossbar came to the rescue when Holmes finally beat him.

Wealdstone; Lightfoot, Fursden, Thomas, Parratt, Barwick, Watson, Brinkman, Furphy, (Griffiths 89), Duck, Ferry, Moss.

Pat Ferry
Player 1977 – 1978

I played for Wealdstone in the 77-78 season. The manager was Alan Fogarty (the 'Brummie') who always managed to get to training from Birmingham quicker than Chris Lightfoot, Bobby Moss and I who only travelled across London from Romford.. We found that ironic. So did he........

Chris was my best friend at the time and when he found out that my contract was terminated at Romford, he tried to persuade me to sign for the 'Stones. We taught at the same school, he was Head of PE and I taught Physics and Chemistry. Before I signed I went to see them play at Chelmsford City and I was impressed by the style of play – Chris also saved a penalty from Jimmy Greaves,

Anyway I signed and my first game was against Geoff Hurst and Telford. I came off the bench and scored in our win. The front three was George Duck, Bobby Moss and I – we had a great blend- Ducky was a great goal scorer, Mossy never stopped running and I was the target man setting the play up. It was a pleasure to play with them.

Steve Brinkman impressed me too with his skill wide on the right. Willie Watson (the nutter!) was a great player, a ball winner who could play as well. I enjoyed linking up with him. The defence was good too with Dave Parratt playing centre half after being converted from centre forward. Young Paul Thomas played at right back and Fursdon at left back. We lacked a really good experienced centre back to play alongside Dave Parratt, and there was Keith Furphy, son of the then Watford manager at left midfield. A good player but too greedy!

The FA Cup against Hereford is my greatest memory. We could only draw 0-0 at home in a very competitive match so it was off to Hereford for the replay the following Wednesday.

Chris and I had to go to the headmaster to ask for time off to play. He said whatever happened we were not to tell anyone what the time off was for, he had informed the local authority that it was for "a relevant course!" We got to Wealdstone around lunchtime, Mossy and I went into the Fish and Chip shop and bought lunch and a couple of cokes. It was a long and boring journey, throughout which we both slept most of the way, spread out across two seats each.

The atmosphere when we arrived was tremendous. The crowd was about 12,000 and we were the sacrificial lambs as far as the home supporters were concerned. The game started and after about a minute we were a goal down. Sheedy rifled in a shot from about 25 yards into the bottom corner giving Chris Lightfoot no chance. We slowly got back into the game and just before half time we won a free kick on the right touchline. Keith Furphy took the kick and I met it perfectly on the volley about ten yards out. It was a goal as soon as I hit it.

The second half started with Mellor their goalkeeper playing like an extra sweeper, eagerly coming out to clear any forthcoming danger. Keith Furphy again got the ball on the left wing and crossed it towards the edge of their 18 yard box. It was an inviting ball which I anticipated better than their centre halves and it was a race between Mellor and I to see who would get their first. I won and headed it over him into an empty net.

Mossy later scored the third and I think Davey pulled one back late on to make it 3-2 to us. It made for the longest twelve minutes ever. It was like the Alamo as they besieged our goalmouth with Chris Lightfoot producing a magnificent performance in the dying moments. When the final whistle went in signalled great celebrations and a memorable evening was had by all!

The next day the headline in the Sun read "FERRY, FERRY GOOD! – Teacher scores two and puts Hereford United out of the FA Cup"

After the celebrations of the night before, Chris and I had to return to teaching and the Headmaster was angry because I'd blown his cover!

The following week we were brought back down to earth losing to Harrow Borough in the Trophy, and later that year the Headmaster got his revenge as neither Chris or I could play in the away legs of the Anglo Italian Tournament as the Head wouldn't allow us to take the time off!

Cardew Robinson
Supporter, 1920's to 1980's, (written in 1977)

Two things a man never forgets - his first sweetheart and his first football team. Even if I had moved too far from Lower Mead to ever actually see the 'Stones again, I would, at the drop of a whistle, be able to recall those first seasons.

I am none to keen to pinpoint the first year I actually watched the side, but doubtless some other supporters of long standing will get some idea when I remind them that the colours then were Black & White Hoops, the captain was a half back named Joe Archer.

The 'Stones played in the Spartan League in those days and can't have enjoyed uninterrupted success because I have a vivid memory of a critical voice calling out plaintively "what about some changes, Joe?"

Of course I was very young. Honestly, I caught the football bug very early indeed. Long before I went to Harrow County School, where they played rugby, but the oval ball had little chance with me even though I played and got into the First XV, my heart remained round shaped.

In this I was not alone and we even had an unofficial school soccer team which played several friendlies including one against rival John Lyon. During this period the names I remember from Wealdstone and my Saturday visits were Champion who was a clever wing half, Hannam who was an amusing looking inside left with his long shorts and Hoslins, a tiny terrier of a centre forward, and a marvelous Outside-right called Maskell. I not only remember with gratitude his electric dashing up the wing, but also his abbreviated shorts – a real rarity in those days.

Later came Arthur Loveday and Charlie Bunce. During the war I played a little for my unit and scored the only goal assisted by a land mine. It had fallen on the camp overnight and was taken away and detonated by the bomb disposal boys. The explosion came just as I took a corner and the players of both teams and supporters were almost turned to stone by the noise – as the inswinging ball sailed over the goalkeepers' head into the net! After the war the Polish forwards Mikrut and Wegrzyk were two really brilliant players.

Among the giants of more recent times, I still treasure the images of our internationals, Charlie Townsend and Hugh Lindsay and the games against our local rivals Hendon, especially the blood tingling holiday matches.

As far as the cup, there was an amazing 7–7 scoreline against Dulwich Hamlet, and of course as far as 'Stones supporters are concerned the Amateur Cup took on some of the elusiveness of the Holy Grail. Year after year being defeated at various stages despite the fans having cheered the lads on to a hoped victory, then when we won the semi final at Chelsea, how disappointed I was to be filming in Venice instead of cheering the team on at Wembley.

But we did it didn't we?

And how appropriate it was that we should at last win the cup at the expense of the old enemy, Hendon. Sadly, I recall the subsequent unsuccessful semi final against Chesham – we had all thought it was going to be such a cinch.

What a contrast to recent events. I was one of a not very inspired or inspiring crowd at Lower Mead for the first Hereford match and quite honestly I thought that our chance had gone and that we were more than a little fortunate to get another one, luck and great defence.

When I heard the result of the replay on the car radio I whooped out loud and nearly drove into a wall. I have been thrilled ever since. All those previous frustrating odd goal defeats can now be forgotten – Port Vale, Aldershot and Reading. What an unbelievable opportunity for quick revenge! Lets hope too that the crowd is bigger than the 2,500 at the Hereford game and that it makes a lot more noise because we're proud of the 'Stones aren't we?

The Reading match in the next round was sweet revenge for the defeat the previous year, Wealdstone winning a nail biting tie by 2–1 with goals from Keith Furphy and George Duck.

An official crowd of 4,044 saw Keith Furphy's inswinging corner beat Reading goalkeeper Steve Death on its way straight into the net after five minutes and on 63 minutes George Duck scored from a penalty at the third attempt – the first hit a post and bounced away to ' safety' only for the referee Alan Turvey to indicate an infringement and point again to the spot.

The second nestled in the back of the net but again referee pointed to the spot as he hadn't blown his whistle for the kick to be taken, but thankfully the third (scoring) attempt counted.

Reading then pulled one back almost immediately to ensure a tense last twenty minutes, but Wealdstone held on to victory.

Twenty minutes after the game and with the celebrations in full swing, the draw was made for the next round and Wealdstone's prize was assured with a visit to First Division Queens Park Rangers in the third round.

After the win over Hereford, Wealdstone had lost in the FA Trophy 3-0 to local rivals Harrow Borough to end their unbeaten run. There had, in common with previous seasons, again been a dip in the league form after the cup exploits as well.

This continued after the Reading match and was highlighted at Christmas when they lost twice to Hillingdon Borough, once in the league cup and once in the league, before a Jimmy Greaves inspired Barnet won 2-1 at Lower Mead at the end of December, Greaves scoring both goals.

With the match against QPR firmly in everyone's minds there was one other piece of business that had to be completed by the club, and that was their application to join the Football League at the end of the season. There was no automatic promotion, nor any guarantee that an applicant would succeed. It was just an opportunity to 'cast a hat into the ring' and for the last four placed clubs in Division Four to have opposition when re-election was on the agenda.

Wealdstone were one of eight Southern League teams, alongside Bath, Gravesend, Maidstone, Nuneaton, Kettering, Telford and Yeovil that had applied. The FA Cup success had been an important part of the decision, not just because of the results, but the match against QPR alone was expected to earn the club in the region of £8,500 that would allow the club to carry out the necessary ground works to meet the Football League regulations. It had also long been thought that Harrow, with a population in excess of 250,000 had the means to support a Football League side.

On the day, Wealdstone were beaten 4-0 by a QPR side that were less than convincing. In many areas the discussions were more about the referee and some of the decisions he made than the match itself.

QPR had taken an early lead after seven minutes but in a similar fashion to the match at Hereford, for the next half hour Wealdstone competed well in front of a crowd of 16,159, Furphy's powerful drive deflected for a corner and a Watson shot, spilled by Phil Parkes in the QPR goal, only for Ferry's shot then to be blocked on the goalline.

The second half saw QPR start brighter, Givens having a header come back off the crossbar before excellent skill from Stanley Bowles, beating three players, set up Leighton James for the second goal.

Wealdstone though continued to battle and create chances until the match turned away from them on the hour when the referee adjudged that Dave Parratt had fouled Micky Leach, Bowles scoring the resulting penalty. Shortly afterwards, Ernie Howe scored the home side's fourth goal and Wealdstone's FA Cup season was over for another year.

Keith Furphy
Player.

I have some great memories of the FA Cup run in 1977-8 but the QPR defeat was tough as we all felt we could have done better on the day.

I went on to play for 13 years and felt my time at the 'Stones taught me a lot about the importance of not taking anything for granted. It made me appreciate every moment of my career.

Steve Paull
Supporter since the 60's

I remember Leighton James, then of QPR, throwing a lump of mud at us. He got a load of stick when he'd crossed the ball out of the ground for the third time, and I remember at the same game Eric Clapton was sitting behind us with the then Mrs George Harrison.

Alan Fursdon
Player 1976 - 1981

I had six happy years at Wealdstone, five as a player and one as an assistant to Ken Payne on the coaching staff. We had some excellent players at that time, John Watson, George Duck, Dave Parratt, Billy Byrne, John Arnold, Bobby Moss and of course Stuart Pearce.

The FA Cup provided some of the best memories, playing Reading twice, Hereford and QPR when their side had eight Internationals playing, Parkes, Clement, Gillard, Bowles, Francis, Givens, James and Hollins!

One of the funniest moments looking back (certainly not at the time) was at Reading when we were losing 1-0. I got sent off for a bad tackle on Robin Friday. I had just got into the dressing room and was feeling sorry for myself when the door opened and in walked John Arnold - he had been sent off sixty seconds after me. As you can imagine we weren't very popular.

Wealdstone were always known for trying to play good football, with players like Watson, Brinkman, Barwick and Furphy but we could hold our own with most teams in a battle. We had some very hard men in the various sides, Vince O'Kane, Stuart Pearce and Bobby Finch for example.

There is one final memory that springs to mind - it was an away match at Barnet in midweek - and the whole of the back four was left footed! Me at right back, Pearce and Paul Bowgett in the centre and Steve Hockham at left back. At the time there was a shortage of left footed players as well!

League form, as had become the norm during a cup run, had suffered and it was soon to become a critical situation. Wealdstone, by the end of January had lost their last seven Premier league matches and had become firmly entrenched in the bottom three of the division. Injuries were partly to blame, but the club was quick to point out that there were seven players in the first team squad under the age of 21; their inexperience was a factor.

Despite their poor form though, Wealdstone were one of six Southern league clubs invited to take part in the third annual Anglo Italian Tournament, to start in March. Selected on the strength of their FA Cup exploits in recent years and 'Stones were pleased to accept and entered the tournament.

They were drawn in the Midland Zone, having two home matches against Paganese on March 22nd and Udinese the following Saturday. Their away matches saw them based in the costal town of Viareggio during June, facing Reggiana and Arezzio.

The announcement that Wealdstone were to take part in the

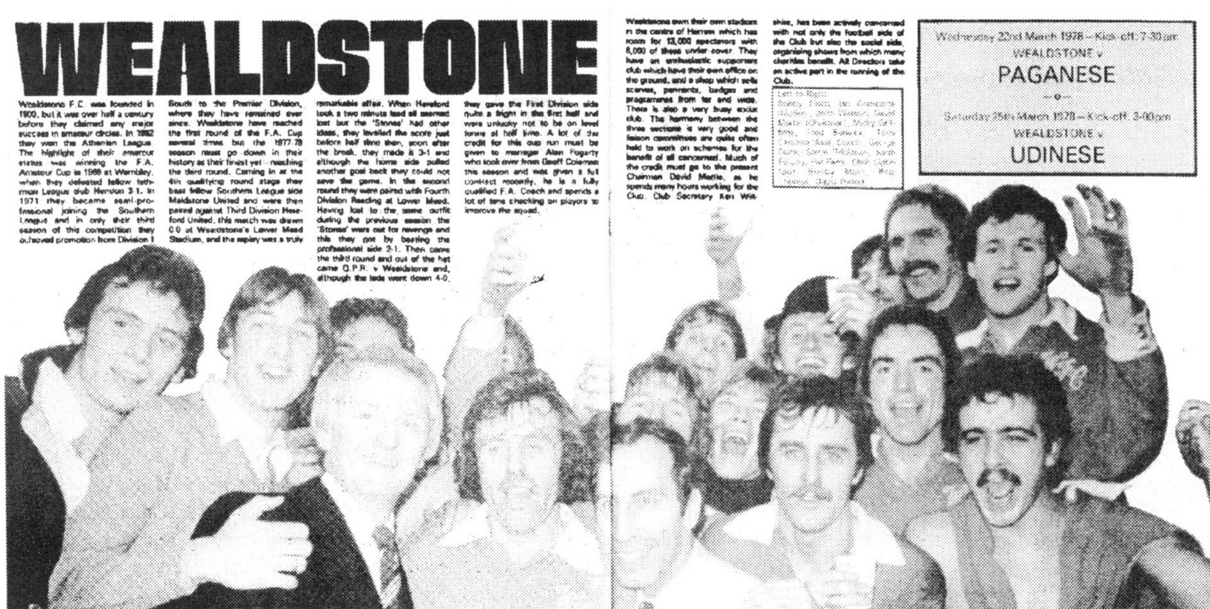

WEALDSTONE

Wealdstone F.C. was founded in 1900, but it was over half a century before they claimed any major success in amateur circles. In 1952 they won the Athenian League. The highlight of their amateur status was winning the F.A. Amateur Cup in 1966 at Wembley, when they defeated fellow Isthmian League club Hendon 3-1. In 1971 they became semi-professional joining the Southern League and in only their third season of this competition they achieved promotion from Division I South to the Premier Division, where they have remained ever since. Wealdstone have reached the first round of the F.A. Cup several times but the 1977-78 season must go down in their history as their finest yet – reaching the third round. Coming in at the 4th qualifying round stage they beat fellow Southern League side Maidstone United and were then paired against Third Division Hereford United, this match was drawn 0-0 at Wealdstone's Lower Mead Stadium, and the replay was a truly remarkable affair. When Hereford took a two minute lead all seemed lost but the 'Stones' had other ideas, they levelled the score just before half time then, soon after the break, they made it 3-1 and although the home side pulled another goal back they could not save the game. In the second round they were paired with Fourth Division Reading at Lower Mead. Having lost to the same outfit during the previous season the 'Stones' were out for revenge and this they got by beating the professional side 2-1. Then came the third round and out of the hat came Q.P.R. v Wealdstone and, although the lads went down 4-0, they gave the First Division side quite a fright in the first half and were unlucky not to be on level terms at half time. A lot of the credit for this cup run must be given to manager Alan Fogarty who took over from Geoff Coleman this season and was given a full contract recently, he is a fully qualified F.A. Coach and spends a lot of time checking on players to improve the squad.

Wealdstone own their own stadium in the centre of Harrow which has room for 13,000 spectators with 6,000 of these under cover. They have an enthusiastic supporters club which have their own office on the ground, and a shop which sells scarves, pennants, badges and programmes from far and wide. There is also a very busy social club. The harmony between the three sections is very good and liaison committees are quite often held to work on schemes for the benefit of all concerned. Much of the credit must go to the present Chairman David Martle, as he spends many hours working for the Club. Club Secretary Ken Wiltshire, has been actively concerned with not only the football side of the Club but also the social side, organising shows from which many charities benefit. All Directors take an active part in the running of the Club.

Wednesday 22nd March 1978 – Kick-off 7-30pm
WEALDSTONE v
PAGANESE
—o—
Saturday 25th March 1978 – Kick-off 3-00pm
WEALDSTONE v
UDINESE

Wealdstone feature from the Anglo Italian Tournament programme

to R: Bobby Finch, Ian Cranstone, (hidden John Watson). David Martle, Micky Griffiths, Fred Barwick, Tony Caruana, George Duck, Steve Brink Keith Furphy, Pat Ferry, Chris Lightfoot, Bobby Moss, Paul Thomas, Dave Parrot.

tournament also seemed to lift the players as a whole to the extent that prior to the two home matches in March, Wealdstone's league form improved with a succession of wins. After 12 matches without a win slipping to second from bottom 'Stones won five and drew two from seven matches to reach mid table.

League matches against Gravesend and Bath were postponed to fit in the Italian matches;

A fine attacking second half display, which produced three goals from Parratt, Moss and Whymark, gave Wealdstone a thoroughly deserved victory in their first taste of Italian football at Lower Mead on Wednesday.

The pattern was set early on, with Paganese defending in depth and breaking quickly and effectively when the opportunity arose. 'Stones quickly accepted the challenge to attack with relish and Ferry should have given them an early lead when he shot wide from close range after three minutes.

George Duck was just wide with a scorching volley Whymark headed over and Duck nearly turned Brinkman's through ball in as 'Stones pressed forward. Paganese replied with sporadic breaks but Ferry turned in Briscoe's cross in the 25th minute to break the deadlock. The lead was short lived. Two minutes later a quick break caught the home defence on the hop and Lanueel crashed home a shot from 20 yards.

Spurred on by Brinkman in the middle and Watson at the back 'Stones continued to come forward but again were they were caught by another break and Cranstone had to make a very brave save at the feet of Sylvestri.

As the second half started, it poured with rain and the Italian skills were stifled temporarily by the slippery conditions. Parratt took advantage by thumping home a header from a corner to restore Wealdstone's lead in the 46th minute.

Watson and Moss went close before Wealdstone paid the penalty for their attacking style, Zana and Giuri combined well on the left, Sylvestri centred and Rossi nipped in to settle the scores. Undaunted and heartened by more rain, 'Stones replaced Barwick with Boyle and continued to attack. After 76 minutes Boyle fed Brinkman on the edge of the box and his intelligent pass allowed Moss to score from close in.

A brief spell of Italian pressure allowed 'Stones to break and Whymark, on his debut, nodded in number four at the far post following a corner. Coco should have pulled one back in the dying moments but Wealdstone were well worth the two goal lead.

Three days later, the match and the result were very different, Wealdstone losing 1–0 to Udinese in a game where they were physically battered by the Italians during the game.

Returning to their league programme the good run of form extended to ten matches unbeaten and 13 unbeaten in the Southern Premier League, including a 4–1 win at Bedford which was the best result of the season.

As May started, Wealdstone had not only fought off any thought of relegation, which in January had seemed likely, they had risen to ninth place in the league table.

Colin Murphy
Supporter

As a lad of about 9 or 10 in 1976/77 I remember living about 400 yards from Lower Mead, above Eric's Auto's.

I've moved on since but I still look out for the results.

I remember as a kid sneaking in without paying – on occasions we used to go right to the end of High Mead and slide under the gate. Then at half time on cold days we used to pay 5p for a Bovril at the Tea Bar.

One match that stands out in the memory was against Clapton, I think. Wealdstone won about 5-1, Byrne and Duck scoring for fun.

It was the queue at the chip shop at the end of the game and then later in the week scouring the Harrow Observer to see if you were in any of the crowd shots.......

It had also been a good year for another element of the club, as despite some indifferent league form, Wealdstone Ladies had also shown good cup form and had won the Presidents Cup, their first trophy, their second honour was to come just a few days later when they beat Aylesbury Harlequins in the final of the Jubilee Cup.

By the end of the season the run of league form had extended to 18 games unbeaten, what should have been excellent preparation for the trip to Italy for the second phase of the Anglo Italian Tournament. It was not to be as a draw and a defeat saw 'Stones finish bottom of their group, Bath and Udinese contesting the final.

During the close season there were to be more changes as Tony Caruana left Wealdstone to join Brian Hall as Assistant Manager at Walton & Hersham.

Pre-season 1978-1979 saw mixed fortunes, with an opening win against Leatherhead followed by defeats in the league cup at Hillingdon and the league at Gravesend.

Stumbling form almost saw the season effectively over in October as there had been no win in eight games since a replay victory over Cambridge City after two attempts in the FA Trophy and a 1-0 win in a match described as a total bore against Kempston Rovers in the FA Cup. Both competitions were to see defeats in the next rounds, losing 2-1 at home to Harlow in the Trophy and 5-0 at home to Enfield in the FA Cup.

By mid December with the situation no better, fans collected their newspapers only to see splashed across the front page the headline:

Entire soccer squad for sale.

Wealdstone FC has placed its entire squad up for sale. This surprise announcement came over the weekend following an emergency board meeting on Wednesday. The decision to do this was made, it is understood, by Manager Alan Fogarty after he had been told by the club's directors that his wage bill had been slashed.

Mr Bill Emerson said in a statement yesterday "This does not mean that we are promoting a giant clearance sale. Our dismissal from two major competitions has aggravated the cash flow position, and it is necessary for us to review our income and expenditure situation.

Undoubtedly, this move will attract enquiries, and we shall probably make strategic transfers bearing in mind that we must always consolidate our position. We must explore every avenue of income.

We would like to see more public support in taking up shares or giving financial support. We are determined to get the club on a sound financial footing and also to improve our playing image."

Mr Emerson then said that the Manager had been given a much reduced budget from which to work but the board had no plans to terminate Mr Fogarty's contract. It had over a year to run.

The New Year again saw some slight improvement in results, although relegation was yet again a distinct possibility. By early March, injuries again weakened the side to the extent that defeats at bottom club Dorchester and at home to Enfield increased the relegation jitters.

There was some unrest in the boardroom as well. Having resigned and then rejoined five months earlier, Chairman David Martle was to resign again.

His reasons were stated at the time to be the opposition of some members of the board to Wealdstone's entry into the new Alliance Premier League, and the refusal of the officers of the Lower Mead Social Club (who were Directors of Wealdstone FC) to allow it's financial affairs to be controlled by Wealdstone Football Club. David Martle was to join the board of Kettering Town FC.

After the meeting had closed an informal meeting was held to discuss the club's situation regarding the Alliance League and Ken Wiltshire announced to the meeting that the Board of Directors had voted against joining as it would be financial suicide for the club, costing an extra £300 per week in wages and between £5000 and £7000 overall.

It was a decision that was eventually overturned and Wealdstone joined as founder members of the new league at the end of the season.

George Duck
Player 1972 – 1979

I flatly refused to join Wealdstone when Sid Prosser asked me. When I left school I went to Millwall as an apprentice pro and did four years there. I didn't make it and got a free transfer and went to Southend for a year. That didn't work out so I came out of football like a lot of young players do, with a chip on their shoulder.

Sid Prosser phoned me and I told him I wasn't interested and he was wasting his time. He came round to where we lived in Tottenham and I still thought he was wasting his time. However he persuaded me to sign, I went to training and it turned out to be the best thing I have ever done.

It changed my whole attitude towards the game. I hated the pro game but non-league football was different. At training sitting there in the dressing room was one of my idols Terry Dyson. After training we would go into the bar have a drink and a bag of crisps and this was unheard off. I thought this was great. I couldn't wait for Saturdays to come around.

I signed for Wealdstone for £14 per week, £4 appearance and £2 if we won. So on a good week if you won you'd come home with a score.

There were some strange times – penalties seem to come to the fore. The Hastings game - Their manager took the team off. They were blatant penalties, no two ways about it. Their manager was so incensed that he threatened to take the team off. I got four that day, 3 penalties. It was even mentioned on Grandstand.

And Reading! We're 1-0 up through Keith Furphy, Mossy gets brought down and it's a penalty. I'm on penalties, It's a big crowd, and it's the FA Cup, terrified really. Normally, penalties would never bother me but this was a big occasion and I was terrified.

I remember the referee was Alan Turvey, who's now chairman

YESTERDAYS HEROES George Duck

George Duck is a man who will need very little introduction to most at Lower Mead, a legend in the true sense of the word he remains probably the most popular player to have ever pulled on a Wealdstone shirt and spent an amazing seven seasons here averaging a goal every 1½ games.

George joined Wealdstone in the 1972/73 season from the then 4th Division side Southend United, he had made a handful of first team appearances in his one season with the Essex club and previously had been at Millwall, although he never broke into the first team. George has since said that having set his heart on a career as a professional footballer, he took a lot of persuading to drop into non-league football with the 'STONES' and it was only the persistence of Wealdstone boss Syd Prosser that stopped him from "chucking in" the game for good, but said he was very soon won over by the warmth of everybody at the club. In seven seasons George made (370) appearances (2) as substitute and scored (251) goals (47) of which were penalties.

He is quite obviously Wealdstones leading goalscorer of all time and 62 goals in all competitions 1973/74 will be a record which is unlikely to be ever beaten, although George was a prolific goalscorer his only major success at Wealdstone was a championship medal (Southern League Division One South) 1973/74, but says the F.A. Cup runs were also just as memorable particularly the 3rd round proper against Q.P.R 1977/78 when he overcame illness in the nick of time to play. Another highpoint was the day he scored his 200th goal for the Stones and it took minutes to clear the pitch of hundreds of fans all wanting to congratulate him.

In 1979 when Wealdstone entered the newly formed Alliance League, he made it clear that he would be unhappy with all the extra travelling, so his association with Wealdstone was ended when he was sold to Isthmian League side Dagenham.

Dagenham gave him the chance to link up with his old boss at Lower Mead, Eddie Presland. A great non-league career was crowned when he scored at Wembley to help the 'DAGGERS' win the F.A.Trophy.

George returned to Harrow the following season with Harrow Borough continuing to score with the same unique ease, before finally completing a truly great career at Hendon.

Georges main interest in football now is coaching his 8 year old son Christopher (a junior stone) who he says could be quite useful and recently attended the F.A.Cup match against Hayes in his own words "To show the boy where the old man used to play".

George is still living in Harrow and is a self-employed London Taxi Driver, and is some one who will always be most welcome at Lower Mead.

Layne Patterson.

From the Wealdstone FC match programme 29th October 1988

of the Isthmian League, Steve D'eath was the goalkeeper. I put the ball down there was a big din, lots of noise. Ref blew his whistle ... ran up... took the penalty ... hit the post. I couldn't believe it.

*I never missed really. Before anyone moved, the referee blew his whistle. Take it again, the goalkeeper moved. So I'm relieved I've got another chance. Sh*****g myself even more! Put the ball down ... ran up ... side footed it into the corner and scored. Started running to the crowd ... NO! ... The referee's blown his whistle again! I'd taken the penalty before he'd blown his whistle! So I've got to take it again.*

What do I do now? I've hit the post and I've sent him the wrong way, So I ran up and for the first time I just shut my eyes and smashed it ... It flew in!

Then after Dagenham and Harrow Borough - I went to the enemy – I nearly came back to Wealdstone.

The season that Wealdstone won the 'double' Brian Hall contacted me during the closed season and wanted to sign me. I met Brian Hall at the John Lyon and we sat down and discussed everything. Everything was fine, The money was no problem and I was going to go back there.

The only problem was how the money was going to be paid. When I was at Wealdstone the first time they had this peculiar way of paying the players. You'd get a certain amount of cash in your packet and you'd be given a cheque for the rest.

After a training session all the players would be in the bar cashing their cheques and some weeks they didn't always have the money. That side of things didn't seem to have changed. I said I'd had all that before and wasn't going through all that again. Where I'd been after Wealdstone you had all your money paid at once and you get used to that. That was what it was all about really.

Former 'Stones Manager, Eddie Presland wanted me at Hendon and because Wealdstone couldn't agree on how the money was paid I agreed to join him.

During the season, I got in a collision with a goalkeeper, the ball got played through, I went up to head it over him and he came out, punched me straight in the face and broke my nose and cheekbone.

I was out for about 3 months that was the worst injury I ever had in the game. That left me with numbness down that side of my face for about 2 years. I came back after the injury and finished the season and then when it was over I packed up.

Mark Snell
Supporter

George Duck is also more than worthy of a mention. He was a bit like Greavsie – he was always in the right place to score yet didn't seem to do too much anywhere else on the field. Still, Its goals that win games, eh!

Wealdstone's form continued to be inconsistent, the defeats still causing concern as the club slipped down the table. There were some good wins to restore the balance and a number of changes to the side were also to have a bearing on the future of the team.

For the home match against Bridgend in April 1979, Jimmy McVeigh failed a fitness test for the 'Stones, so 16 year old Stuart Pearce came back into the defence.

He had made his debut in March away to Dorchester, and had figured in a dozen or so games however this time, he had an immediate impact.

His youth and pace helped him outrun his opponents on numerous occasions and on the hour, he capped his performance when he swung a perfect corner onto the head of Nigel Johnson, who nodded the ball beyond the 'keepers reach for the second goal in a 3–0 win.

The match was followed by three defeats, the third away to Bridgend before a home match with fellow strugglers Yeovil. Wealdstone won 4–0 in front of new Chairman Fred Deanus. George Duck also scored his 250th goal for the club in the win, which lifted 'Stones in the table, eventually finishing in fifteenth position.

Philip Smith
Supporter since 1976

I was born in 1934 in Bransgrove Road, Edgware which is next to Prince Edward Playing Fields. I am a Wealdstone FC Supporter and have been since I moved into Wealdstone in 1976. I used to support Edgware FC (besides Chelsea FC) from when I was a schoolboy; so supporting Wealdstone FC at the White Lion ground brings back memories of long ago.

I will always have memories of Val Shearer, (our sub) taking the clock-hands off at the end of a match at Lower Mead. It was always one of those strange sites that summed up non-league football.

When I first saw Stuart Pearce play, I was in the main stand at Lower Mead, he made a strong but fair tackle on an opponent and they nearly both finished up in the Main Stand – an outstanding player.

The close season saw Wealdstone's membership of the new Alliance Premier League confirmed despite the club's earlier reservations but when the new season started, it was not the immediate success that had been hoped.

After a number of defeats in pre-season, the first league match had a similar result, a 2–1 defeat away to Worcester City the first match, a fair result on the performance. This was followed by a home draw with Nuneaton and the first win was in the Alliance Cup on Bank holiday Monday, 3-0 over Maidstone.

Always looking for ways to raise funds for the Club, Wealdstone agreed to host a floodlight Cricket Match between Middlesex CCC (Past & Present) and a Harrow 'Select' XI at Lower Mead, the funds raised being split three ways.

On Wednesday 19th September, three days before a home league match with A P Leamington, Lower Mead was converted to a cricket square.

Disappointing results heralded the start of the new era and in late September, Manager Alan Fogarty resigned. He left to join Tamworth with Wealdstone second from bottom in the table, with 4 points from 8 games, Ken Payne taking over initially on a Caretaker basis.

There was an immediate change in fortunes as Wealdstone only lost one of their next six matches, a run of form that was good enough for Payne to be confirmed in the Managers role. He appointed Alan Fursdon as his assistant.

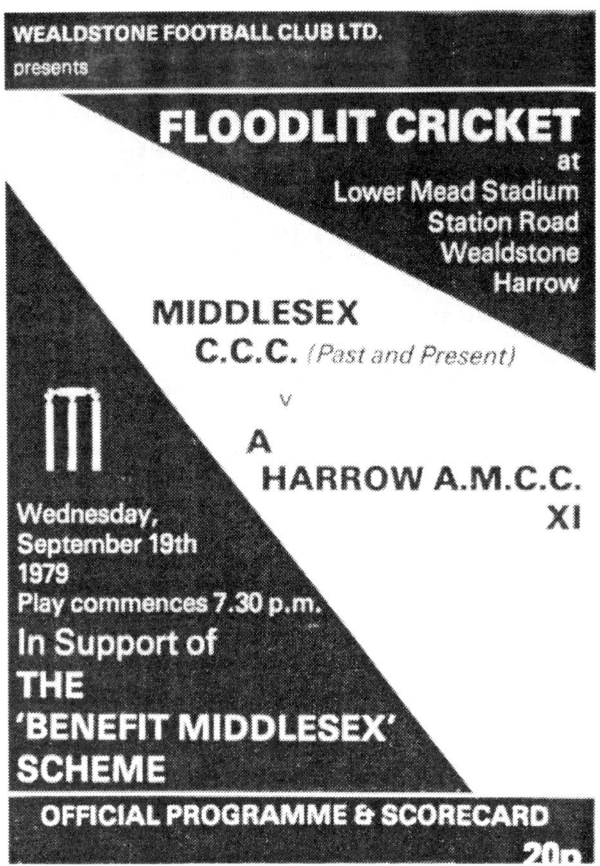
WEALDSTONE FOOTBALL CLUB LTD.
presents
FLOODLIT CRICKET
at
Lower Mead Stadium
Station Road
Wealdstone
Harrow
MIDDLESEX
C.C.C. *(Past and Present)*
v
A
HARROW A.M.C.C.
XI
Wednesday,
September 19th
1979
Play commences 7.30 p.m.
In Support of
THE
'BENEFIT MIDDLESEX'
SCHEME
OFFICIAL PROGRAMME & SCORECARD
20p

The away match at Bath saw a 4–4 draw, a valuable point for Wealdstone, but it could so easily have been two. Wealdstone fell two goals behind early on but four minutes into the second half they were winning 4–2, only for a penalty on 68 minutes to bring Bath back into the game. Their equaliser coming just two minutes from time.

It highlighted the inconsistency in the Wealdstone performances at the time.

October saw the return to the club of an 'old favourite' all be it in a different role. Charlie Townsend returned to the club as Reserve Team Manager, looking after the side in the Suburban League. His first match saw a 2–0 win away to Chertsey.

At the end of October, Yeovil again were visitors to Lower Mead, this time as highflying challengers in the Alliance League (in third place) rather than a struggling Southern League side as they had been the previous season.

Wealdstone were third from bottom, but defied the odds and played to the top form to record a 5–0 victory. They came off at half time 4–0 to the good and received a standing ovation from everyone in the ground. An own goal started the rout on fourteen minutes, Nigel Johnson and Neil Cordice (2) scoring before half time. Bobby Moss added the fifth just two minutes into the second half.

A 1–0 win over Woking in the FA Cup saw Wealdstone drawn at home to Southend, but that match saw 'Stones defeated at home 1–0.

The turn of the year saw some better results but by March Wealdstone had lost 3–0 at home to Enfield in the Middlesex Cup semi-final, in a run of six games where 'Stones only scored once.

As had become a habit, relegation loomed again and it was not until the end of April when a home draw, 1-1 with Bath City ensured that Wealdstone would not finish in the bottom three and be relegated back into the Southern League after just one season.

There were more changes during the summer as Ken Payne tried to improve the squad, and things started well for the 1980-81 season.

The signing of Clevere Forde meant the 'Stones could field two wingers for the first time since the successful Amateur Cup winning side of 1966, and this brought some immediate results as Forde and Alan Cordice destroyed the Finchley defence in the Middlesex Cup.

This was followed by a 4–0 home win over Gordon Banks' Telford side, to see Wealdstone head the Alliance Premier League (for the first time) at the start of the season.

'Stones had started the season full of confidence and had ripped through their opponents, but perhaps they had peaked to early. There was only one way to go from the top of the table and it soon became evident that that was the course Wealdstone's season was to take, not helped by losing centre back Paul Bowgett after the game.

He had broken his arm in two places in a first half tussle and had played on but he was to miss a number of matches with the arm in plaster.

By September the shine was definitely beginning to dull on 'Stones season as three defeats saw the slide down the table begin despite a draw at table topping Kettering and a league cup win over second placed Nuneaton. These were followed by an infamous trip to Scarborough;

The stark details could not reveal the grim realities of Wealdstone's nightmare trip to Scarborough on Saturday. The game ended with goalkeeper Ian Cranstone in hospital and skipper John Watson, Tom Murphy and Paul Bowgett already in the dressing room, having been shown the red card.

The even exchanges of the opening minutes promised an even struggle with the visitors often looking the sharper. After 15 minutes however fate took a hand and promise gave way to nightmare. Cranstone went down for a ground shot which he gathered competently, when Gauden rushed in from ten yards and contested for a ball he had no chance of winning.

The crack as his boot met Cranstone's head was audible in the stand. After treatment, Cranstone gallantly carried on until half time, but between the incident and half time when he collapsed, he remembered nothing. On the half hour, Wainwright went down with an injured leg and Harris the home forward went on unchallenged to score the opening goal past the bemused Cranstone.

Referee Mr Peck's apparent leanings towards the home side were highlighted a few minutes later when after an incident involving the home right back, he summarily waved a red card at Watson despite motions from the linesman to indicate the player was over-reacting as he fell.

'Stones overcame the deficit until five minutes before the break when a free kick enabled Dixie to head past the helpless Cranstone. During the break he collapsed and was rushed to hospital with concussion and shock, Stuart Pearce taking over an unfamiliar role in the green short when play resumed.

Fifteen minutes into the second half, Murphy challenged strongly on the half way line and was penalised, Mr Peck adjudging his patent dissatisfaction as dissent and the second sending off occurred. Frustrated with the tide running against his side Bowgett tangled with Gauden a few minutes later and felled the home striker, earning the third early bath of the game.

Strength in numbers then prevailed and Scarborough scored two more goals for a comfortable looking victory.

Stuart Pearce - Goalkeeper

Further defeats followed and 'Stones were eliminated from the league cup losing the home leg of the tie with Nuneaton 3-0 with a side missing the four regulars. They also went out of the FA Trophy against Southern League Oxford City by 4-2 in a truly woeful performance. The league record dipped to an all time low after a good start, showing only one win in nineteen matches.

The FA Cup too was a disappointment. After a draw 1-1 away from home, 'Stones were expected to beat Harlow at Lower Mead, but they managed to lose the replay 1-0 missing out on a home tie with Charlton Athletic, to a goal scored in the last minute, which prompted Ken Payne to offer his resignation.

By November the Supporters Club Committee resigned en bloc citing dissatisfaction with the current board, a lack of communication and concerns over what had happened to money donated by the Supporters Club to the main club. It added to the disarray, which was even more evident a week later when Chairman Fred Deanus told Ken Payne he had accepted his resignation, made verbally after the Harlow match!

The club already had a replacement in place, Allen Batsford taking over having moved from Hillingdon Borough, and coach Alan Fursdon reverted back to just a player, replaced as coach by Brian Hall.

At Christmas the club were second bottom with 14 points having won 4 and drawn 6 matches out of 21. Director Brian Bennett wrote a 'Half Term Report' for the Harrow Observer but there was little in it to cheer the fans, despite the new appointment.

The job of turning around the fortunes of the club was not going to be easy, starting from second bottom in the league with 14 points from 21 games, having only won four times.

There was no magical turn around in form as Allen Batsford began to make changes and stamp his authority on the side, although the Middlesex Charity Cup Semi Final did see Wealdstone make a little progress. The match at Hendon in mid February saw an interesting prospect as the home side were managed by Ken Payne, who Wealdstone had 'sacked' in November.

The match saw 'Stones dominate from the kick off but fail to score before half time. They then took the lead only three minutes into the second period, Alan Cordice heading home.

'Stones continued to dominate but failure in the 18 yard box allowed Hendon to capitalise, and they equalised on 72 minutes. Six minutes later, Drummy seized on a defensive error and shot around Cranstone, only to see Stuart Pearce punch the ball clear, conceding a penalty which McGleish hit wide.

In extra time, Hendon took the lead just before the break only for Nigel Johnson to equalise with four minutes left to force a replay.

At Lower Mead the following Tuesday, goals from Robin Wainwright and Alan Cordice with only a single reply saw 'Stones reach their first cup final for eleven years – a rare high spot in a season where by the end of March Wealdstone shared the bottom of the league table with Yeovil, both teams on 20 points. After the match between the two strugglers at Lower Mead, nothing changed as they played out a 1-1 draw.

The beginning of April was crisis time for Wealdstone. In previous seasons, form had always improved to stave off the fear of relegation, but this year Wealdstone stared it straight in the face for the first time in their history.

A minimum of eight points were required from the last six games to prevent what was seen as demotion to the relative obscurity of the Southern League. Despite the pressures of the league fixtures, there was a little better cheer as the reserves won through to the final of the Suburban League Cup with a 2–1 victory away to Slough.

There was another distraction for the first team as, with no league fixtures over the Easter weekend, they faced a Millwall side featuring mainly reserve players in a friendly at Lower Mead, running out winners by 7-0, all seven Wealdstone goals coming in the second half as the side played to their capabilities rather than their league form.

Wins against Boston, away to Kettering (who needed a win to maintain their Championship challenge), and at home to Barrow meant that a draw in the last match at home to fellow strugglers AP Leamington would guarantee 'Stones safety.

The sea of tight-lipped grim faces streaming away from Lower Mead on Saturday bore witness to 30 of the most tragic minutes in the long history of Wealdstone Football Club. They had just seen a 1-0 lead turned into an astonishing 2-1 defeat in the final half hour of the final match of the season. In the process Wealdstone waived goodbye to the Alliance Premier League.

The 'Stones needed only a draw to escape relegation. Three straight wins had brought the fans through the turnstiles confident of success against a far from invincible Leamington side, and when Robin Wainwright gave Wealdstone the lead from Jimmy Sweetzer's cross after 61 minutes their joy bubbled to the surface.

"We're staying up this year," sang the crowd behind the goal, a

view seemingly confirmed when Alan Cordice was upended four minutes later and a penalty was awarded. Two nil would have sealed the win and Jimmy Sweetzer, taking only his second penalty for the club looked confident as he ran up to take the kick.

But he missed. The crowd looked on in numbed silence as the ball rebounded from the wall to the right of the goal.

Leamington, who needed to win to avoid the drop suddenly realised their plight was not as hopeless as at first thought. They pushed centre half Gary Brown into attack and in the 77th minute they won their first corner of the second half. Cranstone missed his punch and Tommy Gorman headed in. In the 86th minute, Dennis Byatt failed to clear a hopeful knock on and Doug Hickton raced in to shoot gleefully past Cranstone.

The striker did a victory jig while Wealdstone came into the shocked realisation that their Alliance League life was slipping away. Four minutes later it had done.

For the first time in the club's history Wealdstone FC had been relegated.

There had been a number of matches over the season where 'Stones had played football as good as anyone in the league and had earned wins to match. The relegation was a result of their inability to score goals consistently despite the changes made by Allen Batsford since he had taken over at the club.

COME ON YOU 'STONES'

ARIOLA RECORDS WISH WEALDSTONE THE BEST OF LUCK

ariola

Ariola Records, 48 Maddox Street, London W.1.

An advertising flyer produced by Ariola Records as part of their sponsorship of Wealdstone FC

Ian Cranstone
Goalkeeper 1975/6 – 1980/81

I came out of professional football with Colchester United the season before joining Wealdstone, having spent most of it with my arm in a plaster cast. Alan Foggarty signed me, and he used to travel down from the Midlands to take the training on Tuesdays and Thursdays. I actually took over from Chris Lightfoot.

During my spell with the club I made a record number of consecutive appearances and in 1977-1978 I was voted 'Sportsman of the Year' receiving the Leadbeatter trophy. The following season I was voted Player of the Year and received the Jock Law trophy.

Outside of the players, there is one person who sticks in my mind. Eddie the Coach Driver for away games. He was as mad as a march hare, not just in attitude, but in his driving as well!

The club were going through some financial difficulties as well. It got to the extent that players didn't get paid, but things did improve when the owner of Ariola Records became involved. There was a cash injection and they were our sponsors for a while.

There are three matches that stand out in my mind, all away from home. The first was not so much for the game but the town. We visited Barrow. It was like walking back to the 1950's.

Away to Bangor, we travelled by train on a Sunday. Not a good idea by the organisers!. The train was delayed and for a 3:00pm kick off, we arrived at about 2:45pm. We lost and also had a lousy journey home.

Scarborough will be remembered for all the wrong reasons. I was kicked in the head and I sustained concussion, playing on for five minutes without knowing where I was. I conceded a goal and the team where so incensed by the actions of the Scarbortough forward they decided on retribution.

I was in York Hospital when I heard we had finished with eight men. Needless to say 'Willie' Watson led the retaliation, but he was a great influence on me. The leadership, motivation, enthusiasm, wit and respect that he used to command. His contribution to the team and the club was always 100%.

Tim Parks
Supporter since the late 1960's

My name is Tim Parks and I'm a Wealdstone fan.

There. I've said it. There can be worse addictions, but certainly none you have to explain so many times.

Tony Adams, Paul Merson and Gazza probably get less quizzical looks than when a non-league supporter comes out of the closet. You know the scene, a bunch of workmates talking about the World Cup, for example, when the Arsenal and Man Utd fans get ribbed about their players' contributions.

Then it's; "Who do you follow, Tim?"
"Wealdstone".
"Yeah, but a proper team, you know".
"Well actually, moron, Wealdstone are a proper team".

To be honest, my workmates (on the sportsdesk at The Mirror) are pretty enlightened about the 'Stones. We've even been known to run the odd Wealdstone story (the goalpost fiasco at Grays being the most recent) and we would undoubtedly expose the Ryman League's ground-grading shenanigans if we had more space.

But to be a Wealdstone fan is to invite The Roger Moore Eyebrow. I am in the lucky position to go to any Premier League match on a Saturday with my Carling press pass (I am always in the office, doing my writing headlines and designing pages bit on a Sunday) yet you will normally find me standing with Mick, Nick, Spaull, Wobbly, Swervin' Irvine, Ken, Jon Taffel etc etc at some non-Taylor report stadium complaining about the 'Stones instead.

It is habit, I suppose. A glorious habit, fostered over 30 years since I first saw a Wealdstone team of Andy Williams, Dave Swain, Bernie Bremer et al lose 1-0 at home to Sutton United in September 1969. I was 12. I'd been taken to watch Chelsea with season-ticket-holding relatives (never wanted them to win, perversely); Watford with school pals (terminally dull); and QPR with my mate Derek (Bowles, Francis and Thomas; too flamboyant) but something about Lower Mead and its amateur ethos attracted me back.

It was probably also something to do with the freedom of being able to hop on a train from my home in Hatch End to Harrow & Wealdstone. Oh, the joy of those liberating Saturdays and occasional Tuesdays!

The gleam of the faraway floodlights as you mounted the Wealdstone railway bridge; the ghostly walkways at Harrow & Wealdstone station where our schoolboy imaginings ran riot on freezing December nights, remembering the awful train crash there some 17 years before.

In between the games, of course, the Harrow Observer was our saviour. Its purple prose merchant of those days, Leslie Jones, told tales of Isthmian League daring-do in the exotic, unheard-of quarters of Woking, Leytonstone and Wycombe Wanderers (who always seemed to attract huge crowds, even for meaningless Tuesday games in the Premier Midweek Floodlight League).

Where was Hemel Hempstead? Could I cycle to Ruislip Manor for the Middlesex Senior Cup-tie that coming Saturday - yes I could, unfortunately - and was Leighton Town in East London, or in Leighton Buzzard? I actually made it to that particular away game - an early FA Cup Qualifying Round tie in 1970- thanks to a caravan outing with my parents, and began to realise just what a big club Wealdstone were, and still are.

I had chanced upon them in the fag end of their amateur days. There was an aura about this Middlesex club named after an obscure Harrow suburb... a legend almost. It emanated from winning the 1966 Amateur Cup and the near miss in '68, and this Wealdstone side arrived with a swagger in deepest Bedfordshire four years on to face what was little more than a village outfit.

Sadly, for all the posturing and the legions of blue & white support, it was a poor Wealdstone team. The stars of the mid-Sixties had moved on to Enfield, Hendon and Wycombe, and our team of youngsters and honest triers were held 1-1. In the replay, the Harrow Observer reported the disaster of a 0-1 giant killing.

It was heart-rending, but I can still recall the pride of seeing all those fans urging on a team that did not deserve such support. It could only get better.

Come the summer of 1971 and Wealdstone went semi-professional. And how! It had cost 9d (4p) to get in at Lower Mead to watch our final Isthmian League game in April - a glorious 3-0 win over Woking - and now we were being asked 15p to watch our side (now bolstered by ex-league lags like Cliff Jones, Gary Townend and Mickey Brown) take on the might of the Southern League First Division (North). But it was worth it.

In the rest of the world it was post-Vietnam and Cuban crisis, post-man-on-the-moon and post-England-flop-to-West Germany-in-Mexico-World-Cup, yet the thoughts of this naive 13-year-old were concentrated squarely on Lower Mead.

Our climb to footballing prominence, it seemed to me, were summed up by the results pages of the Sunday Express, the paper we had taken at home since we realised my dad was more right wing than David Beckham. When you couldn't get to an away game, it was a real chore to find out how Wealdstone had fared in the smudgy, almost-too-small-to-read minor results.

Oh to have your name up in lights among the SOUTHERN LEAGUE PREMIER DIVISION scores, where the paper faithfully recorded not only the result in bold type but also the goalscorers and attendance.

It seemed a dream too far, but finally we made it. The wonderful 1973-74 season, with George Duck's 64 goals, saw the "pluckly little Wealdstone team", our Amateur Side Made Good, promoted to the big league. And there, in the Sunday Express after that first game in the Premier Division was proof of our arrival among the elite;

WEALDSTONE 2 WEYMOUTH 1
Duck, Henderson
Att; 1,720

Surely life couldn't get any better than this.

It could, of course. Pan forward 11 years and suddenly you are in the realms of fantasy as Wealdstone (and please stop me if you've heard this before) become the first team to win the non-league double.

But what made it all the sweeter for me, looking back, was my inside track on those glory years after launching a career in journalism that took me from the Watford Observer in 1977, to the Harrow Observer (covering Wealdstone between 1980-81) and on to the Enfield Gazette (covering the 'Stones arch-rivals from 1981-85).

Our reporters on The Mirror today talk about the privilege of covering a World Cup Final; reporting on a British success at The Open; Botham's one-man destruction of the Aussies in 1981; Nigel Mansell and Damon Hill winning the British Grand Prix at Silverstone, but nothing, nothing, can compare with the peaks and troughs of following your own team in print.

Imagine; watching Wealdstone and being paid for it. Interviewing Micky Tomkys after the 'Stones had beaten Harrow Borough 4-0. Commiserating with Enfield boss Eddie McCluskey after Wealdstone had clinched their place in the FA Trophy Final at Wembley. - Priceless!

The deepest trough came when Wealdstone were relegated from the Alliance Premier League (Conference) in 1981. We thought we had escaped when Stuart Pearce's goal brought a 1-0 win at Championship-chasing Kettering two weeks from the end of the season - but we fell through the trapdoor in desperate circumstances on the final Saturday.

In those days, we reporters made ends meet by filing copy for the "Sporting Pink" papers during the game. For this vital match, against fellow relegation strugglers AP Leamington at Lower Mead, it meant phoning over regular reports to the Birmingham evening and Sunday papers.

I had at least three on the go at the same time. (You don't mind when things are going well. We only had to draw to stay up, and when Robin Wainwright gave us the lead I was gleefully passing on the information to the good folk of Leamington.) Then we were awarded a penalty, with 20 minutes to go. It was all over. Jimmy Sweetzer (we'll never forget you) stepped up and failed miserably with the spot kick.

Nevertheless, I was just summing up my match reports for the Birmingham Evening Argus with the immortal lines; "And so, sadly, AP Leamington must re-group in the Southern League after this afternoon's relegation" when the visitors twice caught our goalkeeper Ian Cranstone in no-man's land in the final few minutes.

It was crazy, but we had lost 2-1. The crowd seemed in a trance, making their way numbly out of the ground, and so was I.

The 'phone was ringing in the press box as I left. Did the Evening Argus or Sunday Mercury ever discover the final score? Perhaps we'll never know.

But that was the darkest hour before the dawn, as they say in the posh papers. History records that Wealdstone were winning everything on offer in the Southern League the following season, under Allen Batsford and his assistant Brian Hall, while I had left the Observer for pastures new in the summer of '81.

I landed the Sports Editor's job at the flourishing Enfield Gazette - largely on my knowledge of Alliance League football, as Enfield FC were co-incidentally taking the plunge into the Alliance that same season. Unfortunately, my reputation as a rabid Wealdstone fan went before me.

On my first meeting with Enfield chairman Tommy Unwin, he brandished a copy of Long Ball Down the Middle (the ground-breaking Wealdstone fanzine of the day) which I had edited in the late 1970s. It featured an attack on Enfield's supporters, calling them small-minded. I was prepared for the worst but genial Tom simply said; "You're right. If they had any larger minds they'd be dangerous".

And on the whole, I think the Es fans were kept quiet by the extensive coverage they got in the Gazette. In fact the only abuse I remember getting was on New Year's Day 1983, when Wealdstone recorded a brilliant 1-0 win at Southbury Road to keep on course for the Championship.

I was admirably restrained during the game, but was caught leaping in the air, clicking my heels in the car park at about 5.30pm just as the door at the back of the stand swung open. And coming out were Eddie McCluskey, Lee Holmes and about six other Enfield players.

My most embarrassing moment, however, came while I was covering my first-ever Wealdstone game for the Harrow Observer. Who were the opponents? Yes, Harrow Borough, at Earlsmead, in a Middlesex Charity Cup-tie that kicked off the 1980-81 season.

There I was, at the front of the stand, seeking to ingratiate myself with the Borough officials in an attempt to show how objective I was going to be throughout the season. They knew of my Wealdstone links and I was attempting to put their minds at rest.

Then, drifting over from the terraces behind the Borough goal came the distinctive chant, growing in decibels until it seemed to fill the whole ground; "Tim Parks is biased, Tim Parks is biased". Thanks, fellas.

Steve Paull
Supporter since the 60's

I remember a 2–1 defeat at Burton. The referee gave a last minute penalty when the players of both sides were lining up for a corner. My oldest friend Mick Fishman has only gone onto the pitch twice to remonstrate with the officials. This was one of them. He had heard scorer Ian Storey-Moore apologise to our Manager, Eddie Presland. Once again it was a relegation season and the point from a draw would have kept us up.

Ray Kemp was another that went on the pitch once as well. I remember him going up to International referee Clive Thomas at Bath and telling him to his face what he thought of him.

He had allowed the game to go on for about three minutes with our keeper, Ian Cranstone, knocked out in the penalty area. Cranstone was allowed treatment after Bath had scored into an unguarded net.

The final injustice? How about the game where we were leading 1–0, Jimmy Sweetzer missed a penalty with ten minutes to go, and then A P Leamington scored twice – we lost 2–1 and got relegated. Once again to find out that with the other results as they were, yet again a draw would have kept us up..........

THE EIGHTIES

The 1981 - 1982 season started with a 2-2 draw with Wembley in the held over Middlesex Charity Cup Final, the trophy being shared by the two clubs for the following season. A 5-1 win over Chelmsford City in the first round of the Southern League Cup also showed the fans that this season was to be better than the last.

By the end of August, the Wealdstone side who had problems in front of goal in the previous season, scored their 19th goal winning 4-0 against Fareham. This was followed by two more high scoring results as Thanet were beaten 6-1 and Salisbury were beaten 4-0 in the FA Cup.

Off the field there were further changes as David Morrittt took over as Chairman of Wealdstone FC from Fred Deanus. He had, as a Director, put in £20,000 before the club were relegated from the Alliance League and he promised another £30,000 to help with a major expansion programme at the club stating that "there were plans to return immediately to the Alliance. There is potential at the club, presently standing at the top of the league having scored almost 40 goals".

And so the season continued, big wins at home and away became the norm in both the League and the cup competitions, none more so than a win by 6-1 away to Newbury in the FA Cup at the end of September. It was a match the Wealdstone players almost missed as their coach had broken down in Harrow and after frantic phone calls a replacement was eventually found, the team not arriving at Newbury until just before the three o clock kick off.

Remaining at the top of the league there were disappointments too, as Wealdstone lost 4-1 at home to Harrow Borough to exit the FA Cup competition, only to face the same opponents in their next match in the FA Trophy, this time winning by 4-0.

By the start of November, a 5-0 win at Canterbury meant that 'Stones had already scored more goals than in the whole of the previous season.

The wins continued and in February, a 2-0 win at Dover put 'Stones through to the Southern League Cup semi final. Their league position was a comfortable third, with games in hand over both sides above them. Off the field there was an early warning of what the future was to hold, although it wasn't realised at the time.

Chairman Dave Morrittt told a meeting of Officials and Supporters to 'toe the line or else' - at the end of the meeting he received a standing ovation from the 150 or so people present.The meeting had been called to discuss the rumours that his company, Morrittt Homes had intended to buy the ground for £200,000, possibly to build on the site. It was denied by all present who re-iterated their intention to develop the sporting side of the facility with the addition of Squash Courts and a Gym. It was announced that Alan Clifton would be appointed Clubhouse Manager and from March 1st the bar would be run full time.

By the beginning of March, Wealdstone were firm favourites to win the league despite being in third place in the table.

	P	W	D	L	F	A	Pts
Dorchester Town	31	17	11	3	57	24	45
Waterlooville	34	18	6	10	56	30	42
Wealdstone	**26**	**18**	**5**	**3**	**64**	**23**	**41**
Poole Town	33	14	11	8	63	41	39

Another semi final was the Middlesex Cup, Wealdstone reaching the final with a 2-0 win over Enfield, but there were two league defeats as form stumbled slightly.

At the end of March a 4-0 victory over Andover put 'Stones back on track, Paul Bowgett scoring a hat trick of penalties in the match bringing his tally to 22 for the season, making him second highest goal scorer after Alan Cordice with 27.

Cup Finals were then the order of play, with two 1-0 victories, goals from Stuart Pearce (away) and Paul Bowgett with a penalty at home, securing the first trophy of the current season, the Southern League Cup, over opponents, Gloucester City. The Middlesex Cup Final though saw a defeat, 2-0 to Hayes, but the league form continued to support 'Stones title challenge, which concluded with a 3-0 win at home to Ashford.

With one foot in the Alliance Premier League thanks to Thursday's win over chief rivals, Hastings Wealdstone crossed the border back into non-league soccer's elite and clinched the Southern section championship on Saturday.

Ashford's goal looked to have divine protection for almost half the match as a combination of hard to believe misses and sound covering from a packed visitors defence saw a goalless first half, 'Stones needing only one point to secure the title. When Roy Davies shipped in a fine cross after ten minutes skipper Paul Bowgett powered in a header that had 'goal' written all over it until it was cleared by defender Ireland, entrenched on his own goalline.

Other 'Stones first half raids proved similarly fruitless, as another Davies cross found on-rushing Alan Cordice, but his effort went tamely into the goalkeepers' arms. Ashford's biggest let off came 10 minutes from the interval as a deft touch from Cordice sent Davies rushing clear on a diagonal path to the near post, however with just the keeper to beat, Davies tried to hard and sent a shot spiralling over the Elmslie End.

Ashford began to show signs of cracking after the break and when Carmen let a harmless looking ball slip through his hands in the 64th minute, sowing the seeds for the goal which was to set 'Stones on a Championship winning path.

As Roy Davies' very deep corner came across, out of reach of the waiting attack, Ray Knowles had spotted a gap and he sent a high floating ball into the roof of the net over the despairing defence from 20 yards.

Ashford fell away after that. Three minutes after the goal, Alan Cordice streaked goalwards, and to keep him on a par with most other Southern League defenders this season, Ashford's Hogben brought him down. Ace penalty taker Paul Bowgett blasted the kick high into the left hand corner only for the referee to order it to be retaken. Unruffled as ever, Bowgett this time sent the ball low to the right for his 27th goal of the season.

With the game as any sort of contest over, it only remained to be seen if 'Stones could put the icing on the championship cake by scoring their 100th league goal of the season. The answer came via Roy Davies, who atoned for his earlier miss when he sent a cross in from the left that Carmen could only help into the roof of the net.

All that remained at the final whistle was for 'Stones ever faithful band of supporters to cheer the players back to the dress-

Wealdstone FC – Southern League Champions 1981 – 82
Back; Dr Len Goodchild, Brian Hall (Asst. Manager), Allen Batsford (Manager) Graham Harris (Physio), Peter Braxton (Secretary) Middle; Nigel Johnson, Alan Cordice, Dennis Byatt, Steve Perkins, Ray Goddard, Robin Wainwright, Neil Cordice, Ray Knowles. Front; Fred Barwick, Stuart Pearce, Paul Bowgett, Paul Waites, Roy Davies, Mark Graves
Trophies; SL Champions Cup, Merit Cup, SL Championship Shield, SL South Championship Cup, Southern League Cup

ing room, but, crowd pleasers to the last, they returned for one final bow, tossing their shirts to the frenetic supporters as mementoes of a triumphant season.

Wealdstone; Ray Goddard, Steve Perkins, Stuart Pearce, Dennis Byatt, Paul Bowgett, Fred Barwick, Paul Waites, Robin Wainwright, Alan Cordice, Ray Knowles, Roy Davies, Sub not used, Gary Churchouse.

There was more to celebrate a week later as 'Stones completed a clean sweep in the Southern League with their victory over Nuneaton Borough in the Southern League Shield. Despite losing 1–0 at Nuneaton, a 2–1 victory at home saw the tie go to extra time and then penalties, where Wealdstone won 3–2.

Graham Clark
Supporter since 1960

A follow up from Roy Davies duly collecting his fiver after scoring in an earlier match. Bill Cowan and I made the same offer to the team, via Roy Davies, for the match against Hastings. We won 2–0 and the recipient was to be Alan Cordice who had scored both goals.

We duly paid the money over to Roy to pass on to Alan, however it transpired that Roy had not actually told the rest of the players about the offer and he pocketed the money for himself. The only redeeming factor in this saga was that the players where apparently overwhelmed by Roy's offer to buy them a celebratory drink in the bar afterwards. (With OUR money!)

Despite the success of the previous season, during the summer Wealdstone yet again decided to disband their Suburban League Reserve side, stating that there was too great a difference in standard between this and the first team to be a benefit.

Allen Batsford also indicated that there was talk of a new Midweek League (which was to become the Capital League), containing reserve teams from league and Alliance sides. The standard of this was perceived to be higher, and Wealdstone hoped to join.

Paul Waites
Player 1981-83

In my time with the club, I suppose the greatest memories are the last few games leading up to winning the Southern league Championship.

Hastings at home on the Tuesday night when we won 2-0 and Ashford Town at home on the Saturday. The last home game of the season.

We won 3-0 and then we were all up in the stand throwing our shirts to the crowd – I wonder what happened to my number 7? Then there were Pearcey's shorts – he just kept going after his shirt had gone!

I can still remember the party in the clubhouse afterwards as well.

In all my time at Wealdstone, I only ever knew success so most of the memories are good. Very good. Without Roy Davies though, I'm not sure if any of the success would have been achieved. He brought the players together as he really was the spirit of the team. His character, his singing and always buying the sweeties for the away games on the coach.

The return to the Alliance League the following season started off with a fairytale beginning – three away wins and ten points out of the first twelve was more than could be hoped for, but 'Stones were brought down to earth with a 2-0 home defeat by Bath in the league Cup.

It was only a minor 'blip' however and just one week later, after beating Dagenham at Lower Mead, Wealdstone were top of the Alliance League for the first time. Their record was five wins and two draws from seven league games.

In October, Wealdstone had added a further win and draw to their record, but had slipped to fourth in the table, with four games in hand on the leaders after their exploits in the FA Cup. They were also set to face Gloucester City in the Southern League Championship match.

Only Gloucester City will know how they forced Tuesdays Southern League Championship match, the Southern League equivalent of the Charity Shield, into extra time.

The West Country side, selected to meet Wealdstone thought they'd stumbled into an inferno as the 'Stones came forward with fiery commitment for 90 minutes.

Wealdstone's tally of 24 corners to Gloucester's two was an accurate reflection of a one sided match. The City hero was undoubtedly keeper Glynn Jones who threw his considerable bulk in all directions to thwart Mark Graves and the two Cordice's.

With Stone splaying some delightful approach football, Alan Cordice's 49th minute goal from close range, following a half blocked Bowgett header was long overdue, but immediately afterwards Gloucester drew level by virtue of an own goal, Byatt's back pass from 20 yards appearing to go through Goddard's legs.

'Stones tried to settle the game in normal time with Bowgett and Graves striking the woodwork, but just two minutes into the extra period, Graves finally made the breakthrough with a firm header.

In the 105th minute Stuart Pearce ensured another addition to the 'Stones trophy cabinet by sending a 20-yard free kick past the motionless Jones.

Wealdstone; Ray Goddard, Steve Perkins, Stuart Pearce, Dennis Byatt, Paul Bowgett, Fred Barwick, Roy Davies, Paul Waites, Alan Cordice, Mark Graves, Neil Cordice, Sub Ray Knowles (for Alan Cordice, 70 mins)

The following Saturday and 'Stones still with their unbeaten league record intact, were back in FA Cup action. The previous rounds had seen a 5–0 drubbing of Hertford Town, and then a 3–2 victory over Hendon in a replay. The match at former Manager Eddie Presland's Dulwich Hamlet was to finish in a draw, 'Stones continuing their run with a 2–1 win in the replay at Lower Mead.

It was a match missed by Allen Batsford however as he was in America, talking to two football clubs. Chairman David Morrittt had connections in Florida and had set up meetings at Tampa Bay Rowdies and Tulsa Roughnecks. The intention was for 'Stones to form links with the Tampa club allowing the upcoming stars to come over to Wealdstone for training and coaching to ease the financial strain on the club during the close season, and to gain some first team experience during the season.

The visit to Tulsa was a little different though as the intent was to try and sign former Leeds United player Duncan McKenzie, who was playing for the American side.

The FA Cup saw further progress from the 'Stones as they beat Sutton 3–1 in the next round, to reach the first round proper for the sixth time in eight years, this time eventually losing 2–0 to Swindon Town at the County Ground.

The first defeat in the Alliance league as to come in the 13th game played on the 13th of November, Wealdstone losing 4–2 at home to Weymouth who were also challenging at the top of the table.

These two defeats were the start of a poor run of form that saw Wealdstone only take two points from the next 12 to end a dismal November before form improved again through December, culminating in a 6–0 win over Barnet in front of a crowd of 1,242, the best of the season.

This was followed by a win at local rivals, Enfield and a run of 12 points claimed from 16 possible saw Wealdstone climb from eighth to third in the league table. 'Stones also made progress in the Middlesex Cup. Wins against Kingsbury and Hillingdon Borough on the way to the final against Harrow Boro.

In March, successive away wins at Yeovil (5–1) and Worcester City (3–1) saw 'Stones reach second in the table and a further away win at Maidstone (3–0) at the beginning or April saw 'Stones return to the top for the first time since the start of the season. They were no match though for Harrow Borough on Easter Monday, going down by 2–0.

It was the first time Harrow Borough had won the trophy and came during a very successful period for the club, as they reached the FA Trophy semi final only to lose to eventual winners Telford. Boro' won the first leg at Telford by 2–0 only to lose the return at Earlsmead by 5–1 after extra time.

By some quirk of fate, Wealdstone's next league match was against Telford at Lower Mead and Wealdstone ran out winners, 2–0.

David Mather
Player, Telford United

THAT semi final was amazing. We lost 2-0 at home to Harrow Borough in the first leg and I remember all their players singing songs at us in the dressing room, about going to Wembley and all that.

Then in the second leg we went a goal down and looked down and out. I got one back which gave us a bit of incentive, then got another early in the second half. You could see them wilting and Colin Williams got four as we beat them in extra time. Then on the Tuesday we came to your place and we were cheered onto the pitch!

Wealdstone's Championship dream finally came to an end in mid April, after a draw against Bath and a defeat against Enfield at home, in front of 1,725 people.

The Wealdstone Supporters FC (SFC Wealdstone) did manage to bring a trophy to the club, as they won the Marathon League Division 5, the first Championship in their history. They also reached the Junior Cup Final but had to be content with runner up to seal a successful season for them.

The season finished with Wealdstone in a very creditable third place, behind Enfield and Maidstone. The Supporters Club as ever had made a major financial contribution to the club during the season, and this was extended with a further £500 towards a new tannoy system.

Even in the close season Supporters Club Chairman Ray Kemp was to continue his fundraising, reaching even greater heights than the team as he made a parachute jump from 2,000 feet to raise more money for the club.

Stephen Bird
Supporter since the 1960's

I carried on going to Lower Mead but there was a time when my appearances became a little sporadic as matches clashed with things like the Scouts! This was rectified when I found so many of my school friends were regulars, and I joined them behind the goal.

Dad always discouraged me from joining 'the rowdies' behind the goal but as he wasn't there, I was, and I enjoyed the atmosphere - out of all of those people who used to go together only Martin Lacey still attends matches, Russell Newmark used to report on 'Stones games for the 'Observer and he now works on a national paper, but I wonder what happened to Brian Maynard, John Holter, Jonathan Rose and Nick Rowe..........

Bobby Moss was my favourite in the 70's - he never gave less than 110% - I remember one game where he knocked the ball out of the Goalkeepers hands, took it around him and shot into the empty net and amazingly the referee allowed the goal to stand!

Later in the 70's University meant I couldn't get to either of the 'Hereford' matches though you should have seen my reaction when the replay result was broadcast on the news!! The other occupant of the University Halls TV room must've thought I'd gone mad!! Luckily I did see both Reading and QPR as those games were during the Christmas break.

By the start of the 1980-81 season I had finished University and was back home for good but it was something of a transitional season.

Ken Payne was sacked and in came Allen Batsford and with him, Brian Hall as assistant. By the end of the season we were looking a reasonable side but we were still involved in the relegation battle on the final day when we needed to draw at home to A P Leamington, our rivals for the last relegation spot.

We were leading 1-0 mid way through the second half when Jimmy Sweetzer missed a penalty. Unfortunately the heads then dropped and we let A P Leamington back into the game - they went on to win 2-1 and Wealdstone were relegated.

I always thought Sweetzer was unfairly vilified for the miss - he'd been a decent enough player in his short time with us and God knows we've missed some penalties since then!!

That relegation really was a blessing in disguise as we stormed to the Southern League title pushed all the way by the late lamented Hastings United and we also won the Southern league Cup on a memorable evening at Gloucester City's old Horton Road ground - a vast 'bowl' of a stadium but with a tremendous atmosphere.

There were many occasions during that period that spring to mind - Stuart Pearce's last game, at home in the FA Cup against Basildon United, when he was made captain for the day, and Wealdstone played in Red!

There was a Boxing Day local derby, again at Lower Mead against Barnet - a side at the time who were normally mid-table in the Alliance Premier League.

At centre half on this occasion was a tall gangly youth whose kit looked a size or two too small for him. Needless to say, the fans behind the goal soon singled him out and he was baited mercilessly from behind the goal with comments about his similarity to ET. He had an absolute nightmare as Wealdstone ran out winners, 6-0!

His name? Simon Webster. He was on loan from Spurs and he went on to have a distinguished career with Huddersfield Town and as captain of Charlton Athletic, joining West Ham briefly before retiring through injury!

Andy Waddock
Player 1982 -1983

Wealdstone FC will always be a club that I hold fond memories for as I was something of a supporter myself during my youth and I visited Lower Mead as often as possible when not involved with QPR Schoolboys or the Youth Team on Saturdays.

I remember during one game I was standing behind the goal (Cinema End), which Wealdstone were attacking. All the home fans were singing and chanting when Dennis Byatt hit one of his famous Pile-driver shots.

Unfortunately the effort was not only off target, but was heading at a rather rapid pace for my face, so, quick as a flash, instead of heading or catching the ball, I decided to duck out of the flight of this Byatt-launched missile only to smash my head against the small white fence which surrounded the pitch. A trip to Northwick Park for stitches ensued and I never did get my own back on Dennis for that one!!

Well, just a few years later, just before my eighteenth birthday, QPR decided not to offer me professional terms and released me.

A work colleague of my father, Ray Corner, was a Wealdstone fanatic and he introduced me to the then 'Stones boss, Allen Batsford. Allen felt his squad needed a fresh face at the time and decided to give me a chance.

I made a dream start for the 'Stones, scoring the winner in a Middlesex cup-tie against Kingsbury Town, but I had to wait a while for my league debut which came in a 0-0 draw at Boston United, but I eventually moved to Hendon after making only 14 appearances for the 'Stones in a nine month spell at Lower Mead.

It was a great experience for a young player like myself to be at a club with so many great players. I was able to watch, listen and learn during my time at Wealdstone and I have never forgotten this part of my football career.

There were so many highlights during my time at Wealdstone, but one that immediately springs to mind was an end of season trip to Harrow's twin town, Douai in France. A great time was had by all on that trip and we drew with the French 3-3.

Another really memorable event was an amazing match that I played in, the marvelous 3-3 draw at Northwich Victoria. The Vics were FA Trophy finalists that season and we traveled up there on a wet May Monday (2nd) in 1983, still with an outside chance of winning the Alliance Premier League Championship.

The game started at a furious pace with both sides playing with bundles of passion and no shortage of skill. The home side took the lead in the fifth minute from the penalty spot after a foul by 'Stones skipper, Paul Bowgett, but we powered back and created numerous chances. Big Dennis Byatt missed a penalty before Alan Cordice leveled just prior to the interval.

Allen and his assistant Brian Hall were full of confidence and praise for our efforts in the half time team talk and the feeling was we could go on and win the game.

The second half was every bit as good as the first with Northwich retaking the lead after 56 minutes only for us to equalise again some five minutes later when a certain Stuart Pearce struck a wonderful goal from outside the box.

The game continued to ebb and flow but just as it seemed that both sides had settled for a well earned point, Northwich's 'Super Sub' Steve Cravan popped up in injury time and put his side in front.

There were only seconds remaining and we took the ball back to the centre circle almost in despair. It seemed our efforts would be for nothing and our title bid all but gone.

However from the restart the ball went to the feet of Roy Davies who decided to embark on one of his customary silky runs. The ball looked to be glued to his feet as he went past one player, then another and then another, indeed it seemed as if he beat the entire Northwich side before arriving at the edge of the area.

He then fired a low drive beyond the despairing keepers dive, into the bottom corner of the net for a wonderful goal and the final whistle blew immediately on the restart.

Passion was still riding high as both teams walked off and a few right hooks were exchanged in the tunnel.... Still, no harm done.

We eventually finished third that year behind Enfield and Maidstone but many of that team went on to play a major part in the historic 'Double' two years later.

Dave Morrittt ensured that the club was back in the news during the summer. On July 1st, the Harrow Observer carried a story that he had given a 'thumbs up' to a merger between Wealdstone FC and Harrow Borough FC. Informal talks had taken place between him and Boro Chairman, Peter Rogers with a view to the clubs joining as one, playing at Earlsmead while Lower Mead was developed.

The intention was to combine the support of two clubs and halve the cost – it seemed that the move was supported by the board at the time, the aim to guarantee crowds in excess of 1000 every week and for the new club to use the resources to progress to the Football League.

At the same time he also decided to change the club's colours from Royal Blue which had been used since the change from Blue and White Quarters in 1962, to 'a brighter, cleaner image' of broad Yellow and Blue stripes.

Both decisions were met with some disdain by the fans and neither was supported, although the kit did change!

The end of the season didn't see the visit to Florida for winning

ALLEZ DOUAI

JOURNEES DES JEUNES AU SPORTING CLUB de DOUAI

WEALDSTONE - DOUAI

the title, but there was still an overseas trip for the club to Douai to play the local team as part of the twinning celebrations between Douai and Harrow.

The match ended in a 3-3 draw in front of a large traveling contingent of Wealdstone fans, both fans and players alike then enjoying the local 'hospitality'.

Season 1983-1984 followed a similar pattern to the previous year, although there was one major difference.

With Allen Batsford hospitalised to have a heart by-pass operation, team matters were handed to Brian Hall, Allen taking the General Manager role, although he was to be absent for over two months.

In September, after six league matches, 'Stones had won 5 and drawn 1, and were lying in second place in the league. By the middle of October, seven wins and four draws in eleven games had maintained a second place, two points behind Nuneaton with two games in hand.

The financial situation received a boost with the transfer of Stuart Pearce to Coventry for £25,000 plus the usual 'sell-ons' and additional payments if Stuart was to play for his country.

The deal was done on a Friday, and Stuart signed after passing a medical the following Tuesday. On the intervening Saturday, he captained Wealdstone in the FA Cup against Basildon United at Lower Mead.

The Harrow Observer reported on Stuart's last match;

Three first half goals saw Wealdstone progress to the final qualifying round of the FA Cup at the expense of a spirited Basildon side in monsoon type conditions at Lower Mead last Saturday. Fittingly, it was Stuart Pearce in his final appearance for the 'Stones, who led the team out as Captain for the day, and he responded with a characteristically accomplished performance at left back.

The match began in wet and blustery conditions, and after a quiet opening, the home side took the lead with their first attack on 11 minutes. Goalkeeper Wilson slipping as he tried to intercept Pearce's cross from the left, and Brian Greenaway touched in from close range.

'Stones then increased their lead on the half-hour, courtesy of their prolific striking partnership, with Alan Cordice supplying the cross for Mark Graves to swivel and score from 12 yards. Five minutes later it was Cordice's turn, latching on to a through ball and finishing emphatically with a powerful angled drive into the roof of the net.

To their credit, the visitors refused to fold and with conditions becoming quite appalling, they battled back after half time. Bob Iles did well to thwart Hubbard and then produced a stunning save to tip Hull's fierce volley over the bar. He was helpless though on 71 minutes when the persistent Heritage buried his shot in the far corner after the 'Stones failed to clear a free kick from the right.

Mark Graves, who had earlier hit a post was then twice foiled by the acrobatic Wilson before the end, which the crowd greeted with a standing ovation for their departing hero, Stuart Pearce.

Wealdstone; Bob Iles, Fred Barwick, Stuart Pearce, Dennis Byatt, Paul Bowgett, David Price, Brian Greenaway, Gary Donellen, Nigel Johnson, Alan Cordice, Mark Graves.

Stuart had made 242 appearances for the club, scoring 15 goals.

Stuart Pearce
Player 1979 - 1983

I had no options when I joined Wealdstone. I'd been released from QPR and it was either playing in the park with my mates or joining Wealdstone. It wasn't a big decision though as I hadn't really enjoyed what I'd been doing.

I was a late developer and at Wealdstone, the first year was difficult. I wasn't playing particularly well for the Youth or reserves and the training was difficult as I'd just got a job. It was a bit of a surprise when I got my chance in the first team, I hadn't really expected it. I happened to be the left back in the reserves and that's why I got called up.

I remember early on we played Dartford in the Trophy and I remember the crowd coming on the field. The Chairman came straight over and pushed the fan back off the pitch, so I learnt that he wasn't taking any messing about.

There were a lot of characters in the club, a lot had come out of the league into non-league - I remember playing against Alex Stepney - when I tell people that they can't believe it because he was a hero in the sixties - before my time - I think he was about 41 and I was 16 or 17!

It gave me a great grounding, tremendous experience - it was physically very hard.

Players who have been around the game a long time were worldly wise and knew how to handle themselves, there were a few who tried to sort me out, that's just the way it was in non-league football.

You had to learn quickly about how to look after yourself. I remember Bowg coming over and having a pop at Steve Regan

Stuart Pearce (top left) celebrating with the rest of the squad and Manager Allen Batsford after winning the Southern League Championship.

once. I've gone in for the ball and nicked it past him, so he's come back to sort me out and Bowg then came over to me and told me – I hadn't seen it as I'd gone past him.

The dressing room was dominated by two players in my time at the 'Stones. I think they overlapped by about two weeks – Willie Watson, before he joined Scarborough was club captain – he controlled the atmosphere, then just as he was about to go in came Roy Davies, he was top quality.

I still keep in touch with Fred Barwick too. Dennis Byatt was always an influence but we all used to meet up twice a week and then play on a Saturday.

There were always some people you didn't mix with but it was more because of ages and different tastes than not liking people – we all had football in common and that's what mattered. We had a mix and we worked for each other – everyone wanted the same outcome so we worked towards it.

I remember twice I think we got to the FA Cup 1st round proper they were always big games for us. We lost at home to Southend once and then later we lost 2-0 at Swindon. We'd already played about four rounds to get that far. Against Southend I thought we were unlucky to lose 1-0 at home, there was nothing in it.

At Swindon, I thought I had a really good first half, I came in at half time having done well and the second half I got taken apart by the forward. As a youngster it gave me quite a jolt. From thinking I was playing well against a league club, the second half he came into his own and I didn't know what to do about it.

I remember Paul Rideout played in that game – he was the wonder boy at the time, and we had words in the first half. He told me to get back to my 9 to 5 job and I always remembered it. A few seasons later he was sat on the bench at the first game of the season at Coventry, I was playing. I nearly went over and mentioned it, but I bit my lip. I thought there would be a better time later.

I'm still involved but I don't know where he is now.............

'Stones had achieved a 16 match unbeaten run in all competitions, including the next round of the FA Cup against Bishops Stortford, which saw 'Stones drawn at home to Enfield.

The match at Lower Mead finished 1–1 with Bob Iles the 'Stones star. The replay the following Tuesday saw a tremendous fight back, Wealdstone having taken an early lead before falling behind 2–1, then equalising and forcing the tie into extra time.

The following Monday, the replay at Lower Mead saw 'Stones through with a goal in each half in front of over 1,500 fans to secure a trip to Colchester United where they were beaten 4–0 in the second round.

Despite the repeated promise from Chairman Dave Morritt that he would take the team to Florida to play Rodney Marsh's Tampa Bay Rowdies if they won the league title, the unbeaten run came to an end with a 3–1 defeat at home to Barnet in the Bob Lord Trophy. This was the first of three defeats on the trot in three separate competitions – a defeat at Dagenham in the league was followed by a home defeat to Hendon in the Middlesex Senior Cup.

'Stones maintained a Championship challenge into December and Allen Batsford returned to resume his role, only for the club to sack him just before Christmas, three weeks after his return from hospital. The reasons given were that the club could no longer afford a General Manager.

An unbeaten spell over Christmas and the New Year kept 'Stones well in contention in the title race despite being 11 points behind leaders Runcorn. They had five games in hand as a result of their FA Cup run.

By the beginning of February, 'Stones were third having only lost twice in 23 matches, winning 13 but a run of six matches without a win in March virtually ended the title chance.

The small squad had been stretched to the limit by injuries and Manager Brian Hall had not been allowed to sign any more players despite agreeing terms with at least two.

It resulted in Chairman Dave Morrittt calling a meeting with angry fans to answer criticism aimed at him from the terraces. The position did not change, though, as there was no more money available to sign new players to rescue what had become a disappointing season.

The summer saw little transfer activity, although the groundsman at the club's pre-season training 'home' in Bushey did ask if he could join in. He did, subsequently leading the team on their cross-country run, winning the shuttles and also showing some ability with the ball, so he was signed as an addition to the squad.

'He' was Vince Jones, a nineteen year old taking his first steps into senior football.

Pre-season matches are rarely a guide to the forthcoming season, but the first two of this year saw Reading's first team and a strong Crystal Palace side well beaten, in total five goals were scored without reply and the 'Stones team did look very sharp.

An unbeaten start to the season saw 'Stones take over at the top of the table at the end of August after a 4–2 win over Gateshead. Their first defeat came at the end of September when Boston United scored an 88th minute winner at Lower Mead. They had become a very difficult side for 'Stones to beat – seven of the previous nine meetings between the clubs ending in draws.

At the same time, Wealdstone were heavily involved in the organisation of the Capital League. After months of hard work and planning, eight teams were to be involved, Wealdstone, Barnet, Dagenham, Enfield, Brentford, Gillingham, Orient and Wimbledon.

This meant an additional seven league fixtures as each club was to play each other only once. The Cannon League clubs would visit their non-league counterparts as this was expected to increase the gate receipts. Wealdstone's first two fixtures were to be at home to Brentford and Wimbledon.

The league position was strengthened with away wins at Yeovil and Worcester, but 'Stones then failed to win any of their next five league matches into November. They remained at the top of the table with a four point advantage over Enfield who had a game in hand. Wealdstone were making the most of the 'new' league rule that saw away wins rewarded with an extra point.

Another three matches without a win saw Enfield take over at the top, 'Stones problems mounting as injuries increased as Wealdstone still had a squad of only fifteen or sixteen players. They traveled to Telford, where they lost 4–2 missing Iles and Goddard, their two first choice goalkeepers, Perkins, McCargo,

Dibble, Holmes and Johnson, Dennis Byatt playing despite suffering from the flu.

As the missing players returned to fitness and the first team, 'Stones form took an upturn, starting with another three point win away to Weymouth and later in the month, at Frickley. It was a match that stuck in the mind of many traveling fans as it was played in thick fog. The first Wealdstone goal, Neil Cordice scoring from thirty yards against the run of play, was the first time that many of the fans saw the ball during the game.

The second half saw the fog thicken. On the hour Greenaway scored from a corner to seal the win. With only ten minutes to go and the fog still thick, a nearby allotment owner decided it was a good time to burn his rubbish and as well as the fog, the pitch was soon engulfed in smoke. The referee wasn't going to be fooled by the situation, and having found the Frickley bench he told them to ensure the fire was put out as he was not going to abandon the game.

By the end of January, 'Stones were still in a challenging position at the top of the table, Altrincham, Enfield and Kidderminster seen as the rivals (all were to drop away eventually), Wealdstone were set to stage the Gola League Conference at the end of the season, and everyone determined that they should stage it as Champions.

There were also some new developments 'off the field', Chairman David Morrittt announcing details of his plans for a new £1 million super-stadium to bring league football to Harrow. The new stadium would be built on the Lower Mead site and plans were already being drawn up for a 10,000 capacity stadium with seating for 7,000. Planning permission was to be sought by the end of the current season, the plans also included a merger (again) with Harrow Borough FC where Wealdstone would play while the work was carried out, the 'new' club returning to Lower Mead for the start of the 1986 – 1987 season.

Wealdstone started their FA Trophy season with possibly their worst display of the year, a 0–0 draw away to Harlow, although they rectified matters winning the replay by 5–0. They also made progress in the Middlesex Senior Cup coming back from 2–0 down against Hillingdon Borough to ensure a semi-final meeting with Harrow Borough.

The 2–1 defeat of Wycombe Wanderers at home saw further progress in the Trophy and a third round tie with Welling, also at home.

An Andy Graham goal that would have graced Wembley itself brought Wealdstone's dream a little closer on Saturday. Graham, who replaced the injured Mark Graves for the third round tie capped a superb all round performance with one of the best goals ever seen at Lower Mead.

It came after 21 minutes when he took a Roy Davies pass on his chest and in one movement turned and rifled an unstoppable volley into the top corner of the net. "You very rarely see goals like that" said 'Stones boss Brian Hall, "It was so good the poor lad blushed. You will wait a long time to see a better one".

Despite a rare error from Iles gifting Welling an equaliser, 'Stones eventually ran out winners by 3–1, the same score by which Frickley were dispatched in the next round to see Wealdstone drawn against Enfield in the two legged Semi Final.

A victory over Harrow Borough saw 'Stones reach the Middlesex Cup Final also against Enfield and although the league position had suffered, 'Stones dropping to sixth, they were still very much in the race with games in hand.

The Trophy draw meant that there would be four fixtures between Wealdstone and Enfield in the space of three weeks, the Middlesex Cup Final being played in between the two legs of the FA Trophy semi-final and a league match between the two sides was scheduled for the following week!

The fixture congestion was a major concern as Wealdstone had already played three matches in six days, were expected to play on the Saturday, Sunday and Tuesday prior to the first leg of the semi final, and still had matches to arrange, so it was a relief when the Middlesex FA agreed to postpone the County Cup Final until the following August Bank Holiday.

Ever mindful of the cost of running a successful side, Wealdstone also arranged a Rugby League game at Lower Mead, on April 14th Fulham hosting Whitehaven. The match was a league game and the profits set to benefit the Mayor Of Harrow's Charity, Wealdstone hopeful of securing a deal for Fulham RFC to play at Lower Mead the following season.

In the Trophy semi-final 'Stones took a 2–0 lead in the first leg at Southbury Road, the following week surviving 90 heart stopping minutes at Lower Mead as Enfield laid siege to the 'Stones goal.

They were only to score once, on 17 minutes through Nicky Ironton. It had been a real 'backs to the wall' performance but it was the result that counted, Wealdstone returning to Wembley almost twenty years on from their previous Amateur Cup victory, and the dream of becoming the first club to achieve the non-league double of FA Trophy and Gola League in the

From the early 1980's, another supporters magazine, *Long Ball Down The Middle.*

same season one step closer.

Stephen Yearley
Supporter since 1960's

I've supported the 'Stones ever since the Amateur Cup Final, and up until the early eighties attended the majority of games home and away. My first child, a girl, was born on 5th April 1985 – the day of the semi Final first leg away at Enfield and I celebrated with some friends in the bar at Lower Mead prior to the game.

I really wanted to go to the match but I had promised my wife that I would visit her and the baby in hospital in the afternoon after a few drinks. Sometimes there are more important things in life than football, and this was one of those.

Well, I got so carried away with the atmosphere and the joy of having a baby that I got absolutely plastered. Someone drove me home and when I came round it was 9:30pm in the evening, too late to visit my wife and child, however I did ring the hospital and left a grovelling apology.

To this day, my wife still thinks I went to the match, and because of the 2-0 win, celebrated after the match. That bit's almost true because at 10:00pm I found out the score, so I went out to celebrate and got drunk all over again.

Wealdstone FC is in my heart and soul. The club has been such an influence on my life and the supporters are so special. As the song goes; "You'll never know how much I love you, until you've taken my Wealdstone away".

A difficult run of fixtures saw Wealdstone touring the country over one week, five games being played in seven days. The victories in these lifted 'Stones right back into the title race although defeats in three of the next four league matches meant that nothing was certain.

'Stones finally returning to the top of the league with a 1–0 home win over Kettering with five games remaining. It was in the return at Kettering at the beginning or May that the title was finally won.

It was by no means a vintage Wealdstone performance, but the massed ranks of 'Stones fans that had made the trip to Rockingham Road could not have cared less. They had traveled to Northamptonshire to salute the new Gola League Champions, and when referee Brian Couldrey blew the final whistle that is exactly what they did.

Kettering's pitch was swamped by the delirious fans who swept over the advertising hoardings like a Blue and Yellow wave. They were given an added bonus when the 'Championship Trophy' was presented ahead of schedule by Kettering Chairman John Murphy.

The presentation was due to be held on the following Monday at Barnet but Alan Clifton had persuaded League Secretary Peter Hunter to hand it over early. He traveled down to Kent to collect it and had smuggled it to Kettering!

When Mr Murphy handed the trophy to Paul Bowgett who had missed the game through suspension the celebrations really started. After the customary hugs and kisses on the sidelines, the players took to the stand to receive the adulation of the fans, and that's when the fun really started.

The champagne that had been laid on in the dressing room cascaded down in a celebratory shower over the jubilant mob. It was quickly followed by players throwing their Shirts, Shorts and even socks to be snapped up as treasured souvenirs by the fans.

Dennis Byatt who had probably had his best game for the club finished the celebrations wearing just his jock strap, which he was preparing to launch into the crowd before he was reminded that he would need it for the Barnet match!

Even though 'Stones new cult hero Andy Graham had hit a 78th minute winner – a goal with Championship quality written all over it – the name on the lips of the Wealdstone faithful was that of Manager, Brian Hall.

The strain of the title race had seemed to get to the 'Stones boss over the season, but when the trophy appeared on Saturday his face cracked into a smile wide enough to have toothpaste companies fighting to sign him up, a mixture of sheer joy and untold relief.

It was a day when Wealdstone seemed prepared to simply roll up their sleeves and make sure they put the title in the bag without worrying too much about how they did it.

Paul Bowgett with the Gola League Trophy

Sandwiched between Kettering strikes in a first half hour, which saw 'Stones defend resolutely on a hard, bumpy pitch Lee Holmes headed just wide, Alan Cordice miscued in front of goal and a Cordice effort skimmed to safety off of Fee's head.

Wealdstone put a stranglehold on the match in the second half, dictating the play but never really raising the tempo.

Holmes should have put them ahead on the hour after good work by Roy Davies, Graham and Alan Cordice, but headed wide. Then eight minutes later a quick break involving Graham and Brian Greenaway saw Cordice beat Kettering keeper Willie Boyd to the cross but he poked the ball just wide.

Wealdstone's traveling army had to wait another ten minutes for Graham's super strike. A Byatt free kick was powered over the waiting cluster in the penalty area to Graham, standing on the corner of the box, who met it with a vicious, first time, left foot volley that arrowed into the opposite bottom corner.

Kettering struck back briefly, with Iles twice called into action within a minute but the last strike came from Wealdstone with Greenaway hitting a shot which bounced off the inside of a post, along the goalline and into the arms of a grateful Boyd who held onto the ball as firmly as Hall held on to the trophy after the game.

Wealdstone; Bob Iles, Neil Cordice, Roy Davies, Dennis Byatt, Steve Perkins, Robin Wainwright, Brian Greenaway, Lee Holmes, Alan Cordice, Andy Graham, Gary Donnellan, Subs; Nigel Johnson, Vince Jones.

Mark Snell
Supporter

There is one last memory, and it's a little more recent. When Wealdstone won the league away to Kettering and we all ran on the pitch, Matthew (Snell) was with me, as a young boy.

He got very upset and still reminds me to this day that Dennis Byatt took his yellow and blue Wealdstone scarf and put it round his own neck as they went to receive the trophy.

So Dennis, can he have it back?

The following Monday, a Wealdstone side showing eight changes, lost 7-0 at Barnet where they were officially presented with the Championship trophy.

It seemed to some that they were determined to win the league with a negative goal difference, but the hard work had been done. The following Saturday there was the small matter of a trip to Wembley for the FA Trophy final.

Tony O'Rourke
Supporter since 1974

I am a common or garden supporter who, having followed Wealdstone FC to one degree or another over 26 years finally, last season, took the major leap to Supporters' Club membership.

Having lived within earshot of Lower Mead for 25 years in 1989 I moved 120 miles out of the area to Alvaston, Derbyshire, I continued to support the 'Stones from afar during that period as was most visibly evidenced by my Sharon & Tracy type car visor with "Wealdstone FC" emblazoned across it.

This visor became quite well-known locally with individuals commenting on its harmonious relationship with my R registration 1.6 Ford Capri.

With hindsight I am truly apologetic for this period of my life which, as you can imagine did nothing for the image of Wealdstone fans abroad, never mind 'southerners' in general.

After four happy years in the East Midlands my job with one of the major high street banks (not the Chinese one, the glorified building society, or the one with South African connections) took me to the North East where I settled in Whitley Bay.

Here I represented Wealdstone FC in the unofficial form of a Fantasy League team in the Whitley Bay FC fantasy league, under the name of "Wealdstone - We Were Great Once". This as you can probably tell from the title of the team was during the period when Wealdstone FC's fortunes were sinking like a stone with no light at the end of the tunnel.

The lads in the North East warmed to me as a cockney far from home and were well aware of the stature of Wealdstone FC despite our demise at the time. In fact it was Whitley Bay FC who lost to Hayes in the 1966 Amateur Cup Semi-Final the year that Wealdstone went on to win it at Wembley.

Believe it or not some of the Whitley Bay lads are now irregular attendees of Wealdstone matches as they always want to take in a match when they visit me in sunny Essex.

I should at this point perhaps mention that my protestations that we played a higher standard of football than Whitley Bay's Northern Division 1 rubbish took a bit of a knock when a couple of the lads attended 'that' Grays FC away match, only to be greeted with the sight of the groundsman digging a trench in the goalmouth.

The day of the FA Trophy final sticks in my mind as the small shops of Harrow where bedecked in our Blue & Yellow colours and the 'Stones fans marched en masse through the Streets of Harrow from Lower Mead to Harrow on the Hill tube.

From there, there was a raucous journey on the Met Line to Wembley Park tube and a thoroughly enjoyable walk down Wembely Way hurling abuse at the in bred Boston fans on the way.

The game itself is a bit of a blur (no doubt due to the subsequent all night celebrations at the marquee on the Lower Mead pitch) but the recollection of Andy Graham scoring that semi-overhead peach of a goal from the edge of the penalty area will stay with me forever (much in the same way as the beer stain I generated on the unfortunate part-time supporters clothes who was sitting in front of me as it went in),

Other fond memories include another Andy Graham goal which sealed the league at Kettering and Paul Bowgett lifting the GOLA League trophy after we had been thrashed 7-0 (or was it 1) at Barnet.

I've never seen so many people so happy after such an odd result (albeit achieved with half the team out the week before we went on to lift the FA Trophy at Wembley).

Another fond memory involves the FA Trophy Semi final 2nd leg against Enfield There was a bit of argy-bargy (nothing more) in the crowd behind the Wealdstone goal and one of the boys in blue at the match decided to make an example of the smallest, youngest, member of the crowd.

As the PC tried to haul the youth out (I seem to remember him being pulled by the ear, but I'm sure that's my memory playing tricks on me) assorted Wealdstone supporters above a certain age (a certain pensionable age) steamed in and freed the youth whilst telling the surly office to pick on someone his own size/age.

It brought a lump to my throat (and the policeman's cheekbone).

Roy Davies
Player mid 1980's

I was born in Perivale in 1953 and from the hospital window I could see the Lower Mead stadium.

I promised myself that one day I'd escape from the asylum and play for the illustrious 'Stones' of Wealdstone.

However, affecting my release proved a lot more difficult that at first anticipated. As I was told that I wouldn't be able to take my football home with me - so I disguised myself as a Linesman (referee's Assistant) and made my exit over the back fence. Onto British Rail land there alongside. Unwittingly the flag that was part of the Linesman's regalia came in very handy as I hailed a northbound push and pull to a stop and thus procures a ride to Greenford Station. Unfortunately ticketless, and inappropriately dressed I was apprehended by the London transport militia and sentenced to twenty years hard labour on the chain gang.

Being away from the breast, with no food life was really tough, but it was amongst the sleepers, the rail tracks and ironically the 'Stones' I was able to hone the skills that would stand me in good stead in later life, when I would realise my one ambition.

My eventual connection with Wealdstone was at the hip, as a player. I would probably have been a better player but for the extra attached encumbrance.

My appearances varied from Post New Romantic to Neo-Martinique, with a hint of Club Blazer and fetching Grey Slacks thrown in. My goal was to get out of the Blazer and Slacks and head off to my other 'club', that being Tudors Night club on Wealdstone Bridge.

Some of my fondest memories of the club? - Les Scott is the memory of Wealdstone FC that I hold closest, in fact it's right next to me as we speak. (Who's speaking - I'm writing!)

As I write, I'm reminded of Les's vaudevillesque demeanor, when, as we were changing prior to a game he would burst in at the far end of the dressing room, the end nearest his domain, the kit room, and deliver the most abysmal one-liners and then disappear back to his lair, The jokes were always crap, but I for one was always totally enamored because it was the perfect distraction from the team talks!

Morritt; What was that all about??

Talking again of team talks, pushing Les Scott a close second in the memory stakes was the always immaculate timing of the games tannoy man who had the uncanny knack of playing 'We Are the 'Stones' just as Brian Hall would be down in the dressing room espousing his long ball strategies. The raising of his eyebrows and the shaking of his head, always intimated to me Brian's thoughts about my persona, still, c'est la vie!

A couple of matches spring to mind -firstly scoring my first goal for the club against Basingstoke. Taking my usual amount of abuse from a regular section of the crowd, I was goaded into action with the 'promise' of a fiver if I scored.

Low and behold, I dropped my shoulder, cut in from the left and rifled one into the bottom right hand corner or the net. I raced over to the aforementioned section of the crowd, jumped over the fence, and duly collected my money from the perpetrator of the promise (Postman Mick) who in all fairness was ready and willing to hand it over. - I played the remainder of the match with the fiver down my shorts.

Another occasion was away to Yeovil. We were awarded a free kick on the Halfway line on top of the notorious slope. Myself and 'fatty' Byatt were in charge with strict instructions to hit the far post. Yeovil's keeper, having dealt with two or three previous efforts was already moving in that direction anticipating more of the same.

Both 'fatty' and myself noticed this and he said to me " have you got any food?" - I replied "No - I gave you my last lot!" "OK" he countered "I'm going to smash this in the top corner at the near post".

Checking his aim he took his obligatory four paces back and then rasped the shot exactly where he said he would, with Yeovil's keeper floundering across the goal from the far post.

Probably the best goal I ever witnessed.

"One Nil" I shouted, and then I told him I was only joking about the food, and handed him an egg sandwich that I'd been saving for just such an occasion. We went on to 'muller' them five or six nothing, with me giving a running commentary as goal after

A pre-match visit to Wembley for Byatt, Jones, Wainwright, Johnson and Davies

goal went in. "It's a rout, it's a rout" was my last oration.

Finally, if Vinnie Jones couldn't get in the double winning side, and then a year later was playing in the First Division, can I tell my grandchildren that if I'd been born ten years later, I'd have been a Premiership player, and they wouldn't have been my grandchildren!!

Gary Donellan
Player mid 1980's

Wealdstone FC or rather Lower Mead had two distinct atmospheres. On Saturdays it could be a quiet, even genteel place, but for night matches it was made a very intimidating place to visit for away teams by a hard core of 50-100 fans. The club lost its soul when Lower Mead was sold, but its heart was and is going strong - it's that loyal band of supporters.

There are two great memories from the many games, Nuneaton v Wealdstone the year that we won the double. It was a top of the table clash between two very strong, very powerful teams and both needed the points. We went 1-0 up after about 25 minutes, after a spell when Nuneaton had dominated but not threatened our goal, the remainder of the half being fairly even with no more goals.

After 10 or 15 minutes of the second half Polly (Steve) Perkins was elbowed when going up for a header and was knocked out. All hell broke loose -Byatt and Bowgett were first in and everybody else followed. Bob Iles the goalkeeper ran 40 yards to join in and all twenty-two players got involved. The referee eventually restored order, sending of both Byatt and Bowgett and one of the Nuneaton players.

Polly Perkins eventually came round, to be told that he's now playing centre half with Robin Wainwright, Mark Graves at right back, and three in midfield with one up front.

What Happened?

Probably the greatest mass-brawl ever just showed the spirit of the side - as a team we looked after our own. Wealdstone was never about a player but about a team. We weren't the best players but we most definitely were the best team.

Bob Iles in goal - the best one on one keeper I ever played with, I would still say if the opposition broke through ten times they would score no more than one. His goal kicking was atrocious!

Polly Perkins was a great man for man marker, he must have been one of the fastest runners ever going backwards and no-one ever seemed to 'get to him', and yet this was a man playing with a crippled back.

Roy Davies - famed for that single 'Down at The Wealdstone' and 'We Are the 'Stones' with the supporters as a backing group. Most of the vocals were recorded in the dressing room to make it appear there were more of them.

Paul Bowgett and Dennis Byatt, at their peaks no doubt the best centre half pairing in the league.

Robin Wainwright, the sixties throwback - the first and only hippie I ever played football with. He was in his mid thirties when I first met him but I'll bet he's still playing, still the fittest and at least 45 by now. Generally, he was the quiet man, but once that shirt went onto his back his whole persona changed - nothing but nothing would get past him or beat him if there was any way he could stop it.

Mark Graves, position - goal scorer. He couldn't head, shoot, pass, or tackle, he had no stamina and no pace but he would always be in my team. I was amazed that Brian Hall didn't pick him for the Trophy Final - he didn't even get on the bench.

Alan Cordice. The man dictated the way we played because of his blistering pace. He was a fabulous and great asset to the team, but because of the team he never received the plaudits he deserved.

Brian Hall. The manager - he was critical to our success at Wealdstone, having to take over from Allen Batsford and all of his successes to produce the Double Team.

This was achieved because he created a team that stuck together, that played the managers way even when most people didn't believe it was the right way but mostly a team that gelled together for some reason. He made decisions and selections that many did not agree with but he always had the respect of those around him.

The Squad preparing to leave for Wembley

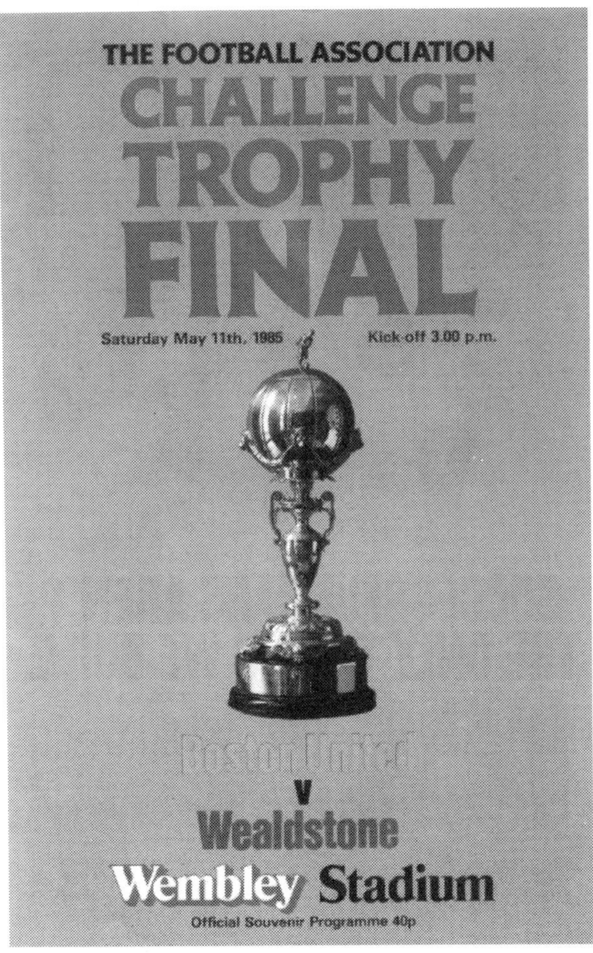

Wealdstone's third Wembley visit also brought success with the 2-1 win over Boston United in the FA Trophy.

The second memory? Trophy Final Day, the 11th of May 1985. Traveling down from the hotel, coming down the A1 passing all the Boston United Supporters coaches, all decorated in orange - we were amazed how many were traveling down.

Our team bus headed for Lower Mead before heading onto Wembley Stadium to pick someone up.

As the bus was going down the main road to the ground no one in Wealdstone appeared to know what was going on - none of the shops were decorated in Wealdstone's colours and nor were the people.

Arriving at Wembley all we could see were Boston coaches, Boston supporters and there was orange all around the car parks. When we went up the Wembley tunnel before kick off, stepping onto the pitch all you could see were Boston people and fans and more orange. Were we going to have anyone watching us?

Then, at kick off time we came out of the tunnel to be met by a sea of Blue. I knew then we couldn't be beaten.

11th May 1985,
FA Trophy Final Wealdstone 2 – 1 Boston United

Wealdstone saved their best football of the season for the opening 45 minutes of Saturday's Trophy Final with Boston. The Pilgrim's voyage to Wembley looked to have taken its toll on the players and as they held back, Wealdstone took full advantage.

Playing with great confidence, composure and a fair amount of style, the 'Stones put a grip on the first half that Boston simply couldn't break.

'Stones could count themselves unlucky to be only two goals ahead at half time, but it was just as well that they had succeeded with two of their first half strikes on the Boston goal. It turned out to be enough to land them the Gola League and FA Trophy double – the first time the feat has ever been achieved.

Boston threw everything bar the corner flags at Wealdstone as they staged a second half comeback but the 'Stones defence held out. Surviving some late scares, with a resolute rear guard action to send Paul Bowgett up the 39 steps to the Royal Box to receive the trophy from Joe Mercer.

Ironically it was Boston that made the first foray on goal. Ray O'Brien whipping in a cross from the left on 35 seconds which Bob Iles gathered at the second attempt under pressure from Bob Lee.

Only another 49 seconds had passed when Wealdstone went ahead, with "supergoal" specialist Andy Graham adding yet another superb strike to his impressive list.

'Stones won a corner, which Brian Greenaway floated in. The ball fell to Graham with his back to goal, and he flicked it up in the air, half turned and hooked the ball over his shoulder and past the despairing dive of goalkeeper Kevin Blackwell into the far corner – a goal worthy of the Wembley stage.

Wealdstone suffered a minor scare barely a minute later when Gary Simpson's free kick floated agonisingly across the face of the goal and out for a goal kick. Then, Wealdstone moved up a gear. Robin Wainwright and Lee Holmes were having outstand-

A section of the Wealdstone support at Wembley

The victorious Wealdstone squad on the Wembley pitch after the FA Trophy Final *ing games in midfield, Greenaway and Gary Donnellan made excellent use of the flanks and the 'Stones defence was rarely troubled.*

The first time Dennis Byatt was troubled was after 19 minutes and that was when he was summoned forward to take a penalty! Another Greenaway corner was met by Bowgett who powered a header past Blackwell only to see O'Brien palm the ball over the crossbar.

Byatt hammered a right foot kick that was arrowing toward the bottom right hand corner but Blackwell was equal to it, pulling off a magnificent save by flinging himself to his left to push the ball around the post

Three minutes later and Alan Cordice should have put Wealdstone further ahead. He was put clear by Donnellan's long through ball and as Blackwell raced out of his area, Cordice skipped round him, but lost his nerve on the edge of the box and screwed a tame shot well wide.

Greenaway flashed a shot just wide in the 23rd minute after Holmes had won an aerial challenge and it was simply a case of sitting back and waiting for 'Stones to score the second goal that was always on the cards. The only way poor Boston could have kept the rampant 'Stones at bay would have been to erect a fence around their penalty area.

Boston's defence was finally cracked again in the 28th minute and again it was a Greenaway corner that led to the goal. His kick found Holmes rising on the penalty spot to send a header into the roof of the net. Although the ball took a deflection on the way, Holmes' name flashed on the Wembley scoreboard and there was no way he was going to be denied his moment of glory!

Boston burst briefly into life in the 38th minute. They won two corners in quick succession and from the first, Lee shot into the side netting. Gilbert gathered the ball from the second corner and found Chris Cook who flicked the ball on for Simpson to drive a shot from the edge of the area that just whistled past the post.

On the stroke of half time, Wainwright should have given Wealdstone an unassailable lead. Donnellan played a short free kick to Roy Davies and the left back cut inside to try a shot, which turned into a superb cross. The ball went straight to Wainwright, totally unmarked just three yards from goal, but somehow, he managed to head the ball over the bar when it may have been easier for him to blow it in.

Wealdstone looked to have done enough in the first half to be safe, but they were sent reeling after the break. Boston skipper, Simpson, who had tried unsuccessfully in the first half to stamp his authority on the game, suddenly snatched the initiative from the Wealdstone midfield men to conduct the game.

He was instrumental in most of what Boston did as they staged a revival, turning the second half into the exact opposite of the first.

In the 48th minute he poked a ball through, that Iles just beat Cook to and then, just 30 seconds later he put in a deep cross which had Lee lining up a shot before Steve Perkins races over to hook the ball off of his toe.

Boston had to wait only four minutes into the second half to get the goal they were desperate for. Simpson, playing a true captain's role, found Cook with a through ball and the blonde striker beat Byatt to lob the ball over Iles. It was now all Boston.

In the 50th minute Iles did well to fist away a Brain Thompson cross under extreme pressure and three minutes later Creane came forward to power a header just over the top. In the 59th minute, Bowgett came to 'Stones rescue with a last ditch tackle on Gilbert.

Wealdstone's first break into Boston territory didn't come until the 67th minute when Byatt's long clearance put Cordice free, but Ladd hauled the striker to the ground and was promptly booked.

Wealdstone thought they had sealed the match with a goal in the 77th minute. Cordice put in a cross that Donnellan met with a first time shot that turned into an up and under. As the ball looped up Blackwell rose to gather but Donnellan had followed up to head the ball home, flattening the Boston keeper in the process. It looked a good goal but referee J E Bray ruled it out, surprisingly, as he had given both 'keepers scant protection during the match.

Boston immediately sent on Gary Mallender for Mick Laverick to mount a late assault. In the 83rd minute, Bowgett wrestled Cook to the ground on the edge of the area, with Byatt clearing Simpsons kick as Gilbert threatened.

Five minutes before the end of normal time, Boston thought they had snatched an equaliser. Lee centered to Cook but the ball ran away from him to Gilbert who poked it home. As Cook turned to celebrate he was greeted by the Linesman's billowing red flag, signaling that Gilbert was offside and the goal ruled out.

Mr Bray added on three and a half agonising minutes of stoppage time as Boston pressed forward. Two minutes into stoppage time Byatt was adjudged to have pushed Lee on the edge of the penalty area and Boston lined up their final strike, but O'Brien's free kick curled harmlessly over the crossbar. There was only time for Neil Cordice to replace Graham before Mr Bray signaled the end of Boston's brave fight.

Bowgett took a tumble on the way up to collect the Trophy but the cut on his face was soon forgotten as he paraded the trophy in front of the Wealdstone fans.

The true spirit of the game came, however, when Wealdstone trooped up to the other end to be greeted by warm applause by the Boston throng. They and put up a barrage of noise in the second half and would have seen lesser teams wilt.

They still had the grace to acknowledge the part both teams had played in a truly memorable final.

Wealdstone; Bob Iles, Steve Perkins, Roy Davies, Dennis Byatt, Paul Bowgett, Robin Wainwright, Brian Greenaway, Lee Holmes, Alan Cordice, Andy Graham, (Neil Cordice 90), Gary Donnellan.

Robin Wainwright
Player 1979 -1988, Club record of over 450 appearances

My memories of Wealdstone FC are the fondest of my thirty-year career with nine different clubs. There were obviously more highs than lows as Wealdstone were a very successful club whilst I was there.

We'd won the Southern League Premier Division, the Southern League Championship, cups, the Gola League (now the

Football Conference), Middlesex Senior and Charity cups and of course the never to be forgotten FA Trophy at Wembley.

There were three of us that made our Wealdstone debuts on the same day away to Worcester in 1979-Stuart Pearce, Neil Cordice and myself, and I remember not long after Roy Davies signed for us we played Kettering at home.

I made what he thought were a couple of mistakes and he wasn't slow in coming forward to tell me about them!! I didn't take to kindly to this and at half time we had to be separated in the dressing room by the other lads.

Funnily enough we went on to win 4-0 and Roy and I never had another crossword, only a unique bond between us. What a character he was. Who else wrote a song and the recorded it? We played it on the coach going down Wembley Way before the Trophy Final.

There are many memories but above all was the team spirit in that season when we won the Double.

That season we played in five games in a week towards the end of the season, and we won every one. This certainly was a feat, which went a very long way to helping us win the league. We played on Saturday at home then Altrincham away on the Monday, away to Gateshead on the Wednesday and then at home again the following Saturday and Sunday!

When we played at Gateshead on the Wednesday, Dennis Byatt was sent off toward the end of the game. This meant a suspension and Brian Hall was not a happy man and the thought of it. After the game he stormed along the corridor at the National Stadium at Gateshead, and went to go into the referee's room to see him, only to find that in his rage he'd walked into the broom cupboard instead.

On the second from last league game of that season, we played Kettering away and if we won we knew that we had definitely won the league. With about 20 minutes to go Andy Graham scored with a low shot from the edge of the area into the bottom corner. I can remember running in front of our supporters nearly the length of the pitch, knees pumping high in celebration!

What tremendous supporters we had - they were the best in non-league football. They were always there at the midweek matches - away to Yeovil, Scarborough, Bath and Gateshead - phenomenal!

Two weeks later we were playing in the FA Trophy Final at Wembley, versus Boston United. Another great day never to be forgotten. We stayed at a hotel on the Friday night; I think it was in Cheshunt. The atmosphere and the spirit of the lads was brilliant - totally unforgettable.

Were we really going to be the first team that won the 'Double'? - Yes!! we were!!

The big day arrived, 'We Are the 'Stones' being played and played on the coach. Wembely Way and into the dressing room, then out onto the pitch. Funnily, I didn't feel nervous. I couldn't wait for the game to start - I loved it.

Within minutes, Andy Graham scored an overhead kick from a corner and then Dennis (Byatt) missed a penalty. Then we went two nil up from a Lee Holmes header, and just before half time I should have scored from a header from another of Roy's crosses, but it went just over.

In the second half Boston scored to make it two - one, and they then had a goal disallowed. Soon after 'Donners' (Gary Donellan) had a goal disallowed then the final whistle.

We'd done it.

There was jubilation, excitement and then sheer mental exhaustion.

Then the celebrations began - we went to the club and all hell broke loose. We were dancing on the tables, Roy Davies was walking round with a broken egg on his head - it was dripping down his face and he was completely oblivious to this. Nigel Johnson was 'scoring' in the penalty area at the Cinema End - a tremendous evening.

Then we repeated it all at the end of season Dinner and Presentations where the awards were given and more speeches made. It really was a season never to be forgotten.

The following season, I remember on a personal note scoring four goals against Boston United again in a home league match - we went on to win 7-2.

There are so many other matches and memories I could write a book of my own, but even now I often sit and chat with my brother and we reminisce about the Wealdstone days as he was an ardent fan, and also now with my four children.

One player stands out for me from all my time at Wealdstone, Polly Perkins. I had the great pleasure of playing with Polly - what a person. Nobody messed with Polly on the pitch and if they did it was at their own peril. A superb tackler, a great defender and a good passer of the ball. He gave absolutely everything in every game and I might add, he was a smashing bloke.

Angela Hall
Brian's Wife

There was one real memory I had of trophy day, was all of us wives – Dave Morritt's wife, Dianne Saxby Liz Clifton and myself were asked to buy matching outfits. David wife made sure he paid for them and off we went.

We arrived at Wembley all in Blue only to be told 'it wasn't the done thing' to wear your teams colours in the Directors Box at Wembley! By then it was too late.

Brian often said that they weren't the best team in the league, but they had the best understanding, each and every one of them knew what the others would do in a situation. Brian always said that's why they won.

The Trophy Final was a very stressful day – it was difficult to really let go in the evening, that's why the Celebration a few days later was better, by then the tension had gone and everyone was able to take in the moment, but I think those players were the last of 'the old style'. Money has made such a difference the whole attitude has changed now............

Henry Wizgier
Supporter in the 1980's and again on his return from Australia. The following is an article he wrote for The Australian British Soccer Weekly, Published 06/02/96

Ten years ago, Wealdstone Football Club were the name on everyone's lips in the thriving world of English non-league foot-

ball.

Had their tiny dilapidated ground been up to scratch, they may well have been playing in the Endsleigh Second Division today along with 'old rivals' Wycombe Wanderers and, who knows - they may even have been living in the same exalted company as another former rival, Wimbledon.

Yet, neither of these two former non-league giants managed to achieve what Wealdstone did, namely, win the great 'double' of the non-league pyramid, The Vauxhall Conference and FA Trophy in the same season.

How fortune smiles on some and rains down on others! While their aforementioned former opponents now bask in the sunshine of England's booming Football Leagues, poor old Wealdstone languish way down at the base of the pyramid which they once conquered in the most spectacular fashion and from which they should have climbed up onto the great professional plateau.

Make no mistake - it's as sad a story as any in recent English football-lore.

Founded in 1900, Wealdstone Football Club hail from the north west London Borough (Australian Municipality) of Harrow and were always a top Amateur club in the days when non-league footballers were not supposed to receive any payments officially, but regularly found bulging envelopes inside their jackets or shoes in the changing rooms.

Then when English football decided to 'come clean' and get rid of that word amateur, the 'Stones became one of the founder members of the Alliance League, now better known as the Vauxhall Conference League.

They had no success until that memorable and soon to be historic, season of 1984-85.

Almost from the beginning they headed the table but, owing to a combination of bad weather and cup commitments, with just six weeks of the season remaining they found themselves back in eighth place and seven points adrift of the leaders. (Only two points for a win then...)

However, they did have games in hand and the way they made up ground was spectacular. It began on Saturday 23rd March 1985 when the 'Stones beat Weymouth 3-2 at home. Two days later on Monday, they bussed it up the M6 to Manchester and beat Altrincham 2-1.

They stayed up north in a hotel, as their next game was just another two days away again, on Wednesday at Gateshead. Their third win in five days and their third win, 2-1.

Now, the 'Stones had a whole three days in which to get back to Harrow and prepare for the visit of Runcorn which was their fourth game in exactly one week. It became their fourth win too, 1-0.

The following day, on Sunday 31st March, Wealdstone recorded their fifth win on the trot in just eight days - as Scarborough were beaten 1-0. If somebody can tell me of a better record than that at a high level of football, I would be interested to hear about it.

With the Gola League (previous name for the Vauxhall Conference) now safely under their belt, the 'Stones then had to make the short hop down the road to Wembley Stadium to wrap up the second leg of that elusive non-league double, the FA Trophy.

Gallant Boston United could not halt the unstoppable 'Stones who won 2-1 in front of over 20,000. (Incidentally, sitting on the bench that day was a promising and likable young 20 year old by the name of Vinnie Jones. Where did it all go wrong Vinnie?)

What should have been the beginning of a glorious new chapter for Wealdstone FC became the first page of a catalogue of disasters.

I left England for Australia soon afterwards but I have gathered since that that the fact that Lower Mead stood on the very edge of the expanding Harrow shopping centre didn't help. Especially as their Chairman happened to be a property developer!

When I visited the Old Dart a few years ago I stood where the old goalmouths would have been at The Elmslie End of the ground - to reach for a packet of sausages.

Ray Goddard
Player 1982 – 1985

After a 'Pro' career at Chelsea, Fulham, Orient, Morton, Millwall and Wimbledon in over 20 years, I thoroughly enjoyed my association over four years at Wealdstone.

Brian Hall in particular stood out, but I had three good seasons with a good crowd of players.

Two great games stand out. Beating Gloucester City in the cup final and then the Trophy Final at Wembley..............

Paul Hanna
Supporter 1973-1985

I lived in Wealdstone from 1973 to 1985 and went to Lower Mead for most of that period. My uncle first started taking me and my main memory is of not knowing what to do when the Stones played away!

I think the Trophy Final was about my last game give or take a few, but I do remember one year when at the end of the season Dave Morritt came round and shook the supporters by the hand and said "sorry lads, we didn't win anything, but there's always next year". I never did trust him.

I lost touch when I moved away though I do keep a look out for the results. Living in Birmingham makes it difficult to get down but at least there is now the internet.

Les Bull
Kit-man and supporter 1960's to present.

I first saw 'Stones play in 1959 with my Grandad who went everywhere watching Wealdstone. He could even recall our first FA Cup 1st Round match away to Port Vale in 1949.

My time as Kit-man coincided with our FA Trophy winning year, which must remain my highlight. The Hotel in Cheshunt the night before, driving up Olympic Way in the Team Coach – all an experience I'll never forget and one that so few actually get to achieve.

At the other end of the scale, there is taking the kit to Rayners Lane in my own car for a Middlesex Senior Cup match, although at least I had Vinnie Jones as a passenger that day.

I also had the privilege to see Stuart Pearce play in our Youth Team and saw him progress through the club to the senior tea. We also shared a dormitory when we played in France against Harrow's Twin Town, Douai in 1983. It was a 3-3 draw and superb hospitality from our French hosts.

Two other players too, stand out. Robin Wainwright and Alan Cordice. Not only two great Wealdstone players, but two gentlemen off the pitch as well, who always had time for a chat.

Alan & Neil Cordice
Players

Joining the club in 1979 / 1980, we both played for Allen Batsford and Brian Hall and it's difficult to pick between them. Allen started the ball rolling but Brian's record speaks for its self.

All through our times at the club, the fans were so special. From the minute we first arrived everyone made us feel part of the club, the players, management and the fans all made it special.
During the double season, that week away – beating Altrincham and then Gateshead. It's was down to Brian Hall.

He'd got us so fit we could play that number of matches and that week won us the season. To travel over a week and see the same fans at all of those games. Just to hear them out-shout and out-sing the away fans was a great lift for us as a team.

People said we played the long ball game, even before Wimbledon, but we played football as well. The long ball was a get out clause if we were in trouble. We did exploit it better than anyone at the time though.

Look at the first half of the final at Wembley, we outplayed Boston with football, second half we didn't play as well, but it wasn't a case of kick and run.

(Neil) My personal low point was not playing I the final at Wembley.

I found out on the Friday at the hotel we were all staying at before the game that I wouldn't be playing. I knew I was sub, but there was no guarantee that I would play. It was just a case of if I got on I got on. That was the way it should be though.

I knew Andy Graham would score at Wembley, and I told him on the way to the ground. We were playing cards on the coach and he won £100 on the way.

Another low was the injury at Maidstone – when I damaged a cruciate ligament, I was due to go to Jersey with the England side the following week.

(Alan) The worst injury? The one against Dover. I should blame Brian Hall for that. I told him I didn't want to play, and he said "Go on, just go and have a run out". I did and I ran straight into the wall.

When I came back against Banbury after a long lay, the fans were superb. Absolutely brilliant, I couldn't believe it – the applause for me and I hadn't played for ages. It would have been great if that overhead kick had gone in.

There were characters in the squad as well. Dennis Byatt was always a big influence, and Vinny Jones and Nigel Johnson too had an effect.

Roy Davies used to supply the videos for the coach on away trips. There was one trip where the driver's wife had come along, but it didn't stop Roy. On went the blue videos, and there we were all watching. I think Roy enjoyed them more than most!

Neither of us suffered to much with racism. There were a couple of occasions with taunts and one with bananas being thrown, but we didn't react. If you do react they win. It's far better to go on and score.

One other thing that stands out – the last match at Lower Mead. It was so sad to see so many people crying. It tells another story of Wealdstone on its own.

We both left, but there was always a part of us at Wealdstone. It's still the first result we look for.

There were no regrets from either of us when we returned to Wealdstone. We had played in a successful side and there had been a number of chances to move on, but Wealdstone had taken us in so we stayed to repay the club.

Then, after we had both left and there was a chance to return, even to a struggling side, we did. We both still loved the club.

James Wiseman
Supporter since the Sixties

Though many would deny it there were other history-making events taking place on the day that Wealdstone clinched the double at Wembley.

At the time I was serving with the Royal Navy deployed to the Falkland Islands on what was known as Peace Patrol. During the earlier pre-Christmas part of the season I had managed to attend a number of matches but since our departure south I had been kept in touch with events by way of letters and a regular supply or programmes and match reports by Matthew Gloor and my brother Tom.

On the Saturday of the final, the major event in our part of the world was the opening of the newly-built Mount Pleasant Airport. Intelligence reports suggested that the Argentinians were planning some form of military demonstration to mark the event and we were tasked to cruise the San Carlos to Stanley area where it was felt that we could make the best use of our long-distance search radar. However I had my own plans for that afternoon.

We used to receive the British Forces Broadcasting Service radio sports programme on Saturdays, which was pretty much a presentation in the Radio 5 format. I stationed myself next to a speaker in one of our maintenance rooms from lunchtime onwards and prepared for ecstasy or misery.

DURING THAT WHOLE AFTERNOON THERE WAS ABSOLUTELY NO MENTION OF THE TROPHY FINAL WHATSOEVER!

When the ceremony at the airport was over, we made a quick stop at Port Stanley and then headed north to begin the long voyage home. Of course I still had no idea of the result of the match.

Organising mail collection was not, as you can imagine, always a straightforward task and it was fully ten days before we were able to arrange a pick-up by helicopter from Bermuda.

ROY'S MESSAGE

Hi, Pals,
Calling all Birmingham City fans! Followers of Brum will be delighted with the Sign Please in next week's issue (June 29th). He's their, and England Under-21 goalie, David Seaman. David made a tremendous impact last season and helped the club to win promotion. Well done, David and City, on your return to the top flight! It may be a bit late, but I must congratulate Gola League Wealdstone on their magnificent achievements during 1984/85. They became the first club to do the Non-League "double" . . . winning the title and F.A. Trophy. It's a challenge that's been open to the "minnows" since 1970, when the initial Final took place. The Middlesex side are the first to "crack it"! Well done, Wealdstone! At the other end of the scale, it's sad to see once proud Preston and Burnley having to kick-off next season in Division Four. When you are down, there's only one way to go . . . up! See you all in seven days!

Roy Race

Roy of The Rovers, May 1985

As fate would have it, the first item out of the pile was a copy of the Harrow Observer, sent by my Parents, with that once-in-a-lifetime headline "WEALDSTONE MAKE HISTORY". - Was I the very last person to know?

There was another financial boost to the club during the summer as well, when Stuart Pearce was transferred to Nottingham Forest – Wealdstone's sell-on clause coming into effect and adding £55,000 to the transfer fee of £25,000 already collected from Coventry City, who had also sent a team down to Lower Mead to play a lucrative friendly match.

John Willard
Supporter since 1933

What is the strength of this great Club? Surely it is the depth and loyalty of devoted supporters who turn out in great numbers for every fixture whether it be a friendly on a murky winter's night or it clashes with an International on the box, whether we are on a run for promotion or fighting to stave off relegation - the team always have the benefit of their vociferous support!!

Why has Wealdstone been so inspirational for me from a lad of 7 years of age to a great grandfather coming up to 73? Well, how's this for starters - what other team of our status has produced 2 full International Captains through its ranks? Stuart Pearce and Vince Jones provided us with endless pleasure as we watched them mature - genuine home-grown stock!

Internationals? Well, part from our many amateur internationals, how about our Polish full Internationals, Mikrut the one-eyed tank of a centre-forward and Wesgryk, a silky smooth forward with a shot straight out of Beckham's repertoire and all this happened years before foreign imports swamped the British game - Wealdstone were surely innovators.

Our greatest player? Even Solomon would be hard pressed to choose one jewel from the necklace of talent that has worn the blue and white quarters.

Bert Dyke - the prolific striker on Arsenal's books but transferred to an All-High team before his ambition could be recognised. The Poles - Mikrut and Wesgryk, George Duck - Predator extraordinaire a literal goal-scoring machine, Hugh Lindsay - The amateur with the Beckham boots....

The 3 Charlies; Charlie Barker, Charlie Edmonds and Charlie Townsend.

Charlie Barker & Charlie Edmonds - bastions in defence who likened their trade to the legendary Gunners' brick wall and matched them in their years too and Charlie Townsend - surely the Peter Pan of Wealdstone and a half back of pure genius, so mild mannered and totally a gentlemen who consistently won the ball without need of a foul and finally Viv Evans - a quicksilver winger who played on and on into the sunset of his brilliant career.

Dave Bassett
Opponent 1966-74 and subsequently a Football League and Premiership Manager

There were a lot of connections between the clubs as well with players and staff going between the two - I knew Hally (Brian Hall) and Allen Batsford from their time at Wimbledon, and some of the players as well - Vinnie Jones who I signed and Paul Bowgett and Ray Goddard as well.

Later on as a Manager, still at Wimbledon I tried to sign Stuart Pearce and I think it was with Brian Hall, but we'd agreed a fee with Wealdstone of £10,000 we just couldn't agree terms with Pearcey - he wouldn't come for the money we were prepared to pay him and then a short while later he went and signed for Coventry.

Still Wimbledon didn't do too badly - we signed Nigel Winterburn on a 'free' from Oxford, and they made a few quid when he went to Arsenal.

G McAlister
Supporter Since 1936

My Connection with Wealdstone is as a supporter since 1936 but I was unable to support them during the war years due to service in the Royal Navy. I started to support them again in 1947.

Always remember the local derbies on Christmas day with Hendon FC and the return at Hendon on Boxing Day. Their best player was Lorrie Toff, and one supporter that did stand out at these and every match was Eric the taxi driver, who was always, home and away, dressed in the Club colours. A real character.

The club's visits to Wembley - when the 'Stones got to the Amateur Cup Final against Hendon in 1966, winning 3-1 against all the odds and also when we played Boston United at Wembley in the FA Challenge Trophy final in 1985 following closely on winning the Gola League to make the 'Stones the first Club to win the double. The FIRST.

At the end of August, the new season opened with a convincing 4–0 win over Barrow, which was the perfect rehearsal for the held over Middlesex Cup Final against local rivals Enfield, to be played on the Bank Holiday Monday.

Monday's Middlesex Senior Cup Final had all the makings of a classic struggle. It's just a pity that no one bothered to tell Harrow referee Mr David Elleray wrote the Harrow Observer, continuing;

This over officious referee had his notebook out more often than a zealous traffic warden and as a result the game was never allowed to develop any sort of pattern. In all nine players were booked, Gary Donnellan, Robin Wainwright and Bob Iles of Wealdstone and Enfield's Carl Richards, Steve King, Mark Poultner, David Howell, Noel Ashford and Dave Flint. Howell and Richards were then sent off, both for speaking out of turn to the referee.

With both sides playing at full strength, 'Stones took the lead on 35 minutes and extended it a minute later, Lee Holmes and Alan Cordice the scorers. Enfield pulled one back from a penalty and five minutes later Graves scored again for Wealdstone before Howell and Richards were both sent off. Nine man Enfield then pulled another goal back from another penalty, although Neil Cordice sealed the victory late on with a fourth goal.

It was another trophy for the collection from the previous season for 'Stones, but there was still one more attainable, The Gola Championship Shield, where Runcorn were to be the visitors to Lower Mead. Three wins and a draw from five league matches plus the County cup win seemed to be a good grounding for Wealdstone, the home draw was a bonus,

Paul Bowgett's penalty miss cost Wealdstone in Tuesday's action packed Gola Championship Shield match at Lower Mead. All conquering 'Stones were gunning for their sixth trophy in as many months but were sent reeling in a dramatic penalty shoot-out. It was a shame that such a match - the best seen at Lower Mead for a number of years – had to be decided that way.

The scores were level at 2-2 after 90 pulsating minutes and again at the end of extra time, leaving the two sides to shoot it out from the penalty spot. Brian Kettle, Graham Jones, Frank Carradus and Steve Skeete were all successful for the visitors, Robin Wainwright, Vince Jones and Lee Holmes for Wealdstone when skipper Paul Bowgett stepped up to take his kick. He hammered it wide of the left hand post and then could only watch as John Imrie stepped up to score Runcorn's fifth to give them the shield.

It was a cruel way to lose, but it was an exciting climax for the 529 fans present.

Runcorn rocked 'Stones in the fourth minute, Imrie lashing the ball home after Jones' free kick cannoned off the defensive wall. Barely 30 seconds later Wealdstone were awarded a penalty when Fraser handled but Greenaway's kick was smothered by Eales in goal.

Runcorn should have stretched their lead in the 13th minute when Fraser's header from a Carrodus corner hit Imrie on the goal line and then cleared the bar, but Wealdstone struck back in the 27th minute when Holmes powered home a header from Greenaway's corner.

Ten minutes into the second half they took the lead following a sweet move down the right. It ended with Mark Graves sending a deep cross to the far post where Derek Doyle bundled the ball in. That lead though, lasted only 40 seconds. A high cross into the box was not cleared by the Wealdstone defence and Alan Crompton looped the ball past Bob Iles.

'Stones still had opportunities to win the game. The best fell to Lee Holmes, who had raced the length of the field before meeting a Steve Tapley cross but he headed just over with the goal at his mercy.

Extra time saw the return of fans favourite, Andy Graham who had re-signed for the club on his return from Tokyo, but the only chance in the extra thirty minutes fell to Graves, his shot flashing inches wide.

Wealdstone; Bob Iles, Steve Tapley, Steve McCargo, Steve Perkins, (Jones 100), Paul Bowgett, Robin Wainwright, Brian Greenaway, Lee Holmes, Alan Cordice, Mark Graves (Andy Graham 104), Derek Doyle.

Inconsistencies had returned to 'Stones league performances and in mid October, home defeats to Enfield (2-4) and Dagenham (0-4) left Brian Hall to state that it was the worst week of his footballing career at the club. It was time to change, he said, threatening that if the players he had couldn't do the job then he would go and get some that could.

The week had started with a presentation to Alan Cordice, he received his non-league Player of the Year trophy before the Enfield defeat.

Midweek saw the worst performance by far, the defeat against a Dagenham side that had lost its previous six away matches, 'Stones looking a poor second best all night. Then to rub salt in the wounds, 'Stones lost for the third time in a week away to Stafford.

A week later, and it seemed the strong words had had the desired effect as 'Stones tore Boston United apart at home. An excellent team performance saw 'Stones to a 7-2 victory, with four of the goals coming from Robin Wainwright as he added his name to the list of players that had scored a hat trick from the penalty spot.

'Stones had taken a ninth minute lead, equalised by Boston just before half time, but a second half demolition started by a Mark Graves overhead kick and thirty five minutes later it was 7-1, Boston only scoring a consolation second at the death.

With league form a little better, Wealdstone faced Reading again in the FA Cup, their first match being the first round proper. Again the trip to Elm Park was to be memorable.

An even match, despite 'Stones missing key players, saw Reading take the lead on 57 minutes from a disputed penalty that turned out to be the only goal of the game.

A mass brawl on 67 minutes soured the atmosphere and resultant sendings off finished the game as far as 'Stones were concerned but they gave the papers plenty to talk about.

A heavy challenge by Reading captain Martin Hicks felled 'Stones substitute Vince Jones on the half way line, and then all hell let lose as 18 outfield players all became involved.

The result was sendings off for Paul Bowgett and Derek Doyle of Wealdstone and Glen Burvill of Reading and a booking for the home side's Stuart Beavon. Neither of the players involved in the original incident instrumental in the following melee.

The match was to see 'Stones branded as thugs by the majority of the press, especially as they had repeated the dual sending off at Reading from 1976. Although 'Stones had let themselves down, there were no excuses for either side, Reading too had been involved and it was a challenge by one of their players that had ignited the incident.

It was another bad week – three days later the holders were dumped out of the Middlesex Senior Cup 3-1 at home to Kingsbury and the following Saturday they suffered another defeat at Kettering.

Form improved enough that by mid February 'Stones were still in with a chance of league honours, having moved up to third place, nine points behind the leaders.

Wins in the FA Trophy also saw 'Stones reach a third round tie with South Bank as the freeze set in and conditions prevented football being played at all for a few weeks.

When the match was finally played, after *ten* postponements it resulted in a 0-0 draw, South Bank winning the replay 2–1 after extra time.

Steve Paull
Supporter

Nick Symmons was working at stores all over the country at the time and had a supply of open ended air tickets, including some to Teeside.

He was working in the vicinity then anyway (he fixed his store visit so he could be in the area for the game) and decided that Mick Fishman and I should use these tickets. The only provision was that as they had his name on we shouldn't fly together.

I completed a night shift, went straight to Heathrow, and fell asleep in the terminal at Teeside after the flight. Mick did a half days work and then flew up.

Nick's timekeeping can go awry sometimes and he was late arriving at the airport to pick us up and take us to the game. We decided to get the train into Sunderland (I think).

Nick just missed us and saw the train pulling away. He drove like a lunatic and was at Sunderland station in time to greet us there.

That result started the worst run of form for a number of years, as in the remaining fourteen league matches, 'Stones only won once and drew four times as they slipped to an eventual tenth place in the league table.

The final ignominy coming as a 1-0 defeat at Enfield saw their hosts seal the league championship at the end of April.

During the close season, Vince Jones traveled to Sweden to play, while at home a combined Harrow Borough & Wealdstone team played the return match with twin town Douai at Lower Mead.

The friendly spirit was not over extended during the match as the 'combination' team won by 5–0, Wealdstone's Andy Graham (2), Keith Tonge, Robbie O'Keefe and Lee Holmes the goalscorers.

There were some additions to the squad during the summer and by the first friendly, a changed Wealdstone side took the field. Andy Wallace, Steve Rutter and Steve Regan all playing their part in beating First Division Charlton Athletic 1–0 with a goal from Wallace.

A week later, the 'Stones pre-season preparations were destroyed totally in a friendly at Wycombe Wanderers, the 1-0 defeat being incidental as a string of injuries stretched the squad to the limit. Brian Greenaway lasted only ten minutes before departing with a groin strain, goalkeeper Bob Iles was injured in a clash with defender Doug McClure and had to be replaced.

Derek Doyle departed at half time, Dennis Byatt suffered an Achilles tendon injury and skipper Paul Bowgett struggled on with a damaged calf.

Bowgett, Iles and Doyle recovered sufficiently to start the following week but despite dominating for long periods, 'Stones lost their opening match at home 3–0 to Stafford Rangers. It was to set the scene for the season as three defeats in succession were followed by three draws before the first win in the seventh league match.

So unsettled was the line up that two seasons previously when 'Stones won the title, they had used only 20 players in the league all season. Three of those were goalkeepers and three more only made one appearance. This season, after seven games, 'Stones had already used 15 players in the league.

After 18 league matches 'Stones had won three and drawn six but the FA Cup provided the best performance of the season to date, away to Dagenham, where 'Stones secured a 3–0 victory, the first round draw pairing them with Swansea City.

Swansea sent officials to watch the 'Stones the week before the tie, in a match at home to Nuneaton and they must have left worried. Despite the poor form overall, Wealdstone recorded their best league win of the season, 6–0 despite a shaky start.

Doug McClure had to clear a Frank Murphy lob off the goalline after six minutes and Gary Donnellan missed a simple chance on twelve minutes.

Nuneaton did make Wealdstone's job a little easier when Shearer turned round after a challenge and punched Doug McClure to receive a red card after 19 minutes, which allowed Wealdstone to take charge of the game. Three goals in five minutes just before half time (Wallace, Wainwright, Galloway) rocking the visitors and Wallace, Galloway and Graves completing the scoring in the second half.

The Harrow Observer reported on the Swansea match;

Andy Wallace kept Wealdstone's FA Cup dreams alive with a last minute equaliser, and it was no more than ten man Wealdstone deserved. In fact 'Stones should have had the high-flying Swans dead and buried by half time.

It was a mixture of bad luck and poor finishing that let Swansea off the hook, With Manager Terry Yorath saying as he left "We were very lucky to get a replay, Wealdstone should have won the game.

Wealdstone were reduced to ten men in the 70th minute, Gary Donnellan – until then one of 'Stones most influential players – was dismissed for felling Swans full back Chris Harrison in an off the ball incident, but 10 man 'Stones fought back bravely after falling behind in the 86th minute.

Rampant 'Stones, spurred on by a 2,576 crowd, tore into Swansea from the start and after seven minutes Harrison's appalling back pass put Mark Graves in the clear but Swansea keeper Mick Hughes smothered the ball at the strikers feet.

Five minutes later the hapless Harrison and Hughes were all at sea as they failed to cut out Brian Greenaway's cross with Gary Donnellan tantalisingly close to applying the finishing touch at the far post. Donnellan went close again in the 20th minute when Dennis Byatt's free kick was flicked on by Robin Wainwright but Hughes blocked his close range shot, with Swansea then scrambling the ball clear.

Wealdstone must have known it was not going to be their day in the 25th minute when Paul Bowgett rose magnificently to meet Greenaway's corner, only to see his header crash against the post.

Donnellan saw a long-range effort finger-tipped over the crossbar by Hughes for 'Stones eighth corner in the first half. Swansea – who won just one corner in the first 45 minutes – were restricted to a single strike on goal in the first half. In the 16th minute Gary Emmanuel's chip was flicked on by Phil Williams to Sean McCarthy but Bob Iles saved bravely at the strikers' feet.

Swansea came more into the game at the beginning of the second half and Iles was forced to block McCarthy's effort as the visitors won an early corner, but Wealdstone soon regained their grip on the game, and in the 63rd minute, Donnellan beat the Swansea offside trap to meet Byatt's free kick only to see his header drift narrowly wide.

A minute later, Wealdstone's best chance fell to Mark Graves. Wainwright sliced open the visitors defence with a glorious ball to Derek Doyle and his cross found Graves unmarked in front of goal but he miscued his shot and the ball flew wide.

For all Wealdstone's dominance however, there was always the danger that Swansea would sneak a goal and they did with just four minutes remaining.

Steve Tapley's miss hit clearance was gathered by Terry Phelan and he found McCarthy, who squared for Williams to slide the ball past Iles.

It was the only mistake the Wealdstone defence had made all afternoon and it looked like it would be enough to give Swansea an undeserved victory, but Wealdstone were not to be denied.

Byatt's free kick was only half cleared by Nigel Stevenson and Greenaway crossed for Wallace to head home off the underside of the crossbar. It was no more than Wealdstone deserved, but Manager Brian Hall was understandably disappointed. "We should have won the game in the first 45 minutes" he said "but I was pleased with the draw at the end of the day as we were down to ten men.

We produced a creditable performance to come back like we did. We had our chance today and did not take it and I do not relish the thought of going to Swansea. We will not go there with a negative attitude because we played enough football today to show them we can play a bit!"

Swans Manager, Terry Yorath was also full of praise for the 'Stones performance "It was a big day for them, they played very well and did themselves proud. Even when they equalised I thought they were going to go on and win. It will be another very difficult match on Tuesday – I just hope we can play better"

Wealdstone; Bob Iles, Steve Tapley, Doug McClure, Dennis Byatt, Paul Bowgett, Robin Wainwright, Brian Greenaway, Andy Wallace, Gary Donnellan, Mark Graves, (Neil Cordice 77), Derek Doyle.

The first replay was postponed, the second abandoned after 54 minutes with 'Stones trailing 2–1. Swansea had missed a first minute penalty but were still two goals in front at half time when a thunderstorm hit The Vetch and the players were forced to wade through a foot of water in the tunnel on their return to the pitch.

Vinnie Jones 63 appearances and 8 goals, 1984-1986

The second half started also with a penalty, this time Doyle converting to bring 'Stones back into the game before conditions became farcical and the match was abandoned.

The 'second' replay saw the result follow the form book as Swansea ran out winners by 4–1 although 'Stones did open the scoring on 8 minutes through Gary Donnellan but it wasn't to be and Swansea progressed.

Vince Jones had returned to the club from Swedish club IFK Holmsund, and in the week before the FA Cup-tie he played his last match for the club. His only appearance of the season, the defeat by Sutton United in the GMAC Cup.

By the end of November he was a Wimbledon player, sold by Wealdstone for £10,000. In his first two games for his new club he certainly made an impression – on his debut at Nottingham Forest he gave away a penalty as the Dons lost 3–2 and the following week, his home debut, he scored the only goal as Wimbledon were to beat Manchester United 1–0.

Summing up 'Stones form at the time, Vinnie returned to Lower Mead before the home match with Weymouth clutching a bottle of Champagne which he handed to Manager Brian Hall, telling him not to open it until 'Stones won which they did on the Saturday afternoon!

Doug McClure
Player 1986-1987

There was one specific memory that stands out from Wealdstone. We had to attend a Testimonial – I'm not sure who for – and we were informed that we had to wear a collar and tie.

I did wear a collar and tie and a jacket as instructed, but I was wearing shorts and a peach coloured pair of Converse baseball boots! I remember that it didn't go down too well with the

Chairman!

There was always a great team spirit as well, it made for an excellent social life while I was with the club especially as Wealdstone always included the wives and girlfriends as well. I actually proposed to my girlfriend at a club disco in front of Dennis Byatt. He couldn't believe what I'd done and spent the rest of the evening trying to talk me out of it!

Despite a brief rally over Christmas, 'Stones league form was poor and defeat by Maidstone in the FA Trophy and Wembley in the Middlesex Senior Cup effectively ended Wealdstone's season, only the fight against relegation likely to maintain interest.

So it seemed too for the Manager as in early January, Brian Hall resigned to take up the vacant Manager's position at Yeovil, ending a six year association with the club. Coach Les Reed also quit the club at the same time as he was offered a position with the Football Association where he remains today, as a part of the England set-up.

Brian Hall
Manager 1983 – 1986, 1991 – 1992

The partnership with Allen Batsford suffered over the problem with Allen's health. Once he went into hospital and it was agreed and I took over as Team Manager.

I just did the job that he wanted me to do and then, when he returned to the club he naturally wanted to take over again – that was fair enough – but there were some remarks made that were hurtful. I wasn't sure that Allen would ever be fit enough to go back into the stressful environment that Management was.

I offered to stand down and I actually had another job, but Allen told me not to resign. He then had a fall out with the Board, all of a sudden they decided that he would stay as General Manager and I would stay as well, but that soon became a problem. Allen left and I remained Team Manager. We fell out for a while – it was one of those things that happen in football, but I'm pleased to say we're friends now. We even still laugh about the fact that we're both deaf in the same ear!

I also had a lot of help from Tony Caruana. He came down and did some of the coaching, he had a spell in charge of the reserves and he did a lot of scouting. He was one of the back-room boys who often gets forgotten, but he was important to what we achieved.

Roy Davies was a tremendous motivator in the dressing room and at the same time he was a good footballer who wanted to do well. Once he realised that Steve McCargo had broken his toe, he knew he had a chance to play at Wembley and he was going to take that chance. There was no way he was going to let anyone else come in.

I picked the side about a couple of weeks before Wembley – there were certain things that were happening – Andy Graham was scoring regularly and Mark Graves was out of the side, but I couldn't tell anyone.

Andy Graham had played at Lancaster City but quite literally he walked in and asked if he could train with us. He trained and then he played in the Capital league against Leyton Orient when he scored a hell of a goal. The following Saturday, Mark Graves still wasn't fit so he played again.... all of his goals were classics, he never scored a tap in. Once he had got into the side, he stayed there.

Neil Cordice was his own worst enemy. His ability as a utility player meant he was always the perfect substitute – he could do a job in a number of positions, covering half the team. Gravesie was an out and out striker. A very difficult decision. Neil though has followed me and still been my super sub.

There seemed to be very little recognition of the match as we traveled to Wembley. Debenhams had talked about putting something in their window, but it never happened. It wasn't until we went out on the pitch that we saw the 'Stones fans............

I was strict with the players before the game as well. I said there would be no waving to the crowd – nothing like that before the game. I said we'd do all our waving at the end when we'd won. It all helped keep the players focused. Half time was the most difficult because I felt we were so far in front. Having gone 2-0 up and missed a penalty it was difficult to keep the team motivated. I didn't want them to think it was already won.

I wanted to get Neil on sooner at Wembley. The referee wouldn't blow the whistle. I thought we'd won it 3–1. I still think Donnellan's goal should have counted and I thought the referee was making an epic out of it. At least by making the change, I slowed the game down a bit and burnt up a little more time, but I'm glad he played at Wembley.

The others, Vinnie for example, I thought he was too inexperienced to play at Wembley with the likes of Holmes and Wainwright. His enthusiasm was incredible – he was first over the fence when we won the game. Like it or not, playing at Wembley, experience counts for a lot and I thought we needed the Bowgett's and the Byatt's on the day.

On the day Gary Donnellan was outstanding. He worked like a Trojan, up and down the field in attack and in defence. The goal would have crowned his day.

When we got back to the Club afterwards, I made all the players stay on the coach – we went round to the back car park and dropped off all the kit and everything and then got back on the coach to go round the front. I wanted everyone to get off the coach together and for them all to enjoy the moment.

It didn't take long for the celebrations to get going but there was so much happening it was difficult to take it all in. A few days later when we went back to the club it was better. We could then take in the atmosphere and the effect of what we've done.

I would have liked to go back and do it all again without the nerves and the tension. To go back and enjoy it. There's one photograph that never did come out properly. It was the Scoreboard with the result on, Les Reed and myself stood in front of it with the Trophy, but I'm sure the time is wrong!

There was one of the Dinners or Celebrations that still makes me smile. It was the day that became my celebration. Robin made a speech after the beer had flowed – he never did translate it, and I got up and sang Send In The Clowns. I think it was Dennis that had a whoopee cushion that he made use of when I got up to speak. I thoroughly enjoyed the occasion that was when I really celebrated.

The following season, breaking up the team was difficult. I knew why it had to happen, but David Morritt didn't. It had to be broken up to allow the new side to develop, but he probably felt this team would last forever. It doesn't happen.

Brian Hall with Paul Bowgett and the FA Trophy

My decision to move came about from a phone call – at first I said I wouldn't go then another call from Yeovil............

I spoke to Dave Bassett about it, Yeovil were a big club. He said if you say no, you regret it forever – he also said I'd taken Wealdstone as far as they could go, whereas Yeovil at least had the potential to go into the league.

Wealdstone or at least the board, wouldn't allow me to break up and rebuild the side, Yeovil wanted me to. In the end I went.

Looking back, I'm convinced David Morritt wanted one club in Harrow, so he could develop the other ground and I'm convinced that Alan Clifton wanted to ensure that the 'one' was Wealdstone. I'm sure he was going to be well looked after while he was doing it as part of the development.

When I came back for the second spell it was difficult. Not only the problems off the field, but I couldn't believe the number of players who were there who didn't care at all about the club. They were only there for the money. There were very few who wanted to do their best all the time.

Barry Nevill who had played twice for the club in 1985–86 and had been part of Brian Hall's back room team was appointed Caretaker. He was expected to be appointed as Manager in due course, but as always there was still a twist to the tale.

At the beginning of February former Arsenal, Watford, Reading and York City player Colin Meldrum was appointed, a decision that resulted in Barry Nevill walking out despite being offered a role 'on the staff'.

Dave Morritt again sought and gained publicity to keep the club profile in the public eye. He announced his plans (again) for Wealdstone to move into a new £2,000,000 Harrow Super Stadium within two years. He announced that he had earmarked two potential sites and he promised to funds the project.

The two sites were the Aldenham Bus Garage, (who later commented that there had been an initial approach from one potential purchaser of the site, but that this had not been followed up), and the second was the Prince Edward Playing Fields in Canons Park.

He also promised new manager Colin Meldrum the one thing he had denied the previous regime – the money to buy players to strengthen the squad to lift 'Stones back up the table, as part of his dream to see the club progress into the Football League playing in the new stadium.

A number of new players did appear for the club in the remaining games and a number of players also left – three joining Hall at Yeovil (Wallace, Donnellan and Rutter) while one (Tonge) joined Dagenham.

The results did not improve, Wealdstone only winning two and drawing three of the ten matches. It was not until the last match of the season that they confirmed their position in the Conference for the following year. Despite losing 3-0 at home to Kidderminster, Welling's defeat at Cheltenham had settled the final relegation place.

In mid July there was worse news for Wealdstone fans and for the club when a safety inspection carried out the fire department and Harrow Council revealed a number of problems that were likely to shut Lower Mead permanently.

Wealdstone were granted a 'stay of execution' for twelve months to allow them to bring the ground up to standard, but the Chairman was determined not to do the work. He was quoted as saying

"I will not revamp Lower Mead to meet the regulations. Why should I spend hundreds of thousands of pounds bringing the ground up to standard when we are going to move anyway?. I am working so hard towards a new stadium that it has got to be built in the next two years. Wealdstone will have a new stadium to walk into at that time"

He had set his sights firmly on Prince Edward Playing Fields, but no agreement had been reached with the Inner London Education Authority who owned it. He had also made a bid for the Ellis Franklin playing fields nearby, which he intended to make into a Training Ground for the club and a Leisure Centre for the local community.

The club also announced their intention to remain at Lower Mead for the one year period and then to look at a groundshare – at the time Barnet FC was suggested – until the new ground was ready.

Two weeks later, the club announced that it would fund some of the required works to allow Wealdstone to continue to play at Lower Mead until 1990, then to move into the new stadium.

This change of heart had been brought about by indications from the Conference that they would be unlikely to allow the club to groundshare for two whole seasons. Behind the scenes, there were also discussions going on regarding other potential sites, not all of which met with the Chairman's agreement or plans;

Reg (Johnny) Johns
Supporter, Director and Commercial Manager 1970's and 1980's.

I Left the RAF and married in 1958, and bought a home in Harrow and became a Wealdstone Supporter. Eventually I became a shareholder and was then elected to the board as Commercial Director although my 'day job' was as a Sales Manager of William Olds.

At the club, I was instrumental in the introduction of sponsored advertising boards around the ground and these helped us out financially by raising about £10,000 per annum at their peak, along with programme advertising.

I also helped set up the weekly Market in the car park and the tea bar as well as many other fund-raising schemes introduced including the letting of the hall for outside functions.

During my time at the club we also 'up-marketed' the programme to a 16 page glossy with various features and general information including a Managers Column and information from The Supporters Club and also a young Roy Couch's statistics.

I became a member of the Harrow Sports Council, and as Chairman and sitting on the Leisure Committee, with Wealdstone FC in mind, I managed to get the offer of the property between the Leisure Centre and the old Railway Line for the site of a new ground.

For some reason better known to himself, the Chairman at the time, David Morritt would not pursue the matter.

I enjoyed a close relationship with Wealdstone FC and regrettably resigned from the board when the financial policy became untenable to me.

The last straw was the Chairman's wish to employ Dave Webb as manager at a salary of £30,000 per annum. Fortunately I won the support of Micheal Macario and David Webb himself to defeat the idea.

There were some great days in my time at the club some specific memories - there was Hugh Lindsay scoring from the centre circle to beat Stevenage, and later, Stuart Pearce and that great player and Captain, John Watson.

I also remembers the stalwarts of the supporters club, Tom Verral and his wife, The Dugards, The Couch's, Alan Jenkins and not forgetting that 'old war-horse' Bill Locke - without these people and others like them there would not be a club.

How can anyone forget that 2-1 victory over Boston United at Wembley, the whole of that season to win the Double and in total five trophies, but I must give pride of place to my wedding day.

After enjoying our wedding breakfast with a couple of dozen relatives and friends the bride and the rest of the family were sent home to prepare for the evening, whilst I took my three sons to the Quarter Final match against Frickley, which we won 3-1. Jean (my wife) and I were presented with a Crystal Decanter etched with WFC - still being treasured not just as a memento of our marriage, but also our very own Trophy.

The 1987–88 season saw 'Stones make their worst league start ever, their first win coming in mid September, a 1–0 at home to Enfield – and their next (league win), Boxing Day away to Dagenham, where a 2–1 victory followed a 1–0 home victory against Banbury in the FA Trophy replay.

At times, injuries and not a little disorganisation had resulted in Wealdstone almost failing to put out a side. This had been worsened as half the squad had left since the departure of Brian Hall and there had been no money available for replacements despite the promises.

For the third match of the season, away to Altrincham 'Stones had been so short that two players were called up from the supporters club team, SFC Wealdstone.

Don Cross and Phil Jackson traveled with the team not as substitutes, (where for the second match in succession, Goalkeeper Andy Haxton was to take his place), but to start, both taking their places in the 'first team' line up.

Despite a 1–0 defeat, Don Cross retained his place for the following week, making his home debut against Runcorn, another 1–0 defeat. These were to be just two of a number of players who only appeared in less than a handful of matches for Wealdstone at the time.

By the middle of September, the inevitable decision had been made. Colin Meldrum was sacked after only seven months in charge, a third of which had been the close season!

He was quoted as saying that there had been no justification for his sacking and he left the club with his head held high, firmly blaming the Board for the lack of money and this, coupled with injuries, for a lack of players and results.

From the club's point of view, the reasons were clear. Wealdstone were bottom of the league and it seemed had little prospect of an immediate change of fortune.

Managerless however, Wealdstone did manage to get their first win of the season, beating Enfield with club captain Dennis Byatt taking charge and Byron Walton scoring the only goal.

Arnie Reed
Physio 1982 – 1988

I joined the club when Brian Hall took over from Allen Batsford. My son Les soon followed as Coach. One of the first memories was the change with Brian and Allen. We played over at Enfield. It was a tight game, I think it was 1-0 at half time as the players came off.

Brian was just about to start his team talk in the dressing room when Allen walked in and took over. With that, Brian Hall asked Les (Reed) to takeover and he took Allen Batsford outside. They had a hell of a row in the corridor.

The following day the press had written that Allen Batsford said "we're having a few problems, but I'm back and this will all be sorted out." It forced the issue for the club and it meant whatever happened only one of them would stay.

I've got some great memories of my time with the club on and off the field. Not only did we have some good players, we had a load of scallywags as well!. There were some real characters.

Not least Polly Perkins who was a great player and loved the club. The most influential footballer was probably Dennis Byatt. He had an infectious attitude in the dressing room and he didn't suffer fools gladly. He was part of what made that team special, he helped pull them together.

Roy Davies too, a comedian and a clown but a great player. We all got bought new blazers and grey slacks. For about six weeks he walked about with the label still on his blazer, he refused to take it off! He called us all clones, but he was a really likeable fellow.

Andy Graham – wherever he was, when ever it was, Andy Graham walked around in a pair of green football socks.

*I don't think I ever saw him in anything else and I don't think he had two pairs. When he scored the first goal at Wembley, Brian just said "F*** me. He's scored" almost without any emotion. It was like he'd just noticed.*

It is a bit unfair to pick players out though. They were a team. If one was in trouble, they were all in trouble and they would all have fought for each other on the field.

The end of the 84 – 85 season was a good time, but we tried to soldier on the following year with the same players. We should have looked at three or four new signings for the following year but it didn't happen.

Even on occasions after that when I stood in between managers, I knew what we needed to do to change things but it didn't happen. I had one spell of 12 games, we won, drew and lost 4 each but the side still needed to change. We went to a cup game, Yeading I think, and they outplayed us totally.

I was trying to sign players but just couldn't get them in. We did mange to drag ourselves off the bottom. With 14 games left we had a chance of survival and Tony Jennings came in. I don't think we won another game.

I had stood in between Colin Meldrum and Jennings. Meldrum was Dave Morritt's biggest mistake. He applied for the job, and he was interviewed. When he had first started in the building trade, Morritt had a clerk of works who basically had built the company up very successfully, and in appearance, Colin Meldrum was his double. That was enough reason for him to get the job.

I was almost Meldrum's assistant taking training with him and looking after the injuries and such like. His idea of coaching was to send me over to the college with the players and a couple of balls to play five a side and then he would take the two strikers away with him and tell them how he wanted them to play.

When they came back, the rest of the players had no idea what he said and he never told them.

Off the field, David Morritt never made a secret of his wish to build on the ground, but there was always going to be another new ground built. Whichever way you look at it, the club has gone down a bit since he left. He'd also brought a lot of important people into the club because of what he did and who he was.

After David's time it was such an unhappy time for the club, but now it seems stable. We should be thankful that it has survived. Its ironic that the club are now looking to move to the playing fields that David first tried to get twenty years ago.

Two days after his dismissal, replacements for the departed Colin Meldrum were named. Former Arsenal first team coach Terry Burton was appointed Manager. He immediately appointed Tommy Coleman as his assistant.

As before the board promised to make money available for new signings to strengthen the squad but despite the addition of players to the squad, it was not a happy partnership and by the end of the year, club and manager had parted company.

It had taken until Christmas, their 21st and 22nd matches in charge, for Wealdstone to record the wins against Banbury and Dagenham. Even under new manager Tony Jennings, they could not sustain a run of results.

After 29 matches, 'Stones had won 3, drawn 12 and lost 14 matches to find themselves at the bottom of the GM Vauxhall Conference, out of the FA Cup at the first attempt, out of the League cup and out of the Middlesex Senior Cup.

The second half of the season was no better either as in he remaining 20 matches, 'Stones won 3, drawing 7 and losing 10.

March had seen the resignation of Chairman David Morritt. He had resigned under a challenge from Alan Clifton, at the time, his Vice-Chairman.

On the field, the inevitable relegation was confirmed late in April in a match away at Lincoln City. True to form, even this was not as straightforward as the 'Observer' recorded;

Wealdstone have launched a furious attack on referee John Morley and opponents Lincoln City, claiming they were 'cheated' out of vital relegation points at Sincil Bank on Saturday.

Referee Morley awarded a penalty that never was; allowed one act of retaliation to escalate into a fifteen man brawl; then sent off the wrong player while only booking the original culprit.

It all happened in eight mad minutes before half time. Until then the 4,159 crowd – the largest Wealdstone had played in front of in the Conference – had seen 'Stones likely to pick up a point.

Wealdstone are now making an official protest to the league about the incident that started it all off – a very debatable penalty awarded in the 36th minute.

Wealdstone are complaining that the referee awarded the spot kick after a disagreement with Paul Bowgett. The centre half alleges he was told by the official "you'll see what I mean by my next decision".

Within seconds he had awarded the penalty against Bowgett for climbing at a corner. Morley appeared to see something no-one else in the whole ground could see, and when he blew his whistle most people thought it was for a free kick to Wealdstone. Instead, he pointed to the spot.

John McGinley scored from the spot kick, and Mike Pittaway was immediately booked for a furious outburst at the referee, pursuing him 40 yards up the pitch in protest.

From the kick off, Danny Bailey attempted a back-pass that was intercepted and Phil Brown ran on to chip the ball past Kevin Foster in goal.

Then all hell broke loose. Lincoln's former Derby defender Steve Buckley, who had already made a number of bad challenges and got away with them went one step too far with the inspirational Tony Lynch. He went in on Lynch from behind and as Lynch retaliated, a brawl developed around him involving most of the players.

Players punched, kicked and hacked at each other in a sickening show of violence. When it was all over, Wealdstone's Samson Olaleye who was behind Lynch and Buckley at the time of the incident and seemed to have nothing to do with it was sent off, while Buckley was only booked.

Despite two draws and a win in their last four games, Wealdstone finished the season second bottom of the table and were relegated into the Beazer Homes (Southern) League Premier Division.

Paul Bowgett
Player 1980 – 1988

Ken Payne signed me in the second season in the Alliance and we got relegated! My first appearance was against Gordon Banks' Telford – we won 4-1 and I broke my arm. The next match was against Altrincham I think and they complained about me playing with the plaster cast on in case I started swinging it about!

That was my first memory. The following year we won everything in the Southern League and won the Challenge Shield. Stuart Pearce was left back that season. When he left us I said to a few people he'd play for England and he has. Even as a seventeen year old he was class. He would tackle anything that moved then and a nice bloke with it.

The day he got 'picked up' by Coventry, Bobby Gould came and watched us at Yeovil. Dennis and Polly both got sent off so he saw me and Pearcie playing at the back and it was like the Alamo. I think we got beaten about 3-0. After that Bobby Gould decided to sign him.

There was one game where we ended up staying in a hotel in Blackpool on the Friday night.. Allen Batsford was the Manager.

We turned up at this hotel, there were nearly fifty of us on the coach. As we're going in we noticed that the manager was, shall we say, a little over friendly. He must have thought all his Christmas's had come at once.

Alan Batsford was probably the manager who turned it around for me. After my first year I didn't have a bad season, but the following year I was having a bad time.

Alan said to me that I had two choices, either to get on with it and play through the problems or he would let me go. I decided I wanted to try and prove him wrong, and then John Watson left and Alan made me skipper. He gave me the kick up the backside I needed.

Alan and Brian were different managers though. Alan was a total disciplinarian, if his opinion was different from yours it was tough. Both he and Brian were very professional. They always knew everything about the opposition. Brian was a little different, he was very much his own man but he would listen to the senior players.

He was very well organised – it was what made us a team – we were based on organisiation.

I played alongside Dennis Byatt for five or six years. He was one of the best one on one defenders I ever played with. Neither of us had great pace. We had some up's and down's but we were a good partnership. It was a good back four with Polly and Steve McCargo or Roy Davies.

My first recollection of Vinny Jones was when he was driving the tractor watching us training – he asked to join in and Brian Hall let him. Next session he was there and he was the fittest thing you've ever seen. Brian Hall liked his cross country runs in training – he loved fit players – Vinny was first in his first session and Brian gave him a game the following week!

There are lots of stories about Vinny – funnily enough I watched the incident in the Gateshead Disco but that was the week that won us the Championship.

The fans were brilliant. We always had 100 or so following us but to see them on a Monday in Altrincham and then to see them all again two days later at Gateshead. It was amazing.

As a team we had a good crack off the park as well. I think that made a lot of the difference. Team spirit was excellent, we all used to have a drink afterwards and a chat about the game. That week on our travels in Gateshead, all sixteen of us went out to the Disco after the game.......

There were always some tough games. Leo Skeets at Altrincham was always a difficult opponent because he took no prisoners on the field. The first challenge I went up for against him I got splattered. I thought if that was the way it was, so b it. It was always hard but we'd get together in the bar afterwards and have a drink.

I had 422 appearances over 8 years and seven or eight sendings off but I scored 65 goals as well. 26 of them were penalties. I always said to Dennis I should have taken the penalty in the Trophy Final. It was my header that was hand balled on the line.

I cant tell you what I thought when Dennis missed the penalty!

The whole of that double year is a great memory. I can't describe the feeling to walk up the steps at Wembley and pick up the Trophy. You don't remember the game until afterwards. I remember saying to Brian Hall just after 'that' picture was taken " now you've stepped out of Alan Batsford's shoes". He'd always said he had to win something and he had!

I remember that game at Altrincham when we had to play to of the supporters. It was disgraceful management by Colin Meldrum.

It should never have happened, but fair play to the two lads, they did alright. They were a bit in awe of players on the pitch but they did well. It just summed up the club at the time. We'd go training and there would be four or five there. He should never have allowed that to happen.

I finally left because the time was right. I'd had enough of different managers coming and going and none of them were doing me any good. I left and went to Baldock.

It wasn't Wealdstone anymore. I had played for the club when players stayed in the most part for a few seasons.

By the time I left most players were lucky if they stayed a year. There was no loyalty. It hurt me because I loved the club and the memories. It was a great club to play for.

Roy Couch
Supporter, Official, Statistician and Programme Editor

I was born at 25 Crawshay Road (this road no longer exists) Brixton on the 23rd December, 1930 and saw my first Wealdstone match during the Second World War.

It was towards the end of the 1973/74 season that I first became involved with Wealdstone on a volunteer basis. At the time Colin Pope was the Programme Editor and the league table that appeared in our programme was the basic second column one, P W D L FA Pts.

As we were going for the Southern League (First Division South) championship, I suggested we print a more detailed table in our remaining programmes showing each Club's home and away record. Colin agreed and from that day right up to the present I have been compiling the league table for our matchday programme.
Around about the middle of the 1970's I also became one of the Club's programme sellers, a job I still do today. In 1991, just after we left Lower Mead I took over from Steve Marshall as Programme Editor and this is another of the roles I still carry out for the Club.

Regarding specific memories of Wealdstone FC and our supporters, several spring to mind.

First of all the supporters. Back in the 70's there were two brothers, I think they were twins who used to stand on the High Mead terrace continually criticising our players even when they were three or four goals up. One such player who came in for this abuse was Danny Light who left us in February 1977 to join Dartford.

Two months later Dartford visited Lower Mead for a Southern League (Premier Division) match and Danny was in their line-

up. The match ended 1-1, Bill Byrne giving us a 52nd minute lead only for Danny Light to equalise in the 79th minute. Immediately after he had scored Danny ran over to the touch-line seeking out those two brothers and taunted them about the goal saying something along the lines of "what about that then".

Another incident that is recalled with much mirth by some of my fellow supporters occurred prior to one of our matches at Hounslow.

A supporter who is now very much part of the Wealdstone set-up, propelled a fan in a wheelchair into the ground. Although he was probably only helping the disabled supporter the story has been embellished over the years into one of him grabbing a poor unfortunate who happened to be passing the ground in his wheelchair and wheeling him into the ground so as to avoid paying the admission price!

With regard to individual matches there are several that stand out.

The 1966 Amateur Cup Final victory over Hendon, the win a Kettering Town in 1985 to clinch the Conference (Gola League) championship followed by the FA Trophy Final victory again Boston United. The first of only three clubs to achieve this "non-League double".

Incidents recalled include one during a Southern League (Southern Division) match versus Basingstoke Town at Lower Mead on Thursday, 1st April, 1982. We were going for the championship and were heading the table just two points clear of second placed Dorchester Town.

A victory for us in this game was essential but as play progressed during the second half the game remained goalless. Suddenly long-time supporter Bill Cowan shouted to Roy Davies that if he scored he would give him £5. Considering Roy hadn't scored all season Bill's money looked safe, however with just two minutes of the game remaining Roy Davies found the net to give us a valuable 1-0 victory. As soon as he scored he ran over to the High Mead terrace, collected his fiver, and ran back to the centre circle waving the note above his head.

Three other incidents recalled are Boston United's late arrival at Lower Mead for an Alliance Premier league fixture in October, 1983 when their coach broke down at Welwyn. They eventually arrived at 4.30 p.m. with the game kicking off 13/4 hours after the schedule 3.00 p.m. start.

We had to wait until the final four minutes before Nigel Johnson opened the scoring but in the final minute Jimmy Lumby scored from the penalty spot to earn Boston a 1-1 draw.

In December 1987 Dennis Byatt scored an "own goal" after just 7 seconds of our home Conference game with Weymouth, the Dorset side going on to win 2-0.

Then in September, 1989 during a 1-1 draw with Woking Town in the Capital league at Lower Mead, Tony Lynch's 29th minute penalty for Wealdstone not only cleared the crossbar, but also the roof of the Elmslie Stand!

Nick Woolford
Supporter since 1966

The era of the Cordice brothers is also etched in my memory. Our forwards struck terror into many a defence with their speed and clinical finishing.

The double-winning team has to warrant a mention for some momentous games. The semi final against Enfield was so full of tension that it was a great relief to make the Wembley game. The egg-throwing incident still causes me to chuckle. I recall the keeper being asked at subsequent games "How do you want your eggs today?"

The visit to Wembley was just fantastic. I missed the Amateur Cup Final in 1966 (as I was still a committed Gooner then!) and so to see MY team not only play but win a cup final at Wembley was just a great feeling. I will never forget Andy Graham's goal in the opening minutes.

In the early 80's my niece expressed an interest in seeing a football match (she is sport crazy) and so I started taking her with me to Lower Mead. Her first game was (I think) against Boston United in a League match.

The visiting team coach got delayed and the game kicked off almost one hour late. As this was before the era of the mobile phone I was not able to advise my sister that we would be late home and so I left after the first half to get her home.

Subsequently Catherine would stand by the fence and I would be on my usual perch on the second step of the Elmslie Stand. Catherine would regularly call out to me with questions such as "Uncle Nicky, what's offside?"

*Usually I was able to give her the benefit of my experience in footballing terms but I was completed floored on days when at the top of her voice she shouted "Uncle Nicky, What's a w****r??"*

My niece then went to Oxford University where she got a full blue for rugby and a half blue for rowing. Subsequently based in Nottingham, she remains a member of the Wealdstone Supporters' Club.

The Elmslie Ender had become a forthright 'voice' from the terraces within the club, and certainly at the end of the eighties, with a regular sale through the Supporters Club, direct to fans, by subscription and by being available through a number of specialist shops, 500 copies frequently sold out.

It was funny, sometimes hard hitting and sometimes a little controversial, after all it was written by supporters for supporters. After comments made in Wealdstone's last Conference season, the Elmslie Ender was banned.

Comments had been made about Dagenham FC, and they had complained. The Conference Secretary, Mr Peter Hunter and the Conference Committee, in dispute with magazine editors Martin Lacey and Sudhir Rawal, had informed Wealdstone FC via Secretary Peter Braxton that the magazine could no longer be sold in or around the ground.

Both the Club and the Supporters Club also withdrew their support for the publication.

On relegation, the matter was then put before the Pyramid Joint Liaison committee, and they too banned the publication. Effectively, The Elmslie Ender was banned from the Conference, the Beazer Homes League and all other feeder leagues to the Conference.

Previously sold in the Club Shop, the magazine could not now be sold anywhere in the ground or the surrounding area – it lead to copies being sold in the road opposite the ground.

Suffice to say, that the ban was eventually lifted and the Elmslie Ender saw out the 20th Century, which is something that Dagenham FC certainly did not!.

The close season saw manager, Tony Jennings start to stamp his identity on the 'Stones team with a number of new signings. One of these was the signing of Paul Morris from neighbours Harrow Borough for a club record £5,000, against competition from Sutton United and Aylesbury among others.

Jennings was also able to confirm the signing of striker Paul Wilkins from Chelmsford City and brothers Dennis and David Greene had been invited along to train with the side after a couple of successful Capital League matches at the end of the previous year.

Rarely, if ever, can Wealdstone have started a new season with such a bizarre game.

This match could have ended 4-2 to the visitors instead of 4-0 to the 'Stones, but it would also be true to say that it could have finished as a 4-4 draw or a 6-0 home win!

The final result was probably an injustice to the visitors. They had missed two penalties, two more open goals and had a shot cleared off the line........

So ran the match report after the game.

In the first minute, Skipper Everard La Ronde saw a shot flash just over the bar. Ten minutes later, and 'Stones had the lead, Lynch scoring from a Steve Browne free kick.

These in fact were the only two chances Wealdstone had in the first half as the visitors had by far the better of the play. Darren Williams proving his worth and paying back some of his £4,000 transfer fee.

Dennis Byatt increased 'Stones lead with a trademark free-kick just after the start of the second half and immediately from the restart, Moor Green pressed forward and earnt a penalty. Williams, who had conceded the kick then saved the shot to make amends.

A second penalty was awarded later, only for the ball to rebound of the post, before Wealdstone further increased their lead through Tony Lynch before Mark Harrison finished the scoring, with a penalty just before then end.

A draw at Gosport and then a victory at Bedworth saw 'Stones, with almost a completely new side, take five points from their first three games.

It was the end of the 'David Morritt era' at Wealdstone.

A High Court victory by Chairman Alan Clifton at the end of August 1988 saw all of the previous directors' shareholding returned to Wealdstone FC, along with the ownership of the Lower Mead Car Park. At the same time, the club also purchased the Chest Clinic and two properties in the adjoining Hindes Road.

The cost of these purchases, some £2,000,000 was immediately recouped for the club by the sale of the properties to Harrovian Estates.

It meant that Wealdstone were immediately freed of the £200,000 charge Morritt had on it and the car park became the club's property for the first time since 1935.

It was all supposed to strengthen the club's position as far as selling the site and the car park as one item to at the time, an unnamed Supermarket chain, for £7,000,000.

Morritt had purchased the car park for £50,000 from EMI Cinemas in 1984 and had always stated that this was for the club, however the purchase had been made by Leveloak Developments, one of his companies.

When he resigned from the Wealdstone FC Board in March, he had refused to return the lease of the car park to the club and thus the court challenge had occurred.

As part of the victory, the lease was bought back by the club, a sum in the region of £200,000 was returned to David Morritt, this being the money he had invested in the club, along with an interest payment.

He was released from his guarantees to Charringtons Breweries and Barclays Bank on behalf of the club.

It meant a sum approaching £800,000 would be paid over when the ground and surrounding property was finally sold.

A record of 8 wins, three draws and two defeats up to the middle of November had seen Wealdstone go top of the Beazer Homes League, after a 2-0 home win over Alvechurch but it was very much the 'peak' of the season.

'Stones suffered six defeats and four draws in the ten matches before their next win and there were only seven more in the remaining eighteen matches as 'Stones slipped to an 11th place finish.

Nigel Waterfield
Supporter

There are two memories of Lower Mead that remain with me. Waiting in the queue outside the Supporter Club shop as the half time whistle blew on a cold winter's day, with the aim of going in to browse to keep warm and standing by the exit at the corner of the main stand just before the end of matches listening to Val Shearer summing up the game to the nearby spectators.

The close season again saw a record transfer fee as the club paid £10,000 for Tony Kelly and amid concern at the spiralling fees generally, Tony Jennings also spent £9,000 on defender Sean Norman from Wycombe Wanderers and another £7,000 on Steve Tapley.

These figures paled into obscurity though a week later as Chairman Alan Clifton 'held court' on the back pages of the local paper under the headline ***"Why 'Stones are £1m in the red"***

Wealdstone FC Chairman Alan Clifton has laid the blame fairly and squarely on the shoulders of past administrations for the acute financial plight which led to the club's decision this week to sell their Lower Mead ground for an estimated £7m and take up temporary residence at Willesden Stadium.

'Stones are over £1m in debt and the move to Willesden while the search for a new permanent ground goes on, is seen as the salvation of the club and the very key to their continued existence.

Said Mr Clifton " In my search of the archives, the start of the club's basic financial problems can be traced back to 1972 when the club turned professional and joined the Southern League.

Coupled with this expense and the drop in attendances the club's financial resources were acutely overstretched.

From then on, with a succession of different chairmen and directors over the years, they only succeeded in compounding the issue until today, we have this terrible price to pay." He added "It also became patently obvious that the majority of my predecessors had little or no commercial experience. I believe that this lack of experience encouraged most to allow their hearts to rule their heads"

Mr Clifton's plans to quit Lower Mead were given the go-ahead on Saturday at a three hour meeting of the members and shareholders.

"My major task now is to build on the groundwork that has been established, continue with my negotiations and secure and build a new stadium as a permanent home for our team and supporters" he said.

Wealdstone's move to Willesden came as a surprise to many. Most observers expected the club to groundshare while awaiting re-location with Harrow Borough always the likely favourite to accommodate their neighbours.

'Stones plumped for the less costly option at Willesden where they will play on Astro-turf and will be the only team in the league with an artificial pitch.

The following week, the Observer Letters page carried a questioning response from former Chairman, David Morrit. He agreed that when he 'left' there were debts of £622,000 accumulated over the previous 14 years, but he also pointed out that during this period, not only had the club had some great success, but the value of the ground *"had increased from £1,000,000 to £10,000,000"*.

Further questions were raised as to how and why the club had accrued an additional £500,000 of debt in just over one year, while being relegated.

Questioning the sale of the ground to Harrovian, the club sponsors, Morritt queried the actions of the trustees and...

...their duty to market the site fully so as to be sure the club received the highest price available.

He went on: *When I resigned, Mr Clifton assured me and the members that he had £1m available to loan the club, interest free for three years, during which period he was hopeful of finding a new ground. Why then has a deal been rushed through in 16 months? A deal which gives no assurance that the club will ever have it's own ground again.*

It was an opinion that was to rankle with parts of the club over a number of years as the club moved closer to the wilderness, but the deal was done.

Stephen Bird
Supporter since the 1960's

The season following the 'Double' started well enough but then midway through, the club went into a steep decline, starting with an FA Trophy defeat at South Bank, and it was around this time that I took my place back on the High Mead terrace.

'Hally' left a year later and was replaced by Colin Meldrum, in my opinion surely the worst Manager the club ever had. To lose most of the team was bad enough but to leave them unreplaced was madness - why then Chairman Dave Morrittt didn't take matters into his own hands and get rid of him during the summer of 1987 I'll never know.

Eventually succeeded by Terry Burton, all too briefly, which was a pity. He brought in several useful players and we started to play like a team again - I don't know what got to him in the end - whether he thought it was too much for him or the team being booed off the pitch after the first really poor performance under his management I don't know, but his subsequent record as a coach at Wimbledon speaks for itself.

Then in came Tony Jennings a big name and former England Semi Pro captain, he managed to stabilise things but not in time to prevent us being relegated in 1988, a lack of new ideas saw him replaced by Alan Gane and under his management we started playing some of the best football seen at Lower Mead since the days of Allen Batsford and possibly since the mid 70's.

Unfortunately although there was nothing wrong with his abilities on the pitch, he had no financial control and allowed the clubs cost to spiral excessively and get completely out of hand. Although he had eventually gone and been replaced by a returning Brian Hall, the financial situation was so bad that it eventually forced the sale of Lower Mead.

A sad tale to end the 80's but there were some memorable moments. There was Dennis Byatt's moment of pure comedy and THAT own goal - if you don't know about it try and find a copy of "When Saturday Comes", Issue 13.

Suffice to say for timing alone it was only beaten by Pat Kruse of Torquay in the 70's.

Despite the spending spree during the summer which had seen the club spend more in one summer on players than its entire history, on the field results were poor.

After eight league matches reaped only eight points ('Stones slipped to fourth from bottom is mid September) and a disappointing FA Cup exit to Wivenhoe, it was no surprise that after a meeting with the Chairman, Tony Jennings resigned.

The Wivenhoe match did leave one memory for the Wealdstone FC Folklore library however;

'Lifelong' Wealdstone fan Cardew Robinson suffered an embarrassing case of colour blindness on Saturday when he watched the club's 1-0 defeat at home to Wivnehoe.

Cardew, watching 'Stones for the first time this season was unaware that they had changed their colours to white, and when the visitors played in 'Stones traditional blue and scored late in the game, he thought Wealdstone had won.

He said "I didn't recognise any of the players other than Dennis Byatt who waved to me during the kick about. He was wearing a Blue tracksuit top, so I spent the entire game under the impression that Wealdstone were in blue.

I leapt to my feet when the goal went in because I thought Wealdstone had scored. It was only when Dennis came on as a substitute that I realised I'd been cheering the wrong team. I've never felt such a nana in my life".

Alan Gane was appointed manager and despite a six match unbeaten run soon afterwards, he could not lift 'Stones to the required level – from an early season average of one point per game, it did improve slightly to three points from every two games. A long way short of mounting a challenge at the top of the division.

There had been another change-around as the new manager brought in new players, and other players left the club during the same period. The final analysis showed Wealdstone one place and one point worse off than at the end of the previous season, in 12th place.

The end of the season saw Alan Gane 'forced' to retain all of his squad despite the wishes of most people that the team was dismantled and rebuilt in the hope of forcing a championship challenge for the following year.

The decision was actually out of his hands as there was no more money available. He had to sell before he could bring in new faces to strengthen the side, despite the initial promises from the Chairman and the Board.

Yet again the club decided that a reserve team would be run to increase the potential development of young players, and Roy Davies was named as the Manager and the side was accepted into the Suburban League.

The club had also set in place an agreement with Belmont United that a number of their players would form the basis of the Reserve side. Indeed, before the season had ended, three, Mark Culverhouse, Pat A'Mara and Mark Kelly appeared for Wealdstone in the Capital League, but to no avail as by the end of April Wealdstone were rooted firmly at the bottom of the table.

Graham Brown
Supporter since the early 1960's

I was born in 1949, physically in Camberley, but have lived all my life in and around Wealdstone. I have supported Wealdstone since the early 1960's, although as my refereeing career progressed I was unable to see them as often as in the early days. For example, in 1966 I saw all the Amateur Cup games and was pleased to be at the Harrow Granada after the game when the team paraded the trophy

My own particular memories, which may provide a different slant are about refereeing. Firstly I was lucky enough to "line" on a couple of Middx Cup games, including one which Steve Hibberd refereed. As a 'Stones supporter it was a great honour to walk out at Lower Mead as an official.

The game I really want to talk about was a "Veterans" game, held on a Sunday morning at Lower Mead, between an ex-Wealdstone team and a team from the North East captained by an ex-'Stones player from the sixties, Tony Knox.

At the time, I played on Sundays, for Hatch End F.C. who were managed by an old 'Stones player, George Mowle. Because of that I was invited to referee.

The 'Stones team included most of my "heroes" from 1966, Hugh Lindsay, Charlie Townsend, Bill Fowler, Arthur Peel, (my old PE teacher), George himself, and several others my memory can't recall. What the 'Stones team did not know was that the North East team contained several players from the Bishop Auckland and West Auckland teams of the same era, and more importantly, they regularly played together as a "Vets" team in the North East.

To cut a long story short the 'Stones got "stuffed" about 9-1, I don't remember the exact score, but I know I gave a last minutes penalty against Wealdstone, which Bill Fowler saved! He was undoubtedly the happiest Stone after the game.

After the bath in the referees room, there were no showers, only a standard domestic bath, we all had a good drink in the old bar under the stand (the Vice-Presidents bar) and I was honoured to have been able to referee the players who had been my heroes as a boy.

My favourite Wealdstone player of all time? To my mind there is no doubt, Hugh Lindsay. He scored goals from open play and free-kicks which were the equivalent of Peter Lorimer in his heyday. To see the ball hit the back of the net from a Hughie free kick remains one of my happiest memories.

1990–91 started with similar form as the previous season had ended, three wins, two draws and two defeats from the first seven matches. The FA Cup saw victories over Saffron Walden Town and Wivenhoe, but not without cost, as sendings off were to take their toll.

Coupled with injuries the squad began to get stretched but for one player it was more unfortunate than most, Ian Fergusson returning after a six match ban, only to break his leg on his comeback as 'Stones lost in the FA Cup at Ruislip Manor.

This and other injuries meant that by mid October 'Stones had five first choice midfield players unavailable for the visit of Weymouth, which despite the problems, brought another win.

Despite the calls of the first team on the squad, the reserves had started well and by November were leading the Suburban League table, confirmed with a victory over local rivals Edgware Town reserves.

Peter John-Baptiste
Supporter

I started watching Wealdstone around 1980, when I went along with school friends. At first it was just something I used to do to pass the time on a Saturday afternoon, but pretty soon I was hooked.

The thing I remember most from the early days were the crowds and the level of excitement that used to build up on match days. In those days we were regularly pulling in crowds in excess of 1000 and the atmosphere in Lower Mead was as good as anything I've experienced in twenty years watching football at home and abroad.

The biggest memory is the Trophy final. The month leading up to the game was a joy for a 14 year old boy who had to take stick from his class mates all year for supporting a local non-league team. Suddenly, all these kids were asking me where and how they could get tickets and everyone in school was pledging their undying loyalty to the club.

They were all planning to attend every game leading up to the final. My club was thrust into the spot light and everybody wanted a piece of the reflected glory. The game and the celebrations that day will remain forever in the memories of all the 'Stones fans that were there.

Later on, I marked Corey Browne in an SFC V Wealdstone FC reserves game match in 1990. He didn't score but I did. Unfortunately it was an own goal.

If I'm not mistaken this was the game where Mike Kane shouted out after about 10 minutes ' Come on SFC, lets start hitting a few of these bastards'.

It didn't go down too well with their manager, Roy Davies.

In mid December there was another shock for the fans as the entire management team – Alan Gane, his assistant Frank Dotson, coach Richard Parkin and Reserve Team Manager Roy Davies – were sacked. It was the fourth change of management in under four years.

Despite topping the Suburban League and being involved in the Beazer Homes League Championship, the chairman sited the cost of the squad and unsuccessful transfer dealings as the reasons for the sackings.

Mark Harrison took over for one game, but the popular return of Brain Hall who had recently left Yeovil was anticipated to see Wealdstone return to the top.

It wasn't the case however. With limited funds and injuries preventing drastic changes to the squad, Wealdstone's form faltered. By mid January, 'Stones had dropped to 12th in the table, twelve points behind the leaders, Worcester City.

In February, a public meeting was called to discuss another potential move for the club, this time to the Willesden Stadium in Brent. The club had been forced to look outside the Borough of Harrow as all possible avenues seemed to be closing around them. There was little help from the council.

It was suggested that this would be a permanent rather than a temporary move, with the club hoping, if all went well, to secure a 99 year lease on the site.

The following week, the front page of the Observer broke the news that Tesco had bought the Lower Mead ground, and that the deal had been completed before Christmas. As part of the deal it was agreed that 'Stones could remain in situ – but only until the end of the season, some three months away.

The news had come hard on the back of the public meeting in which the local residents and present users of Willesden Stadium had had emphatically voted against Wealdstone moving in.

There was worse to come as well as Wealdstone began to investigate a possible groundshare in light of the Willesden decision. They were informed that any potential groundshare – the one under consideration was an agreement with Harrow Borough – would only be allowed for a maximum of one year.

With an EGM planned Club Chairman Alan Clifton released another statement to the press dismissing fears that the club was likely to 'go under'. He emphasised the strength of the club and the number of options available, but as was repeated at the EGM, none of the options were identified.

Enough was said though for the supporters and members at the meeting to give the board a vote of confidence.

There was contention between the Board and the Supporters Club. The supporters had issued their own statement after the meeting and had expressed serious concerns over the future of the club as a whole. This resulted in a difference of opinion become ever more public as the Harrow Observer carried commentary from both sides.

The board, standing their corner were defending their actions and confirming their progress while the Supporters Club were questioning the progress being made, both sides stating that they had the best interests of the club at heart.

The on field activities of the club almost seemed to pale into insignificance. They must certainly have been affected by the off-field wrangling but at the beginning of April there was some potentially good news that healed the rift. Wealdstone FC announced that they had purchased a half share of a 127 year lease on Vicarage Road, the home of Watford FC.

Watford Director, Charles Lissack represented the league club, while David Pollock of Greene and Co, Estate Agents, instigated the proceedings on behalf of Wealdstone FC.

Under the agreement, the Stadium was to be run by an umbrella committee, made up of representatives of both clubs to ensure that all costs except match day expenses would be shared, with the two clubs playing at home on alternate weeks.

The Supporters Club too confirmed that, after the initial shock as the announcement came out of the blue, it was an exciting prospect for the club.

April 27th 1991 saw the last league match played at Lower Mead, the home of Wealdstone FC for some seventy years.

It was an emotional day with may of the 'Stones supporters, players and officials shedding tears as the final whistle was blown and the crowd thronged onto the pitch. Most with camera's at the ready, taking photographs of the final moments of the ground.

The last match had not been memorable but the occasion most certainly was, even the Cambridge newspaper was taken in by what it described as a bizarre atmosphere for a football match, where the crowd for most of the afternoon was totally oblivious to what was happening on the pitch.

The reserve team was to be disbanded after its one season return, as the groundshare at Vicarage Road would not allow them to use the pitch as well, but they did at least sign off with a win, in the match against Harefield United reserves by 1–0 triumphantly winning the Suburban League Championship.

Wayne Roach
Player 1990-1992

I fondly remember my time at Wealdstone and the fans. Looking back at some of the photo's, I now know why I gave up football and came home to New Zealand!

Seriously though, I now keep in touch via the internet and often look for the Stones results. It has been good to see the progress lately.

J R S Whitehead (Roger)
Supporter 1950-1988

I was a Long-term supporter 1950-1988, when I moved to Cheltenham and took a significant financial stake in Cheltenham Town Football Club. What a success story there!

The two Poles stick in my mind - Mikrut and Wegrzyk. Not for-

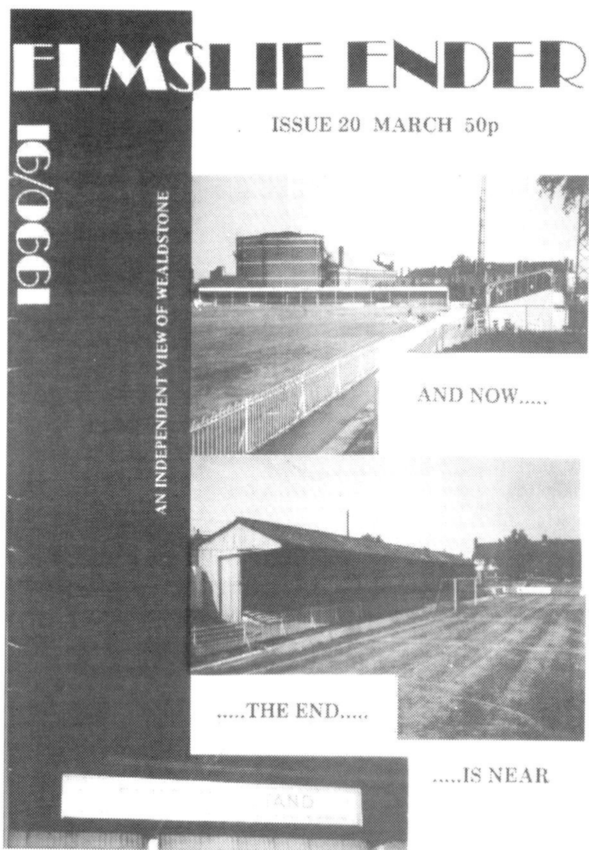

The front cover of the Elmslie Ender at the time that Lower Mead was sold.

getting Gilbert Gaze (the milkman) from very early days and subsequently Charlie Barker, Charlie Edmonds and Eddie Smith.

The Christmas day matches against Hendon were always a highlight. The Amateur Cup Final at Wembley against Hendon and of course, the final against Boston Utd at Wembley.

I am still waiting to hear though, what happened to the proceeds of the sale of Lower Mead!

J L Field
Supporter since 1940's

My parents moved in 1935 to Kenton, Harrow where I grew up. My eldest sister married in the early 1940's and she and her husband occupied a flat in High Mead with a view immediately over Wealdstone's ground. In fact in line with the centre line.

As a result during the early 1940's in the days of the war and thick smog's my father and I would visit my sister on match days and have a superb view of the matches.

Christmas Day Wealdstone played Hendon at home and I would go along with my father and brother-in-law into the ground. They would pay, but I was still small enough to walk in under the turnstiles.

Come 1947 my sister and brother-in-law emigrated to New Zealand so thereafter I paid to see home games from the terraces.

I lost touch as a result of marrying, but renewed contact in the late 1960's when I would take my son along to watch; be quickly became addicted and he joined the Supporters' Club, which became his second home.

As a result of his contact with the Supporters' Club I still felt an affinity with the team and also all of the friends of my son.

It was with sadness I saw the disposal of Lower Mead, but I am very pleased that you are making progress towards a ground of your own again, and although I do not watch on a regular basis I still look for the results at weekends.

The last ever match at Lower Mead was a fitting farewell from Wealdstone supporters.

The final match at Lower Mead was played between SFC Wealdstone's supporters teams. The match, played on Thursday was between the first team and reserves. The score was of no real consequence but a near full strength first team beat a depleted reserves side 8-2.

Mike Kane (3) Don Cross (3) and Paul Williams (2) scored for the first team while James Knightsbridge and an own goal from Peter John-Baptiste after sterling work from Paul Ryan, replied for the reserves. John-Baptiste's own goal will be remembered as the last ever scored at the loved, revered and infamous home end, the Elmslie End.

The match was a personal triumph for Paul 'Fingers' Fruin who has had to face many years of ridicule for his efforts between the posts. But having been drafted in at a late hour to go in goal for the reserves, Fingers played probably his greatest ever game, holding back the first team side. His most glorious moment was a penalty save from Sudhir Rawal.

Steve Marshall blew the final whistle to bring down 69 years of football at Lower Mead and more than a few tears were shed on this final night.

A superb programme was issued for the occasion, Sateesh Khanna producing a 40 page extravaganza with a full colour cover for a mere 50p without an advert in sight!

First team; Sudhir Rawal, Gordon McKay, Wayne McMillain, Matthew Ansell, Peter John-Baptiste, Don Cross, Roger Slater, Mike Kane (Paul Williams), Steve Goody, Steve Hobbs, Mark Storey.

Reserves; Steve Marshall (Paul Fruin), Steve Johnson (Tony Platt), Roy Sharpe, Phil Clegg, Ken Pegg, Sateesh Khanna, Layne Patterson, Paul Ryan, Dominic Whyley (Mark Chamberlain), James Knightsbridge, Andy Fall.

Layne Patterson
Former Director, and Official of the Club & Supporters Club

Wembley in 1985 will remain with me as a memory for ever, but my best memories are of the last days of Lower Mead.

That last League game there against Cambridge City was a very sad occasion. Strange as it seems, I was intent on enjoying the day and being surrounded by so many people who shared a common interest it made it one hell of an experience.

People still tell me about things that happened that day and the fact that it is still talked about at all shows how much it meant to people.

I was also lucky enough to play in the last actual match on the ground, when SFC Wealdstone's first and reserve teams brought the curtain down on seventy years of history. Everyone involved was keen to do something there for the last time – the last goal, the last own goal, the last penalty save.

I managed to concede the last penalty, happy that my name would be written in the history of the ground forever. Except that a few minutes later, there was another penalty – my place in history was disappearing fast!

I did reclaim it though when punching clear a corner for yet anther spot kick to be awarded.

James Smith
Supporter and General Assistant

My first time watching the "'Stones" was at Lower Mead when I was just five years old in the successful season of 1981 –1982. My dad was just a supporter at the time and he took me along as many games as he could. I can remember parking the car a few streets away and walking up Station Road to the ground, I would normally stand to the left of the main stand or in front of it. The ground it self had so much character which really amazed me and especially being a five year old, it was like Old Trafford to me.

The main things I remember about it were quite funny. The ball boys room had the tiniest of doors that you had to crouch down low to get into. There were about five or six boys crammed into this room and at half time drinking our coke and eating stale crisps.

There was the floodlight switch box, positioned next to the Elmslie Stand on the junction of the High Mead terrace. It meant walking all the way round to turn the lights on if the referee asked during a game - it could take ten minutes !

During the school holidays I would always be at the ground helping out in anyway under the supervision of Peter Braxton. I remember painting the crush barriers on the High Mead terrace on hot summer days and not getting home until late.

I would always ride by bike there and back so I was really tired when I got home, and then when Tony Lynch was groundsman I would help him do the pitch or clean out the dressing rooms.

I will never forget the day when I arrived at the ground to find someone had painted some obscene words about Alan Clifton all over the fence surrounding the ground and guess what "Lynchie" and I had to do, yes you've guessed it, we had to "blue wash" the fence to cover those messages. It took forever and I was covered in blue paint.

Being small, I also had one of the worst jobs at Lower Mead - about two or three times a season, my dad and I had to crawl under the Elmslie Stand and clear out all the rubbish to prevent a fire as the Elmslie Terrace was made from wooden blocks.

The Fire Brigade had ordered us to clear it after the Bradford fire incident which ironically was the same day Wealdstone completed the first non-league double by beating Boston United in the F.A Trophy at Wembley.

I also started to clean "Lynchies" boots from about 1988 to 1992. I got paid one pound for every pair. Then other players got into the act and they included Tony Kelly, Danny Bailey, Steve Tapley amongst others so I made quite a lot of money back then and I'm sure with a few of the players there's a few debts still to settle !

On Sunday lunchtimes I would go into the ground and see Val Shearer cleaning up the terracing and a chap called Henry who used to do the washing of the kit. On some occasions the kit was so dirty that it was put into the massive bath that the players used. Of course the bath would not be used for players these days with the ruling on showers only in the dressing rooms.

I will always remember the small kit room we had, I tried to keep it tidy and in order and felt like an apprentice doing all the mucky jobs including sweeping up cleaning boots and many more things.

The Board Room and the VP Bar had a lot of character about it, the trophy cabinet made me think that I was with one of the best teams in England!. (Well I was only young then and to me Wealdstone was one of the best teams !).

I loved being in the VP Bar after games mixing with the players and just enjoying myself with my idols. I would always be the first to ask Karen Fletcher for the teletext control so I could see how everyone else had got on, in the end I didn't have to ask for it when I went into the bar she had it ready for me.

The most terrifying day at Lower Mead was when I was mascot for the day, it was against Telford in the "Double " season. I had the worst butterflies and felt sick. Once I had met all the players and had to wait for Brian Hall had finished his team talk then I would go out with the team on to the pitch for a kick about. Neil Cordice helped through the warm up just kicking the ball to me and he tried to teach me a few things but I was too nervous to notice.

Obviously on the football side my happiest memory was Wealdstone winning the "Double".

I had the best two weeks in my footballing life at the end of that season 1984/85. Wealdstone had gone to Kettering and won the Gola League (now the Conference) then made history by winning the F.A. Trophy and Manchester United won the F.A.Cup. I was on cloud nine and don't think I'll ever be that excited again.

My only regret was not seeing the second leg of the F.A.Trophy semi-final at Lower Mead. My mum made me go to my Aunt's. I was not impressed. Dad phoned me up to tell me the score and I was so happy that we had gone through, I screamed down the phone.

Winning the League Titlte at the Kettering match itself, I can still see Andy Graham firing the ball home from the edge of the area and Vinnie Jones spraying Champagne all over us, my hat is still covered with stains.

The journey home was one of jubilation, Ted Brazier who sadly is no longer with us drove us back and his son Adam and I had our scarves out of the window along the motorway for all to see.

The day of the F.A Trophy my dad and I put banners and scarves on house windows. I went with a couple of mates in Dad's car and just could not believe that Andy Graham scored only after just 74 seconds. We went on to win 2-1 against Boston United even though missing a penalty. Wealdstone had done what no other non-league club had done and that was to win the Gola league and the F.A. Trophy in the same season.

The saddest day was leaving Lower Mead, it had become my second home and I still miss it dearly. The last game against Cambridge City was so emotional that I had to hold back my tears, now I wish I had cried because I never felt I said goodbye

properly.

I could not believe that anyone would take away the place where I had spent some of my happiest times as a youngster. After that day I still went down to the ground to watch the demolition work. I just sat in the main stand watching work men knock down the Cinema end with a tear in my eye.

I thought the world had come to an end.

My photos of it all are one of greatest souvenirs, I have a photo of the main stand knocked down with the home dressing room door still standing while everything was in bits, It's quite funny when you think about, maybe it was trying to say something!

The final completion of the deal to move to Vicarage Road was not signed until late June. It was not as smooth a transition as had been hoped.

Despite their support for the potential move, the Supporters Club again had voiced their concerns for the future of the club. After a meeting with Club Directors, Trustees and their Legal Advisors, the Supporters Club demanded that the remaining money from the sale of Lower Mead was handed over.

It resulted in the board of the Football Club disowning its own Supporters Club in a public statement, although the Supporters Club responded by re-iterating its duty to represent its members and to voice its concerns where necessary.

Nick Dugard
Supporter, SC Chairman, Club Vice-Chairman

I started following the 'Stones around 1973 and I couldn't tell you my first game but I do know that I was introduced to the club by a college friend, George Pinkney whose enthusiasm for one George Duck, related to me during Sociology classes bordered on the obsess ional.

I can tell you that my first ever away game was when we played Aldershot in the cup and I was well and truly hooked on the pure excitement and drama that I realised could be generated through the game of football.

My official role at the club started with the supporters club when I joined the committee under the chairmanship of Bert Wakefield, in the late seventies. Also on the committee at that time was Barbara Robson, Tom and Julia Verrall, Alan Couch and Phil Tricker amongst others. I had the utmost respect for these people but times were changing at the club and many changes on the committee where to happen.

My problem is that I'm useless on dates but I was on the committee for over 10 years - I know this because I've got an award to prove it!

I suppose I was considered a bit of a young upstart on the committee (around 1975 ish) and other present stalwart supporters were starting to get involved ie Tim Parks, Mark Chamberlain, and others including my brother Bob.

This was the period in my sad life when I would spend virtually whole summers at Lower Mead doing maintenance jobs, burning back the weeds was always a good laugh, with people like the late Steve Field and Ron Davies, Dan Helen, Tony Hayes and Dave Heath who worked tremendously hard for the club and was on the committee for a long period -unfortunately disappeared off the scene when he got married.

My brother Bob was a fantastic organiser who enjoyed planning and running things and he took over the Lower Mead tea-bars when Julie Verrall retired. When we entered the Alliance Premier and crowds started to get bigger we reopened the old cinema end tea-bar and kept in touch with walkie-talkies!

Bob and myself were fairly critical of the club during these and earlier times and we started various fundraising initiatives. One of these were Saturday morning Jumble sales and we organised a Fete on the pitch which despite our efforts was not very well attended – no change there then! Bob also organised a car boot sale.

These were to me the carefree halcyon days when I wasn't dragged down with the awesome burdens of helping keep the club afloat and the dread behind the scenes machinations of the board that I must confess can be purgatory.

There were still problems though and the supporters club was a very powerful group in those days, partly because we ran the place on match days and raised considerable funds through our efforts (we did sponsored walks in those days – I have a photo somewhere of one when we walked around Harrow)

We flexed our muscles sometimes- particularly when we didn't like what was happening to our large fundraising monies - dur-

Lower Mead 1922 - 1991

ing the seventies and much of the early eighties there was a kind of shop floor union (we provided the labour) and Management mentality.

I once resigned from the committee with my brother when I had a major falling out with Ken Wiltshire, and Frank Ryder when Fred Deanus had just taken over as Chairman.

I had no real problem with Fred but we couldn't abide the attitude which prevailed of 'them and us' at that particular time. If my memory serves me correctly the whole supporters club committee resigned under the leadership of Bert and Barbara Robson – a lady I have a huge amount of respect for and was a huge stalwart of the club at that time. Unfortunately I don't think Barbara ever got over the departure of Dave Martle as Chairman.

The committee did return to support the club after this well publicised episode but some of the older stalwarts started to leave and a much younger element took over the reins on the supporters club committee.

Ray Kemp took over as Chairman in around 1983/84 and this saw the dawn of our best and positively worst experiences at the club as Ray, myself and others formed an effective combative close knit group which, whether we liked it or not, became the focus of a massive power struggle to come.

This would culminate in the use of lawyers, incoming threats of varying descriptions and crisis meetings the likes of which we had never seen before.......

An appeal from the supporters club to the main board for a meeting to resolve the dispute was carried by the local press alongside pictures of Lower Mead as the demolition and clearance started. It seemed whatever happened, there was no way back.

Graham Smith
Club Official since 1986

The saddest of my life where Wealdstone was concerned came on the April 27th. 1991 the last league game played at Lower Mead, the Club going to groundshare with Watford F.C.

The Club was so much in debt that they sold their ground to Tesco's which is another very long and difficult story to understand.

I remember Tony Kelly scoring that last league goal at Lower Mead then just before the end Wealdstone supporters bringing on the "Elmslie Stand" sign onto the pitch, it was very moving but the Cambridge City supporters were not amused.

At the final whistle I just went on the pitch holding back my tears. I could not come to terms with the fat that it really was the end of an era.

I could not go down to my favourite ground to help out and not going in the Bar on a Sunday lunchtime with the rest of the family for a few pints and discussing the previous day's match.

Nick Woolford
Supporter since 1966

I began to get more involved with the Supporters' Club and actually served on the committee for a couple of years.
It was at this time that I learned of the difficulties that the club was experiencing and the financial shenanigans that had seemingly be going on for years.

The Morrittt era, followed by the man whose name I cannot bring myself to write, all has left a very nasty taste in the mouth.. I was absolutely devastated when I learnt that in order to survive the club would have to sell Lower Mead !

The misdemeanours which followed the sale are well catalogued do I will not go into them any further, just to say that I hated our time at Watford. I still hold a massive grudge against that club for what they did to us.

Quentin Fox
Director

I was brought up in Harrow, not far from Lower Mead, and our family home was in Northwick Park Road behind the old Granada cinema.

I used to hang around outside the gates at the age of 11 or so, but I didn't have enough money to go in – my mother refused to pay for me because 'football hooliganism' was rife and she thought I'd get hurt. I did however, manage to persuade my father to buy me an occasional programme and that was as close as I got to being there. Sad or what!

By about 1970 I had worked out how to sneak into the ground through those gaps at the back of the stand and I also occasionally had enough money to pay! I became a dedicated supporter at home games, watching from underneath the big clock opposite that stand.

I was there in the era of George Duck, Billy Byrne and John Henderson, and George remains my favourite player of all time. I remember the fans behind the goal singing 'Georgie, Georgie' whilst waving their scarves over their heads.......

At that time the entrances at both sides of the Cinema end were in use and I remember buying a half time Bovril from the tea bar at the side.

I drifted away from the club after I went to university in 1975 and I didn't return until David Pollock (later to become Chairman) persuaded me to come and watch a match at Lower Mead on a wet Tuesday evening in about 1988.

He failed to mention that it was only a Capital League match, but it re-awakened the dormant Wealdstone virus in my bloodstream and I was hooked once more. Needless to say I missed the glory years of Alan Cordice and Stuart Pearce which is now a source of great regret.

Memories from my return to the club include Samson Olaleye's unique style of play. Paul Gbogidi's neck-high tackling and Tony Lynch's mazy dribbles from the half way line, usually ending in a screaming shot onto or just over the cross bar.

I also remember a splendid 35 yard drive into the top corner from Danny Bailey at the Cinema End when I was behind the goal.

ROLLING STONES

There was almost no way forward either as the final agreement was not in fact signed until 1:40am on Saturday 3rd August, just two weeks before the new season was to start. There were still calls from supporters and members for the details of the whole deal to be disclosed as in many quarters there was a growing disquiet that was to result in a move to oust the Chairman of the club at an EGM in late August.

The result, seen as a vote of confidence from those present, led to a call to support the chairman and the board or to 'go elsewhere'.

With an ever increasing sense of the dramatic, just two weeks later, Alan Clifton resigned, citing ill health, allowing David Pollock to take over, just two weeks after he was appointed to the board.

New surroundings they may have been but there was no immediate improvement on the field either. The imposing surroundings of Vicarage Road – a 20,000 plus capacity stadium – looked at times desolate and empty when holding a gate of a mere 800 as Wealdstone took the field for their home fixtures.

It was certainly to add impetus to the opponents as well, the opportunity to play on an excellent surface seemed to spur on many opposing sides as Wealdstone struggled to create an atmosphere to give them a home advantage.

Lower Mead had been a tight and compact ground, with supporters a few feet from players and at night it really was an intimidating environment. Vicarage Road with (relatively) small crowds was soulless.

By Christmas, 31 matches had been played in all competitions. Wealdstone had won only 13 of these with six draws, which had resulted in a mid table position.

There did seem to be some promise as a seven game unbeaten run (four wins, three draws) through December had lifted spirits and the league position. The run was ended in the first fixture of the New Year and a run of five defeats and a win in six games saw 'Stones fortunes change again.

By mid February the alarm bells were ringing as *'Stones demonstrated an inability to score goals and a decided panache for conceding them'* as the report on another home defeat began.

It was a familiar tale as Wealdstone could not make the most of their possession or pressure and contrived to concede goals at any time.

By the beginning of April, relegation had become a distinct possibility as they slipped to just one place above the relegation zone with a one point advantage over two clubs, Crawley and Waterlooville, both of whom had two games in hand.

Their record of ten wins and seven draws from 36 matches seemed all the worse when it was realised that the recent record was one win and two draws from the last ten matches.

Two wins and two defeats from the next four fixtures did not bode well and the eventual relegation was confirmed win the second to last match of the season, at home to Gravesend, who were bottom of the table. The visitors taking the points with a 1-0 win.

It was almost expected as poor form against the 'lower' clubs was the main reason for the drop. Wealdstone had failed to beat any of the other three relegated clubs home or away during the season.

With finances still uncertain after the sale of Lower Mead and with gates lower than had been hoped for, no doubt as a result of the relegation, it was not entirely a surprise when in June the club called in the administrator.

It was a move intended to stabilise the club's finances and to ensure it's continuance, but it was not an easy path, the first application was adjourned in the High Court to enable the club to obtain further evidence to support the claim.

The sale of Lower Mead and the purchase of a half share of the Vicarage Road lease was expected to have secured a bright future for the club, but there were still some internal problems regarding the management and transfer of the outstanding monies that were to haunt the club for some time to come.

A crisis meeting was held at Vicarage Road in August. The Harrow Observer reported

"Carry On Wealdstone!" was the message from members at Tuesday's crisis meeting. They voted unanimously for the much troubled club to continue it's existence, and set it off on the long road to recovery by approving a new set of club rules, electing a new committee to handle club affairs, and also backed litigation to get back money lost in the tangled web surrounding the sale of Lower Mead.

The committee was to include club Chairman, David Pollock and Secretary Peter Braxton, together with David Buchler and Peter Phillips of Buchler Phillips the club's administrators.

The meeting heard from Philip Reuben of the club's solicitors, Finers Ltd, the 'full story' of events that had led to the club's current plight, events which began in December 1990 with the sale of Lower Mead and periphery property owned by Mr W Johnson to TESCO Stores Limited. The £12.1m was to be shared between Mr Johnson and the club.

The meeting then heard of further agreements between Mr Johnson and his company, Harrovian Group plc for sponsorship of the club and construction of a new ground, then intended to be at Willesden, which resulted in Wealdstone only receiving £3.5m from the sale instead of £6.05m. It was believed by this deal that there would be a considerable saving in Capital Gains Tax on the Lower Mead sale.

Mr Johnson is now bankrupt, and Harrovian Group plc is in liquidation.

Commenting on the events, Mr Pollock said "we want to make it clear that the board feel in hindsight, that the deal was ridiculous".

Wealdstone have now begun legal action against their former solicitors Minet Perring, alleging negligence. Their claim is for an unlimited sum said Mr Reuben. He was "cautiously optimistic" over the chances of success of the action which was expected to cost over £100,000 to pursue. Loss of the action, which could not be heard for 18 months was expected to cost the club £75,000.

Litigation has also commenced for the sum of £350,000 against TESCO Stores Ltd. This complicated issue relates to a periph-

ery property owned by Mr Johnson on which there was a mortgage charge which was never redeemed and a deduction was made from money the club was due to receive. A date for that action is likely to be 6-9 months.

Wealdstone will also be defending an action brought by Watford FC who have issued a writ in excess of £100,000 for ground charges at Vicarage Road. Wealdstone have paid £2m of a sum of £2.5m agreed for a half share of the 127 year lease of the ground, but it seems certain their future now lies away from Watford.

Mr Pollock said "One of the things we are looking at is selling our share of Vicarage Road to raise assets to relocate to another ground, hopefully within the borough of Harrow. But it is early days and we have to give Watford notice".

The intention would be to sell the ground back to Watford FC but if they chose not to buy it, it would be put on the open market.

Wealdstone went into administration two months ago when the company found themselves in the position of having no cash with which to trade and lots of liabilities, a situation complicated by the club having three arms, the club, the limited company and the Trustees.

This move came after the Trustees, faced with a £2.4m Capital Gains Tax assessment from the Lower Mead sale. Agreement has now been reached with the Inland Revenue that the Trustees are not personally liable, the remaining money, around £300,000 has now been handed over by the Trustees.

The administrators believe there will be sufficient assets to pay the club's debts. Sorting it out, they estimate, will take about a year.

The biggest financial noose around Wealdstone's neck is the wage bill that David Pollock revealed was £185,000. This included contractual obligations to players and he praised club manager Brian Hall for his efforts over the last year in endeavouring to trim this figure down.

Support from fans joining the club's Blue Ribbon lottery scheme and support also from patron Russell Grant, backed by the ongoing commercial activities were hoped to increase the available funds with a new season approaching.

Toby Jackson
Former Trustee, Company Secretary & Supporter

I began supporting by playing truant from Boarding School on Saturday afternoons in 1965 after moving to the Harrow area. From there things moved on and I ended up setting up a Club shop on the High Mead Terrace with the help of Colin Pope, then Commercial & Publicity Director and Ron Davies' electrical skills.

I was co-opted onto the Supporters Club committee and helped manage the Club Shop until 1991 and the move to Watford. In fact, it continued at Watford for a while despite the best efforts of the Watford officials who seemed oblivious to the fact that we had 'equal rights' to any part of Vicarage Road.

I was invited to become a Trustee of Wealdstone by David Morritt. It was just after he found out that it was me that took the phone calls at Barclays Bank Local Head Office whenever the Morritt Homes or Wealdstone FC accounts went 'out of order'.

Later I was invited onto the board and I resigned after the 'Harrovian' deal went through, then the dealings with Watford FC and then having received a £2,400,000 tax demand in my personal name for the Capital Gains Tax on the sale of Lower Mead.

Endless hours were spent on what seemed the less bad of two options to provide a future for the club. Now I prefer the quiet life back on the terraces watching the 'Stones and producing the badges sold in the Supporters Club shop and for numerous other clubs.

There are so many memories – I remember Dinky and Wendy who used to keep an eye on all of us 'youngsters' when I started watching Wealdstone and making sure we behaved. Remember Barbara Robson's Coach trips with Derek (Mapley?) buying all the tickets to make sure he won.

There was Hell's Granny at Stourbridge – an old lady who was just returning from a ban for assaulting a Linesman with her umbrella, but didn't appreciate a response from Tall Martin after telling us all to shut up cheering behind the goal.

Then her two burly sons materialised to flank Martin and the police then warned us that we would be ejected from the ground if we caused any more trouble.

I used to take my dog, "Mick the Mascot" to matches before I ran the club shop, resplendent in his blue coat with badges from his visits and his Wealdstone silk scarf.

His dinner got launched at a myopic linesman at Leatherhead and then there was a slide down a thistle-strewn bank at Margate as he chased after another hound......

There was a disappointment in the first match of the new season as it resulted in a 4–1 home defeat by Margate, although consecutive away wins, followed by draws at home and away put 'Stones in a strong position near the top of the league table.

Late September saw 'Stones record improve to five wins and three draws to one defeat in all competitions as the beleaguered club, at least on the field, seemed strong.

Then there was a further bombshell, as with finances dwindling still further, both Peter Braxton and Brian Hall were axed buy the administrator.

It was a dramatic cost cutting exercise and was accompanied by a bleak warning, The problems with Watford FC over the jointly owned ground meant that simply, there was no guarantee that the club would be able to see out the season at Vicarage Road.

The warning also detailed the possibility of Wealdstone FC suspending its activities and resigning from the Beazer Homes League.

The club was failing by some way to match income with expenditure, and as the position became clear to the administrator, dramatic action had to be taken.

An increasing push to 'sell' memberships of the Blue Ribbon scheme at least offered a 'stay of execution' as the supporters and friends rallied round to help.

On the field, with Dennis Byatt taking charge after the departure of Brian Hall, the club's fortunes were still on the up. Never more so than a sparkling win by 3–0 over league leaders

Gravesend, the club that had relegated the 'Stones the previous year. It came on the back of an FA Cup replay win away to Wivenhoe, which assured a home tie with Dagenham and Redbridge. This too was to be a welcome boost to the ailing finances.

Good form continuing, 'Stones had risen to fourth place in the league table by the beginning of December, but there were still major concerns over the finances and the clubs ability to complete it's season.

Supporters organised 'The Walk To Fisher' for the fixture on December 5th in the hope of raising £5,000 towards the day to day running of the club.

It was originally the idea of Neale Harvey, at the time a long distance supporter as he travelled regularly from Bath to support the 'Stones. 74 people were actually set to walk from Harrow & Wealdstone Station to the Fisher ground in Rotherhithe via Kenton, through central London and across London Bridge and down Jamaica Road with the intent of arriving around 12:30pm.

71 people set off on time, Steve and Sue Marshall about an hour behind due to a car breakdown and Steve Paull leaving at 12;30 and running all the way. Everyone arrived tired but safely and after the money had all been collected, over £5,500 was handed to the club.

The team also thanked those that took part - both by winning the match at Fisher and by presenting the walkers with a couple of cases of beer after the match.

It did enough to ensure that the club would see out the season.

Steve 'Hughie' Marshall
Supporter, Official and former Director

I nearly made two league appearances for Wealdstone in the Capital League, but the goalkeepers were found on both occasions! I did manage a few Capital league sides when they were strongly comprised of SFC Wealdstone players though.

There are literally thousands of memories and characters in the club, There always has been. It is what makes the club what it is. The best memory is probably the Walk To Fisher, which was very special. My own memories and those of my wife, Sue were different from everyone else's, as the British Rail car that we were driving down in broke down on the M1.

Sue's father came out and rescued us but we didn't arrive at Harrow & Wealdstone Station before everyone else had left. We followed about 50 minutes behind and caught up with absolutely no-one! I almost had to carry Sue through the gates at Fisher. It took us all of six hours but it was all worthwhile. I'm still convinced it was more than 16 miles.

The result too came in the middle of a good run of form as the year ended. 'Stones winning seven and losing two of the league

The Walkers at London Bridge – 5/12/92
Those involved in alphabetical order; Dave Albert, Jeremy Albert, Steve Ball, Steve Batty, Stephen Bird, Nick Brown, Mark Chamberlain, Tim Chamberlain, Brian Collins, Nicholas Conway, Steve Corner, Wayne Corner, Don Cross, Ken Davis, Louise Davies, Terry Dollman, Peter Drew, Steve Drew, Andy Fall, Mick Ferguson, Steve Field, Mark Fowler, Paul Fruin, Stephen Fry, Adam Gloor, Chris Halsey, Neale Harvey, Mark Hobbs, Michael Ivers, Toby Jackson, Phil Jefferson, James Jenner, Graham Jones, Matthew Kelsall, Darren Linden, David Lloyd, John Lloyd, Mark Lloyd, Patrick Lovett, Tony Maidment, Jamie Maloney, Steve Marshall, Sue Marshall, Simon Mitchell, Paul Morton, Paul McGreal, Alan McHugh, Mark McManus, Alan O'Connor, Michael O'Connor, Danny O'Haloran, Dave Parish, Layne Patterson, Steve Paull, Simon Pickering, Sarin Rawal, Sudhir Rawal, Martin Read, Declan Rickard, Alan Robins, Doug Robinson, Paul Rumens, Paul Ryan, Rob Saville, Roger Slater, Ian Spicer, Gus Stanners, Mark Stewart, Dave Thomas, Jenny Thomas, Rowland Thompson, Chris White, Dominic Whyley, Adam Williams, Stephen Williams

matches up to 28th December to maintain a challenge at the head of the Southern League table, the club looking to make an immediate return to the Premier Division.

Despite the results, some of the performances may not have been all that was expected. In hindsight, the indications were not as bright as the results seemed to indicate as the report on a 4-1 win over Fareham Town in the week before Christmas showed;

A well taken hat-trick from David Venables saw 'Stones to a victory on Saturday which maintained their push for a quick return to the Premier Division.

But despite the scoreline, it was a far from convincing performance against a depleted Fareham side who had seven players absent through suspension and injury and were forced to play their back-up 'keeper as a striker, and they had their Manager on the sub's bench.

'Stones had the better of an uninspiring first half and should have gone ahead in the 12th minute when Venables challenged defender Aniello Iannone for an Andy Hedge cross and the ball broke to Jim Watson who blazed wildly over with just keeper Bloxham to beat.

Venables however showed Watson how to finish four minutes later. Neil Cordice's challenge on Bloxham from a Hedge free kick saw the ball fall loose to Venables and with the keeper grounded the planted it firmly into the net to give 'Stones the lead.

Only a late challenge prevented Sean Pearson from adding to the lead after a great run and cross by Cordice, but right on half time Pearson did find the net. Venables won possession in midfield and a superb chip over the visiting defence sent Pearson free. He rounded Bloxham before finding the net from an acute angle.

Iannone, for whom confrontation with Wealdstone players in the past have not been entirely unknown, was clearly upset with Pearson over the goal and was booked for airing his views at referee Bullivant.

Iannone was lucky he didn't get a red card when he set about Pearson as the teams came off at half time and only Mr Bullivant knows why the Fareham player wasn't despatched to the dressing room midway through the second half when he brought down Venables as he had a clear run on goal.

Fareham started the second half brightly and they got back in contention in the 52nd minute when Jon Pettifer knocked the ball back to Rob Tenkorang who had already left his goal. The ball evaded him and left Taylor the simple task of slipping it into the empty net.

Only a flying save from Bloxham denied Colin Tate as 'Stones looked to regain the initiative and the keeper's bravery kept Cordice out after a good move involving Pettifer and Venables.

However two Fareham infringements in their own penalty area in the final 15 minutes saw 'Stones finally sew up the points. Under pressure, Bloxham picked up Rutherford's back pass in the 75th minute and from the ensuing free kick by Tate, just six yards from goal, Venables drove the ball low into the net.

Five minutes later, Iannone obstructed Tate in the area and an almost identical free kick brought similar reward as Tate set up Venables for his hat-trick.

Wealdstone; Rob Tenkorang, Jon Pettifer, Sean Pearson, Jim Watson, Jim Hicks, Neil Cordice, Dermott Drummy, Mick Garratt, Andy Hedge, Dave Venables (Johnson Hippolyte) Colin Tate. Sub not used; John Shanahan.

As January 1993 broke, Wealdstone were in second place in the table, seven points behind Gravesend, but with one game in hand. Dennis Byatt was named a Manager of the Month for December and the team celebrated with a win 4-3 away to Baldock, 'Stones having led 4-1 with only three minutes remaining.

Martin Blackler
Player 1991 - 1993

I never wanted to leave Wealdstone after Denis Byatt took over. I thought the world of Denis but with the overall situation and the wage cuts, coupled with the fact that Big Den wanted me to travel up from Swindon three times a week for training and matches, it was a better option to play locally.

*When I joined the club at the beginning of 1992, a few days after the defeat at Cheltenham in the Trophy. There were a few players on unbelievable money, who really didn't give a toss about the club and the atmosphere within the team was s**t".*

There was confirmation 'off the field' that 'Stones were to finalise the agreement to move out of Vicarage Road and to sell back their share of the lease to Watford FC.

It was to cost Wealdstone in excess of £2,000,000 to leave as Watford held on to the money already paid over and then added the maintenance charge - in excess of £175,000 in settlement of all outstanding claims Watford had over Wealdstone.

This meant that the club would not have to hand over the remaining £500,000 of the originally agreed figure.

Chairman at the time, David Pollock was quoted at the AGM as saying *"I think it is the very best deal we could hope to do in very bad circumstances. With the limited options available to us I think we are doing the right thing"*

With the deal worked out between the club administrator David Buchler and Watford Chairman Jack Petchey there was little option but for the club to agree with the deal. There were still the outstanding court cases related to the original sale of Lower Mead.

The case against Tesco was set to be heard by March 1993 while the case against Minet Perrin had been set for March 1994 as there was a lack of available court time to schedule a case expected to last for two weeks.

With the club still unsure of where the next groundshare would be, there was though, a surprise offer from Watford when they offered Wealdstone a further year's groundshare at a reduced rate of 25% (from 50%) of the maintenance charge, if they were unsuccessful in reaching a suitable agreement elsewhere.

Leaving Vicarage Road seemed to be the only solution, despite Watford's offer, that would allow the club any chance of a brighter future, and so it was that the decision was made, although there was still a stumbling block.

The meeting at Watford had agreed, less than enthusiastically to meet the costs, not to exceed £30,000, of the solicitors bill accrued on behalf of the Trustees of Wealdstone FC, yet one of the Trustees, Les Hobbs received the papers relating to the transfer back to Watford and declined to sign them.

As was reported at the time;

He promptly said "I shall decline to sign them. It's a joke. How can I sign away the club's future just like that. With all the clauses to go through it can't possibly be done in the time (2 days)"

Mr Hobbs said that he wanted to call a meeting of the shareholders; "I want to tell them exactly what is going on and what the alternatives are. They weren't told them at the last meeting"

Mr Hobbs is convinced that the salvation of the club is to accept the £500,000 takeover bid made by Morris Nixon of Countrywide Markets, which was initially rejected by the Wealdstone board of directors in January, but still remains on offer.

The club responded the following week by announcing that they were to take legal action for damages against Les Hobbs following his refusal to sign the papers.

Commenting on the 'takeover' David Pollock indicated that there had been some indirect approaches but nothing formal to the club, the board or the administrator. He did say though that were anyone to deposit £500,000 in the Finers Bank Account for the use of Wealdstone FC he felt that he and his directors would have no problem relinquishing control.

All of this, and further cost cutting did have an effect on the field as well and results began to suffer as the new year progressed,. By Mid March Wealdstone had slipped to ninth place, having won only four and drawn two of fourteen league matches.

At the same time, Les Hobbs finally relented and signed the documents to allow Wealdstone to leave Vicarage Road and a groundshare was announced with Yeading FC at The Warren.

It was announced at the same time, that the proposed takeover bid from Countrywide Markets had been rejected by the club's administrators. This however did not stop negotiations being carried out by representatives involved in the takeover to secure an alternative groundshare at Wembley FC's Vale Farm. The Wealdstone board had already agreed to the Yeading move and the Club pointed out that the people who were actively involved in the Countrywide Markets takeover were not authorised to negotiate on behalf of the club, at Wembley FC or anywhere else.

This was not the only disruption caused by the move. David Pollock, who had initially only wanted to take on the Chairmanship of the club on a temporary basis, did eventually resign from the board over the move to Yeading, which he was against.

His preferred option was a move to Wembley, which did have certain geographical advantages. In his resignation letter to the board he accepted that he was in the minority. He accepted the decision and felt it was the time to stand down.

David W. Pollock
Supporter and former Club Chairman

My main connection with Wealdstone Football Club was as its Chairman in the mid-nineties. I suppose my all-time favourite Wealdstone player would have to be Bob Iles, mainly because of all the rubbish he had to put up with, being shouted at from supporters behind the goal like myself.

I started initially following the Club in the early seventies. I was trying to think recently of my favourite anecdote or incident that I was involved with the Club and the one that keeps coming to my mind is the story I set out below;

When I became Chairman of the club it was in severe financial difficulties and didn't have the money to complete the transaction of buying half of Vicarage Road Football Club from Watford FC, even though they were contracted to do so.

I was advised by a number of individuals and advisors that my best route was the put the Club into administration , thus putting a protective cloak around it from any creditors until Wealdstone could resolve its problems.

Shortly after these administrators became involved they told me that I would have to dispose of the services of our Manager, Brian Hall as he was on a contract which was too costly for the Club to maintain. Therefore with great reluctance I had to terminate Brian's employment.

A month or so later I was driving to work through Willesden and found a number of policemen doing spot checks on people's tax discs.

I had totally forgotten to renew mine and therefore it was no surprise when a policeman pulled me over the front of a churchyard where his team were carrying out the checks.

The policeman directed me to one of the officers who was wearing a yellow fluorescent jacket and cap. He looked strangely familiar to me.

It was only as I got closer that I realised that it was Brian. His face seemed light up with excitement at gaining some revenge for his recent sacking.

Not only was I fined for not displaying my tax disc but I had to drive away afterwards with Brian's words ringing in my ear "See Mr. Chairman, that's another 3 points I have got for you this season".

On a personal note Brian and I made our peace and spoke on a number of occasions since then. His premature death was a very sad day for everyone who knew him.

Paul Rumens, the Vice-Chairman was appointed to take on the position of Chairman. He thanked David Pollock for the work he had done for the club and he re-iterated that the move to Yeading was financially better. The facilities available to Wealdstone were also far better.

As the season closed on the field, a run of two draws and four defeats saw Wealdstone slip further down the table eventually to finish in 11th place.

The last match at Vicarage Road was against struggling Andover and 'Stones scored a comprehensive five goal victory. Andover had fielded a number of youth team and reserve players, as they had resigned from the league. Despite Wealdstone's emphatic victory, they too were applauded of the field at the end of the match.

There was certainly none of the sadness and emotion that had been evident for the last match at Lower Mead. In fact very few of the Wealdstone faithful even turned back to glance around as they left the stadium.

A bitter taste in the mouth all that remained of over £2,000,000.

Dave Venables
Player 1990-1993

Despite only having a relatively short stay at the club, I still have many fond memories of Wealdstone FC, and I still look for the results every week.

The main memory is of the fantastic outstanding support, not so much in terms of the numbers, but the loyalty - especially away from home. These were fans who had once supported the best non-league team and club in the country and were now trying to cheer on, encourage and support an average team in a weaker league - but still they had the same passion and pride - BRILLIANT!

I remember the last game at Vicarage Road, Watford, all the players were there and we were trying (Dennis Byatt especially) to drink as much of Watford FC's booze as we could - Dennis was doing the serving - but we thought they owed us!!

I was with the club at an extremely difficult time but through the support of so many people I am thrilled to see the club slowly regaining it's former status.

There was a little good news in May, when the litigation with Tesco was successfully concluded with a payment of £369,000 made to the club. The matter was settled 'out of court' after a meeting of the Solicitors Compensation Fund.

Much as it was good news it was tempered by outstanding debts of £300,000, which included the final £175,000 payment to Watford FC. It wasn't going to help the funds available for players either, as the money would be required to finance the litigation against Minet Perrin.

There was the small matter of the £1.5m Capital Gains Tax hearing as a result of the Lower Mead sale, despite the club being hopeful that the liability would be reduced.

The situation worsened once again when Watford FC insisted that interest was charged on the £175,000 – it meant that another sum of almost £10,000 had to be found. It meant that over two years, the deal had cost Wealdstone over £35,000 per game to play at Vicarage Road.

Andy French
Reporter, Watford Observer

I reported on Wealdstone from the time they moved into Vicarage Road for the two years they were there. Subsequently my visits have been limited as I'm now involved at Watford FC.

As soon as I could kick a ball, I realised football was never a career for me although I did manage one substitute appearance for SFC Wealdstone Reserves (and a booking for a pretty awful foul). Reporting became the next best option.

I have lots of memories of the two years covering the Stones. Mainly the friendliness of the people involved in the club, both officials and supporters was particularly striking.

In the two years I made some good friends and I had many days out at godforsaken places watching away matches. I immensely enjoyed those days and even now working at a 'pro' club I still fondly recall those trips.

I was always impressed and a little amazed at the Stones fans.

The passion and dedication was beyond what any non-league club could or should expect.

One particular match that I really enjoyed is perhaps one that not many people will even bother to recall. An F A Cup replay away to Witham. I just made kick off after Pete Worby decided on the scenic route via Clapton seafront!

The home fans were so blinkered it was beyond belief and they were hot favourites to win. However, Johnson 'Draks' Hippolyte scored two cracking goals which brought the fans onto the pitch. 'Stones then survived a sending-off and an onslaught from the home team to reach the next round.

When the second goal went in, as a reporter, I lost my neutrality for a second. Long enough for me to jump up and dislodge my glasses which fell to the ground and broke. I spent the rest of the match holding part of one lens up to my eye.

My two years with the Stone sis a very small part of a long history. They were not good years for the club. Many fans would gladly forget the time spent at Vicarage Road and the problems the club suffered as a consequence.

I learned a lot during that period and have nothing but the best wishes for everyone at the club. I hope they soon get positive news about the ground and start to regain the stature in non-league football that they deserve.

There were no auspicious beginnings at Yeading for the 1993-1994 season.

Five league defeats were followed by a 3–1 defeat to local rivals Harrow Borough in the FA Cup. That in turn was followed by the club axing long time servant Dennis Byatt as Manager, being replaced by former Fulham player and a non-league manager with a good reputation, Fred Callaghan.

A draw and a win in his first two league matches in charge seemed to indicate that under their new manager, Wealdstone may at last start to reach their potential, but this was followed by a run of five defeats and a draw in the next six games, leaving 'Stones firmly rooted at the bottom of the table, as Callaghan began to change his squad and struggled to find a settled side.

By the end of November, and a chance for revenge in the FA Trophy against Harrow Borough, only five players in the squad for that match had been at the club in September when Dennis Byatt was sacked.

On the back of a league win against Weymouth, Wealdstone finally seemed to be on form and Andy Hedge duly gave 'Stones a first half lead only to see Graham Westley, who had been on loan at Wealdstone some four years earlier, equalise for the visitors.

Richard Mellor restored 'Stones advantage with fifteen minutes to go but there was to be no deserved victory as substitute Tony Knight equalised just before then end. Harrow Borough it was that were to progress in the competition, winning the replay 3-0.

It was the start of the worst run of results in Wealdstone's history. Between the beginning of December and the beginning of

April, Wealdstone's only victories were recorded in the Middlesex Senior Cup, against Hayes and Feltham, both 2–1. Defeat in the semi final to Staines Town ended their interest in that competition as well.

The league form had seen 'Stones lose thirteen matches on the trot in a run that saw four draws and fourteen defeats in eighteen matches, and in that time a further twenty three players were tried in the first team.

The last ten matches of the season saw four wins and a draw – the draw on April 21st, was 0-0 away to Buckingham. It was the first time all season that Wealdstone had managed a clean sheet away from home. There was no surprise that Wealdstone could only finish above just one club, Bury Town, as the season ended.

'Stones were only saved the ignominy of relegation back into the 'feeder' system by the fact that Dunstable Town and Canterbury City went out of business. As if to amplify the problems the club had on the field, sixty-three players had been used during the season, and twenty-nine of those had started less than five games.

Roger Slater
Supporter, Club Secretary & Director,

Harrow Civic Centre at 7:20am, Saturday 7th May, was strangely quiet. In the Car Park on a mild but grey Saturday, a small car boot fair was setting up.

In the middle of the old vases, roller skates, brassware and general junk was a burger van doing quite a steady trade to heavy legged and bleary eyed football fans (almost all showing signs of an excessively liquid Friday night), buying a varying array of bacon and sausage sandwiches. In some cases, even the burgers seemed attractive.

Tony Platt, to name but one seemed to find the food generally a good idea. At least until the first mouthful, when suddenly the procession started to the waste bin.........

*At 7;30 the coach arrived, as had all the expected travelers, in itself testimony to the constitution of Wealdstone fans, but what would you expect after some of the c**p stomached in the previous year?*

The journey to Weymouth started fairly quietly, with a few people trying to get their heads down for a sleep, and others trying to get their heads together and actually convince themselves (and their bodies) that they were actually awake. Little did we know that our driver was no Sherpa Tensing (and our coach may well have been faster had it been pulled by horsepower rather than driven by it), at least, not until we were on the M25 traveling at our top speed of about 50 mph, when the driver asked if he should take the M3.

This turned out to be the first of many requests for directions, some of which were requested late enough for us to end up traveling towards Portsmouth on the M27 rather than Bournemouth, and then via Wimbourne and Hamworthy on the way to Poole.

Eventually, at 11;15 we finally arrived at Weymouth FC to be met by the opposition for our supporters game, already changed and looking a lot healthier and somewhat more professional than us. With them, a lonely and extremely worried looking Mike Kane who had driven down, arriving well in front of us.

Hurriedly changing as the starting XI was announced, Deadly Doug made his way to the bar and the rest of us to the pitch, an hour late for kick off.

As the game started, one or two ooh's and aaah's were heard, not from either set of fans, but from players (ours) straining 'well oiled' and unwilling limbs, as well as heavy lidded almost closed eyes, wondering if the impending header was a good idea. (It wasn't!)

After a short while, as lungs expanded and greater quantities of both oxygen and water we were taken on board, the game began to turn in Wealdstone's favour. By half time, we were 4-0 up, a pair each for Mike Kane and Gordon McKay.

The second half was played at a slightly more leisurely pace, with the only really notable points being a further two goals from Mike Kane and one in reply from Weymouth. A certain 'Kanie' also maliciously won the ball from the Weymouth FC Chairman, unfortunately breaking his ankle in the process. It did give us something else to sing about in the afternoon!

The final score, 6–1 to Wealdstone, keeping up an impressive record of no more than three or four defeats in 50-odd supporters matches. The Team; Sudhir Rawal, Mark McManus, Tony Platt, Mark Fowler, Roger Slater, Sateesh Khanna, Gordon McKay, Paul Fowler, Jezz Albert, Mike Kane, Neale Harvey. The Subs (all played a part); Trevor Davies, James Smith, David Lloyd, 'A Goalkeeper', Adrian 'Marathon Man and Swindon Town fan.' All ably supported by Deadly Doug and Louise Davies.

Quickly showered we hit the bar and were met by a great buffet and a card from the Weymouth supporters wishing WFC good luck in the Court Case's as well as a speedy return, with them, to the Conference. A nice touch and well appreciated, more so when we told them of the out of court settlement.

As the two sets of fans split across the bar, strengthened by more of their traveling friends, the odd football chant and song was heard, until common ground was found in that both sets of supporters hate Salisbury, and would both be impressed should Yeovil be relegated!

As game time approached, yet more beer flowed and then in the ground the team changes were met with the usual bored acceptance and the comment Steve who is second sub?

The game started brightly, 'Stones and particularly Andy Hedge missing a few sitters, but with the fans in great voice. The chants of 'We'll score again, don't know where don't know when' did Vera Lynn proud and caused some amusement, even the players grinned!

Then it happened.

A through ball met (and controlled) by Hedgie on the edge of the box and a sharp half volley beat the home keeper. After some 520 minutes Wealdstone had scored again.

Hedgie and John Shanahan seemed to enjoy some celebratory on-pitch shagging, as a rousing chorus of Allelulyah, alleylulyah broke out from behind the goal.

Just before half time, 'Stones went further ahead thanks to hero of the day, Vic Schwartz, whose looping header deceived the home keeper before settling in the corner of the net. As Vic turned with an arm raised in celebration, doing a cross between the Maori Haka and Knees Up Mother Brown, a new song sprang forth from behind the Wealdstone chorus - "Ava Beer, ava fag, score a goal" was born and sung throughout the remainder of the match.

The second half continued in much the same way both on and off the field as the 'Stones team received congratulatory chants, a whole season's misery forgotten in one afternoon.

Then, frustration and disgust on Roger Jashek's face as his close range header just went wide and he punched the ground. Strangely, we didn't expect him to score!

With twenty minutes to go, the fans were treated to a moment of sheer class as Dermot Drummy stepped aside a challenge and sweetly chipped in Wealdstone's third goal.

With Paul Brown replacing Shanahan with only fifteen minutes to go, a great deal of chanting encouraged Steve Frangou (assistant manager and second sub!) to strip off his tracksuit and, jokingly, prepare to enter the fray.

This was noticed by the players, and amid the continuing chants of "We want Frangou on....", suddenly Dermot Drummy indicated that he had pulled a hamstring. As he walked to the bench, rapturous applause welcomed Steve Frangou to the field.

Only as the game restarted, with Dermot doing an Irish jig on the touchline did it become evident that he'd stitched Steve up and played to the crowd.

Weymouth did score in the last few minutes, then supporters home and away and players ventured off to the bar for a top up prior to a long and equally indirect (but happy) journey home.

Graham Smith
Club Official since 1986

The two years at Yeading was one of the worst periods Wealdstone have experienced and yet the omens were there from the very beginning - for the first league game, away to Poole Town, the coach arrived at Yeading's car park late, we were then held up in traffic and we did not turn up at Poole until 10 minutes before kick-off.

To top it all we went 1-0 down in the first 10 minutes eventually losing 5-1 and having a player, Paul Swales, sent off in the process !

I remember an evening match at Dunstable in the Doctor Martens Cup, there was a floodlight failure and our own Defender Mick "Sparks" Garrett repaired the fault during a 50 minute half time (we drew 3-3 that night and won 4-3 on aggregate)

Just before season 1994-95 Wealdstone took part in the Arlington Cup - a Tournament at Aldershot FC with teams from Farnborough Town, Aldershot, Camberley and ourselves.

In our second game we played Farnborough and the ex West Ham player Tony Gale guested for us and I remember that I could not find a pair of shorts big enough for him! a week later he signed for Blackburn Rovers and played his first in the F.A.Charity Shield at Wembley - I wonder if their kit-man had the same problem......

The summer saw the 'Stones agree an out of court settlement, this time in their case against Minet Perrin, when 'Stones agreed a settlement of £987,500 which was again to ease some of the pressure. It was not the maximum that could have been achieved but it was very close, and had in turn reduced the costs applicable to the club in pursuing he matter.

Yet again, there was not to be a major input to the funds available for players. The board were determined to put the club on a firm financial footing and to relocate again, back into the Borough of Harrow.

Shaun Lawson
Supporter since the late 1980s.

Season 1993/4, Newport IOW (h). For me, this was the day the club hit rock bottom. This was the worst season in our history, as we finished 2nd bottom in the Southern League, Southern Division, and were only saved from relegation to the undreamt of status of park football by the resignations of Dunstable and Canterbury City (the second time in our history that Dunstable had come to our rescue).

The team was hopeless. And the club seemed set firmly in self-destruct mode. Newport - an unbelievable 6-0 home defeat - marked the nadir of this shocking season, with a 4-0 thrashing by the might of Bury Town earlier in the term pushing it very close.

At the Bury game, the Wealdstone supporters had resorted to high sarcasm every time a 'Stones player touched the ball, and Chairman Paul Rumens was practically foaming at the mouth by the end.

The Newport game saw many fans retire to the bar for the entire second half, unable to take any more humiliation. On the bright side, this really did mark the club's lowest point; an out-of-court settlement with Minet Perrin was achieved in May, and Wealdstone have slowly but surely been on the up ever since.

The groundshare at Yeading had only been for one year with a one year option and falling gates and poor performances on the field had reduced the income and the profile of the club.

Both had been damaged firstly by the move to Watford and had not recovered at Yeading. It was generally felt that a move back into Harrow, even in a groundshare initially, would at least help the gates to recover.

There was an immediate effort to re-establish the club back in the borough, as the Club announced that it was considering the purchase of a Pub. This was to give the fans a base in Harrow and was also intended to generate income that had been lacking since the move away from Lower Mead. It was eventually to come to nothing, although the Club did establish a small shop in Harrow, used as a base for the commercial activities.

In July, an approach was made by the former chairman of Hendon FC for Wealdstone to buy that club and to move into the Claremont Road ground.

Victor Green had moved to take over at Stevenage Borough, leaving his wife in charge at Hendon, but the couple still owned the club in its entirety.

It would have meant an amalgamation of the two teams taking up the Hendon place in the Diadora Premier League. At a hastily arranged board meeting, the opportunity was rejected as it was felt that a move out of the borough, and this time a permanent one, would have resulted in the loss of the club's identity and history.

The new season started with a win and another opportunity to lay the ghost of Harrow Borough – a win at Tring in the FA Cup Preliminary round would see 'Stones host Harrow Borough in the 1st Qualifying Round.

It also saw the announcement of the plans for a new stadium, to include a number of other sporting facilities available to the local community and other sporting organisations.

It was seen as a positive step and a number of sites had been identified by Kip Hewitt, who had been brought into the club to progress the works.

On the field, the match against Harrow Borough resulted in another defeat, this time by 1–0. The league form was no better than average as again players failed to deliver in an unsettled side.

New players were tried out, some with greater success than others. One in particular was Tim Buzaglo. Famous for his earlier FA Cup goalscoring exploits with Woking it was six matches before he broke his duck with the 'Stones, but he then went on to score in five consecutive matches.

In January of 1995 Wealdstone announced that they would be groundsharing with Edgware Town for the 1995 – 96 season, finally getting their wish of moving back into the borough of Harrow. It was initially to be a two year groundshare as the club hoped to have its own new stadium in place by the end of this period.

It wasn't a great surprise to the fans, as the ground had been used in December for a Middlesex Charity Cup-tie, Wealdstone facing North Greenford United and winning 8-1.

More startling was the news that due to the increasing costs of running the side, Wealdstone members were to be asked to vote on a move across the Pyramid to the Diadora League, based more firmly in London and the South East.

The AGM voted to transfer but there were reservations about the drop in status. Wealdstone would have to drop into the Diadora League Division Three as opposed to the equivalent Division One status held in the Beazer Homes League. After a long and detailed discussion the vote was carried.

It was this vote that in the future was to give many 'Stones fans the response "I didn't vote for it" to many a question.

At the end of February, 'Stones were away to Tonbridge, a match that resulted in one of the high points of the season;

Gerry Solomon's first ever goal for the club, just three minutes from time, gave 'Stones all three points and a league double over Tonbridge on Saturday.

It was a splendid win for Wealdstone who fought back superbly after being 2–1 down at half time in this thriller.

Tonbridge had opened the scoring in the 12th minute when a corner was half cleared to Emblem who hit a firm shot past Jon Franklin.

'Stones responded with Steve Browne putting Tim Buzaglo clear but a good tackle from Boyton prevented the striker from scoring. Then Tonbridge keeper Wright fumbled a Mark Biggins corner but Campfield managed to clear before 'Stones could take advantage.

However, with 31 minutes gone, the visitors drew level as Buzaglo latched onto a bad back pass and went round the keeper to score, and 'Stones almost scored again soon afterwards but Simon Quail's shot on the turn was well saved by Wright.

Mark Hill had to clear a Tonbridge effort off the line on 39 minutes and then Freeman's header hit a post, but two minutes later, while 'Stones were down to ten men as Mark Brown was off the field receiving treatment, Tonbridge took the lead when Freeman's cross was hit home by Mawson.

Early in the second half, Franklin made a fine save to deny Mawson, but it was 'Stones who struck next, equalising in the 53rd minute when Buzaglo found Quail who cleverly beat the advancing keeper and saw his shot hit Boynton's legs and enter the net.

Five minutes later and Quail scored again. Taking a pass from man of the match, Biggins, and beating Wright to put Wealdstone ahead for the first time.

The lead lasted 15 minutes before Jarvis's long cross was met by substitute Colbran whose excellent overhead kick was headed home by Freeman for Tonbridge's equaliser.

The home side thought they had taken the lead on 80 minutes, but a linesman's flag ruled out their 'goal' for offside and with just three minutes left it was 'Stones who struck the vital blow after Solomon had had a shot well saved by Wright at the expense of a corner.

Super sub, Roddy Braithwaite, who came on for Steve Browne in his first game since Boxing Day, took the kick which was punched by Wright to Solomon, twenty yards out.

The defender cleverly controlled the ball with his chest and then sent a great shot whistling past Wright into the net to send the traveling 'Stones fans wild and the team home with the points.

Wealdstone; Jon Franklin, Mark Brown, Gerry Solomon, Mark Hill, Rod Findlay, Tommy Mason, Steve Browne (Roddy Braithwaite) John Shanahan, Tim Buzaglo, Simon Quail, Mark Biggins, Subs not used; Terry Birch, Lee Brown.

In early March, Wealdstone entertained and beat league leaders, Waterlooville by 2–1. It was Tim Buzaglo's day as he became the first Wealdstone player to score in nine consecutive league and cup matches.

He had scored 16 goals in his last fifteen league and cup matches beating a record set by George Duck in 1975–1976, and his achievement of scoring in eight consecutive league matches beat Sean Pearson's record from the 1992–1993 season.

Tim's goalscoring run was to end with a cynical challenge away to Clevedon Town that resulted in a broken leg for Tim, finishing his season, although he did win Player of the Year despite only playing twenty league matches.

The board by February were already cutting the wage bill in preparation for the change.

This season had seen 46 players used in the first team and an early casualty was popular assistant manager Steve Frangou who was to leave the club. Manager Fred Callaghan took an immediate 50% drop in wages, all with the intention of being able to retain the current squad to play in Division Three of the

This is how it's done, Vinnie

Vinnie Jones and new signing Val Shearer photographed as publicity for the signing. It was featured on Carlton TV.

Diadora League the following season.

Wealdstone also had to wait for the decision of the Beazer Homes League to whether their resignation would be accepted, and this decision would then have to be further ratified by the joint liaison committee to ensure that the Diadora League would then accept the club.

By the end of March Wealdstone announced a new signing under the banner headline "Shearer Signs For Wealdstone" but it was 83 year old Val, not England's Alan.

It was an action taken by the club to register a protest in the ongoing dispute with the league, who had not accepted Wealdstone's registration.

The club had applied to transfer to reduce the traveling costs and to enable the club to sign more local players. It would also give the club more opportunity for local derbies to attract support.

In refusing the transfer, the Beazer Homes league were almost sealing the fate of the club. Currently in administration and losing money, there was no way that the club would survive. The signing of Val Shearer was intended to illustrate the likelihood that there would be a number of similar signings as the club could not sign players it could not afford.

After the injury to Tim Buzaglo, Wealdstone's season and form dropped away. Only two wins and three draws gaining points from the last 14 league games, as the 'Stones attack struggled to score as many goals as the shaky defence conceded.

It had been a mark of the years of Fred Callaghan's management. In two seasons the club had finished in 21st place conceding 95 league goals, scoring 45, the following year conceding 94 league goals, scoring 76. There was certainly some entertainment to be had but there was no base on which to build success.

Barbara Robson
Supporter and Former Supporters Club Secretary

I'm now over 70 years old (born 1927), and at 4 weeks old I was taken by my mother to watch Wealdstone FC, bottle and dummy included.

I think we were in the Spartan League. I have supported them ever since, though not in person these days.

For sixteen seasons I never missed a match, home or away and for many seasons I was secretary of the Supporters Club. I also worked for the main club for a while and in one of those seasons we actually made a profit - Mr David Martle was the Chairman in those days.

I have lots of happy and frustrating memories of our club. One of my busiest times was organising 15 coaches to take us to Stamford Bridge - what a day that was! especially coming home after a victory, but one of many characters of my time was "The Man In The Blue", Eric Metcalfe - he stood behind the goal come rain or shine, he did his best to cut out bad language and hooligan behaviour and everyone respected him.

Two very memorable matches were when we won the Amateur Cup (1966) and the FA Trophy (1985) - how proud we were.

Frustration set in when a certain Mr David Morritt became Chairman and started to tear our club apart, bit by bit, was everybody blind or maybe they just didn't want to know.......

Thankfully the club now has a hopefully better attitude. The Club has a Chairman in Mr Paul Rumens who is Wealdstone through and through. I can recall when he used to sneak out of school to catch the coach to away matches. I don't know how he got back in at night.

Rob Saville
Supporter

(Former Stone Simon Quall apparently retired for two years after a family death and was working 'On The Buses')

Simon Quail driving a bus;
Overtake a car, reverse, overtake it again.
Stop.
Reverse.
Overtake it on the inside.
Fail to notice three passengers waiting to get off.
Reverse.
Get overtaken by the car.
Give up, and return, head down, to the depot.

In May Wealdstone finally won their right to transfer to the Diadora League when the decision by the tribunal of the pyramid committee to uphold the Beazer Homes League's decision to refuse to accept the resignation was dramatically overturned on appeal.

At the end of the month after discussions with the board, Fred Callaghan tendered his resignation as Manager and this was accepted, as the club needed to strengthen their management structure and their squad to challenge for immediate promotion out of the third division of the Diadora league.

One week later, Gordon Bartlett, until then manager of Wealdstone's landlords Yeading was appointed to take over, and he was joined shortly afterwards by his assistant Leo Morris.

Nick Woolford
Supporter since 1966

One memory I have of our time at Yeading was of Attic Man, standing on his own behind the goal, in the pouring rain (we were all under the little area of cover at the side of the ground by the changing rooms). Taking off his brand new leather jacket and tucking it under his arm to protect it, he was thus in just a T-shirt in the tanking-down rain.

You can (I am sure) remember the chant!

We had experienced some miserable lows during our nomadic years - remember Fred Callaghan at Yeading and the enormous number of players we used one season? - I remember one substitute coming on – no-one knew his name so we called him "man from t'pub").

The Isthmian League AGM in June saw Wealdstone's membership recommended by the management committee. It was expected to be no more than a formality that Wealdstone were elected by the members.

It was not to turn out quite that simple. While the other two clubs seeking membership, Yeovil Town and Wingate & Finchley were both elected unopposed, Wealdstone were made to sweat.

The club representatives were asked to leave the meeting while their election was debated.

Finally – almost an hour later – voted upon. The club were elected by just four votes.

As part of the pre-season build up, Wealdstone were involved in the formation of a new competition, the Harrow Senior Cup.

Harrow Borough, Edgware Town and Rayners Lane were involved in the tournament with Wealdstone, who met Harrow Borough in the final. Yet again the result went the way of the Boro, only adding to the period since Wealdstone had last beaten their local rivals.

More details also became available of the proposals for a new home for Wealdstone FC, with the proposed site on disused allotments on The Ridgeway in North Harrow.

It was to be a community multi sports and leisure facility with a 3000 capacity stadium. It was to contain administration offices, function halls, a restaurant, bar and sports shops as well as a crèche facility. There was to be a Sports Hall that would contain squash courts and a fitness room.

It was going to be a long two months before the plans were put in front of the Harrow planning sub-committee for approval in September.

Despite the best intentions of the Directors and management, and promises and commitments from a number of players, only three of the previous seasons squad remained at Wealdstone for the new campaign, an entirely new squad having been brought together in a short space of time by Gordon Bartlett..

It was no surprise that the start to the season was a little inconsistent, ranging from the spectacular, a 9–1 opening day win away to Cove and a 10–0 victory in Wealdstone's first ever FA Vase match, countered by defeats at home to Horsham in the league and away to Feltham in the Middlesex Senior Cup.

It was evident that the side was capable of matching anyone on their day – a draw at Premier Division Grays, followed by a 4-3 win at home in the FA Cup showed that, but it meant nothing as a defeat at Hertford Town saw Wealdstone eliminated in the next round.

The anticipated increase in support also seemed to have been realised, when in the first home league fixture, 502 turned out to watch a 2–2 draw with Wingate & Finchley. Although a number of these were only there because it was the first game, a good majority were retained as the season progressed.

Four league wins and two draws from their first ten matches were followed by five wins and a draw from the next seven to leave 'Stones in third place at Christmas.

There was disappointment off the field however when the planning application for The Ridgeway was rejected and 'Stones were forced to look elsewhere for the site of their new home.

In January of 1996 a proposal was announced to develop the Prince Edward Playing Fields.

Not for the first time, the site's owners, Camden Council were considering it's sale, and also not for the first time, Wealdstone FC were looking toward the site for their future. There was likely to be opposition from the local residents who had already stated that they wished to keep the site as it was.

The legacy of Watford and subsequently Yeading was to come to light at the AGM as well, when the club announced a loss of £249,971 on the previous season.

Having lost £2m in two years at Watford and a further £81,929 the previous year at Yeading, it only amplified the board's reasons for wanting to move across the pyramid and back into the borough of Harrow.

There were some significant amounts included in the figures. Payouts to former Manager Brian Hall and Secretary Peter Braxton in lieu of their contracts, cancelled by the clubs administrators, totaled over £43,000.

There were also fees (mainly to the administrator) of £30,000, the cost of the groundshare at Yeading and over £60,000 in wages, with more than half spent on players.

There was some dissent from the floor at the meeting, but a proposal that the board should resign was defeated once explanations and details were known.

On the field the club had maintained more stability than in recent years, and despite losing to promotion rivals Northwood and Harlow at Christmas, and only gaining a draw away to Kingsbury on a Boxing day ice rink, Wealdstone had maintained a challenge at the top of the table. They were in fifth place at the end of February with all to play for.

The fifteen league matches played in March and April saw the club lose only once – away to Horsham who were also in the promotion race, but it seemed that five draws had cost 'Stones enough points to prevent the promotion wanted so much in the first year.

By the time of the last match of the season, a 2–0 home defeat to Harlow Town, the result didn't matter and Wealdstone were to finish fourth.

Damian Irisarri
Occasional supporter

I am an irregular supporter although I attended almost half the games in the 1996 – 97 season when I was 'between' being an Arsenal season ticket holder, and moving up to Lancashire. Since then I have seen the team on a few occasions but I'm waiting for them to go up a division or two so they might come up North and I can see them again.

The first match I saw was back in 1990 in Gloucester of all places. I found that watching football 'live' was quite enjoyable and totally different to watching it on TV. (I had previously been to Highbury in the mid 80's but I was intimidated and too shy to really enjoy it.)

Another memory was of going to Clapton in 1997 and being greeted by the welcome of "Here they come. We always get a good crowd when Wealdstone play us!" Its nice to be part of a team that's appreciated for it's loyal fan base, despite whatever division its in. And then we beat them 10–1!

They had started brightly with a record away win and they had exceeded it during the season with a 10-1 win away to Clapton. Ironically they also scored Clapton's goal, as the unlucky Roy Marshall scored for the home side.

Southall had been beaten by 9–0 at home and 7–0 away and Hertford Town had also come across Wealdstone on a 'good day' when they were defeated by 7–0 at the White Lion Ground. Wealdstone had scored 104 league goals, the second highest in the division, and they had conceded only 39, which was the second lowest in the division but to no avail.

There was some good news in early May when it was announced that Wealdstone FC had come out of administration after almost four years. It had cost almost £200,000 in fees for solicitors, administrators and accountants, but it meant at last that the club were solvent as a company and a football club, capable of running and managing their own affairs.

It was to signal the quietest summer at Wealdstone for a number of years!

Tony O'Rourke
Supporter since 1974

One specific memory, although definitely not a fond memory, involved popping down from Derbyshire and taking in a 'Stones match at Vicarage Road. I went with the expectation of bursting with pride at the size of "our" new stadium only to find it was virtually empty, the team was unrecognisable, and they seemed to be playing in see-through shorts (all right for some, but not for me).

A more pleasurable memory involved breaking down on my way home on the Western bypass outside Newcastle and being given a lift to a local hotel to call the AA.

Up to that point it wasn't pleasurable at all but whilst waiting for the 4th emergency service to arrive I sat in the foyer and picked up the days "Times".

Turning to the Sports page I was amazed to see a reasonably sized article detailing not only Wealdstone FC but a 10-0 (TEN - as they do on the Teleprinter on Saturdays) win. It's not often the AA get a chance to pick up a stranded motorist who thinks he's died and gone to heaven.

Paul Cooke
Supporter

Being a northerner and from Liverpool you can guess what team I was brought up on, I used to go to Anfield a lot with my dad and I still go to matches when I can. My family moved down to Harrow in 1981.

I had never heard of Wealdstone Football Club until the trophy final of 1985, but that was about it, I had no interest in non-league football, seeing my team where the European champions, non-league footie wasn't too attractive.

I first watched the 'Stones in the final year at Lower Mead. A friend of mine was a fan I went along, I don't remember much of the game but I do remember it raining constantly and I wasn't impressed with the standard of football, so I never did return to the ground.

I started going now and again when Wealdstone were at Yeading, when my sister used to go there with her boyfriend (Richard Harries), and I used to tag along when I had nothing better to do, and I wasn't seeing Liverpool play.

Most people would have been put off by the standard of football Wealdstone were producing in our final days in the Southern League but not me. I started to get sucked in and eventually when we where playing 'the scum' in a cup match replay I was bitten by the 'Wealdstone bug'. I loved it, the abuse the atmosphere, ok we were beaten 3-0 (I think) but I loved it.

I started university, the money dried up so Liverpool was becoming an expensive option, that and me working on a Saturday morning meant actually getting to see Liverpool play was getting harder - I needed the 'footie fix' so I started to go to see the 'Stones more and more.

Our first season in the Isthmian League was what I regard as my first 'proper' year, I missed few home games, but I still wasn't a regular away fan, yet by the end of the season I was feeling all the ups and downs that go with being a 'Stones fan and the away game at Windsor was when I realised I was never going to give up Wealdstone FC.

It wasn't until our second season in the Isthmian League that I started going away regularly. In that season I missed 4 games home and away in all competitions, and what a year to start doing that, champions, and a cup final.

Liverpool are still a big part of my life, but I enjoy going to see Wealdstone a lot more than going to Anfield, you feel apart of a the club not just a 'customer' that the big clubs of this country are turning their fans into.

I know I'm not the only 'big' league convert, and I'm not going to be the last. But non-league football, and for me Wealdstone, are the future for English football, if you love football to the core and love the game for what it is really about, you couldn't choose a team any better then Wealdstone Football Club.

The 1996–97 season seemed destined to start with a stuttering, even under-performing side when 'Stones went a goal behind in their first league match at home to Camberley.

This time they fought back to gain a 3–1 win. It was followed with a 4–0 defeat at Flackwell Heath as the frailties returned, but only for one match.

In early September objections to various elements of the proposal, lead the Sports Council's London Regional Officer, David Lawrence and the Department of the Environment to inform the club that it would not secure the required planning approval for the Prince Edward Playing Fields development.

Changes in government policy related to the use of such sites had *'moved the goalposts'* as far as Wealdstone FC and their plans were concerned.

Undaunted the Club was to continue with its efforts to secure a site to develop a stadium of its own.

Perhaps galvanised by the news, the 'Stones team won its next twelve games to lead the division, breaking the run at promotion rivals Braintree Town with a 2–0 defeat.

Martin Lacey
Supporter and Elmslie Ender Co-editor.
From The Elmslie Ender' Issue 39.

The idea of a club fanzine was first discussed on the terraces at Scarborough while Wealdstone were losing a GMVC fixture early in the 1986/87 season.

I had fond memories of Long Ball Down The Middle and was at the time involved in the production of the early issues of When Saturday Comes. Sudhir had also been partly responsible for a 'one-off' magazine called Wemberlee, Wemberlee, celebrating (guess what!). Together we made a dream team!

When the first issue appeared it was one of the first club based fanzines and among the most professionally produced; although in the subsequent ten years the arrival of the ubiquitous Desk Top Publishing has made our early efforts look amateur, they were highly admired at the time and played a significant part in the de-mystifying of the publishing business. The message was 'anyone can do it'.

Writing in "El Tel Was A Space Alien" in 1989 I said "The magazine was not a reaction to the depressing events on the pitch – as football fans we are used to the up's and downs – but the inertia which seemed to grip the club at boardroom level. Wealdstone were sinking obviously and inexorably and nobody seemed to care". Rings true doesn't it?

Within a year or so we'd run into trouble, not for our outspoken criticism of events at Wealdstone, but for slagging off rival teams, Dagenham in particular. There were in the non-league world, some very tiny and paranoid minds at work. The Elmslie Ender played little part in the removal of David Morritt, events moving rather quicker than our production schedules, though we were supportive of Alan Clifton. However, even at that point we said his promises were too good to be true and he'd obtained power by simply telling us what we wanted to hear.

Still, Lower Mead was reprieved – little did we know how temporary that would be – and money made available for the team – little did we know how badly it would be spent!

Clifton was briefly flavour of the month. In truth, despite our reputation as troublemakers, my main regret over the years is that the magazine has been far too reticent in criticising those who deserved it. Though we have been informally accused of libel, we've actually been very cautious.

Too cautious. I've lost count of the times we've been in possession of crucial information from 'behind the scenes' or rumours which turned out to have a deal of truth, but not printed them because we were advised it would "not be in the best interests of the club"

Its still happening! Could we have made a difference? We'll never know. After one editorial suggesting in the mildest possible terms that the Chairman at the time wasn't facing up to the club's dire position, I was taken aside by a director who suggested that if I didn't tone down the criticism, the chairman in question may quit! Some threat!

When the club went into administration and Paul Rumens arrived on the scene, it signalled the end of the 'us and them' divide which made the Elmslie Ender essential in the first place.

Since then the magazine has appeared fitfully due to the other commitments of myself and Sudhir, and some would say with declining relevance.

These ten years have been a time of unmitigated catastrophe for Wealdstone FC and it would not be hard for someone to persuade me that the Elmslie Ender has put a jinx on the club, and if we'd only give up, everything would come good again.

On the other hand, I'm looking forward to our twentieth anniversary issue too much............

Four wins followed before the return match with Braintree Town at the White Lion Ground in mid February. The evening was a far more pleasing occasion for the Harrow Observer to report;

They can put the champagne on ice at Wealdstone FC. After their remarkable 6–0 annihilation of title rivals Braintree Town at the White Lion Ground on Tuesday night, the ICIS League Third Division Championship is surely destined to become 'Stones first major honour since they achieved the non league double in 1985.

'Stones boss, Gordon Bartlett said in his programme notes that he didn't think that the Braintree game would be the match that decided the championship, but that a victory could make the task much easier.

Yes there are still 13 games to go, including tough home and away clashes with promotion rivals Northwood and Harlow Town, but with his side now holding a massive 13 point lead at the top of the table, the manager must be supremely confident that the title race is now all but over – even if he steadfastly refuses to admit it publicly.

"We haven't got one hand on the trophy – we've now got one hand on promotion" was his guarded comment afterwards. Of his team's performance, which saw Braintree not only beaten, but thoroughly outclassed, he said "We were absolutely magnificent. It was easily the best we have played since I joined the club".

And there was praise too from the manager for the vociferous Wealdstone supporters who made up the bulk of the 411 crowd, the club's best gate of the season. "They were magnificent. They don't realise just how influential they can be to the team".

Marvelous, magnificent 'Stones made a total mockery of the title race with this sound thrashing of second placed Braintree Town.

It was unbelievably one-sided, it was almost untrue as the league leaders and champions elect simply played the visitors off the park.

Doubtless still reeling from the weekend departure of their Manager, and with their leading scorer Wade Falana injured, Braintree were clearly not up for the job.

They did have some good fortune as they got away with a six goal thrashing, Had 'Stones finishing been better it could easily have been double figures.

Wealdstone dominated right from the start and with the Braintree goal often resembling the Alamo, it was only a matter of time before the goal avalanche began.

'Stones opener came in the 13th minute. Bryan Hammatt turning in a Simon Garner shot following a Steve Bircham corner, but a host of chances went begging before they added to their lead a minute from the break, Roy Marshall netting with a bullet header at the far post from a Bircham cross.

Set up by the impressive Paul McKay, Terry Hibbert quickly killed off any thoughts of a Braintree comeback when he drilled home Wealdstone's third goal five minutes into the second half.

Ten minutes later and Garner followed up to score the fourth after keeper Paul Catley had failed to hold a blockbuster from inspirational skipper Fergus Moore, after he had made one of numerous surging runs into attack.

Garner hit his second from a Hammatt cross after 72 minutes, and three minutes from time, Tony Smith rifled home a great 25 yarder to complete the rout.

Wealdstone; Darren Bonfield, Tony Smith, Dominic Sterling (John Massey), Fergus Moore, Ian Waugh, Roy Marshall, Paul McKay, Terry Hibbert, Simon Garner (Peter Green), Bryan Hammatt, Steve Bircham, Sub not used; Mark Weedon.

Two draws and three wins from the next five matches kept 'Stones at the top of the table. They also progressed to the final of the Associate Members Trophy, after a draw at Leatherhead in the semi-final, the home win by 2–1 in the replay secured the final place.

At the beginning of April, Harlow, Northwood and Kingsbury were to cause serious concerns for Wealdstone, just as they had the previous year. Home defeats to Harlow Town and Northwood and another draw at Kingsbury reduced Stones' lead at the top of the table, and with away matches at both Harlow and Northwood in the remaining four games, Wealdstone were certainly under pressure as Braintree gained ground.

A win at home to Epsom followed by a 1–0 win at Clapton with a Lee Walker goal were followed by defeat at Harlow Town. Wealdstone were still top but had to win their last game of the season, away to third placed Northwood to ensure their championship. Braintree Town were at home to Harlow who also needed to win to pip Northwood for the final promotion place.

In a nail biting finish to the season Wealdstone clinched the ICIS League Division Three Championship in their final game of the season.

But neighbours Northwood certainly made it difficult for them and it took two goals in the last nine minutes of a tension packed match to finally give 'Stones victory and the coveted title.

Keeper Darren Bonfield with a cloud hanging over him from the Harlow game three days earlier made amends with a fine diving save to keep out a stinging drive from Elroy Richardson early on, but after that it was 'Stones who made most of the running although goals were not forthcoming before the break.

Their best effort came from Simon Garner who had a superbly struck angled drive magnificently tipped over by Les Carroll although Dominic Sterling should have done better than blazing wildly over from 10 yards after Roy Marshall's header from Terry Hibbert's cross had been blocked.

Chris Walton was narrowly wide with a diving header early in the second half before Wealdstone finally made the breakthrough in the 49th minute.

With the Northwood defence dithering over a clearance, garner latched onto the loose ball on the edge of the area and laid it off for Bryan Hammatt who waltzed round Carroll and fired low into the corner of the net.

However, with the game now there for the taking, 'Stones were then guilty of total and utter complacency which handed Northwood an equaliser just two minutes later. Fergus Moore conceded a needless free kick 30 yards out from which extremely poor marking allowed Tony Millard to bullet a header past Bonfield

That goal proved a considerable body blow for 'Stones, and knowing that rivals Braintree were winning and a draw was not enough, the next 25 minutes saw them in a decidedly dejected mood.

But the all or nothing move by manager Gordon Bartlett that saw strikers Lee Walker and Peter Green thrown into the action 15 minutes from time proved the turning point of the game and with nine minutes to go the gamble paid off. The challenges of Garner and Walker caused Carroll to only flap away a Green corner and Roy Marshall followed up to head 'Stones in front.

Wealdstone weren't going to let it slip now and with three minutes remaining they sealed victory with a third goal from another Green corner. Garner headed it goalwards, Hammatt hooked it home and the massed ranks of Wealdstone fans amongst the 700 crowd began celebrating in earnest.

Wealdstone; Darren Bonfield, John Massey (Tony Smith), Dominic Sterling (Lee Walker), Fergus Moore, Ian Waugh, Roy Marshall, Chris Walton Terry Hibbert (Peter Green), Paul McKay, Simon Garner Bryan Hammatt.

Graham Smith
Club Official since 1986

The 1996-97 season was one of the best for a very long time as we became Division III Champions.

The most memorable matches were beating Wingate and Finchley 3-2 after being 2-0 down at half time, beating Tring 7-0 and Braintree 6-0. The best day came on the last game of the season at Northwood as we beat them 3-1 to clinch the title - what a night of celebration that was.

The other highlight for me was the signing of Simon Garner the ex Blackburn Rovers record goal scorer. Apart from being a class act, I found him to be a most pleasant person to speak to.

Funnily enough he has achieved promotion with Blackburn, Wycombe and Woking but has never been in a Championship team until he played for Wealdstone.

Shaun Lawson
Supporter since the late 1980s.

Season 1996/7, Northwood (a). At long last, reward for the club's incredible supporters. Without them, there is little doubt that Wealdstone would have long been a mere footnote in the history of non-league football.

Champions!

The fans ARE the club. And one wonderful Saturday afternoon in early May 1997 made it all worthwhile. the 'Stones had blown a 13-point lead over Braintree, who had been slaughtered 6-0 on a never-to-be-forgotten evening at Edgware. Now, to clinch the title, and their first piece of silverware for 12 years, the Blues had to win at Chestnut Avenue, Northwood - where the home side had been undefeated in the league all season.

Manager Gordon Bartlett evidently told his players to keep things tight; it was goalless at half-time. Amid scenes of euphoria, Bryan Hammatt put 'Stones ahead, but barely 90 seconds later, hesitation between Bonfield and his defence let in Northwood to equalise.

Despair reigned; were Wealdstone to be denied at the very last? Bartlett made 3 substitutions. Minutes later, Tony Smith, on for Terry Hibbert, swung in a corner, and from the resulting melee, Roy Marshall, a colossus all season, bundled the ball into the net. Now, surely, Wealdstone would not be denied. Sure enough, from another corner, Hammatt volleyed in Simon Garner's flick on.

BEDLAM.

Delirium took over the Wealdstone supporters. Years of despair and frustration poured out amid scenes of jubilation. Grown men were practically having sex with each other in front of their wives and children. (Okay, so maybe I exaggerated that last one a bit. But you get the idea.)

Moments later, the referee blew for full-time, the 'Stones fans invaded the pitch, and the championship trophy was ours. The sleeping giant, virtually comatose for twelve long years, had finally stirred.

Bryan Hammatt
Player

I played for the club for only one season (the first time) - that of Champions of ICIS League Division III, and I think I was top scorer with 28 goals that year.

There were some very good players in that side - players from higher divisions dropping to Division III because of the management team, Gordon Bartlett, Leo Morris and Frank O'Brien and their ambitions, and also the ambitions of the club. It all made for an excellent team spirit aided all the way by the likes of Lee Walker and 'Fergie' The management really were a brilliant team - who will ever forget Frank's 'Bish, Bash, Bosh' team talks?

That last day of the season and the match against Northwood, away. we had to win, and we did, and then the celebrations began, but there is one final memory of that day - Fergus Moore, in the dressing room after the match, doing to Lee Walker, what is now generally known as 'a Monica!!'.

Good luck, 'Stones

There was to be no fairytale double though, as three days after the Northwood match Wealdstone were beaten 1–0 by second division Leighton Town in the Associate Members Trophy Final at Hitchin. It was a lacklustre performance by the 'Stones, who had achieved their main target on the Saturday.

Kevin Williams
Supporter since mid 1980's

I remember,
Do you remember?
That day,
The one in May,
Wealdstone went away to play.
Come on I said,
For we had to win,
For celebrations to begin,
With the 90 closing in ....
I yelled and yelled some more,
"Come on Wealdstone, Can't you Score"?
If we won, we won the league,
If we lost, we wouldn't succeed.
Then a ray of light,
For it was so very bright, the cheers were there,
The sun was out,
But then disaster came about.
"Oh dear" I said, "1-1 and 90 near",
Can we still have the last cheer?
Then I yelled "save the beer, ' cos we are getting very N E A R ....
"Yes 2-1" I yelled, for we had scored,
The fans went mad,
The opposition looking sad.
Some people were on the pitch, did they have a certain itch?
Apparently they thought it was all over ......
"It is now", I cried,
I could have died.
The referee reached for his whistle,
We won and won the league,
I always knew we would succeed.
Then a man said "here, take this",
The Silver cup,
"And don't forget, you're going up".
I remember,
Do you remember?
That day,
The one in May,
Wealdstone went away to play.

Manager Gordon Bartlett and Captain Fergus Moore with the Championship Trophy

James Keen
Player 1996-1997

An obvious memory for me is the day that the club secured the Division III title by beating Northwood away, 3-1. It was a momentous occasion as they too were pushing for promotion, which they still achieved.

The atmosphere in the dressing room afterwards is something I had never experienced before. The team and the whole squad must have been in the dressing room for at least an hour after the presentation of the Trophy on the pitch - we went through about three cases of lager and god knows how much Champagne.

Although I had not been involved in that particular game it was still a very special day for myself and more importantly, the club. I also remember how fanatical the supporters were and still are. They would give you confidence and a certain amount of pride in playing for the team. It wasn't only other players and the management you'd let down if you lost but also those supporters that would be there week in and week out regardless of distance, weather conditions or cost to themselves!

Another thing that struck me as vital to the team's success was the dedication of the manager and his backroom staff. Gordon Bartlett was (and hopefully still is) the Manager, and along with Leo, Frank and Alan their enthusiasm for the game is tremendous and as this was my first introduction to senior non-league football they helped me personally develop as a player.

Then there was the presentation evening - a great night out held at Wasps RFC and Roy Marshall swept the board with the Player of The season trophies from the players and supporters.

I'd like to thank Wealdstone FC for the season I had there, and I wish them every success in the future, especially in securing somewhere to build a new home ground. It's long overdue, and in the long term the club will reap the benefits of having this.

Quentin Fox
Director

Good footballing memories from the 1990's are few and far between.

The highlight for me was the 3-1 victory at Northwood to win the Isthmian League Division 3 title.

Unusually, my family were there and they were very surprised to see tears rolling down my cheeks at the end.

Roberto Puzzi
Supporter since 1997

My name is Roberto Puzzi, I live in Soragna, (Parma - Italy). My passion for Wealdstone began a few years ago when Matteo Tonna (the first 'Stones Italian fan) showed me the promotion videotape (Northwood v Wealdstone, 1-3).

Since that moment I have supported to follow the results and fixtures every week on the Internet thanks to my membership of the Mailing List, but my limited knowledge of English doesn't allow me to actively participate on the list, even though sometimes I can by pushing myself, understand some of what is said.

I would really like one day to be able to answer "any particular match memory?" but I know that this will remain a dream for now.

Matteo Tonna
Supporter since 1996

Like Roberto, I also live in Soragna. I played in the Youth Teams of Soragna FC and once in the first team in 1984-85. Since then I have been Secretary & Chairman and I am now Programme Editor and Club Statistician. I have also been the Soragna football reporter for the local paper "Gazzetta di Parma" since 1992.

I first visited London in the summer of 1986. As I was already interested in Non League football in Italy, I purchased a copy of the Non League Directory, which had on the cover a photo taken at Wembley from the Trophy final, and inside the book was full of information on Wealdstone FC – The first non league 'Double' winners!

Once home, I wrote to the club asking for a sticker or a team photo. I received a parcel with so many items inside and a letter from then Club Shop manager, Toby Jackson who has since become a good friend.

The following year, I made a visit to Lower Mead (on a Wednesday morning) and I decided that Wealdstone had become my favourite club. With it's long, proud history and a lively band of dedicated supporters – I even realized that you could 'feel' the atmosphere in the ground even when empty!

Wishing to keep more up to date with Wealdstone, in 1989 I became a subscriber to the home programmes and on the 18th August 1990 I finally had the opportunity to watch the 'Stones play for the first time.

It was against V S Rugby, the first match of the season. The atmosphere was so much more that I had expected.

The programme, the Elmslie End in full cry, the beautiful chaos in the Club Shop and everyone drinking in The Elmslie Tavern....

And on the pitch! For Italian standards it was 'kick and run' at terribly high speed – even if Wealdstone's goalscorer that day was 'Stroller' Mark Harrisson – but it was technically very good as well. Everything was so different from Italy where Non League football is generally more important for the players than the supporters.

I was so excited by that first match that on the following Tuesday I traveled down to the New Forest to watch Wealdstone play at Bashley. Tony Kelly scored the only goal of the game and sent the singing 'Stones fans home wondering what would be achieved in a season that had started so well.

There was no success though at the end of the season. Just the last ever match at Lower Mead. When I heard that the final decision had been made (I remember getting the Elmslie Ender through the post one morning, - it had the title "The End Is Near") I felt I couldn't miss the opportunity of saying the last farewell as the ground was one of the main reasons I chose to support the club.

I flew to London for two days just to watch the match, but what a match! I firmly believe that no other football occasion, at Non league level at least, can generate as much passion, noise, love and pride from the supporters as on that last day.

The following season I traveled back again and watched three matches over Easter – one was the match where relegation was finally confirmed at Fisher Athletic.

There were some 'positives' though. I saw David Venables play and I still think he must be the best Wealdstone player I have ever seen (Stuart Pearce is still my hero though) and I first met Alan and Roy Couch. Both have helped me immensely in my goal of gathering as much information as possible on the past of Wealdstone FC.

My connection continued through the Yeading years and my subscriptions now include the Elmslie Ender and the Harrow Observer as well but I didn't see the club again until the first season at Edgware.

It was in the December I saw Wealdstone 4-0 Hornchurch, and in the bar in the evening Gordon Bartlett presented me with a shirt autographed by the squad. It was very much appreciated.

Since then, with the birth of the Internet and e-mail and the discussion groups, I have been able to follow what happens around the club on a daily basis. Even now this is going strong and I can keep in touch.

Towards the end of the nineties I had begun to transmit my 'Wealdstone Fever' to Roberto Puzzi who is a co-editor on the Soragna programme. He took an interest, following the up's and down's through my programme collection and via the internet.

In 1999 we both came to London and we were able to visit most of the Stadiums – we saw matches at Highbury, White Hart Lane and Stamford Bridge but the atmosphere was so much better at the White Lion Ground. If not for the friendly with Walton & Hersham, then definitely for the first league match against Harlow Town.

Roberto is also now a programme subscriber and we are now WFCSCUIB – the Wealdstone FC Supporters Club Unofficial Italian Brach – not everyone knows that there are more Wealdstone supporters in Italy that Harrow Borough fans in Harrow!!!

More seriously, I am proud to be a life member of the Supporters Club. Wealdstone FC has allowed me to share a passion and grow an interest. I also owe Wealdstone FC the vast majority of friends I have in London.

Toby Jackson and his family are close friends and contact is kept up through the phone and e-mail with Roy and Alan Couch and Roger Slater.

I know I chose a very difficult time to become a Wealdstone fan, but the special spirit that lives through the 'Stones as a club and especially as a band of supporters is unbelievable and it really does keep the blue flag flying high.

Now we can see the light at the end of the tunnel, as I think that the PAPF development will be a new dawn for the club.

I am more than ready to be a part of it.

Despite the previous obstacles set in the way of Wealdstone FC, the summer of 1997 saw a chink of light appear in the tunnel that was 'Stones intent to move to the Prince Edward Playing Fields.

The owners, Camden Council, were busily trying to reach agreement with the other London Boroughs that would allow them to dispose of the site.

Approval from 13 Boroughs would allow the land to be transferred to the London Playing Fields Society with the likelihood that Wealdstone and the LPS could then reach a deal to allow the club to develop the site, which had become derelict since a lack of funds meant that the cost of upkeep was prohibitive.

Wealdstone's proposal was to build a small non-league ground on the site with a revenue earning facility which would fund the upkeep of the site as a whole. Given agreement from the London Playing Fields Society, The Sports Council and the required Planning Permission, Wealdstone were hopeful that they could have a ground up and running within two years.

The new season in Division 2 started with an away defeat at Wivenoe, and then an opportunity, at home, for revenge over Cup winners Leighton Town, 'Stones running out winners by 2–1.

By the end of October, 5 wins, 5 draws and two defeats saw Wealdstone in the top half of the table, but they too had suffered revenge, being knocked out of the FA Cup at Leatherhead, who they had defeated on the way to the previous years cup final.

A defeat at the beginning of November, 4–1 to Ashford Town (Middlesex) in the Senior Cup and Hampton in the Charity Cup were the only defeats in a month where the club won 6 and drew once at Hitchin Town in the Guardian Insurance Cup;

Dennis Greene blasted home a spectacular 25 yard volley with the last kick of normal time to earn 'Stones a dramatic draw at premier Division Hitchin Town on Tuesday night.

And with extra time failing to break the deadlock, this second round tie goes to a replay at the White Lion Ground. Hitchin must have thought that they had won it with just a minute remaining, Williams headed them into a 4-3 lead. But almost immediately, Simon Garner put Greene in for his remarkable late saving goal for Wealdstone.

Earlier the home side had taken the lead after 4 minutes when James Bush failed to gather a corner and could only parry the ball to Williams who volleyed home. Hitchin almost scored again minutes later but Scott's shot hit the post.
However, after 12 minutes 'Stones drew level. Paul McKay's free kick found Keith Boreham who laid the ball off for Brian Jones to fire an excellent low shot past keeper Palfreyman.

Bush made amends for his earlier error with two fine saves to deny Parker and then Dellar, but he was beaten again after 52 minutes when McKay was adjudged to have fouled Parker in the box. Bush half saved the penalty by ex-Stone Rudi Hall, but the ball trickled under his body into the net.

Boreham should have leveled for 'Stones soon after but his soft goal bound effort was cleared off the line.

Gordon Bartlett's 66th minute double substitution of Simon Garner and Mario Celaire for Boreham and McKay seemed to have backfired unkindly on the Wealdstone boss when, within a minute, Hitchin made it 3–1. Jones lost possession to Scott who found Dellar and although his effort hit the post, Barr followed up to net the rebound.

But 'Stones hit back four minutes later when Ian Waugh's shot was deflected off the home keeper as he tried to gather and Jones smartly fired home the lose ball. After 76 minutes Jones completed his hat-trick, leveling the score by beating Palfreyman with a 20 yard shot after a fine run.

After Greene cancelled out Hitchin's fourth goal in the dramatic finale, the tie went to extra time which was rather tame by comparison. Bush saved superbly from Barr but in the closing minutes only a good save from Palfreyman prevented Garner from giving 'Stones a famous victory.

Wealdstone; James Bush, Stephen Kelly, Steve Bircham, Fergus Moore, Ian Waugh, Roy Marshall, Chris Walton, Brian Jones (Terry Hibbert), Keith Boreham (Simon Garner), Dennis Greene, Paul McKay (Mario Celaire).

The league form continued to be good with three wins and a draw in December, but defeats in the replay with Hitchin Town and at Great Wakering Rovers in the FA Vase were disappointing.

By February, 'Stones were again looking to secure promotion, holding third place with a record of fifteen wins and eight draws from 26 matches.

Off the field, some thirteen months after the Prince Edward playing Fields had closed down, it seemed that Wealdstone were moving ever closer to their aim for a new stadium on the site.

Pressure from Harrow Council and Harrow East MP, Tony McNulty raised the question of ownership of the site in the House Of Commons, in a question to Sports Minister, Tony Banks. The result was that the site was finally set to change hands.

It was another step in the right direction ass the club had been informed in talks with David Lawrence of the London Playing Field Society that the deal would be thrashed out once they had appointed their new Chairman within two weeks. The club then hoped to be in a position to go for Outline Planning permission by the end of the season.

The run-in saw Wealdstone win 11 and draw 4 of their remaining nineteen games, the last victory of the season with a depleted side at Marlow, promotion having already been guaranteed.

The all-important win had been 'away' at the White Lion Ground, against landlords Edgware Town.

It was the fourth time that the clubs had met during the season, and Wealdstone had won all four matches, but none were greeted with as much celebration as the league victory by 2–0 that sealed Wealdstone's second consecutive promotion.

Long time league leaders Braintree were expected to secure the Championship, but a defeat to bottom of the table Cheshunt saw Canvey Island take the title on goal difference.

Off the field Wealdstone renewed their groundshare agreement with Edgware Town, at least securing the short term future of the club.

At the same time design work was being done to put into place a planning application for what had become a £4m Community Sports Complex on the Prince Edward Playing Fields.

The scheme was unveiled by the club in early August and included 12 football pitches, an all weather surface and six tennis courts.

More importantly for the club, it included a new stadium which would end the nomadic experience of the previous seven years.

There were to be state of the art changing facilities, seating for 600 people and a capacity of over 3000.

The 1998–1999 season saw Wealdstone in their third division in four years. Division One of the Ryman League was at last equal to the status the club had held before transferring across the pyramid but it wasn't expected to be a season where 'Stones would compete for promotion.

With so much happening with regard to the new ground and with further delays, the ever dwindling funds had to be conserved, so there wasn't a great deal for the Manager, Gordon Bartlett to spend on his team.

Fergus Moore
Player and Club Captain 1995 to 1999

When I first arrived at W.F.C I had a rough idea of the great support that the club had, but never experienced it at first hand. When I did, I was totally amazed.

It sank in on pre-season of my first year at the Club when 40-50 supporters turned out for a trial game between the players that Gordon had got together after about 2 or 3 training sessions. Then again they turned out, about 100 of them, for our first proper Friendly at the Polytechnic Ground, Stanmore. Frightening!

I remember thinking to myself, "If this is what it is like in Friendlies, what would it be like when we get down to the real nitty-gritty of competitive matches?" To the supporters' credit and everybody else involved in the Club, I was not to be let down.

That first season 1995-96, we kicked off with a game at Cove, ICIS League Division 3. Even though I had played in a higher level of football the previous 4 seasons, I hadn't sampled an atmosphere quite like it.

The fans during our 9-1 win that day were magnificent. To be honest, after this win and with the supporters' enthusiasm, I along with the Chairman, thought at the time that we could win the FA Vase, FA Cup, league, the lot, so fast was my adrenaline pumping at the time, as the season progressed, obviously we, the team, weren't good enough and finished fourth in the league, but as usual the fans were superb and finished top of their league by a mile. With their tremendous vociferous support you couldn't expect anything else.

The highlights of that season were when we, the team, and supporters worked in tandem. Notably Leighton Town (A) 2-0, Windsor (A) 2-0 and Grays Ath. (A) 3-3 in the FA Cup. Grays, at the time, were in the Premier Division.

The disappointment of that year made everyone connected with the club all the more determined to gain promotion the next year, for the special fans. We achieved our aim by winning the ICIS Div 3 Championship. In doing so, giving the Club its first major trophy for a long spell. On a personal note, I was privileged enough to be captain who picked up the trophy. I felt on that particular day that I wasn't just representing the Club, but I was representing the great supporters who more than anyone had helped us achieve our goal. Their loyalty was being repaid for the times they had cheered on their team during the long barren years previously. Long may they keep up that fanatical support.

During my reign at the 'Stones', I was delighted to lead the team as skipper to the ICIS Div 3 Championship and also 3rd place in Div 2, so gaining promotion to Div 1. Also, in this spell, we were runner up in Associate Members Final 96-97, semi finalists the following year and also gained re-entry into the FA Trophy after a number of years absence, it all meant that the 3_ years that I spent at the Club would be hard to match for success and also memories, in fact there are so many happy memories and I find it hard to separate them, I like to keep them as a whole.

Winning the 3rd Div Championship was definitely a personal high. I hadn't won anything major with my previous clubs, so to win something with a Club of Wealdstone's tradition was a great thrill. OK, there were some people at the time who were envious of Wealdstone were saying "It's only Division 3", but I knew that it would be the start of something special for the Club. In winning that "only Div 3" trophy, it would be a major stepping stone along the way of bringing more major honours to the Club.

That season ran along quite smoothly up to about the last furlong of the race. Eventually, due to other results not involving us, we clinched promotion, but even that didn't stop us getting Championship jitters. It was compounded in the penultimate game of the season on a Wednesday night away to Harlow. The season was to finish on the Saturday so we could have clinched the title that night, but lost 2-1.

So the stage was set for the final game of the season at Northwood FC. Northwood were 99% certain of promotion themselves, being in 3rd spot. Only a freak result involving Harlow would see them losing out. Also, our task was not made any easier by the fact that Northwood had not lost a home game all season and also they had reached the _ finals of the FA Vase after some very good victories and Braintree, our nearest rivals, were playing at home to mid-table East Thurrock. I can't recall the exact circumstances, but a draw wouldn't have been good enough – we HAD to win.

Going into the game it was very tense, but Gordon did his best to relax us. He said something along the lines of "Go out there and enjoy yourselves and try to play to the best of your ability. I'm sure the crowd will help you along as well".

The first half, as you would expect, was a tight, nervy, squalid affair, but the 2nd half more than made up for it. We took the lead through Brian Hammett after about 50 minutes.

I remember thinking to myself that would be the winner – I was proved decisively wrong! Sixty seconds later, Northwood equalised through a headed goal, from a free kick conceded by me. I was devastated. They hadn't threatened our goal, but now they were endangering our title dreams. For the next 30 odd minutes we battled gamely on, searching for that elusive goal, with the crowd giving us tremendous backing.

Then mass hysteria broke out with about 10 minutes to go. Roy Marshall, our best player all season, scored with a scrambled headed goal from a Tony Smith corner. I felt at that stage, surely we were going to be Champions and the feeling was unreal.

My legs and brain had gone at this stage, but somehow I mustered enough energy to jump into our supporters behind the goal. It took what seemed an eternity to get the match re-started, due to the celebrations. Luckily for me, as all my energy had been totally drained, Brian Hammett scrambled in another goal about 2 minutes to go. The final whistle blew. Music to my ears. Cue mass pandemonium.

The scenes that followed were amazing. A thousand hugs and kisses were given out by everyone and the champagne started flowing. The whole game and after-match celebrations were captured on video. I don't think I will ever get bored watching that video. I only wish that the night could have been caught on video as most of it is a blur to me! Tough luck Braintree!

Another major highlight of that title-winning year was when we played our nearest rivals throughout that season, Braintree at home - we had lost to them in December so for the return match in February (I think) we were fired up for revenge. It was one of those matches where the 11 players who played, played at their peak and 10 times better. We were absolutely phenomenal and annihilated them 6-0. At half time, we had a two-goal lead, so the 3rd goal was going to be crucial. If my memory serves me correctly, it was Terry Hibbert who got the 3rd goal about 5 minutes into the 2nd half.

I was ecstatic and dived into the supporters who congregated at the far corner of Edgware's ground and seemed to get thrown to the back of the stand. The referee would have been in this rights to have booked me for over zealous celebrations, but I wouldn't have cared! From that moment on, and till the final whistle, I was in heaven. We scored another 3 goals before the end. We had totally overrun our nearest rivals on a truly memorable night. Any time we played Braintree after that, you could see fear in their eyes.

It wasn't to end either, as the following season was another great season.

A lot of people around the scene had predicted that we wouldn't achieve another promotion as the 2nd Div was a much harder league, but again we came up trumps, and the turning point without a doubt that season was in the last week of March, when we visited, you guessed it, Braintree!

We were going there on a dodgy run, we had the jitters again, culminating on the previous Saturday when we lost to lowly 10 man Barking. It was a game we were desperate to win. If we had lost, I don't think we would have got that promotion.

To make matters even harder, Braintree were on a 32 match unbeaten run that season and were carrying over something like a 20 match run from the previous season. What a task we had to perform. (Braintree, I think I recall, were already up, but we were fighting for 3rd place with the hard pressing Bedford Town.)

The match kicked off and we proceeded to play our best football of the season to earn a tremendous 1-0 victory, thanks to a first half goal by Dennis Greene.

Not only did we shatter Braintree's fine record, but it was a victory that set us up for an unbeaten surge that would lead us to Division 1. Again, the joy of such a great win led me into the terraces with our supporters but by the time I got there, the majority of fans were on the pitch, joining in the euphoric celebrations of the players.

Promotion was clinched on the penultimate game of the season, this time when we beat our landlords, Edgware, for the fourth time that season. Tough luck Bedford Town.

One particular story, which I feel is relevant to divulge in, is about our Championship Party. I was so overwhelmed when we clinched victory against Northwood.

The changing room for the ensuing couple of hours was sheer bedlam. For once, us the players and backroom staff were out-singing our supporters. In fact, at one stage, the supporters got all jealous and wanted to join us in the dressing room! Beers were flowing, and there was plenty of high-jinx on a few others and my behalf. I don't think I emerged from the dressing room for about two hours after the game and I definitely wasn't sober!

I took it upon myself that no-one, and I mean no-one, was gonna take that cup out of my grasp! I travelled down to Wasps Rugby ground for the 'End Of season Dinner', along with Gordon, Super Val Shearer and Lee Walker, cup in tow.

We reached Wasps and were the last there and received a rapturous welcome. People started taking photos, but had to have them taken with me. Nobody cared, such was the high spirits.

The presentation finished and then I had a song and dance with the supporters to the Queen anthem "We are the Champions", with the cup in the middle.

Next stop for Gordon, Leo and us the players, was Middlesex and Herts Night Club. Again, the cup and I were taking centre stage, but to outsiders looking in, there were some looks of sheer disbelief! The night finally came to an end at a pub, whose Landlord we had met in the Night Club.

The Landlady invited us back for an extension to the jovial proceedings. At this stage, things were obviously becoming a blur and somehow I managed to get myself home in the very early hours.

You can imagine my horror when I woke up and there was no cup lying beside me. I went into a frightful panic. I managed to finally get hold of Gordon, sometime late Sunday morning. He, like me, wasn't feeling at his best. I asked him did he have the cup – he replied "No" and there was a deafening silence before he broke out in laughter, saying that I had left it in the pub, but luckily Stevie Bircham picked it up. I didn't live it down for quite a time.

Great night and memory, though.

It was a major honour in my career to have played for Wealdstone for many different reason, not just football and I have made many friends during my spell there; supporters, players, directors alike. There must be a special mention to Lee Walker, Paul Lamb and Paul McKay whose friendship I value very highly.

Also, I would like to thank Gordon Bartlett for bringing me to the Club. I left a Club 2 divisions higher to join Wealdstone, based on Gordon's promises that I would be guaranteed to win things. After the first year, things didn't look too rosy, but everything turned out how he said it would in the end, and even better. He must surely go down as Wealdstone's best Manager and it was an honour to have played under him.

Finally, I had a great rapport with the supporters at Wealdstone, who loved my passion on the pitch. I was only showing on the pitch what they showed off it. A great will to win and an undying passion not to lose.

Long Live the 'Stones.

Mark Lloyd
Supporter

I wonder if the gates to the White Lion will become a shrine to the late and genuinely lamented Fergus Moore.

I suppose he (note past tense) represented all we wanted from a defender in the lower reaches of the Ryman League; Committed, hearty, scary and occasionally ill-timed. Most of all I think he will be fondly remembered as he seemed to understand what Wealdstone was all about ; Yes, it's that word again, Passion. Goals and victories always celebrated wildly. Defeats with tears. Our very own Gazza.

It became obvious at the start of the season that he was going to struggle. Many of the goals we conceded appeared to be down to Fergie and mutterings from the bench (notably at Potters Bar) indicated that all was not well. I'm sure he'll be an asset to some team but if he thinks he's getting an easy ride when he plays us...

As we all know, players are inter-changeable, here today gone tomorrow, that's the way it is. The fans ARE the club and, as a result, reserve the right to slaughter anyone not playing for us that day.

*My own favourite Fergie moment? Hmm lots to choose from...but I think I'll go for him baring his backside at (I think) his Marlow adversary in the home game after Greene scored our 3rd goal. This after already being booked. Off-the-wall and pure a***. Err - I mean class.*

Good Luck Fergie - you were alright.

There were some high points, particularly beating league leaders Bognor in January. The match had shown what Wealdstone were capable of 'on their day' and there was another chance to slay the recent poor record against Harrow Borough, when they were to visit the White Lion Ground early in February in the Middlesex Senior Cup.

The match ended in a 2–2 draw. The replay was certainly not a 'classic' but it will last in the memories of 'Stones fans for a very long time. Two goals from Mick Swaysland finally secured a 'Stones win after fourteen years.

Boro keeper David Hook had been sent off for a foul on 27 seconds and Manager Alan Paris had taken over in goal as the ten men fought hard to take a first half lead against a poor Wealdstone side. The second half was a different matter as 'Stones finally started to produce, Mick Swaysland opening the scoring on 63 minutes but they couldn't increase their lead. Harrow Borough equalised in the 88th minute to take the tie to extra time.

Just before the interval Swaysland scored his second, heading home unchallenged from a Brian Jones free kick and 'Stones maintained their lead to the end.

It was not a great victory, nor a momentous performance but at last a Wealdstone team had beaten their local rivals!

The players who will by dint of this volume will go down in history were;

Noel Imber, Steve Dell, Phil Dicker (Shaun Fleming), Dominic Sterling, Ian Waugh, Paul Lamb, Lewis Reid, Brian Jones (Barry Forshaw), Mick Swaysland, Carl Holmes, Paul McKay and the other sub (not used), Paul Benning.

The victory had been met with tremendous celebration from the 'Stones fans, almost as though they had won the cup itself.

Mat Tarrant
Supporter since 1995

Around 1995/96, after more than 20 years watching Derby County I became disillusioned with Premiership football. My best days as a Derby fan were spent in the old 3rd division and the final straw came when they left the famous old Baseball Ground for a soulless, all-seater, non smoking ground with special singing areas and charged over £20 a go for the privilege of being there. There were no longer any links with the players, few of whom could even speak English.

So I went off in search for the heart and soul of football and after brief flirtations with Chesterfield, Slough Town, Gresley Rovers and St Albans I found it with Wealdstone. Initially attracted to the club via the internet I was looking for a local team following a move to Bushey Heath. My first fixture was a home match with Barking in the Ryman's 2nd division in Oct 1997 v Barking.

The 'Stones ran out comfortable winners with a hat-trick from Keith Boreham but the star man was Brian Jones. Steve Bircham got himself sent off for chinning a Barking player. The two factors that impressed me were the quality of the football and the camaraderie of the fans.

It was obvious that Gordon Bartlett was attempting to achieve success by playing good football and many of that side are still at the club as I write. Jones, Bircham, Stirling, MacKay, Imber and of course Chrissy Walton. It was Jones who grabbed my attention and I loved to watch him play, he has scored some truly memorable goals, a solo effort in a night match against Windsor and Eton later that season stands out in my memory.

Of course the season ended in high drama and excitement as Dennis Greene scored the goals against our landlords which ensured promotion. There were some magnificent performances throughout the year but special mention has to go to Roy Marshall and Fergus Moore at the back who showed composure and commitment in abundance.

The 'Stones fans are superb. I was warmly welcomed to the club as a new supporter and very soon felt at home. There is a fantastic belief in the club and after what they have been through and survived it is the supporters who will ensure that the club moves forward.

After a little over 2 years as a fan I entered the London Marathon to raise funds for the club. Something I would never have dreamed of doing for Derby County.

This is real football. Roll on the next 100 years.

It was no real surprise when defeat at Oxford City in mid February saw 'Stones in mid table. The record of 9 wins, 5 draws and 9 defeats from 23 matches was better than relegation, but unlikely to challenge the leaders.

Three wins on the trot though saw 'Stones leap to seventh place in the Division by the end of the month, but they were still 13 points behind now third placed Bognor Regis Town with only one game in hand.

Four more wins to make it 21 points out of 21 had seen 'Stones rise still further, to the edge of the promotion battle, but there was still an immense mountain to climb if 'Stones were to compete, particularly as their next match was away to promotion rivals Grays Athletic.

The match ended in a draw and it seemed as though 'Stones were finally serious contenders for promotion.

So unlikely had promotion seemed only a month before, the board had agreed with the manager to cut the playing budget to preserve funds still further as there was no chance of relegation.

A supporters collection had been organised and with donations from £5 to £300 had managed to raise its target of £3500 to make up the shortfall in the budget for the remaining eight weeks of the season.

Late March also saw another Wealdstone Supporters Sponsored Walk, this time to a fixture at Leyton Pennant, starting at Baker Street, early on the Saturday morning. Yet again the 'Stones fans had answered the call, far above what was expected, to help out the club as it strived to make ends meet with no income, whilst trying to develop a new home for the team.

By the time of the match at Grays, Wealdstone had realised that there were only six days in which to bring the White Lion Ground up to an A grade in readiness for promotion, should the excellent run of form continue.

Worse still, the deadline fell on Easter Weekend and outside help was almost entirely unavailable, so yet again it was supporters and officials that started the work, which included the addition of 42 seats, a new turnstile and some fencing.

Four more wins saw 'Stones in the thick of the promotion race as their rivals form stumbled but the visit to Canvey Island on 10th April caused serious concerns for the club.

Canvey too had had a ground inspection and had been informed that they had passed the A grade despite the fact that on the day Wealdstone visited, some work was still being carried out.

They also commiserated with their visitors, informing Wealdstone that they had been unsuccessful and would not be promoted. The concern at Wealdstone was with regard to the new seating. The Ryman League had stated that it had to be covered, and at the time of the inspection, sprung on the club at short notice on the Easter weekend, it had not been possible to complete the cover. It was in fact completed on April 4th, some three days after the deadline.

There was certainly an 'atmosphere' at Canvey on that afternoon, but it didn't seem to affect the players if they were aware of it as Brian Jones put Wealdstone into a slightly fortunate 2-0 lead at half time. The result though was eventually to go the islanders way as they scored 4 without reply in the second half.

'Stones directors and officials were frantically trying to contact the league to find out officially what the outcome of the grading had been. They were met with delays and no real answers, being told that they would receive a phone call later in the evening with the outcome.

The call finally came and confirmed 'Stones worst nightmare. The grading had been turned down and a top three finish would not see Wealdstone promoted.

'Stones Chairman Paul Rumens was quoted as saying *"It was an absolutely ludicrous decision"* and *"the club has been led up the garden path by the league"*.

He claimed that when the ground had been inspected on April 3rd, the league had verbally agreed to a six day extension to enable the installation of a permanent roof over the seating in question.

As Paul Rumens continued, *"If we had not achieved the grading, why didn't the league tell us there and then? Why give us an extension and cause us to spend thousands of pounds?"*

Ryman League Chairman, Alan Turvey disputed the club's claims saying *"That is simply not true. I was one of the two league officers at the inspection and I did not say that.*

Wealdstone's Vice-Chairman and another Director were told that we would have to report to the committee that the work required was not completed in time. It was definitely not said that if they completed the outstanding work they would qualify. Clive Moyse happened to be nearby on the Friday and called in to see if it had been done."

Wealdstone counter claimed that the return of Mr Moyse had been pre-arranged to receive pictures of the completed structure from Vice-Chairman Nick DuGard, which had been requested to show the management committee.

The club also stated that a wooden structure over the seats could have been completed by the April 1st deadline, but the decision to delay and to put up a better and longer lasting steel roof had been sanctioned by the league.

Wealdstone were to appeal the decision to the Football Association if they maintained a promotion place at the end of the season.

Six wins in their remaining six matches ensured that 'Stones did finish in a promotion place. From 13 points behind third place, a run of 14 wins, 1 draw and 1 defeat saw 'Stones in third place with three matches remaining.

The last week of the season was surrounded by greater tension than usual. A win away at Worthing would guarantee Wealdstone third place, but not promotion, just the opportunity to appeal to the FA.

In a tense atmosphere, where 'Stones made up well over half of the crowd of around 400.

Two players sent off, an equaliser by Worthing followed by a dramatic winner for Wealdstone, both from the penalty spot, all in the space of a remarkable ten minutes of added time, made for a sensational finish to this match at Woodside Road on Saturday.

It was an amazing conclusion that would have been simply impossible to script.

Leading with a superbly struck goal from Carl Holmes, a minute into first half stoppage time, and having dominated the second period, Wealdstone were seemingly heading for three comfortable points as the game ended its closing stages.

But then referee Mr Stoneham lit the fuse on an explosive finale. The Maidstone official had already distinguished himself with a succession of inept decisions, notable when he disallowed an apparently valid Worthing goal in the 23rd minute.

He ruled that Noel Imber had been fouled as he grasped thin air in an attempt to keep out a speculative lob from Miles Rutherford that ended up in the net, but in truth there was no-one near the keeper.

When Mr Stoneham instantly pointed to the spot after Paul Lamb clearly fouled Ben Carrington OUTSIDE the 'Stones area with the game five minutes into injury time, those who felt the official was attempting to even things up seemed to have a good case.

Rutherford fired home the penalty, and it looked like a point a piece, but the drama was far from over.

Two minutes later, Wealdstone sub Brian Jones chased a ball through to Worthing's Philip Reid and just clipped the keeper as he gathered the ball. Reid's response was to totally lose control and launch a head butt at the 'Stones striker who went down like the proverbial sack of manure.

In the mayhem that followed, Wealdstone defender Phil Dicker was shown the red card for foolishly expressing his less than subtle observations to Mr Stoneham and when order was finally restore, Reid, not surprisingly was dispatched.

For his part, Jones received a Yellow Card when many felt that an Oscar would have been more appropriate.

Mr Stoneham's final ruling was a spot kick to 'Stones for Reid's aberration and having scored from a penalty at one end, Rutherford took over in goal in an attempt to prevent one at the other end.

He did get a hand to Rocky Baptiste's shot but was unable to keep it out and Wealdstone dramatically regained the lead.

Two minutes later Mr Stoneham blew the final whistle and the large 'Stones contingent raced onto the pitch to join the team in celebration.

Wealdstone; Noel Imber, Eddie Boxford, Dominic Sterling, Nathan Copeman (Phil Dicker), Ian Waugh, Paul Benning, Chris Walton, Carl Holmes, Rocky Baptiste, Steve Bircham (Brian Jones), Paul McKay (Paul Lamb).

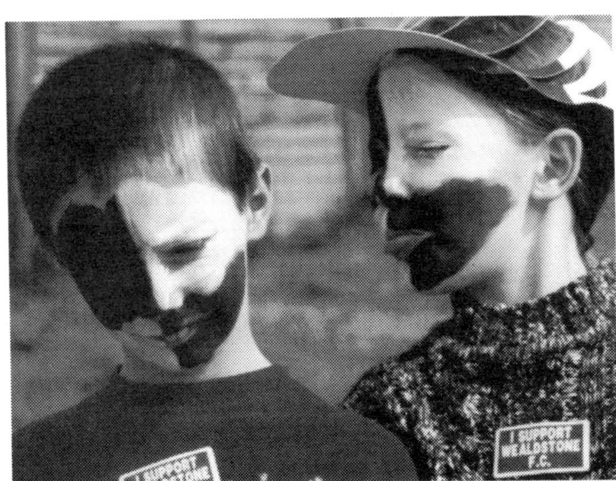

Shane and Sinead

Shane (aged 9)

My favourite match was against Barton Rovers in 1999 on Saturday March 13th. Wealdstone were 2-0 down at half time. The match changed round in the second half because just before half time, Barton Rovers had a player sent off because he hurt Jonah. The second half was amazing. First, Rocky Baptiste rounded the 'keeper and placed the ball in the back of the net, then Benning headed home to make it two all. Then Paul Lamb was next on the score sheet when he tapped the ball into the net.

Then Brian Jones was at it again by scoring his wonderful goal. Finally Carl Holmes scored by smacking the ball in the back of the net.

My man of the match was Brian Jones who later on, was voted Player of the season. He's my best player because I like the way he scores goals. I did all of the walk to Leyton Pennant too.

Sinead (aged 10)

"We're all off to the seaside......" I sang happily. We were on the train heading towards Worthing station to see if Wealdstone could win another promotion. A few minutes later I was asking how much longer it would be before we got there.

"Hurry" I shouted "We're finally here!"
"Quiet down" my mum replied. "Can we go to the beach?" I asked. "First things first" mum replied.

We hunted around for a nice place to eat. Eventually we managed to find a Pizza Hut, although it was very busy we still jumped in the queue. "at last!" I whispered. The waitress came over and took our order. After lunch we went for an Ice Cream. Shane and I got a double cone and my Mum and Steve got a single.

We walked all the way to Worthing's ground (it's a long way from the station). The referee blew his whistle and the game began. The players passed the ball to one another and suddenly the crowd started yelling because Wealdstone had scored. The rest of the half was a load of rubbish from the Worthing players but the Wealdstone players played very well as usual.

The second half was the best of all, everyone sang and shouted amusing Wealdstone songs because it was a very important match. The fun went on until a few minutes into injury time when the referee gave a penalty to Worthing, which they scored.

Even later in injury time, Brian Jones, who had come on late in the second half though he could barely walk, let alone run, went to hassle the goalkeeper who was trying to take a goal kick.

The keeper went mad and swung a punch at Jonah who hit the deck holding his (already bruised) eye. He should come and take part in my school play! The Wealdstone fans started shouting at the Ref. Suddenly, Phil Dicker ran over and said a few words to him regarding the situation and the referee pulled out a red card. Then he booked Jonah and the crowd went very mad.

Then he sent off the Worthing goalkeeper and gave Wealdstone a penalty. Ian Waugh stepped up to take the penalty but instead Rocky Baptiste took it and scored.

Finally, the referee blew his whistle. Everyone jumped on the pitch and a piece of concrete fell on my mum's foot When people came off the pitch they went into the bar to have a drink and greet the winning team.

A midweek win over second placed Hitchin Town and a victory over Staines Town saw 'Stones finish the season on a high, having won 17 of their last 19 matches with only one defeat, but there was still nothing that could be done until the appeal had been heard at the Football Association.

Later in the month Wealdstone's appeal was heard and the decision of the Ryman League was upheld by the FA. 'Stones though were not finally defeated and would appeal to the AGM and Members of the Ryman League in June.

'Stones fans also became involved as the AGM at Harrow Borough, when they held a peaceful protest outside the entrance to Harrow Borough FC where the AGM was to be held, asking for support from the representatives from the other league clubs in attendance.

They were supported by fans from other clubs, Bishops Stortford and Maidenhead being two that were represented. The fans had also written to club Chairmen asking them to write to the league in support of the 'Stones and letters had been published in the press in support of their case, but it was all to no avail, as, in front of the Football Association representatives and legal advisors at the meeting, 'Stones were defeated again and the decision to deny the team promotion was upheld.

Rob Saville
Supporter

I was raised in North Harrow and soon became a supporter. I also launched the 'Original Wealdstone FC website'. My Uncle was once a Vice President ie he fixed Morritt's radiators once, so I got in free.

There are some good memories of the supporters, Duncan Towell made hundreds of funny comments and always kept me coming back for more. Tony Platt " You could eat an apple though a tennis racket" etc and 'deadly' - three lines on a chart.

If I supported another club who were playing Wealdstone, I'd think "Their supporters are far ruder, and far more abusive than our fans. And it looks more fun."

There was nothing for it other than to prepare for another season in Division One. It was difficult to understand the decision and it made a very long summer for people involved with the club.

Terry Dollman
Supporter

Megaphone & I were on our way home from Barton, and got to talking about football teams in general. I got on my high horse and started talking about how Wealdstone FC were very rarely recognised by people in Wealdstone.

For a team that was founded over 100 years ago, WFC doesn't get the support it deserves. We have had some great players over the years, & after all we've been through, there is still a Wealdstone.

Taking all this into account, it hurts me to think that there are only a handful of us, who are still here & will be here no matter what.

Wealdstone is the only team I have ever supported. I don't glory hunt & go to Chelsea, or even Watford for that matter, for me Wealdstone is enough!!!

Its very difficult to express how much Wealdstone means to me., but here's to another 100 years.

The summer had also seen the birth of the Independent Wealdstone Action Group as a result of the decision by the Ryman League to deny Wealdstone's promotion.

They handed out leaflets to raise support at a non-league International, played at St Albans prior to the league AGM, and subsequently decided, after the lack of support from other league clubs to hit them where it hurts – in the pocket.

The following season was to see a number of 'Stones traveling fans shun club bars, tea bars and match programmes at away matches. Most clubs were happy to see 'Stones excellent away following as invariably it added money to the coffers, but their lack of support was not to be forgotten.

There was one small bright spot at the end of the season. The launch of a new Youth System at Wealdstone, intended to bring young players on to the verge of the first team.

The Programme For Academic and Sporting Excellence, run in conjunction with the Bedford College would see players from 16 – 19 taken on full time, spending 4 hours a day training or playing football and four hours a day schooling as they studied for various BTEC sports related qualifications.

The Club had joined the Allied Counties Youth League for the younger players (U18) and would compete in the Nationwide PASE Conference for the U19 as part of the scheme. By the end of June a first year intake of more than 30 players had been confirmed.

After the disappointments of the previous year, pre-season started with a boost to the finances at least as Graham Taylor brought Watford FC to play Wealdstone at the White Lion Ground.

The result was a defeat by 7–0 against a fairly strong Watford side that were about to start their first season in the Premiership. The match was played in front of almost 1400 paying spectators.

Three wins and a draw from the first four matches saw 'Stones head the table early in the season but it soon proved to be a false dawn. Again the side struggled to get any consistency, often losing when a win was expected and winning against all the odds on other occasions.

It was a season more memorable for personal performances than for those of the team. One of these was an enigma in his own right, Rocky Baptiste.

Rocky had had a chequered career with Wealdstone, before it had started. He signed for the club in the previous season in October and made his debut in the league cup against Berkhamstead, scoring twice.

The next day he was the subject of a protest, as it turned out he was already a contracted player at another club. Wealdstone were removed from the competition and Rocky wasn't to appear in a Wealdstone shirt again until the following January.

At the end of the season and the start of the next, he proved he had the ability to destroy teams on his own, on other occasions people would wonder how.

It was the FA Cup that was to prove his forte in 1999-2000. He played but didn't score in the Preliminary round and missed the home first qualifying round match at home to Ford United that finished in a draw.

The replay at Ford saw him turn the game as he scored a hat-trick. 'Stones against the odds, ran out winners by 3-2.

The next round was away to Staines; *Rocky Baptiste has done it again* ran the Harrow Observer headline as he scored another hat-trick to give 'Stones a 3-0 win away from home;

After his three goals at Ford United his latest hat-trick began after just eight minutes when he hit a splendid 20 yard shot past the home keeper from a Brian Jones pass.

'Stones extended their lead in the 21st minute when Dominic Sterling found Brian Jones whose pass to Baptiste allowed him to fire into the roof of the net.

Early in the second half David Greene blasted just over and a Rocky Baptiste run ended with a fine lob that Lovett just got a touch to at the expense of a corner. From the resulting kick, Brian Jones hit the crossbar.

After 52 minutes it was Jones, who had had a hand in all three goals that put Baptiste clear. He went inside Lovett to slot home his hat-trick..

He was to score for 'Stones in the next round as well, but a 1-1 draw with Rothwell Town saw them eliminated in the replay. With seven goals he remained the competitions top scorer for a long period.

By the end of the season Rocky had decided he wanted to leave the club, and he was eventually transferred to Staines Town. He played for them against Wealdstone at the end of the season, and of course, scored twice.

His short career at the 'Stones had seen him make 48 starts and thirteen subs appearances, scoring 35 goals.

Two weeks after the cup exit at Rothwell, it was Ian Waugh's turn to achieve a personal goal, in more ways than one!

Yes it was only against bottom of the table Chertsey, and it wasn't particularly impressive either, but it was a win. Something Wealdstone haven't achieved in the league for two months...........

..............'Stones desperately needed a spark of inspiration to turn the game having gone in at half time a goal behind, but it was difficult to see where it would come from as they were so badly out of sorts.

However 13 minutes into the second half, Wealdstone got the break they required – but it owed little to inspiration and a great deal to a slice of good fortune.

Paul McKay fed Ian Waugh down the right, and the defender, without a goal in over 150 appearances for the club, cut inside and let fly from 25 yards out.

With Chertsey keeper Graham Benstead well positioned it was doubtful whether the shot would have scored until it cannoned off the head of full back Cooper, standing on the penalty spot................

The Harrow Observer commented that it may well have normally have been credited as an own goal, but for the fact that it was Ian Waugh who scored.

It was to be his only goal for the club in 169 appearances and resulted in the supporters club, with their usual humour, producing a celebration tee-shirt in honour of the moment.

The club celebrated its centenary season, the records at the time had dated the foundation of the club to the 1899–1900 season, but there wasn't a great deal to celebrate.

There was a Centenary Dinner at which a number of former players attended. There were hero's from all of the popular era's of the club, the oldest being Jack Russell, who had scored in the 1942 cup final at Wembley. Also there, the clubs two most capped Amateur Internationals, Charlie Townsend and Hugh Lindsay.

From the seventies, George Duck, John Morton, John 'Willie' Watson and Ray ' Ginger' Fulton where in attendance as where Freddie Barwick and Paul Waites. From the eighties Dennis Byatt, Robin Wainwright, Steve Perkins and Paul Bowgett.

From the fans one group stood out – occasional player sponsors the Four Skinless Bangers attended in matching tux's....

Terry Stern, Nick Symmons, Steve Paull and Mick Fishman in matching skins.

The dinner was a bright spot in a disappointing year.

Not to be outdone on personal honours, later in the season Paul McKay was to inspire 'Stones to a much needed win away to Leatherhead.

Having beaten Romford in December, 'Stones had not won for ten league games and found themselves only four points above the relegation positions in the table.

At half time at Leatherhead the score had been 0-0 but it took only four minutes of the second half for Paul to break the deadlock, chesting down a partly cleared corner, he fired a vicious dipping volley over the home keeper from fully thirty five yards.

After 72 minutes, he doubled the lead after a long clearance from Darren Watts was headed on by Mickie Swaysland and McKay outpaced a defender to the ball and then delicately chipped over the goalkeeper to seal the 2-0 victory and to ease the pressure a little.

No mean feat for a defender cum midfield player who was not normally on the score sheet.

By early March there was some good news regarding the relocation of the club following a decision by the Secretary of State for the Environment not to issue a directive, either restricting the granting of planning permission that had been granted two earlier, nor to 'call in' the application.

It meant that 'Stones could continue to develop the plans at local level and also, the fundraising efforts. The major part of the funding was hoped to come from the National Lottery and an application for funding was being prepared.

As things at last seemed to move forward on the new ground, there were problems with the groundshare at Edgware Town when it was realised that there were complications with the lease.

The requirements of Scottish & Newcastle Breweries were different to those conditions insisted on by the Ryman League. With a planned hotel development at the site entrance it seemed that Wealdstone and Edgware Town were both likely to become homeless at the end of the season.

It was a black cloud over the club for the return of Stuart Pearce who was guest speaker at the Sportsman's Dinner, another part of the ongoing fundraising effort.

Nick Woolford
Supporter since 1966

The return to the Borough has been welcomed but in all honesty I do not like the White Lion Ground. It is definitely a sad and decrepit stadium and I think it is to the credit of our board and supporters that we managed to bring it up to the standard we did, even though all our hard work was in vain.

I have thoroughly enjoyed the reign of Gordon and his management team at the Club. The last few years in which we have seen the club achieve promotion statues three seasons in a row is testament to Gordon's guidance.

Long may he stay.

I am truly grateful to him for turning down the opportunities that have been extended to him by other clubs in the recent past.

The Sportsman's Dinners that Paul Rumens has instigated have also become a regular feature of my annual calendar. Every year I have supported this event by arranging a table for friends and colleagues who have to suffer my diatribes each Monday about the fortunes (or otherwise) of Wealdstone FC.

The best (by far) was 2001 when we arrived after having a few beers en-route!

The auction was just hysterical. I subsequently discovered that I had been bidding (from the bar) against my colleagues at the table who were buying the item for me! Apparently I pushed to price of the item up by £50 just to ensure that I bought it and they didn't .

Wealdstone looked to be on the move once again. With league rules insisting that any groundshare agreement had to be in place and ratified by April 1st, there was little time to act and more importantly, there were very few offers from clubs who could or would accommodate the 'Stones for the following season.

It meant for many clubs that they would have to forgo their reserve sides. As remaining at Edgware Town and the White Lion Ground was the preferred option, any new arrangement would have to have a 'get out' clause. This put any prospective host as risk of losing revenue.

One club who did offer to accommodate the 'Stones was Chesham United. The problem was that the rental payment would be payable quarterly. There was a 90 day notice period.

The season finished somewhat quietly on the field, 'Stones avoiding relegation, but with no agreement reached on the lease at Edgware, it looked as though both clubs would be moving on.

It meant a great deal of disruption during pre-season – Manager Gordon Bartlett had difficulty in signing players as the club were still unsure if their home was to be Edgware or Chesham.

It also meant that some of the existing players would move on, as the travelling to Chesham in midweek was likely to prove very difficult. One player who did leave was Paul McKay. He joined his local club. Ironically, Leatherhead, who had been the victims of his two goal onslaught the previous year.

In the background meeting were held between Wealdstone, Edgware, Chesham, Scottish & Newcastle Breweries and the Ryman League to try and reach an amicable solution. It was to cost Wealdstone money as during May, the first quarterly payment was due on the provisional lease at Chesham United.

As time progressed with no resolution, Wealdstone prepared for the new season at Chesham United, even playing their home pre-season matches there. At one point, the White Lion Ground was closed by the league, which would have meant the end of Edgware Town as they had no fall back option, but with four days to go to the start of the new season, an acceptable lease was produced and signed.

Wealdstone had already paid two instalments on their 'provisional' lease at Chesham and the host club insisted that the 90 day notice period had to be served. This meant that another payment would have to be handed over. The disruption and changes at the White Lion Ground had cost Wealdstone, the innocent party, over £9000 at a time when every penny was precious.

The disruption to the squad was immeasurable. A number of players had left the club and signed for other sides as the travel for 'home games' would have been impractical. Others had refused to sign for the same reason. Four days before the first match, the situation changed.

Christer Svan
Supporter in Sweden

I have just joined the 'Stones mailing list (on the internet). I am living in Sweden .My connection with the 'Stones? I have followed the 'Stones since the early eighties when I was in London, and watched several football games including West Ham, Chelsea and the 'Stones.

I have been a non-league lover for over twenty years now, so going to a non-league game in London was just something I could not miss. By a coincidence the game was Crawley v the

One of the most exciting players to appear in a Wealdstone shirt in recent years, Brian Jones. Caught in action by David Saunders.

'Stones.

Wealdstone looked like a nice friendly club, with a great bunch of lads.

The game was played in the 81-82 season, when Wealdstone got promotion from the Southern section of the Southern League to the Alliance Premier League.

I followed the 'Stones during the eighties and the early part of the nineties, but have not followed them frequently since then. Information about non-league football was hard to find in Sweden, but i could at least get the results in the English Sunday papers.

With the internet, information is now very easy to find and to start follow the 'Stones again is just natural.

It was a strange dressing room that welcomed the start of the new campaign, as manager Gordon Bartlett had made seven signings in the two days leading up to the match and the dressing room was the first time that many of the players had met. Far from ideal preparations.

When a phone call was received forty minutes before kick off to tell the club that one of his new signings and selected starting line up was actually due to serve a four match ban and was therefore unavailable, all of the frustrations, released when the ground situation had been (in the short term) resolved, returned.

One win and three draws in the first ten league games did not help the situation as the squad struggled to gel together.

When an inglorious suicide saw the club throw away a two goal lead at home against Belper to go out of the FA Cup it became apparent again that it was not to be a good year for the 'Stones.

All the disruptions of the summer had taken a great effect and the reduced playing budget had severely limited the options available. One chance of raising money had been the FA Cup but two unnecessary sendings-off had put paid to that as well.

Worse was to come when it was announced that the bid for National Lottery funding for the new stadium had been rejected.

The Sport England Lottery Panel rejected the proposals, but instructed the 'Stones to submit the application to the new Football Foundation, as the scheme was more than 85% football based. It was as though the application, which had been under review for a number of months, had been rejected as the guidelines for funding had changed. Something that was out of the club's control.

It meant there was to be a further delay. There were no means of application available for the Football Foundation as the body was 'too new' and the forms had not even been developed. It was hoped though that the delay would only be a few months and the application could soon be progressed.

The prospect of a run in the FA Trophy was to go a similar way to the FA Cup as again 'Stones squandered a 2 goal lead to draw 3-3 with Weston Super Mare, but again the second chance was squandered as Wealdstone lost the replay 2–0.

The proposed application to the Football Foundation was rocked further when it was realised that their maximum grant was to be limited to £1m – approximately 20% of what Wealdstone required for the development that they had worked so hard towards, and it caused a major re-think to the plans.

Not only did additional funding have to be sought, but a new planning application also had to be submitted.

The board worked tirelessly behind the scenes to salvage what they could from the situation, at the same time putting a brave face on the public front of the club. If the supporters had become disheartened the project would fail.

By the AGM the club were able to announce that a number of options were being considered. Private funding had been investigated and there were a number of potential investors for the project from the Health and Leisure Industry.

The whole project had been revised and a presentation was made for the facility to include a Health Club. This would be separately funded and would allow much of the project to be developed as part of the same package. Wealdstone were bringing to the table the site, the potential to renew their planning application that made the prospect attractive.

On the field, there was little change. By the end of February, Wealdstone had played 26 league matches, winning six and drawing seven. There was a serious danger of relegation to add to their problems, but wins in their next two matches again eased the pressure. Six wins and two draws in their remaining sixteen matches was enough to ensure safety by a slim margin.

There was something to put a few smiles back on faces though as a fundraising match at the end of the season saw a number of former Wealdstone players unluckily lose 2–1 to a 'Showbiz' XI.

There weren't too many of the hoped for stars in the Showbiz XI but it didn't matter. Wealdstone fans had turned out to see their former heroes play once again.

John Morton
Wealdstone Past XI

Another match?

I have only just recovered from the last game. Whilst lining up for the 'team photo' Chris Lightfoot asked me if I realised that our combined ages was 108. A sobering thought.

I would be delighted to be involved again although I'm not sure if my wife will be as keen. I think I'd better start training now.

I've promised George Duck I'll wear a tie this time, as he gave me a bollocking for being incorrectly dressed on a match day at the last game.

Darren Linden
Lifelong supporter.

Specific memories of WFC? Incredibly loyal support. Seeing the same faces now that I saw when I first started watching the team when around 8 years old, and now I'm drinking with some of them!

There has always been excellent vocal support, the social side of the club (away matches especially!) has developed lifelong friends, no matter what the age. People like Val Shearer are more than supporters, They're part of the club, they really are 'the fixtures and fittings'.

A new planning application was prepared, based on the new design criteria and in partnership with Stadia Management, it was presented to the Council. The increase in building was at the cost of some of the external features but it did offer the project as a whole a more business like potential.

The Outline Planning Application was granted and again it was passed by the respective Greater London Authority and the Secretary of State for the Environment, without need for further

Wealdstone Past XI 2001
Back; Mark Graves, Alan Cordice, Vic Schwartz, Chris Lightfoot, John Morton, Paul Bowgett, Alan Fursdon, Robin Wainwright Front; Fred Barwick, George Duck, Nell Cordice, Doug McClure, Paul Waites.

examination.

A great deal of work on Business and Operational Plans, detailed costing's and detailed design finally secured a loan from the Bank Of Scotland to cover the major cost of the development and to ensure that an application of an acceptable level could be made to the Football Foundation.

Phil Spencer,
Supporter

When I tell people in Nottingham that I'm travelling to London to see the 'Stones the mystified look is normally accompanied by the question "why?"

Why indeed. I'm a lifelong Notts County supporter with no ties to the Borough of Harrow, but the answer lies in that hallowed strip of land between Harrow Hill tube and Harrow and Wealdstone station, plus the unremarkable Arnold Library.

At one my interest was nurtured after I first stumbled across Lower Mead in 1988, in the other I found a book about London's villages which described some of Middlesex's ancient communities and their potential for further exploration. Once I had been to some of these places and the High mead terracing, smelt the decaying heaps of grass and absorbed the whole experience that was Lower Mead, I was hooked.

I have no weight of historical association. My time is now, if only because the period between 1988 and 1996 was so unbelievably bleak!

My favourite match took place as recently as 1996, a 3-2 win over Wingate and Finchley.

Two down at half time, 'Stones responded with all guns blazing snatching a late winner amid great scenes of jubilation and high emotion, not least in the portion of the White Lion Ground where I was standing. When Bryan Hammatt rifled in the winner, it was the first time in six years that I'd seen Wealdstone win in around fifty matches!

The funniest incident came in a drab goalless draw with Camberley. Their number three, having already planted a number of free kicks into touch became the target for the Wealdstone Boo-Boys who seemed fascinated both by his cheerlessness and by his error-strewn method of playing the beautiful game.

Had he possessed one iota of humour, had he reacted to the taunts with a merry quip of his own, then he might've been accepted as 'one of the lads'.

Instead he maintained a sullen silence as his latest farcical attempt sailed into tough, whereupon he would turn and attempt a snarling, invariably obscene repost to the growing band of detractors.

Finally, something snapped as 'our hero' prepared to launch another Camberley free kick downfield., to a chorus of caustic comments from the crowd.

As he walked back, he shouted "Why are you doing this? You don't know me. You've never seen me before. Why don't you get off my back?"

In the eerie silence that followed he hoofed the ball high. Indeed so high that it sailed, almost in slow motion, over the bar, over the perimeter fencing, over a hedge and into a neighbours garden.

Now you don't often see Spurs or Man United players consumed with mirth when there best laid plans go awry. They are too well paid to enjoy playing the game.

At Ryman ' three', when a full back commits a deed of perfectly glorious footballing slapstick that the whole crowd can enjoy, the least he can do in join in. But No! our hero, surely released from his contract at the Tottenham Empire or Edgware Metropole for our delectation and delight, merely scowled again and replaced an imaginary piece of turf.

There wasn't a dry eye in the house........

Paul Conroy
Youth Player and Supporter since the 1970's

Having just returned from shopping at Tesco's and being half way through a nice glass of Chianti I take time to open a large official looking letter which through the address window I can see is from Wealdstone Football Club.

As I glance through the assorted documents regarding shares, letters of support for the new ground and the team draw one letter catches my attention. A letter from the Club secretary, enquiring about memories from the past for inclusion in the Centenary History book.

As I read through the letter my mind begins to wander back to Wealdstone Football Club and how we met over thirty years ago.

I was about six or seven when my old man took me to watch the 'Stones at Lower Mead. Evans, Townsend and all. Fairly large crowds in those days and good memories at that. The tea bar at the Elmslie stand end of the ground, the balls hit over the stand and down the side alley of the ABC cinema never seemed to come back and players, hero's on the pitch and to me later in life friends.

My first memory is of going home to tell my mum that I had touched the match ball seven times as I leant over the railings alongside the cinder track.

I felt as though I had played my part in the game and at the end asking my hero Viv Evans to take my programme into the dressing room for autographs. I didn't think I was being cheeky, but about ten minutes latter Mr. Evans returned with my programme covered in scribble, what terrible hand writing these footballers have.

Time went on and more visits to Lower Mead and autograph hunting became, it seemed, a regular occurrence.

One thing amused me at all the games. The half time ritual change of ends via the old corrugated toilet behind the main stand by all the 'Stones supporters carrying out away team goalkeeper barracking duties. I can remember the 'Stones walked around the chest hospital side of the ground, and if there were any away supporters, they would join in with the ritual and embark in their own repositioning via the High Mead side of the ground. Happy times.

Time moved on, myself and Wealdstone parted company and I wasn't to go back to Lower Mead until 1975 when I returned for trials with the club for the Youth team, managed by my hero Viv Evans. As I approached the ground from the bus stop outside the fish and chip shop the large white letters painted on the back of the main stand stood out like an old friend.

Through the small gate and now I was going into the players entrance to change in the away teams dressing room. Success, I was asked back every Tuesday and Thursday for a number of weeks.

Then that day....... when signing on forms were given out by the senior team manager Mr Eddie Presland via Mr. Tom Macdonald upon the instructions of Viv Evans.

It was a tension filled dressing room as a lot of hopeful young lads waited to know their fate.

As Eddie and Tom moved around the room Viv would say yes or no, if yes Tom handed a form to Eddie who shook your hand and welcomed you to Wealdstone Football Club and then moved on to the next. To the lads given a form it was instant relief to those bypassed total sadness and rejection as I was to find out a couple of years later.

The squad was chosen and training was stepped up. Brian Jacks was strutting his stuff on the BBC Superstars programme and squat thrusts became part of our training programme. Training that also included the senior team and youth team squad being mixed together.

Goalkeeper from the senior side, defence from the youth side, midfield from the senior side, forwards from the youth team and visa versa. Now at times I was in the same team as George Duck and my old PE teacher Paul Fairclough and trying not to upset John Watson.

A league was entered and top of the list was Luton Town F.C. A chance to play at Kenilworth Road we thought. No chance. They played their home matches at a local ground in Luton on a Saturday morning with a kick off at 10.30 so that their team could attend the first team matches to carry out duties applicable to their apprenticeship.

Two players from that Luton side stuck in my mind. Ricky Hill latter to play for England and Godfrey Ingram who had already played for England schoolboys at Wembley. There I was on the same pitch as them. Occasionally I touched the ball when they didn't want it.

In a friendly match played before the start of the season we played against the Qatar national youth team. It seemed strange my old man now coming to Lower Mead to watch me and having to pay for the privilege.

As we lined up before the kick off the Qatar team all rushed towards us and gave each Wealdstone player a medal. Then as another gesture of good will they then beat us 3-1. That's as near as we got to playing in Europe but that's proof that at least one international match was played at Lower Mead.

Then came my moment, Andy Warhol's " everybody is famous for 15 minutes" thing, we were playing Cambridge City in a cup match at home and losing 2-0 in the second half. I was kicking my heels on the subs bench.

Then came the call, get warmed up, a couple of sprints along the cinder track in front of the main stand is all the energy I could spare as I wanted as much time on that pitch as possible.

On I went, first couple of minutes I ran around like a headless chicken, then it happened. A short back pass that wasn't going to reach the Cambridge goalkeeper and there quick as a flash was me, my chance 2-1 a goal, my first, at home, no more a headless chicken. We pushed forward, a corner a low cross, ball at my feet 2-2 ...super sub. Replay, headlines in the Harrow Observer. Wow.!

Replay one Thursday night in Cambridge before the M25 was built, not the easiest of journeys. We lost, out of the cup, no more a hero.

During my time at Wealdstone I saw about seventy lads trial, stay and go but at the end only one that I am aware of made it through to league football - Francis Joseph, now back coaching at the club. A couple made appearances for the senior team - Steve Hanson and Ian Forrest. I don't know what ever happened to them or where they ended up but both were good players. Then the fateful day for me it was goodbye, sorry son, we don't want you.

The memory of that day although sad had its funny side. Training had finished and players changed, bathed and left for an orange juice in the bar. Hang about at the end I was asked. The changing room emptied all but my mate Colin Weaver who was still in the bath, Viv Evans and me.

For anyone who knew the changing rooms at Lower Mead you will remember the bench seating being about 2 foot six high. There I was sitting on my own looking at the floor waiting for ....I didn't know what.

Then Viv started talking to me and walking around the dressing room, eventually he was standing in front of me across the other side of the room stark naked telling me that they wouldn't be signing me on at the end of the season. I looked up then straight back down at the floor, totally devastated but trying not to picture in my mind the situation that I was being given the news in.

So that's how Wealdstone and me parted company for a second time at the end of a training session and having to walk in the rain to catch my bus home. Now the circles gone around again, me and Wealdstone are back together again I now help to coach one of the junior teams and my son Daniel who I had taken to watch Wealdstone aged six plays.

Its strange how things come around again he now plays for the juniors and we watch the senior team just as me and my old man did. Those days at Lower Mead will remain forever, that was the best pitch I have ever played on, I was lucky to play with and against some very good players and to have met and befriended one of my hero's. Viv Evans a flying winger who was totally committed and a winner. I hold nothing against him for saying "Sorry son we don't want you" but I thank him for the chance he gave me in the first place.

It's strange but as I get to the bottom of the second glass of Chianti and my mind wanders back to Tesco's I can just imaging that failed back pass to the Cambridge 'keeper just coming across and past the bread counter...happy days.

As the 2001 – 2002 season began, so did the preparation of all the required documentation for the Football Foundation and New Opportunities Fund applications. It eventually reached over 400 pages of detailed documentation, examining the past as well as the present and future of the club.

It was to be the most detailed examination of every area of the project from demographics and potential users to viability and cost.

The season on the field started brightly. With a number of new players and a young feel to the side, again brought about by budget cuts as the club preserved its dwindling funds, initial results were good. Six wins in the first nine games showed the ability within the side but a lack of experience and injuries were the reason for the three defeats.

It was eleven league games before the side won in the league again, and this became part of the worst run in club history as the side managed only one win in 23 league matches, breaking the record set a few years previously.

It was a strange season all round as there was to be no relegation. It meant that the club could try and preserve as much money as possible for the future while trying to maintain a level of performance that would give hope and develop the younger players, but for a very long winter, it didn't work.

The win in the ninth game against Uxbridge was against the odds as 'Stones fought a rearguard action for 90 minutes, yet it was followed by one of the best performances of the season, away to Aylesbury, where they were unlucky to draw 2-2 as the home side scored a 90th minute equaliser.

From then, October 9th, it was December 15 at Bromley that the next league win was recorded and then March 9th, at home to league leaders Aylesbury when they won again.

In a match that they were expected to lose, 'Stones battled hard hassled for 90 minutes to a deserved three points. Another stoic performance in the next match against fourth placed Bognor also saw a 'Stones victory and a spirit return to the side.

With planning to detailed design stage ongoing, the first pictures and a model of the proposed new ground were shown at the AGM.

A new style and a larger premises split in to three distinct areas, one for the Health Club and swimming pool, one for the Football Club and the third to support all of the outside pitches and services.

The funding application was presented to the Football Foundation for their funding in February, and this was closely followed by an application to the New Opportunities Fund for a smaller amount relating to other services on the site.

For the remaining three months of the season there were a number of meetings, discussions and revised submissions in response to questions from both funds relation to the project proposals.

Nick Woolford
Supporter since 1966

I have one lasting memory of two particular players.

My abiding memory of them is an off the pitch one. I went to an England International at Wembley wearing my Blue & White quartered shirt.

*The Wembley surrounds were heaving with people trying to buy posters/scarfs/etc. Standing in the queue for programmes I was scared shitless by this scream of "Wealdstone t*sser! We're gonna get you!" And there were Paul Lamb and Lee Walker screaming in my ear and laughing their socks off!*

On the field there was little change as results continued to be poor as the season drew to a close. The only highlights a fortunate win at Uxbridge in the Middlesex Charity Cup semi-final, and a few days later, a win in the final league game of the season.

Off the field, there were also some indications of progress towards the final funding decision in early May, but these had to remain within the board as any public discussion of the progress could not only have been detrimental, but it may have highlighted areas that objectors could try to use to their advantage.

It meant that May 2002 was to become a very important month in the history of the club.

The Charity Cup Final was scheduled for Thursday 10th May, against Enfield Town FC, formed as a breakaway from old rival Enfield. It was hoped that by this day, the board of Wealdstone FC would be able to share some of the information they had already received about the Foundation application.

On May 2nd, the club had found out verbally that the application had been successful, but were not allowed to publicise or discuss it, even with the fans.

They were told in no uncertain terms that should the information 'leak out' in advance of the publicity from the Foundation themselves, the decision could be reversed. It meant a period on tenterhooks for the members of the board.

On Sunday 4th May, SFC Wealdstone, the team founded by supporters of Wealdstone FC in 1978 also took part in their Middlesex Cup Final, winning the Junior Trophy with a 2–0 victory over Apex Bulldogs at Yeading FC.

It was the first cup the team had ever won, and it was hoped that this would be the start of a hat-trick of wins to celebrate the start of a new era for Wealdstone FC.

Thursday 9th May saw the Wealdstone side complete their season in the Middlesex Charity Cup Final at Brook House FC, against Enfield Town.

They could not follow on from where the supporters team had left off however. Despite dominating the match for long periods, 'Stones eventually lost on penalties, the match having finished 1-1 after extra time.

On Friday 10th May, the U19 PASE team competed in the PASE National Cup Final – a tremendous achievement for the side, marshalled well by former 'Stones player Francis Joseph. He too had started his career in the 'Stones youth team, before going on to play professionally.

'Stones had started brightly to take a 2-0 lead but injuries and a sending off disrupted the side, and they were eventually to lose 3–2.

Five of the squad from the PASE final had been involved in the Middlesex Charity Cup Final on the previous evening. It was a young 'Stones side, and despite the defeats, it showed promise for the future.

The summer brought the final decisions on the funding for the Prince Edward Playing Field project that was key to the future of the club.

The Football Foundation confirmed that their grant would be £800,000.

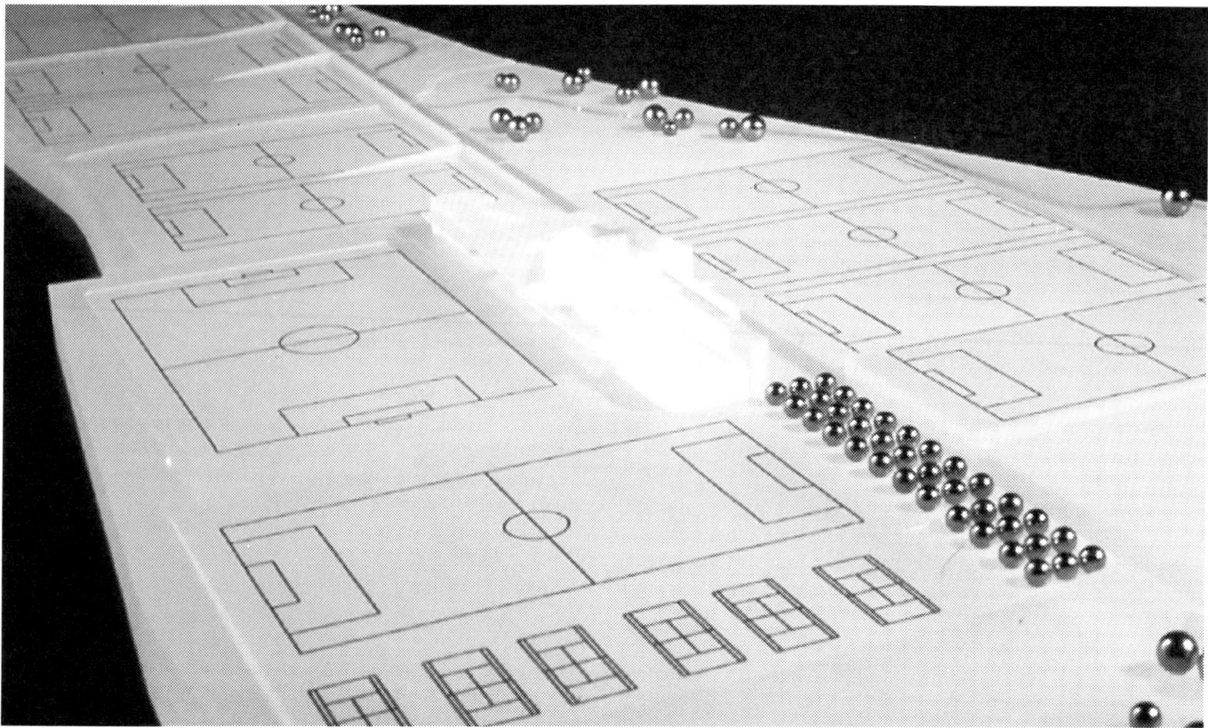

A photograph of the architects model of the new Prince Edward Playing Field Stadium and buildings.

The New Opportunities Fund confirmed a grant of £500,000.

The Stadia Improvement Fund confirmed a grant of £250,000.

With the John Lyon Trust and other grants, the loan detail agreed with the Bank Of Scotland, the legal agreements could finally be put in place. Hopefully by the time you are reading this, the new ground will be well under way.

Howard Krais
Former Supporters Club Chairman and current Director

I have no doubt that the supporters of Wealdstone FC are a class apart. In traveling to over 250 other grounds, I have never come across a group of people anything like so passionate and dedicated that the followers of Wealdstone are The passion is infectious and there are so many examples of Wealdstone supporters going over and beyond "the call of duty".

To represent and lead the Official body of Wealdstone supporters is a position not taken lightly and it was one that gave a great amount of pride and satisfaction, as does my present role on the board.

Given the adversities which have befallen the club over the last ten or twelve years, starting from the 'sale' of Lower Mead.

The Supporters Club was the only body to make a concerted public stand against the board, and right up until the present day it is simply a wonder that our club has not gone to the wall.

There have been plenty of opportunities for this to happen, but so often, when both barrels of a shotgun have been pointed squarely at us, it is the supporters who continually respond with fantastic contributions.

And when there is success on the field to celebrate, seeing the joy and pride which runs through the whole club makes it worthwhile.

I have often thought that if the definitive history of Wealdstone FC were ever written and submitted to a publisher it would be returned as being simply impossible. Yet we fight on, on and off the field.

One of the by-products of the constant turmoil has been that in reality it is the fans who run the club. Each member of the Board was and is a supporter, the Supporters Club remains strong and a crucially independent voice within the club.

Fortunately these days most people at the club are pulling in the same direction so there is little need for the Supporters Club to do anything other than support the club, especially financially.

Sportsman's Dinners and a multitude of other events help raise crucial moneys and donations continue to run at record levels.

Helping to pan and organise some of these events and activities, and having some say in the future direction of the club is as source of great pride.

The main ambition however remains playing some part (however small) in ensuring the club has a future which is secure in terms of ground and finance.

When that is all settled, perhaps it will be time to let others play their part, however with Wealdstone Football Club, no doubt there are only another 2500 crises to happen before that day.......

Mick Fishman
Supporter since 1963

It is always tempting to recount great games, famous victories or favourite players, but supporting a non-league club is more than that, and supporting Wealdstone is even more.

I would offer the view that there is no supporter in football more passionate about his or her club than one who supports Wealdstone. No supporter is more loyal. Results matter. Success Matters. In that, we are like those that follow the very biggest of full time pro clubs, but we also enjoy the moments of humour. We have a keen sense of the absurd. In that, we are like the supporters of the very smallest non-league sides. We may not be unique but we are as near as damn it.

Lots of players have captured my imagination and there have also been 16 or so managers in 'my time' – only five of those have actually delivered, Vin Burgess under whom we won the Amateur Cup in 1966, Sid Prosser who put together the 1973/74 Southern league Championship side, Allen Batsford who compiled the 1981/82 Southern league Champions, the team that was to form the basis of Brian Hall's Double Winners, and Gordon Bartlett.

Given the different circumstances under which each has had to operate (standard of players, resources available, training facilities etc) I think Gordon just about comes out on top.

There have been numerous players that have made an impression, some good and some inevitably bad and some OPPONENTS! I realise that Harrow Borough have become THE local rivals, but pre 1980 it was Enfield. They were both arrogant and good and they invariably beat us. Hendon were a great side in the sixties, but I cannot recall disliking David Hyde or Jimmy Quail. Maybe that is because, as good as they were we beat them as often as they defeated us.

And of course Hendon did not employ Alf D'Arcy. Around thirty years after I last saw Alf play, he still raises the heckles. An excellent, cool defender, he was the most cynical footballer it has ever been my privilege to see.

A back four of Tardelli, Gentile, Scheitlecker and D'Arcy would have been a dream come true! I hated Alf. I really hated him. My word did I hate him. GREAT PLAYER!!

Some of the other E's players who still make me see red are John Connell (when he wasn't playing for us of course), Roger Day, Ken Gray, Ron Howell, Tony Bass (scored four in one game against us) and many, many members of the loathsome McClusky sides – Steve 'Fatty' King, Noel Ashford, Nicky Ironton, Dave Howell – the list goes on and on.

There are a number of others worthy of a mention too – Anny Ianone, Reg Leather, Kim Casey, Kevin Millet – some of these are names that will mean nothing to many people, but to those who remember.........

As I suggested, supporting a non-league club is more than just the great moments. Equally memorable are the moments of high comedy. I recall the play being held up at Leighton Town in 1970 as players scrambled around the pitch looking for one of Rob Williams' contact lenses

There was a fifty yard own goal at Hillingdon Borough in the seventies, the Wainwright / Iannone scraps and Hughie Dowe. Just Hughie Dowe. There was an amazing swallow dive by goalkeeper Ray Bullen against, I think, Bath City.

As the ball was half cleared from a corner, Ray came rushing from his line, leapt into the air while describing a foetal position, fists clenched, eyes closed, and as the ball dropped to earth Ray passed it by while on the way up. As the ball bounced, he passed it again when on the way down.

The pain in the ribs from laughing was appalling. All great stuff.

The standard and level of abuse in non-league, apart from unfortunate degeneration into thoughtless expletives, is truly magnificent. When though out properly, presented well and times to perfection it invariably elicits a response from players, whether it's anger, confusion or amusement.

Stuart Pearce, Vince Jones and mascot, Nottingham Forest and Wealdstone fan, Iain Devenish.

Several examples spring to mind, most from my friend, super wit and director Nick Symmons. There was a match at Lower Mead against loathed rivals Enfield in the mid 80's. Two 'Stones players lay prostrate on the pitch. While Arnie Reed attended to one, Dave Jones, the Enfield physio (who was by the way blessed with one of the largest noses I have ever seen) very kindly treated our other injured player.

When finished he gathered his things and ran off the pitch towards the High Mead terrace where he was greeted by "Stop peeing about mate and take your mask off" and "Halloween seems to have come early" He then ran a gauntlet of abuse as he made his way past the Elmslie Stand and the terraces on the other side. Very cruel but at the time very funny.

The thread of appalling humour runs up to the present day – who could forget Tony Platt asking the Buckingham No 7 "who scares the birds off the fields while you're playing football, mate?" or Nick again, asking a coloured goalkeeper with a peroxide blonde (aka David James) hairstyle "Are you a natural blonde?"

The existence of Long Ball Down The Middle and The Elmslie Ender since the mid 70's – way before many other irreverent fanzines is testimony both to the passion and the love of humour that sit side by side within the club.

My small contribution to this, in combination with Steve Paull, Nick Symmons and Terry Stern was the Sausage of the season award under the nom de plume The Four Skinless Bangers. We also designed the Board Game "Away Match" for one edition of Long Ball Down The Middle.

Ridiculous and totally unplayable, but it was good fun.

One final moment of humour – an away match at Dunstable and a 'home' player was being treated on the pitch for an injury, when one bright spark – Paul Fingers Fruin I think – spotted a wheelbarrow. He collected it and strolled onto the pitch towards the injured player as if to cart him off. Very quick thinking and visually very funny.

I am proud to be a 'Stones devotee, but I didn't choose them, they chose me. My brother took me to Spurs. It was quite enjoyable. My Uncle took me to Arsenal once or twice. Very pleasant. Then my brother Barrie took me to Lower Mead to see a match against Sutton. As soon as I walked in I recognised, even as a ten year old, that I had found my spiritual home.

I have made arrangements for my death. I have asked Nick and Spaull and others to place my corpse in a coffin with a Perspex window at eye level so that I can be propped up level with the penalty area at whichever end Wealdstone are attacking.

A taped recording of me hurling abuse would offer completeness.

Appendix 1

First Team League Tables

1898 - 2002

This section includes all of the league tables for Wealdstone FC since it first entered league football in 1898.

The exceptions to this are quasi-reserve leagues such as the various Midweek leagues and the Capital League. These fixtures are recorded in Appendix 3.

In some early instances, it has not been possible to obtain final league tables, so the latest available table has been included with any other known information.

Willesden & District League 14/04/1899	P	W	L	D	F	A	Pts
Hyde & Kingsbury	12	9	1	2	33	11	20
Willesden Green Reserves	10	8	1	1	22	11	17
Roxeth Reserves	11	6	2	3	21	21	15
Willesden Town	11	3	3	5	38	15	11
Wealdstone Albion	11	5	6	0	21	19	10
Kensal Albion	11	1	10	0	5	23	2
East Acton Athletic	10	0	9	1	3	43	1
** Stonebridge withdrew from League, record expunged							

Willesden & District League 07/04/1900	P	W	D	L	F	A	Pts
Brigade Institute	15	11	3	1	48	19	25
Roundwood Rangers	13	9	3	1	47	14	21
Wealdstone	**14**	**8**	**3**	**3**	**41**	**20**	**19**
Metropolitan Railway	13	6	4	3	20	24	16
Harlesden Primrose	11	5	2	5	**21**	14	12
Roundwood Swifts	11	5	1	5	20	10	11
Queens Park Rovers	12	3	1	8	4	14	7
Stanmore	13	2	0	11	11	40	4
Queens Park Congress	15	1	1	13	5	57	3

Willesden & District League 1900 - 1901	P	W	D	L	F	A	Pts
Brigade Institute	18	14	2	2	54	17	28
Wembley	18	13	1	4	49	16	27*
Harrow Weald	18	12	3	3	37	14	27*
Shepherds Bush	18	10	1	7	37	30	21
Roundwood Rangers	17	6	4	7	33	32	16
Wealdstone	**18**	**5**	**4**	**9**	**16**	**37**	**14**
Ealing St Johns	18	5	3	10	30	35	13
Haven Green	18	5	2	11	21	40	12
Northwood	18	3	4	11	15	35	10
Willesden Highfield	17	3	2	12	19	59	8
* Harrow Weald lost Play Off 3 - 0 to Wembley for 2nd Place							

Willesden & District League 1901 - 1902	P	W	D	L	F	A	Pts
Brigade Old Boys	20	18	1	1	80	13	37
Harrow Weald	20	14	4	2	73	13	32
Wealdstone	**20**	**13**	**5**	**2**	**41**	**17**	**31**
Kensal Rise Athletic	20	12	1	7	43	46	25
Willesden Green United	20	9	2	9	43	25	20
Willesden Highfield	20	9	2	9	31	44	20
Ealing St Johns	20	6	6	8	33	27	18
Shepherds Bush	20	6	2	12	23	49	14
Neasden Reserves	20	4	3	13	20	76	11
Wembley	20	2	2	16	16	48	6
Metropolitan Electric	20	1	4	15	14	57	6

Willesden & District League 11/04/1903	P	W	D	L	F	A	Pts
Brigade Old Boys	13	11	2	0	51	5	24
Pinner	16	8	3	5	49	37	19
Wealdstone	**15**	**7**	**4**	**4**	**36**	**14**	**18**
Allens Athletic	16	8	2	6	38	35	18
Willesden Highfield	15	7	1	7	30	39	15
Clare Hampstead	16	6	3	7	30	31	15
Stanmore	16	5	4	7	21	30	14
Ealing St Johns	15	3	4	8	20	45	10
Great Western Railway	16	2	1	13	14	53	5

Willesden & District League 25/03/1904	P	W	D	L	F	A	Pts
Wealdstone	**12**	**10**	**0**	**2**	**36**	**5**	**20**
Pinner	13	9	2	2	31	16	20
Willedsen Oakdene	12	8	1	3	34	17	17
Willesden Invicta	10	8	0	2	26	9	16
Stanmore	12	6	1	5	17	18	13
Ealing St Johns	11	2	1	8	13	32	5
Clare Hampstead	9	1	2	6	5	17	4
Allens Athletic	12	1	1	10	17	45	3
Benjamin Brothers	11	1	0	10	9	32	0*
* Two points deducted for ineligible player							
Willesden Invicta eventually won the League and it seems Wealdstone finished the season as Runner Up							

Willesden & District League 1904 - 1905	P	W	D	L	F	A	Pts
Wealdstone	**10**	**7**	**1**	**2**	**20**	**11**	**15**
Ealing St John's	10	6	2	2	28	19	14
Harrow United Reserves	10	5	1	4	19	20	11
Stanmore	10	4	2	4	11	21	10
Kilburn	10	3	3	4	20	15	9
Clare Hampstead	10	0	1	9	10	19	1
Wealdstone won their first Championship.							

Willesden & District Division 1 07/04/06	P	W	D	L	F	A	Pts
Kilburn	16	11	3	2	49	15	25
Hyde & Kingsbury	12	8	2	2	53	38	18
Old Lyonians	16	8	2	6	51	38	18
Wealdstone Church Athletic	**15**	**7**	**3**	**5**	**36**	**23**	**17**
Ealing St John's	12	7	2	3	29	23	16
Stanmore	16	5	3	8	43	35	13
Allen's Athletic	13	3	2	8	10	28	8
Victoria Halls	14	2	4	8	13	40	8
Hampton United	16	3	1	12	13	63	7
Hyde & Kingsbury won their last four matches to win the League.							

Willesden & District Division 1 1906 - 1907 23/02/07	P	W	D	L	F	A	Pts
Mayfield Rovers	11	7	2	2	36	20	16
Wealdstone Church Athletic	**12**	**6**	**3**	**3**	**32**	**17**	**15**
Hyde & Kingsbury	8	5	2	1	35	16	12
Kilburn	7	6	0	1	17	6	12
Stanmore	10	3	5	2	10	17	11
Old Lyonians	8	4	2	2	23	12	10
Ealing St John's	12	4	1	7	25	28	9
Board of Education	11	2	3	6	25	38	7
Sudbury Institute	9	1	4	4	7	17	6
Allen's Athletic	10	0	0	10	11	50	0
Wealdstone Church Athletic finished in 4th place at the end of the season.							

Willesden & District Division 1 1907 - 1908	P	W	D	L	F	A	Pts
Kilburn	16	13	1	2	60	13	27
Hyde & Kingsbury	16	10	1	5	39	17	21
Ridge Athletic	16	10	1	5	25	18	21
Mayfield Rovers	16	9	3	4	30	23	21
Wealdstone Church Athletic	**16**	**8**	**2**	**6**	**22**	**22**	**18**
Old Lyonians	16	7	3	6	40	19	17
Pinner	16	7	1	8	23	20	15
Stanmore	16	1	0	15	4	34	2
Allen's Athletic	16	1	0	15	5	77	2

Willesden & District Division 1 1908 - 1909	P	W	D	L	F	A	Pts
Hyde & Kingsbury	20	15	2	3	54	28	30 *
Old Lyonians	20	12	5	3	56	23	29
Kilburn	20	13	0	7	40	23	26
Mayfield Rovers	20	12	2	6	38	39	26
Wealdstone	**20**	**9**	**4**	**7**	**25**	**28**	**22**
Pinner	20	5	5	10	24	30	15
Harrow Association	20	6	3	11	24	46	15
MHC United	20	6	2	12	17	22	14
St Gabriels	20	5	4	11	15	34	14
Northwood	20	4	6	10	37	41	14
Hampstead Corporation	20	2	3	12	29	41	13
* 2 points deducted - inelligible player							

Willesden & District Division 1 1909 - 1910	P	W	D	L	F	A	Pts
Lotus	10	8	1	1	29	5	17
Kilburn	10	6	2	2	28	12	14
Hyde & Kingsbury	10	5	2	3	30	20	12
Wealdstone	**10**	**5**	**0**	**5**	**18**	**17**	**10**
MHC United	10	2	1	7	5	21	5
West Hampstead Reserves	10	1	0	9	6	39	2

Willesden & District Premier Division 18/04/1911							
	P	W	D	L	F	A	Pts
Pinner	10	6	3	1	21	8	15
Wealdstone	**10**	**6**	**2**	**2**	**24**	**5**	**14**
Hampstead Town	9	6	0	3	23	13	12
Hyde & Kingsbury	10	5	2	3	23	14	12
Kilburn	9	1	1	7	3	32	3
MHC United	10	1	0	9	13	35	2

Willesden & District Premier Division 1911 - 1912							
	P	W	D	L	F	A	Pts
Hampstead Town	9	6	2	1	27	6	14
Deerfield Social	9	5	2	2	14	5	12
Hyde & Kingsbury	8	3	2	3	12	13	8
Kilburn	8	2	0	6	7	13	4
Hendon Town	8	2	0	6	5	28	4
Wealdstone	**1**	**1**	**0**	**0**	**2**	**0**	**2**

Wealdstone withdrew from the League unable to complete their fixtures.
Top two played a decider won 1 - 0 by Hampstead Town

London League Division 2 1911 - 1912							
	P	W	D	L	F	A	Pts
Ilford	12	9	0	3	33	12	18
Wealdstone	**12**	**7**	**2**	**3**	**39**	**15**	**16**
West Norwood	12	7	2	3	23	21	16
Hampstead Town	11*	6	0	5	23	21	12
Braleys Ironworks	12	5	0	7	21	30	10
Nunhead	12	2	2	8	15	35	6
West London Old Boys	11*	2	0	9	14	34	4

* Final game remained unplayed.

Willesden & District Premier Division 08/03/1913							
	P	W	L	D	F	A	Pts
Wealdstone	**13**	**10**	**2**	**1**	**52**	**10**	**22**
L & NW Railway AC	11	8	0	3	37	13	16
Willesden Green	11	6	2	3	29	23	14
Harrow Weald	12	5	1	6	32	33	11
St Gabriels	11	4	1	6	22	27	9
St Marylebone Institute	11	3	1	7	21	38	7
Paddington Technical Institiute	11	3	1	7	17	31	7
Neasden Hotspur	12	3	0	9	16	52	6

London League Division 2 1912 - 1913							
	P	W	D	L	F	A	Pts
Wealdstone	**12**	**9**	**1**	**2**	**37**	**11**	**19**
Braleys Ironworks	12	9	0	3	16	10	18
West Norwood	12	6	4	2	22	13	16
Custom House Reserves	12	7	0	5	24	23	14
West London Old Boys	12	3	3	6	17	19	9
Fulham St Andrews Reserves	12	3	1	8	14	26	7
Tufnell Park	12	0	n	9	10	38	3

London League Division 1 1913 - 1914							
	P	W	D	L	F	A	Pts
West London Old Boys	14	11	3	0	38	8	25
Charlton Athletic Reserves	14	12	1	1	42	10	25
Wealdstone	**14**	**6**	**2**	**6**	**30**	**30**	**14**
Barking Reserves	14	6	2	6	30	31	14
Hampstead Town Reserves	14	4	2	8	24	26	10
Tufnell Park	14	5	0	9	27	44	10
Custom House Reserves	14	4	1	9	30	46	9
Ilford	14	1	3	10	14	40	5

Middlesex & District League 1913 - 1914							
	P	W	D	L	F	A	Pts
Bronze Athletic	12	8	3	1	30	8	19
Hampstead Town	12	9	0	3	33	15	18
Wealdstone	**12**	**6**	**2**	**4**	**21**	**12**	**14**
2nd Scots Guards	12	4	4	4	24	21	12
Page Green Old Boys	12	5	1	6	19	17	11
Liberty	12	4	2	6	29	31	10
East Ham	12	0	0	12	7	67	0

Willesden & District Premier Division 10/04/1914							
	P	W	L	D	F	A	Pts
St Gabriels	8	6	2	0	19	9	12
Hyde & Kingsbury	6	5	1	0	11	6	10
Wealdstone	**8**	**3**	**4**	**1**	**8**	**10**	**7**
St John's Hendon	8	2	5	1	9	16	5
Wembley Institute	4	1	1	2	7	5	4
Mapleleaf	7	1	5	1	12	16	3

Season 1914 - 1915 saw the outbeak of War and all football was suspended until the leagues reformed in 1919 - 1920

Middlesex & District League 1919 - 1920							
	P	W	D	L	F	A	Pts
Gnome Athletic	16	13	2	1	62	10	28
Handley Page	16	11	0	5	73	26	22
Wealdstone	**16**	**7**	**4**	**5**	**35**	**28**	**18**
Enfield	16	7	4	5	31	25	18
Chiswick Town	16	7	3	6	32	41	17
Leyton	16	5	3	8	12	28	13
Islington Town	16	5	0	11	23	44	10
Hammersmith	16	4	2	10	25	53	10
Polytechnic	16	2	4	10	19	58	8

London League Division 1 1919 - 1920							
	P	W	D	L	F	A	Pts
London Generals	16	13	1	2	57	17	27
Harrow Weald	16	11	1	4	57	17	23
Sterling Athletic	16	11	0	5	54	14	22
Wealdstone (Reserves)	**16**	**9**	**2**	**5**	**41**	**18**	**20**
Grays Athletic Reserves	16	10	0	6	42	24	20
Charlton Athletic Reserves	16	6	3	7	28	34	15
Catford Southend Reserves	16	5	1	10	26	44	11
Pearl Assurance	16	2	0	14	15	92	4
Great Northern Railway	16	1	0	15	14	74	2

Middlesex & District League 1920 - 1921							
	P	W	D	L	F	A	Pts
Wealdstone	**22**	**16**	**3**	**3**	**57**	**23**	**35**
Gnome Athletic	22	17	0	5	70	27	34
Hyde & Kingsbury	22	14	2	6	74	39	30
Hertford Town	22	15	0	7	59	34	30
R A F Uxbridge	22	14	2	6	57	34	30
Luton Amateurs	22	11	3	8	53	34	25
Old Lyonians	22	11	1	10	52	45	23
Leyton	22	8	3	11	42	57	19
Hammersmith	22	6	0	16	36	43	12
Willesden Town	22	5	2	15	30	63	12
1st Coldstream Guards	22	3	3	16	42	87	9
Croydon South End	22	2	1	19	24	110	5

London League Division 1 1920 - 1921							
	P	W	D	L	F	A	Pts
Sterling Athletic	30	24	4	2	136	30	52
Temple Mills	30	17	7	6	81	37	41
Harrow Weald	30	17	5	8	90	49	39
Cray Wanderers	30	14	9	7	88	54	37
Catford Southend Reserves	30	16	5	9	77	50	37
Harlesden Town	30	14	5	11	74	54	33
Ordinance	30	14	3	13	64	64	31
Summerstown Reserves	30	12	6	12	47	64	30
Blackwall & Thames Ironworks	30	9	11	10	64	60	29
Hampstead Town Reserves	30	12	3	15	59	69	27
Metropolitan Railway	30	9	7	14	70	82	25
Bexley Heath Labour	30	11	2	17	59	87	24
Waterlow's	30	9	5	16	47	69	23
Old Alaysians	30	8	5	17	66	104	21
Wealdstone	**30**	**8**	**4**	**18**	**32**	**76**	**20**
Willesden Town	30	4	3	23	33	138	11

Middlesex & District League 1921 - 1922							
	P	W	D	L	F	A	Pts
Wealdstone	**18**	**13**	**2**	**3**	**36**	**18**	**28**
Luton Fricker Athletic	18	11	3	4	36	14	25
R A F Uxbridge	18	8	4	6	40	32	20
Old Lyonians	18	8	2	8	35	27	18
Luton Amateurs	18	7	4	7	34	28	18
Harrow Weald	18	8	2	8	47	39	18
Hyde & Kingsbury	18	6	3	9	23	38	15
Lensbury	18	5	2	11	27	49	12
Willesden Town	18	2	3	13	22	61	7
L & NW Railway	18	7	5	6	28	22	19

London League Division 1 1921 - 1922	P	W	D	L	F	A	Pts
Barking Town Reserves	30	25	1	4	96	29	51
Grays Athletic Reserves	30	22	4	4	95	31	48
Cray Wanderers	30	21	3	6	87	40	45
Summerstown Reserves	30	18	3	9	82	53	39
S T D Athletic	30	16	5	9	59	38	37
Cheshunt	30	15	3	12	73	53	33
Harlesden Town	30	13	6	11	62	56	32
Custom House Reserves	30	12	6	12	59	58	30
Catford Southend Reserves	30	11	5	14	57	57	27
Blackwell & Thames Ironworks	30	11	2	17	62	83	24
Wealdstone	**30**	**8**	**7**	**15**	**45**	**69**	**23**
Metropolitan Railway	30	8	5	17	51	83	21
Hampstead Town Reserves	30	7	6	17	52	68	20
Old Alaysians	30	7	6	17	65	102	20
H M SO Press	30	6	5	19	49	99	17
Transport Workers	30	4	5	21	26	101	13

Spartan League 1922 - 1923	P	W	D	L	F	A	Pts
Chesham United	26	20	3	3	106	29	43
Wealdstone	**26**	**16**	**3**	**7**	**72**	**44**	**35**
Slough	26	15	2	9	68	51	32
Maidenhead United	26	12	8	6	47	51	32
Leavesden Mental Hospital	26	13	3	10	50	40	29
G E R (Romford)	26	13	3	10	52	50	29
Walthamstow Avenue	26	11	6	9	58	51	28
Wood Green	26	11	2	13	48	68	24
Hertford Town	26	9	5	12	55	50	23
Aylesbury United	26	10	2	14	47	60	22
Old Latymerians	26	10	0	16	65	80	20
Polytechnic	26	8	4	14	35	59	20
Finchley	26	6	3	17	36	61	15
Old Lyonians	26	3	6	17	38	83	12

Spartan League 1923 - 1924	P	W	D	L	F	A	Pts
Leavesden Mental Hospital	26	21	1	3	66	14	43
G E R (Romford)	26	18	3	5	77	29	39
Slough	26	18	2	6	90	33	38
Aylesbury United	26	15	4	7	70	46	34
Wealdstone	**26**	**14**	**5**	**7**	**71**	**47**	**33**
Chesham United	26	14	1	11	68	59	29
Wood Green	26	10	3	13	67	62	23
Hertford Town	26	11	1	14	61	77	23
Polytechnic	26	11	1	14	42	57	23
Walthamstow Avenue	26	7	8	10	52	65	22
Old Lyonians	26	7	4	15	39	68	18
Maidenhead United	26	7	3	16	44	67	17
R A F Uxbridge	26	5	3	18	39	95	13
Old Latymerians	26	3	1	22	33	100	7

Spartan League 1924 - 1925	P	W	D	L	F	A	Pts
Chesham United	26	21	4	1	107	32	46
G E R (Romford)	26	17	4	5	74	37	38
Slough	26	17	1	8	90	54	35
Botwell Mission	26	13	3	10	69	42	29
Staines Lagonda	26	12	5	9	57	51	29
Walthamstow Avenue	26	11	5	10	59	64	27
R A F Uxbridge	26	11	5	10	56	73	27
Hertford Town	26	11	4	11	56	52	26
Maidenhead United	26	9	2	15	55	66	20
Wealdstone	**26**	**7**	**6**	**13**	**48**	**62**	**20**
Wood Green	26	8	4	14	53	73	20
Aylesbury United	26	8	3	15	51	79	19
Old Latymerians	26	6	3	17	37	81	15
Polytechnic	26	5	3	18	38	84	13

Spartan League 1925 - 1926	P	W	D	L	F	A	Pts
G E R (Romford)	28	21	3	4	97	47	45
Botwell Mission	28	20	3	5	109	51	43
Maidenhead United	28	19	3	6	122	64	41
Walthamstow Avenue	28	17	5	6	103	61	39
Chesham United	28	15	6	7	100	59	36
Slough	28	17	2	9	81	50	36
Wealdstone	**28**	**13**	**4**	**11**	**79**	**80**	**30**
Aylesbury United	28	13	2	11	78	86	28
Wood Green Town	28	9	7	12	62	83	25
Colchester Town	28	10	4	14	63	94	24
Staines Town	28	6	6	16	75	90	18
Polytechnic	28	6	5	17	60	98	17
Hertford Town	28	7	3	18	73	120	17
Sutton Court (Old Latymerians)	28	5	2	21	59	111	12
RAF Uxbridge	28	4	1	23	74	141	9

Spartan League 1926 - 1927	P	W	D	L	F	A	Pts
Maidenhead United	28	19	5	4	116	51	43
Chesham United	28	18	4	6	83	41	40
Slough	28	18	4	6	96	53	40
Wealdstone	**28**	**18**	**3**	**7**	**100**	**67**	**39**
Great Eatern Railway (Romford)	28	16	4	8	85	68	36
Walthamstow Avenue	28	15	5	8	97	61	35
Botwell Mission	28	14	2	12	71	57	30
Aylesbury United	28	12	5	11	79	86	29
Lyons Club	28	10	8	10	64	55	28
Staines Town	28	10	6	12	84	93	26
Colchester Town	28	10	4	14	64	74	24
Wood Green	28	6	3	19	57	92	15
Hertford Town	28	6	3	19	61	119	15
Polytechnic	28	4	6	18	54	102	14
Old Latymerians	28	1	4	23	38	130	6

Spartan League 1927 - 1928	P	W	D	L	F	A	Pts
Botwell Mission	28	22	2	4	106	46	46
Walthamstow Avenue	28	21	2	5	106	48	44
Chesham United	28	18	5	5	101	44	41
Wealdstone	**28**	**17**	**3**	**8**	**90**	**62**	**37**
Maidenhead United	28	15	4	9	103	57	34
Great Eastern Railway (Romford)	28	11	8	9	74	67	30
Staines Town	28	12	6	10	65	76	30
Aylesbury United	28	13	2	13	89	69	28
Slough	28	12	4	12	82	73	28
Lyons Club	28	11	6	11	47	58	28
Colchester Town	28	10	5	13	69	74	25
Berkhamsted Town	28	10	1	17	52	82	21
Hertford Town	28	7	4	17	52	114	18
Polytechnic	28	2	2	24	33	101	6
Wood Green	28	2	0	26	46	144	4

Athenian League 1928 - 1929	P	W	D	L	F	A	Pts
Leyton	26	19	5	2	78	33	43
Hampstead	26	16	3	7	64	39	35
Sutton United	26	13	7	6	73	50	33
Southall	26	12	5	9	66	47	29
Enfield	26	11	7	8	47	51	29
Bromley	26	11	6	9	68	63	28
Barnet	26	12	3	11	67	55	27
Wealdstone	**26**	**11**	**3**	**12**	**81**	**63**	**25**
Redhill	26	9	6	11	70	59	24
Barking Town	26	11	2	13	52	55	24
Kingstonian	26	10	1	15	61	71	21
Uxbridge Town	26	7	3	16	59	71	17
Windsor & Eton	26	5	6	15	33	94	16
Cheshunt	26	4	5	17	52	120	13

Athenian League 1929 - 1930	P	W	D	L	F	A	Pts
Walthamstow Avenue	26	19	3	4	94	39	41
Barnet	26	17	3	6	75	35	37
Leyton	26	15	7	4	58	35	37
Barking Town	26	14	3	9	66	60	31
Wealdstone	**26**	**12**	**5**	**9**	**59**	**50**	**29**
Enfield	26	11	5	10	53	50	27
Redhill	26	11	3	12	72	67	25
Sutton United	26	9	6	11	49	51	24
Uxbrdige Town	26	11	2	13	60	65	24
Bromley	26	11	1	14	65	68	23
Hampstead	26	9	5	12	46	51	23
Finchley	26	7	5	14	53	74	19
Southall	26	5	4	17	45	74	14
Cheshunt	26	4	2	20	42	118	10

Athenian League 1930 - 1931	P	W	D	L	F	A	Pts
Barnet	26	22	2	2	103	30	46
walthamstow Avenue	26	14	6	6	73	47	34
Leyton	26	15	4	7	62	44	34
Enfield	26	12	5	9	75	52	29
Wealdstone	**26**	**12**	**5**	**9**	**79**	**60**	**29**
Southall	26	13	2	11	59	51	28
Hayes	26	12	4	10	66	58	28
Hampstead	26	11	6	9	68	60	28
Bromley	26	11	4	11	57	73	26
Barking Town	26	10	5	11	69	60	25
Sutton United	26	9	4	13	45	57	22
Uxbridge Town	26	6	4	16	53	88	16
Redhill	26	5	5	16	53	89	15
Cheshunt	26	1	2	23	32	125	4

Athenian League 1931 - 32	P	W	D	L	F	A	Pts
Barnet	26	17	5	4	90	56	39
Hayes	26	16	4	6	74	56	36
Leyton	26	15	4	7	74	46	34
Hampstead	26	14	4	8	72	52	32
Barking Town	26	13	6	7	71	54	32
Wealdstone	**26**	**12**	**3**	**11**	**65**	**70**	**27**
Enfield	26	12	2	12	81	65	26
Romford	26	10	6	10	64	61	26
Sutton United	26	9	7	10	65	56	25
Wealthamstow Avenue	26	10	5	11	57	65	25
Southall	26	8	4	14	52	72	20
Redhill	26	7	3	16	59	83	17
Bromley	26	7	2	17	65	91	16
Uxbridge Town	26	4	1	21	29	97	9

Athenian League 1932 - 1933	P	W	D	L	F	A	Pts
Walthamstow Avenue	26	16	6	4	80	29	38
Hampstead	26	15	6	5	82	35	36
Barnet	26	15	4	7	74	48	34
Barking	26	14	6	6	54	48	34
Leyton	26	8	11	7	58	54	27
Sutton United	26	10	5	11	54	66	25
Romford	26	8	8	10	50	66	24
Enfield	26	10	3	13	55	51	23
Redhill	26	9	5	12	53	66	23
Wealdstone	**26**	**9**	**4**	**13**	**38**	**56**	**22**
Southall	26	7	7	12	53	75	21
Hayes	26	7	6	13	53	57	20
Uxbridge Town	26	8	3	15	46	80	19
Bromley	26	7	4	15	68	87	18

Athenian League 1933 - 1934	P	W	D	L	F	A	Pts
Walthamstow Avenue	26	20	1	5	80	34	41
Romford	26	16	4	6	61	39	36
Golders Green	26	16	2	8	80	37	34
Enfield	26	12	5	9	56	51	29
Barnet	26	13	2	11	66	55	28
Sutton United	26	12	2	12	58	56	26
Barking	26	12	2	12	59	64	26
Hayes	26	11	3	12	66	69	25
Leyton	26	10	4	12	55	60	24
Uxbridge Town	26	10	3	13	55	56	23
Southall	26	9	4	13	50	69	22
Redhill	26	9	3	14	55	71	21
Wealdstone	**26**	**5**	**6**	**15**	**54**	**78**	**16**
Bromley	26	4	5	17	42	98	13

Athenian League 1934 - 1935	P	W	D	L	F	A	Pts
Barking	26	15	5	6	57	40	35
Enfield	26	15	3	8	51	33	33
Leyton	26	13	7	6	57	39	33
Walthamstow Avenue	26	13	5	8	50	38	31
Romford	26	11	7	8	62	46	29
Golders Green	26	12	5	9	70	56	29
Bromley	26	12	4	10	44	50	28
Southall	26	10	5	11	43	57	25
Sutton United	26	10	3	13	69	63	23
Barnet	26	9	3	14	41	53	21
Hayes	26	8	5	13	45	59	21
Uxbridge Town	26	7	6	13	54	66	20
Redhill	26	7	5	14	51	69	19
Wealdstone	**26**	**5**	**7**	**14**	**47**	**72**	**17**

Athenian League 1935 - 1936	P	W	D	L	F	A	Pts
Romford	26	15	8	3	79	36	38
Bromley	26	16	5	5	52	26	37
Walthamstow Avenue	26	16	4	6	81	41	36
Enfield	26	13	6	7	49	42	32
Golders Green	26	13	5	8	73	60	31
Southall	26	13	3	10	57	60	29
Redhill	26	11	5	10	48	47	27
Leyton	26	10	6	10	45	49	26
Barking	26	8	7	11	65	48	23
Sutton United	26	9	5	12	40	61	23
Hayes	26	7	7	12	45	61	21
Barnet	26	6	3	17	53	83	15
Wealdstone	**26**	**6**	**2**	**18**	**48**	**80**	**14**
Uxbridge	26	3	6	17	45	86	12

Athenian League 1936 - 1937	P	W	D	L	F	A	Pts
Romford	26	24	1	1	102	35	49
Walthamstow Avenue	26	17	5	4	101	45	39
Wealdstone	**26**	**17**	**3**	**6**	**66**	**44**	**37**
Sutton United	26	11	5	10	47	45	27
Bromley	26	12	3	11	51	63	27
Barnet	26	11	3	12	66	82	25
Leyton	26	10	4	12	56	51	24
Redhill	26	7	9	10	56	66	23
Hayes	26	7	9	10	49	58	23
Golders Green	26	8	5	13	58	56	21
Barking	26	9	2	15	56	64	20
Southall	26	8	4	14	54	76	20
Enfield	26	8	2	16	57	68	18
Uxbridge	26	3	5	18	31	97	11

Athenian League 1937 - 1938	P	W	D	L	F	A	Pts
Walthamstow Avenue	26	19	4	3	96	32	42
Barnet	26	15	3	8	62	46	33
Romford	26	13	5	8	73	49	31
Wealdstone	**26**	**11**	**7**	**8**	**58**	**45**	**29**
Golders Green	26	11	6	9	61	56	28
Sutton United	26	10	6	10	56	63	26
Leyton	26	12	1	13	49	46	25
Bromley	26	10	4	12	38	49	24
Barking	26	8	7	11	45	55	23
Hayes	26	10	3	13	50	67	23
Redhill	26	9	4	13	44	63	22
Tooting & Mitcham	26	9	4	13	44	63	22
Enfield	26	5	8	13	38	62	18
Southall	26	7	4	15	40	75	18

Athenian League 1938 - 1939	P	W	D	L	F	A	Pts
Walthamstow Avenue	26	19	4	3	79	28	42
Romford	26	18	1	7	81	35	37
Wealdstone	**26**	**15**	**5**	**6**	**70**	**49**	**35**
Hayes	26	14	6	6	63	36	34
Barnet	26	10	5	11	62	68	25
Barking	26	11	2	13	53	48	24
Bromley	26	8	8	10	50	49	24
Golders Green	26	9	6	11	42	57	24
Leyton	26	10	3	13	44	50	23
Sutton United	26	9	4	13	45	57	22
Tooting & Mitcham	26	8	3	15	38	50	19
Southall	26	7	5	14	31	66	19
Redhill	26	6	6	14	48	83	18
Enfield	26	6	6	14	33	63	18

Season 1939 - 1940 saw the outbeak of War and the Athenian League was suspended

Herts & Middlesex League 1940 - 1941	P	W	D	L	F	A	Pts
Hitchin Town	20	17	1	2	82	27	35
Metroploitan Police	20	12	4	4	72	33	28
Wealdstone	**20**	**13**	**2**	**5**	**84**	**39**	**28**
St Albans City	20	10	1	9	63	58	21
Southall	20	9	2	9	58	58	20
Enfield	20	7	3	10	64	72	17
Slough Town	20	6	4	10	49	72	16
Golders Green	20	6	3	11	50	69	15
Barnet	20	6	3	11	41	57	15
Finchley	20	5	3	12	29	62	13
Tufnell Park	20	6	0	14	27	71	12

Herts & Middlesex League 1941 - 1942	P	W	D	L	F	A	Pts
Walthamstow Avenue	24	22	1	1	71	27	45
Barnet	24	16	3	5	66	36	35
Leyton	24	15	3	6	61	39	33
Hitchin Town	24	13	6	5	75	52	32
Southall	24	10	2	12	71	72	22
Slough Town	24	8	6	10	58	71	22
St Albans City	24	9	2	13	59	64	20
Golders Green	24	8	4	12	59	71	20
Enfield	24	8	3	13	54	60	19
Wealdstone	**24**	**9**	**1**	**14**	**58**	**68**	**19**
Finchley	24	8	3	13	56	67	19
Wood Green Town	24	5	6	13	47	67	16
Tufnell Park	24	4	2	18	37	81	10

Herts & Middlesex League 1942 - 1943	P	W	D	L	F	A	Pts
Walthamstow Avenue	22	14	5	3	71	36	33
Southall	22	15	1	6	72	36	29 *
Finchley	22	12	5	5	73	49	29
Hitchin Town	22	11	4	7	57	40	26
Golders Green	22	9	5	8	46	54	23
Tufnell Park	22	9	4	9	47	42	22
St Albans City	22	8	6	8	60	66	22
Barnet	22	8	5	9	66	51	21
Leyton	22	9	3	10	50	45	21
Slough	22	3	7	12	35	67	13
Wood Green Town	22	5	2	15	37	86	12
Wealdstone	**22**	**5**	**1**	**16**	**46**	**88**	**11**
* Southall 2 point deducted - ineligible player							

Herts & Middlesex League 1943 - 1944	P	W	D	L	F	A	Pts
Walthamstow Avenue	26	19	5	2	108	33	43
Slough United	26	16	4	6	75	41	36
Hitchin Town	26	12	8	6	58	29	32
Leyton	26	14	4	8	63	46	32
Tufnell Park	26	14	4	8	66	56	32
Finchley	26	14	3	9	77	56	31
Barnet	26	12	2	12	75	62	26
Clapton	26	9	6	11	57	59	24
Southall	26	10	3	13	56	68	23
Golders Green	26	9	4	13	47	66	22
Grays Athletic	26	8	3	15	60	74	19
Wealdstone	**26**	**7**	**5**	**14**	**62**	**84**	**19**
St Albans City	26	8	1	17	44	93	17
Wood Green Town	26	4	0	22	42	123	8

Herts & Middlesex League 1944 - 45	P	W	D	L	F	A	Pts
Walthamstow Avenue	26	21	2	3	98	32	44
Tufnell PArk	26	18	1	7	79	45	37
Slough United	26	16	3	7	63	49	35
Southall	26	16	2	8	78	58	34
Barnet	26	15	2	9	84	52	32
Finchley	26	14	3	9	70	59	31
Hitchin Town	26	12	5	9	63	46	29
Golders Green	26	10	4	12	58	59	24
Leyton	26	10	3	13	63	64	23
Clapton	26	10	2	14	83	73	22
Grays Athletic	26	9	3	14	71	84	21
Wealdstone	**26**	**6**	**4**	**16**	**46**	**82**	**16**
St Albans City	26	6	0	20	45	97	12
Wood Green Town	26	2	0	24	42	143	4

Athenian League 1945 - 1946	P	W	D	L	F	A	Pts
Sutton United	26	17	6	3	100	44	40
Leyton	26	17	5	4	80	35	39
Tooting & Mitcham	26	17	2	7	103	53	36
Hayes	26	16	4	6	68	45	36
Bromley	26	16	1	9	92	55	33
Wealdstone	**26**	**10**	**9**	**7**	**64**	**55**	**29**
Southall	26	12	3	11	62	60	27
Barnet	26	10	5	11	73	70	25
Finchley	26	8	6	12	59	71	22
Hitchin Town	26	10	1	15	61	68	21
Enfield	26	7	4	15	55	84	18
Golders Green	26	7	3	16	56	84	17
Barking	26	5	3	18	40	93	13
Redhill	26	2	4	20	39	135	8

Athenian League 1946 - 1947	P	W	D	L	F	A	Pts
Barnet	26	15	4	7	88	45	34
Sutton United	26	15	4	7	59	37	34
Bromley	26	13	4	9	79	54	30
Wealdstone	**26**	**12**	**6**	**8**	**58**	**46**	**30**
Southall	26	13	4	9	66	62	30
Hitchin Town	26	11	5	10	64	63	27
Tooting & Mitcham	26	12	3	11	72	78	27
Hendon	26	12	2	12	62	59	26
Hayes	26	11	3	12	48	63	25
Redhill	26	11	1	14	59	69	23
Finchley	26	9	4	13	59	67	22
Barking	26	8	6	12	42	52	22
Enfield	26	8	3	15	52	77	19
Leyton	26	6	3	17	36	72	15

Athenian League 1947 - 1948	P	W	D	L	F	A	Pts
Barnet	26	18	2	6	86	38	38
Hendon	26	14	5	7	45	30	33
Bromley	26	12	6	8	60	50	30
Tooting & Mitcham	26	12	4	10	46	41	28
Wealdstone	**26**	**9**	**8**	**9**	**44**	**36**	**26**
Enfield	26	10	6	10	55	60	26
Hayes	26	9	7	10	43	43	25
Sutton United	26	9	7	10	32	38	25
Leyton	26	10	5	11	48	59	25
Finchley	26	10	5	11	38	52	25
Hitchin Town	26	10	4	12	43	61	24
Redhill	26	8	5	13	32	39	21
Barking	26	6	9	11	27	37	21
Southall	26	6	5	15	37	52	17

Athenian League 1948 - 1949	P	W	D	L	F	A	Pts
Bromley	26	18	5	3	88	35	41
Hendon	26	15	7	4	55	33	37
Tooting & Mitcham	26	15	4	7	64	42	34
Wealdstone	**26**	**12**	**5**	**9**	**56**	**54**	**29**
Sutton United	26	9	8	9	32	33	26
Finchley	26	9	8	9	47	50	26
Hitchin Town	26	9	7	10	44	46	25
Hayes	26	9	7	10	48	52	25
Barnet	26	10	3	13	46	53	23
Barking	26	7	7	12	46	48	21
Redhill	26	9	2	15	51	64	20
Enfield	26	7	6	13	32	52	20
Southall	26	6	7	13	46	63	19
Leyton	26	7	4	15	37	67	18

Athenian League 1949 - 1950	P	W	D	L	F	A	Pts
Tooting & Mitcham	26	16	7	3	51	26	39
Hayes	26	15	4	7	51	29	34
Bromley	26	12	9	5	59	39	33
Barking	26	14	5	7	51	46	33
Wealdstone	**26**	**11**	**7**	**8**	**55**	**42**	**29**
Hitchin Town	26	12	5	9	44	50	29
Hendon	26	13	2	11	54	48	28
Barnet	26	10	2	14	53	56	22
Finchley	26	8	6	12	40	49	22
Southall	26	7	8	11	36	51	22
Enfield	26	8	5	13	43	47	21
Sutton United	26	9	2	15	37	48	20
Redhill	26	6	4	16	39	56	16
Leyton	26	5	6	15	29	55	16

Athenian League 1950 - 1951	P	W	D	L	F	A	Pts
Bromley	30	24	1	5	90	34	49
Walton & hersham	30	21	3	6	77	42	45
Hayes	30	17	10	3	88	38	44
Hendon	30	15	6	9	45	40	36
Sutton United	30	15	5	10	63	51	35
Redhill	30	14	7	9	56	60	35
Tooting & Mitcham	30	14	2	14	59	57	30
Barnet	30	13	3	14	82	69	29
Wealdstone	**30**	**11**	**5**	**14**	**52**	**52**	**27**
Finchley	30	12	3	15	68	82	27
Southall	30	10	6	14	41	53	26
Barking	30	10	4	16	54	65	24
Cambridge City	30	8	7	15	49	72	23
Enfield	30	8	4	18	36	64	20
Hitchin Town	30	6	6	18	47	75	18
Leyton	30	4	4	22	36	89	12

Athenian League 1951 - 1952	P	W	D	L	F	A	Pts
Wealdstone	**30**	**23**	**4**	**3**	**81**	**29**	**50**
Hendon	30	20	8	2	84	32	48
Bromley	30	15	8	7	74	53	38
Sutton United	30	15	8	7	70	53	38
Hayes	30	15	7	8	65	40	37
Southall	30	12	11	7	71	49	35
Walton & Hersham	30	14	4	12	56	51	32
Finchley	30	12	6	12	64	62	30
Redhill	30	12	6	12	55	63	30
Barking	30	11	4	15	56	86	26
Leyton	30	8	7	15	51	52	23
Barnet	30	7	8	15	53	72	22
Tooting & Mitcham	30	6	9	6	64	71	21
Cambridge City	30	6	8	15	44	70	20
Enfield	30	6	7	17	47	77	19
Hitchin Town	30	5	1	24	36	111	11

Athenian League 1952 - 1953	P	W	D	L	F	A	Pts
Hendon	26	18	6	2	68	21	42
Wealdstone	**26**	**17**	**3**	**6**	**58**	**38**	**37**
Southall	26	17	2	7	55	28	36
Tooting & mitcham	26	11	6	9	42	34	28
Leyton	26	12	4	10	59	58	28
Finchley	26	12	2	12	52	57	26
Walton & Hersham	26	11	3	12	42	36	25
Cambridge City	26	11	2	13	38	38	24
Barnet	26	10	3	13	39	46	23
Hayes	26	9	4	13	41	51	22
Hitchin Town	26	8	4	14	37	56	20
Enfield	26	7	5	14	51	65	19
Sutton United	26	7	4	15	44	60	18
Redhill	26	6	4	16	41	82	16

Athenian League 1953 - 1954	P	W	D	L	F	A	Pts
Finchley	26	17	4	5	61	37	38
Hitchin town	26	16	3	7	58	32	35
Southall	26	15	3	8	56	40	33
Tooting & Mitcham	26	12	5	9	49	35	29
Hendon	26	12	5	9	40	32	29
Hayes	26	9	10	7	49	42	28
Cambridge City	26	11	6	9	45	49	28
Sutton United	26	8	7	11	35	42	23
Redhill	26	9	4	13	44	40	22
Walton & Hersham	26	9	4	13	32	55	22
Leyton	26	9	3	14	38	56	21
Wealdstone	**26**	**8**	**4**	**14**	**51**	**60**	**20**
Barnet	26	8	4	14	36	54	20
Enfield	26	4	8	14	40	60	16

Athenian League 1954 - 1955	P	W	D	L	F	A	Pts
Tooting & Mitcham	26	15	8	3	65	32	38
Southall	26	16	5	5	64	39	37
Enfield	26	12	9	5	51	39	33
Sutton United	26	11	8	7	57	45	30
Hendon	26	8	11	7	51	45	27
Finchley	26	11	5	10	47	44	27
Hayes	26	9	7	10	47	43	25
Redhill	26	8	8	10	45	52	24
Leyton	26	10	4	12	36	47	24
Walton & Hersham	26	8	7	11	51	53	23
Barnet	26	6	11	9	39	48	23
Hitchin Town	26	6	9	11	44	60	21
Cambridge City	26	9	1	16	37	53	19
Wealdstone	**26**	**4**	**5**	**17**	**36**	**70**	**13**

Athenian League 1955 - 1956	P	W	D	L	F	A	Pts
Hendon	28	18	5	5	63	35	41
Hounslow Town	28	15	8	5	67	42	38
Enfield	28	16	5	7	60	39	37
Tooting & Mitcham	28	17	2	9	60	47	36
Redhill	28	12	5	11	45	37	29
Walton & Hersham	28	13	3	12	59	68	29
Barnet	28	11	6	11	53	58	28
Finchley	28	8	12	8	52	62	28
Southall	28	10	7	11	50	46	27
Wealdstone	**28**	**11**	**3**	**14**	**64**	**60**	**25**
Hayes	28	8	6	14	55	56	22
Sutton United	28	9	4	15	56	64	22
Leyton	28	8	6	14	46	67	22
Cambridge City	28	7	4	17	39	61	18
Hitchin Town	28	7	4	17	47	74	18

Athenian League 1956 - 1957	P	W	D	L	F	A	Pts
Hayes	28	18	4	6	73	38	40
Finchley	28	18	4	6	75	43	40
Hounslow Town	28	17	4	7	78	49	38
Hendon	28	15	4	9	85	51	34
Leyton	28	13	6	9	59	47	32
Southall	28	14	1	13	57	54	29
Enfield	28	9	9	10	46	58	27
Carshalton Athletic	28	9	8	11	53	59	26
Cambridge City	28	11	4	13	48	62	26
Hitchin Town	28	10	5	13	67	73	25
Sutton United	28	10	5	12	40	51	25
Redhill	28	7	9	17	46	65	23
Wealdstone	**28**	**10**	**1**	**17**	**61**	**69**	**21**
Walton & Hersham	28	8	3	17	43	74	19
Barnet	28	4	7	17	41	79	15

Athenian League 1957 - 1958	P	W	D	L	F	A	Pts
Sutton United	30	18	7	5	64	37	43
Maidstone United	30	19	4	7	63	45	42
Hendon	30	15	7	8	73	40	37
Barnet	30	16	5	9	78	52	37
Hounslow Town	30	16	4	10	60	55	36
Finchley	30	13	9	8	64	46	35
Hayes	30	14	3	13	76	70	31
Wealdstone	**30**	**11**	**8**	**11**	**64**	**65**	**30**
Hitchin Town	30	12	6	12	52	65	30
Southall	30	13	3	14	66	55	29
Enfield	30	10	8	12	47	49	28
Leyton	30	9	6	15	59	80	24
Carshalton Athletic	30	9	6	15	48	67	24
Redhill	30	6	7	17	53	71	19
Cambridge City	30	7	5	18	47	82	19
Walton & Hersham	30	5	6	19	45	80	16

Athenian League 1958 - 1959	P	W	D	L	F	A	Pts
Barnet	30	20	4	6	85	44	44
Wealdstone	**30**	**19**	**6**	**5**	**74**	**39**	**44**
Maidstone United	30	16	6	8	53	37	38
Hendon	30	15	6	9	69	56	36
Grays Athletic	30	11	11	8	67	52	33
Hounslow Town	30	13	7	10	62	49	33
Hayes	30	13	7	10	61	58	33
Finchley	30	13	3	14	61	70	29
Enfield	30	10	7	13	63	55	27
Sutton United	30	10	6	14	49	60	26
Carshalton Athletic	30	8	10	12	41	61	26
Southall	30	8	9	13	50	56	25
Leyton	30	10	4	16	49	65	24
Hitchin Town	30	8	8	14	37	52	24
Walton & hersham	30	9	4	17	39	61	22
Redhill	30	5	6	19	35	80	16

Athenian League 1959 - 1960	P	W	D	L	F	A	Pts
Hounslow Town	30	21	4	5	80	43	46
Barnet	30	17	9	4	79	35	43
Enfield	30	14	7	9	65	46	35
Wealdstone	**30**	**16**	**3**	**11**	**64**	**51**	**35**
Hornchurch & Upminster	30	15	5	10	56	47	35
Sutton United	30	16	1	13	66	60	33
Southall	30	12	7	11	58	49	31
Hendon	30	9	12	9	48	39	30
Hayes	30	11	7	12	52	51	29
Hitchin Town	30	11	6	13	55	57	28
Grays Athletic	30	10	5	15	59	64	25
Redhill	30	9	6	15	45	66	24
Finchley	30	8	6	16	50	69	22
Walton & Hersham	30	8	6	16	49	75	22
Leyton	30	8	5	17	39	75	21
Carshalton Athletic	30	7	7	16	37	75	21

Athenian League 1960 - 1961	P	W	D	L	F	A	Pts
Hendon	30	18	56	6	72	38	42
Wealdstone	**30**	**18**	**5**	**7**	**78**	**44**	**41**
Barnet	30	17	5	8	69	43	39
Sutton United	30	17	3	10	71	55	37
Hitchin Town	30	15	6	9	81	52	36
Enfield	30	14	6	10	76	49	34
Hounslow Town	30	16	2	12	73	66	34
Hornchurch & Upminster	30	13	6	11	65	57	32
Walton & Hersham	30	11	8	11	66	57	30
Hayes	30	13	3	14	63	65	29
Southall	30	9	11	10	48	64	29
Leyton	30	8	6	16	45	79	22
Finchley	30	9	3	18	43	81	21
Redhill	30	8	4	18	46	85	20
Grays Athletic	30	7	5	18	46	74	19
Carshalton Athletic	30	8	1	21	50	83	17

Athenian League 1961 - 1962	P	W	D	L	F	A	Pts
Enfield	30	25	2	3	97	36	52
Barnet	30	23	3	4	85	30	49
Wealdstone	**30**	**16**	**5**	**9**	**76**	**52**	**37**
Hayes	30	16	4	10	58	63	36
Walton & Hersham	30	14	6	10	70	55	34
Hitchin Town	30	15	4	11	85	71	34
Hendon	30	13	5	12	54	56	31
Grays Athletic	30	13	3	14	56	65	29
Sutton United	30	13	2	15	70	69	28
Hounslow Town	30	11	6	13	56	62	28
Finchley	30	10	7	13	49	46	27
Leyton	30	9	9	12	60	79	27
Redhill	30	7	4	19	51	75	18
Carshalton Athletic	30	6	5	19	45	71	17
Hornchurch	30	4	9	17	37	77	17
Southall	30	6	4	20	41	83	16

Athenian League 1962 - 1963	P	W	D	L	F	A	Pts
Enfield	30	26	2	2	130	28	54
Barnet	30	22	3	5	90	39	47
Wealdstone	**30**	**19**	**4**	**7**	**62**	**39**	**42**
Sutton United	30	16	4	10	75	47	36
Hitchin Town	30	16	3	11	74	61	35
Walton & Hersham	30	15	4	11	66	49	34
Hendon	30	12	5	13	60	60	29
Finchley	30	13	2	15	55	46	28
Hayes	30	13	2	15	52	62	28
Hounslow Town	30	10	7	13	49	63	27
Hornchurch	30	12	3	15	59	77	27
Southall	30	9	6	15	48	53	24
Grays Athletic	30	9	3	18	54	88	21
Carshalton Athletic	30	7	3	20	34	95	17
Leyton	30	7	2	21	34	82	16
Redhill	30	6	3	21	36	89	15

Athenian League 1963 - 1964	P	W	D	L	F	A	Pts
Barnet	26	17	4	5	82	34	38
Finchley	26	14	6	6	61	39	34
Carshalton Athletic	26	15	4	7	42	28	34
Hayes	26	9	12	5	50	39	30
Wealdstone	**26**	**12**	**5**	**9**	**54**	**47**	**29**
Dagenham	26	12	4	10	57	42	28
Walton & Hersham	26	13	2	11	52	54	28
Redhill	26	9	9	8	39	40	27
Maidenhead United	26	12	2	12	54	48	26
Hornchurch	26	7	8	11	35	49	22
Grays Athletic	26	9	4	13	27	43	22
Leyton	26	4	9	13	33	62	17
Hounslow Town	26	7	1	18	38	76	15
Southall	26	5	4	17	36	59	14

Isthmian League 1964 - 1965	P	W	D	L	F	A	Pts
Hendon	38	28	7	3	123	49	63
Enfield	38	29	5	4	98	35	63
Kingstonian	38	24	8	6	86	44	56
Leytonstone	38	24	5	9	115	62	53
Oxford City	38	20	7	11	76	50	47
St Albans City	38	18	9	11	63	43	45
Sutton United	38	17	11	10	74	57	45
Wealdstone	**38**	**19**	**6**	**13**	**93**	**68**	**44**
Bromley	38	14	11	14	71	80	39
Tooting & Mitcham United	38	15	7	16	71	66	37
Hitchin Town	38	13	9	16	71	66	35
Walthamstow Avenue	38	15	5	18	63	82	35
Wycombe Wanderers	38	13	7	18	70	85	33
Corinthian Casuals	38	13	7	18	56	77	33
Barking	38	10	8	20	58	80	28
Ilford	38	8	8	22	43	89	24
Maidstone United	38	8	6	24	49	86	22
Dulwich Hamlet	38	8	5	25	45	79	21
Clapton	38	8	3	27	43	91	19
Woking	38	7	4	24	44	113	18

Isthmian League 1965 - 1966	P	W	D	L	F	A	Pts
Leytonstone	38	27	7	4	98	33	62
Hendon	38	27	5	6	111	55	59
Enfield	38	24	8	6	104	54	56
Wycombe Wanderers	38	25	6	7	100	65	56
Kingstonian	38	24	5	9	94	55	53
Wealdstone	**38**	**20**	**6**	**12**	**90**	**64**	**46**
Maidstone United	38	19	6	13	74	61	44
St Albans City	38	19	5	14	57	56	43
Sutton United	38	17	7	14	83	72	41
Tooting & Mitcham United	38	16	7	15	65	58	39
Corinthian Casuals	38	17	5	16	74	67	39
Woking	38	12	10	16	60	83	34
Walthamstow Av.	38	12	9	17	81	75	33
Oxford City	38	10	9	19	49	72	29
Barking	38	10	7	21	51	72	27
Bromley	38	10	5	23	69	101	25
Ilford	38	7	10	21	50	84	24
Hitchin Town	38	6	8	24	57	118	20
Clapton	38	5	6	27	46	103	16
Dulwich Hamlet	38	5	5	28	30	95	15

Isthmian League 1966 - 1967	P	W	D	L	F	A	Pts
Sutton United	38	26	7	5	89	33	59
Walthamstow Avenue	38	22	12	4	89	47	56
Wycombe Wanderers	38	23	8	7	92	54	54
Enfield	38	25	2	11	87	33	52
Hendon	38	20	9	9	64	37	49
Tooting & Mitcham United	38	19	10	9	76	60	48
Leytonstone	38	19	9	10	67	38	47
St Albans City	38	16	12	10	59	45	44
Kingstonian	38	18	8	12	60	49	44
Oxford City	38	15	9	14	74	61	39
Woking	38	13	10	15	65	71	36
Wealdstone	**38**	**13**	**8**	**17**	**72**	**73**	**34**
Barking	38	11	12	15	56	61	34
Bromley	38	12	7	19	50	67	31
Clapton	38	10	8	20	49	92	28
Ilford	38	8	10	20	43	77	26
Corinthian Casuals	38	9	7	22	45	68	25
Maidstone United	38	6	10	22	43	90	22
Hitchin Town	38	8	6	24	39	89	22
Dulwich Hamlet	38	3	4	31	33	107	10

Isthmian League 1967 - 1968	P	W	D	L	F	A	Pts
Enfield	38	28	8	2	85	22	64
Sutton United	38	22	11	5	89	27	55
Hendon	38	23	6	9	90	36	52
Leytonstone	38	21	10	7	78	41	52
St Albans City	38	20	8	10	78	41	48
Walthamstow Avenue	38	19	9	10	81	64	47
Wealdstone	**38**	**19**	**8**	**11**	**80**	**45**	**46**
Tooting & Mitcham United	38	19	5	14	57	45	43
Barking	38	17	8	13	75	57	42
Oxford City	38	17	4	17	59	58	38
Kingstonian	38	14	10	14	56	61	38
Hitchin Town	38	14	9	15	61	73	37
Bromley	38	12	10	16	58	80	36
Wycombe Wanderers	38	13	5	20	73	85	31
Dulwich Hamlet	38	10	7	21	39	66	27
Clapton	38	10	7	21	51	88	27
Woking	38	8	8	22	50	90	24
Corinthian Casuals	38	7	10	21	40	80	24
Ilford	38	7	7	24	41	77	21
Maidstone United	38	3	4	31	26	131	10

Isthmian League 1968 - 1969	P	W	D	L	F	A	Pts
Enfield	38	27	7	4	103	28	61
Hitchin Town	38	23	10	5	67	41	56
Sutton United	38	22	9	7	83	29	53
Wycombe Wanderers	38	23	6	9	70	37	52
Wealdstone	**38**	**20**	**11**	**7**	**73**	**48**	**51**
Hendon	38	22	5	11	69	47	49
St Albans City	38	17	13	8	75	44	47
Barking	38	20	7	11	69	46	47
Oxford City	38	18	8	12	76	64	44
Tooting & Mitcham United	38	16	10	12	68	55	42
Leytonstone	38	18	4	16	71	53	40
Kingstonian	38	15	8	15	62	56	38
Walthamstow Avenue	38	10	10	18	47	71	30
Maidstone United	38	10	8	20	47	75	28
Clapton	38	10	7	21	52	76	27
Woking	38	8	7	23	45	77	23
Bromley	38	8	7	23	52	95	23
Dulwich Hamlet	38	6	9	23	31	77	21
Ilford	38	6	8	24	33	77	20
Corin. Casuals	38	2	4	32	23	120	8

Isthmian League 1969 - 1970	P	W	D	L	F	A	Pts
Enfield	38	27	8	3	91	26	62
Wycombe Wanderers	38	25	11	2	85	24	61
Sutton United	38	24	9	5	75	35	57
Barking	38	21	9	8	93	47	51
Hendon	38	19	12	7	77	44	50
St Albans City	38	21	8	9	69	40	50
Hitchin Town	38	19	10	9	71	40	48
Tooting & Mitcham United	38	19	5	14	88	62	43
Leytonstone	38	17	7	14	57	41	41
Wealdstone	**38**	**15**	**10**	**13**	**53**	**48**	**40**
Oxford City	38	15	7	16	61	78	37
Kingstonian	38	13	9	16	55	57	35
Ilford	38	8	15	15	42	73	35
Dulwich Hamlet	38	8	12	18	46	66	28
Woking	38	10	7	21	46	69	27
Walthamstow Avenue	38	11	5	22	52	81	27
Clapton	38	9	7	22	45	87	25
Maidstone United	38	7	8	23	48	84	22
Corinthian Casuals	38	6	3	29	30	99	15
Bromley	38	3	4	31	28	111	10

Isthmian League 1970 - 1971	P	W	D	L	F	A	Pts
Wycombe Wanderers	38	28	6	4	93	32	62
Sutton United	38	29	3	6	76	35	61
St. Albans City	38	23	10	5	87	26	56
Enfield	38	24	7	7	67	24	55
Ilford	38	21	7	10	74	51	49
Hendon	38	18	11	9	81	37	47
Barking	38	20	4	14	89	59	44
Leytonstone	38	17	10	11	68	50	44
Woking	38	18	6	14	57	50	42
Walthamstow Avenue	38	14	11	13	63	52	39
Oxford City	38	13	10	15	51	48	36
Hitchin Town	38	12	9	17	46	60	33
Wealdstone	**38**	**12**	**8**	**18**	**45**	**64**	**32**
Tooting & Mitcham United	38	11	9	18	44	66	31
Kingstonian	38	11	8	19	53	71	30
Bromley	38	10	6	22	34	77	26
Dulwich Hamlet	38	7	10	21	30	66	24
Maidstone United	38	7	6	25	42	84	20
Clapton	38	5	7	26	33	101	17
Corinthian Casuals	38	2	8	28	23	103	12

Southern League Division 1 North 1971 - 1972	P	W	D	L	F	A	Pts
Kettering Town	34	23	6	5	70	27	52
Burton Albion	34	18	13	3	58	27	49
Cheltenham Town	34	20	4	10	72	51	44
Rugby Town	34	18	7	9	52	36	43
Wellingborough Town	34	15	10	9	73	44	40
Stourbridge	34	13	14	7	59	42	40
Kings Lynn	34	14	11	9	62	45	39
Corby town	34	15	9	10	47	35	39
Ilkeston Town	34	14	11	9	44	38	39
Banbury United	34	14	5	15	54	46	33
Bury Town	34	14	5	15	47	44	33
Wealdstone	**34**	**14**	**5**	**15**	**51**	**58**	**33**
Lockheed Leamington	34	15	3	16	41	52	33
Gloucester City	34	8	8	18	46	61	24
Stevenage Athletic	34	8	8	18	41	69	24
Bletchley	34	7	7	20	36	70	21
Dunstable Town	34	5	7	22	29	75	17

Southern League Division 1 South 1972 - 1973	P	W	D	L	F	A	Pts
Maidstone United	42	25	12	5	90	38	62
Tonbridge AFC	42	26	7	9	70	44	59
Ashford Town	42	24	7	11	90	40	55
Bideford	42	19	14	9	70	43	52
Minehead	42	20	12	10	65	47	52
Gravesend & Northfleet	42	22	7	13	81	55	51
Bath City	42	18	11	13	56	54	47
Wealdstone	**42**	**16**	**12**	**14**	**81**	**61**	**44**
Bletchley Town	42	14	13	15	54	51	41
Hastings United	42	14	13	15	53	53	41
Andover	42	15	11	16	62	70	41
Canterbury City	42	14	12	16	51	59	40
Basingstoke Town	42	14	12	16	48	57	40
Crawley Town	42	14	11	17	59	76	39
Metropolitan Police	42	15	8	19	82	75	38
Bexley United	42	12	14	16	54	64	38
Trowbridge Town	42	15	8	19	65	77	38
Salisbury	42	14	10	18	49	60	38
Bognor Regis Town	42	12	9	21	41	66	33
Dorchester Town	42	10	12	20	47	73	32
Winchester City	42	7	11	24	41	79	25
Dunstable Town	42	4	10	28	38	105	18

Southern League Division 1 South 1973 - 1974	P	W	D	L	F	A	Pts
Wealdstone	**38**	**26**	**7**	**5**	**75**	**35**	**59**
Bath City	38	20	8	10	55	34	48
Waterlooville	38	16	15	7	55	38	47
Minehead	38	16	15	7	69	52	47
Bideford	38	17	12	9	61	51	46
Poole Town	38	18	9	11	67	47	45
Bexley United	38	18	7	13	50	42	43
Hastings United	38	16	9	13	45	36	41
Basingstoke Town	38	14	11	13	55	44	39
Gravesend & Northfleet	38	13	13	12	58	52	39
Bognor Regis Town	38	13	12	13	48	54	38
Ashford Town	38	14	8	16	41	42	36
Ramsgate	38	13	9	16	46	44	35
Dorchester Town	38	10	13	15	40	48	33
Canterbury City	38	9	12	17	37	46	30
Trowbridge Town	38	8	14	16	44	61	30
Salisbury	38	10	9	19	40	60	29
Metropolitan Police	38	9	11	18	37	61	29
Andover	38	11	3	24	38	70	25
Crawley Town	38	6	9	23	35	79	21

Southern League Premier Division 1974 - 1975	P	W	D	L	F	A	Pts
Wimbledon	42	25	7	10	63	33	57
Nuneaton Borough	42	23	8	11	56	37	54
Yeovil Town	42	21	9	12	64	34	51
Kettering Town	42	20	10	12	73	41	50
Burton Albion	42	18	13	11	54	48	49
Bath City	42	20	8	14	63	50	48
Margate	42	17	12	13	64	64	46
Wealdstone	**42**	**17**	**11**	**14**	**62**	**61**	**45**
Telford United	42	16	13	13	55	56	45
Chelmsford City	42	16	12	14	62	51	44
Grantham	42	16	11	15	70	62	43
Dover	42	15	13	14	43	53	43
Maidstone United	42	15	12	15	52	50	42
Atherstone Town	42	14	14	14	48	53	42
Weymouth	42	13	13	16	66	58	39
Stourbridge	42	13	12	17	56	70	38
Cambridge City	42	11	14	17	51	56	36
Tonbridge AFC	42	11	12	19	44	66	34
Romford	42	10	13	19	46	62	33
Dartford	42	9	13	20	52	70	31
Barnet	42	10	9	23	44	76	29
Guildford & Dorking United	42	10	5	27	45	82	25

Southern League Premier Division 1975 - 1976	P	W	D	L	F	A	Pts
Wimbledon	42	26	10	6	74	29	62
Yeovil Town	42	21	12	9	68	35	54
Atherstone Town	42	18	15	9	56	55	51
Maidstone United	42	17	16	9	52	39	50
Nuneaton Borough	42	16	18	8	41	33	50
Gravesend & Northfleet	42	16	18	8	49	47	50
Grantham	42	15	14	13	56	47	44
Dunstable Town *	42	17	9	16	55	43	43
Bedford Town	42	13	17	12	52	51	43
Burton Albion	42	17	9	16	52	53	43
Margate	42	15	12	15	62	60	42
Hillingdon Borough	42	13	14	15	61	54	40
Telford United	42	14	12	16	54	51	40
Chelmsford City	42	13	14	15	52	57	40
Kettering Town	42	11	17	14	48	52	39
Bath City	42	11	16	15	62	57	38
Weymouth	42	13	9	20	51	67	35
Dover	42	8	18	16	51	60	34
Wealdstone	**42**	**12**	**9**	**21**	**61**	**82**	**33**
Tonbridge AFC	42	11	11	20	45	70	33
Cambridge City	42	8	15	19	41	67	31
Stourbridge	42	10	9	23	38	72	29

* Dunstable Town were relegated. Wealdstone were reprieved.

Southern League Premier Division 1976 - 1977	P	W	D	L	F	A	Pts
Wimbledon	42	28	7	7	64	22	63
Minehead	42	23	12	7	73	39	58
Kettering Town	42	20	16	6	66	46	56
Bath City	42	20	15	7	51	30	55
Nuneaton Borough	42	20	11	11	52	35	51
Bedford Town	42	17	14	11	54	47	48
Yeovil Town	42	15	16	11	54	42	46
Dover	42	13	16	13	46	43	42
Grantham	42	14	12	16	55	50	40
Maidstone United	42	13	14	15	46	50	40
Gravesend & Northfleet	42	13	13	16	38	43	39
AP Leamington	42	12	15	15	44	53	39
Redditch United	42	12	14	16	45	54	38
Wealdstone	**42**	**13**	**12**	**17**	**54**	**66**	**38**
Hillingdon Borough	42	14	10	18	45	59	38
Atherstone Town	42	14	9	19	41	49	37
Weymouth	42	16	5	21	53	73	37
Dartford	42	13	10	19	52	57	36
Telford United	42	11	12	19	36	50	34
Chelmsford City	42	9	13	20	56	68	31
Burton Albion	42	10	10	22	41	52	30
Margate	42	9	10	23	47	85	28

Southern League Premier Division 1977 - 1978	P	W	D	L	F	A	Pts
Bath City	42	22	18	2	83	32	62
Weymouth	42	21	16	5	64	36	58
Maidstone United	42	20	11	11	59	41	51
Worcester City	42	20	11	11	67	50	51
Gravesend & Northfleet	42	19	11	12	57	42	49
Kettering Town	42	18	11	13	58	48	47
Barnet	42	18	11	13	63	58	47
Wealdstone	**42**	**16**	**14**	**12**	**54**	**48**	**46**
Telford United	42	17	11	14	52	45	45
Nuneaton Borough	42	15	14	13	38	36	44
Dartford	42	14	15	13	57	65	43
Yeovil Town	42	14	14	14	57	49	42
Hastings United	42	15	9	18	49	60	39
Cheltenham Town	42	12	14	16	43	52	38
Hillingdon Borough	42	13	9	20	45	54	35
Atherstone Town	42	10	15	17	41	56	35
Redditch United	42	15	5	22	40	55	35
AP Leamington	42	11	13	18	34	57	35
Minehead	42	11	12	19	43	48	34
Dover	42	9	13	20	41	63	31
Bedford Town	42	8	13	21	51	75	29
Grantham	42	11	6	25	40	66	28

Southern League Premier Division 1978 - 1979	P	W	D	L	F	A	Pts
Worcester City	42	27	11	4	92	33	65
Kettering Town	42	27	7	8	109	43	61
Telford United	42	22	10	10	60	39	54
Maidstone United	42	18	18	6	55	35	54
Bath City	42	17	19	6	59	41	53
Weymouth	42	18	15	9	71	51	51
AP Leamington	42	19	11	12	65	53	49
Redditch United	42	19	10	13	70	57	48
Yeovil Town	42	15	16	11	59	49	46
Witney Town	42	17	10	15	53	52	44
Nuneaton Borough	42	13	17	12	59	50	43
Gravesend & Northfleet	42	15	12	15	56	55	42
Barnet	42	16	10	16	52	64	42
Hillingdon Borough	42	12	16	14	50	41	40
Wealdstone	**42**	**12**	**12**	**18**	**51**	**59**	**36**
Atherstone Town	42	9	17	16	46	65	35
Dartford	42	10	14	18	40	56	34
Cheltenham Town	42	11	10	21	38	72	32
Margate	42	10	9	23	44	75	29
Dorchester Town	42	7	11	24	46	86	25
Hastings United	42	5	13	24	37	85	23
Bridgend Town	42	6	6	30	39	90	18

Alliance Premier League 1979 - 1980	P	W	D	L	F	A	Pts
Altrincham	38	24	8	6	79	35	56
Weymouth	38	22	10	6	73	37	54
Worcester City	38	19	11	8	53	36	49
Boston United	38	16	13	9	52	43	45
Gravesend & Northfleet	38	17	10	11	49	44	44
Maidstone United	38	16	11	11	54	37	43
Kettering Town	38	15	13	10	55	50	43
Northwich Victoria	38	16	10	12	50	38	42
Bangor City	38	14	14	10	41	46	42
Nuneaton Borough	38	13	13	12	58	44	39
Scarborough	38	12	15	11	47	38	39
Yeovil Town	38	13	10	15	46	49	36
Telford United	38	13	8	17	52	60	34
Barrow	38	14	6	18	47	55	34
Wealdstone	**38**	**9**	**15**	**14**	**42**	**54**	**33**
Bath City	38	10	12	16	43	69	32
Barnet	38	10	10	18	32	48	30
AP Leamington	38	7	11	20	32	63	25
Stafford Rangers	38	6	10	22	41	57	22
Redditch United	38	5	8	25	26	69	18

Alliance Premier League 1980 - 1981							
	P	W	D	L	F	A	Pts
Altrincham	38	23	8	7	72	41	54
Kettering Town	38	21	9	8	66	37	51
Scarborough	38	17	13	8	49	29	47
Northwich Victoria	38	17	11	10	53	40	45
Weymouth	38	19	6	13	54	40	44
Bath City	38	16	10	12	51	32	42
Maidstone United	38	16	9	13	64	53	41
Boston United	38	16	9	13	63	58	41
Barrow	38	15	8	15	50	49	38
Frickley Athletic	38	15	8	15	61	62	38
Stafford Rangers	38	11	15	12	56	56	37
Worcester City	38	14	7	17	47	54	35
Telford United	38	13	9	16	47	59	35
Yeovol Town	38	14	6	18	60	64	34
Gravesend & Northfleet	38	13	8	17	48	55	34
AP Leamington	38	10	11	17	47	66	31
Barnet	38	12	7	19	39	64	31
Nuneaton Borough	38	10	9	19	49	65	29
Wealdstone	**38**	**9**	**11**	**18**	**37**	**56**	**29**
Bangor City	38	6	12	20	35	68	24

Southern League Southern Division 1981 - 1982							
	P	W	D	L	F	A	Pts
Wealdstone	**46**	**32**	**8**	**6**	**100**	**32**	**72**
Hastings United	46	31	9	6	79	34	71
Dorchester Town	46	21	18	7	76	41	60
Gosport Borough	46	26	8	12	76	45	60
Fareham Town	46	20	14	12	58	48	54
Poole Town	46	19	15	12	92	63	53
Waterlooville	46	22	9	15	75	53	53
Welling United	46	19	13	14	70	48	51
Addlestone & Weybridge	46	17	17	12	71	53	51
Chelmsford City	46	20	11	15	64	53	51
Aylesbury United	46	19	12	15	79	61	50
Basingstoke Town	46	18	12	16	75	61	48
Dover	46	19	8	19	61	63	46
Ashford Town	46	16	14	16	52	56	46
Tonbridge AFC	46	19	7	20	62	70	45
Dunstable	46	18	8	20	63	68	44
Salisbury	46	16	10	20	64	81	41
Hounslow	46	15	11	20	59	83	41
Hillingdon Borough	46	14	10	22	46	58	28
Canterbury City	46	10	16	20	49	78	36
Crawley Town	46	9	12	25	46	81	30
Folkestone	46	10	6	30	49	101	26
Andover	46	4	11	31	39	100	19
Thanet United	46	5	7	34	37	110	17

Alliance Premier League 1982 - 1983							
	P	W	D	L	F	A	Pts
Enfield	42	25	9	8	95	48	84
Maidstone United	42	25	8	9	83	34	83
Wealdstone	**42**	**22**	**13**	**7**	**80**	**41**	**79**
Runcorn	42	22	8	12	73	53	74
Boston United	42	20	12	10	77	57	72
Telford United	42	20	11	11	69	48	71
Weymouth	42	20	10	12	63	48	70
Northwich Victoria	42	18	10	14	68	63	64
Scarborough	42	17	12	13	71	58	63
Bath City	42	17	9	16	58	55	60
Nuneaton Borough	42	15	13	14	57	60	58
Altrincham	42	15	10	17	62	56	55
Bangor City	42	14	13	15	71	77	55
Dagenham	42	12	15	15	60	65	51
Barnet	42	16	3	23	55	78	51
Frickley Athletic	42	12	13	17	66	77	49
Worcester City	42	12	10	20	58	87	46
Trowbridge Town	42	12	7	23	56	88	43
Kettering Town	42	11	7	24	69	99	40
Yeovil Town	42	11	7	24	63	99	40
Barrow	42	8	12	22	46	74	36
Stafford Rangers	42	5	14	23	40	75	29

Alliance Premier League 1983 - 1984							
	P	W	D	L	F	A	Pts
Maidstone United	42	23	13	6	71	34	70
Nuneaton Borough	42	24	11	7	70	40	69
Altrincham	42	23	9	10	64	39	65
Wealdstone	**42**	**21**	**14**	**7**	**75**	**36**	**62**
Runcorn	42	20	13	9	61	45	62
Bath City	42	17	12	13	60	48	53
Northwich Victoria	42	16	14	12	54	47	51
Worcester City	42	15	13	14	64	55	49
Barnet	42	16	10	16	55	58	49
Kidderminster Harriers	42	14	14	14	54	61	49
Telford United	42	17	11	14	50	58	49
Frickley Athletic	42	17	10	15	68	56	48
Scarborough	42	14	16	12	52	55	48
Enfield	42	14	9	19	61	58	43
Weymouth	42	13	8	21	54	65	42
Gateshead	42	12	13	17	59	73	42
Boston United	42	13	12	17	66	80	41
Dagenham	42	14	8	20	57	69	40
Kettering Town	42	12	9	21	53	67	37
Yeovil Town	42	12	8	22	55	77	35
Bangor City	42	10	6	26	54	82	29
Trowbridge Town	42	5	7	30	33	87	19

Gola League 1984 - 1985							
	P	W	D	L	F	A	Pts
Wealdstone	**42**	**20**	**10**	**12**	**64**	**54**	**62**
Nuneaton Borough	42	19	14	9	85	53	58
Dartford	42	17	13	12	57	48	57
Bath City	42	21	9	12	52	49	57
Altrincham	42	21	6	15	63	47	56
Scarborough	42	17	13	12	69	62	54
Enfield	42	17	13	12	84	61	53
Kidderminster Harriers	42	17	8	17	79	77	51
Northwich Victoria	42	16	11	15	50	46	50
Telford United	42	15	14	13	59	54	49
Frickley Athletic	42	18	7	17	65	71	49
Kettering Town	42	15	12	15	68	59	48
Maidstone United	42	15	13	14	58	51	48
Runcorn	42	13	15	14	48	47	48
Barnet	42	15	11	16	59	52	47
Weymouth	42	15	13	14	70	66	45
Boston United	42	15	10	17	69	69	45
Barrow	42	11	16	15	47	57	43
Dagenham	42	13	10	19	47	67	41
Worcester City	42	12	9	21	55	84	38
Gateshead *	42	9	12	21	51	82	33
Yeovil Town	42	6	11	25	44	87	25

* Gateshead deducted 1 point for playing an ineligible player.
2 points for a home win, 3 for an away win and 1 for a draw

Gola League 1985 - 1986							
	P	W	D	L	F	A	Pts
Enfield	42	27	10	5	94	47	76
Frickley Athletic	42	25	10	7	78	50	69
Kidderminster Harriers	42	24	7	11	99	62	67
Altrincham	42	22	11	9	70	49	63
Weymouth	42	19	15	8	75	60	61
Runcorn	42	19	14	9	70	44	60
Stafford Rangers	42	19	13	10	61	54	60
Telford United	42	18	10	14	68	66	51
Kettering Town	42	15	15	12	55	53	49
Wealdstone	**42**	**16**	**9**	**17**	**57**	**56**	**47**
Cheltenham Town	42	16	11	15	69	69	46
Bath City	42	13	11	18	53	54	45
Boston United	42	16	7	19	66	76	44
Barnet	42	13	11	18	56	60	41
Scarborough	42	13	11	18	54	66	40
Northwich Victoria	42	10	12	20	42	54	37
Maidstone United	42	9	16	17	57	66	36
Nuneaton Borough	42	13	5	24	58	73	36
Dagenham	42	10	12	20	48	66	36
Wycombe Wanderers	42	10	13	19	55	84	36
Dartford	42	8	9	25	51	82	26
Barrow	42	7	8	27	41	86	24

GM Vauxhall Conference League 1986 - 1987	P	W	D	L	F	A	Pts
Scarborough	42	27	10	5	64	33	91
Barnet	42	25	10	7	86	39	85
Maidstone United	42	21	10	11	71	48	73
Enfield	42	21	7	14	66	47	70
Altrincham	42	18	15	9	66	53	69
Boston United	42	21	6	15	82	64	69
Sutton United	42	19	11	12	81	51	68
Runcorn	42	18	13	11	71	58	67
Telford United	42	18	10	14	69	59	64
Bath City	42	17	12	13	63	62	63
Cheltenham Town	42	16	13	13	64	50	61
Kidderminster Harriers	42	17	4	21	77	81	55
Stafford Rangers	42	14	11	17	58	60	53
Weymouth	42	13	12	17	68	77	51
Dagenham	42	14	7	21	56	72	49
Kettering Town	42	12	11	19	54	66	47
Northwich Victoria	42	10	14	18	53	69	44
Nuneaton Borough	42	10	14	18	48	73	44
Wealdstone	**42**	**11**	**10**	**21**	**50**	**70**	**43**
Welling United	42	10	10	22	61	94	40
Frickley Athletic	42	7	11	24	47	82	32
Gateshead	42	6	13	23	48	95	31

GM Vauxhall Conference League 1987 - 1988	P	W	D	L	F	A	Pts
Lincoln City	42	24	10	8	86	48	82
Barnet	42	23	11	8	93	45	80
Kettering Town	42	22	9	11	68	48	75
Runcorn	42	21	11	10	68	47	74
Telford United	42	20	10	12	65	50	70
Stafford Rangers	42	20	9	13	79	58	69
Kidderminster Harriers	42	18	15	9	75	66	69
Sutton United	42	16	18	8	77	54	66
Maidstone United	42	18	9	15	79	64	63
Weymouth	42	18	9	15	53	43	63
Macclesfield Town	42	18	9	15	64	62	63
Enfield	42	15	10	17	68	78	55
Cheltenham Town	42	11	20	11	64	67	53
Altrincham	42	14	10	18	59	59	52
Fisher Athletic	42	13	13	16	58	61	52
Boston United	42	14	7	21	60	75	49
Northwich Victoria	42	10	17	15	46	57	47
Wycombe Wanderers	42	11	13	18	50	76	46
Welling United	42	11	9	22	50	72	42
Bath City	42	9	10	23	48	76	37
Wealdstone	**42**	**5**	**17**	**20**	**39**	**76**	**32**
Dagenham	42	5	6	31	37	104	21

Beazer Homes League Premier Division 1988 - 1989	P	W	D	L	F	A	Pts
Merthyr Tydfil	42	26	7	9	104	58	85
Dartford	42	25	7	10	79	33	82
VS Rugby	42	24	7	11	64	43	79
Worcester City	42	20	13	9	72	49	73
Cambridge City	42	20	10	12	72	51	70
Dover Athletic	42	19	12	11	65	47	69
Gosport Borough	42	18	12	12	73	57	66
Burton Albion	42	18	10	14	79	68	64
Bath City	42	15	13	14	66	51	58
Bromsgrove Rovers	42	14	16	12	68	56	58
Wealdstone	**42**	**16**	**10**	**16**	**60**	**53**	**58**
Crawley Town	42	14	16	12	61	56	58
Dorchester Town	42	14	16	12	56	61	58
Alvechurch	42	16	8	17	56	59	56
Moor Green	42	14	13	15	58	70	55
Corby Town	42	14	11	17	55	59	53
Waterlooville	42	13	13	16	61	63	52
Ashford Town	42	13	13	16	59	76	52
Fareham Town	42	15	6	21	43	68	51
Leicester United	42	6	11	25	46	84	29
Redditch United	42	5	7	30	36	105	22
Bedworth United	42	4	7	31	36	102	19

Beazer Homes League Premier Division 1989 - 1990	P	W	D	L	F	A	Pts
Dover Athletic	42	32	6	4	87	27	102
Bath City	42	30	8	4	81	28	98
Dartford	42	26	9	7	80	35	87
Burton Albion	42	20	12	10	64	40	72
VS Rugby	42	19	12	11	51	35	69
Atherstone United	42	19	10	13	60	52	67
Gravesend & Northfleet	42	18	12	12	44	50	66
Cambridge City	42	17	11	14	76	56	62
Gloucester City	42	17	11	14	80	68	62
Bromsgrove Rovers	42	17	10	15	56	48	61
Moor Green	42	18	7	17	62	59	61
Wealdstone	**42**	**16**	**9**	**17**	**55**	**54**	**57**
Dorchester Town	42	16	7	19	52	67	55
Worcester City *	42	15	10	17	62	63	54
Crawley Town	42	13	12	17	53	57	51
Waterlooville	42	13	10	19	63	81	49
Weymouth	42	11	13	18	50	70	46
Chelmsford City	42	11	10	21	52	72	43
Ashford Town	42	10	7	25	43	75	37
Corby Town	42	10	6	26	57	77	36
Alvechurch	42	7	5	30	46	95	26
Gosport Borough	42	6	5	31	28	93	23
* Worcester City: 1 point deducted							

Beazer Homes League Premier Division 1990 - 1991	P	W	D	L	F	A	Pts
Farnborough Town	42	26	7	9	79	43	85
Gloucester City	42	23	14	5	86	49	83
Cambridge City	42	21	14	7	63	43	77
Dover Athletic	42	21	11	10	56	37	74
Bromsgrove Rovers	42	20	11	11	68	49	71
Worcester City	42	18	12	12	55	42	66
Burton Albion	42	15	15	12	59	48	60
Halesowen Town	42	17	9	16	73	67	60
VS Rugby	42	16	11	15	56	46	59
Bashley	42	15	12	15	56	52	57
Dorchester Town	42	15	12	15	47	54	57
Wealdstone	**42**	**16**	**8**	**18**	**57**	**58**	**56**
Dartford	42	15	9	18	61	64	54
Rushden Town	42	14	11	17	64	66	53
Atherstone United	42	14	10	18	55	58	52
Moor Green	42	15	6	21	64	75	51
Poole Town	42	12	13	17	56	69	49
Chelmsford City	42	11	15	16	57	68	48
Crawley Town	42	12	12	18	45	67	48
Waterlooville	42	11	13	18	51	70	46
Gravesend & Northfleet	42	9	7	26	46	91	34
Weymouth	42	4	12	26	50	88	24

Beazer Homes League Premier Division 1991 - 1992	P	W	D	L	F	A	Pts
Bromsgrove Rovers	42	27	9	6	78	34	90
Dover Athletic	42	23	15	4	66	30	84
VS Rugby	42	23	11	8	70	44	80
Bashley	42	22	8	12	70	44	74
Cambridge City	42	18	14	10	71	53	68
Dartford	42	17	15	10	62	45	66
Trowbridge Town	42	17	10	15	69	51	61
Halesowen Town	42	15	15	12	61	49	60
Moor Green	42	15	11	16	61	59	56
Burton Albion	42	15	10	17	59	61	55
Dorchester Town	42	14	13	15	66	73	55
Gloucester City	42	15	9	18	67	70	54
Atherstone United	42	15	8	19	54	66	53
Corby Town	42	13	12	17	66	81	51
Waterlooville	42	13	11	18	43	56	50
Worcester City	42	12	13	17	56	59	49
Crawley Town	42	12	12	18	62	67	48
Chelmsford City	42	12	12	18	49	56	48
Wealdstone	**42**	**13**	**7**	**22**	**52**	**69**	**46**
Poole Town	42	10	13	19	46	77	43
Fisher Athletic	42	9	11	22	53	89	38
Gravesend & Northfleet	42	8	9	25	39	87	33

Beazer Homes League Southern Division 1992 - 1993	P	W	D	L	F	A	Pts
Sittingbourne	42	26	12	4	102	43	90
Salisbury	42	27	7	8	87	50	88
Witney Town	42	25	9	8	77	37	84
Gravesend & Northfleet	42	25	4	13	99	63	79
Havant Town	42	23	6	13	78	55	75
Sudbury Town	42	20	11	11	89	54	71
Erith & Belvedere	42	22	5	15	73	66	71
Ashford Town	42	20	8	14	91	66	68
Braintree Town	42	20	6	16	95	65	66
Margate	42	19	7	16	65	58	64
Wealdstone	**42**	**18**	**7**	**17**	**75**	**69**	**61**
Buckingham Town	42	16	11	15	61	58	59
Baldock Town	42	15	9	18	59	63	54
Poole Town	42	15	7	20	61	69	52
Fareham Town	42	14	8	20	67	65	50
Burnham	42	14	8	20	53	77	50
Canterbury City	42	12	10	20	54	76	46
Newport Isle of Wight	42	9	16	17	44	56	43
Fisher Athletic	42	8	9	25	38	98	33
Andover	42	7	9	26	42	99	30
Dunstable	42	5	14	23	42	92	29
Bury Town	42	8	5	29	46	119	29

Beazer Homes League Southern Division 1993 - 1994	P	W	D	L	F	A	Pts
Gravesend & Northfleet	42	27	11	4	87	24	92
Sudbury Town	42	27	8	7	98	47	89
Witney Town	42	27	8	7	69	36	89
Salisbury City	42	26	10	6	90	39	88
Havant Town	42	27	4	11	101	41	85
Ashford Town	42	24	13	5	93	46	85
Baldock Town	42	26	7	9	76	40	85
Newport Isle of Wight	42	22	8	12	74	51	74
Margate	42	20	8	14	76	58	68
Weymouth	42	18	9	15	71	65	63
Tonbridge AFC	42	19	5	18	59	62	62
Buckingham Town	42	14	14	14	43	42	56
Braintree Town	42	16	7	19	72	84	55
Fareham Town	42	12	12	18	54	75	48
Poole Town	42	13	6	23	54	86	45
Burnham	42	10	9	23	53	92	39
Fisher 93	42	9	10	23	52	81	37
Dunstable	42	9	7	26	50	91	34
Erith & Belvedere	42	9	5	28	40	72	32
Canterbury City	42	8	7	27	35	80	31
Wealdstone	**42**	**6**	**7**	**29**	**45**	**95**	**25**
Bury Town	42	3	5	34	36	121	14

Beazer Homes League Southern Division 1994 - 1995	P	W	D	L	F	A	Pts
Salisbury City	42	30	7	5	88	37	97
Baldock Town	42	28	10	4	92	44	94
Havant Town	42	25	10	7	81	34	85
Waterlooville	42	24	8	10	77	36	80
Ashford Town	42	21	12	9	106	72	75
Weston-super-Mare	42	18	13	11	82	54	67
Bashley	42	18	11	13	62	49	65
Weymouth	42	16	13	13	60	55	61
Newport Isle of Wight	42	17	10	15	67	67	61
Witney Town	42	14	14	14	57	57	56
Clevedon Town	42	14	13	15	73	64	55
Tonbridge Angels	42	14	12	16	74	87	54
Margate	42	15	7	20	60	72	52
Braintree Town	42	12	13	17	64	71	49
Wealdstone	**42**	**13**	**8**	**21**	**76**	**94**	**47**
Yate Town	42	11	13	18	57	75	46
Fisher 93	42	9	16	17	54	70	43

ICIS League Division 3 1995 - 1996	P	W	D	L	F	A	Pts
Horsham	40	29	5	6	95	40	92
Leighton Town	40	28	5	7	95	34	89
Windsor & Eton	40	27	6	7	117	46	87
Wealdstone	**40**	**23**	**8**	**9**	**104**	**39**	**77**
Harlow Town	40	22	10	8	85	62	76
Northwood	40	20	9	11	76	56	69
Epsom & Ewell	40	18	14	8	95	57	68
Kingsbury Town	40	15	16	9	61	48	61
East Thurrock Utd	40	17	8	15	61	50	59
Aveley	40	16	10	14	62	53	58
Wingate & Finchley	40	16	7	17	74	70	55
Lewes	40	14	7	19	56	72	49
Flackwell Heath	40	14	5	21	60	84	47
Hornchurch	40	11	8	21	55	77	41
Harefield United	40	11	7	22	49	89	40
Tring Town	40	10	8	22	40	78	38
Camberley Town	40	9	9	22	45	81	36
Hertford Town	40	10	5	25	72	103	35
Cove	40	8	10	22	37	89	34
Clapton	40	9	6	25	48	89	33
Southall	40	9	5	26	34	104	32

ICIS League Division 3 1996 - 1997	P	W	D	L	F	A	Pts
Wealdstone	**32**	**24**	**3**	**5**	**72**	**24**	**75**
Braintree Town	32	23	5	4	99	29	74
Northwood	32	18	10	4	60	31	66
Harlow Town	32	19	4	9	60	41	61
Aveley	32	17	6	9	64	39	57
East Thurrock Utd	32	16	6	10	58	51	54
Camberley Town	32	15	6	11	55	44	51
Wingate & Finchley	32	11	7	14	52	63	40
Hornchurch	32	11	6	15	35	51	39
Clapton	32	11	6	15	31	49	39
Lewes	32	10	8	14	45	53	38
Kingsbury Town	32	11	4	17	41	54	37
Hertford Town	32	10	6	16	55	65	36
Epsom & Ewell	32	8	5	19	62	78	29
Flackwell Heath	32	8	5	19	36	71	29
Tring Town	32	7	3	22	33	74	24
Southall	32	6	4	22	28	69	22

Ryman League Division 2 1997 - 1998	P	W	D	L	F	A	Pts
Canvey Island	42	30	8	4	116	41	98
Braintree Town	42	29	11	2	117	45	98
Wealdstone	**42**	**24**	**11**	**7**	**81**	**46**	**83**
Bedford Town	42	22	12	8	55	25	78
Metropolitan Police	42	21	8	13	80	65	71
Wivenhoe Town	42	18	12	12	84	66	66
Edgware Town	42	18	10	14	81	65	64
Chalfont St Peter	42	17	13	12	63	60	64
Northwood	42	17	11	14	65	69	62
Windsor & Eton	42	17	7	18	74	72	58
Tooting & Mitcham	42	16	9	17	58	56	57
Barking	42	15	12	15	62	75	57
Banstead Athletic	42	15	9	18	60	63	54
Marlow	42	16	5	21	64	78	53
Horsham	42	13	9	20	67	75	48
Bracknell Town	42	13	8	21	68	93	47
Leighton Town	42	13	6	23	45	78	45
Hungerford Town	42	11	11	20	66	77	44
Witham Town	42	9	13	20	55	68	40
Tilbury	42	9	12	21	57	88	39
Egham Town	42	9	5	28	47	101	32
Cheshunt	42	4	10	28	31	90	22

Ryman League Division 1 1998 - 1999	P	W	D	L	F	A	Pts
Canvey Island	42	28	6	8	76	41	90
Hitchin Town	42	25	10	7	75	38	85
Wealdstone	**42**	**26**	**6**	**10**	**75**	**48**	**84**
Braintree Town	42	20	10	12	75	48	70
Bognor Regis Town	42	20	8	14	63	44	68
Grays Athletic	42	19	11	12	56	42	68
Oxford City	42	16	14	12	58	51	62
Croydon	42	16	13	13	53	53	61
Chertsey Town	42	14	16	12	57	57	58
Romford	42	14	15	13	58	63	57
Maidenhead United	42	13	15	14	50	46	54
Worthing	42	13	13	16	47	61	52
Leyton Pennant	42	13	12	17	62	70	51
Uxbridge	42	13	11	18	54	51	50
Barton Rovers	42	11	15	16	43	49	48
Yeading	42	12	10	20	51	55	46
Leatherhead	42	12	9	21	48	59	45
Whyteleafe	42	13	6	23	51	72	45
Staines Town	42	10	15	17	33	57	45
Molesey	42	8	20	14	35	52	44
Wembley	42	10	10	20	36	71	40
Berkhamsted Town	42	10	7	25	53	81	37

Ryman League Division 1 1999 - 2000	P	W	D	L	F	A	Pts
Croydon	42	25	9	8	85	47	84
Grays Athletic	42	21	12	9	80	44	75
Maidenhead United	42	20	15	7	72	45	75
Thame United	42	20	13	9	61	38	73
Worthing	42	19	12	11	80	60	69
Staines Town	42	19	12	11	63	52	69
Whyteleafe	42	20	9	13	60	49	69
Bedford Town	42	17	12	13	59	52	63
Bromley	42	17	9	16	62	65	60
Uxbridge	42	15	13	14	60	44	58
Bishop's Stortford	42	16	10	16	57	62	58
Barton Rovers	42	16	8	18	64	83	56
Oxford City	42	17	4	21	57	55	55
Braintree Town	42	15	10	17	65	74	55
Yeading	42	12	18	12	53	54	54
Wealdstone	**42**	**13**	**12**	**17**	**51**	**58**	**51**
Bognor Regis Town	42	12	13	17	47	53	49
Harlow Town	42	11	13	18	62	76	46
Romford	42	12	9	21	51	70	45
Leatherhead	42	9	13	20	47	70	40
Chertsey Town	42	9	5	28	50	84	32
Leyton Pennant	42	7	9	26	34	85	30

Ryman League Division 1 2000 - 2001	P	W	D	L	F	A	Pts
Boreham Wood	42	26	7	9	82	49	85
Bedford Town	42	22	16	4	81	40	82
Braintree Town	42	25	6	11	112	60	81
Bishop's Stortford	42	24	6	12	103	76	78
Thame United	42	22	8	12	86	54	74
Ford United	42	19	12	11	70	58	69
Uxbridge	42	21	5	16	73	55	68
Northwood	42	20	8	14	89	81	68
Whyteleafe	42	20	6	16	62	69	66
Oxford City	42	16	13	13	64	49	61
Harlow Town	42	15	16	11	70	66	61
Worthing	42	16	9	17	69	69	57
Staines Town	42	16	8	18	60	66	56
Aylesbury United	42	17	4	21	65	55	55
Yeading	42	15	9	18	72	74	54
Bognor Regis Town	42	13	11	18	71	71	50
Walton & Hersham	42	14	8	20	59	80	50
Bromley	42	14	6	22	63	86	48
Wealdstone	**42**	**12**	**9**	**21**	**54**	**73**	**45**
Leatherhead	42	12	4	26	37	87	40
Romford	42	9	4	29	53	113	31
Barton Rovers	42	2	9	31	30	94	15

Ryman League Division 1 2001 - 2002	P	W	D	L	F	A	Pts
Ford United	42	27	7	8	92	56	88
Bishop's Stortford	42	26	9	7	104	51	87
Aylesbury United	42	23	10	9	96	64	79
Bognor Regis Town	42	20	13	9	74	55	73
Northwood	42	19	11	12	92	64	68
Carshalton Athletic	42	17	16	9	64	53	67
Harlow Town	42	19	9	14	77	65	66
Slough Town	42	17	11	14	68	51	62
Uxbridge	42	18	6	18	68	65	60
Oxford City	42	17	9	16	59	66	60
Thame United	42	15	14	13	75	61	59
Tooting & Mitcham United	42	16	11	15	69	70	59
Walton & Hersham	42	16	10	16	75	70	58
Yeading	42	16	10	16	84	90	55
Worthing	42	15	8	19	69	65	53
Staines Town	42	12	11	19	45	60	47
Dulwich Hamlet	42	11	13	18	64	76	46
Wealdstone	**42**	**11**	**12**	**19**	**60**	**81**	**45**
Bromley	42	10	11	21	44	74	41
Whyteleafe	42	10	11	21	46	86	41
Barking & East Ham	42	8	7	27	61	123	31
Windsor & Eton	42	7	5	30	53	93	26

Appendix 2
First Team Appearances (where known)
1887 - 2002

This section includes all of the first team fixtures, appearances and goalscorers where known.

In a number of early seasons, as the clubs were Junior clubs, it was often the case that fixtures and results were not reported although some do occasionally appear.

Up to 1898, all of the fixtures recorded are friendly matches and cup competitions, as the club did not enter a league until 1898.

Between 1898 and 1919, various leagues and cups were entered and in a number of years Wealdstone ran two sides, both of equal status, in different leagues. As many of these fixtures as could be obtained are included.

A number of friendlies were also played during the season in the early 1900's. Some of these were originally intended to be league fixtures but due to conditions or non arrival of officials etc. these were played as friendly matches. Others were not identified. To this end, a number of friendlies have been included in these lists up to 1919.

Subsequent to 1919, friendly match details are listed in Appendix 4.

1887-88
The Oaks

Date	Opponent	Result	Scorers	Hole T	Gill S	Jones H	Parker S	Matthews S	Whatmore J	Thorogood W	Norris A	Blake T	Waghorn H	Poole J	Darville H	Bindon H	Stephenson W	Browne G	Short T	Darville A	Parker W	Passmore C	Wright E	Tooms	Hughes
Friendly Matches																									
Oct-01	(h) Grosvenor	L 0-1		1	2	3	4	5	6	7	8	9	10	11											
Oct-08	(a) Harrow Rovers	L 0-8		1	3	10		5		4	6	8	9	7	2	11									
Oct-29	(a) Tavistock	L 1-3	Poole		3	8	6		5	4	9		11	10				2	1			7			
Nov-05	(h) Arrow	W 7-0	og, Matthews 4, Jones 2			8		5		4							3								
Nov-19	(a) Cogswell & Harrison	W 3-0	Waghorn 2, Norris	1	2	7		9			8		10	11	6		3	4			5				
Dec-03	(a) Cogswell & Harrison	W 1-0	Poole		9	8	4	11	6					7	5		3	2		1			10		
Dec-10	(a) Kings Langley	D 0-0				8		11				9						2							
Jan-07	(a) Watford Rovers	L 2-3	Norris, Poole	1		7	4	8			10	11		9	5									2	3
Jan-28	(h) Cogswell & Harrison	L 1-2		6	3	7		9			8		10	11	2				1	4	5				
Feb-04	(h) F G Cooper- Brown's XI	L 1-5																							

1888-89
The Oaks

Date	Opponent	Result	Scorers	Crook W	Hills H	Gill S	Starkey J	Branston R	White J	Darville H	Jones H	Cook	Norris A	Matthews S	Harding J	Darville A	Hole T	Bentley W	Hughes	Parker	White G	Gibson	Waghorne	Fazakerly H	Warden
Friendly Matches																									
Oct-20	(a) Harrow Town																								
Oct-27	(h) Tavistock	W 5-2		1	2	3	4	5	6	7	8	9	10	11											
Nov-03	(h) Watford Swifts	W 2-1	Matthews, Darville			3				7	8			11									9		
Nov-17	(a) Watford Rovers 2nd XI	L 0-1			2	3	8			9	10		11	7		4	5		1	6					
Nov-24	(a) Webb-Crawfords XI	D 1-1			2	3	11		4	9	10		8	7		1	5			6					
The Oaks (Wealdstone)																									
Friendly Matches																									
Dec-01	(h) Harrow Rovers	L 1-5	Jones		2	3		6		9	10		8	7	1	4	5	11							
Dec-15	(h) Watford Church Institute	D 0-0			2	3	7		6	9	10		8			5					1	4		11	
Jan-19	(a) Harrow Town	L 2-4			2	3			4	7	9	10				8					6	1		5	11
Mar-16	(a) Harrow Rovers	L 0-4								7	9														
Mar-30	(h) Harrow Town																								

1889-90
Wealdstone FC

Date	Opponent	Result	Scorers	Horton G	Hills H	Whitehouse E	Hughes T	Hole T	Morris A	Dickenson T	Astle G	Williamson J	Perry G	Poole J
Friendly Matches														
Oct-05	(a) Harrow Town	L 0-6												
Oct-12	(h) Victoria Halls	L 1-2												
Nov-23	(a) Harrow Colts	W 3-2												
Nov-30	(h) Harrow Colts	W 3-1		1	2	3	4	5	6	7	8	9	10	11
Dec-21	(a) Harrow Rovers	L 0-5												
Dec-28	(a) Victoria Halls	L 1-2												
Feb-01	(h) Harrow Town	L 1-2												

1890-91
Wealdstone FC

Date	Opponent	Result	Scorers	Horton G	Hills H	Whitehouse E	Hughes T	Hole T	Morris A	Dickenson T	Astle G	Williamson J	Perry G	Poole J	Castle	Simons
Friendly Matches																
Nov-08	(a) Victoria Halls															
Feb-21	(h) Cogswell & Harrison	W 4-0														
Mar-14	(a) Kings Langley	D 2-2														

1891-92
Wealdstone FC

Date	Opponent	Result	Scorers	Gill W	Isabell E	Gill T	Pearce	Darville H	Perry	Castle	Poole J	Dickenson	Simons	Bentley W	Astle G
Friendly Matches															
Oct-10	(a) Harrow Athletic	W 2-0	og, Astle	1	2	3	4	5	6	7	8		10	11	9

1892-93
Wealdstone FC

Rd	Date	Opponent	Result	Scorers	Hills H	Darville H	Pearce J	Lea G	Isabell E	Bentley W	Smith P	Norris A	Justice D	Stevens A	Simons G	Stanislaus	Bates W	Poole G	Lavender J	Poole J	Justice D	Williamson J	Crook W	Darville A	Perry G
Friendly Matches																									
	Oct-01	(-) Watford St Mary's	W 11-0																						
	Oct-08	(-) Croxley Green	W 4-2																						
	Oct-15	(h) Stanmore	W 5-1																						
	Oct-22	(-) Rickmansworth	L 0-2																						
	Oct-29	(h) Soho (Crosse & Blackwell's)	W 7-0	Smith 2, Norris 2, Lea, Bentley, Poole		X	X	X		X	X	X			X		X	X	X	X					
	Dec-10	(a) Stanmore	D 0-0		X		X				X			X	X				X	X	X	X	X	X	
	Dec-17	(h) Willesden	W 2-0																						
	Dec-26	(-) Foxes Reserves	W 4-0																						
	Jan-21	(a) Harrow Athletic	D 1-1	Smith							7														
	Feb-11	(h) Harrow Athletic	L 0-2			2			5		7			10											
	Mar-25	(-) Holborn Circus	W 2-1																						
	Apr-01	(-) Stanmore	W 3-2																						
	Apr-03	(-) Watford St Mary's	D 1-1																						
Middlesex Junior Cup																									
1	Dec-03	(a) Southall Reserves	W 2-1																						
2	Jan-28	(-) G N Railway Athletic	W 1-0																						
QF	Feb-18	(a) Uxbridge Reserves	D 1-1		1	2	3	4	5	6	7	8	9	10	11										
QFr	Feb-25	(a) Uxbridge Reserves	W 2-0	Bentley, Smith	1	2	3	4	5	6	7	8	9	10	11										
SF	Mar-18	(a) Old Argyle *	W 4-2	Norris, Darville A, Perry, Justice	X	X	X	X			X	X	X	X	X									X	X
F	Apr-08	(a) Robin Hood **	L 0-3		1	2	3	4	5	6	7	8	9	10	11										

1893-94
Wealdstone FC

	Date	Match	Result	Scorers	Hills H	Pearce F	Darville H M	Dove E	Burcham	A Doctor !	Simons G	Bentley W	Williamson J	Stevens A	Smith P	Lea G	Perry G	Hughes	Stanislaus	Fisk	Pearce	Crook	Blizzard G	Norris A	Williamson A
Friendly Matches																									
	Sep-30	(h) Watford Church Institute	D 0-0		1		2				11	10			7	4	6	3	9	8	5				
	Oct-07	(a) Old Argyle	W 3-0		1	2		6			11	3	4		7				10	8		5	9		
	Oct-14	(h) Harrow Athletic Reserves	L 0-2		1	5	2				11	3		10	7		6		9			4		8	
	Oct-28	(h) Soho	W 4-0	Darville 2, Stanislaus 2		2										9									
	Nov-11	(h) Queens Park Albion																							
	Nov-18	(h) West Herts Reserves																							
	Nov-25	(a) West Herts Reserves																							
	Dec-02	(a) Rickmansworth Rovers	W 2-0																						
	Dec-09	(a) Acton	W 2-0	Williamson A 2	1	3	2	6			11	10	4	8	7		5								9
	Dec-16	(a) Melrose																							
	Dec-23	(h) Harrow Athletic	L 0-1		1	3	2	4	5	6	7	8	9	10	11										
	Dec-30	(a) London Walsall																							
	Jan-06	(h) Stanmore																							
	Jan-20	(a) Queens Park Albion																							
	Jan-27	(a) Watford Church Institute																							
	Feb-03	(h) London Walsall																							
	Feb-10	(h) Harrow Athletic	D 1-1												11										
	Feb-17	(h) Holborn Circus																							
	Feb-24	(a) Soho																							
	Mar-03	(h) Great Northern Athletic																							
	Mar-10	(h) Acton																							
	Mar-17	(h) Melrose																							
	Mar-23	(h) Brixton																							
	Mar-24	(h) Rickmansworth																							
	Mar-31	(h) Old Argyle																							
	Apr-14	(a) Harrow St Mary's																							
Middlesex Junior Cup																									
1	Oct-21		W																						
2	Nov-04		W																						
3	Jan-13	(a) Uxbridge Reserves	L 1-2	Bentley	1	2	3	6			11	8	10	9	7	4	5								

1894-95
Harrow Athletic FC

	Date	Match	Result	Scorers	Hills H	Kay	Smith S	Bentley W	Hone F	Page C	Cooke E	Hartley J	Darville H	Fisk E	Kavanagh W	Woodbridge H	Barber	Carter	Hunt	Stogden	Barker	Bosworth-Smith	Rosveare	Bentley E	Page W	Fieron	Parker A	McMillain	Page J	Cater G	Enthoven
Friendly Matches																															
	Sep-22	(h) Bowes Park	W 3-0	Hartley 2, Fisk	1	2	3	4	5	6	7	8	9	10	11																
	Sep-29	(h) West End	W 5-1	Hartley, Cooke, Darville, Fisk, Hone	1		2		6	4	11	10	9	8	7	3							5								
	Oct-06	(h) Hampstead	W 5-1	Page, Darville 2, Cooke, Hartley	1		2	6		4	11	10	9	8	7	3							5	4							
	Oct-13	(h) St Bartholomew	W 3-2																												
	Oct-27	(h) Oberon																													
	Nov-03	(h) Minerva	W 2-0	Cooke, Hartley	1		2	6			11	10	4		7	3							5			8	9				
	Nov-11	(h) Old Westminsterians																													
	Dec-08	(a) Watford St Mary's	W 3-0																												
	Dec-15	(a) Olympian			1																										
	Jan-05	(h) Old Harrovians	W 2-1	Hunt, Parker	1		2	6		4	11		9		7	3		5	10						8						
	Mar-09	(h) Old Brightonians	W 8-0	Page 2, Parker 4, Stogden, Hunt	1		2	6			11		5			3		4		7	10				8		9				
	Mar-23	(h) R A Cooke's XI	W 4-0	Darville, Kavanagh 2, Boswell-Smith			2						5		8	3	4	6	7	10		11					9	1			
Middlesex Senior Cup																															
1Q	Oct-20	(a) Caledonian Athletic	W 2-0	Hartley, Darville	1		2	6			11	10	9		7	3	4						5			8					
2Qr	Nov-24	(a) Hounslow	D 1-1	Page	1		2	6	8		11	10	4		7	3			9				5								
2Qr	Dec-07	(h) Hounslow	W 4-0	Cooke, Carew-Hunt, Page, og	1		2	6		4	11		9		7	3			10				5		8						
1		(h) QPR	W																												
2		(a) Brentford	W																												
SF	Mar-31	(h) 2nd Scots Guards	D 0-0				2						5		10	3	4	6	7	8	9	11							1		
SFr	Apr-06	(a) 2nd Scots Guards	L 1-10	Parker			2	6					5		10	3			7	8	9	11							1	4	
West Middlesex Cup																															
2Q	Jan-19	(h) Hayes	W 13-1		1		2	6		4	11				7	3		5	10						8		9				
1			W																												
2	Mar-02	(a) Southall	W 3-2	Cooke 2, Parker	1		2	6			11		5		7	3		4		10					8		9				
SF			W																												
F	Apr-13	(-) 8th Hussars	L 1-2	Boswell-Smith				6	5				2		10	3			7	8	9	11				4					1

1895-96
Wealdstone Athletic FC

	Date	Match	Result	Notes	Gibson A	Little F	Gill	Bentley W	Smith G	Cooper H	Beckley A	Wells G	Meadows W	Poole J	Livy	Larkham	Smith P	Grafe F	Brown A	Rogers C	Ainsworth	Welsh F	Hills H	Smith A	Harrison	Williamson A	Dove E	Welch J	Cozens A	Cozens W	Rosson W	Wells C	Seymour G	Hole H	Fulcher	Hill	Ealing	Cousins	Bowles	Barnes T	Darville A
Friendly Matches																																									
	Sep-27	(a) Eagle Wanderers	L 1-4		1	2	3	4	5	6	7	8	9	10	11																										
	Oct-25	(a) Acton Rovers	L 0-1			6				11		9		8		1	2	3	4	5	7	10																			
	Nov-02	(h) Wembley	L 2-6	Poole ?		4			5				9					6	8				1	2	3	7	10	11													
	Nov-09	(h) Stanmore	L 0-5	(only 9 players arrived)		4				3		6		5					7				1	2		9		8													
	Nov-16	(a) Bushey Rovers	W 2-0	Little, W Cozens		10			6			9	3						4				1	2				11	7	8	5										
	Nov-23	(h) Imperial Rovers				6			5			9	3						4				1	2		7		11		8		10									
	Jan-04	(h) Rickmansworth	L 1-3																																						
	Jan-18	(h) Byng	D 2-2			6			5				3						4			11	9	2		7				1			8	10							
	Feb-08	(h) Bushey Rovers	L 1-2	(only 10 players arrived)	5	8					6																		4	2					1	3	7	9	10		
	Feb-15	(h) Wembley	L 0-11																																						
	Mar-01	(h) Imperial Rovers																																							
	Mar-15	(h) Acton Rovers																																							
	Apr-04	Harrow Athletic *	D 1-1	Meadows		10			6		4		11							5			1			9	3							8						2	7

*Match played as F Little's XI

1896-97
Wealdstone Rovers FC

Friendly Matches				Cozens H	Cozens W	Bowles C	Gibson	Payne	Luckman	Rogers	Beckley	Frankum	Poole J	Livy	Latimer	Ling	Cozens E	Little F
Sep-05	(h) South Hackney Clarence	W 5-0		1	2	3	4	5	6	7	8	9	10	11				
Sep-12	(a) Bushey Rovers	W 4-2																
Sep-19	(h) Willesden Presbyterians	W 3-0			2	11	3	5	9	4	8		10		1	6	7	
Oct-31	(a) Wembley Reserves																	
Dec-25	(a) Harrow Athletic *	L 3-5				X					X		X	X				X
	*Match played as F Little's XI																	

1897-98
Wealdstone Rovers FC

Friendly Matches				Ward	Gibson	Bowles	Pain	Alnott	Royce	Livy	Poole	Bowles	Cozens W	Cozens E	Beckley	Begley	Good 'un A	Barnes	Franklin	Little A	House A
Sep-04	(a) Kings Langley	W 2-1	Poole,Livy	1	2	3	4	5	6	7	8	9	10	11							
Sep-18	(a) Harrow Reserves	L 3-4	og, Couzins, Beckley		2	1	4	5	6	11	10	9	8	3	7						
Sep-25	(a) Pinner	W 3-0	Poole, Begley, Livy		1	3	4		5	11	10	6	7	2	8	9					
Oct-09	(a) Telephone Athletic	D 1-1			2	3			8	11	10	5	9		4		1	6	7		
Oct-30	(a) Edgware	W 3-1					4			11	10	9									
Nov-06	(a) Wembley	L 2-4	Poole, Franklin		1	3	4	5		11	10	6	7	2	8				9		
Nov-27	(h) Wembley	D 1-1	Beckley		1	3		6		7	8		11	2	10				9	4	5

1897-98
Wealdstone Juniors FC

Friendly Matches				Smither	Matthews T	Thompson	Leadale	Armstrong	Hayes	Cersell	Baldwin	Crowsley	Hillier	White	James J	Sherlock
Jan-08	(a) Watford Rovers	L 0-6		1	2	3	4	5	6	7	8	9	10	11		
Jan-29	(h) Wealdstone Wanderers	L 0-3		1	2	3	4	11	5		6		10	9	7	8

1897-98
Wealdstone Wanderers FC

Friendly Matches				Franklin	Bellchambers V	Cozens E	Bowles	Alnott	Dymock H	Livy H	Norman H	Dear E	Cozens W	Roeb C	Farmborough F	Perry W	Butland T	James J	Nash S	Barrett H	Butland J	Widows C	Matthews T	Johnson	Booker	Norman G	House A	Brown H	Perry E	Hillier G	Little A	Hayes A	Dear S
Oct-23	(h) Polytechnic	W 6-0	Poole 3 Dear 3	1	2	3	4	5	6	7	8	9	10	11																			
Dec-04	(a) Roxeth Rovers	W 6-1	Bellchambers, Dear 3 Dymock 2		2				9			8			1	3	4	5	6	7	10	11											
Dec-18	(a) Harrow Weald Rec	W 3-0	Barrett, Dear, Alnott					8	9		7				1	3	4	5		11	10	6	2										
Dec-25	(h) Harrow Old Boys	L 1-3													1	3																	
Dec-26	(a) Stanmore Reserves	L 0-4																															
Jan-08	(h) Hamilton Club				2				9		5	7			4	3	5			11				1	8	10							
Jan-22	(h) Oakley Casuals	W 3-0	Norman 2 Brown		2						9	7				3	6			8	11				10	4	1	5					
Jan-29	(a) Wealdstone Juniors	W 3-0	H Norman, Dear, G Norman		2						11	8				3	4			10	6				7	9	1	5					
Feb-05	(a) Oakley Casuals	W 4-1	Dear 3 Norman		3				11		8	9			5	2	4			7	6			1	10								
Feb-12	(h) Sudbury Wranglers	W 7-2	Booker 2, Dymock 3, Barrett, Norman						9		5				11	2	4			7	6				10	8			1	3			
Feb-19	(h) Roundwood Park	D 4-4	Barrett, Dymock, Johnson 2						10						6	2				7	4			9		3			11	8	1	5	
Feb-26	(a) Wealdstone Juniors	W 2-0	Dear Alnutt					4			7	9			1	2				8	6				11	5		3					10
Mar-19	(h) Watford Juniors	W 5-4																															

1898-99
Wealdstone Albion FC

Willesden & District League Div II - 5th				Smither	Matthews	Moffat	Leadale	Hayes	Elmslie	Beckley	Thompson	White S E	Cozens H	Armstrong	Dymock	Woodward	Marshall F	Goodfellow A	Hawkins	Kirby	Welch	Poole	Royce	Baldwin	Hillier	Batten	Burfitt	Snelling	Almond	Smith	Key	Payne	Bowles	Dear S	Livy	Gibson	Cozens W	Franklin	Dart
Sep-10	(h) Wealdstone Wanderers	L 0-8			4	3		5		8	7	6	2	9	11	10	1							12* sub used															
Sep-17	(a) Roxeth Rovers	L 0-5		1	2	3	4	5	6	7	8	9		11	10																								
Sep-24	(h) Willesden Green	L 3-4																																					
Oct-01	(a) Kensal Albion																																						
Oct-22	(a) Stonebridge	W 4-0																																					
Nov-12	(h) East Acton Reserves	W 6-0	Dear 4, og, Livy				4				8	6	7			3						9										5		11	10	1	2		
Nov-19	(h) Kensal Albion	W 2-1	Pool, Beckley			4		6		9	8		7			3						10										5			11	1	2		
Nov-26	(a) Watford Rovers	L 1-4	Pool (9 men)		3		4			5			7	6								10										5		9	11	1	2		
Dec-03	(a) Hyde & Kingsbury	L 0-3					4			8		6	7			3						10										5		9	11	1	2		
Dec-10	(a) Pinner	L 1-2				4					2	6	7			3						10										5		9	11	1	8		
Dec-12	(a) Metropolitan Railway	W 1-0	Dear		2	8	4	6				10	7			3						11										5		9		1			
Dec-31	(h) Watford Rovers	D 1-1	Pool		2	3	4					6	7									10				1						5	8	9	11				
Jan-07	(a) Willesden Green	L 0-1			11		4	6				9	7			3																5		8		1	2	10	
Jan-07	(h) Sepia	W 7-2													3					2	9		10	11		1	4	5	6	7	8								
Jan-14	(h) Willesden Town B																																						
Jan-28	(h) Brigade Old Boys																																						
Feb-04	(h) Harrow	L 2-5	Livy, Cozens		5		4			8		6	7			3																		9	11	1	2	10	
Feb-18	(a) Sudbury Poplars	W 6-2	Baldwin 3, Poole, Royce, Moffat (10pls)			4				9					2			1	3	6	7	8	10	11															
Feb-25	(a) Willesden Green	L 0-1			3		4			8			7									11										5		9	10	1	2	6	
Mar-04	(a) East Acton Reserves	W 4-0	Dear, Pool, Payne 2		3	6	4								1							9										5		8			2	7	
Mar-11	(a) Stanmore Reserves	L 1-3	Franklin		10		4					6	7									11						5						9		3	2	8	1

1898-99
Wealdstone Wanderers FC

Friendly Matches				Bellchambers	Perry	Bowles	Butland J	Alnutt	Butland T	Barrett	Norman	Johnson	Baker	Dear E	Brown	Norman	Butland
Sep-03	(a) Roxeth Rovers																
Oct-08	(a) Neasden St Andrews	W 5-1	Barratt, Booker 2, Johnson, Dear	1	2	3	4	5	6	7	8	9	10	11			
Nov-12	(h) Harrow Reserves	L 1-3															
Nov-19	(h) Old Palmerians	W 2-0	Gowers, Johnson	1	3	2		10	6	11	4	8			5	7	9
Nov-26	(a) Stanmore Reserves	L 2-3			2	3					4					1	

1899-00

	Date	Willesden & District League Div II - 3rd	Result	Former Club	Bellchambers	Cozens W	Johnson	Matthews	Payne	White	Cozens H	Livy	Dear E	Dear S	Hillier	Welsh	Pool	Farmborough	Dymock	Welch W	Welch H	Keetch	Welch W	Moffat	Key	Royce	Baldwin	Kirby	Hawkins	Burfitt	Snelling	Merridew	Almond	Buckley
				Former Club	*W*	*R*	*W*	*A*	*R*	*A*	*A*	*R*	*W*	*W*	*A*	*A*	*A*	*W*	*A*	*A*				*A*	*A*	*A*	*A*	*A*	*A*	*A*	*A*		*A*	
F	Oct-07	(a) Northwood	W 6-1	Cozens 2 Dear S 3, Dear E	1	2	3	4	5	6	7	8	9	10	11																			
F	Oct-14	(a) Roundwood Swifts	W 6-0	Dear S 4, Pool 2	1	2	3	10	5	6	7		9	8		4	11																	
	Oct-28	(a) Metropolitan Railway	W 4-1	Dear E, Dear S, Pool, Cozens	1	2	3	10	5	6	7		9	8		4	11																	
	Nov-04	(h) Stanmore	W 5-0	Dear E 2, Dear S 2, Pool	1	X	X		5	x	7	8	9	10		X	11																	
F	Nov-11	(h) Roundwood Swifts																																
	Jan-20	(h) Brigade Institute	D 2-2	Dear, White	X		X			X				X																				
	Jan-27	(a) Stanmore																																

Former Club: A = Wealdstone Albion, R = Wealdstone Rovers, W = Wealdstone Wanderers Players with no appearance were known to have played in the 'Reserves'

1900-01

	Date	Willesden & District League Div I - 6th	Result	Scorers	Bellchambers	Cozens W	Livy	Welch Wm	Bowles	Keetch	Cozens H	Matthews	Henderson	White	Hillier	Woodward	Poole	Welch W	Dymock	A N Other	Doman	Farmborough	Almond	Payne H	Johnson	Carmalt J	Carmalt H	Burgess	Kirby	Bradbury	Stevens
Fr	Sep-15	(h) Harrow Athletic Reserves	W 2-0	Hillier, White	1	2	3	4	5	6	7	8	9	10	11																
Fr	Sep-22	(a) Roxeth Rangers	W 1-0	Dymock	1	2		3			9	5			11	8	7	6	4		10										
Fr	Sep-29	(h) West Hampstead	L 0-2								7		9				10					1									
	Oct-06	(a) Harrow Athletic Reserves	L 0-3			2		3	5		6	9		11	8		10	7					1	4							
	Oct-12	(a) Brigade Old Boys	L 2-7	Hillier 2	1									10	11										9						
	Oct-22	(h) Wembley	W 1-0	Cozens W	1	2	3	4		6	7			11											9	5	10	8			
	Nov-10	(h) Shepherds Bush	L 1-2	Cozens W	1	2	3	4		6	7			10	11			8								5	9				
Fr	Nov-17	(h) Pinner	L 1-2	White										10																	
	Nov-24	(h) Brigade Old Boys	L 1-2	Cozens H		2	3	4		6	7	1		11	10										9	5	8				
	Dec-01	(a) Stanmore	L 0-1		1	2	3	4			7	5		11	10		9	6						8							
	Dec-08	(a) Haven Green	W 2-0	??	1	2	3	4		6	7			11	10		9									5	8				
	Dec-15	(h) Harrow Weald	L 0-4		1	2	3	4		6	7			11	10					9						5	8				
	Dec-22	(h) Ealing St Johns				2	3	4		6	7	1		11	10		9	5											8		
	Jan-05	(a) Wembley	L 0-5			2	3	4		6	7	1		11	10		9	5											8		
	Jan-19	(h) Roundwood Rangers	D 1-1																												
	Jan-26	(a) Harrow Weald		*Postponed due to the death of Queen Victoria*																											
	Feb-15	(a) Northwood	D 1-1	og																											
	Feb-22	(a) Roundwood Rangers																													
	Mar-09	(h) Northwood										1																			
	Mar-16	(a) Harrow Weald	L 1-2	Stevens		2	7	3		5	8	1		11	10			4												6	9
	Mar-23	(h) Haven Green			4	2	11	3		6	7	1		10	8			5													9
	Apr-06	(a) Ealing St Johns	L 1-3	(only 8 players arrived)																											
	Apr-13	(a) West Hampstead																													
	Apr-25	(h) Willesden Highfield	W 2-1																												
			Selected for Willesden League Representative Side:			X	X	X		X		X																			

1901-02

	Date	Willesden & District League Div I - 3rd	Result	Scorers	Bellchambers	Cozens W	Matthews T	Rowe	Keetch	Welch Wm	Beckley E	Cozens B	Welch W	Livy	White	Matthews W	Hawkins	Dawes E	Beckley	Carmalt W
F	Sep-28	(a) Pinner	L 0-2																	
	Oct-05	(h) Neasden Reserves	W 3-1																	
	Oct-12	(a) Harrow Weald	W 2-1	Livy 2	1	2	3	4	5	6	7	8	9	10	11					
	Oct-26	(h) Shepherds Bush	W 4-2	Livy 2, White, Beckley E		2		4	5	6	7		9	10	11	1	3	8		
	Nov-02	(a) Willesden Highfield	W 2-0		1	2	5	6			7	8	9	10	11		3		4	
	Nov-09	(h) Ealing St Johns	W 1-0	Beckley E	1	2	6	5				7	9	10	11		3	8	4	
	Nov-16	(a) Wembley	D 2-2																	
	Nov-30	(a) Metropolitan Electric Co.	D																	
	Dec-07	(h) Harrow Weald	D 1-1	Livy	1	2		6	5		8		9	10	11		3	7	4	
	Dec-14	(a) Neasden Reserves	W 7-0	????? Carmalt 2	1	2		6				8	9	10	11		3	7	4	5
	Dec-21	(h) Brigade Old Boys	L 1-4	Livy	1	2	6				8		9	10	11		3	7	4	5
	Dec-28	(h) Metropolitan Electric Co	W																	
	Jan-04	(a) Kensal Rise Athletic	W																	
	Jan-11	(a) Shepherds Bush	W																	
	Jan-18	(h) Wembley	W 2-0																	
	Jan-25	(h) Willesden Green United	D																	
	Feb-08	(a) Ealing St Johns	D 0--0																	
	Mar-01	(h) Willesden Highfield	W																	
F	Mar-08	(a) Harrow Athletic Reserves	W 2-1																	
	Mar-15	(h) Kensal Rise Athletic	W																	
	Mar-29	(a) Brigade Old Boys	L 2-3																	
	Apr-05	(a) Willesden Green United	W																	

1902-03

	Date	Willesden & District League Div I - 3rd	Result	Scorers	Barrett	Cozens W	Hawkins	Carmalt W	Welch	Rowe	Dawes	Brown C	Todd	Glidle	Livy	Keetch	Beckley E	Cozens H	Sadler	Matthews T	Welch W	Ferguson	Bellchambers E	Perry
F	Sep-13	(h) Great Central Loco	W 5-0	Brown, ????	1	2	3	4	5	6	7	8	9	10	11									
F	Oct-04	(a) Pinner	W 2-0																					
	Oct-11	(a) Allens Athletic	L 1-2	Dawes	1	2	3	4	5		9				11	6	7	8	10					
	Oct-18	(a) Ealing St Johns	L 0-1		1	2	3	4	5	9	7				11	6	8			10				
	Nov-01	(a) Great Western Railway	L 1-2																					
	Nov-21	(a) Northwood	W 4-1	Beckley E 2, Carmalt, Dawes				X			X						X							
	Nov-28	(h) Civil Service	W 5-1	Welch 2, Beckley, Dawes, Ferguson	1	2	3	4		8	7					5	10			6	11	9		
	Dec-13	(h) Stanmore	W 1-0																					
	Dec-27	(h) Brigade Old Boys	D 0-0		1	2	8	4	3	10	7			9	11	5							6	
	Jan-03	(h) Allens Athletic	W 4-0	Livy, Dawes, ??							X				X						X		X	
	Jan-17	(a) Pinner	D 0-0																					
	Jan-24	(a) Stanmore																						
	Feb-14	(a) Allens Athletic	L 0-4																					
F	Mar-07	(a) Allens Athletic	W 6-2	Beckley E 3, Glidle, Livy, Perry										X	X		X							X

1903-04

Rd	Date	Opponent	Result	Scorers	Barrett	Welch J	Welch W	Keetch	Wolters F	Beckley W	Lane A	Dawes	Glidle	Beckley A	Perry	Wolters A	Beckley E	Bellchambers B	Little A	Matthews T	Higgins E	Gibson C	Brown	Rhodes E
Willesden & District League Div I - 2nd																								
	Sep-12	(h) Benjamin Brothers	W																					
	Sep-19	(a) Clare Hampstead	W 5-1	Beckley A, Welch J 3, Dawes																				
	Sep-26	(a) Willesden Invicta	D 0-0		1	9	3	4	5	6		7		10	11	2	8							
	Oct-03	(h) Brigade Old Boys	W 3-1		1	9	3	4	5	6		7		10	11	2	8							
	Dec-25	(a) Alperton																						
	Jan-02	(h) Pinner	W 4-0	Beckley A, Rhodes, Perry, Glidle																				
	Jan-09	(h) Willesden Oakdene	W 2-0	Rhodes 2			3		9	6	5	8		10	11					2		1	4	7
	Jan-16	(h) Benjamin Brothers	W				3		9	6	5	8		10	11					2		1	4	7
	Jan-30	(a) Stanmore	W 1-0				3	4	5	11	9	8		10						2		1	6	7
	Feb-06	(h) Willesden Invicta	L				3	4	5	11	9	8		10						2		1	6	7
	Feb-20	(h) Allens Athletic	W				3	4	5	6	9			10			8			2		1	7	11
	Mar-05	(h) Clare Hampstead																						
	Mar-19	(a) Pinner	L 0-1			11	3	4	5	6		7	10				8			2		1	9	
	Mar-26	(a) Allens Athletic					3	5		6	10	7	10		11					2	9	1	4	8
	Apr-02	(h) Stanmore					3	5		6	10	7			11					2	9	1	4	8
London Junior Cup																								
2	Oct-24	(a) Great Central Railway	D 2-2	Lane, ?	1	3		4	5	6	9	7		10	11	2	8							
2r	Oct-31	(h) Great Central Railway	W 9-0	Lane 2, Dawes, Beckley A 2, Beckley E 2, Perry, Wolters F	1		3	4	5	6	9	7		10	11	2	8							
2r2*	Nov-14	(h) Great Central Railway	W 7-0	Lane 2, Welch W, Wolters F 3, Keetch	1	8	3	4	5	6	9	7		10	11	2								
3	Nov-21	(h) Holloway Ramblers	W 3-1	Beckley A 2, Lane	1	8	3	4	5	11	9	7		10		2		6						
		* Unknown reason for a further replay after a 9-0 win.....																						
Middlesex Junior Cup																								
1	Oct-17	(h) Hyde & Kingsbury	W 4-1	Welch W, Beckley A 2, Welch J	1	9	3	4	5	6		7		10	11	2	8							
2	Nov-28	(h) Stanmore	W 4-1	Lane, Beckley W, Beckley A, Glidle	1	2	3	4	5	11	9	7	8	10					6					
3	Dec-12	(a) Belgrave	D																					
3r	Dec-19	(h) Belgrave			1		3	4	5	6	9	7		10	11					2	8			

1904-05

Rd	Date	Opponent	Result	Scorers	Gibson C	Welch W	Petley	Matthews T	Gregory V	Wolters F	Dawes H	Bowell H	Lines A	Beckley A	Stevens T	Randall C	Keetch G	Brown J	Cozens W	Lane A	Tibbs	Moffat G	Bellchambers B	Welti A	Jones	Little A	Beckley E	Baldwin	Livy	Saunders F	Woods S	Henderson	Auld	Darville
Willesden & District League Div I - 1st																																		
F	Sep-10	(h) Cameron Rangers	W 5-1	Dawes, Lines 2, Tibbs, Beckley	1	2	3				7		9	10			5	11	4	6	8													
	Sep-17	(h) Willesden Invicta	W 2-1	Dawes, Lines	1	2	3	6		4	7		9	10			5			11	8													
F	Sep-24	(h) Queens Park Athletic	W 6-0	Beckley 4, Tibbs, Lines		2	3	1			7		9	10			5		4	6	8	11												
F	Oct-08	(h) Verditure	W 2-1			2	3	11	5		7		9						4			8	1	6	10									
	Oct-15	(h) Stanmore	W 5-0																															
	Dec-17	(h) Harrow United	W 2-0	Beckley, Bowell	1	2	3	6		4	7	8	9	10		5		11																
	Dec-24	(h) Willesden Radicals	W 2-0		1	2		3	5	4	7	8	9	10		6		11																
	Dec-26	(h) Cleveland Athletic	W		1	2				3	7	8		10		6	5										4	9	11					
	Jan-15	(a) Kilburn	W 3-1	Bowell 2, Dawes	1	2		3	5	4	7	8	9	10	6			11																
D/H	Jan-28	(h) Clare Hampstead	W		1	2	3	11	5	6	7	8	9	10		4																		
	Feb-04	(h) Margurite			1	2	3	6		4	8	9	10		11	7	5																	
	Feb-11	(h) Willesden Radicals	W 14-1	Gibson 2, Bowell 2, Brown, Lines 5, Welch 2, Dawes 2	1	2	3	6		4	8	9	10			7	5	11																
	Feb-18	(a) Stanmore	W 2-0	Bowell, Randall	1	2		3	6		8	9				10	5	11								4				7				
	Feb-25	(h) Kilburn	W 1-0	Lines	1	2		3	5		7	8	9			6		11								4				10				
	Mar-04	(a) Ealing St Johns	D 2-2	Wolters Dawes	1	2	3	6	5	4	7	8	9					11												10				
F	Mar-18	(h) Ravensbourne	D 3-3	Dawes, Welch, Bowell	2	5			3		7	9				4		6												8	1	10	11	
F	Apr-22	(a) Harrow United	L 1-2	Dawes	X	X					X																							X
London Junior Cup																																		
2	Oct-22	(a) Sutton Court	W		1	2	3		6	4	7		9	10	8		5	11																
3			W																															
4			W																															
5	Jan-08	(h) Belgrave	W 3-1	Wolters, Dawes, Beckley	1	4		3	5	6	7	8	9	10		2		11																
6	Jan-21	(a) Holborn Circus	L 0-2		1	2		3	6	4	7	8	9	10			5	11																
Middlesex Junior Cup																																		
1	Oct-01	(a) Grove House	W 3-2	Lines, Gregory, Stevens	1	2	3		6	4	7		9	10	8		5	11																
2	Oct-15	(a) Breakspear Institute	L 0-5			2	3		6	4	7		9	10	8		5	11								1								

1905-06

Rd	Date	Opponent	Result	Scorers	Butler	Matthews	Welch	Beckley W	Gregory	Jones	Butler	Randall	Bowell	Beckley A	Gliddle	Webb	Evans	Little	Cozens	Saunders
(Willesden & District League Div I)																				
	Sep-09	(a) Wealdstone Church Athletic	D		1	2	3	4	5	6	7	8	9	10	11					
	Sep-16	(h) Shepherds Bush			X		X		X	X	X	X	X	X		X	X	X		
		* No further matches played as Wealdstone. Wealdstone Church Athletic took over the fixtures.																		
Middlesex Junior Cup																				
1	Sep-30	(h) Sudbury Institute	D 0-0				2	4	5	1	9	6	10	8	11				3	7

* Match not replayed as Wealdstone had become Defunct before the replay was Scheduled. Wealdstone Church Athletic were already entered in the Competition.

1905-06
Wealdstone Church Athletic FC

No.	Date	Match	Result	Scorers	Pluck F	Bellchamners B	Spooner J	Wolters F	Humphries	Elmslie G	White S	Bennett	Todd	Wickes J	Dawes E	Dodd	Hawkins	Biggs	Courtney	Dickinson	Lane A	Lingfield H	Hales G	Robinson	Whittle	Robertson	Bunker	Matthews
Willesden & District League Div I - 3rd																												
	Sep-09	(h) Wealdstone FC	D		1	2	3	4	5	6	7	8	9	10	11													
	Nov-24	(a) Victoria Hall	W 4-1	Dodd, White, Dawes, Bellchambers		X					X			X	X	X	X											
	Dec-01	(h) Old Lyonians	W 2-1	Bellchambers, Spooner	X	X	X				X																	
	Dec-08	(a) Stanmore	D 3-3	Todd 2, og,	X						X		X			X												
	Dec-15	(a) Allens Athletic	W 3-1	Biggs 2, Wickes	X		X				X			X		X		X	X									
	Dec-26	(h) Ealing St Johns	L 1-4		X	X		X												X								
	Dec-30	(h) Brigade Old Boys	D 1-1	Biggs														X										
	Jan-13	(a) Old Lyonians	D 3-3	Biggs, Bellchambers, Lane	X	X	X	X		X	X			X				X			X							
	Jan-20	(h) Hyde & Kingsbury	L 0-1		1	2	3	4			X			10							9	8						
	Jan-27	(a) Hampton United	W 11-0	Lane 5, Lingfield 3, Bellchambers, Wickes 2	1	2	3	5			7			10	11	6					9	8	4					
	Feb-10	(a) Hyde & Kingsbury	L 4-6	Dawes 3, Lane	X		X	X			X		X	X	X			X			X			X	X			
	Feb-24	(a) Stanmore			1	2	3	5		4	7		9	10	11						6					8		
	Mar-03	(a) Kilburn	D 0-0		X			X		X					X												X	
	Mar-10	(h) Shepherds Bush Res.	D 1-1	Lane																	X							
	Mar-31	(h) Allens Athletic	W 3-0	Lingfield, Wickes, Dawes		X	X							X	X							X						X
	Apr-07	(a) Ealing St Johns	L 1-3	Robinson	X																			X				
	Apr-28	(h) Victoria Halls	W 1-0	Hawkins	X						X				X		X											
London Junior Cup																												
1	Oct-07	(h) Leyton Athletic	L 2-0																									

1906-07
Wealdstone Church Athletic FC

No.	Date	Match	Result	Scorers	Parsons F	Wilson A	Spooner J	Bishop F	Wolters F	Robinson	Dodd A	Tew F	Shadwick J	Wickes J	Howman	Pluck F	White S	Bussey	Dodd (T)	Bellchamners B	Martin	Whittle	Robertson	Sub	Lawrence	Steele	Clow	Newton	Richardson	Dickinson	Lane A	Todd	Varcoe F	Elmslie G	Bunker	Matthews	Hales G	Lingfield H	Dawes E	Hawkins	Biggs	Biggs	Courtney
Willesden & District League Div I - 4th																																											
	Sep-15	(h) Ridge Athletic	D 2-2	Robinson 2,	X	X	X	X	X	X	X	X	X	X	X																												
	Sep-22	(h) Mayfield Reserves	W 4-3	Robinson, Howman, Tew 2			X		X	X	X	X		X	X	X	X	X	X																								
	Oct-20	(h) Board Of Education	W 4-3	Howman 2. Spooner, ?			X		X						X	X	X			X	X																						
	Nov-03	(h) Victoria Halls	W 4-0	og, Newton, Spooner 2,		X	X							X	X							X	X	X	X	X	X	X			<---- Known Reserves ---->												
	Nov-24	(a) Leavesden Asylum				X	X		X					X	X	X	X				X		X				X	X	X														
	Dec-01	(h) Sudbury Institute	D 0-0			X	X		X					X	X	X	X				X		X				X	X															
	Dec-08	(a) Stanmore	L 0-1			X	X		X					X	X	X	X				X		X				X			X													
	Dec-15	(h) Mayfield Reserves	L 2-3	Tew, Clow			3		5			9				1	7			4	2		8				10		11		6												
	Jan-05	(h) Kilburn				X	X	X	X			X		X		X	X				X		X									X											
	Jan-12	(a) Board of Education	W 2-1	og, White		X	X	X	X			X		X		X	X				X		X									X											
	Jan-19	(h) Hyde & Kingsbury				X	X	X	X			X		X		X	X				X		X									X											
	Jan-26	(a) Mayfield Rovers	D 1-1	White		X	X	X	X			X		X		X	X				X		X									X											
	Feb-02	(a) Hyde & Kingsbury	D 1-1	Robertson		X	X		X			X	X	X		X	X				X		X									X											
	Feb-09	(h) Ealing St Johns	W 3-1	Wickes, Shadwick, Bellchambers		2	3	4	5		7		11			1				6			10				9				8												
	Feb-16	(a) Kilburn	L 0-2			2	3	4	5		7		10			1				6			9				11				8												
	Feb-23	(h) Old Lyonians	W 3-0	Lane, Clow, Robertson		2	3	6	5					11		1	7				4		8				10				9												
	Mar-16	(a) Old Lyonians	D 2-2	White 2		2	3		5				9	10		1	7			6	4		8				11																
	Mar-23	(h) Soho United					3						9	10	7	1				6	4	2	8				11				5												
	Apr-06	(h) Stanmore	D 1-1	Wickes			3		5				9	10		1	7			6		2	8				11						4										
	Apr-13	(a) Ealing St Johns	D 0-0				3		5				9	10	4	1	7			6		2	8				11																
	Apr-20	(h) Hyde & Kingsbury	D 2-2																																								
Middlesex Junior Cup																																											
1	Sep-29	(a) Old Lyonians	D 2-2	White 2												X	X																										
1r	Oct-06	(h) Old Lyonians	D 2-2							X		X			X	X	X	X																									
1r2	Oct-13	(a) Old Lyonians	L 1-4	Robinson						X						X																											

1907-08
Wealdstone Church Athletic FC

No.	Date	Match	Result	Scorers	Pluck F	Spooner J	Martin F	Case F	Wolters F	Bellchambers B	White S	Lawrence P	Shadwick P	Steeles W	Bird H	Bowell H	Scotton W	Wickes J	Lane A	Elms W	Robertson A	Theobold F	Rordan W	Clow W	Lordan W	Howman W
Willesden & District League Div I - 5th																										
	Sep-14	(h) Wealdstone Juniors			1	2	3	4	5	6	7	8	9	10	11											
	Sep-28	(h) Shepherds Bush	L 1-3	White	1	2	3		5	4	7		6			8	9	10	11							
	Oct-19	(h) Hyde & Kingsbury	L 0-2		1	2	3		5	6	7					8	9		4	11	10					
	Nov-23	(a) Ridge Athletic	L 0-2		1	2	3		5	4	7		6				9		8		11	10				
	Dec-21	(a) Harrow Association	L 1-5	(9 men only) Shadwick							X		X													
	Jan-25	(a) Stanmore	W 2-0	Lordan, Scotton	X																				X	
	Feb-01	(h) Kilburn			X												X								X	
	Feb-15	(h) Old Lyonians	W 3-1	Theobold, Clow, Case	1	2	3	5		4	7								6			10		11	9	8
	Apr-11	(a) Old Lyonians																								
London Junior Cup																										
2	Oct-26	(a) Twickenham Town	L		1	2	3		5	6	7					8	9		4			10	11			
Middlesex Junior Cup																										
1	Oct-12	(h) L&NW Athletic	W 7-1	Scotton 2, og, Robertson 3, White	1	2	3		5	6	7					8	9		4	11	10					
2	Nov-09	(a) Pinner	D 1-1		1	2	3		5	6	7					8	9		4	11	10					
2r	Nov-16	(h) Pinner	L 1-2 **	Bowells	1	2	3		5	6	7					8	9		4		10			11		
2r2	Nov-30	(h) Pinner	L 1-2	Scotton 2, og, Robertson 3, White	1	2	3		5	6			10			8	9		4	11				7		

** Wealdstone protested over a Pinner player and the match was ordered re-played

1908-09

	Date	Opponent	Result	Scorers	Pluck F	Padley	Martin	Spooner J	Bellchambers	Cane F	Miller H	White S	Bowells H	Lane A	Theobold F	Roberts	Courtin J	Bishop E	Howman W	Farmborough	Collas	Meens	Else S	Coombers	Brown J	Skilton A	Tew F	Wolters F	Beckley
Willesden & District League Div I - 5th																													
	Sep-05	(h) West London Old Boys	W 2-0	Howman, Farmborough	1	2	3			5	6	7			10	11		4	9	8									
	Sep-12	(h) Rotherhithe Invicta	W 11-0	Lane, Bowells, Cane ???	1			2		5	6	7	8	9	10		3	4	11										
	Sep-19	(h) Pinner	W 3-1	Theobold 2, Cane	1		3		2	5	6	7	8	9	10	11		4											
F	Sep-26	(h) Radlett	W 6-1	Howman 4, Bowells, Lane	1		3	2	4	5	6		8	9	10				11		7								
	Oct-10	(h) Kilburn					3	2	4	5	6	7	8		10			9	1				11						
	Nov-14	(a) Mayfield Rovers			1		3		2	5			8	4	10				11					6	7	9			
	Nov-21	(a) Old Lyonians	L 0-3		1		3	2	4	5	6		8	9	10				11						7				
	Dec-05	(a) St Gabriels	W 1-0	Bowells	1		3	2	4	5	6		8	9	10				11						7				
	Dec-12	(h) Mental Hospital United			1		3		2	5	6		8	9	10				11					4	7				
	Jan-09	(a) MHC United	L 1-2	Theobold	1		3		2	9	6		5		10			7	11								8	4	
	Jan-23	(h) Uxbridge			1		3		2	5	6				10			7	11							9	8	4	
	Apr-13	(a) Pinner	W 3-1	?, Beckley, Theobold	X			X		X	X				X														X
F	May-03	(h) Mr P Skilton's XI																											
London Junior Cup																													
1	Oct-03	(a) Shepherds Bush United	L				3	2	4	5	6	7	8	9	10				11			1							
Middlesex Junior Cup																													
1	Nov-07	(a) Hendon	W 3-2	Bowells, Theobold, Lane	1		3	2	4	5			8	9	10				11					6	7				
2	Dec-19	(a) Breakspear United	Ab 4-3 **		1		3	2			6		5		10			7	11							9	8	4	
2r	Jan-01	(a) Breakspear United	W 2-1	Tew, Skilton	1		3		2	5	6				10			7	11							9	8	4	
DSF	Jan-16	(h) Kilburn	L 0-1																										

** Abandoned for bad light

1909-10

	Date	Opponent	Result	Scorers	Bradberry	Spooner	Davy	Bellchambers	Cane F	Miller H	White S	Tew	O'Brien	Theobold	Roberts	Robertson	Howman	Wilson	Elms	Payne	Balkwill	Martin	Burton	Pangbourne	Flack
Willesden & District League Premier Div - 4th																									
	Sep-11	(h) Romford	L 2-3		1	2	3	4	5	6	7	8	9	10	11										
	Sep-18	(a) Willesden Rangers	D 1-1	Theobold	1	3		2	5	6		8	4	10	11	7	9								
	Oct-02	(h) Willesden Amateurs			1	2	3		5	6	7	8	9	10			11								
	Oct-09	(h) London Caledonian Strollers																							
	Jan-15	(a) Kilburn	L 0-3										X				X								
	Jan-29	(h) Willesden Rangers	W 3-2	Balkwill 3	1	3		2	5	6	7	8	4	10			11				9				
	Feb-05	(a) Deerfield Social	W 5-2	Theobold 2, Tew, Burton, Balkwill	1			2	5	6		8	4	10			11				9	3	7		
	Feb-12	(h) Hyde & Kingsbury	W 4-1	Balkwill, Tew, Theobold 2	1	3		2	5	6	7	8	4	10			11				9				
	Feb-19	(a) MHC United	L 0-2		1	3		2	5	6	7	8	4	10			11				9				
	Feb-26	(h) Lotus	W 3-1	Theobold 2, Howman	1	3		2	5	6	7	8	4	10			11				9				
	Mar-05	(h) West Hampstead Reserves	W 2-0	Balkwill, Tew,	1	3		2	5	6		8	4	10			11				9		7		
	Mar-12	(h) Brondesbury	W 7-0	Balkwill 4, Tew, Spooner, og	1	3		2	5	6	7	8	4	10			11				9				
	Mar-26	(a) Kilburn	L 1-3	Balkwill	1			2	5	6	7	8	4								9		10	3	11
	Apr-09	(a) Hyde & Kingsbury	W 2-0	Theobold, Balkwill	1			2	5	6	7	8	4	10			11				9	3			
	Apr-16	(a) Lotus	L 0-4		1	2		4	5	6	7	8									9	3	10		11
	Apr-30	(a) MHC United	L 0-1																						
Middlesex Junior Cup																									
1		Bye																							
2	Nov-12	(h) Harlesden Amateurs	D																						
2r1	Nov-19	(h) Harlesden Amateurs	D																						
2r2	Nov-27	(h) Harlesden Amateurs	D 0-0		1	2			5	6	7	8	4	10				9	11	3					
2r3	Dec-04	(a) Harlesden Amateurs	L																						
West Middlesex FA Cup																									
	Oct-23	(h) Gramaphone Sports Club	L																						

1910-11

Rd	Date	Opponent	Result	Scorers	Bradberry T	Bellchambers B	Martin F	O'Brien P	Andrews P	Miller H	White S	Tew F	Page G	Theobold	Howman	Cane F	Shadwick P	Beckley	Meens	Burton	Robertson	Richardson H	Shadwick J	Bird	Rogers P	Poole
Willesden & District Premier League - 2nd																										
	Sep-10	(h) Hendon Town	W 1-0	Theobold	1	2	3	4	5	6	7	8	9	10	11											
	Sep-11	(h) Hampstead Town	W 5-0	Theobold 2, Page, Tew, Cane								X	X	X	X	X										
	Sep-18	(h) Harrow Association	W 8-3	Howman, Tew 4, Blakeney 2, Shadwick P	1	2	3	4	5	6	7	8			11		9	10								
	Oct-08	(a) Star United	W 4-1	Bellchambers, Howman 2, Shadwick P	1	2	3	4	5	6	7	8	9		11		10									
	Oct-15	(h) Deerfield Social Club	L 0-1		1	2	3	4	5	6	7	8	9		11		10									
	Dec-10	(a) Hyde and Kingsbury	L 0-2			2	3	4	10	6	7	8	9		11	5			1							
	Dec-31	(a) North Paddington	W 4-0	Burton 2, Page, Shadwick		X							X		X		X		X	X	X		X			
	Jan-21	(a) MHC United	W 3-0	Page, Shadwick, Martin		2	3	4	10	6	7		9		11	5			1		8					
	Jan-28	(a) Hendon Town	D 1-1	Robertson	X		X								X		X				X	X		X		
	Feb-11	(h) Hyde and Kingsbury	D 1-1	Tew	1		3	4		6	7	8	9		11	5	10					2				
	Feb-18	(a) Kilburn	W 2-0	Tew, Andrews	1	2	3	4	10	6	7	8	9		11	5										
	Mar-25	(h) MHC United	W 5-0	Richardson 2, Andrews, Page, Cane	1	2	3	4	10	6		8	9		11	5						7				
	Apr-01	(a) Hampstead Town			1	2	3		10	6	7	8	9			5						11			4	
	Apr-17	(a) Pinner	D 0-0		1	2	3		10	6		8	9		7	5						11			4	
London Junior Cup																										
1	Oct-01	(a) Westley Athletic	W 3-1	Shadwick P, Tew, Page	1	2	3	4		6	7	8	9		11	5	10									
3	Nov-12	(h) City Of Westminister	W 3-1		1	2	3	4	10	6	7	8	9		11	5										
4	Dec-03	(h) West Kensington	W 3-1	Tew 2, White	1	2	3	4	10	6	7	8	9		11	5										
5	Jan-07	(a) Harrow Weald	W 2-1	Shadwick, Page	1	2	3	4		6	7	8	9		11	5	10									
Div F	Feb-04	(h) Lorne Athletic	W 3-0	White, Andrews, Howman	1	2	3	4	10	6	7	8	9		11	5										
SF	Mar-04	(a) Silvertown Rubber Works	L 0-2		1	2	3	4	10	6	7	8	9			5						11				
Middlesex Junior Cup																										
1		Bye																								
2	Nov-05	(h) Harrow Association	W 5-1	White, Howman, Tew 2, Miller							X				X	X										X
3	Nov-26	(h) Harrow Weslyans	W 1-0	Andrews	1	2	3	4	10	6	7	8	9		11	5										
4	Jan-14	(a) Hampstead Town	W 1-0	Page	1	2	3	4	10	6	7	8	9		11	5										
Div F	Feb-25	(a) Deerfield Social	L 0-1		1	2	3	4	10	6	7	8	9		11	5										
West London Charity Cup																										
1		Bye																								
2	Oct-22	(a) Harlesden Amateurs	D 2-2		1	2	3	4	10	6	7	8	9		11	5										
2r	Nov-19	(h) Harlesden Amateurs	W 3-0		1	2	3	4	10	6	7	8	9			5	11									
3	Dec-16	(h) Napier	W 6-0		1	2	3	4	10	6	7	8	9			5	11									
4	Mar-11	(h) Mission Social	W 3-0	Richardson, Tew, Andrews	1	2	3	4	10	6	7	8	9			5						11				
SF	Mar-18	(a) West Kensington	L		1	2	3	4	10	6	7	8	9			5						11				

1911-12

Rd	Date	Opponent	Result	Scorers	Bradbury	Bellchambers	Davey	Pluck	Cane	Miller	White	Tew	Shadwick P	Andrews	Robertson	Kirby R	Rogers	Shadwick J	Pride H	Martin	Howman
Willesden & District Premier League - W/D																					
London League Div II - 2nd																					
	Sep-02	(h) Pinner	L 0-1		1	2	3	4	5	6	7	8	9	10	11						
	Sep-06	(h) Wealdstone Wanderers																			
	Sep-23	(a) Hampstead Town	W 1-0	Andrews	1	2	3	4	5	6	7	8	9	10		11					
	Oct-07	(h) Brailey Ironworks			1	2	3	4	5	6	7	8	9	10		11					
	Oct-28	(h) Hampstead Town	W 7-5	Davey, Andrews 4, Kirby, Tew	1	2	3		5	6	7	8	9	10		11	4				
	Nov-11	(h) Nunhead	D 2-2	Andrews, Shadwick P	1	2	3		5	6	7	8	9	10		11	4				
	Dec-30	(h) Hyde and Kingsbury	W 2-0	Shadwick P, Tew	1	2	3		5	6	7	8	9			11	4	10			
	Jan-20	(h) Shepherds Bush Reserves	W 6-3	Andrews 3, Shadwick J, Shadwick P, Cane	1	2	3		5	6	7		9	10		11	4	8			
	Feb-17	(a) N L Old Boys	W 5-2	White, Pride, Shadwick J, Shadwick P, Cane	1	2	3		5	6	7		9			11	4	8	10		
	Feb-24	(a) Nunhead	W 5-1	Shadwick J, Pride, Kirby 2, Miller		2	3		5	6	7		9			11	4	8	10	1	
	Mar-16	(h) West Norwood	L 1-2	Pride	1	2	3		5	6	7		9	10		11	4		8		
	Mar-09	(a) West Norwood	D 0-0		1	2	3			6			9	10		11	4	8	7	5	
	Apr-13	(h) Ilford	L 0-1		1	2			5	6	7			10		11	4	8	9	3	
London Junior Cup																					
3	Nov-18	(h) Oadby Hall	W 2-1	Bellchambers, White	1	2	3		5	6	7	8	9	10		11	4				
4	Dec-08	(a) West Kensington	W 3-2	Shadwick J, Andrews, Miller	1	2	3		5	6	7		9	10		11	4	8			
Div F	Feb-02	(h) Hyde and Kingsbury	W 3-1	Shadwick P, Andrews, Pluck	1	2	3	4	5	6	7		9	10		11		8			
SF	Mar-02	(a) Walthamstow Avenue	W 2-1	Andrews 2	1	2	3		5	6	7		9	10		11	4	8			
F	Apr-08	(-) Silvertown Rubber Works	L 0-2		1	2	3	9	5	6	7			10		11	4	8			
Middlesex Junior Cup																					
1	Oct-14	(a) Roxeth Brigade Old Boys	D 0-0		1	2	3		5	6	7	8	9	10		11	4				
1r	Oct-21	(h) Roxeth Brigade Old Boys	W 1-0	Rogers	1	2	3		5	6	7	8	9	10		11	4				
2	Nov-04	(h) Harrow Association	W 3-1	Andrews 2, Cane		2	3		5	6	7	8	9	10		11	4				1
3	Nov-25	(a) Harrow St Mary's	W 3-1	Cane, Shadwick P, Andrews	1	2	3		5	6	7	8	9	10		11	4				
4	Jan-13	(h) Neasden Hotspurs	W 2-1	Shadwick J, Pluck	1	2	3	8	5	6	7		9			11	4	10			
Div F	Jan-27	(h) Ivanhoe	D 1-1	Cane	1	2	3		5	6	7		9	10		11	4	8			
Div Fr	Feb-10	(a) Ivanhoe	W 5-1	Cane, Shadwick J, Kirby, Andrews, Bellchambers		2	3		5	6	7		9	10		11	4	8			1
SF	Mar-23	(-) Clapton Warwick	L		1	2	3		5	6	7		9	10		11	4	8			

1912-13

Rd	Date	Opponent	Result	Scorers	Bradberry T	Martin	Bellchambers	Rogers	Cane	Miller	White	Mallett	Walker	Andrews	Kirby	Howman	Cant	Balkwill	Honeyborn	Southwood	Fox	Shadwick P	Rolfe	Robertson
Willesden & District Premier League - 1st																								
London League Div II - 1st																								
	Sep-07	(h) Tower Hamlets	W 8-2	Mallett 4, Walker 3, andrews	1	2	3	4	5	6	7	8	9	10	11									
	Sep-14	(h) Neasden Hotspurs	W 8-0	Mallett 4, Andrews 2, Walker 2	1	2	3	4	5	6		8	9	10	11	7								
	Sep-21	(a) Braleys Ironworks	W 3-1	Mallett, Walker, Andrews	1		3	4	5	6	7	8	9	10	11		2							
	Oct-26	(a) Tufnell Park	W 2-0	Balkwill, Andrews	1	2	3	4	5	6	7	8		10	11			9						
	Nov-01	(h) Chelsea	L 0-2		1	2	3	4	5	6	7	8	9	10	11									
	Dec-14	(h) Fulham St Andrews	W 3-1	Andrews 2, White	1	2	3	4	5	6	7	8		10	11				9					
	Jan-25	(a) West London Old Boys			1	2		4	5	6	7	8		10					9	3	11			
	Feb-22	(h) Tufnell Park	W 10-0	Honeyborn 3, Mallett 3, Cane, Andrews, Kirby, Miller	1	2	3	4	5	6	7	8		10	11				9					
	Mar-15	(a) Fulham St Andrews	W 8-0	Mallett 3, Shadwick 3, Kirby, Balkwill		2		4		6		8			11	1		10	9	3	5	7		
	Apr-19	(a) West Norwood	W 3-0	Kirby, Andrews, Honeyborn	1	2	3	4		6				10	11			9	8		7		5	
	Apr-26	(a) Custom House			1	2	3	4		6				10	11			9	8		7		5	
London Junior Cup																								
1	Nov-16	(a) Turnham Green Garage	L		1	2	3	4	5	6	7	8	9	10	11									
Middlesex Junior Cup																								
1	Nov-08	(h) Harrow Weald	W 8-0	Andrews 2, Kirby, Rogers 2, Cane, Mallett 2	1	2	3	4	5	6	7	8		10	11			9						
2	Nov-30	(a) Harefield	W		1	2	3	4	5	6	7	8	9	10	11									
			W																					
			W																					
5	Feb-01	(h) Talbot	W 1-0	Honeyborn	1	2	3	4	5	6	7	8		10	11			9						
Div F	Feb-08	(h) Harrow Gas Works	W 4-0	Andrews 2, Balkwill 2	1	2	3	4	5	6	7	8		10	11			9						
F	Apr-12	(-) NLP	W 3-1	Shadwick, Balkwill, Southwood	1		3	4	5	6		8		10	11			9		2	7			
Middlesex Charity Cup																								
1	Oct-05	(h) Harrow St Mary's	W 7-1	Bellchambers, Walker 5, Andrews	1	2	3	4		6	7	8	9	10									5	11
2	Oct-19	(a) Roxeth Brigade Old Boys	W 5-1	Walker 3, Andrews, Mallett	1	2	3	4	5	6	7	8	9	10	11									
			W																					
SF	Mar-01	(a) Uxbridge	L 1-3 aban		1	2	3	4	5	6	7	8		10	11			9						
SFr	Mar-08	(a) Uxbridge	D 2-2		1	2	3	4	5	6	7	8		10	11			9						
SFr	Mar-22	(h) Uxbridge	L																					

1913-14

Rd	Date	Opponent	Result	Scorers	Bradberry T	Bellchambers B	Martin F	Rogers F	Rolfe R	Miller H	Butler F	Andrews P	Balkwill W	Theobold F	Howman	Ryder E	Everitt F	May H	Harding A	Baker J	Pierce E	Hillyer G	Shadwick JJ	Shadwick JR	Olibbens H	Smerdon J	Kirby	Fox G	White	Goodege	Walker B	Burton	Tann	Tew	Cane	Gallagher	Simper	Gibbons	Bastin	Deeley	Ward	Andrews D	Robertson A	Baldwin
London League Div I - 3rd																																												
Middlesex League - 3rd																																												
Willesden & District Premier League - 3rd																																												
	Sep-20	(a) Liberty	W 2-1	Balkwill 2	1	2	3	4	5	6	7	8	9	10	11																													
	Sep-20	(h) Tufnell Park														1	2	3	4	5	6	7	8	9	10	11																		
	Sep-27	(h) Ilford	W 4-1	Kirby, Balkwill, Fox	1	2	3	4	5	6		8	9	10													7	11																
	Oct-04	(h) Charlton Athletic Reserves	L 0-1		1	2	3	4	5	6	8	10	9				11										7																	
	Nov-08	(h) Hampstead Town			1	2	3			6		5		9									8				10	11	7															
	Dec-06	(h) East Ham	W 5-0	Kirby 2, Fox 3	1	2	3			6		8	4	10			5										11	9	7															
	Dec-20	(a) Hampstead Town	D 0-0		1	2	3			6		8	4	10			5										11	9	7															
	Jan-03	(a) Page Green Old Boys			1	2	3			6		8	4	10			5										11	9	7															
	Jan-10	(a) East Ham	W 1-0	Fox	1	2	3			6		8		10			5										11	9	7	4														
	Jan-17	(h) Bronze Athletic	L 0-2		1	2	3			6			8	10			5										11	9		4	7													
	Jan-24	(a) Bronze Athletic	D 0-0		1	2	3			6			4	10			5											11	7	9		8												
	Jan-31	(a) West London Old Boys	L 0-2		1		3			6		8	4	10			5											11	7	9		2												
	Feb-06	(h) 2nd Scots Guards	W 3-1	Kirby 2, Andrews	1	2	3			6		8	4	10			5										9	11	7															
	Feb-28	(h) Custom House	W 6-2	Kirby, Theobold 2, Everitt, Andrews, Fox	1	2				6		9	4	10			5										8	11	7	3														
	Mar-07	(a) Tufnell Park	W 5-2	Andrews 3, Fox 2	1	2	3			6		9	4	10			5										8	11	7															
	Mar-14	(h) West London Old Boys	D 0-0 aban		1	2	3			6		9		10			5										8	11	7	4														
	Mar-18	(a) Hampstead Town	L 2-3	Andrews, Fox	1	2	3			6		9		10			5										8	11	7	4														
	Mar-21	(h) 2nd Scots Guards	D 1-1	Kirby	1	2				6		9		10			5									3	8	11	7	4														
	Mar-26	(h) Hampstead Town	L 0-2			2				6		9		10		1	5									3		11	7	4			8											
	Mar-28	(a) Ilford	D 1-1	Andrews	1	2	3			6		9		10			5										8	11	7	4														
	Apr-01	(a) West London Old Boys	L 2-4	Andrews. Kirby		2				6		9		10		1	5									3	8	11		4			7											
	Apr-04	(a) Custom House	W 2-0	White, Gallagher	1	2	3							10							6					8		11	7					4	5	9								
	Apr-11	(h) Barking	W 6-4	Fox 2, Theobold 3, Gallagher						2				10		1	5				6					3		11						4		9	7	8						
	Apr-13	(h) Clifton View	W 2-1	Everitt, Fox						2				10		1	5				6					3		11						4		9	7	8						
	Apr-18	(h) Page Green Old Boys	W 1-0	Theobold	1	2	3			6				10			5											11	7	4						9		8						
	Apr-25	(a) Charlton Athletic Reserves	L 0-1		1	2	3			6				10			5											11		4						9	7	8						
	May-01	(h) Liberty	W 5-0	Goodege, Theobold, Tann 2, Simper						6				10			5									3		11		9			8				7		1	2	4			
The English Cup																																												
1	Sep-13	(h) Page Green Old Boys	L 0-3		1	2	3	4	5	6	7	8	9	10														11																
Amateur Cup																																												
2	Oct-18	(h) Sutton Court	W 5-1	Balkwill 2, White, Shadwick, Andrews	1	2	3			6		5	9		4								8					11	7													10		
3	Nov-01	(a) 3rd Coldstream Guards	L 0-4		1	2	3	4		6		5	9	10														11	7														8	
London Senior Cup																																												
1	Nov-22	(h) Page Green Old Boys	W 5-1	Fox 3, Theobold, Martin	1	2	3			6		10	4	8			5										11	9	7															
2	Nov-29	(a) Tooting	L 1-2	Andrews	1	2	3			6		10	4	8			5										11	9	7															
Middlesex Senior Cup																																												
1	Nov-15	(h) Pinner	L 1-2		1	2	3			6		5		9									8				10	11	7															4

1913-14 to 1918 - 1919 Wealdstone FC ceased playing for the duration of the First World War

1919-20

	Date	Opponents	Result	Scorers	Jacobs G	Kirby H	Smerdon J	Durham J	Harbud F	Tann A	Gallagher W	Wentworth H	Theobold T	Kirby R	Honeybom G	Veale J	Rogers F	Hardy F	Ward W	White S	Ambridge	Burroughs	Miller H	Mascall F	Howman	Stock	Hobbs	Bellchambers	Gawn	Tann	Tew	Shadwick
London League Div I - 4th																																
Middlesex League - 3rd																																
	Aug-30	(h) Catford Southend	W 3-1	Gallagher, Ward, Harbud	1	2	3	4	5	6	7	8	9	10	11																	
	Sep-06	(h) Chiswick Town	L 1-2	Wentworth		2	3	6			9	7	10	11		1	4	5	8													
	Sep-20	(a) Chiswick Town	W 5-4	Wentworth, Ambridge 2, White, Theobold			3	6	5	4		8	10	11		1		2		7	9											
	Oct-25	(h) Islington					3		5			10	9	8		1		4		7		2	6	11								
	Nov-01	(a) Hammersmith	W 5-0	Wentworth 2, Theobold, Kirby 2,								10	9	8																		
	Jan-10	(a) Chiswick Town	D 1-1	Hobbs			3		5			9	10	8				4				2	6		1	7	11					
	Jan-31	(a) Polytechnic	D 2-2	Kirby, Theobold			3		5			9	10	8				4				2	6		1	7	11					
	Feb-07	(h) Charlton Athletic	W 3-0	Kirby, Hobbs, Durham			3	10	5			9		8				4				2	6			7	11	1				
	Mar-20	(h) Handley Page	W 3-2	Wentworth, Kirby, Hobbs					5			7	9	10													11					
	Mar-27	(a) Handley Page	L 1-3	Kirby										10																		
	Mar-31	(h) Harrow Weald	L 0-1				3		5			9	10	8								2	6		1	7	11				4	
	Apr-28	(a) Harrow Weald	D 1-1	Theobold			3		5			9	10	8				4				2	6		1	7	11					
The English Cup																																
Pr																																
Amateur Cup																																
	Oct-17	(a) Chesham United	L 2-4	Wentworth, Kirby			3					9	10	8		1				7		2										
London Senior Cup																																
1	Oct-03	(a) Ravensbourne	D				3		5			9	10	11		1		4		7		2	6									8
1r	Oct-10	(h) Ravensbourne	W																													
2	Nov-15	(a) Kingstonians	L 0-2						5			8	9	10								7			1	11						
Middlesex Senior Cup																																
1	Dec-13	(h) Page Green Old Boys	W 8-0	Kirby 2, Stock 2, Wentworth 2, Theobold, og,			3		5			9	10	8				4				2	6		1	7	11					
2	Jan-17	(a) Enfield	L																													

1920-21

	Date	Opponents	Result	Scorers	Bates R	Burroughs J	Smerdon J	Durham C	Harbud F	Miller H	Stock B	Theobold F	Kirby R	Theobold E	Hobbs W	Smith	Samuels	Burton	Tew	Welch	Gallagher	Pearce	Latham	Craker	Wilson	Cooper	Shadwick J	Hampton	Lavender	Pratt	Smith A	Booth	Wartnaby	Pulker	O'Connell	Mascall	Gibbons	Steele	Tann	White	Gibbs	Henderson	Morgan	I'Hnasen	Butler	Bowman	Holley	Wentworth
London League Div I - 15th																																																
Middlesex League - 1st																																																
	Sep-04	(h) Hyde & Kingsbury	D 3-3	Theobold E, Kirby 2	1	2	3	4	5	6	7	8	9	10	11																																	
	Sep-04	(a) Bexley Heath	L 0-2													1	2	3	4	5	6	7	8	9	10	11																						
	Sep-11	(a) Blackwell & Thames Ironworks	D 1-1	Shadwick		2	3	4	5	6	7	8		10		1										11	9																					
	Sep-18	(a) Leyton	D 1-1	Miller pen	1	2	3	4	5	6		8	7	10												11	9																					
	Sep-18	(h) Waterlows	W 1-0	Hobbs pen											11	1	2	3			5		10	9	8								1	6	7													
	Sep-25	(a) Ordanance	LO 0-6								10				7	1	2	3			5		8		9	11									6													
	Oct-02	(h) Catford Southend	L 0-1													1	2	3		5		7		9	10	11									4	8	6											
	Oct-15	(a) Willesden Town	L 2-3	Wilson, Latham												1	3	9			5	7	8		10										4			2	6	11								
	Nov-06	(h) Hammersmith	W 4-1	Kirby 2, Latham, og	1	2	3	4	5	6		10	9	8									11								7																	
	Nov-13	(a) Harlesden Town	L 1-3													1	2	3			5	11			8	7									4			6	10				9					
	Nov-20	(a) Hampstead Town	L 1-6													1	2	3			5	11			8	7									4			6	10				9					
	Nov-27	(h) Old Lyonians	W 3-1	Smith, Latham, Kirby	1	2	3	4	5	6		10	9	8									11								7																	
	Dec-04	(h) Willesden Town	W 1-0	Theobold E	1	2	3	4	5	6		10	9	8									11								7																	
	Dec-11	(a) RAF Uxbridge	L 0-2		1	2	3	4	5	6		10	9	8									11								7																	
	Jan-15	(h) Coldstream Guards	W 6-2	Kirby 3, Theobold E, Smith, Theobold F	1			4		5		10	9	8				3			3		11								7		6															
	Feb-05	(h) Willesden Town	W 4-0	Kirby 2, Theobold E, og	1	2		4	5	6		10	9	8				3					11								7																	
	Feb-12	(a) Gnome Athletic	L 0-6		1	2		4	5	6		10	9	8				3					11								7																	
	Feb-26	(a) Luton Amateurs	W 2-1	Kirby 2	1		3	4	5	6			9	8			2						11																					7	10			
	Mar-05	(h) Luton Amateurs	W 2-0	Butler, Kirby	1		3	4	5	6			9	8			2						11																					7	10			
	Mar-12	(h) Leyton	W 4-0	Theobold E, Theobold F 2, Latham	1	2	3	4	5	6		10	9	8									11																					7				
	Mar-19	(h) Coldstream Guards	W 3-2	Kirby 2, Theobold E	1		3	4	5	2		10	9	8									11										6											7				
	Apr-09	(a) Hyde & Kingsbury	L 1-3	Smith	1	2	3	4	5	6		10		8							9		11																					7				
	Apr-16	(a) Hertford Town	W 2-0	Kirby, Smith	1	2	3	4	5	6		10	9	8									11								7																	
	Apr-20	(h) Hertford Town	W 3-0	Durham, Theobold F 2	1	2	3	4	5	6		10	9	8									11								7																	
	Apr-23	(a) Croydon South End	W 4-0	Kirby 2, Theobold, Miller	1		3	4	5	6		10	9	8							2		11								7																	
	Apr-30	(a) Old Lyonians	W 3-0	Kirby 2, Theobold F	1	2	3	4	5	6		10	9	8									11								7																	
	May-04	(h) Gnome Athletic	W 2-0	Theobold F 2	1	2	3	4	5	6		10	9	8									11								7																	
The English Cup																																																
Pr	Sep-25	(h) Cheshunt	D 1-1	og	1	3	2	4	5	6		10	11	8													9				7																	
Prr		(a) Cheshunt	L																												7																	
Amateur Cup																																																
P	Oct-02	(a) Harrow Weald	D 1-1	Theobold F	1	3	2	4		6		10	9	8	11																7															5		
Pr	Oct-09	(h) Harrow Weald	W 2-1	Shadwick, og	1	2	3		4	6		10		8	11												9				7															5		
1	Oct-16	(h) Willesden Town	W 3-0	Smerdon, Smith, og	1	2	3	4	5	6		10	11	8													9				7																	
2	Oct-30	(h) Hyde & Kingsbury	W 3-1 aet	Theobold F, Kirby, Smith	1	2	3	4	5	6		10	9	8								11									7																	
3	Nov-20	(h) Uxbridge	W 4-3	Kirby 3, Theobold E	1	2	3	4	5	6		10	9	8									11								7																	
4	Dec-31	(h) Tufnell Park	D 0-0 aet		1	2		4	5	6		10	9	8				3					11								7																	
4r	Jan-01	(a) Tufnell Park	L 1-2 aet	Kirby 3, Theobold E	1	2		4	5	6		10	9	8				3					11								7																	
London Senior Cup																																																
1	Oct-22	(h) Willesden Town	W 4-2	Pierce, Smith, Miller, Theobold E	1	2	3	4	5	6		10	9	8								11									7																	
2	Oct-30	(a) Polytechnic	L 1-7 **	Latham												1		2			5		8		10	11									4			3	6								7	9
		** Reserves fulfilled fixture as 1st Team had a League Game																																														
Middlesex Senior Cup																																																
2Q	Nov-13	(h) Sutton Court	W 2-1	Theobold E 2	1	2	3	4	5	6		10	9	8									11								7																	
1	Jan-22	(a) Wood Green Town	W 4-0	Kirby 2, Latham 2	1			4		5		10	9	8				3			3		11								7		6															
QF	Feb-19	(a) Barnet	L 0-2		1		3	4	5	6			9	8			2						11																					7	10			

1921-22

Rd	Date	Opponent	Result	Scorers	Bates R	Martin H	Smerdon J	Burroughs J	Gibbon	Miller H	Smith A	Theobold E	Kirby R	Theobold F	Latham C	Haskell A	Burton	Samuels	Fleet	Tew	Kemp	I'Anson	Ball	Marsh	Stock	Morgan D	Durham	Harbud F	Butlin J	Gallagher	Davenport	O'Connell	Smith V	Pearce E	Welch B	Randall H	Cracker C	Wentworth	Wilson	Shadwick J	Randall A	Wright E	Bird	Mitchell	Clements	Brett	Wright	Dalby	Deeley	Crowden	Peed	Simper	Mascall F
London League Div I - 11th																																																					
Middlesex League - 1st																																																					
	Sep-03	(a) Willesden Town	W 3-2	Kirby 2, Theobold F	1	2	3	4	5	6	7	8	9	10	11																																						
	Sep-03	(h) Cray Wanderers	L 1-2	Morgan												1	2	3	4	5	6	7	8	9	10	11																											
	Sep-10	(h) Frickers Athletic	D 0-0		1	2	3			6	7	8	9	10	11												4	5																									
	Sep-17	(a) Luton Amateurs	W 2-1	Kirby 2	1	2	3			6		8	9	10	11							7					4	5																									
	Oct-15	(a) Transport Workers	L 1-3		1												2	3			6	7	9			11			4	5	8	10																					
	Oct-22	(h) Cheshunt	L 0-1		1			3									2				6	7				11			4	5	9		8	10																			
	Oct-22	(a) Old Lyonians	L 1-4	Wentworth		2	3			6	7			10		1																			4	5	8	9	11														
	Oct-29	(a) Cheshunt	L 0-3																																																		
	Nov-05	(a) Lensbury	D 1-1	Smith		2	3			6	7	4		10		1												5												11	8	9											
	Nov-05	(h) Transport Workers	W 3-2	I'Anson, Morgan, Davenport				3									2					9				11			4		10			6	5				7				1	8									
	Nov-12	(a) Catford South-End	L 1-2	Mitchell	1			3									2					9				11					10	7	6			5								8									
	Nov-19	(h) Willesden Town	W 2-0	Wright 2		2	3			6	8	4			7	1										11	10	5											7			9											
	Nov-26	(h) Harlesden Town	D 0-0																																																		
	Dec-03	(a) Hyde and Kingsbury	L 0-1			2	3			6				10		1										11	4	5											7			8			9								
	Dec-10	(a) C T D Athletic	L 0-2					3									5	2				9			11				6					4					7				1	8		10							
	Dec-17	(h) Barking Town	W 4-1	og, Mitchell, Wright, Brett		2	3			6						1									11		4									5			7					8		10	9						
	Dec-24	(h) Metropolitan Railway	W 2-0	Theobold F, Wright			3	2			8	6		10													4									5			7				1			11	9						
	Dec-26	(a) HMSO Press	W 6-2	Brett 4 Morgan, Deeley		2	3			6						1										11			4							5			7							10	8		9				
	Dec-31	(a) Metropolitan Railway	W 2-0	Theobold E 2		2	3					4		10		1						9							6							5			7			8				11							
	Jan-07	(a) Harrow Weald	W 5-0	Theobold E 2, Theobold F 2, Brett		2	3			6	9			10		1											4									5			7			8				11							
	Jan-07	(h) Old Aloysians	W 4-1	Davenport 2, Mitchell, Stock	1			3									2	4				8			11				5		10	6	9															7					
	Jan-14	(h) Old Lyonians	W 1-0	Wright		2	3			6		9		11		1											4									5			7			8							10				
	Jan-14	(a) Harlesden Town	L 2-3	Mitchell, Brett													2				3	9			7				4		10	6		5									1	8		11							
	Jan-28	(h) Lensbury	W 1-0	Theobold E	1		3	2		6		10		11													4									5			7			8							9				
	Feb-04	(h) RAF Uxbridge	W 1-0	Deeley		2	3			6				11		1											4	5											7			8				10			9				
	Feb-04	(h) Summerstown	D 2-2	Mitchell 2	1												2	3			6	7				11			4		9						10							8						5			
	Feb-11	(a) Blackwell & Thames Ironworks	L 2-4		1												2	3			6	7				11			4		9													8		10				5			
	Feb-11	(h) Harrow Weald	W 3-0	Deeley 2, Theobold E		2	3			6		10		11		1											4	5											7			8							9				
	Feb-18	(a) L & N W Railway	W 1-0	Deeley		2	3			6		10		11		1											4	5											7			8							9				
	Feb-18	(h) Grays Athletic	D 3-3	Morgan, Randall, Smith	1						8						2	3				7				11			4		9					5										10				6			
	Mar-04	(h) L & NW Railway	W 5-2	Deeley 2, Theobold E 2, Wright		2	3			6	7	10		11		1												5								4						8							9				
	Mar-04	(a) Cray Wanderers	L 2-5																																																		
	Mar-11	(h) Luton Amateurs	W 2-1	Deeley, Wright		2	3			6	7	10		11		1												5								4						8							9				
	Mar-18	(h) Stanmore	D 2-2	Davenport, I'Anson	1												2	3				7				11			4		9	6												8		10				5			
	Mar-18	(h) Hyde and Kingsbury	W 4-3	Deeley 2, Theobold E, Wright		2	3			6	7	10		11		1												5								4						8							9				
	Mar-25	(a) Barking Town	L 0-4				3							11		1		2										5	6		4								7			8				10			9				
	Apr-01	(a) Old Lyonians	W 3-1	Wright 2, Deeley			3		2	6		10		11		1												5											7			8				4			9				
	Apr-08	(h) C T D Athletic	W 2-1	Wright, Miller	1	6						8					2	3				10				11			4		9								7	5													
	Apr-14	(h) Transport Workers	L 1-2	Stocks	1		9	3		5							2				6	7			8	11			4		10																						
	Apr-15	(h) Blackwall & Thames Ironworks	L 1-2	Wilson		2	3									1	9				6					11			4										7							10	8			5			
	Apr-17	(h) Hampstead Town	W 3-1	Peed 2, Wright	1	2	3		5	6		10		11															4													8									9		
	Apr-19	(h) Custom House	D 2-2	Theobold E 2								8		10																	x																		9				
	Apr-22	(a) Summerstown	L 0-8																																																		
	Apr-22	(a) Frickers Athletic	L 1-3	Miller		2	3			6		10		11		1												5	4										7			8							9				
	Apr-26	(h) RAF Uxbridge	L 1-3	Deeley		2	3								10	1										11		5	4										7								8		9			6	
The English Cup																																																					
Pr	Sep-24	(h) Luton Clarence	D 0-0			2	3			6	7	8		10		1										11		5			4									9													
Prr	Sep-28	(a) Luton Clarence	W 3-0	Theobold F, Draper, Latham		3	2			6	7	8		10		1										11		5												9													
1	Oct-08	(a) Hampstead Town	L 0-1			2	3			6	7	8		10		1												5			4								11			9											
Amateur Cup																																																					
P	Oct-01	(a) Chiswick Town	W 1-0	Theobold F		2	3			6	7	8		10	11	1												5													4												9
1	Oct-15	(a) Southall	L 0-1			2	3			6	7	8		10		1												5			4							9	11														
London Senior Cup																																																					
1	Nov-26	(a) Leyland Motors	1-2 aban Fog	Theobold F		2	3			6	8			10		1										11	4	5											7			9											
1r	Dec-10	(a) Leyland Motors	L 0-1			2	3			6	7			10		1										11	4									9					5	8											
Middlesex Senior Cup																																																					
Q	Nov-12	(h) Metropolitan Railway	W 2-0	Wright, Harbud		2	3			6	8	4		10	11	1												5											7			9											
1	Jan-21	(a) RAF Uxbridge	L 2-3	Wright, Theobold E		2		3		6		10		11		1											4	5											7			8							9				

1922-23					Haskell A	Martin G	Spencer V	Gibbons F	Randall E	Deeley P	Wilson E	Theobold F	Peed E	Spencer F	Edwards A	Miller H	Harbud F	Wright	Kirby	Theobold E	Moxon H	Wray	Mold J	Mason C	Beard H	Springthorpe	Shouler	Downing P	Burroughs	Smerdon	Randall E	Hobbs W	Saunders	Butlin	Thompson A	Deeley H	Cole S A	Mascall R	Esser G	Jackson L	Fleet P	Rogers L	Pritchard A	Walden H	Hall R	Pratt J	I'Anson A	Latham C	Simper H
Spartan League - 2nd																																																	
	Sep-16	(h) Wood Green Town	L 1-2	Wright		2	3			6	7		9	10	11		5	9		4	1																												
	Sep-20	(a) Wood Green Town	L 2-5																																														
	Oct-07	(a) Old Lyonians	W 4-2	Mold, Mason 2, Edwards		2	3			6	7				11		5	8		4	1		10	9																									
	Dec-02	(a) Old Latymerians	L 1-3	Peed			3				7		9		11	6	5													2			8	4	10														
	Dec-09	(h) Aylesbury	W 3-0	Mason 2, Saunders			3			6	7				11		5			4				9	1								8		10	2													
	Dec-16	(a) Slough	W 4-0	Downing, Saunders, Edwards, Wilson		2	3			6	7				11		5			4				9	1			10					8																
	Dec-23	(h) Slough	W 6-3	Edwards 3, Mason 2, Downing		2	3				7				10		5			4				9	1			6					8				11												
	Dec-30	(a) Polytechnic	W 3-0	Wilson, Saunders, Edwards		2	3				7				10		5			4				9				6				11	8																
	Jan-06	(h) Polytechnic	W 3-0	Saunders, Edwards, Mason	1	2	3			6	7				10		5			4				9	1			3					8				11												
	Jan-13	(a) Aylesbury	W 5-1	Edwards 2, Mason 2, Wright		2				6	7				10		5	8		4				9	1			3									11												
	Jan-20	(h) Walthamstow Avenue	W 3-1	Wright 2, Edwards		2				6	7	11			10		5	8		4				9	1			3																					
	Feb-10	(a) Maidenhead Unitel	L 0-3			2				6	7						5	9						10	1								8	4			11		3										
	Feb-17	(a) Leavesden Mental Hospital	L 0-2			2	3			6	7						5	8						9	1			10						4			11												
	Mar-10	(a) Finchley	L0-4							6	7				10		5	8						9	1									4						3		2	11						
	Mar-17	(h) Finchley	W 5-0	Walden, Edwards 3, Mason		2	3			6	7				10		5							9	1			11												4				8					
	Mar-24	(a) Great Eastern Railway	W 5-2	Mason 2, Edwards 2, Theobold E		2	3			6	7				10		5	8		4				9	1			11																	8				
	Apr-03	(a) Chesham United	D 2-2	Mason, Walden		2				3	7				10		5							9	1			6			4													8					
	Apr-05	(h) Leavesden Mental Hospital	W 3-1	???		2				3	7				10		5			4				9	1			6																	8				11
	Apr-07	(a) Hertford Town	D 2-2	Hall, Edwards		2				3	7				10		5			4				9	1			6																	8			11	
	Apr-12	(a) Walthamstow Avenue	L 2-6	???		2				5	7				10					4				9	1			6											3						8				11
	Apr-14	(h) Hertford Town	D 2-2	Simper, Mason		2				5	7				10					4				9	1			6											3						8				11
	Apr-18	(h) Old Lyonians	W 2-1																																														
	Apr-21	(h) Great Eastern Railway	W 2-1	Edwards 2		2	3			4	7				10		5							9	1			11																6	8				11
	Apr-28	(h) Chesham United	W 3-1	Mason 2, Edwards		2	3			6	7				10		5			4				9	1			11																	8				
	May-05	(h) Old Latymerians	W 5-0	Hall, Edwards 3, Mason		2	3			6					10		5			4				9	1			11																	8		7		
The English Cup																																																	
Pr	Sep-09	(h) Berkhamstead Town	W 2-0	Spencer, Peed	1	2	3				7		9	10	11	6	5			4																													
1Q	Sep-23	(a) Biggleswade	L 1-2	Deeley		2	3			6	7		9		11		5			4	1	10																											
Amateur Cup																																																	
1P	Sep-30	(h) Polytechnic	W 2-0	Wright, Kirby		2	3			6	7				11		5	8	9	4	1		10																										
2P	Oct-14	(h) Egham Town	W 6-0	Wright 2, Mason 2, Mold, Edwards		2	3			6	7				11		5	8		4			10	9	1																								
3P	Oct-28	(h) Southall	D 1-1	Mason		2	3			5	7				11		5			4	1		10	9				8																					
3Pr	Nov-04	(a) Southall	L 0-6		1					6	7				11		5	8					10	9					2	3	4																		
London Senior Cup							3																																										
1	Oct-21	(h) Railway Clearing House	W 2-1	Wright, Edwards			3			6					11		5	8		4		10		9	1	7	2																						
2	Nov-18	(h) Harlesden	W 9-0	Mason 3, Saunders 3, Downing 3			3			6	7						5			4				9	1			10		2		11	8																
3	Nov-25	(a) Kingstonians	L 0-2							6	7						5			4				9	1			10		2		11	8																
Middlesex Senior Cup																																																	
1	Nov-11	(h) Wood Green Town	W 4-1	Wright, Mason 2, Deeley			3			6	7						5	8		4				9	1			10		2		11																	
2	Jan-27	(h) Hounslow	W 3-1	Edwards 2, Mason		2				6	7				10		5	8		4				9	1			3									11												
3	Feb-24	(a) Botwell Mission	L 1-2	Edwards 2, Mason		2	3			6	7				10		5		8	4				9	1			11																					

1923-24

Rd	Date	Opponent	Result	Scorers	Beard H	Deeley H	Martin G	Glasscock A	Randall E	Deeley P	Wright W	Mascall A	Hall R	Edwards A	Downing A	Theobold E	Mason C	Harbud F	Mold J	Pratt W	Williams J	Wilson E	Moore F	Bird G	Miller H	Hart K	Esser C	Haskell A	Smerdon J	Nightingale L	Rogers E	Gregory H	Hulett R	Proud J	I'Anson A	Firmer H	Melhuish J	Davis A	Sims G	Goodman	Tilley	Evershed	Wallace	Mascall F	Beale	Theobold F
Spartan League - 5th																																													
	Sep-01	(h) Leavesden	W 3-1	Edwards 2, Mascall	1	2	3		5	6	7	8		10	11	4	9																													
	Sep-15	(a) RAF Uxbridge	W 6-4	Edwards 4, Mason, Wright	1	2	3		6		7	8		10	11	4	9	5																												
	Sep-29	(a) Maidenhead	D 2-2	Mason 2	1	2				6	7	8		10	3	4	9	5	11																											
	Nov-10	(a) Great Eastern Railway (Romford)	D 1-1	Mascall	1					6	7	8	11		3	4	9	5		2	10																									
	Dec-01	(h) Old Lyonians	L 2-3	Hall, Mascall	1	2		5		6		8	9		3				10		4	7	11																							
	Dec-08	(a) Hertford Town	L 1-2	Williams		2				6	8		10		3	4					4	7		1	6	11																				
	Dec-15	(h) Walthamstow Avenue	D 1-1	Hall, Mascall						5	8		10		3	4					4	7	11	1	6																					
	Dec-22	(a) Slough	L 3-11	Wright 2, Hall						5	7	8	9		6	4				2	10		11	1			3																				
	Dec-29	(h) Great Eastern Railway (Romford)	D 2-2	Edwards, Hall		2				6	7	8	9	10	3	4		5				11		1																							
	Jan-05	(a) Walthamstow Avenue	D 1-1	Edwards		2				5	7	8	9	10		4							11			6			1	3																		
	Jan-12	(h) Wood Green Town	W 2-1	Edwards 2		2				5	7	8	11	10		4							9			6			1	3																		
	Feb-23	(h) Old Latymerians	W 4-1	Edwards, Mascall, Wilson, Miller		2				5	7	8	11	10		4							9			6			1		11																	
	Mar-01	(a) Polytechnic	W 3-0	Hall, Wilson, Edwards		2				5	7	8	11	10							4	9			6			1			3																
	Mar-15	(a) Old Latymerians	W 7-0	Wilson 3, Mascall 3, Edwards		2					7	8	11	10	3	4		5				9			6			1			3																
	Mar-20	(a) Chesham United	W 4-0	Theobold, Wilson, Edwards		2					7	8	11	10	3	4		5				9			6			1																			
	Mar-22	(a) Leavesden Mental Hospital	L 1-4	Edwards		2			5		7	8	11	10	3	4							9			6			1																			
	Apr-05	(h) Maidenhead	W 3-0	Edwards 2, Wilson		2			5		7	8	11	10	3	4							9						1				6														
	Apr-12	(a) Old Lyonians	W 2-0	Edwards, Mascall		2			5		7	8	11	10	3	4							9									6	1														
	Apr-16	(h) Slough	W 3-1	Wilson 3,			2			5	7	8	11		3	4				10			9			6			1																			
	Apr-19	(h) Aylesbury	L 1-2	Firmer			2		5			11								10		8											3	6	1	4	7	9										
	Apr-26	(h) Chesham United	W 5-1	Wilson 3, Wright, og					5		7	8			3	4							9			6			1											2	10	11							
	Apr-30	(a) Aylesbury	L 0-4				2		5		7	8	9		3	4				10							6																			1	11					
	May-03	(a) Wood Green Town	L 2-3				2					7	8			3					10							6			1																4	5	9	11		
	Unknown	(h) Hertford Town	W 4-1																																												
	Unknown	(h) RAF Uxbridge	W 4-0																																												
	Unknown	(h) Polytechnic	W 4-1																																												
FA Cup																																													
XPr	Sep-08	(h) Arlesey Town	W 4-1	Edwards 3, Mason	1	2	3		5	6	7	8		10	11	4	9																													
Pr	Sep-22	(h) Biggleswade	W 2-1	Edwards, Mascall	1	2	3			6	7	8		9	11	4		5	10																											
1Q	Oct-06	(a) Hertford Town	D 0-0		1	2				6	7	8		10	3	4	9	5	11																											
1Qr	Oct-10	(h) Hertford Town	W 5-3	Hall 3, Beale, Edwards	1	2		9		6	7	8		10	3		9	5			4																								11	
2Q	Oct-20	(h) Tufnell Park	L 0-1		1	2	3			6	7	8	11	10		4	9	5																												
Amateur Cup																																													
1	Oct-13	(h) 12th London Regiment	W 22-0	Mason 7, Edwards 6, Mascall 4, Hall 3, Deeley P, og	1	2	3			6	7	8	11	10		4	9	5																												
2	Oct-27	(h) RAF Uxbridge	W 6-0	Theobold F 3, Hall 2, Mason	1	2	3			6	7		11		9		10	5			4																									8
3	Nov-17	(a) Staines Lagonda	L 0-2		1	2	3				7	8	11		10		9	5			4																									6
London Senior Cup																																													
3Q	Nov-03	(a) Summerstown	W 4-0	Williams 2, Mason 2	1	2	3			6	7		11		9		10	5			4																									8
4Q	Nov-24	(h) Finchley	L 0-3		1	2	3				7	8	11		10		9	5			4																									6
Middlesex Senior Cup																																													
1	Jan-26	(a) Wood Green Town	D 2-2	Hall, Mascall		2				5	7	8	9	10	3	4										6			1																			
1r	Feb-02	(h) Wood Green Town	W 4-2	Edwards 3, Wilson		2				5	7	8	11	10	3	4							9			6			1																			
2	Feb-16	(a) Cheshunt	W 4-3	Edwards 3, Wilson			2			5	7	8	11	10	3	4							9			6			1																			
SF	Mar-29	(n) Bush Hill Park	W 1-0 *	Wilson		2				5	7	8	11	10	3	4							9			6			1																			
F	Apr-21	(n) Southall	L 1-3 **	Mascall			2			5	7	8	11	10	3								9			6			1				4														
	* Played at Old Lyonians ** Played at RAF Uxbridge																																												
Middlesex Charity Cup																																													
1	Jan-19	(h) Tufnell Park	W 3-1	Wilson, Deeley P, og		2				5	7	8	11	10		4							9			6			1	3																		
2	Mar-08	(a) Botwell Mission	L 1-2	Edwards		2	3			5	7	8	11	10		4							9			6			1																			

1924-25

Rd	Date	Opponent	Result	Scorers	Bastin	Deeley H	Martin A	Harbud F	Randall	Miller H	Wright	Mascall	Wilson	Edwards	Hall G	Haskall A	Pratt W	Kemp S	Theobold E	Gregory A	Williams J	Summer A	Groves E	Sims	Bird G	L'Anson A	Weaver J	Downing A	Biddle W	Creasey E	Mold J	Wartnaby R	Morton W	Deeley P	Smith R	Jackson H	Rogers C	Johnson	Dellow J	Jones	Davis G	Willis J	Latham C
Spartan League - 10th																																											
	Aug-30	(h) Botwell Mission	L 1-4	Edwards	1	2	3	4	5	6	7	8	9	10	11																												
	Sep-06	(a) Hertford Town	L 0-2					5				8	9		11	1	2	3	4	6	7	10																					
	Sep-10	(a) Botwell Mission	L 0-2																																								
	Sep-13	(h) Staines Lagonda	D 2-2	Groves 2				5				8	9		10	1	2	3	4	6			7	11																			
	Sep-03	(a) RAF Uxbridge	L 1-2	Edwards	1	2	3	4	5	6		8	9	10	11						7																						
	Nov-03	(h) Slough	W 4-1	Groves 3, Mascall		2		5				8			10			3	4	6			9		1	7	11																
	Dec-06	(h) Walthamstow Avenue	D 2-2	Wilson 2		10		5				8	9					2	4	6					1	7	11	3															
	Dec-20	(h) Maidenhead United	W 7-1	Theobold, Hall 3, Groves 3		2		5							10			3	8				9		1	7	11		4	6													
	Dec-27	(a) Chesham United	L 0-5			2		5							10			3	8				9		1	7	11		4	6													
	Jan-03	(a) Slough	L 0-4			2		8		6								3		4			9		1	7			5		10	11											
	Jan-17	(h) Aylesbury United	W 4-1	Wilson 3, Williams		2		5					9					3	4	6	8				1	7	11				10												
	Jan-31	(a) Great Eastern Railway Romford	L 0-2			2		5					9					3	4	6	8		10		1	7	11																
	Feb-14	(h) Old Latymerians	W 4-1	Theobold, I'Anson 2, Johnson													4	3	10		8		9		1	7							2	5	6	11							
	Feb-28	(h) Hertford Town	W 2-1	Groves, Deeley		8		5					9					2	4				10		1	7	11	3							6								
	Mar-07	(a) Staines Lagonda	W 2-1	Wilson, Smith		2		5					9					3	10	6	8				1		10								11								
	Mar-14	(h) Wood Green Town	L 1-2	Wilson		2			5				9					3	4	6	8						11								10		1						
	Mar-25	(a) Polytechnic	L 0-4				2		5								4			6	8		9		1		11	3										7	10				
	Apr-04	(a) Old Latymerians	D 2-2	Wilson, Weaver				5				8	9					2	4	6				10		7	11	3									1						
	Apr-08	(h) RAF Uxbridge	L 1-5	Wilson																																							
	Apr-13	(h) Polytechnic	W 6-1	Jones 3, Mascall 2, og		2						8			10			6	4	5	7			11				3									1			9			
	Apr-18	(h) Chesham United	D 2-2	Edwards, Wilson		2		5				8	9	10					4	6						7	11										1			3			
	Apr-25	(a) Wood Green Town	L 1-6	Weaver		2	1		5				9	10					4	6				11			7	3													8		
	Apr-29	(h) Great Eastern Railway Romford	D 2-2	??																																							
	May-01	(a) Aylesbury United	L 1-2	Groves																																							
	Unknown	(a) Walthamstow Avenue	D 2-2	??																																							
	Unknown	(a) Maidenhead United	L 1-3	?																																							
FA Cup																																											
Pr	Sep-20	(a) Tufnell Park	W 2-1	Groves 2		2		5			7	8			10			3	4	6			9				11										1						
1Q	Oct-04	(a) Waterlows (Dunstable)	L 1-2	Hall		2	2	5			7	8			10		4	3		6			9				11										1						
Amateur Cup																																											
1	Oct-11	(h) Ashford Town	W 5-0	Groves 3, Hall 2			2					8			10			3	4	6			9			7	11		5								1						
2	Oct-25	(h) Uxbridge Town	L 1-3	Groves								8			10			2	4	6			9		1	7	11	3						5									
London Senior Cup																																											
1Q	Sep-27	(h) Latymer Old Boys	W 5-1	Groves 2, Hall 2, Mascall			2	5			7	8			10		4	3		6			9				11										1						
2Q	Oct-18	(h) Hendon Town	D 3-3 aet	Gregory, Groves 2			2	5				8			10			2	4	6			9			7	11	3									1						
2Qr	Nov-01	(a) Hendon Town	L 1-2	Groves				5							10		2	3		6			9		1	7	11				10											4	
2Qr*	Nov-15	(a) Hendon Town	W 3-1	Groves, Hall, Mascall				5				8			10			2	4	6			9		1	7	11	3															
3Q	Nov-22	(h) Polytechnic	W 3-2	Groves, Hall 2		2		5				8			10			3	4	6			9		1	7	11																
4Q	Nov-29	(a) Hounslow	W 4-0	Groves 3, Hall				5				8			10			2	4	6			9		1	7	11	3															
5Q	Dec-13	(h) Finchley	W 2-0	Mascall 2		2		5				8			10			3	4	6			9		1	7	11																
1	Jan-10	(h) Bromley	W 3-2	Wilson 3		2		5					9		10			3	4	6	8				1	7	11																
2	Feb-07	(h) London Caledonians	L 1-2	Hall		2		5					9		10		4	3		6	8				1	7	11																
	2Qr* Match replayed. Wealdstone protested about the size of the pitch.																																										
Middlesex Senior Cup																																											
1	Jan-24	(a) Bush Hill Park	L 0-1			2		5		6			9					3	4	10	8				1	7																	11
Middlesex Charity Cup																																											
1	Feb-21	(h) Old Lyonians	W 2-0	Theobold 2				5					9					2	4		8			11	1	7		3							6						10		
2	Mar-28	(a) Uxbridge Town	L 0-4					5				8	9		10			2	4	6					1	7	11	3															

1925-26

Date	Opponent	Result	Scorers	Rogers J	Kemp L	Martin W	Williams James	Downing A	Gregory R	I'Anson A	Mascall A	Wilson E	Smith H	Edwards A	Martin G	Pratt A	Leetch W	Williams John	Hart G	Dutton H	Harbud F	Weaver J	Deeley H	Davis G	Berryman W	Randall E	Clark H	Champion A	Bird G	Leigh F	Walker	Riley C	Groves N	Whitting H	Hall G	Goodall R	Smith R	Ramsey J	Church A	Kettle H	Tilley A	Russell F	Kohl H	Sims G	Dawe H
Spartan League - 7th																																													
Aug-29	(h) Slough	L 2-4	Edwards 2	1	2	3	4	5	6	7	8	9	10	11																															
Sep-02	(a) Botwell Mission	L 1-6																																											
Sep-05	(a) GER Romford	L 1-5	Edwards	1	3				5	7		9	10	11	2	4	6	8																											
Sep-09	(a) RAF Uxbridge	W 5-4																																											
Sep-12	(a) Wood Green Town	W 3-2	Smith 3	1	2			3	6	7			9	11		4		10	5	8																									
Sep-25	(a) Maidenhead United	L 1-4	Harbud	1	2			3	6	7			9	10		4		8			5	11																							
Nov-07	(h) Chesham United	D 4-4	Wilson 2, I'Anson, Downing	1	3			11	6	7		9						4		8	5		2	10																					
Nov-14	(h) Botwell Mission	L 0-2		1	3			11	6	7		9						4		8	5		2	10																					
Nov-21	(a) Staines Town	L 1-11	Weaver	1				11	6	7		9						4		8	5	10	2		3																				
Dec-05	(h) Aylesbury United	W 3-2	og, Clark, I'Anson	1	2				6	7		9				4				8		11			3	5	10																		
Dec-12	(h) Maidenhead United	L 1-4	Champion	1	3			6		7		9						4				11	2			5	10	8																	
Dec-19	(a) Chesham United	L 0-2			3			6		7	9							4			5		2				10	8	1	11															
Jan-02	(a) Walthamstow Avenue	D 2-2	Champion, Leigh	1				3		7		8														8	10	9		11		2	4	6											
Jan-09	(h) Staines Town	W 5-2	Clark, Leigh, Wilson 2, Champion	1				3		7		8				2		4								8	10	9		11				6											
Jan-23	(h) Sutton Court	W 6-2	Mascall 2, Champion 2, Wilson 2	1	2			3		7	8		6					4								5	10	9							11										
Jan-30	(a) Sutton Court	W 4-1	Clark, Champion 2,Wilson	1	2			3		7		8	6			4										5	10	9							11										
Feb-06	(a) Hertford Town	L 3-7	Clark, Leigh, Champion, Wilson 2	1	3					7		8						4					2			5	10	9						6	11										
Feb-13	(h) Hertford Town	W 11-1	Wilson 5, Champion 4, Clark 2	1	3			11		7		8						4					2			5	10	9						6											
Feb-20	(h) Wood Green Town	w 4-0	Champion 2, Clark, Wilson	1	3			11		7		8				2		4								5	10	9						6											
Feb-27	(a) Aylesbury United	W 3-0	Clark, og, Champion	1	3			11		7		8				2		4					5				10	9						6											
Mar-06	(h) Colchester Town	W 3-2	Smith, Downing	1				11					6			2		4					3			5	10	9								7	8								
Mar-13	(a) Colchester Town	L 1-2	Champion	1				11		7		8	6			2		4					5				10	9										3							
Mar-20	(a) Polytechnic	W 4-0	Champion 2, Clark 2	1	2							8	6					4					5				10	9								7		3	11						
Apr-02	(h) Walthamstow Avenue	W 3-2	Champion 2, og	1				3		7		8				5		4					2				10	9											11		6				
Apr-09	(a) Slough	L 0-3		1	3			11		7	8		4			5							2				10	9														6			
Apr-16	(h) GER Romford	D 1-1	I'Anson							7	8		6			5		4					2				10	9										3			11				
Unknown	(h) Polytechnic	D 1-1																																											
Unknown	(h) RAF Uxbridge	W 5-3																																											
FA Cup																																													
Pr Sep-19	(h) Hitchin Blue Cross	W 4-1	Smith 3, Pratt	1	2			3	6			7	9	10		4		8			5	11																							
1Q Oct-03	(h) Baldock Town	D 1-1	Smith	1	2			3	6		10	7	9			4		8			5	11																							
1Qr Oct-08	(a) Baldock Town	L 0-2		1		2		3	6	7	8	9				4		10			5																						11		
Amateur Cup																																													
1 Oct-10	(h) Staines Town	L 2-3	Williams, Wilson	1	2			3	6	7		8				4		9			5	10																						11	
London Senior Cup																																													
1 Oct-31	(a) Finchley	L 0-5		1	2			3	6	7		10	9			4		8				11																							5
Middlesex Senior Cup																																													
1 Oct-17	(a) Finchley	L 1-3	Williams	1	2			3	6	7		8	10			4		9			5	11																							
Middlesex Charity Cup																																													
1 Jan-16	(a) Botwell Mission	L 2-5	Champion 2	1				3		7		8				2		4								5	10						6												

1926-27

Rd	Date	Opponent	Result	Scorers	Berry W	Pratt WW	Downing A	Williams J	Randell E	Smith R	Goodall RS	Donleavy H	Tansley RW	Champion A	Church A	Ryder E	Deeley H	Smith H	Short J	Cantrell A	Wilson E	Martin G	L'Anson A	Hoskins L	Kemp L	Alford B	Lee E A	Caslake J	Rogers J	Mascall A	Buckingham J	Johnson A	Groves L	Wright A	Wilcox A	Groves R	Stebbing H	Ellis A J	Tilley E	Hunt J	Butland W
Spartan League - 4th																																										
	Sep-04	(a) Wood Green Town	W 2-1	Tansley, Williams	1	2	3	4	5	6	7	8	9	10	11																										
	Sep-08	(h) Polytechnic	W 4-1	Ryder, Champion 2, Goodall	1	2	3	4	5	6	7		8	10	11	9																									
	Sep-11	(h) Sutton Court	W 5-0	Tansley 2, Ryder, Goodall 2	1	2	3	4	5	6	7		9	8	11	10																									
	Sep-16	(a) Aylesbury	W 4-3	Tansley 2, Ryder 2	1	2	3	4		6	7		8			9	5	10	11																						
	Sep-25	(a) Hertford Town	W 6-2	Tansley 5, H Smith	1	2	3	4		6	7		9	8	11	5		10																							
	Sep-28	(h) Aylesbury	W 6-0	Tansley 2, H Smith 3, Ryder																																					
	Dec-11	(h) Maidenhead	L 0-3		1	2	3			6	7		9	10	11	5				4	8																				
	Dec-18	(a) Sutton Court	W 6-2	Champion, Tansley 3, Hoskins 2	1		3	4		6			9	10	11	5						2	6	7																	
	Dec-25	(h) Hertford Town	W 16-2	Champion 3, Tansley 7, H Smith 2, Church 3, L'Anson	1	2	3	4		6			9	10	11	5		8					6																		
	Jan-15	(a) Slough	L 1-3	Tansley	1	2		4		6	7		9	10	11	5		8							3																
	Feb-05	(h) Walthamstow Avenue	W 5-3	Champion, Wilson, Downing, Alford 2,	1	2	11	4		6	7			10		5					8				3	9															
	Feb-26	(h) Wood Green	W 4-1	Champion 2, Alford 2	1	2	3	4		6				10		5					8			7		9	11														
	Mar-05	(a) Great Eastern Railway	L 2-5	Alford, Wilson	1	2	3	4		6				10		5					7			8		9	11														
	Mar-12	(h) Slough	D 2-2	Champion, Alford	1	2		4		6	7			10		5					8					9	11	3													
	Mar-16	(a) Polytechnic	D 2-2	?																																					
	Mar-31	(a) Chesham United	L 2-5	Hoskins 2		2	11	4		6			9			5		10						8				3	1	7											
	Apr-09	(a) Staines Town	L 1-5*	Champion	1			4		6			9	10		5					7	2		8	3																
	Apr-13	(a) Lyons Athletic	W 3-2	Hoskins 2, Champion	1			4		6			8	10		5	2				7			9	3						11										
	Apr-16	(a) Walthamstow Avenue	W 3-2	Tansley, Wilson, Ryder	1		3	4		6			10			5	2				9						11			8		7									
	Apr-18	(a) Maidenhead United	L 1-7	Tansley	1					6			8			5			4			2		9				3				7	10	11							
	Apr-23	(h) Chesham United	W 4-2	Tansley 2, Downing 2	1	2	11	4		6			9	10				5			8		7		3																
	Apr-25	(h) Great Eastern Railway	D 1-1	Ryder	1	2	3							10		5			6	4	8		7	9									11								
	Apr-30	(h) Colchester	L 3-4	Wilcox, Lee 2	1	2		4		6			10			5				8			7		3		11								9						
	May-02	(h) Staines Town	W 5-2	Tansley 2, Hoskins 2, Smith R	1	2	11	4		6			8			5		10					7	9	3																
	May-04	(h) Botwell Mission	W 2-1	Lee, Hoskins	1	2	3	4		6			8			5		10					7	9			11														
	May-07	(a) Colchester	W 4-3	Groves R 2, Downing 2	1	5	10	4		6			8				2						7		3								11			9					
	Unknown	(h) Lyons Athletic	W																																						
	Unknown	(a) Botwell Mission	W																																						
		* played with 10 men																																							
FA Cup																																										
Pr	Sep-18	(h) Leavesden Mental Hospital	W 2-0	Tansley, Ryder	1	2	3	4		6	7		8	10	11	9	5																								
1Q	Oct-02	(h) Apsley	W 3-1	Ryder 2, H Smith	1	2	3	4		6	7		8	11		9		10		5																					
2Q	Oct-16	(h) Waterlows	L 1-5	Champion	1	2	3	4	5	6	7		9	8	11	10																									
Amateur Cup																																										
1Q	Oct-09	(a) Civil Service	W 2-1 aet	Champion 2	1	2	3	4	5	6	7		8	10	11	9																									
2Q	Oct-23	(h) Polytechnic	W 2-1	Champion, Goodall	1	2	3	4	5	6	7		8	10	11	9																									
3Q	Nov-20	(h) RAF Uxbridge	W 9-3	Tansley 3, Ryder, Church 2, Champion, H Smith, og,	1	2	3	4		6	7		9	10	11	5		8																							
4Q	Dec-04	(a) Hendon	W 4-1	Champion 3, Wilson, Goodall	1	2		4		6	7		9	10	11	5					8							3													
1	Jan-01	(h) Maidenhead	L 1-2	H Smith	1	2		4		6			9	10	11	5	3	8					7																		
London Senior Cup																																										
3Q	Oct-30	(a) Great Eastern Railway	D 1-1	Ryder	1	2	3	4		6	7		8	10	11	9																					5				
3Qr	Nov-06	(h) Great Eastern Railway	W 7-1	Champion 2, Tansley 3, H Smith 2	1	2	3	4		6	7		9	8	11	5		10																							
4Q	Nov-27	(h) Metropolitan Police	W 3-1	Champion, Tansley, Church	1	2		4		6	7		9	10	11	5		8										3													
5Q	Jan-08	(h) Savoy	W 6-3	Champion (pen), Tansley 4, Goodall	1	2		4		6	7		9	10	11	5		8							3																
1	Jan-29	(a) Barking Town	L 0-6		1		3	4		6	7		9	10	11	5		8							2																
Middlesex Senior Cup																																										
1	Jan-22	(h) Hounslow	W 6-2	Champion 2, Tansley, H Smith 2, Goodall	1	2	11	4		6	7		9	10		5		8							3																
2	Feb-12	(h) RAF Uxbridge	W 8-2	Champion 3, Wilson 3, H Smith, Short	1		3	4		6	7			10		5		8	11		9				2																
SFr	Mar-19	(h) Uxbridge Town	D 1-1	Champion	1	2	3	4		6			8	10		9		5			7						11														
SFr	Mar-26	(a) Uxbridge Town	L 1-6	og	1	2	11	4		6			8	10		9		5			7							3													
Middlesex Charity Cup																																										
	Feb-19	(h) Tufnell Park	W 5-2	Champion, Alford 2, Wilson, Goodall	1	2	3	4		6	7			10		5					8					9												11			
SF	Apr-02	(a) Barnet	L 2-12	Tansley 2	1					4			9	10		2		5										3		8									6	7	11

1927-28

Rd	Date	Opponent	Result	Scorers	Berry W	Deeley H	Bowtle H	Williams J	Kemp L	Smith R	I'Anson A	Tansley R	Hannam E	Groves R	Eagle A	Gates A	Halford F	Cochran J	Downing A	Ryder E	Groves N	Pratt W	Collins F	Hoskins L	Bradshaw AA	Maskell T	Hill R	Allcock W	Fraser L	Short J	Groves L	Sims G	Miall H	Stocks A	Carey A	Davis G	Vance A	Welch F	Harbud F	Smith H	Puddephatt W	Caslake J	Rogers L
Spartan League - 4th																																											
	Sep-03	(a) Maidenhead U	L 0-3		1	2	3	4	5	6	7	8	9	10	11																												
	Sep-07	(h) Berkhamsted T	W 2-1	Tansley, R Groves	1		2	4	3	6		8		9	11	5	7	10																									
	Sep-10	(h) Polytechnic	W 8-2	R Groves 2, N Groves 3, Ryder (pen), og 2	1			4	2	6		10		8	11		7		3	5	9																						
	Sep-14	(a) Berkhamsted T	L 1-3	Eagle	1		3	4		6		9		8	11		7	10		5		2																					
	Oct-01	(h) Wood Green Town	W 4-1	Hoskins, Bradshaw, Collins, Ryder	1		2					8		4	11				3	5	6		7	9	10																		
	Oct-15	(a) Slough	W 2-0	Collins 2	1		2			6		9			11				3	5		4	10		8	7																	
	Nov-05	(a) Aylesbury U	L 2-8	Tansley, Ryder	1			4		6		9			11				3	5		2	10		8	7																	
	Dec-03	(a) Polytechnic	W 4-1	Tansley 4 (2 pens)					2	6		9		4	11				3	5					10	7	1	8															
	Dec-10	(h) Aylesbury U	W 3-0	Tansley, Collins, Allcock			2			6		9		4	11				3	5			10			7	1	8															
	Dec-17	(h) Wood Green Town	W 3-2	Tansley, Maskell, Ryder			2			6		9		4	11				3	5			10			7	1	8															
	Dec-24	(a) Botwell Mission	L 2-4	Tansley, Bowtle			8			6		9		4	11					5			10			7	1		2	3													
	Dec-31	(h) Hertford Town	W 6-1	Tansley 3, Collins 3 (1 pen)			2			6		9		4	11				3	5			10	8		7	1																
	Jan-14	(h) Slough	D 4-4	Tansley 3, Hannam			2			6		9	8	4					3	5			10			7	1				11												
	Jan-21	(h) GE Railway	W 7-3	Tansley 3, Collins 2 (1 pen),Hannam,og			2			6		9	8	4	11				3	5			10			7	1																
	Feb-11	(h) Walthamstow Ave	L 2-3	Tansley, Collins			2			6		9	8	4					3	5			10			7	1					11											
	Feb-25	(a) GE Railway	D 2-2	Hannam, R Groves						6		9	8	4	11				3	5			10			7							1	2									
	Mar-10	(a) Hertford Town	W 8-2	Tansley, Hannam 2,Maskell,Bowtle 3,L Groves			10					9	8	4					3	5			6			7					11		1	2									
	Mar-24	(a) Chesham U	L 1-7	Maskell								9	8	4					3	5			2			7					11		1		6	10							
	Mar-31	(a) Colchester T	W 2-1	Tansley 2								9	8	4					3	5			10			7				6	11		1	2									
	Apr-06	(h) Lyons Club	W 3-0	Tansley, Hannam, R Groves								9	8	4					3	5			10			7				6	11		1	2									
	Apr-07	(h) Maidenhead U	W 5-4	Tansley 2,Hannam,Collins, R Groves (pen)								9	8	4						5			10			7				6	11		1	3			2						
	Apr-09	(a) Lyons Club	W 6-0	Tansley 2,Hannam 2,Ryder,R Groves (pen)								9	8	4					3	5			10			7				6	11		1	2									
	Apr-14	(h) Chesham U	W 3-2	Tansley 2, Maskell								9	8	4					3	5			10			7					11		1	2				6					
	Apr-18	(h) Staines	W 4-1	Tansley 3, Hannam								9	8	4					3	5			10			7				6	11		1	2									
	Apr-23	(a) Walthamstow Ave	L 1-2	Ryder								9	8	4					3	5			10			7				6	11		1	2									
	Apr-26	(a) Staines	D 2-2	Collins, Hoskins								9		4					3	5			10	8		7			2	6	11		1										
	Apr-28	(h) Botwell Mission	L 0-2									9	8	4					3				10			7				6	11		1	2				5					
	May-05	(h) Colchester T	W 3-1	Tansley, Hannam, Collins								9	8	4					3				10			7					11		1	2					5	6			
FA Cup																																											
Pr	Sep-17	(h) Waterlow's (Dunstable)	L 2-7	R Groves, H Smith	1			4		6		8		9	11		7		3	5		2																		10			
Amateur Cup																																											
	Oct-08	(h) Uxbridge Town	W 4-3	Tansley 2, H Smith, Maskell	1		2			6		9		4	11				3	5					8	7														10			
	Oct-22	(a) Hendon T	W 6-4	Tansley 3, Collins 2, Eagle	1		2			6		9			11				3	5		4	10		8	7																	
3Q	Nov-12	(a) Civil Service	L 2-3	Collins, Ryder	1				2	6		9		4	11				3	5			10			7															8		
London Senior Cup																																											
3Q	Oct-29	(h) Walthamstow Ave	W 4-1	Tansley 2, Maskell, Eagle	1		2			6		9			11				3	5		4	10		8	7																	
	Nov-19	(a) Summerstown	L 4-6	Tansley, Bowtle 2, Maskell			8		2	6		9		4	11				3	5					10	7	1																
Middlesex Senior Cup																																											
1	Jan-28	(h) Old Lyonians	D 3-3 aet	Hannam, Maskell, Bowtle			2			6		9	8	4	11				3	5			10			7	1																
1r	Feb-04	(a) Old Lyonians	W 5-4 aet	Tansley, Hoskins 2, L Groves, Ryder					2	6		9		4					3	5			10	8		7	1				11												
2	Feb-18	(h) Met. Police	L 3-6	Hannam 2, Collins	1					6		9	8	4						5			10			7			2		11											3	
2r†	Mar-03	(h) Met. Police	L 3-7 aet	Tansley 2, L Groves						6		9	8	4					3	5			10			7					11			2									1

†Game replayed as Met. Police fielded ineligable player in 1st match.

1928-29

Rd	Date	Opponent	Result	Scorers	Grafton W	Deeley HM	Stocks A	Groves R	Ryder EE	Harbud F	Maskell T	Hannam A	Hoskins L	Clark RL	Groves L	Downing A	Short DJ	Smith H	Champion AE	Pyle EJ	Turner TJ	Davies C	Dunn RV	Wilson E	Whiting	Foster R	Gardner V	Leach W	Burrows R	Hill R	Clifford A	Poulson W	Vance J	Dale F	Wheeler A	Marks Sgt	Massey JA	Welch FW	Clark R	Bollen R	Ayres R
Athenian League - 8th																																									
	Aug-25	(h) Enfield T	L 3-4	Clark 2, L Groves	1	2	3	4	5	6	7	8	9	10	11																										
	Sep-01	(h) Sutton U	L 2-4	L Groves 2	1	2		4	5		7	8		9	11	3	6	10																							
	Sep-08	(a) Sutton U	L 1-2	Clark	1	2		4	5		7	8		9		3	6	11	10																						
	Sep-22	(h) Southall	L 1-3	Clark (pen)	1	2	3	4	5		7	8		9	11		6		10																						
	Oct-13	(h) Kingstonians	W 2-1	R Groves, Hannam	1			9			7	8		3		11	6	5	10	2	4																				
	Nov-24	(a) Windsor & E	W 5-1	R Groves, Champion 2, Hannam, Downing	1			9			7	8		2		11	6	5	10		4	3																			
	Dec-25	(h) Hampstead T	L 2-3	Hannam, Whiting			2	9				8		3			6	5	10		4		1	7	11																
	Dec-26	(a) Hampstead T	L 1-3	Champion	1		2					8		6		3	5		10		4			7	11	9															
	Dec-29	(h) Windsor & E	W 10-1	Champion 3,Foster 2,Hannam 2,Maskell,Whiting,Clark	1	2					7	8		6			5		10		4	3			11	9															
	Jan-05	(h) Cheshunt	W 7-3	Champion 2, Foster 3, Maskell, Short	1					5	7	8		2			6		10		4	3			11	9															
	Jan-19	(a) Southall	L 4-8	R Groves, Smith (pen), Whiting 2	1		2	9			7			10			6	5			4	3			11		8														
	Feb-02	(a) Leyton	L 2-4	Hoskins, Hannam	1	2					7	8	9				6	5	10		4	3			11																
	Feb-09	(a) Cheshunt	W 9-2	Champion 3, Smith 4, Hannam, Maskell	1						7	8		2			6	9	10		4	3			11			5													
	Mar-02	(h) Bromley	L 2-3	Hannam 2	1						7	8		2			6				4	3		9	11			5	10												
	Mar-09	(a) Bromley	D 3-3	Clark, Hannam, Maskell							7	8		9			6		10		4	3			11			5		1	2										
	Mar-16	(a) Barking T	L 2-3	Smith, Hannam							7	8		2			6	9	10		4	3			11			5				1									
	Mar-23	(h) Barnet	W 5-1	Smith, Hannam, Champion, Whiting, og				2			7	8					6	9	10		4	3			11			5				1									
	Mar-29	(h) Uxbridge Town	W 5-1	Smith 2, Hannam, Champion, ??				2			7	8					6	9	10		4	3			11							1	5								
	Mar-30	(a) Kingstonian	D 1-1	Champion								8	7				6	5	10		4	3			11							1	2	9							
	Apr-01	(a) Uxbridge Town	W 3-1	Ayres 2, Leach																																					
	Apr-06	(h) Barking T	D 2-2	Hannam, Marks							7	8							6		4	3			11						2	1	5		9	10					
	Apr-17	(a) Redhill	W 2-1	??																																					
	Apr-22	(a) Enfield	L 1-2	Dale				2			7	8					6	5	10		4	3			11							1		9							
	Apr-25	(h) Redhill	W 2-0	Hannam 2 (1 pen)				2				8					6	9	10		4	3			11			5				1					7				
	Apr-27	(a) Barnet	L 2-5	Smith, Maskell				2			7	8					6	9	10		4	3			11			5				1									
	May-01	(h) Leyton	W 2-1	Hannam, Whiting				2			7	8					6	9	10		4	3			11			5				1									
FA Cup																																									
Pr	Sep-15	(a) Leavesden Mental Hospital	W 2-1	Clark, Hannam	1	2		4	5		7	8		9	11		6		10												3										
1Q	Sep-29	(h) Chesham U	L 1-4	Clark (pen)	1	2	3		5		7	8		9	11		6		10																			4			
FA Amateur Cup																																									
	Oct-06	(a) Hounslow	D 2-2 aet	RL Clark, R Groves	1	2	4	9			7			10	11		5		8			3																	6		
R	Oct-20	(h) Hounslow	W 3-2	Clark (pen), R Groves, L Groves	1			9			7	8		3	11			5	10	2	4																			6	
	Oct-27	(h) Botwell Mission	W 5-3	R Groves,Champion,Hannam,Maskell,og	1			9			7	8		3		11	6	5	10		4	2																			
	Nov-10	(h) RAF (Uxbridge)	W 4-1	R Groves 2, Hannam, Champion	1			9			7	8		3		11	6	5	10		4	2																			
	Dec-01	(a) Uxbridge Town	W 4-3	R Groves, Champion, Gardner 2	1			9			7			2		11	6	5	10		4	3					8														
1	Dec-15	(h) Ilford	D 3-3	R Groves 2, Maskell	1			9			7	8		2		11	6	5	10		4	3																			
R	Dec-22	(a) Ilford	L 0-8		1			9			7	8		2		10	6	5			4	3																			11
London Senior Cup																																									
3Q	Nov-03	(h) Wood Green Town	W 7-1	Ryder 2, Hannam 3, Champion, Maskell	1				9		7	8		3		11	6	5	10		4	2																			
4Q	Nov-17	(h) Erith & Belvedere	W 3-1	Champion, Downing 2	1			9			7	8		2		11	6	5	10		4	3																			
5Q	Dec-08	(a) Walthamstow Ave	L 1-2	Champion	1			9			7			2			6	5	10		4	3					8														11
Middlesex Senior Cup																																									
1	Jan-26	(a) Enfield	L 1-2	Hannam				9		5	7	8		2			6				4	3	1		11	10															
Middlesex Charity Cup																																									
1	Feb-23	(a) Enfield	W 2-0	Hannam 2	1			9			7	8		2			6				4	3			11			5	10												
SF	Apr-13	(h) Botwell Mission	L 2-4	Hannam, Marks				2			7	8					6	5	9		4	3			11							1				10					

1929-30

Rd	Date	Opponent	Result	Scorers	Poulson F	Groves RD	Davies C	Turner TJ	Leach W	Short DJ	Maskell T	Hannam EH	Clark RL	Champion AE	Whiting G	Smith HR	Davies TC	Dunn RV	McGowan J	Hoskins LCR	Flint HH	Woodbridge DJ	Chaston	Webb FT	Burrows R	Dale J	Hester S	Stokes C R	Smith LB	Welch FW	Minter WH	Turnbull G	McDermott J	Brown CG	Downing A	Ellis R	Deeley HM	Harbud F	Beagent AS	Mortimer V	Hill RE
Athenian League - 5th																																									
	Aug-31	(h) Finchley	D 2-2	Clark, Maskell	1	2	3	4	5	6	7	8	9	10	11																										
	Sep-14	(a) Barking	L 2-3	Maskell 2	1	2	3	4		6	7	8	9	10		5	11																								
	Sep-28	(a) Sutton U	W 1-0	Clark		2	3	4		6	7	8	9	10		5	11	1																							
	Dec-25	(h) Hampstead	D 1-1	Hoskins			3	4		6		8	2	10		5		1	7	9	11																				
	Dec-26	(a) Hampstead	W 3-2	Hoskins, McGowan, Woodbridge			3	4		6		8	2	10				1	7	9	11	5																			
	Feb-01	(h) Barnet	L 2-3	Clark 2 (1 pen)			3	4		6	7	8	2	10		5				9	11		1																		
	Feb-08	(a) Cheshunt	W 6-5	Hoskins 3, Flint 2, Hannam	1		6	4			7	8	3	10		5				9	11			2																	
	Feb-22	(h) Cheshunt	W 5-1	Hannam 2, Maskell 2, McGowan			3	4			7	8	2			5		1	10	9					6	11															
	Mar-01	(h) Redhill	W 4-3	Hannam 2, Dale, Hester	1		3	4			7	8	2			5				9					6	10	11														
	Mar-08	(h) Bromley	L 1-2	Clark			3	4		6	7	8	2			5		1		9						10	11														
	Mar-27	(a) Walthamstow Ave	D 1-1	?	1		3	4			7	8				5				9					6		11	2	10												
	Mar-29	(h) Southall	W 3-0	Hannam 2 (1 pen), Maskell		2	3	4		6	7	8	10			5		1		9							11														
	Apr-02	(h) Walthamstow Ave	L 0-3		1	2	3	4		6	7	8				5				9						10	11														
	Apr-05	(a) Bromley	W 3-1	Hoskins, Hannam 2 (1 pen),	1		3	4		6	7	8	2			5				9						10	11														
	Apr-07	(h) Sutton U	L 1-2	Hannam	1	2	3	4		6		8								7						10	11			5	9										
	Apr-10	(a) Barnet	L 0-2				3	4																																	
	Apr-12	(a) Enfield	L 2-4	Clark 2	1	2	3	4		6	7	8	10			5				9							11														
	Apr-14	(h) Enfield	W 2-0	Clark 2	1		3	4			7	8	10			5				9	11			2	6																
	Apr-16	(a) Finchley	L 1-3	Hannam (pen)			3	4		6	7	8	2			5		1		9	11									10											
	Apr-18	(h) Uxbridge Town	W 5-2	Hoskins 2, Maskell 2, Smith	1	2	3	4		6	7	8	10			5				9							11														
	Apr-19	(a) Uxbridge Town	D 2-2	McDermott, Turnbull			3	4		6	7	8						1							5	11	9					2	10								
	Apr-24	(a) Leyton	D 2-2	Hoskins 2	1		3	4		6	7	8				5				9							11					2	10								
	Apr-26	(h) Leyton	W 2-1	Clark 2	1	2	3	4		6	7	8	10			5				9							11														
	Apr-28	(h) Barking	W 6-0	Hoskins 3, Hannam, Maskell 2	1		3	2		6	7	8	10			5				9							11							4							
	Apr-30	(a) Redhill	L 0-4																																						
	May-03	(a) Southall	W 2-1	Hannam, Dale	1	2	3	4			7	8				5					11				6	9							10								
FA Cup																																									
EP	Sep-07	(a*) Waltham Com	W 6-1	Clark 3, Champion 2, Hannam (pen)	1		3	4	2	6	7	8	9	10		5																			11						
Pr	Sep-21	(h) St Albans	W 4-0	Clark, Champion, Hannam, TC Davies		2	3	4		6	7	8	9	10		5	11	1																							
1Q	Oct-05	(h) Apsley	W 3-1	Clark, Champion, Hannam		2	3	4		6	7	8	9	10		5	11	1																							
2Q	Oct-19	(h) Chesham	W 2-0	Hannam 2 (1 pen)		2	3	4		6	7	8	9	10		5		1									11														
3Q	Nov-02	(a) Cheshunt	D 1-1	Hannam		2	3	4		6	7	8	9	10		5	11	1																							
3Qr	Nov-06	(h) Cheshunt	W 4-0	Champion 2, Hoskins, Hannam		2	3	4		6	7	8		10		5		1		9							11														
4Q	Nov-16	(a) Dulwich Hamlet	D 7-7	Champion 2,Hoskins 2,Hannam(pen),og 2		2	3	4		6	7	8		10		5		1		9							11														
4Qr	Nov-20	(h) Dulwich Hamlet	L 1-2	Hannam		2	3	4		6	7	8		10		5		1		9							11														
		*Played at Lower Mead																																							
FA Amateur Cup																																									
	Oct-12	(a*) RAF Uxbridge	W 3-0	Clark, Ellis, Smith		2	3	4		6	7	8	9			5	11	1																		10					
	Oct-26	(h) Old Latymerians	W 8-1	Clark 4,Champion,Hannam (pen),Smith 2		2	3	4		6	7	8	9	10		5	11	1																							
	Nov-09	(a) Staines Town	W 4-1	Champion 2, Hoskins, Hannam			3	4		6		8		10		5		1		9							11										2	7			
	Nov-23	(a) Hounslow	L 1-4	Maskell		2	3	4		6	7	8				5				9							10								11				1		
		*Played at Lower Mead																																							
London Senior Cup																																									
3Q	Dec-07	(a) Mitcham W	W 2-0	Maskell, Smith			3	4		6	7	8	2			5		1		9	11																			10	
4Q	Dec-14	(a) Erith & Belvedere	D 4-4	Hoskins, Champion 2, Hannam			3	4		6	7	8	2	10		5				9	11																		1		
4Qr1	Dec-21	(h) Erith & Belvedere	D 4-4 aban	Champion 2, Hannam, Hester			3	4		6		8	2	10		5		1		9	11						7														
4Qr2	Dec-28	(n*) Erith & Belvedere	W 5-0	Hoskins 4, Smith			3	4		6	7	8	2			5		1		9	11						10														
5Q	Jan-04	(a) Hayes	L 2-4	Clark 2			3	4		6	7		10					1		9	11				5		8										2				
		*Played at Clapton FC																																							
Middlesex Senior Cup																																									
	Nov-30	(a) Cheshunt	W 4-3	Hoskins 2, Hannam, Maskell			3	4		6	7	8	2			5				9	11					10													1		
	Jan-25	(h) Great Western Railway	W 10-5	Hoskins 4, Champion 2, Flint 3, Smith			3	4			7	8	2	10		5				9	11				6																1
	Feb-15	(h) Uxbridge Town	W 3-1	Hoskins, Hannam 2			3	4			7	8	2	10		5		1		9	11				6																
SF	Mar-15	(n*) Barnet	W 3-1	Hoskins 2, Hester	1	2	3	4		6	7	8	10			5				9							11														
F	Apr-21	(n*) Haywards Sports	D 2-2	Hannam 2	1	2	3	4			7	8	10			5				9					6		11														
Fr	May-07	(n*) Haywards Sports	W 3-1	Hoskins 2, Clark	1	2	3	4		6	7	8	10			5				9							11														
		*Played at Hampstead Town FC																																							
Middlesex Charity Cup																																									
1	Jan-18	(a) Hayes	W 4-3	Hoskins 3, Flint			3	4			7		2	10		5		1	8	9	11				6																
SF	Mar-22	(h) Southall	W 5-3 aet	Hoskins 3, McGowan 2	1	2	3	4		6	7		10			5			8	9							11														
F	May-10	(n*) Hampstead T	W 3-1 aet	Hoskins, Clark, Hannam	1	2	3	4		6	7	8	10			5				9							11														
		*Played at Brentford FC																																							

1930-31

	Date	Opponent	Result	Scorers	McLeod AJ	Groves RD	Davies C	Brown CG	Smith HR	Turner TJ	Maskell T	Vanner HJ	Spurr SC	Bowyer C	Groves LG	Poulson F	Burrows R	Shorland J	Hoskins LR	Baxter SC	Clifford AJ	Loveday AW	Harris HH	Champion AE	Welch FW	Palmer ?	Lemarie R	Woodham CE	Hester SL	Wilson EC
Athenian League - 5th																														
	Aug-30	(h) Cheshunt	W 8-2	Bowyer 5, Spurr 3	1	2	3	4	5	6	7	8	9	10	11															
	Sep-06	(a) Enfield	D 3-3	Bowyer, Spurr 2		2	3	4	5	6	7	8	9	10	11	1														
	Sep-13	(a) Redhill	W 2-1	Groves, Vanner			3	4	5	2	7	8	9	10	11	1	6													
	Sep-20	(h) Hayes	W 5-3	Bowyer 2, Spurr 2, Groves,	1		3	4	5	2	7	8	9	10	11		6													
	Sep-27	(a) Walthamstow Ave	L 0-3				3	4	5	2	7	8	9	10	11	1	6													
	Oct-04	(h) Enfield	D 4-4	Bowyer, Spurr, Vanner, Maskell			3	4	5	2	7	8	9	10	11	1	6													
	Oct-18	(h) Leyton	L 2-3	Bowyer (pen), Hoskins			3	4	5		7		8	10	11	1	6	2	9											
	Nov-15	(a) Bromley	D 1-1	Bowyer			3	4			7	8	9	10	11	1		2		5	6									
	Nov-29	(a) Barnet	D 2-2	Spurr 2			3	4		6	7		8	10	11	1		2	9						5					
	Dec-06	(h) Redhill	W 5-4	Bowyer 2, Spurr, Hoskins, Groves			3	4			7		8	10	11		6	2	9						5	1				
	Dec-13	(h) Sutton U	D 3-3	Groves 2, Maskell			3	5		4	7	10	8	6	11	1		2	9											
	Dec-20	(a) Southall	L 0-2				3	5		6		7	8	10	11			2	9							1	4			
	Dec-25	(h) Hampstead	W 5-2	Hoskins 2, Spurr, Maskell, Groves			3	5		4	7		8	10	11	1		2	9								6			
	Dec-26	(a) Hampstead	L 0-3				3	5		4	7		8	10	11	1		2	9								6			
	Dec-27	(a) Barking	L 1-6	Maskell			3	5		?	7	?	?		11	?	?	2	?											
	Jan-03	(h) Southall	W 3-0	Hester 2, Maskell			3	4			7		9		11	1		2	8								6	5	10	
	Jan-31	(a) Sutton U	L 0-2				3	4			7		8		11	1		2	9								6	5	10	
	Feb-07	(h) Bromley	W 6-0	Hester 3, Hoskins, Spurr (pen), Groves			3			4	7		8		11	1		2	9								6	5	10	
	Feb-21	(h) Barnet	L 0-3				3	4			7		8		11	1			9			2			6			5	10	
	Mar-07	(a) Leyton	L 0-1				3	4		6	7				11	1		2	9									5	10	8
	Mar-14	(a) Cheshunt	W 6-3	Hoskins 2,Hester 2 (1 pen),Groves,Maskell			3	4		6	7				11	1		2	9									5	10	8
	Mar-28	(h) Walthamstow Ave	W 3-1	Hoskins 3			3	4		6	7			10	11	1		2	9									5		8
	Apr-03	(h) Uxbridge Town	W 6-1	Bowyer 2, Wilson, Maskell 3			3	4		6	7			10	11	1		2	9									5		8
	Apr-07	(a) Uxbridge Town	W 3-2	Bowyer, Groves 2			3	?		?	?			10	11	1		?	?									5		8
	Apr-22	(a) Hayes	L 1-5	Bowyer			3	4		?	?			10	11	1		?	9									5		?
	May-02	(h) Barking	W 10-0	Bowyer 5 (1 pen), Champion, Groves, Wilson, Maskell, Woodham			3	4		6	7			9	11	1		2						10				5		8
FA Cup																														
FA Amateur Cup																														
2Q	Oct-25	(h) RAF	W 12-0	Bowyer 4,Spurr 2,Vanner 4,Groves,Smith			3	4	5	6	7	8	9	10	11	1		2												
3Q	Nov-08	(a) Southall	W 3-2	Spurr 2, Groves			3	4	5		7	8	9	10	11	1	6	2												
4Q	Nov-22	(h) Hayes	L 2-4	Groves 2			3	4			7	8	9		11	1	6					2	5	10						
London Senior Cup																														
	Nov-01	(a) Hayes	L 2-3	Bowyer, Maskell			3	4	5	6	7	8		10	11	1		2	9											
Middlesex Senior Cup																														
1	Jan-24	(a*) Met. Police	W 3-1	Hoskins, Groves, Maskell			3	4			7		8		11	1		2	9								6	5	10	
2	Feb-14	(a) Hayes	L 0-4				3	4			7	8			11	1		2	9								6	5	10	
		*played at Lower Mead																												
Middlesex Charity Cup																														
1	Feb-28	(h) Hayes	W 5-4	Hoskins, Hester, Groves 3			3	4		6	7				11	1		2	9									5	10	8
SF	Mar-21	(h) Staines	W 9-1	Hoskins 3, Groves 3, Wilson 2, Maskell			3	4			7				11	1	6	2	9									5	10	8
F	May-09	(n*) Hampstead T	W 3-2	Bowyer, Champion, Groves			3	4		6	7			9	11	1		2						10				5		8
		*played at Finchley FC																												

1931-32

Rd	Date	Opponent	Result	Scorers	Poulson FR	Loveday AW	Davies C	Brown CG	Woodham CE	Turner TJ	Hester SL	Crossley BJ	Morgan JM	Bowyer CE	Groves LG	Darvill B	Butcher AG	Maskell T	Prestwich RC	Booker S	Russell F	Beach G	Wilson EC	Shorland J	Brooks JC	Stephen J	Wyatt SF	George V	Seddon CE	Champion A	Hill H	Bishop RC	Hoskins LR	Taber AW	Halcombe WE
Athenian League - 6th																																			
	Aug-29	(h) Bromley	W 3-2	Morgan, Crossley, Groves	1	2	3	4	5	6	7	8	9	10	11																				
	Sep-12	(a) Redhill	L 2-4	Crossley, Prestwich		2	3			4		10	9		11	5	6	7	8	1															
	Sep-26	(a) Walthamstow Ave	L 4-6	Bowyer 2 (1 pen), Maskell,Groves	1	2	3			4	10			9	11	5		7			6	8													
	Oct-03	(h) Barnet	L 2-5	Bowyer 2 (1 pen)	1	2	3			4				9	11	5		7	10		6		8												
	Oct-10	(h) Hayes	W 3-2	Bowyer, Brooks 2	1	2	3							10	11	5		7			6	8		4	9										
	Oct-17	(h) Redhill	L 0-2		1	2	3							10	11	5		7			6	8		4	9										
	Oct-31	(a) Barnet	D 1-1	Darvill		2	3			4				10	11	5				1	6				9	8	7								
	Nov-07	(a) Hayes	L 4-6	Bowyer (pen),Brooks,Groves,Wyatt		2	3			4				10	11	5				1	6				9		7	8							
	Nov-21	(h) Leyton	D 2-2	Bowyer, Champion		2	3			4				9	11	5				1	6						7			8	10				
	Dec-05	(a) Barking	L 1-5	Hill			3			4				9	11	5				1	6	8		2			7				10				
	Dec-25	(a) Hampstead T	L 1-6	Wyatt	1	2			4					10	11	5		7			6						9					3	8		
	Dec-26	(h) Hampstead T	L 3-4	Bowyer 2, Wyatt	1	2			4					9	10	5		7			6						11					3	8		
	Jan-02	(h) Barking T	D 2-2	Bowyer, Wyatt	1	2			4					9	10	5		7			6						11					3	8		
	Jan-09	(h) Sutton U	L 4-6	Bowyer 2, Maskell, Wyatt (pen)	1	2			4					9	10	5		7			6						11					3	8		
	Jan-16	(a) Bromley	W 5-3	Bowyer 2, Hoskins 2, Wyatt	1	2	3		4					10	11												7				8		9	5	6
	Feb-06	(h) Southall	W 4-1	Hoskins 3, Hill	1	2	3		4					10	11	5		7			6										8		9		
	Feb-13	(a) Southall	W 3-2	Bowyer, Maskell, Darvill	1	2	3		4			8		10		5		7			6						11						9		
	Feb-20	(h) Romford	W 1-0	Hoskins	1	2	3		4					10		5		7			6						11				8		9		
	Feb-27	(h) Walthamstow Ave	W 6-1	Bowyer, Hoskins 3, Groves 2	1	2	3		4					10	11	5		7			6										8		9		
	Mar-05	(a) Sutton U	L 1-2	Maskell	1	2	3		4			8		10	11	5		7			6												9		
	Mar-12	(a) Enfield	W 3-1	Hoskins, Groves, Maskell	1	2	3		4			8		10	11	5		7			6												9		
	Mar-25	(h) Uxbridge	W 2-1	Bowyer, Hoskins	1	2	3		4			8		10	11	5		7			6												9		
	Mar-28	(a) Uxbridge	W 2-1	Maskell 2	1	2	3		4			8		10	11	5		7			6												9		
	Apr-09	(a) Leyton	W 1-0	Groves (pen)	1	2	3		4			8		10	11	5		7			6												9		
	Apr-16	(a) Romford	L 1-5	Hoskins	1	2	3		4	8				10	11	5		7			6												9		
	Apr-27	(h) Enfield	W 4-0	Bowyer 2, Crossley, Maskell	1	2	3			4		8		10	11	5		7			6												9		
FA Cup																																			
EP	Sep-05	(h) Thame	W 12-4	Bowyer 6 (1 pen), Morgan 2, Prestwich 2, Turner, Groves	1	2	3			4			9	10	11	5	6	7	8																
Pr	Sep-19	(h) Hampstead T	D 1-1	Bowyer (pen)	1	2	3			4			9	10	11	5	6	7	8																
R	Sep-24	(a) Hampstead T	L 2-5	Bowyer (pen), Groves	1	2	3			4				10	11	5	6	7	8			9													
FA Amateur Cup																																			
1	Dec-12	(a) Kingstonians	L 1-6	Brooks		2	3			4		8		10	11	5				1	6				9		7								
London Senior Cup																																			
3Q	Oct-24	(a) Park Royal	W 3-2	Brooks 2, Groves	1	2	3			4				10	11	5					6	8			9	7									
4Q	Nov-14	(h) Beddington Corner	W 5-2	Bowyer 2, Brooks, Wyatt, Maskell	1	2	3			6				10	11	5		7							9		8		4						
	Dec-19	(h) Met. Police	L 1-3	Champion		2	3		4					10	11	5				1					9		7		6	8					
Middlesex Senior Cup																																			
	Jan-23	(a) Enfield	L 0-5		1	2	3		4					10	11												7				8		9	5	6
Middlesex Charity Cup																																			
1	Nov-28	(h) Hampstead T	W 6-3	Bowyer 4 (1pen), Hill, Wyatt		2	3			4				9	11	5				1	6						7			8	10				
SF	Mar-19	(h) Enfield	D 1-1	Bowyer	1	2	3		4			8		9	11	5		7			6										10				
R	Apr-02	(a) Enfield	L 1-2 aet	Beach	1	2	3		4			8		10	11	5		7			6	9													

1932-33

	Date	Opponent	Result	Scorers	Booker S	Loveday AW	Davies C	Woodham CE	Darvill B	Russell F	Maskell T	Crossley B	Hoskins L	Schofield A	Groves LG	Reeve AG	Cushway L	Hill H	Turner TJ	Ryder RJ	Bradley AC	Groves R	Miles DJ	Cox A	Parker H	Underwood C	Pratt A	Cox AE	Cox AF	Payne A	Short DJ	Beach G	Wyatt S	Phillips C	Ives P	Vale A	Poulson FR
Athenian League - 10th																																					
	Aug-27	(h) Bromley	D 1-1	Hoskins	1	2	3	4	5	6	7	8	9	10	11																						
	Sep-10	(h) Enfield	W 2-1	Hoskins, L Groves	1	2	3		5	6	7		9	10	11	4	8																				
	Sep-24	(a) Sutton U	W 3-2	Hoskins 2, Maskell	1	2	3		5	6	7		9	10		4			8	11																	
	Oct-01	(a) Enfield	W 2-1	Hoskins, Schofield	1	2	3		5	6	7		9	10		4			8	11																	
	Oct-15	(h) Southall	L 1-2	Hoskins	1	2	3		5	6	7		9	10		4			8	11																	
	Nov-19	(a) Walthamstow Ave	L 1-6	Underwood		2	3		9	6	7		8							11			1	4	5	10											
	Dec-03	(h) Uxbridge Town	W 5-1	Beach 2, Ryder 2, Schofield		2	3		5	6	7			10						11			1			8					4	9					
	Dec-17	(a) Barnet	L 1-3	Underwood		2	3		5	6	7			10						11			1			8					4	9					
	Dec-24	(h) Hampstead	L 1-3	Wyatt		2	3		5	6				10						11			1			8					4	9	7				
	Dec-26	(a) Hampstead	L 1-5	?		2	3		5	6	7			10						11			1		8						4	9					
	Dec-31	(h) Barnet	D 2-2	Beach, Russell		2	3		5	6	7			10					8	11			1								4	9					
	Jan-07	(h) Romford	W 3-2	Beach 2, Underwood	1	2	3		5	6	7									11						8					4	9		10			
	Jan-14	(a) Bromley	W 3-0	Beach 2, Underwood	1	2	3		5	6	7									11						8					4	9		10			
	Jan-28	(a) Southall	L 0-2		1	2	3		5	6	7									11						8					4	9		10			
	Feb-18	(h) Barking T	D 1-1	Underwood	1	2	3		5	6	7									11						8					4	9			10		
	Feb-25	(h) Hayes	W 2-1	Underwood, Maskell	1	2	3		5	6	7			10						11						8					4	9					
	Mar-04	(h) Sutton U	L 1-2	Underwood	1	2	3		5	6	7			10						11						8					4	9					
	Mar-11	(a) Uxbridge Town	L 0-4		1	2	3			6	7									11					5	8					4	10			9		
	Mar-18	(a) Hayes	L 1-3	Ryder		2	3			6	7		9	10						11		4	1		5	8											
	Mar-25	(h) Walthamstow Ave	W 2-1	Hoskins, Ryder			3				7		9							11		4	1		5	10	2				6	8					
	Apr-08	(a) Romford	L 2-4	Underwood 2		2	3				7		9	10						11		4	1		5	8					6						
	Apr-14	(h) Redhill	L 0-2			2	3				7		9							11		4	1		5	8					6					10	
	Apr-17	(a) Redhill	L 0-1				3				7			9					8	11		4	1		5						6			2		10	
	Apr-20	(a) Leyton	D 1-1	Underwood			3				7															#										#	1
	May-03	(h) Leyton	W 2-1	Underwood, Schofield	1	2	3				7			10						11		4			5	9					6					8	
	May-06	(a) Barking T	L 0-4			2	3				7			10					4	11			1		5	9					6					8	
FA Cup																																					
EP	Sep-03	(a*) Abingdon	W 9-0	Hoskins 6, Maskell 2, L Groves	1	2	3		5	6	7		9	10	11	4	8																				
Pr	Sep-17	(a) Maidenhead U	L 0-4		1	2	3		5	6	7		9	10	11	4		8																			
		*played at Lower Mead			2	2	2		2	2	2		2	2	2	2	1	1																			
FA Amateur Cup																																					
	Oct-08	(a) Civil Service	W 1-0	Schofield	1	2	3		5	6	7		9	10		4			8	11																	
	Oct-22	(h) Staines Town	W 4-2	Hoskins 3, Bradley	1	2	3		5	6	7		9	10		4				11	8																
	Nov-05	(a) Southall	L 0-5		1	2	3		5	6	7		9	10		4				11	8																
London Senior Cup																																					
	Oct-29	(h) Sutton U	W 4-0	Hoskins 3, Maskell	1	2	3		5	6	7		9	10		4				11	8																
	Nov-12	(a) Casuals	L 2-4	Hoskins, Darvill	1		3		5	6	7		9	10		4				11	8	2															
Middlesex Senior Cup																																					
	Jan-21	(a) Finchley	W 2-1 aban	Phillips, Wyatt	1	2	3		5	6										11						8					4	9	7	10			
R	Feb-04	(h) Finchley	L 1-3	Underwood	1	2	3		5	6	7			10						11						8					4	9					
Middlesex Charity Cup																																					
1	Nov-26	(a) Hayes	L 0-2									10	9			8			2		7		1		5		3	4	6	11							

1933-34					Miles DJ	Gorman V	Davies C	Groves RD	Parker H	Bloxham J	Potts K	Beach G	Christmas L	Vale G	Ryder RJ	Russell F	Smith JE	Booker S	Morris A	Shores AJ	Wyatt SF	Evans G	Sampson W	Shorland J	Hoskins L	Maskell T	Woodham C	Norton F	Wylde CH	Wilton J	Porter W	Hansard P	Payne A	Phillips C	Underwood C	Barnett L
Athenian League - 13th																																				
	Aug-26	(h) Leyton	D 2-2	Potts, Christmas	1	2	3	4	5	6	7	8	9	10	11																					
	Sep-09	(h) Barking	D 2-2	Shores 2 (1 pen)		2	3	4	5	6	9				11		7	1	8	10																
	Sep-16	(h) Romford	L 1-3	Ryder		2	3	4	5	6	9				11			1		8	7	10														
	Sep-23	(a) Leyton	L 0-4			2	3	4	6	5		10			11			1		8	7		9													
	Sep-30	(a) Redhill	L 2-3	Potts, Hoskins			3	4	5	6	10	8			11			1			7			2	9											
	Oct-14	(h) Hayes	L 0-7				3	4	5	6	10				11			1		8				2	9	7										
	Dec-02	(h) Bromley	D 3-3	Potts (pen), Ryder, Maskell		2				5	8				11	6								3	9	7	4		1	10						
	Dec-09	(a) Bromley	W 4-3	Hoskins 3, Wilton				2		5	8				11	6								3	9	7	4		1	10						
	Dec-25	(h) Golders Green	L 0-2					2		5	8				11	6								3	9	7	4		1	10						
	Dec-26	(a) Golders Green	L 2-3	?				2		5	8				11	6								3	9	7	4		1	10						
	Dec-30	(h) Southall	L 3-5	Russell 2, Hansard					4	5	8				11	6								2	9	7			1	3		10				
	Jan-13	(a) Southall	L 0-3			3		4		5	8	7				6								2	9				1			10	11			
	Jan-27	(a) Uxbridge Town	L 1-3	Bloxham		2			5	4	9	7			11	6	8							3					1			10				
	Feb-03	(h) Redhill	D 3-3	Potts 2, Bloxham	1	2			5	8	9	7			11	6								3								10		4		
	Feb-10	(a) Hayes	W 3-0	Beach 2, Phillips	1	2			5	4	9	7			11	6								3								10		8		
	Feb-24	(h) Walthamstow Ave	W 3-1	Potts 2 (1 pen), Beach	1	2			5	4	9	7			11	6								3								10		8		
	Mar-03	(a) Sutton U	L 3-4	Potts 2 (1 pen), Phillips	1	2			5	4	9	7			11	6								3								10		8		
	Mar-17	(h) Sutton U	D 3-3	Beach 2, Ryder	1	2			5	4	9	7			11	6								3								10		8		
	Mar-24	(a) Barnet	L 1-3	Potts	1	2			5	4	9	7			11	6								3								8			10	
	Mar-31	(h) Uxbridge Town	W 5-0	Potts 3, Phillips, Ryder	1				5	4	9	7			11	6								2								3		8	10	
	Apr-07	(a) Enfield	L 1-6	Potts	1	2			5	6	9	7			11	10								3								4			8	
	Apr-14	(a) Romford	L 1-3	Potts	1				5	4	9	7			11	6				10				2	8							3				
	Apr-21	(a) Barking	L 1-4	Potts	1				5	4	9	7				6				10				2	8							3	11			
	Apr-23	(h) Enfield	W 6-1	Potts 3 (1 pen), Russell 2, Payne	1				5	6	9	7				10								2	8							3	11			4
	Apr-28	(h) Barnet	D 4-4	Potts, Beach 2, Payne	1				5	6	9	7				10								2	8							3	11			4
	May-01	(a) Walthamstow Ave	L 0-3		1				5	6	9	7				10								2	8							3	11			4
FA Cup																																				
EP	Sep-02	(a) Hounslow	L 3-4	Potts, Christmas, Beach	1	2	3		5	4	10	8	9		11	6	7																			
FA Amateur Cup																																				
1Q	Oct-07	(a*) Ealing Association	W 4-0	Potts 2, Hoskins, Maskell			3	4	5	6	10	8			11			1						2	9	7										
2Q	Oct-21	(a) Tufnell Park	L 2-3	Potts, Ryder		2				5	10				11	6		1		8				3		7	4	9								
		*played at Lower Mead																																		
London Senior Cup																																				
	Nov-11	(h) West Norwood	W 3-1	Potts, Wilton, Ryder		2		9		5	8				11	6								3			4		1	10	7					
	Nov-18	(a) Nunhead	L 0-4			2		9		5	8				11	6								3					1	10	7	4				
Middlesex Senior Cup																																				
1	Nov-04	(a) Hounslow	W 3-1	Potts, Ryder 2		3		9		5	8				11	6								2		7	4		1	10						
2	Jan-20	(h) Uxbridge Town	W 3-2 aet	Potts, Beach, Russell		2			5	4	9	7			11	6				8				3					1			10				
3	Feb-17	(a) Park Royal	L 2-3	Potts, Phillips	1	2			5	4	9	7			11	6								3								10		8		
Middlesex Charity Cup																																				
1	Nov-25	(h) Golders Green	D 2-2	Potts (pen), Hoskins		2				5	8				11	6								3	9	7	4		1	10						
R	Dec-16	(a) Golders Green	L 2-3	Hoskins 2				2		5	8				11	6								3	9	7	4		1	10						

1934-35

Rd	Date	Opponent	Result	Scorers	Cutbush RE	Godman F	Shorland J	Bloxham J	Barnett LH	Russell F	Lawrence JC	Welsh TD	Potts K	Henson F	Ryder RJ	Scott D	Hansard P	Cook A	McKenzie D	Cannell B	Wilson J	Beach G	Masters F	Parker H	Crump A	Miles D	Groves RD	Shores AJ	Payne A	Hannam EH	Whiting W	Rasor L	Beach C	Cooper A	Clark L	Jarrett A	Mills F	Gorst W	Gordon C	Green A	Poulson FR	Nurton A
Athenian League - 14th																																										
	Aug-25	(h) Barnet	L 1-2	Ryder	1	2	3	4	5	6	7	8	9	10	11																											
	Sep-01	(a) Bromley	L 1-2	Lawrence	1	2	3	4	5	6	7	8		10	11	9																										
	Sep-08	(h) Barking	L 1-4	Ryder (pen)	1	2		4		6					11	9	3	5	7	8	10																					
	Sep-29	(a) Hayes	D 3-3	Potts 2, Masters	1	2		4		6			8		11		3				10	7	9	5																		
	Oct-13	(a) Southall	L 1-3	Wilson	1	2	3	4		6			9		11						10	7	8	5																		
	Oct-27	(a) Barnet	W 1-0	Scott		2	3						9			7				6	10			5		1	4	8	11													
	Nov-10	(h) Romford	L 0-2			2	3		4				9			7		6			10			5		1		8	11													
	Dec-15	(h) Southall	D 2-2	Hannam 2		2	3						10							6	11	8		5		1	4			9	7											
	Dec-22	(a) Redhill	L 0-4			2	3						20							6	11	8		5		1	4			9		7										
	Dec-25	(h) Golders Green	W 6-4	Potts 3, Beach 2, Rasor		2	3			6			11								10	8		5		1	4			9		7										
	Dec-26	(a) Golders Green	L 0-6			2	3			6			10								11	8		5		1	4			9		7										
	Dec-29	(h) Hayes	W 3-0	Hannam 3		2	3		4	6			11								10	8		5		1				9		7										
	Jan-05	(a) Romford	D 1-1	Potts		2	3		4	6			11								10	8		5		1				9		7										
	Jan-12	(h) Redhill	D 3-3	Masters 2, Wilson		2	3		4	6			11								10	8	9	5		1							7									
	Jan-19	(a) Leyton	L 1-4	Wilson		2	3		4	6			11								10	8		5		1				9		7										
	Feb-02	(a) Uxbridge	L 2-4	Wilson, Hannam	1	2	3			6			11			4					10			5						9		7			8							
	Feb-16	(a) Walthamstow Ave	L 2-3	Wilson, Mills	1	2	3			6			11			8					10			5						9						4	7					
	Feb-23	(a) Sutton U	L 1-7	Wilson	1	2							11			6					10			5											3	4	8	7	9			
	Mar-02	(a) Enfield	D 1-1	Hannam	1	2				6						11					10			5						9					3	4	8	7				
	Mar-09	(a) Barking	L 2-5	Mills, Potts	1	2				6			11			7					10			5						9					3	4	8					
	Mar-23	(h) Walthamstow Ave	D 3-3	Hannam, Scott 2		2	3			6			11			8					10			5						9						4	7			1		
	Mar-30	(h) Sutton U	L 3-4	Mills, Clark 2		2	3			6						8					10			5						9					11	4	7			1		
	Apr-06	(h) Bromley	D 1-1	Clark		2	3			6						8					10			5						9					11	4	7				1	
	Apr-19	(h) Uxbridge	L 2-3	Clark 2		2	3			6						8					10			5						9					11	4	7				1	
	Apr-27	(h) Enfield	W 3-0	Mills 2, Masters		2	3									8					10		9	5			4								11	6	7				1	
	May-01	(h) Leyton	W 2-1	Wilson, Mills		2										8					10		9	5			4								3	6	11				1	7
FA Cup																																										
Pr	Sep-15	(a) Enfield	L 0-4		1	2		4	5	6			9	10	11		3		7			8																				
FA Amateur Cup																																										
ExP	Sep-22	(h) Old Owens	W 3-2	Potts, Ryder, Hansard	1		2	6		3			9		11		5			4	10	7	8																			
Pr	Oct-06	(h) Park Royal	L 1-5	Beach	1	2		4		6			9		11						10	7	8	5	3																	
London Senior Cup																																										
2Q	Oct-20	(h) Beddington Corner	W 7-1	Payne 5 (1 pen), Wilson, Scott		2	3						9			7				6	10			5		1	4	8	11													
3Q	Nov-24	(h) Colney Hatch	W 2-1	Potts, Payne		2	3			6			9			8					10	7		5		1	4		11													
1	Dec-08	(a) Clapton	L 0-2			2	3	6					8									7		5		1	4	10	11	9												
Middlesex Senior Cup																																										
Q	Dec-01	(h) Old Johnians	W 3-1	Beach 2, og		2	3	6					9								10	7		5		1	4		11	8												
1	Jan-26	(h) AEC	W 9-2	Potts 3, Wilson 3, Hannam 2, Scott		2			4	6			11			8					10			5						9		7		1	3							
2	Feb-09	(h) Finchley	L 1-2	Payne	1	2	3		4	6			9			8					10			5					11			7										
Middlesex Charity Cup																																										
1	Nov-17	(h) Old Lyonians	W 5-2	Potts 2, Beach 2, Payne (pen)		2	3			6			9								10	7		5		1	4	8	11													
SF	Mar-23	(a) Finchley	L																																							

1935-36

					Martindale S	Wheatley JW	D'Arcy L	Scott MD	Barrett J	Jarrett A	Nurton AC	McCaffrey J	Jones R	Wilson J	Clark RL	Godman F	Pullen J	Whiting W	Pugh L	Groves R	Potts K	Poulson F	Pickford N	Sutton H	Roche P	Allin B	Masters F	Parker H	V Hayward	Davies J	Roche J	Holly A	Hansard PV	Groves L	Friday S	Richardson T	Dunne T	Fowler P	Reece S	Mills F
Athenian League - 13th																																								
	Aug-31	(a) Walthamstow Ave	L 1-3	Nurton	1	2	3	4	5	6	7	8	9	10	11																									
	Sep-14	(h) Sutton U	W 2-0	Potts 2	1	3		6	5		8			10		2	7		11	4	9																			
	Nov-23	(a) Enfield	L 1-4	Pickford	1	3		6	5		8					2	7		11				9	10	4															
	Dec-07	(h) Hayes	W 2-0	Wilson, og	1	3		4	5		7	8		10					11							2	9	6												
	Dec-21	(a) Leyton	L 1-2	Masters	1	3		4	5		7	8		10												2	9	6	11											
	Dec-25	(h) Golders Green	L 3-6	Nurton, Pickford 2	1	3		4	5		8			10			7						9			2		6	11											
	Dec-26	(a) Golders Green	L 1-3	Wilson		3		4	5		8			10			7						9			2		6	11	1										
	Dec-28	(h) Enfield	D 2-2	Pickford, Clark		3		10	5		8				11					4			9			2		6		1	7									
	Jan-04	(a) Hayes	L 0-3			3		4	5			8					7		11	2			10				9	6		1										
	Jan-11	(h) Redhill	L 3-6	Nurton (pen), Masters, Pugh		3		6	5		8			10					11	2						4	9			1	7									
	Jan-18	(h) Bromley	L 2-3	Hansard 2				6	5		8				3				11	2							9			1	7	4	10							
	Feb-01	(a) Redhill	L 2-4	Nurton (pen), L Groves				6	5		8				3					2			10							1	7	4	9	11						
	Feb-15	(h) Southall	L 1-3	Barrett					5							3	7			2										1		4	10	11	6		8	9		
	Feb-22	(a) Barnet	L 4-5	Fowler 2, Pullen, Dunne				6	5						3	2	7			4										1			10	11			8	9		
	Feb-29	(a) Romford	L 2-3	Wilson, L Groves										10		3	7			2								4		1			6	11	5		8	9		
	Mar-07	(h) Barking	W 1-0	Dunne	1			6						10		2	7																3	11	5		8	9	4	
	Mar-14	(a) Leyton	L 1-2	L Groves	1			6						10		2	7																3	11	5		8	9	4	
	Mar-28	(a) Barking	L 0-6		1			6						10	11	2	7																3		5			9	4	8
	Apr-04	(h) Romford	W 4-3	Fowler 2, Pullen 2	1			6						10	11	2	7																3		5		8	9	4	
	Apr-10	(h) Uxbridge	D 3-3	Fowler, Pullen, Barrett	1			6	5					10	11	2	7																3				8	9	4	
	Apr-11	(h) Sutton U	L 0-2		1			6	5					10	3	2	7						11														8	9	4	
	Apr-13	(a) Uxbridge	L 2-6	Fowler, Dunne	1			6	5					10	3	2	7						11														8	9	4	
	Apr-18	(a) Bromley	L 0-3		1			6	5					10		3	7			2													11				8	9	4	
	Apr-20	(a) Southall	L 0-4																																					
	Apr-25	(h) Barnet	W 6-1	Wilson 4, Fowler 2	1				5			8		10		3	7			2													6					9	4	11
	May-02	(h) Walthamstow Ave	W 4-3	Wilson 3, Masters	1				5					10						2							9	6			7		3					8	4	11
FA Cup																																								
EP	Sep-07	(a) London Labour	D 1-1	Nurton	1	3		4	5	6	8			10		2	7	9	11																					
R	Sep-11	(h) London Labour	W 2-0	Nurton, Potts	1	3		6	5		8			10		2	7		11	4	9																			
Pr	Sep-21	(h) Tufnell Park	D 4-4	Potts, Scott, Pugh 2	1	3		6	5		8			10		2	7		11	4	9																			
R	Sep-26	(a) Tufnell Park	W 2-1	Nurton, Pugh		9	2	6	5		8				3		7		11	4	10	1																		
1Q	Oct-05	(a) St Albans C	L 1-3	Groves		9		6	5		8				3	2	7		11	4	10	1																		
FA Amateur Cup																																								
	Sep-28	(h) Old Owens	W 6-0	Nurton 3, Wheatley 2, Groves		9	2	6	5		8				3		7		11	4	10	1																		
	Oct-12	(a) London Labour	D 3-3	Nurton, Groves, Pugh		3		6	5		8					2	7		11	4	10	1	9																	
	Oct-19	(h) London Labour	W 4-0	Wilson, Pickford 2, Potts	1	3		6	5		8			10		2	7			4	11		9																	
	Oct-26	(a) Southall	L 0-7		1				5		8			6	3	2	7		11	4	10		9																	
London Senior Cup																																								
	Nov-09	(h) Polytechnic	W 7-0	Nurton 2,Pickford 2,Pugh 2,Pullen	1	6	2	4	5		8					3	7		11				9	10																
	Nov-16	(h) Old Lyonians	W 6-1	Nurton,Pickford 2,Sutton 2, og	1	6	2	4	5		8			11		3	7						9	10																
	Nov-30	(a) Enfield	L 2-5	Nurton, Masters	1	3		4	5		8						7		11					10	6	2	9													
Middlesex Senior Cup																																								
	Nov-02	(h) Lyons Club	W 4-3	Pickford 2, Pullen, og	1	3	2	6	5		8						7		11	4			9	10																
	Jan-25	(a) Enfield	W 3-0	Nurton, Masters, Scott	1			6	5		8				3					2			10				9	4			7			11						
	Feb-08	(a) Golders Green	L 0-4		1			6	5		9				3		7			2			10											11	4	8				
Middlesex Charity Cup																																								
1	Dec-14	(h) Old Lyonians	W 7-2	Nurton(pen), Masters 2, Wilson 3,Pullen	1	3		4	5		8			10			7		11							2	9	6												
SF	Mar-21	(h) London Caledonian	L 0-1		1			6	5					10		2	7																3	11			8	9	4	

1936-37

	Date	Opponent	Result	Scorers	Martindale S	McPherson A	Ellis RC	Reece S	Jearrad LM	White RC	Brown C	Bidewell S	Bunce CE	Wilson J	Balaam RC	Loveday AW	Holding	Parker H	Hansard P	Masters F	Barrett H	Scott D	Friday S	Roche J	Potts K	Walker E	Reeves AG	Lloyd J	Showler W	Mills F	Metson L	Whyman J	Catton J
Athenian League - 3rd																																	
	Aug-29	(h) Uxbridge	W 8-0	Bunce 5, Wilson, Bidewell 2	1	2	3	4	5	6	7	8	9	10	11																		
	Sep-05	(a) Southall	W 3-2	Bunce, Brown 2	1		3	4	5	6	7	8	9	10	11	2																	
	Sep-12	(a) Barnet	L 1-5	Masters			3	4			7	8		10	11	2	1	5	6	9													
	Oct-03	(a) Walthamstow Ave	L 1-2	Wilson	1	6	3				7	8	9	10	11	2						4	5										
	Oct-31	(h) Romford	L 1-3	Loveday	1		3			6		8	9	10	11	2						4	5		7								
	Dec-05	(a) Leyton	W 3-2	Bunce, Potts, Roche			3	6				8	9	10		2						4	5	7	11	1							
	Dec-12	(h) Bromley	L 0-1				3				7	8	9			2						4	5		11	1	6	10					
	Dec-19	(a) Redhill	D 1-1	Wilson			3				7	8	9	10		2						4	5		11	1	6						
	Dec-25	(h) Golders Green	W 1-0	Bunce			3				7	8	9	10		2						4			11	1	6		5				
	Dec-26	(a) Golders Green	W 4-3	Wilson 3, Bidewell			3		5		7	8		10		2						11			9	1	6		4				
	Jan-02	(a) Hayes	D 3-3	Potts, Showler, og			3				7	8		10		2						11	5		9	1	6		4				
	Jan-16	(h) Southall	W 4-0	Bunce 2, Potts 2			3				7	8	9	10		2							5		11	1	6		4				
	Mar-13	(a) Romford	D 2-2	Bunce, Masters		3					11	8	7	10				6		9		4	5						2		1		
	Mar-20	(h) Barking	W 2-1	Bidewell, Ellis		2	3					8	7	10						9			5			1	6	11	4				
	Mar-26	(h) Enfield	W 4-1	Wilson 2, Bidewell, Masters			3					8	7	10		2		5		9		4			11	1		6					
	Mar-27	(h) Hayes	W 1-0	Catton		3			4				7	10		2						6	5			1		11				8	9
	Mar-29	(a) Enfield	W 3-2	Bunce, Wilson 2		3					7		8	10		2		6		9		4			11	1			5				
	Apr-03	(a) Barking	W 2-1	Brown 2			3				11	8	7	10		2				9			5			1	6		4				
	Apr-10	(h) Barnet	W 5-2	Bunce 4, Potts			3				7	8	9	10		2						4			11	1	6		5				
	Apr-14	(h) Leyton	W 4-2	Bunce 3, Ellis			3				7	8	9	10		2						4			11	1	6		5				
	Apr-17	(a) Uxbridge	W 4-2	Bunce, Bidewell, Potts, Ellis			3				7	8	9	10		2						4			11	1	6		5				
	Apr-21	(a) Sutton U	W 2-1	Wilson, Bidewell			3				7	8	9	10		2						4			11	1	6		5				
	Apr-24	(h) Redhill	W 4-1	Brown, Potts, Showler, Ellis (pen)			3				7	8		10		2			9			4			11	1	6		5				
	Apr-26	(a) Bromley	L 1-6	Wilson			3		5			8		10		2			9			4			11	1		6					7
	Apr-28	(h) Walthamstow Ave	L 0-1				3		5		7		9	10		2			8			4			11	1	6						
	May-01	(h) Sutton U	W 2-0	Bunce 2			3		5				9	10	11	2			8			4				1	6		7				
FA Cup																																	
Pr	Sep-19	(h) Tufnell Park	L 0-3		1		3	4			7	8	9	10	11	2		6			5												
Amateur Cup																																	
	Sep-26	(h) Old Lyonians	W 9-0	Bunce 4, Bidewell 2, Wilson 2, Scott	1	6	3				7	8	9	10	11	2						4	5										
	Oct-10	(a) Ealing Assoc.	W 2-1	Bunce, Wilson	1	6	3			5		8	9	10	11	2						4		7									
	Oct-24	(a) Hounslow	W 3-1	Bunce 2, Balaam	1	4	3			6	7	8	9	10	11	2							5										
	Nov-07	(h) Hayesco	W 6-2	Bunce 3, Potts 2, Wilson	1		3	4		6	7	8	9	10		2							5		11								
	Nov-21	(h) Frosts Athletic	W 3-0	Bunce 2, Bidewell	1		3	4		6	7	8	9	10		2							5		11								
1	Jan-09	(h) Chesham U	W 4-0	Bunce 2, Showler, Ellis (pen)			3				7	8	9	10		2							5		11	1	6		4				
2	Feb-06	(a) Uxbridge	W 3-1	Bunce, Potts, og			3				7	8	9	10		2							5		11	1	6		4				
3	Feb-20	(h) Dulwich Hamlet	D 1-1	Bidewell	1		3					8	9	10		2							5	7	11		6		4				
3r	Feb-27	(a) Dulwich Hamlet	L 0-4		1		3					8	9	10		2							5		11		6		4	7			
London Senior Cup																																	
	Oct-17	(h) CWS Silvertown	W 7-0	Potts 3, Hansard 2, Scott(pen), Wilson	1	6	3			5	7			10	11	2			9			4			8								
	Nov-28	(a) Erith & Belvedere	L 2-3	Bunce, Wilson	1		3	4		6	7	8	9	10		2							5		11								
Middlesex Senior Cup																																	
	Jan-23	(a) Uxbridge	W 4-2	Bunce 2, Bidewell, og			3				7	8	9	10		2							5		11	1	6		4				
	Feb-13	(h) Finchley	W 6-1	Bunce 3, Bidewell, Wilson, Roche		2	3					8	9	10									5	7	11	1	6		4				
	Mar-06	(a) Southall	L 2-6	Wilson, Ellis (pen)	1		3				7	8	9	10		2							5		11		6		4				
Middlesex Charity Cup																																	
1	Nov-14	(a) Golders Green	L 0-2		1		3	4		6	7	8	9	10		2							5		11								

1937-38

	Date	Opponent	Result	Scorers	Walker E	Loveday AW	Ellis RC	Showler WF	Friday S	Green LF	Brown C	Ette C	Bunce CE	Lloyd J	Downing AR	Reeves AG	Potts K	Wilson J	McPherson A	Hopper W	Roche J	Catton J	Masters F	Dyke H	D'Arcy L	Scott D	Balaam A	Soden EW	Gaze AG	Baldwin K	Bidewell R	Porter K	Lavender F	Martindale G	Wilson R	Morris T	Jearrad LM	Lewis R
Athenian League - 4th																																						
	Aug-28	(h) Enfield	W 8-0	Bunce 4, Ette, Downing, Lloyd 2	1	2	3	4	5	6	7	8	9	10	11																							
	Sep-04	(a) Enfield	D 3-3	Bunce, Potts, Ellis (pen)	1	2	3	4	5	10		8	9		11	6	7																					
	Sep-08	(h) Barnet	W 3-1	Bunce 2, Ellis	1	2	3	4	5	6	7		9	8	11			10																				
	Sep-11	(h) Barking	W 1-0	Lloyd	1		3	4	5	6	7	8		10	11				2	9																		
	Sep-23	(a) Barnet	L 2-4	Catton 2	1	2	3	5		4			9	10	11	6					7	8																
	Sep-25	(a) Barking	L 0-1		1	2	3		5	4			9	8	11	6		10			7																	
	Oct-09	(a) Hayes	L 0-1		1	2	3		5	4	7	8			11	6		10					9															
	Oct-23	(h) Sutton U	W 6-1	Showler, Ette 2, Lloyd 2, Downing	1	2	3	4	5	6		8		9	11		7							10														
	Oct-30	(h) Romford	D 2-2	Dyke, og	1	2	3	4	5	6	7	8		9	11									10														
	Nov-06	(a) Walthamstow Ave	L 0-5		1	2	3	4	5	6	7	8		9	11		10																					
	Nov-13	(a) Redhill	L 1-2	Potts (pen)	1	3		4	5		7	8			11		9	10							2	6												
	Nov-27	(a) Romford	D 2-2	Ette, Soden	1	2	3	4	5		7	8					9	10								6		11										
	Dec-25	(h) Golders Green	W 4-1	Gaze 2, Baldwin 2	1	2	3	4	5		7						11	10								6			9	8								
	Dec-27	(a) Golders Green	D 2-2	Baldwin, Catton	1	2	3							4			11	10				7				6			9	8	5							
	Jan-29	(h) Tooting & Mitcham United	W 4-3	Bunce 2, Gaze, Potts	1	2	3		5		7		9				11									6			8	10		4						
	Feb-05	(a) Tooting & Mitcham United	D 1-1	Gaze	1	2	3	4	5				9				11	10								6			7	8								
	Feb-19	(a) Sutton U	L 2-5	Bunce 2	1	2	3	4	5				9				11	10								6			8				7					
	Feb-26	(h) Hayes	W 1-0	Gaze	1		3		5				9				11							8		6			7	10		4		2				
	Mar-05	(a) Leyton	L 0-3		1	3		4	5		7		9				11									6			8	10				2				
	Mar-26	(h) Leyton	W 2-0	Gaze, J Wilson	1	3		2	5								11	10						8		6			9			4			7			
	Apr-02	(h) Redhill	W 2-1	Showler, J Wilson	1	2	3	4	5				9				11	10								6			8						7			
	Apr-09	(h) Walthamstow Ave	D 1-1	Scott	1	2	3	4	5				7				11	10						8		6										9		
	Apr-15	(a) Southall	D 2-2	Bunce, Dyke	1	2	3	4			7		9				11	10						8		6					5							
	Apr-18	(h) Southall	W 5-1	Scott 2, Ellis (pen), Dyke, Wilson	1	2	3	4					9				11	10						8		6					5		7					
	May-02	(h) Bromley	W 3-1	Bunce, Potts, Showler	1	2	3	4	5		7		9				11	10						8		6												
	May-04	(a) Bromley	L 1-2	Bunce	1	2	3						9				11	10						8		6				7	5						4	
FA Cup																																						
Pr	Sep-18	(a*) Pinner	W 4-0	Bunce 2, Potts, Downing	1	2	3	4	5		7		9	8	11	6	10																					
1Q	Oct-02	(a) Bishops Stortford	W 3-2	Bunce, Ette 2	1	2	3		5	4	7	8	9		11	6		10																				
2Q	Oct-16	(h) Enfield	L 2-3	Bunce 2	1	2	3	4	5		7	8	9		11	6								10														
		*played at Lower Mead																																				
FA Amateur Cup																																						
4Q	Nov-20	(a) Hersham	W 4-1	Potts 3, Wilson	1	2	3	4	5		7		9				8	10								6	11											
1	Jan-15	(a) Sutton U	L 0-2		1	2	3	4	5		7	10	9				11									6			8									
London Senior Cup																																						
1	Dec-18	(h) Epsom	L 0-2		1	2	3	4	5		7	8					11	10								6			9									
R†	Jan-01	(h) Epsom	W 3-2	Bunce 2, Wilson	1	3		2	5	4		8	7				11	10								6			9									
2	Jan-08	(a) Ilford	L 2-3	Ette, Ellis	1	2	3	4	5		7	10	9				11									6			8									
		†replayed following Wealdstone protest (ineligible player)																																				
Middlesex Senior Cup																																						
1	Jan-22	(h) Brentham	W 7-2	Bunce3, Gaze, Showler,Potts,Wilson	1	2	3	4	5		7		9				11	10								6			8									
2	Feb-12	(h) Southall	W 3-2	Bunce, Gaze, Lloyd	1	2	3	4	5		7		9	10			11									6			8									
SF	Mar-12	(n*) Uxbridge	W 6-0	Bunce 2, Wilson 2, Porter, Potts	1	2	3	4	5				9				11	10								6			7			8						
F	Apr-23	(n*) Tufnell Park	W 3-1	Bunce, Potts, Ellis (pen)	1	2	3	4	5		7		9				11	10						8		6												
		*played at Golders Green FC																																				
Middlesex Charity Cup																																						
1	Dec-04	(h) Southall	W 7-1	Potts 4, Wilson, Gaze, Scott(?)	1	3			5	4	7	8					11	10							2	6			9									
SF	Mar-19	(h) Hayes	W 2-0	Potts 2	1	2	3	4	5				9				11	10								6			7	8								
F	May-14	(h) Golders Green	W 4-0	Dyke, Potts, Morris, Ellis (pen)		2	3	4	5		7						11	10						8		6										9		1

1938-39

Rd	Date	Opponent	Result	Scorers	Lewis R	Loveday AW	Ellis R	Showler WF	Friday S	Scott D	Brown C	Dyke H	Bunce CE	Wilson J	Potts K	Gaze AG	Baldwin K	Balaam RC	Walker E	Green L	Bassett E	Nicholson R	Barker C	Bidewell R	Porter K	Whiting W	Wilson R	Schofield F	Morris T	Howdon W
Athenian League - 3rd																														
	Aug-27	(h) Leyton	W 3-2	Bunce 2, Wilson	1	2	3	4	5	6	7	8	9	10	11															
	Sep-03	(a) Leyton	W 4-0	Bunce, Baldwin 2, Gaze	1	2	3	4	5	6			9	10	11	7	8													
	Sep-07	(h) Barnet	L 0-2		1	2	3	4	5	6			9	10	11	7	8													
	Sep-10	(h) Barking	W 3-2	Balaam, Baldwin, Wilson	1	2	3	4	5	6			9	10		7	8	11												
	Sep-24	(h) Enfield	W 4-1	Bunce, Baldwin, Wilson 2,	1	2	3	4	5	6			9	10		7	8	11												
	Oct-08	(a) Barking	L 1-3	Bunce	1	2	3	4	5	6			9		11	8					7	10								
	Oct-15	(a) Bromley	W 3-0	Gaze 2, Potts	1	2		4		6	7		9		11	8						10	3	5						
	Oct-29	(a) Enfield	W 1-0	Bunce	1	2	3	4	5	6	7		9		11	10	8													
	Nov-05	(h) Romford	W 3-2	Bunce, Baldwin (pen), Gaze	1	2	3			6	7		9	10		11	8			4				5						
	Nov-12	(h) Bromley	W 3-2	Bunce, Baldwin, og	1	2	3	4	5	6	7		9	10		11	8													
	Nov-19	(a) Romford	L 1-2	Gaze	1	2	3	4	5	6	7		9	10		11	8													
	Nov-26	(a) Redhill	D 3-3	Bunce, Wilson 2	1	2	3	4	5	6			9	10		7	8						11							
	Dec-10	(h) Tooting & Mitcham United	W 9-2	Bunce 2,Baldwin 2,Barker 2,Wilson 2,Gaze	1	2	3	4	5	6			9	10		7	8						11							
	Dec-31	(h) Hayes	W 4-1	Baldwin, Wilson, Scott, Bidewell	1	2	3		5	6			9	10		7	8						11	4						
	Feb-25	(a) Barnet	D 4-4	Baldwin, Wilson 2, og	1	2	3		5	6	7		9	10			8			4								11		
	Mar-11	(h) Sutton U	W 5-2	Bunce 2, Baldwin 2, Wilson	1	2	3		5	6	7		9	10			8			4								11		
	Mar-18	(a) Golders Green	D 3-3	Bunce 2, Baldwin	1	2	3			6			9	10		7	8			4				5				11		
	Apr-01	(h) Golders Green	W4-2	Bunce 3, J Wilson	1	2	3		5	6	7		9	10			8			4							11			
	Apr-07	(h) Southall	D 1-1	Barker	1	2	3			6	7			10			8			4			11	5					9	
	Apr-08	(a) Sutton U	W 2-1	Baldwin 2	1	2			5	6				10		7	9			4		8	3				11			
	Apr-15	(h) Redhill	W 4-1	Baldwin 2, Wilson, Schofield	1	2	3			6				10			9			4		8	11	5				7		
	Apr-20	(a) Hayes	L 1-6	Baldwin	1	2				6			9	10		7	8			4			3	5				11		
	Apr-22	(a) Southall	L 0-2		1	2			5	6			9	10		7				4		8	3					11		
	Apr-27	(a) Walthamstow Ave	D 2-2	Bunce, Baldwin	1				5	6			9	10		7	8			4			3					11		2
	Apr-29	(a) Tooting & Mitcham United	L 0-3		1	2	3		5	6			9	10		7	8			4								11		
	May-03	(h) Walthamstow Ave	W 2-0	Bunce, og	1	2			5	6			9	10		7	8			4			3					11		
FA Cup																														
Pr	Sep-17	(h) London Caledonians	W 6-0	Bunce 3, Wilson 2, Gaze,	1	2	3	4	5	6			9	10		7	8	11												
1Q	Oct-01	(a) Golders Green	D 0-0		1	2	3	4	5	6		10	9		11	7	8													
1Qr	Oct-05	(h) Golders Green	L 1-2	Bunce		2	3		5	6		10	9		11	7	8		1	4										
FA Amateur Cup																														
1	Jan-14	(a) Walthamstow Ave	L 2-4	Wilson, Barker	1	2	3	4		6	7		9	10			8						11	5						
London Senior Cup																														
1	Dec-17	(a) Tooting & Mitcham United	W 3-1	Bunce, Gaze, og	1	2	3	4	5	6			9	10		7	8						11							
2	Jan-07	(a) Ilford	W 4-3	Bunce 3, Scott	1	2	3	4	5	6	7		9	10			8						11							
3	Jan-28	(h) Dulwich Hamlet	L 1-2	Wilson	1	2			5	6	7		9	10		11	8						3		4					
Middlesex Senior Cup																														
1	Feb-04	(a) Wood Green Town	D 3-3 aet	Bunce 2, Wilson	1	2	3		5	6			9	10			8				7		11		4					
1r	Feb-11	(h) Wood Green Town	W 5-2	Gaze 2, Whiting, Scott, Barker	1	2	3		5	6				10		7	8			4			11			9				
2	Feb-18	(a) Southall	W 3-0	Bunce, Baldwin, J Wilson	1		3		5	6	7		9	10			8			4			2				11			
SF	Mar-25	(h) Enfield	W 2-1	Baldwin, Barker (pen)	1	2	3		5	6			9	10		7	8			4			11							
F	Apr-10	(n*) Golders Green	L 0-4		1	2	3		5	6	7		9			10	8			4			11							
		*played at Finchley FC																												
Middlesex Charity Cup																														
1	Dec-03	(h) Finchley	W 3-2	Bunce, Wilson, Gaze	1		3	4	5	6			9	10		7	8				11		2							
SF	Mar-04	(h) Enfield	W 4-0	Baldwin, Wilson, Brown 2	1	2	3		5	6	7		9	10			8			4			11							
F	May-13	(h) Hayes	W 4-1	Bunce 2, Wilson, Schofield	1	2	3			6			9	10		7	8			4				5				11		

Season 1939 - 1940 saw the outbeak of War and the Athenian League was suspended

1939-40

	Date	Opponent	Result	Scorers	Lewis R	Loveday A	Barker C	Green L F	Friday S	Scott D	Brown C	Baldwin K	Bunce C	Wilson J	Schofield F	Bidwell R W	Gaze A	Parr W W	Bunyan	Nicholson R	Haydon F	Gordon	Wright	Dyke H	Edmonds C	Thompson R	Doig	Walker E	Morton
Friendlies																													
	Aug-26	(h) Rest of the League	L 3-4	Baldwin, Bunce, Barker (pen),	1	2	3	4	5	6	7	8	9	10	11														
	Sep-16	(h) Southall	W 8-4	Bunce 4, Wilson2, Baldwin 2,	1	2	3	4		6		8	9	10	11	5	7												
	Sep-23	(h) Golders Green	W 2-1	Bunce, Barker (pen)	1	2	3	4		6		8	9	10	11	5	7												
	Sep-30	(h) Hitchin Town	W 3-0	Baldwin, Bunce, Gaze	1	2	3	4		6		8	9	10	11	5	7												
	Oct-07	(h) Dartford	W 5-1	Bunce 2, Gaze 2, Wilson	1	2	3	4		6		8	9	10	11	5	7												
	Oct-14	(a) Chesham	W 8-1	Baldwin, Bunce, Barker (pen), Parr 3, Wilson, Bidewell	1	2	3	4	5	6		8	9	10		11		7											
	Oct-21	(h) Chesham	W 7-2	Baldwin 2, Bunce 4, Parr	1	2	3	4	5	6		8	9	10		11		7											
	Oct-28	(h) Wycombe W	W 4-2	Baldwin, Bunce, Wilson, Schofield	1	2	3	4		6		8	9	10	11	5													
	Nov-04	(h) Brentford Res	L 2-5	Barker, Schofield	1	2	3	4	5	6		8	9	10	11		7												
	Nov-11	(h) Tunbridge Wells R	L 2-3	Scott, Schofield	1	2	3	6		4		8	9	10	11	5													
	Nov-18	(a) Woking	W 6-2	Barker 2, Bunce 2, Baldwin, Nicholson	1	2	3		5	6		8	9	10	11				4	7									
	Nov-25	(h) Woking	W 5-1	Barker, Bunce, Wilson, Schofield, Parr	1	2	3			6		8	9	10	11	5		7	4										
	Dec-02	(h) Fulham	W 4-3	Barker 2, Bunce, Schofield	1		3			6		8	9	10	11	5			4	7	2								
	Dec-09	(a) Dulwich Hamlet	W 2-1	Wilson 2,	1	2	3			6		8	9	10	11	5			4	7									
	Dec-16	(h) Dulwich Hamlet	W 3-2	Baldwin, Bunce, Haydon	1	2	3			6		8	9	10	11	5		7	4										
	Dec-23	(h) Golders Green	W 2-1	Scott, Nicholson	1	2	3			6		8	9	10	11	5			4	7									
	Dec-26	(a) Golders Green	W 4-2	Barker, Wilson, Schofield, Nicholson	1		3	6		2		8	9	10	11	5			4	7									
	Jan-06	(h) Leyton	L 0-1 aban		1	2	3			6		8	9		11	5		7	4			10							
	Jan-13	(h) Chelsea Res	W 2-1	Schofield, Bunce	1	2	3			6		8	9		11	5		7	4			10							
	Jan-20	(a) Wycombe W	W 4-0	Bunce 2, Gordon 2		2	3	6		5			9		11				4	7		10	1	8					
	Feb-10	(h) Cambridge Univ.	W 2-1	Schofield, Dyke	1	3		6		5		9			11				4	7	2	10		8					
	Mar-02	(h) Oxford Univ.	W 6-2	Baldwin 3, Bunce 2, Parr	1	2	3	6		5		8	9		11			7	4					10					
	Mar-22	(a) Crystal Palace	D 3-3	Baldwin, Gordon, Bunce	1	2	3			5		8	9		11				6	7		10			4				
	Mar-23	(h) Nunhead	W 6-1	Schofield, Bunce 3, Baldwin, Nicholson	1	2	3	5		6		8	9		11					7				10	5**	4			
	Mar-25	(h) Crystal Palace	W 3-2	Bunce, Gordon, Baldwin	1	2	3		6			8	9		11					7		10			5	4			
	Apr-11	(h) Gillingham	W 10-0	Bunce 4, Schofield 2, Parr 2, Nicholson 2	1	2	3			6		8	9		11			7		10**				10	5		4		
	Apr-18	(h) Leyton	W 3-2	Bunce 2, Wilson	1	2	3			6		8	9	10	11			7							5		4		
	May-11	(h) Met. Police	W 5-4	Barker, Bunce, Wilson, Schofield, Nicholson		2	3			5		4	9	10	11					7		8					6	1	
	May-13	(h) Southall	W 5-0	Wilson 2, Barker, Baldwin, Schofield		2	3			6		8	9	10	11			7							5		4		1
	May-22	(h) Kodak	W 7-0																										
	May-25	(h) Briggs Sports	W 5-3	Barker, Dyke 2, Bunce 2		2	3			6		4	9		11			7		8				10	5			1	
	May-29	(h) Pinner				2	3			6		4	9		11			7				8		10	5			1	
	Jun-01	(h) Tooting & Mitcham United	D 6-6			2	3			6		8	9		11			7						10	5		4	1	
	Jun-08	(a) Tooting & Mitcham United																											
FA Cup																													
EP	Sep-02	(h) Old Johnians	W 7-3	Wilson 4, Bunce, Schofield 2	1	2	3	6		5		4	9	10	11		7			8									
London Senior Cup																													
1	Jan-27	(a*) West Norwood	W 2-0 aban	Dyke 2	1	2	3	6		5		8	9		11			7	4					10					
1	Feb-17	(a*) West Norwood	W 6-0	Barker, Bunce, Baldwin 3, Parr	1	2	3	6		5		8	9		11			7	4					10					
	Feb-24	(h) Wimbledon	W 4-2	Baldwin 3, Bunce	1	2	3	6		5		8	9		11			7	4					10					
	Mar-09	(h) Bromley	W 7-4	Parr 2, Baldwin 2, Bunce 2, Bunyan	1	2	3	6		5		8	9		11			7	4					10					
SF	Mar-30	(?) Barnet	W 2-1	Bunce 2	1	2	3			6		8	9		11			7	4					10	5				
F	Apr-27	(n**) Walthamstow Ave	L 0-5		1	2	3			6		8	9	10	11			7							5		4		
		*played at Lower Mead																											
		**played at West Ham FC																											
Middlesex Red Cross Cup																													
	Dec-30	(h) Polytechnic	W 7-0	Baldwin, Parr 2, Schofield 2, Bunce, Gordon	1		3	6				8	9		11	5		7	4		2	10							
	Mar-16	(h) Pinner	W 7-0	Baldwin 2, Bunce 3, Parr 2	1	2	3	6		5		8	9		11			7	4					10					
	Apr-04	(h) Enfield	W 7-3	Scott, Baldwin 2, Bunce 3, Schofield	1	2	3			6		8	9		11			7	4					10	5				
F	May-04	(h) Golders Green	W 4-1	Baldwin 2, Bunce, Barker (pen)	1	2	3			6		8	9	10	11			7							5		4		

** Sides agreed to the use of Substitutes

1940-41					Walker E	Loveday A	Conniff G	Green L	Scott D	Gadsden R	Kennett F	Butterworth F	Gale H	Dyke H	Dolding L	Upchurch G	Nicholson R	Allen T	Bruce A	Baldwin K	Doherty M	Leeming B	Charlton H	Chat K	Webb F	Bunyan P	Barker C	Wilson J
Herts and Middlesex League - 3rd																												
Fr	Aug-31	(h) Erith & Belvedere	W 4-1	Scott, Gale, Dolding, Butterworth	1	2	3	4	5	6	7	8	9	10	11													
	Sep-07	(a) Tufnell Park	W 5-0	Allen 3, Dolding, Dyke	1	2	3	4	5			8		10	11	6	7	9										
	Sep-14	(h) Tufnell Park	W 7-0	Scott 2, Gale 3, Butterworth 2	1	2	3	4	5			8	9	10	11	6	7											
	Sep-21	(h) Met Police	W 3-1?	?	1	2	3	4	5			8	9	10	11	6	7											
Fr	Sep-28	(h) QPR Reserves	W 8-0	Dyke 2, Nicholson, Gale 3, Dolding, Scott	1	2	3	4	6			8	9	10	11	5	7											
	Oct-05	(h) St Albans	W 6-2	Bunce 3, Nicholson, Dyke, Dolding	1	2	3	4	6			8		10	11	5	7		9									
	Oct-12	(a) St Albans	L 1-3	Dyke 2, Nicholson, Gale 3, Dolding, Scott	1	2	3		6			8	9	10	11		7		9									
	Oct-19	(a) Barnet	W 3-1		1	2	3	4	6			8		10	11	5	7			9								
	Oct-26	(h) Barnet	W 8-1	Butterworth 3, Dyke 2, Gale 2, Scott	1	2	3	4	6			8	9	10	11	5	7											
	Nov-02	(h) Enfield	W 8-2	Dolding 3, Baldwin 2, Butterworth, Gale, Nicholson	1	2	3	4	6			10	9		11	5	7			8								
	Nov-23	(h) Slough	W 5-0	Butterworth 2, Nicholson, Dyke, Gale		2	3	4	6			8	9	10	11	5	7				1							
	Dec-07	(h) Met. Police	D 2-2	Gale, Butterworth		2	3	4	6			8	9	10	11	5	7				1							
Fr	Dec-14	(h) Walthamstow Avenue	D 1-1	Gale		2	3	4	6			8	9	10	11	5	7				1							
	Dec-28	(h) Finchley	W 6-2	Nicholson 2, Dolding 2, Butterworth 2	1	2		4	3			10	9		11	5	7					6	8					
	Jan-04	(a) Finchley	W 2-1																									
	Jan-11	(a) Hitchin Town	L 2-3																									
	Jan-25	(h) Hitchin Town	W 4-3	Butterworth 3, Gale		2	3	6	4			8	9	10	11	5	7				1							
	Mar-01	(a) Enfield	L 3-5	Gale 2, Nicholson		2		4	3			6	9	10	11	5	8				1			7				
	Mar-15	(h) Golders Green	D 4-4	Dyke 3, Charlton				4				6		10									9					
	Mar-22	(a) Met. Police	L 1-2																									
	Apr-05	(a) Golders Green	L 3-4	Gale 2, Charlton				4				6	9		11	5	7				1	3	10		2	8		
	Apr-12	(h) Southall	W 7-1	Nicholson 3, Gale, Dolding, Bunyan		2			3				9		11		7						10					
	Apr-14	(a) Southall	W 1-0	Dyke		2							9				7					3						
	Apr-21	(h) Slough	W 6-3	Butterworth 4, Dolding, Bunyan		2						8			11	5										4		
Fr	May-17	(h) Irish Guards	W 7-3	Barker 6, Butterworth								10															9	
Fr	May-21	(h) Watford	W 4-2	Dolding 2, Butterworth, Charlton								10			11								9					
Fr	May-31	(h) Harrow Town	W 8-1	Butterworth 3, Dolding 2, Dyke 2, Nicholson								8		10	11		7											
Fr	Jun-07	(h) RAF XI	W 9-0			2		4				8		10	11	5	7				1	3	9			6		
London Senior Cup																												
	Dec-21	(h) Hounslow	W 4-2	Scott 3, Butterworth		2	3	6	4			8	9	10	11	5	7				1							
	Feb-15	(h) Met. Police	D 2-2	Butterworth, Gale		2	3	4	6			8	9	10	11	5	7				1							
	Feb-22	(a) Met. Police	L 1-4																									
Middlesex Senior Cup																												
2	Feb-08	(h) Finchley	W 7-3	Nicholson 2, Dyke 2, Gale 2, Dolding		2	3	4	6			8	9	10	11	5	7				1							
SF	Mar-08	(h) Southall	W 10-2	Wilson 3, Charlton 3, Butterworth, Dyke, Nicholson 2				6	3			4		10	11	5	7				1	2	9					8
F	Apr-26	(h) Pinner	W 5-1	Butterworth 2, Dyke, ??		2		6	3			10		8	11	5	7				1		9			4		
Middlesex Red Cross Cup																												
1	Feb-01	(h) RAF	W 4-1	Butterworth, Barker, Dyke, Gale		2		6	4			8	9	10	11	5	7				1						3	
SF	Mar-29	(h) Enfield	W 3-1	Nicholson, Dolding, Butterworth				3				6			11	5	7				1							
F	May-03	Wood Green Town	D 2-2*																									
Fr	May-24	Wood Green Town	W 2-0 *	Butterworth								8																
		* Played at Golders Green FC																										
Cambridge Hospital Cup																												
	May-10	(a) Cambridge T	W 3-2	Dolding, Gale, Nicholson		2						8	9		11		7											

1941-42

Rd	Date	Opponent	Result	Scorers	Doherty M	Loveday A	James E	Green L	Upchurch G	Hay F	Nicholson R	Leeming B	Barker C	Dyke H	Wright H	Bunyan P	Charlton H	Butterworth F	Thompson J	Conniff D	Dolding L	Winterbottom	Kay T	Kay S	Lewis L	Waymouth	Wilson J	Russell J	Fayers J	Ayres D	Scott D	Wheatley	Smith P	Crosby J	Morris T	Wilson R	Stanton R	Viggins	Kay H	Moore J	Edmonds W	Witchire	Faggoter
Herts and Middlesex League - 10th																																											
Fr	Aug-30	RAF Bentley Priory	L 3-4	Barker 2, Nicholson	1	2	3	4	5	6	7	8	9	10	11																												
	Sep-06	(h) Walthamstow Ave	L 0-3		1	2		4	5		7	3	9	10		6	8	11																									
	Sep-13	(h) Enfield	W 4-1	Nicholson 2, Barker, Dolding	1				5		7	6	9	10		4	8		2	3	11																						
	Sep-20	(h) Wood Green Town	W 1-0	?	1	2			5			4	9	10		6	8			3	11	7																					
	Sep-27	(a) Tufnell Park	W 5-2	Lewis 2, Kay S, Dyke, Bunyan	1				5			4	3	10		6					11	7	2	8	9																		
	Oct-04	(h) St Albans	L 2-3	?	1	2			5			4		10		6	7				11			8	9	3																	
	Oct-11	(a) St Albans	L 2-5	Wilson 2	1				5			3		8		6	9				11	7	2	4			10																
	Oct-18	(a) Enfield	L 0-6		1	2			5			3		8		6					11	7		4			10	9															
	Oct-25	(h) Leyton	L 2-4	Russell, Fayers	1				5	7		4	3	10		8					11		2	6				9															
	Nov-01	(a) Leyton	L 0-5		1				5	7		6		10		4			3		11		2					9	8														
	Nov-08	(h) Tufnell Park	W 4-2	?	1				5			6		8			7		3		11		2					9	10	4													
	Nov-15	(a) Finchley	L 1-6	?	1				5	7		6		8					2		11		3					9	10	4													
	Nov-22	(h) Finchley	W 6-0	Dyke 2, Russell 2, Dolding, Charlton	1	2			5				3	8			7		6		11		4					9	10														
	Nov-29	(a) Hitchin Town	L 0-3		1								3	8					6		11							9		2													
	Dec-13	(a) Slough	L 1-4	?																																							
	Dec-20	(h) Slough	W 4-0	?																																							
Fr	Dec-25	(h) Harrow Fire Service	W 6-1	Scott, Lewis, Charlton 2, Bunyan, Wheatley												X	X								X						X	X											
	Dec-27	(a) Wood Green	L 3-5	Dolding, Russell, Crosby			2					5	3				7				11		4					9					1	10									
	Jan-17	(a) Southall	L 2-4	?																																							
Fr	Feb-28	(h) RAF Bassingbourne	W 4-2	Barker, Russell, Charlton, Lewis									3	8		4	7				11				9			10															
	Mar-21	(h) Hitchin Town	W 5-3	Dolding, Charlton 2, Lewis, Russell	1			4	5			2	3				7		6		11				9			10							8								
	Apr-11	(a) Golders Green	D 2-2	?																																							
	Apr-18	(h) Golders Green	L 0-3		1				5			2	3		6	4					11				9		8	10								7							
	Apr-25	(h) Barnet	L 2-3	?																																							
	May-09	(a) Walthamstow Avenue	W 8-1	Butterworth 3, Morris 4, Russell		2			5			4	1					10			11						7	9							8		6	9					
	May-16	(a) Barnet	L 2-3	Dolding, Morris	1				5			4	3								11		2		9			10							8	7			6				
	May-23	(h) Southall	W 2-0	Russell 2																			4					9								10	6						
Herts & Middlesex League Cup																																											
1	Apr-04	(a) Golders Green	W 2-1	Lewis 2	1				5			2	3			4	7		6		11				9						10				8								
SF	May-02	(h) Southall	D 4-4 aet	Dolding 2, Morris, Russell	1	2			5			6	3								11		4					9							8	10				7			
SFr	May-25	(a) Southall	L 0-6																		11		3									3			10				1				
London Senior Cup																																											
2	Jan-03	(h) Erith & Belvedere	W 4-2	Dyke 2, Dolding, Charlton	1				5			4	3	8			7		6		11							10													9		
3	Mar-14	(a) Southall	L 4-5	Barker 2, Dyke, Charlton	1				5			2	3	8		4	7	10	6		11				9																		
Middlesex Senior Cup																																											
2	Dec-06	(h) Enfield	W 5-1	Dyke 3, Russell 2	1	2			5			6	3	8			7		10		11		4					9															
3	Jan-10	(h) Pinner	W 6-2	?	1	2			5			4	3	8			7		6		11							10													9		
SF	Feb-21	(h) Uxbridge	W 2-1	?	1				5			2	3	8		4	7		6		11							9													10		
F	Apr-06	(h) Finchley	W 4-1	Russell 3, Barker (pen)	1				5			2	3			4	7		6		11				9			10							8								
Middlesex Red Cross Cup																																											
1	Feb-14	(h) Napier Athletic	W 4-3	Barker, Russell, Charlton, Dyke	1				5			2	3	8		4	7		6		11							9													10		
2	Mar-07	(A) Finchley	W 4-3	Dolding 2, Russell, Charlton					5			2	3	8		4	7		6		11							9															
SF	Mar-28	(h) Southall	W 5 -2	Dolding 2, Barker, Lewis, Morris	1				5				3				7				11				9										8								
F	Jun-03	RAF Uxbridge (Wemb)	W 5-2 aet	Russell 2, Morris, Wilson, og	1				5			4	3								11		2					9							8	10	6			7			

1942-43

	Date	Opponent	Result	Scorers	Kay H	Carter T	Barker C	Townsend H	Wright F	Leeming B	A N Other	Anderson G	Russell J	Bunyan P	Dolding L	Doherty M	Vickers T	Kay T	Stanton R	Moore J	Wilson R	Upchurch G	Dyke H	Brown C	Edgard R	Wheatley W	Morris T	Harle F	Frost F	Mogridge S	Bidwell R	Field S	Wheeler F	Bexon	Parish G
Herts and Middlesex League - 12th																																			
	Aug-29	(h) RAF Bentley Priory	W 3-2	Dolding 2, Russell	1	2	3	4	5	6	7	8	9	10	11																				
	Sep-05	(a) Wood Green	W 4-2	Russell 3, Barker			3		5				9	10	11	1	2	4	6	7	8														
	Sep-12	(h) Walthamstow Ave	L 1-2	Dyke			3			4			9		11	1		2	6		7	5	8												
	Sep-19	(a) Walthamstow Ave	L 1-6	Russell		3			5			4	9		11	1		2			8		10	6	7										
	Sep-26	(h) Finchley	L 2-4	Russell, Morris			3			5		4	9		11	1		2	6		8					7	10								
	Oct-03	(a) Tufnell Park	D 2-2	Mogridge 2		3				4			10					2	6	7	8				11			1	5	9					
	Oct-10	(h) Hitchin	L 3-5	Dolding, Mogridge 2											11			3	6		4				7		8	1	5	9	2	10			
	Oct-17	(a) Leyton	L 1-4	Mogridge						4					11	1		3	6		7	5								9	2	10	8		
	Oct-24	(h) Wood Green Town	W 6-2	Stanton 2, Wilson R 2, Mogridge, Field						4					11	1	3	2	6	7	8	5								9		10			
	Oct-31	(a) St Albans	L 2-4	Stanton, Mogridge									8		11		3	2	6	7		5								9		10		1	4
	Nov-07	(h) St Albans	L 1-6	Box						3			8		11			2	6			5								7		10		1	4
	Nov-14	(a) Finchley	L 3-7	Box 3		3				6			7		11		3	2	8			5						1				10			4
	Nov-21	(a) Barnet	L 1-9	Russell									9		11		3	4										1				10			5
	Nov-28	(h) Barnet	L 0-2							4			7		11	1	3	2	6								8					10			5
	Dec-25	(h) Golders Green	L 2-3	Box, Dolding			3								11			2		7								1				10			
	Dec-26	(a) Golders Green	L 2-9	Wilson R, Baldwin											11						8							1							
	Jan-02	(h) Southall	W 3-1	Morriss 3						6			9		11	1		2				5							10						4
	Jan-09	(a) Hitchin Town	L 0-6							6			9			1						5					10								4
	Jan-23	(h) Leyton	L 1-4	Field			3																									8			
	Jan-30	(a) Southall	L 1-3	Barker 2			3			6		4	9		11	1						5										10			
	Feb-13	(h) Slough	W 4-2	Haydon 2, Yates, Baldwin			3						9			1		4				5													6
Fr	Feb-20	(h) Gloster Aircraft	W 4-3	Russell 2, Dyke, og			3			2								4				5	9												6
	Feb-27	(a) Slough	W 5-1	Dolding 3, Parish, Hardie											8																				6
	Mar-06	(h) Tufnell Park	L 1-4	Box						4						1		3				5													6
Fr	Apr-03	(h) Worcester Regiment	W 4-3	Russell 4			3						4					2													5				6
Fr	Apr-07	(h) Royal Navy Training Unit	W 5-1	Yates 2, Barker 2, Field			9											4														7			
Fr	Apr-10	(h) Liason Regiment	W 6-2	Russell 3, Hardie 2, Haynes			3						9			1		2		7							10								5
Fr	Apr-17	(h) RAF Halton	L 2-3	Boshell, Vaughan												1		2				5													6
Herts & Middlesex League Cup																																			
	Feb-06	(a) St Albans	W 4-2	Haydon 2, Moore, Hardie			3						9			1		4		7		5													6
2	Mar-27	(a) Wood Green Town	W 2-1	Barker 2			8						9			1		2														11			5
SF	Apr-24	(a) Tufnell Park	L 1-4	Moore									9					2		7		5													
London Senior Cup																																			
	Dec-12	(h) Southall	L 2-7	Vickers, Wilson J											11		3	2									8					7			5
Middlesex Senior Cup																																			
1	Dec-05	(h) Harrow Town	W 3-2	Morris, Dolding, Field						4					11	1		2	6								10					7			5
2	Jan-16	(h) Yiewsley	W 6-2	Haynes 3, Dolding, Morriss, Parish									9		11	1		4				5					8								6
SF	Mar-13	(a) Hounslow	W 2-1	Russell, Dolding			3						9		10	1		2		7		5													6
F	Apr-26	(a) Finchley	D 3-3	Russell 2, Morris									9			1		2		7							10								
Fr	May-01	(h) Finchley	W 3-0	Morris, Moore, Baldwin						10			9		11			2		7		5					10								6
Middlesex Red Cross Cup																																			
1	Feb-19	(h) Pinner	W										9					2									10							1	3
2	Mar-20	(h) Golders Green	L 0-3				3						9		10	1		2		8		5													6

	Date	Opponent	Box G	East L	Young A	Floyd A	Butterworth F	Baldwin K	Bamborough	Pearson K	Hardie G	King	Branford A	Haynes L	Welch S	Yates A	Haydon F	Bird G	Williams J	Mainwaring	Horn	Boshell J	Vaughn A	De Lucas	Phillips	Allen W	Wilson J	Cummings A	Jones W	Saunders B	Hancock W	Green L	Barrow D	Gamble L
Herts and Middlesex League - 12th																																			
	Aug-29	(h) RAF Bentley Priory																																
	Sep-05	(a) Wood Green																																
	Sep-12	(h) Walthamstow Ave																																
	Sep-19	(a) Walthamstow Ave																																
	Sep-26	(h) Finchley																																
	Oct-03	(a) Tufnell Park																																
	Oct-10	(h) Hitchin																																
	Oct-17	(a) Leyton																																
	Oct-24	(h) Wood Green Town																																
	Oct-31	(a) St Albans																																
	Nov-07	(h) St Albans	9																															
	Nov-14	(a) Finchley	9																															
	Nov-21	(a) Barnet		1	6	7																												
	Nov-28	(h) Barnet	9																															
	Dec-25	(h) Golders Green	9				8																											
	Dec-26	(a) Golders Green						9																										
	Jan-02	(h) Southall							3	7	8																							
	Jan-09	(a) Hitchin Town								9		11																						
	Jan-23	(h) Leyton							11				9	10																				
	Jan-30	(a) Southall									7			8	2																			
	Feb-13	(h) Slough						10			7				2	8	11																	
Fr	Feb-20	(h) Gloster Aircraft		1				10			7					8	11																	
	Feb-27	(a) Slough																																
	Mar-06	(h) Tufnell Park	9					8			7			10	2		11																	
Fr	Apr-03	(h) Worcester Regiment						4			7			10		8	11	1																
Fr	Apr-07	(h) Royal Navy Training Unit		1					3					10	2	8			5	6	11													
Fr	Apr-10	(h) Liason Regiment						4			8			11								6												
Fr	Apr-17	(h) RAF Halton						4			7			10	3							8	9	11										
Herts & Middlesex League Cup																																			
	Feb-06	(a) St Albans									8			10	2		11																	
2	Mar-27	(a) Wood Green Town		1				4			7			10								6			3									
SF	Apr-24	(a) Tufnell Park						4			8						3							11										
London Senior Cup																																			
	Dec-12	(h) Southall	9	1															6							4	10							
Middlesex Senior Cup																																			
1	Dec-05	(h) Harrow Town	9																3									8						
2	Jan-16	(h) Yiewsley									7			10	3														2					
SF	Mar-13	(a) Hounslow						4			8						11																	
F	Apr-26	(a) Finchley						4									3																	
Fr	May-01	(h) Finchley		1				4									3																	
Middlesex Red Cross Cup																																			
1	Feb-19	(h) Pinner									7																			4	5	6	8	11
2	Mar-20	(h) Golders Green						4			7						5																	

1943-44					East L	Kay T	Welsh S	Baldwin K	Saunders B	Parish G	Hill H	Hardie G	Gregg E	Morris T	Lane E	Haynes L	Leeming B	Mainwaring	De Luca D	Rowell S	Upchurch G	Moore J	Russell J	Blond	Green L	Preston S	Barker C	Hancock W	Wiltshire S	Westray	Chappel D	Williams R	Gamble L	Armstrong A	McIntosh A	Dyke H	Horne	Stanton R	O'Neill W	Smith L	Burrows	Barrow B	Hardie A	Thorpe A	Pratt A	Baysford L	Allen	Bidewell R	Scott D	Perrin K	Williams J
Herts and Middlesex League - 12th																																																			
Fr	Aug-28	(h) Irish Guards	L 2-3		1	2	3	4	5	6	7	8	9	10	11																																				
	Sep-04	(h) Wood Green Town	W 5-3	Baldwin 3, Welch, Hardie	1	2	3	4	5	6		7	9	8		10	11																																		
	Sep-11	(a) Wood Green Town	L 1-3	Mainwaring	1	2			5	6		7		9		8	3	4	10	11																															
	Sep-18	(h) Tufnell Park	L 1-4	Russell	1	2			4	6		8		10		11	3				5	7	9																												
	Sep-25	(a) Grays Athletic	L 4-10	Morris 2, Upchurch, Hardie		2		4	5	6		7		8		10					9			1	3	11																									
	Oct-02	(h) Barnet	W 9-7	Barker (pen), Morris 4, Parrish, Baldwin 2, Hardie	1	2		8	5	6		7		9		10									4	11	3																								
	Oct-09	(a) Tufnell Park	L 0-1		1	2		8	5	6		7					4		10		9					11	3																								
	Oct-16	(h) Grays Athletic	D 2-2	Hardie, Moore	1	2			5	6		7		9								8				11		4	10																						
	Oct-23	(a) Barnet	L 1-5	Morris	1	2			5	6		7		9			3									11		4		8	9	10																			
	Oct-30	(h) St Albans	L 1-2	Chappell	1	2			5	6		7		8											4	11	3	10			9																				
	Nov-06	(a) Hitchin Town	D 1-1	Chappell	1	2			5			7													6	11	3	4			9		8	10																	
	Nov-13	(h) Hitchin Town	L 0-2		1	2			5	10		7		8											4		3	6			9		11																		
	Nov-20	(a) St Albans	W 7-2	Morris 3, Gamble 2, Barker, Parish	1	2			5	10		7		9											4	11	3	6					8																		
	Nov-27	(h) Southall	W 1-0	Parish	1	2		8	5	10				9			7								4		3	6					11																		
	Dec-04	(h) Walthamstow Avenue	L 0-4		1	2			5	10		7		8											6		3	9					11		4																
	Dec-25	(h) Golders Green	D 3-3	Dyke, Horne, Stanton																																X	X	X													
	Dec-27	(h) Golders Green	L 3-4	Russell 3, ?																			X																												
	Jan-01	(a) Slough	L 2-4	Russell, Smith	1				3	6		7		8					10				9		2			5											4	11											
	Jan-08	(h) Leyton	D 3-3	Russell 2, Hardie	1				2	3		7		10									9		6			5					11						4		8										
	Jan-15	(a) Leyton	L 0-3 aban		1	2			5	3		7		10									9		6								11			8				4											
	Jan-22	(a) Clapton	D 2-2	Morris, Gamble	1	2			4	3		7		10									9		6			5					11									8									
	Feb-05	(a) Finchley	L 2-5	Russell, Gamble	1	2			4	3		7		8					10				9		6			5					11																		
	Feb-12	(h) Finchley	L 4-5	Hardy, Russell 2, Gamble	1	2			6	3		7		10									9		4			5					11									8									
	Feb-26	(h) Clapton	W 3-1	Hardie, Morris, Russell	1	2	3	8	5	6		7		10									9					4					11																		
	Mar-11	(a) Southall	W 4-1	Welch, Morris, Russel, Gamble			7							8									9					5					10																		
	Mar-18	(h) Slough	W 2-1	Welch 2	1		7			6													9		4		3	5					10																		
	Apr-01	(a) Leyton	L 0-4		1	2	7		4	6				10			3						9					5					8										11								
Fr	Apr-08	(h) Austrian FC	W 4-0	Gamble 3, Saunders	1				4	6				10			2	3	11			7						5					9											8							
	Apr-29	(a) Walthamstow Avenue	L 1-5	Kay T	1	2	10		4	6									8				9					5															7		3	11					
Fr	May-03	(h) Army Pay Corps	L 2-3	Russell																			X																												
Herts & Middlesex League Cup																																																			
1	Mar-25	(h) Golders Green	W 6-2	Russell 4, Hardie 2	1	2	7			6				8									9				3	4					10										11				5				
2	Apr-11	(a) Slough	W 2-1	Russell 2	1				3	6								2	11			4	9					5					10										7	8							
SF	Apr-22	(h) Clapton	L 3-5	Morris, Russell, Bidwell	1	2				6				8								7	9					5					10										11					4	3		
London Senior Cup																																																			
	Dec-11	(a) Southall	L 2-6	Kay T, Chappell		2	3			6		7																			10																			8	
Middlesex Senior Cup																																																			
1	Dec-18	(h) Uxbridge	L 3-4	Kay T, Green, Gamnble	1	2			5	10		7		8											6			9					11																	4	3
Middlesex Red Cross Cup																																																			
1	Feb-19	(h) Pinner	W 6-2	Hardie 2, Russell 2, Gamble 2	1	2	4		5	6		7		8					11				9		6		3						10																		
SF	Mar-04	(a) QPR Juniors	L 1-4	Russell	1			8						10									9		7		3	4					11																		

1944-45

	Date	Opponent	Result	Scorers	Stanhope	Kay T	Pratt A	Vessey P	Hancock W	Parish G	Basford C	Garrigon G	Russell J	Haynes L	Hardie A	Cooke H	Coxon R	Brown L	Currie E	Green L	Upton E	Taylor W	Preston S	Baynham A	Arnold W	Tann J	Jones D	Hewson T	Poxon J	East L	Williams R	Twigg W	Baldwin K	Horn N	Edmunds C	Mainwaring T	Moore J	Dolding L	Jones D	Dyke H	Parish E	Hewlett A	Jennings H	Saunders B	Warner B	Harrison C	Heathcote S	Mortemore F	Floyd F	Driver K	Barker C	D'Arcy J	A N Other	Dallingin A	De Luca D	Dyke S	Cooke H	Christmas W	Garrison G	Emmott K	Hawson K	Walton F
Herts and Middlesex League - 12th																																																														
Fr	Aug-26	(h) Ringley	L 2-3	Russell	1	2	3	5	6	7	4	8	9	10	11																																															
Fr	Sep-02	(h) Royal Navy XI	W 8-0	Russell 5, Parish, Barford, Brown		2		4	5	6	11	8	9		3	1	7	10																																												
	Sep-09	(h) Hitchin Town	D 1-1	Hardie		2		4	5	6	10	8			11	1	7		3	9																																										
	Sep-16	(a) Barnet	L 2-4	Russell 2		2		8	5	6	10		9		11	1	7		3	4																																										
	Sep-23	(a) Walthamstow Avenue	L 2-5	Currie, og		2			5	6		8				1	7		10	4	3	9	11																																								
	Sep-30	(h) Clapton	D 4-4	Hardie 3, Arnold			3		5	6		8			11	1	7			4	2			9	10																																				
	Oct-07	(a) Finchley	L 0-6			2			5	6		8	9		11	1	7			4	3				10																																				
	Oct-14	(a) Wood Green Town	W 2-0	Russell, Hardie					5	6	10		9		11	1			3	4	2	7				8																																			
	Oct-21	(h) St Albans	L 1-2	Russell		2			5	6	11	8	9			1			4		3	7						10																																		
	Oct-28	(a) Tufnell Park	L 0-2			2			6	5	11	8	9			1	7		3	4							10																																		
	Nov-04	(h) Leyton	W 5-3	Hardie 3, Garrigon, Russell		2			6	5		8	9		11	1	7			4	3						10																																		
	Nov-11	(a) St Albans	W 2-1	Russell					6	5		8	9		11	1	7			4	3						10	2																																	
	Nov-18	(h) Barnet	W 3-1	Jones 3					6	5		8	9		11	1	7			4	3						10		2																																
	Nov-25	(a) Slough	L 1-2	Hardie					6	5		8	9		11	1	7			4	3						10		2																																
	Dec-02	(h) Southall	L 1-6	Russell					6	5		8	9		11	1	7			4	3						10	2																																	
	Dec-25	(h) Golders Green	D 2-2	Garrigan, Baynham		2				5		7			3									9					8	1	4	6	10	11																											
	Dec-30	(h) Walthamstow Avenue	L 1-3	Poxon		2			4	6		7	9							11	3								8	1			10		5																										
Fr	Jan-06	(a) Leytonstone	W 4-3	Mainwaring 3, Hewson		2			6	4		8			3		7				2						8		10		1					5	9																									
	Jan-13	(h) Wood Green Town	W 5-3	Dolding, Poxon 2, Russell, Jones		2			4	6			9									3							10		8	1					5		7	11	10																							
	Feb-03	(h) Grays Athletic	L 3-4	Poxon, Dyke, Jones		2			4	6												3							10		7	1			11		5				10	8	9																					
	Feb-17	(h) Slough	L 1-3	Twigg						2	6		7			11	3														8			4			5					10		1	9																				
	Feb-24	(a) Clapton	L 2-8	Dyke, Jennings		2			9	5												3									7				4									10		1	8	5																			
Fr	Mar-03	(h) Gloster Aircraft	W 4-1	Garrigan 2, Hancock, og		2			9	6		8			11						3											7			4			5					10		1																						
	Mar-24	(h) Finchley	D 2-2	Hancock 2		2			8	6		7	9									3														4			5							1				10	11																
	Mar-31	(a) Hitchin Town	L 0-1			2			9	6		8			11						3														4			5							1					7	10															
	Apr-07	(a) Leytonstone	L 1-4	Russell		2			6	5			9		8						3														4								10		1					11																
	Apr-21	(a) Southall	L 1-3	Heathcote		2			9	6		7									3										8			4			5					10		1						11														
Fr	Apr-28	(h) Leytonstone	L 1-4	Mortemore 2		2			11	5		7									3										8			4								10		1						6	9													
Fr	May-02	(h) Pinner	L 3-6	Russell 2, Mortemore		2				6			9									3										8			4										1						11	10	5	7											
Fr	May-09	(h) RAOC	L 1-2	Dyke																																																											
	May-12	(a) Grays Athletic	L 1-7	Barker																																																	3												
	May-19	(h) Tufnell Park	L 1-4			2				6		7									3														4		11	5							1						10					8	9										
	May-26	(a) Golders Green	W 2-1	Heathcote 2		2				6		8									3						4	9										5						10														1	7							
Herts & Middlesex League Cup																																																														
1	Feb-10	(a) Slough	L 0-3			2			4	6											3										8						5						10	9										11	1		7						
London Senior Cup																																																														
2	Dec-09	(a) Edgware Town	L 0-14						6	5			9						4	3																				10																			1	2	8	7	11	
Middlesex Senior Cup																																																														
1	Dec-16	(h) Acton United	D 2-2	Russell 2					4	6		7	9		11					2	3						10		8	1					5																											11
1r	Dec-23	(h) Acton United	W 3-2	Russell 2, Baldwin		2				5		8	9		11		7			4	3									1		6	10																													
2	Jan-20	(h) Polytechnic	W 2-0	Hancock, Jones		2			4	6		8										3						10	7	9	1					5			11																								
3	Mar-17	(a) Southall	L 1-3	Russell		2				6		7	9									3										8			4			5					10		1				11																
Middlesex Red Cross Cup																																																														
1	Mar-10	(a) Pinner	W 3-0	Poxon 2, Harrison		2			9	6		8									3										7			4			5					10		1				11																
2	Apr-14	(h) Edgware Town	W 2-1	Mortemore 2		2			8	6		7									3														4			5					10		1					11	9															
3	May-05	(h) Golders Green	L 2-3	Dyke, Mortemore		2				6		7									3										8			4								10		1							9			11												

1945-46

Rd	Date	Opponent	Result	Scorers	Lewis R	Upton EG	Shervington D	Twigg W	Edmonds C	Pratt TE	Garrigan G	Hancock W	Berthelemy WB	Lawrence HR	Burgess SC	Barker C	Parish G	Young SW	Dyke H	Haydon F	Hewlett W	Scott D	Jennings V	Hardie A	Saunders B	Heathcote S	Buller W	McDonald L	Moore J	Gaze G	Williams G	Dolding L	Ward C	Jocelyn R	Newbury F	Hardie G	Doig A	Morris T	Wilson J	Marjoram R	Brown F	Rouse A	Capon GS	Boyle L	Clark EA	Kay T	Duffell G	A N Other
Athenian League - 6th																																																
	Aug-25	(h) Southall	D 2-2	Pratt (pen), Berthelemy	1	2	3	4	5	6	7	8	9	10	11																																	
	Sep-01	(a) Hitchin	W 2-1	Lawrence, Berthelemy	1	2		4	5	6	7	8	9	10	11	3																																
	Sep-15	(h) Redhill	D 0-0		1	2		4	5	10	7	8	9		11	3	6																															
	Sep-29	(h) Sutton	L 2-3	Dyke, Berthelemy	1	2			5	6	7		9	10	11		3	4	8																													
	Oct-27	(a) Southall	L 0-3		1	3		4	5	6	7			10	11				8				9	2																								
	Nov-03	(a) Barking	W 4-1	Lawrence 3, A Hardie		2		4	5	6	7			10					8		1	3	9	11																								
	Nov-10	(a) Enfield	D 1-1	Lawrence	1	2		4		6	7			10					8			3	9	11																								3
	Nov-17	(h) Hitchin	D 3-3	Lawrence, Jennings, Garrigan	1	2		4	5		7			10	11				8			3	9		6																							
	Nov-24	(h) Leyton	D 0-0		1	2			5	6	7			10		11			8			3	9		4																							
	Dec-01	(a) Leyton	L 0-3		1	2		9	5	6	7				11	10			8			3			4																							
	Dec-08	(a*) Barking	W 3-0	Dyke, Heathcote 2	1	2		7	5	9	8					3			10			6			4	11																						
	Dec-22	(a) Hayes	L 1-4	Barker		2			5	6						3			10			4				11	8	1	7	9																		
	Dec-25	(h) Golders Green	W 4-0	Gaze 2, Dyke, Garrigan		2			5	6	8					3			10			4						1	7	9	11																	
	Dec-26	(a) Golders Green	W 3-2	Gaze, Heathcote, Barker (pen)		2			5	6	8					3			10			4				11		1	7	9																		
	Dec-29	(h) Enfield	W 6-0	Lawrence 2,Heathcote 2,Gaze,Moore		2				6				11		3			10			5			4	7		1	8	9																		
	Jan-05	(a) Barnet	W 5-2	Lawrence 2, Dolding 3		2			5	6				10		3			8			4					7				11	9											1					
	Feb-02	(h) Tooting & Mitcham United	L 2-3	Moore 2				4	5	6				10					8			3						1	9				11	2	7													
	Feb-23	(a) Redhill	W 5-3	Dyke 2, Morris, Moore 2		2			5	6				11		3			10			4						1	7						8			9										
	Mar-02	(h) Barnet	D 1-1	Moore				4	5	6						3			10			2		11				1	9				7						8									
	Mar-09	(a) Tooting & Mitcham United	L 3-5	Morris 2, Barker (pen)					5							3			10			6		2				1	7							11	4	9	8									
	Mar-23	(a*) Finchley	D 3-3	Wilson 2, R Marjoram					5	6				11		3			10			2						1	7								4		8	9								
	Apr-13	(a) Sutton U	L 3-6	Dyke 2, Wilson												3			10			2			5				7	9						11	4		8		1	6						
	Apr-20	(h) Finchley	D 2-2	Gaze, Wilson						6				11		3						2			5			1	7	9							4	8	10									
	Apr-25	(a) Bromley	W 1-0	Gaze					5	6				11		3			10											9						7	4	8						1	2			
	May-01	(h) Bromley	D 5-5	Lawrence, Gaze 2, Dyke, Barker(pen)					5	6				11		3			8			2						1	7	9							4		10									
	May-04	(h) Hayes	W 3-2	Gaze 2, Dyke					5	6				11		3			8			2						1		9						7	4		10									
		*played at Lower Mead																																														
FA Cup																																																
Pr	Sep-08	(a) Pinner	W 2-1	Pratt, Berthelemy	1	2		4	5	10	7	8	9		11	3	6																															
1Q	Sep-22	(a) St Albans	D 2-2	Pratt (pen), Young	1	2		4	5	3	7		9	10	11		6	8																														
1Qr	Sep-26	(h) St Albans	W 3-0	Pratt, Berthelemy 2	1	2		4	5	6	7		9	10	11		3	8																														
2Q	Oct-06	(a) Harrow T	D 1-1	Berthelemy	1	2			5	6	7		9	10	11		3	4	8																													
2Qr	Oct-10	(h) Harrow T	W 6-1	Pratt (pen), Berthelemy 4, Burgess	1	3			5	6	7		9	8	11		4	10		2																												
3Q	Oct-20	(a) Barnet	L 0-3																																													8
FA Amateur Cup																																																
1	Jan-19	(a) Hayes	L 0-3					4	5	6				10		3			8			2				7		1					11					9										
London Senior Cup																																																
1	Jan-26	(a) Bromley	L 0-4			2		4	5	6				10					8									1	9				11													3	7	
Middlesex Senior Cup																																																
1	Jan-12	(h) Rayners Lane	W 4-3	Dyke 2, Ward, Buller		2			5		7			10		3			8			4			6		9	1					11															
2	Feb-16	(h) Wood Green Town	W 7-1	Lawrence,Dyke 2,Morris 3,Barker (pen)					5	6				11		3			10			4		2				1	7								8	9										
SF	Mar-16	(h) Pinner	W 5-1	Dyke, Morris 2, Moore, Barker					5	6				11		3			10			2						1	7								4	9	8									
F	Apr-22	(n*) Edgware	W 2-0	Dyke, Wilson					5	6						3			10			2						1	7	9							4	8	11									
		*played at Golders Green FC																																														
Middlesex Charity Cup																																																
1	Dec-15	(h) Yiewsley	D 1-1 aban	Dyke	1	2		4	5	9	7				11				10			3			6		8																					
1r	Feb-09	(a) Yiewsley	W 3-1	Lawrence, Moore 2				4	5	6	8			10		3						2		7				1	9				11															
2	Mar-30	(h) Southall	L 2-4	Dyke, Wilson					5	6				11		3			10			2							7								4	9	8					1				
Wealdstone FC Hospital Cup																																																
	May-08	(h) Golders Green	W 4-0	Gaze 2, Dyke 2					5	6				11		3			10			4						1		9						7	8								2			
Northwood War Memorial Cup																																																
	May-11	(a) Pinner	W 2-1	Gaze, Barker (pen)					5	6				11		3			10			4						1		9						7	8								2			

1946-47

	Date	Opponent	Result	Scorers	McDonald LA	Clark EA	Barker CA	George RW	Edmonds C	Young SW	Moore J	Dyke HH	Gaze AG	Fowler JW	Hardie G	Hill RA	Pratt TE	Lawrence HR	Doig A	Morris T	Boston F	Haydon F	Boyle L	Holben G	Scott D	Beasley SJ	Marjoram R	Kay T	Hunt DA	Benn A	Franklin RS	Jocelyn R	Stevens A	Hardie A
Athenian League - 4th																																		
	Aug-31	(a) Hitchin Town	D 4-4	Gaze 2, Hardie, Moore	1	2	3	4	5	6	7	8	9	10	11																			
	Sep-07	(h) Leyton	W 2-1	Gaze, Dyke		2	3	4	5	10	7	8	9			1	6	11																
	Sep-14	(a) Sutton U	L 0-2			2	3	4	5	10	7	8	9			1	6	11																
	Sep-28	(a) Hayes	W 5-3	Gaze, Dyke 2, Boston, Moore		2	3		5	8	7	10	9			1	6		4		11													
	Oct-12	(h) Enfield	W 4-1	Gaze, Dyke, Boston, Morris		2	3		5		7	10	9				6			8	11	4		1										
	Oct-19	(a) Barnet	L 2-3	Moore 2			3		5	4	7	10	9	8		1	6				11	2												
	Oct-26	(h) Tooting & Mitcham United	W 6-1	Gaze 2,Dyke,Fowler,Boston,Barker(pen)			3		5	4	7	8	9	10		1	6				11	2												
	Nov-02	(a) Redhill	W 6-4	Gaze 3, Dyke, Moore, Pratt			3		5	4	7	8	9	10		1	6				11	2												
	Nov-09	(h) Bromley	D 0-0				3		5	4	7	8	9	10		1	6				11	2												
	Nov-16	(a) Enfield	W 3-1	Gaze 2, og			3		5	6	7	8	9	10		1	4				11	2												
	Nov-23	(h) Southall	W 4-2	Gaze, Fowler 2, Barker (pen)			3		5	4	7	8	9	10		1	6				11	2												
	Nov-30	(a) Tooting & Mitcham United	L 3-4	Boston 3			3		5	4	7	8	9	10		1	6				11	2												
	Dec-07	(h) Barnet	W 2-1	Gaze 2			3		5	4	7	8	9	10		1	6				11	2												
	Dec-14	(a) Barking	D 0-0				3		5	4	7	8	9	10		1	6				11	2												
	Dec-25	(h) Hendon	L 1-4	Moore			3		5		7	8	9	10		1	6				11	2											4	
	Dec-26	(a) Hendon	W 2-0	Dyke, Hardie	1		3		5			8	9	10	7		6				11	2			4									
	Dec-28	(a) Bromley	L 1-5	Fowler	1		3		5		7	8	9	10			6				11	2			4									
	Mar-08	(h) Hitchin Town	W 4-2	Gaze 3, Hunt			3		5	6	7	10	9			1						2				11			8	4				
	Mar-15	(a) Southall	W 2-0	Gaze, Beasley			3		5	4	7	10	9			1	6					2				11			8					
	Mar-22	(a) Finchley	D 1-1	Hunt			3		5	4	7	10	9			1	6					2				11			8					
	Mar-29	(h) Barking	D 0-0				3		5	4	7	10	9			1	6					2				11			8					
	Apr-05	(h) Finchley	D 1-1	Hunt			3		5	4	7	10	9		11	1	6					2							8					
	Apr-19	(h) Hayes	L 1-2	Gaze			3		5	4	7	10	9			1	6					2							8		11			
	Apr-26	(a) Leyton	W 3-0	Barker 3 (1 pen)		3	11		5	4	7	10	9			1	6					2							8					
	May-03	(h) Redhill	L 1-3	Pratt		3	11		5	4	7	10	9			1	6					2							8					
	May-17	(h) Sutton U	L 0-1			3	9		5	11		10	7			1	6					2							8	4				
FA Cup																																		
Pr	Sep-21	(h) Tufnell Park	W 6-1	Gaze 3, Dyke 2, Moore		2	3		5	6	7	10	9			1			4	8	11													
1Q	Oct-05	(a) Harrow T	L 3-4	Boston, Pratt, og		2	3		5		7	10	9				6	8			11	4	1											
FA Amateur Cup																																		
	Jan-18	(a) Hounslow	L 1-3	Boston		2	3		5		7	10	9			1	6				11	4					8							
London Senior Cup																																		
1	Jan-11	(a) Kingstonian	L 2-3	Boston 2			3		5		7	8	9	10		1	6				11	2			4									
Middlesex Senior Cup																																		
1	Jan-04	(a) Hendon	D 1-1 aban	Barker (pen)			3		5		7	8	9	10		1	6					2			4	11								
R	Jan-25	(h) Hendon	L 1-2	G Hardie			3		5		9	10	7		8	1	6								4	11		2						
Middlesex Charity Cup																																		
1	Dec-21	(h) Pinner	W 3-0	Dyke, Boston, R Marjoram		3					7	8	9			1	6				11	2					10					4	5	
SF	Apr-12	(a) Hendon	L 1-3 aet	G Hardie			3		5	4	7		9		11	1	6					2							8		10			
Wealdstone F C Hospital Cup																																		
	Jun-14	(h) Harrow T	L 1-5	Gaze		3			5	4		10	9			1	6					2							8		7			11

1947-48

Rd	Date	Opponent	Result	Scorers	Hill RA	Haydon FJ	Barker CA	Hill WG	Edmonds CA	Francis ET	Gaze AG	Nicholson RW	Bryant BL	Attwood RH	Ray WH	Dyke HH	Moore JA	MacDonald LA	Hardie G	Franklin RS	Marjoram RA	Scott DH	Marjoram TH	Hardie A	Munday AJ	Pratt TE	Hooker R	Boston F	Durban C	Kay T	Norton EH	Westray F	Davison F	Shakeri PL	Wright H
Athenian League - 5th																																			
	Aug-23	(h) Leyton	W 5-2	Bryant 2, Attwood, Ray, Nicholson	1	2	3	4	5	6	7	8	9	10	11																				
	Aug-30	(a) Sutton U	D 0-0		1	2	3	4	5	6		7	9	10	11	8																			
	Sep-06	(h) Bromley	W 5-1	Attwood 2, Dyke, Moore, Barker (pen)	1	2	3	4	5	6			9	10	11	8	7																		
	Sep-13	(a) Barking	W 3-0	Bryant 2, Ray	1	2	3	4	5	6			9	10	11	8	7																		
	Sep-27	(a) Tooting & Mitcham United	W 3-0	Attwood 2, Ray	1	2	3	4	5	6			9	10	11	8	7																		
	Oct-11	(a) Enfield	D 1-1	Moore	1	2	3	4	5	6			9	10	11	8	7																		
	Oct-25	(h) Barnet	L 2-3	Dyke, Ray	1	2	3	4	5	6			9	10	11	8	7																		
	Nov-08	(h) Barking	D 0-0			2	3	4	5	6	9	7		10	11	8		1																	
	Nov-29	(a) Hitchin Town	L 1-2	Ray	1	2	3	4	5				9	8	11	10			7							6									
	Dec-06	(h) Sutton U	D 0-0		1	2	3	4	5	6					11	10	7			8	9														
	Dec-20	(h) Hitchin Town	W 3-1	Moore 2, Barker (pen)	1	2	3	4	5	10			9		11	8	7								6										
	Dec-25	(h) Hendon	W 2-1	Dyke 2	1		3	4	5	6				10	11	8	7					9		2											
	Dec-27	(a) Hendon	D 1-1	Dyke	1		3	4	5	6				10	11	8	7					9	2												
	Feb-28	(a) Hayes	W 2-1	R Marjoram 2	1		3	4	5	6				10		8	7				9		2				11								
	Mar-20	(a) Leyton	L 1-2	Dyke	1	2	3	4	5	6						8	7				9		10					11							
	Mar-26	(a) Finchley	L 1-2	Dyke		5	3	4		6					11	8	7	1			9		2			10									
	Mar-27	(h) Hayes	D 2-2	Barker, Pratt			2			6					11	8	7	1			9			3	4	10				5					
	Mar-29	(h) Finchley	L 0-1				2	4		6					11	8	7	1			9			3		10				5					
	Apr-03	(h) Tooting & Mitcham United	W 2-0	Dyke, R Marjoram	1	5	3			6					11	8	7				9		2		4	10									
	Apr-07	(a) Barnet	L 0-2			5	3			6					7	8		1			9		2	11	4	10									
	Apr-10	(a) Redhill	D 1-1	Dyke	1	5	3								11	8				10	9		2		4	6					7				
	Apr-17	(h) Enfield	L 2-4	Dyke, Barker (pen)		5	3	4								8	7	1		10	9		2			6			11						
	Apr-21	(h) Southall	D 1-1	Dyke	1	5	3	8		6						9	7				4					10			11	2					
	Apr-24	(a) Southall	L 2-3	Durban 2	1	5	3	9		6						8				10				2					11				4	7	
	Apr-28	(a) Bromley	L 1-4	Franklin	1	2	3			6							7			10	9	8							11				4		
	May-01	(h) Redhill	W 3-1	Moore, Ray 2	1	2	3			6					9	10	7				5											8	4		11
FA Cup																																			
Pr	Sep-20	(h) Enfield	W 2-0	Bryant, Ray	1	2	3	4	5	6			9	10	11	8	7																		
1Q	Oct-04	(h) Finchley	W 5-4 aet	Bryant,Attwood,Dyke,Barker(pen),Ray	1	2	3	4	5	6			9	10	11	8	7																		
2Q	Oct-18	(a) Edgware T	W 2-1	Barker (pen), Attwood	1	2	3	4	5	6			9	10	11	8	7																		
3Q	Nov-01	(a) Leavesden Mental Hospital	W 3-1	Dyke, Ray 2	1	2	3	4	5	6				10	11	8	7				9														
4Q	Nov-15	(h) Bromley	L 0-2		1	2	3	4	5	6	7		9	10	11	8																			
FA Amateur Cup																																			
4Q	Nov-22	(h) Uxbridge Town	W 3-1	Bryant 2, Attwood	1	2	3	4	5	6			9	8	11	10			7																
1	Jan-17	(h) Sutton U	D 0-0		1	2	3	4	5	6				10	11	8	7				9														
1r	Jan-24	(a) Sutton U	W 4-3	R Marjoram 2, Ray, Barker (pen)	1	2	3	4	5	6				10	11	8	7				9														
2	Jan-31	(a) Wimbledon	W 1-0	R Marjoram	1	2	3	4	5	6				10	11	8	7				9														
3	Feb-14	(h) Leytonstone	L 0-1		1	2	3	4	5	6				10	11	8	7				9														
London Senior Cup																																			
1	Jan-10	(a) Walthamstow Ave	W 1-0 aban	R Marjoram	1	2	3	4	5	6				10	11	8	7				9														
1r1	Feb-21	(h) Walthamstow Ave	L 1-4	Attwood	1	2	3	4	5	6				10	11	8	7				9														
1r2†	Mar-13	(h) Walthamstow Ave	L 1-2	Dyke		2	3	4	5	10					11	8	7	1			9				6										
		†match replayed following Wealdstone protest																																	
Middlesex Senior Cup																																			
1	Jan-03	(h) Hounslow T	W 4-2	R Marjoram 3, Barker (pen)	1	2	3	4	5					10	11	8	7				9				6										
2	Feb-07	(a) Edmonton B	W 3-2 aet	R Marjoram, Dyke, Barker (pen)	1	2	3	4	5	6				10	11	8	7				9														
SF	Mar-06	(a) Edgware T	L 0-2				3	4	5	6				10	11	8	7	1			9		2												
Middlesex Charity Cup																																			
	Dec-13	(a) Hayes	L 0-1		1	2	3	4	5	6			9	10	11		7			8															
Slough Hospital Cup																																			
	May-08	(a) Slough U	L 1-2 aet	Dyke	1	2	3			6					9	10	7				5								11			8	4		

1948-49

Rd	Date	Opponent	Result	Scorers	MacDonald LA	Haydon FJ	Barker CA	Hardie A	Hill WG	Edmonds CA	Francis ET	O'Boyle CJ	Rogers PA	Smith EW	Dyke HH	Ray WH	Durban C	Walker RW	Franklin RS	Gadsden D	Hill RA	Moore JA	Brown WS	James RA	Latimer JS	Norman GD	Marjoram TH	Attwood RH	Davison F	Hardie GR	Rowe RT	Weston LH	Hill BS	Shailer G	Hayes CS	Wiltshire DW	Lievens G	Biggerstaff F	Roberts W	O'Brien MH	Saunders W
Athenian League - 4th																																									
	Aug-21	(a) Sutton U	D 0-0		1	2		3	4	5	6	8	10		9	11						7																			
	Aug-28	(h) Bromley	L 0-3		1	2	3		4	5	6	7	10		8	9	11																								
	Sep-04	(a) Redhill	W 4-0	Smith 2, Rogers, O'Boyle	1		3		4	5	6	7	10	9	8			11									2														
	Sep-11	(h) Barnet	W 7-1	Smith 6, Dyke	1	2	3		4	5	6	7	10	9	8			11																							
	Sep-25	(a) Enfield	W 2-1	Smith, Dyke	1	2	3		4	5	6	7	10	9	8			11																							
	Oct-09	(h) Tooting & Mitcham United	L 2-4	Smith, Barker (pen)	1	2	3		4	5	6	7	10	9				11	8																						
	Oct-23	(h) Enfield	W 3-0	Dyke, Smith, O'Boyle	1	2	3			5	6	7	10	9	8				4	11																					
	Nov-06	(a) Hayes	W 5-3	Smith 3, Moore, Rogers		3			4	5	6		10	9	8			11			1	7					2														
	Nov-13	(h) Finchley	L 2-5	Dyke 2		2	3		4	5	6		10	9	8						1		7	11																	
	Nov-20	(h) Sutton U	L 1-2	Smith		2			4	5	6		10	9	8						1		7	11										3							
	Dec-04	(h) Barking	D 1-1	Franklin		2		3			6			9	10			11	8				7		1	4								5							
	Dec-11	(a) Tooting & Mitcham United	L 1-5	Barker (pen)		2	3		4	5	6			9	8			11				7			1			10													
	Dec-18	(a) Bromley	L 0-7					3	4	5	6			9	8						1	7		11			2	10													
	Dec-25	(h) Hendon	D 2-2	Norman, James		2	3			5	6			9					8		1			11		10			4	7											
	Dec-27	(a) Hendon	D 1-1	James		2	3			5	6			9	10				8		1			11					4	7											
	Feb-19	(a) Finchley	W 4-2	Dyke 2, Smith, Barker (pen)		2	3			5	6			9	10							7								8	1	11	4								
	Mar-19	(a) Hitchin Town	D 0-0			2	3			5	6			9	10				7					11		4							8			1					
	Apr-02	(h) Southall	W 4-3	Smith 3, Hayes		2		3						9	10							7		11		4					1		6	5	8						
	Apr-09	(a) Leyton	W 1-0	Smith		2	3				6			9	10							7		11		4					1			5	8						
	Apr-15	(h) Leyton	W 5-0	Dyke 2, Hayes 3		2	3							9	10							7		11		4			6		1				8		5				
	Apr-16	(h) Hayes	W 4-2	Hayes 3, James		2	3							9	10							7		11		4			6		1				8		5				
	Apr-20	(a) Southall	L 0-5			2	3				6			9	10							7		11					4		1			5	8						
	Apr-26	(a) Barnet	L 2-3	Dyke, Franklin		2	3				6				10				8					11					4	9	1			5					7		
	Apr-30	(a) Barking	L 1-2	Hayes		2	3				6			9	10									11					4		1			5	8			7			
	May-04	(h) Hitchin Town	W 1-0	Hayes		2	3				6				10									11					4		1			5	8			7	9		
	May-07	(h) Redhill	W 3-2	Smith, Dyke, James		5								9	10				6					11			2		4	7	1				8					3	
FA Cup																																									
Pr	Sep-18	(h) Willesden	W 4-0	Smith, Dyke, Rogers, O'Boyle	1	2	3		4	5	6	7	10	9	8			11																							
1Q	Oct-02	(h) Harrow T	W 2-1	Smith, Barker (pen)	1	2	3		4	5	6	7	10	9	8			11																							
2Q	Oct-16	(a) St Albans C	W 5-0	Dyke, Smith 3, Walker	1	2	3		4	5	6	7	10	9	8			11																							
3Q	Oct-30	(a) Hendon	L 2-4 aet	Dyke, Smith	1	2	3		4	5	6	7	10	9	8			11																							
FA Amateur Cup																																									
1	Jan-15	(h) Walthamstow Ave	W 2-0	Dyke, Franklin		2	3	11		5	6				10				8		1	7				4				9											
2	Jan-29	(h) Met. Police	D 1-1 aet	Smith		2	3			5	6			11	10				8		1	7				4				9											
2r	Feb-05	(a) Met. Police	W 3 -1	Smith, Hardie, Barker (pen)		2	3			5	6			11	10				8		1	7				4				9											
3	Feb-12	(h) Thameside Amateurs.	W 2-0 aet	Smith 2		2	3			5	6			11	10				8			7				4				9						1					
4	Feb-26	(a) Leytonstone	D 0-0 aet			2	3			5	6			9	10				8											7	1	11	4								
4r	Mar-05	(h) Leytonstone	L 0-4			2	3			5	6			9	10				8							4				7	1	11									
London Senior Cup																																									
	Jan-01	(a) Ilford	L 1-2	Norman		2	3			5	6			9	10				8		1					11			4	7											
Middlesex Senior Cup																																									
1	Jan-08	(h) Finchley	W 1-0	Smith		2	3			5	6			9	10				8		1			11		4				7											
2	Mar-12	(a) Hayes	L 1-2	Franklin		2	3			5	6				10				8		1	7		11		4				9											
Middlesex Charity Cup																																									
1	Mar-26	(h) Hounslow	L 0-1			2				5	6			9	10				7					11		4	3						8			1					
Wycombe Hospital Cup																																									
	May-14	(a) Wycombe W	L 2-3	Hayes, Saunders		2	3				6			9										11					4					5	10	1		8			7

1949-50					Wiltshire DW	Haydon FJ	Barker CA	Hill BS	Shailer G	Francis ET	Saunders W	Attwood RH	Smith EW	Dyke HH	Maloney WP	Hardie A	Hayes CS	Norman GD	Rogers PA	Tillyer H	Roberts W	Neville D	Padina G	Thomas C	Franklin RS	Benningfield A	Slade R	Edmonds C	Harmer E	Tur J	Pyne D	Hutchings A	Forest N	Reeves W	Cook W	Bristow A
Athenian League - 5th																																				
	Aug-20	(h) Redhill	W 4-1	Attwood, Dyke, Francis, Maloney	1	2	3	4	5	6	7	8	9	10	11																					
	Sep-03	(a) Enfield	L 1-2	Attwood	1	2		4	5	6	7	10	9		11	3	8																			
	Sep-10	(h) Barnet	W 4-1	Hayes, Maloney, Smith, Barker (pen)	1	2	3		5	6	7	10	9		11		8	4																		
	Sep-24	(a) Southall	D 0-0		1	2	3		5	6	7		9				8	4	10	11																
	Oct-22	(h) Sutton U	W 3-1	Francis, Hayes, Norman	1	2	3		5	6	11						8	4	10		7	9														
	Nov-05	(a) Hitchin Town	L 1-3	Neville	1	2	3	11	5	6							8	4	10		7	9														
	Nov-19	(h) Leyton	D 2-2	Attwood, Saunders	1	2	3		5	6	11	10		8				4			7	9														
	Dec-03	(h) Tooting & Mitcham United	D 2-2	Barker, Smith	1	2	3	6	5		9		11	8				4	10				7													
	Dec-10	(a) Barking	L 1-2	Roberts	1	2	3		5			8	9					4			7			6	10	11										
	Dec-26	(a) Hendon	L 1-2	Smith	1	2	3			6	8		9		7			4	10							11		5								
	Dec-27	(h) Hendon	L 2-3	Benningfield, og					5		8										7					11										
	Dec-31	(a) Hayes	D 1-1	Hill	1	2	3	10		6	8		9					4			7					11		5								
	Jan-28	(a) Tooting & Mitcham United	D 0-0			2	3	4		6	7		8						10							11		5		1	9					
	Feb-04	(h) Enfield	W 5-0	Smith 2, Dyke, Rogers, Barker (pen)		2	3	4		6	7		8	9	11				10									5		1						
	Feb-11	(h) Hitchin Town	W 5-3	Smith 2, Dyke 2, Saunders		2	3	4		6	7		8	9	11				10									5		1						
	Mar-04	(a) Bromley	D 2-2	Smith 2	1	2	3	4		6	7		8	9	11				10									5								
	Mar-11	(a) Sutton U	L 0-5		1	2	3	4			7		8	9	11				10					6				5								
	Mar-18	(h) Southall	D 3-3	Barker, Dyke, Maloney	1	2	3	4		6	7		8	9	11				10									5								
	Mar-25	(a) Barnet	L 0-2		1	2	3	4		6	7		8	9	11				10									5								
	Apr-01	(h) Finchley	W 2-1	Saunders 2	1	2	3	4			11				7				10					6				5				8	9			
	Apr-08	(h) Hayes	W 1-0	Smith	1	2	3	4		6	11		8	10	7													5					9			
	Apr-15	(h) Barking	L 0-3		1	2	3	4		6	7		8	9					10							11		5								
	Apr-22	(a) Leyton	W 1-0	Benningfield	1		2	4		6	7		8						10		9					11		5						3		
	Apr-26	(h) Bromley	W 4-0	Dyke 2, Roberts, Smith	1	2	3	4		6			8	9					10		7					11		5								
	Apr-29	(a) Redhill	W 4-2	Benningfield, Hill, Rogers, Saunders	1	2	3	4		6	8			9					10		7					11		5								
	May-06	(a) Finchley	W 6-1	Roberts 2,Rogers 2,Benningfield,Bristow	1	2		6			8								10		7					11		5						3	4	9
FA Cup																																				
Pr	Sep-17	(a) Hendon	W 4-0	Smith 2, Hayes, Maloney	1	2	3		5	6	7	10	9		11		8	4																		
1Q	Oct-01	(a) Enfield	D 0-0		1	2	3		5	6	7		9				8	4	10	11																
1Qr	Oct-08	(h) Enfield	W 2-0	Smith, Saunders	1	2	3		5	6	7	8	11					4	10		9															
2Q	Oct-15	(a) St Albans C	W 1-0	Smith	1	2	3		5	6	7		11				8	4	10		9															
3Q	Oct-29	(a) Edgware T	W 1-0	Smith	1	2	3		5	6	7	8	11					4	10		9															
4Q	Nov-12	(h) Colchester U	W 1-0	Saunders	1	2	3		5	6	7		11	8				4	10		9															
1	Nov-26	(a) Port Vale	L 0-1		1	2	3		5	6	7		11	8				4	10		9															
FA Amateur Cup																																				
1	Jan-14	(a) Salisbury	L 1-4	Rogers	1	2	3			6	8		9		11			4	10		7							5								
London Senior Cup																																				
1	Jan-07	(a) Sutton U	L 0-3		1	2	3	10		6	7							4			9				8	11		5								
Middlesex Senior Cup																																				
1	Jan-21	(h) Willesden	W 1-0	Roberts		2	3	4		6	7		8						10		9					11		5	1							
2	Feb-18	(a) Uxbridge	L 1-2	Saunders	1	2	3	4		6	7		8	9	11				10									5								
Middlesex Charity Cup																																				
1	Dec-17	(h) Edgware T	W 2-0	Franklin, Hill		2	3	10			11		9		7			4						6	8		1	5								
2	Feb-25	(a) Enfield	W 1-0	Maloney	1	2	3	4		6	7		8		11				10		9							5								
SF	Apr-19	(h) Uxbridge	W 2-1	Benningfield, Saunders	1	2	3	4		6	7		8						10		9					11		5								
F	May-10	(n*) Finchley	W 3-1	Barker (pen), Dyke, Rogers	1	2	3	4		6	7		8	9					10							11		5								
		*played at Hendon FC																																		
Wealdstone Cup																																				
	May-13	(h) Maidstone	W 6-1	Bristow 3, Rogers 2, Smith	1	2	3	4		6			8						10		7					11		5								9

1950-51

Rd	Date	Opponent	Result	Scorers	Tur J	Ward E	Barker C	Cook W	Edmonds C	Francis E	Roberts W	Doucy A	Bristow A	Rogers P	Benningfield A	Wiltshire D	Reeves W	Franklin R	Bow D	Molloy W	Norman G	Walls J	Langdale F	Harman G	Batchelor R	O'Boyle J	Beattie J	Hornsby E	Hudson W	Wigginton C	Roeder V	Edghill F	Mason C	Garden T	Banham C	O'Leary M	White P
Athenian League - 9th																																					
	Aug-19	(a) Barking	L 0-2		1	2	3	4	5	6	7	8	9	10	11																						
	Aug-26	(h) Sutton U	L 1-2	Bow		2	3		5	6		8			11	1			7	10	4	9															
	Aug-30	(a) Southall	L 1-2	Bow		2	3		5	6		8			11	1			7	10	4	9															
	Sep-02	(a) Cambridge C	L 0-1			2	3		5	6			9		11	1			7	8	4	10															
	Sep-06	(h) Barnet	W 3-2	Bristow 2, Batchelor		2	3		5	6	7		9		11	1					4	8			10												
	Sep-09	(h) Walton & H	D 2-2	Batchelor, Barker (pen)		2	3		5	6			9		11	1			7		4	8			10												
	Sep-23	(h) Hayes	L 1-4	Bristow			3		5	6			9		11	1					4	7	2	8	10												
	Oct-07	(a) Bromley	L 0-2			4	3	6	5	10			9		11	1					8		2			7											
	Oct-14	(h) Redhill	L 2-3	Hornsby, Barker		2	3		5	6			9		11	1					4	7					8	10									
	Oct-21	(a) Sutton U	D 0-0			2	3		5	6			9		11	1					4						7	10	8								
	Oct-28	(a) Hayes	D 1-1	Bow		2	3		5	6			9		11	1			7		4							10	8								
	Nov-04	(h) Cambridge C	W 4-0	Benningfield, Bristow, Hornsby, Barker (pen)		2	3		5	6			9		11	1			7		4							10	8								
	Nov-11	(h) Hitchin Town	D 1-1	Bristow		2	3		5	6			9			1			7		4							11	8	10							
	Nov-18	(a) Hitchin Town	W 4-0	Bristow 2, Hornsby, Molloy		2			5	6	7		9			1	3			8	4							11	10								
	Nov-25	(h) Leyton	W 3-1	Bristow 2, Molloy		2	3		5	6	7		9			1				8	4							11	10								
	Dec-02	(a) Walton & H	L 0-1			2	3	6	5		7		9			1				8	4							11	10								
	Dec-09	(h) Bromley	L 2-4	Bristow, Hornsby		2	3		5	6			9			1				8	4	7						11	10								
	Dec-16	(a) Barnet	L 1-4	Molloy	1		3		5	6			9							10	4	8	2					11			7						
	Dec-25	(h) Hendon	L 1-3	Molloy			3		5	6	9		8							10	4	7	2					11				1					
	Dec-26	(a) Hendon	W 5-2	Bristow 2, Roberts 2, Norman (pen)		2			5		9		8								4	6	3					11	10			1	7				
	Jan-27	(a) Leyton	W 2-1	Benningfield, Hornsby		2	3		5	6	9		8		11						4	7						10				1					
	Feb-03	(h) Tooting & Mitcham United	W 2-0	Benningfield, Roberts		2	3		5	6	9		8		11						4	7						10				1					
	Mar-03	(h) Southall	W 2-0	Bristow, Hornsby		2	3		5	6			9		11						4	7						8				1		10			
	Mar-10	(a) Redhill	L 1-3	Garden		2	3		5	6	7		9		11						4							10				1		8			
	Mar-17	(h) Finchley	W 3-2	Francis, Molloy, Wall		2	3		5	6					11					8	4	7						9				1		10			
	Mar-24	(a) Tooting & Mitcham United	W 3-2	Garden 2, og		2	3		5	6					11					8	4	7						9				1		10			
	Mar-26	(h) Enfield	W 3-0	Garden, Hornsby, og		2	3		5	6					11					8	4	7						9				1		10			
	Apr-07	(a) Finchley	L 1-3	Bristow.		2	3		5	6			8		11							7						9				1		10	4		
	Apr-21	(a) Enfield	D 1-1	Garden		2	3	4	5	6			8		11							7						9				1		10			
	May-05	(h) Barking	L 2-3	Bristow, Hornsby		2	3		5	6			8		11	1					4	7						9						10			
FA Cup																																					
Pr	Sep-16	(a) Hertford Town	W 3-1	Bristow, Batchelor, Wall		2	3		5	6			9		11	1					4	7		8	10												
1Q	Sep-30	(h) St Albans C	L 1-5	Norman	1	4	3		5	6			9		11						8	7	2	10													
FA Amateur Cup																																					
1	Jan-13	(a) Leytonstone	L 2-3	Benningfield, Roberts		2	3			6	9		8		11					10	5	4										1	7				
London Senior Cup																																					
1	Dec-30	(a) Cheshunt	D 1-1	Roberts	1	2			5	6	9		8								4	7	3					11	10								
1r	Jan-20	(h) Cheshunt	L 0-2		1	2	3		5	6			9		11				7		4	10					8										
Middlesex Senior Cup																																					
1	Feb-24	(h) Hayes	L 2-3	Hornsby, Barker (pen)		2	3		5	6	9		8		11						4	7						10				1					
Middlesex Charity Cup																																					
1	Aug-23	(a) Edgware T	D 1-1	Bow		2			5	6		8	9		11	1	3	4	7	10																	
1r	Jan-06	(h) Edgware T	W 3-1	Molloy, Roberts, Bow	1	2	3		5	6	9		8						7	10	4	11															
SF	Apr-19	(h) Hendon	W 3-1	Wall, O'Leary, Garden		2	3		5				8		11	1					4	7						6						10		9	
F	May-19	(n) Finchley ‡	L 2-3	Bristow, Roberts		2	3		5	6	9		8		11	1					4													10			7

‡played at Hayes

1951-52

Rd	Date	Opponent	Result	Scorers	Wiltshire D	Ward E	Barker C	Norman G	Edmonds C	Wastell J	White P	Wegrzyk H	Mikrut H	Hornsby E	Benningfield A	Palmer J	Cross F	Garden T	Wall J	McGhee T	Wilson F	Ferris R	Bennett F	Roberts W	Hynd A	Payne A	Gadsden R
Athenian League - 1st																											
	Aug-18	(a) Barnet	W 2-0	Benningfield, Mikrut	1	2	3	4	5	6	7	8	9	10	11												
	Aug-25	(h) Walton & H	W 2-0	White, Hornsby	1	2	3	4	5	6	7	8	9	10	11												
	Aug-29	(h) Hitchin Town	W 6-0	Cross 2, Benningfield, Mikrut, White, Barker (pen)	1	2	3	4		6	7	8	9		11	5	10										
	Sep-01	(h) Leyton	W 5-2	White 3, Wegrzyk, Barker (pen)	1	2	3	4	5	6	7	8	9		11		10										
	Sep-08	(h) Bromley	L 1-2	Garden	1		3	4	5	6	7	8	9		11	2		10									
	Sep-13	(a) Barking	W 4-1	Mikrut 2, Wegrzyk 2	1		3	4	5	6	7	8	9		11	2		10									
	Sep-22	(a) Sutton U	D 1-1	Mikrut	1		3	4	5	6	7	10	9		11				8	2							
	Oct-06	(a) Hitchin Town	W 3-1	Garden, Benningfield, Mikrut	1		3	4	5	6	7	8	9		11			10		2							
	Oct-20	(h) Tooting & Mitcham United	W 5-1	Mikrut 4, Ferris	1		3	4	5	6	7	8	9		11					2		10					
	Nov-03	(a) Redhill	W 5-1	Mikrut, Ferris, Wegrzyk, White, Benningfield	1	3		4	5	6	7	8	9		11	2						10					
	Nov-24	(h) Barnet	W 3-1	Bennett, Mikrut, Wegrzyk	1	3		4	5	6	7	8	9		11					2			10				
	Dec-08	(h) Redhill	L 0-1		1	3		4	5	6	7	8							10	2			11	9			
	Dec-15	(a) Southall	L 1-2	Bennett	1	3		9	5	6	7	8			11								10		2	4	
	Dec-25	(h) Hendon	D 0-0		1	2			5	6	7	8	9		11								10			4	3
	Dec-26	(a) Hendon	D 2-2	Barker 2 (1 pen)	1	2	3		5		7	8	9		11								10			4	6
	Dec-29	(a) Hayes	W 3-1	Barker, Benningfield, White	1	2	9	4	5	6	7	8			11								10				3
	Jan-12	(a) Tooting & Mitcham United	D 2-2	Mikrut, Wegrzyk	1	2		4	5	6	7	8	9		11								10				3
	Feb-09	(h) Enfield	W 4-2	Mikrut 2, Ferris 2	1	2		4	5	6	7	8	9									10	11				3
	Feb-23	(h) Barking	W 3-0	Mikrut 2, Bennett	1	2		4	5	6	7	8	9									10	11				3
	Mar-01	(a) Cambridge C	W 2-1	Wegrzyk 2	1	2		4	5	6		8	9									10	11	7			3
	Mar-08	(h) Cambridge C	W 2-1	Mikrut, Wegrzyk,	1	2		4	5	6		8	9									10	11	7			3
	Mar-15	(a) Walton & H	W 1-0	Wegrzyk	1	2			5	6	7	8	9									10	11			4	3
	Mar-22	(a) Bromley	W 2-0	Wegrzyk, Wall	1	2		4	5	6	7	8	9						10				11				3
	Apr-05	(a) Enfield	W 2-1	Wegrzyk (pen), White	1	2		4	5		7	8	9						6			10	11				3
	Apr-14	(h) Southall	W 2-1	Bennett, White	1			4	5	6	7	8	9						10	2			11				3
	Apr-19	(h) Sutton U	W 2-0	Wall 2	1	3		4	5	6	7	8	9						10	2			11				
	Apr-23	(h) Finchley	W 2-1	Bennett, White	1			4	5	6	7	8	9						10	2			11				3
	Apr-28	(a) Finchley	W 5-0	Mikrut 2, Wegrzyk 2, Wall	1			4	5	6	7	8	9						10	2			11				3
	Apr-30	(a) Leyton	W 3-2	Mikrut, Wegrzyk 2	1				5	6	7	8	9						10	2			11			4	3
	May-03	(h) Hayes	W 6-2	Mikrut, Wegrzyk, Bennett 3, White	1			4	5	6	7	8	9						10	2			11				3
FA Cup																											
Pr	Sep-15	(h) Southall	W 2-1	Mikrut, Barker (pen)	1	2	3	4	5	6	7	8	9		11			10									
1Q	Sep-29	(h) Uxbridge	W 2-1	Garden, Benningfield	1			4	5	6	7	8	9		11			10		2	3						
2Q	Oct-13	(h) Hayes	W 2-0	White, og	1	2	3	4	5	6	7	8	9		11			10									
3Q	Oct-27	(h) Slough T	W 5-0	Mikrut 2, Wegrzyk, Ferris, Norman	1		3	4	5	6	7	8	9		11					2		10					
4Q	Nov-10	(a) Tonbridge	L 0-2		1	3		4	5	6	7	8	9		11					2		10					
FA Amateur Cup																											
4Q	Nov-17	(h) Corinthian C	L 0-1		1	3		4	5	6	7	8	9		11					2		10					
London Senior Cup																											
1	Dec-01	(a) Bromley	W 3-0	Wegrzyk, White 2	1	3		4	5	6	7	8	9		11				10	2							
2	Jan-26	(a) Dagenham	W 1-0	Wegrzyk	1			4	5	6	7	8	9		11					2			10				3
3	Feb-02	(h) Southall	W 1-0	og	1			4	5	6	7	8	9		11					2		10					3
SF	Apr-12	(n*) Hounslow T	W 2-1	Mikrut, Bennett	1	2		4	5	6	7	8	9						10				11				3
F	May-10	(n**) Finchley	L 0-1		1	3		4	5	6	7	8	9						11	2		10					
		*played at QPR																									
		**played at Arsenal																									
Middlesex Senior Cup																											
1	Jan-19	(h) Edgware T	W 4-1	Wegrzyk 3, Benningfield	1	2		4	5	6	7	8	9		11								10				3
2	Feb-16	(a) Hayes	L 3-5 aet	Wegrzyk 2, White	1			4	5	6	7	8	9							2		10	11				3
Middlesex Charity Cup																											
1	Sep-05	(h) Hounslow T	W 3-0	Benningfield, Garden, White	1		3	4	5	6	7	8	9		11	2		10									
SF	Dec-22	(h) Enfield	W 2-0	Mikrut, Wegrzyk (pen)	1	3		4	5	6	7	8	9		11								10		2		

1952 - 53					Wiltshire D	McGhee T	Gadsden R	Comben A	Edmonds C	Wastell J	White P	Wegrzyk H	Mikrut H	Hussey L	Bennett F	Littlejohn A	Wall J	Roberts W	Cross F	Palmer J	Francis E	Ward E	Bloxham P	Bristow A	Bow D	Wakefield J	Nairn A	Hopkins V	Haydon F	Morris T	Doak P	Ayres R
Athenian League - 2nd																																
	Aug-23	(a) Cambridge C	W 4-1	Mikrut, Wegrzyk, Bennett, Hussey	1	2	3	4	5	6	7	8	9	10	11																	
	Aug-30	(h) Finchley	D 2-2	Wegrzyk, Bennett	1	2	3	4	5	6	7	8	9	10	11																	
	Sep-06	(a) Leyton	W 3-2	Mikrut, Hussey 2	1		3			6		8	9	10	11		4	7		5		2										
	Sep-20	(h) Sutton U	D 1-1	Mikrut	1		3	4				8	9	10	11	2	7			5	6											
	Oct-04	(a) Redhill	W 3-1	Bennett 2, Cross	1		3			6	7		9	8	11	2	4		10	5												
	Oct-11	(h) Southall	W 2-1	Bennett 2	1		3			6	7	8	9	10	11	2	4			5												
	Oct-18	(a) Tooting & Mitcham United	L 0-3		1		3			6	7	8	9	10	11	2	4			5												
	Oct-25	(h) Walton & H	L 1-3	Wegrzyk		2	3	6	5		7	8	9		11		4		10							1						
	Nov-01	(a) Hitchin Town	W 3-2	Mikrut, Wall, White	1		3	10	5	6	7	8	9		11		4					2										
	Nov-08	(a) Walton & H	W 1-0	Bennett	1		3	4	5	6	7	8	9		11		10					2										
	Nov-15	(h) Barnet	W 4-0	Mikrut 3, Wall	1		3	4	5	6	7	8	9		11		10					2										
	Nov-22	(h) Cambridge C	W 2-0	Mikrut, og	1		3	4	5	6	7	8	9		11		10					2										
	Nov-29	(h) Redhill	W 4-1	Wegrzyk, Bennett, Hussey 2	1		3	4	5	6	7	8	9	10	11												2					
	Dec-25	(h) Hendon	W 2-0	Mikrut, Wegrzyk	1		3	4	5	6	7	8	9	10	11							2										
	Jan-17	(h) Tooting & Mitcham United	D 2-2	White 2 (2 pens)	1		3		5	6	7	8	9	10	11		4			2												
	Feb-21	(a) Hendon	L 0-2		1		3	4	5	6	7	8	9	10	11		2															
	Mar-07	(a) Enfield	W 3-1	Wegrzyk 2, Morris	1		3	4	5	6	7	8	9															11	2	10		
	Mar-14	(h) Hitchin Town	W 1-0	Mikrut	1		3	4	5	6	7	8	9		10													11	2			
	Mar-21	(h) Leyton	W 4-1	Wegrzyk 2, Ayres 2	1		3	4	5	6		8	10		11														2		7	9
	Apr-04	(h) Hayes	W 3-0	Wegrzyk, Bennett, Ayres	1		3	4	5	6	7	8	10		11														2			9
	Apr-06	(a) Finchley	L 1-2	Wegrzyk (pen)	1		3		5	6	7	8	10		11		4												2			9
	Apr-23	(a) Barnet	L 1-4	Ayres	1		3	4	5	6	7	8	10		11												2					9
	Apr-25	(a) Sutton U	W 3-1	Bennett 2, Wastell	1		3	4	5	6	7	8	10		11												2					9
	Apr-28	(h) Enfield	W 2-0	Wegrzyk (pen), Wall	1		3	4	5	6	7	8	9		11		10										2					
	Apr-29	(a) Hayes	W 4-2	Mikrut, Ayres 3	1		3	4	5	6	7	8	10		11														2			9
	May-02	(a) Southall	L 2-3	Ayres, Gadsden	1		3	4	5	6	7	8	10		11														2			9
FA Cup																																
Pr	Sep-13	(a) Windsor & E	W 4-0	Wegrzyk 2, Hussey, White	1	2	3			6	7	8	9	10	11		4			5												
1Q	Sep-27	(h) Hendon	L 0-1		1	2	3			6	7	8	9	10	11		4			5												
FA Amateur Cup																																
1	Dec-13	(h) Moor Green	D 1-1	Wegrzyk	1		3	4	5	6	7	8	9		11		10					2										
1r	Dec-20	(a) Moor Green	W 6-1	Mikrut, White 3, Hussey, Comben	1		3	4	5	6	7	8	9	10	11							2										
2	Jan-24	(a) Walthamstow A	D 0-0		1		3	4	5	6	7	8	9	10	11					2												
2r	Feb-07	(h) Walthamstow A	W 1-0	Mikrut	1		3	4	5	6	7	8	9	10	11					2												
3	Feb-14	(a) Southall	L 0-3		1		3	4	5	6	7	8	9	10	11		2															
London Senior Cup																																
1	Jan-03	(a) Wembley	W 3-0	Mikrut 2, Hussey	1		3	4	5	6	7	8	9	10	11					2												
2	Jan-10	(a) Dulwich H	W 2-1	Mikrut, Bennett	1		3	4	5	6	7	8	9	10	11					2												
3	Feb-28	(h) Ilford	W 1-0	Hopkins	1		3	8	5	6	7	10	9				4										2	11				
SF	Mar-28	(a*) Walthamstow A	D 1-1	Wegrzyk	1		3	4	5	6		8	10		11														2		7	9
SFr1	Apr-11	(a**) Walthamstow A	D 1-1 aet	Wall	1		3		5	6	7	8	10		11		4	9											2			
SFr2	Apr-18	(a***) Walthamstow A	L 1-2	Bennett	1		3	4	5	6	7	8	10		11														2			9
		*played at Ilford FC																														
		**played at Southall FC																														
		***played at Hendon FC																														
London Challenge Cup																																
1	Oct-06	(a) Crystal Palace	W 3-1	Wegrzyk 2, Bennett	1		3			6	7	8	9	10	11	2	4			5												
2	Oct-20	(a) Brentford	L 1-3	Bennett	1		3			6	7	8	9	10	11	2	4			5												
Middlesex Senior Cup																																
1	Jan-31	(h) Hayes	L 0-2†		1		3	4	5	6	7	8		9	11		10			2												
Middlesex Charity Cup																																
F	Sep-10	(n*) Southall	L 0-1		1		3		5	6		8	9		11	2	4	7	10													
1	Sep-29	(h) Uxbridge	W 1-0	Bristow	1		3		5							2		7	10		8	4	6	9	11							
SF	Apr-20	(a) Hendon	L 0-3		1				5					8		3	4	9					6				2	11		10	7	
		*played at Hayes FC																														

1953 - 54

Rd	Date	Opponent	Result	Scorers	Wiltshire D	Nairn A	McGhee T	Payne AT	Littlejohn A	Francis E	Bodfish K	O'Connor T	Roberts W	Hussey L	Hopkins V	Haydon F	May C	Treheam S	Bristow A	Millerd W	Rogers PA	Mikrut H	Muller J	Bicknell E	Meadows H	Ogan D	Ward C	Rogers PJ	Porter R	Franklin R	Bignall K	Wilkinson G	Glennon P	Cross J	Thomas E	Stewart R	Wynn P	Travis C	Duley R	Bennett E	Warwick J	Forbes T	Kenny G	Key K	Gaughan J	Bloxham P	Bloxham V
Athenian League - 12th																																															
	Aug-22	(h) Southall	L 1-2	Payne	1	2	3	4	5	6	7	8	9	10	11																																
	Aug-29	(a) Sutton U	D 3-3	Hopkins 2, Hussey		3	2	4	5		7		9	10	11		6			8			1																								
	Sep-05	(h) Tooting & Mitcham United	W 2-1	Bodfish, Bristow	1		2	4	5		7			10	11	3	6	8	9																												
	Sep-19	(h) Leyton	W 5-1	Hopkins 2, Hussey 2, Rogers	1		2	4		5				10	11	3	6			7	8	9																									
	Oct-03	(a) Barnet	L 1-2	Hopkins	1	2		4	5		7		9	10	11	3	6				8																										
	Oct-17	(a) Finchley	L 1-3	Millerd	1		2	6	5		8				11	3	4			7	10	9																									
	Oct-31	(h) Walton & H	W 5-0	Mikrut, Bodfish 3, Payne			2	4	5		8				11	3	6			7	10	9	1																								
	Nov-14	(a) Hayes	L 1-2	Hopkins			2		5		7				11	3	6	8	9		10		1	4																							
	Nov-21	(h) Enfield	D 3-3	Bristow, Littlejohn, Rogers			2	4	5		7				11	3	6		10		8		1		9																						
	Dec-05	(a) Leyton	L 2-4	Bristow, Rogers		3	2	4	5		7				11		6		9		8		1		10																						
	Dec-12	(h) Hitchin Town	L 2-4	Bristow, Rogers		3	2		5		7						6		9		8		1	4		10	11																				
	Dec-25	(h) Hendon	W 4-2	Bodfish 2, Haydon (pen), Ward		2		4			8					3	6		9	7			1	10			11	5																			
	Dec-26	(a) Hendon	L 0-2			2					8						6		10	7			1	11				5	3	4	9																
	Jan-16	(h) Barnet	W 3-2	Millerd, Ward, Haydon (pen)		2					8					3			9	7	10		1		4		11	5		6																	
	Jan-23	(a) Enfield	L 0-2				2		5		8					3				7	10		1				11					4	6	9													
	Jan-30	(h) Finchley	L 1-2	Meadows			2	4			7					3					8		1		10					11		5	6	9													
	Feb-06	(a) Cambridge C	L 1-3	Ward		2		4			8					3					10		1		9		11			6		5					7										
	Feb-20	(a) Redhill	L 0-4																		8				4		11	2		6		5				3	9	1	7	10							
	Feb-27	(h) Cambridge C	W 4-0	Bristow 2, Bodfish, Ward		2					8							10	9					4			11			6		5			1	3	7										
	Mar-06	(a) Hitchin Town	L 0-4			2					8								9		10			4			11			6		5			1	3	7										
	Mar-13	(a) Southall	L 1-4	Bristow		2					8							11	9		10		1	4						6		5					7				3						
	Mar-20	(h) Redhill	W 3-2	Bristow, Rogers 2		3												10	9	7	8		1	4			11	2		6		5															
	Mar-27	(a) Tooting & Mitcham United	L 1-2	Bristow		3					8								9	7	10		1	4			11	2		6		5															
	Apr-03	(h) Hayes	D 4-4	Rogers 2, McGhee, Payne		3	2	4			8									7	10	9	1				11			6		5															
	Apr-10	(a) Walton & H	D 1-1	Bodfish		2		4		5	8									7	10	9	1						3	6												11					
	Apr-24	(h) Sutton U	W 2-1	Millerd, Rogers		3		4				8								7	10		1				11	2		6		5											9				
FA Cup																																															
Pr	Sep-12	(a) Barnet	W 2-1	Bodfish 2	1		2	4	5		7			10	11	3		8				9																								6	
1Q	Sep-26	(h) Southall	W 2-1	Hussey 2 (1 pen)	1		2	4	5		7			10	11	3	6				8	9																									
2Q	Oct-10	(h) St Albans C	W 2-0	Mikrut, Hussey	1		2	4	5		7			10	11	3	6				8	9																									
3Q	Oct-24	(a) Yiewsley	W 3-0	Millerd 2, Rogers	1		2	6	5		8				11	3	4			7	10	9																									
4Q	Nov-07	(h) Headington U	L 0-3				2		5		8				11	3	6		9	7	10		1	4																							
FA Amateur Cup																																															
1	Dec-19	(h) Hendon	D 3-3	Bristow 2, Bicknell		11	2	4	5		8					3	6		9	7			1	10																							
1r	Jan-02	(a) Hendon	L 1-3	Rogers		2		4	5		8					3	6		9	7	10		1							11																	
London Senior Cup																																															
1	Nov-28	(h) Sutton U	W 2-0	Hopkins, Rogers			2	4	5		7				11	3	6		9		8		1		10																						
2	Jan-09	(a) Hounslow T	L 3-4	Bristow, Bodfish, Rogers		3	2	4			8					5			9	7	10		1		6					11																	
London Challenge Cup																																															
1	Oct-05	(a) Walthamstow A	W 1-0	Bristow	1	2		4	5		8				11	3	6		9	7	10																										
2	Oct-19	(h) Finchley	W 3-0	Mikrut, Hopkins, Bodfish	1	2		4	5		8				11	3	6			7	10	9																									
SF	Nov-02	(a) Arsenal	L 1-4	Hopkins (pen)		2		4	5		8				11	3	6			7	10	9	1																								
Middlesex Senior Cup																																															
1	Feb-13	(h) Edgware T	L 1-3	Bodfish			2	4			7					3			10		8		1		9		11	5		6																	
Middlesex Charity Cup																																															
1	Sep-23	(h) Edgware T	D 1-1 aet	Hussey	1	2		4	5					10	11	3	6		8	7		9																									
1r	Sep-30	(a) Edgware T	L 1-3	Bloxham		2										3		8		9			1	6						4														5	7	10	11

1954 - 55

Rd	Date	Opponent	Result	Scorers	Roberts E	Nairn A	Dickinson H	Payne A	Lievens G	Bicknell E	Millerd W	O'Connor T	Donovan J	Trehearne S	Ward C	Muller J	Stone A	Rogers PJ	Franklin R	Kenny G	Bristow A	Luck P	Wood G	Porter R	Glennon J	Longman K	Gee K	Evans V	Knapp G	Littlejohn A	Bodimeade B	Lovett J	Coldwell W	Archer D	Hussey L	Warrick J	Gomersall D	Mulley D	Stephen G	Bowen J	Ogan D	Wastell W	Pluckrose R
Athenian League - 14th																																											
	Aug-21	(a) Sutton U	L 0-5		1	2	3	4	5	6	7	8	9	10	11																												
	Aug-28	(h) Enfield	D 1-1	Franklin		2		4				8	9		11	1	3	5	6	7	10																						
	Sep-04	(a) Barnet	L 2-3	O'Connor, Trehearne				4				8	9	10	11	1	3	5	6		7	2																					
	Sep-18	(a) Hayes	L 3-4	Donovan, Evans, Longman		2						8	9					5	6				1	3	4	7	10	11															
	Sep-25	(h) Southall	L 1-3	Franklin (pen)		2						8	9					5	6				1	3	4	7	10	11															
	Oct-02	(a) Walton & H	D 2-2	Donovan, Evans		2			6			10	9					5					1		4	7		11	3					8									
	Oct-09	(h) Tooting & Mitcham United	L 2-5	Kenny, Longman		2		4				10						5		9	8		1		6	7		11	3														
	Oct-16	(h) Leyton	W 2-1	Bristow 2				4				10				1		5		9	8			3	6	7		11	2														
	Oct-23	(a) Finchley	L 0-2					4				10				1		5		9	8			3	6	7		11	2														
	Oct-30	(h) Hitchin Town	D 1-1	Bristow				4				8	9			1					10			3		7		11	2	5	6												
	Nov-06	(a) Redhill	D 4-4	O'Connor, Evans, Coldwell, Glennon				4				8				1					9			3	10		7	11	2		6		5										
	Nov-13	(h) Barnet	W 3-1	Payne 2 (2 pens), Glennon				4				8				1								3	10		7	11	2	5	6	9											
	Nov-20	(h) Hayes	L 0-3					4				8				1					10			3			7	11	2	5	6	9											
	Nov-27	(a) Tooting & Mitcham United	L 0-3									8				1					10			3			7	11	2	5	4	9							6				
	Dec-11	(h) Finchley	W 3-1	Evans, Glennon, Archer												1					10			3	6	9	7	11	2		4		5	8									
	Dec-25	(h) Hendon	D 1-1	Archer												1								3	6	9	7	11	2	5	4			8	10								
	Dec-27	(a) Hendon	L 1-5	Lovett												1			4		10				6			11	2			9	5	8		3	7						
	Jan-08	(a) Enfield	L 0-4																				1	3	8		7	11	2	5	4			9	10				6				
	Feb-05	(a) Leyton	L 1-2	Bristow										10		1		2			9				6		7	11		5	4			8					3				
	Feb-19	(a) Cambridge C	L 1-2	Evans												1		2		7	9				6			11		5					10				3	4	8		
	Mar-05	(h) Redhill	L 1-4	og												1		2		9					6		7	11		5					10				3	4	8		
	Mar-12	(a) Hitchin Town	L 0-2													1		2		9					6		7	11		5					10				3	4	8		
	Mar-19	(h) Sutton U	L 3-4	Evans, Archer, Wastell								8				1					7				6			11		5				10				2	3	4		9	
	Apr-09	(h) Walton & H	W 4-2	Evans 2 (1 pen), Glennon, Wastell										6		1									4		7	11		5	3			10				2				9	8
	Apr-23	(a) Southall	L 0-4													1					10				6		7	11		5				8				2	3	4		9	
	Apr-30	(h) Cambridge C	L 0-1									8				1				9					6		7	11		5				10				2	3	4			
FA Cup																																											
Pr	Sep-11	(h) Wimbledon	L 2-4	Glennon, Donovan								8	9	10	11	1	3	5	6	7					4					2													
FA Amateur Cup																																											
1	Dec-18	(a) Wycombe W	D 1-1	Evans												1								3	6	9	7	11	2	5	4			8	10								
1r	Jan-01	(h) Wycombe W	L 1-2	Evans												1								3	6		7	11	2	5	4	9		8	10								
London Senior Cup																																											
1	Dec-04	(h) Harris Lebus	W 4-2	Evans 2, O'Connor, Coldwell								8				1					10			3	6		7	11	2	5	4		9										
2	Feb-12	(h) Walthamstow A	L 2-3 aet	Evans 2								8				1		2	6		9				4		7	11		5					10				3				
Middlesex Senior Cup																																											
1	Jan-29	(h) Rayners Lane	W 3-0	Evans 2, Archer										10		1		5			9				6		7	11			4			8				2	3				
2	Feb-26	(h) Edgware T	L 0-2													1		2		9					6			11		5				7	10				3	4	8		
Middlesex Charity Cup																																											
1	Sep-29	(a) Hounslow T	W 2-0	Donovan, Longman									9	10				5	6			2	1		4	7		11	3					8									
SF	Apr-02	(h) Enfield	D 1-1 aet	Hussey												1									6		7	11		5					10			2	3	4		9	8
SFr1	Apr-19	(a) Enfield	D 1-1 aet	Wastell												1					10				6		7	11		5				8				2	3	4		9	
SFr2	May-06	(h) Enfield	L 2-4 aet	Evans, Trehearne										10		1									6		7	11		5				8				2	3	4		9	

1955 - 56

	Date	Opponent	Result	Scorers	Muller J	Mulley D	Stephen G	Comben A	Littlejohn A	Glennon J	Gee K	Wegrzyk H	Mikrut H	Harper I	Evans V	Wood G	Bodimead B	Pluckrose R	Randall J	Halward G	Moss R	Morris T	Kelly R	Saffery G	Archer D	Bowen J	Porter R	Lovell E	Reeves W	Knapp G	Longman K	Farmer E	Coster J	Gomersall D	Naim A	Stevens B	Harrison K	Lattimore J
Athenian League - 10th																																						
	Aug-20	(h) Sutton U	L 0-5		1	2	3	4	5	6	7	8	9	10	11																							
	Aug-24	(a) Enfield	L 0-4				3	4	5		7	8		9	11	1	2	10	6																			
	Aug-27	(a) Barnet	L 2-3	Wegrzyk, Harper				4		6		8		9		1	2		3	5	7	10	11															
	Aug-31	(h) Southall	W 4-1	Wegrzyk, Evans 2, Harper				4		6	7	8		9	11	1	2		3	5		10																
	Sep-03	(h) Hounslow T	D 2-2	Harper 2				4		6		8		9	11	1	2		3	5				7	10													
	Sep-17	(a) Hitchin Town	D 2-2	Wegrzyk, Harper	1			4		6		8		9	11		2		3	5				7		10												
	Oct-01	(h) Barnet	W 4-0	Harper, Evans, Archer, Bowen	1			4		6		8		9	11		2		3	5					7	10												
	Oct-29	(h) Leyton	W 2-0	Wegrzyk, Harper	1			4				8		9	11				2	5					10	6	3	7										
	Nov-05	(a) Tooting & Mitcham United	L 0-2		1			4		6		10		9	11				3	5					8			7	2									
	Nov-12	(h) Redhill	W 4-2	Wegrzyk (pen), Evans, Bowen 2	1			4		6		10		8	11				3	5						9		7	2									
	Nov-19	(a) Walton & H	L 1-2	Wegrzyk				4		6		10		8	11	1			3	5						9		7	2									
	Nov-26	(h) Cambridge C	W 3-0	Evans 2, Bowen				4		6		10		8	11	1			3	5						9		7	2									
	Dec-10	(a) Hayes	L 1-7	Longman								10		9	11	1			6	5					8	4	3		2		7							
	Dec-26	(a) Hendon	L 0-4					4	2			10	9	7	11	1			6	5												3	8					
	Dec-27	(h) Hendon	L 1-2	Harper				4				8	9	10	11	1			6	5									2	7		3						
	Dec-31	(a) Redhill	L 1-2	Mikrut				4				10	9	7	11	1			6	5									2			3	8					
	Jan-14	(h) Hayes	W 4-2	Wegrzyk, Evans, Harper, Gomersall				4				10		7	11	1			6	5									2				8	9	3			
	Jan-21	(a) Leyton	L 0-2									10		7	11	1			6	5						4				2		3	8	9				
	Jan-28	(h) Tooting & Mitcham United	L 1-2	Wegrzyk (pen)				4				10		7	11				6	5									2			3	8	9		1		
	Feb-11	(a) Sutton U	W 5-2	Wegrzyk, Evans, Harper 2, Randall				4				10		7	11	1			6	5										2		3	8				9	
	Feb-25	(h) Walton & H	W 5-0	Wegrzyk 2, Coster, Harrison, Reeves				4		6		10		7	11	1			3	5									2				8				9	
	Mar-03	(a) Cambridge C	W 3-2	Harrison 2, Mulley		2		4		6		10		7	11	1			3	5													8				9	
	Mar-17	(h) Hitchin Town	W 7-1	Wegrzyk, Evans, Harper, Harrison 3, Comben				4		6		10		7	11	1			3	5									2				8				9	
	Apr-02	(a) Finchley	L 1-3	Wegrzyk				4		6		10		7	11	1			3	5												2	8				9	
	Apr-07	(a) Hounslow T	L 2-4	Harper, Coster				4		6		10		7	11				3	5												2	8			1	9	
	Apr-14	(h) Enfield	D 1-1	Wegrzyk		2		4				10		7	11	1			6	5												3	8				9	
	Apr-21	(h) Finchley	W 8-1	Wegrzyk,Harper,Harrison 2,Coster 2,Comben,Gomersall				4				10		7		1			6	5									2			3	8	11			9	
	Apr-28	(a) Southall	L 0-2					4				10		7		1			6	5									2			3	8	11			9	
FA Cup																																						
Pr	Sep-10	(a) Wembley	W 3-2	Wegrzyk, Evans, OG	1			4		6		8	9	10	11		2		3	5				7														
1Q	Sep-24	(a) Harrow T	W 7-0	Wegrzyk(pen),Evans 3,Harper,Bowen,OG	1			4		6		8		9	11		2		3	5				7		10												
2Q	Oct-08	(h) Southall	L 1-2	Evans	1			4		6		8		9	11		2		3	5				7		10												
FA Amateur Cup																																						
1Q	Oct-15	(a) Yiewsley	D 3-3	Wegrzyk 2, Evans	1			4		6		8		9	11		2		3	5				7		10												
1Qr	Oct-22	(h) Yiewsley	L 0-1		1			4				8		9	11				2	5				7	10	6	3											
London Senior Cup																																						
1	Dec-03	(a) Wimbledon	L 1-4	Wegrzyk				4				10		8	11	1			3	5						6		7		2	9							
Middlesex Senior Cup																																						
1	Jan-07	(h) Southall	W 3-0	Harper 2, Evans				4				10		7	11	1			6	5							3		2				8	9				
2	Feb-18	(a) Hayes	W 2-1	Gomersall, Lattimore				4		6		10		7	11	1			2	5												3		9				8
SF	Mar-10	(n*) Wembley	L 1-2 aet	Evans				4		6		10		7	11	1			3	5									2					9				8
Middlesex Charity Cup																																						
1	Sep-14	(h) Hayes	W 2-0	Harper 2	1			4		6		8		9	11		2		3	5				7		10												
SF	Mar-24	(a) Edgware T	W 4-1	Wegrzyk (pen), Evans, Harrison 2				4		6		10		7	11	1			3	5												2	8				9	
F	May-12	(a*) Hounslow T	L 0-1					4				10		7		1			6	5									2			3	8	11			9	
		*at Hayes FC																																				

1956 - 57

				Wood G	Reeves W	Randall J	Comben A	Halward G	Glennon J	Furnues G	Wall J	Tombs D	Coster J	Wegrzyk H	Evans V	Naim A	Harrison K	Littlejohn A	Farmer E	Harper I	Mulley D	Hannam J	Bennett T	Knox G	Teevan D	Bates A	Norman G	Conroy M	East D	Packham D	Seabrook F	Fogden E	Gomersall D	Birch J	Thomlinson D	Bodfish K	Williams F	Valentine J	Horler D
Athenian League - 13th																																							
Aug-18	(a) Enfield	W 3-1	Wegrzyk, Wall, Tombs	1	2	3	4	5	6	7	8	9	10	11																									
Aug-22	(h) Leyton	W 5-0	Wegrzyk, Evans,Glennon, Coster, Comben	1	2	3	4	5	6	7	9		10	8	11																								
Aug-25	(h) Southall	L 1-3	Furnues	1	2	3	4	5	6	7	9		10	8	11																								
Aug-29	(a) Finchley	L 2-5	Furnues, Halward	1		3		5	6	7	4		8	10	11	2	9																						
Sep-01	(a) Walton & H	L 1-5	Wall	1	2	3	4		6	7	8			10	11		9	5																					
Sep-15	(a) Redhill	L 1-2	Harrison	1	2	5	4		6		10	8	11				9		3	7																			
Sep-22	(h) Sutton U	L 0-1		1	2	3		5	6		8		11	10			9			7			4																
Sep-29	(a) Hitchin Town	W 3-2	Wegrzyk 2, Knox	1	2	3		5	6		4		10	8	11					7				9															
Oct-06	(h) Carshalton Athletic	W 5-2	Wegrzyk, Evans, Harper, Harrison 2	1	2	3		5	6		4		10	8	11		9			7																			
Oct-20	(a) Cambridge C	W 4-1	Harrison 2, Bates, Coster		2	3	4	5			6		10	8	11		9								1	7													
Nov-03	(h) Hitchin Town	W 5-2	Evans 3, Harrison, Bates		2	3	4	5			6		10	8	11		9								1	7													
Nov-10	(h) Finchley	L 3-4	Evans, Harrison 2		2	3	4	5			6		10	8	11		9								1	7													
Nov-17	(a) Southall	L 1-3	Evans		2	3		5			6		10	8	11		9			7					1		4												
Dec-08	(h) Hayes	L 2-3	Harper, Randall (pen)		2	6	8		4		10		11		7				3	9							5		1										
Dec-15	(a) Hounslow T	L 2-3	Evans, Wall		2	6			4		10		11	8	7				3	9							5		1										
Dec-22	(h) Redhill	L 0-2				6			4		10		11	8	7				3	9							5		1	2									
Dec-25	(h) Hendon	W 2-0	Evans, Wall			3			4		10		7	8	11					9		6					5		1	2									
Dec-26	(a) Hendon	L 0-2				3		5	4		8		10		11					9		6							1	2	7								
Dec-29	(h) Enfield	L 1-5	Harper	1		5			4		10		7	8	11				3	9		6								2									
Jan-05	(h) Hounslow T	W 2-1	Wall 2			3		5	4		8		9	10	11					7		6							1	2									
Jan-12	(a) Barnet	L 1-2	Coster			3		5	4		8		9	10	11					7		6							1	2									
Jan-26	(a) Carshalton Athletic	L 0-3				3			4						11					7		10	6					8	1	2		5	9						
Feb-09	(a) Leyton	L 1-4	Evans	1		3			6						11					7		10	4				5	8		2			9						
Feb-16	(h) Cambridge C	L 2-4	Evans, Harper	1		3			4				10		11					7		6		9				8		2		5							
Feb-23	(a) Sutton U	D 2-2	Harper, Knox	1		3	4								11					10		6		9			5	8		2				7					
Mar-09	(h) Walton & H	W 8-2	Harper 3, Conroy 2, Gomersall, Knox, OG	1		3	4								11					10		6		9			5	8		2			7						
Mar-30	(a) Hayes	W 3-0	Bodfish, Conroy, Knox	1		3	4								11					10		6		9			5	8		2						7			
Apr-30	(h) Barnet	L 1-5	Comben			3	4								11					10		6		9			5	8		2					1	7			
FA Cup																																							
Pr Sep-08	(h) Hayes	L 2-4	Evans, Harrison	1	2	5	4				6		10	8	11		9		3	7																			
FA Amateur Cup																																							
1Q Oct-13	(h) Pinner	W 5-0	Wegrzyk 3, Harrison 2		2	3	4	5			6		10	8	11		9			7					1														
2Q Oct-27	(a) Willesden	W 2-1	Harrison, Coster		2	3	4	5			6		10	8	11		9								1	7													
3Q Nov-24	(a) Yiewsley	L 2-3	Wegrzyk, Evans		2	3	4	5			6		10	8	11		9								1	7													
London Senior Cup																																							
1 Dec-01	(a) Clapton	L 0-6				2		5			6		10	7	11				3	9					1		4	8											
Middlesex Senior Cup																																							
1 Jan-19	(a) Yiewsley	L 0-4				3			4		8			10	11		9			7		6							1	2		5							
Middlesex Senior Cup																																							
1 Sep-12	(h) Finchley	L 1-2	Wegrzyk (pen)				5		4			9	11	10	1		8		3	7	2	6																	
North West Middlesex Invitation Cup																																							
SF Apr-13	(a) Harrow Town	D 1-1	Randall	1		3	4								11					10		6		9			5	8		2						7			
SF Apr-22	(h) Harrow Town	L 1-4	Randall (pen)			3	4								11							6	10				5						9			7	1	2	8

1957 - 58					Culver E	Hurrell R	Randall J	Gibbons R	Kingsland R	Hannam J	Moore C	Birrell K	Townsend C	James B	Evans V	Harper I	Packham D	Reeves W	Low J	Comben A	Coster J	Russell R	Knox G	Rogers P	Bennett T	Littleales D	Norman G	Martin D	Rolph E	Adkins B	Bennett J	Gomersall D	Darling T	Gordon W	Kay D	Moran J	Hills L	Brown R	Sells C	Hatton R	Hall D	Beament R	Sanders J	Lindsay H	Walkinshaw W
Athenian League - 8th																																													
	Aug-24	(h) Cambridge C	W 5-2	Evans 2, Randall (pen), Moore, James	1	2	3	4	5	6	7	8	9	10	11																														
	Aug-28	(a) Hayes	W 3-0	Harper 2, Moore	1	2	3	4	5	6	7	8	9		11	10																													
	Aug-31	(a) Redhill	W 2-1	Townsend 2	1	3		4	5	6	7	8	9		11	10	2																												
	Sep-11	(h) Leyton	W 6-1	Harper, Evans, Moore 2, Hannam 2 (1 pen)	1	3		4	5	6	7		9		11	10		2			8																								
	Sep-14	(a) Hitchin Town	D 1-1	Harper	1	3		6	5		7		9		11	10			2	4	8																								
	Sep-21	(h) Maidstone U	L 1-2	Coster (pen)	1	3		6	5		7		9		11	10			2	4	8																								
	Oct-05	(h) Carshalton Athletic	D 2-2	Hannam, Moore	1	2	3	4	5	6	7				11	8					10	9																							
	Oct-19	(a) Sutton U	W 3-0	Evans 2, Moore	1	2	3	4	5	6	7				11	10								8	9																				
	Nov-02	(a) Maidstone U	D 1-1	Evans	1	2	3	4	5	6	7				11	10								8		9																			
	Nov-23	(h) Hounslow T	D 1-1	Hannam,	1	2	3		5	6	7				11	10										9	4	8																	
	Dec-07	(h) Enfield	W 4-2	Evans 2, Harper, Martin	1	2	3		5	6			9		11	10											4	8	7																
	Dec-14	(a) Southall	L 0-3		1	2	3		5	6			9		11	10											4	8	7																
	Dec-21	(a) Hounslow T	L 0-1		1	2	3		5	6			9		11	10								8			4		7																
	Dec-25	(h) Hendon	D 2-2	Evans 2	1	2	3		5	6			9		11	10								8			4		7																
	Dec-26	(a) Hendon	W 2-1	Evans, Townsend	1	2	3		5	6			9		11	10											4	8	7																
	Dec-28	(h) Sutton U	L 0-2		1	2	3		5	6			9		11	10								8			4		7																
	Jan-04	(a) Barnet	L 0-3		1	2	3		5	6			8			10											4		11	9	7														
	Jan-11	(h) Redhill	W 4-3	Harper 2, Hurrell (pen), Gomersall	1	2	3	4	5	6			10		11	8														7		9													
	Feb-22	(h) Walton & H	W 4-1	Evans, Gorden, Harper, Martin	1	2	3	4							11	9											6	8	7					10	5										
	Mar-01	(h) Hayes	L 4-7	Hills 2, Harper, Randall	1	2	3	4	5						11	10											6	8								7	9								
	Mar-08	(a) Cambridge C	L 0-4		1	2	3	4	5						11	10													7							8	9				6				
	Mar-15	(h) Finchley	D 1-1	Hills	1			4	5						11	10			2								6	8							3	7	9								
	Mar-22	(a) Leyton	W 2-1	Hills 2,		2		4	5						11	8											6								3	7	9	1	10						
	Mar-29	(a) Carshalton Athletic	L 1-4	Harper		2		4	5						11	8											6								3	7	9	1	10						
	Apr-12	(a) Walton & H	L 5-6	Evans, Hills 2, Harper, Kingsland (pen)		2		4	5				8		11	7																			3	10	9	1			6				
	Apr-19	(h) Southall	L 2-5	Hills, Townsend		2		4	5				8		11	7																			3	10	9				6	1			
	Apr-21	(a) Finchley	D 1-1	Townsend		2			5				9		11														7						3	10				1	6		4	8	
	Apr-23	(a) Enfield	L 0-5			2	3	4	5				8		11													7								10	9			1	6				
	Apr-26	(h) Hitchin Town	D 1-1	Evans		2		4	5				8		11	7																			3	10	9						6		1
	Apr-30	(h) Barnet	W 6-1	Evans, Hills 3, Townsend, Kingsland (pen)		2	3	4	5				8		11																						9		10				6	7	1
FA Cup																																													
Pr	Sep-07	(h) Hendon	L 0-5		1	3		4	5	6	7	8	9		11	10		2																											
FA Amateur Cup																																													
Pr	Sep-28	(a) Wingate	W 4-1	Evans 2, Harper, Moore	1	2	3	4	5	6	7				11	8					10	9																							
1Q	Oct-12	(a*) Willesden	W 3-2	Hannam, Knox, Moore	1	2	3	4	5	6	7				11	8					10		9																						
2Q	Oct-26	(h) Harrow T	W 5-2	Harper 3, Littleales 2	1	2	3	4	5	6	7				11	10								8		9																			
3Q	Nov-09	(a) Uxbridge	D 1-1	Gibbons	1	2	3	4	5	6					11	10								8		9	7																		
3Qr	Nov-16	(h) Uxbridge	L 1-2	Littleales	1	2	3		5	6					11	10							7			9	4	8																	
		*played at Lower Mead																																											
London Senior Cup																																													
1	Nov-30	(a) Finchley	L 1-3	Evans	1	2	3		5	6	10				11								9			8	4	7																	
Middlesex Senior Cup																																													
1	Jan-18	(h) Willesden	D 1-1 aet	Evans	1	2	3	4	5	6			9		11	10												8		7															
1r	Feb-01	(h) Willesden	W 3-2	Harper, Hannam, OG	1	2	3		5	6			8		11	9											4						7	10											
2	Feb-15	(a) Hendon	L 1-6	Gomersall	1	2	3		5						11	9				4							6					8	7	10											
Middlesex Charity Cup																																													
1	Sep-30	(a) Yiewsley	L 1-2	Harper	1	2	3	4	5	6	7				11	8					10			9																					
North West Middlesex Invitation Cup																																													
SF	Feb-08	(a) Wembley	W 7-3	Harper 4, Darling 2, Townsend	1	2	3		5				8		11	9				4							6						7	10											
SF	Apr-07	(h) Wembley	W 4-1	Evans, Harper, Hills 2		2			5	4			8		11	7																		10	3		9			1	6				
F	May-02	(a) Harrow T	D 1-1	Hills		3		4	5				8		11				2																		9		7				6	10	1
F	May-03	(h) Harrow T	W 3-2 aet	Hills 3				3	5				8		11				2	4																	9		7				6	10	1

1958 - 59

Athenian League - 2nd

Rd	Date	Opponent	Result	Scorers	Culver T	Hurrell R	Gibbons R	Comben A	Kay D	Saunders J	Martin D	Townsend C	Farrell M	Moran J	Evans V	Matthews J	Ash A	Ware R	Sells C	Mowle G	Nicholls J	Parfitt P	Hall J	Hills L	Waldheim J	Murphy T	Davies J	Elliott L	Farmer E	Nash G	Gordon W	Green B	McLoughlin N	Conniff T	Dunk M	Hughes M	Quinn M	Emerson M	Leadbetter J	Stone C
	Aug-23	(a) Walton & H	W 3-1	Farrell, Comben, Moran	1	2	3	4	5	6	7	8	9	10	11																									
	Aug-30	(h) Grays Athletic	D 0-0		1	2	3	4	5	6	7	8	9	10	11																									
	Sep-03	(h) Barnet	L 0-2		1	2			5	4		8	9		11	7	6	3													10									
	Sep-06	(a) Finchley	L 1-2	Martin	1	2	3	4	5		8	10	9		11	7	6																							
	Sep-13	(h) Sutton U	W 3-0	Farrell 2, Townsend (pen)	1	3	4		5	6		8	9	10	11	7		2																						
	Sep-17	(a) Hayes	D 2-2	Farrell, Moran	1	3	4		5	6		8	9	10	11	7		2																						
	Sep-27	(a) Maidstone U	W 4-0	Farrell 2, Sells, OG	1	3	6		5			4	9	10	11	7			8	2																				
	Nov-22	(a) Barnet	L 1-3	Moran (pen)	1	2	4		5	6		8	9	11			3				7	10																		
	Dec-06	(h) Enfield	W 2-1	Hills, Townsend	1	2				6		4			11		3		8		7	10	5	9																
	Dec-13	(a) Enfield	W 5-2	Moran 2, Hills, Nicholls, Sells	1	2			5	6		4		10	11		3		8		7			9																
	Dec-20	(h) Southall	W 2-1	Evans, Sells	1	2				6		4		10	11		3		8		7		5	9																
	Dec-25	(h) Hendon	D 3-3	Hills 2, Sells	1	2				6		4		10	11		3		8		7		5	9																
	Dec-27	(a) Hendon	W 4-3	Evans, Hills, Moran, Nicholls	1	2				6		4		10	11		3		8		7		5	9																
	Jan-10	(h) Leyton	W 3-1	Hills, Sells 2	1	2	4			6				10	11		3		8		7		5	9																
	Feb-21	(a) Leyton	W 4-1	Hills 2, Sells, Moran	1	2				6				10	11		3		8			4	5	9	7															
	Feb-28	(h) Hounslow T	D 1-1	Parfitt	1	2				6			9	10	11		3		8			4	5		7															
	Mar-07	(a) Hitchin Town	W 2-1	Hills, Moran	1	2				6				10	11		3		8			4	5	9	7															
	Mar-21	(h) Maidstone U	W 1-0	Hills	1	2				6				10	11		3		8		7	4	5	9																
	Mar-27	(h) Hayes	W 3-1	Hills 3	1	2						4		10	11		3		8		7	6	5	9																
	Mar-28	(a) Carshalton Athletic	W 3-1	Evans, Moran, Nicholls	1	2						4		10	11		3		9		8		5		7	6														
	Mar-30	(h) Finchley	W 6-1	Farrell 3, Parfitt, Sells, Moran (pen)	1	2						4	9	10	11		3		8		7	6	5																	
	Apr-04	(h) Redhill	W 4-0	Moran 2, Evans, Hills	1	2								10	11		3		8		7	4	5	9		6														
	Apr-11	(a) Grays Athletic	L 3-5	Evans, Hills, Moran	1	2				6				10	11		3		8		7		5	9		4														
	Apr-18	(a) Hounslow T	W 3-1	Farrell 2, Moran	1	3	4			6			9	10	11				8	2			5		7															
	Apr-22	(a) Southall	D 1-1	Hills	1	3	4			6			7	10	11				8	2			5	9																
	Apr-28	(a) Redhill	W 4-2	Farrell 3, Evans	1	3	4			6			7	10	11				8	2			5	9																
	Apr-29	(h) Walton & H	W 1-0	Moran	1	3	4		5	6			7	10	11				8	2				9																
	May-02	(h) Hitchin Town	W 3-0	Evans, Hills, Hurrell	1	3	4		5	6			7	10	11				8	2				9																
	May-06	(h) Carshalton Athletic	D 0-0		1	3	4		5	6			7	10	11				8	2				9																
	May-09	(a) Sutton U	L 2-3	Farrell, Moran (pen)	1	3	4		5	6			9	10	11				8	2	7																			

FA Cup

Rd	Date	Opponent	Result	Scorers	Culver T	Hurrell R	Gibbons R	Comben A	Kay D	Saunders J	Martin D	Townsend C	Farrell M	Moran J	Evans V	Matthews J	Ash A	Ware R	Sells C	Mowle G	Nicholls J	Parfitt P	Hall J	Hills L	Waldheim J	Murphy T	Davies J	Elliott L	Farmer E	Nash G	Gordon W	Green B	McLoughlin N	Conniff T	Dunk M	Hughes M	Quinn M	Emerson M	Leadbetter J	Stone C
1Q	Sep-20	(h) Uxbridge	W 2-1	Farrell, Evans	1	3	4		5	6		8	9	10	11	7				2																				
2Q	Oct-08	(h) Hayes	W 2-1	Moran 2 (2 pens)	1	3			5	6		4	9	10	11	7	2		8																					
3Q	Oct-18	(a) Yiewsley	W 2-1	Nicholls, Sells	1	2			5	6		4	9	10	11		3		8		7																			
4Q	Nov-01	(h) Headington U	L 2-4	Sells 2	1	2			5	6		4	9	10	11		3		8		7																			

FA Amateur Cup

Rd	Date	Opponent	Result	Scorers	Culver T	Hurrell R	Gibbons R	Comben A	Kay D	Saunders J	Martin D	Townsend C	Farrell M	Moran J	Evans V	Matthews J	Ash A	Ware R	Sells C	Mowle G	Nicholls J	Parfitt P	Hall J	Hills L	Waldheim J	Murphy T	Davies J	Elliott L	Farmer E	Nash G	Gordon W	Green B	McLoughlin N	Conniff T	Dunk M	Hughes M	Quinn M	Emerson M	Leadbetter J	Stone C
1Q	Oct-11	(h) Ruislip Manor	D 2-2	Sells, Moran (pen)	1	3			5	6		4	9	10	11	7			8	2																				
1Qr	Oct-25	(a) Ruislip Manor	W 4-0	Farrell 2, Evans, Saunders	1	2			5	6		4	9	10	11		3		8		7																			
2Q	Nov-08	(h) Twickenham	W 2-1	Farrell, Parfitt	1	2			5	6		4	9				3		8		7	10					11													
3Q	Nov-15	(h) Harrow Town	L 2-3	Farrell, Parfitt	1	2			5	6		4	9			11	3		8		7	10																		

London Senior Cup

Rd	Date	Opponent	Result	Scorers	Culver T	Hurrell R	Gibbons R	Comben A	Kay D	Saunders J	Martin D	Townsend C	Farrell M	Moran J	Evans V	Matthews J	Ash A	Ware R	Sells C	Mowle G	Nicholls J	Parfitt P	Hall J	Hills L	Waldheim J	Murphy T	Davies J	Elliott L	Farmer E	Nash G	Gordon W	Green B	McLoughlin N	Conniff T	Dunk M	Hughes M	Quinn M	Emerson M	Leadbetter J	Stone C
1	Nov-29	(a) Leyton	W 4-3	Moran, Nicholls, Parfitt, Sells	1	2			5	6		4		10	11		3		8		7	9																		
2	Jan-03	(h) Borehamwood	W 7-1	Evans 2, Hills 2, Moran 2(1 pen), Nicholls	1	2				6		4		10	11		3		8		7		5	9																
3	Feb-07	(a) Dulwich Hamlet	L 1-3	Moran	1	2	4			6				10	11		3		8		7		5	9																

Middlesex Senior Cup

Rd	Date	Opponent	Result	Scorers	Culver T	Hurrell R	Gibbons R	Comben A	Kay D	Saunders J	Martin D	Townsend C	Farrell M	Moran J	Evans V	Matthews J	Ash A	Ware R	Sells C	Mowle G	Nicholls J	Parfitt P	Hall J	Hills L	Waldheim J	Murphy T	Davies J	Elliott L	Farmer E	Nash G	Gordon W	Green B	McLoughlin N	Conniff T	Dunk M	Hughes M	Quinn M	Emerson M	Leadbetter J	Stone C
1	Jan-24	(a) Edgware T	D 1-1	Farrell	1	2				6		4	9	10	11		3		8		7		5																	
1r	Jan-31	(h) Edgware T	W 4-1	Farrell 3, Evans	1	2	4			6			9	10	11		3		8		7		5																	
2	Feb-14	(h) Harrow T	W 2-1	Moran (pen), Parfitt	1	2				6		4		10	11		3		8		7	9	5																	
SF	Mar-14	(n*) Finchley	W 3-2	Evans, Moran, Sells	1	2				6			9	10	11		3		8		7	4	5																	
F	Apr-25	(n) Enfield	W3-1 aet	Farrell 2, Evans	1	3	4			6			9	10	11				8	2	7		5																	

*played at Hounslow FC

Middlesex Charity Cup

Rd	Date	Opponent	Result	Scorers	Culver T	Hurrell R	Gibbons R	Comben A	Kay D	Saunders J	Martin D	Townsend C	Farrell M	Moran J	Evans V	Matthews J	Ash A	Ware R	Sells C	Mowle G	Nicholls J	Parfitt P	Hall J	Hills L	Waldheim J	Murphy T	Davies J	Elliott L	Farmer E	Nash G	Gordon W	Green B	McLoughlin N	Conniff T	Dunk M	Hughes M	Quinn M	Emerson M	Leadbetter J	Stone C
1	Sep-15	(a) Hendon	D 2-2 aban	Nash, Sells								8					6		10	2	7		5			4		1	3	9	11									
1r	Apr-20	(h) Hendon	W 2-1	Comben, Nicholls				8	5								3	2			11					4						1	6	7	9	10				
SF	May-04	(h) Enfield	L 1-2	Hughes	Reserve Team played fixture																																			

North West Middlesex Invitation Cup

Rd	Date	Opponent	Result	Scorers	Culver T	Hurrell R	Gibbons R	Comben A	Kay D	Saunders J	Martin D	Townsend C	Farrell M	Moran J	Evans V	Matthews J	Ash A	Ware R	Sells C	Mowle G	Nicholls J	Parfitt P	Hall J	Hills L	Waldheim J	Murphy T	Davies J	Elliott L	Farmer E	Nash G	Gordon W	Green B	McLoughlin N	Conniff T	Dunk M	Hughes M	Quinn M	Emerson M	Leadbetter J	Stone C
SF	May-02	(a) Edgware T	L 1-4	Conniff	Reserve Team played fixture																																			
SF	May-09	(h) Edgware T	L 2-3	Conniff, Dunk														2							11	4						1		7	9	8	3	5	6	10

1959-60

Rd	Date	Opponent	Result	Scorers	Culver E	Mowle G	Hurrell R	Townsend C	Hall J	Saunders J	Massey B	Sells C	Farrell M	Moran J	Evans V	Gibbons R	Murphy T	Conniff T	Kay D	Stone C	ash A	Fowler B	Comben A	Parfitt P	Hills L	Spong L	Quinn M	Hughes M	Gordon B	Pert R	Peake R	Formoy B	Aldridge D	Keen P	Jenner A	Timberlake D	Riddy G	Hatton P
Athenian League - 4th																																						
	Aug-22	(h) Leyton	W 3-1	Farrell, Evans 2	1	2	3	4	5	6	7	8	9	10	11																							
	Aug-26	(h) Southall	L 1-2	Conniff	1	2	3		5			8	9	10	11	4	6	7																				
	Aug-29	(a) Walton & H	W 2-0	Massey, Moran	1	2	3	4			7		9	10	11	6			5	8																		
	Sep-02	(a) Enfield	L 3-6	Farrell 2, Moran	1	2	3			6	7		9	10	11	4			5		8																	
	Sep-12	(a) Hounslow T	L 1-5	Evans			2	4		6	7	8	9		11				5			10	3	1														
	Sep-19	(h) Walton & H	W 3-1	Hills, Moran, Sells				4	5			8		10	11	6		7					2	1			9		3									
	Sep-26	(a) Finchley	W 2-1	Evans, Hills				4	5			8		10	11	6		7					2	1			9		3									
	Oct-03	(h) Carshalton Athletic	D 2-2	Sells 2				4	5			8		10	11	6		7					2	1			9		3									
	Oct-10	(a) Sutton U	L 1-2	Sells				4	5			8		10	11	6		7					2	1			9		3									
	Oct-17	(h) Hitchin Town	L 1-2	Conniff	1		5	4				8		10	11	6		7					2				9		3									
	Oct-24	(a) Hayes	L 0-2		1		2		5	6		8		10	7	4		11					3				9											
	Oct-31	(h) Finchley	W 3-1	Farrell , Moran, Conniff	1	2		4	5	6		7	9	10				11					3							8								
	Nov-07	(a) Hitchin Town	W 5-3	Farrell, Sells, Parfitt 2, og	1	2		4	5	6		7	9	8	11								3			10												
	Nov-14	(h) Hayes	W 5-0	Farrell, Sells, Evans, Parfitt, Moran (pen)	1	2		4	5	6		7	9	8	11								3			10												
	Dec-12	(a) Barnet	L 2-4	Moran 2	1	2			5	6		7	9	8	11	4										10						3						
	Dec-19	(h) Hounslow T	W 1-0	og	1	2			5	6		7	9	8	11	4										10						3						
	Dec-25	(h) Hendon	D 2-2	Farrell 2	1	2		10	5	6		7	9	8	11	4																3						
	Dec-26	(a) Hendon	L 0-1		1	2		10	5	6		7		8	11	4		9														3						
	Jan-23	(h) Grays Athletic	W 6-0	Farrell 3, Evans, Moran, og		2		4	5	6		7	9	8	11									1								3	10					
	Jan-30	(a) Hornchurch U	W 4-2	Farrell 2, Evans, Moran		2		4	5	6		7	9	8	11									1								3	10					
	Feb-06	(h) Hornchurch U	W 2-1	Farrell, Moran		2		4	5	6		7	9	8	11									1								3	10					
	Feb-13	(a) Grays Athletic	L 2-4	Evans, Peake		2		4	5	6		7	9	8	11									1								3	10					
	Feb-20	(h) Enfield	L 1-4	Farrell		2		4		6		7	9	8	11									1								3	10			5		
	Feb-27	(h) Sutton U	W 2-1	Formoy, Sells		2		4	5	6		10	9	8	11									1					3					7				
	Mar-05	(a) Leyton	W 1-0	Farrell		2			5	6		8	9		11									1					3				10	7	4			
	Mar-12	(a) Redhill	L 2-3	Farrell, Sells		2			5			10	9	8	11	6								1									3	7	4			
	Mar-19	(h) Redhill	W 3-0	Farrell 3		2		4	5	6		7	9	8	11									1									3		10			
	Mar-26	(a) Southall	D 1-1	Aldridge		2		4	5	6		8	9		11			7						1									3		10			
	Apr-02	(a) Carshalton Athletic	W 2-0	Farrell 2		2		4	5	6		7	9	10	11									1									3		8			
	Apr-09	(h) Barnet	W 1-0	Moran (pen)		2		4	5	6		7	9	10	11									1									3		8			
FA Cup																																						
Pr	Sep-05	(a) Hayes	L 1-2	Massey	1		2	4		6	7	8	9	10	11				5				3															
FA Amateur Cup																																						
4Q	Nov-21	(h) Oxford C	W 3-2	Farrell, Evans, Saunders	1	2		4	5	6		7	9	8	11								3			10												
1	Jan-09	(a) Bromley	L 1-5	Sells	1	2	3	10	5	6		7	9	8		4																					11	
London Senior Cup																																						
1	Nov-28	(a) Wood Green Town	D 1-1	Gordon	1	2		4	5	6		7	9	8	11								3								10							
1r	Dec-05	(h) Wood Green Town	W 2-1	Farrell, Evans	1	2		4	5	6		7	9	8	11								3			10												
2	Jan-02	(h) Sutton U	L 1-3	Sells	1	2		10	5	6		7	9	8	11	4																3						
Middlesex Senior Cup																																						
1	Jan-16	(h) Willesden	L 1-2 aet	Farrell	1	2	3	4	5			7	9	8												6				10							11	
Middlesex Charity Cup																																						
1	Sep-08	(h) Hounslow T	L 1-3	Moran (pen)			2		5					10				7				8	3	1	4	6	9	11										
North West Middlesex Invitation Cup																																						
SF	Apr-15	(h) Edgware T	W 3-0	Farrell, Evans, Aldridge		2		4	5				9		11	6		7		10				1									3		8			
SF	Apr-16	(a) Edgware T	W 9-0	Farrell 3, Evans 2, Aldridge, Gibbons, Moran (pen),og		2		4	5				9	10	11	6								1									3	7	8			
F	May-04	(h) Harrow T	W 3-1	Evans, Aldridge 2 (1 pen)			2	4	5	6		8	9		11									1									3	7	10			
F	May-06	(a) Harrow T	W 5-1	Hatton 4, Aldridge		2		4	5			10			11	6		7						1									3		8			9

1960-61

Rd	Date	Opponent	Result	Scorers	Fowler W	Pike B	Peake R	Townsend C	King R	Saunders J	Aldridge K	Sells C	Farrell M	Aldridge D	Evans V	Hall J	Illsley L	Timberlake D	Mowle G	Riddy G	Hughes M	Moran J	Parfitt P	Quinn M	Culver T	Jarmin D	Pluck T	Hooper R	Hatton P	Emmings B	Low J	Bolton D	Palmer M	Shannon T	Pearce C
Athenian League - 2nd																																			
	Aug-20	(a) Hornchurch & U	W 4-2	Farrell, Evans 2, Sells	1	2	3		5	6	7	8	9	4	11						10														
	Aug-25	(a) Barnet	W 5-3	Farrell 3, Evans 2	1	2	3	4	5	6	7	8	9	10	11																				
	Aug-27	(h) Finchley	W 4-1	Farrell, Sells 2, Aldridge(D)	1	2	3	4	5	6	7	8	9	10	11																				
	Aug-31	(h) Hayes	W 2-1	Sells, Aldridge(D)	1	2	3	4	5		7	8	9	10	11	6																			
	Sep-03	(a) Sutton U	L 1-2	Evans	1	2	3	4	5	6	7	8	9	10	11																				
	Sep-24	(a) Enfield	L 0-5		1	2	3	4	5		7	8	9	10	11	6																			
	Oct-01	(h) Grays Athletic	W 6-0	Farrell 2, Aldridge(D) 2, Aldridge(K), Illsley	1	2	3	4	5	6	7		9	8	11		10																		
	Oct-08	(a) Hayes	L 3-4	Aldridge(D), Timberlake, og	1	2	3	4	5		7	8	9	6			10	11																	
	Oct-15	(h) Hounslow T	L 4-5	Farrell, Aldridge(D) (pen), Aldridge(K), og	1	2	3	4			7	8	9	6			10	11		5															
	Oct-22	(a) Leyton	W 4-0	Farrell 4	1		3	4			7	8	9	6	11				2	5	10														
	Oct-29	(a) Hounslow T	W 4-2	Farrell, Sells, Townsend, Aldridge(K)	1		3	4	5		7	8	9	6	11				2			10													
	Nov-05	(h) Redhill	W 4-1	Farrell 2, Aldridge(K), Moran	1		3		5	6	7	8	9		11				2			10	4												
	Nov-12	(a) Southall	D 2-2	Farrell, Moran	1		3	4	5		7	8	9		11				2			10	6												
	Nov-19	(h) Barnet	W 3-0	Farrell, Aldridge(K) 2	1			4	5		11	8	9						2			10	6	3		7									
	Dec-11	(h) Enfield	W 4-1	Farrell, Evans 2, Moran	1			4	5		7	8	9		11				2			10	6	3											
	Dec-27	(h) Hendon	D 4-4	Farrell 2, Aldridge(K) 2	1			4	5		7	8	9	6	11				2			10		3											
	Jan-14	(a) Finchley	L 2-3	Farrell, Moran	1			4	5		7	8	9	6	11				2			10		3											
	Feb-04	(h) Hornchurch & U	W 1-0	Farrell				4	5	3	7	8	9	10	11				2				6		1										
	Feb-11	(a) Walton & H	W 1-0	Parfitt	1			4	5	3	7	8	9	10	11				2				6													
	Mar-18	(a) Grays Athletic	W 2-1	Farrell, Sells	1			4	5	3	7	8	9		11				2			10	6													
	Mar-25	(h) Southall	D 0-0		1			4	5	3	7	8	9	6	11				2			10														
	Apr-01	(a) Hendon	L 0-1		1			4		3		8	9	6	11				2	5		10				7										
	Apr-03	(h) Leyton	W 4-2	Farrell 2, Sells, Evans	1			4				8	9	6	11				2	5		10		3		7										
	Apr-08	(h) Carshalton Athletic	W 2-1	Evans, Moran (pen)	1			4	5			8	9	6	11				2			10		3		7										
	Apr-15	(a) Redhill	W 2-0	Farrell 2	1			4	5	6		8	9		11			7	2			10		3											
	Apr-19	(a) Hitchin Town	D 1-1	Pluck	1			4	5	6			9		8			11	2			10		3				7							
	Apr-22	(h) Walton & H	W 5-0	Farrell 3, Evans, Sells	1			4	5	6		8	9		11			7	2			10		3											
	Apr-26	(h) Sutton U	L 1-2	Farrell	1					6		8	9		4			11	2	5		10		3				7							
	Apr-29	(a) Carshalton Athletic	W 3-0	Hatton 2, Moran	1					6		8			11				2	5		10		3		7		4	9						
	May-06	(h) Hitchin Town	D 0-0		1			4	5	6		8	9		11				2			10		3		7										
FA Cup																																			
1Q	Sep-10	(h) Harrow T	L 1-2	Aldridge(K)	1	2	3	4	5	6	9	8	10		7			11																		
FA Amateur Cup																																			
4Q	Nov-26	(a) Wood Green Town	W 8-0	Farrell 3, Aldridge(K), Townsend, Sells, Moran 2 (1 pen)	1			4	5		7	8	9		11				2			10	6	3											
1	Jan-21	(h) Enfield	L 1-2	Farrell	1			4	5		7	8	9		11				2			10	6	3											
London Senior Cup																																			
1	Dec-17	(h) Dulwich Hamlet	W 6-2	Farrell 3, Evans 2, Aldridge(K)	1			4	5		7	8	9		11				2			10	6	3											
2	Dec-31	(a) Edgware T	W 1-0	Farrell	1			4	5		7	8	9	6	11				2			10		3											
3	Jan-28	(h) Kingstonians	W 7-0	Farrell, Evans 2, Aldridge(K) 2, Aldridge(D), Sells	1			4	5	3	7	8	9	10	11				2				6													
SF	Feb-25	(a) Carshalton Athletic	W 4-1	Evans, Aldridge(K) 2, Aldridge(D)	1			4	5	3	7	8	9	10	11				2				6													
F	May-13	(n*) Enfield	L 0-3		1			4		6		8	9		11				2	5		10		3		7										
		*played at Highbury																																	
Middlesex Senior Cup																																			
1	Jan-07	(h) Chalfont N	W 8-0	Farrell 4, Townsend 2, Moran 2 (2 pens)	1			4	5		7	8	9	6	11				2			10		3											
2	Feb-18	(h) Uxbridge Town	W 3-0	Farrell, Aldridge(K), Aldridge(D) (pen)	1			4	5	3	7	8	9	10	11				2				6													
SF	Mar-11	(a) Hendon	L 0-1		1			4	5	3	7	8	9	10	11				2				6													
Middlesex Charity Cup																																			
1	Sep-07	(h) Hendon	W 2-1	Aldridge(K), Aldridge(D)	1					6	9	8		4	7	5	10	11	2					3											
2	Mar-04	(h) Harrow T	W 6-2	Evans,Aldridge(K) 2,Sells 2,Townsend	1			4	5	3	7	8	9	10	11				2				6													
AFA Invitation Cup																																			
1	Sep-02	(h) Pegasus	W 3-1																																		
		Wealdstone eliminated due to fixture congestion																																	
North West Middlesex Invitation Cup																																			
SF1	Apr-10	(a) Harrow T	W 2-1	Evans, Sells	1							8			10			7	2	5				3						9	4				6	11
SF2	Apr-19	(h) Harrow T	D 0-0		1										7			11		5							8		9		2	3	4	6	10

1961-62

Rd	Date	Opponent	Result	Scorers	Fowler W	Mowle G	Quinn M	Townsend C	King R	Saunders J	Peel A	Sells C	Farrell M	Moran J	Evans V	Low J	Jarmin D	Appleton N	Emmins A	Pillinger B	Brennan M	Knox T	Cazaly S	Rowley G	Buchanan M	Timberlake D	Merry K	Riddy G	Good R	Rocknean G	Davies G	Groves R	Emerson M	Morley J	Young A	Gilhooley M	Illsley L	McDonald B
Athenian League - 3rd																																						
	Aug-19	(h) Grays Athletic	D 1-1	Moran	1	2	3	4	5	6	7	8	9	10	11																							
	Aug-26	(a) Walton & H	L 1-2	Farrell	1	2		4	5	6	7		9	10	11	3	8																					
	Aug-30	(a) Southall	W 2-1	Farrell, Saunders	1	2		4	5	6	7	8	9	10	11			3																				
	Sep-02	(h) Hornchurch	L 2-3	Farrell, Peel	1	2		4	5	6	7	8	9	10	11			3																				
	Sep-06	(h) Carshalton Athletic	W 4-1	Farrell 2, Evans 2	1	2		4	5	6	7	8	9	10	11			3																				
	Sep-16	(a) Leyton	W 6-0	Evans 2, Pillinger 3, Moran	1				5	6	7	8		10	11	2		3	4	9																		
	Sep-30	(a) Hendon	W 5-0	Farrell 2, Moran 2 (1 pen), Rowley	1	2							9	10		3	8				6	5	4	7		11												
	Oct-07	(h) Southall	W 2-1	Evans, Jarmin	1	2		4	5					10	11	3	8			9			6	7														
	Oct-14	(a) Barnet	D 1-1	Evans	1	2		4	5		7			10	9	3	8					6				11												
	Oct-21	(h) Finchley	D 2-2	Knox 2 (1 pen)	1	2		4	5		11					3	8				9	10	6	7														
	Oct-28	(a) Sutton U	W 4-3	Evans 2, Merry 2	1			4	5		7				11	3	8	2			10	6					9											
	Nov-04	(a) Redhill	W 2-1	Evans, Jarmin	1	2		4			7			10	11	3	8					6					9	5										
	Nov-11	(h) Hounslow T	W 5-3	Evans 2, Merry, Moran, Townsend	1	2		4	5		7			10	11	3	8					6					9											
	Nov-18	(a) Carshalton Athletic	L 0-1		1	2			5		7			10	11	3	8					6	4				9											
	Nov-25	(h) Enfield	L 1-2	Evans	1			4	5		7			10	11	2	8					6					9		3									
	Dec-09	(h) Sutton U	W 5-1	Knox 2, Merry 2, Jarmin	1			4	5		7			10	11	2	8					6					9		3									
	Dec-16	(a) Hornchurch	W 3-0	Merry 2, Moran	1			4	5		7			10	11	2	8					6					9		3									
	Dec-25	(a) Hayes	L 2-4	Moran, Peel	1			4	5		7			10		2	8					6				11	9		3									
	Dec-26	(h) Hayes	L 1-2	Moran	1			4	5		7			10		2	8					6		11			9		3									
	Dec-30	(a) Grays Athletic	W 5-0	Merry 3, Moran, Townsend	1	2		8	5					10									4	7		11	9		3	6								
	Jan-27	(h) Walton & H	W 6-3	Evans 2, Merry 2, Knox, Peel	1	2	3	4	5		7				11		8					10	6				9											
	Feb-17	(h) Leyton	D 4-4	Evans 3, Knox (pen)		2		4	5		7				11							8	6				9		3		10	1						
	Feb-24	(h) Hendon	L 2-4	Evans, Jarmin	1	2		4			7			10	11		8					5	6				9		3									
	Mar-24	(h) Barnet	W 1-0	Knox	1			4	5		7				11	3	8					10	6				9							2				
	Apr-07	(a) Hitchin Town	L 1-7	Davies	1	2			5		7				11	3	8					6	4				9				10							
	Apr-14	(a) Finchley	W 2-0	Young 2	1			4	5						11	2	7						6				9		3		10				8			
	Apr-21	(h) Redhill	W 2-1	Evans, Low	1			4	5		7				11	2	8					6					9		3		10							
	May-02	(a) Hounslow T	D 2-2	Knox, Moran	1			4	5		7			10	11	2						8	6				9		3									
	May-03	(a) Enfield	L 1-2	Knox	1	2		4	5		7				11		10					8					9		3					6				
	May-05	(h) Hitchin	W 1-0	Jarmin					5		7				11	2	10					6	4						3				8		9	1		
FA Cup																																						
1Q	Sep-09	(a*) Ware T	W 5-0	Evans 3, Sells, Moran (pen)	1	2		4	5	6	7	8	9	10	11			3																				
2Q	Sep-23	(h) Barnet	D 1-1	Sells	1	2		4	5	6	7	8		10	11			3		9																		
2Qr	Sep-28	(a) Barnet	L 0-9		1				5			8		10	11	2		3		9			4	7	6													
		*played at Lower Mead																																				
FA Amateur Cup																																						
4Q	Dec-02	(h) Aveley	W 5-0	Evans, Merry 2, King, Peel	1		3	4	5		7			10	11	2	8					6					9											
1	Jan-20	(a) Maidenhead	L 1-3	Evans	1	2	3	4	5		7				11		10					8	6				9											
London Senior Cup																																						
1	Jan-06	(h) Barking	W 2-1	Evans, Merry	1	2								10	11		8					5	4	7			9		3	6								
2	Feb-03	(a) Erith & Belvedere	W 4-2	Evans 2, Knox, Davies	1	2		4	5		7				11		8					6					9		3		10							
3	Mar-17	(a) Bromley	D 1-1	Merry	1			4			7				11	3	8					5	6				9				10			2				
3r	Mar-31	(h) Bromley	W 5-2	Evans, Jarmin, Knox, Merry, Peel	1	2		4	5		7			10	11	3	8					6					9											
SF	Apr-28	(n*) Enfield	W 3-1	Peel 2, Cazaly	1			4	5		7			10	11	2						8	6				9		3									
F	May-12	(n**) Wimbledon	D 1-1 aet	Peel	1				5		7			10	11	2						8	4				9		3					6				
		*played at Barnet FC																																				
		**played at Dulwich Hamlet FC																																				
London Challenge Cup																																						
1	Oct-02	(a) Brentford	L 3-6	Farrell, Moran (pen), og	1	2		6					9	10	11	3	8					5	4	7														
Middlesex Senior Cup																																						
1	Jan-13	(h) Uxbridge Town	W 3-2	Evans, Merry, Townsend	1	2		8	5		7			10	11							6	4				9		3									
2	Feb-10	(a) Finchley	D 1-1 aet	Knox		2		4	5		7				11		8					10					9		3	6		1						
2r	Mar-03	(h) Finchley	W 3-1	Evans 2, Merry	1	2		4			7				11	3	8						6				9				10		5					
SF	Mar-10	(n*) Hayes	W 5-2	Evans 2, Merry, Davies 2	1	2		4			7				11	3						8	6				9				10		5					
F	Apr-23	(n**) Enfield	L 1-4	Merry	1			4	5		7				11	2	8						6				9		3		10							
		*played at Southall FC																																				
		**played at Finchley FC																																				
Middlesex Charity Cup																																						
SF†	Aug-22	(h) Enfield	L 1-3	Timberlake	1	2	3	4	5	6			9	10	11		8									7												
1	Jan-30	(h) Finchley	W 2-1	Knox 2 (1 pen)				4			7				11	2	8					6					9		3		10	1	5					
SF	Apr-11	(a) Enfield	L 2-3	Young 2	1	2			3						11	9							4				8						5	6	10		7	
		†Held over from 1960-61 season																																				
AFA Invitation Cup																																						
1	Jan-23	(h) Wycombe W	D 1-1	Evans	1	2	3	4	5						11		10					6		7			9				8							
1r	Apr-18	(a) Wycombe W	L 0-2		1	2	10	4	5						11	6	7												3						8			9

1962-63

Rd	Date	Opponent	Result	Scorers	Fowler W	Low J	Good R	Richards D	King R	Townsend C	Peel A	Lindsay H	Norman D	Knox T	Evans V	Merry K	Smith B	Jones C	West P	Davies S	Gilhooley M	Ashworth J	Cazaly S	Hughes M	Houston P	Groves R	Pearce C	Watts B	Mowie G	Emerson M	Williams A	Morley J	Bennett J	Donaghue L	Knox G	McPhee S
Athenian League - 3rd																																				
	Aug-18	(a) Walton & H	W 5-2	Lindsay 3, Evans, Norman	1	2	3	4	5	6	7	8	9	10	11																					
	Aug-25	(h) Southall	L 0-1		1	2	3	4	5	6	7	8	9	10	11																					
	Aug-28	(h) Hendon	W 2-1	Lindsay, og	1	2	3	4	5	6		8	9	10	11		7																			
	Sep-01	(a) Sutton U	W 3-2	Lindsay, Evans, Merry	1	2	3	4	5		7	8	9	10	11	6																				
	Sep-06	(a) Finchley	W 2-0	Lindsay 2	1	2	3	4	5	6	7	8		10	11	9																				
	Sep-15	(h) Grays Athletic	W 6-0	Evans 3, Knox 2, Jones	1	2	3	4	5		7			10	11	6	8	9																		
	Sep-29	(h) Hornchurch	W 4-2	Lindsay, Knox 3 (1 pen)	1	2	3	4	5		7	8		10	11	6	9																			
	Oct-13	(a) Hitchin Town	L 0-1		1	2	3	4	5		7	8		10	11	6			9																	
	Oct-20	(h) Finchley	D 1-1	Lindsay	1	2	3	4	5		7	8		10	11	6			9																	
	Nov-03	(a) Redhill	W 4-1	Lindsay, Evans 2, Knox	1	2	3	4	5	10	7	8		6	11				9																	
	Nov-10	(h) Carshalton Athletic	W 2-1	Lindsay 2	1	2	3	4	5	10	7	8		6	11				9																	
	Nov-24	(h) Barnet	D 3-3	Lindsay, Evans, Knox (pen)	1	2	3	4	5	6	7	8		10	11					9																
	Dec-08	(h) Leyton	W 4-0	Lindsay 3, Merry		2	3	4	5		7	8			11	9		10		6	1															
	Dec-15	(a) Southall	W 2-1	Lindsay, Merry		2	3	4	5		7	8			11	9		10		6	1															
	Dec-25	(h) Hayes	W 3-0	Lindsay, Townsend, Ashworth		2	3	4		6	7	8			11	9				10	1	5														
	Dec-26	(a) Hayes	L 1-2	Evans		2	3	4	5	6	7	8			11	9				10	1															
	Mar-09	(a) Hornchurch	L 0-3		1	2	3	4		6	7	8			11	9		10				5														
	Mar-12	(a) Hendon	W 3-2	Evans, Merry, Low	1	2	3	4		6	7	8			11	9		10				5														
	Mar-19	(h) Enfield	W 2-0	Lindsay, Jones	1	2	3	4		6	7	8			9	10		11				5														
	Apr-02	(h) Hounslow T	D 1-1	Peel	1	2	3	4		6	7	8			11	10	9					5														
	Apr-06	(a) Hounslow T	D 1-1	Lindsay	1	2	3	4		6	7	8			9	10		11				5														
	Apr-13	(a) Grays Athletic	W 1-0	Evans	1	2	3	4		6	7	8			9	10		11																		
	Apr-15	(h) Sutton U	W 2-0	Evans, Peel	1	2	3	4		6	7	8			9	10		11				5														
	Apr-20	(a) Carshalton Athletic	L 1-3	Evans	1	2	3	4		6	7	8			11		9	10				5														
	Apr-23	(a) Leyton	W 1-0	Evans	1	2	3	4		6	7	8			11		9	10				5														
	Apr-30	(h) Hitchin Town	W 2-0	Evans, Ashworth	1	2	3	4		6	7	8			11	9		10				5														
	May-04	(h) Redhill	W 3-1	Lindsay 2, Jones	1	2	3	4		6	7	8			11	9		10				5														
	May-07	(a) Enfield	L 0-4		1	2	3	4			7				11	10						5	6	8							9					
	May-14	(h) Walton & H	W 2-1	Peel, og	1	2	3	4			7				11			10				5	6	8	9											
	May-23	(a) Barnet	L 1-5	Houston	1		3	4			7	8			11	6						5		10	9											2
FA Cup																																				
1Q	Sep-08	(a) Harlow Town	W 2-0	Evans 2	1	2	3	4	5		7	8	9	10	11	6																				
2Q	Sep-22	(a) Bishops Stortford	W 2-0	Evans, W Smith	1	2	3	4	5	6	7	8		10	11		9																			
3Q	Oct-06	(h) Enfield	L 1-5	Lindsay	1	2	3	4	5		7	8		10	11	6	9																			
FA Amateur Cup																																				
4Q	Dec-01	(a) Letchworth	L 1-2	Evans	1	2	3	4	5	6	7	8		9	11	10																				
London Senior Cup																																				
1	Nov-17	(a) Southall	W 3-1	Evans, West 2	1	2	3	4	5		7	8			11	6		10	9																	
2	Feb-16	(a) Ford U	D 1-1	Townsend		2	3	4		6	7	8			11	9		10			1	5														
2r	Mar-02	(h) Ford U	W 2-1 aet	Jones, Merry		2	3	4		6	7	8			11	9		10			1	5														
3	Mar-16	(a) Leytonstone	L 0-1		1	2	3	4		6	7	8			11	9		10				5														
London Challenge Cup																																				
1	Oct-01	(h) Millwall	W 3-0	Lindsay 2, Knox		2	3	4	5		7	8		10	11	6			9							1										
2	Oct-15	(h) West Ham U	W 4-1	Lindsay 2, West 2	1	2	3	4	5		7	8		10	11	6			9																	
SF	Oct-29	(h) Arsenal	D 1-1	West	1	2	3	4	5		7	8		10	11	6			9																	
SFr	Nov-12	(a) Arsenal	L 1-3	og	1	2	3	4	5		7	8		10	11	6	9																			
Middlesex Senior Cup																																				
1	Mar-05	(h) Finchley	W 2-0	Evans, Merry (pen)	1	2	3	6	4		7				9	8		10				5					11									
2	Mar-23	(a) Uxbridge	D 1-1 aet	Jones	1	2	3		4	6	7	8			9	10		11				5														
2r	Mar-30	(h) Uxbridge	W 4-2	Lindsay, Evans 2, Smith	1	2	3	4		6	7	8			11	10	9					5														
SF	May-11	(n*) Hayes	W 4-1	Peel, Hughes, Jones 2 (1 pen)	1	2	3	4		6	7	8			11			10				5		9												
F	May-21	(n**) Enfield	W 2-0	Houston, Jones	1		3	2			8					5	7	11					6	10	9										4	
		*played at Hendon FC																																		
		**played at Finchley FC																																		
Middlesex Charity Cup																																				
1	Nov-27	(h) Willesden	W 5-2 aet	West 2, Williams, Knox, og			3	4						8	7	6		11	10		1									5	9	2				
SF	May-24	(a) Finchley	W 2-1	Evans 2	1	2	3	4			8	10			11	5	7						6		9											
Mithras Cup																																				
1	Dec-11	(h) Maidenhead	W 3-2	Evans, Merry, og		2	3	4	5	6		8			11	9	7	10			1															
1	Dec-18	(a) Maidenhead	L 3-5 aet	Lindsay 2, Townsend		2	3	4		6		7			11	9					1		10							5				8		
Battle of Britain Cup																																				
	Sep-04	(h) Chelsea	L 1-3	Evans	1	2	3	4	5		7		9	6	11	10	8																			
East Anglian Cup																																				
2	Apr-04	(a) Hertford Town	L 0-1							4	8				11	6	7				1							3	2	5	9		10			
AFA Senior Cup																																				
1	Oct-27	(h) Eastbourne	W 5-0	Townsend, West 2, Smith, Evans	1	2	3			4	7	10		5	11	6	8		9																	

1963-64

	Date	Opponent	Result	Scorers	Fowler W	Creasey WA	Good R	Richards D	Ashworth J	Townsend C	Peel A	Lindsay H	Jenkins B	Jones C	Evans V	Stanley M	Merry K	Devine H	Cazaley S	Millington J	Bell D	Durdle R	Farrell M	Goldsby B	McKendry L	Doyle M	Haydon T	Bremer B	McKenzie E	McPhee S	Morley J	Smith W	Housten W	Saunders J
Athenian League - 5th																																		
	Aug-24	(a) Grays Athletic	W 1-0	Jenkins	1	2	3	4	5	6	7	8	9	10	11																			
	Aug-31	(h) Redhill	D 3-3	Lindsay, Evans, Jenkins	1	2	3	4			7	8	9		11	5	6	10																
	Sep-14	(a) Hornchurch	L 0-1		1	2	3				7		9	8	11	5	6		4	10														
	Oct-05	(h) Walton & H	L 1-2	Jenkins	1	2	3	4	5	6	7	8	9	10						11														
	Oct-12	(h) Finchley	L 2-4	Bell 2	1	2	3	4	5	6	7	8	9	11							10													
	Oct-19	(a) Dagenham	L 1-2	Evans	1	2	3	6	5	4		8	9		7			11			10													
	Oct-26	(h) Leyton	D 1-1	Townsend		2	3	6	5	4	7	8			11			9			10	1												
	Nov-02	(a) Hayes	D 2-2	Jenkins, Bell		2	3	6	5	4	7	8	9		11						10	1												
	Nov-09	(a) Southall	L 1-2	Evans		2	3	6	5	4	7	8	9		11						10	1												
	Nov-16	(h) Carshalton Athletic	W 4-3	Farrell 2, Evans, og		2	3	6	5	4	7	8			11						10	1	9											
	Dec-21	(a) Barnet	D 2-2	Evans, Lindsay		2	3	6	5	4	7	10			11								9		8									
	Dec-28	(a) Hounslow T	W 4-2	Farrell 2, Lindsay, og		2	3	6	5	4	7	8			11							1	9		10									
	Jan-04	(h) Grays Athletic	W 5-0	Farrell 3, Lindsay, Evans		2	3	6	5	4	7	8			11							1	9		10									
	Feb-01	(h) Maidenhead U	W 2-1	Farrell, Bell			3	6	5	4		10			11						7	1	9		8	2								
	Feb-08	(a) Carshalton Athletic	D 1-1	Townsend (pen)			3	6	5	4		8			11						7	1	9			2		10						
	Feb-22	(a) Redhill	W 2-1	Lindsay, Bell	1		3	6	5			8			11						7		9	4	10	2								
	Feb-29	(a) Walton & H	W 2-1	Lindsay, Evans	1		3	6	5	9		8			11						7			4	10	2								
	Mar-07	(h) Hayes	L 1-2	Bell	1		3	6	5	9		8			11						7			4	10	2								
	Mar-21	(a) Maidenhead U	W 1-0	Bremer	1		3	6	5	4		8									7				10	2	9	11						
	Mar-28	(h) Hornchurch	W 7-2	Lindsay 2, Evans 4, Haydon			3	6	5	4		10			9						7	1				2	8	11						
	Apr-04	(a) Leyton	L 1-2	Bell			3	6	5	4		10			9						7	1				2	8	11						
	Apr-07	(h) Southall	W 3-1	Haydon, McKenzie, Bell			3	6							11						7	1		4	5	2	9	10	8					
	Apr-14	(h) Hounslow T	W 5-2	Lindsay 2, Evans, Townsend, Haydon			3	6	5	4		10			9						7	1				2	8	11						
	Apr-18	(h) Dagenham	W 2-1	Townsend, McKenzie			3	6	5	4		10			9							1				2	8	11	7					
	Apr-21	(a) Finchley	L 0-4				3	6	5	4		10			9						7	1				2	8	11						
	May-01	(h) Barnet	L 0-5		1		3	6	5	4		10			11						7		9			2	8							
FA Cup																																		
1Q	Sep-21	(h) Hertford Town	L 0-1		1	2	3	4		6	7	8	9	10	11	5																		
FA Amateur Cup																																		
4Q	Nov-30	(a) Vauxhall Motors	W 4-0	Lindsay, Evans 2, Townsend		2	3	6	5	4	7	8			11						10	1	9											
1	Jan-11	(h) Carshalton Athletic	D 1-1	Farrell		2	3	6	5	4	7	8			11							1	9		10									
1r	Jan-18	(a) Carshalton Athletic	L 1-3	Evans		2	3		5	4	7	10			11						8	1	9		6									
London Senior Cup																																		
1	Dec-07	(h) Hendon	D 1-1	Evans		2	3	6	5	4	7	10			11	9						1		8										
1r	Dec-14	(a) Hendon	L 2-3	Lindsay, Townsend (pen)		2	3	4		8		7			11	5						1		10	9									6
London Challenge Cup																																		
1	Oct-07	(h) Arsenal	L 1-2	Bell	1	2	3	4		6	7	8	9	11		5					10													
Middlesex Senior Cup																																		
1	Jan-25	(h) Hendon	W 3-2	Farrell, Lindsay, Bell		2	3	6	5	4		10			11						7	1	9		8									
2	Feb-15	(h) Hounslow T	W 2-0	Lindsay, Evans	1		3	6	5		10	8			11						7		9		4	2								
SF	Apr-11	(a) Enfield	W 6-4 aet	Lindsay 3, Bremer, Townsend, Haydon			3	6	5	4		10			9						7	1				2	8	11						
F	May-09	(h) Finchley	W 2-0	Townsend, Haydon	1		3	6	5	4		10			9						7					2	8	11						
Middlesex Charity Cup																																		
F†	Sep-04	(a) Hayes	L 1-4	Jones	1		3	2			8			10	11		6		4												5	7	9	
SF	Mar-30	(a) Southall	W 2-1	Evans, Haydon			3	6	5	4		10			9						7	1				2	8	11						
F	May-05	(h) Hayes	W 3-1	Lindsay, Bremer, Haydon	1		3	6	5	4		10			9						7					2	8	11						
		†Held over from 1962-63 season																																
Mithras Cup																																		
SF1	Feb-18	(h) Hemel Hempstead	W 2-0	Evans, og	1			6				8			11						7		9	4	5	2		10		3				
SF2	Mar-10	(h) Hemel Hempstead	W 4-1	Lindsay 2, Bell, Haydon	1		3	4	5			8			11						7				6	2	9	10						
F1	Apr-08	(a) Maidenhead	D 1-1	Bell			3	6							9						7	1		4	5	2	8	11	10					
F2	Apr-23	(h) Maidenhead	W 3-2	Bremer, Haydon 2			3	6	5	4		10			11							1	9			2	8	7						
Battle of Britain Cup																																		
F	Oct-22	(h) Leyton Orient	W 4-2	Townsend 3 (1 pen), Devine		2	3	6	5	4	7	8			11			9			10	1												
East Anglian Cup																																		
Pr	Sep-17	(h) Edgware T	W 4-2	Jenkins 3, Jones	1	2	3	4		6	7	8	9	10	11	5																		
2	Oct-29	(h) Uxbridge	D 0-0			2	3	6	5	4	7	8	9		11						10	1												
2r	Dec-17	(h) Uxbridge	W 6-1	Lindsay 4, Farrell 2		2	3	6		4	7	10			11	5					8	1	9											
3	Mar-24	(h) Bishops Stortford	W 5-0	Lindsay, Farrell 2, Bremer, Haydon			3	6	5	4		10									7	1	9			2	8	11						
4	Apr-15	(h) Stevenage	L 0-3				3	10	5	4					9						7	1			6	2	8	11						
London Charity Cup																																		
1	Oct-01	(h) Hayes	W 2-1	Jones 2	1	2	3	4	5	6	7		9	10	8					11														
SF	Apr-28	(a) Hounslow T	W 1-0	Evans	1		3	6	5	4		10			9						7					2	8	11						
Hitchin Centenary Cup																																		
1	Oct-15	(h) Loughborough C	W 3-1	Lindsay 2, Townsend			3		5	4	7	8	9			6		11			10	1				2								

1964-65

Rd	Date	Opponent	Result	Scorers	Fowler W	Doyle M	Good R	Townsend C	Ashworth J	Richards D	Bell D	Haydon T	Jones C	Lindsay H	Evans V	Connell J	McPhee S	Farrell M	Bremer B	Dillsworth E	Smith R	McKendry L	Jones A	Wilson D or J?	Hughes M	Emerson M	Wyatt A	Bennett J	Childs B	Smith J	Adamson J	McKenzie E
Isthmian League - 8th																																
	Aug-22	(h) Tooting & Mitcham United	W 2-1	Lindsay, Bell	1	2	3	4	5	6	7	8	9	10	11																	
	Aug-26	(a) Kingstonian	L 1-2	Townsend (pen)	1	2	3	4	5	6	7	9		10	11	8																
	Aug-29	(a) Ilford	D 2-2	Lindsay, Haydon	1	2	3		5	6	7	9		10		8			11			4										
	Sep-05	(h) Wycombe W	W 4-2	Lindsay, Farrell, Connell 2	1		3	4	5	6		7		10		8	2	9	11													
	Sep-09	(a) Oxford C	D 1-1	Farrell	1	2		4	5	6		7		10		8	3	9	11													
	Sep-12	(h) Bromley	W 7-2	Lindsay,Bremer 2,Connell,Ashworth,Townsend(pen),og	1	2	3	4	5	6	7			10		8		9	11													
	Sep-15	(h) Kingstonian	L 2-5	Lindsay, Dillsworth		2		4	5	6	7			10		8	3		11	9	1											
	Sep-19	(a) Tooting & Mitcham United	W 3-1	Bell, Connell, Haydon	1	2	3	4	5		7	9		10		8			11			6										
	Sep-22	(h) St Albans C	W 3-0	Dillsworth 2, Jones	1	2		4	5			6	11	10		8			7	9		3										
	Sep-26	(h) Maidstone U	W 1-0	Connell	1	2			5		7	8				10	3		11	9		6		4								
	Sep-30	(a) Wycombe W	W 3-0	Bremer, Connell(pen), Bell	1	2		4	5		7	9		10		8	3		11			6										
	Oct-05	(h) Woking	W 6-0	Bremer 2, Dillsworth 3, Connell (pen)	1	2		4	5		7			10		8	3		11	9		6										
	Oct-10	(a) Sutton U	L 1-3	Lindsay	1	2	3	4	5		7			10					11	9		6			8							
	Oct-13	(h) Oxford C	L 0-1		1	2	3	4	5		7			10		8			11	9		6										
	Oct-17	(h) Dulwich Hamlet	W 3-1	Farrell 2, Bell	1	2	3	4	5		7			10		8		9	11			6										
	Oct-24	(h) Corinthian C	W 4-2	Farrell 2, Lindsay, Wyatt	1	2	3	4						10	11	8		9				6				5	7					
	Oct-31	(a) Bromley	D 2-2	Evans, Townsend	1	2	3	4	5		8			10	11			9				6					7					
	Nov-07	(h) Sutton U	D 1-1	Evans	1	2	3	4	5			8		10	11			9				6					7					
	Nov-17	(a) Corinthian C	L 4-5	Farrell, Evans 2(Connell 1 per ho), Haydon	1	2				4	7	10			11	8	3	9				6				5						
	Nov-26	(a) Woking	L 1-2	Bell	1	2		4	5	3	7			10	9	8			11			6										
	Dec-05	(a) Walthamstow Ave	L 1-2	Bremer	1	2		4	5	3	7			10		8			11	9		6										
	Dec-12	(a) Hitchin Town	L 0-4		1	2		4	5	3	10					8			11	7		6						9				
	Dec-19	(h) Barking	W 4-0	Bremer 2, Connell 2 (1 pen)	1	2		4	5	6		9		10	11	8			7			3										
	Dec-25	(h) Hendon	L 3-6	Lindsay 2, Childs	1	2		4	5	6				10	11	8			7			3							9			
	Dec-26	(a) Hendon	L 1-2	J Smith		2		4	5	6				10	11	8			7		1	3								9		
	Jan-16	(h) Walthamstow Ave	W 5-0	Lindsay 3 (1 pen), Bremer, Childs	1	2		8	5	4				10			3		11			6					7		9			
	Jan-30	(a) Maidstone	D 2-2	Bremer, Childs	1	2		8	5	4				10			3		11			6					7		9			
	Feb-06	(h) Ilford	W 5-3	Lindsay 2 (1 pen), Bremer, Childs 2	1	2		8	5	4				10			3		11			6					7		9			
	Feb-20	(a) Barking	W 3-1	Childs 2, Wyatt	1	2		8	5	4				10			3		11			6					7		9			
	Feb-27	(h) Clapton	W 4-0	Bremer 3, Childs	1	2			5	4	10					8			11			6					7		9		3	
	Mar-02	(a) Leytonstone	L 1-3	Bremer	1	2		8	5	4	10					7			11	9		6									3	
	Mar-13	(a) Enfield	L 1-3	Childs	1	3		8	5	2				10		7			11	4		6							9			
	Mar-23	(h) Leytonstone	W 3-1	Childs 3	1	3		8	5	2				7					11	4		6							9	10		
	Mar-27	(a) St Albans C	L 0-3		1	3		8	5	2				7					11	4		6							9	10		
	Apr-03	(h) Enfield	D 3-3	Lindsay, Connell, McKenzie	1	3		6	5	2				10		8			7	4									9			11
	Apr-10	(a) Clapton	W 2-0	Childs 2	1	2		6	5					10		8			7	4									9	3		11
	Apr-16	(h) Hitchin Town	W 2-1	Childs 2	1	3		6	5	2				10		8			11	4									9			7
	Apr-17	(a) Dulwich Hamlet	W 2-1	Lindsay, Dillsworth	1	2		6	5					10		8			11	4			3				7		9			
FA Cup																																
		Wealdstone were excluded as their entry was late																														
FA Amateur Cup																																
4Q	Nov-28	(a) Didcot	W 2-1	Bremer, Ashworth	1	2		4	5	3	7	8		10					11	9		6										
1	Jan-02	(h) Grays Athletic	W 3-0	Lindsay (pen), Childs, Connell	1	2		4	5	6				10	11	8			7			3							9			
2	Jan-23	(a) Bishop Auckland	W 4-2	Lindsay, Townsend, Ashworth, og	1	2		8	5	4				10			3		11			6					7		9			
3	Feb-13	(a) Alvechurch	L 1-4	Bremer	1	2		8	5	4	10						3		11			6					7		9			
London Senior Cup																																
1	Nov-21	(h) Enfield	W 2-0	Farrell, Bell	1	2	3		5	4	7	10			11	8		9				6										
2	Jan-09	(h) Carshalton Athletic	L 0-4		1	2		4	5	6				10	11	8			7			3					9					
London Charity Cup																																
F†	Sep-01	(h) Barnet	W 2-1	Farrell, Haydon	1		3		5	6	7	8		10			2	9	11			4										
1	Nov-23	(a) Dagenham	W 3-2	Connell, Dillsworth, Haydon						4		8				10	2		11	9	1			6	7	5					3	
SF	Apr-26	(a) Finchley	L 1-6	McKenzie	1	3		6	5	2						8			11	4									9	10		7
		†Held over from 1963-64 season																														
Middlesex Senior Cup																																
1	Nov-14	(a*) C.A.V.	L 1-2	Farrell	1	2	3	4						10	11	8		9				6				5	7					
		*played at Lower Mead																														
Hitchin Centenary Cup																																
SF†	Oct-20	(h) Stevenage	W 6-1	Farrell 2,Bell,Haydon,Townsend,Wyatt	1	2	3	4	5		10	8			11			9				6					7					
F1†	Jan-12	(h) Hitchin Town	W 4-2	Lindsay, Childs, Townsend, Wyatt	1	2		8	5	4				10			3		11			6					7		9			
F2†	Mar-16	(a) Hitchin Town	W 3-1	Bremer 2, McKenzie	1	3			5	2						8			7	4		6							9	10		11
		†Held over from 1963-64 season																														

1965-66

Rd	Date	Opponent	Result	Scorers	Goymer B	Doyle M	Sedgeley G	Richards D	Ashworth J	Dillsworth E	Allen B	Cooley J	Childs B	Lindsay H	Bremer B	Townsend C	McKendry L	McKenzie E	Smith J	Searle K	Wortley J	Lavender R	Smith R	Paisley A	Hogg P	Stanley M	Hughes M	Pearce S	Rapley C	Sidey D	Morris P	Goldsby B	Kinsey F	Snelling P
Isthmian League - 6th																																		
	Aug-21	(a) Maidstone U	W 2-1	Lindsay, Cooley	1	2	3	4	5	6	7	8	9	10	11																			
	Aug-26	(h) Enfield	L 1-3	Lindsay	1	2	3	4	5	6	7	8	9	10	11																			
	Aug-28	(h) Barking	D 0-0		1	2	3	4	5	6	7	8	9	10	11																			
	Sep-01	(a) Kingstonian	W 4-1	Lindsay, Cooley, Childs, Townsend	1	2	3		5		7	8	9	10	11	4	6																	
	Sep-09	(h) Dulwich Hamlet	W 4-0	Dillsworth 2, Bremer, Allen	1	2	3		5	9	7	8		10	11	4	6																	
	Sep-11	(h) Clapton	W 6-1	Childs 3, Cooley 3	1	2			5	3	7	8	9	10	11	4	6																	
	Sep-21	(a) Hitchin Town	W 2-1	Childs, Cooley(Bremer per ho)??	1	2		4	5	3	7	8	9		10		6	11																
	Sep-25	(h) Ilford	W 3-1	Childs 2, McKenzie	1	2		4	5	3	7	8	9		10		6	11																
	Sep-29	(a) Wycombe W	L 1-2	Lindsay	1			2	5	3	10	9		8	11	4	6	7																
	Oct-05	(h) Oxford C	D 1-1	Cooley		2	3	4	5	9	7	8		10	11		6						1											
	Oct-09	(a) Walthamstow Ave	D 1-1	Dillsworth		2	3	4	5	9	7	8			11	10	6						1											
	Oct-19	(a) St Albans C	L 0-1		1		3	2	5	8	7		9	10	11	4	6																	
	Oct-23	(a) Sutton U	W 2-1	Childs, Allen	1		3		5	8	7		9	10	11	4	6		2															
	Oct-30	(h) Kingstonian	L 0-2		1	2			5	8			9	10	11	4	6		3	7														
	Nov-02	(h) Walthamstow Ave	L 1-3	Townsend		2			5	8			9		7	4	6		3		11		1				10							
	Nov-06	(a) Tooting & Mitcham United	L 0-2			2			5	3		8	9	10		4	6				11		1					7						
	Nov-23	(h) Leytonstone	L 1-3	Childs(Cooley or og - per ho)	1	2	3		5	4	10	8	9		7		6				11													
	Dec-11	(h) Corinthian C	W 3-2	Lindsay 2 (1 pen), Wortley	1	2	3		5	6	7	8	9	10		4					11													
	Dec-18	(a) Enfield	L 2-5	Lindsay, Cooley	1	2	3		5	6	7	8	9	10		4					11													
	Dec-25	(a) Hendon	L 2-5	Childs 2	1	2	3		5	6	7	8	9	10		4					11													
	Jan-25	(a) Corinthian C	W 3-1	Lindsay, Townsend 2	1	4	3		5	6	7			10		8				9	11	2												
	Jan-29	(h) Hendon	L 2-3	Childs, Allen	1	2	3		5	6	7		9	10		4				8	11													
	Feb-19	(h) Maidstone U	W 3-1	Lindsay, Childs, Ashworth	1	2	3		5	6	7	8	9	10	11	4																		
	Feb-28	(a) Leytonstone	W 4-1	Childs, Bremer 3	1	4	3		5	6	7	8	9		10						11	2												
	Mar-08	(a) Barking	W 5-3	Searle 3, Bremer, Dillsworth		2			5	8	7				10					9	11	3					4		6					1
	Mar-21	(h) Wycombe W	D 1-1	Bremer		4	3		5	6		8			10					9	11	2		1				7						
	Mar-28	(h) Hitchin Town	W 6-1	Lindsay 3 (1 pen),Cooley,Bremer,Allen		2	3		5	6	7	9		8	10	4					11			1										
	Mar-31	(a) Oxford C	W 3-1	Lindsay 2, Allen		2	3		5	6	7	9		10	8	4					11			1										
	Apr-02	(a) Bromley	W 3-2	Childs 2, Wortley		2	3		5	6	7	9	8	10		4					11			1										
	Apr-08	(h) St Albans C	L 0-3		1	2	3		5	6	7	9	8	10	11	4																		
	Apr-09	(a) Woking	W 5-2	Lindsay, Cooley 3, Wortley(Childs?? -ho)	1	2	3		5	6	4	9	8	10	7						11													
	Apr-25	(h) Tooting & Mitcham United	W 2-1	Searle 2	1		3		5		7	9			8	4				10	11	2							6					
	Apr-28	(a) Clapton	D 1-1	Searle	1				5	3	7	9		10	11	4				8		2							6					
	Apr-30	(a) Dulwich Hamlet	W 3-0	Bremer, Wortley, og	1	2	3		5		4	9	8	6	7					10	11													
	May-03	(h) Sutton U	W 4-0	Cooley 3, Allen	1	2			5		4	9	8	6	7					10	11						3							
	May-07	(h) Bromley	W 5-2	Lindsay (pen), Cooley 3, Townsend	1	2	3		5		6	9	8	10	7	4					11													
	May-10	(a) Ilford	D 2-2	Bremer, Townsend	1	2	3		5	6	7				10	4				9	11						8							
	May-12	(h) Woking	L 2-3	Searle 2		2	3		5	6		9		10	8	4				7	11			1										
FA Cup																																		
1Q	Sep-04	(a) Hertford Town	W 2-1	Cooley, Allen	1	2	3		5		7	8	9	10		4	6													11				
2Q	Sep-18	(h) Harlow Town	W 5-1	Bremer 2, Childs 2, Cooley	1	2			5	3	7	8	9	10	11	4	6																	
3Q	Oct-02	(h) Stevenage T	W 6-5	Lindsay 4 (2 pens), Cooley, Dillsworth		2		3	5	9	7	8		10	11	4	6						1											
4Q	Oct-16	(h) Oxford C	W 2-0	Cooley, Allen			3	2	5	9	7	8		10	11	4	6						1											
1	Nov-13	(a) Millwall	L 1-3	Cooley	1		3		5	6	7	8	9	10	11	4	2																	
FA Amateur Cup																																		
1	Jan-01	(h) Hitchin Town	W 4-1	Lindsay 2 (2 pens), Cooley, Bremer	1		3		5	6	7	8	9	10	11	4						2												
2	Jan-22	(h) Tow Law T	W 2-1	Lindsay, Wortley	1	2	3		5	6	7	8	9	10		4					11													
3	Feb-12	(a) Barking	W 3-1	Childs 2, Townsend	1	2	3		5	6	7	8	9	10		4					11													
4	Mar-05	(h) Leatherhead	W 2-1	Cooley, Townsend		2	3		5	6	7	8	9	10	11	4								1										
SF	Mar-19	(a) Alvechurch *	W 1-0	Allen		2	3		5	6	7	8	9	10	11	4								1										
F	Apr-16	(a) Hendon **	W 3-1	Childs 2, Bremer	1	2	3		5	6	7	9	8	10	11	4																		
		* played at Chelsea FC																																
		** played at Wembley																																
London Senior Cup																																		
1	Nov-20	(h) Corinthian C	W 2-0	Wortley 2	1	2	3		5	4	10	8	9		7		6				11													
2	Jan-08	(a) Ford U	W 4-0	Lindsay (pen), Cooley 3	1		3		5	6	7	8	9	10		4					11	2												
3	Feb-05	(a) Hendon	D 2-2	Lindsay, Wortley	1	2	3		5	6	7	8	9	10		4					11													
3r	Mar-12	(h) Hendon	W 2-1	Lindsay (pen), Cooley		2			5	6	7	8	9	10	11	4						3		1										
SF	Mar-26	(a) Leytonstone	L 0-2			2	3		5	6		8		10	11	4					7			1	9									
London Charity Cup																																		
1	Oct-26	(a) Finchley	D 3-3	Lindsay, Childs, Ashworth					5	8			9	10			4	11	3	7			1			2	6							
Middlesex Senior Cup																																		
1	Nov-27	(h) Hampton	W 6-1	Childs 3,Dillsworth,Townsend,Ashworth	1	2	3		5	10	7	8	9			4	6				11													
2	Jan-15	(h) Wingate	W 3-0	Lindsay, Wortley 2	1		3		5	6	7	8		10		4				9	11	2												
SF	Apr-23	(a) Hendon	D 2-2	Lindsay, Bremer	1		3		5	6	7	9		10	8	4					11	2												
SFr	May-05	(a) Hendon	W 4-2	Lindsay,Bremer,Childs,Townsend(pen)	1	2	3		5	6	7	9	8	10	11	4																		
F	May-14	(h) Enfield	L 0-2		1	2	3		5	6	7	9	8	10		4					11													
F	May-24	(a) Enfield	L 1-2	Cooley	1	2	3			6	7	9	8		11	4				10						5								
East Anglian Cup																																		
Pr	Sep-27	(h) Letchworth T	L 0-4															11	3	9		2	1				6	7		8	4	5	10	

1966-67

Rd	Date	Opponent	Result	Scorers	Goymer B	Doyle M	Townsend C	Riddy G	Stanley M	Allen B	Dillsworth E	Lindsay H	Drake R	Childs B	Searle K	McKurk K	Jones A	Bremer B	Lavender R	Garman M	Leonard D	Blyth M	Paisley A	Fulks K	Wilkinson C	Lambert D	Peel A	Warman B	Harper J	Anderson P	Shallet C	McCoy F	Harper R	Quick T	Praede M	Howard M	Smith J	Cronshaw A
Isthmian League - 7th																																						
	Aug-20	(h) Corinthian C	D 2-2	Lindsay, Drake	1	2	3	**4**		6	7	8	9	10	11	12	5																					
	Aug-23	(a) Enfield	L 0-2		1	2	4		5	7	6	8	9	10			3	11																				
	Aug-27	(a) Clapton	L 1-2	Childs	1	2	4		5		6	8	9	10				11	3	7																		
	Aug-29	(h) Hitchin Town	W 7-0	Lindsay 3,Childs 2(1 pen),Bremer,Stanley	1	2	4		5	7	**6**	8	9	10				11	3	12																		
	Sep-06	(h) Tooting & Mitcham United	D 2-2	Lindsay 2	1	2	4	5	3	7	6	10	9		8			11																				
	Sep-10	(h) Kingstonian	L 0-1		1	2	**4**	5	3	7	6	10	9		8			11			12																	
	Sep-17	(a) Leytonstone	L 0-4		1	2	4	**5**	6	7	10	11	8	9						12	3																	
	Sep-24	(h) Barking	W 4-3	Searle 2, Bremer, Childs	1	2			5	10	6		7	9	8			11		4	3																	
	Oct-01	(a) Dulwich Hamlet	W 3-2	Searle 2, Bremer		2		5			6		7	9	8			11		4	3		1	10														
	Oct-06	(a) St Albans C	L 0-2				4	5	2	10	6		7	9	8			12			3		1	11														
	Oct-08	(a) Maidstone U	W 3-2	Searle, Townsend, Wilkinson			4		2	7	6			9	8			11			3		1	10	5													
	Oct-11	(h) Oxford C	D 1-1	Searle		2	4			12	6		7	9	8			11			3		**1**	10	5													
	Oct-15	(h) Walthamstow Ave	L 0-1			2	4			10	6		7	9	8			11			3		1		5													
	Oct-17	(h) Clapton	W 4-0	Townsend 2, Bremer, Childs (pen)		2	4			10	6		7	9	8			11			3		1		5													
	Oct-22	(a) Woking	D 1-1	Searle		2	4			10	6			9	8			7			3		1	11	5													
	Oct-29	(h) Leytonstone	D 0-0		1	2	4			10	6		7	9	8						3			11	5													
	Oct-31	(h) Ilford	W 3-0	Bremer 2, Fulkes		2	4		5	10	6			9	8			7			3		1	11														
	Nov-05	(a) Sutton U	L 2-3	Searle 2		2	4		5	10	6		8		9			7			3		1	11														
	Nov-08	(a) Wycombe W	W 5-2	Searle 3, Bremer, Childs	1		4		5	10	6			9	8			7			3			11		2												
	Dec-28	(a) Hendon	L 1-2	OG		2	4				6	10	7	9	8			11			5	1						3										
	Dec-31	(a) Hitchin Town	W 2-0	Lindsay 2		2	4			8	6	10	7	9				11			3	1						5										
	Jan-31	(h) Enfield	L 2-6	Childs 2 (1 pen)		2	4				6	10		9				7			3	1		**11**				5	8			12						
	Feb-04	(h) Bromley	W 2-1	Childs (pen), J Harper		2	4			6	3	10	7	9	8							1						5	11									
	Feb-14	(h) Sutton U	L 0-3			2	4			8	6	10	7		9			11			5	1				3												
	Feb-18	(a) Corinthian C	W 2-1	Searle, Childs		2	4				6	10		9	8			11			3	1						5		7								
	Feb-25	(a) Barking	W 4-2	Searle, Lindsay, Bremer, Childs (pen)			4				6	10		9	8			11				1			5	2		3		7								
	Feb-28	(h) Hendon	D 2-2	Childs (pen), OG			4				6	10		9	8			11				1			5	2		3		7								
	Mar-11	(h) Woking	L 1-2	Searle		**2**						10		7	8			11			3	1			5			4		12	6	9						
	Mar-21	(a) Oxford C	L 2-4	Searle 2			4			6					9			11			3	1						5		7	2	10	8					
	Mar-25	(h) St Albans C	L 1-6	Lindsay		2	4			8	6	10			9						3	1								7	5	11						
	Mar-27	(a) Tooting & Mitcham United	L 0-7			2	4				6	10		8	**9**			11			3	1		12				5		7								
	Mar-30	(a) Walthamstow Ave	L 0-1			2					6	10									3			11						7	4		8	5	9			1
	Apr-01	(h) Maidstone U	D 1-1	Praede		2	4				6	10						11				1						3		7			8	5	9			
	Apr-05	(a) Kingstonian	L 1-2	Lindsay		2	4				6	10		9				11			3	1						8		7				5				
	Apr-08	(a) Ilford	D 1-1	Searle			4				6	10		9	8			11			3	1						2		7				5				
	Apr-15	(h) Wycombe W	W 7-0	Dillsworth 4, Lindsay, Childs 2		2	4				12	**10**		9	7			11			3	1						6					8	5				
	Apr-29	(h) Dulwich Hamlet	W 4-0	Searle,Bremer,Warman 2 (2 pens)		2	8								9			11			3	1						6		7	4		10	5				
	May-06	(a) Bromley	L 1-2	Lindsay		2	4			8	10				9			11			3	1						6		7				5				
FA Cup																																						
1	Nov-26	(h) Nuneaton	L 0-2			2	4		5	12	6	10	7	9	8			11			3	1																
FA Amateur Cup																																						
1	Jan-14	(h) Stowmarket	D 1-1	Lindsay		2	4				6	10	7	9	8			11			3	1						5										
1r1	Jan-21	(a) Stowmarket	D 1-1 aet	Searle		2	4			6		7	8	10	9			11			5	1						3										
1r2	Jan-24	(a) Stowmarket	W 5-2 aet	Searle, Bremer 2, Childs 2		2	4			6		7	8	10	9			11			5	1						3										
2	Jan-28	(a) Brook S	W 3-0	Searle 2, Childs		**2**	4			6		10	7	9	8			11			3	1						5	12									
3	Feb-11	(a) Skelmersdale	L 0-1			2	4			6		10	7	9	8			11			3	1						5										
London Senior Cup																																						
1	Nov-19	(h) Corinthian C	D 0-0			2				4	3	6	7	9	8			10			5	1		11														
1r	Dec-17	(a) Corinthian C	W 2-0	Searle, Fulkes		2	4				6		7	9	8			10			3	1		11	5													
2	Jan-07	(a) Carshalton	W 3-1	Lindsay 2, Searle		2	4			8	6	10	7		9			11			3	1						5										
3	Mar-04	(h) Kingstonian	D 1-1	og		2	4			7	6	10		9	8			11				1			5			3										
3r	Mar-18	(a) Kingstonian	L 1-3	Bremer			5			6	4	10		9	7			11			3	1						2				8						
London Challenge Cup																																						
Pr	Sep-19	(h) Walthamstow Ave	W 2-0	Lindsay, Searle	1	2	4		5	11	6	10	7	9	8						3																	
1	Oct-03	(h) Arsenal	L 1-4	Childs		2	4		5	10	6		7	9	8			11			3	1																
Middlesex Senior Cup																																						
1	Nov-12	(h) Hampton	L 1-4	Fulkes	1	2	4			10	6			9	8			7			3			11	5													
East Anglian Cup																																						
1	Sep-28	(a) Hemel H	W 3-0	Childs 2. Fulkes		2		5		10	6			9	8					4	3	1		11			7											
2	Oct-27	(h) Stevenage T	W 1-0	Searle	1	2			6	10	4		7	9	8						3			11	5													
3	Mar-07	(a) Hitchin Town	W 1-0	Childs (pen)		2				6		10		7				8				1		11	5			3			4	9						
4	Mar-13	(h) Hertford Town	D 1-1	Childs (pen)			5			6	4	10		9	7			11			3	1									2	8						
4r	Apr-03	(a) Hertford Town	W 3-0	Lindsay, Bremer, Howard		2	4					10						11			3	1						6	8	7				5		9		
SF	Apr-24	(h) Dagenham	W 4-1	Searle, Bremer 2, Dillsworth		2	4				10				8			11			3	1						6		7		**9**		5			12	
F	May-11	(a) Kings Lynn	L 2-3	Searle, Bremer		2	4				10				8			11			3	1						6		7		9		5				
Hitchin Centenary Cup																																						
SF	Sep-13	(h) Stevenage T	W 1-0	Drake	1	2	4	5	6	7	8	10	9					11			3																	
F1	Dec-13	(h) Hillingdon B	L 2-3	Childs 2		2	4				6	10	7	9	8			11			3	1						5										
F2	Apr-10	(a) Hillingdon B	L 1-2	Bremer		2	4				6	10			8			11				1						3		7				5		9		
Alaway Memorial Trophy																																						
	Nov-14	(h) Middlesex W	W 3-2	Lindsay 2, Searle		2	4				6	10	7	9	8			11			3	1						5										

1967-68

Rd	Date	Opponent	Result	Scorers	Blythe M	Warman B	Leonard D	Townsend C	McGuiness T	Slade T	Lindsay H	Montague D	Swain D	Smart D	Bremer B	Thomas T	Desmond D	Hutchinson J	McCormack J	Williams A	McCoy F	Greenhalgh G	Williams R	Jones D	Praede M	Pettitt D	Day R	Gill B	Clary M	Harper R	Somers K	Phillips A	Rapley C	McKenzie E	Quick T
Isthmian League - 7th																																			
	Aug-19	(a) Kingstonian	W 3-0	Swain 2, Smart	1	2	3	4	5	6	7	8	9	10	11																				
	Aug-22	(h) Leytonstone	L 1-2	Smart	1	6	3	4	5	8	7		9	10	11	2																			
	Aug-26	(h) Barking	W 4-2	Swain, Smart, Bremer, Townsend	1	2	3	8	5	6	7	4	9	10	11																				
	Aug-29	(a) Enfield	L 1-3	Swain	1	8	3	4	5		7		9	10	6	2					11														
	Sep-05	(h) Oxford C	W 1-0	Townsend	1	2	3	4	5	6			9	7	10		8	11																	
	Sep-09	(h) Dulwich Hamlet	W 3-1	Swain, Lindsay, Bremer	1	2	3	4	5	6	7		9	12	10		8	11																	
	Sep-12	(a) St Albans C	W 1-0	Smart	1	2	3	4	5	6	10		9	7		12		11	8																
	Sep-23	(a) Bromley	D 1-1	Slade	1	2	3		5	6		4	9	7	10			11	8																
	Sep-26	(h) Hitchin Town	W 4-0	Swain, Lindsay, McCormack,Montague (pen)	1	2	3	4	5	10	7	6	9		11				8																
	Sep-30	(h) Wycombe W	W 2-0	Lindsay, Bremer	1	2	3	4	5	10	7	6	9		11				8																
	Oct-02	(h) Woking	D 1-1	Lindsay		2	3	4	5	10	7	6	9		11				8	1															
	Oct-07	(a) Maidstone U	W 6-0	Swain 2,Lindsay,Bremer 2,McCormack (pen)		2	3	4	5	10	7	6	9	12	11				8	1															
	Oct-10	(a) Corinthian C	D 2-2	Bremer, McCormack (pen)		2	3	4	5	6	7	10	9		11				8	1															
	Oct-14	(h) Clapton	W 5-1	Swain 2, Lindsay, Leonard, McCormack		2	3	4	5	10	11	6	9		7				8	1															
	Oct-17	(a) Sutton U	D 2-2	Bremer, McCormack		2	3	4	5	10		6	9	11	7				8	1															
	Oct-21	(a) Ilford	W 2-0	Swain 2		2	3		5	4	11	6	9	7	10				8	1															
	Oct-28	(h) St Albans C	D 1-1	Swain		2		4	5	6	11	3	9	7	10				8	1															
	Nov-11	(h) Maidstone U	W 7-1	Lindsay 3, Bremer, Slade 2, Townsend		2	3	4	5	6	11	10	9		7				8	1															
	Nov-25	(a) Hitchin Town	D 2-2	Bremer, McCormack		2	3	4	5	6	11	10	9	12	7				8	1															
	Dec-21	(a) Woking	L 0-3			6	3	4	12	5	9			10				11		1						2		7		8					
	Dec-25	(a) Hendon	L 1-3	Slade		6	3	4	5	10	11		9	7	8					1						2									
	Dec-30	(h) Hendon	D 1-1	Swain		3	6	4	5	10	8		9		7		12	11		1						2									
	Jan-06	(h) Tooting & Mitcham United	W 4-1	Lindsay 2, Bremer, Slade			3	4	5	6	11	10	9		7				8	1						2									
	Jan-20	(a) Tooting & Mitcham United	L 0-1			2	3	4	5	6	11	10	9		7				8	1						12									
	Mar-05	(a) Barking	W 3-2	Swain, Bremer, Somers	1	2	3		5			6	9		7			11	8												10	4			
	Mar-09	(h) Ilford	W 2-0	Lindsay 2,		2	3	4	5		11	10			7				8	1						6					9				
	Mar-19	(a) Oxford C	D 1-1	Lindsay				4	5	3	11		9					10	7	1						2					8	6			
	Mar-23	(h) Kingstonian	W 5-0	Lindsay 2, Bremer, Hutchinson, Montague (pen)					5	3	10	4	9		7			11	8	1						2						6			
	Mar-26	(a) Clapton	L 1-4	Montague					5	3	10	6	9		7				8	1						2			11			4			
	Mar-30	(a) Walthamstow Ave	W 3-0	Bremer, Clary 2		3		4	5		8	6	9		7			11		1			2						10						
	Apr-02	(h) Enfield	L 0-2						5	4	10	6	9		7			11		1			2						8			3			
	Apr-06	(h) Walthamstow Ave	L 1-2	Slade			3		5	10	11	6	8		7					1						2					9	4			
	Apr-09	(h) Sutton U	L 0-2			3			5	7	10	6	9		8			11		1										4	12	2			
	Apr-13	(a) Dulwich Hamlet	L 0-1			3		4	5		10	6	9		7			11		1									8			2			
	Apr-27	(h) Bromley	W 3-1	Lindsay 2, Hutchinson			3	4	5		10	6			7			11		1										8	9	2			
	May-04	(a) Wycombe W	W 3-1	Bremer 3		3		4	5		10	6	9		7			11		1										8		2			
	May-14	(a) Leytonstone	L 0-1				3	4	5	8	11		9		7					1			6			2					10				
	May-16	(h) Corinthian C	W 3-0	Bremer, Townsend, McCormack	1		3	7					9		11				10				4			2					8	5	6		
FA Cup																																			
Pr	Sep-02	(a) Wembley	L 0-2		1	6	3	4	5				9	10	11	2	8				7														
FA Amateur Cup																																			
1	Jan-13	(a) Torpoint A	W 4-2	Swain 2, Bremer, McCormack			3	4	5	6	11	10	9		7				8	1						2									
2	Feb-03	(h) Kingstonian	W 2-0	Bremer, McCormack		3	4		5	6	11	10	9		7				8	1						2									
3	Feb-10	(a) Eastwood T	D 1-1	Swain		2	3	4	5	6	11	10	9		7				8	1															
3r	Feb-17	(h) Eastwood T	W 4-1	Swain, Lindsay, Somers, Townsend		2	3	4	5	6	11	10	9		7								1								8				
4	Feb-24	(h) Barking	W 3-1	Swain, Lindsay, Somers		2	3	4	5	6	11	10	9		7								1								8				
SF	Mar-16	(a) Chesham *	L 0-2			2	3	4	5	6	11	10	9		7				12				1								8				
		* played at Fulham FC																																	
London Senior Cup																																			
1	Dec-02	(h) Hampton	W 4-0	Lindsay, Bremer, Townsend, og		2	3	4	5	6	8	10	9		7			11		1															
2	Jan-27	(h) Dagenham	D 0-0				3	4	5	6	11	10	9		7			12	8	1						2									
2r	Feb-12	(a) Dagenham	L 1-4	Montague (pen)		3	4		5	6	11	10			7			8	9	1						2							12		
Middlesex Senior Cup																																			
1	Nov-18	(h) Hounslow T	W 3-1	Lindsay 2, Smart		2	3		5	4	11	6	9	7	10				8	1															
2	Dec-16	(h) Staines Town	W 3-1	Swain, Lindsay, Bremer			3	4	5	6	11	10	9	12	7				8	1						2									
SF	Mar-02	(h) Hendon	W 1-0	Bremer	1	2	3	4	5	6		10	9		7				11												8				
F1	Apr-15	(h) Hayes	W 2-1	Townsend 2			3	4	5		10	6	9		7			11		1									8			2			
F2	May-11	(a) Hayes	W 1-0	Somers	1		3	4	5	10		6	9		11								2							7	8				
Middlesex Charity Cup																																			
1	Oct-30	(h) Uxbridge	W 5-1	Swain,Lindsay,Townsend,McCormack 2 (1 pen)		2	3	4	5	10	11	6	9		7				8	1															
SF	May-19	(h) Hayes	D 0-0 aet				3	4	5		11	6	9		7				10	1											8	2			
SF	May-21	(a) Hayes	W 3-0 aet	Swain, Leonard, McCormack			3	8	5	10		6	9		7			11	12	1			2									4			
F	May-25	(h) Wembley	D 2-2 aet	Swain, Williams			3	8	5	10		6	9		7				11	1			2								12	4			
East Anglian Cup																																			
2	Oct-24	(h) Edgware T	D 1-1	Lindsay	1	2			5		10	6		7				11	8			3	4	9	12										
2r	Nov-07	(h) Edgware T	W 5-0	Swain, Lindsay, Bremer, Slade, McCormack		2	3		5	4	11	6	9	7	10				8	1															
3	Nov-21	(h) Letchworth T	W 4-1	Swain, Lindsay 3	1	2	3	4	5	6	11	10	9		7				8																
F†	Jan-15	(a) Stevenage T	L 0-7		1									8		2		11				3	4	7						10			6	9	5
		†Area Final																																	
Presidents Cup																																			
	Nov-29	(a) Wembley	D 2-2	Smart, Harper			3	4				6	9	7	10			11		1						2	5	7		8					
	Dec-19	(h) Wembley	L 1-4	og		2	3	4	5	6			9		10			11		1						12			7	8					

1968-69

Rd	Date	Opponent	Result	Scorers	Williams A	Perrett G	Leonard D	Townsend C	McGuinness A	Bromley D	Searle K	Lindsay H	Swain D	Montague D	Bremer B	Hutchinson I	Bullock D	Doyle M	Franks C	Carter S	Blythe M	Smith T	Davis A	Hand G	Lavin J	McCoy F	Barnard M	Rapley C	Fowler W	Gerrard K	Whitlock P	Ritchie J	Evans V	Murphy M	Underwood D	Steele T
Isthmian League - 5th																																				
	Aug-10	(h) St Albans C	W 3-2	Lindsay, Bremer, Hutchinson	1	2	3	4	5	6	7	8	9	10	11	12																				
	Aug-17	(a) Sutton U	W 2-0	Swain, Hutchinson	1	2	3	4	5	6	7	8	9		11	12		10																		
	Aug-20	(a) Kingstonian	D 0-0		1	2	3	4	5		7	8	9			12	6	10	11																	
	Aug-24	(h) Walthamstow Ave	L 0-4		1	2	3	4		5	7	8	9			12	6	10	11																	
	Aug-27	(a) Oxford C	D 2-2	Swain, Searle	1	11	3	4	6	5	7	8	9	10		12		2																		
	Aug-31	(a) Ilford	D 1-1	Bromley	1	11	3	4	5	6	7		9	10		8		2																		
	Sep-07	(h) Bromley	W 6-1	Searle,Montague 2 (1 pen),Doyle,Carter,McGuiness			3	10	5	4	9	8		7			6	2		11	1	12														
	Sep-11	(h) Kingstonian	W 3-2	Lindsay, Bromley, Montague (pen)	1		3	10	5	4	9	8		7			6	2		11																
	Sep-14	(a) Enfield	L 0-4		1		3	10	5		9	8		4		7		2	6				11													
	Sep-17	(h) Oxford C	W 4-1	Lindsay, Searle, Carter 2	1		3		5		9	8		4		11		2	6	10		7														
	Sep-28	(a) Corinthian C	W 5-0	Swain 2, Lindsay 2, Hutchinson	1		3		5	4	7	8	9			11		2	6			10														
	Oct-01	(h) Wycombe W	W 2-0	Lindsay, Hutchinson	1		3		5	4	7	8	9			11	10	2	6																	
	Oct-08	(h) Woking	W 2-1	Hutchinson, Smith	1		3	4	5		12	8	9			11		2	6	7		10														
	Oct-12	(a) Dulwich Hamlet	L 1-2	Searle	1		3	9	5	4	7	8				11	10	2	6																	
	Oct-15	(h) Corinthian C	W 4-1	Swain, Searle, Hutchinson, Bullock	1	2			5	4	7		9			11	8					10						6					12			
	Oct-22	(a) Hitchin Town	D 0-0		1	2	3	6	5	4	10	8	9		7	11																				
	Oct-26	(h) Tooting & Mitcham United	D 1-1	Lindsay	1		3	4	5		9	8	7			11	6	2	10			12														
	Nov-09	(a) Barking	W 2-0	Searle, Hutchinson	1		3	4	5		9	12	7		10	11		2	6						8											
	Nov-23	(h) Enfield	L 1-3	Lindsay	1		3	4	5		9	8		10	7	11		2	6			12														
	Dec-07	(a) Wycombe W	W 1-0	Franks	1		3	8	5	4			9	10	7	11		2	6																	
	Dec-25	(h) Hendon	L 1-2	Swain	1				6	5	10	8	9	4	7	12		2	11					3												
	Feb-17	(h) Hitchin Town	D 1-1	Lavin	1		3	6	5		10	8	9	4		11		2							7											
	Feb-25	(a) Leytonstone	W 3-1	Swain, Searle 2	1		3	2	5	6	10	8	9	4	7	11																				
	Mar-04	(h) Sutton U	D 2-2	Bromley 2	1		3	2	5	4	10	8	9	6		11									7											
	Mar-08	(h) Ilford	W 1-0	Searle	1	2		12	5	4	9	8		6		11			10					3		7										
	Mar-11	(a) Hendon	D 2-2	Searle, Montague	1	2	3		5	6	10	8	9	4										11		7										
	Mar-20	(a) Walthamstow Ave	W 2-1	Searle, Bullock	1	2			5	4	10		9			11	7					8					3	6								
	Mar-25	(h) Dulwich Hamlet	W 1-0	Searle			3			4	10		9	6	7	11	8										2	12	1	5						
	Apr-09	(h) Leytonstone	L 1-2	Evans						5	10		9	6	8	11	4	2									3		1				7			
	Apr-11	(a) Clapton	W 3-1	Searle 3		2			5		9				7	10	4		6			8					3				1	11	12			
	Apr-17	(a) St Albans C	D 1-1	McGuiness	1				5		10		9	6	7	11	4	2				8					3					12				
	Apr-19	(a) Bromley	W 4-0	Hutchinson 2, Ritchie, Montague (pen)	1				5		10		9	6	7	11	4					2					3					8				
	Apr-22	(h) Barking	D 0-0		1				5		10		9	6	7	11	4					2					3					8				
	Apr-26	(h) Maidstone U	D 1-1	Searle	1				5		10	8	9	6		11	4	2				7					3									
	Apr-30	(a) Woking	W 3-2	Lindsay, Searle 2	1				5		10	8	9	6	7		4	2				3										11				
	May-03	(a) Maidstone U	W 2-0	Swain, Ritchie	1		3		4		9		12	7		10	5	2						6								11			8	
	May-05	(h) Clapton	W 4-3	Searle 2, Bremer, Ritchie	1		3				10	8	9	6	7		5	2				4										11				
	May-10	(a) Tooting & Mitcham United	L 1-4	McGuiness	1		3		5		10		9	4	7			2				8		6								11			12	
FA Cup																																				
1Q	Sep-21	(h) Dunstable T	W 3-2	Swain, Searle, Hutchinson	1		3		5	4	7	8	9	10		12		2	6	11																
2Q	Oct-05	(h) Banbury U	W 3-1	Swain 2, Searle	1		3	10	5	4	7	8	9			11		2	6																	
3Q	Oct-19	(h) Aylesbury U	W 2-1	Lindsay, Hutchinson	1		3		5	4	7	8	9			11	10	2	6																	
4Q	Nov-02	(a) Slough T	D 1-1	Searle	1		3	6	5	4	9	8	7		10			2							11											
4Qr	Nov-06	(h) Slough T	W 2-0	Searle, og	1		3	6	5	4	9	8	7		10	12		2							11											
1	Nov-16	(h) St Albans C	D 1-1	Lindsay (pen)	1		3	6	5		9	8	7		10	11		2	4																	
1r	Nov-19	(a) St Albans C	L 0-1		1		3	6	5		9	8	7		10	11		2	4																	
FA Amateur Cup																																				
1	Dec-14	(a) Hertford Town	D 0-0		1		3	8	5	4	10		9	6	7	11		2																		
1r1	Dec-21	(h) Hertford Town	D 3-3 aet	Swain, Searle, og	1		3		5	4	8	12	9	10	7	11		2	6																	
1r2	Dec-28	(h) Hertford Town	D 1-1 aet	Lindsay (pen)	1		3	10	5		8	7	9					2	6							11								4		
1r3	Jan-01	(a*) Hertford Town	D 1-1 aet	Leonard	1		5	8	4		10	9	11	3		7		2	6																	
1r4	Jan-04	(a) Hertford Town	W 1-0	Swain	1		3	7	5	4	10	8	9			11		2	6																	
2	Jan-11	(h) Cirencester T	W 3-1	Lindsay, Hutchinson, og	1	2	3	7	5	4	10	8	9			11			6																	
3	Feb-01	(h) Hayes	W 1-0	Lindsay (pen)	1		3	5		4	10	8	9		7	11		2	6																	
4	Mar-01	(a) North Shields	L 0-1		1		3	2	5	6	10	8	9	4	7	11			12																	
		*played at Wembley FC																																		
London Senior Cup																																				
1	Nov-30	(h) Clapton	W 3-1	Swain 2, Doyle	1		3	8	5	4		12	9	10	7	11		2	6																	
2	Jan-25	(a) Kingstonian	D 1-1	Searle	1		3	5		4	10	8	9	6	7	11		2																		
2r	Feb-04	(h) Kingstonian	W 2-1	Swain, Bremer	1		3		5		10	8	9	4	7	11		2	6																	
3	Mar-15	(h) Barking	D 1-1	Montague (pen)	1	2			5	4	10	8	9	6		11								3		7										
3r1	Mar-29	(a) Barking	D 2-2 aet	Searle, Bremer							10		9	6	7	11	8	2				4					3		1	5						
3r2	Apr-05	(h) Barking	L 0-1 aet							5	10	12	9	6	7		4	2				8			11		3		1							
Middlesex Senior Cup																																				
1	Jan-18	(h) Edmonton	W 4-3	Swain, Bremer, Hutchinson, McGuiness	1				5	4	10	8	9		7	11		2	6															3		
2	Feb-15	(h) Feltham T	W 3-1	Lindsay, Bremer, Montague (pen)	1		3	9	5		10	8		4	7	11		2	6							12										
SF	Mar-22	(a) Enfield	L 1-3	Doyle	1		2		5	4	10		9	6		11	8	7									3									
Presidents Cup																																				
	May-08	(a) Wembley T	D 0-0		1		3				10		9	4	7		5	2				8		6								11			12	
	May-11	(h) Wembley T	W 2-1	Lindsay, Lavin							10	8	9		2							4		3	11				1					5	6	7

1969-70

	Date	Opponent	Result	Scorers	Williams A	Sedgley G	Leonard D	Montague D	Bullock D	Draper J	Bremer B	Lindsay H	Swain D	Searle K	Mitchell B	Thomas A	Hutchinson J	Doyle M	Moxon H	Connell J	Thompson B	Smith M	Ritchie J	Hand G	Smith T	Barnard M	Underwood D	Evans V	Williams B	Pullman F	Hay R	Szemerenyi S	Booth G	Smith Peter	Carter S	Peddie L	Jackett A	Williams G	Barrett P
Isthmian League - 13th																																							
	Aug-09	(h) Maidstone U	W 3-0	Lindsay, Bremer, og	1	2	3	4	5	6	7	8	9	10	11																								
	Aug-12	(a) Wycombe W	D 2-2	Swain, Searle		2	3	4	5	6	7	8	9	10	11	1	12																						
	Aug-16	(a) Bromley	W 6-1	Swain 2, Lindsay, Bremer,Draper,Hutchinson	1	2		4	5	6	7	8	9		11		10	3																					
	Aug-19	(h) Oxford C	D 1-1	Searle	1	2		10	5	6	7		8	9	11			3	4																				
	Aug-23	(h) Sutton U	L 0-1		1	2		10	5	6	7		11	9			12	3	4	8																			
	Aug-27	(a) Oxford C	L 1-2	Swain	1	2		10	5	6			11	9			7	3	4	8																			
	Aug-30	(a) Dulwich Hamlet	L 1-3	Searle	1	3		10	5	6			11	9	7		12	2	4	8																			
	Sep-02	(h) Tooting & Mitcham United	W 3-1	Swain 2, Hutchinson	1	3		4	10	6			11	9			7	2	5	8																			
	Sep-09	(h) Corinthian C	W 3-1	Searle, Ritchie, Hand	1	3		6					11	9				2			4	5	7	8	10														
	Sep-13	(a) Leytonstone	D 0-0		1	3		4	12	6			11	9	10		7	2	5					8															
	Sep-16	(h) Walthamstow Ave	W 2-1	Searle, Mitchell	1	3		4		6			11	9	8		7	2	5					10															
	Sep-27	(a) Hitchin Town	L 0-2		1				4	6			9		8		7	2				5		12		3	10	11											
	Sep-30	(h) St Albans C	W 2-0	Swain, Bullock	1				10		7		9		8		11	2	4			5		6		3													
	Oct-07	(h) Hitchin Town	W 2-1	Swain, Hutchinson	1			4	10		7		9		8		11	2				5		6		3													
	Oct-11	(a) Ilford	W 3-0	Swain, Hutchinson, Montague	1			8	10		7		9		12		11	2	4			5		6		3													
	Oct-21	(a) Tooting & Mitcham United	L 0-3		1			5	9	7					8		11				4		12	6		3			2	10									
	Oct-25	(h) Kingstonian	W 2-1	Bremer, Hutchinson	1				5	6	7		9		8		11		4					10		3			2		12								
	Nov-08	(a) Kingstonian	L 0-2		1			5		6	7		9		10		11	2	4					8		3													
	Nov-15	(a) Clapton	W 2-1	Doyle, Bullock (pen)	1			5	10		7		9				11	2	4			6		8		3													
	Nov-22	(h) Barking	L 0-4		1			6	10		7		9				11	2	4			5		8		3													
	Dec-20	(a) Corinthian C	W 1-0	Draper	1				9	6					12				3					8		5		11	4			2	7	10					
	Dec-25	(a) Hendon	L 1-2	Swain	1				6	7	10		9						4					8		3		11	5			2							
	Dec-27	(h) Hendon	L 0-1		1				7	6			10					4	3					8		5		11				2			9				
	Jan-03	(a) Woking	W 1-0	Bullock (pen)	1			8	7	6			10					2	3							5			4					11	9				
	Jan-24	(a) Walthamstow Ave	D 1-1	og	1			10	12	6	7		9					2	3					8		5			4							11			
	Feb-07	(h) Clapton	W 3-0	Peddie 2, og	1			6	12		7		9					2	3				10	8		5			4							11			
	Feb-10	(a) St Albans C	L 0-1		1			8	6		7		9					2	5				10	12		3			4							11			
	Feb-28	(h) Woking	W 4-3	Bremer, Peddie 2, og	1			11	6		7		9						3				10	5		2			4							8			
	Mar-17	(a) Barking	L 0-3		1			11	4	12	7		9					2	3				10	5					6							8			
	Mar-21	(h) Bromley	D 1-1	Swain	1			11	8		7		9					2	6			5		3		12			4							10			
	Mar-24	(h) Enfield	W 3-2	Swain, Peddie 2 sub=Hay.Play?	1			6		7			9					2				5	10	8		3			4							11			
	Mar-27	(a) Maidstone U	D 2-2	Peddie, Ritchie	1					10			9									5	7	3		2			4		6					11	8		
	Mar-31	(h) Ilford	D 1-1	Swain	1				8	7			9						4			5	10	3		2			6							11			
	Apr-08	(h) Leytonstone	L 0-1		1			8		7	11		9					2	6			5	10	3					4										
	Apr-10	(a) Sutton U	D 0-0		1			10	2	7									4			5	8	3		11												6	9
	Apr-14	(h) Wycombe W	D 0-0		1			8	4	7	12		9						6			5	10	3					2							11			
	Apr-18	(h) Dulwich Hamlet	D 2-2	Swain, Bullock	1				6	12	8		9									5	10	3		2			4							11	7		
	Apr-20	(a) Enfield	L 0-1		1			8	4	7			9						5			6	10	3					2							11			
FA Cup																																							
Pr	Sep-06	(h) Bletchley T	W 2-1	Searle, Montague (pen)	1	3		4	10	6			11	9				2	5				7	8															
1Q	Sep-20	(h) Aylesbury U	D 0-0		1	3		4	12	6			11	9	8		7	2	5					10															
R	Sep-25	(a*) Aylesbury U	W 3-1	Doyle, Hutchinson, Mitchell	1				4	6			9		8		7	2				5				3	10	11											
2Q	Oct-04	(h) Banbury U	W 1-0	Hand	1				10		7		9		8		11	2	4			5		6		3													
3Q	Oct-18	(h) Dunstable T	W 4-0	Swain 2, Hutchinson 2	1			5	10	6			9		7		11		4					8		3			2										
4Q	Nov-01	(h) Enfield	L 0-1		1			5	10	6	7		9		12		11	2	4					8		3													
		*played at Chesham FC																																					
FA Amateur Cup																																							
1	Dec-14	(h) Vauxhall Motors	W 3-2	Bremer, Moxon, P Smith	1				6	8	10							4	3					7		5		11	2					9					
2	Jan-10	(h) Bromley	W 3-2	Bremer 2, Bullock	1			10	8	6	7		9					2	3							5		11	4										
3	Jan-31	(h) Wycombe W	L 0-1		1			10	12	6	7		9					2	3					8		5			4							11			
London Senior Cup																																							
1	Dec-06	(a) Ilford	L 1-2	Bullock (pen)	1			6	3	10	7		9		11			2	4			5		8															
Middlesex Senior Cup																																							
1	Jan-17	(a) Kingsbury Town	W 3-1	Swain, Bremer, Bullock (pen)	1			10	8	6	7		9					2	3					12		5		11	4										
2	Feb-21	(h) Hampton	W 1-0	Bremer	1			8	6		7		9					2	3				10			5			4							11			
SF	Mar-14	(a) Finchley	W 4-0	Swain, Bremer 2, Peddie	1			11	6		7		9					2	3				10	5					4							8			
F1	May-02	(h) Enfield	W 2-0	Peddie, Ritchie	1			8	12	7	6		9						4			5	10	3					2							11			
F2	May-16	(a) Enfield	L 0-3		1			8		6	7		9						4			5	10	3					2							11			
Presidents Cup																																							
	Apr-25	(h) Wembley	L 1-2	Swain	1			8		7	4		9						6			5	10	3					2							11			
	May-05	(a) Wembley	W 2-0	Peddie, Ritchie	1			8	7		4		9									5	10	3		2			6							11			

1970-71

Rd	Date	Opponent	Result	Scorers	Swain C	Mahon T	Thompson W	Williams R	Holt P	Draper J	Worley L	Wilson J	Daffom A	McRae B	Ritchie J	Smith M	Booth G	Somers P	Barnard M	Olson G	Carter B	Shufflebotham	Bullock D	Bennett B	Johnson W	Townsend C	Thomas A	Allen P	Yerby D	Chapman J	Hand G	Pentecost A	Hazell J	Charker L	Rapley C	Bunker N	Austin G
Isthmian League - 13th																																					
	Aug-15	(a) Tooting & Mitcham United	L 0-2		1	2	3	4	5	6	7	8	9	10	11	12																					
	Aug-18	(h) Wycombe W	L 1-6	Draper	1	2	4			6	7	8	5	10	9	12	3	11																			
	Aug-22	(h) Dulwich Hamlet	W 2-1	McRae, Thompson	1	2	6	4		12	7	11		9	10				3	5	8																
	Aug-26	(a) Oxford C	L 1-2	Ritchie	1	2		6		8	7	11		9	10				3	4		5	12														
	Aug-29	(a) Bromley	L 0-1		1	2	12	8		6	7	11			10				3	5		4	9														
	Sep-01	(h) Leytonstone	L 0-1		1	2		4			11	7		9					3			5	6	8	10												
	Sep-08	(a) Sutton U	L 1-2	Booth	1	2		4				11					9		3	7		5	6	8					10								
	Sep-12	(h) Barking	L 1-3	Townsend		2		5			8	11					9			10		3	4			7	1		6	12							
	Sep-15	(h) Kingstonian	D 1-1	Worley		2		4			7	11					10		3	9		5	6			8	1		12								
	Sep-22	(h) Tooting & Mitcham United	D 2-2	Ritchie, Worley		2					7	11			9		8		3	6		5	4			10	1										
	Sep-26	(h) Ilford	W 2-0	Ritchie, Allen		2		4			7	11			9		12		3	6		5				10	1	8									
	Sep-28	(a) Wycombe W	L 1-2	Booth		2		4				11			9		8		3	6		5	7			10	1										
	Oct-03	(a) Leytonstone	D 2-2	Barnard, Wilson (pen)		2		4			7	11			9		12		3	6		5				8	1	10									
	Oct-06	(h) Oxford C	D 0-0		1	2		4			7	11			9		8		3	6		5				10			12								
	Oct-17	(h) Sutton U	L 0-2			2		4				11							3	6		5		9		8	1	10	7								
	Oct-24	(a) Maidstone U	L 0-1			2		4				7	12		11		9		3	6		5		10		8	1										
	Oct-31	(a) Corinthian C	W 4-1	Ritchie, Hazell 2, Shufflebotham		2		4				7			10				3	6		5				8	1					11	9				
	Nov-07	(h) Walthamstow Ave	W 3-2	Hazell 2, Pentecost		2		4				7			10				3	6		5				8	1					11	9				
	Nov-14	(a) Enfield	L 0-4			2		4				7			10					5		6				8	1				3	11	9	12			
	Nov-21	(h) Bromley	W 4-0	Ritchie 2, Yerby, Olson (pen)	1	2		4				11	3		9					5						7			10		6	8					
	Nov-28	(a) Dulwich Hamlet	W 1-0	Pentecost	1	2		4				7	3		9					5		12				10			11		6	8					
	Dec-12	(a) Clapton	L 0-3		1	2		4					3		9					5					7	8			11	12	6	10					
	Dec-19	(h) Enfield	W 1-0	Olson	1	6		4					2		9					5						7			11		3	10			8		
	Dec-25	(h) Hendon	D 1-1	Pentecost	1	6		4					2		9					5					12	7			11		3	10			8		
	Jan-11	(a) St Albans C	L 0-5		1	8		4					2		9				12	5					11	7					3	10			6		
	Feb-02	(a) Hitchin Town	W 1-0	Bunker																																	
	Feb-06	(a) Woking	W 2-1	Hazell, Pentecost		2		3							11					6		5				7	1			4		8	9			10	
	Feb-13	(a) Barking	L 0-2			2		3							11					5		6				4	1			7		8	9			10	
	Feb-20	(h) Hitchin Town	L 1-2	Bunker		2		3							11					5		4				7	1			12	6	8	9			10	
	Feb-27	(h) Maidstone U	W 3-2	Pentecost, Townsend, Olson (pen)		2		4							9				3	5						10	1		8		6	11				7	
	Mar-06	(a) Walthamstow Ave	L 1-4	Ritchie		2		4					3		10				12	5						7	1		6	8		11				9	
	Mar-13	(h) Clapton	D 2-2	Pentecost, Bunker				4					2		7				3	5				9		8	1					10				11	6
	Mar-20	(a) Kingstonian	W 2-1	Ritchie, Bunker		8		4					2		9				3	5				12		7	1					10				11	6
	Mar-23	(h) St Albans C	L 0-3			6		3					2		10				5					12		7	1			9		8				11	4
	Mar-27	(h) Corinthian C	D 0-0			8		4					2		9				3					12		6	1		7			10				11	5
	Apr-03	(a) Ilford	L 1-2	Ritchie		6		4					2		9				3							8	1		7			10				11	5
	Apr-13	(h) Woking	W 3-0	Ritchie 2, Pentecost	1	2		4					5		9				3							8			7			10				11	6
	Apr-20	(a) Hendon	D 1-1	og		6							2		9				3	4				12		8	1		7			10				11	5
FA Cup																																					
Pr	Sep-05	(h) Hatfield T	W 2-0	Bennett, McRae	1	2		4				11		9			7		3			5	6	8	12				10								
1Q	Sep-19	(a) Wembley T	W 2-0	Ritchie, Booth		2		4			7	11			9		10		3	6		5				8	1										
2Q	Oct-10	(a) Leighton Town	D 1-1	Williams	1	2		4				11			9		8		3	6	7	5				10			12								
R	Oct-13	(h) Leighton Town	L 0-1			2		4				7			11				3	6	12	5	9			8	1		10								
FA Amateur Cup																																					
1	Jan-09	(a) Wycombe W	L 0-1		1	8		4					2		9					5					12	7			11		3	10			6		
London Senior Cup																																					
1	Dec-05	(h) Cheshunt	W 3-2	Hand, Johnson, Olson	1	2		4					3		10					5				9	7				11		6	8					
2	Jan-23	(a) Tooting & Mitcham United	L 0-1			2		4							9					6		5					1		11	8	3	10		7			
Middlesex Senior Cup																																					
1	Jan-16	(a) Ruislip Manor	D 3-3 aet	Yerby, Shufflebothom, Olson	1	2		4					6		10					5		9			12	7			11		3	8					
R	Jan-30	(h) Ruislip Manor	L 1-3	Chapman																																	
Presidents Cup																																					
	May-04	(a) Wembley T	L 0-1			7		4					2		9					6						8	1		12		3	10				11	5
	May-07	(h) Wembley T	W 5-1	Ritchie 2, Mahon, Williams, Yerby		2		4							9				3	5						12	1		7		8	10				11	6

1971-72

Rd	Date	Opponent	Result	Scorers	Barr J	Mahon T	Bielkus D	Furie J	Gibbs D	Bailey B	Watson T	Brown M	Townend G	Cockell D	Jones C	Hale D	Cooper J	Hand G	Urquhart G	McPhee I	Swain D	Whitaker R	Knight B	Austin G	Pearce J	Presland E	Beyer J	Owen K	Latham P	Livingstone R	Dyson T	Byrne W	Brown A	Vint R
Southern League Division 1 North - 12th																																		
	Aug-24	(a) Stourbridge	L 1-4	Townend	1	2	3	4	5	6	7	8	9	10	11																		
	Sep-11	(a) Kings Lynn	L 1-2	Townend	1	2		4		5	10	8	9	12	11	7	6	3																	
	Sep-25	(h) Gloucester C	W 2-1	Hale 2	1	3		2		5	8	7	9	6	11	4	12	10																	
	Oct-02	(a) Ilkeston T	D 0-0		1	2					8	11	9	6		4		3	10	5	7													
	Oct-16	(a) Wellingborough T	L 0-3		1			3		2		7		4		6			8	5	9	11	10												
	Oct-23	(h) Cheltenham	L 2-3	Brown, Swain	1	3		2		6		7		4	10	8				5	9	11												
	Nov-06	(h) Wellingborough T	L 1-2	Swain	1	3		2		4		7	9	5	10	6					8	11												
	Nov-20	(a) Corby T	L 0-1		1	2		6		12	10	7	9			4		3			8	11			5									
	Nov-27	(h) Kettering T	W 3-2	Brown 2, Hale	1			6			8	7	10	2		4		3			9	11			5									
	Nov-30	(a) Bletchley U	W 1-0	Townend	1			4		2	8	7	10	6				3			9	11			5									
	Dec-04	(h) Stourbridge	L 0-5		1			4			8	7	10	2				3			9	11			5	6								
	Dec-11	(a) Banbury U	W 1-0	Swain	1			6		3	8	7	10	2		4					9	11			5									
	Dec-18	(h) Burton Albion	D 1-1	Hale	1			6		3	8	7	10	2		4					9	11			5									
	Dec-27	(a) Dunstable T	L 1-2	Brown	1			6		12	8	7	10	2		4					9	11			5	3								
	Jan-01	(h) Dunstable T	W 3-1	Brown 2, Swain	1			6			8	7		2		4					9	11			5		3	10						
	Jan-08	(a) Gloucester C	W 3-1	Brown, Hale, Swain	1			6			8	7		2		4					9	11			5	3		10						
	Jan-22	(a) Lockheed L	L 0-2		1			6		12		8	9	2		4						11			7	5	3	10						
	Jan-29	(h) Ilkeston T	L 1-3	Brown	1			6			8	7		2		4					9	11			5	3		10						
	Feb-12	(a) Cheltenham	L 0-4		1			6			10	7		2		4					9	11			8	3	12		5					
	Feb-19	(h) Stevenage A	D 3-3	Dyson, Livingstone,Watson	1			6			8	7		2		12						10			5	3			4	9	11			
	Feb-26	(a) Bury Town	W 1-0	Watson	1			2			6	8		4		7						10			5	3	12			9	11			
	Mar-04	(h) Bletchley U	W 2-0	Byrne, Livingstone	1			4			8	7	12	6											5	3	2			10	11	9		
	Mar-11	(h) Corby T	D 1-1	Byrne	1			10			4	8		6								11			5	3	2				7	9		
	Mar-14	(h) Barry T	W 5-1	Byrne, Dyson, Brown 3 (1 pen)	1			10			4	8	12	6								11			5	3	2				7	9		
	Mar-18	(a) Kettering T	L 0-1		1			10			4	8	7	6											5	3	2				11	9		
	Mar-21	(h) Bury Town	W 2-1	Beyer, A.Brown	1			10			4	8		6											5	3	2				11	9	7	
	Mar-25	(h) Kings Lynn	W 2-1	Byrne, Brown (pen)	1			10			6	8		4											5	3	2				11	9	7	
	Apr-01	(h) Banbury U	W 3-0	Brown 3	1			10			6	8	12			4						11			5	3	2				7	9		
	Apr-03	(a) Rugby T	L 1-3	Furie	1			10				7	8	4		6									5	3	2				11	9		12
	Apr-04	(h) Rugby T	L 0-3		1			10		6	4	8														5	3	2				11	9		7
	Apr-08	(a) Burton Albion	W 2-1	Byrne, Presland	1			6				9											11			5	3	2		4		8	10	7	12
	Apr-13	(a) Barry T	D 2-2	Livingstone, Presland	1			6					10			7						11			5	3	2		4	9			8	
	Apr-15	(h) Lockheed L	W 5-2	Brown 2, Byrne, Whitaker, og	1			7				10											11			5	3	2		4		8	9	6	
	Apr-22	(a) Stevenage A	L 1-2	Byrne	1			6				10				12						11			5	3	2		4		7	9	8	
FA Cup																																		
1Q	Sep-18	(a) Harrow Borough	W 1-0	Townend	1	2					5	10	8	9	4	11	7	3	6															
2Q	Oct-09	(a) Borehamwood	D 1-1	Brown	1	2					3	8	7	9	6	11	4				5			10										
2Qr	Oct-12	(h) Borehamwood	L 0-2		1	2		3		6	7	11	9	4		8	12			5			10										
Southern League Cup																																		
1Q	Aug-14	(h) Banbury U	W 3-1	Jones 2, Townend	1	2	3	10	5	6	7	8	9	4	11																		
2Q	Aug-17	(h) Stevenage A	L 0-1		1	2	3	10	5	6	7	8	9	4	11										12									
3Q	Aug-21	(a) Lockheed L	W 1-0	Brown	1	2	3	10	5	6	7	8	9	4	11																		
4Q	Aug-28	(a) Dunstable T	W 2-0	Brown, og	1	2	3			6	7	8	9	4	11		5	10															
5Q	Sep-04	(h) Bletchley U	W 3-1	Brown 2, Townend	1	2		4		5	10	8	9		11	7	6	3															
1	Oct-05	(a) Cambridge C	L 1-2	Swain	1	2		12		3	10	7	9	6	11	4				5	8													
1r	Oct-19	(h) Cambridge C	L 0-1		1	3		2		6		7		4	10	8				5	9	11												
London Challenge Cup																																		
1	Sep-27	(h) Arsenal	L 0-3		1	2					5	8	7	9	6	10	4		3	11														

1972-73

Rd	Date	Opponent	Result	Scorers	Barr J	Burgess E	Presland E	Cockell D	Furie J	Dyson T	Duck G	Pearce J	Brown A	Livingstone R	Whitaker R	Hale D	Brown M	Byrne W	Vafiadis S	Beyer J	Connell J	Franklin N	Haynes J	Doherty P	Gozney D	Fairclough P	Kinnear C	McMullan E	Hopkins K	McKenzie R	Watson J	Smith J	Dennis A
Southern League Division 1 North - 8th																																	
	Aug-12	(a) Bath C	L 1-3	Burgess	1	2	5	4	7	8	10	3	6	9	11																		
	Aug-15	(a) Dunstable T	W 3-0	Hale, Brown 2 (1 pen)	1	2	3	5	7	8	10	4			11	6	9			12													
	Aug-19	(h) Tonbridge	W 1-0	Brown	1	2	3	4	7	8	10	5			11	6	9																
	Aug-26	(a) Gravesend & Northfleet	L 0-2		1	2	3	4	7	8		5			11	6	10	9															
	Sep-02	(h) Bideford	W 4-0	Byrne 2, Duck, og	1	2	3	4	7	10	8	5			12	6		9	11														
	Sep-05	(h) Dunstable T	W 3-0	Byrne 2, Brown	1	2		4	7	8	11	5				6	9	10		3													
	Sep-19	(a) Maidstone U	D 3-3	Duck 2, Brown	1	2	3	4	7	8	11	5	6				9	10															
	Sep-23	(a) Bexley U	D 2-2	Duck, Hale	1	4	3	7			11	5	8			6	9	10	12	2													
	Oct-14	(a) Minehead	L 0-1		1	9	3	4	6	7	10	5	8			12			11	2													
	Nov-04	(h) Met. Police	W 4-2	Duck 2, Burgess, Dyson	1	5	3	4	7	11	9		8			6				2	10												
	Nov-14	(h) Maidstone U	L 2-3	Burgess, Franklin	1	5	3	4		8	9		7	11		6					10	2											
	Nov-18	(h) Dorchester T	L 2-3	Duck, Dyson	1	5	3	4		8	9					6				2	11	7	10										
	Nov-25	(a) Canterbury City	D 1-1	Gozney	1	3	7	6		8	10		12			4				2	9			5	11								
	Dec-02	(h) Bognor Regis T	D 1-1	Connell	1	3	7	6		8	10					4	9			2	11			5									
	Dec-05	(h) Andover	D 2-2	Brown 2	1		7	6		8	10		3			4	9	12		2	11			5									
	Dec-09	(a) Winchester C	D 1-1	Duck	1	6	3	4		7	10		8					11		2	9			5		12							
	Dec-16	(h) Trowbridge T	W 4-1	Duck 2, Byrne, Connell	1	3	12			8	10					4	9	7		2	11			5		6							
	Dec-23	(a) Bognor Regis T	W 3-0	Byrne, Connell, Duck	1	2	3			8	11		9			4		10			6			5		7							
	Dec-26	(h) Bletchley T	L 0-1		1	2	3			8	10		12				9	11		4	7			5		6							
	Dec-30	(a) Tonbridge	L 1-2	Duck	1	2	3			7	11					6	9	10			8			5		4							
	Jan-06	(h) Bexley U	W 5-1	Duck 3, Presland 2 (1 pen)	1	3	2			8	11		12			4	9	10			6			5		7							
	Jan-09	(h) Salisbury	W 4-0	Duck 3, Byrne	1	3	2			8	11					5	9	10			7			4		6							
	Jan-13	(a) Hastings U	L 0-2		1	2	3			11	10		12				7	9		6	8			5		4							
	Jan-20	(a) Bideford	L 1-4	Kinnear	1	3	5			8	10		11			4	9			2	12					6	7						
	Jan-27	(h) Ashford Town	W 3-0	Brown, Duck, Fairclough	1	2	3			7	11		8			4	9	10						5		6							
	Feb-03	(h) Crawley Town	W 4-1	Byrne,Docherty,Duck,Fairclough	1	2	3			7	11		8			4	9	10						5		6							
	Feb-06	(h) Gravesend & Northfleet	W 4-2	Duck 2, Brown, Presland (pen)	1	2	3			7	11		8				9	10						5		6	4						
	Feb-10	(a) Andover	D 1-1	Byrne	1	2	3			7	11		8				9	10						5		6	4						
	Feb-24	(h) Hastings U	D 1-1	Brown	1	2	3			8			7				9	10						5		6	4	11					
	Mar-03	(a) Salisbury	D 0-0			3				7			8				9	10		2				5	12	6	4	11	1				
	Mar-14	(a) Basingstoke T	L 0-1			8	3			7	10		9				6	11		2				5			4		1				
	Mar-17	(a) Met. Police	W 2-1	Byrne, Duck		2	3			7	11						9	10						5		8	4	6	1				
	Mar-20	(a) Crawley Town	D 2-2	Duck 2		2	3			8	11						9	10						5		6	4	7	1				
	Mar-24	(h) Basingstoke T	D 2-2	Duck 2		2	3			8	11						9	10		12				5		7	4	6	1				
	Mar-31	(h) Canterbury City	W 5-1	A.Brown 2, Byrne, Brown, og	1	2	3			8	11		6				9	10						5		7	4						
	Apr-04	(a) Ashford Town	L 0-5		1	2	3			8	11							10		9				5		6	4	7					
	Apr-07	(a) Trowbridge T	L 1-2	Duck	1	2	3			8	11		7					10		6				5			4	9					
	Apr-14	(h) Winchester C	W 1-0	Byrne		5	3			9	11		4					10		12				6	7	8	2			1			
	Apr-17	(h) Minehead	D 3-3	Dyson,Fairclough,Presland (pen)		2	3			8	11		10											5		6	4			1	7	9	
	Apr-21	(a) Dorchester T	L 1-2	Smith	1	2	12			8	11		10											5		6	4				7	9	3
	Apr-23	(a) Bletchley T	W 2-0	Kinnear, Smith			3			10			7	11						4				5		6	8			1		9	2
	Apr-24	(h) Bath C	L 1-2	Dyson			3			8			10	11						2				5		7	4			1	6	9	
FA Cup																																	
1Q	Sep-16	(h) Windsor & Eton	D 0-0		1	2	3		7	8	11	5	12			6	9	10		4													
1Qr	Sep-21	(a) Windsor & Eton	W 3-0	Brown, Duck, Byrne	1	2	3	4	7	8	11	5	6				9	10		12													
2Q	Oct-07	(a) Finchley	W 2-0	Brown 2	1	2		4	12	10	11	5	7			6	9	8		3													
3Q	Oct-21	(a) Hayes	L 1-3	Burgess	1	7	3	6		10	9	5	8		11	7			12	2													
F A Trophy																																	
Pr	Sep-09	(h) Waterlooville	W 1-0	Cockell	1	2		4	7	8	11	5				6	9	10		3													
1Q	Sep-30	(a) Andover	W 4-2	Duck 3, A.Brown	12	2	3	4		10	11	5	7			6	9	8		1													
2Q	Oct-28	(a) Winchester C	W 2-0	Duck 2	1	5	3	4	7	11	9		8	10		6				2													
3Q	Nov-11	(a) Banbury	L 1-3	Connell	1	2	3	4	7	8	10		6	11		5					9												
Southern League Cup																																	
1	Aug-22	(h) Stevenage Ath.	D 1-1	Brown	1	2	3	4	6	8	10	5			11	7	9	12															
1r	Aug-28	(a) Stevenage Ath.	L 0-3		1	2	3	4	7	8		5			11	6	10	9															
London Challenge Cup																																	
Pr	Sep-11	(a) Kingstonian	W 3-0	Duck 2, Brown	1	4			2	8	11	5	6			7	9	10		3													
1	Sep-27	(a) Millwall	D 2-2	Hale, Presland	1	2	3	4		8	11	5	9			6		10	7														
1r	Oct-09	(h) Millwall	W 3-1	A.Brown, Duck, Presland (pen)	1	4	3	6	8	11	10	5	7				9		2	12													
2	Oct-16	(h) Enfield	L 2-3	Duck 2	1	4	3	6		10	9	5	8		11	7			12	2													

1973-74

Rd	Date	Opponent	Result	Scorers	MacKenzie R	Presland E	Watson J	Kinnear C	McCormick J	Burgess E	Fairclough P	Godfrey J	Fulton R	Dyson T	Byrne W	Duck G	Henderson J	Brown A	Barnes J	Brodie C	Baker J	Bristow K
Southern League Division 1 North - 1st																						
	Aug-11	(a) Salisbury	W 2-1	Barnes, Byrne	1		2	4	5		7	8	3		9	10	11	12	6			
	Aug-18	(h) Minehead	W 2-1	Duck 2 (1 pen)	1	2	7	4	5		6		3	8	9	10	11					
	Aug-25	(a) Bexley U	W 2-0	Duck, og	1	2		4	5		7	8	3		9	10		11	6			
	Sep-08	(a) Canterbury City	L 0-3				8	4	5	2	7	6	3		9	10	11			1		
	Sep-22	(a) Ramsgate	L 2-2	Duck 2,	1		11	4	5	2	6	7	3	12	9	10		8				
	Sep-29	(h) Salisbury	W 2-1	Byrne, og	1	2	3	4	5	6	8	12		7	9		10	11				
	Oct-06	(a) Dorchester T	W 2-1	Duck, Fairclough	1	2	3	4	5	6	11			7	9	8	10					
	Oct-20	(h) Bath C	W 3-0	Duck 2, Byrne	1			4	5	2	7	6	3	8	9	11	10					
	Oct-27	(a) Bideford T	D 0-0		1	2		4	5		7	6	3	8	9	11	10	12				
	Nov-03	(h) Poole Town	W 2-0	Godfrey, Henderson	1	2		4	5		7	6	3	8	9	10	11					
	Nov-24	(h) Andover	L 1-5	Duck (pen)	1	2		4	5		6	8	3	7	9	10	11					
	Dec-08	(h) Waterlooville T	D 1-1	Duck	1	2	3	6	5	4	7			8	9	10	11					
	Dec-15	(h) Met. Police	W 3-0	Henderson, Duck 2 (1 pen)	1	2	3	6	5	4	7			8		9	11					10
	Dec-22	(a) Minehead	W 4-3	Duck 2, Byrne, Kinnear	1	2	3	6	5	4	7		8		12	10	11					9
	Dec-26	(h) Gravesend & Northfleet	W 2-1	Henderson, Kinnear	1	2	3	6	5	4			7	8	12	10	11					9
	Dec-29	(h) Hastings	W 2-1	Duck, Byrne	1	2	3	6	5	4	7		8		9	10	11					
	Jan-01	(h) Ashford Town	W 4-1	Duck 2 (1 pen),Byrne,Henderson	1	2	3	6	5	4			8	7	9	10	11					
	Jan-06	(h) Bognor Regis T	D 0-0		1	2	3	6	5	4			8	7	9	10	11					12
	Jan-19	(h) Ramsgate	L 0-1		1	2	3	6	5	4			7	8	9	10	11					12
	Jan-26	(a) Waterlooville T	D 0-0		1	2	3	6	5	4	8		7		9	10	11					
	Feb-16	(a) Hastings	D 0-0		1	2	3	7	5	8			6		9	10	11					4
	Mar-09	(h) Bideford T	W 3-1	Duck (pen), Byrne, Fairclough	1	2		3	5	4	7	8	6		9	10	11					
	Mar-17	(a) Poole Town	W 3-2	Duck, Henderson, Presland	1	3		2	5	4	7	8	6		9	10	11					
	Mar-19	(a) Crawley Town	W 3-0	Duck 2, Byrne	1	3		2	5	4	7	8	6		9	10	11					
	Mar-23	(h) Crawley Town	W 4-1	Duck 2, Byrne, Fairclough	1		3	2	5	4	7	6	8		9	10	11					
	Mar-27	(a) Basingstoke T	W 2-0	Byrne 2	1		3	2	5	4	7	6	8		9	10	11					
	Mar-30	(a) Bath C	L 0-2		1		3	2	5	4	7	6	8	12	9	10	11					
	Apr-02	(h) Canterbury City	W 3-1	Duck 2 (1 pen), Byrne	1	3		2	5	4	7	6	8		9	10	11					
	Apr-06	(a) Andover	W 3-0	Duck 2, Henderson	1		3	2	5	4		6	8	7	9	10	11					12
	Apr-09	(a) Bognor Regis T	W 2-1	Duck, Godfrey	1		3	2	5	4		6	8	7	9	10	11					
	Apr-12	(a) Ashford Town	W 1-0	Duck (pen)	1		3	2	5	4		6	8	7	9	10	11					
	Apr-13	(h) Dorchester T	W 2-0	Fulton, Henderson	1		3	2	5	4		6	8	7	9	10	11					
	Apr-15	(a) Gravesend & Northfleet	W 2-0	Byrne, Henderson	1		3	2	5	4	7	6	8		9	10	11					
	Apr-20	(h) Basingstoke T	W 2-0	Burgess, Dyson	1		3	2	5	4		6	8	7	9	10	11					
	Apr-23	(a) Met. Police	W 4-0	Duck (pen),Byrne,Fairclough,og	1		3	2	5	4	6		7	8	9	10	11					
	Apr-27	(a) Trowbridge T	D 1-1	Duck	1		3	2	5	4	8	6	7	12	9	10	11					
	Apr-30	(h) Bexley U	W 3-0	Duck 3	1		3	2		4		6	8	7	9	10	11				5	
	May-04	(h) Trowbridge T	D 3-3	Duck, Byrne, Henderson	1		3	2		4	5	6	8	7	9	10	11					
FA Cup																						
Pr	Sep-01	(h) Marlow	W 2-0	Duck, Henderson	1			4	5	2	6		3	7	9	10	11	12	8			
1Q	Sep-15	(a) Chesham U	D 1-1	Duck	1	2		4	5	6	12	7	3	11	9	10		8				
1Qr	Sep-18	(h) Chesham U	L 2-4	Duck, Dyson	1		2	4	5	6	12	7	3	11	9	10		8				
FA Trophy																						
Q1	Oct-13	(h) Hatfield T	W 4-0	Duck,Henderson,Fairclough,og	1	2	3	4	5	6	7			8		11	9	10				
Q2	Nov-10	(h) Dunstable T	W 3-0	Dyson, Fairclough, og	1	2		4	5		6	8	3	7	9	10	11					
Q3	Dec-05	(h) Boston	W 6-1	Duck 4 (2 pens), Byrne 2	1	2	3	6	5	4	7			8	9	10	11					
1	Jan-12	(a) Wimbledon	W 1-0	Presland	1	2	3	6	5	4	12		8	7	9	10	11					
2	Feb-02	(h) Hastings	W 5-2	Duck 4 (3 pens), Henderson	1	2	3	6	5	4			7		9	10	11					8
3	Feb-23	(h) South Shields	D 1-1	Henderson	1	2	3	7	5	4	12		6	10	9		11					8
3r	Mar-02	(a) South Shields	L 1-2 aet	Henderson	1		3	2	5	4	7	8	6	12	10	9	11					
Southern League Cup																						
1	Aug-21	(h) Bletchley U	W 4-1	Duck 3 (1 pen), Dyson		2		4	5		6	7	3	11	9	10	8			1		
1	Aug-28	(a) Bletchley U	W 4-1	Duck (pen),Henderson 2, Godfrey		2		4		5	6	7	3	8		10	11	9	12	1		
2	Oct-16	(h) Wimbledon	D 1-1	Duck	1		2	4	5		7	6	3	8	9	11	10	12				
2r	Nov-06	(a) Wimbledon	D 2-2 aet	Henderson, McCormick	1	2	12	4	5		6	8	3	7	9	10	11					
2r2	Nov-13	(h) Wimbledon	D 3-3 aet	Duck, Byrne, Presland	1	2	12	4	5		6	8	3	7	9	10	11					
2r3	Nov-28	(a) Wimbledon	L 0-3		1	2	3	4	5	6	7		12		9	10	11	8				
London Challenge Cup																						
	Sep-10	(h) Barnet	W 4-1	Duck 3 (1 pen), Presland	1	2		4	5	6	12	7	3	11	9	10		8				
	Sep-24	(a) Tottenham H	L 0-4			2	3	4	5		7	6		11	8	10	9			1		

1974-75

	Date	Opponent	Result	Scorers	Morton J	Kinnear C	Presland E	Burgess E	McCormick J	Evans D	Dyson T	Evans T	Byrne W	Duck G	Henderson J	Fulton R	Fairclough P	Godfrey J	Watson J	Eglite A	McKenzie R	Moss B	Kitchener W	O'Kane V
Southern League Premier Division - 8th																								
	Feb-00	(h) Weymouth	W 2-1	Duck, Henderson	1	2	3	4	5	6	7	8	9	10	11									
	Aug-20	(h) Dartford	W 4-1	Byrne 2, Fulton, Godfrey	1	2		4	5	6		8	9	10	11	7	12	3						
	Aug-24	(a) Tonbridge	L 0-1		1	2		4	5	6		8	9	10	11	7	12	3						
	Aug-31	(h) Margate	L 0-3		1			4	5	2		8	9	10	11	6	12	7	3					
	Sep-07	(a) Kettering T	W 3-2	Duck, Henderson, Godfrey	1	2		4	5	6			9	10	11		8	7	3					
	Sep-11	(a) Yeovil T	L 1-4	Godfrey	1	2		4	5	6			9	10	11		8	7	3					
	Sep-24	(h) Stourbridge	W 3-0	Duck (pen), Fulton, Godfrey	1	2		4	5	8			9	10	11	6		7	3					
	Sep-28	(h) Atherstone T	W 2-0	Duck, Watson	1	2		4	5	8			9	10	11	6		7	3					
	Oct-12	(a) Maidstone U	L 1-3	Duck	1	2		4	5	8		12	9	10	11	7		6	3					
	Oct-22	(h) Yeovil T	L 1-2	Duck	1	2		4	5	3		11	9	10	8	7		6						
	Oct-26	(h) Maidstone U	D 1-1	Byrne	1			4	5	2		8	9	10	11	3	7	6						
	Oct-29	(h) Bath C	D 0-0		1	2		4	5				9	10	8	3	7	6		11				
	Nov-06	(h) Romford	W 3-2	Byrne, Eglite, Fairclough	1				5	2	8		9	10	7	3	4	6		11				
	Nov-09	(h) Telford U	L 1-3	Henderson		2			5			8	10	11	7		4	6	3	9	1			
	Nov-16	(a) Guildford C	W 2-1	Duck, Godfrey	1	2			5				9	10	7	8	4	6	3	11				
	Nov-23	(h) Tonbridge	W 4-1	Eglite 3, Henderson	1	2				5			9	10	7	8	4	6	3	11				
	Nov-30	(a) Stourbridge	D 1-1	T Evans	1	2			5	10		12	9		8	7	4	6	3	11				
	Dec-07	(a) Bath C	L 0-2		1	2			5	10	12	9			8	7	4	6	3	11				
	Dec-14	(h) Guildford C	D 1-1	Henderson	1	2			5				9	10	8	7	4	6	3	11				
	Dec-21	(a) Dover Athletic	W 2-0	Moss, Godfrey	1	2	5				6			10	8	3	4	9		11		7		
	Dec-26	(a) Barnet	D 1-1	Duck	1	2			5					10	8	7	4	9	3	11		6		
	Jan-01	(h) Wimbledon	W 1-0	og	1	2			5					10	8	7	4	6	3	11		9		
	Jan-04	(a) Chelmsford City	D 3-3	Duck 2 (1 pen), Henderson	1	2			5					10	8	7	4	6	3	11		9		
	Jan-11	(h) Cambridge C	W 4-1	Duck, Moss, Eglite, McCormick	1	2			5					8	10	7	4	6	3	11		9	12	
	Jan-25	(h) Grantham	W 1-0	Eglite	1	2			5				9	8	10	7	4	6	3	11				
	Feb-03	(a) Nuneaton B	L 0-2		1	2							5	10	8	7	4	6	3	11		9		
	Feb-08	(h) Burton A	L 1-2	Moss	1	2							9	10	11	7	4	5	3	6		8		
	Feb-12	(a) Weymouth	L 0-4		1	2							6	10	8		4	7	3			9	5	11
	Feb-15	(a) Grantham	D 1-1	Eglite	1	2								10	8	7	4		3	11		9	5	6
	Feb-22	(h) Dover Athletic	D 0-0		1	2							11	10	8	7	4		3	12		9	5	6
	Mar-01	(a) Telford U	W 2-0	Eglite 2	1	2							5	10	8	7		4	3	11		9		6
	Mar-08	(h) Kettering T	W 2-1	Byrne, Moss	1	2							5	10	8	7		4		11		9	3	6
	Mar-15	(a) Atherstone T	W 2-1	Duck 2	1	2							5	10	8	7		4		11		9	3	6
	Mar-18	(a) Romford	D 3-3	Duck (pen), Moss, Kitchener	1	2							5	10	8	7		4		11		9	3	6
	Mar-22	(h) Chelmsford City	W 2-1	Moss, Kitchener	1	2							5	10	8	7		4		11		9	3	6
	Mar-29	(a) Cambridge C	L 1-2	Duck (pen)	1	2							5	10	8	7		4	6	11		9	3	
	Mar-31	(h) Barnet	D 1-1	Moss	1	2							5	10	8	7		4	6	11		9	3	
	Apr-03	(a) Wimbledon	W 2-1	Duck, Moss,	1	2							5	10	8	7		4	6	11		9	3	
	Apr-05	(a) Dartford	L 1-3	Moss	1	2							5	10	8	7		4	6	11		9	3	
	Apr-12	(h) Nuneaton B	D 0-0		1	2			4				5	10	8	6		7	3	11		9		
	Apr-19	(a) Burton A	L 1-3	Duck	1	2			4				9	10	8	6		7	3	12		11	5	
	Apr-25	(a) Margate	L 1-2	Eglite	1	2	12		5		7		9	10		6			3	11		8	4	
FA Cup																								
1Q	Sep-14	(a) Hampton T	D 2-2	Duck, og	1	2		4	5	7			9	10	11		8	6	3					
1Qr	Sep-17	(h) Hampton T	W 2-0	Duck, Fairclough	1	2		4	5	8			9	10	11	12	7	6	3					
2Q	Oct-05	(h) Uxbridge	W 2-0	Byrne, Fulton	1	2		4	5	8			9	10	11	6	7		3					
3Q	Oct-19	(a) Tooting & Mitcham United	L 0-1		1	2		4	5	8		12	9	10	11	7		6	3					
FA Trophy																								
Pr	Sep-21	(a) Finchley	L 0-1		1	2		4	5	7		12	9	10	11	3	8	6						
Southern League Cup																								
1	Aug-27	(h) Bury Town	W 7-1	Duck 2,T Evans 2,Fairclough 2,Henderson				4	5	2		8	9	10	11		7	6	3		1			
1'	Sep-04	(a) Bury Town	W 2-1	Godfrey, og		2		4		6	9			10	11	5	8	7	3		1			
	Oct-07	(a) Chelmsford City	L 0-2			2		4	5			8	9	10	11	6	7		3		1			
Middlesex Charity Cup																								
	Feb-24	(a) Wembley	W 2-1	Duck 2		2							8	10	12	7	4		3	11	1	9	5	6
SF	Apr-17	(h) Southall	L 1-3	Duck	1	2					11		5	10	8	6		7	3	12		9	4	

1975-76

	Date	Opponent	Result	Scorers	Morton J	Kinnear C	Watson J	Fairclough P	McCormick J	Lewis J	Godfrey J	O'Kane V	Duck G	Henderson J	Eglite A	Fulton R	Kitchener W	Byrne W	Moss B	McHale S	Hanson S	Dyson T	Edmundson S	Dyson B	Light D	Halliday K	Bullen R	Forrest I	McKenzie R
Southern League Premier Division - 19th																													
	Aug-16	(h) Stourbridge T	D 1-1	Eglite	1	2	3	4	5	6	7	8	9	10	11														
	Aug-19	(h) Maidstone U	W 2-1	Henderson, og	1	2		4			7	6	10	8	11	3	5	9											
	Aug-23	(a) Dunstable T	L 0-2		1	2		4			6	10	9	8	11	3	5	7	12										
	Aug-30	(h) Telford U	W 3-2	Lewis, Moss, Duck	1	2	3			6	4		10	11		7	5	9	8										
	Sep-06	(a) Atherstone T	L 1-3	Byrne	1	2	3			7	4		10	11		6	5	9	8										
	Sep-09	(h) Chelmsford City	W 4-0	Moss 2, Duck (pen), Fulton	1	2	3		5	7	4		10	11	12	6		9	8										
	Sep-20	(a) Margate	L 1-2	Godfrey	1	2		6	5	7	4	3	10	11	9				8										
	Sep-27	(a) Cambridge C	L 1-4	Eglite	1	2		11	5	6		3	10		9	7	4		8										
	Oct-13	(a) Bath C	D 2-2	McCormick, Duck	1	2	3	4	6	8	5		10	11	12	7		9											
	Oct-25	(a) Nuneaton B	D 0-0		1	2	7	4		6	5	3	10	11		12		9	8										
	Oct-28	(h) Weymouth	W 3-1	Duck, Byrne 2	1	2	3	4	5	7			10	11		8		9	6										
	Nov-15	(h) Bath C	W 3-1	Duck, Watson, Fulton	1	2	3	4	5	6			10	11		8		9	7										
	Nov-18	(h) Hillingdon B	W 2-1	Moss, Duck	1	2	3	4	5	6			10	11		8		9	7										
	Nov-25	(h) Gravesend & Northfleet	W 7-1	Byrne 2,Lewis,Kinnear,Moss,Duck,Henderson	1	2	3	4		6			10	11	12	8		9	7	5									
	Dec-06	(a) Yeovil T	D 1-1	Henderson,	1	2	3	4	5	7			10	11		8		9	6										
	Dec-13	(h) Tonbridge	W 2-1	Lewis, Duck	1	2	3	4		6			10	11		7		9	8	5									
	Dec-20	(a) Grantham T	L 0-3		1	2	3	4	5	7			10	11	12	8		9	6										
	Dec-26	(h) Wimbledon	L 0-2		1	2	3	4	5	6			10	11	12	8		9	7										
	Dec-27	(a) Telford U	L 0-4		1	2	3	12		7	4		10	11	6	8		9		5									
	Jan-01	(h) Margate	L 1-4	Duck	1	2	3	7		6	4		10	11	12	8		9		5									
	Jan-03	(h) Kettering T	W 1-0	Byrne	1	2	3	5		6	4		10	11		8		9	7										
	Jan-05	(a) Stourbridge T	L 1-2	Kinnear (pen)	1	2	3	4		6	7		9	10	12	11		8	5										
	Jan-17	(h) Atherstone T	L 1-2	og	1	2	3	10		6	4		12	11	8	7		9	5										
	Jan-19	(a) Bedford Town	L 1-2	Godfrey	1	2	3	12	5	6	4		10	11	8			9	7										
	Jan-24	(a) Tonbridge	D 3-3	Eglite, Duck, Moss	1	2	5	3			4		10	7	11	8		9	6										
	Feb-04	(a) Dover A	L 1-4	Duck (pen)	1	2	3	4	5	7	6		10	11	9	8				12									
	Feb-07	(h) Cambridge C	L 0-1		1	2		5		6	4		10	9	11	7		8			3								
	Feb-14	(h) Dover A	L 3-4	Moss 2, Dyson	1		6	5			4		10	11	7	3		9	8			2							
	Feb-21	(a) Gravesend & Northfleet	L 0-2		1		3			8	5		10	11	12	7		9	6				2	4					
	Feb-25	(a) Burton A	L 1-2	Godfrey	1	2	8				9		10	11		3			7	5			6	4					
	Feb-28	(h) Burton A	D 1-1	Duck	1	2	6				9		10	11		3			8	5				4	7				
	Mar-13	(h) Nuneaton B	L 1-4	McHale	1	2				7			10	11	9			12	8	5			6	3	4				
	Mar-16	(a) Maidstone U	D 1-1	Eglite	1	3				7			12	10	11			9	8	5			2	4	6				
	Mar-20	(h) Bedford Town	D 1-1	Eglite	1	2	7			12				11	10			9	8	5			6	3	4				
	Mar-27	(h) Yeovil T	W 2-1	Duck 2	1	2	6				9		10	11	12				8	5			3	4	7				
	Mar-30	(a) Hillingdon B	L 1-4	Duck	1	2	9				11		10		12				8	5			3	6	4	7			
	Apr-03	(a) Kettering T	L 0-2		1	2	7			12	9		10	11				5	8					3	4	6			
	Apr-07	(a) Weymouth	W 2-0	Moss, Light	1	2	3						10	11	12			9	8	5				6	4	7			
	Apr-10	(h) Dunstable T	W 3-0	Duck, Moss, Byrne		2	3						10	11				9	8	5				6	4	7	1		
	Apr-17	(a) Chelmsford City	L 0-4				3						10	11				9	8	5			2	6	4	7	1		
	Apr-19	(h) Grantham T	D 2-2	Watson, Duck (HO says Duck 2?)			3						10	11				9	7	5			2	4	6	8	1		
	Apr-27	(a) Wimbledon	L 1-4	Light			3			12			10	11				9	8	5			2	6	4	7	1		
FA Cup																													
1Q	Sep-13	(h) Woking	D 1-1	Henderson	1	2			5	7	4	3	10	11		6		9	8										
1Qr	Sep-16	(a) Woking	W 5-3 aet	Fulton 2,Byrne,Duck(pen),Godfrey	1	2		12	5	7	4	3	10		11	6		9	8										
2Q	Oct-04	(a) Burnham	W 2-0	O'Kane, Duck	1	2		4		8	5	3	10		11	7		9	6										
3Q	Oct-18	(h) Dagenham	W 2-0	Moss, Duck	1	2	3	4	6	8	12	7	10	5				11	9										
4Q	Nov-01	(h) Southwick	W 3-1	Henderson, Duck, Byrne	1	2	3	4	5	7		12	10	11		8		9	6										
1	Nov-22	(a) Aldershot T	L 3-4	Duck 2 (1 pen), Lewis	1	2	3	4	5	7			10	11	12	8		9	6										
F A Trophy																													
1Q	Oct-11	(a) Cheshunt	W 2-1	Duck, Eglite	1	2	4	5		6		3	10	11	12	7		9	8										
2Q	Nov-08	(h) Oxford C	W 4-0	Duck 2, Byrne, McCormick	1	2	3	4	5	6			10	11	12	8		9	7										
3Q	Nov-29	(h) Leatherhead	D 2-2	Moss, Duck	1	2		4	5	6		3	10	11	12	8		9	7										
3Qr	Dec-02	(a) Leatherhead	L 0-1		1	2	3	4	5	6			10	11	12	8		9	7										
Southern League Cup																													
1	Aug-25	(a) Stevenage Ath	W 3-1	Byrne 2, Duck (pen)		2	3			7	4		10	11		6	5	9	8										1
1	Sep-02	(h) Stevenage Ath	W 4-1	Moss 2, Duck, Eglite		2	3			8	7		10	12	11	6	4	9	5										1
2	Oct-21	(h) Dunstable T	W 3-1	Byrne 2, Duck (pen)	1	2	3	4		7	5	6	10	11		12		9	8										
3	Dec-16	(a) Cambridge C	D 0-0			2	3	4	5	7			10	11		8		9	6										1
3r	Jan-10	(h) Cambridge C	W 2-0	Moss, Godfrey	1	2	3	10		6	4			11	7	8		9	5										
4	Feb-09	(a) Dover Ath	L 1-2	Lewis	1	2	3	4		7	5		10	11	6	8		9			12								
Middlesex Charity Cup																													
D	Aug-05	(h) Harrow Borough	D 2-2	Henderson 2			2		5	11	4	6	10	8		7	3	12	9										1
D	Aug-09	(a) Hendon	L 1-2	Godfrey	1	2	5	3	4	8	7	6	9	11	10	12													

1976-77

	Date	Opponent	Result	Scorers	Morton J	Kinnear C	Woolgar S	Edmundson S	Lawrence K	Byrne W	Arnold J	Hanson S	Fulton R	Duck G	Halliday K	Light D	Moss R	Watson J	Bullen R	Prince L	Stagg W	Lightfoot C	Parratt D	Fursdon A	Keenaghan D	Lucas D	Downes J	Griffiths M	Thomas P	O'Kane V	Brinkman S	Gayle D	Hogg D	Joseph F	Hill K
Southern League Premier Division - 14th																																			
	Aug-28	(a) Margate	W 2-0	Lawrence, Woolgar	1	2	3	4	5	6	7	8	9	10	11																				
	Aug-30	(a) Minehead	L 1-2	og	1	2	3		5	6	7		9	10	11	4	8	12																	
	Sep-04	(h) Bath C	L 0-2			2	6		5		7		12	10	11	9	8	4	1	3															
	Sep-11	(a) Wimbledon	L 1-5	og		2	6	4	5		7		12	10	11	9	8		1	3															
	Sep-14	(h) A.P.Leamington	W 7-2	Fulton 2,Moss 2,Byrne,Light,Kinnear	1	2			5	4			7	10	11	9	8	12		3	6														
	Sep-25	(a) Nuneaton B	L 0-2			2			5	4			7	10	11	9	8	12		3	6	1													
	Oct-02	(h) Telford U	W 4-2	Duck 3, Watson					5	4			6	10	11	8	7	2		3	9	1	12												
	Oct-05	(h) Kettering T	L 0-3							4			6	10	11	8	7	2		3	9	1	12	5											
	Oct-16	(a) Burton A	L 1-2	Duck		2			5	4			11	10		8	7	6				1	9	3	12										
	Nov-02	(h) Dover	W 3-1	Duck, Parratt, og					5	4	11		7	10		8	6	2				1	9	3											
	Nov-13	(a) Atherstone T	D 1-1	Duck (pen)					5	4			11	10		8	7	2		3		1	9	6											
	Dec-04	(a) Grantham	D 1-1	Duck				6	5				11	10		8		2		3	7	1	4			9									
	Dec-06	(a) Hillingdon B	L 0-1		1			6	5				11	10		8	12	2		3	7		4			9									
	Dec-11	(h) Grantham	D 1-1	og	1				5	4			11	10		8	6	2		3	7					9									
	Dec-27	(a) Dartford	W 1-0	Duck					5	6			11	10		8		4		3	7	1	9	2											
	Jan-01	(h) Maidstone U	L 1-2	Lawrence					5	6			11	10		8		4		3	7	1	9	2											
	Jan-08	(a) Bedford Town	L 0-2		1			5		4			11	10		8	6	2		3			9	7											
	Jan-18	(h) Chelmsford City	L 2-4	Duck, Byrne	1			12	5	4			11	10		8	7	2		3	6		9												
	Jan-22	(a) Dover	D 1-1	Parratt				4		5			11	10		8	7	2		3		1	9	6											
	Jan-29	(h) Minehead	L 1-4	Duck				4		5	7		11	10		8		2		3		1	9	6											
	Feb-05	(h) Margate	D 1-1	Duck					5	11				10	12	8	7	2		3		1	9	6			4								
	Feb-12	(a) Bath C	L 0-2						5	11	12			10		8	7	2		3		1	9	6			4								
	Feb-23	(a) Yeovil T	L 1-3	Duck					5	11	9			10		8	7	2		3		1		6			4	12							
	Feb-26	(a) A.P.Leamington	L 0-1		1				5	11				10			7	2		3			9	6			4	8							
	Mar-01	(h) Hillingdon B	D 1-1	Duck	1				5	11			12	10			8	2		3			9	6			4	7							
	Mar-05	(h) Nuneaton B	D 1-1	Duck	1				5	11			12	10			8	2		3			9	6			4	7							
	Mar-15	(h) Weymouth	W 2-1	Duck 2					5	11			12	10				4		3		1	9	6			8	7	2						
	Mar-19	(a) Kettering T	L 0-2						5	11				10			12	4		3		1	9	6			7	8	2						
	Mar-22	(h) Bedford Town	L 2-3	Griffiths 2					5	11				10			8					1	9	6			4	7	2	3					
	Mar-26	(h) Burton A	W 2-1	Duck, Moss						11			12	10			5					1	9	6			4	7	2	8	3				
	Mar-29	(a) Gravesend & Northfleet	W 2-1	Moss 2									12				10	4				1	9	6			7	8	2	5	3	11			
	Apr-02	(a) Weymouth	L 0-2						12				11				9	7				1	5	3			6		2	8	4	10			
	Apr-05	(h) Yeovil T	D 1-1	Brinkman (pen)									11				9	6		8		1	5	7			4		2		3	10	12		
	Apr-09	(a) Maidstone U	W 2-1	Moss, Byrne					12	10			7				11	5		8		1	9	6			4		2		3				
	Apr-11	(h) Dartford	D 1-1	Byrne	1					9			10				8	3					5	7			4	6	2		11				
	Apr-19	(h) Redditch United	W 1-0	Watson						9			11				10	6				1	5	3			4	8	2		7				
	Apr-23	(h) Atherstone T	W 4-3	Brinkman, Parratt, Griffiths, Fursdon						9			11				10	6				1	5	3			4	8	2		7				
	Apr-25	(a) Telford U	D 2-2	Byrne 2						9		6	10				8	3				1	5				4	7	2		11				
	May-07	(h) Gravesend & Northfleet	W 1-0	Moss						9							10	4		5		1		3			6	11	2	8	7				
	May-10	(a) Redditch United	D 0-0							9							10	4		3		1	5				6	11	2	8	7				
	May-12	(h) Wimbledon	D 0-0							9							7	6		3		1	5				4	11	2	8	10				
	May-14	(a) Chelmsford City	W 2-1	og 2						9							10	4				1	5	3			6	11	2	8	7				
FA Cup																																			
1Q	Sep-18	(h) Clapton	W 5-1	Duck 2, Byrne 3	1	2			5	4			7	10	11	9	8			3	6														
2Q	Oct-09	(a) Kingstonian	W 2-0	Duck (pen), Byrne	1	3			5	4			6	10	11	8	7	2					9												
3Q	Oct-23	(a) Dulwich H	W 2-0	Duck, Arnold	1			12		4	6		7	10		8	11	5		3			9	2											
4Q	Nov-06	(h) Bishops Stortford	W 3-2	Duck 2, Arnold	1				5	4	7		11	10		8	6	2		3			9												
1	Nov-20	(a) Reading	L 0-1		1				5	4	12		11	10		8	7	2		3			9	6											
FA Trophy																																			
1Q	Oct-30	(h) Wellingborough T	W 3-1	Duck 2, Parratt					5	4	7		11	10		8	6	2		3	12	1	9												
2Q	Nov-27	(a) Croydon	W 2-1	Byrne 2					5	4	12		11	10		8	7	6		3		1	9	2											
3Q	Dec-21	(a) Barnet	D 1-1	Lawrence					5	4			11	10		8	6	2		3	7	1	9												
3Qr	Jan-05	(h) Barnet	L 0-3		1				5	4			11	10		8	6	2		3	7		9	12											
Southern League Cup																																			
1	Aug-21	(h) Barnet	L 0-2		1	2		4	5	6	7	9	8	10	11					3	12														
1	Aug-24	(a) Barnet	L 0-2			2	4		5	6	7	12	9	10	11				1	3	8														
Middlesex Senior Cup																																			
1	Jan-11	(a) Willesden	D 1-1	Joseph	1			4	5	9	8		7	10			12	2					6	3								12		11	
1r	Jan-25	(h) Willesden	W 3-0	Byrne, Parratt 2				4		5	13		11	10		8	7	2		3		1	9	6											
2	Feb-15	(h) Hendon	W 1-0	Duck				12	5	11	9		4	10		8	7	2		3		1		6											
SF	Mar-12	(a) Hampton	L 2-3	Byrne, Watson					5	9			6	10			2	4		3		1		8			7								11

1977-78

Rd	Date	Opponent	Result	Scorers	Lightfoot C	Thomas P	Fursdon A	Watson J	Parratt D	O'Kane V	Barwick F	Brinkman S	Furphy K	Duck G	Moss R	Ferry P	Cranstone I	Griffiths M	Hockham S	Webster P	Horgan S	Finch B	Boyle T	Briscoe S	Waymark M	McVeigh J	Byrne W	Dennison P	Stratford K	Martin C	Doyle
Southern League Premier Division - 8th																															
	Aug-27	(a) Yeovil T	W 2-1	Duck 2	1	2	3	4	5	6	7	8	9	10	11	12															
	Aug-31	(a) Kettering T	D 1-1	Moss	1	2	3	4	5	6	7	8	9	10	11																
	Sep-03	(h) Dartford	L 0-2			2	3	4	5	6	7	8	9	10	11	12	1														
	Sep-10	(a) Telford U	L 1-3	Duck		2	3	4	5	6	7	8	9	10	11		1														
	Sep-17	(h) Grantham	W 3-0	Ferry, Moss, og	1	2	3	4	5	6	7		12	10	11	8		9													
	Sep-24	(a) Redditch United	L 0-1		1	2	3	4	5		7	6		10	11	8		9	12												
	Oct-01	(h) A.P.Leamington	D 0-0		1	2	3	4	5		6	8	7	10	11	9		12													
	Oct-04	(a) Hastings U	D 0-0		1		3	4	5		6	8		10	11	9		7	2												
	Oct-08	(h) Bedford Town	W 3-2	Duck, Parratt, Griffiths	1		3	4	5		6	8	12	10	11	9		7	2												
	Oct-22	(h) Atherstone T	W 4-0	Duck 2, Ferry, Watson	1		3	4	5		6	8	9	10	11	7		12	2												
	Oct-29	(a) Maidstone U	D 2-2	Duck 2 (1 pen)	1		3	4	5		6	8	9	10	11	7		12	2												
	Nov-01	(h) Bath C	D 2-2	Moss 2	1		3	4	5		6	8	9	10	11	7			2												
	Nov-19	(h) Cheltenham T	D 0-0		1		3	4	5		6	8	9	10	11	7			2												
	Dec-05	(a) Nuneaton B	L 0-1		1	11	3	4	5		6	8	12	10		7		9	2												
	Dec-10	(a) Weymouth	L 1-2	Moss	1	2	3	4	5		6	8	9	10	11	7															
	Dec-26	(a) Hillingdon B	L 2-3	Ferry, Furphy (pen)			3	4			6		9			7	1	8	11	10	5	2	12								
	Dec-27	(h) Barnet	L 1-2	Furphy	1	2	3	4			6		9	10		7			11	12	5	8									
	Jan-02	(a) Minehead	L 1-4	Moss	1	2	3	4	5		6	8		10	11	7			9			12									
	Jan-14	(h) Dover	L 1-3	Barwick	1		2	4	5		6	8	9		11	7		12	3			10									
	Jan-21	(a) Dartford	L 1-2	Furphy	1		2				6	8	9		11			10	3		4	5		7							
	Feb-04	(h) Telford	D 1-1	Moss	1		2	4			6	8			11	7		12	3		5	9		10							
	Feb-06	(a) Bath C	L 1-3	Ferry	1		2	4			6	8			11	7			3		5	9		10							
	Feb-18	(h) Redditch United	W 2-1	Briscoe, Horgan				4	5		6	8		11	12	7	1		3		2	9		10							
	Feb-25	(a) A.P.Leamington	L 0-2		1			4	5		6	8		11	12	7			3		2	9		10							
	Feb-28	(h) Maidstone U	W 1-0	Briscoe			2	4	5			8		10	7	12	1		3		6	9		11							
	Mar-04	(a) Worcester City	W 2-1	Duck 2			2	4	5			8		10	7	12	1		3		6	9		11							
	Mar-07	(h) Kettering T	W 1-0	Moss			2	4	5			8		10	7	3	1				6	9		11							
	Mar-11	(h) Hastings U	W 2-0	Duck 2				4	5		2	8		10	7	3	1				6	9		11							
	Mar-14	(h) Minehead	W 1-0	Moss		12		4	5		2	8		10	7	3	1	6				9		11							
	Mar-18	(a) Atherstone T	D 0-0			6		4	5		2	8		10	7	3	1				9			11							
	Mar-20	(h) Gravesend & Northfleet	D 0-0			2		4	5		9	8		10	7	3	1				6			11	12						
	Mar-27	(h) Hillingdon B	W 2-1	Duck (pen), Moss			3	4	5		2	8		10	7	9	1						12	11	6						
	Apr-01	(a) Cheltenham T	D 1-1	McVeigh		12	3	4	5		6	8		10	7		1					2		11		9					
	Apr-04	(h) Worcester City	W 2-1	Duck, og			3	4	5		6	8		10	9	2	1							11		7					
	Apr-08	(h) Nuneaton B	D 0-0				3	4	5		6	8		10	7	9	1							11	12	2					
	Apr-11	(h) Yeovil T	D 1-1	Duck (pen)			3	4	5		6	8		10	7		1		9			12		11		2					
	Apr-15	(a) Bedford Town	W 4-1	Duck, Briscoe, Fursdon 2			3	4	5		6	8		10	12		1		9			7		11		2					
	Apr-18	(a) Barnet	W 2-1	Duck 2			3	4	5		6	8		10	7		1		9					11		2					
	Apr-24	(h) Weymouth	D 0-0				3	4	5		6	8		10	7		1		9					11		2					
	Apr-29	(a) Gravesend & Northfleet	W 2-1	Duck 2		2	3	4	5		6	8		10		12	1		9					11		7					
	May-01	(a*) Grantham	W 2-0	McVeigh, Briscoe			3	4	5		6	8		10		12	1		9				7	11		2					
	May-03	(a) Dover	D 2-2	Moss, Hockham			3	4	5		6	8		10	7		1		9					11		2					
		*Played at Kettering Town FC																													
FA Cup																															
4Q	Nov-05	(h) Maidstone U	W 2-1	Duck 2	1		3	4	5		6	8	9	10	11	7		12	2												
1	Nov-26	(h) Hereford U	D 0-0		1	2	3	4	5		6	8	9	10	11	7															
1r	Nov-30	(a) Hereford U	W 3-2	Moss, Ferry 2	1	2	3	4	5		6	8	9	10	11	7		12													
2	Dec-17	(h) Reading	W 2-1	Furphy, Duck (pen)	1	2	3	4	5		6	8	9	10	11	7		12													
3	Jan-07	(a) QPR	L 0-4		1	2	3	4	5		6	8	9	10	11	7															
FA Trophy																															
1Q	Oct-15	(h) Walton & H	D 1-1	Furphy			3	4	5		6	8	11	10		9	1	7	2	12											
1Qr	Oct-18	(a) Walton & H	W 2-1	Duck, Ferry	1			3	5		6	8	9	10		11		7	2	4	12										
2Q	Nov-12	(h) Dulwich Hamlet	W 4-2	Duck, Ferry, Furphy 2	1		3	4	5		6	8	9	10	11	7			2												
3Q	Dec-03	(a) Harrow Borough	L 0-3		1	2	3	4	5		6	8	9	10	11	7						12									
Southern League Cup																															
1	Aug-20	(h) Barnet	W 1-0	Duck	1	2	3	4	5	6	12	8		10	11			7									9				
1	Aug-23	(a) Barnet	W 1-0	Brinkman	1	2	3	4	5	6	7	8		10	11												9				
2	Sep-27	(h) A.P.Leamington	W 1-0	Parratt	1	2	3	4	5		6	8	7	10	11	9															
3	Nov-21	(h) Hillingdon B	D 2-2	Duck (pen), Ferry	1	2	3		5		6	8	9	10	11	7		12				4									
3r1	Dec-21	(a) Hillingdon B	D 3-3	Duck (pen), Ferry, Watson	1	2	3	4	5		6		9	10	11	7		8	12												
3r2	Dec-24	(h) Hillingdon B	L 1-3	Duck (pen)	1	2	3	4			6		9	10	11	7		8	12		5										
Middlesex Senior Cup																															
2	Dec-31	(a) Hayes	L 1-4	Webster					5			8					1		11	10	4	7	6		12			9	2	3	
Anglo-Italian Tournament																															
	Mar-22	(h) Paganese	W 4-2	Moss, Briscoe, Parratt, Waymark		2		5	6		3	4		8	7	9	1						12	11	10						
	Mar-25	(h) Udinese	L 0-1				3	5	6		2	4		8	7	9	1							11	10						
	Jun-20	(a) Reggiana	L 0-1			12		4	5			7		10			1		11		6	2		3	12	8					9
	Jun-23	(a) Arezzo	L 0-2			3		4				7		10			1		11		5	2	9	6	12	8					

1978-79

	Date	Opponent	Result	Scorers	Cranstone I	McVeigh J	Fursdon A	Watson J	Parratt D	Barwick F	Thomas P	Hockham S	Moss R	Duck G	Briscoe S	Doyle A	Lightfoot C	Boyle T	Horgan S	Arnold J	Plaskett J	Brinkman S	Wilkinson A	Johnson N	Knight T	Brannigan P	Mount R	Pearce S	Clarke A	Bookman J	Abel P	Gilbert P
Southern League Premier Division - 15th																																
	Aug-26	(a) Gravesend & Northfleet	L 2-5	Duck, Parratt	1	2	3	4	5	6	7	8	9	10	11	12																
	Sep-02	(h) Telford	W 3-0	Duck, Moss 2		7	3	4	5	6		8	9	10	11		1	2	12													
	Sep-09	(h) Redditch United	W 3-0	Duck (pen), Parratt, Doyle	1	2	3	4	5	6			9	10	11	8		12	7													
	Sep-11	(a) Hillingdon B	W 1-0	Duck	1	2	3	4		6			9	10	11	8		7	5													
	Sep-16	(a) Weymouth	L 1-2	Moss	1	2	3	4	5	6			9	10	11	8		7	12													
	Sep-23	(a) Bath C	L 0-1		1	2		4	5	6		7	8	10	11	9			3													
	Sep-30	(h) Hastings U	L 1-2	Duck (pen)	1	2	3		5	6		7	9	10	11			4		8												
	Oct-07	(h) Weymouth	D 0-0		1	2	3			6			9	10	11	7		4	5	8	12											
	Oct-21	(h) Witney Town	L 0-1		1	2		4	5	6		3	10		11			12	9	8		7										
	Oct-28	(a) Barnet	L 2-3	Moss, Doyle	1	2			5	6			9		11	10		3	4	8		7										
	Nov-18	(h) Atherstone T	W 1-0	Moss	1	2	3		5	6			9		11				4			7	8	10								
	Dec-04	(a) Worcester City	L 1-3	Duck	1	2	3	4					9	6	11				5	12		7	8	10								
	Dec-09	(h) Margate	W 1-0	Johnson	1	2	3	4	7	6			9		11				5			8	12	10								
	Dec-16	(a) Yeovil T	L 1-4	Johnson	1	2	3	7	5	6			9		11				4	8			12	10								
	Dec-23	(h) Kettering T	D 1-1	Brinkman (pen)	1	2	3	7	5	6			9		11				4			8		10								
	Dec-26	(a) Dartford	L 0-1		1	2			5	6			9		11			7	4			8	3	10	12							
	Jan-13	(h) Gravesend & Northfleet	W 2-1	Johnson, McVeigh	1	2	3			6			7	10				12	4			8	11	9		5						
	Feb-03	(h) Bath C	D 0-0		1	2	3	4		6			9	10					5			8		11		7						
	Feb-06	(a) Maidstone U	D 0-0		1	2	3	4		6			9	10				12	5			8		11		7						
	Feb-10	(a) Hastings U	W 4-2	Duck (pen), Moss, Wilkinson, og	1	2	3			6			9	10				4	5			8	12	11		7						
	Feb-21	(a) Telford U	D 2-2	Duck, McVeigh	1	2	3	6						10				4	5			8		9		7	11					
	Feb-24	(h) Hillingdon B	W 1-0	Duck	1	2	3	6						10				4	5			8	11	9		7						
	Feb-27	(h) Barnet	D 1-1	Mount	1	2	3	4						10				6	5			8	11	9		7	12					
	Mar-03	(a) Dorchester T	L 1-5	Johnson		2	3	4										6	5		11			9		7	10	8	1			
	Mar-20	(h) Dorchester T	D 2-2	Duck, Johnson	1		3	4						10				6	5				8	9		7		11		2		
	Mar-24	(h) Maidstone U	W 2-1	Johnson, Brannigan	1	2	3	4					6	10				12			5		11	9		7				8		
	Mar-26	(a) Nuneaton B	L 0-4		1	2	3						6	10				12	5		4		11	9		7				8		
	Mar-31	(a) A.P.Leamington	D 0-0		1	2	3	4						10				8	5				11	9		7	12			6		
	Apr-03	(h) Cheltenham T	D 0-0		1	2	3	4					5	10				8			12		11	9		7	6					
	Apr-05	(a) Redditch United	L 0-1		1		3	4						10				5			2			9		7	6	8			11	
	Apr-07	(h) Nuneaton B	D 0-0		1	2	3	4					8	10				6	5				11	9		7				12		
	Apr-12	(a) Witney Town	L 1-3	Johnson	1		3	4					6	10				11	2		5			9		7	12			8		
	Apr-14	(h) Dartford	L 3-4	Duck (pen), Moss 2	1	2	3						8	10				6			4			9		7	12	5		11		
	Apr-16	(a) Cheltenham T	W 4-2	Duck (pen), Moss, Johnson 2	1	2	3						8	10				11			4		12	9		7	6	5				
	Apr-18	(h) Worcester City	D 0-0		1	2	3						8	10				6	5					9		7		4		11		
	Apr-21	(h) Bridgend T	W 3-0	Duck (pen), Johnson 2	1		3	4		11			8	10				6	5					9		7		2		12		
	Apr-25	(a) Kettering T	L 0-1		1		3	4		11			8	10				6	5					9		7		2		12		
	Apr-28	(a) Margate	L 0-1		1	2	3	4		6			8	10				7			12			9				5		11		
	Apr-30	(a) Atherstone T	D 2-2	Moss, Brannigan	1		3			6			5	10				4	12		2			9		7	11				8	
	May-02	(a) Bridgend T	L 1-3	Brannigan	1		3	4		6				10				11	5					9		7	8	2				
	May-05	(h) Yeovil T	W 4-0	Duck 2, Moss, Boyle	1	2	3	4		6			8	10				7	5					9		11						
	May-07	(h) A.P.Leamington	L 0-1		1	2	3	4		6			8	10				7	5					9		11	12					
FA Cup																																
4Q	Nov-04	(h) Kempston Rovers	W 1-0	Horgan	1	2	5			6			9		11	10		4	3	8		7										
1	Nov-25	(h) Enfield	L 0-5		1	2	3		5	6			9		11				4	12		7	8	10								
FA Trophy																																
1Q	Oct-14	(a) Cambridge C	D 2-2	Brinkman (pen), Horgan	1	2			5	6		7	9		11	12		4	8	10		3										
1Qr1	Oct-17	(h) Cambridge C	D 0-0 aet		1	2			5	6		7	10		11	12		4	9	8		3										
1Qr2	Oct-23	(h) Cambridge C	W 2-1	Moss, Brinkman	1	2		4	5	6			10		11	7		12	9	8		3										
2Q	Nov-11	(h) Harlow Town	L 1-2	Doyle	1	2	3		5	6			9		11	10			4	8		7										
Southern League Cup																																
1	Aug-19	(a) Hillingdon B	L 1-2	McVeigh	1	2	3	4	5	6	11		8	10	9	7		12														
1	Aug-22	(h) Hillingdon B	W 3-0	McVeigh, Parratt 2	1	2	3	4	5	6	12		9	10	11	7		8														
2	Sep-26	(a) Barnet	L 0-1		1	2	3	4	5	6		10	9		11	8		12	7													
Middlesex Senior Cup																																
2	Dec-30	(a) Harringay Borough	W 1-0	Moss		2				6			9		11			7	4		3	8	12	10		5			1			
3	Jan-22	(a) Finchley	W 1-0	Duck		2		11		5			8	10					4			7	6	9		3			1			
SF	Mar-10	(h) Enfield	L 0-4			2	3	4						10				6	5		8			9		7		11	1			
Stones Trophy																																
	Aug-08	(a) Maidstone U	W 1-0	Boyle	1	2	3		5	6	12	11	8		10	9		4				7										12
	Aug-15	(h) Maidstone U	W 3-1	Duck 3 (1 pen)	1	2	3	4	5	6	12	8	9	10	11	12		12	12			7										

1979-80					Cranstone I	Brannigan P	Fursdon A	Wainwright R	Horgan S	Barwick F	Moss R	James T	Johnson N	Cordice N	Johnson C	Pearce S	Watson J	Boyle T	Pearce D	Adams M	Toogood J	Robinson P	Filby M	Bennett A	Greenhalgh B	Tutt G	Taylor B	Davie M	Cordice G	Abell P
Alliance Premier League - 15th																														
	Aug-18	(a) Worcester City	L 1-2	Cordice	1	2	3	4	5	6	7	8	9	10	11	12														
	Aug-22	(a) Kettering T	L 0-2		1		2	10	5	6	7	8	9	11		3	4													
	Aug-25	(h) Nuneaton B	D 2-2	Moss, Horgan	1		3	7	5	6	8		10	9		2	4	11												
	Sep-01	(a) Maidstone U	L 0-3		1	12	3	7	5	6	8		10	9	11	2	4													
	Sep-03	(h) Kettering T	D 2-2	Cordice, S Pearce	1		3	7	5	6	8		10	9		2	4	11	12											
	Sep-08	(h) Stafford Rangers	W 2-1	Cordice, S Pearce	1	7	3		5	6	8		10	9		2	4	11		12										
	Sep-15	(a) Weymouth	L 0-4		1	7	3	11	5	6	8		10	9		2	4													
	Sep-22	(h) A.P.Leamington	L 1-2	N Johnson		3		7	5	6			10	9	8	2	4	11			1									
	Oct-06	(a) Nuneaton B	W 1-0	og	1	2	12	6	5		8		10	9	11	3	4	7												
	Oct-09	(a) Gravesend & Northfleet	L 0-3		1	2	12	6	5		8		10	9	11	3	4	7												
	Oct-20	(a) Bath C	D 4-4	Cordice, Moss, Horgan 2 (1 pen)	1	12		6	5	2	8		10	9		3	4	7		11										
	Oct-27	(h) Yeovil T	W 5-0	Cordice 2, N Johnson, Moss, og	1	2	12	6	5		8		10	9	11	3	4	7												
	Nov-10	(a) Boston U	D 0-0		1	2	5	6			8		10	9	11	3	4	7												
	Nov-13	(h) Bangor C	D 0-0		1	2	5	6			8		10	9	11	3	4	7												
	Dec-01	(h) Scarborough	L 2-4	Horgan, og	1	2		6	5	7	8		10	9	11	3	4	12												
	Dec-08	(h) Altrincham	L 1-4	Cordice	1	2	3	6	5	7			10	9		11	4	8				12								
	Dec-15	(a) Telford U	W 3-1	Horgan, Wainwright, Watson	1	2	5	6	7		12		10	8		3	4			11		9								
	Dec-26	(a) Barnet	W 3-1	Cordice, Robinson, Horgan (pen)	1	2		6	5		8	12	10	7		3	4			11		9								
	Dec-29	(a) Barrow	L 0-1		1	2		6	5			8	10	7		3	4	12		11		9								
	Jan-05	(h) Telford U	D 0-0		1	2	5	6					10	8	11	3	4	7				9								
	Jan-08	(h) Barnet	W 2-1	N Johnson, Wainwright	1	2	5	6	7	8			10	9	12	3	4			11										
	Jan-12	(h) Redditch United	W 2-0	N Johnson, Brannigan	1	2	5	6		7		8	10			3	4			11		12	9							
	Jan-26	(h) Barrow	W 2-1	N Johnson, Adams	1	2	7	6	5	8			10	9		3	4			11										
	Feb-16	(a) Bangor C	L 0-1		1	7	4	6	8	2			10	9		3		12		11				5						
	Feb-23	(a) A.P.Leamington	D 0-0			8	4	6	7	2			10	9		3				11				5	12	1				
	Mar-01	(h) Worcester City	L 2-4	Cordice, N Johnson		8	5	6	7	2			10	9		3	4			11						1				
	Mar-15	(h) Gravesend & Northfleet	D 0-0		1	7		6	5	2			10	9		3	4	8							11					
	Mar-22	(a) Stafford Rangers	W 1-0	Horgan (pen)	1	11	5	6	8	2	9		10	7		3	4													
	Mar-26	(a) Scarborough	D 0-0			2	5	6	8	4			10	7		3						11		12	9		1			
	Mar-29	(h) Weymouth	D 1-1	Moss,		2	5	6		4	9			7		3	8					11			10		1			
	Mar-31	(a) Altrincham	L 1-2	Cordice		2	5	6	7	4				9		3				11		8			10		1			
	Apr-05	(a) Redditch United	L 1-4	Moss		2	5	6	8	4	7			9		3				11		12			10		1			
	Apr-12	(h) Maidstone U	D 0-0		1	2	5	6		4	10			9		3	8			11		7								
	Apr-16	(h) Northwich V	L 0-1		1	8	3	6		2	10			9		7	4					11		5	12					
	Apr-19	(h) Bath C	D 1-1	Horgan (pen)	1		4	6	5	2	8		10	9		3				11		7								
	Apr-26	(a) Northwich V	D 0-0		1	7		6		2	8		10	9		3	4			11				5	12					
	Apr-29	(h) Boston U	D 1-1	Wainwright (pen)	1	7		6		2	8		10	9		3	4			11				5	12					
	May-03	(a) Yeovil T	D 1-1	N Johnson	1	7	4	6		2	8		10	9		3				11				5						
FA Cup																														
4Q	Nov-03	(h) Woking	W 1-0	Moss	1	2	5	6			8		10	9	11	3	4	7												
1	Nov-24	(h) Southend	L 0-1		1	2		6	5	7	8		10	9	11	3	4													
FA Trophy																														
1Q	Oct-13	(a) Barnet	D 0-0		1	2	5	6			4		10	9		3		7	8	11								12		
1Qr1	Oct-16	(h) Barnet	D 1-1	Cordice	1	2	5	6			8		10	9		3	4	7	12	11										
1Qr2	Oct-22	(a) Barnet	L 0-2		1	5	2	6			8		10	9		3	4	7	11	12										
Alliance Premier League Cup																														
1	Aug-27	(h) Maidstone U	W 2-0	N Johnson, Moss	1		3	7	5	6	8	4	10	9		2		11	12											
2	Sep-29	(a) Boston U	D 1-1	Cordice	1	12		6	5	2	8		10	9	11	3	4	7												
2r	Oct-03	(h) Boston U	W 3-2 aet	N Johnson 2, Moss	1	12		6	5	2	8		10	9	11	3	4	7												
3	Dec-17	(a) Altrincham	L 1-2	N Johnson	1	2	5	6	7				10	8		3	4			11		9								
Middlesex Senior Cup																														
2	Dec-12	(h) Harefield United	W 5-0	Cordice 2, Horgan 2, Abell	1	2	5	6	7		12		10	8		3	4			13									9	11
3	Jan-22	(h) Hillingdon B	W 1-0	Horgan (pen)	1	2		6	5	8	7		10	9		3	4			11		12								
SF	Mar-08	(h) Enfield	L 0-3		1	7		6	5	2			10	9		3	4	8		11					12					
London Senior Cup																														
1	Jan-15	(h) Kingstonian	W 3-2	Cordice, Moss, Adams	1		5	6		2	7		10	9		3	4			11		8								
2	Feb-05	(a) Woking	L 0-3		1	2	4	6	5	7	8		10	9		3				11		12								

1980-81

Rd	Date	Opponent	Result	Scorers	Cranstone I	Brannigan P	Pearce S	Barwick F	Bowgett P	Murphy T	Cordice A	Watson J	Baldwin T	Johnson N	Forde C	Bennett A	Larner K	Wainwright R	Fursdon A	Adams M	Sperrin M	Evans D	Cordice N	Harriot L	Hardman C	Perkins S	Byatt D	Sweetzer J	Robinson P	Johns S	Pemberton M	Carlton D
Alliance Premier League - 19th																																
	Aug-16	(h) Telford U	W 4-0	Johnson,Forde,A Cordice,Bowgett(pen)	1	2	3	4	5	6	8	7	9	10	11	12																
	Aug-23	(a) Northwich V	D 0-0		1	11	3	4		2	7	8	9	10		5	6															
	Aug-25	(h) Frickley A	L 0-2		1	2	3	4		6	8	7	9	10	11	5	12															
	Aug-30	(h) Altrincham	L 1-2	Watson	1	7	3	4	5	2	9	8		10	11	12		6														
	Sep-06	(a) Altrincham	L 0-2		1	2	3	4	9	12	7	8		10	11	5	6															
	Sep-13	(h) Weymouth	D 1-1	Johnson	1	2		4		6	7	8		10		5	9	12	3	11												
	Sep-20	(h) Kettering T	D 1-1	Watson	1	2	3	4	5	6	7	8		10	9					11												
	Sep-27	(a) Scarborough	L 0-4		1		3	4	5	7	9	8		10	11	12		6	2													
	Oct-18	(h) Bangor C	D 1-1	Bowgett (pen)	1	7	3	4	8	12	9			10		5		6	2	11												
	Oct-20	(h) Gravesend & Northfleet	W 3-1	Sperrin 2, Bowgett (pen)	1	12	3	4	8	7	9			10		5		6	2		11											
	Oct-25	(a) Barrow	L 0-1		1		3	4	8	7	9	11		10		5		6	2													
	Nov-08	(a) Maidstone U	L 0-4		1	7	3	4	8		9			10	12	5		6	2	11												
	Nov-15	(h) Worcester City	L 1-2	Brannigan	1	9	3	4	5		7			10	11	6		8	2													
	Nov-22	(a) Frickley A	D 1-1	Johnson	1	7	3	4	5	12	9			10	11			6	2			8										
	Nov-29	(h) Nuneaton B	D 0-0		1	8	3	4	5	7					11	10		6	2	12		9										
	Dec-06	(a) Gravesend & Northfleet	W 1-0	N Cordice	1	6	3	4	5	11	7				8				2			9	10									
	Dec-13	(h) Bath C	L 0-1		1	6	3	4	5	12	7			11	8				2			9	10									
	Dec-26	(a) Barnet	L 0-3		1	7	3	4	5		8				11				2			9	10	6								
	Dec-27	(a) Stafford R	L 0-3		1	7	3	4	5					10	11	2						9	8	6								
	Jan-01	(h) Barnet	W 2-0	N Cordice, Bowgett	1	9	3	4	5		7			8						11			10	6	2							
	Jan-03	(a) Weymouth	L 1-2	N Cordice	1	11	3	4	5		7			9	8	6			2				10									
	Jan-17	(h) Maidstone U	W 2-1	Johnson, Bowgett (pen)	1		3	4	5		7			10		6			2	12		9	8	11								
	Jan-24	(a) Worcester City	L 1-4	N Cordice	1		3	4	5		7			11				8		12		9	10	6	2							
	Jan-31	(a) A.P.Leamington	D 1-1	Bowgett	1	11	3	4	5		7				12			8				9	10		2	6						
	Feb-07	(a) Nuneaton B	L 0-2		1	7	3		5		11				4			8		12		9	10		2	6						
	Feb-21	(a) Bath C	L 0-2		1	6	3		5		11			12				8		7		9	10		2	4						
	Feb-28	(h) Stafford R	D 1-1	N Cordice	1	4	3	12	5		11			10				8		7			9		2	6						
	Mar-08	(a) Bangor C	W 2-0	A Cordice, Bowgett (pen)	1	4	3	8	5		11			9						7			10		2	6						
	Mar-17	(h) Yeovil T	D 1-1	Johnson	1	8	3	4	5		11			10	12			7					9		2	6						
	Mar-21	(h) Northwich V	D 1-1	Barwick	1	11	3	4	5		7			10	12			8					9			2	6					
	Mar-25	(a) Yeovil T	L 0-4		1		3	4	5		11			9	7			8					10			2	6					
	Mar-28	(a) Telford U	L 1-2	A Cordice	1		3	4	5		11			9	6			8					10		2			7				
	Apr-04	(h) Scarborough	D 2-2	N Cordice 2	1		3	4			7			12	11			8					9		2	6	5	10				
	Apr-11	(a) Boston U	L 1-2	A Cordice	1	9	3	4			11			12				8					10		2	6	5	7				
	Apr-14	(h) Boston U	W 3-0	N Cordice 2, Bowgett	1		3	4	11		9							8					10		2	6	5	7				
	Apr-25	(a) Kettering T	W 1-0	Pearce	1		3	4			9				11			8					10		2	6	5	7				
	Apr-28	(h) Barrow	W 2-0	Pearce, Sweetzer (pen)	1		3	4	11		10							8					9		2	6	5	7				
	May-02	(h) A.P.Leamington	L 1-2	Wainwright	1		3	4	11		10				12			8					9		2	6	5	7				
FA Cup																																
4Q	Nov-01	(a) Harlow Town	D 1-1	Sperrin	1		3	4	5	7	9	8		10		2		6			11											
4Qr	Nov-03	(h) Harlow Town	L 0-1		1		3	4	5	7	9	8		10		2		6		12	11											
FA Trophy																																
1Q	Oct-11	(h) Oxford C	L 2-4	Johnson, Robinson	1		3	4	5	8	7			10	11	9		6											12	2		
Alliance Premier League Cup																																
2	Sep-22	(a) Nuneaton B	W 1-0	Brannigan	1	7	3	4		6	9	8		10	11	5			2													
2	Sep-29	(h) Nuneaton B	L 0-3			7	3	4			9			10	11	5		6	2	8											1	
Middlesex Senior Cup																																
2	Jan-20	(a) Hillingdon B	L 0-2		1		3	4	5		7			9		6		12		11			10	8	2							
Middlesex Charity Cup																																
B	Aug-02	(h) Edgware T	D 1-1	Barwick	1	2		4	5	3	7	8		10	11			6											9			
B	Aug-04	(h) Finchley	W 2-0	Fursdon, Murphy	1	2		4	5	6	7	8		10	11				3													9
B	Aug-09	(a) Harrow Borough	D 1-1	Murphy	1	2		4	5	3	7	8		10	11			6	12										9			
SF	Feb-17	(a) Hendon	D 2-2 aet	A Cordice, Johnson	1	6	3		5		11			12				8		7		9	10		2	4						
SFr	Feb-24	(h) Hendon	W 2-1	A Cordice, Wainwright	1	4	3		5		11			10				8		7			9		2	6						

1981-82

Rd	Date	Opponent	Result	Scorers	Goddard R	Hardman C	Pearce S	Byatt D	Bowgett P	Wainwright W	Cordice A	Knowles R	Cordice N	Johnson N	Forde C	Morris J	Waites P	Barwick F	Geddis P	Perkins S	Davies R	Churchouse G	Ferguson I	Cranston I	Adams M
Southern League Southern Division - 1st																									
	Aug-15	(a) Hastings U	D 0-0		1	2	3	4	5	6	7	8	9	10	11										
	Aug-22	(h) Dorchester T	L 1-2	Wainwright	1	2	3	5	6	7		8		9	11	4	10	12							
	Aug-29	(a) Basingstoke T	W 3-2	Johnson, Knowles, Wainwright	1	2	3	4	5	6		9	8	10			11	7							
	Sep-01	(h) Fareham Town	W 4-0	Johnson 2, N Cordice, Bowgett (pen)	1	2	3	4	5	7		9	10	11			8	6							
	Sep-05	(h) Crawley Town	W 4-1	Johnson 2, N Cordice, Knowles	1	2	3	4	5	8		9	10	11		12	7	6							
	Sep-08	(a) Dover	D 0-0		1	2	3	4	5	8	9		10	11			7	6							
	Sep-12	(a) Chelmsford City	W 2-0	N Cordice 2	1	2	3	4	5	6	10		9	7			11	8							
	Sep-15	(h) Thanet U	W 6-1	Johnson,N Cordice, A Cordice 2,Wainwright,Hardman	1	2	3	4	5	8	9		10	11	12		7	6							
	Sep-26	(h) Salisbury	W 4-1	N Cordice, A Cordice, Wainwright, Bowgett (pen)	1	2	3	4	5	7	9		8	11			10	6							
	Oct-10	(h) Dunstable	W 4-0	N Cordice, A Cordice 3	1	2	3	4	5	8	9		10	11			7	6							
	Oct-12	(a) Poole Town	W 2-1	A Cordice 2	1	2	3	4	5	8	9		10	11			7	6							
	Oct-20	(h) Aylesbury U	W 6-1	Johnson 2, N Cordice, A Cordice 2, Bowgett(pen)	1	2	3	4	5		9		10	11		8	7	6							
	Oct-31	(a) Canterbury City	W 5-0	Johnson, N Cordice 3, Bowgett	1	2	3	4	5			9	10	11	8		7	6							
	Nov-07	(a) Folkestone T	L 1-2	N Cordice	1	2	3	4	5	12		9	10	11	8		7	6							
	Nov-17	(h) Poole Town	W 4-1	Knowles, Wainwright, Bowgett, Waites	1	2	3	4	5	8		9	10	11			7	6							
	Nov-21	(a) Waterlooville	W 1-0	Wainwright	1	2	3	4	5	8		9	10	11			7	6							
	Nov-24	(a) Aylesbury U	L 0-3		1	2	3	4		8	12	9	10	11			7	6	5						
	Dec-05	(a) Ashford Town	D 0-0		1	2	3	4	5	8	9		10	11			7	6							
	Jan-02	(h) Dover	W 1-0	Waites	1	2	3	4	5	8	9	11	10				7	6							
	Jan-23	(a) Tonbridge	W 2-0	A Cordice, Perkins	1	2	3	4	5	8	9	10	11				12	6		7					
	Jan-27	(h) Addlestone & W	D 0-0		1	2	3	4		8	9	11	10				7	6		5					
	Jan-30	(a) Crawley Town	W 2-1	Knowles, Byatt (pen)	1	2	3	4		8	9	7	10					6		5	11				
	Feb-09	(a) Hounslow	W 5-3	N Cordice, A Cordice, Byatt, Wainwright, Bowgett (pen)	1		3	4	5	8	9	11	10					6		7	2				
	Feb-13	(a) Salisbury	W 4-2	A Cordice, Knowles 2, Bowgett (pen)	1	2	3	4	5	8	9	10						6		7	11				
	Feb-27	(a) Dunstable	W 2-1	Knowles, Bowgett (pen)	1	2	3		5	8	9	11	10					6		4	7				
	Mar-02	(h) Welling U	D 1-1	Bowgett	1	2	3	4	5	8		11	9					6		10	7				
	Mar-06	(h) Gosport B	L 0-1		1		3	4	5	8	9	10	12				7	6		2	11				
	Mar-16	(h) Tonbridge	L 1-2	A Cordice	1		3	4	5	8	9	10	12				7	6		2	11				
	Mar-18	(a) Gosport B	W 3-1	A Cordice, Knowles, Bowgett	1		3	4	5	8	9	11					7	6		2	10				
	Mar-20	(h) Canterbury City	W 2-0	N Cordice, Wainwright	1		3	4	5	8		10	9				7	6		2	11				
	Mar-23	(h) Andover	W 4-0	Bowgett 3 (3 pens), Wainwright	1		3	4	5	8	9	10				6	7			2	11				
	Mar-25	(h) Hounslow	W 3-0	A Cordice, Pearce, Byatt	1	12	3	4	5	8	9	10					7	6		2	11				
	Mar-27	(h) Folkestone T	W 6-0	A Cordice 4, Waites, Bowgett (pen)	1		3	4	5	8	9	10					7	6		2	11				
	Mar-30	(a) Dorchester T	D 2-2	A Cordice, Pearce	1	2	3	4	5	8	9	10						6		7	11				
	Apr-01	(h) Basingstoke T	W 1-0	Davies	1		3	4	5	8	9	10					7	6		2	11				
	Apr-03	(a) Welling U	D 0-0		1		3	4	5	8	9	10					7	6		2	11				
	Apr-07	(a) Fareham Town	W 1-0	Morris	1	2	3		5		9	11	8			7		6		4	10				
	Apr-10	(a) Hillingdon B	D 1-1	Knowles	1	2	3		5		9	10	8			12	7	6		4	11				
	Apr-17	(h) Waterlooville	W 2-1	A Cordice 2	1	12	3	4	5	8	9	10					7	6		2	11				
	Apr-20	(a) Thanet U	W 2-0	A Cordice, Bowgett	1		3	4	5	8	9	10				12	7	6		2	11				
	Apr-22	(h) Hillingdon B	W 1-0	Bowgett (pen)	1		3	4	5	8	9						7	6		2	11	10			
	Apr-24	(a) Andover	W 1-0	Churchouse	1		3	4	5	8	9					11	7	6		2		10			
	Apr-27	(h) Chelmsford City	W 1-0	Knowles	1		3	4	5	8	9	10					7	6		2	11				
	Apr-29	(h) Hastings U	W 2-0	A Cordice 2	1		3	4	5	8	9	10					7	6		2	11	12			
	May-01	(h) Ashford Town	W 3-0	Knowles, Davies, Bowgett (pen)	1		3	4	5	8	9	10					7	6		2	11				
	May-03	(a) Addlestone & W	L 0-1		1		3	4	5	9						8	7	6		2	11	10			
Southern League Championship																									
	May-08	(a) Nuneaton B	L 0-1		1		3	4	5	8	9	10					7	6		2	11	12			
	May-10	(h) Nuneaton B	W 2-1†	Churchouse, og	1	2	3		5	8	9						7	6		4	11	10			
		†After extra time(Agg 2-2). Wealdstone won 3-2 on penalties																							
FA Cup																									
1Q	Sep-19	(h) Salisbury	W 4-0	Johnson, A Cordice 2, Waites	1	2	3	4	5	7	9		8	11			10	6							
2Q	Oct-03	(a) Newbury Town	W 6-1	Johnson 2, N Cordice, A Cordice 2, Bowgett	1	2	3	4	5	8	9		10	11			7	6							
3Q	Oct-17	(h) Harrow Borough	L 1-4	Johnson	1	2	3	4	5	8	9		10	11	12		7	6							
FA Trophy																									
1Q	Oct-24	(a) Harrow Borough	D 2-2	Forde 2	1	2	3	4	5		9		10	11	12	8	7	6							
1Qr	Oct-27	(h) Harrow Borough	W 4-0	Johnson, N Cordice 2, Pearce	1	2	3	4	5			9	10	11	8		7	6							
2Q	Nov-28	(a) Bedworth U	D 1-1	Bowgett (pen)	1	2	3	4	5	8	7	9	10	11				6							
2Qr	Dec-02	(h) Bedworth U	W 5-1	Johnson, A Cordice 2, Bowgett (pen), og	1	2	3	4	5	8	9		10	11			7	6							
3Q	Jan-04	(a) Sutton Coldfield T	D 0-0		1	2	3	4	5		9	11	10				7	6		8					
3Qr	Jan-06	(h) Sutton Coldfield T	W 2-1	Perkins, og	1	2	3	4	5		9	11	10				7	6		8					
1	Jan-20	(h) Gloucester C	W 3-1	N Cordice, A Cordice, Bowgett	1	2	3	4	5	8	9	11	10				7	6							
2	Feb-06	(h) Dagenham	L 1-2	A Cordice	1	2	3	4	5	8	9	11	10					6		7					
Southern League Cup																									
1	Aug-18	(h) Chelmsford City	W 5-1	Johnson, A Cordice,Wainwright, Forde, Bowgett(pen)	1	2	3	5	6	7	8	9		4	11		10								
1	Aug-24	(a) Chelmsford City	W 4-2	Johnson 2, Knowles, Byatt	1	2	3	4	5	7		9		11			10	6					8		
2	Nov-10	(h) Hillingdon B	W 2-1	N Cordice, Knowles	1	2	3	4	5	8		9	10	11		12	7	6							
3	Feb-03	(a) Dover	W 2-0	Knowles, Byatt (pen)	1	2		4		8	9	11	10			7		6		5	3				
SF	Feb-16	(a) Dorchester T	W 3-1	Wainwright, Bowgett 2	1	2	3	4	5	8	9	10						6		7	11				
SF	Feb-24	(h) Dorchester T	W 2-0	A Cordice, Wainwright	1	2	3	4	5	8	9	11						6		10	7				
F	Apr-05	(a) Gloucester C	W 1-0	Pearce	1		3	4	5	8	9	10					7	6		2	11				
F	Apr-14	(h) Gloucester C	W 1-0	Bowgett (pen)	1	12	3	4	5	8	9	10	7					6		2	11				
Middlesex Senior Cup																									
2	Jan-25	(a) Edgware	W 5-0	Knowles 2, Barwick, Pearce, Bowgett (pen)	1	2	3		5	8	9	10	15			12	7	6		4	11				
3	Feb-20	(a) Hillingdon B	D 0-0		1	2	3	4	5	8	9	11	10					6			7				
3r	Feb-22	(h) Hillingdon B	W 2-1	Knowles 2	1	2	3	4	5	8	9	11	10					6			7				
SF	Mar-13	(h) Enfield	W 2-0	A Cordice, Waites	1	15	3	4	5	8	9	10					7	6		2	11				
F	Apr-12	(n*)Hayes	L 0-2		1	4	3		5			10	8			9	7	6		2	11				
		*played at Southall FC																							
Middlesex Charity Cup																									
F	Aug-08	(h) Wembley	D 2-2 aet	Knowles, Bowgett (pen)		2	3		5	7	10	9	8		11			4						1	6
		‡Final held over from 1980-81 season.																							

1982-83

Rd	Date	Opponent	Result	Scorers	Goddard R	Perkins S	Pearce S	Byatt D	Bowgett P	Barwick F	Davies R	Wainwright R	Cordice N	Graves M	Johnson N	Knowles R	Cordice A	Waites P	Elliott M	Priddy P	Margerrison J	Waddock A	Crooks A
Alliance Premier League - 3rd																							
	Aug-14	(a) Altrincham	W 1-0	Graves	1	2	3	4	5	6	7	8	9	10	11								
	Aug-16	(a) Dagenham	W 2-1	N Cordice 2	1	2	3	4	5	6		8	7	9	11	10							
	Aug-21	(h) Boston U	D 0-0		1	2	3	4	5	6		8	10	7	11		9						
	Aug-28	(a) Scarborough	W 2-1	A Cordice, Byatt	1	2	3	4	5	6		8		7	11	10	9						
	Sep-04	(a) Trowbridge T	D 0-0		1	2	3	4	5	6	11	8	9	7		10							
	Sep-07	(h) Dagenham	W 3-1	N Cordice, Johnson, Wainwright	1	2	3	4	5	6	10	8	9	7	11								
	Sep-11	(h) Northwich Vic	W 2-1	Johnson, Pearce	1	2	3	4	5	6		8	10	9	11			7	12				
	Sep-25	(a) Telford U	D 0-0			2	3	4	5	6	7	8	10		11		9			1			
	Oct-09	(h) Worcester City	W 2-0	N Cordice, A Cordice	1	2	3	4	5	6	7		11	10			9	8					
	Oct-23	(h) Stafford R	W 3-2	A Cordice, Bowgett, Davies	1	2	3	4	5	6	7		11	10			9	8					
	Nov-06	(a) Frickley Ath	D 2-2	A Cordice, Davies	1	2	3	4	5	6	7	8	11	10			9						
	Nov-08	(a) Nuneaton B	D 1-1	Graves	1	2	3	4	5	6	7	8	11	10			9						
	Nov-13	(h) Weymouth	L 2-4	A Cordice, Pearce	1	2	3	4	5	6	7	8	11	10	12		9						
	Nov-27	(a) Runcorn	L 1-2	Graves	1	2	3	4	5		7	6	11	10	8	12	9						
	Dec-04	(h) Frickley Ath	W 2-0	Johnson 2	1	2		4	5		3	6	11	10	8		9	7					
	Dec-11	(h) Nuneaton B	L 1-2	Graves	1	3		4	5	2	7	6	11	10	8		9						
	Dec-18	(a) Barrow	W 2-0	N Cordice, Johnson	1	3		4	5	2	7	6	11	10	8		9						
	Dec-27	(h) Barnet	W 6-0	Graves 2, A Cordice, N Cordice, Johnson, Bowgett(pen)	1	3		4	5	2	7	6	11	10	8		9						
	Jan-01	(a) Enfield	W 1-0	Graves	1	2		4	5	3	7	6	11	10	8		9						
	Jan-04	(h) Maidstone	D 0-0		1	3		4	5	2	7	6	11	10	8		9						
	Jan-08	(h) Barrow	W 4-0	Graves, A Cordice, N Cordice, Johnson	1	3		4	5	2	7	6	11	10	8		9	12					
	Jan-22	(h) Bangor C	W 2-0	Graves, Byatt (pen)	1	2	3	4	5	8	7	6	11	10			9	12					
	Feb-02	(a) Bath C	L 2-3	A Cordice, og	1	2	3	4	5	6		8	11	10			9				7		
	Feb-19	(a) Kettering T	W 3-1	N Cordice, Johnson, Byatt	1	2	3	4	5	6			11	10	7		9				8		
	Feb-26	(h) Trowbridge T	W 4-0	Graves, A Cordice, Margerrison, Davies	1	2	3	4	5	6	7		11	10	12		9				8		
	Mar-05	(a) Bangor C	D 2-2	N Cordice, Davies	1	2	3	4	5	6	7	8	11	10	9								
	Mar-12	(h) Yeovil T	W 2-0	N Cordice, A Cordice	1	2	3	4	5	6	7		11	10			9				8		
	Mar-15	(a) Stafford R	L 1-2	Graves	1	2	3	4	5	6	7		11	10			9				8		
	Mar-19	(a) Yeovil T	W 5-1	Graves 3, N Cordice, A Cordice	1	2	3	4	5	6	7		11	10			9				8		
	Mar-21	(a) Worcester City	W 3-1	Graves, A Cordice, Margerrison	1	2	3	4	5	6	7		11	10			9				8		
	Mar-24	(a) Barnet	D 0-0		1	2	3	4		6	7	5	11		10		9				8		
	Mar-29	(h) Runcorn	W 1-0	Johnson	1	4	3		5	2	7		11	10	6		9				8		
	Apr-02	(a) Maidstone U	W 3-0	Graves 2, Margerrison	1	2	3	4	5	6	7	12	11	10			9				8		
	Apr-09	(h) Bath C	D 1-1	Graves	1	2	3	4	5	6	7			10	11		9				8		
	Apr-12	(h) Enfield	L 1-3	Graves	1	2	3	4	5	6	7	11		10			9				8		
	Apr-16	(a) Weymouth	L 1-4	Byatt (pen)	1	2	3	4	5	6	7	11		10			9				8		
	Apr-19	(h) Telford U	W 2-0	Margerrison, Byatt (pen)	1	2	3	4	5	6	7			10	11		9				8		
	Apr-23	(h) Scarborough	D 2-2	Graves, Johnson	1	2	3	4	5	6	7	12		10	11		9				8		
	Apr-30	(a) Boston U	D 0-0		1		3	4	5	6	7			10	11		9				8	2	
	May-02	(a) Northwich Vic	D 3-3	A Cordice, Pearce, Davies	1		3	4	5	6	7			10	11		9				8	2	
	May-04	(h) Kettering T	W 4-0	Graves 3, Pearce (pen)	1		3	4	5		7	6		10	11		9	12			8	2	
	May-07	(h) Altrincham	D 1-1	Johnson	1		3	4	5		7	6		10	11		9				8	2	
FA Cup																							
1Q	Sep-18	(h) Hertford Town	W 5-0	Graves, N Cordice 3, A Cordice	1	2	3	4	5	6		8	10	9	11		12	7					
2Q	Oct-02	(a) Hendon	D 1-1	Byatt	1	2	3	4	5	6	7	8			11	10	9						
2Qr	Oct-05	(h) Hendon	W 3-2 aet	Graves 2, N Cordice	1	2	3	4	5	6	7	8	12	10	11		9						
3Q	Oct-16	(a) Dulwich Hamlet	D 0-0		1	2	3	4	5	6	7		11	10			9	8					
3Qr	Oct-18	(h) Dulwich Hamlet	W 2-1	Graves, Bowgett	1	2	3	4	5	6	7		11	10			9	8					
4Q	Oct-30	(h) Sutton U	W 3-1	Graves, N Cordice, A Cordice	1	2	3	4	5	6	7		11	10			9	8					
1	Nov-20	(a) Swindon T	L 0-2		1	2	3	4	5	6	7	8	11	10			9						
FA Trophy																							
1	Jan-18	(a) Wycombe W	L 1-2	N Cordice	1	5	3	4		2	7	6	11	10	8		9						
Bob Lord Trophy																							
1	Aug-25	(a) Bath C	W 1-0	Barwick	1	2	3	4	5	6		8		7	11	10	9						
1	Aug-31	(h) Bath C	L 0-2		1	4	3		5	2		8	6	7	11	10	9						
Middlesex Senior Cup																							
2	Dec-14	(a) Hampton	W 3-2	A Cordice 2, og	1	3		4	5	2	7	6	11	10	8		9						
3	Jan-29	(a) Kingsbury Town	W 2-1	Waites, Waddock	1	2	3	4	5		7	6	9	10				8				11	12
SF	Mar-01	(a) Hillingdon B	D 1-1	Margerrison	1	2		4	5	6	3		11	10	9			7			8	12	
SFr	Mar-08	(h) Hillingdon B	W 1-0 aet	N Cordice	1	2	3	4	5	6	7		9	10	11						8		
F	Apr-04	(n*) Harrow Borough	L 0-2		1	2	3	4	5	6	7	11		10	14		9				8		
		*played at Hillingdon Borough FC.																					
Southern League Challenge Match																							
	Oct-12	(h) Gloucester C	W 3-1 aet	Graves, A Cordice, Pearce	1	2	3	4	5	6	7		11	10		12	9	8					

1983-84					Iles B	Waddock A	Pearce S	Morris M	Bowgett P	Price D	Donellan G	Barwick F	Cordice A	Graves M	Johnson N	Waites P	Richardson J	Byatt D	McCargo S	Greenaway B	Cordice N	Perkins S	Wainwright R	Dibble C	Goddard R
Alliance Premier League - 4th																									
	Aug-20	(a) Gateshead	D 1-1	Donellan	1	2	3	4	5	6	7	8	9	10	11	12	14								
	Aug-23	(h) Yeovil T	W 1-0	Bowgett	1	2	8		5	4	7	6	9	10	11		3								
	Aug-27	(h) Kidderminster H	W 2-0	A Cordice 2	1	2	8		5		7	6	9	10	11	12	3	4	13						
	Aug-30	(a) Trowbridge T	W 2-1	Graves 2	1		3		5	6	8	2	9	10	11	12		4		7					
	Sep-03	(a) Telford U	W 1-0	Graves	1		3		5	6	8	2	9	10				4	11	7					
	Sep-10	(h) Bangor C	W 5-0	Graves 2, Johnson, Bowgett, Donellan	1		3		5	6	8	2		10	11			4	9	7	12	13			
	Sep-20	(a) Bath C	D 0-0		1		3		5	6			9	10	11			4		7	8	2	12		
	Sep-24	(h) Altrincham	W 3-1	Graves 3	1		3		5	6	8		9	10	11			4		7		2	12		
	Sep-28	(a) Yeovil T	D 0-0		1		3		5	6	8		9	10	11			4		7	13	2	12		
	Oct-08	(h) Boston U	D 1-1	Johnson	1		3		5	6	8		9	10	11			4		7		2	12		
	Oct-22	(a) Weymouth	W 4-0	Greenaway 2, Bowgett, Barwick	1				5	6	8	2	9	12	11			4		7		3	10		
	Nov-12	(a) Dagenham	L 0-1		1				5	6	8	2	9	10				4		7	12	3		11	
	Nov-26	(h) Nuneaton B	D 0-0		1				5	6	8	2	9	10				4		7	11	3	12		
	Dec-03	(a) Worcester City	D 1-1	Dibble	1				5		6	2	9	10				4		7	8	3	12	11	
	Dec-17	(h) Maidstone U	L 1-2	Bowgett	1				5	4	3		9	10	8					12	11	2	6	7	
	Dec-21	(a) Boston U	D 1-1	Graves					5	4			9	10	8				3	12	11	2	6	7	1
	Dec-26	(a) Kettering T	W 2-1	A Cordice, Graves (pen)					5	4			9	10	8				3	7		2	6	11	1
	Dec-31	(a) Enfield	W 2-0	Greenaway, Dibble					5				9	10	8			4	3	7		2	6	11	1
	Jan-02	(h) Kettering T	W 4-2	Graves 3, Dibble					5		14		9	10	8			4	3	7		2	6	11	1
	Jan-07	(a) Scarborough	D 1-1	Bowgett					5	2	12		9	10	8			4	3	7			6	11	1
	Jan-10	(h) Barnet	W 3-0	Graves 2 (1 pen), Greenaway	1				5	2	12		9	10	8			4	3	7			6	11	
	Jan-21	(h) Weymouth	W 2-0	Johnson, A Cordice	1				5				9	10	8			4	3	7		2	6	11	
	Feb-04	(h) Enfield	W 2-1	Graves, Johnson	1				5				9	10	8			4	3	7		2	6	11	
	Feb-11	(a) Kidderminster H	L 1-3	Johnson	1				5		3		9	10	8			4		7		2	6	11	
	Feb-14	(h) Trowbridge T	W 6-0	Graves,Greenaway 3(1 pen),Bowgett,McCargo	1				5		13		9	10	8			4	3	7		2	6	11	
	Feb-18	(a) Northwich Vic	D 1-1	Graves	1				5				9	10	8			4	3	7		2	6	11	
	Feb-28	(h) Bath C	L 0-3		1				5	12			9	10	8			4	3	7		2	6	11	
	Mar-03	(h) Scarborough	D 1-1	Graves (pen)	1				5	6	7		9	10	8			4	3			2		11	
	Mar-06	(a) Barnet	D 1-1	og	1				5	6	7		9	10	8			4	3			2		11	
	Mar-10	(a) Nuneaton B	D 1-1	Graves	1				5	6	7		9	10	8			4	3			2		11	
	Mar-17	(a) Maidstone U	L 1-2	Donellan	1				5	7	9			10	8			4	3		12	2	6	11	
	Mar-20	(a) Bangor C	D 0-0		1				5	7	11		9	10	8			4	3	12		2	6		
	Mar-24	(h) Runcorn	W 4-2	Graves 2 (2 pens), A Cordice, Greenaway	1					5	11		9	10	8				3	7		4	6	2	
	Mar-31	(h) Worcester City	W 3-1	Graves 2 (1 pen), og	1					6			9	10	8			4	3	7	14	5	11	2	
	Apr-07	(a) Runcorn	L 2-4	Graves, Bowgett	1				5	6			9	10	8			4	3	7	12		11	2	
	Apr-11	(h) Telford U	W 4-0	Johnson 2, Greenaway, Dibble	1				5		11		9		8			4	3	7		2	6	10	
	Apr-17	(a) Frickley Ath	W 5-2	Graves 4 (1 pen), Greenaway	1						11		9	10	8			4	3	7		5	6	2	
	Apr-21	(h) Gateshead	W 4-0	Graves, A Cordice, N Cordice, Bowgett	1				5		11		9	10	8			4	3	7	12	2	6		
	Apr-24	(h) Dagenham	W 1-0	Donellan	1				5		11		9	10	8			4	3	7	12		6	2	
	Apr-28	(h) Frickley Ath	D 0-0		1				5		11		9	10	8			4	3	7		2	6		
	May-01	(h) Northwich Vic	W 1-0	Graves	1				5		11		9	10	8			4	3	7		2	6		
	May-05	(a) Altrincham	L 0-1		1				5	14	11		9	10	8			4	3	7		2	6		
FA Cup																									
1Q	Sep-17	(a) Cambridge C	W 2-1	Graves, Johnson	1				5	6	8		9	10	11		3	4		7	12	2			
2Q	Oct-01	(a) Aveley	D 1-1	Byatt (pen)	1		3		5	6	8		9		11			4		7	10	2	12		
2Qr	Oct-04	(h) Aveley	W 2-0	Johnson, Byatt (pen)	1		3		5	6	7		9		11			4			10	2	8		
3Q	Oct-15	(h) Basildon U	W 3-1	Graves, A Cordice, Greenaway	1		3		5	6	8	2	9	10	11			4		7					
4Q	Oct-29	(h) Bishops Stortford	W 1-0	A Cordice	1				5	6	8	2	9	10	11			4		7		3			
1	Nov-19	(h) Enfield	D 1-1	Graves	1				5	6	8	2	9	10				4		7		3	11	12	
1r1	Nov-22	(a) Enfield	D 2-2 aet	Graves, Byatt (pen)	1				5	6		2	9	10				4		7	11	3	12	8	
1r2	Nov-28	(h) Enfield	W 2-0	Graves, N Cordice	1				5		6	2	9	10				4		7	8	3		11	
2	Dec-10	(a) Colchester U	L 0-4		1				5	12	3		9	10				4		7	11	2	6	8	
FA Trophy																									
1	Jan-14	(a) Yeovil T	L 3-4	Byatt 2, Wainwright	1				5	2	3		9	10	8			4		7			6	11	
Bob Lord Trophy																									
2	Nov-08	(h) Barnet	L 1-3	Johnson	1				5	6		2		10	11			4		7	9	3		8	
2	Dec-13	(a) Barnet	W 3-2	Graves, Johnson, Byatt	1					5	3		9	10	8			4	14	7	11		6	2	
Middlesex Senior Cup																									
2	Nov-15	(h) Hendon	L 1-2	Barwick	1				5	6	8	2		10				4		12	9	3	11	7	

1984-85

Rd	Date	Opponent	Result	Scorers	Iles B	Davies R	McCargo S	Byatt D	Bowgett P	Wainwright R	Greenaway B	Holmes L	Cordice A	Graves M	Donellan G	Wedderburn K	Cordice N	McGuinness W	Goddard R	Johnson N	Dibble C	Perkins S	Baddeley K	Jones V	Graham A	Cotter P	Dowe H	Ascensao J
Gola League - 1st																												
	Aug-18	(a) Northwich Vic	W 2-0	Graves, Holmes	1	2	3	4	5	6	7	8	9	10	11													
	Aug-21	(h) Dartford	D 0-0		1	2	3	4	5	6	7	8	9	10	11													
	Aug-25	(h) Kidderminster H	W 5-2	Graves 3, Wainwright, Holmes	1	2	3	4	5	6	7	8	9	10	11	12												
	Aug-27	(a) Dagenham	W 2-1	Graves, Donellan	1	2	3	4	5	6		8	9	10	11		7											
	Sep-01	(h) Gateshead	W 4-2	Graves 2, N Cordice, Holmes	1	2	3	4	5	6	14	8	9	10	11		7											
	Sep-08	(a) Boston U	D 1-1	Greenaway	1	2	3	4	5	6	7	8	9	10	11		12											
	Sep-11	(h) Nuneaton B	W 3-1	Graves (pen), Bowgett, McCargo		2	3	4	5	6	7	8	9	10	11			1										
	Sep-19	(a) Yeovil T	W 2-0	Graves, Byatt		2	3	4	5	6	7	8	9	10	11		12		1									
	Sep-22	(a) Worcester City	W 4-0	Graves, A Cordice, Donellan, Greenaway		2	3	4	5	6	7	8	9	10	11		12		1									
	Sep-25	(h) Boston U	L 0-1			2	3	4	5	6	7	8	9	10	11		12		1									
	Oct-02	(a) Dartford	W 3-2	Graves, N Cordice, McCargo		2	3	4	5	6	7	8	9	10	11		12		1	14								
	Oct-06	(h) Telford U	D 2-2	Graves, McCargo		2	3	4	5		7	8		10	11		9		1	6	14							
	Oct-09	(a) Bath C	L 1-3	Johnson			3	4	5	6	7	8	9	10	11				1	14	2							
	Oct-20	(h) Worcester City	D 3-3	A Cordice 3		3		4	5	6	7	8	9	10	11		12		1		2							
	Oct-27	(h) Barrow	D 2-2	A Cordice, Donellan		3		4	5	6	7	8	9	10	11				1			2						
	Nov-03	(a) Telford U	L 2-4	Graves, Wainwright		2		4	5	6	7		9	10	11		8	1					3	12				
	Nov-10	(a) Enfield	L 0-2			2		4	5	6	7	8	9	10	11			1					3	12				
	Nov-24	(h) Bath C	L 0-1		1	2			5	6	7	4	9	10	11		8						3					
	Dec-01	(a) Weymouth	W 3-0	Graves 2, Holmes	1	2			5	6	7	4	9	10	11		8						3					
	Dec-15	(a) Frickley Ath	W 2-0	N Cordice, Greenaway	1	2	3		5	6	7		9	10	11		8							4				
	Dec-22	(h) Altrincham	W 1-0	A Cordice	1	2	3		5	6	7	4	9	10	11		8											
	Dec-29	(h) Maidstone U	D 1-1	Donellan	1	2	3		5	8	7	4	9	10	11		6			12								
	Jan-01	(h) Barnet	L 1-2	A Cordice	1	2	3		5	8	7	4	9	10	11		6			12				14				
	Jan-05	(a) Scarborough	D 1-1	Johnson	1	3		4	5	6	7	8	9	10	11					12		2						
	Mar-02	(a) Barrow	L 1-2	Holmes	1	3		4	5	6		8	9		11		12			7		2			10			
	Mar-09	(a) Maidstone U	W 1-0	Graham		11	3	4	5	6		8	9	10								2		7	14	1		
	Mar-19	(h) Yeovil T	L 0-3			2	3	4	5	6			9		14		8			11				7	10	1		
	Mar-23	(h) Weymouth	W 3-2	N Cordice, Johnson, Donellan		2	3		5		7	8		14	9		6			11		4		12	10	1		
	Mar-25	(a) Altrincham	W 2-1	Graham, A Cordice	1		3	4	5	6		8	9		11					12		2		7	10			
	Mar-27	(a) Gateshead	W 2-1	N Cordice 2	1	11	3	4	5	6	7		9	14			8					2			10			
	Mar-30	(h) Runcorn	W 1-0	A Cordice	1		3	4	5	6			9	12	11		8			14		2		7	10			
	Mar-31	(h) Scarborough	W 1-0	A Cordice	1	2	3	4		6	7		9	12			8			11		5			10			
	Apr-02	(a) Runcorn	L 0-2		1	2	3	4		6			12	10	9		8			11		5		7				
	Apr-16	(h) Northwich Vic	D 1-1	A Cordice	1	14	3	4	5	6	7	12	9	10	11		8					2						
	Apr-18	(h) Enfield	L 1-2	N Cordice	1	3		4	5	6		8	9	12	11		7					2			10			
	Apr-20	(a) Nuneaton B	L 0-1		1	3		4	5	6	7	8	9	10	11		12					2						
	Apr-22	(h) Kettering T	W 1-0	og	1	3		4	5	6	7	8	9	10	11							2						
	Apr-27	(h) Dagenham	D 0-0		1	3			5	6	7	8	9	10	11		2							4	14			
	Apr-29	(a) Kidderminster H	W 3-0	Graham, Holmes, og	1	3		4	5	6	7	8	9		11		2			14					10			
	May-01	(h) Frickley Ath	D 1-1	Holmes	1	3		4	5	6	7	8	9		11		2								10			
	May-04	(a) Kettering T	W 1-0	Graham	1	3		4		6	7	8	9		11		2					5			10			
	May-06	(a) Barnet	L 0-7			12		4	5		7	8		10	9					11		2		6		1	3	
FA Cup																												
1Q	Sep-15	(a) Hounslow	W 5-2	N Cordice, Holmes, Bowgett, Greenaway, Donellan		2	3	4	5	6	7	8	9	10	11		12	1										
2Q	Sep-29	(h) Dunstable	W 6-0	Graves(pen), Holmes 2,N Cordice,Donellan,McCargo		2	3	4	5	6	7	8	9	10	11		12		1									
3Q	Oct-13	(a) Grays Athletic	L 1-2	A Cordice			3	4	5	6	7	8	9	10	11				1	12	2							
FA Trophy																												
1	Jan-28	(a) Harlow Town	D 0-0		1	2	3		5	6	7	8	9	10	11							4						
1r	Jan-30	(h) Harlow Town	W 5-0	Graves 3, A Cordice, Greenaway	1	2	3		5	6	7	8	9	10	11					12		4						
2	Feb-02	(h) Wycombe W	W 2-1	Bowgett, Greenaway (pen)	1	5		3	4	6	7	8	9	10	11					12		2						
3	Feb-23	(h) Welling U	W 3-1	Graham, A Cordice, Johnson	1	3		4	5	6		8	9		11		12			7		2			10			
4	Mar-16	(h) Frickley Ath	W 3-1	Graham, A Cordice 2	1	12	3	4	5	6			9				8			11		2		7	10			
SF	Apr-06	(a) Enfield	W 2-0	Graham, N Cordice	1	12	3	4	5	6	7		9				8			11		2			10			
SF	Apr-13	(h) Enfield	L 0-1		1		3	4	5	6			9		7		8			12		2		11	10			
F	May-11	(n*) Boston U	W 2-1	Graham, Holmes	1	3		4	5	6	7	8	9		11		12					2			10			
		*Played at Wembley Stadium																										
Bob Lord Trophy																												
2	Nov-06	(h) Enfield	L 1-2	Bowgett		2		4	5	6		12		10	11		8	1			7		3	9				
Middlesex Senior Cup																												
2	Nov-17	(a) Rayners Lane	W 3-2	Graves 2 (1 pen), Donellan		2				6	7	8	9	10	11		4		1				3	5				
3	Feb-07	(h) Hillingdon B	W 3-2	N Cordice, Holmes, Davies	1	2	3	4	5			6			11		8			12				7	9			10
SF	Feb-26	(a) Harrow Borough	W 1-0	Holmes	1	4	3		5	6		8	9		11		12			7		2		14	10			

1985-86

	Date	Opponent	Result	Scorers	Iles B	Perkins S	McCargo S	Byatt D	Bowgett P	Wainwright R	Greenaway B	Holmes L	Cordice A	Graves M	Donnellan G	Doyle D	Cordice N	Tapley S	Jones P	Jones V	Graham A	Davies R	Seagraves C	O'Keefe R	McClure D	Tong K	Cleaveley L	Elliott T
Gola League - 10th																												
	Aug-24	(h) Barrow	W 4-0	Graves, Holmes 2, Greenaway	1	2	3	4	5	6	7	8	9	10	11	12	14											
	Aug-31	(a) Northwich Vic	D 2-2	Donnellan, McCargo	1	2	3	4	5	6	7	8	9	10	11		12											
	Sep-04	(a) Boston U	L 0-1		1		3	4	5	6	7	8	9	10	11		12	2										
	Sep-07	(h) Frickley Ath	W 2-0	Holmes 2	1	4	3		5	6	7	8	9	10		11	12	2										
	Sep-14	(a) Cheltenham T	W 2-1	A Cordice, Doyle	1	4	3		5	6	7	8	9			11	10	2		12								
	Sep-21	(a) Nuneaton B	D 0-0		1	4	3		5	6	7	8	9	10		11		2		14	12							
	Sep-25	(a) Maidstone U	W 1-0	Doyle	1		3	4	5	6	7	8	9	12		11		2		14	10							
	Sep-28	(h) Altrincham	D 2-2	Graves, Doyle (pen)		4	3		5	6	7	8	9	10		11	12	2	1	14								
	Oct-01	(h) Maidstone U	W 3-2	Graves, N Cordice, Wainwright		4	3		5	6	7	8	9	10		11	12	2	1	14								
	Oct-05	(a) Runcorn	D 1-1	Holmes		4	3		5	6	7	8		10	14	11	9	2	1	12								
	Oct-08	(a) Dartford	W 2-1	N Cordice, Bowgett	1	4	3		5	6		8		10	7	11	9	2										
	Oct-12	(h) Enfield	L 2-4	Graves, Graham	1	4	3		5	6			9	10	11	7	8	2			12							
	Oct-15	(h) Dagenham	L 0-4		1	4			5	6			9	10	11	7	8	2			12	3						
	Oct-19	(a) Stafford R	L 1-2	Graham	1		3		5	6	7	8	9	12	11		2	4			10							
	Oct-22	(h) Boston U	W 7-2	Graves 2,Wainwright 4(3 pens),Greenaway	1		3		5	6	7	8	9	10	11		2	4		14								
	Oct-26	(a) Altrincham	L 0-1		1		3		5	6	7	8	9	10	11		2	4										
	Nov-02	(h) Northwich Vic	D 0-0		1	14	3		5	6	7	8		10	9		11	4		2	12							
	Nov-09	(h) Wycombe W	W 2-0	Graham, V Jones	1	12	3	4	5	6	7	8			11	14		2		9	10							
	Nov-23	(a) Kettering T	L 1-2	N Cordice	1		3	4	5	6				10	11	7	9	2		8				14				
	Nov-30	(h) Barnet	W 2-0	Greenaway, Wainwright	1		3	4		6	7	8			11		10	2		5	9							
	Dec-14	(h) Kettering T	W 3-1	Graham, N Cordice, Wainwright (pen)	1		3	4		6	7	8			11		10	5			9		2					
	Dec-28	(a) Barnet	L 0-1		1		3	4	5	6	7	8		10	11		9	2		14								
	Jan-01	(h) Nuneaton B	W 1-0	Bowgett	1		3	4	5	6	7	8		10	11		9	2		14								
	Jan-04	(a) Telford U	L 1-2	Holmes	1		3	4	5	6		8		10	11		9	2		12				7				
	Jan-06	(a) Dagenham	W 2-0	Donnellan, Byatt	1		3	4		6		8		10	11	7	9	5		12	14		2					
	Jan-11	(a) Scarborough	W 1-0	N Cordice	1		3	4	5	6	7	8		10		11	9	2		12								
	Jan-25	(h) Dartford	W 2-1	N Cordice, V Jones	1		3	4	5	6	7			10		11	9	2		8								
	Feb-01	(a) Bath C	W 3-2	Wainwright (pen), Greenaway, Doyle	1		3	4	5	6	7	8		10		11	9	2		12								
	Mar-08	(h) Cheltenham T	D 0-0		1		3		5	6	7	8		10	11		9	2		4	14							
	Mar-11	(a) Weymouth	L 2-4	Graves, Greenaway	1		3		5	6	7			10	11	8	9	2		4								
	Mar-15	(a) Kidderminster H	L 1-3	Graves	1		3		5	6	7			10	11	8	9	2		4	12							
	Mar-22	(h) Kidderminster H	L 0-3		1		3	4	5	6	7		9	10	11		8	2										
	Mar-29	(a) Frickley Ath	L 1-2	Doyle	1			4	5	6	7	9		10	11	8		2		3			14	12				
	Mar-31	(h) Bath C	L 0-1		1		3	4	5	6	7	10	9			11	8	2		12				14				
	Apr-05	(h) Scarborough	L 0-3		1			4	5	6	7	8		10		11	9	2		14					3	12		
	Apr-08	(h) Weymouth	W 1-0	Graham					5	6	8	7		10		11		2		4	9				3	14	1	
	Apr-12	(h) Telford U	D 1-1	Graham	1				5	6	8	7		10		11		2		4	9				3	14		
	Apr-19	(a) Wycombe W	L 0-1		1			4	5	6	7	8		10		11		2			9				3	14		
	Apr-26	(a) Barrow	D 1-1	Holmes	1		14	4	5	6	7	8		10		11		2			12				3	9		
	Apr-29	(a) Enfield	L 0-1		1		14	4	5	6	7	8		10		11		2			9				3			
	May-01	(h) Stafford R	L 2-3	Graves, McCargo	1		3		5	6	7	8		10		11		4			9				2	12		
	May-03	(h) Runcorn	D 1-1	Graham	1		3		5	6	7	8		10	11			4			9				2	12		
FA Cup																												
1	Nov-16	(a) Reading	L 0-1		1		3	4	5	6	7	8			9	11		2		12	10							
FA Trophy																												
1	Dec-21	(h) Welling U	W 1-0	Wainwright	1		3	4	5	6	7	8		12	11		9	2			10							
2	Jan-18	(h) Frickley Ath	W 2-1	Wainwright, Holmes	1		3	4	5	6	7	8		10		11	9	2		12								
3	Mar-03	(h) South Bank	D 0-0		1		3	4	5	6		8		10	11	7	9	2										
3r	Mar-06	(a) South Bank	L 1-2 aet	Graves	1		3		5	6		8		10	11	7	9	2		4						12		
Bob Lord Trophy																												
2	Nov-06	(h) Weymouth	D 1-1	N Cordice	1		3	4	5	6	7	8			11		10	2		14	9							
2	Nov-26	(a) Weymouth	L 2-3	Holmes, Wainwright (pen)	1		3	4	5	6		9			11	7	10	2		8								
Gola Championship Shield																												
	Sep-17	(h) Runcorn	D 2-2†	Holmes, Doyle	1	4	3		5	6	7	8	9	10		11		2		14	12							
		†After extra time lost on penalties 3-5																										
Middlesex Senior Cup																												
F	Aug-26	(a) Enfield	W 4-2†	Graves, A Cordice, N Cordice, Holmes	1	14	3	4	5	6	7	8	9	10	11		12	2										
1	Nov-19	(h) Kingsbury Town	L 1-3	Donnellan	1		14	4		6		8			11	9	12	2		5	10			7				2
		†Held over from 1984-85																										

1986-87

	Date	Opponent	Result	Scorers	Iles B	Tapley S	McClure D	Rutter S	Bowgett P	Wainwright R	Doyle D	Wallace A	Cordice N	Graves M	Donnellan G	Holmes L	Byatt D	Greenaway B	Ragan S	Miller P	Tonge K	Haxton A	Galloway S	Dolling G	Maddison L	Hatter S	Hirst M	McCarthy P	Smurthwaite T	Walton B	Meadows T	Jones V
GM Vauxhall Conference - 19th																																
	Aug-16	(h) Stafford Rangers	L 0-3		1	2	3	4	5	6	7	8	9	10	11	12																
	Aug-20	(a) Maidstone U	L 0-1		1	2	3		5	6	12		9	10	11	8	4	7	14													
	Aug-23	(a) Scarborough	L 1-2	Wainwright	1	2	3	4	5	6	7		9	10	11	8		12	14													
	Aug-26	(h) Dagenham	D 2-2	Graves, Doyle	1	2	3	4	5	6	7		9	10	11	8		12	14													
	Aug-30	(h) Northwich Vic	D 1-1	Doyle (pen)	1		3	4	5	6	7	2	9	10	11	8			14													
	Sep-02	(a) Sutton U	D 2-2	Donnellan, Holmes	1	2	3		5	6	8		9	10	11	7	4															
	Sep-06	(a) Cheltenham T	W 1-0	Graves	1	2	3		5	6	7	14	9	10	11	8	4	12														
	Sep-09	(h) Sutton U	W 2-1	Holmes, Doyle (pen)	1	2	3		5	6	7	4	9	10	11	8		12														
	Sep-13	(h) Altrincham	L 0-2		1	2	3		5	6	7	14	9	10	11	8	4															
	Sep-17	(a) Boston U	L 0-2		1	2	3	12	5	6	7	14	9	10	11	8	4															
	Sep-20	(a) Nuneaton B	D 1-1	Holmes	1	2	3		5	6	7	8	9			10	4	11	14													
	Sep-23	(h) Maidstone U	D 0-0		1	2	3	12	5	6	7	10		9		8	4	11	14													
	Sep-27	(h) Telford U	L 0-1		1	2	3	4	5	6	10			9	11	8		7	14		12											
	Sep-30	(a) Barnet	L 1-2	Ragan	1	2	3	4	5	6	11			10		8		7	9		12											
	Oct-04	(a) Gateshead	D 1-1	Wainwright	1	2	3	4	5	6	11			10		8		7	9		14											
	Oct-07	(h) Welling U	W 3-1	Graves 2, Miller	1	2	3	4	5	6	11			10		8		7	9	12	14											
	Oct-11	(a) Weymouth	L 2-3	Wainwright, Doyle	1	2	3	4	5	6	11			10		8	14	7		9	12											
	Oct-18	(h) Bath C	L 1-2	Graves		2	3	4	5	6	11	8		10				7			12	1	9									
	Nov-01	(a) Northwich Vic	L 1-2	Wallace	1	2	3	5	14	6	11	8		10			4	7			12		9									
	Nov-08	(h) Nuneaton B	W 6-0	Graves, Wallace 2, Galloway 2, Wainwright	1	2	3	5	12	6	11	8		14	9		4	7					10									
	Nov-22	(h) Runcorn	L 0-3		1	2	3		5		11	8	6	10	9		4	7			12			14								
	Nov-29	(a) Enfield	L 2-4	Doyle (pen), Rutter	1	2	3	4	5	6	11	8	7	10						9	14			12								
	Dec-06	(h) Weymouth	W 3-1	Donnellan 2, Wallace	1	2	3	5		6	10	8	14	12	11		4	7		9												
	Dec-13	(a) Kidderminster H	L 2-5	Graves, Miller	1	2	3		5		10	8	14	6	11		4	7		9												
	Dec-26	(h) Kettering T	W 2-1	Wainwright, Wallace	1	2			5	6	10	8	3	12	11		4	7		9	14											
	Jan-01	(a) Kettering T	W 2-0	Wallace 2	1	2	3			6		8	14		11			7		9	10				4	5						
	Jan-03	(h) Frickley Ath	W 2-1	Cordice, Tonge		2	3			6		8	5		11			7		9	10	1			4							
	Jan-10	(a) Welling U	D 1-1	Greenaway (pen)	1	2	3			6		8	5		11			7		9	10				4							
	Jan-24	(a) Telford U	W 3-1	Graves, Miller, Greenaway	1	2	3		11	6		8	5	14				7		9	10				4							
	Jan-31	(a) Frickley Ath	L 1-3	Miller	1		3	4	11	6		8	5	14				7		9	10				2							
	Feb-07	(h) Boston U	L 0-4		1	2	3	12	5	6		8	10	9	11		4	7														
	Feb-17	(h) Scarborough	L 1-3	Graves	1		3		5	6	11		10	9			4	7							2		8					
	Feb-21	(h) Cheltenham T	W 1-0	Bowgett	1				5	6	11		9	10			4	7							2	3	8					
	Feb-28	(a) Runcorn	D 1-1	Byatt	1				5	6	11		9	10			4	7							2	3	8			12		
	Mar-10	(a) Bath C	L 0-2		1	2	4		3	6	11		10	9				7								5	8			12		
	Mar-21	(a) Stafford Rangers	L 0-1		1	2	12		3	6	11		9				4	14							8	5			7	10		
	Mar-28	(h) Gateshead	D 2-2	Graves 2	1	2	4		3	6	11		9	10				7							8	5	14					
	Apr-04	(a) Altrincham	W 2-1	Graves, Walton	1	2	4		3	6				10				7								5	8	11		9		
	Apr-11	(a) Dagenham	L 0-1			2	11		3	6				10				7				1			8	5		4		9	12	
	Apr-18	(h) Enfield	L 0-3			2	11		3	6				10			14	7				1			8	5		4		9		
	Apr-20	(h) Barnet	D 0-0			2	11		3	6				10			4	7				1				5		8		9		
	Apr-25	(h) Kidderminster H	L 0-3		1	2	11		3	6			12	10			4	7								5		8		9		
FA Cup																																
4Q	Oct-25	(a) Dagenham	W 3-0	Graves, Greenaway, Wallace	1	2	3	5	14	6	11	8		10			4	7		9												
1	Nov-15	(h) Swansea C	D 1-1	Wallace	1	2	3		5	6	9	8	14	10	11		4	7														
1r	Nov-24	(a) Swansea C	L 1-4	Donnellan	1	2	3		5	6	11	8	14	12	9		4	7		10												
FA Trophy																																
1	Dec-20	(h) Maidstone U	D 1-1	Tapley	1	2	3			6	10	8	5	12	11		4	7		9	14											
1r	Dec-28	(a) Maidstone U	L 1-2 aet	Doyle	1	2	3			6	10	8	12	11			4	7		9	14				5							
GMAC Cup																																
1	Nov-11	(h) Sutton U	L 2-4	Graves, Wainwright		2	3	14	5	6	11	8		10	12			7			9	1										4
Middlesex Senior Cup																																
1	Dec-02	(a) Hampton	D 2-2	Miller, Greenaway	1	2	3	4	5	6	11	8	14	10				7		9				12								
1r	Dec-08	(h) Hampton	W 4-2	Graves, Miller, Donnellan, Cordice	1	2	3		5		10	8	12	6	11		4	7		9	14											
2	Feb-03	(a) Wembley	L 1-3	Cordice	1			2	5	6	14	8	9	10	11		4	7			12				3							

1987-88

	Date	Opponent	Result	Scorers	Welsh A	Pittaway M	Dowe H	Byatt D	Hatter S	Wainwright R	McCarthy P	Hirst M	Perry M	Walton B	O'Keefe R	Cordice N	Lowe B	King G	Meadows T	Cross D	Bowgett P	Jackson P	Kotey P	Hirst S	Ferguson M	Rivero F	Isaacs T	Solomon G	Evans T	English T	Bate F	Turner P	Stagg B	Lynch T	Devlin M	La Ronde E	Olaleye S	Cordice A	Davis B	Harrison M	Davis P	Bailey D	Zacharia G	Foster K	Haxton A
GM Vauxhall Conference - 21st																																													
	Aug-22	(a) Cheltenham T	D 1-1	Walton	1	2	3	4	5	6	7	8	9	10	11	12																													
	Aug-25	(h) Sutton U	D 0-0		1	2	3		5	6	7	8		10	11	9	4	12																											
	Aug-29	(a) Altrincham	L 0-1		1	2				6	7	8		11		10			3	4	5	9	14																						
	Sep-05	(h) Runcorn	L 0-1		1	2	3	12		6	7	8		10		9				4	5			11																					
	Sep-09	(a) Welling U	L 0-4		1		3	4	2	6	7	8		10						14	5			11	9																				
	Sep-12	(a) Telford U	D 1-1	Ferguson	1			4	5	6	2		7	10	8	11					3				9																				
	Sep-15	(h) Enfield	W 1-0	Walton	1			4	5	6	2	12	7	10	8	11					3				9																				
	Sep-19	(h) Macclesfield T	D 1-1	Walton	1				5	6	2	12	7	10	8	11			4		3				9																				
	Sep-23	(a) Maidstone U	D 1-1	McCarthy	1	2	11		5	6	7	8		10					12		3				9	4	14																		
	Sep-26	(a) Runcorn	L 0-1		1	2			5	6	7	8		10		11					3				9	4	14																		
	Sep-29	(h) Dagenham	L 2-3	Wainwright (pen), Hatter	1	2			5	6	7	8		10		11					3				9	4																			
	Oct-03	(h) Kettering T	L 0-2		1	14			5	6	7	8		12		11			2		3				9	4		10																	
	Oct-10	(a) Bath C	D 0-0		1			4		6	7	8		10					3						9	2		11	5																
	Oct-17	(h) Lincoln C	D 0-0		1	4				6	7	8	10	11							3					2	9		5																
	Oct-31	(a) Stafford Rangers	L 2-5	Bate, Ferguson	1	2				6	7	8	10				14				3				12	5	9			4	11														
	Nov-07	(h) Telford U	D 2-2	English, Bate	1	5				6	2		12		8		10		14		3					9	4			7	11														
	Nov-14	(a) Enfield	L 2-5	Bate 2	1	2				12	7	6			8		14		4		3					5		10		9	11														
	Nov-17	(h) Cheltenham T	L 1-4	English	1	5				14	2	8	12				10				3					9		6		7	11	4													
	Nov-21	(h) Kidderminster H	D 1-1	Ferguson	1				4	6	7	8	12				11				5				10	2		3		9															
	Nov-28	(a) Barnet	L 1-5	English	1				4	6	7	8	12				11		14		5					2		3		9	10														
	Dec-05	(h) Weymouth	L 0-2		1	2		4		5	7	8	9	14					12		3					6		11		10															
	Dec-12	(a) Sutton U	D 1-1	English (pen)	1	4			5		7	8		10												2		3		9			6	11	12										
	Dec-26	(a) Dagenham	W 2-1	English, A Cordice	1	10				6	7										3					2		12		9				11		4	5	8							
	Dec-28	(h) Boston U	D 1-1	English	1	2				6	7	4														8				10			12	11		3	5	9							
	Jan-02	(a) Fisher Ath	L 1-3	English	1	4				6	7	12	5													2				9			14	11		3	8	10							
	Jan-09	(h) Wycombe W	D 0-0		1	4				6	14	12									5					2				9				11		3	8	10	7						
	Feb-06	(a) Wycombe W	L 0-1		1	4				6	7	8	14								5									9			12	11		3	10			2					
	Feb-17	(a)† Weymouth	L 1-2	Lynch	1	4		12		6		8									5													11		3	10	9		2	7				
	Feb-20	(h) Welling U	D 1-1	Olaleye	1	4				6		8									5													11		3	10	9		2	7				
	Feb-27	(a) Boston U	W 1-0	Byatt	1	8		4			6										5					9								11		3		10		2	7				
	Mar-12	(h) Altrincham	D 0-0		1			4			6										5					9				12				11		3		10		2	7	8			
	Mar-19	(h) Barnet	L 0-6		1			4			6	12									5									9				11		3	10			2	7	8	14		
	Mar-22	(a) Macclesfield T	L 2-3	Lynch 2	1	4				14	6	9									5													11		3	10			2	7	8	12		
	Mar-26	(a) Kettering T	L 2-3	Harrison, M Hirst	1						6	9									5									12				11		3	10			2	7	4	8		
	Mar-29	(h) Stafford Rangers	W 4-2	English, Olaleye 3	1						6	9									3									10				11		4	14			5	2	7	8		
	Apr-02	(a) Kidderminster H	L 1-2	La Ronde	1			4			6										5									9				11		3		12		2	7	10	8		
	Apr-05	(h) Bath C	D 1-1	A Cordice	1			4			6	14									3									10				11			12	9		5	2	7	8		
	Apr-16	(a) Lincoln C	L 0-3			4					6										5					14				12				11		3	10			2	7	8	9	1	
	Apr-19	(h) Northwich Vic	D 2-2	English, Bowgett		8					6										3									10				11		4	9			5	2	7	14	1	
	Apr-23	(h) Fisher Ath	W 2-1	English, Zacharia		2		4			6										3									10				11			9	12		5		7	8	1	
	May-02	(a) Northwich Vic	D 0-0			2		4		14	6										5									9				11				10		3		8	7	1	
	May-05	(h) Maidstone U	L 1-3	A Cordice		2		4			6										3					12				9				11				10		5		8	7	1	
		†Played at Bournemouth FC																																											
FA Cup																																													
4Q	Oct-24	(a) Tamworth	L 0-2		1	9		4		6	7	8	10	11							5					2	3	14																	
FA Trophy																																													
1	Dec-19	(a) Banbury U	D 2-2	English 2	1	2		4		6	7	12									5					8		3		10				11				9							
1r	Dec-22	(h) Banbury U	W 1-0	Lynch	1	2				6	7	4									5					8		3		10				11				9							
2	Jan-23	(h) Telford U	L 0-3		1	4				6	8	12	10								5					2				9				11		3	14		7						
GMAC Cup																																													
1	Oct-14	(a) Maidstone U	L 1-4	Rivero		12		4		6	7	8	9						3						14	10	2	11	5																1
Middlesex Senior Cup																																													
1	Nov-30	(h) Yeading	D 1-1	English	1	2		4		6	7	8	3	14							5				9			11		10					12										
1r	Dec-08	(a) Yeading	L 1-3	Bowgett	1	2		4	5		7	6	9	10							3					8				11					12										

1988-89

Rd	Date	Match	Result	Scorers	Williams D	Corbin K	Harrison M	Byatt D	O'Brien L	Morris P	La Ronde E	Browne S	Wilkins P	Cordice A	Lynch T	Browne C	Olaleye S	Bailey D	Rowe T	Risk A	Eriemo S	Lawrence M	Foster K	Wright C	Pedlar L	Goyette P	Margerrison J	DaSilva T	Jones R
Beazer Homes League - Premier Division - 11th																													
	Aug-20	(h) Moor Green	W 4-0	Lynch 2, Byatt, Harrison (pen)	1	2	3	4	5	6	7	8	9	10	11	12	14												
	Aug-23	(a) Gosport B	D 2-2	Lynch 2	1	2	3		7	6	5	4	9	8	11	12	10	14											
	Aug-27	(a) Bedworth U	W 2-1	Lynch, Cordice	1	2				8	6	5	9	12	11	14	10	7	3	4									
	Sep-03	(h) Redditch United	W 4-0	Lynch, Rowe, C Browne, Olaleye	1	2	3			8	6		9	7	11	14	10		5	4	12								
	Sep-06	(h) Dartford	L 1-3	Wilkins	1	2	3			6	5	11	9	7		14	10		8	4									
	Sep-10	(a) Worcester City	D 1-1	Harrison	1		3			8	6		9			11	10	2	5	4		7							
	Sep-24	(h) Bromsgrove R	W 3-2	Lynch, Harrison, C Browne	1	5	3			8	6			9	11	7	10	2		4									
	Oct-08	(h) Leicester U	W 2-1	Olaleye, C Browne	1	5	3			8	6		7	12	11	14	10	2		4		9							
	Oct-22	(h) Burton A	W 2-1	Olaleye 2	1		3			8	7	6		9	11	14	10	2		4	5								
	Oct-29	(h) Bedworth U	W 3-1	Olaleye 2, C Browne			3			8	7	6	5		11	14	10	2			9	4	1	12					
	Nov-05	(a) Fareham Town	L 1-2	Morris		5	3			8	7			12	11	14	10	2		4	9	6	1						
	Nov-12	(a) Waterlooville	D 0-0		1	5	3			8	7			9	11	6	10	2			4								
	Nov-19	(h) Alvechurch	W 2-0	Cordice, Bailey	1	5	3			8			7	9	11	6	10	2			4								
	Nov-26	(a) VS Rugby	L 0-2		1	5	3	4		8			7	9	11	12	10	2			6								
	Dec-10	(a) Moor Green	L 1-3	Lynch	1	5	3				6		12	14	11	7	10	2		4	8				9				
	Dec-17	(a) Bromsgrove R	L 1-2	Harrison (pen)	1	5	3	4			6		12	9	11	7	10			2	14				8				
	Dec-26	(h) Cambridge C	D 0-0		1	4	3			8	6		5	9	11	7	10			2					14				
	Dec-31	(h) Bath C	L 1-2	Cordice	1	4	3	12		8	6	7	5	9	11		10			2					14				
	Jan-02	(a) Ashford Town	L 2-3	Harrison (pen), Pedlar	1	5	3	4			6	11		9		7	10			2				12	8				
	Jan-07	(h) Dorchester T	D 0-0		1	5	3			4	6	11		9			14			2					8	7	10		
	Jan-21	(h) Dover Ath	D 0-0		1	5	3			4	6	14	7	9			10	12		2						11	8		
	Jan-28	(a) Merthyr Tydfil	D 1-1	Wilkins	1	5	3			8	6	11	10	9			12	4			14					2	7		
	Feb-08	(a) Corby T	L 0-2			2	3			4	6	11				9	10	7		5	14		1	12			8		
	Feb-11	(a) Leicester U	W 2-0	Byatt, La Ronde		2		5		4	6	3	9		11		7	10					1				8		
	Feb-14	(a) Redditch United	L 0-2			2		4		5	6	3	9		11		10	8			14		1	12			7		
	Feb-18	(a) Crawley Town	D 1-1	Lynch		2	3	5		4		10	9		11		6	7			14		1				8		
	Feb-25	(h) Corby T	W 2-1	Wilkins, Harrison (pen)	1	2	3			4	7	6	9		11	12	10			5							8		
	Feb-28	(a) Burton A	D 2-2	C Browne, Harrison (pen)	1	2	3			4		10	9		11	6		7		5							8		
	Mar-11	(h) Worcester City	L 0-2			2	3			5		6	9		11	12		7		4			1			10	8	14	
	Mar-13	(h) Waterlooville	D 1-1	Bailey		2	3	5			6				11		10	7		4			1			8	9	12	
	Mar-18	(a) Bath C	L 0-1			2	3			4	6		12		11		10	7		5			1			9	8		
	Mar-25	(h) Ashford Town	W 4-1	Olaleye 2, Bailey, Goyette (pen)		2				5	6		3		11		10	7		4			1			9	8		
	Mar-27	(a) Cambridge C	L 1-2	Olaleye		2	14			5	6		9		11		3	7		4			1			10	8		
	Apr-01	(a) Dorchester T	W 3-1	Lynch, Wilkins, og		2	3			5	6		9		11		8	7		4						10		14	1
	Apr-08	(h) Crawley Town	L 1-3	Lynch		2	3	12		5	6				11	9	8	7		4						10		14	1
	Apr-15	(h) Fareham Town	W 3-0	Lynch, Olaleye, Harrison		2	3			5	6		9		11		8	7		4			1			10		14	
	Apr-20	(h) Gosport B	W 3-0	Wilkins 2, Risk		2	3			5	6		9		11		8	7		4			1			10			
	Apr-22	(a) Alvechurch	L 1-2	Lynch		2		5			6		9		11	14	3	7		4	12		1			10	8		
	Apr-25	(h) VS Rugby	W 2-0	Bailey, Lynch		2	3	5					9		11		8	7		4			1			10	6		
	Apr-29	(h) Merthyr Tydfil	L 0-3			2		5			3		9		11		8	7		4			1			10	6	14	
	May-01	(a) Dartford	W 1-0	Olaleye		2	3			5	12		9		11		6	7		4			1			10	8		
	May-06	(a) Dover Ath	L 0-2			2	3	14		5	12		9		11		6	7		4			1			10	8		
FA Cup																													
1Q	Sep-17	(h) Vauxhall Motors	W 2-1	Olaleye, La Ronde	1	4	3			8	6		9	12		11	10	2	5			7							
2Q	Oct-01	(h) Arlesey T	W 1-0	Lynch	1	5	3			8	7		14	9	11		10	2		4		6							
3Q	Oct-15	(h) Hayes	L 1-2	S Browne	1	5	3			8	7	6		14	11	9	10	2		4									
FA Trophy																													
1	Jan-14	(a) Bromley	W 2-1	Wilkins, La Ronde	1	5	3			4	6	11	7	9			10			2							8		
2	Feb-04	(h) Wycombe W	L 0-1			2	3			5	6	11	9			14	10	7		4			1				8		
Westgate Insurance Cup																													
1	Oct-11	(a) Ruislip	W 6-0	Harrison 2 (1pen), Bailey, Cordice, Wright, Olaleye	1	2	3			8	14			9	11	7	10	6		4	5			12					
1	Oct-18	(h) Ruislip	L 1-2	La Ronde					3		7	8		12	11	9	14	2		4	5	6	1	10					
2	Nov-08	(a) Rushden Town	D 4-4	Lynch, Cordice, Morris, C Browne	1	5	3		6	8				9	11	12	10	2			4		14	7					
2	Nov-14	(h) Rushden Town	W 2-1	Lynch, Cordice	1	5	3			8	7	14		9	11	6	10	2			4								
3	Dec-13	(a) Dartford	L 0-3		1	2	3				6		8	9	11	7	10			4	5				14				
3	Dec-19	(h) Dartford	D 1-1	Cordice	1		3	4		8	6		14	9	11	7	10			2					5				
Premier Inter League Cup																													
1	Oct-04	(h) Aylesbury U	W 2-0	Lynch, Olaleye	1	5	3			8	6		14		11	7	10	2		4		9							
2	Oct-25	(h) Hayes	W 3-2	Morris, Olaleye, og	1	5	3			8	7	6			11		10	2		4	9								
3	Nov-29	(h) Sutton U	L 0-4		1	5	3	4		8	6		7	9	12	14	10	2			11								
Middlesex Senior Cup																													
1	Jan-10	(a) Hendon	D 1-1	Harrison (pen)	1	5	3			8	6	11		9		7	10			2	14			4					
1r	Jan-17	(h) Hendon	W 2-1	Cordice, Risk	1	5	3			4	6	11	7	9		10		8		2									
2	Jan-24	(a) Hayes	D 2-2	Harrison (pen), La Ronde	1	5	3			4	6	11	7	9				2								10	8		
2r	Jan-31	(h) Hayes	W 2-1	Harrison (pen), Wilkins		5	3			4	6	11	7			9	10	8		2			1						
SF	Mar-04	(a) Kingsbury Town	D 1-1	Wilkins		2	3			5		6	9		11	10	12	7		4			1				8		
SFr	Mar-07	(h) Kingsbury Town	L 1-2	Wilkins		2	3			5		6	9		11	14	12	7		4			1			10	8		

1989-90

Rd	Date	Opponent	Result	Scorers	Foster K	Tapley S	Norman S	Findley R	Morris P	Harrison M	Rowe T	Goyette P	Wilkins P	Kelly T	Lynch T	Margerrison J	Mason P	Browne S	Hall C	Cosby A	Byatt D	Campbell J	Risk A	Poole G	Olaleye S	Rivero F	Smart S	Williams D	Gbogidi P	Collins J	Flint D	Price N	Johnstone C	Westley G	Collins K	Eccles R	Watson J	Price G	Fergusson I	Shanks D	Jawandha B
Beazer Homes League Premier Division - 12th																																									
	Aug-19	(a) Alvechurch	W 2-0	Wilkins, Harrison (pen)	1	2	3	4	5	6	7	8	9	10	11																										
	Aug-22	(h) Ashford Town	L 0-1		1	2	3	4	5	6	7	8	9	10	11	12	14																								
	Aug-26	(h) Burton Albion	L 0-1		1	2	3	4	5	6	7	8		10	11	9	12																								
	Sep-02	(a) Bromsgrove R	L 0-1		1	2	3	4	5	6	9	8		10	11	7		12																							
	Sep-05	(a) Dorchester T	D 1-1	Margerrison	1	2	3	4	5	6	7	8		10	11	9		12																							
	Sep-09	(h) Weymouth	W 2-1	Harrison 2 (2 pens)	1	2	3	4	5	6	7	8	9	10	11	14																									
	Sep-11	(a) Gosport B	L 0-1		1	2	3	4	5	6		8	9	10	11	12		7	14																						
	Sep-23	(h) Cambridge C	D 2-2	Browne 2	1	2	3	4		6	14	8	9	10	12	5		7		11																					
	Oct-07	(a) Worcester City	L 0-1		1	2	3	4	5			8	9	10	11	7		6				12																			
	Oct-14	(h) Corby T	W 2-1	Kelly 2	1		3	4	5			8		10	11	6		7		9				2																	
	Oct-21	(h) Gravesend & Northfleet	L 2-3	Kelly, Goyette	1		7	2	5	3		8	14	10	11	9		12					4		6																
	Oct-28	(h) Dover Ath	W 3-2	Margerrison, Cosby, Campbell	1		3	4	5			8			11	6		2		10		14	7		9	12															
	Nov-04	(a) Moor Green	D 2-2	Browne, Goyette	1	2		4	5			8			11	6		9	12	10	14	7					3														
	Nov-11	(a) Gloucester C	D 2-2	Kelly 2	1	2			5			8	9	10	11	6		7			4						3														
	Nov-18	(h) VS Rugby	W 5-1	Margerrison 2, Goyette 2 (2 pens),Gbogidi	1	2			5	14		8	12	10	11	6		7			4				9				3												
	Nov-25	(a) Dartford	D 1-1	Kelly	1	2			5	3		8		10		6		7					4		9		12		11												
	Dec-02	(h) Atherstone U	W 3-1	Lynch, Olaleye, Gbogidi	1	2			5	3		8		10	14	6		7					4		9				11												
	Dec-09	(a) VS Rugby	L 0-2		1	2			5	3		8		10	12	6		7			4				9				11												
	Dec-16	(a) Gravesend & Northfleet	L 0-2		1				5	3		8		10		6		7				14	4				2		11	9											
	Dec-26	(h) Crawley Town	W 4-0	Browne 3 (1 pen), Goyette	1				5	3		8		10		6		7					4				2		11	12	9	14									
	Dec-30	(h) Waterlooville	W 1-0	Browne	1				5	3		8		10		6		7					4				2		11		9										
	Jan-01	(a) Chelmsford City	W 3-1	Browne, Margerrison, Collins	1				5	3		8	12	10		6		7					4				2			11	9	14									
	Jan-06	(a) Bath C	L 1-2	Wilkins	1					3		8	14	10		6		7					4				2			11	9	5									
	Jan-20	(h) Alvechurch	W 1-0	Goyette (pen)	1				11	5		8		10		6		7					4				2				9	3									
	Jan-27	(a) Weymouth	L 0-1		1				5	3		8		10		6		7					4				2		11	12	9	14									
	Feb-10	(h) Gloucester C	L 2-3	Johnstone, Flint	1				11	5		8		10	12	6							4				2			14	9	3	7								
	Feb-13	(h) Gosport B	W 2-1	Kelly, Goyette (pen)	1				5	4		8		10	11	6											2				9	3	7								
	Feb-17	(a) Cambridge C	L 1-3	Kelly	1				5	3		8		10	11	6							4				2				12	14	7	9							
	Feb-24	(h) Dartford	D 1-1	Goyette					5	3		8	12	10	11	6							4				2	1						9	7						
	Mar-03	(a) Burton Albion	L 0-4						5	3		8		10	11	6							4				2	1			12		14	9	7						
	Mar-06	(a) Ashford Town	W 1-0	Westley					5	3		8			11	6							4				2	1			10		7	9							
	Mar-10	(a) Corby T	D 0-0			12			5	3		8			11								4				2	1			10		7	9	6	14					
	Mar-17	(h) Worcester City	W 4-1	Browne, Margerrison, Lynch, Eccles					5	4		8			11	6		7									2	1	10			3		12		9					
	Mar-24	(h) Bath C	L 0-1			4				5		8	14		11	6		7									2	1	10			3				9					
	Mar-31	(a) Atherstone U	L 0-2			4			5	3		8	14		11	6		7										1	10							9	2				
	Apr-07	(a) Waterlooville	L 1-4	Eccles		4			5			8			12	6		7									2	1	10							9	3	11			
	Apr-14	(h) Chelmsford City	W 2-1	Browne, Goyette (pen)		4			5	3		8			14	6		7									2	1	10		12					9		11			
	Apr-16	(a) Crawley Town	D 0-0			4				3		8			11												2	1	10		12	5				9		7	6		
	Apr-21	(a) Dover Ath	L 0-2			4				3		8			12			7									2	1	10			5				9	14	11	6		
	Apr-24	(h) Bromsgrove R	D 0-0			4				3		8			11			7									2	1	6			5				9		10			
	May-01	(h) Dorchester T	W 2-0	Lynch, G Price		4				3		8			11	10		7									2	1	6			5						9			
	May-05	(h) Moor Green	W 2-1	Lynch, G Price		4			12	3		8			11	6		7									2	1				5	14			10		9			
FA Cup																																									
1Q	Sep-16	(a) St Albans C	W 2-1	Kelly, Lynch	1	2	3	4	5	6		8	9	10	11	12		7																							
2Q	Sep-30	(h) Wivenhoe Town	L 0-1		1	2	3	4	6			8	9	10	11	5		7	12		14																				
FA Trophy																																									
1	Jan-13	(h) Harrow Borough	D 1-1	Morris	1	6			5	3		8	11	10				7				12	4				2				9										
1r	Jan-16	(a) Harrow Borough	L 0-1		1	6			5	3		8	12	10				7					4		14		2				9		11								
Westgate Insurance Cup																																									
1	Oct-17	(a) Burnham	W 5-1	Cosby 3, Findley, og	1		7	2	5	3		8		10	11	6			12	9			4		14																
1	Oct-31	(h) Burnham	D 1-1	Goyette (pen)		2	3	4	5			8			11			6	14	10	12	9				7		1													
2	Nov-14	(h) Dartford	L 0-4		1	2			5			8	9	10	11			7			4				12		3		6												
2	Dec-04	(a) Dartford	L 0-5					4	5	3					11	6		7		10					9		8	1												2	
Premier Inter League Cup																																									
1	Oct-10	(h) Weymouth	D 1-1 aet	Goyette	1		3	4	5			8		10	11	6		7		9		12	14	2																	
1r	Oct-25	(a) Weymouth	W 2-0	Kelly, Margerrison	1		3	4	5			8	14	10	11	6		2				12	7		9																
2	Nov-08	(h) Bognor Regis T	W 6-0	Kelly 3, Tapley 2, Byatt	1	2		4	5			8	14	10	11			7	12		6	9					3														
3	Feb-01	(a*) Ashford Town	L 0-1		1	4			5	3		8	14	10		6						7			12		2				9		11								
		* Played at Lower Mead																																							
Middlesex Senior Cup																																									
1	Dec-06	(a) Edgware T	W 2-0	Kelly, Lynch	1	2			5	3		8		10	11	6		7			4				14		12		9												
2	Jan-22	(a) Hounslow T	D 1-1	Collins	1				5	14		8		12		6		7					4				2		11	10	9	3									
2r	Feb-05	(h) Hounslow T	W 4-0	Kelly 2, Goyette, Flint	1				11	5		8		10		6							4				2				9	3	7								
SF	Mar-13	(h) Yeading	L 1-2	Flint					5	6		8		14	11			12					4				2	1			10	3	7	9							
Middlesex Charity Cup																																									
1	Nov-28	(a) Finchley	L 0-2		1			10		3						6			7			14	4		9		11		8											2	5

1990-91

Rd	Date	Opponent	Result	Scorers	Vagg C	Donnellan L	Smart S	Tapley S	Fergusson I	Harrison M	Browne S	Goyette P	Jenkins S	Blackman B	Lynch T	Kelly T	Robinson C	Gipp D	Roach W	Bartlett P	Lewis S	Olaleye S	Hendry I	Eriemo S	Gbogidi P	Brown M	Donnellan G	Watson J	Morris P	Browne C	Waugh I	Coles D	Johnson M	Cordice N	Goodison P	Howard R	Martin A	Hopson M	Hudson D	Hayrettin H	Ferguson J	Dixon A
Beazer Homes League Premier Division - 12th																																										
	Aug-18	(h) VS Rugby	D 1-1	Harrison	1	2	3	4	5	6	7	8	9	10	11	14																											
	Aug-22	(a) Bashley	W 1-0	Kelly	1	6	2	4	5	3	7	8	9	10	12	11																											
	Aug-25	(a) Burton Albion	L 2-3	S Browne, Lynch	1	6	2	4	5	3	7	8	9	10	12	11								14																			
	Aug-28	(h) Gravesend & Northfleet	W 3-0	S Browne, Goyette, Blackman	1	6		4	5	3	7	8		10	14	11	2	9																									
	Sep-01	(h) Moor Green	W 2-1	S Browne 2		6		4	5	3	7	8		10	14	11	2	9	1	12																							
	Sep-04	(a) Dorchester T	D 1-1	Fergusson		6		4	5	3	7			10		11	2	9		8	1	12																					
	Sep-08	(a) Halesowen Town	L 0-1			6		4	5	3	7	8		10	12	11	2	9			1																						
	Sep-11	(h) Gloucester C	W 2-1	Kelly, Blackman	1	6		4	5	3	7	8		10	14	11	2	9																									
	Sep-22	(a) Dartford	W 2-1	Kelly 2	1	6	5	4		3	7	8			14	11		9		2			10																			
	Oct-06	(h) Worcester City	L 0-1		1	6	5			3	7		12	8		11		10		2		14		4	9																		
	Oct-20	(h) Weymouth	W 4-2	Blackman, Gbogidi, Eriemo, Brown	1		3			6				10		9				2		7	5	4	8	11																	
	Nov-03	(h) Poole Town	W 4-1	Gbogidi, Blackman, Brown 2	1		3			6				10		9	12			2		7	5	4	8	11																	
	Nov-10	(h) Atherstone U	L 1-3	Kelly	1		3			6			14	10		9				2		7	5	4	8	11																	
	Nov-17	(a) Bromsgrove U	L 0-1		1		14			6			12	10		9	3			2			5	4	8	11	7																
	Nov-24	(a) Waterlooville	D 2-2	Gbogidi, Brown	1		3			6				10		9				2		12	5	4	8	11	7																
	Dec-15	(a) Moor Green	L 0-2		1	6	3	4		5		8		12		9							11					2	7	10	14											
	Dec-22	(h) Chelmsford City	L 0-3			6	12	4		5		8		11		9		14											7	10	2	1	3									
	Jan-01	(h) Rushden Town	W 2-1	Kelly, Goyette (pen)		6	3	4		5		8		10		9		14										2		12		1	7	11								
	Jan-05	(a) Gravesend & Northfleet	D 1-1	Kelly		6	3	4		5		8		10		9													2	7			1		11								
	Jan-19	(h) Dartford	W 2-1	Blackman, Gipp		6	3			5		8		10		12		9		4									2	7			1		11	14							
	Jan-26	(h) Halesowen Town	L 1-2	Blackman		6	3	4		5		8		10		12		9											2	7			1		11								
	Jan-30	(a) VS Rugby	L 1-2	Cordice		6	3	4	8	5				10		14		9											2	7			1		11								
	Feb-02	(a) Atherstone U	W 2-1	Cordice, Smart		6	3	4		5				10		9		8		12									2	7			1		11								
	Feb-23	(a) Poole Town	L 2-3	Goyette, Martin		6	3	4			7			10		9		8		5															1		11	14	2	12					
	Feb-26	(a) Gloucester C	L 1-2	Blackman		6	3	4			14			10		9		12		5															1		11		2	8	7				
	Mar-02	(h) Dorchester T	W 2-1	Blackman, Cordice		6		4	14			3		10		9		12		5								2				1		11			7	8				
	Mar-16	(a) Farnborough T	W 3-2	Harrison, Donnellan, Goodison		6	3	4		5				10		12		9		7																11	14	2		8	1			
	Mar-19	(h) Dover Ath	L 2-3	Hopson, Goodison		6	3	8		5		4		10		12		14		2																11	9			7	1			
	Mar-23	(h) Waterlooville	L 1-3	Kelly		6	3	8		5		4		10		9		14		2																11				7	1			
	Mar-26	(h) Bashley	D 1-1	Donnellan		6	3	8		5				10		12				2									4						11				7	1	9		
	Mar-30	(h) Crawley Town	W 2-0	Goyette, og		6		8		5		3		10		12				2									4						11				7	1	9		
	Apr-01	(a) Rushden Town	W 1-0	Cordice		6		8		5		3		10		9				2									4						11	12			7	1		14	
	Apr-03	(a) Weymouth	W 2-0	Tapley, og			3	8		5		6		10		9				4									2						11	12			7	1			
	Apr-09	(h) Farnborough T	L 0-2				3	8		5		6		10		9		14		4									2											1	7		
	Apr-13	(h) Burton Albion	D 0-0			7	3	8		5		6		10		9		14		4									2											1	11	12	
	Apr-16	(a) Crawley Town	L 0-1				3	4		5				10		9		11	1	8									2							7		14			6		
	Apr-20	(a) Worcester City	L 2-3	Smart, og			3	4		5				10		9		7	1										2						14	11		8			6		
	Apr-22	(a) Chelmsford City	D 0-0				3	4		5		7		10		9		11	1	8									2							12		14			6		
	Apr-24	(h) Bromsgrove R	L 0-1				3	8				11		10		9		7	1	4									2							5		14	12		6		
	Apr-27	(h) Cambridge C	D 1-1	Kelly			3	4		5				10		9		12	1	8									2						11	14			7		6		
	May-01	(a) Cambridge C	L 1-2	Goodison			3	4		5		6		10		9		12	1	8									2						11	14			7				
	May-04	(a) Dover Ath	W 2-1	Hopson, Hayrettin		14	3	4		5				10					1	8									2						11	9			7		6		
FA Cup																																										
1Q	Sep-15	(a) Saffron Walden T	W 4-0	S Browne 2, Gipp 2	1	6	5	4		3	7	8		10	12	11	2	9		14																						
2Q	Sep-29	(a) Wivenhoe Town	D 0-0		1	6	5			3	12	8		14		11		9		2			10	4	7																	
2Qr	Oct-02	(h) Wivenhoe Town	W 2-1	S Browne, Goyette (pen)	1	6	5			3	7	8				11				2			10	4	9																	
3Q	Oct-13	(a) Ruislip Manor	L 0-1		1	6		4	5	3				7		11		12		2		10		9	8	14																
FA Trophy																																										
3Q	Dec-01	(a) Leyton-Wingate	W 1-0	Gbogidi	1	10	3	4		6	7						9				2			5		8	11																
1	Jan-12	(a) Wycombe W	L 0-1			6	3	4		5		8		10		9		12		14									2	7			1		11								
Larchimage Windows Cup																																										
1	Oct-17	(a) Burnham	D 2-2	Donnellan, Harrison (pen)	1	6				3				10		11		9		5		7		4	8	14																	2
1	Oct-30	(h) Burnham	D 2-2†	Brown, Goyette (pen)	1		3			6		8		10		9	12	14		2		7	5	4		11																	
Premier Inter League Cup																																										
1	Oct-08	(a) Dagenham	L 0-1		1	6		5		3			8	10		11		14		2		7		4	9																		
Middlesex Senior Cup																																										
1	Dec-04	(h) Hounslow	W 2-0	Kelly, Blackman	1	10	3	4		6	7	5		15		9				2					8	11		14															
2	Jan-15	(a) Hendon	L 1-2	Blackman		6	3			5		8		10				14		4									2	7	9	12	1		11								

†After extra time - lost 4-5 on penalties

1991-92

Rd	Date	Opponent	Result	Scorers	Hudson D	Watson J	Smart S	Tapley S	Bartlett P	Lowe T	Hopson M	Donnellan L	Goyette P	Blackman B	Cordice N	Harrison M	Gipp D	Kelly T	Richards R	Gore S	Wilson R	Roach W	Hedge A	Ferguson J	Lay W	Browne S	McGuire M	Hippolyte J	Pearson S	Drummy D	Payne D	Quinn J	Blackler M	Venables D	Lynch T	McPherson G	Gallacher G	Moussaddik C	Tate C	Walford S	Cawley P	Adamson S
Beazer Homes League Premier Division - 19th																																										
	Aug-17	(a) Gloucester C	L 2-3	Hopson, Donnellan	1	2	3	4	5	6	7	8	9	10	11	12	14																									
	Aug-21	(h) Dartford	D 2-2	Hopson 2	1	2	11	4	5	3	7	8			6		10	9	14																							
	Aug-24	(h) Moor Green	W 1-0	Smart	1	2	11	4		3	7	9			10	6		8		5	14																					
	Aug-26	(a) Cambridge C	L 1-2	Wilson	1	2	11	4		3	7	9	12		10	6		8		5	14																					
	Aug-31	(a) Halesowen Town	D 1-1	Gore		2		4		3	7	6	12		11	8		9		5	10	1	14																			
	Sep-04	(h) Trowbridge T	W 3-1	Hopson 2, Wilson		2		4	3		7	12			10	6		8		5	11	1	9																			
	Sep-07	(a) Corby T	W 6-2	Hopson 3(1 pen), Kelly, Wilson, Hedge		2		4		3	7		12		10	6		8		5	9	1	11																			
	Sep-11	(h) Crawley Town	L 0-2			2		4		3	7	12			11	6		8		5	10	1	9																			
	Sep-21	(a) Dover Ath	L 0-3		1	2		4	5	3	7		12		10	14		8		6	9		11																			
	Oct-05	(a) Dorchester T	L 0-2		1	2		4		3	7		12	9	10	6		8					11	5	14																	
	Oct-12	(h) Atherstone U	W 1-0	Lowe		2			5	3		7	11	12	6	10					9	1	8	4		14																
	Oct-19	(a) Worcester City	L 0-1			2		4		3		12	8		10	6					9	1	11	5		7																
	Oct-26	(h) Waterlooville	W 2-0	Browne, Wilson		2		4		3		6	8		10	12				5	9	1	11			7																
	Oct-29	(a) Dartford	L 1-4	Hippolyte		2		4		3					11						9	1		5		7	6	8	10													
	Nov-02	(h) Bashley	L 1-2	Wilson		2		4	5	3		11	8		6						10	1				7		9	12													
	Nov-09	(a) VS Rugby	L 2-3	Hippolyte, og		2			5	3		10	8		11	6						1	4			7		9	12													
	Nov-16	(h) Gloucester C	W 3-2	Hippolyte 2, Watson		2			5	3		8	11		6						14	1				7		9		4	10											
	Nov-20	(h) Cambridge C	L 2-3	Wilson, Donnellan		2			5	3		8	11		6						14	1				7		9	12	4	10											
	Nov-23	(a) Waterlooville	W 1-0	Browne		2				3		6			11						10	1				7	12	9	8	5	4											
	Dec-07	(a) Poole Town	D 0-0		1	2				3			11		6				5		10					7		9	14	4	8											
	Dec-21	(a) Burton Albion	D 1-1	Lowe		2			4	3		12	11		6						10	1	14			7		9		5	8											
	Dec-26	(h) Fisher Ath	D 4-4	Cordice, Lowe (pen), Hippolyte, Wilson		2			5	3		8	11		6						10	1	12				14	9	7	4												
	Dec-28	(h) Halesowen Town	W 2-1	Donnellan, Goyette		2		5		3		9	11		6						10	1	14					12	7	4		8										
	Jan-01	(a) Chelmsford City	L 0-3			2		5		3		8	11		6						10	1	14					12	7	4		9										
	Jan-04	(h) Poole Town	L 0-1			2		5	3		14	9	11		6							1	7					10	12	4		8										
	Jan-18	(h) Corby T	W 3-0	Blackler, Quinn, Donnellan		2				3	14	10	11		6						9	1	5						7	12		8	4									
	Feb-01	(h) Burton Albion	L 1-3	Cordice		2				3		9	11		5						10	1	4						7	6			8									
	Feb-08	(a) Trowbridge T	L 2-3	Lowe, Blackler		2				3		10	11		6						9	1	5					14	7	4			8									
	Feb-15	(h) Bromsgrove R	L 1-3	Pearson		2		11		3		10			6						9	1	5					14	7	4			8									
	Feb-22	(a) Gravesend & Northfleet	D 1-1	Hopson	1	2		7	9	3	12	10	11		6						14		8							4			5									
	Mar-04	(a) Atherstone U	L 0-2		1	2		4		3		10			6						9		12				14		7			8	5	11								
	Mar-07	(a) Bashley	D 1-1	Venables	1	2		4		3		12			6													14	7			8	5	11	9	10						
	Mar-14	(a) Crawley Town	W 1-0	Lynch	1	2		4		12		10			6													14	7			8	5	11	9		3					
	Mar-18	(h) VS Rugby	L 0-3		1	2		4				10			6								12					14	7			8	5	11	9		3					
	Mar-21	(h) Dover Ath	L 0-2			2				3		10			6														11	4		8	5	7	12			1	9			
	Mar-28	(a) Bromsgrove R	L 0-1			2		4		3	10												6						7			8	5	11	12			1	9			
	Apr-04	(h) Worcester City	L 1-4	Lowe		2		4		3	10				12						14		6						7			8	5	11				1	9			
	Apr-11	(a) Moor Green	W 1-0	Blackler				2		6		12			5								3					14	11	7			8	10				1	9	4		
	Apr-18	(h) Chelmsford City	W 2-0	Blackler, Donnellan				2		6		7	11		4						12		3										8	10				1	9	5		
	Apr-20	(a) Fisher Ath	L 0-1			12		2		6		7	11		5						10		3					14					8					1	9	4		
	Apr-25	(h) Gravesend & Northfleet	L 0-1			2				6	14	7	11		4						12		3										8	10				1	9	5		
	Apr-30	(h) Dorchester T	W 2-1	Tate, Goyette		2				6	10		11		5						12		3										8				7	1	9	4		
FA Cup																																										
1Q	Sep-14	(a) Witham Town	W 3-1	Kelly, Wilson, Donnellan		2		4		3	7	14	12		11	6		8		5	9	1	10																			
2Q	Sep-28	(h) Chesham U	L 2-4	Blackman (pen), Hedge	1	2	4		12	3	7			10	11	6		9		5			8		14																	
FA Trophy																																										
3Q	Nov-30	(a) Hendon	D 0-0			2			5	3	12	8	11		6						9	1				7				4	10											
3Qr	Dec-04	(h) Hendon	W 4-1	Wilson 2, Lowe 2		2			5	3	12	8	11		6						9	1				7				4	10											
1	Jan-11	(a) Cheltenham T	L 2-3	Donnellan, Lynch				3	5		7	9	11		6							1	12							4	14	8			10						2	
Barclays Challenge Cup																																										
1	Oct-09	(h) Baldock Town	W 2-0	Payne, Donnellan		2			4			12	7	9	6		14			5		1	8	3		11					10											
1	Nov-05	(a) Baldock Town	W 5-0	Hippolyte 2, Goyette, Browne, Pearson		2			5	3		8	6		11						10	1	4			7	14	9	12													
2	Nov-27	(a) Dunstable	L 1-2	Hippolyte		2			5	3		8			6						10	1				7	4	9	11													14
2	Dec-16	(h) Dunstable	W 4-1	Payne 2, Pearson, Browne (pen)		2			5				11		6				3		10	1				7		9	14	4	8											
3	Jan-28	(h) Cambridge C	D 1-1	Donnellan		2				3	14	10	11		6						9	1	5						7	8			4									
3	Feb-04	(a) Cambridge C	L 1-2	Cordice		2					7	9	11		6							1	3				12	8	10	4			5									
Middlesex Senior Cup																																										
1	Jan-07	(a) Hendon	D 1-1	Donnellan (pen)		2		3	5		10	8	11		6							1	12				7	9	15	4												
1r	Jan-15	(h) Hendon	L 1-3	Hedge				3			10	8	11		6				5			1	2				7	12	9	4												15

1992-93

Rd	Date	Opponent	Result	Scorers	Hudson D	Shanahan J	Hedge A	Watson J	Tapley S	Cordice N	Drummy D	Blackler M	Hippolyte J	Venables D	Gallacher G	Tate C	Pearson S	Hopson M	Finch J	Gayle K	Adamson S	Tonge K	Garratt M	Tenkorang R	Pettifer J	Hicks J	Barrowcliff P	Papa M	Lovegrove R	Short C	Maclennan J	Wilkerson P	Chandler R	Sim G	Fowell J
Beazer Homes League Southern Division - 11th																																			
	Aug-22	(h) Margate	L 1-4	Drummy	1	2	3	4	5	6	7	8	9	10	11	14																			
	Aug-26	(a) Burnham	W 3-1	Hippolyte, Gallacher, Hopson	1	4		2	5	6	7	8	9	10	11		3	14																	
	Sep-02	(a) Bury Town	W 4-0	Hippolyte 2, Venables, Drummy	1	2	12	4	5	6	7	8	9	10	11		3	14																	
	Sep-05	(h) Sittingbourne	D 2-2	Venables 2	1	2	8	4	5	6	7		9	10	11		3																		
	Sep-08	(a) Witney Town	D 1-1	Drummy	1	2	8	4	5	6	7	12	9	10	11		3																		
	Sep-19	(h) Canterbury City	W 3-1	Pearson, Drummy, Finch	1	2	11	4		6	7	8	9	10		14	3	12	5																
	Oct-03	(h) Gravesend & Northfleet	W 3-0	Hippolyte, Drummy, Tate	1	2	11	4	5		7	8	9	10		3	12			6	14														
	Oct-17	(h) Erith & Belvedere	D 2-2	Venables, Blackler	1		6	4	5			8	9	10		11	3			7		2													
	Oct-24	(a) Poole Town	W 2-1	Pearson, Hedge	1	2	7	4	5			8	9	10		11	3			6															
	Oct-31	(h) Ashford Town	L 2-3	Hippolyte, Venables	1	2	7	4	5		12	8	9	10		11	3			6															
	Nov-03	(a) Sudbury Town	L 1-3	Blackler	1	2	3	4	5		7	8	9	10		11				6	14														
	Nov-07	(a) Margate	W 2-1	Hippolyte, Pearson	1	2	10	4			7	8	9			11	3			6	14		5												
	Nov-14	(a) Braintree Town	L 1-4	Pearson	1	2	6	4		10	7		9	12		11	3			5			8												
	Nov-21	(h) Salisbury	W 4-3	Venables,Pearson,Cordice,Tate (pen)		14	9	4		6	7		12	10		11	3			8			5	1	2										
	Dec-01	(h) Bury Town	W 3-1	Venables 2, Cordice	1		3	4		6	7		9	10		11				8	14		5		2										
	Dec-05	(a) Fisher Ath	W 1-0	Pearson			4	2		6	7		12	10		11	3			8				1	9	5									
	Dec-08	(a) Sittingbourne	L 1-2	Pearson		14	9	4		6	7		12	10		11	3			8				1	2	5									
	Dec-19	(h) Fareham Town	W 4-1	Venables 3, Pearson		14	9	4		6	7		12	10		11	3						8	1	2	5									
	Dec-26	(h) Dunstable	W 2-0	Hippolyte, Pearson			9	4		6	7	12	8	10		11	3			14				1	2	5									
	Dec-28	(a) Buckingham Town	W 4-0	Hippolyte, Venables, Tate, Cordice			9	4		6	7	12	8	10		11	3			14				1	2	5									
	Jan-03	(h) Havant Town	L 1-2	Pearson			9	4		6	7	12	8	10		11	3							1	2	5									
	Jan-05	(a) Baldock Town	W 4-3	Venables, Pearson 2, Blackler		14	9	4		6	7	8	11	10			3			12				1	2	5									
	Jan-16	(a) Salisbury	L 0-1			3	9	4		6	7	8	10			11				12	14			1	2	5									
	Jan-30	(a) Gravesend & Northfleet	L 0-3					4		6	7	8	12	10		11	3			9				1	2	5									
	Feb-06	(h) Fisher Ath	W 2-0	Pearson, Blackler		4	9				7	8	11	10			3			6				1	2	5									
	Feb-10	(h) Burnham	L 1-2	Gayle		4	9			14	7	8	11	10		12	3			6				1	2	5									
	Feb-13	(a) Canterbury City	L 0-3			4	9			6	7		8	10		11	3			5				1	2										
	Feb-16	(a) Ashford Town	L 1-2	Hippolyte		4	9			6	7		10			11	3			8				1	2	5									
	Feb-20	(h) Baldock Town	L 0-3			4	11				7		10	9		8	3			12	14			1	2	5	6								
	Feb-27	(h) Braintree Town	W 2-1	Tate, og		4	9			11	7			10		8	3			6	14			1	2	5									
	Mar-06	(a) Havant Town	L 2-4	Drummy, Tate		4	9			6	7		12			11	3				10			1	2	5	8	14							
	Mar-09	(a) Andover	W 2-0	Adamson, Tate			9				7		10			11	3			6	4			1	2	5		12	8	14					
	Mar-13	(a) Erith & Belvedere	D 1-1	Drummy		4	9			6	7		11			10	3			14	8			1	2	5			12						
	Mar-17	(h) Newport (IOW)	D 0-0			4	9				7			10		11	3			8				1	2	5			12		6				
	Mar-20	(h) Poole Town	W 2-1	Tate 2 (1 pen)		4	9			14	7			10		11	3			8	6			1	2	5			12						
	Mar-27	(h) Sudbury Town	D 0-0			4	9			6	7		8	10		11	3							1	2	5			12						
	Apr-07	(h) Witney Town	L 0-1			4	9			6	7		8	10		11	3				12			1	2	5									
	Apr-10	(a) Dunstable	L 1-2	Venables		4	9			12		7	8	10		11	3				14				2	5			6			1			
	Apr-12	(h) Buckingham Town	L 3-4	Hippolyte, Venables, Drummy			9			6	7	5	8	10		11	3				12				2				4			1			
	Apr-17	(a) Fareham Town	L 1-5	Venables			9			6	7	8	5	10		11	3			14	12			1	2				4						
	Apr-24	(a) Newport (IOW)	D 1-1	Cordice		4	9			6	7	8	5	10		11	3				12			1	2										
	May-01	(h) Andover	W 5-0	Venables, Pearson 3, Blackler		4	5			6	7	8	9	10		11	3							1	2										
FA Cup																																			
Pr	Aug-30	(h) Tiptree United	W 2-1	Venables, Drummy	1	2	12	4	5	6	7	8	9	10	11		3	14																	
1Q	Sep-13	(h) Witham Town	W 2-1	Venables, Hedge	1	2	12	4	5	6	7	8	9	10	11		3																		
2Q	Sep-27	(h) Wivenhoe Town	D 1-1	Venables	1	2	3	4	5		7	8	9	10		12				14	11												6		
2Qr	Sep-30	(a) Wivenhoe Town	W 2-0	Hippolyte 2	1	4	3	2	5		7	8	9	10		11				6															
3Q	Oct-11	(h) Dagenham & Redbridge	L 1-6	Tate (pen)	1	2		4		6	7	8	9	10		3	11			5															
FA Trophy																																			
3Q	Nov-28	(h) Solihull Borough	W 5-2	Pearson, Tate 2, Gayle, og			9	4		6	7			10		11	3			8			5	1	2										
1	Jan-18	(h) Bashley	L 1-2	og				4		6	7	10	8			11	3			9	14			1	2	5									
Barclays Challenge Cup																																			
1	Oct-07	(h) Buckingham Town	L 2-5	Tate, Adamson		2	3	4			7		9			11	5			6	10	14											8	1	
1	Oct-27	(a) Buckingham Town	L 0-1		1	2	11	4	5				12	10		14	3			7	9												6		8
Middlesex Senior Cup																																			
Pr2	Nov-11	(h) Harrow Borough	L 0-3		1	2	5	4			7		9	10		11	3			6	8												14		

1993-94

	Date	Opponent	Result	Scorers	Tenkorang R	Perry M	Cordice N	Shanahan J	Richards R	Gayle K	Drummy D	Hedge A	Barham L	Tate C	Sweales P	Lovegrove R	Nolan A	Johnson R	Adamson S	Williams A	Pettifer J	Hicks J	Randall L	Holohan P	Robinson C	Garratt M	Fernandes T	Kinnear C	Mellor R	Hall J	Duncan I	Keane M	McGrath I	MacPherson G	Saunders E	Hopping A	Dennis F	Lawrence C	Waltman G	Frankland T	Seabrook D	Augustine P	Buckley M	Anglin T	Jashek R	Webb P	Walsh S	Devitt J	Chewins J	Elward G	Gibson C	Brown P	Steward J	Schwartz V	English A	Brathwaite R	Brown M	Hill D	Gartell B	Williams D	Meakin G	Drury M	Frangou S	Chambers A	Johnson E	Papa M	Kent T
Beazer Homes League Southern Division - 21st																																																																		
	Aug-21	(a) Poole Town	L 1-5	Sweales	1	2	3	4	5	6	7	8	9	10	11	14																																																			
	Aug-25	(h) Canterbury City	L 1-2	Tate		2	9	4			7	8	6	10	5	3	1	11	14																																																	
	Aug-28	(h) Margate	L 1-3	Perry		2	3	4	12		7	8	6	10	9	5	1	11		14																																																
	Aug-30	(a) Tonbridge	L 0-3			2	9	4	12			8	6	10	7	3	1	11		14	5																																													
	Sep-04	(a) Sudbury Town	L 2-3	Cordice, Adamson			5		2			8	6	10			1	11	9		4	3	7																																												
	Sep-18	(a) Newport (IOW)	D 1-1	Hedge	1		9		5		2	8	6	10				11	12		4		3	7																																											
	Sep-22	(h) Fisher 93	W 3-0	Tate (pen), Hedge, Johnson	1		7				2	9	8	10				6	14		3	4	5	11																																											
	Oct-02	(h) Salisbury City	L 2-3	Tate (pen), Cordice	1		7	12			2	9	8	10				6	14		3	4	5	11																																											
	Oct-09	(h) Braintree Town	L 3-4	Tate (pen), Cordice, Adamson	1		7		14			5	8	10				6	9		3			11	2	4																																									
	Oct-16	(a) Burnham	L 0-3					7	5			3	8	10				6	14					11	2	4	1	9																																							
	Oct-23	(a) Havant Town	L 0-2				5	9		7	3	8	12							14			6	2	4	1	11	10																																						
	Oct-30	(h) Erith & Belvedere	D 1-1	Holohan			6	5			7	3	8	10							2			11		4	1			9																																						
	Nov-06	(h) Witney Town	L 1-4	Kinnear			6	5			7	3	8								2			11		4	1	12	10	9																																						
	Nov-20	(h) Weymouth	W 3-0	Mellor, McGrath, Duncan			6	4					8											11		5	1		10	9	2	3	7																																	
	Dec-04	(h) Fareham Town	D 2-2	Mellor, MacPherson			6	4			2	14												11		5	1		10			3	8	7	9																																
	Dec-11	(a) Bury Town	L 0-4					2			10	6	9				12			14			11		5						3	7	8		1	4																													
	Dec-18	(h) Ashford Town	D 0-0				7	14				6	9								2						5						3	11	8		1	4	10																												
	Jan-01	(h) Buckingham Town	L 2-5	Hall, Hedge			7				12	6									2			11		5				8		3	14			1	4	10	9																											
	Jan-15	(a) Erith & Belvedere	L 0-2				7	4			6											2										9	8		3	11			1	12			5	10																									
	Jan-22	(a) Sudbury Town	L 0-1				7	4														2												9			8		11	1	6			5	10	3	12	14																							
	Jan-29	(a) Margate	L 1-4	Mellor			7					6									5						12				9				11		8	1	4	14			10	3		2																							
	Feb-05	(h) Newport (IOW)	L 0-6				7	4													5					3				9	8			11		6	1	14	12			10			2																							
	Feb-12	(a) Salisbury City	L 0-4				7				6										5					12					8						9	1	3	11						2	4	10																					
	Feb-15	(a) Gravesend & Northfleet	L 1-4	Cordice			7				2	11									5					12											1	4	9			10	3		14	6	8																					
	Feb-19	(h) Poole Town	L 1-2	Dennis (pen)							7	8													14					9								1	5	11				3		2	4	10	6	12																		
	Feb-26	(h) Havant Town	L 0-4																								11					9				8		10	1	4							2	5	7			3	6	14															
	Mar-05	(a) Ashford Town	L 0-2								14														10					9							1	4	12						2	5	11			3	7	6	8														
	Mar-12	(h) Gravesend & Northfleet	L 0-3						4			10	11										2																	1						3				5	7	8				6	9														
	Mar-16	(h) Tonbridge	L 1-2	Drummy							7										2			11													1	4	12				3			5					8	6		9	10	14												
	Mar-23	(h) Baldock Town	L 1-2	Dennis (pen)				6				3												11													1	4							2	5	7				8		9	10	14													
	Mar-26	(a) Braintree Town	D 2-2	Schwartz, Dennis (pen)							10										12			6													1	4							2	5	11			3	7	14	9		8														
	Mar-29	(a) Fisher 93	D 1-1	Shanahan				12			6	14											11													1	4							2	5				3	8	7	9				10											
	Apr-02	(h) Dunstable	W 4-0	Brathwaite 3, Schwartz							8	14											6													1	4								5				3	7		12		10		9	2	11									
	Apr-09	(a) Baldock Town	L 0-1								10	12																										4					11		5					3	7		14		9		8	2		1	6							
	Apr-13	(a) Canterbury City	W 2-1	Schwartz 2							7	9																										4					3		2		11				14	8		5	10			12		1		6						
	Apr-16	(h) Bury Town	W 5-1	Brathwaite 2, Meakin, og 2,							9	11																										4								7					3		12			10		8	2		1	5	6	14					
	Apr-19	(a) Dunstable	L 0-1								8	11																										4					3		7	5						12		9	10			2		1	6		14					
	Apr-21	(a) Buckingham Town	D 0-0					12																														4					11		7	5	10			3			9	14	8			2		1		6						
	Apr-23	(a) Witney Town	L 0-2					2				12																									4								7	5	8			3		11	9		10			14		1		6						
	Apr-27	(a) Fareham Town	L 0-1					12				9																									4								7	5	11			3		14			10		8	2		1		6						
	Apr-30	(h) Burnham	L 0-3								4	10																										12					3		7	5	8					14	9						2		1	11	6						
	May-07	(a) Weymouth	W 3-1	Drummy, Schwartz, Hedge				11			8	9																										4								2	5				3		7	12		10					1		6		14				
FA Cup																																																																		
1Q	Sep-11	(a) Harrow Borough	L 1-3	Cordice	1	2	9				7	8	6	10					11		5	4	3																																													
FA Trophy																																																																		
3Q	Nov-27	(h) Harrow Borough	D 2-2	Hedge, Mellor			9	4			7	6	8												11	2	5	1		10			3																																				
3Qr	Dec-01	(a) Harrow Borough	L 0-3				9	4			7	6	8					12			14			11	2	5	1		10			3																																				
Dr Martens Cup																																																																		
1	Oct-20	(h) Dunstable	W 1-0	Kinnear				5	9		6	3	8	12										11	2	4	1	7	10																																					
1	Oct-25	(a) Dunstable	D 3-3	Tate 2, Hall			7	5			6	3	8	12							2			11		4	1		10	9																																				
2	Nov-24	(h) Waterlooville	L 0-2				6	4			2	11	8					7			5				12							3		9																														1	10	14	
London Challenge Cup																																																																		
1	Jan-11	(a) Tooting & Mitcham United	L 2-5	Hall, Lawrence								6									2			11		5			14	9		3	8			1	4	10					7																									
Middlesex Senior Cup																																																																		
Pr2	Nov-10	(h) Hanwell Town	D 2-2	Hall, Johnson			6	5				3						7			14			11	2	4	1		9	10																																					8
Pr2r	Nov-16	(a) Hanwell Town	W 5-1	Mellor 3, Kent 2			6	5			2	3	7					12			14			11		4	1		9	10																																					8
1	Feb-02	(h) Hayes	W 2-1	Cordice, Dennis			7	4				6									5										9	8			11		12	1	14				10	3		2																						
2	Feb-09	(h) Feltham & H	W 2-1	Hall, og			7				2										5										9	8			6		11	1	4	12	14		10			3																						
SF	Mar-08	(a) Staines Town	L 2-4 aet	Elward, Webb							14													11					9							1	4	12						2	5	8			3	7	6	10														

1994-95

Rd	Date	Opponent	Result	Scorers	Gartell B	Anglin T	Birch T	Hill M	Shanahan J	Mason T	Elward G	McGrath I	Pedlar L	Mattis S	Hudson B	Schwartz V	Findley R	Brownlie L	Griffiths S	Kent T	Parkinson I	Goodison P	Wilson M	Solomon G	Quail S	Brathwaite R	Webb P	Jukes A	Page D	Buzaglo T	Robbins K	Buzaglo R	Biggins M	Brown M	Hill D	Bettaccini N	Browne S	Frankland T	Franklin J	Hall M	Brown L	O'Neill D	Milne S	Pepperall M	Drummy D	Francis K	Frangou S	Meakin G	Gnahore S	Brindou J
Beazer Homes League Southern Division - 15th																																																		
	Aug-20	(a) Fareham Town	W 2-0	Pedlar, Mattis	1	2	3	4	5	6	7	8	9	10	11	12	14																																	
	Aug-24	(h) Margate	L 0-1		1	2	3		5	6	7		9	10	8		4	11	12	14																														
	Aug-29	(a) Baldock Town	L 1-2	Goodison	1	2	3		5		7			10	11	12	4		6		8	9	14																											
	Sep-03	(h) Yate Town	W 2-0	McGrath, Kent	1	2				4	6	11		10	7	12	5		9	8			14	3																										
	Sep-06	(a) Bury Town	W 3-2	Goodison, Findley, Kent	1	2	3			6	7	4			11		5		9	8		10	14																											
	Sep-24	(a) Witney Town	W 2-0	Elward 2	1			4	2	6	7			12	11		5			8				3	9	10																								
	Oct-08	(a) Poole Town	L 0-3		1		14	4	2		8	6		12	11		5					10		3	9		7																							
	Oct-22	(a) Havant Town	D 1-1	Kent	1			4	8	6					11		14			7				3	9			2	5	10																				
	Oct-25	(a) Margate	L 1-3	Shanahan	1		14	4	8	6				10	11		12			7				3				2	5	9																				
	Oct-29	(a) Braintree Town	W 3-0	Quail, Kent, R Buzaglo			3	4	8	6										7					10			2	5	9	1	11																		
	Nov-05	(h) Tonbridge	W 3-2	Quail 2 (1 pen), Findley				4	5	6		8			12		14			7				3	10			2		9	1	11																		
	Nov-12	(a) Weymouth	L 1-5	Quail				4	8	6							14			7				3	10	12		2	5	9	1	11																		
	Nov-16	(h) Baldock Town	L 2-6	Brathwaite 2				4	8	6										7				3	10	11		2	5	9	1																			
	Nov-26	(h) Erith & Belvedere	L 1-2	Findley			3	4	6		8				14		12			7					10	11		2	5	9	1																			
	Dec-03	(a) Ashford Town	L 2-3	T Buzaglo, Elward			3	4	6		9				14		11			7					10	8		2	5	12	1																			
	Dec-10	(h) Fareham Town	W 3-0	T Buzaglo, Quail, Brathwaite				4		5	7						14			12				3	10	11		2	6	9	1		8																	
	Dec-14	(h) Clevedon Town	D 1-1	T Buzaglo				4		6	7						14							3	10	11			5	9	1		8	2																
	Dec-17	(a) Weston Super Mare	L 2-4	T Buzaglo, Page				4		6	8									14				3	10	11			5	9			7	2	1															
	Dec-21	(h) Ashford Town	L 4-5	Quail, Brathwaite, Browne, Page			4			6	11						12			14				3	10	9			5				8	2	s	1	7													
	Dec-26	(h) Burnham	D 1-1	Quail				4	14	6	11													3	10	12			5	9			8	2	1		7													
	Jan-07	(h) Salisbury City	L 1-2	T Buzaglo				3		6	11				7		12			14					10				5	9			8	2	1			4												
	Jan-14	(h) Bashley	W 1-0	T Buzaglo				3	8	6	11				7		12								10				5	9				2				4	1											
	Jan-28	(h) Braintree Town	W 3-1	T Buzaglo 2, Quail				4		6	11				7		12							3	10				5	9			8	2					1											
	Feb-04	(a) Bashley	D 2-2	T Buzaglo, Quail				4		6	8													3	10				5	9			11	2			7		1											
	Feb-11	(h) Witney Town	L 1-2	T Buzaglo				4		6	8													3	10				5	9			11	2			7		1	12										
	Feb-25	(a) Tonbridge	W 4-3	T Buzaglo, Quail 2, Solomon				4	8	6							5							3	10	12				9			11	2			7		1											
	Mar-04	(h) Fisher 93	D 2-2	T Buzaglo, Brathwaite			14	4	6								5							3	10	8				9			11	2			7		1	12										
	Mar-11	(h) Waterlooville	W 2-1	T Buzaglo, Browne (pen)				4	8	6														3	12	10			5	9			11	2			7		1											
	Mar-14	(a) Clevedon Town	L 2-4	Quail, Hall			12	4	6						11		5							3	10	14				9				2			7			8	1									
	Mar-18	(a) Yate Town	L 0-4				2	4	6						11		12							3	10	9			5					14			7		1	8										
	Mar-25	(a) Fisher 93	D 2-2	Brathwaite, Biggins			3				11				12									8	10	9			4				6				7		1			2	5							
	Apr-01	(h) Poole Town	D 2-2	Brathwaite, Hudson			3	4							11										10	9						14	8	6			7				1	2	5							
	Apr-05	(h) Newport (IOW)	L 1-2	Quail	1		3	4									5							11	10	9						14	8	6			7			12		2								
	Apr-08	(a) Erith & Belvedere	D 1-1	Biggins			3	4									10							8		9							6	11	1		7			14		2	5							
	Apr-11	(a) Waterlooville	L 0-5				3			4														8	10	9						14	11	6	1		7			12		2	5							
	Apr-15	(h) Havant Town	L 2-6	Quail, Browne			3		4						12									8	10	9						14	11	2	1		7			6			5							
	Apr-17	(a) Burnham	W 4-0	Browne (pen),Biggins,R Buzaglo, og			4								12									3	10	9						8	11	2			7		1	6			5							
	Apr-22	(h) Weston Super Mare	L 4-6	Quail, Brathwaite, R Buzaglo, M Hill			14	4							12									3	10	9						8	11				7		1	6		2	5							
	Apr-25	(a) Newport (IOW)	L 1-2	Birch			5	4							11									3	10	9						8		6			7		1				12	2	14					
	Apr-29	(h) Weymouth	W 4-1	Brathwaite,Hudson,Browne(pen),Brindou			2	1	6						11									3	10	9							8				7								4				5	12
	May-01	(h) Bury Town	L 1-2	Hall			12	4	2															3	10	9							8				7		1	14					6				5	11
	May-06	(a) Salisbury City	L 1-3	Brathwaite			3	4	2						11										10	9							8				7		1	14					6				5	12
FA Cup																																																		
Pr	Aug-27	(a) Tring Town	W 1-0	Findley	1	2	3		5		7	8		10	11	9	4			6		12																												
1Q	Sep-10	(h) Harrow Borough	L 0-1		1	2			4	6	7				11		5		9	8		10		3			14																							
FA Trophy																																																		
1Q	Sep-17	(h) Bromley	W 3-0	Quail, Brathwaite, Kent	1		12	4	2	6	7				11		5			8		14		3	9	10																								
2Q	Oct-16	(h) Purfleet	L 0-3		1			4	2	6		7			11		5			8		14		3	9																				10					
Dr Martens Cup																																																		
1	Oct-04	(a) Sudbury Town	D 3-3	Quail, Elward, Mattis	1		4		2	6	8	12		10	11		5					9		3	14		7																							
1	Oct-19	(h) Sudbury Town	L 1-2	Quail	1			4	7	6		8		10	11							14		3	9			2	5																					
Middlesex Senior Cup																																																		
1	Nov-14	(h) Bedfont	D 2-2 aet	Hudson, Shanahan			3	14	4			6		12	8		5								10	11	7	2		9	1																			
1r	Nov-29	(a) Bedfont	L 1-2	Quail (pen)			3	4							10		8			7					11			6	5	9	1															2				
Middlesex Charity Cup																																																		
1	Nov-22	(a) Waltham Abbey	W 2-0 aet	Quail (pen), Shanahan			3	4	8	6	11						14			7					10	9		2	5			12			1															
2	Dec-07	(h*) North Greenford United	W 8-1	T Buzaglo 2, Quail 4, Findley 2			2	4		6	8						11			7				3	9		14		5	10					1												12			
3	Feb-27	(a*) Ruislip Manor	W 3-0	T Buzaglo, Browne 2 (1 pen)	1		14	4	12	6							5							3	10	8				9			11	2			7													
QF	Mar-28	(a) Wembley	L 4-6	Brathwaite 2, Biggins, Browne (pen)	1		3	4							8		5							11	10	9						14	6	2			7											12		

1995-96

Rd	Date	Opponent	Result	Scorers	Wild R	Marskell B	Moore F	Bhatia P	Croad S	Brathwaite R	Walton C	Yates N	Fraser S	Sheldrick P	Birch T	Shanahan J	Ivers M	Tekell L	Tenkorang R	Hall M	Moore J	Smith A	Hart G	Stone K	Marshall R	Smart L	Barnard L	Hibbert T	Walker L	Waugh I	Buzaglo T	Hoare A	Tarry M	Kirby D	Knight T	Bircham S	Brown L	Clark H	Bullman P	Ramsey D	McCluskey	Boreham K
Icis League Division 3 - 4th																																										
	Aug-19	(a) Cove	W 9-1	Sheldrick 3,Fraser 3 (2 pens),Yates 2,Croad	1	2	3	4	5	6	7	8	9	10	11	12	14	15																								
	Aug-30	(h) Wingate & Finchley	D 1-1	Sheldrick,		2	3	4	5	6	7	8	9	12	11		10		1	14																						
	Sep-16	(a) Harefield United	W 2-1	Birch (pen), Hart		2	3		5	6	7	8	12	10	11		9		1		4	14	15																			
	Oct-14	(h) Horsham	L 0-1				3	4	5	6	7		15	10	11		12	2	1		14	8		9																		
	Oct-17	(a) Flackwell Heath	D 0-0				3	4	5	6	7	8		12			10	2	1				11	9																		
	Oct-21	(h) Windsor & Eton	L 1-5	Sheldrick,			3	4	5	6	7	8	12	10			9	2	1					11																		
	Oct-24	(h) Aveley	L 3-4	Sheldrick, Brathwaite, Fraser			3	4	5	6	7		12	10	11		9	14	1		2			15	8																	
	Nov-01	(a) Lewes	W 4-0	Marshall, Smith, Stone, Moore(J)			3		5	14	7	8	10					2	1		11	6		9	4																	
	Nov-04	(h) East Thurrock United	W 3-0	Smith 2, Stone			3		5	14	7	8	10		15			2	1		11	6		9	4	12																
	Nov-11	(a) Tring Town	L 0-1				3		5	6	7	8		12	11			10	1			4		9		2																
	Nov-14	(h) Southall	W 9-0	Tekell 3,Birch,Smith 2,Yates,Smart,Moore(J)				14	5		7	8		9	11			10	1		6	4	15	12		2	3															
	Nov-18	(a) Camberley Town	W 2-1	Walker, Moore(F)			3		5		7	8						10	1		6	11				2		4	9													
	Nov-25	(h) Clapton	W 2-1	Smith, Croad			3		5		7	8		10				12	1		14	11			4	2		6	9													
	Dec-02	(a) Leighton Town	W 2-0	Sheldrick 2			3		5		7	8		10				6	1			11				2		4	9													
	Dec-09	(h) Hornchurch	W 4-0	Walker, Sheldrick, Croad, Tekell			3		5	14	7	8		10				6	1		12	11				2			9	4												
	Dec-16	(a) Harlow Town	L 0-3				3		5	10	7	8			12			6	1		15	11				2		4	9	14												
	Dec-26	(a) Kingsbury Town	D 0-0				3		5	14	7	8		10				12	1		15	11				2		6	9	4												
	Jan-01	(h) Northwood	L 0-4				3		5			8	10	14				12	1		7	11			4	2		6	9	15												
	Jan-06	(a) Southall	W 7-0	Walker 2 (1 pen), Sheldrick 4, Croad			3		5			8		10				11	1		12		14		7	2		6	9	4												
	Jan-20	(h) Cove	W 4-0	Sheldrick (pen),Hibbert,Walton,Moore(F)			3		5		7		15	10				14	1			12			4	2	8	11		6	9											
	Feb-03	(h) Flackwell Heath	W 4-0	Walker, Fraser, Tekell, Moore(F)			3				7		6	14				8				11			4		12	2	10		9	1	5	15								
	Feb-10	(a) Wingate & Finchley	L 0-2				3				7		14	12				8				11			4		6	15	9		10	1	5		2							
	Feb-17	(h) Harefield United	W 3-1	Walker, Tekell, Moore(F)			3		5		7			12				8	1						4	2	6		9		10				11							
	Feb-24	(h) Lewes	W 3-2	Sheldrick, Walton, Tekell			3		5		7		14	12				8	1						4	2	6	15	9		10				11							
	Mar-02	(a) Windsor & Eton	W 2-0	Walker, Sheldrick			3		5		7		11	12				14	1							2	6	4	9	15	10				8							
	Mar-09	(a) Horsham	L 1-2	Fraser			3		5		7		9	10				8	1			12			4	2		6	14	15					11							
	Mar-16	(h) Epsom & Ewell	D1-1	Fraser			3		5		7		11	12				8	1			15			4	2		6	9	14	10											
	Mar-19	(h) Hertford Town	W 7-0	Walker,Sheldrick 3,Fraser,Smith,Smart			3		5		7		11	10				14	1			15			4	2		8	9						6							
	Mar-23	(h) Tring Town	W 3-1	Walker, Buzaglo, Croad			3		5		7		11	10				14	1			8				2		4	9		12				6							
	Mar-27	(h) Camberley Town	D 0-0				3				7		11	10				12	1			8				2		4	9	5					6							
	Mar-30	(a) East Thurrock United	W 3-0	Walker 3			3				7		11	10					1							2		4	9	5					6	8						
	Apr-06	(a) Northwood	W 5-0	Knight,Walton,Fraser,Sheldrick,Buzaglo			3		5		7		10	12				8	1			15				2			9	4	14				6	11						
	Apr-08	(h) Kingsbury Town	W 2-0	Walker (pen), Tekell			3		5		7		10					8	1			14				2			9	4	12				6	11						
	Apr-11	(a) Aveley	D 1-1	Walker			3		5		7		10	12				8	1			15			4	2		6	9							11						
	Apr-13	(a) Clapton	W 10-1	Walker (pen), Smart, Marshall, Hibbert, Sheldrick 2, Buzaglo, Fraser, Tekell, Knight			3		5				10	12				8				15			4	2		6	9		14				7	11	1					
	Apr-16	(a) Hertford Town	W 2-1	Walker (pen), Smith			3		5		7			10				8				14			1	2			9	4	12				6	11						
	Apr-20	(h) Leighton Town	D 1-1	Walker			3		5		7			12				8	1			14			4	2		15	9	6					10	11						
	Apr-27	(a) Hornchurch	D 1-1	Sheldrick							7		9	10				8	1			14			4	2		3		6	12				5	11						
	Apr-30	(a) Epsom & Ewell	W 2-0	Buzaglo, Knight			3		5		7			12				8	1			11			4					2	9				6	10						
	May-04	(h) Harlow Town	L 0-2				3		5		7		15	12				8	1			11			4	14			9	2					6	10						
FA Cup																																										
Pr	Aug-26	(a) Cheshunt	W 1-0	Birch		2	3	4	5	6	7	8	9	10	11				1	14																						
1Q	Sep-09	(a) Grays Athletic	D 2-2	Sheldrick 2			3	4	5	6	7	8		10	11		9		1		2																					
1Qr	Sep-12	(h) Grays Athletic	W 4-3	Sheldrick 2, Brathwaite, Birch			3	4	5	6	7	8		10	11	14	9		1		2																					
2Q	Sep-23	(a) Hertford Town	L 0-1				3		5	6	7	8	9	10	11	15	12		1		2	4	14																			
FA Vase																																										
1Q	Sep-02	(h) East Ham United	W 10-0	Fraser 3, Sheldrick 2, Birch 2, Tekell, Walton, Brathwaite			3	4	5	6	7	14	9	10	11	2	12	8	1		15																					
2Q	Sep-30	(h) St Margaretsbury	D 1-1 aet	Brathwaite			3	4	5	6	7	8	12	10	11		9		1		2	14	15																			
2Qr	Oct-07	(a) St Margaretsbury	W 2-0	Brathwaite, Birch (pen)			3	4	5	12	7	8	14	10	11		9	2	1			6																				
1	Oct-29	(h) Hampton	L 0-3				3	4	5	6	7	8		12	11			2	1					9	10																	
Guardian Insurance League Cup																																										
1	Aug-22	(a) Wivenhoe Town	W 5-2	Ivers 2, F Moore, Bhatia, Croad	1	2	3	4	5	15	7	8	9		11		10	6		12																						
2	Sep-05	(a) Tooting & Mitcham United	L 3-4	Sheldrick, Yates, Birch (pen)		2	3	4	5	12	7	6	9	10	11		14	8	1		15																					
Carlton Associate Members Trophy																																										
2	Nov-28	(h) Bedford Town	W 1-0	Walker			3					14		10				8	1			11			4	2	6	7	9	5												
3	Jan-30	(a) Northwood	W 2-0	Buzaglo, Tekell			3		5		7			12				8				11			4		10	6		2	9		14	15			1					
4	Mar-05	(h) Hungerford Town	L 1-2	Sheldrick			3		5		7			10				8	1			11	15			2	6	4	9	12												
Middlesex Senior Cup																																										
1	Nov-08	(a) Feltham	L 1-2 aet	Sheldrick			3	4		6	7			10	12			2	1		15	8	11	9	5																	
Middlesex Charity Cup																																										
2	Oct-10	(a) Brimsdown Rovers	W 1-0	Tekell	1	2		4					10			5		8		9	7	6	11															3				
3	Dec-19	(a) Hanwell Town	L 0-2				3				7			10				2			5	11					8	6	9	4									1			
Harrow Senior Cup																																										
SF	Aug-05	(a*) Rayners Lane	W 3-1	Sheldrick 2 (1 pen), Birch		15	3	4			7	8	12	10	11			14	s	9	2		16																	1	5	6
F	Aug-06	(h) Harrow Borough	L 1-3	Birch		2	3	4		9	7	6	10	12	11	5		8	s																				1			14
		*played at Harrow Borough FC																																								

1996-97

Rd	Date	Opponent	Result	Scorers	Bonfield D	Smart L	Smith A	Moore F	Croad S	Marshall R	Hibbert T	Hall R	Hammatt B	Sheldrick P	Bircham S	Ross D	Tekell L	Walker L	Walton C	Massey J	Waugh I	McBride D	Fraser S	Jones S	London P	Zefi A	McDaid P	Green P	Knight T	Williams O	McKay P	Sterling D	Garner S	Keen J	Weedon M	Kelly S	Miller S	Yaku L
Icis League Division 3 - 1st																																						
	Aug-17	(h) Camberley Town	W 3-1	Moore 2, Hibbert	1	2	3	4	5	6	7	8	9	10	11	12	14	15																				
	Aug-24	(a) Flackwell Heath	L 0-4		1	2	3	4	5	6	8		9	10	11	12	15	14	7																			
	Sep-17	(h) Hertford Town	W 5-1	Fraser 2, Hibbert, Walker, Tekell	1		14	4		6	3		12		11		8	9	7	2	5	10	15															
	Sep-21	(a) Tring Town	W 3-0	Walker 2, Fraser	1			4		6			10		11		8	9	7	2	5	12	3	14														
	Oct-12	(h) Aveley	W 1-0	Walker	1			4		6	8		12		11			9	7	2	5		10		3													
	Oct-19	(a) Lewes	W 1-0	Walton	1		6	4	15		8		12		11			9	7	2	5		10		3													
	Oct-22	(h) Wingate & Finchley	W 3-2	Walton, Bircham, Hammatt	1		3	4		6	8		12		11			9	7	2	5		10															
	Oct-26	(a) Camberley Town	W 3-0	Walker (pen), Moore, Bircham	1		3	4		6	8		10	14	11			9	7	2	5			12		15												
	Nov-09	(a) Hornchurch	W3-0	Marshall, Zefi, Bircham	1		3	4		6			10		11				7		5			8		9	2											
	Nov-16	(h) Southall	W 1-0	Hammatt (pen)	1		3	4		6	11		10						7		5			8		9	2	14	12	15								
	Nov-23	(h) Hornchurch	W 2-0	Green, Bircham	1		3	4	5	6			10	12	11				7	15				8			2	9										
	Nov-30	(h) Kingsbury Town	W 5-0	Smith 2, Hibbert, Bircham, Sheldrick	1		3	4		6	8		10	15	11				7	2	5			14			12	9										
	Dec-07	(a) Epsom & Ewell	W 3-2	Hibbert 3	1		3	4		6	8		10		11			15	7	2	5							9										
	Dec-14	(h) Clapton	W 2-0	Hibbert, og	1		3	4		6	8		10		11				7	2	5							9										
	Dec-21	(a) Braintree Town	L 0-2		1		3	4		6	8		10		11			12	7	2	5			15			14	9										
	Jan-25	(h) Flackwell Heath	W 3-0	Walker, Hibbert, Hammatt	1		3	4			8		10		11			9	7		5						2	14			6							
	Feb-01	(a) Hertford Town	W 2-0	Walker, Sterling	1		12	4		6	8		14		11			9		2	5			15							7	3	10					
	Feb-08	(h) Tring Town	W 7-0	Garner,Hammatt 2,Green,Hibbert,Smith, Sterling	1		2	4		6	8		11							12							15	9			7	3	10	5	14			
	Feb-15	(a) East Thurrock United	W 1-0	Hammatt	1		2	4		6	8		11								5							9			7	3	10					
	Feb-18	(h) Braintree Town	W 6-0	Garner 2,Hammatt,Hibbert,Marshall,Smith	1		2	4		6	8		10		11					14	5							12			7	3	9					
	Mar-01	(a) Aveley	D 1-1	Bircham	1		2	4		6	8		10		11						5							12			7	3	9					
	Mar-08	(h) Lewes	W 2-1	Garner, Moore	1			4		6	8		11		9					2	5							3			7		10					
	Mar-15	(a) Wingate & Finchley	W 3-0	Green, Hibbert 2	1		2	4		6	8		10		11					12	5							9			7	3			14	15		
	Mar-22	(a) Southall	D 1-1	Hammatt	1		11				8		10						14	2	5							9			7	3	12	4		6		
	Mar-25	(h) East Thurrock United	W 4-1	Hammatt 2, Hibbert, McKay	1		3	4		6	8		11						9		5										7		10	12		2		
	Apr-05	(h) Harlow Town	L 0-2		1		12	4		6	8			15	11			14	7		5										2	3	10				9	
	Apr-08	(h) Northwood	L 0-2		1		2	4		6			8	14	11			12	7		5										3		10				9	
	Apr-12	(a) Kingsbury Town	D 0-0		1		14	4		6	8		11		9				7	12	5										2	3	10				15	
	Apr-19	(h) Epsom & Ewell	W 2-1	Walker, Bircham (pen)	1			4		6			14		11			12	7	2											8	3	10		5		9	
	Apr-26	(a) Clapton	W 1-0	Walker (pen)	1			4			8		10		11			12	7	2	5										6	3					14	9
	Apr-30	(a) Harlow Town	L 1-2	Hammatt	1			4		6	8		10		11			12	7	3	5										2		14				15	9
	May-03	(a) Northwood	W 3-1	Hammatt 2, Marshall	1		14	4		6	8		11					12	7	2	5							15			9	3	10					
FA Cup																																						
Pr	Aug-31	(a) Shoreham	W 1-0	Hibbert	1			4	5	6	3		10		11	12	8	9	7	2																		
1Q	Sep-14	(a) Horsham	L 0-1		1		15	4	5	6	3		10	12	11		8	9	7	2	14																	
FA Vase																																						
1Q	Sep-08	(h) Kempston Rovers	W 4-0	Walker, Hammatt 2, Smith	1		15	4	5	6	3	12	10		11		8	9	7	2		14																
2Q	Oct-05	(h) Hoddesdon Town	W 1-0	Walker (pen)	1		2	4		6	3		10		11		12	9	7	14	5		15	8														
1	Nov-02	(a) Spalding U	D 1-1 aet	Hammatt	1		3	4		6	8		10		11			9	7	2	5			14		15												
1r	Nov-06	(h) Spalding U	L 1-2 aet	Walker (pen)	1		3	4		6	8		10	12	11			9	7	2	5			14		15												
Guardian Insurance League Cup																																						
Pr	Aug-27	(h) Kingsbury Town	W 1-0	Moore	1			4	5	6	15	8		12	11	10	3	9	7	2																		
1	Sep-11	(h) Horsham	W 4-2 aet	Hibbert 2, Massey, Marshall	1		12	4	5	6	3		10	14	11		8	9	7	2		15																
2	Nov-26	(a) Banstead Ath	L 0-6		1			4	5	6			10	7	11					12				8	3		2	9										
Associate Members Trophy																																						
1	Dec-17	(a) Dorking	W 7-0	Walker,Hammatt 3,Sheldrick,Moore,Smith	1		3	4		6	8		10	14				9	7	15				5			2	12				11						
2	Jan-28	(h) Bracknell T	W 3-1	Walker, Sterling, og	1			4			8		10		11			9	7	2	5			15			14	12			6	3						
3	Feb-06	(h) Met. Police	W 4-2	Green 3, Hammatt (pen)	1		3	4		6	8		10		11					2				15				9			7				5			
4	Mar-18	(a) Egham T	W 2-1	Green, Hammatt	1		11	4		6	8		10								5							9			7	3				2		
SF	Apr-17	(a) Leatherhead	D 0-0		1		3	4		6			11	15	9			12	7	2	5										8	14	10					
SFr	Apr-22	(h) Leatherhead	W 3-1	Hammatt 2, Yaku	1		3	4			8		9	14	11				7	2											6	5	10	12				15
F	May-06	(a*) Leighton Town	L 0-1		1		14	4		6	8		11					12	7	2	5										9	3	10					
		*at Hitchin FC																																				
Middlesex Senior Cup																																						
Pr	Sep-24	(a) Viking Sports	W 2-0	Fraser, Hammatt	1		3	4	5				15		11			12	7	2	6	9	10	8														
1	Nov-14	(a) Hendon	L 1-3 aet	Williams	1		2	4	5		8			10	11						6				14	9			7	15		3		12				
Middlesex Charity Cup																																						
2	Nov-12	(a) Edgware T	L 1-2	Jones	1		3	4		6			10		11				7		5			8		9	2		12	14		15						

1997-98

Rd	Date	Opponent	Result	Scorers	Imber N	Bowder S	Edmunds A	Moore F	Atkins S	Marshall R	Walton C	McKay P	Boreham K	Garner S	Bircham S	Hibbert T	Sterling D	Celaire M	Galloway A	Lamb P	Waugh I	Jones B	Bonfield D	Kelly S	Greene D	Bush J	Corbould M	Beckett N	Walker L	Gayle K	Horner R	Yaku L	Roberts G	Benning P	Peaks A	Dobson R	Smith T	Bissah K	Gomes U	Cordery S
Ryman League Division 2 - 3rd																																								
	Aug-16	(a) Wivenhoe Town	L 1-2	McKay	1	2	3	4	5	6	7	8	9	10	11	12	14	15																						
	Aug-19	(h) Leighton Town	W 2-1	Garner, og	1	2		4	5	6		8	9	10	11	12	15		3	7																				
	Aug-23	(h) Bracknell T	W 2-0	Boreham, Celaire	1	2			5	6	12	8	9	10	11	14	4	15	3	7																				
	Sep-02	(a) Chalfont St Peter	D 1-1	Moore		2	5	4	15			7		10	11	12	3	9			6	8	1																	
	Sep-20	(h) Cheshunt	W 5-1	Jones 3, Boreham 2	1	2		4	15	6	12	7	14	10	11	8	3				5	9																		
	Sep-23	(a) Met. Police	L 0-1	who went off? sb thinks bircham	1	2		4		6		7	10		11	14	3			8	5	9																		
	Sep-30	(a) Tilbury	W 2-1	Boreham 2 (1 pen)	1	2		4		6	12	7	9		11	14	3			8	5	10																		
	Oct-07	(a) Hungerford Town	D 1-1	Boreham (pen)	1			4		6	7	8	9		10	12	3		5	2		11																		
	Oct-11	(h) Canvey Island	D 1-1	Walton		14		4		6	7	8	9		10	15	3		12	2	5	11	1																	
	Oct-18	(h) Barking	W 4-2	Boreham 3, Bircham	1			4		6	7	8	9	14	10	12			3	2	5	11		15																
	Oct-25	(a) Bedford Town	D 0-0		1			4		6	7	11	9	12	10		3	15		2	5	8																		
	Oct-28	(h) Banstead Ath	D 1-1	Boreham	1			4		6	7	11	12		10		3	15		2	5	8		14	9															
	Nov-08	(a) Egham T	W 5-3	Greene 4, Boreham				4		6	7	11	9					14	15	3	5	8		2	10	1														
	Nov-15	(h) Tooting & Mitcham United	W 2-0	Jones, Bircham	1			4		6	7	11	12		9		3			2	5	8			10															
	Nov-29	(h) Marlow	W 5-0	Greene 2, Garner, Boreham, McKay	1			4		6	7	2	9	12	11	15	3				5	8		14	10															
	Dec-06	(a) Leighton Town	W 1-0	Garner	1	12				6	7	11	9	10		14	3				5	8		2			4													
	Dec-16	(a) Horsham	W 2-0	Jones, Bowder		2				6	7	11			9		12			3	5	8	1		10		4	14												
	Dec-20	(h) Edgware T	W 3-1	Greene, Jones, Beckett		2		4		6	7	11			12		14	15		9		8	1		10		3	5												
	Dec-27	(a) Northwood	D 0-0			2		4		6	7	11	9				3	15		8	5		1		10															
	Jan-10	(a) Banstead Ath	L 1-4	Greene	1	2		4		6	7	11	9		8		12	14		3	5				10			15												
	Jan-17	(h) Wivenhoe Town	D 1-1	Moore		2		4		6	7	11					3	15		9	5	8	1		10		14													
	Jan-24	(a) Bracknell T	W 4-3	Boreham 2, Greene, Jones				4		6	7		9	12	11		3			2	5	8	1		10		14	15												
	Jan-31	(h) Chalfont St Peter	W 2-0	Yaku, Marshall				4		6	7		9		11		3	10		2	5	8	1									14								
	Feb-07	(a) Cheshunt	W 2-0	Garner, Jones				4		6				12	11		3	9		2	5	8	1		10			7	14											
	Feb-14	(h) Braintree Town	D 1-1	Garner				4		6		7		11	9		3			2	5	8	1		10					14										
	Feb-17	(h) Windsor & E	W 2-0	Jones, Sterling				4		6			12	11	9		3			2	5	8	1		10					7										
	Feb-21	(a) Canvey Island	L 0-2							6			12	11	9		3			2	5	8	1		10		14			7	4									
	Feb-24	(a) Witham Town	W 4-3	Boreham 3, Celaire						6			9	12	11		3	14		2	5	8	1		10					7	4									
	Feb-28	(h) Hungerford Town	W 3-1	Jones 2, Lamb (pen)										12	11		3	9		2	5	8	1						15	7	4		6	10						
	Mar-07	(a) Windsor & E	W 2-1	Boreham, Bircham				4		6		12	9		11		3	15		2	5		1		10					7				8						
	Mar-10	(h) Witham Town	D 1-1	Boreham (pen)				4		6		8	9	15	11		3	12		2			1		10				14	7				5						
	Mar-14	(h) Met. Police	L 0-2					4		6		12	9	15	11		3			2	5	8	1		10									7						
	Mar-21	(h) Bedford Town	L 0-1					4		6			12		9		3	14		2	5	8	1		10						7			11						
	Mar-24	(h) Tilbury	W 3-1	Greene 2, Moore				4		6		7		12	9					2	5	8	1		10						3			11						
	Mar-28	(a) Barking	L 1-2	Walker				4		6		7	15	14	9		3			2		8	1		10				12		5			11						
	Mar-31	(a) Braintree Town	W 1-0	Greene	1			4		6			14	11	9		15			2		8			10						3			12	5	7				
	Apr-04	(h) Egham T	W 4-2	Boreham 2, Jones, Dobson	1			4				7	9							2		8							12	11		14		5	6	10			15	3
	Apr-13	(h) Northwood	D 1-1	Greene (pen)	1			4		6	15	7	12	14	9							8			10						5			11	3	2				
	Apr-18	(a) Tooting & Mitcham United	D 2-2	Greene (pen), Garner	1			4		6	14	2	9	12	7						15	8			10						3			11	5					
	Apr-25	(h) Horsham	W 4-2	Walton, Lamb, Horner, Bircham	1						7	12		8	9		3			2	4				10						5			11	6	15				
	Apr-28	(a) Edgware T	W 2-0	Greene, Sterling	1					6	7	12	14	8	9		3			2	4				10									11	5	15				
	May-02	(a) Marlow	W 2-0	Walker, Sterling	1	14				6	7	10	9				3			2	4								12					11	5	8				
FA Cup																																								
Pr	Aug-30	(a) Leatherhead	L 0-2			2		4	5		7			12	11	14		9	3	8	6	10	1														15			
FA Vase																																								
1Q	Sep-09	(a) Hornchurch	W 5-4 aet	Boreham 2, Garner, Jones, Sterling	1	2		4	14	6	12	7	15	10	11	8	3				5	9																		
2Q	Oct-04	(a) Harefield United	W 4-1	Boreham, Jones, Walton, McKay	1	14		4		6	7	8	9		11	15	3		12	2	5	10																		
1	Nov-01	(a) Whitton U	W 3-1 aet	Jones, Celaire, Moore	1	14		4		6	7	11	9	12				15	3	10	5	8		2																
2	Nov-22	(a) Ramsgate	W 1-0	Greene (pen)	1			4		6	7	11		12	9		3			2	5	8			10															
3	Dec-13	(a) Great Wakering R	L 1-2	Greene (pen)		2				6	7	11	9				3	12		4	5	8	1		10															
Guardian Insurance League Cup																																								
Pr	Aug-26	(h) Edgware T	W 2-1	Celaire, McKay	1	2		4	5		12	7		10	11		3	9		8	6	15																		
1	Oct-21	(h) Barton Rovers	W 4-1	Jones 2, Garner, McKay	1	12		4				7	9	10	6	14	3	15		11	5	8		2																
2	Nov-11	(a) Hitchin Town	D 4-4 aet	Jones 3, Greene				4		6	7	11	9	12	3	15		14			5	8		2	10	1														
2r	Dec-02	(h) Hitchin Town	L 2-6	Garner, Walker	1	2				6	7	4	9	11			3					8			10				5									12		
Vandanel Trophy																																								
2	Nov-25	(a) Tilbury	W 2-1	Garner, Greene (pen)	1	2		4			7	11		8	9				3	6	5				10				12											
3	Jan-13	(a) Edgware T	W 2-1	Lamb, Greene		14		4			15			12	11		3	9		7	5	8	1		10		2	6												
4	Feb-10	(a) East Thurrock United	W 2-1	Greene, Yaku	1			4		6	7							9		2	5	8			10		3	12		11		14								
SF	Mar-17	(h) Epsom & Ewell	L 0-1					4		6		2	12	10				9			5	8	1						3	7		14		11					15	
Middlesex Senior Cup																																								
1	Nov-04	(h) Ashford Town (Middlesex)	L 1-4 aet	Greene	1	11		4			7	6	12			8		10	3	5		14		2	9				15											
Middlesex Charity Cup																																								
2	Nov-18	(a) Hampton	L 1-3	Garner	1	15		4				11	9	10	8	7	3	14	2	6									5											

1998-99

Rd	Date	Opponent	Result	Scorers	Imber N	Lamb P	Sterling D	Moore F	Benning P	McKay P	Walton C	Jones B	Kellman D	Holmes C	Kent S	Bircham S	Dell S	White D	Celaire M	Waugh I	Dale S	Dicker P	Yaku L	Swaysland M	Homer R	Fleming S	Forshaw B	Reid L	Brennan G	Baptiste R	Boxford E	Copeman N	James C	Hayward T	Walker L
Ryman League Division 1 - 3rd																																			
	Aug-22	(h) Romford	W 1-0	Kent	1	6	3	4	5	10	7	8	12	14	9	11		2	15																
	Sep-01	(h) Braintree Town	D 2-2	Jones, Walton	1	6	3	4	5	11	7	8	9			10	2		14	12															
	Sep-12	(a) Molesey	L 0-2		1	2		4	5	3	7	8	15	10	12	11					14	6	9												
	Sep-15	(a) Bognor Regis T	L 0-2		1	11	3	4	5	2	7	8			9						10	6	12												
	Sep-22	(a) Chertsey T	W 1-0	Holmes	1	11		4	5		7	8		10			2			3		6		9											
	Sep-26	(a) Barton Rovers	W 3-0	Holmes, Jones, Swaysland	1	11		4	5	12	7	8		10			2			3	14	6	15	9											
	Sep-29	(h) Whyteleafe	W 2-1	Holmes 2	1	11	15	4	5	7		8		10			2			3		6	12	9											
	Oct-11	(h) Croydon	L 0-1		1	11	3	4	5	12	7	8		10	9					2	14	6													
	Oct-17	(a) Yeading	W 1-0	Walton	1	11	3	4	5	2	7	8		10	9		12			15		6	14												
	Oct-31	(a) Hitchin Town	L 1-3	Swaysland (pen)	1	11	3	4		8	7	12		15	10	14	2			5		6		9											
	Nov-07	(h) Canvey Island	W 3-0	Swaysland, Jones, Dicker	1	2	3	4		11	7	8		12		10	15			5		6	14	9											
	Nov-14	(a) Uxbridge	W 1-0	Sterling	1		4		5	11	7	8			12	10	2				14	6		9		3									
	Nov-28	(a) Staines Town	D 2-2	Swaysland (pen), Jones	1	6	5		4	11	7	8				10	12					2		9		3									
	Dec-05	(h) Molesey	D 2-2	Swaysland, Walton	1	6	4		11	10	7	8			15		14					2		9	5	3	12								
	Dec-12	(a) Wembley	W 2-0	Swaysland, Sterling	1		4		11	10					14	15	2			6		7		9	5	3	8								
	Dec-19	(h) Leatherhead	D 1-1	Forshaw	1	6	4	12	7	11					14	10				5		2		9		3	8								
	Dec-28	(a) Berkhamsted T	L 1-4	Sterling	1		4		6	11	7			14	8	10				5		2	15	9		3		12							
	Jan-02	(h) Maidenhead U	L 0-3		1	6	4		14	11	7				12	10	15					2		9	5	3		8							
	Jan-09	(h) Bognor Regis T	W 2-0	Swaysland, Jones	1		4			11	7	8					2			5		12		9		3	14	10	6						
	Jan-23	(h) Grays Athletic	L 1-2	Swaysland	1		4			11	7	8		15		12	2			5		14		9		3		10	6						
	Jan-30	(a) Braintree Town	L 0-1		1				4	11	7	8		14		12	2			5		3		9				10	6	15					
	Feb-06	(h) Chertsey T	D 2-2	Swaysland, Holmes	1	2	4			11				8		7				5		3		9			15	12	6	10					
	Feb-13	(a) Oxford C	L 1-3	Swaysland	1	2	4			11	7	8		10		12				5				9		3			6	15					
	Feb-16	(h) Leyton Pennant	W 1-0	Jones	1	8	4				7	12		14		10	2					5		9		3		15	6	11					
	Feb-20	(a) Croydon	W 3-2	Swaysland, Jones, McKay	1	5	3			6	7	8		10		11				2				9		14		12	4	15					
	Feb-23	(h) Worthing	W 4-1	Swaysland, Bircham 2, Walton	1	5	3			6	7	8				10				2		4		9				11		14					
	Mar-06	(a) Whyteleafe	W 2-0	Baptiste 2	1	2	4		12	11	7	8								5		3						10	6	9					
	Mar-13	(h) Barton Rovers	W 5-2	Jones,Baptiste,Benning,Lamb,Holmes	1	5	3		6	11	7	8		12		10				2		4						15		9					
	Mar-20	(a) Leyton Pennant	W 2-1	Jones, Sterling	1	5	3		6	11	7	8		10		12				2		4				15				9					
	Mar-23	(h) Oxford C	W 2-0	Jones, Baptiste	1		3		6	11	7	8		10		5						2				12			4	9					
	Mar-25	(a) Grays Athletic	D 1-1	Jones	1		3		6	11	7	8		10		5				12		2							4	9					
	Mar-27	(h) Yeading	W 2-0	Jones, Benning	1		3		6	11	7	8		10		5				2						12			4	9	15				
	Apr-03	(a) Maidenhead U	W 2-0	Baptiste, Bircham	1		3		6	11	7	8		10		12						2							4	9	5	14			
	Apr-05	(h) Berkhamsted	W 5-2	Jones 3, Baptiste, Walton	1		3		6	11	7	8		12		10						2							4	9	5	14	15		
	Apr-07	(a) Romford	W 4-0	Jones, Baptiste 2 (1 pen), Holmes	1		3			6	7	8		11		10				5						12			4	9	2				
	Apr-10	(a) Canvey Island	L 2-4	Jones 2	1		3		6	11	7	8		12		10				5		2				14			4	9			15		
	Apr-14	(h) Wembley	W 1-0	Baptiste (pen)	1		3		6	11	7	8		14		10				5		12							4	9	2		15		
	Apr-17	(h) Uxbridge	W 2-1	Benning, Holmes	1		3		6	11				8		10				5		7							4	9	2		15		
	Apr-22	(a) Leatherhead	W 1-0	Holmes	1	12	3		6	11	7			8		10				5		4								9	2				
	Apr-24	(a) Worthing	W 2-1	Holmes, Baptiste (pen)	1	15	3		6	11	7	12		8		10				5		14								9	2	4			
	Apr-28	(h) Hitchin Town	W 2-1	Holmes, Walton	1	8	3		6	11	7			10						5		4								9	2		14		
	May-01	(h) Staines Town	W 3-1	Holmes, Walton, Walker	1	14	3		6	11	7			8		10						5							4	9	2		15		12
FA Cup																																			
Pr	Sep-05	(a) Potters Bar T	D 2-2	Kent, Yaku	1	6	3	4	5	8	7		9		10		2		15	11			12												
Prr	Sep-09	(h) Potters Bar T	W 5-3	Yaku 2, Holmes 2, Kent	1	11	3	4	5	10	7	8	9	16	12		2			6			14												
1Q	Sep-19	(a) Buckingham Town	W 1-0	Walton	1	11	3		4	10	7	8		17	9				14	2		6	15		5										
2Q	Oct-03	(h) Newport (IOW)	D0-0		1	11	3	4	8	14	7	12		10	9		2			5		6	15												
2Qr	Oct-06	(a) Newport (IOW)	L 2-3†	Jones, og	1	11	3	12	5	14	7	8		10	16		2			4		6		9											
FA Trophy																																			
1	Oct-27	(a) Dagenham & Redbridge	D 1-1	Kent	1	11	3	4		10	7				9	12	2			5		6	17	8											
1r	Nov-09	(h) Dagenham & Redbridge	L 0-5		1	2	3	4			7	8		11	16	10				5		6		9											
Puma Full Members Cup																																			
1	Dec-01	(a) Grays Athletic	W 1-0	Jones	1	6			4	11	7	12				10	2					3	15	9	5		8								
2	Dec-08	(a) Yeading	W 5-2	Swaysland 3, Forshaw, Yaku	1	6	4	12	11	10							2			14		7	15	9	5	3	8								
3	Jan-26	(a) Oxford C	W 4-2	Swaysland 2 (1 pen), Bircham, Jones	1		3		12		7	8		11		10	2			5		4		9				6							
4	Mar-09	(a) Dulwich Hamlet	L 0-1		1	5	3		6	11	7	8		12		10				2		4								9					
Isthmian Football League Cup																																			
Pr	Aug-25	(h) Northwood	W 4-1	Holmes 3, Sterling	1	6	3	4	5		7	8	9	12	10	11	2		15		14														
1	Oct-21	(h) Berkhamsted	W 4-1	Baptiste 2, Holmes, Yaku	1			4		7		12		14		9	2	3			8	6	10		5					11					
Middlesex Senior Cup																																			
1	Nov-03	(h) Feltham	W 5-1	Swaysland, Holmes, Homer, Bircham, Lamb	1	11		4		7	15	8		10	14	3		2			12	6		9	5										
2	Feb-02	(h) Harrow Borough	D 2-2	Holmes 2	1	6	4			12	7	8		11		10	14			5		2		9		3									
2r	Feb-09	(a) Harrow Borough	W 2-1	Swaysland 2	1	6	4			11		8		10			2			5		3		9		15	12	7							
3	Feb-18	(a) Hayes	W 2-1	Swaysland, McKay	1	5	3			6	7	8		10		11				2		4		9		14									
SF	Mar-02	(a) Hendon	L 0-3		1		3		12	5	7	8		10		11				2		4					14	6		9					
Middlesex Charity Cup																																			
2	Feb-25	(a) Ruislip Manor	L 0-2		1	2				7		14		10						5		6				3	11	8	4	9				15	

1999-2000

Rd	Date	Venue / Opponent	Result	Scorers	Imber N	McKay P	Lyons J	Boxford E	Tilbury D	Lamb P	Holmes C	Jones B	Baptiste R	Bircham S	Reid L	Walton C	Valenti F	Campbell M	Sterling D	Walker L	Dicker P	Gustave D	Waugh I	Greene D	Timberlake M	Randall K	Hall J	Dobson R	O'Connor S	Rutherford I	Sofo-Yarabi F	Stanislas S	Spencer W	Rowlands K	Nesbitt J	Murphy M	Maynard S	Prutton A	Coktas M	Hodson B	Benning P	Richmond A	Hamdouche S	Behzadi B	Swaysland M	Coffey G	Watts D	Peaks A	Robinson S	Gough M	Morgan M	Tarrant B	Roche M	Cooper V
Ryman League Division 1 - 16th																																																						
	Aug-14	(h) Harlow Town	W 3-1	Baptiste 2 (2 pens), Bircham	1	2	3	4	5	6	7	8	9	10	11																																							
	Aug-17	(a) Yeading	D 1-1	Baptiste	1	2	3	4	5	6	11	8	9	10	14	7	12	15																																				
	Aug-24	(h) Thame U	W 1-0	Holmes	1		3	6	5	2	11	8	9	10		7			4	12																																		
	Aug-28	(a) Grays Athletic	W 1-0	Jones	1	14	3	6	5	2	11	8	9	10		7		15	4	12																																		
	Sep-01	(h) Bishop's Stortford	L 0-2		1	14	3	6	5	2	11	8	9	10		7		15	4	12																																		
	Sep-11	(h) Bognor Regis T	D 0-0		1	3			5	2	10	8			11	7			4	12	15	14	6	9																														
	Sep-25	(a) Braintree Town	L 1-2	Baptiste (pen)	1	3			5	2		8	9			7	15		4	12	6		14	10			11																											
	Oct-16	(h) Bedford Town	D 1-1	Holmes	1	3	15		5	9	10	8	14			7			4	12	6		2				11																											
	Oct-23	(a) Chertsey T	W 3-1	Waugh, Holmes, Walker	1	3	15		5	2	10	8	9			7			4	12	6		11																															
	Oct-30	(h) Uxbridge	D 1-1	Jones			3	14	5	11	10	8	9			7			4	12	6		2						1																									
	Nov-06	(h) Bromley	L 1-3	Jones	1	11	3	2	5		10	8	12			7			4		6		14							9	15																							
	Nov-12	(a) Oxford C	L 1-2	Holmes	1	3	15	14	5	2	10	8		12		7			4		6		11					9																										
	Nov-20	(h) Barton R	W 4-1	Jones, Baptiste, Sofo-Yarabi 2	1	3		4	5	6		8	10	11		7		14		9	2							12			15																							
	Dec-04	(a) Bishops Stortford	L 0-3		1	3		11	5	2	12		9	8		7			4		6												10				14																	
	Dec-08	(h) Whyteleafe	W 3-1	Jones, Baptiste 2	1	3	14	9		2	10	8	12	11		7			4		6																5																	
	Dec-11	(h) Romford	W 2-0	Jones, Holmes	1		3	2	5		10	8	14	11					4		6																9	7																
	Dec-18	(a) Worthing	D 1-1	Maynard	1	3	14	9	5	2	10	8	12	11					4		6																15	7																
	Dec-27	(h) Staines Town	L 0-2		1	3		9	5	2	10	8	12	11					4		6														15		14	7																
	Jan-03	(a) Bromley	L 1-4	Baptiste	1	3	10	12	5	2	15		9	11					4		6														14		8	7																
	Jan-08	(h) Grays Athletic	L 0-2		1	3	14	6	5	2	12	8	9					15	4																11			7		10														
	Jan-22	(a) Thame Utd	D 1-1	Lamb	1	3	11	6	5	2	10	8	12						4	14																15	7			9														
	Jan-29	(h) Leyton Pennant	D 2-2	Holmes, Sterling	1		3		5	2	10	12	9						4		6									11							7							8										
	Feb-05	(a) Harlow Town	D 0-0		1	3		6	5	2	10		14						4											9							15	12			11			7	8									
	Feb-08	(h) Yeading	L 1-3	Swaysland (pen)	1	3			5	2	10	12		15					4		6									9								14			11			7	8									
	Feb-12	(h) Croydon	L 1-2	Swaysland	1	3				2		8		11					4	5	6									9						7								15	10									
	Feb-19	(a) Bognor Regis	D 1-1	Rutherford		3				2		8		11						5	6									10						4					7			12	9		1							
	Feb-22	(a) Leatherhead	W 2-0	McKay 2		3				2		8		11					4	5	6									9						7								15	10		1							
	Feb-26	(a) Bedford Town	L 0-4			3				7	12	8		10					4		5									9						2					14			15	11		1	6						
	Mar-04	(h) Maidenhead U	L 0-1			3			9	2	12	8		11					4	5										14						15					7				10		1	6						
	Mar-08	(a) Croydon	D 2-2	Jones, Swaysland		3			4	7	11	8		10						5																					2				9		1	6						
	Mar-11	(a) Uxbridge	D 1-1	Jones		3			4	7	11	8		10						5																					2				9		1	6						
	Mar-18	(h) Braintree Town	W 2-0	Jones, Swaysland		3			4	7	11	8		10					5																	2					12				9		1	6						
	Mar-21	(a) Leyton Pennant	W 2-0	Jones, Swaysland		3			14	7	11	8							4																	10					2				9		1	6	5					
	Mar-25	(a) Whyteleafe	L 1-2	Holmes		3			5	7	11	8							4												15					2					10				9		1	6	12	14				
	Apr-01	(h) Chertsey T	L 0-1			3			5		11					7																				10					2	4			9		1	6	8		12	14	15	
	Apr-08	(h) Worthing	W 2-1	Swaysland, Jones		3			5	7	11								4																	10					2				9		1	6			8		12	
	Apr-19	(a) Maidenhead U	L 0-2			3			5	7		8							4																	2					11				9		1	6	14		12	15	10	
	Apr-22	(h) Oxford C	W 2-1	Swaysland 2		3			5	7		8							4																	10					2				9		1	6	11		12			
	Apr-24	(a) Staines Town	L 1-2	Swaysland (pen)		3			5	7		8						12	4																	10					2				9		1	6	11		14			15
	Apr-29	(h) Leatherhead	D 1-1	Morgan		3			5	7	11								4																	10					8				9		1	6			12		15	2
	May-01	(a) Romford	W 3-1	Swaysland, Morgan, Tilbury		3			5	4	11							15																		7					2				9		1	6	12		10		14	8
	May-06	(a) Barton R	L 1-2	Robinson		3				7								12													15					10					2	5			9		1	6	4		8		14	11
FA Cup																																																						
Pr	Aug-21	(h) Clacton T	W 1-0	Holmes	1	11	3	6	5	2	10		9	8	15	7	14		4	12																																		
1Q	Sep-04	(h) Ford U	D 1-1	Sterling	1	11	3		5	2	10	8				7	17		4	9	6	15																																
1Qr	Sep-07	(a) Ford U	W 3-2	Baptiste 3	1	3			5	2	10	8	11			7			4	9	6																																	
2Q	Sep-18	(a) Staines Town	W 3-0	Baptiste 3		3			5	2	11	8	9			7	14		4	12	6			10	1	16																												
3Q	Oct-02	(h) Rothwell T	D 1-1	Baptiste	1	3			5	10		8	9			7			4		6		2				11																											
3Qr	Oct-05	(a) Rothwell T	L 0-2		1	3			5	10	11	8	9			7			4	12	6		2	14			17																											
FA Trophy																																																						
2	Nov-27	(a) Crawley Town	W 2-0	Jones, Bircham	1	3		6	5	11	14	8	9	10		7			4		2																																	
3	Jan-15	(h) Kingstonian	L 0-5		1	11	3	2	5	7	15	8	12						4		6														17		10			9														
Full Members Cup																																																						
1	Nov-22	(a) Hendon	D 2-2*	Baptiste, Rowlands	1	3		2	5		7		10	8					4		6							14			12		9	11	15																			
2	Nov-30	(h) Borehamwood	W 3-0	Jones, Holmes, Rowlands	1	3	15	6	5		7	8		11					4		2												9	10	14	12																		
3	Jan-25	(a) Gravesend & Northfleet	L 1-3	Holmes	1	3	11	6	5	2	10	8	9						4	12																15				14				7										
		*after extra time. Won 7-6 on pens.																																																				
Ryman Football League Cup																																																						
1	Sep-14	(a) Hertford Town	W 4-3	Hall, Greene 2, Gustave		3				7	8		9			12	2		4	5	6	15		10	1		11																											
2	Nov-09	(h) Leyton Pennant	W 1-0	Lamb	1	11			5	8			9	14		7			4		6		2					3		10																								
3	Dec-14	(h) Oxford C	L 0-1		1		3	11	5			8	9			7		14	4		6							12								2		10	15															
Middlesex Senior Cup																																																						
1	Nov-03	(h) Harefield United	W 3-1	Baptiste, Holmes, Dobson		3		2	5	7	10	8	9					15	4	1	6		14					11				16																						
2	Jan-11	(a) Uxbridge	L 2-3	og, Jones		3	7	6	5		10	8						4		1														9	2		11				12	15	16											
Middlesex Charity Cup																																																						
1	Oct-06	(h) Waltham Abbey	W 2-0	Baptiste, Holmes	1	14	3		5	4	12	8	10	11						9	6		2				7	17																										
2	Feb-15	(h) Brook House	W 5-0	Jones, Swaysland 2, Coffey 2	1	3			14	11		8							4	5	6															2					7			15	10	9								
3	Mar-28	(h) Wembley	D 0-0*			3			5	7	11	8						16	4																						2	10			9		1	6	14					
		*after extra time. Lost 0-3 on pens.																																																				

2000-01

Rd	Date	Opponent	Result	Scorers	Watts D	Carter W	Murphy M	Tucker R	Reeve D	Lamb P	Boyce R	Tilbury D	Swaysland M	Holmes C	Totton C	Bircham S	Maynard S	Morgan M	Robinson S	Norman P	Williams G	Greene D	Cooper V	Walker L	Dicker P	Doherty L	Toppin A	Joyce T	Jones B	Ravenscroft C	Keane K	Clarke D	Leary C	Burgess J	Leenders A	Domi S	James S	Cenolli M	Perry M	Reed N	Amartelfio B	Barima M	Butterfield T	Hingley A	Alexander B	Towle S	Mentore E	Fry J
Ryman League Division 1 - 19th																																																
	Aug-19	(h) Whyteleafe	L 1-2	Swaysland	1	2	3	4	5	6	7	8	9	10	11	12	14	15																														
	Aug-22	(a) Thame U	L 0-4		1	8	3	4	5	6	11	7	9	10	14	12	15		2																													
	Aug-26	(a) Braintree Town	D 1-1	Boyce	1	12	3	4	5	6	7	8	9	10		11	15			2	14																											
	Aug-28	(h) Uxbridge	W 1-0	Tilbury	1	10	3	4	5	6	7	8	9	12		11				2	14	15																										
	Sep-05	(a) Bishops Stortford	D 2-2	Boyce, Cooper	1	8	2	4	5	6	11	7	9		12	10				3	15		14																									
	Sep-09	(h) Boreham Wood	L 2-3	Boyce, Reeve (pen)	1	7	3	8	5		11				12	10				2	9		15	4	6	14																						
	Sep-19	(h) Northwood	D 2-2	Swaysland (pen), Carter	1	7	3	2		6	11		9	10	14										4	8	15	5	12																			
	Sep-23	(a) Ford U	L 1-2	og	1	7	2		5	6	11		9		15										8	14	4	3	12	10																		
	Oct-06	(h) Aylesbury U	L 1-3	Swaysland	1	7	3		5	6	11	15	12	9				14									4	2	8	10																		
	Oct-10	(a) Staines Town	L 1-4	Holmes	1	14	3		5	6	11	8	9	10				7									4	2	12	15																		
	Oct-17	(h) Bognor Regis T	W 2-0	Holmes, og	1	12	3		5	6		7	9	10				14						4			11	2	8	15																		
	Oct-21	(h) Romford	D 3-3	Jones, Tilbury, Joyce	1	12	3	5		6		11	9	10										4				2	8		7																	
	Oct-28	(a) Walton & H	W 2-0	Swaysland, Jones	1	7		2		6	3	11	9	10				12						4			15		8			5																
	Nov-11	(h) Worthing	L 0-1		1	7	3	4	5	6		11		10				9										2	8			12																
	Nov-18	(a) Yeading	D 2-2	Swaysland, Reeve	1	7	3	4	5	6		11	9	10				15										2	8					14														
	Dec-02	(a) Oxford C	L 0-3		1	7		4	5	6		11	9							3								2						8	10													
	Dec-16	(a) Uxbridge	W 2-0	Swaysland, Holmes	1	7		4	5		6	11	9	10				12										2	8							3	14											
	Dec-23	(h) Barton R	W 2-0	Jones, Carter	1	7		4	5		6	11	9	10				12										2	8					14	15	3												
	Jan-13	(h) Thame U	L 0-4		1	7		4	5		6	11	9	10														2	8					15		3	14											
	Jan-23	(a) Bedford Town	L 1-4	og	1	7		4	5			11		10				9		s								2	8					6	s	3				s								
	Jan-27	(h) Braintree Town	L 2-3	Jones, Burgess	1				5	12		11		10				9		4								2	8					6	14	3				7	15							
	Jan-30	(a) Worthing	W 1-0	Carter	1	7			5	12		11						9		4									8					10	3					6	2							
	Feb-03	(a) Northwood	L 1-3	Reeve	1	7		15	5	12		11						9		3								2	8					6	10	14					4							
	Feb-10	(h) Staines Town	D 1-1	Jones	1	7		10		9		11								3					12			2	8					6						5	4							
	Feb-17	(a) Borehamwood	L 1-2	Walker	1	7		3		6		11						14		9				12	4			2	8					10						5		15						
	Feb-24	(h) Bedford Town	D 1-1	og	1	7		3		6		11								9					4			2	8					10									5					
	Mar-03	(a) Aylesbury U	W 2-0	Jones 2	1	7		3		6		11		10						9				12	4			2	8											5		15						
	Mar-10	(a) Bognor Regis T	W 3-2	Carter, Morgan, Holmes	1	7		3	5	6		11		10				14		9					4			2	8					15														
	Mar-14	(a) Harlow Town	L 1-3	Tilbury	1	7		3	5	6		11		10				15		14				9	4				8														2					
	Apr-03	(h) Leatherhead	L 0-1		1	7		s	5	6		s		10										4					8					s							2		3	9	11			
	Apr-07	(h) Yeading	D 0-0		1	7		3	5	6		11		10				9						4				2						12									8	15				
	Apr-10	(h) Bishops Stortford	L 1-2	Tilbury	1				5	6		11		10				12		2														7						3	4		8	9	14			
	Apr-12	(h) Bromley	W 4-1	Holmes 3, Hingley	1	7			5	6				10						3				4				2	12					14									8	9	11			
	Apr-14	(a) Barton Rovers	W 1-0	Holmes	1	7			5	6				10				9		2				4					8					14						3	15		11					
	Apr-16	(h) Harlow Town	D 2-2	Jones, Holmes	1	7			5	6		11		10				14						12				2	8					3							4				9			
	Apr-19	(h) Ford U	W 3-1	Holmes, Carter, Hingley	1	7			5	6		11		10				8						4				12						14						3	2			9	15			
	Apr-21	(a) Leatherhead	L 0-1		1	7			5			11		10				12		2				4					8					14						3			6	9	15			
	Apr-23	(a) Whyteleafe	L 0-2			7		4	5			11						9		3								2					1	6						12		10	8			14		
	Apr-28	(h) Oxford C	L 0-1		1	7		3		6		11		10				9						4				2	8					5									14			15		
	Apr-29	(a) Romford	W 2-0	Holmes, Butterfield	1	7		3		6		11		10				9		2				4										12						5			8					
	May-03	(h) Walton & H	L 2-3	Holmes, Walker		7		5		6		11		10				9						4				2					1	12									3		8		14	
	May-05	(a) Bromley	L 0-4		1	7		5		6				10				9		3				4				2						11					12						8			14
FA Cup																																																
Pr	Sep-02	(a) Brackley T	W 3-0	Tilbury, Carter, og	1	7	2	3	5	6	11	8	9		16	10							14	4			17																					
1Q	Sep-16	(h) Ware	W 4-0	Swaysland 2 (1 pen),Holmes,Murphy	1	7	3		5	6	11		9	15	10					2				4		8	17		14																			
2Q	Sep-30	(a) Stowmarket	W 2-1	Carter 2	1	7		2	5	6	11		9	15		10		17									4	3	12	8																		
3Q	Oct-14	(h) Belper Town	L 2-3	Swaysland, Jones	1	7	3	14	5			11	9	10										4			6	2	8																			
FA Trophy																																																
1	Nov-05	(h) Weston Super Mare	D 3-3	Jones, Carter, Reeve (pen)	1	7	14	2	5	6	3	11		10				9						4			12		8																			
1r	Nov-07	(a) Weston Super Mare	L 0-2			7	3	2	5	6	4	11		10				9											8		14	12	1															
Full Members Cup																																																
2	Feb-15	(h) Hitchin Town	L 0-3			7		3		6								14						12	9			2	8				1	10						5	4		11					
Ryman Football League Cup																																																
1	Sep-12	(a) Thame U	L 3-4	Carter, Reeve, Doherty	1	7	2	8	5		11				9	10				3	15			14	6	4																						
Middlesex Senior Cup																																																
1	Dec-05	(a) Ashford Town (Middlesex)	L 1-4	Reeve		7		4	5			6	9	10				14		2								3	8						11	15		1	16									
Middlesex Charity Cup				Competition cancelled																																												

2001-02

Rd	Date	Opponent	Result	Scorers	Carter A	Bryson T	Moore F	Amartellio B	Reeve D	McDonagh R	Somers V	Shaw J	Walker L	Hammatt B	Tilbury D	Pither R	Greene D	Chandler S	Tucker R	Lamb P	Connelly R	Leary C	Gibbs D	Bamgbola O	Deadman J	Morgan M	Perry M	Carter M	Homer R	Chamberlin T	Hunt C	Reed N	Ramsay K	O'Reagan J	Scarlett A	Drahe B	Swaysland M	Moore K	Wright D	Hercules T	McCarthy A	Godfrey D	Marie-Sainte J	Bowen J	Fenemore D	Beckford J	Adan G	Duncan J	Cobb N
Ryman League Division 1 - 18th																																																
	Aug-18	(h) Bromley	W 4-1	Somers, Shaw, Moore, Reeve (pen)	1	2	3	4	5	6	7	8	9	10	11	12	15																																
	Aug-21	(a) Walton & H	W 2-1	Walker, Chandler	1	2	3	4	5	6	7	8	9	10	11	12	15	14																															
	Aug-25	(a) Harlow Town	L 0-2		1	2	3	4	5	6	7	8	9	10	12		15	14	11																														
	Aug-27	(h) Oxford C	W 3-0	Hammatt 2, Pither	1	15	3			6	7	8		10	11	12	9	5	2	4																													
	Sep-08	(h) Slough T	W 2-1	Walker, og	1			14		4	7	8	12	10	11	15	9	5	2	6	3																												
	Sep-12	(h) Bognor Regis T	L 2-3	Walker, Shaw	1		3	5		4	7	8	12	10	11	14	9		2	6	15																												
	Sep-22	(a) Dulwich Hamlet	L 2-3	Hammatt, Moore			3	14		11	7	8	9	10		15	12	5	2	6	4	1																											
	Sep-25	(a) Worthing	W 2-0	Greene, Tilbury	1		3	5	6	4	7	8		10	11	14	9		2																															
	Oct-02	(h) Uxbridge	W 2-1	Hammatt (pen), Tilbury	1		3		5		7	8	12	10	11	14	9	4	2	6			15																										
	Oct-09	(a) Aylesbury U	D 2-2	Hammatt (pen), Lamb	1		3	4	5		7	8		10	11	15	9		2	6																													
	Oct-13	(a) Thame U	L 2-4	Reeve, Shaw	1		3	4	5			8	12	10	11	7	9		2	6	14		15																										
	Oct-16	(h) Whyteleafe	D 1-1	Walker	1		3	12	5	9		8	4	10	11				2	6	14		7	15																									
	Oct-20	(a) Carshalton Athletic	L 0-3		1		3	4				8		10	11	15	9		2	6	5			14	7																								
	Oct-23	(a) Bishops Stortford	L 1-7	Deadman	1		3	4	5		15	8		10	11	14	9		2	6					7																								
	Oct-27	(h) Barking & E Ham	D 2-2	Walker, Hammatt	1		3				7	8	4	10	11	12			2	6	14			15	5	9																							
	Nov-10	(a) Staines Town	D 1-1	Somers	1		3				11	8		14		10			4	12				9	6		2	7	5																				
	Nov-17	(h) Tooting & Mitcham United	L 0-1		1		3				7	8		10	12	14				6				15	4	9	2	11	5																				
	Nov-24	(a) Ford U	L 1-2	M Carter	1		3			9	7	8			11	15				6				12	4		2	10	5																				
	Dec-08	(h) Yeading	L 0-2		1		3			9	7	8		12	11	14				6					4		2	10	5	15																			
	Dec-15	(a) Bromley	W 2-1	Moore, Chamberlin	1		3				12	8	4		11	6								15	7	10	2		5	9																			
	Dec-29	(h) Walton & H	D 3-3	Tilbury, Morgan, Homer	1				2	12	7	8			11	4								9		10			5		14	3	6	15															
	Jan-05	(h) Bishops Stortford	D 2-2	Pither, Reeve	1				4		15	8		10	11	14								7		9	2		5	6		3																	
	Jan-12	(a) Slough T	L 0-6		1						7	8	12	10		15								14		9	2	6	5	4	11		3																
	Jan-19	(h) Dulwich H	L 1-3	Shaw	1		3		14			8		10		15									2	12			5				4		6	7	9	11											
	Jan-29	(h) Windsor & E	D 1-1	Homer	1		3					8		10	2	12								14					5				4		6		9		7	11									
	Feb-02	(a) Yeading	L 1-2	Tilbury	1		3							10	11	15								14	2		12		5				4		6		9		8	7									
	Feb-09	(h) Ford United	D 1-1	Tilbury	1		3							10	11										2			14	5				4		6		9		8	7									
	Feb-12	(a) Oxford City	L 2-4	Hammatt 2	1		3							10	11									14	2		4	12	5						6		9		8	7									
	Feb-16	(a) Windsor & Eton	D 3-3	Swaysland 2, Hercules			3							10	11				4			1			2		5	12			15				6		9		8	7									
	Feb-23	(h) Worthing	D 1-1	Swaysland	1		3							10	11				2						4			8			7				6		9			14	5								
	Feb-26	(h) Northwood	D 2-2	Swaysland 2	1		4							10	11				2					14				8	12		7		5		6		9			3									
	Mar-02	(a) Uxbridge	L 0-1		1		4							10	11				2					15			14	8	12		7		5		6		9			3									
	Mar-09	(h) Aylesbury United	W 1-0	Morgan			4							10	11				2							7		8	5						6		9			3		1							
	Mar-12	(a) Bognor Regis Town	W 1-0	Carter M			4																			10	2	8	5		14		11		6		9			3		1	7						
	Mar-23	(h) Thame United	L 1-3	Morgan	1	2	4								11				3					15		10		8	5		14		12		6		9						7						
	Mar-26	(a) Whyteleafe	W 2-1	Swaysland, Morgan	1	14	4							3	11				2							10		8	12		15		5		6		9						7						
	Mar-30	(h) Harlow Town	D 1-1	Tilbury	1	12	4							3	11											10		8			14		2		6		9						7	5					
	Apr-06	(a) Barking & East Ham United	L 1-2	Hammatt	1	15						2	4	3	11											10	14	8			12		6				9						7	5					
	Apr-09	(a) Northwood	L 1-3	Hammatt	1							2	12	3	11				4							10		8			7		6				9							5		14	15		
	Apr-13	(h) Carshalton Athletic	L 1-2	Hunt	1		4					14	12		11											10	3	8			7		2				9						6	5	15				
	Apr-20	(a) Tooting & Mitcham United	L 2-3	Hammatt, Perry (pen)	1		4					14	12	11									15		10	3	8			7		2				9						6	5					
	Apr-27	(h) Staines Town	W 1-0	Walker			4					6	9		11				2					7		10	3	8						5			12					1						14	
FA Cup																																																
Pr	Sep-01	(a) Tilbury	D 1-1	Greene				4	5		7	8	12	10	11		9	3	2	6	15	1																											
Prr	Sep-03	(h) Tilbury	W 2-1	Somers, og	1					5	7	8	12	10	11	16	9	3	2	6	4																												
1Q	Sep-19	(a) Ware	W 5-1	Hammatt, Walker(pen), Pither, Somers, Moore	1		3		15	4	7	8	9	10	11	17	12	5	2	6																													
2Q	Sep-29	(a) Purfleet	L 2-3	Hammatt, Tilbury	1		3	6	5	4	7	8		10	11	16	9	12	2				14																										
FA Trophy																																																
1	Nov-04	(h) Bishops Stortford	D 1-1	Tilbury	1		3	5			15	8			11	14			4	6				9	7	10	2																						
1r	Nov-06	(a) Bishops Stortford	L 2-3	Deadman, Moore	1		3	5			14	8			11	10			4	6				9	7		2																						
Ryman Football League Cup																																																
Pr	Oct-30	(h) Edgware T	W 5-2	Morgan 2, Pither 2, Lamb	1		3					8	4		12	14	9		2	6				11	5	10	15	7																					
1	Nov-27	(h) Tilbury	W 6-1 aet	Bamgbola 3, Tilbury 2, Somers	1		3			9	7	8			11	12				6				14	4		2	10	5	15																			
2	Dec-18	(a) Met. Police	W 2-1 aet	Bamgbola, Hunt	1		3		5	8	7		4		11	6				12				14		10	2			9	15																		
3	Jan-22	(h) Ford U	W 3-2	Hammatt 3 (1pen)	1		3		4			8		10		11								14	7	9	2		5						6			12											
4	Feb-19	(h) Tooting & Mitcham United	L 0-1		1		4							10	11				2					9			12	8	5		7				6			3					15		14				
Middlesex Senior Cup																																																
1	Nov-14	(h) Hanwell Town	W 2-1	Hammatt, Somers			3	5		4	7	12		10	11	9				6				15	8		2																						1
2	Nov-29	(a) Potters Bar T	W 3-0	Walker, Reed, Tilbury	1		3		5			8	12	10	11	2				6				9				7			17	4		14															
3	Jan-07	(a) Enfield T	L 1-3	Hammatt	1				4			8	15	10	11	17								12		9	2		5	7	6	3																	
Middlesex Charity Cup																																																
1		Bye																																														
2	Mar-21	(a) Northwood	W 3-1	Swaysland, Tucker, Beckford		2	4								11				3							10		8	5		7				6		9					1	15			16	17		
3	Apr-11	(a) Yeading	D 2-2 †	Walker, Moore	1		5					6	4		11	7										10	16	8			17		3				12								2		9			
SF	Apr-23	(a) Uxbridge	W 2-1	Moore, Perry	1		5					10	4		11				6							12	7	8			16		3				9								2					
F	May-09	(n*) Enfield Town	D 1-1 ††	Perry	1		4					6			11				2					7		10	3	8			16			5			12								14		9			

* Played at Brook House FC

† After extra time - won 4-2 on penalties

†† After extra time - lost 4-3 on penalties

Appendix 3

First Team Other League Matches

1967 - 1994

Competitions included here are as follows:

Bucks Border League
M1 Floodlight League
Premier Midweek Floodlight League
Mid-Surrey Floodlight League
Capital League
Capital League Presidents Cup
Arlington Gold Cup

WEALDSTONE IN OTHER COMPETITIONS

Bucks Border League

1967-68

Dec 5 v Wellingborough (h) 2-2 *Lindsay, Smart*
A Williams, Warman, Leonard, Townsend, McGuinness, Slade, B Gill, Lindsay, Swain, Montague, Smart
Jan 16 v Bedford T (h) 2-1 *Bremer, Lindsay*
A Williams, Pettit, Leonard, Townsend, McGuiness, Slade, Bremer, Lindsay, Swain, Montague, Hutchinson
Jan 30 v Wellingborough (a) 3-2 *Praede, McKenzie, Clary*
Blythe, Barnard, Warman, R Day, Phillips, C Rapley, M Praede, M Clary, Somers, E McKenzie, Smart
Feb 6 v Bletchley (a) 0-1
Blythe, Barnard, G Greenhalgh, R Williams, Phillips, Rapley, M Praede, M Clary, Somers, E McKenzie,P Jordan
Feb 13 v Bletchley (h) 1-0 *Clary*
Blythe, R Williams, G Greenhalgh, Phillips, T Quick, Rapley, P Jordan, Smart, Somers, M Clary, Hutchinson
Apr 22 v Bedford (a) 0-2
A Williams, Pettit, G Greenhalgh, Townsend, P Snell, Rapley, M Praede, M Clary, Somers, E McKenzie, Hutchinson
Apr 29 v Watford (a) 1-0 *Phillips*
A Williams, Phillips, Warman, Townsend, McGuiness, Montague, Bremer, Slade, Somers, Lindsay, Hutchinson Sub: Swain
May 6 v Watford (h) 3-2 *Bremer, Townsend, Somers*
A Williams, Phillips, Leonard, Townsend, McGuinness, Montague, Bremer, Slade, Somers, Lindsay, Hutchinson Sub: M Clary

M1 Floodlight League

1968-69

Oct 30 v Bletchley (a) 4-1 *Underwood,Roebuck,Evans,Lavin (pen)*
Edwards, Praede, Barnard, Smith, Rapley, Lavin, F McCoy, D Underwood, B Roebuck, Bremer, V Evans
Nov 12 v Wellingborough T (a) 1-1 *Carter*
K Pickard, K Gerrard, Barnard, T Smith, G Perrett, C Rapley, F McCoy, Bullock, B Roebuck, S Carter, V Evans
Dec 3 v Bletchley (h) 3-1 *Swain 2, McKenzie*
B Fowler, G Perrett, G Hand, M Murphy, Montague, Bromley, Bremer, Lindsay, Swain, Bullock, E McKenzie
Dec 9 v Wellingborough T (h) 5-0 *McCoy 2, Searle 2, Hutchinson*
Fowler, Doyle, Hand, Murphy, Gerrard, Montague, McCoy, Lindsay, Searle, Evans, Hutchinson
Mar 17 v Watford (a) 1-1 *T Smith*
Fowler, Doyle, Barnard, T Smith, K Gerrard, Bullock, Underwood, Searle, Swain, C Rapley, Hutchinson
May 12 v Watford (h) 0-2
A Williams, Doyle, Hand, Bullock, K Gerrard, Montague, Bremer, Lindsay, Swain, Searle, Ritchie

Premier Midweek Floodlight League

1970-71

Oct 20 v Hemel Hempstead (h) 1-1 *Booth*
Thomas, Mahon, Barnard, Bullock, Dafforn, Olson, Yerby, Chapman, Booth, Wilson, Bennett
Oct 27 v Maidenhead (a) 0-1
Thomas, Mahon, Barnard, Dafforn,Olson, Yerby, Wilson, Townsend, Ritchie, Bennett, Johnson
Nov 3 v Chesham U (h) 3-1 *Ritchie, Hazell, Charker*
Swain, Mahon, Hand, Dafforn, Olson, Williams (Johnson), Charker, Townsend, Hazell, Ritchie, Pentecost
Nov 11 v Oxford C (a) 1-1 *Ritchie*
Swain. Mahon, Hand, Dafforn, Olson, Pentecost, Charker, Wilson, Hazell, Ritchie, Johnson
Nov 17 v Slough T (h) 0-0
Swain, Mahon, Dafforn, Williams,Olson, Hand, Wilson, Pentecost, Price, Ritchie, Charker (Yerby)
Nov 24 v Marlow (a) 1-2 *Yerby*
Swain, Mahon, Barnard, Shufflebotham, Olson, Hand, Yerby, Pentecost, Hazell, Ritchie, Charker
Dec 1 v Marlow (h) 4 –3 *Ritchie, Hazell, Pentecost, Johnson*
Swain, Mahon, Barnard, Shufflebotham, Olson, Hand, Johnson, Pentecost, Hazell, Ritchie, Johnson
Dec 22 v Wycombe W (h) 1-0 *Johnson*
Thomas, Dafforn, Hand, Williams, Olson, Rapley, Yerby, Mahon, Ritchie, Pentecost, Johnson
Feb 16 v Hemel Hempstead (a) 1-3 *Bunker*
Swain (Shufflebotham), Mahon, Hand, Williams, Olson, Yerby, Chapman, Pentecost, Hazell, Ritchie, Bunker
Feb 23 v Maidenhead U (h) 0-1
Thomas, Mahon, Williams, Shufflebotham, Olson, Townsend, Chapman, Hand, Bunker, Ritchie, Pentecost
Mar 2 v Chesham U (a) 2-0 *Bunker, Chapman*
Thomas, Dafforn, Williams, Austin, Olson, Yerby, Townsend, Chapman, Ritchie, Bunker, Pentecost
Mar 9 v Oxford C (h) 2-0 *Bunker, Olson (pen)*
Thomas, Dafforn, Barnard, Williams, Olson, Austin, Yerby, Townsend, Ritchie, Pentecost, Bunker
Mar 31 v Wycombe W (a) 0-4
Thomas, Austin, Dafforn, Williams, Price, Townsend, Yerby, Mahon, Bunker, Webb, Pentecost
Apr 6 v Slough T (a) 3-6 *Ritchie, Bennett, Bunker (pen)*
Rose, Dafforn, Barnard, Williams, Price, Austin, Yerby (Bennett), Mahon, Ritchie, Bunker, Townsend

1971-72

Oct 27 v Hampton (a) 0-1
Barr, Beyer, Mahon, Morris, Cockell, Watson, D Walker, Gallagher, Swain, Townend, Livingstone
Nov 2 v Southall (a) 0-0
Barr, Beyer, Furie, Cockell, Latham, D Walker, Gallagher, Watson, Vint, Swain, Brown. Sub: Evans
Nov 9 v Kingstonian (a) 1-0 *Brown*
Barr, Furie, Hand, Hale, Latham, Cockell, Watson, Brown, Townend, Whitaker, Jones
Nov 16 v Southall (h) 5-1 *Townend 2,Bailey,Brown,Hale*
Dempsey, Mahon, Hand, Hale, Latham, Furie, Brown, Swain, Townend, Watson, Whitaker (Bailey)
Dec 7 v Addlestone (h) 2-0 *Brown, Swain*
Barr, Mahon, Presland, Hale, Pearce, Furie, Brown, Watson, Swain, Townend, Whitaker
Dec 14 v Croydon Amateurs (a) 1-0 *Gallagher*
Barr, Beyer, Furie, Bailey, Pearce, Cockell, Watson, Brown, A Brown, Gallagher, D Walker Sub: Evans
Dec 21 v Hampton (h) 0-2
Dempsey, Beyer,Presland, Furie, Hale, Cockell, Watson, Brown, Swain, Pearce, Whitaker
Jan 19 v Addlestone (a) 1-1 *Swain*
Barr, Beyer, Presland, Hale, Furie, Cockell, K Owen, Brown, Swain, Pearce, Whitaker,
Feb 8 v Wembley (h) 1-1 *Swain*
Barr,Beyer,Presland,Cockell, J Walker, Furie, Brown, Swain, Livingstone, (Watson), Pearce, Whitaker
Mar 9 v Wembley (a) 1-1 *Townend*
Dempsey, Beyer, Evans, Furie, Latham, Hale, Townend, Watson, Byrne, Bailey, Vint
Apr 11 v Croydon Amateurs (h) 2-1 *Byrne, Livingstone*
Barr, Beyer, Presland, Latham, Pearce, Furie, Dyson, Livingstone, Byrne, A Brown, Vint
Apr 17 v Hayes (a) 1-1 *Dyson*
Barr, Furie, Beyer, Latham, Pearce, Hale, Whitaker, A Brown, Byrne, Livingstone, Dyson
Apr 24 v Kingstonian (h) 1-0 *A Brown*
Barr, Beyer, Furie, Latham, Pearce, Reed, Dyson, A Brown, Byrne, Livingstone, Whitaker

May 5 v Hayes (h) 1-0 *Byrne*
Barr, Lawrence, Presland, Hale, Pearce, Cockell, Dyson, A Brown, Byrne, Livingstone, Whitaker

Mid-Surrey Floodlight League

1972-73
Nov 7 v Basingstoke (h) 3-2 *Hale 2, Whitaker*
Coleman, Doherty, Presland, Cockell, Burgess, Hale, Furie, Whitaker, Duck, Connell, Dyson
Nov 21 v Met. Police (a) 0-2
Barr, Furie, Burgess, Cockell, Doherty, Presland, Hale, A Brown, Duck, Connell, Gozney
Nov 28 v Crawley (h) 1-0 *Presland*
Barr, Beyer, Burgess, Hale, Doherty, Cockell, Presland, A Brown, M Brown, Duck, Gozney (Connell)
Dec 11 v Guildford (a) 2-3 *Duck, A Brown*
Barr, Beyer, Presland, Fairclough, Doherty, Kinnear, A Brown, Dyson, Byrne, Duck, Connell
Dec 19 v Wimbledon (h) 1-2 *Connell*
Barr, Presland, Burgess, Doherty, Kinnear, Haynes, Fairclough, A Brown, Byrne, Duck, Connell
Jan 2 v Hillingdon B (a) 0-0
Barr, Beyer, Presland, Burgess, Doherty, Fairclough, A Brown, Connell, Byrne, Haynes, Duck
Jan 16 v Crawley (a) 5-4 *Duck 2, Burgess, Dyson, Presland(pen)*
Currell, Burgess, Presland, Beyer, Kinnear, Fairclough, A Brown, Collier, Byrne, Duck, Dyson
Jan 30 v Guildford (h) 1-4 *Duck*
Hopkins, Burgess, Presland, Beyer (Kinnear), Doherty, Fairclough, Dyson, A Brown, M Brown, Byrne, Duck
Feb 20 v Basingstoke (a) 0-1
Hopkins, Beyer, Presland (Burgess), Kinnear, Doherty, Fairclough, Dyson, A Brown, M Brown, Byrne, Gozney
Feb 27 v Met. Police (h) 3-0 *M Brown, Fairclough, OG*
Hopkins, Burgess, Presland, Kinnear, Doherty, Fairclough, A Brown, Dyson, M Brown, Beyer, Gozney
Mar 27 v Wimbledon (a) 0-1
Barr, Burgess, Presland, Kinnear, Doherty, Fairclough, A Brown, Dyson(Byrne), M Brown, Beyer, Duck
Apr 10 v Hillingdon B (h) 0-0
McKenzie, Dennis, Presland, Kinnear, Doherty, Burgess, A Brown, Dyson, Watson, Gozney, Duck

1973-74
Oct 9 v Crawley T (a) 1-1 *Duck*
Mckenzie, Burgess, Presland, Kinnear, McCormick, Watson, Dyson, A Brown, Duck, Henderson, Godfrey

1974-75
Oct 1 v Crawley T (a) 0-2
Mckenzie, D Evans, Fulton, Burgess, McCormick, Fairclough, Dyson, Godfrey, T Evans, Henderson, Kinnear
Oct 15 v Basingstoke T (h) 2-1 *Duck, Dyson*
Mckenzie, D Evans, Fulton, Baker, Burgess, Fairclough, Dyson, Godfrey, Byrne, Duck, T Evans
Nov 2 v Basingstoke T (a) 4-0 *Duck, T Evans 2, Eglite*
Mckenzie, D Evans, Fulton, Burgess, McCormick, Godfrey, Dyson, T Evans, Eglite, Duck, Henderson Sub: Fairclough
Nov 19 v Met. Police (h) 1-2 *Henderson*
Mckenzie, D Evans, Fulton, Fairclough, McCormick, Baker, Dyson, T Evans, Henderson, Eglite, Kinnear

Dec 10 v Met. Police (a) 2-3 *Duck, McCormick*
Morton, J Turner, Watson, Fairclough, McCormick, Godfrey, Fulton, Dyson, Byrne, Duck, Eglite Sub: Baker
Jan 14 v Crawley T (h) 3-1 *Duck, Byrne, OG*
Mckenzie, Kinnear, Watson, Fairclough, Kitchener, Presland, Fulton, Duck, Moss, Byrne, Dyson
Jan 21 v Hillingdon Boro (h) 4-2 *Duck 2, Byrne 2*
Mckenzie, Kinnear, Watson, Fairclough, McCormick, Godfrey, Fulton, Duck, Byrne, Moss, Eglite Sub: Henderson

Mar 25 v Dartford (a) 0-5
Mckenzie, Kinnear, Kitchener, Godfrey, Byrne, Watson, Fulton, Henderson, Moss, Duck, Eglite
Apr 7 v Hillingdon Boro (a) 1-2 *OG*
Mckenzie, Kinnear, Kitchener, Godfrey, Byrne, Watson, Fulton, Henderson, Moss, Duck, Dyson Sub: Eglite
Apr 21 v Dartford (h) 5-3 *Duck, Byrne, Dyson, Henderson, Moss*
Morton, Kinnear, Watson, Kitchener, Byrne, Godfrey, Fulton, Henderson, Moss, Duck, Dyson Sub: I Forrest

Capital League

1984-85
Oct 16 v Brentford (h) 10-0 *Graves, Johnson, Jones, Donnellan 2, Dibble 2, Holmes 3 (1 pen)*
Goddard, Perkins, Davies, Byatt, Bowgett, Johnson, Greenaway, Holmes Dibble, N Cordice, Donnellan Subs: Graves, V Jones
Oct 30 v Wimbledon (h) 3-1 *N Cordice, Jones 2*
Goddard, Perkins, Baddeley, Byatt, Bowgett, Holmes, Dibble, V Jones, A Cordice, N Cordice, Donnellan, Subs: Greenaway, Davies
Nov 26 v Orient (h) 1-0 *N Cordice*
Iles, Davies, Baddeley, H Dowe, Johnson, Dibble,Greenaway, N Cordice, A Cordice, Graham, Donnellan, Sub: V Jones
Mar 7 v Gillingham (h) 3-0 *Graves, Jones, Bowgett (pen)*
Iles, Perkins, McCargo, Byatt, Bowgett, N Cordice, Greenaway, Holmes, A Cordice, Graves, Johnson Subs: Graham, V Jones
Apr 10 v Dagenham (a) 2-3 *O'Brien, Pedlar*
P Cotter, P Williams, J Taffel, H Dowe, D Cross, Holmes, G McKay, T Bunce, N Harvey, L Pedlar, J O'Brien Subs: T Parks, M Allen
May 7 v Barnet (h) 5-0*McKay, Pedlar 3, Allen*
Goddard, P Williams, J Taffel, D Cross, M Chamberlain, M Allen, G McKay, B Kelly, L Pedlar, T Parks, J O'Brien Subs: G Jones, T Davies
May 16 v Enfield (h) 5-1 *Graham, Greenaway, Tonge 3*
Goddard, Perkins, Dowe, Byatt, Bowgett, V Jones, P Waites, Holmes, K Tonge, Graham, Greenaway, Subs: L Pedlar, D Hoare

1985-86
Aug 8 v Orient (h) 5-1 *Graves 3, V Jones, Iles*
Iles, Tapley, McCargo, Byatt, Bowgett, N Cordice, Greenaway, Holmes, A Cordice, Graves, Donnellan, Subs: V Jones, Perkins
Oct 9 v Wimbledon (h) 2-1 *N Cordice, Graham*
P Jones, Tapley, McCargo, V Jones, Doyle, Wainwright, Davies, N Cordice, Graham, Tonge, D Empson, Subs: T Elliott, L Reed
Oct 28 v Barnet (a) 4-0 *Donnellan 2, O'Keefe 2*
Iles, Tapley, McCargo, V Jones, Perkins, O'Keefe, Greenaway, Holmes, Doyle, Donnellan, D Hoare, Subs: N Harvey, T Elliott
Oct 30 v Gillingham (h) 1-0 *Holmes*
B Neville, Perkins, McCargo, V Jones, T Elliott, O'Keefe, Graham, Holmes, A Cordice, Graves, N Harvey Subs: Byatt, L Cleaveley
Mar 17 v Southend U (h) 3-3 *Graham, Donnellan 2*
Iles, Tapley, McCargo, Byatt, Bowgett, N Cordice, Greenaway, C Seagraves, Graham, A Cordice, Donnellan, Sub: Tonge
Mar 27 v Wycombe W (a) 3-4 *Donnellan, Wainwright 2 (1 pen)*
Iles, Tapley, V Jones, Byatt, Bowgett, Wainwright, Greenaway, Holmes, Graham, Doyle, Donnellan, Sub: Tonge
Apr 17 v Enfield (h) 2-2 *Doyle, Holmes*
Iles, Tapley, McCargo, Byatt, Bowgett, McClure, C Seagraves, Holmes, Graves, Tonge, Doyle, Subs: Graham, A Williams
Apr 22 v Dagenham (h) 7-1 *Graves, Doyle 2, Graham, Tonge 2, OG*
Iles, Tapley, McClure, Byatt, Wainwright, Greenaway, Holmes, Tonge, Graves, Doyle, C Seagraves, Subs: McCargo, Graham
Apr 28 v Brentford (h) 1-11 *Hall*
A Williams, S Graves, P Williams, D Cross, T Parks, M Allen, G McKay, B Kelly, N Hall, J O'Brien, T Platt, Subs: J Taffel, M Chamberlain

1986-87

Oct 28 v Wimbledon (h) 3-2 *Greenaway, Meadows, OG*
A Haxton, Jones, McClure, Byatt, Bowgett, Wainwright, Greenaway, Tonge, Miller, G Dolling, T Meadows, Subs: Doyle, Graves

Dec 10 v Barnet (h) 6-0 *Graves, Donnellan, Tonge 2, Bowgett, Dolling*
A Haxton, L Maddison, McClure, Byatt, Bowgett, N Cordice, Graves, Donnellan, Tonge, G Dolling, A Bell, Sub:T Meadows

Jan 6 v Gillingham (h) 0-0
A Haxton, Tapley, McClure, Hatter, Wainwright, Greenaway, Hirst, N Cordice, Graves, G Dolling, T Smurthwaite, Subs: Tonge, P Miller

Mar 3 v Wycombe W (a) 2-1 *Walton, Hatter*
A Haxton, Tapley, McClure, Byatt, Hatter, Hirst, Greenaway, Walton, G Dolling, T Meadows, N Cordice, Sub: T Smurthwaite

Mar 31 v Southend U (h) 4-1 *Walton 3, Bowgett*
A Haxton, Tapley, L Maddison, McClure, Bowgett, Hatter, T Meadows, McCarthy, N Cordice, T Curtis, Walton, Sub: Graves,

Apr 14 v Orient (h) 2-4 *Curtis, Meadows*
A Haxton, McClure, Byatt, Bowgett, Hatter, Greenaway, McCarthy, T Curtis, T Meadows, G King, G Dolling, Subs: Smurthwaite, Tapley

Apr 30 v Enfield (a) 1-0 *Meadows*
A Haxton, Tapley, McClure, Byatt, Hatter, Greenaway, McCarthy, Graves, T Curtis, T Meadows, Walton, Sub: L Maddison

1987-88

Sep 2 v Brentford (h) 1-1 *S Hirst*
A Haxton, Pittaway, Dowe, Bowgett, M Hirst, McCarthy, D Cross, N Cordice, P Kotey, B Cronin, S Hirst, Subs: P Jackson, K Lawal

Nov 4 v Gillingham (h) 4-2 *English 3, Perry*
A Haxton, Pittaway, Solomon, Bowgett, O'Keefe, Lowe, McCarthy, T Meadows, T Ryan, English, S Durning, Subs: Perry, S Hirst

Nov 10 v Wimbledon (h) 2-3 *Rivero, Perry*
Welsh, Pittaway, Bowgett, McCarthy, O'Keefe, Perry, Walton, T Meadows, M Hirst, M Devlin, Rivero, Subs: Solomon, S Durning

Nov 24 v Enfield (h) 0-3
Welsh, Byatt, Hatter, McCarthy, Walton, T Meadows, T Ryan, G King, M Devlin, B Laryea, S Hirst, Sub: Solomon

Jan 19 v Wycombe W (a) 1-2 *Perry*
A Haxton, McCarthy, Wainwright, Perry, I Bowyer, M Devlin, B Stagg, B Davis, Rivero, Isaacs, Solomon Sub: G King

Mar 2 v Leyton Orient (a) 3-1 *Rivero, McCarthy, Stagg*
Welsh, Byatt, Harrison, McCarthy, I Whiteley, P Lovell, S Dalsan, M Abbott, Stagg, Lynch, Rivero, Subs: P Davis, La Ronde

Mar 8 v Dagenham (a) 2-0 *McCarthy, Lynch*
Welsh, Pittaway, P Davis, Harrison, Byatt, McCarthy, Wainwright, M Hirst, Stagg, Lynch, Rivero Sub: La Ronde

Mar 14 v Barnet (h) 0-2
Welsh, Pittaway, Harrison, P Davis, Bowgett, Wainwright, M Hirst, Bailey, Rivero, English, Zacharia, Sub: Olaleye

May 9 v Welling U (h) 5-0, *Dennis Greene 3, David Greene, McCarthy*
Foster, G Lister, P Davis, Byatt, Lynch, David Greene, Bailey, C Browne, Dennis Greene, R Green, R Brown, Sub: McCarthy

1988-89

Aug 31 v Aylesbury U (a) 2-3, *Morris, Harrison (pen)*
D Boughton, Eriemo, Corbin, Harrison, Morris, A Wright, A Vullo, C Wright, C Browne, G Clarke, A Cordice, Sub: A Ansah

Sep 21 v Gillingham (a) 2-2 *Pamphlet, C Browne*
Foster, Eriemo, D Jacques, Risk, Lawrence, Bailey, M Telfer, Wilkins, A Wright, C Wright, T Pamphlett, Subs: C Browne, A Vullo

Oct 19 v Wokingham T (a) 3-1 *Morris, Olaleye 2*
Williams, Eriemo, Harrison, Olaleye, O'Brien, Morris, A Cordice, Lynch, La Ronde, C Wright, S Browne, Subs: D Brown, T Copeman

Oct 27 v Wycombe W (a) 3-6 *C Wright 3*
D Boughton, Eriemo, Corbin, O'Brien, T Copeman, Morris, Lawrence, C Browne, Wilkins, C Wright, A Wright, Subs: D Brown, S Grimes

Nov 2 v Aylesbury U (h) 2-0 *Cordice, C Browne*
Foster, Bailey, Eriemo, Harrison, O'Brien, Lawrence, La Ronde, Morris, A Cordice, C Browne, Lynch, Sub: Olaleye

Nov 16 v Cambridge U (a) 2-3 *Pedlar, C Wright*
Foster, Bailey, Harrison, Byatt, Corbin, S Browne, C Wright, Morris, Wilkins, L Pedlar, Lynch, Sub: C Browne

Nov 23 v Southend U (h) 1-0 *Pedlar*
Foster, Bailey, A Hedge, Byatt, Corbin, C Browne, Wilkins, S Hedge, L Pedlar, C Wright, Eriemo, Subs: Lynch, D Thomas

Dec 7 v Barnet (h) 2-0 *Pedlar 2*
Foster, Eriemo, C Browne, Byatt, Risk, La Ronde, Olaleye, Wilkins, L Pedlar, A Cordice, Corbin, Sub: C Wright

Dec 15 v Enfield (h) 3-2 *Pedlar, C Browne, C Wright*
Williams, Eriemo, C Browne, Byatt, Harrison, La Ronde, Olaleye, Wilkins, L Pedlar, C Wright, M Telfer, Sub: Risk

Dec 21 v Gillingham (h) 1-5 *C Wright*
Foster, Eriemo, Risk, Byatt, S Thomas, Harrison, Wilkins, Morris, C Wright, L Pedlar, C Browne, Sub: S Hedge

Jan 18 v Leyton Orient (a) 3-2*La Ronde, Olaleye, Goyette (pen)*
Foster, Eriemo, Byatt, Risk, Bailey, Olaleye, Margerrison, La Ronde, Wilkins, C Browne, Goyette, Sub: M Johnson

Jan 25 v Brentford (h) 1-2 *C Browne*
Foster, Bailey, Eriemo, Byatt, Corbin, La Ronde, Olaleye, Margerrison, C Browne, Goyette, S Browne,

Feb 6 v Colchester U (h) 2-5 *Lynch, Hammond*
M Voght, P Blennerhassett, S Graves, Byatt, Eriemo, J O'Brien, R Keegan, S Hammond, C Wright, T Keegan, Lynch, Subs: S Dibley, N Harvey

Feb 15 v Leyton Orient (h) 1-0 *C Wright*
M Vogt, Corbin, P Blennerhassett, Byatt, Eriemo, C Browne, Bailey, C Wright, Wilkins, S Browne, Lynch, Subs: S Rowe, M Botten

Feb 20 v Barnet (a) 2-0 *Lynch, Wilkins*
M Vogt, Corbin, P Blennerhassett, Morris, Eriemo, Harrison, C Conlon, Olaleye, Wilkins, S Browne, Lynch

Mar 20 v Wycombe W (h) 1-4 *Wilkins*
Williams, Eriemo, P Blennerhassett, Byatt, Margerrison, Morris, Da Silva, Goyette, Wilkins, Olaleye, C Browne, Subs: Lynch, R Jones

Apr 4 v Enfield (a) 1-2 *Goyette*
Foster, Eriemo, Blennerhassett, Byatt, Bailey, Olaleye, Morris, C Browne, Goyette, T DaSilva, N Milne,

Apr 19 v Southend U (a) 0-1
R Jones, G Lister, P Blennerhassett, Byatt, Eriemo, W Jackson, Margerrison, C Browne, R Cherry, E Carrick, A Jones, Subs: S Jones, F Carrick

Apr 27 v Welling U (h) 2-1 *C Browne, Eriemo*
R Jones, P Blennerhassett, M Hayden, Risk, Eriemo, Harrison, A Jones, Margerrison, C Browne, R Cherry, Da Silva, Sub: Lynch

May 3 v Wokingham T (h) 1-1 *Blennerhassett*
R Jones, Corbin, P Blennerhassett, Eriemo, Harrison, J Coleman, Lynch, Margerrison, Morris, C Browne, DaSilva, Sub: La Ronde

May 4 v Welling U (a) 6-4 *Wilkins, Bailey, A Jones, Barness 3*
R Jones, M Nicholson, M Reavill, N Lockett, Risk, Bailey, La Ronde, Wilkins, A Barness, A Jones, M Hayden,

May 8 v Brentford (a) 3-0*Lynch 2, Eriemo*
Foster, Eriemo, Harrison, Byatt, Corbin, J Coleman, Margerrison, Morris, C Browne, Lynch, P Mason, Sub: N McSween

May 10 v Colchester U (a) 2-2 *Richards, Cherry*
R Jones, Risk, R Cherry, Bailey, La Ronde, Goyette, A Jones, S Jones, M Nicholson, A Barness, J Richards, Sub: T Jennings

May 12 v Cambridge U (h) 0-6
Foster, La Ronde, Eriemo, P Blennerhassett, Bailey, P Hucker, A Ferguson, J Coleman, L Murphy,Da Silva, M Cranfield, Sub: J Richards

1989-90

Aug 29 v Wokingham T (a) 1-4 *Findley*
Foster, Tapley, Norman, Findlay, Morris, Harrison, T Joseph, Goyette, C Hall, Kelly, Lynch

Sep 20 v Barnet (h) 1-4 *Kelly*
Foster, Tapley, Norman, Findlay, D Martin, T Joseph, C Hall, Kelly, Wilkins, S Browne, Lynch, Subs: P Blennerhassett, M McCabe

Sep 26 v Wokingham T (h) 1-1 *Margerrison*
A Tsitsis, Tapley, Shanks, Risk, Margerrison, C Hall, D Martin, S Browne, Wilkins, Kelly, Lynch, D Brown, J Campbell

Oct 2 v Welling U (a) 2-2 *Lynch, Goyette (pen)*
Foster, K Hills, Norman, Byatt, Risk, D Martin, S Browne, Goyette, Wilkins, Campbell, Lynch, Subs: C Hall, T Macklin

Nov 15 v Wycombe W (h) 5-3 *Wilkins, Olaleye 2, Risk, Campbell*
Williams, D Shanks, Harrison, Campbell, Findley, Risk, C Hall, M McCabe, Olaleye, D Martin, Wilkins, Subs: Byatt, B Williams

Nov 22 v Aldershot (a) 1-1 *Campbell*
Williams, D Shanks, Harrison, Findley, Risk, Tapley, Campbell, D Martin, Olaleye, C Hall, A Cosby, Subs: M McCabe, P Blennerhassett

Dec 13 v Aldershot (h) 3-3 *Campbell, Collins, Gbogidi*
Williams, D Shanks, L Stocker, Byatt, Risk, Johnstone, S Browne, Goyette, Campbell, J Collins, Gbogidi, Subs: C Hall, M McCabe

Dec 18 v Cambridge U (h) 1-1 *Kelly*
Williams, Smart, Harrison, Byatt, D Shanks, Wilkins, Campbell, Goyette, J Collins, Kelly, Gbogidi, Subs: D Brown, Johnstone

Jan 3 v Barnet (a) 1-2 *N Price*
Williams, Rivero, N Price, D Shanks, Tapley, K Collins, Johnstone, L Stocker, Campbell, Olaleye, Wilkins, Subs: J Collins

Jan 10 v Southend U (h) 0-5
Williams, Tapley, Rivero, L Stocker, Wilkins, Olaleye, E Maki, M Graves, J Campbell, C Johnstone, Gbogidi, Subs: J Collins, P Sansom

Feb 7 v Southend U (a) 2-3 *J Collins 2*
Williams, Tapley, N Price, L Stocker, Rivero, Johnstone, D Irving, Goyette, Wilkins, J Collins, D Buckley, Subs: Campbell, Lynch

Feb 20 v Welling U (h) 1-1 *Wilkins*
Williams, Tapley, N Price, K Collins, Morris, Johnstone, Goyette, Smart, Westley, Wilkins, M Butler Sub: Lynch

Feb 27 v Wycombe W (a) 0-3
Williams, Tapley, Harrison, L Stocker, N Price, R Eccles, Lynch, Smart, Wilkins, K Collins, C Johnstone, Subs: G Westley, Margerrison

Mar 20 v Gillingham (a) 4-2 *Browne 3, Kelly*
A Tsitsis, Watson, N Price, Risk, Morris, Johnstone, S Browne, Gbogidi, Wilkins, Kelly, Lynch, Sub: Goyette

Mar 28 v Cambridge U (a) 0-0
Williams, Watson, Harrison, Tapley, Morris, Johnstone, Gbogidi, Goyette, Wilkins, M Abrey, Lynch, Sub: Margerrison

Apr 3 v Brentford (h) 4-0
G Price 3 (1 pen), Goyette (pen)
C Vagg, I Fergusson, N Price, Eriemo, Risk, Smart, R Eccles, Goyette, Wilkins, S Browne, G Price, Sub: Lynch

Apr 9 v Enfield (h) 1-2 *Johnstone*
Williams, Smart, N Price, Tapley, Harrison, Margerrison, Campbell, Goyette, Eccles, Gbogidi, Wilkins, Subs: Watson, Johnstone

Apr 19 v Gillingham (h) 1-2 *Abrey*
Foster, Watson, M Harries, Risk, Morris, Johnstone, Campbell, M Culverhouse, M Dunwoodie, Flint, Lynch, Subs: M Abrey, P Amara

Apr 23 v Enfield (a) 1-2 *Wilkins*
Foster, Watson, P Amara, Risk, Lynch, Margerrison, Campbell, M Culverhouse, Flint, Wilkins, L La-Cumbre, Subs: Smart, M Kelly

Apr 26 v Colchester U (a) 1-4 *OG*
Foster, Watson, Smart, Goyette, M Dunwoodie, M Kelly, Margerrison, C Johnstone, Flint, P Amara, D Lewis, Sub: Lynch

May 3 v Brentford (a) 1-2 *Lynch*
Foster, Watson, Smart, Byatt, Morris, Fergusson, Johnstone, D Lewis, Flint, M Dunwoodie, Lynch, Subs: Campbell, R Davies

May 9 v Leyton Orient (h) 1-2 *Browne*
Vagg, Watson, Smart, R Davies, Harrison, Johnstone, Ferguson, Gbogidi, D Lewis, Margerrison, Lynch, Subs: Campbell, S Browne

May 14 v Colchester U (h) 2-4 *G Price, Smart*
T Phillips, Watson, Smart, P Amara, N Price, Johnstone, Fergusson, Gbogidi, G Price, S Browne, Lynch, Subs: D Butler, Campbell

May 16 v Leyton Orient (a) 2-2 *Lynch, Goyette*
T Phillips, Watson, Smart, Tapley, Fergusson, Margerrison,C Johnstone, Gbogidi, Goyette, S Browne, Lynch, Sub: R Davies

1990-91

Aug 21 v Wycombe W (h) 2-0 *Olaleye, Robinson*
D Matthews, Robinson, Hedge, Bartlett, Eriemo, Olaleye, Gbogidi, J Murphy, P Downes, W Downes, Johnstone, Subs: M Fisher, Kelly

Aug 29 v Slough T (a) 0-1
Roach, Bartlett, Watson, Eriemo, Hedge, Gbogidi, Johnstone, Olaleye,Jenkins, J Murphy, Lynch, Subs: Campbell, O Powell,

Sep 26 v Wycombe W (a) 1-0 *Harrison (pen)*
Vagg, Bartlett, Harrison, Eriemo, Smart, L Donnellan, S Browne, Blackman,Gipp Hendry, Kelly Subs: Jenkins, Lynch

Oct 23 v Sutton U (a) 1-1 *Gipp*
Roach, Richards, Watson, Tapley, P Hayward, Robinson, O Powell, J Murphy, Gipp, J King, J Duviau, Subs: J Luto, R Davies

Nov 6 v Barnet (h) 3-3 *Blackman, Gipp, Gbogidi*
Roach, Robinson, Harrison, Bartlett, Richards, Watson, D Ross, Gbogidi, Jenkins, Gipp, Blackman

Nov 13 v Brentford (h) 4-6 *Kelly 2, Gbogidi, G Donnellan*
Roach, Robinson, Harrison, Hedge, Eriemo, Olaleye, D Ross, Gbogidi, Kelly, Gipp, G Donnellan, Subs: D Field, Watson

Nov 21 v Colchester U (h) 1-2 *Watson*
Roach, A Dixon, Smart, Eriemo, G Maxin, D Field, Olaleye, Watson, Campbell, Gipp, C Browne, Subs: R Maguire, A Wright

Nov 28 v Aldershot (a) 2-4 *Smart, Olaleye*
Roach, A Dixon, Smart, Tapley, Eriemo, Harrison, S Browne, Olaleye, Gipp, Gbogidi, G Donnellan Sub: Goyette

Dec 10 v Southend U (h) 1-2 *Olaleye*
Vagg, Watson, Eriemo, Tapley, Harrison, L Donnellan, Olaleye, Goyette, Campbell, Blackman, M Brown, Subs: C Browne, Morris

Jan 16 v Southend U (a) 0-2
M Pantelli, Smart, Watson, Waugh, I Fergusson, Bartlett, Goyette, Morris,Gipp, Blackman, Goodison, Subs: R Polson

Feb 4 v Barnet (a) 0-5
L Hunter, Tapley, Watson, Smart, Harrison, I Fergusson, Kelly, Donnellan, Blackman, Cordice, Goodison, Subs: R Howard, Gipp

Feb 19 v Cambridge U (h) 1-3 *Gipp*
A Tsitsis, J Ferguson, Smart, A Glucina, Bartlett, I Fergusson, Tapley, Goyette, Kelly, Gipp, N Cordice, Subs: R Howard, A Martin

Mar 6 v Aldershot (h) 1-1 *Gipp*
Roach, Watson, Morris, Goyette, Harrison, L Donnellan, A Martin, Hopson, Gipp, Bartlett, N Cordice, Sub: P Goodison

Mar 11 v Slough T (h) 6-0 *Gipp 3, N Cordice, Smart, Goodison*
Hudson, R Howard, Smart, Morris, Harrison, L Donnellan, Hopson, Tapley, Gipp, Blackman, N Cordice, Subs: Kelly, P Goodison

Mar 13 v Brentford (a) 1-3 *Gipp*
Hudson, Watson, Bartlett, Tapley, Harrison, L Donnellan, P Goodison, Hopson, Kelly, Gipp, R Howard, Subs: Goyette, Smart

Mar 27 v Colchester U (a) 1-1 *Howard*
Hudson, Tapley, Watson, Goyette, Donnellan, Bartlett, Gipp, A Martin, Goodison, R Howard, J Fergusson, Sub: Blackman

Apr 10 v Wokingham T (a) 1-1 *Gipp*
Roach, Harrison, P Hayward, J Fergusson, S Watts, J McMillan, M Milton, A Wright, Gipp, Kelly, Bartlett, Subs: Hedge
Apr 11 v Leyton Orient (a) 1-4 *Tapley*
Hudson, Tapley, J McMillan, Watson, R Richards, Goyette, Blackman, Hedge, Gipp, S Watts, Goodison, Subs: M Milton, T Brady
Apr 17 v Wokingham T (h) 3-2 *Goodison, Harrison, Irving*
Roach, Watson, J McMillan, Tapley, Bartlett, Harrison, D Irving, P Goodison, Kelly, A Wright, Gipp, Subs: A Martin, T Brady
Apr 25 v Leyton Orient (h) 1-5 *Martin*
A Tsitsis, I Waugh, P Hayward, R Richards, J Hawks, A Martin, D Ross, J Murphy, D Irving, T Brady, Hopson, Subs: J Luto, A Wright
May 1 v Cambridge U (a) 0-2
R Hall, Hedge, J Murphy, R Richards, P Hayward, J Luto, D Ross, A Wright, Waugh, M Milton, D Irving, Subs: T Brady, J Richards
May 7 v Sutton U (h) 1-1 *N Cordice*
Roach, Watson, Smart, J McMillan, N Cordice, Harrison, Hopson, J Daly, Richards, Blackman, Bartlett, Sub: Kelly

1991-92
Aug 28 v Slough T (a) 3-1*Hedge, S Browne, Lay (pen)*
Roach, Ferguson, Goyette, J McMillan, Richards, Bartlett, W Lay, Hedge, Gipp, A Wright, R Findley, Subs: S Browne, Cordice
Sep 18 v Sutton U (a) 0-2
Hudson, Watson, Ferguson, Bartlett, Richards, Goyette, W Lay, Harrison, Gipp, A Wright, Blackman, Sub: S Browne
Sep 23 v Wycombe W (a) 1-1 *S Browne*
Hudson, Watson, Ferguson, Bartlett, Gore, Cordice, W Lay, Hedge, Blackman, S Browne, Smart, Subs: Gipp, Harrison
Oct 16 v Colchester U (a) 2-2 *Kelly 2*
Hudson, Watson, Goyette, Richards, Gore, Harrison, S Browne, Gipp, Kelly, Donnellan, Cordice, Sub: Blackman
Oct 30 v Barnet (a) 0-5
Hudson, Bartlett, Goyette, Richards, Gore, Hedge, Kelly, A Wright, Gipp, Donnellan, Pearson Sub: McGuire
Nov 6 v Slough T (h) 2-2 *Pearson, Gipp (pen)*
Hudson, Watson, Harrison, Richards, Bartlett, McGuire, A Wright, Hedge, Gipp, D Reuben, Pearson, Subs: Adamson
Dec 9 v Barnet (h) 2-5 *Cordice, Hippolyte*
Hudson, Hedge, Harrison, Tapley, Bartlett, McGuire, Hopson, Cordice, Hippolyte, Donnellan, Pearson, Subs: A McShannon, N Groves
Dec 18 v Southend (a) 2-2 *Donnellan 2*
Hudson, Hedge, Goyette, Tapley, Bartlett, McGuire, Richards, Cordice, Donnellan, A McShannon, Pearson, Sub: Adamson
Jan 20 v Wycombe W (h) 0-4
Hudson, Drummy, Goyette, Tapley, Bartlett, McGuire, Hopson, Hedge, Hippolyte, Adamson, Richards, Subs: A McShannon, D Reuben
Jan 30 v Crystal Palace (a) 0-0
S Donnelly, Richards, Bartlett, Tapley, Hedge, McGuire, Hopson, Pearson, Hippolyte, A McShannon, Goyette, Subs: A Beyaz, Adamson
Feb 5 v Cambridge U (h) 1-4 *Adamson*
Hudson, Tapley, Goyette, Richards, Bartlett, McGuire, I Farrell, Hedge, A McShannon, Adamson, Pearson, Subs: Hippolyte, Donnellan
Feb 12 v Cambridge U (a) 2-2 *Richards, McShannon*
Hudson, Tapley, Pearson, Bartlett, Watson, Cordice, Richards, McGuire, Hippolyte, Hedge, A McShannon, Subs: Adamson, A Beyaz
Feb 17 v Aldershot (a) 2-0 * *Blackler, Drummy*
S Donnelly, Watson, Tapley, Drummy, Richards, Cordice, Pearson, Hopson, Blackler, Quinn, A McShannon, Subs: Bartlett, McGuire
* Aldershot withdrew from CL so their results were expunged.
Feb 24 v Brentford (h) 3-6 *Adamson 3*
Hudson, Watson, Goyette, Tapley, Gayle, Blackler, Hippolyte, McGuire, Adamson, Hopson, A McShannon, Subs: Richards, A Beyaz
Mar 2 v Southend U (h) 1-4 *Hopson (pen)*
Hudson, Watson, Goyette, Cordice, Bartlett, Quinn, Hopson, McGuire, Hippolyte, Adamson, A McShannon, Subs: Gayle, Donnellan
Mar 23 v Brentford (a) 1-1 *Gallacher*
Hudson, Drummy, Goyette, Watson, Bartlett, Blackler, Hedge, McGuire, Tate, Hopson, Gallacher Subs: Donnellan, Hippolyte
Mar 30 v Wokingham T (h) 0-2
Hudson, Tapley, Goyette, Richards, Bartlett, D Owen, Drummy, Blackler, Hippolyte, Adamson, Donnellan, Sub: Hedge
Apr 1 v Leyton Orient (h) 2-2 *Hopson, Donnellan (pen)*
Moussaddik, Drummy, Hedge, Tapley, Watson, Quinn, Venables, McGuire, Tate, Hopson, Pearson, Subs: Donnellan, Hippolyte
Apr 6 v Sutton U (h) 3-1 *Cordice, Hippolyte, Pearson*
Moussaddik, Tapley, Hedge, Cordice, Bartlett, McGuire, Drummy, Donnellan, Tate, Hopson, Pearson Subs: Hippolyte, Venables
Apr 13 v Colchester U (h) 2-0 *Hopson, Goyette*
Hudson, Watson, Bartlett, Gayle, Walford, Donnellan, McGuire, Hopson, Hippolyte, Adamson, Goyette, Sub: Hedge
Apr 22 v Wokingham T (a) 1-1 *Adamson*
Moussaddik, Watson, Hedge, Bartlett, Walford, Donnellan, Hopson, Blackler, Hippolyte, Adamson, Goyette,.Sub: Gayle
Apr 27 v Crystal Palace (h) 3-0 *Hippolyte, Gallacher, OG*
Roach, Watson, Walford, Bartlett, Shanahan, Cordice, Hopson, McGuire, Adamson, Hippolyte, Gallacher, Sub: Gayle
Apr 28 v Leyton Orient (a) 4-3 *Tate 2, Gallacher 2*
Roach, Richards, Goyette, Shanahan, Gayle, Hedge, McGuire, Hippolyte, Tate, Hopson, Gallacher Subs: Bartlett, Adamson

1992-93
Sep 10 v Reading (a) 0-2
Hudson, Chandler, Hedge, Gayle, Tapley, Blackler, M Green, Tonge, Adamson, J Mannix, Hopson, Subs: Shanahan, K Thomas
Sep 16 v Leyton Orient (a) 2-3 *Pearson, Tate*
A Tsitsis, Robinson, Hedge, Gayle, Shanahan, Cordice, Chandler, Blackler, Hippolyte, Venables, Pearson, Subs: Tate, Adamson
Sep 23 v Wycombe W (a) 3-3 *Hopson, Venables, Blackler*
G Sims, Watson, Hedge, Tapley, J Finch, Cordice, Chandler, Blackler, Tate, Venables, Pearson, Subs: Hopson, Adamson
Note: Wealdstone withdrew from Capital League after 3 fixtures.

Capital League Presidents Cup

1986-87
Oct 14 v Orient (h) 3-3 aet *Greenaway, Tonge, Meadows*
A Haxton, I Dowie, McClure, Byatt, Bowgett, Rutter, Greenaway, N Cordice, Donnellan, T Meadows, Tonge, Subs: Holmes, B Neville
Jan 27 v Orient (a) 1-4 *Miller*
A Haxton, L Maddison, McClure, Byatt, Rutter, Wainwright, M Hirst, G Dollings, Graves, Doyle, D Chalmers, Subs: Tonge, Miller

1987-88
April 6 v Gillingham (a) 1-3 *David Greene*
Foster, P Davis, Harrison, Byatt, Harrison, Wainwright, M Hirst, R Brown, Dennis Greene, David Greene, Lynch

1990-91
Dec 19 v Colchester U (h) 2-0 *C Browne 2*
Vagg, Watson, Blackman, Morris, Hendry, Donnellan, T Martin, Waugh, Gipp, C Browne, M Brown, Subs: Kelly, R Polson
Jan 22 v Sutton U (a) 2-3 aet *Harrison, Blackman*
M Pantelli, Tapley, Watson, Morris, N Cordice, Harrison, Goyette, Kelly, A Cordice, Blackman, Goodison Subs: Bartlett, Gipp

1991-92
Nov 11 v Sutton U (h) 1-2 *Adamson*
Hudson, Drummy, Harrison, Goyette, Richards, Bartlett, Donnellan, McGuire, D Reuben, Adamson, Pearson, Sub: S Browne

Arlington Gold Cup

1994-95
Aug 6 v Farnborough Town 0-2
Gartell, Anglin, Mason, Shanahan, Hill, Elward, Kent, Findley, McGrath, Griffiths, Subs: M Wilson, D Williams
Aug 7 v Camberley T 1-1 (4-2 on pens) *Joseph*
Gartell, Anglin, Birch, Shanahan, Hill, Mason, McGrath, Schwartz, L Pedlar, F Joseph, M Wilson, Subs: Meakin, Findley
NB: Tournament played at Aldershot FC

Appendix 4
First Team Friendlies
1919 - 2002

This section includes all first team friendlies with as much information as it has been possible to obtain.

In recent seasons, a number of trials and squad friendlies have also been played. These matches are recorded by result and scorers only.

WEALDSTONE FC FRIENDLY MATCHES 1919 – 2002

Dec 20 v LGOC (a) Result Unknown
Howman, Burroughs, Smerdon, Hardy, Harbud, Miller, Stock, Kirby, Wentworth, Theobold, Hobbs
Feb 14 v 2nd Scots Guards (a) 0-0
Howman, Burroughs, Smerdon, Bellchambers, Harbud, Miller, White, Gawn, Tann, Durham, Hobbs

1920-21
Sep 11 v Tottenham Gasworks (h) 0-4
Hampton, Samuels, Gallagher, Lavender, Pratt, Pearce, Smith, Wilson, Craker, Booth, Hobbs
Nov 06 v Staines Lagonda (a) Result Unknown
Smith, Burton, Samuels, O'Connell, Gallagher, Tann, Gibbs, Henderson, Shadwick, Wilson, Cooper.

1921-22
Sep 17 v Braby's Athletic (h) 1-1
No further details known
Oct 29 v London Caledonians (h) 1-1 *Theobold F*
Haskell A, Martin H, Smerdon J, Randall H, Harbud F, Miller H, Smith A, Theobold E, Wentworth, Theobold F, Shadwick J.
Dec 17 v Harrow Weald (a) 0-10
Bird, Burton, Burroughs J, Samuels, Butlin J, O'Connell, Dalby, I'Anson A, Smith V, Davenport, Morgan D.
Feb 25 v Hyde & Kingsbury (h) 6-0 *Smith 2, I'Anson 4*
Haskell A, Martin H, Smerdon J, Randall H, Harbud F, Smith A, Wilson, Theobold E, I'Anson, Smith V, Theobold F.
Mar 25 v Old Bancroftians (h) 1-0 *Smith*
Bates R, Burton, Burroughs J, Samuels, Randall H, Butlin J, I'Anson A, Mitchell, Davenport, Brett, Morgan D.

1922-23
Aug 26 v Clapton Orient Res (h) 0-6
Haskell A, Martin G, Spencer V, Gibbons F, Randall E, Deeley P, Wilson E, Theobold F, Peed F, Spencer F, Edwards A.
Sep 02 v Arsenal 'A' (h) 1-2 *Theobold F*
Haskell A, Martin G, Spencer V, Harbud F, Randall E, Miller H, Wilson E, Theobold F, Peed F, Spencer F, Edwards A.
Feb 03 v St Albans (a) 1-5 *Wright*
Beard H, Martin G, Downing P, Theobold E, Harbud F, Deeley P, Wilson E, Wright, Mason C, Mascall R, Cole S.
Mar 03 v Leavesden Mental Hospital (h) 4-0 *Mason 3, Edwards*
Beard H, Martin G, Jackson L, Theobold E, Harbud F, Deeley P, Wilson E, Fleet P, Mason C, Edwards A, Downing P
Mar 31 v West Norwood (h) 3-2 *Mason 3,*
Beard H, Martin G, Deeley P, Pratt J, Harbud F, Deeley H, I'Anson A, Theobold E, Mason C, Edwards A, Downing P.

1923-24
Aug 25 v Fulham Reserves (h) D 1-1 *Edwards*
Beard H, Deeley H, Martin G, Glasscock A, Randall E, Deeley P, Wright W, Mascall A, Hall R, Edwards A, Downing A.
Apr 28 v Southall (a) D 3-3
No further details known

1924-25
-

1925-26
Oct 24 v Tottenham Hotspur (h) 1-3 *Smith*
Rogers J, Kemp L, Downing A, Gregory R, I'Anson A, Smith H, Pratt A, Williams John, Harbud F, Weaver J.
Dec 26 v Tufnell Park (h) 2-2 *Wilson, I'Anson*
Rogers J, Kemp L, Downing A, I'Anson A, Wilson E, Smith H, Williams John, Harbud F, Deeley H, Clark H, Walker
Mar 27 v Ipswich Town (h) 4-1 *Wilson, Kettle 2, Williams John*
Rogers J, Kemp L, Williams James, Downing A, Wilson E, Smith H, Williams John, Clark H, Champion A, Whiting H, Church A, Kettle H.

1926-27
Aug 28 v Clapton Orient Res (h) 2-0 *Champion, H Smith*
Berry, Pratt, Downing, Williams, Randell, R Smith, F Thorne, D Donleavy, Champion H Smith, Church
Sep 1 v Metropolitan Police (h) 1-5 *Short*
R Hill, J Clayton, Kemp, Williams, H Goddard, Whiting, I'Anson, WG Smith, Kettle, H Smith, Short

1927-28
Aug 27 v Fulham 'A' (h) 5-4 *Tansley 2, R Groves 2, Ryder (pen)*
Berry, Pratt, Kemp, Williams, Ryder, R Smith, S Harding, Tansley, R Groves, J Cochrane, Eagle
Sep 24 v Metropolitan Police (h) 1-4 *Tansley*
Berry, Pratt, Downing, R Groves, Ryder, F Shaw, J Hall, F Davison, Tansley, E Batten, Eagle
Jan 7 v Customs House (h) 5-1 *Tansley, Collins 2 (1 pen), L Groves,Ryder*
R Hill, L Fraser, Downing, R Groves, Ryder, R Smith, Maskell, Hannam, Tansley, Collins, L Groves
Mar 17 v Tottenham Hotspur Res (h) 1-3 *R Groves (pen)*
Miall, Stocks, Downing, R Groves, Ryder, Collins, Maskell, Hannam, Tansley, Bowtle, L Groves

1928-29
Jan 12 v Chelmsford Town (a) 1-7 *OG*
Grafton, Deeley, Davies, Turner, R Groves, Short, Maskell, Ayres, Hannam, L Groves, Whiting

1929-30
Sep 11 v Old Lyonians (h) 3-2 *Champion, Hannam 2*
Poulson, R Groves, Davies, Turner, H Smith, Short, Maskell, Hannam, Clark, H Davies

1930-31
Oct 11 v Army Wanderers (h) 2-3 *Maskell, Vanner*
Poulson, Shorland, C Davies, Brown, Turner, G Hall, Maskell, Vanner, Spurr, Bowyer, L Groves
Jan 17 v Northampton Nomads (h) 2-3 *Spurr, Hester*
Poulson, Shorland, C Davies, Brown, Woodham, Lemarie, Maskell, Hoskins, Spurr, Hester, L Groves
Apr 11 v Casuals (a) 3-2 *Hoskins 2, Bowyer*
Poulson, Shorland, C Davies, Brown, Woodham, Turner, Maskell, Wilson, Hoskins, Bowyer, L Groves
Apr 29 v Notts County (h) 3-8 *Hoskins,Maskell, Bowyer*
Poulson, Shorland, C Davies, Brown, Woodham, Turner, Maskell, Wilson, Hoskins, Bowyer, L Groves

1931-32
Apr 23 v Chesham U (h) 3-3 *Bowyer 3*
Poulson, Loveday, Davies, Woodham, Darvill, Russell, Maskell, Turner, Hoskins, Bowyer, Groves

1932-33
Nov 26 v Tunbridge Wells Rgrs (h) 8-3 *Beach 3, Maskell 2, Underwood, Ryder, OG*
W Craft, R Groves, Davies, D Short, Darvill, Russell, Maskell, Underwood, Beach, Schofield, Ryder
Dec 10 v Cray Wanderers (h) 4-1 *Beach, Underwood 2, Darvill*
Miles, Loveday, Davies, Short, Darvill, Russell, Reeves, Maskell, Underwood, Beach, Schofield, Ryder

1933-34
Apr 2 v Old Lyonians (h) 4-1 *Potts 2, Beach, Russell*
Miles, R Groves, Shorland, Bloxham, Parker, Russell, Beach, H Smith, Potts, Hansard, Ryder

1934-35

1935-36
-

1936-37
-

1937-38
Sep 15 v Chelsea (h) 1-2 *Bunce*
Walker, Loveday, Ellis, Showler, Friday, Reeves, Brown, LLoyd, Bunce, Wilson, Downing

Dec11 v Chelsea (h) 3-3 *Gaze 2, Potts*
Walker, Loveday, Ellis, Green, Friday, Scott, Brown, Ette, Gaze, Wilson, Potts
Apr 30 v Dagenham (h) 2-0 *Wilson, Potts*
Lewis, Loveday, Ellis, Showler, Friday, Scott, Baldwin, Dyke, Bunce, Wilson, Potts
May 7 v Tottenham Hotspur Res (h) 2-0 *Bunce, Potts*
Walker, Showler, Ellis, Baldwin, Friday, Scott, Brown, Dyke, Bunce, Wilson, Potts

1938-39
Aug 31 v Fulham (h) 4-3 *Bunce, Scott, Wilson, Ellis (pen)*
Lewis, Loveday, Ellis, Showler, Friday, Scott, Gaze, Baldwin, Bunce, Wilson, Potts
Sep 14 v Chelsea (h) 1-2 *Friday*
Lewis, Loveday, Ellis, Showler, Friday, Scott, Gaze, Baldwin, Bunce, Wilson, Balaam
May 6 v Watford (h) 1-2 *Scott*
Lewis, Loveday, Ellis, Green, R Bidewell, Scott, Gaze, Baldwin, Bunce, Wilson, Schofield

Due to the number of Friendly Matches played during the War Years 1939—1945 these have been included in the main statistics.

1945-46
Oct 13 v Erith & Belvedere (h) 1-0 *Spurr*
Lewis, Upton, R Jocelyn, Twigg, Edmonds Pratt, Lawrence, Dyke, Berthelemy, Young, Spurr
Apr 6 v QPR Reserves (h) 3-3 *Gaze, Moore, G Hardie*
F Brown, Scott, Barker, Doig, Edmonds, Pratt, Moore, Wilson, Gaze, Dyke, G Hardie
Apr 27 v Enfield (a) 2-2 *Gaze 2*
L McDonald, Scott, Barker, Doig, Edmonds, Pratt, Moore, Wilson, Gaze, Dyke, G Hardie

1946-47
Apr 7 v Carpathians (h) 1-3 *Barker (pen)*
Hill, Haydon, Barker, Young, Edmonds, Pratt, Hardie, Hunt, Gaze, Dyke, Beasley
May 10 v Fulham Res (h) 1-2 *Barker (pen)*
Hill, Haydon, Clark, Benn, Edmonds, Pratt, Gaze, Hunt, Dyke, Franklin, Barker

1947-48
-

1948-49
Jan 22 v Boldmere St Michaels (h) 2-1 *Smith, G Hardie*
Hill, Haydon, Barker, Norman, Edmonds, Davison, Moore, Franklin, G Hardie, Dyke, Smith
1949-50
Aug 27 v FC Schaffhausen (h) 1-2 *Barker (pen)*
Wiltshire, Haydon, Barker, Hill, Lieven, Francis, Saunders, Hayes, Smith, Attwood, Maloney, Sub: Shailer
Apr 10 v Walton & H (a) 2-1 *Smith 2*
Wiltshire, Haydon, Barker, Hill, Edmonds, Francis, Maloney, Smith, Forrest, Dyke, Saunders

1950-51
Sep 20 v Chelsea XI (h) 4-1 *Benningfield, Bristow, Harman, Wall*
Wiltshire, Langdale, Barker, Francis, Edmonds, Norman,Walls,Harman,Bristow, Batchelor, Benningfield
Feb 10 v Wycombe W (a) 4-6 *Wall 2, Roberts, Garden*
Edghill, Ward, Barker, Norman, Edmonds, Francis, Wall, Bristow, Roberts, Hornsby, Benningfield, Sub: Garden
Mar 23 v St Albans C (h) 3-0* *O'Leary 2, Bristow*
Edghill, Ward, Reeves, Norman, Littlejohn, Cook, McLaren, Bristow, Roberts, O'Leary, Benningfield
**Abandoned after 80 minutes, because of torrential rain.*
Mar 31 v Grays A (h) 4-2 *Hornsby 2, Garden, Wall*
Edghill, Ward, Barker, Norman, Edmonds, Francis, Wall, Molloy, Hornsby, Garden, Benningfield
Apr 14 v Clacton T (a) 1-3 *Bristow*
Edghill, Ward, Barker, Norman, Edmonds, Francis, Wall, Bristow, Hornsby, Garden, Benningfield
May 12 v Watford (h) 2-4 *Garden, White*
Wiltshire,Ward,Barker,Norman, Edmonds, Francis, White, Milton, Hornsby, Garden, Benningfield
May 16 v RAF(London) (h) 4-1 *Bristow, Benningfield, Hornsby,White*
Wiltshire, Ward, Barker, Norman, Edmonds, Francis, White, Bristow, Hornsby, Garden, Benningfield

1951-52
Jan 5 v Pegasus (h) 3-1 *Wegrzyk, White, Barker (pen)*
Wiltshire, Ward, Gadsden, Norman, Edmonds, Barker, White, Wegrzyk, Mikrut, Bennett, Benningfield

1952-53
Aug 27 v Athenian League XI (h) 2-0 *Hussey 2*
Wiltshire, McGhee, Gadsden, Comben, Edmonds, Wastell, White, Wegrzyk, Mikrut, Hussey, Bennett
Sep 3 v Harrow Town (h) 3-1 *Mikrut, Hussey, Bennett*
Wiltshire, Ward, Gadsden, Wall, J Palmer, Wastell, White, Wegrzyk, Mikrut, Hussey, Bennett
May 6 v Hendon (h) 2-2 *Mikrut, Bennett*
Wiltshire, Haydon, Gadsden, Comben, Edmonds, Wastell, White, Wegrzyk, Ayres, Mikrut, Bennett

1953-54
Sep 2 v Slough T (h) 2-2 *Hussey 2*
Wiltshire, McGhee, Haydon, Payne, K Key, May, Bodfish, O'Connor, J Thatcher, Hussey, Hopkins
Apr 16 v Falmouth T (a) 8-3 *Bodfish 3, Kenny 3, Trehearne 2*
Muller, PJ Rogers, Francis, Payne, Wilkinson, Franklin, Bodfish, O'Connor, Kenny, Trehearne, R Stewart
Apr 17 v Truro C (a) 0-3
Muller, PJ Rogers, J Warrick, Payne, Wilkinson, Franklin, Bicknell, O'Connor, Kenny, Trehearne, R Stewart

Apr 27 v Wembley (h) 2-0 *Kenny, O'Connor*
Nothing further known
May 8 v Slough T (a) 0-2
Muller, PJ Rogers, Porter, Payne, G Catherall, Bicknell, Millard, O'Connor, Kenny, Trehearne, Franklin

1954-55
Sep 8 v Harrow Town XI (h) 2-1 *Evans, MacDuff*
Nothing further known
Jan 22 v Aveley (a) 3-4 *Bristow 2, Archer*
Muller, R Mockler, Stephen, Bodimeade, Littlejohn, Glennon, Gee, Archer, Bristow, Trehearne, Evans
Mar 26 v Leytonstone (h) 5-4 *Wastell 3, Evans, Pluckrose*
Muller, Mulley, Stephen, Bowen, Littlejohn, Glennon, Gee, Pluckrose, Wastell, Archer, Evans
Mar 29 v Yiewsley (a) 0-0
Nothing further known
Apr 20 v RAF Stanmore (h) 2-1 *Ward, O'Connor*
Nothing further known

1955-56
Dec 17 v Pegasus (h) 5-3 *Wegrzyk 2, Comben, Evans, Harper*
Wood, Reeves, Farmer, Comben, Halward, Randall, Harper, Wegrzyk, Bowen, Mikrut, Evans
Mar 31 v Grange A (h) 5-2 *Wegrzyk 2,Comben,Harper, Mikrut (pen)*
Wood, Reeves, Farmer, Comben, Halward, Randall, Harper, Coster, Mikrut, Wegrzyk, Evans

1956-57
Sep 19 v Harrow T (H) 3-2 *Knox 2, Harrison*
Wood, Reeves, Farmer, T Bennett, Halward, Hannam, Harper, Harrison, Knox, Gomersall, Wegrzyk
Sep 26 v Leyton Orient (h) 2-2* *Wegrzyk, Knox*
Teevan, Reeves, Randall, Wall, Halward, Glennon, Harper, Wegrzyk, Knox, Coster, Evans
**Abandoned before end, because of bad light.*
Feb 2 v Pegasus (h) 2-3 *Evans, Randall (pen)*
East, Packham, Randall, Bennett, Norman, Glennon, Harper, Conroy, Gomersall, Hannam, Evans

Mar 16 v Epping T (h) 3-4 *Harper 2, Evans*
Wood, Packham, Randall, Comben, Norman, Hannam, Gomersall, Conroy, Knox, Harper, Evans
Mar 23 v Hounslow T (a) 1-3 *Bodfish*
Wood, Packham, Farmer, Comben, Norman, Hannam, R Bickley, Conroy, Harper, Bodfish, Evans
Apr 6 v St Albans C (h) 3-2 *Knox 2, Evans*
Wood, Packham, Randall, Comben, Norman, Hannam, Bodfish, Conroy, Knox, Harper, Evans
Apr 20 v Grange A (h) 1-0 *Randall (pen)*
F Williams, Packham, Randall, Comben, Norman, Hannam, Bodfish, Conroy, Gomarsall, Harper, Evans

1957-58
Apr 5 v Pegasus (h) 3-1 *Evans, Hills, OG*
G Wood, Hurrell, Kay, Hannam, Kingsland, Hall, Harper, Townsend, Hills, Gordon, Evans

1958-59
-

1959-60
Apr 18 v Ulysses (h) 1-0 *Moran (pen)*
Nothing further known

1960-61
-

1961-62
Feb 6 v ESV (Austria) (h) 5-0 *Merry 3, Davies, Evans*
Groves, Mowle, Good, Townsend, King, Cazaly, Peel, Knox, Merry, Davies,Evans *Att: 2000*
Feb 14 v Watford (h) 2-3 *Evans 2*
Groves, Mowle, Good, Townsend, King, Cazaly, Peel, Jarman, Merry, Rocknean, Evans
Feb 20 v Yiewsley (h) 3-0 *Evans 2, Peel*
Fowler, Low, Good, Cazaly, Emerson, Knox, Peel, Jarman, Davies, Moran,Evans
Mar 6 v Past XI (h) 1-0 *Jarman*
Fowler, Mowle, Low, Townsend, Emerson, Rocknean, Rowley, Davies, Merry, Knox, Evans. Sub: Jarman
Mar 13 v Corinthian Casuals (h) 1-2 *Rowley*
Fowler, Mowle, Low Cazaly, Emerson, Knox, Rowley, Jarmin, Merry, Young, Evans
Mar 21 v Maidenhead (a) 1-3 *Evans*
Fowler, Morley, Low, Townsend, King, Cazaly, Peel, Jarmin, Merry, Davies, Evans
Mar 27 v Clapton (h) 5-1 *Evans 3, Moran, Peel*
Fowler, Mowle, Low, Cazaly, King, Knox, Peel, Jarmin, Merry, Moran, Evans
Apr 3 v Maidenhead (h) 1-2 *Jarman*
Fowler, Mowle, Good, Cazaly, King,Knox, Rowley, Jarmin, Merry, Moran, Evans

1962-63
-

1963-64
Aug 17 v Barnet (a) 1-4 *Smith*
Fowler, Creasey, Good, Richards, J Morley, J Saunders, Peel, F Bennett, Jenkins, D Bell, Evans, Subs: G Hughes, J Millington, Smith
Sep 7 v Wokingham T (h) 3-0 *Jenkins 2, Cazaly*
Fowler, Creasy, Good, Cazaly, Stanley, Merry, Peel, Jones, Jenkins, Millington, Evans
Sep 28 v Chatham T (a) 1-2 *Jenkins*
Fowler, Creasy, Good, Richards, Stanley, Cazaly, Peel, Parsons, Jenkins, Jones, Evans

1964-65
Oct 2 v Loughborough College (h) 6-0 *Farrell 2, Bremer, Connell, Lindsay, OG*
Smith, Doyle, McPhee, Townsend, Ashworth, McKendry, Bell, Connell, Farrell, Lindsay, Bremer
Feb 8 v Watford (h) 1-2 *Childs*
Fowler, Doyle,McPhee,Richards,Ashworth, McKendry, Wyatt, Townsend, Childs, Lindsay, Bremer, Sub: Connell
Mar 30 v Alvechurch (h) 3-2 *Childs, Dillsworth, J Smith*
Fowler, Richards, Doyle, Dillsworth, Ashworth, McKendry, J Smith, Townsend, Childs, Lindsay, Bremer

May 1 v Northern Nomads (h) 3-1 *J Smith 2, McKenzie*
Fowler, Richards, Doyle, Goldsby, Ashworth, Dillsworth, McKenzie, Connell, J Smith, Lindsay, Bremer

1965-66
? v Hampton 4-3
Nothing further known
? v Edgware 3-0
Nothing further known
Aug 14 v Rothwell T (h) 6-1 *Childs 3, Bremer 2, Allen*
Nothing further known
May 11 v Chelsea XI (h) 1-4 *Townsend*
Goymer, Doyle, Sedgeley, Townsend, Dillsworth, Hughes, Allen, Searle, Cooley, Lindsay, Bremer, Sub: Paisley

1966-67
Aug 9 v Borehamwood (a) 3-3
Nothing further known
Aug 12 v Watford (h) 1-2 *Childs*
Goymer, Doyle, McKurk, Garman. Stanley, Dillsworth, Allen, Bremer, Childs, Searle, Messenger , Subs: Patmore, Oria, Jones
? v Edgware (a) 3-1
Nothing further known
Sep 3 v Windsor & Eton (a) 0-1
Goymer, Doyle, Lavender, Townsend, Stanley, Oria, Allen, Lindsay, Drake, Childs, Bremer,
Sep 26 v Hilal SC(Libya) (h) 3-1 *Allen, Peel, Searle*
Paisley,Doyle,Leonard,Garman, Wilkinson, Oria, Bremer, Drake, Searle, Allen, Fulks, Subs: Peel, Dillsworth
Dec 3 v Dagenham (a) 4-0 *Childs 3, Fulkes*
Nothing further known
May 2 v Luton T (h) 1-1 *Searle*
Blythe, Doyle, Leonard, Shalet, Quick, Warman, Anderson, Townsend, Searle, Harper, Bremer
May 19 v Barnet (a) 0-6
Nothing further known

1967-68
Aug 5 v Southall (a) 4-1 *Swain, Lindsay, Smart, Lee*
A Cronshaw, Warman, Leonard, Shalet, McGuiness, T Slade, M Lee, Montague, Swain, D Desmond, Lindsay, Subs: D Smart, T Thomas, Davies, P Anderson, J Harper
Aug 7 v Orient (h) 3-3 *Lindsay 2, Smart*
Blythe, Warman, Leonard, S Shalet, McGuiness, T Slade, P Anderson, Lindsay, Montague, D Smart, Bremer, Subs: M Lee, J Harper
Aug 12 v Hayes (a) 2-4 *Bremer, Smart*
Blythe, T Thomas, Leonard, Warman, McGuiness, T Slade, Lindsay, Montague, D Jones, D Smart, Bremer, Subs: P Anderson, S Shalet, T Quill
Aug 16 v Bedford T (h) 1-3 *Smart*
Blythe, Warman, Leonard, Townsend, McGuiness, Slade, Lindsay, Anderson, Montague, Smart, Bremer
Sep 16 v Leighton T (h) 3-1 *Bremer, Lindsay, Smart*
A Williams, Thomas, Warman, Montague, Day, Slade, Anderson, Smart, McCormack, Lindsay, Bremer
May 12 v J Haynes All Stars (h) 7-7 *Townsend, Clary 3, McCormack,Somers, D Poole*
A Williams, Pettit, Leonard, Townsend, P Snell, Slade, D Poole, Somers, Swain, M Clary, Lindsay, Subs: McCormack, M Praede

1968-69
Aug 3 v Chelsea (h) 0-3
A Williams, G Perrett, D Leonard, Townsend, McGuinness, Bromley, Searle, Lindsay, Swain, Montague, Hutchinson, Subs: R Williams, Cooper, Bremer, Franks, R Sayer

1969-70
Aug 2 v Paget Rangers (h) 2-0 *Bremer, Bullock*
A Williams, Sedgley, Leonard, Montague, Bullock, Draper, Bremer, Lindsay, Searle, Swain, Hutchinson, Sub: Mitchell

Aug 5th v Dagenham (a) 3-2*Swain,Searle,Bullock (pen)*
A Williams, Sedgley, Barnard, Bullock, K Gerrard, Draper, Bremer, Lindsay, Searle, Swain, Mitchell, Sub: Hand
Oct 26 v International Club (h) 1-3 *Bremer*
A Williams, R Williams, Barnard, Doyle, Bullock, Draper, Bremer, Mitchell, Swain, Hand, R Hay, Sub: Evans
Nov 25 v Flitwick (h) 1-0 *Bremer*
A Williams, Doyle, Bullock, Moxon, M Smith, Montague, Bremer, Hand, Swain, P Smith, Hutchinson, Subs: Thomas, R Williams, B Mitchell, Draper
Dec 9 v West Herts (h) 3-1 *Swain 2, Bremer*
A Williams, R Williams, Barnard, Moxon, Doyle, Montague, Bremer, Hand, Swain, Draper, P Smith, Subs: V Evans, S Szereneymi
Feb 24 v Maidenhead U (a) 2-3 *Barrett 2*
Thomas, Barnard, G Booth, M Smith, Moxon, Bullock, Bremer, Montague, Swain, P Barrett, Peddie, Subs: A Williams, Draper, Hand, R Hay
Mar 28 v Amsterdam FC (h) 0-2
Nothing further known
Apr 3 v Whitley Bay (h) 1-1 *Moxon*
A Williams, Barnard, Hand, R Williams, M Smith, Moxon, Draper, P Barrett, Swain, Montague, Peddie, Sub: Bullock
May 9 v International XI (h) 1-1 *Jackett*
A Williams, Barnard, Hand, R Williams, M Smith, Montague, Jackett, Bullock, Swain, Ritchie, Peddie, Sub: P Barrett

1970-71
? v Finchley (h) 3-0 *D Swain, Bullock 2*
Thomas, Mahon, Williams, Dafforn, Thompson, Draper, Johnson, Somers, Bullock, D Swain, Ritchie, Subs: C Swain, Bennett, M Smith
? v Guildford C (h) 2-0 *D Swain, Worley*
C Swain, Mahon, Thompson, Williams, Dafforn, Smith, Somers, Draper, Bullock, D Swain, Ritchie, Subs: Thomas, Worley,
? v Watford XI (h) 2-4
Thomas, Mahon, Thompson, Williams, Dafforn, Draper, Worley, Wilson, Bullock, Ritchie, Somers
Apr 11 v Elmsbuttel (Hamburg) (h) 4-0 *Ritchie 2, Bunker, Townsend*
Thomas, Dafforn, Barnard, Williams, Austen, Mahon, Yerby, Townsend, Ritchie, Pentecost, Bunker

1971-72
Aug 4 v Basingstoke (h) 0-0
Barr, Mahon, Bielkus, Furie, Gibbs, Bailey, Watson, M Brown, Townend, Hale, Jones, Sub: Austin
Aug 7 v Staines (a) 2-1 *Jones, OG*
Barr, Mahon, Bielkus, Furie, Gibbs, Bailey, Watson,M Brown,Townend,Cockell, Jones,
Aug 9 v Hillingdon B (h) 2-2 *Townend, M Brown*
Barr, Mahon, Bielkus, Furie, Gibbs, Bailey, Watson,M Brown,Townend,Cockell, Jones,
Aug 11 v Watford (h) 4-2 *Jones 2, Bailey, OG*
Barr, Mahon, Bielkus, Furie, Gibbs, Bailey, Watson,M Brown Townend,Cockell, Jones, Subs: Austin, Dempsey
Oct 30 v Weymouth (h) 0-2
Barr, Mahon, Bailey, Watson, B Rusher, Cockell, M Brown, Gallagher, Swain, Jones, Whitaker, Sub: Furie
Nov 13 v Barnet (a) 1-2 *Whitaker*
Barr, Hand, Mahon, Hale, Latham, Furie, M Brown, Swain, Townend, Watson, Whitaker
Jan 15 v Barnet (h) 2-1 *M Brown, Pearce*
Barr,Beyer,Cockell,Pearce,Presland,Furie,M Brown, Hale, Townend, K Owen,Whitaker

1972-73
Aug 1 v Harrow Borough (a) 2-1 *Whitaker, Byrne*
Barr, Burgess, Presland, Latham, Pearce, A Brown, L Boughey, M Brown, Byrne, Duck, Whitaker, Sub: Reynolds
Aug 3 v Bishop Stortford (a) 0-3
Barr, Burgess, Presland, Latham, Pearce, Hale, Dyson, M Brown, Duck, A Brown, Whitaker
Aug 9 v Luton Town (h) 3-2 *Reynolds, Presland, Pearce*
Barr, Burgess, Presland, Cockell, Pearce, M Brown, Duck, A Brown, Furie, Whitaker, Vafiadis, Sub: Reynolds

1973-74
Aug 4 v Skelmersdale (h) 1-0 *Duck*
MacKenzie, Watson, Fulton, Kinnear, McCormick, Barnes, Fairclough, Byrne, Duck, Henderson, Dyson, Subs: Brown, Godfrey
Aug 7 v Barnet (h) 3-1 *Duck 2 (1 pen), Presland*
MacKenzie, Presland, Fulton, Kinnear, McCormick, Fairclough, Dyson, Godfrey, Byrne, Duck, Brown, Subs: Barnes, Henderson, Watson
Aug 14 v Leytonstone (h) 2-4 *Byrne, Fairclough*
Brodie, Presland, Fulton, Kinnear, McCormick, Fairclough, Dyson, Watson, Byrne, Duck, Brown, Subs: Godfrey
Oct 29 v Watford (h) 2-5 *Brown, Duck (pen)*
MacKenzie, Watson, Fulton, Kinnear, McCormick, Dyson, Burgess, Presland, Byrne, Brown, Henderson, Subs: Duck, Godfrey, Fairclough
Nov 17 v Bletchley (a) 1-1 *Duck (pen)*
MacKenzie, Watson, Fulton, Kinnear, Doyle,Burgess, Fairclough, Fulton, Dyson, Duck, Brown,
Dec 12 v Gibralter XI (a) 4-1 *Byrne, Fulton, Summers, Ryan*
M Coffey, Baker, Watson, Kinnear, Burgess,Brown, Fulton, M Ryan, V Summers, Byrne, Henderson

1974-75
Aug 6 v Walthamstow Ave (h) 1-0 *T Evans*
Mackenzie, Kinnear, Watson, Burgess, McCormick, D Evans, Fulton, T Evans, Byrne, Godfrey, Henderson, Subs: Morton, Fairclough
Aug 10 v Hendon (h) 3-0 *Duck, T Evans 2*
Morton, Kinnear, Presland, Burgess, McCormick, D Evans, Fulton, T Evans, Byrne, Duck, Henderson, Subs: Mackenzie, Dyson, Watson
Dec 3 v First Tower Jersey (a) 4-1 *Byrne, Watson, Kinnear,Eglite*
Nothing further known
Apr 15 v Wolverhampton W (h) 2-5 *Duck 2 (1 pen)*
Mackenzie, Moss, Kinnear, Watson, Godfrey, Byrne, M Lazarus, Henderson, Duck, J Greaves, Fulton, Subs: Eglite, Burgess,

1975-76
Aug 2 v Boston FC (a) 2-4 *Duck 2*
Bullen, I Forrest, Watson, Kitchener, McCormick, O'Kane, Fulton, Henderson, Eglite, Duck, Lewis, Subs: Godfrey, Moss,

1976-77
Aug 7 v Torquay U (h) 3-1 *Duck 2, Edmundson*
Morton, Watson, Prince, Light, Lawrence, Byrne,Arnold,Hanson,Fulton,Duck,Halliday, Subs:Bullen, Stagg, Moss, Edmundson
Aug 9 v Luton T (h) 3-1 *Duck, Byrne, Moss*
Morton, Kinnear, Prince, Light; Lawrence, Byrne,Arnold,Moss, Fulton, Duck, Halliday, Subs:Hanson, Bullen, Stagg, Edmundson
Aug 12 v Leytonstone (a) 0-1
Morton, Watson, Prince, Hanson, Kinnear, Byrne,Arnold, Light, Duck, Fulton, Halliday, Subs:Bullen, Stagg, Moss, Edmundson
Aug 14 v Croydon A (a) 0-1
Morton, Kinnear, Prince, Light, Lawrence, Byrne, Stagg, Moss,Arnold,Fulton,Halliday, Subs:Watson, Hanson, Bullen, Edmundson
Aug 18 v Watford (h) 2-0 *Moss, Stagg*
Morton, Kinnear, Prince, Edmundson, Lawrence, Byrne, Arnold, Hanson, Fulton, Stagg, Halliday Subs:Watson, Light, Bullen,Moss,Franklin
Apr 30 v Aylesbury (h) 3-1 *Byrne, Griffiths, Parrett*
Lightfoot, Thomas, Watson, Downes, Parratt, Prince, Griffiths, Moss, Byrne, O'Kane,Brinkman, Subs:Morton, Hanson, Fulton
May 20 v Watford (h) 1-2 *Duck*
Lightfoot, Thomas, Fursdon, Downes, Parratt, Watson, Brinkman, Moss, Byrne, Duck, Fulton Subs:Morton, Prince, O'Kane, Griffiths

1977-78

Aug 6 v Slough T (a) 2-2 *O'Kane, Dennison*
Cranstone, Thomas, Fursdon, Barwick, Parratt, Brinkman, Griffiths, O'Kane, Ferry, Duck, Moss, Subs: Hill, Dennison

Aug 9 v Hounslow T (h) 0-1
Cranstone, Thomas, Fursdon, Barwick, Parratt, Moss, Ferry, O'Kane, Hill, Duck, Griffiths, Subs: Gayle, Brinkman

Aug 13 v Dagenham (h) 3-1 *Duck 2 (1 pen), Byrne*
Cranstone, Thomas, Fursdon, Barwick, Parratt, Watson, Moss, Brinkman, Byrne, Duck, Griffiths

Aug 16 v Watford (h) 1-0 *Moss*
Lightfoot, Thomas, Fursdon, Brinkman, Parratt, Watson, Moss, O'Kane, Byrne, Duck, Griffiths, Sub: Barwick

1978-79

Aug 5 v Leatherhead (h) 2-1 *Parratt, Doyle*
Cranstone, Thomas, Fursdon, Gilbert, Parratt, Barwick, B Topiwala, Brinkman, Moss, Doyle, Briscoe

Aug 12 v Carshalton Athletic (h) 0-1
Cranstone, McVeigh, Fursdon, Watson, Parratt, Barwick, Brinkman, Moss, Duck, Briscoe, Hockham, Subs: Boyle, Thomas, Doyle, Clarke

Oct 24 v West Ham U (h) 0-0
Lightfoot, Barwick, Briscoe, Dangerfield, Parratt, Horgan, Arnold, Brinkman, Moss, Duck, Greaves, Subs: Doyle, Hockham, Boyle, McVeigh, Cranstone

1979-80

Aug 4 v Tooting & Mitcham (h) 1-2 *N Johnson*
Cranstone, Brannigan, Fursdon, Watson, Horgan, Barwick, Moss, James, N Johnson, D Pearce, C Johnson, Sub: Boyle

Aug 7 v Hillingdon Borough (h) 2-0 *Horgan 2*
Cranstone, Brannigan, Fursdon, Watson, Horgan, Barwick, Moss, James, N Johnson, D Pearce, Boyle Sub: C Johnson

Aug 11 v Slough T (a) 0-2
Cranstone, Brannigan, Fursdon, Boyle, Wiseman, Barwick, Moss, Cordice, N Johnson, D Pearce, C Johnson

Aug 14 v Barking (h) 0-1
Cranstone, Brannigan, Fursdon, Wainwright, Horgan, Barwick, Moss James, Cordice, N Johnson, C Johnson, Subs: Boyle, D Pearce, S Pearce

Oct 1 v TSV Eching (Munich) (h) 2-0 *D Pearce, N Cordice*
Cranstone, Barwick, Fursdon, Watson, Horgan, Brannigan, Boyle, Moss, C Johnson, N Johnson, D Pearce, Subs: Cordice, S Pearce, Adams

Feb 9 v Wycombe Wanderers (a) 1-1 *Greenhalgh*
Cranstone, Barwick, S Pearce, Fursdon, Bennett, Wainwright, Horgan, Boyle, Cordice, Greenhalgh, Adams, Subs: Moss, N Johnson

Feb 27 v Wimbledon (h) 2-3 *Wainwright, N Johnson*
Tutt, Barwick, S Pearce, Watson, Bennett, Wainwright, Brannigan, Walker, N Johnson, Cordice, Adams, Subs: Moss, Greenhalgh

1980-81

Aug 11 v Luton Town (h) 1-2 *Moss*
Cranstone, Brannigan, Pearce, Barwick, Bowgett, Murphy, Forde, Watson, Moss, Duck, Adams, Subs: Johnson, D Carlton, A Bennett

Oct 3 v Wimbledon XI (h) 0-1
R Walker, N Robinson, Pearce, Barwick, Bowgett, Watson, J Boake, Murphy, A Cordice, Johnson, Forde, Subs: Brannigan, Adams, D Robinson, S Johns

Jan 28 v Chelsea XI (h) 0-1
Cranstone, Hardman, Pearce, Barwick, Bowgett, Perkins, Brannigan, Wainwright, D Evans, N Cordice, Forde, Subs: Adams, D O'Doherty

Feb 3 v Edgware Town (h) 4-1 *Johnson, Brannigan, Bowgett, Forde*
Cranstone, Hardman, Forde, Brannigan, Bowgett, Perkins, Johnson, D O'Doherty, D Evans, N Cordice, A Cordice, Subs: Adams, T Kelly

Feb 14 v Wimbledon XI (h) 1-2 *Adams*
Cranstone, Hardman, Forde, Brannigan, Bowgett, Perkins, Adams, Wainwright, D Evans, Johnson, A Cordice, Sub: N Cordice

Apr 18 v Millwall XI (h) 7-0 *Johnson 4, Pearce, N Cordice, Bowgett (pen)*
P Overton, Hardman, Pearce, Barwick, Byatt, Perkins, Sweetzer, Forde, Johnson, N Cordice, Bowgett, Sub: Adams

Apr 21 v Wycombe Wanderers (h) 2-2 *A Cordice 2*
Cranstone, Hardman, Pearce, Barwick, Byatt, Perkins, Sweetzer, Wainwright, A Cordice, N Cordice, Bowgett

1981-82

Aug 1 v Woking (a) 2-0 *Johnson, A Cordice*
Cranstone, Hardman, S Pearce, D Powell, Bowgett, Adams, A Cordice, Wainwright, Johnson, Waites, Forde

Aug 4 v Walton & Hersham (a) 1-1 *Johnson*
Cranstone, Hardman, S Pearce, Barwick, Bowgett, Adams, A Cordice, Wainwright, Johnson, Waites, Forde

1982-83

July 31 v Hungerford Town (a) 6-0 *Knowles 2, Johnson, Graves, Bowgett, Davies*
Goddard, Perkins, Pearce, Byatt, Bowgett, Churchouse, Davies, Wainwright, Graves, Knowles, Johnson, Subs: Barwick, A Kingston

Aug 3 v Wimbledon (h) 1-1 *Peachey*
Goddard, Perkins, Pearce, Byatt, Bowgett, Churchouse, J Peachey, Wainwright, Graves, Knowles, Johnson, Sub: Barwick

Aug 5 v Charlton Athletic (h) 2-1 *Davies, Byatt*
Goddard, Perkins, Pearce, Byatt, Bowgett, Barwick, Davies, Wainwright, J Peachey, Graves, Johnson

Aug 7 v Fulham (h) 2-2 *Johnson, Knowles*
Goddard, Perkins, Pearce, Byatt, Bowgett, Churchouse, Graves, Wainwright, J Peachey, Knowles, Johnson, Sub: Waites

Aug 12 v Crystal Palace (h) 2-1 *Knowles, N Cordice*
Goddard, Churchouse, Pearce, Byatt, Bowgett, Barwick, Graves, Wainwright, N Cordice, Knowles, Johnson, Subs: Davies, Waites

Feb 5 v Hendon (h) 3-1 *A Cordice 2, Graves*
Goddard, Perkins, Pearce, Byatt, Bowgett, Barwick, Waddock, Margerrison, Graves, A Cordice, Johnson, Sub: A Crooks

May 11 v Sporting Club De Douai (a) 3-3 *Waites, Pentland, Graves*
D Carlyle, Waddock, Pearce, B Edwards, G Bryant, J Richardson, C Fielder, Wainwright, Graves, S Pentland, Waites,
Sub: K Bright

1983-84

Aug 9 v Wimbledon XI (h) 2-2 *A Cordice, Johnson*
Iles, Waddock, J Richardson, Byatt, Bowgett, Barwick, Price, Wainwright, A Cordice, Graves, Johnson, Sub: Waites

Aug 13 v QPR XI (h) 1-5 *Johnson*
Iles, Donnellan, J Richardson, Byatt, Bowgett, Barwick, Price, Wainwright, A Cordice, Graves, Johnson, Sub: Waites

Aug 16 v Luton Town XI (h) 1-1 *Bowgett*
Ward, Barwick, J Richardson, Byatt, Bowgett, Price, Donellan, Wainwright, A Cordice, Waites, Johnson, Sub: Waddock

Sep 12 v Wimbledon XI (h) 6-0 *Graves 5, Bowgett*
Iles, Perkins, Pearce, Byatt, Bowgett, Price, Greenaway, N Cordice, Graves, Johnson, Donnellan, Subs: J Richardson, Wainwright, McCargo

Nov 5 v VS Rugby (a) 3-2 *N Cordice, Bowgett, McCargo*
Iles, Perkins, Dibble, Byatt, Bowgett, Barwick, Price, N Cordice, Johnson, Graves, Greenaway, Sub: McCargo

Feb 23 v Pennant (h) 7-0 *Graves 2, Dibble 2, A Cordice 2, McCargo*
Iles, Perkins, McCargo, Byatt, Bowgett, Price, Greenaway, Dibble, A Cordice, Graves, Donnellan, Sub: Johnson

1984-85

Aug 4 v Reading (h) 3-0 *Bowgett, A Cordice, Greenaway*
Iles, J Williams, McCargo, Byatt, Bowgett, Wainwright, Greenaway, Holmes, A Cordice, Graves, Davies, Subs: K Redguard, W McGuinness

Aug 7 v Crystal Palace (h) 2-0 *N Cordice 2*
Iles, Davies, McCargo, Byatt, Bowgett, N Cordice, Greenaway, Holmes, A Cordice, Graves, D Wintergill, Subs:K Redguard,K Wedderburn, V Jones

Aug 11 v Slough T (a) 5-2 *Graves 2, Donnellan 3*
Iles, Donnellan, McCargo, V Jones, Bowgett, Wainwright, Greenaway, Holmes, N Cordice, Graves, Davies, Sub: L Meade
Aug 14 v Tooting & M (h) 4-1 *Graves, Donnellan 2, Greenaway*
Iles, N Cordice, McCargo, Byatt, Bowgett, Wainwright, Greenaway, Holmes, A Cordice, Graves, Davies, Subs: W McGuinness, V Jones, L Meade, Donnellan

1985-86
Aug 3 v Sutton U (a) 1-2 *Graves*
P Jones, Tapley, McCargo, Byatt, Bowgett, Wainwright, Greenaway, Holmes, Donnellan, Graves, R Codner, Subs: Iles, V Jones, A Cacciapuoti, C Solari, L Pedlar
Aug 6 v Kingstonian (a) 2-3 *Donnellan, Holmes*
Iles, Tapley, McCargo, Perkins, Bowgett, Wainwright, Greenaway, A Cordice, Donnellan, Graves, N Cordice, Subs: P Jones, Holmes, V Jones, C Solari, L Pedlar, T Elliott
Aug 10 v Charlton Ath (h) 1-0 *Graves*
P Jones, Tapley, McCargo, Byatt, Bowgett, Wainwright, Greenaway, Holmes, A Cordice, Graves, Doyle, Subs: R Codner, V Jones, Perkins, N Cordice, T Smart
Aug 13 v Slough T (a) 1-1 *Donnellan*
Iles, Perkins, McCargo, Byatt, Bowgett, Wainwright, Greenaway, Holmes, Donnellan, Graves, N Cordice, Subs: P Jones, Tapley, R Codner, T Elliott, T Smart
Aug 17 v Tooting & Mitcham (a) 1-2 *N Cordice*
P Jones, Tapley, McCargo, Byatt, Bowgett, Wainwright, Greenaway, Holmes, N Cordice, Graves, Doyle, Subs: Iles, Perkins, Donnellan, V Jones
Aug 20 v Wokingham (a) 4-2 *Graves, Holmes, Doyle, V Jones*
Iles, Perkins, McCargo, Byatt, Bowgett, Wainwright, Greenaway, Holmes, Tonge, Graves, Doyle, Subs: Tapley, Donnellan, V Jones
Nov 11 v Coventry City (h) 3-6 *Graham, Donnellan, O'Keefe*
L Cleaveley, V Jones, Tapley, Byatt, Bowgett, Wainwright, Greenaway, R O'Keefe, Donnellan, Graham, Doyle
Jan 21 v Wimbledon (h) 1-1 *Doyle*
L Cleaveley, Tapley, McCargo, V Jones, R O'Keefe, Wainwright, Greenaway, C Seagraves, N Cordice, Doyle, Graham
Subs: Bowgett, Graves
Mar 19 v Dartford (a) 8-1 *Graves 2, A Cordice, N Cordice, Graham, Tonge, Greenaway, Wainwright (pen)*
L Cleaveley, V Jones, Donnellan, Byatt, C Seagraves, Wainwright, Greenaway, Holmes, A Cordice, Graves, Tonge, Subs: Graham, N Cordice
May 18 v SC Douai (h) 5-0 *Graham 2, Tonge, O'Keefe, Holmes (pen)*
Iles, Tapley, McClure, C Seagraves, Bowgett, Wainwright, Greenaway, Tonge, M Adams, Graves, Doyle, Subs: K Lavender, Byatt, Holmes, Graham, R O'Keefe, J Turner

1986-87
July 30 v Wembley (a) 0-0
Iles, Wallace, McClure, Byatt, Rutter, Wainwright, Greenaway, Holmes, N Cordice, Graves, Doyle, Sub: Donnellan
Aug 5 v Charlton Ath (h) 1-0 *Wallace*
Iles, Tapley, Bowgett, Byatt, Rutter, Wainwright, Greenaway, Holmes, N Cordice, Wallace,Doyle, Subs: McClure, Graves, Donnellan, Ragan

Aug 9 v Wycombe W (a) 0-1
Iles, Tapley, McClure, Byatt, Bowgett, Wainwright, Greenaway, Holmes, N Cordice, Graves, Doyle, Subs: Donnellan, Ragan, T Meadows, A Haxton
Mar 17 v Rayners Lane (h) 1-1 *McClure*
Iles, Tapley, McClure, Byatt, Hatter, Wainwright, Greenaway, G Dolling, Walton, L Maddison, Doyle, Subs: N Cordice, Bowgett, A Haxton, T Smurthwaite

1987-88
July 28 v Chelsea (h) 1-1 *Perry*
Welsh, Pittaway, Bowgett, Byatt, McCarthy, Hatter, O'Keefe, Wainwright, Perry, Lowe, Walton
Aug 1 v Rayners Lane (a) 3-1 *Perry, Walton, Byatt (pen)*
Welsh, Pittaway, T Meadows, Byatt, Hatter, McCarthy, M Hirst, E Gibson, Perry, Lowe, Walton
Aug 4 v Arsenal (h) 1-6 *O'Keefe*
A Haxton, Pittaway, Bowgett, Byatt, McCarthy, Hatter, O'Keefe, Wainwright, M Hirst, Lowe, Walton
Aug 7 v Watford (h) 1-4 *Walton*
A Haxton, Pittaway, Bowgett, Byatt, Hatter, Wainwright, McCarthy, M Hirst, Perry, Walton, T Meadows, Subs: E Gibson, G King
Aug 11 v Charlton Ath (h) 0-2
A Haxton, Pittaway, Dowe, Bowgett, Hatter, Wainwright, McCarthy, M Hirst, Perry, Walton, O'Keefe
Aug 15 v Hendon (a) 2-4 *Perry 2*
Welsh, Pittaway, Dowe, Byatt, McCarthy, Hatter, O'Keefe, Wainwright, Perry, Walton, M Hirst
Feb 13 v Harrow Borough (h) 1-1 *English*
Welsh, B Davis, Harrison, Byatt, Bowgett, McCarthy, Stagg, M Hirst, Perry, Rivero, A Cordice, Subs: Pittaway, P Davis, Wainwright, English
Feb 23 v Stevenage Borough (a) 0-2
Welsh, Pittaway, Harrison, Bowgett, McCarthy, Wainwright, P Davis, La Ronde, English, Rivero, Stagg, Subs: G Smith, M Smith

1988-89
Aug 2 v Leyton Wingate (a) 2-2 *Wilkins, R Greene*
Williams, Eriemo, Harrison, Byatt, Corbin, David Green, R Green, Bailey, Wilkins, Olaleye, A Cordice, Subs: Foster, ennis Green
Aug 6 v Witton Albion (h) 2-3 *Wilkins (pen), C Browne*
Williams, Eriemo, Harrison, Byatt, Corbin, Morris, Bailey, Wilkins, C Browne, Olaleye, Lynch, Subs: R Green, La Ronde
Aug 9 v Edgware T (h) 7-1 *Wilkins, Olaleye 2, Lynch 2, Wright, C Browne*
J Jacobs, Corbin, Harrison, Byatt, O'Brien, Morris, La Ronde, C Wright, Wilkins, Olaleye, Lynch, Subs: Eriemo, R Green, C Browne
Aug 11 v Leytonstone & Ilford (a) 1-2 *Lynch*
J Jacobs, Corbin, Harrison, Byatt, Morris, C Browne, C Wright, La Ronde, Wilkins, Olaleye, Lynch, Sub: Eriemo
Aug 16 v Slough T (a) 2-2 *Byatt, S Browne*
Williams, Corbin, Harrison, Byatt, Morris, O'Brien, S Browne, La Ronde, Wilkins, Olaleye, Lynch, Subs: Eriemo, C Browne
Mar 23 v Yeovil T (h) 1-4 *Lynch*
Foster, Corbin, Bowgett, Byatt, Morris, R Davies, C Browne, Olaleye, M Graves, J Margerrison, Lynch, Sub: J Watson

1989-90
Aug 1 v Windsor & Eton (a) 6-3 *Kelly 2, Lynch, Rowe, Mason, Wilkins*
Williams, Tapley, Norman, Findley, Harrison, Morris, Margerrison, Rowe, Wilkins, Kelly, Lynch, Subs:Foster,Byatt,P Mason, G McClelland
Aug 3 v Redbridge Forest (h) 1-2 *Margerrison*
Foster, Tapley, Norman, Findley, Morris, Harrison, Margerrison, Kelly, Wilkins, P Mason, Lynch, Subs: Williams, G McClelland
Aug 5 v Hertford T (h) 3-2 *Kelly, Lynch, Wilkins*
Foster, Tapley, Norman, Findley, Harrison, Morris, Margerrison, M McCabe, Wilkins, Kelly, Lynch, Sub: P Blennerhassett
Aug 8 v Wycombe W (a) 0-2
Foster, Tapley, Norman, Findley, Morris, Harrison, Margerrison, Kelly, J Campbell, Wilkins, Lynch, Subs: M McCabe, P Mason
Aug 12 v Staines T (a) 0-2
Foster, Tapley, Norman, Findley, Morris, Harrison, Margerrison, Campbell, Wilkins, Rowe, Lynch, Subs: Kelly, Goyette, P Mason
Mar 22 v Guernsey FA (h) 0-2
Williams, Watson, Smart, K Collins, Harrison, Margerrison, Johnstone, Goyette, Wilkins, Kelly, Lynch Subs: A Tsitsis, Price, M Abrey, D Irving, S Browne, Risk, R Davies, E Anyan

1990-91

July 26 v Marlow T (a) 1-1 *Lynch*
Vagg, Tapley, Smart, Eriemo, D Lewis, Harrison, S Browne, Goyette, Kelly, Jenkins, Lynch, Subs: Donnellan, Johnstone, Blackman, Gbogidi, K Haag, D Field, C Browne

July 31 v Egham T (a) 3-1 *Lynch, Goyette, Smart*
Vagg, Smart, Donnellan, Eriemo, Tapley, Harrison, S Browne, Goyette, Jenkins, Blackman, Gbogidi, Subs: D Lewis, Kelly, Lynch, K Haag, Olaleye, Fergusson

Aug 4 v Sutton U (h) 1-1 *Goyette (pen)*
Vagg, Donnellan, Smart, Tapley, Fergusson, Harrison, S Browne, Goyette, Blackman, Gbogidi, Lynch, Subs: Kelly, Jenkins, D Field

Aug 7 v Windsor & Eton (h) 2-0 *Goyette (pen), Jenkins*
Vagg, Donnellan, Smart, Tapley, Fergusson, Harrison, S Browne, Goyette, Jenkins, Blackman, Lynch, Subs: Johnstone, Bartlett

Aug 11 v Carshalton Ath (a) 3-3 *Blackman, S Browne, Harrison*
Vagg, Donnellan, Smart, Tapley, Fergusson, Harrison, S Browne, Goyette, Jenkins, Blackman, Lynch, Subs: D Lewis, Gbogidi, Bartlett

Apr 6 v Jersey FA (h) 1-2 *Harrison*
Roach, Watson, Smart, Bartlett, Tapley, Goyette, S Watts, R Howard, Kelly, Harrison, Gipp, Subs: Goodison

1991-92

Aug 8 v Chertsey T (a) 0-1
Hudson, Watson, Goyette, Tapley, Bartlett, Cordice, Hopson, Donnellan, Gipp, Kelly, Smart, Subs: Roach, Richards, Hedge, B Ferns, L Maddison, J McMillan

Aug 10 v Barnet (h) 0-4
Hudson, Watson, Harrison, Tapley, Bartlett, Cordice, Hopson, Donnellan, Kelly, Gipp, Smart, Subs: Roach, Goyette, J McMillan, W Lay, B Ferns, Hedge, L Maddison

Aug 13 v Harefield (a) 0-1
Hudson, J Ferguson, Harrison, Richards, J McMillan, Cordice, W Lay, A Wright, D Irving, Gipp, A Martin, Subs: Goyette, Hedge, M Milton, S Robb, Blackman, G McIntosh

Mar 16 v Watford Observer SL (h) 0-1
Robbins, Drummy, Goyette, Bartlett, McGuire, Richards, Hopson, Hedge, Franklyn Ikeme, Adamson, Gallagher, Subs: Pearson, Hippolyte, Venables

1992-93

Aug 4 v Hitchin T (a) 3-4 *Cordice, Tate, Blackler*
Hudson, Watson, Pearson, Bartlett, Tapley, Blackler, Venables, Cordice, Tate, Hippolyte, Gallacher, Subs: Shanahan, Gayle, Hedge, Hopson, Drummy, Tonge, Chandler, Richards

Aug 8 v Hendon (a) 0-4
Roach, Watson. Hedge, Shanahan, Tapley, Cordice, Venables, Blackler, Tate, Chandler, Pearson, Subs: Hudson, Tonge, Gayle, Hippolyte,

Aug 12 v Edgware T (a) 1-2 *Hippolyte*
Roach, Robinson, Hedge, Tapley, Richards, Cordice, Hopson, Chandler, Hippolyte, Venables, Drummy, Subs: Hudson, K Thomas, Tate, Adamson, Blackler

Aug 15 v Leyton (a) 3-1 *Gallacher 3 (1 pen)*
Hudson, Watson, Hedge, Tapley, Shanahan, Cordice, Drummy, Chandler, Venables, Hippolyte, Gallacher, Subs: Roach, Gayle

Aug 17 v Wycombe W (h) 1-1 *Hedge*
Hudson, Shanahan, Hedge, Tapley, Watson, Cordice, Drummy, Blackler, Hippolyte, Venables, Gallacher, Subs: Gayle, Hopson, Tonge, Chandler, Pearson

1993-94

Aug 7 v Bugbrooke St Michaels (a) 3-0 *Tate, Hedge, Adamson*
Nolan, Perry, Randall, Shanahan, Gayle, C Short, Richards, Hedge, Johnson, Tate, Adamson, Subs: P Herbert, E O'Connor, Tenkorang

Aug 8 v Northampton Spencer (a) 2-1 *Tate, Herbert*
Tenkorang, Perry, Lovegrove, Shanahan, Richards, Gayle, Drummy, Johnson, Tate, Hedge, Adamson, Subs: Herbert, Sweales

Aug 14 v Met. Police (a) 3-3 *Tate, Sweales 2*
Tenkorang, Perry, Lovegrove, Shanahan, Richards, Hedge, Drummy, Gayle, Herbert, Tate, Johnson, Subs: Nolan, Sweales, O'Connor, Denny

Aug 17 v Yeading (a) 0-5
Tenkorang, Perry, Lovegrove, Shanahan, Richards, Barham, Drummy, Hedge, Cordice, Tate, Johnson, Subs: Sweales, Gayle, Williams, Magrone

Sep29 v Feltham & Hounslow B (a) 3-5 *Tate,Johnson 2*
Tenkorang, Shanahan, Perry, Hicks, Pettifer, Barham, Johnson, Papa, Adamson, Tate, Hedge, Subs: Nolan, C Williams, A Williams, Richards, Craven

Dec 8 v Yeading (a) 2-2 *Hedge, OG*
Hopping, Hedge, Pettifer, MacPherson, Lawrence, J Knibbs, M Keane, Barham, Saunders, English, Holohan, Subs: Johnson, J Faucher, McGrath, Dennis, J Donovan

Jan 26 v Camberley T (a) 0-3
Hopping, Anglin, Augustine, Pettifer, S Broadhurst, Hedge, C Lindo, Keane, Mellor, Seabrook, McGrath, Subs: Buckley, Bennett, Papa, Robinson

1994-95

July 26 v Egham T (a) 2-2 *Brathwaite, Wilson*
Gartell, Anglin, Mason, Kent, Jashek, Meakin, R Wilmott, McGrath, Findley, Brathwaite, P Waites Subs: M Wilson, C Warmington, M Hill, Shanahan, R Anderson, F Dennis, Birch

July 30 v Tring T (h) 2-1 *Brathwaite 2 (2 pens)*
Gartell, Anglin, Birch, M Hill, Findley, Mason, Elward, Kent, Griffiths, Brathwaite, McGrath, Subs: D Williams, Shanahan, Waites, R Anderson, M Wilson, C Onwere

Aug 1 v Ruislip Manor (a) 0-2
Gartell, Shanahan, Birch, Findley, Jashek, Anglin, McGrath, Webb, P Brown, Schwartz, P Waites, Subs: D Hill, Meakin, Dean Hill, Augustine, M Wilson, C Lindo, C Onwere

Aug 4 v Hillingdon B (a) 2-1 *T Buzaglo, Elward*
Gartell, Shanahan, Birch, M Hill, Mason, C Warmington, Elward, Brathwaite, Schwartz, T Buzaglo, McGrath, Subs: D Hill, Anglin, Meakins, Findley, Dennis, Jashek, Kent, Wilson, Anderson

Aug 9 v Viking Sports (a) 5-1 *Findley 2, Schwartz, Joseph, Hayward*
D Hill, R Anderson, Birch, Anglin, M Hayward, Meakins, Pedlar, Hudson, F Joseph, Schwartz, McGrath, Subs: Shanahan, M Wilson, Findley

Aug 13 v Rayners Lane (a) 1-1 *M Hill*
Gartell, Anglin, Hill, Mason, M Hayward, McGrath, Elward, Schwartz, Pedlar, F Joseph, Peaks, Subs: Goodison, Findley, Wilson, Shanahan, R Anderson, Birch

Sep 20 v Edgware T (a) 2-2 *Brathwaite, Drummy*
D Hill, Anglin, Birch, Shanahan, Findley, Drummy, Webb, McGrath, Brathwaite, L Brownlie, M Wilson, Sub: D Jones

Sep 29 v Fulham (a) 1-0 *Kent*
Gartell, Shanahan, McGrath, M Hill, Findlay, Mason, Elward, Kent, Quail, Goodison, Birch, Subs: Solomon, M Wilson, Webb

1995-96

July 25 v North Greenford U (h) 4-0 *Fraser, Hall 2, Watson*
D Ramsay, Marskell, Terry Birch, Bhatia, M Tero, D Watson, Walton, Yates, Fraser, Drummy, Gibson, Subs: Troy Birch, Brathwaite, J Moore, Jashek, Hall, Smith, A Giannini

July 29 v Canvey Island (a) 3-1 *Fraser 2, Katsiaounis*
D Ramsay, Marskell, Moore, Francis, Shanahan, Walton, Tekell, Brathwaite, Fraser, K Boreham, Troy Birch, Subs: P Bulliman, Bhatia, Findley, D Watson, N Katsiaounis, Yates

Aug 1 v Bedfont (a) 2-0 *Hall, Bhatia*
Bettacinni, J Moore, Terry Birch, D Wright, Jashek, A Morgan, Gibson, Bhatia, Hall, H Shugaa, Hart Subs: H Clements, M Medal, Sheldrick, F Moore

Aug 3 v Cockfosters (h) 1-2 *Adams*
M Medal, J Moore, H Clarke, K Boreham, R Findlay, T Birch, Bhatia, Tekell, N Katsiaounis, Sheldrick, Hart, Subs: Tenkorang, A Morgan, J Walker, T Adams, M Hutchinson, A Odumboni, M Wilson, T Lawrence

Aug 8 v Molesey (h) 4-0 *Hall 2, Brathwaite, Ivers*
Tenkorang, Marskell, Yates, Bhatia, F Moore, Shanahan, K Boreham, Tekell, Hall, Ivers, Brathwaite, Subs: R Wild, I Hart, T Birch, G Hart, G Boreham

Aug 12 v Chipstead (h) 5-1 *Brathwaite,Ivers,Birch (pen),Boreham, Sheldrick*
R Wild, Marskell, J Moore, Shanahan, Croad, Walton,Tekell, Ivers, Fraser, Brathwaite, Birch, Subs: Bhatia, Drummy, Hall, K Boreham, Sheldrick, Tenkorang

Aug 15 v Bedford T (a) 2-2 *Fraser, Ivers*
R Wild, Marskell, F Moore, Bhatia, Croad, Tekell, Walton, Yates, Fraser, Sheldrick, Hart, Subs: Brathwaite, Ivers, Shanahan, Hall, J Moore

Oct 3 v Maidenhead U (a) 1-0 *Marskell*
R Wild, Marskell, Stone, H Clarke, Shanahan, J Moore, Hart, Tekell, T Smith, Hall, Laye, Subs: F Moore, Yates

Jan 22 v Rushden & Diamonds (a) 0-1
Tenkorang, F Moore, Waugh, Shanahan, M Tarry, T Smith, Walton, T Knight, Walker, E Lomotey, Hibbert, Subs: D Kirby, Sheldrick, Birch

Mar 12 v Burnham (a) 2-1 *Sheldrick, Papa*
G Doolan, F Moore, Tekell, S Tricker, A Nikshigi, M Leite, Papa, A Zefi, Walker, Sheldrick, Hart, Subs: D Dyson, S Thomas,D Gomaz, D Kirby,

1996-97

July 20 v Hayes (a) 3-1 *Sheldrick 2, Moore*
Bonfield, Smart, B Wise, Moore, Waugh, Hibbert, Walton, Tekell, D Ross, Bircham, Miller, Subs: J Bush, F Ramirez, T North, S Jones, J Jervier, Sheldrick, C Gnahore

July 23 v North Greenford U (a) 4-3 *Sheldrick 2, Wise, Antell*
J Bush, S Dell, B Wise, Moore, C Gnahore Hibbert, Knight, S Ross, D Ross, Walker, Miller, Subs: Sheldrick, F Ramirez, J Antell, J Taylor, A Caliskan, A Mills

July 27 v Abington T (a) 0-4
Bonfield, Smart, T North, Moore, S Jones, Hibbert, Walton, Tekell, Walker, D Ross, Bircham, Subs: B Wise, Waugh, F Ramirez, S Dell, Croad, Massey

July 31 v Sutton U (h) 0-1
Bonfield, Massey, J Taylor, Moore, Croad, Hibbert, Walton, M Telfer, I Brathwaite, Sheldrick, Bircham, Subs: Smart, B Wise, Tekell, S Jones, Walker, Hammatt, Zefi

Aug 1 v Rayners Lane (h) 4-1 *Hammatt, Zefi, Leite 2*
J Bush, S Dell, Smith, J Antell, T North, F Ramirez, S Patterson, Zefi, Hammatt, Walker, G Hart, Subs: J Jervier, J Roberts, M Leite, B Finch, F Pineda, D Drury

Aug 3 v Ware (a) 2-1 *Sheldrick, Hammatt*
L Brown, Smart, B Wise, Moore, Croad, S Jones, Walton, Tekell, Walker, Hammatt, Bircham, Subs: Waugh, Sheldrick, Massey, Smith, M Telfer, Marshall

Aug 6 v Walton & Hersham (a) 1-0 *Bircham*
J Holdsworth, Massey, Smith, Moore, Croad, Marshall, Hibbert, Tekell, Walker, Sheldrick, Bircham, Subs: Smart, B Wise, Waugh, D Ross, Hammatt, Zefi, G Hart

Aug 10 v Wimbledon (h) 0-4
Bonfield, Smart, Massey, Moore, Croad, Marshall, Walton, Hibbert, Hammatt, Zefi, Bircham, Subs: Smith, Tekell, D Ross, Walker, Sheldrick

Aug 12 v Bedfont (a) 1-1 *Leite*
J Bush, Massey, B Wise, Hibbert, S Jones, Smith, D Ross, R Hall, Sheldrick, Zefi, Tekell, Subs: S Hawkins, M Leite

Aug 13 v Maidenhead U (a) 1-0 *Ross*
Bonfield, Smart, Smith, Moore, S Jones, Marshall, Walton, Hibbert, Zefi, Sheldrick, Bircham, Subs: Tekell, R Hall, B Wise, D Ross

Sep 2 v Enfield (h) 2-0 *Bircham (pen), Hall (pen)*
J Bush, Smart, London, Moore, Waugh, Smith, Walton, Bircham, McBride, D Ross, R Hall, Subs: Sheldrick, Zefi, M Leite, F Ramirez

Sep 28 v Tring T (a) 3-0 *Tekell, Zefi, McBride*
J Bush, Sterling, Smith, Moore, Waugh, S Jones, Tekell, D McBride, M Leite, Zefi, E Sula, Subs: Bonfield, Massey, J Keen, E Bokpe

Oct 30 v Barnet (h) 2-0 *Williams, Sheldrick (pen)*
J Bush, B Devenney, Sterling, Smith, S Jones, J Keen, London, Sheldrick, Knight, Green, Zefi, Subs: T Welch, McDaid, J Warsame, O Williams, P Paynter

Nov 18 v Harefield U (a) 4-2 *Sheldrick, L Yaku 2, Earle*
J Bush, L Earle, R Wordsworth, J Warsame, C Wright, J Keen, P Green, Hibbert, O Williams, A Kutay, Sheldrick
Subs: T Yaku, L Yaku, E McGuigan

Dec 10 v Hampton (a) 2-4 *Sterling, Walker*
S Middleton, McDaid, Sterling, F Moore, S Jones, A Kutay, E McGuigan, J Keen, M Corbould, Walker, Sheldrick

Dec 28 v Borehamwood (a) 5-3 *Walker 2, Yaku, Hibbert, Zefi*
Bonfield, Massey, Smith, Moore, Waugh, J Keen, Bircham, Sheldrick, Walker, Zefi, L Yaku, Subs: Hibbert, Hammatt

Jan 18 v Camberley T (a) 3-2 *Hammatt 2, Sheldrick*
Bonfield, McDaid, Sterling, Moore, Waugh, Hibbert, Walton, Smith, P Green, Zefi, L Yaku, Subs: Walker, Massey, Hammatt, Sheldrick, Marshall

Feb 10 v Bedfont (a) 4-0 *Yaku 2, Green, McDaid*
J Bush, P McDaid, S Jones, M Weedon, Bircham, S Kelly, Sheldrick, B Devenney, P Green, S Dell, L Yaku
Subs: L Morris, Olajide Williams

1997-98

July 22 v Amersham T (a) 1-1 *Ephgrave*
Bonfield, Galloway, J Reece, P Osahon, Waugh, E Udaw, Smith, Knight, Bircham, Green, Garner, Subs: D Wallace, B Shrimpton, Celaire, S Ephgrave, S Freeman, K White

July 24 v Hitchin T (a) 1-1 *Boreham*
Bonfield, Bowder, Sterling, Moore, Richards, Kelly, Walton, Marshall, Boreham, McKay, Yaku, Subs: Celaire, Lamb, Galloway, E Udaw

July 26 v Chertsey T (a) 4-2 *Garner 2, Green, Bowder (pen)*
Bonfield, Galloway, Bowder, Moore, Lamb, Bircham, Garner, Celaire, McKay, J Keen, G Cooper, Subs: Green, Walton, Marshall, Hibbert

July 29 v London Colney (a) 3-2 *Yaku, Boreham, Smith*
J Bush, Galloway, Smith, Knight, Richards, J Keen, Walton, G Cooper, Boreham, Yaku, Hibbert, Subs: D Wallace, S Ephgrave,

Aug 2 v Chesham U (a) 1-1 *Green*
Bonfield, Bowder, Sterling, Moore, Marshall, Lamb, Walton, Bircham, Garner, Hibbert, N Stevens, Subs: Galloway, Waugh, Smith, Green, Boreham, McKay

Aug 5 v Kingsbury T (a) 0-1
J Bush, Galloway, Sterling, Waugh, Lamb, P Watkins, Knight, Bircham, Hibbert, Celaire, Green, Subs: Richards, Boreham, Yaku, Massey, M Leite

Aug 9 v Hendon (h) 2-2 *Boreham 2 (1 pen)*
J Bush, Bowder, Moore, Marshall, McKay, S Atkins, Walton, A Edmunds, Garner, Bircham, Boreham, Subs: Waugh, Green, Celaire, Hibbert, Lamb

Aug 13 v Milton Keynes (a) 2-1 *Yaku, Massey*
B Parker, Galloway, Sterling, Massey, S Atkins, A Edmunds, Celaire, Yaku, Lamb, Hibbert, M Leite, Subs: K Bissah, S Miller, Smith

Aug 20 v Broadfields U (a) 1-1 *Walker (pen)*
J Bush, Vladimir, Walker, S Freeman, Gayle, R Mason, B McAni, F Affiah, D Burn, Danny ?, Hibbert, Subs: P Burn, M Fletcher, K Bissah, N Kassauf,

Sep 27 v Corinthian Casuals (a) 1-2 *K Boreham*
Bonfield, Waugh, Galloway, G Boreham, Lamb, Moore, Walton, Hibbert, K Boreham, Jones, P Baretta, Subs: C Weston, S Hayes, P Challis, U Nwankokwu, Sterling

1998-99

July 28 v Hertford T (a) 0-3
Imber, D White, J Denton, Moore, Benning, Marshall, Holmes, Jones, Bircham, Kent, Dobson, Subs: Celaire, S Dale, Lamb, Walton, Yaku, D Kingshott, B Fahy

Aug 1 v Borehamwood (h) 4-1 *Kent 2, Holmes, Knight*
Imber, Lamb, Sterling, Moore, Benning, McKay, Walton, Bircham, Yaku, Kent, Holmes, Subs: D White, Dobson, S Dale, Waugh, Knight, A Paris

Aug 4 v Harrow Borough (a) 2-2 *Kent, Walton*
Imber, Lamb, Sterling, Moore, Benning, McKay, Walton, Jones, Holmes, Kent, Bircham, Subs: D White, J Denton, Dobson, Yaku, S Dale, Waugh, K Lamb
Aug 6 v Harpenden T (a) 2-0 *Dale, Kingshott*
Imber, D Kingshott, S Dale, B Fahy, K Lamb, Dobson, C Hague, J Roberts, A Kinsey, A Hawksworth, A Spender
Sub: Yaku
Aug 8 v Ashford T (Mdx) (a) 6-2 *Kent 2, Jones, Kellman 2, Denton*
Imber, D White, J Denton, Moore, Sterling, Holmes, Walton, Jones, Kent, S Dale, McKay, Subs: Benning, Dobson, Lamb, Kellman
Aug 12 v Flackwell Heath (h) 4-1 *Kellman 2, Holmes, Boreham*
Imber, D White, Sterling, Waugh, Benning, McKay, Walton, Lamb, Kellman,Celaire, Holmes, Subs: Moore, Marshall, Boreham, S Dale, B Fahy, A Spender
Aug 15 v Wingate & Finchley (a) 1-3 *Boreham*
D Watts, Dicker, Moore, Benning,Marshall, McKay, Walton, Kent, Kellman, A Spender, K Thomas, Subs: Celaire, S Dale, Waugh, Knight, Boreham
Aug 17 v Bedfont (a) 1-1 *Dale*
D Watts, S Dale, D Kingshott, B Fahy, Knight, A Hawksworth, A Spender, Yaku, N Christie, A Alia, C Brown, Subs: K Bissah, R Dee, E Ismaili, K Kurti
Aug 19 v Camberley T (a) 1-1 *Benning*
Imber, D White, S Dale, Moore, Marshall, Holmes, Bircham, Celaire, Lamb, McKay, A Spender, Subs: Benning, Kent, Walton, Kellman, Sterling, Yaku
Aug 29 v Grays Athletic (a) 0-3
Imber, Dell, Sterling, Moore, Benning, Lamb, Walton, McKay, Kellman, Kent, Holmes, Subs: Jones, Waugh, A Spender

1999-2000
July 17 v Crawley T (a) 2-0 *Baptiste 2*
Imber, Boxford, Lyons, Sterling, Tilbury, Lamb, McKay, Jones, Baptiste, Benning, Vallenti, Subs: Walker, C James, M Graham, A Swaysland
July 20 v Berkhamsted T (a) 0-3
Imber, Walton, Lyons, Lamb, N Copeman, Boxford, McKay, Jones, D Gustaf, Benning, Valenti, Subs: J Courtlidge, Bircham, Holmes, Walker, Baptiste
July 24 v Northwood (a) 0-3
Imber, Boxford, Lyons, Sterling, Tilbury, Lamb, Walton, Holmes, P Halbert, Benning, S Finnan, Subs: Baptiste, Walker, C James, Waugh, M Graham
July 27 v Watford (h) 0-7
Imber, Boxford, Lyons, Sterling, Tilbury, Lamb, Walton, Jones, Baptiste, Holmes, Benning, Subs: McKay, Walker, Waugh

July 31 v Edgware T (a) 5-3 *Jones, Baptiste, Walton, Halbert, Walker (pen)*
Imber, Boxford, Lyons, Valenti, Tilbury, Lamb, Walton, Jones, Baptiste, McKay, J Boadu, Subs: Walker, C James, N Copeman, Bircham, P Halbert, Waugh, Reid
Aug 3 v Flackwell H (a) 2-5 *Walker 2*
C Belson, Waugh, Bircham, P Halbert, Tilbury, Boxford, Holmes, Lamb, Walker, Reid, J Boadu, Subs: L Smith, E Winter, S Cunningham, A McKay
Aug 7 v Ware (a) 2-2 *Holmes, Baptiste*
Imber, Lamb, Lyons, Boxford, Tilbury, Walker, Walton, Holmes, Baptiste, Reid, McKay, Subs: Valenti, C James, Bircham, L Smith, J Boadu
Aug 10 v Walton & H (h) 1-1*Baptiste (pen)*
Imber, Lamb, Lyons, Boxford, Tilbury, Walker, McKay, Bircham, Baptiste, Holmes, Reid, Subs: Halbert, Valenti, B Haxholli, L Smith
Nov 16 v Aylesbury U (a) 3-1 *Jones, Maynard, Walton*
Imber, Boxford, Murphy,Campbell,Waugh, Dicker, Walton, Jones, Sofo-Yarabi, Lamb, Maybanks, Subs:: Lyons, Dobson, Walker, Loshi
Feb 1 v Edgware T (a) 5-0 *Swaysland, Benning, Bircham, Murphy, Coffey*
C Leary, M Murphy, A Richmond, Boxford, Campbell, M Gough, Benning, T Hadhiri, Walker, Bircham, S Hamdouche
Subs: Prutton, G Coffey, V Cave,M Swaysland

2000-2001
July 19 v Hillingdon Boro (a) 0-1
Trial match played over 3 periods
July 20 v Hillingdon Boro (a) 4-1 *G Lippiat, Totton, S Towle, B Hanley*
Trial match played over 3 periods
July 27 v Chesham Utd (a) 0-3
Watts, Murphy, W Barber, A Francis, Chandler, A Leenders, McKay, M Barima, Swaysland, Morgan, B Newby, Subs: B Miles, Peaks, P Ford, Holmes, N Fyfield, J Tarlton
July 30 v Slough Town (h) 1-2 *Fyfield*
Watts, Murphy, J Tarlton, Peaks, Chandler, P Ford, McKay, Cooper, Swaysland, N Fyfield, Boyce, Subs: B Miles, Campbell, Simon Robinson, A Leenders, S Towle, Maynard
Aug 1 v Bedfont (a) 1-7 *Leenders*
Squad friendly
Aug 5 v Burnham (a) 1-3 *Holmes*
Watts, Robinson, W Barber, P Ford, Foster, Peaks, Cooper, Morgan, Swaysland, Holmes, Boyce, Subs: B Miles, Bircham, G Coffey
Aug 8 v Kingsbury Town (a) 3-1 *Boyce, Holmes, Coffey*
Watts, Simon Robinson, W Barber, Peaks, Foster, Steve Robinson, Bircham, Holmes, Swaysland, Morgan, Boyce
Subs: B Miles, B Porter, J Tarlton, K Ridley, Cooper, R Phillips, G Coffey
Aug 12 v Arlesey Town 3-3 *Swaysland 2 (1 pen), Holmes*
Watts, Murphy, K Powell, G Thompson, Maynard, Boyce, Steve Robinson, Holmes, Bircham, Totton, Swaysland Subs: Cooper, Ridley, Morgan, Simon Robinson
Aug 15 v Hillingdon Boro (a) 3-1 *Tilbury, Lamb, J Tarlton*
Squad friendly
Aug 24 v Hillingdon Boro (a) 3-3 *Holmes, Coffey, Towle (pen)*
Squad friendly
Aug 30 v Viking Sports (a) 5-1 *Carter, Swaysland 2 (1 pen), Lamb, OG*
Squad friendly

2001-02
July 21 v Portsmouth RN (a) 2-1 *Morgan, Tilbury*
Carter, Reed, Moore, Amarteifio, Reeves, D Gibbs, Somers, R Ellis, Morgan, McDonnagh, Tilbury, Subs: N Cobb, Tucker, A McGovern, Pither
July 26 v Hillingdon Boro (a) 3-4 *Asombang 2, Oriot*
Squad friendly
July 28 v Brook House (a) 4-1 *Somers, Tilbury, Pither, Lamb (pen)*
Practice match played over 4 periods
July 31 v Burnham (a) 0-1
N Cobb, Lamb, Moore, Tucker, Reeve, R Ellis, Pither, Bryson, Morgan, V Asombang, J Fry, Subs: Tilbury, M Watton, Reed, S Beattie, Amarteifio
Aug 1 v Hillingdon Boro (a) 2-1 *Casey, Sofo-Yarabi*
Squad friendly
Aug 4 v Beaconsfield SYCOB (a) 3-0 *Tilbury 2, Somers*
C Leary, Bryson, Moore, Amarteifio, Reeve, D Gibbs, Tilbury, Lamb, Morgan, Shaw, Somers Subs: N Cobb, Chandler, McDonnagh, V Asombang, Reed, R Ellis, Walker
Aug 7 v Enfield Town (h) 2-2 *Asombang, Walker*
D Godfrey, M Watton, Reed, Tucker, Chandler, J Fry, R Ellis, Bryson, Walker, V Asombang, D Oriot, Subs: N Cobb, Perry, A McGovern, T Hupe, S Towle, Bamgbola
Aug 11 v Berkhamsted (a) 2-2 *Hammatt 2*
N Cobb, Bryson, Moore, Amarteifio, Chandler, McDonnagh, Tilbury, Hammatt, Morgan, Shaw, Somers Subs: R Ellis, Reed, Tucker, Lamb, Walker, V Asombang
Aug 13 v Edgware Town (a) 1-0 *Hammatt*
Carter, Bryson, Moore, Amarteifio, Chandler, Somers, McDonnagh, Shaw, V Asombang, Hammatt, Tilbury, Subs: Perry, J Burgess, T Hupe, Pither, J Kelly
Aug 14 v Kingsbury Town (a) 0-0
Squad friendly
Sep13 v Ruislip Manor (a) 2-0 *Pither, Bryson*
N Cobb, R Walsh, R Connelly, Reeve, Perry, Hunt, Pither, Bryson, Deadman, Morgan, Bamgbola
Oct 11 v Brook House (a) 4-4 *Pither, Alexander, Gibbs, Walker (pen)*

Squad friendly
Nov 20 v Hillingdon Boro (a) 2-1 *Tilbury 2*
Squad friendly
Dec11 v Potters Bar (a) 4-1 *Pither, Hunt, Chamberlin 2*
Squad friendly